A New l ι 1800

A NEW DICTIONARY OF IRISH HISTORY FROM 1800

D. J. Hickey

J. E. Doherty

GILL & MACMILLAN

To the verdant memory of Carmel Doherty and Michael J. Hickey

Gill & Macmillan Ltd
Hume Avenue, Park West, Dublin 12
with associated companies throughout the world
www.gillmacmillan.ie

978 07171 2521 0

Design and print origination by O'K Graphic Design, Dublin
Printed in Malaysia

This book is typeset in 9/10pt Adobe Garamond

*The paper used in this book comes from the wood pulp of managed forests.
For every tree felled, at least one tree is planted, thereby renewing natural resources.*

A CIP catalogue record for this book is available from the British Library.

3 5 6 4 2

Preface

In the first edition of this work we observed that it was the first dictionary devoted solely to the events of Irish history. It remains the only work devoted in such detail to the period since 1800. Its popularity has, we feel, justified our decision to concentrate on the period since the Act of Union. It is a source of great satisfaction to us now to bring our work into the new millennium through the publication of a rewritten and updated edition as *A New Dictionary of Irish History from 1800.*

We have dropped some entries from the original work and added a considerable amount of new material. We continue to define history in the broadest terms possible: in addition to political history we include entries on the arts, associations, economics, folk customs, literature, movements, religious developments, social affairs, societies, and tribunals, as well as a very broad spectrum of personalities. To accommodate new material we have made decisions that may require some explanation. There are fewer entries on purely literary figures, as we believe there are now popular works devoted solely to Irish literature; we have excluded some aspects of contemporary popular culture and sport, as we believe that these are dealt with in other accessible works. As far as possible we have justified our entries on the grounds of their historical significance. The extent to which this has been successful may be debatable, as in works of this genre it always is.

In the nature of developments in Ireland since the publication of the original work (1980), this new edition includes a comprehensive account of events and personalities connected to Northern Ireland. No-one is more conscious than the authors that history continues after a book is published; in short, history is an unfinished business, and there are events to which it is not possible to write *finis.* On the other hand, they could not be excluded merely because they still form part of a developing process.

As in the previous edition, we direct the work at readers who wish to locate historical information in a readily accessible format from 1800 to date. In doing so we have tried to abide by Ralph Waldo Emerson's advice on a dictionary: 'There is no cant in it, no excess of information and it is full of suggestion—the raw material of possible poems and histories.'

Nomenclature, particularly in relation to titled persons, presented some problems of designation. In general, we have chosen to include such persons under the title or name by which they were popularly known.

ACKNOWLEDGMENTS

A work as diverse as this would not be possible without liberal assistance from a variety of institutions and individuals. We wish to express our sincere gratitude to the following: Staff of the National Library of Ireland; the staffs of the Limerick City and Limerick County Libraries (especially Aileen Dillane); Mary Farrell, Westmeath County Librarian; Liam Hamrock, Senior Library Assistant, Mayo County Library, for invaluable assistance in our research on the Annaghdown, Cleggan, Clew Bay, Doolough and Kirkintilloch tragedies; Anna Keavney, Drogheda Library, for information on the Carlingford Lough Disaster; Gearóid O'Brien, Librarian, Westmeath County Library; Margaret O'Shaughnessy, Curator, Foynes Flying Boat Museum; Bob Collins, then Director-General of RTE; Dolores Meaney, Assistant Librarian, RTE Reference Library; P. Moloney, Examiner Publications, Cork, for material on the Drumcollogher Cinema Tragedy; Gerry Slevin, editor of the *Nenagh Guardian*; Seán F. Ó Beirn for his incisive information on the founding of Taibhdhearc na Gaillimhe; the historian Peter Moser for his helpful comments on the founding of Clann na Talmhan; Sinéad McCoole for permission to use material from her *Guns and Chiffon*; Roy Stokes, author of *The Sinking of the Leinster*, for reading and commenting on our entry; Leo Collins, Manager, Land Surveying and Mapping Section, Dublin City Council, for his extremely helpful comments and invaluable assistance on the Dublin of the War of Independence and Civil War; Paddy Reidy, Limerick, for his materials relating to the Shannon Scheme; the author Liz Curtis for a copy of the birth certificate of James Larkin (senior) and for her helpful comments; James Creed, An Grianán, for information on the Irish Countrywomen's Association; James Whelan of the Blood Transfusion Board; Cheryl Forde of the ESRI; the Commissioners of Irish Lights; Donal Morrissey, for information on his uncle Daniel Morrissey; Canon Micheál Liston, Limerick; Paddy O'Halloran, for his observations on the Connaught Rangers Mutiny; and the former Tipperary hurling star Paddy Williams for information on the Modreeney ambush.

For their encouraging comments and advice we wish also to thank Manus Nunan, Aix-les-Thermes, and the author Donal O'Donovan.

As ever, our thanks are due to the staff at Gill & Macmillan, especially Fergal Tobin, who, despite the many vicissitudes that attended this work, remains a very firm friend, and Deirdre Rennison Kunz for her invaluable help and assistance.

Our thanks also to Tom O'Flaherty, Tipperary, for sharing his experience of the lime kiln with us.

Yet again, our inadequate thanks to our wives, Anna and Caithlin, and families, who have lived with this work and us for such a very long time.

Abbreviations

AOH	Ancient Order of Hibernians
c.	circa
CIE	Córas Iompair Éireann
DLitt	doctor of letters
DMP	Dublin Metropolitan Police
DUP	Democratic Unionist Party
EC	European Communities
EEC	European Economic Community
ESB	Electricity Supply Board
EU	European Union
GPO	General Post Office
ICTU	Irish Congress of Trade Unions
INLA	Irish National Liberation Army
IRA	Irish Republican Army
IRB	Irish Republican Brotherhood
IRSP	Irish Republican Socialist Party
ITGWU	Irish Transport and General Workers' Union
LVF	Loyalist Volunteer Force
MD	doctor of medicine
MP	member of Parliament
NILP	Northern Ireland Labour Party
NUI	National University of Ireland
NUIC	National University of Ireland, Cork
NUID	National University of Ireland, Dublin
NUIG	National University of Ireland, Galway
NUIM	National University of Ireland, Maynooth
OECD	Organisation for European Co-operation and Development
PSNI	Police Service of Northern Ireland
QC	Queen's counsel
QUB	Queen's University, Belfast
RBAI	Royal Belfast Academical Institution
RDS	Royal Dublin Society
RHA	Royal Hibernian Academy of Arts
RIA	Royal Irish Academy
RIC	Royal Irish Constabulary
RUC	Royal Ulster Constabulary
RUI	Royal University of Ireland
SDLP	Social Democratic and Labour Party

TCD	Trinity College, Dublin (sole college of the University of Dublin)
TD	teachta Dála (member of Dáil Éireann)
UCC	University College, Cork (now National University of Ireland, Cork)
UCD	University College, Dublin (now National University of Ireland, Dublin)
UCG	University College, Galway (now National University of Ireland, Galway)
UDA	Ulster Defence Association
UDR	Ulster Defence Regiment
UFF	Ulster Freedom Fighters (a name sometimes used by the UVF)
UPNI	Unionist Party of Northern Ireland
UUP	Ulster Unionist Party
UUUC	United Ulster Unionist Council
UVF	Ulster Volunteer Force

A

Abbey Theatre, Dublin. The Irish National Theatre was founded in 1904 from a merger of the National Dramatic Company (directed by the brothers FRANK AND WILLIAM FAY) and the IRISH LITERARY THEATRE. A donation of £1,500 from Annie Horniman (1860–1937) facilitated the adaptation of the Dublin Mechanics' Institute, Abbey Street, as the Abbey Theatre (named from the street). The theatre opened on 27 December 1904 with performances of Yeats's *On Baile's Strand* and Lady Gregory's *Spreading the News.* The Abbey Theatre device, a woodcut of the legendary queen Méabh with a wolfhound on a leash, was designed by Elinor Monsell. The brothers Fay left the Abbey in 1908, and two years later the theatre was forced to become self-supporting when Miss Horniman withdrew her financial assistance. In 1924 the Abbey received an annual grant of £850 from the Free State government. The Peacock Theatre, a small venue for experimental works and intended also as an acting and ballet school, opened adjacent to the Abbey in 1928.

The most famous early writers included JOHN M. SYNGE (*The Playboy of the Western World,* 1907) and SEÁN O'CASEY (*The Shadow of a Gunman,* 1923, *Juno and the Paycock,* 1924, and *The Plough and the Stars,* 1926). The theatre was destroyed by fire on 18 July 1951, after which the company was housed at the Queen's Royal Theatre, Pearse Street, Dublin, until the new Abbey Theatre opened on 18 July 1966. Designed by MICHAEL SCOTT and Partners, the main theatre seated 628 and the Peacock 157.

Actors associated with the Abbey Theatre included F. J. McCormick (stage name of Peter Judge, 1889–1947); Máire Ní Shiubhlaigh (1883–1958), one of a family of five at the Abbey Theatre when it opened, with her brother George on stage and three of her siblings backstage; Sara Allgood (1883–1950) and her sister Molly (1887–1952), who used the stage name Máire O'Neill; Barry Fitzgerald (stage name of William Shields, 1888–1961) and his brother Arthur (1896–1970); Harry Brogan (1905–1977); Cyril Cusack (1910–1993); Éamonn Kelly (1914–2001); Siobhán McKenna (1923–1986); and Ray McAnally (1926–1989).

In addition to W. B. Yeats, Lady Augusta Gregory, Edward Martyn, J. M. Synge, and Seán O'Casey, writers associated with the theatre included GEORGE BERNARD SHAW: *The Shewing-Up of Blanco Posnet* (1909), a season of whose plays, 1916–17, included *John Bull's Other Island* (1904), *Widowers' Houses* (1916), *Arms and the Man* (1916), and *Man and Superman*; T. C. Murray (1873–1959), a member of the 'Cork Realists', whose works included *Birthright* (1910), *Maurice Harte* (1912), *Sovereign Love* (1913), *The Briery Gap* (1917), *Spring* (1918), *Aftermath* (1922), *Autumn Fire* (1925), and *Michaelmas Eve* (1932); Seumas O'Kelly (c. 1875–1918): *The Shuiler's Child* (1909), *Meadowsweet* (1912), *The Bribe* (1914), and *The Parnellite* (1919); Lord Dunsany (1878–1957): *The Glittering Gate* (1909) and *King Agimenes and the Unknown Warrior* (1911); Pádraic Colum (1881–1972): *The Land* (1905, one of the theatre's earliest successes), *The Fiddler's House* (1907), and *Thomas Muskerry* (1910); St John Ervine (1883–1971), manager of the theatre, 1915–16, whose works included *Mixed Marriage* (1911) and *John Ferguson* (1915); Lennox Robinson (1886–1958), manager and director, 1910–23, whose works included *The Clancy Name* (1908), *The Cross-Roads* (1909), *The Dreamers* (1915), *The White-headed Boy* (1916), *The Lost Leader* (1918), *The White Blackbird* (1925) and *The Far-Off Hills* (1928) and who also published *The Irish Theatre* (1939), *Curtain Up* (reminiscences, 1942) and *Ireland's Abbey Theatre, 1899–1950* (1951) as well as editing the *Journals* of Lady Gregory (1946); George Shiels (1886–1949), more than thirty of whose plays at the Abbey included *Bedmates* (1921), *Insurance Money* (1921), *Paul Twyning* (1922), *Professor Tim* (1925), *Cartney and Kevney* (1927), *The New Gossoon* (1930), *Grogan and the Ferret* (1933), *The Passing Day* (1936), *The Rugged Path* (with a record-breaking run in 1940), *The Summit* (1941), *The Fort Field* (1944), and *The Old Broom* (1944); George Fitzmaurice (1887–1963), whose earliest success was with *The Country Dressmaker* (1907), other works including *The Pie Dish* (1908), *The Magic Glasses* (1913), and *Twixt the Giltinans and the Carmodys* (1923); Brinsley MacNamara (1890–1963), an actor with the theatre, 1909–13, whose plays included *The Rebellion in Ballyscullion* (1919), *The Glorious Uncertainty* (1923), *Look at the Heffernans* (1926), and *Margaret Gillan* (1933); Paul Vincent Carroll (1900–1968): *The Watched Pot* (Peacock, 1930), *Things that Are Caesar's* (1932), *Shadow and Substance* (1937), *The White Steed* (1938), and *The Old Foolishness* (1940); Louis D'Alton (1900–1951): *The Man in the Cloak* (1937), *Tomorrow Never Comes* (1939), *The Spanish Soldier* (1940), *The Money*

Doesn't Matter (1941), *Lovers' Meeting* (1941), *They Got What They Wanted* (1947), *The Devil a Saint Would Be* (1951), *This Other Eden* (1953), and *Cafflin' Johnny* (1958); Denis Johnston (1901–1984), who changed the title of *Rhapsody in Green* to *The Old Lady Says 'No'* for a production at the Gate Theatre when Lady Gregory turned it down, *The Moon in the Yellow River* (1931), and *The Scythe and the Sunset* (1958); FRANK O'CONNOR, a director of the theatre, 1935–39, who wrote *In the Train* (1937) and *Moses' Rock* (1938) for the Abbey; Walter Macken (1915–1967): *Mungo's Mansion* (1946), *Vacant Possession* (1948), *Home Is the Hero* (1952), *Twilight of a Warrior* (1955), *Look in the Looking Glass* (1958), and *The Voices of Doolin* (1960); M. J. Molloy (1917–1994): *The Old Road* (1943), *The Visiting House* (1946), *The King of Friday's Men* (1948), *The Wood of the Whispering* (1953), and *Petticoat Loose* (1979); James Plunkett (1920–2003): *The Risen People* (1958); Hugh Leonard (born 1926): *The Big Birthday* (1956), *A Leap in the Dark* (1957), *A Life* (1979), and *Love in the Title* (1999); Brian Friel (born 1929), whose Abbey productions included *The Enemy Within* (1962), *Freedom of the City* (1973), *Aristocrats* (1979), *The Faith Healer* (1979), and *Dancing at Lughnasa* (1990); Thomas Kilroy (born 1934), writer in residence, 1998: *The Death and Resurrection of Mr Roche* (1968), *The O'Neill* (1969), *Tea, Sex and Shakespeare* (1976), *Talbot's Box* (Peacock 1977, Abbey 1978), and *Ghosts* (from Ibsen, 1989); Tom Murphy (born 1935), writer in residence, 1987–89: *Famine* (Peacock, 1968), *A Crucial Week in the Life of a Grocer's Assistant* (1969), *The Morning After Optimism* (1971), *The White House* (1972), *The Sanctuary Lamp* (1975), *The Blue Macushla* (1980), *The Gigli Concert* (1983), *Bailegangaire* (1985), *Too Late for Logic* (1989), *The Patriot Game* (Peacock, 1991), *The Wake* (1998), and *The House* (2000), with a season of his plays in 2001; Bernard Farrell (born 1941), writer in residence, 1996: *I Do Not Like Thee, Dr Fell* (1979), *Canaries* (1980), *All In Favour Said No!* (1981), *Petty Sessions* (1983), *All the Way Back* (1985), *Say Cheese!* (1987), *The Last Apache Reunion* (1993), and *Kevin's Bed* (1998); Frank McGuinness (born 1953), writer in residence, 1992: *The Factory Girls* (Peacock, 1982), *Baglady* (Peacock, 1985), *Observe the Sons of Ulster Marching Towards the Somme* (Peacock and Abbey, 1985), *Carthaginians* (Peacock, 1988), *The Bird Sanctuary* (1994), and *Dolly West's Kitchen* (1999); and Sebastian Barry (born 1955), writer in residence, 1980: *Prayers of Sherkin* (1990), *The Only True History of Lizzie Finn* (1995), and *Hinterland* (2002).

Abdication Crisis (1936), a constitutional crisis provoked by the proposal of King Edward VIII to abdicate the throne of Great Britain in order to marry Mrs Wallis Simpson. As a member of the Commonwealth of Nations, the Irish Free State was affected by the crisis. The President of the Executive Council (head of government), ÉAMON DE VALERA, exploited it to effect changes in the CONSTITUTION OF THE IRISH FREE STATE. On 11 December, the day of the abdication, Dáil Éireann was summoned to debate two bills, under guillotine so as to have them passed by the following night. The Constitution (Amendment No. 27) Act (1936), which removed all references to the King and the GOVERNOR-GENERAL from the Constitution, was passed by 79 to 54; the EXTERNAL RELATIONS ACT (1936), which recognised the King only 'for the purpose of the appointment of diplomatic and consular representatives, and the conclusion of international agreements . . .' was passed by 81 to 5. There were no references to the monarchy in the CONSTITUTION OF IRELAND (1937).

Abercorn, James Hamilton, first Duke of (1811–1885), landowner, politician (Conservative); born in Edinburgh, educated at the University of Oxford. He administered his estates in Cos. Derry and Donegal from the family home at Baron's Court, Co. Tyrone. His perception as a humane and popular landlord is challenged in a letter from Karl Marx to Frederick Engels (2 November 1867), in which the former states that Abercorn had recently 'cleared' his estate of thousands of tenants by forcible evictions and that among those evicted were well-to-do farmers whose improvements and capital investments were confiscated. Lord Lieutenant of Ireland, 1866–68 and 1874–76, during his first term he dealt firmly with the IRB, while his later endeavours on behalf of Catholic children led to the passing of the Intermediate Education (Ireland) Act (1878) (see SECONDARY EDUCATION).

Abercorn, James Hamilton, second Duke of (1830–1913), landlord and politician (Conservative); born in Brighton, educated at the University of Oxford. He was MP for Co. Donegal, 1860–80, where his family owned large estates, but lost his seat during the LAND LEAGUE agitation. He was the founder of the

NORTH-WEST LOYALIST REGISTRATION AND ELECTORAL ASSOCIATION, 1886, and chief spokesman of Ulster unionism. Addressing a crowd of eleven thousand at the Ulster Unionist Convention, 17 June 1892, he said: 'You are fighting for home, for liberty, for everything that makes life dear to you . . . Men of the North, once more I say, we will not have home rule.' His opposition to the measure continued until its ultimate defeat in the House of Lords, 1893. Chairman of Tyrone County Council, he opposed tenant purchase but later sold large tracts of his estate under the Irish Land Act (1903) (see LAND ACTS). His son James Gilbert Edward Hamilton (1869–1953), later third Duke of Abercorn, was MP for Derry city, 1900–13, Lord Lieutenant of Co. Tyrone, 1917–53, and Governor of Northern Ireland, 1922–45.

Aberdeen, John Campbell Gordon, first Marquess of (1847–1934), British politician (Liberal); born in Aberdeenshire, educated at St Andrew's University and the University of Oxford. During his first term as Lord Lieutenant, January–July 1886, W. E. GLADSTONE failed to carry HOME RULE. Aberdeen returned as Lord Lieutenant in the HENRY CAMPBELL-BANNERMAN government, 1905–15, and would hold the office longer than any incumbent. His wife, Ishbel (née Isabel Marjoribanks), forced him to release JAMES CONNOLLY from prison after a plea from Connolly's wife. Though Aberdeen sought the arrest of the leaders of the LARNE GUN-RUNNING, he was not too concerned with political affairs, interpreting his Irish role in a conciliatory way. He did not enjoy the confidence of the Prime Minister, H. H. ASQUITH, who, following the BACHELOR'S WALK incident (26 July 1914), wrote privately: 'I am tempted to regret, that I didn't make the "clean cut" six months ago, and insist upon the booting out of Aberdeen . . . and the whole crew. A weaker and more incompetent lot were never in charge of a leaky ship in stormy weather.' Aberdeen's reminiscences, *We Twa'*, appeared in 1925.

Achill Missionary Herald and Western Witness, a paper founded by Rev. EDWARD NANGLE to further his extreme anti-Catholic views. In the first issue (31 July 1837) he announced that the paper would 'bear a faithful and uncompromising testimony against the superstition and idolatry of the Church of Rome' and 'proclaim the glorious truths of the Gospel.' Printed in Achill Island, Co. Mayo, it was a constant source of irritation to the Catholic Church in Connacht. It ceased to appear in the early 1850s and was replaced by the *Church Advocate* in 1864. (See also SECOND REFORMATION.)

Act of Union (1800). Ireland had its own parliament from 1295 to 1800. Its legislative authority was restricted until 1782 by Poynings' Law (1494) and the 'Sixth of George I' (1719). When these acts were repealed in 1782 'Grattan's Parliament' (called after HENRY GRATTAN) came into existence, and lasted until 1800.

While the achievement of independence in 1782 gave the impression that the idea of Union had been dropped permanently, the situation was changed by the French Revolution (1789) and the insurrection of the UNITED IRISHMEN (1798). The possibility of Ireland becoming a base for an attack on England was demonstrated when General Humbert landed at Killala, Co. Mayo, on 22 August 1798 to aid the United men. The rising, suppressed with great savagery, secured support from influential members of the establishment for a union of the two parliaments. Addressing the Irish Parliament on 22 January 1799, the Lord Lieutenant of Ireland, MARQUESS CORNWALLIS, made no direct reference to a union but did refer to the need to adopt measures that would strengthen the powers and resources of the British Empire. A motion by George Ponsonby (1755–1817) to secure an amendment that the reference be deleted from the address and that the Irish Parliament should maintain 'the undoubted birthright of the people of Ireland to have a free and independent legislature' was defeated (106 to 105) but two days later was carried (111 to 106). Ponsonby failed in an attempt to secure a pledge from the Parliament that it would never again entertain the idea of union.

WILLIAM PITT desired that the Union be carried by a strong majority. An offer of CATHOLIC EMANCIPATION secured the support of the Catholic Church, under THOMAS TROY. Cornwallis and the Chief Secretary for Ireland, VISCOUNT CASTLEREAGH, supported Pitt, but emancipation was strongly opposed by the Lord Chancellor, the EARL OF CLARE. The leading opponents of the Union, with Ponsonby, were the Chancellor of the Exchequer, Sir John Parnell (1744–1801), who lost his post, and the Speaker of the House of Commons, John Foster (1740–1829), later the most heavily compensated member of the Parliament, though unwavering in his opposition to the measure.

Castlereagh and Clare were the prime architects of government victory. Catholic property-owners were won over with promises of law and order and prosperity. Catholic barristers, however, led by DANIEL O'CONNELL, expressed fears (which proved to be groundless) that their position in the judicial system would be compromised. Members of the Protestant churches, alarmed by the 1798 rising, were assured of adequate protection for the established Church of Ireland and the Presbyterian Church. Those who controlled pocket boroughs and rotten boroughs were promised patronage, titles, and generous financial compensation; in addition, support was bought with pensions, offices, and promises of political advancement. In all, £1,250,000 was spent on buying out the boroughs, at an average of £15,000 per seat, paid equally to opponents and supporters of the Union.

After listening to a plea from Henry Grattan that the Union be rejected, the Irish House of Commons voted in favour (138 to 96) on 22 January 1800. On 6 February the proposals were carried (158 to 115). The motion was carried in the British House of Commons on 28 March, and 'An Act for the Union of Great Britain and Ireland' came into force on 1 January 1801. The Union was not, however, immediately followed by Catholic emancipation, as the King, GEORGE III, refused to consider such a measure.

The act, containing eight articles, provided for Irish representation in the British House of Lords of twenty-eight temporal and four spiritual lords and for 100 members in the House of Commons: two for each county, two each for the cities of Dublin and Cork, one each for thirty-one boroughs and towns, and one for the University of Dublin. The established churches of Ireland and England were united and were guaranteed to be 'an essential and fundamental part of the Union.' Article 6 granted equality between England and Ireland in matters of commerce and free trade, save for different rates of duties on certain home-produced goods and foreign imports. (There would, however, be a system of countervailing duties on goods passing from one country to the other.) Selected manufactures, including cotton and woollen goods, would incur customs duties for twenty years. Ireland and England were to have separate exchequers and separate responsibility for their national debts. Ireland was to contribute two-seventeenths to the expenditure of the United Kingdom, subject to periodic review. Under certain conditions the exchequers and national debts could be united (as occurred in 1817). Under article 8, all laws in force at the time of the Union, and in the civil and ecclesiastical courts, unless altered by the imperial parliament, retained their status quo.

Opposition to the Union began during the 1830s when Daniel O'Connell led a group of Repeal MPs in the British House of Commons. The REPEAL ASSOCIATION unsuccessfully sought to regain a national parliament. Later the Union was attacked by ISAAC BUTT, CHARLES STEWART PARNELL, and JOHN REDMOND, all of whom sought—to varying degrees—a national parliament within the United Kingdom. A more radical position, complete political separation of Ireland from England, was taken up by the IRB. In the wake of the EASTER RISING (1916), SINN FÉIN established the first DÁIL ÉIREANN, 21 January 1919. Nationalists rejected the GOVERNMENT OF IRELAND ACT (1920), which established separate parliaments for NORTHERN IRELAND (the six north-eastern counties) and the rest of the country, known briefly as 'Southern Ireland'.

The end of the legislative union between Ireland and Britain was confirmed in the ANGLO-IRISH TREATY (1921), which conferred 'dominion status' on the IRISH FREE STATE.

Adair, General Sir William (1850–1931), soldier and Ulster unionist. A veteran of the Anglo-Boer Wars, he became deputy adjutant-general of the Royal Marines, 1907–11. Prominent in the ULSTER UNIONIST PARTY, he commanded the Antrim unit of the ULSTER VOLUNTEER FORCE and was in charge of the landing and dispersal of guns during the LARNE GUN-RUNNING.

Adams, Gerry (born 1948), politician (Sinn Féin); born in Ballymurphy, Belfast. After leaving school he worked as a barman, 1965, and later supported the Provisional IRA. Arrested on 14 March 1972; his release was one of the IRA's demands as a precondition for talks with WILLIAM WHITELAW (7 July 1972). Believed to be the officer commanding an IRA 'brigade' in Belfast, he was interned 1973–77. While in the Maze Prison, under the pen-name Brownie, he published a series of articles in *Republican News* in which he outlined a strategy that would enable the Provisional IRA to build a political structure through Sinn Féin while pursuing an armed struggle.

With Ivor Bell he reorganised the IRA in a

structure of four-member cells. After organising a Northern take-over of Sinn Féin, with Adams becoming president, 1983, they ended the party's policy of parliamentary abstention in 1986. Adams defeated GERRY FITT to become abstentionist member of the British Parliament for West Belfast, 9 June 1983, held the seat until defeated by Dr Joe Hendron of the SDLP in 1992, and regained it in 1997. He was shot and wounded in Belfast, 14 March 1984, for which a member of the UFF, John Gregg, was sentenced to eighteen years' imprisonment in 1985. In 1987 Adams entered talks with JOHN HUME (see HUME-ADAMS TALKS). While he led opposition to the DOWNING STREET DECLARATION (1993), the IRA ceasefire on 31 August 1994 enabled him to engage more publicly in the PEACE PROCESS. He insisted that the 'decommissioning' of arms could not be a precondition for Sinn Féin's admission to the peace talks. After the new British Prime Minister, TONY BLAIR, announced that Sinn Féin could join the all-party talks at Stormont in the event of an IRA ceasefire, and Blair and the outgoing Taoiseach, JOHN BRUTON, announced that the handing over and decommissioning of weapons was no longer a precondition, Adams attended talks on 15 September 1997, though no unionists were present. Following a meeting with Blair in Belfast he became the first Sinn Féin leader since the ANGLO-IRISH REATY to enter 10 Downing Street, on 11 December 1997. On 10 April 1998 Adams and Martin McGuinness signed the BELFAST AGREEMENT. Adams headed the poll in West Belfast to take a seat in the 108-member Northern Ireland Assembly, in which Sinn Féin had 18 seats. He retained his West Belfast seat with the highest mandate of any candidate in the general election of 7 June 2001, with 27,096 votes. His autobiography, *Before the Dawn,* was published in September 1996.

agitation, the policy adopted by DANIEL O'CONNELL in 1825 when embarking on the mass movement for CATHOLIC EMANCIPATION and again employed during his struggle for Repeal, 1843. It consisted of mass meetings, inflammatory speeches, and a direct appeal to the passions and traditions of his audiences. The initial success of this policy was widely observed; the French novelist Honoré de Balzac commented that O'Connell had 'incarnated a whole people.' The government ended the tactic in 1843 by proscribing O'Connell's 'monster meeting' scheduled for Clontarf, Dublin. (See also REPEAL ASSOCIATION.)

agrarian crime. The law classified crime into four categories: crime against the person, crime against property, crime against public peace, and intimidation by threatening letter. In an effort to combat such crimes, a number of Peace Preservation Acts, commonly called COERCION ACTS, were passed during the second half of the nineteenth century. The figures for certain reported agrarian crimes during the GREAT FAMINE (1845–49) were:

	1845	1846	1847	1848	1849
Burglary	97	269	561	279	134
Robbery	124	257	559	588	460
Murder	95	116	145	117	139
Cattle and sheep stealing	79	368	1,223	821	993

Annualised figures for agrarian violence during the LAND WAR (1879–1903) were:

1879	863	1892	405
1880	2,585	1893	380
1881	4,439	1894	276
1882	3,433	1895	261
1883	870	1896	251
1884	762	1897	247
1885	944	1898	243
1886	1,056	1899	246
1887	883	1900	280
1888	660	1901	246
1889	534	1902	253
1890	519	1903	195
1891	472		

Agricultural and Technical Instruction (Ireland) Act (1899). Prompted by the RECESS COMMITTEE, the act of 9 August 1899 was inspired by Sir HORACE PLUNKETT, first vice-president of the Department of Agriculture and Technical Instruction (established under the act in 1900); the secretary of the department was Plunkett's protégé THOMAS PATRICK GILL. Financed from central and local funds, the new department established a system of technical education to provide opportunities for night classes in larger towns. The function of the schools was to provide education in practical subjects. An Advisory Council of Agriculture of 104 members was established. There were two boards to administer the department's funds, one each for agriculture and technical instruction, on each of which the council was represented. The department also operated an agricultural scheme for the areas under the control of the CONGESTED DISTRICTS BOARD; by 1909, fifty-seven inspectors were employed for these areas.

The functions of the department were taken over by the Department of Education of the Irish Free State in 1923; the schools administered by the department continued as before until reorganised under the Vocational Education Act (1930). In 1931 the Department of Agriculture and Technical Instruction was dissolved, the Technical Instruction Branch was placed under the Department of Education, and the Department of Agriculture took its modern form.

Agricultural Wages Act (1936), an act to fix minimum wages for agricultural workers. Wages varied according to area: they were highest in some parts of Leinster and in Cork and lowest in Connacht and Ulster. The introduction of the act was opposed by the Department of Finance.

Ahern, Bertie (born 1951), politician (Fianna Fáil); born in Dublin, educated at Rathmines College of Commerce and UCD. A member of Dáil Éireann from 1977, he was chief whip, March–November 1982, spokesperson on youth, 1981–82, and spokesperson on labour and the public service, 1983–87. As Minister for Labour, 1987–91, he played a prominent role in securing the national wage agreements that were credited with producing industrial peace and aiding economic prosperity into the late 1990s. He also took part in the negotiations with the PROGRESSIVE DEMOCRATS after the 1989 election and the renegotiation of the pact in 1991, a period during which CHARLES HAUGHEY described Ahern as 'the most devious [and] the most cunning of them all.'

As Minister for Finance from 1991 Ahern presided over the early stages of an unprecedented economic boom that came to be called the 'Celtic Tiger'. He resisted pressure to challenge ALBERT REYNOLDS for leadership of the party when Haughey resigned, February 1992, and remained in Finance; he was unchallenged for the succession to Reynolds, 19 November 1994. In opposition, 1994–97, Ahern concentrated on party unity. He also developed a harmonious working relationship with the leader of the Progressive Democrats, MARY HARNEY. He admitted to the MORIARTY TRIBUNAL that he had signed blank cheques on the party leader's account when Haughey controlled it but claimed he was unaware of the purpose of the money or that some of it had ended up in Haughey's personal account.

Ahern again became Taoiseach in a coalition government of Fianna Fáil and the Progressive Democrats, 26 June 1997. His appointment of Ray Burke as Minister for Foreign Affairs proved embarrassing when Burke admitted to accepting 'political donations' from building developers and then resigned from the Government and the Dáil, 7 October 1997. The Oireachtas then established the FLOOD TRIBUNAL to look into matters involving planning in north Co. Dublin.

Ahern played a prominent role in the PEACE PROCESS that led to the BELFAST AGREEMENT (1998), for which he had worked with determination since assuming office. He was linked during the summer of 2000 to unsuccessful attempts to have the former judge Hugh O'Flaherty appointed to a position in the European Investment Bank, amid widespread disquiet. There were revelations that Ahern had carried out an investigation in 1996 following complaints over a donation of £100,000 to Haughey; he had not revealed this information to the Moriarty Tribunal, which was attempting to uncover the sources of Haughey's wealth. A motion of no confidence on the issue put by the leader of the Labour Party, RUAIRÍ QUINN, was defeated (by 84 to 80).

As the peace process stalled over the summer of 2001, Ahern continued to work with TONY BLAIR to secure a solution to the issues raised by the IRA's failure to decommission its arms, police reform, and demands for demilitarisation. When a general election was called, 17 May 2002, Ahern was heading the longest-serving government since the 1940s. On 6 June he became the first Taoiseach to be re-elected since JACK LYNCH in 1969 when returned with the largest number of votes in the history of the state (ninety-three) to again lead a coalition of Fianna Fáil and the Progressive Democrats. That December his government introduced the first budget deficit in five years.

Aiken, Frank (1898–1983), politician (Fianna Fáil); born in Camlough, Co. Armagh. A member of the Irish Volunteers from 1913 and the Gaelic League from 1914, he was a Sinn Féin organiser from 1917 and commandant of the 4th Northern Division of the IRA during the WAR OF INDEPENDENCE. Opposed to the ANGLO-IRISH TREATY, he wished to remain neutral during the CIVIL WAR but was drawn into the conflict. As chief of staff in succession to LIAM LYNCH he issued the Cease-Fire and Dump Arms Order that ended the war, 23 May 1923. A founder-member of FIANNA FÁIL, he represented Co. Louth, 1927–73, holding several ministerial offices: Defence, 1932–39,

Co-ordination of Defensive Measures, 1939–45, Finance, 1945–48, External Affairs, 1951–54, 1957–68, and Agriculture, March–May 1957. He was Tánaiste from 1965 until his retirement to the back benches in 1969.

At the United Nations, Aiken articulated Ireland's support for the non-proliferation of nuclear weapons and, from 1957, for the admission of China to membership.

Aikenhead, Mary (1787–1858), religious leader, founder of the Sisters of Charity; born in Cork. A convert to Catholicism, 1802, she spent three years in a novitiate at York before returning to Dublin to open the first convent of the Irish Sisters of Charity at the North William Street Orphanage, Dublin. Professed as Sister Mary Augustine, 1 September 1815, she became Mother-General of the new order. Having bought the town house of Lord Meath in St Stephen's Green, Dublin, for £3,000, she opened it as St Vincent's Hospital, with accommodation for twelve female patients, 23 January 1834, the first Catholic hospital in Ireland since the Reformation and the first in Ireland to be served by nuns. She established twelve convents as well as schools and an asylum for penitents, and saw the order extend to England and Australia.

Ailtirí na hAiséirí ('architects of the resurgence'), a right-wing nationalist organisation founded by Gearóid Ó Cuinneagáin, March 1942, after a split in Craobh na hAiseirí of the GAELIC LEAGUE; another Belfastman, Proinsias Mac an Bheatha, established a rival organisation, Glúin na Bua ('generation of victory'). It served as a vehicle for Ó Cuinneagáin in his aim of establishing a 'corporate State based on the 1916 Proclamation.' In the 1943 and 1944 general elections Aiséirí candidates fared poorly: Ó Cuinneagáin secured 607 votes in Dublin North-West, Seán Ó Dubhghaill got 1,019 in Cork, Eoin Ó Coigligh got 585 in Co. Louth, and Tomás Ó Dochartaigh got 926 in Co. Waterford. In the 1944 general election its seven candidates lost their deposits. Supporters in Limerick included SEÁN SOUTH. Some members of the organisation were later active in CLANN NA POBLACHTA.

Alderdice, John, Lord Alderdice (born 1955), psychiatrist and politician, educated at QUB. Alderdice was a consultant psychiatrist at Belfast City Hospital. After joining the ALLIANCE PARTY, 1978, he failed to win a seat in Lisburn in 1981; he was leader of the party, 1987–98. He sought a review of the operation of the ANGLO-IRISH AGREEMENT (1985), believing that the Unionist demand for suspension was unrealistic. In November 1992 he confirmed that the Alliance Party had reached 'broad agreement' with the ULSTER UNIONIST PARTY and the DEMOCRATIC UNIONIST PARTY on a system of devolution. Under his leadership the party enjoyed good relations with FINE GAEL and the PROGRESSIVE DEMOCRATS in the Republic and with the Liberal Democrats in Britain. He expressed interest in the Forum proposal in the DOWNING STREET DECLARATION (1993) and attended the FORUM ON PEACE AND RECONCILIATION in Dublin. In February 1995 he led his party into formal talks with Sinn Féin. The party won seven seats in the Northern Ireland Forum elections, May 1996. Alderdice was made a life peer on the nomination of the Liberal Democrats, August 1996, and supported the BELFAST AGREEMENT (1998). His party won only six seats in the new Northern Ireland Assembly elected under the agreement. Following his resignation from the leadership he was appointed presiding officer of the Assembly.

Aliens Act (1935). Introduced in tandem with the IRISH NATIONALITY AND CITIZENSHIP ACT (1935), it defined as aliens all those who were not citizens of the Irish Free State, including British subjects.

Allan, Fred (1861–1937), Fenian; born in Dublin into a Methodist family, educated at Central Model Schools, Marlborough Street. A clerk with the Great Northern Railway, he was influenced by the writings of Karl Marx and JOHN MITCHEL. He was a leading member of the IRISH REPUBLICAN BROTHERHOOD and the Young Ireland Society and worked on the FREEMAN'S JOURNAL until it became anti-Parnellite, 1891. He joined the Parnellite *Irish Daily Independent* (see IRISH INDEPENDENT), of which he became business manager, turning the newspaper office into a virtual IRB headquarters. While secretary to the IRB Supreme Council he co-ordinated the CENTENARY CELEBRATIONS (1898). He was dismissed from the *Independent,* March 1899, when the paper came under new ownership. As private secretary to the lord mayor of Dublin he was criticised by republicans for organising a children's *fête* during Queen Victoria's visit to Dublin, April 1900, but managed to retain his membership of the IRB and exercised influence in the organisation through the Wolfe Tone Clubs. An able organiser, from 1901 he was secretary of Dublin Corporation's Electric Light Company, Cleansing Department and Public Lighting Committee until 1922.

Increasingly alienated from the younger generation of republicans, Allan resigned from the IRB, March 1912. He supported the IRISH VOLUNTEERS and after the EASTER RISING (1916) was a trustee of the IRISH NATIONAL AID ASSOCIATION and IRISH VOLUNTEERS' DEPENDANTS' FUND. He supported Sinn Féin, working in DÁIL COURTS during the WAR OF INDEPENDENCE, during which he was imprisoned on four occasions. He supported the ANGLO-IRISH TREATY and served on the executive of CUMANN NA NGAEDHEAL. A civil servant in the Department of Industry and Commerce from 1922, he played a prominent role in the establishment of the SHANNON SCHEME.

All-for-Ireland League, founded by WILLIAM O'BRIEN, 31 March 1910, following rejection by the UNITED IRISH LEAGUE of his proposal for a LAND CONFERENCE; its motto was *Conference, conciliation, consent.* O'Brien's belief that a solution to the national question should be sought through conference was not shared by the majority of the IRISH PARTY, from which he resigned. Strongest in O'Brien's Cork hinterland, where it won eight seats in the 1910 general election, the league opposed partition, declaring, 'All for Ireland, Ireland for all.' Prominent Unionist members included the EARL OF DUNRAVEN AND MOUNT EARL and Lord Barrymore (see A. H. SMITH-BARRY). The league was critical of REDMOND's acceptance of the (third) HOME RULE BILL. It became moribund in 1916 following O'Brien's call for support for the British war effort. O'Brien and T. M. HEALY represented the league at the MANSION HOUSE CONFERENCE (1918). Its parliamentary members did not contest the general election of December 1918.

Alliance Party, a political party founded in Belfast, 21 April 1970, by OLIVER NAPIER (who led it from 1972 to 1984) and Robert Cooper. It had its origins in the NEW ULSTER MOVEMENT and sought to provide a middle ground between nationalists and unionists. It had support from the NORTHERN IRELAND LABOUR PARTY. In 1972 three sitting members at Stormont (two unionists and one nationalist) sat for the party. It won sixty-three seats in the district council elections, May 1973. Supporting 'power-sharing' (multi-party government), the party won eight seats in the Northern Ireland Assembly, June 1973 (see NORTHERN IRELAND). It joined with the SOCIAL DEMOCRATIC AND LABOUR PARTY and pro-Assembly unionists, led by BRIAN FAULKNER, to form a power-sharing Executive. The party had one voting member in the Executive, Oliver Napier (Minister of Law Reform), and two non-voting members, Basil Glass (deputy chief whip) and Robert Cooper (Minister of Manpower). It won eight seats in the 1975 Convention election and seventy seats in the 1977 district council elections.

The party failed to gain a seat in the British House of Commons in 1979 and fared poorly in the European Parliament elections. David Cook, an Alliance councillor, became the first non-unionist lord mayor of Belfast, 1978–79. The party supported the 'rolling devolution' initiative of JIM PRIOR in 1982. In October it won ten seats in the Assembly elections. Under its new leader, JOHN CUSHNAHAN, it lost four of its thirty-eight seats in the 1985 district council elections. It lost unionist support when it supported the ANGLO-IRISH AGREEMENT (1985). Cushnahan resigned in September 1987, and DR JOHN ALDERDICE became the new party leader in October. In October 1988 the party called for a devolved power-sharing government, which would have an equal role with the Republic in a new tripartite Anglo-Irish Agreement Conference. The party suffered from the entry of the Conservative Party into Northern politics: in North Down it received less than half the Conservative vote. By 1992 it was in broad agreement with the ULSTER UNIONIST PARTY and DEMOCRATIC UNIONIST PARTY on a scheme for devolution, which resulted in a breach with the SDLP. It had three seats at the FORUM FOR PEACE AND RECONCILIATION in Dublin.

In February 1995 party members had their first formal meeting with SINN FÉIN in Belfast. Supporting the 'twin-track' process, the party made submissions on the decommissioning of arms to GEORGE MITCHELL. It secured seven of the eighteen seats it contested in elections to the Northern Ireland Forum. Having supported the BELFAST AGREEMENT (1998), it fared poorly in the Assembly elections, winning six of the eighteen seats it contested. Alderdice resigned to become presiding officer of the new Assembly and was succeeded by SEÁN NEESON.

The party failed to return any of its ten candidates in the elections to the British House of Commons on 7 June 2001, while in the local elections held on the same day it retained 28 of its 41 seats and, crucially, held the balance of power in Belfast City Council. Under a new leader, David Ford, party members temporarily redesignated themselves 'unionist' to enable DAVID TRIMBLE to be elected First Minister, 7 November 2001.

All-Ireland Committee, founded in February 1897 to seek the return of taxes determined by a Royal Commission as overpaid since the Union. Members included E. J. SAUNDERSON, JOHN REDMOND, T. M. HEALY, HORACE PLUNKETT, and JOHN DILLON. It had little tangible impact.

All-Party Anti-Partition Committee (also called the Mansion House Committee), established in January 1949 and consisting of the Taoiseach, JOHN A. COSTELLO, WILLIAM NORTON, SEÁN MACBRIDE, ÉAMON DE VALERA, and FRANK AIKEN; the treasurer was CEARBHALL Ó DÁLAIGH. It organised a public collection, the Mansion House Fund, for the peaceful reunification of Ireland and sponsored the publication of anti-partition propaganda, including *The Finances of Partition* and *Indivisible Ireland*. With the ANTI-PARTITION LEAGUE it helped finance anti-partition candidates in Northern Ireland and the establishment of an Anti-Partition League in England.

Ambrose, Robert (1855–1940), surgeon and politician (nationalist, anti-Parnellite); born in Limerick, educated at Queen's University. As member of Parliament for West Mayo, 1893–1910, he introduced the first bill for compulsory land purchase in Ireland, 1897. He also introduced a bill to grant county councils compulsory purchase powers to acquire land for reclamation and resale to the landless sons of small farmers, with mineral rights remaining with the councils. He wrote on peasant proprietorship for England, Scotland, and Wales. His best-known work was *A Plea for the Industrial Regeneration of Ireland* (1909).

American Association for the Recognition of the Irish Republic, launched in Washington by ÉAMON DE VALERA, 16 November 1920. It attempted to heal the division within the FRIENDS OF IRISH FREEDOM and to raise money for the Republican cause during the WAR OF INDEPENDENCE. De Valera's representative on the association was JAMES O'MARA. At its peak the association claimed 700,000 members, but, weakened by the split in the republican movement caused by the ANGLO-IRISH TREATY, its influence had declined by 1926.

American Commission of Inquiry on Conditions in Ireland, launched by Dr W. J. Moloney and Frank P. Walsh, August 1920, to investigate alleged excesses by Crown forces during the WAR OF INDEPENDENCE. Drawn from thirty-six American states, the committee was representative of municipalities, education, the press, and leaders of labour and industry. It called witnesses from Ireland and invited EARL FRENCH and HAMAR GREENWOOD to attend, but no British witness attended. The committee's interim report drew world attention to conditions in Ireland, served to increase pressure on the British government to sue for a cessation of hostilities, and led to the founding of the WHITE CROSS, January 1921.

American Land League, founded in New York by CHARLES STEWART PARNELL, MICHAEL DAVITT and JOHN DILLON, March 1880. The majority of the league's seven-member committee, including JOHN DEVOY, were members of CLAN NA GAEL. Through its treasurer, Father Walsh of Waterbury, Connecticut, more than $500,000 was channelled to the LAND LEAGUE.

'American Note', a note delivered by the US government to the Irish government, 21 February 1944, demanding the removal of German and Japanese representatives from Irish soil. The Americans claimed that such diplomats had 'the opportunity for highly organised espionage.' A week later the Irish representative in Washington, ROBERT BRENNAN, called to the State Department (without an appointment) and stated that he personally interpreted the note as an ultimatum; he was assured that the note was not an ultimatum and that no invasion was contemplated. In a reply to the note on 7 March, ÉAMON DE VALERA stated that the Irish government had prevented attempts to use Ireland as a base for spying and restated Ireland's neutrality in relation to the belligerents. The American reply reiterated the original request; but Britain had informed the State Department that Ireland was prepared to provide co-operation in adopting whatever security safeguards the British and Americans desired.

'American wake', the practice of holding a 'wake' for emigrants on the eve of departure to America, common from c. 1830. Describing the practice to a researcher, an old man explained: 'There was very little difference between going to America and going to the grave, one was unlikely to return from either.' It was customary for the departing emigrant to call to the houses of friends and neighbours, inviting them to the 'wake', to be held at his or her home the night before departure. Neighbours brought gifts, usually home-made produce, such as hard-boiled eggs, butter, and bread, to be eaten on the voyage. It was a matter of honour for the parents of the departing that food, tobacco and drink be on hand for the guests. In many instances the food was bought on credit, with payment forthcoming on the arrival of the first 'money from America' letter. The 'wake' lasted until first light, when guests would accompany the traveller on the first leg of the journey, often to a prominent point from which the emigrant could be watched until out of sight. In many areas priests blessed the emigrant at the doorstep before departure.

Amnesty Association, originally the Irish Liberation Society, launched on 29 June 1869 by JOHN 'AMNESTY' NOLAN (secretary) and ISAAC BUTT (first president) to obtain the release of those imprisoned under the TREASON FELONY ACT (1848). Frederick Engels and Karl Marx assisted the efforts of the association through the International Working Men's Association. In response to the agitation, forty-nine prisoners were released. Police reports showed that between July and October 1869 an estimated 638,000 people attended 411 amnesty meetings or demonstrations. When Butt founded the HOME GOVERNMENT ASSOCIATION in 1870 the Amnesty Association provided valuable support. More prisoners were released in January 1871.

The association's agitation continued until 1872, by which time it had secured the release of important Fenians, including JOHN DEVOY and JEREMIAH O'DONOVAN ROSSA. It resumed activities in the 1890s to secure the release from imprisonment of convicted dynamiters, when a leading role was played by MAUD GONNE. (See AMNESTY ASSOCIATION OF GREAT BRITAIN.)

Amnesty Association of Great Britain, founded in London by DR MARK RYAN, 23 January 1892; the various branches amalgamated in Liverpool to form the Amnesty Association of Great Britain, August 1894. The first president was Arthur Lynch; prominent members included JOHN MACBRIDE. It remained in existence until it had fulfilled its task of securing the release of imprisoned Fenians, the last of whom, THOMAS J. CLARKE, was released in 1898.

Ancient Order of Hibernians. The AOH took its modern form in Ireland in 1838 as a Catholic reaction to the Orange Order. Adopting as its motto *Fidelity to Faith and Fatherland* and including King James II, the shamrock and Catholic martyrs among its symbols, it established the fifteenth of August (the feast of the Assumption) as its marching day. Strongest in south Ulster, during the nineteenth century it became one of the leading Irish movements in the United States. In 1878 the order split over the admission of members of Irish descent rather than of Irish birth. The rift spread to Ireland in 1884 and continued until 4 March 1902, when a conference established the BOARD OF ERIN.

The AOH supported the IRISH PARTY in the struggle for HOME RULE. In 1904 JOSEPH DEVLIN became national president of the Board of Erin, which had represented a majority of the AOH membership, and employed the organisation in furthering a nationalist political agenda. As a reward for organising the Ulster nationalist vote the AOH was allowed an increased influence in the affairs of the Irish Party (in the six years from 1903 the AOH delegation to the national convention of the party was increased from 24 to 417). A further split developed in the AOH in 1905 over the decision to register as a friendly society. The order, which opposed WILLIAM O'BRIEN and the ALL-FOR-IRELAND LEAGUE, supported WILLIAM MARTIN MURPHY and the employers' federation in the DUBLIN LOCK-OUT (1913). During the 1920s it was the principal guardian of Catholic rights in NORTHERN IRELAND.

The American AOH, the largest Irish-American organisation, was founded at St James's Church, Oliver Street, New York, in 1836. During the 1880s it was dominated by CLAN NA GAEL, through which it was linked to the MOLLY MAGUIRES. It also financed a detachment of fifty members, the Hibernian Rifles, who were in action during the EASTER RISING (1916). There is a parallel women's organisation, the Ladies' Ancient Order of Hibernians.

Anderson, Sir Robert (1841–1918), civil servant and author; born in Dublin, educated at TCD and called to the bar. A member of the Secret Service from 1867, he became adviser on political crimes to the Home Office, 1868, in which capacity he was the London spymaster of the informer HENRI LE CARON in America. He investigated the FENIANS and the DYNAMITERS of the 1880s; he supplied the *Times* with material for the Parnell Commission (see 'PARNELLISM AND CRIME') and was the author of the second series of articles, using material provided by Le Caron. He was head of the Criminal Investigation Department, 1888–1901. His most enduring work, *Criminals and Crime,* was published in 1907.

Andrews, C. S. [Christopher Stephen] 'Tod' (1901–1985), public servant; born in Dublin, educated at UCD. A participant in the WAR OF INDEPENDENCE, he rejected the ANGLO-IRISH TREATY and served as adjutant to LIAM LYNCH in the CIVIL WAR, when he was wounded and several times imprisoned. He worked for the Irish Tourist Association and the ESB. Joining the Department of Industry and Commerce under SEÁN LEMASS, 1932, he was seconded to the Turf Development Board (later Bord na Móna, of which he became managing director). During the years of the Second World War he served as Fuel Director for the state. A founder-member and president of the Institute of Management, chairman of the Irish Railways Clearing House Committee, chairman of the Board of CIE, 1958–66, and of the RTE Authority, 1966–71, and a member of the Arts Council, he published two volumes of autobiography, *Dublin Made Me* (1979) and *Man of No Property* (1982).

Andrews, John Miller (1871–1956), politician (Ulster Unionist); born in Comber, Co. Down, educated at RBAI. A prominent Unionist and member of the ORANGE ORDER, with CARSON he sat as a non-labour member of the Ulster Unionist Labour Association, 1918. As Minister of Labour, 1921–37, he observed in 1933 that of the thirty-one porters employed at the Parliament Buildings there was only one Catholic—'there temporarily.' His threatened resignation from the cabinet if Northern Ireland was excluded from the free trade element of the Anglo-Irish Agreements (1938) was thwarted by the unilateral acceptance of the agreement by the Prime Minister, Craigavon. As Prime Minister, 1940–43, Andrews faced nationalist hostility to the proposed extension of conscription to Northern Ireland; apprised of his reservations, the British government concluded that conscription in Northern Ireland would be 'more trouble than it was worth.' Replaced as Prime Minister by Sir Basil Brooke (see VISCOUNT BROOKEBOROUGH) in 1943, Andrews remained leader of the UUP until 1946.

Anglesey, Henry William Paget, first Marquess of (1768–1854), Lord Lieutenant of Ireland, 1828–29, 1830–33; born in London, educated at the University of Oxford. Appointed to Ireland by the DUKE OF WELLINGTON, he supported CATHOLIC EMANCIPATION and reforms in the fields of education and TITHES. Though officially recalled in January 1829, he did not leave his Irish post until March. He returned to the post in 1830, but his second term was not successful: he was at odds with O'Connell over the repeal of the Corn Laws, and he introduced COERCION to deal with the increase in crime caused by the anti-tithes campaign. The system of NATIONAL EDUCATION introduced by Lord Stanley in 1831 owed much to the endeavour and influence of Anglesey.

Anglo-Irish Agreement ('Hillsborough Agreement') (1985), signed at Hillsborough Castle, Co. Down, by the British government (Conservative) and Irish government (coalition of Fine Gael and Labour Party), 15 November 1985. It was the first time that a British government had conceded a role to the Republic in the affairs of NORTHERN IRELAND. Registered at the United Nations, the agreement, containing twelve clauses, provided for the establishment of an Intergovernmental Conference, to be headed by the Secretary of State for Northern Ireland and the Minister for Foreign Affairs, to promote cross-border co-operation and to deal with security (including the Northern Ireland Police Authority, the Police Complaints Board, and prisons, including the examination of individual cases of prisoners), legal, administrative and political matters, and a permanent secretariat of Northern and Southern civil servants. This functioned despite Unionist opposition. Under Article 1 (*c*) no change could occur in the constitutional status of Northern Ireland without the consent of a majority in Northern Ireland. Under Article 4, both governments supported a measure of devolution, provided the terms were acceptable to the 'constitutional representatives of both traditions . . .'

The agreement was approved by both parliaments by the end of November 1985. In the House of Commons it was approved by 473 to 47, one of the biggest majorities in the history of the Parliament. However, it provoked violent reactions among Ulster loyalists and was also opposed by FIANNA FÁIL, then in opposition. Condemning it as unacceptable to all sections of unionist opinion, MARY ROBINSON resigned from the LABOUR PARTY. Provisional SINN FÉIN and unionist parties also condemned it. JAMES MOLYNEAUX and IAN PAISLEY united in opposition under the slogan *Ulster says No.* All fifteen Unionist MPs resigned their seats, leading to by-elections, in which Unionists put up dummy candidates all called 'Peter Barry' (the name of the Minister for Foreign Affairs). Loyalists called for a 'day of action' on 3 March 1986, when roads throughout Northern Ireland were barricaded. The APPRENTICE BOYS defied a ban to parade on 31 March 1986 in Portadown, forcing their way through the (Catholic) Garvaghy Road district, leading to further violence when the RUC enforced the ban (using plastic bullets).

The Anglo-Irish Agreement was superseded by the BELFAST AGREEMENT (1998).

Anglo-Irish Agreements (1938). Signed in London by ÉAMON DE VALERA and NEVILLE CHAMBERLAIN, 25 April 1938, the three agreements, covering defence, finance, and trade, marked the end of the ECONOMIC WAR. Chamberlain's decision to return the TREATY PORTS was influenced by his Joint Chiefs of Staff, who concluded that the manpower and logistical arrangements required to hold the ports could best be employed elsewhere. The return of the ports, denounced by WINSTON CHURCHILL, enabled the Irish state to declare itself neutral during the Second World War. Under the economic agreement, Ireland agreed to pay £10 million in full settlement of all British claims (which totalled £104 million); this amount covered the LAND ANNUITIES, the withholding of which had precipitated the Economic War. The commercial agreement reopened the British market to Irish cattle and food products, while Ireland allowed duty-free access to British goods. Generally well received in the British press and in political circles, in Ireland the agreements were considered a triumph for de Valera, assisting him to an electoral landslide some two months later.

Anglo-Irish Free Trade Area Agreement (1965), an agreement that gave Irish industry immediate tariff-free access to the British market. Coming into effect on 1 July 1966, it also guaranteed a market for sheep and store cattle and provided for an increased butter quota. Ireland in return contracted to reduce tariffs against imports from Britain by 10 per cent per annum, setting 1975 as the target for full free trade between the two countries.

The agreement formed an important element of Irish economic policy during the 1960s (see PROGRAMMES FOR ECONOMIC EXPANSION). Irish agricultural and horticultural produce would not be regulated except by intergovernmental commodity agreement or some other arrangement. The British government also undertook to afford opportunities for the growth of imports from Ireland on terms no less favourable than those granted to British farmers. Under the agreement there was to be freedom of access to Irish fish and fishery products. Protective duties on textiles and clothing containing synthetic fibres were to be eliminated. Agricultural exports showed an increase in 1967 as a result of the agreement: store cattle exports were 620,000 head, compared with an annual average of 510,000 in 1962–66, and beef exports were 730,000 head, compared with an annual average of 340,000 in 1963–66.

Anglo-Irish Intergovernmental Council (1982), approved following a meeting in Dublin between the Taoiseach, GARRET FITZGERALD, and the Prime Minister, MARGARET THATCHER, in Dublin, 20 January 1982. The plan envisaged a four-tier structure, at ministerial, official, parliamentary and advisory committee levels. The first ministerial meeting took place on 29 January 1982, when the Secretary of State for Northern Ireland, JIM PRIOR, and the Minister for Foreign Affairs, Jim Dooge, met in London. The conference was superseded by provisions of the ANGLO-IRISH AGREEMENT (1985).

Anglo-Irish Trade Agreement (1948), an agreement under which the prices of Irish cattle and sheep were linked to prevailing British market prices. (See also ANGLO-IRISH FREE TRADE AREA AGREEMENT.)

Anglo-Irish Treaty (1921), the name generally given to the Articles of Agreement for a Treaty between Great Britain and Ireland, 6 December 1921. The WAR OF INDEPENDENCE, which had broken out on 21 January 1919, the same day on which SINN FÉIN representatives formed the first DÁIL ÉIREANN and reaffirmed the Irish Republic, ended with a TRUCE on 11 July 1921. Three days later ÉAMON DE VALERA, President of Dáil Éireann, met DAVID LLOYD GEORGE, the British Prime Minister, in London. De Valera found Lloyd George's proposal of dominion HOME RULE STATUS unacceptable. This rejection was endorsed by Dáil Éireann and relayed to Lloyd George on 24 August.

As President of the Irish Republic (since August), de Valera accredited five members of his government to open negotiations with Britain in October on the basis of the 'GAIRLOCH FORMULA' proposed by Lloyd George:

In virtue of the authority vested in me by Dáil Éireann, I hereby appoint Arthur Griffith, T.D., Minister for Foreign Affairs; Michael Collins, T.D., Minister for Finance; Robert C. Barton, T.D., Minister for Economic Affairs; Edmund J. Duggan, T.D., and George Gavan Duffy, T.D., as Envoys Plenipotentiary of the Republic of Ireland to negotiate and conclude on behalf of Ireland, representatives of His Majesty George V, a treaty or treaties of settlement, association and accommodation between Ireland and the community of nations known as the British Commonwealth. In witness thereof I hereunder subscribe my name as President.

Éamon de Valera.

Griffith, Collins, Barton, Duggan and Gavan Duffy were given the following written instructions:

1. The Plenipotentiaries have full powers as defined in their credentials.
2. It is understood, before decisions are finally reached on main questions, that a dispatch notifying the intention to make decisions will be sent to members of the cabinet in Dublin, and that a reply will be awaited by the Plenipotentiaries before the final decision is made.
3. It is also understood that a complete text of the draft Treaty about to be signed will be submitted to Dublin, and reply awaited.
4. In case of a break, the text of the final proposals from our side will be similarly submitted.
5. It is understood that the Cabinet in Dublin will be kept regularly informed of the progress of the negotiations.

Full negotiations with the British representatives began in London on 11 October. The British side consisted of Lloyd George, the EARL OF BIRKENHEAD, WINSTON CHURCHILL, SIR HAMAR GREENWOOD, Austen Chamberlain, L. Worthington-Evans, and Gordon Hewart. During the negotiations de Valera continued to press the Irish delegates to seek his formula of EXTERNAL ASSOCIATION, which had earlier been rejected by Lloyd George.

The draft of the Treaty (or Articles of Agreement) discussed throughout October and November was presented to the Ministry (government) in Dublin, and rejected on 3 December. There was dissatisfaction about the status Ireland would have (dominion status), the form and degree of association with the British Empire, the OATH OF ALLEGIANCE, and the question of the future of the six counties of NORTHERN IRELAND (established since June 1921). The delegates understood, as they returned to London, that the document would not be signed until it had once more been referred back to the Ministry in Dublin.

Negotiations with the British were resumed on 4 December and continued throughout the next day. On the evening of 5 December, Lloyd George confronted Griffith with an ultimatum: the Irish must sign the document, or the war would be resumed within three days. Following further discussions among the Irish delegates the Treaty was signed at 2:20 a.m. on 6 December. 'Southern Ireland' was to become a Free State with full dominion status within the British Empire.

At a Ministry meeting on 8 December the Treaty was accepted by four votes to three: for acceptance were Griffith, Collins, Barton, and W. T. Cosgrave; against were de Valera, CATHAL BRUGHA, and AUSTIN STACK. De Valera then published a repudiation of the document. The Dáil debates on the Treaty continued throughout the Christmas period until 7 January 1922, when it was accepted by 64 votes to 57.

De Valera and his followers refused to recognise the PROVISIONAL GOVERNMENT, which was then established under the chairmanship of Collins. They did recognise the government of Dáil Éireann, of which Griffith was elected President in place of de Valera. The British government recognised only the Provisional Government for the purpose of handing over authority in the IRISH FREE STATE, which came into existence on 6 December 1922.

In the general election of 16 June 1922, the 'PACT ELECTION', 620,283 votes were cast: 239,193 pro-Treaty, 133,864 anti-Treaty, and 247,226 for others. Fifty-eight pro-Treaty candidates were returned, thirty-five anti-Treaty, seventeen for the Labour Party, seven Farmers, four Unionists, and seven independents. At the end of the month the attack by Provisional Government forces on the Republican garrison in the FOUR COURTS, Dublin, precipitated the CIVIL WAR. Over the protests of the British government, the Treaty was registered as an international instrument with the League of Nations in Geneva (11 May 1924).

The text of the Treaty is as follows:

1. Ireland shall have the same constitutional status in the community of Nations known as the British Empire as the Dominion of Canada, the Commonwealth of Australia, the Dominion of New Zealand, and the Union of South Africa, with a parliament having powers to make laws for the peace, order and good government of Ireland and an Executive responsible to that parliament, and shall be styled and known as the Irish Free State.

2. Subject to the provisions hereinafter set out, the position of the Irish Free State in relation to the Imperial parliament and government and otherwise shall be that of the Dominion of Canada, and the law, practice and constitutional usage governing the relationship of the Crown or the representative of the Crown and of the Imperial parliament to the Dominion of Canada shall govern their relationship to the Irish Free State.
3. The representative of the Crown in Ireland shall be appointed in like manner as the Governor-General of Canada, and in accordance with the practice observed in the making of such appointments.
4. The oath to be taken by members of the parliament of the Irish Free State shall be in the following form: I . . . do solemnly swear true faith and allegiance to the Constitution of the Irish Free State as by law established and that I will be faithful to H.M. King George V, his heirs and successors by law in virtue of the common citizenship of Ireland with Great Britain and her adherence to and membership of the group of nations forming the British Commonwealth of Nations.
5. The Irish Free State shall assume liability for the service of the Public Debt of the United Kingdom as existing at the date hereof and toward the payment of War Pensions as existing at that date in such proportion as may be fair and equitable, having regard to any just claims on the part of Ireland by way of set-off or counter-claim, the amount of such sums being determined in default of agreement by the arbitration of one or more independent persons being citizens of the British Empire.
6. Until an arrangement has been made between the British and Irish governments whereby the Irish Free State undertakes her own coastal defence, the defence by sea of Great Britain and Ireland shall be undertaken by His Majesty's Imperial Forces. But this shall not prevent the construction or maintenance by the government of the Irish Free State of such vessels as are necessary for the protection of the Revenue or the Fisheries. The foregoing provisions of this Article shall be reviewed at a conference of Representatives of the British and Irish governments, to be held at the expiration of five years from the date hereof with a view to the undertaking by Ireland of a share in her own coastal defence.
7. The government of the Irish Free State shall afford to His Majesty's Imperial Forces:
   (*a*) In time of peace such harbour and other facilities as are indicated in the Annex hereto, or such other facilities as may from time to time be agreed between the British government and the government of the Irish Free State; and
   (*b*) In time of war or of strained relations with a Foreign Power, such harbour and other facilities as the British government may require for the purposes of such defence as aforesaid.
8. With a view to securing the observance of the principle of international limitation of armaments, if the government of the Irish Free State establishes and maintains a military defence force, the establishments thereof shall not exceed in size such proportion of the military establishments maintained in Great Britain as that which the population of Ireland bears to the population of Great Britain.
9. The ports of Great Britain and the Irish Free State shall be freely open to the ships of the other country on payment of the customary port and other duties.
10. The government of the Irish Free State agrees to pay fair compensation on terms not less favourable than those accorded by the Act of 1920 to judges, officials, members of Police Forces, and other Public Servants who are discharged by it or who retire in consequence of the change of government effected in pursuance hereof.

    Provided that this agreement shall not apply to members of the Auxiliary Police Force or to persons recruited in Great Britain for the Royal Irish Constabulary during the two years next preceding the date hereof. The British government will assume responsibility for such compensation or pensions as may be payable to any of these excepted persons.
11. Until the expiration of one month from the passing of the Act of Parliament for the ratification of this instrument, the powers of the parliament and the government of the Irish Free State shall not be exercisable as respects Northern Ireland, and the provisions of the Government of Ireland Act, 1920, shall, so far as they relate to Northern Ireland, remain in full force and effect, and no election shall be held for the return of members to serve in the parliament of the Irish Free State for constituencies in Northern Ireland, unless a resolution is passed by both houses of the parliament of Northern Ireland in favour of holding such election before the end of the said month.
12. If, before the expiration of the said month, an address is presented to His Majesty by both houses of parliament of Northern Ireland to that effect, the powers of the parliament and government of the Irish Free State shall no longer extend to Northern Ireland, and the provisions of the Government of Ireland Act, 1920 (including those relating to the Council of Ireland) shall, so far as they relate to Northern Ireland, continue to be of full force and effect, and this instrument shall have effect subject to the necessary modifications.

    Provided that if such an address is so presented a Commission consisting of three persons, one to be appointed by the government of the Irish Free State, one to be appointed by the government of Northern Ireland and one who shall be Chairman to be appointed by the British government shall determine in accordance with the wishes of the inhabitants, so far as may be compatible with economic and geographic conditions, the boundaries between Northern Ireland and the rest of Ireland, and for purposes of the Government of Ireland Act, 1920, and of this instrument, the boundary of Northern Ireland shall be such as may be determined by such Commission.

13. For the purpose of the last foregoing article, the powers of the parliament of Southern Ireland under the Government of Ireland Act, 1920, to elect members of the Council of Ireland shall, after the parliament of the Irish Free State is constituted, be exercised by that parliament.

14. After the expiration of the said month, if no such address as is mentioned in Article 12 hereof is presented, the parliament and government of Northern Ireland shall continue to exercise as respects Northern Ireland the powers conferred on them by the Government of Ireland Act, 1920, but the parliament and government of the Irish Free State shall in Northern Ireland have in relation to matters in respect of which the parliament of Northern Ireland has not power to make laws under that Act (including matters which under the said Act are within the jurisdiction of the Council of Ireland) the same powers as in the rest of Ireland, subject to such other provisions as may be agreed in manner hereinafter appearing.

15. At any time after the date hereof the government of Northern Ireland and the Provisional Government of Southern Ireland hereinafter constituted may meet for the purpose of discussing the provisions subject to which the last foregoing article is to operate in the event of no such address as is therein mentioned being presented and those provisions may include:

(*a*) Safeguards with regard to patronage in Northern Ireland;

(*b*) Safeguards with regard to the collection of revenue in Northern Ireland:

(*c*) Safeguards with regard to import and export duties affecting the trade or industry of Northern Ireland:

(*d*) Safeguards for minorities in Northern Ireland:

(*e*) The settlement of the financial relations between Northern Ireland and the Irish Free State:

(*f*) The establishment and powers of a local militia in Northern Ireland and the relations of the Defence Forces of the Irish Free State and of Northern Ireland respectively:

and if at any such meeting provisions are agreed to, the same shall have effect as if they were included amongst the provisions subject to which the powers of the parliament and government of the Irish Free State are to be exercisable in Northern Ireland under Article 14 hereof.

16. Neither the parliament of the Irish Free State nor the parliament of Northern Ireland shall make any law so as either directly or indirectly to endow any religion or prohibit or restrict the free exercise thereof or give any preference or impose any disability on account of religious belief or religious status or affect prejudicially the right of any child to attend a school receiving public money without attending the religious instruction at the school or make any discrimination as respects State aid between schools under the management of different religious denominations or divert from any religious denomination or any educational institution any of its property except for public utility purposes and on payment of compensation.

17. By way of provisional arrangement for the administration of Southern Ireland during the interval which must elapse between the date hereof and the constitution of a parliament and government of the Irish Free State in accordance therewith, steps shall be taken forthwith for summoning a meeting of members of parliament elected for constituencies in Southern Ireland since the passing of the Government of Ireland Act, 1920, and for constituting a Provisional Government, and the British Government shall take the steps necessary to transfer to such Provisional Government the powers and machinery requisite for the discharge of its duties, provided that every member of such Provisional Government shall have signified in writing his or her acceptance of this instrument. But this arrangement shall not continue in force beyond the expiration of twelve months from the date hereof.

18. This instrument shall be submitted forthwith by His Majesty's Government for the approval of parliament and by the Irish signatories to a meeting summoned for the purpose of the members elected to sit in the House of Commons of Southern Ireland, and if approved shall be ratified by the necessary legislation.

On behalf of the Irish Delegation.
Signed
Art Ó Griobhtha [Arthur Griffith]
Micheál Ó Coileáin [Michael Collins]
Riobárd Bartún [Robert Barton]
Eudhmonn Ó Dugáin [Éamonn Duggan]
Seórsa Ghabháin Uí Dhubhthaigh [George Gavan Duffy]

On behalf of the British Delegation.
Signed
D. Lloyd George
Austen Chamberlain
Birkenhead
Winston S. Churchill
L. Worthington-Evans
Hamar Greenwood
Gordon Hewart
6th December 1921

ANNEX

1. The following are the specific facilities required:

Dockyard port at Berehaven

(*a*) Admiralty property and rights to be retained as at the date hereof. Harbour defences to remain in charge of British care and maintenance parties.

Queenstown

(*b*) Harbour defences to remain in charge of British care and maintenance parties. Certain mooring buoys to be retained for use of His Majesty's ships.

Belfast Lough

(*c*) Harbour defences to remain in charge of British care and maintenance parties.

Lough Swilly

(*d*) Harbour defences to remain in charge of British care and maintenance parties.

Aviation

(*e*) Facilities in the neighbourhood of the above ports for coastal defence by air.

Oil Fuel Storage

(*f*) Haulbowline, Rathmullen. To be offered for sale to commercial companies under guarantee that purchasers shall maintain a certain minimum stock for Admiralty purposes.

2. A Convention shall be made between the British government and the government of the Irish Free State to give effect to the following conditions:

(*a*) That submarine cables shall not be landed or wireless stations for communication with places outside Ireland be established except by agreement with the British government; that the existing cable landing rights and wireless concessions shall not be withdrawn except by agreement with the British government; and that the British government shall be entitled to land additional submarine cables or establish additional wireless stations for communication with places outside Ireland.

(*b*) That lighthouses, buoys, beacons, and any navigational marks or navigational aids shall be maintained by the government of the Irish Free State as at the date hereof and shall not be removed or added to except by agreement with the British government.

(*c*) That war signal stations shall be closed down and left in charge of care and maintenance parties, the government of the Irish Free State being offered the option of taking them over and working them for commercial purposes subject to Admiralty inspection, and guaranteeing the upkeep of existing telegraphic communication therewith.

3. A Convention shall be made between the same governments for the regulation of civil communication by air.

Annaghdown Tragedy (4 September 1828). Eleven men and eight women lost their lives when an old rowing-boat foundered opposite Menlo Graveyard on Lough Corrib while transporting thirty-one passengers, ten sheep and a quantity of timber from Annaghdown to the fair at Fair Hill, Galway. When a sheep drove its leg through a plank, a passenger placed his coat over the hole and stamped on it, thus driving the plank from the bottom of the boat, which sank almost immediately. The event was the subject of the poem 'Eanach Dhúin' by Raiftearaí (Antaine Ó Reachtaire, 1779–1835), translated by DOUGLAS HYDE as 'The Drowning of Annach Doon'.

Ansbacher Inquiry, 1997–2002, an inquiry into an unlicensed banking system operated from 1971 by DES TRAYNOR, an employee of Guinness and Mahon Bank, Dublin. His Guinness Mahon Cayman Trust was bought by Henry Ansbacher of the Cayman Islands and renamed Ansbacher (Cayman) Ltd. In essence, Traynor's select list of wealthy customers opened offshore trusts and lodged money to offshore accounts through Traynor, who facilitated them in making withdrawals from their accounts in Dublin and organising loans backed by the secret offshore accounts. While the money was nominally abroad, it was actually available in Dublin. Many of those availing of this illegal banking system evaded paying tax.

The existence of the Ansbacher deposits became public on 30 June 1997, when the MCCRACKEN TRIBUNAL announced that, while examining the financial affairs of CHARLES HAUGHEY, it had uncovered offshore deposits lodged in Ireland and accessible to the depositors. In September 1997 the Minister for Enterprise, Trade and Employment, Mary Harney, authorised an accountant in her department, Gerry Ryan, to investigate the Ansbacher scheme. The MORIARTY TRIBUNAL was also established to investigate payments to politicians, including Haughey and the former Fine Gael minister Michael Lowry. The report, believed to contain 120 names, could not be published. While identifying £50 million placed on deposit in Guinness and Mahon in 1989, the investigator estimated that the offshore trusts could amount to hundreds of millions of pounds.

On the minister's application the High

Court appointed three inspectors to investigate the activities of Ansbacher, 22 September 1999: Declan Costello, a retired High Court Judge, Noreen P. Mackey, a barrister, and Paul F. Rowan, a retired accountant. Later Mr Justice Costello was replaced by Seán O'Leary, a judge of the Circuit Court, and Michael Cush, a barrister.

The inspectors' 10,000-page report, containing 190 names, including some of the most prominent in business circles, was presented to the High Court on 10 June 2002 and published on 6 July 2002. Mr Justice Finnegan directed that copies of the report be sent to the revenue authorities in Britain and the United States. The inspectors issued a *caveat* with the report, pointing out that 'a finding that any particular individual is a client of Ansbacher is *not* a finding that that person may have evaded tax.' They found that the failure of the Central Bank to gather information available to it resulted in the Ansbacher scheme continuing undetected for longer than it ought to have been. They also found evidence that certain companies and individuals conducted their financial affairs so as to defraud the Revenue Commissioners, or conspired with companies to do so.

Anti-Coercion Association, founded in 1880 by H. M. Hyndman (1842–1921) and other British radicals to gather support for the LAND LEAGUE. It used its paper, the *Radical,* to attack the Liberal government on its Irish policies, in which COERCION played a central part.

Anti-Partition League, established in 1947 to protest against the continuing partition of Ireland, supported by the NATIONALIST PARTY OF NORTHERN IRELAND. (See also ALL-PARTY ANTI-PARTITION COMMITTEE.)

Aontacht Éireann, a political party launched by KEVIN BOLAND and Seán Sherwin, 19 September 1971, after they left Fianna Fáil in protest at the government's handling of affairs in relation to Northern Ireland. It sought support for a united Ireland, and proposed that the Republic should assist republicans in Northern Ireland in attempts to end the British presence and partition. Until 1973 the party had one member in Dáil Éireann. Through Boland the party unsuccessfully challenged the SUNNINGDALE AGREEMENT in the High Court, claiming that the agreement violated articles 2 and 3 of the Constitution of Ireland. Following Boland's resignation in 1976 from the leadership of the party, it quickly faded away.

Appeal to the Irish Race for the Sustainment of the Irish National Land Movement, issued by the LAND LEAGUE at its inaugural meeting in the Imperial Hotel, Dublin, 21 October 1879. Directed to the Irish in America as well as to 'all whom evil laws have scattered the world over, as well as to all other nationalities who sympathise with a wronged and impoverished people,' the appeal was supported by JOHN DEVOY and resulted in financial assistance that enabled the Land League to continue its fight against the landlord system. $250,000 was pledged at a meeting in New York should an Irish MP visit America—which CHARLES STEWART PARNELL did two months later.

Apprentice Boys of Derry, a Protestant organisation founded in Derry in 1814, named for the apprentices who locked the gates of the city against King James II, thus precipitating the siege of the city (April–July 1689). It is closely associated with the ORANGE ORDER, and its annual march on 12 August attracts Orangemen from overseas. A demonstration on 18 December has as its purpose the burning in effigy of Colonel Lundy, who attempted to negotiate the surrender of the city during the siege. The parades sometimes provoke violence, as part of the route takes the marchers around the city walls overlooking the mainly Catholic Bogside area. (See also ROYAL BLACK PRECEPTORY.)

Arbitration Courts. During the agitation for repeal of the Union, DANIEL O'CONNELL proposed the establishment of arbitration courts to frustrate the operation of the Crown courts, and they operated for a brief period in 1843. The idea was revived during the WAR OF INDEPENDENCE, when British administration in Ireland was hampered by the SINN FÉIN takeover of local government. The Republicans also established Land Arbitration Courts to settle disputes over land division. (See also DÁIL COURTS.)

Arbour Hill, Dublin, a military detention centre, with accompanying church and graveyard, built in 1842. The executed leaders of the EASTER RISING (1916) are buried there. Closed after the evacuation of the twenty-six counties by the British army and the establishment of the Irish Free State, 1922, during the CIVIL WAR it was used to hold anti-Treatyite prisoners. Members of the IRA were held there during the 1930s in what were described as 'grim' conditions. It was reopened as a high-security civil prison in 1975.

Ardagh Chalice, an eighth-century silver chalice, 7 in. (180 mm) high, part of a hoard uncovered in 1868 by a labourer, Patrick Flanagan, while digging potatoes on the lands of James Quin at Reerasta Rath, Ardagh, Co. Limerick. The find, examined by Bishop Butler of Limerick and Lord Dunraven and Mount Earl, was sent to the Royal Irish Academy, which had it cleaned and assessed by the silversmiths Johnson and Donegan. Flanagan received a reward of £10 for the find. The hoard consisted of the silver chalice, a smaller bronze chalice, and four silver brooches. Considered one of the finest examples of Irish metalwork and one of the most outstanding artefacts from the golden age of Irish art, it was presented to the RIA in 1878 and later given to the National Museum.

Armagh Railway Disaster (12 June 1889), the greatest disaster in Irish railway history, in which eighty people died and almost four hundred were injured. The accident occurred on the annual Armagh–Warrenpoint excursion of the Armagh Methodist Sunday School. The engine stalled near the end of its climb on the Dobbin's Bridge gradient, and it was uncoupled and the train divided to facilitate the climb. During the uncoupling the front part of the train touched the rear portion, which careered down the steep incline and smashed into the 10:35 Armagh–Newry train. Following a *nolle prosequi* entered at Green Street Court, Dublin, Justice O'Brien discharged all concerned, 25 October 1889. As a consequence of the accident, legislation was enacted for the compulsory fitting of automatic brakes on passenger trains. (See also BUTTEVANT RAIL CRASH.)

Armour, Rev. James Brown ('Armour of Ballymoney') (1841–1928), clergyman (Presbyterian); born in Lisboy, Ballymoney, Co. Antrim, educated at Queen's College, Belfast. A Presbyterian minister in Ballymoney from 1869 and a prominent member of the Ulster Liberal Association, he was a strong opponent of sectarianism. Founder of the Intermediate School in Ballymoney and a lecturer at Magee College, Derry, he campaigned in support of tenant right (ULSTER CUSTOM) and HOME RULE and for a Catholic university. He condemned Ulster unionism as a device for maintaining the Protestant Ascendancy in its privileges. He opposed the ULSTER UNIONIST PARTY and the establishment of self-government in part of Ulster.

Arms Trials (1970), a series of trials following the dismissal by the Taoiseach, JACK LYNCH, of CHARLES HAUGHEY (Minister for Finance) and NEIL BLANEY (Minister for Agriculture). Charges against the latter were dropped when Judge Dónal Kearney in the District Court ruled that there was not enough evidence linking him to the charge of conspiring to import weapons. Haughey, Captain James Kelly (a former army intelligence officer), Albert Luykx (a Belgian businessman domiciled in Ireland for twenty years) and John Kelly (a Belfast republican) were charged in the Central Criminal Court with conspiring to illegally import arms (500 pistols and approximately 180,000 rounds of ammunition) on various dates between 1 March and 24 April 1970.

The first trial, which began on 22 September, collapsed when Mr Justice Aindrias Ó Caoimh dismissed the jury on 29 September. A new trial began before Mr Justice Séamus Henchy on 6 October. Three of the four defendants admitted attempting to import arms illegally, on the understanding that the Minister for Defence, Jim Gibbons, had sanctioned the operation. Haughey denied knowledge of the operation and claimed he had played no part in it; his counsel claimed that others giving evidence—Captain Kelly, Anthony Fagan (personal secretary to Haughey in the Department of Finance), Peter Berry (secretary of the Department of Justice), and Gibbons—should not be believed. The jury retired on 23 October and returned a verdict of not guilty in relation to all four defendants.

The trials led to a crisis in Fianna Fáil. Lynch, then in the United States, returned to Dublin on 26 October to a display of solidarity from government colleagues and leaders of the party, while enthusiastic crowds greeted Haughey and Blaney, calling for Lynch's resignation. Lynch won a confidence vote from the parliamentary party, 70 to 3, while a subsequent motion of no confidence in Dáil Éireann was defeated, 74 to 67 (his supporters including Blaney and Haughey). However, when Blaney and Paudge Brennan voted with the opposition in a motion of no confidence in Gibbons on 10 November, they were expelled from the Fianna Fáil parliamentary party. (Haughey voted with the government.) The subsequent Fianna Fáil ard-fheis on 19–21 February 1971 was a triumph for Lynch, whose policy on Northern Ireland was vindicated.

Army Comrades' Association, founded by Commandant Edmund (Ned) Cronin following a meeting in Wynn's Hotel, Dublin, 10 February 1932. The meeting decided to organise former members of the Free State army with the aim of upholding the Free State and commemorating those who died during the WAR OF INDEPENDENCE. Its first president was Colonel Austin Brennan; its first convention was held on 17 March. During the general election of March 1932, which was won by FIANNA FÁIL, the association gave support to CUMANN NA NGAEDHEAL. Membership, opened to the public from August under its new president, Thomas F. O'Higgins, was claimed at thirty thousand. During the violent campaign of the general election of January 1933 the association provided protection to CUMANN NA NGAEDHEAL candidates harassed by the IRA. The organisation declared itself opposed to communism, which it attributed to Fianna Fáil and the IRA. The movement was now remodelled with a view to greater discipline, and in April 1933 its members took to wearing uniform blue shirts, and the organisation came to be known as the BLUESHIRTS. From 20 July 1933, under the presidency of EOIN O'DUFFY, it was known as the NATIONAL GUARD.

Army Conventions (26 March and 9 April 1922). The Army Convention of 26 March 1922 was demanded by officers of the IRA who were concerned that the establishment of the PROVISIONAL GOVERNMENT and the acceptance of the ANGLO-IRISH TREATY meant the abrogation of the Irish Republic declared by the first Dáil. The Minister for Defence, RICHARD MULCAHY, acceded to the demand, but the Ministry (government) proscribed the convention, which was attended only by the anti-Treaty IRA (soon to be known as the New IRA). More than 230 delegates, representing 52 of the 73 brigades, appointed a sixteen-member executive as the supreme command of the IRA. The convention resolved that the IRA should affirm its allegiance to the Irish Republic, and that it was the only legal army; it also called on the Provisional Government to cease recruiting for the National Army and the CIVIC GUARD. The executive was granted authority 'if it considered fit' to suppress the general election scheduled for 16 June. It concluded by repudiating the authority of the Minister for Defence and his Chief of Staff (General EOIN O'DUFFY). The section of the IRA that supported the Free State became known as the Old IRA.

On 9 April, 217 delegates attended a further convention. A new army constitution was drafted, affirming the aims of the IRA and placing it under the control of an executive that included LIAM LYNCH (Chief of Staff), LIAM MELLOWS, SEÁN MOYLAN, RORY O'CONNOR, PEADAR O'DONNELL, and ERNIE O'MALLEY. Before the end of the month Republican units seized the FOUR COURTS and other buildings in Dublin, leading to the CIVIL WAR. (See also ARMY MUTINY.)

Army Mutiny (1924). A crisis for the government of the Irish Free State arose in 1924 when W. T. COSGRAVE and his colleagues were presented with an ultimatum from the Old IRA element within the Free State army. The 'Ultimatum to the government of Saorstát Éireann', signed by Liam Tobin and C. F. Dalton and presented on 6 March, was prompted by two factors. The government had announced a reduction of almost half in the 55,000-strong army and a consequent reduction in its 3,300 officer complement. The other factor was the resentment of the Old IRA at the influence within the army of the IRB, to which the Minister for Defence, RICHARD MULCAHY (as a former member), was thought to be sympathetic. The ultimatum demanded an end to demobilisation, the abolition of the Army Council established by Mulcahy, and a declaration that the government was still committed to the ideal of an independent Irish republic. In the absence of the President of the Executive Council, W. T. Cosgrave, who was ill, the crisis was handled by the Minister for Justice, KEVIN O'HIGGINS.

The affair affected the government immediately. The Minister for Industry and Commerce, JOSEPH MCGRATH, who was sympathetic to the Old IRA, resigned on 7 March in protest at the manner in which the Department of Defence had neglected the army's grievances; eight backbenchers followed his example. General EOIN O'DUFFY was appointed to the command of the army on 10 March.

The two signatories of the ultimatum were arrested. A committee of three, established to inquire into the origins of the mutiny, reported on 17 June. Though now a private citizen, McGrath assured the mutineers that their grievances would be investigated and the Army Council remodelled to their satisfaction. Shortly afterwards, when Free State soldiers attempted to arrest armed mutineers, McGrath prevented bloodshed. The soldiers had acted without the authorisation of O'Duffy but on the orders of the Adjutant-General, Gearóid O'Sullivan, who had consulted Mulcahy. The Adjutant-General and two other senior officers were forced to resign, as did Mulcahy (19 March).

The mutiny came to an end when the legitimate grievances of the army had been conceded. Those who did not return to their posts were deemed to have retired. The mutiny resulted in the resignation of two ministers, three major-generals, seven colonels, thirty commandants, forty captains, and nineteen lieutenants. It had demonstrated the strength of Republican sentiment among Free State supporters but had also shown the determination of the government to subordinate the army to the civil authority. In the words of O'Higgins, 'those who take the pay and wear the uniform of the state . . . must be non-political servants of the state.'

Arranmore Disaster. Nineteen out of twenty islanders from Árainn Mhór, Co. Donegal, were drowned while returning from seasonal work in Scotland when their open boat struck a rock on the night of 9 November 1935. Patrick Gallagher, the sole survivor, lost six members of his family. (See CLEW BAY TRAGEDY.)

Arrears Act (1882). An act to enable tenants in arrears with their rent to benefit from the Land Law (Ireland) Act (1881) was promised to CHARLES STEWART PARNELL by W. E. GLADSTONE under the terms of the 'KILMAINHAM TREATY'. Some 130,000 tenants were excluded from the working of the act. After the introduction of the Arrears Act, 15 May 1882, there was a fall in the number of agrarian outrages. The act provided £800,000 for paying off arrears, enabling tenants to benefit from the fair rent clause of the 1881 act.

Arts Council (An Chomhairle Ealaíon). The Taoiseach, JOHN A. COSTELLO, commissioned Dr Thomas Bodkin (1887–1961), who had submitted a previous report on culture and the arts (1923), to prepare another, and *Report on the Arts* was published in 1951. Steered through Dáil Éireann by Costello, the Arts Act (1951) was enacted on 8 May 1951. The Fianna Fáil government, replacing the coalition, established the first Arts Council, which held its inaugural meeting under its director, PATRICK J. LITTLE, on 25 January 1952. Its first offices were at 45 St Stephen's Green, Dublin; in 1959 it moved to 70 Merrion Square, where it opened its Exhibition Room on 27 October. The Arts Acts (1951 and 1973) were repealed in 2002 in legislation that reduced the size of the Arts Council from sixteen to nine members.

The Arts Council administers Aosdána, the organisation for writers and artists considered worthy of support by the state for outstanding contributions to the arts, launched on 5 March 1981. The first eighty-nine members were elected in December. *Toscairí* (delegates) are elected by the membership; five are appointed to the grade of *saoi* (expert or wise man). A *cnuas* (a means-tested annuity for up to five years) is available to members. Aosdána reached its quota of 150 members in 1992.

Ascendancy. The term 'Ascendancy' was first applied by John Gifford (1746–1819) to the Anglo-Irish Protestant landowning class that dominated social, political, cultural and economic life during the eighteenth and nineteenth centuries.

Asgard, a 28-ton gaff-rigged ketch designed in Norway by Colin Archer of Larvik. Dr Hamilton Osgood of Boston and his wife presented it to their daughter, Mary, on her marriage to ROBERT ERSKINE CHILDERS. Crewed by Childers and his wife, with Gordon Shephard, Mary Spring Rice (1880–1924), and two Co. Donegal fishermen, it sailed for the Rötigen lightship, 29 June 1914, to rendezvous with the German-registered ship *Gladiator* on 12 July. It took on board 900 rifles and 29,000 rounds of ammunition, bought by DARRELL FIGGIS in Hamburg for the IRISH VOLUNTEERS. A second yacht, the KELPIE, sailed a few days later to take some of the cargo. Mary Childers sold the boat in 1926, and it was later bought by the Government for use as a training vessel. From 1968 until it became unseaworthy in 1974 it was used as a sail-training vessel for young people; it was later placed on display at Kilmainham Jail, Dublin. *Asgard II,* a sail-training brigantine built by John Tyrrell and Sons at Arklow, Co. Wicklow, was commissioned on 8 March 1981. (See also HOWTH GUN-RUNNING.)

Ashbourne, Edward Gibson, first Baron (1837–1913), politician (Unionist); born in Dublin, educated at TCD and called to the bar. Member of Parliament for the University of Dublin, he was Attorney-General, 1877–80. As chief Conservative spokesman on the Irish land question he led the attack on W. E. GLADSTONE's Irish policy, 1880–85. He was made a peer and appointed Lord Chancellor of Ireland, with a seat in the cabinet, 1885. In the same year he drew up a LAND ACT introduced by the Salisbury caretaker government. He was the author of *Pitt: Some Chapters in His Life and Times* (1898). His son, William Gibson, second Baron Ashbourne (1868–1942), was a scholar and member of the GAELIC LEAGUE, of which he was for a time president. In addition to contributions to a variety of scholarly journals he published *The Abbé Lemennais and the Liberal Catholic Movement* (1896).

Ashe, Thomas (1885–1917), republican; born in Kinnard, Lispole, Co. Kerry; educated at De La Salle Training College, Waterford, and became a national school teacher, 1905. A poet, singer, musician, and painter, he was principal of Corduff National School, Lusk, Co. Dublin, 1908–16. He was active in the GAELIC LEAGUE and the IRISH VOLUNTEERS, on whose behalf he went to the United States on a fund-raising mission in 1914. He supported JAMES LARKIN in the DUBLIN LOCK-OUT (1913) and was also a friend of SEÁN O'CASEY. During the EASTER RISING (1916) he led the local Volunteers at the BATTLE OF ASHBOURNE, Co. Meath, for which he was sentenced to life imprisonment. Following his release, 17 June 1917, he was an organiser for SINN FÉIN and the Volunteers. Re-arrested on charges of inciting the civil population, he was sentenced to two years' imprisonment in August. After failing to secure recognition of the Republicans' claim for political status in Mountjoy Jail he organised a hunger strike among the prisoners, 20 September. On 25 September he died while being forcibly fed. An inquest, 27 September to 1 November, censured those responsible for the treatment inflicted on him. Some thirty thousand people attended his funeral, at which MICHAEL COLLINS briefly spoke. While in Lewes Prison, Isle of Wight, 1917, Ashe wrote the poem 'Let Me Carry Your Cross for Ireland, Lord!'

Asquith, Herbert Henry, first Earl of Oxford and Asquith (1852–1928), British politician (Liberal); born in Morley, Yorkshire, educated at the University of Oxford. Home Secretary, 1892–1904, he was Chancellor of the Exchequer from December 1905 and introduced old-age pensions in 1908. Prime Minister, 1908–16, he gained the support of the IRISH PARTY in his struggle with the House of Lords when he made a public commitment to HOME RULE, 10 December 1909, before the general election of January 1910. Having removed the absolute veto of the House of Lords in 1911, Asquith introduced the (third) Home Rule Bill (1912). It was bitterly opposed by the Ulster Unionists. The ULSTER VOLUNTEER FORCE was established, January 1913; the IRISH VOLUNTEERS came into existence during the following November.

In March 1914 Asquith's government sought an undertaking from the British army at the Curragh that it would he prepared to act in Ulster, provoking the CURRAGH INCIDENT. Another attempt to solve the crisis over home rule by bringing unionists and nationalists together in the BUCKINGHAM PALACE CONFERENCE ended in failure, July 1914. Asquith secured a suspension of the Home Rule Act for the duration of the Great War, with the proviso that the question of Ulster would be considered before the act would come into force. During the EASTER RISING (1916) he sent GENERAL JOHN MAXWELL to Ireland to restore order. Asquith came to Dublin for six days on 12 May and prevented any further executions. Having informed the cabinet that government in Ireland had broken down, he instructed DAVID LLOYD GEORGE to begin negotiations with the unionists and the nationalists (see IRISH CONVENTION). In December 1916 virulent criticism of his 'wait and see' policy on the war effort led to his replacement as Prime Minister by Lloyd George. He entered the House of Lords as Earl of Oxford and Asquith in 1925.

Assembly of the Northern Irish People (1971), held on 26 October 1971 at Dungiven, Co. Derry, by non-Unionist MPs opposed to the governing ULSTER UNIONIST PARTY at Stormont. It met as an 'alternative Assembly' to show, in the words of JOHN HUME, that 'no system of government can survive if a significant section of the population is determined that it will not be governed.' The Assembly held only two plenary sessions but was regarded as a successful propaganda exercise.

Association for Legal Justice, established in 1971 and closely associated with the NORTHERN IRELAND CIVIL RIGHTS ASSOCIATION. It investigated allegations of ill-treatment by the RUC and British army and monitored the reform programme reluctantly inaugurated by the Stormont government. It published *Know Your Legal Rights* (1971) and campaigned to end political appointments to the judiciary. It accused the Northern Ireland courts of anti-Catholic bias, claiming that Catholics received longer sentences. Opposed to internment, it accused the RUC in 1974 of using torture to secure confessions from Provisional IRA accused. The association claimed in 1982 that the RUC and British army were shooting suspected terrorists in what were in effect 'summary executions'.

Aud. The steamship *Libau,* previously the British auxiliary cruise ship *Castro* (seized by a German destroyer early in the First World War), was disguised as the Norwegian vessel *Aud,* April 1916, to carry guns for the IRISH VOLUNTEERS for use in the EASTER RISING (1916). The ship, commanded by Captain Karl Spindler with a crew of twenty-one, left Lübeck on 9 April with a cargo of 20,000 rifles and machine-guns and ammunition. Sailing under the Norwegian flag, the vessel carried a camouflage cargo of timber. It was intended that the *Aud* would rendezvous off Fenit, Co. Kerry, with the German submarine *U19,* carrying ROGER CASEMENT and ROBERT MONTEITH. The ship carried no wireless and so was unaware that the date for its arrival had been altered from Thursday 20 April to Sunday 23 April, the date of the proposed rising. As a result of the alteration no preparations had been made by AUSTIN STACK and the Kerry Volunteers to meet the ship, which hove to for nearly twenty-four hours, attracting the attention of a British patrol vessel, the *Bluebell,* which forced Spindler to make for Queenstown (Cóbh). Rather than allow his ship to fall into enemy hands, Spindler and crew scuttled the vessel and boarded a lifeboat, 22 April. They were interned for the duration of the war. In his memoir *The Mystery of the Casement Ship* (1931), Spindler claimed that copies of documents containing the entire plans of the Irish venture were stolen from the office of Wolf von Igel, a secretary at the German embassy in Washington, on 18 April 1916, and that President Wilson personally apprised British officials of the plans.

Auxiliaries, unofficial name of the Auxiliary Police Force, recruited mainly from among demobilised officers of the British army from 27 July 1920. The Auxiliaries were intended to augment the ROYAL IRISH CONSTABULARY, from which there had been nearly six hundred resignations within three months. The IRA campaign during the WAR OF INDEPENDENCE had been directed mainly at the RIC. In all, about 1,500 'cadets', as they were officially known, were involved in supporting the RIC. Ranked equal to senior RIC sergeants and nominally under RIC command, they were in fact separate from it and from the other auxiliary force, the BLACK AND TANS. Divided into companies of about a hundred men, they were stationed in designated trouble areas. Their pay of £1 per day plus expenses made them the highest-paid uniformed force of their time. Operating under the RESTORATION OF ORDER IN IRELAND ACT (1920), which allowed for internment without trial, trial by military courts, the suppression of coroners' inquests, and additional waivers from normal jurisprudence, the Auxiliaries were given a virtual *carte blanche,* which they fully exercised. By mid-1921 there were fifteen companies operating in Cos. Clare, Cork, Dublin, Kerry, Kilkenny, Longford, Meath, and Roscommon. Feared and despised by the nationalist population and resented by members of the regular British forces, the 'Auxies' were identified with the burning and looting of Cork and the sacking of Balbriggan, Co. Dublin, and Trim, Co. Meath. One of the most hated of the force, Major Arthur Percival, operated in the west Cork area; directly responsible for several killings and the torture and maiming of prisoners, he survived three attempts on his life by the Cork No. 3 Brigade, commanded by TOM BARRY. On 15 February 1942 Percival, then a lieutenant-general, surrendered Singapore to Lieutenant-General Yamasita of the Japanese army.

B

Bachelor's Walk Incident. On 26 July 1914 Assistant Commissioner W. V. Harrell, backed by a hundred soldiers of the King's Own Scottish Borderers under Captain Cobden, halted some eight hundred members of the Irish Volunteers at Bachelor's Walk, Dublin, returning from the HOWTH GUN-RUNNING at Clontarf. DARREL FIGGIS and THOMAS MACDONAGH engaged Harrell in discussion, enabling the Volunteers to disperse with the arms. A crowd gathered and harangued the soldiers; on their return journey, now commanded by Major Haig, they were subjected to further abuse and missile-throwing. At the corner of Liffey Street, Haig, unaware that the soldiers' weapons were loaded, gave a command that brought them face to face with the crowd. While he was addressing the gathering a shot was fired, followed by a volley in which twenty-one weapons were used and twenty-nine shots discharged. Three people were killed and at least thirty-eight injured, fifteen of whom were admitted to hospital.

A commission of inquiry censured the use of the military. Its report (4 September 1914) stated: 'In our view—and apart from the fundamental illegality as to the seizure of rifles—there was in the events and circumstances set forth no case warranting military intervention . . . We are convinced that many of the victims who suffered by the firing in Bachelor's Walk were innocent of all connection with the unseemly and outrageous and provocative action of the crowd, but were passive spectators or ordinary pedestrians . . .' Harrell was dismissed for 'provocatively calling out the military to deal with the situation,' and General Cuthbert, Brigadier-General of the Infantry Brigade in Dublin, was censured for allowing soldiers to be used without written order and for not having 'more scrupulously' considered the nature of their proposed duty. The incident fuelled nationalist feelings, especially as the perpetrators of the LARNE GUN-RUNNING, which involved the seizure and imprisonment of Customs and Excise officers, remained unpunished.

Baird, Ernest (born 1930), politician (Unionist); born in Ballycampsie, Co. Donegal. He left the ULSTER UNIONIST PARTY and became a joint founder and first chairman of ULSTER VANGUARD, 1972, which he left following William Craig's advocacy of a coalition with the SDLP, 1976. He established the UNITED ULSTER UNIONIST MOVEMENT to promote unity among unionists. Elected for Fermanagh-South Tyrone to the Northern Ireland Assembly, 1973, and to the Convention, 1975, he was active in the ULSTER WORKERS' COUNCIL, 1974, and associated with REV. IAN PAISLEY in the UNITED UNIONIST ACTION COUNCIL, May 1977. He was leader of the United Ulster Unionist Party, 1977–84. Following defeat in the 1982 Assembly elections he left politics for business and in 1997 rejoined the Ulster Unionist Party.

Baker Report (1984). Reviewing the Emergency Provisions Act, Sir George Baker recommended the retention of the DIPLOCK COURTS and the continued controversial use of INFORMERS. He also recommended that the paramilitary ULSTER DEFENCE ASSOCIATION not be proscribed, and that victims of Provisional IRA violence should be entitled to legal aid to sue Sinn Féin for damages.

Baldwin, Stanley, first Earl Baldwin of Bewdley (1867–1947), British politician (Conservative); educated at the University of Cambridge. Baldwin succeeded ANDREW BONAR LAW as Prime Minister, 1923–24, and was Prime Minister again, 1924–29, 1935–37. During negotiations on the BOUNDARY COMMISSION he successfully argued that the Irish Free State should be released from the financial obligations of article 5 of the ANGLO-IRISH TREATY. He engineered a tripartite agreement between the Irish Free State, Britain and Northern Ireland for shelving the report of the BOUNDARY COMMISSION, 1925. He argued against a proposal by SIR WINSTON CHURCHILL that a restrictive clause be inserted to prevent the Free State from repudiating the Treaty, claiming that it would offend all Irishmen, and other dominions within the British Commonwealth. Resigning in May 1937, he was succeeded by NEVILLE CHAMBERLAIN.

Balfour, Arthur James, first Earl Balfour (1848–1930), British politician; born in Whittingehame, East Lothian, a nephew of the Prime Minister, Lord Salisbury. His period as Chief Secretary for Ireland, 1887–91, was distinguished by a mixture of COERCION and conciliation. The 'MITCHELSTOWN MASSACRE' (September 1887) earned him the name 'Bloody Balfour'. He described the Irish land system as 'essentially and radically rotten,' formed a poor opinion of the greedier landlords, and condemned absentee landlords. He made constructive efforts to deal with land problems. The Light Railways Act (1889) established a system of railways that linked the west of Ireland with the east, and he established the CONGESTED DISTRICTS BOARD to deal with the particular problems of the west. He introduced the Land Purchase Act (1891) (see LAND ACTS), which was modified by his brother, Gerald Balfour (1853–1945). As Prime Minister, 1902–05, he resolutely opposed HOME RULE. Replaced as leader of the Conservative Party by ANDREW BONAR LAW, 1911, he remained an important influence within the party.

Ball, Francis Elrington (1863–1928), historian; born in Portmarnock, Co. Dublin, third son of the Lord Chancellor, JOHN THOMAS BALL, educated privately because of poor health. He contributed papers to learned societies and was a fellow, 1899, and vice-president, 1901–04, of the Royal Society of Antiquaries of Ireland. He was awarded a DLitt degree by the University of Dublin for his *Correspondence of Jonathan Swift* (6 vols., 1910–14); other works included *History of the County of Dublin* (1902–20) and *The Judges in Ireland, 1221–1921* (1926), which assumed critical importance when historical records and documents were destroyed in the FOUR COURTS, 1922.

Ball, John Thomas (1815–1898), jurist and writer, Lord Chancellor of Ireland, 1875–80; born in Portmarnock, Co. Dublin, educated at TCD. He was president of TCD Historical Society and closely associated with prominent figures of the era, including ISAAC BUTT. Member of Parliament for University of Dublin, 1865–75, he was Queen's Advocate from 1865, Solicitor-General, 1868, and Attorney-General from 1868. Though opposed to the Irish Church Act (1869), he helped frame the constitution for the DISESTABLISHMENT of the Church of Ireland. He was a frequent contributor to DUBLIN UNIVERSITY MAGAZINE; his books included *The Reformed Church of Ireland, 1537–1886* (1886) and *Historical Review of the Legislative Systems* (1889). FRANCIS ELRINGTON BALL was his son.

Ballingarry, Co. Tipperary, scene of an abortive rising, 29 July 1848. Former members of YOUNG IRELAND who had formed the IRISH CONFEDERATION (and were now the Irish League) held a conference at Ballingarry, July 1848, to determine policy. The majority favoured avoiding an armed rising but were opposed by WILLIAM SMITH O'BRIEN and JAMES STEPHENS. Their undisciplined and poorly armed following of approximately one hundred forced forty-five members of the RIC commanded by Inspector Trent to take refuge in the home of a Mrs McCormack, whose five children were also in the house. Stephens and TERENCE BELLEW MCMANUS removed smouldering hay from around the cabin when informed of the presence of the children. When called on to surrender, Trent, aware of impending reinforcements, requested time to consider his response. During a lull in the fighting some of the attackers hurled stones, smashing the back windows of the cabin; the RIC opened fire, killing two of the attackers and wounding several others. Further casualties were inflicted on the fleeing rebels when reinforcements arrived. Stephens (who was wounded), JOHN BLAKE DILLON, MICHAEL DOHENY and JOHN O'MAHONY escaped, while O'Brien and THOMAS FRANCIS MEAGHER, who were later arrested, had their initial death sentence commuted to transportation to Van Diemen's Land (Tasmania).

Ballinglass Evictions (13 March 1846). Outrage was caused by the decision of a landowner, Mrs Gerrard, to evict the entire population of the village of Ballinglass, Co. Galway, to turn the land over to grazing. The tenants were not in arrears with rent and in fact had improved their holdings by reclaiming some 400 acres of adjoining bogland. The incident received wide publicity and was investigated by Lord Londonderry, who, in a statement to the House of Lords, 30 March 1846, said:

> I am deeply grieved, but there is no doubt concerning the truth of the evictions at Ballinglass. Seventy-six families, comprising 300 individuals had not only been turned out of their houses, but had even—the unfortunate wretches—been mercilessly driven from the ditches to which they had betaken themselves for shelter . . . these unfortunate people, had their rents actually ready.

Despite widespread condemnation, the eviction order was not rescinded.

Ballot Act (1872). Introducing the secret ballot, the act was of particular importance to Ireland, as it enabled tenants to vote against the wishes of their landlord in parliamentary elections. This became evident by the general election of 1880, which marked the end of landlord influence in the Irish Party and gave the new chairman of the party, CHARLES STEWART PARNELL, a greater measure of control over its members, the majority of whom lacked independent means.

Ballymun. The Housing Committee of Dublin City Council agreed, 29 January 1965, that the Minister for Local Government should authorise the National Building Agency to enter into a contract for a housing estate to be built at Ballymun, Dublin. The completed estate consisted of 2,814 units, made up of seven fifteen-storey blocks, nineteen eight-storey blocks, and ten four-storey blocks. In 1996 Dublin City Council announced that it intended to take down the blocks and rehouse the tenants in more conventional housing.

Baptist Society, founded in London, 1814, to promote the education of the poor. It established more than sixty schools in Connacht and was considered a proselytising agency for the established Church of Ireland.

Baring Brothers, an English mercantile house controlled by Thomas Baring (1799–1873). It was entrusted by SIR ROBERT PEEL with the purchase of Indian corn on the American market for supply to Ireland between November 1845 and July 1846 during the GREAT FAMINE. It refused any commission for work performed in the cause of famine relief, during which fourteen ships were employed. The company declined to act beyond 1846, when the British government instructed it to restrict purchases to within the United Kingdom, and it was replaced as agents by the corn-factors Erichson of London. In 1847 Thomas Baring became chairman of the BRITISH ASSOCIATION FOR THE RELIEF OF DISTRESS. The Baring Group collapsed in February 1995 with losses of $2.2 billion caused by the trading activities of Nick Leeson, employed by the subsidiary company Baring Futures (Singapore).

Barrett, Michael (died 1868), Fenian. He was closely associated with Captain John Murphy, who, with Jeremiah O'Sullivan, was responsible for the CLERKENWELL EXPLOSION. Barrett was in Glasgow at the time of the explosion and was arrested for discharging firearms on Glasgow Green. False evidence was presented at his trial, when he was charged with responsibility for the Clerkenwell explosion. In the last public execution in England he was hanged by William Calcraft at Newgate, London, 26 May, before a crowd estimated at two thousand.

Barry, John Milner (1769–1822), physician; born in Bandon, Co. Cork, educated at Edinburgh, graduating as MD, 1792. He introduced vaccination into Ireland in 1800 and two years later founded Cork Fever Hospital. A contributor to the leading medical and scientific journals of the day, he wrote on the physical dangers of alcoholism (he sought the imprisonment of habitual drunkards). He was also a strong advocate of women's emancipation. In the *Transactions of the Association of the College of Physicians* he expounded the idea that intestinal parasites might have an external origin, rather than resulting from spontaneous internal generation, as was then believed. His works included *An Account of the Nature of the Cow-Pock* (1800) and *Report of the Fever Hospital of the City of Cork* (1818).

Barry, Kevin (1902–1920), republican soldier; born in Dublin, educated at UCD. He joined the IRISH VOLUNTEERS, October 1917. While a medical student at UCD, having previously participated in minor engagements, he took part in an IRA attack on a British army detachment at Monk's Bakery, Upper Church Street, Dublin, 20 September 1920. Following the attack, in which three British soldiers were killed, he was discovered lying under a van with an automatic pistol in his possession; he was court-martialled and sentenced to death. Despite international pleas for clemency on the grounds of his youth, supported by the Irish Lord Chancellor, James Campbell, and Chief Justice, T. F. Moloney, he was hanged at Mountjoy Jail, Dublin, on 1 November, the first Volunteer to be executed. A fact generally lost in the political climate of the time was that a British soldier killed by the IRA during the raid was slightly younger than Barry. Barry's interrogation and execution became the subject of some twenty-six ballads, the most famous of which, with the opening line 'In Mountjoy Jail one Monday morning,' was written anonymously by a Glasgow Irishman, November 1920.

Barry was one of ten Republican soldiers whose remains were accorded a state funeral when he was re-interred in Glasnevin Cemetery, Dublin, 14 October 2001.

Barry, Tom (1897–1980), republican soldier; born in Ross Carbery, Co. Cork. He learnt of the EASTER RISING (1916) more than three months after the event while serving with the British army in Mesopotamia (Iraq) and was appalled at the executions of the leaders and at the shelling of Dublin. Demobilised in January 1919, he joined the IRA as intelligence officer and later training officer of Cork No. 3 (West Cork) Brigade from which he formed one of the leading FLYING COLUMNS of the WAR OF INDEPENDENCE, responsible for the ambushes at Kilmichael and Cross Barry. Opposing the ANGLO-IRISH TREATY (1921), he supported the Republican side during the CIVIL WAR. Several times arrested for IRA activities in the 1930s, he called for a war against England. He rejected the call by FRANK RYAN for Republican volunteers to defend the Spanish Republic (see CONNOLLY COLUMN), resigned his position on the Army Council in 1937, and ceased to be an IRA activist in 1940. He was unsuccessful as an independent candidate for Dáil Éireann in Cork, 1946. He was the author of *Guerilla Days in Ireland* (1949) and *The Reality of the Anglo Irish War, 1919–21* (1974), a pamphlet contradicting much of Liam Deasy's *Towards Ireland Free* (1973).

Barry's wife, Leslie de Barra, née Price (1893–1984), was an internationally recognised humanitarian. She had a long association with Gorta, the famine relief organisation, and was the first woman recipient of the Henri Dunant Medal, 18 December 1979, for her services as chairwoman of the Irish Red Cross Society, 1950–84.

Barter, Richard (1802–1870), physician; born in Cooldaniel, Co. Cork, educated at London College of Physicians. His experiences during the cholera epidemic of 1832 convinced him of the curative powers of water and prompted him to open the first Turkish baths in Ireland, the Hydropathic Institution at St Anne's, Blarney, Co. Cork, 1842. He was honorary secretary of the County of Cork Agricultural Society for many years.

Barton, Robert Childers (1881–1975), politician (Sinn Féin); born in Glendalough, Co. Wicklow, where he was raised with his cousin (ROBERT) ERSKINE CHILDERS, educated at the University of Oxford. He was a member of the committee of the Irish Agricultural Organisation Society from 1910. Commissioned in the British army during the Great War, he was sent to Dublin during the EASTER RISING (1916) and resigned to join the Irish Volunteers. Returned to the first Dáil for Wicklow West, as first Minister for Agriculture, 1919–21, he was responsible for the Irish Land Bank. Several times imprisoned for his activities, he was released from Portland Prison during the TRUCE and was a member of the team that negotiated the ANGLO-IRISH TREATY (1921). Though he signed the Treaty and voted for it in the Dáil, he took the anti-Treaty side in the CIVIL WAR, during which he escaped from Portobello Barracks, Dublin. He retired from politics at the end of the hostilities to manage his extensive estate in Co. Wicklow. He headed the Agricultural Credit Corporation, 1934–54, and Bord na Móna, 1946.

Bates, Richard Dawson (1876–1949), lawyer and politician (Ulster Unionist Party); born in Belfast. Secretary of the ULSTER UNIONIST COUNCIL, he was a founder-member of the ULSTER VOLUNTEER FORCE. During the LARNE GUN-RUNNING (1914) he intercepted the *Clyde Valley* at the entrance to Belfast Lough to advise of a change in landing orders. As a member of Parliament, 1921–43, he was Minister of Home Affairs in the first Northern Ireland government. He was responsible for the SPECIAL POWERS ACT, the principal weapon used by the Northern government to fight against the IRA. In 1934 he prompted the Prime Minister of Northern Ireland, Sir James Craig (see VISCOUNT CRAIGAVON), to introduce the gerrymander that ensured that in Derry 9,961 nationalist voters returned eight councillors while 7,744 Unionist voters returned twelve.

Battle of Ashbourne (28 April 1916). During the EASTER RISING (1916) the 5th Battalion of the Dublin Brigade, under THOMAS ASHE, with RICHARD MULCAHY second in command, attacked the RIC barracks at Ashbourne, Co. Meath. Having captured two RIC members as they erected a barricade, the attacking party laid siege to the barracks. Ashe was unaware that in response to similar attacks throughout the country, barracks now held fifteen men, rather than the usual six. Firing had continued for approximately half an hour when some fifty motorised police reinforcements arrived and engaged the attackers. The fighting lasted several hours, ending with the surrender of the reinforcing party, followed immediately by the capitulation of the defenders. RIC casualties were eight dead and fifteen wounded, while the IRA lost two men and had five wounded.

'Battle of Baltinglass' (1950). Baltinglass, Co. Wicklow, became a centre of political controversy in 1950 when JAMES EVERETT, Minister for Posts and Telegraphs in the inter-party government and a member of Dáil Éireann for the county, appointed Michael Farrell to the office of sub-postmaster. The office had been held by Helen Cooke, deputising for her invalid aunt, whose family had held it since 1870. Amid allegations of political jobbery, members of the community, supporting the Cooke family, objected to Farrell's appointment. Gardaí were brought in to transfer the telephone lines to Farrell's shop; telegraph wires in Baltinglass were cut, and Farrell's shop was boycotted. In the village a shop licensed to sell stamps became a rival 'post office', with local people taking turns to bring the post to post offices in other towns. As a result of the agitation Farrell resigned the office, 20 December 1950, and Miss Cooke was appointed.

It was believed that the Baltinglass affair contributed to the downfall of the inter-party government, 1951, also involved in controversy over the MOTHER AND CHILD SCHEME. A humorous ballad, 'The Siege of Baltinglass', became popular; attributed to 'Sylvester Gaffney', it was the work of Leo Maguire (died 1985).

Bean na hÉireann ('the Irishwoman'), journal of INGHINIDHE NA HÉIREANN, 1908–11, and the first nationalist feminist journal produced in Ireland. It was edited by HELENA MOLONEY, who described it as 'a mixture of guns and chiffon,' and its voluntary staff included Sydney Gifford Czira, MAUD GONNE, BULMER HOBSON,

PATRICK MCCARTAN, Seán McGarry, CONSTANCE MARKIEVICZ, and Madeline Ffrench-Mullan.

Béaslaí, Piaras (1883–1965), journalist and soldier; born in Liverpool. In Dublin from 1904, he joined the Gaelic League and the Irish Volunteers. Editor of the Gaelic League paper *An Fáinne,* 1917–22, and active in the Volunteers during the WAR OF INDEPENDENCE, he was member for East Kerry in the first Dáil. Supporting the ANGLO-IRISH TREATY (1921), he visited the United States in 1922 to win Irish-American support for the agreement. A major-general in the Free State army during the CIVIL WAR, he resigned in 1924 to devote his time to the Irish-language movement. His works include *Michael Collins and the Making of the New Ireland* (2 vols., 1926) and *Michael Collins, Soldier and Statesman* (1937). He edited Arthur Griffith's *Songs, Ballads and Recitations* (n.d.) and translated Goldsmith's *She Stoops to Conquer* to Irish (1939).

Beaufort, Sir Francis (1774–1857), mathematician, seaman, and inventor of the Beaufort scale; born in Navan, Co. Meath. An admiral in the British Navy, while recovering from wounds he assisted his brother-in-law Richard Lovell Edgeworth (father of MARIA EDGEWORTH) in the construction of a system of telegraph signals from Dublin to Galway, 1803. He devised the scale that bears his name in 1805, which classifies wind speed by the reaction of common outdoor features, such as smoke and trees; it was adopted by the Admiralty in 1838 and internationally in 1874. Beaufort conducted various nautical surveys for the British Navy, for which he was Hydrographer from 1829.

Beckett, J. C. [James Camlin] (1912–1996), historian; educated at QUB, after which he taught history at the Royal Belfast Academical Institution 1934–45. A member of the history department at Queen's University, he published *Protestant Dissent in Ireland, 1687–1780* (1948) and *A Short History of Ireland* (1952). He was joint author (with T. W. Moody) of a two-volume history of Queen's University. Reader in history, 1952, he was awarded the chair of Irish history, 1958. *The Making of Irish History* (1966) was a standard text for several decades.

Beckett, Samuel (1906–1984), novelist, poet, and dramatist; born in Dublin, educated at TCD. With a degree in modern languages (French and Italian), he taught for a short period in Belfast before moving to France to teach at the École Normale Superieure, Paris, 1920–30. He was a lifelong friend of Thomas McGreevy (1893–1967), who introduced him to JAMES JOYCE in Paris; Beckett occasionally worked as Joyce's secretary on the manuscript of *Finnegans Wake.* He returned to Dublin in 1930 to lecture in French at TCD but resigned after two years to return to Paris. After the fall of France to Germany, 1940, he joined the Resistance, for which he was awarded the Croix de Guerre, 1945, returning to Paris in 1946. He was awarded the Nobel Prize for Literature in 1969. *En Attendant Godot* (*Waiting for Godot,* 1952) brought him international acclaim and established him as a leading figure in the theatre of the absurd.

Beef Tribunal, the Tribunal of Inquiry into the Beef-Processing Industry, chaired by Mr Justice Liam Hamilton (1928–2000), established by the Oireachtas, 31 May 1991, to investigate allegations of irregularities in the beef industry made in an ITV documentary, 'World in Action', 13 May. The programme, concentrating in particular on companies controlled by Larry Goodman and using information supplied by a former Goodman accountant, Patrick McGuinness, alleged widespread corruption, tax evasion, and fraud, apparently carried out with the collusion or knowledge of senior politicians and civil servants. The scope of the tribunal was limited through a number of court actions, including a Supreme Court ruling that confidentiality within the Government was absolute. During the hearings a conflict between evidence given by ALBERT REYNOLDS, the Taoiseach and a former Minister for Industry and Commerce, and that given by DESMOND O'MALLEY, the incumbent Minister for Industry and Commerce, led to the fall of the Government.

Having sat for a record 226 days, during which seventy-four legal teams examined more than four hundred witnesses, and at an estimated cost of £36 million, the tribunal reported on 29 July 1994. Mr Justice Hamilton commented that 'an awful lot of money and time would have been saved,' and the need for an inquiry obviated, if questions asked in Dáil Éireann 'were answered in the way they were answered here.' He ruled that large financial donations passed by the beef industry to politicians were within the scope of 'normal political contributions'; however, by the end of the decade such payments were the subject of three further tribunals of inquiry (see FLOOD TRIBUNAL, MCCRACKEN TRIBUNAL, and MORIARTY TRIBUNAL).

beggars. The number of beggars in Ireland during the nineteenth century was continually increased by the evicted and famine-stricken. Several efforts were made to contain the numbers entering towns, including a licence system, under which badges were issued to 'official' beggars, who were in turn empowered to drive away all 'foreign' beggars. Beggars flocked to Dublin in the wake of the famine of 1817, taxing the city's charitable institutions beyond capacity. A group of public-spirited people made several efforts to alleviate the problem, including the launching of an appeal to the citizens of Dublin. When their efforts met with little success it was decided that more drastic action was needed. Accordingly, processions of beggars were led forth daily to howl outside the doors of the wealthy; more than £1,000 was speedily collected in this fashion. The Dublin Mendicity Institution was founded to organise the distribution of the fund. ANNA MARIA HALL and her husband recalled an incident at Newmarket, Co. Cork, when ninety-two beggars queued for several hours for a promised half-penny.

Behan, Brendan (1923–1964), dramatist, novelist, and raconteur; born in Dublin, educated at Brunswick Street Christian Brothers' School. A member of a strongly republican family and a nephew of PEADAR KEARNEY, he joined FIANNA ÉIREANN and the IRA in 1937. From the age of twelve he published work in the *Farmer's Journal, Wolfe Tone Weekly,* and *United Irishman.* He left school at fourteen to become an apprentice house-painter. After the IRA's 'declaration of war' on Britain, 1939, he was arrested in Liverpool in possession of explosives, December 1939, for which he was sentenced to three years' borstal detention. His experiences in the borstal institution at Hollesley Bay, Suffolk, 1939–41, provided him with the material for his best-selling novel *Borstal Boy* (1958). Four months after his return to Dublin, 22 April 1942, he was sentenced to fourteen years' imprisonment for the attempted murder of a garda but was released under the general amnesty of December 1946. His term of imprisonment in Mountjoy and Arbour Hill Prisons, Dublin, and the Curragh Camp, during which time he worked at perfecting his Irish and his reading and writing, provided the inspiration for his play *The Quare Fellow* (first produced at the Pike Theatre, Dublin, 9 November 1954).

He spent some time in London and Paris, supporting himself as a house-painter. He broadcast on Radio Éireann, where he contributed scripts to a variety of programmes as well as having plays performed. *An Giall* was first produced at the Damer Theatre, Dublin, 16 June 1958; a longer English-language version, *The Hostage,* was produced in London by Joan Littlewood later the same year. His other works include *Brendan Behan's Island* (1962), *Hold Your Hour and Have Another* (1963, from his *Irish Press* articles and illustrated by his wife, the artist Beatrice Salkeld), *Brendan Behan's New York* (1964), *Confessions of an Irish Rebel* (1965), and the play *A Garden Party* (1967). His last work, *Richard's Cork Leg,* was completed by Alan Simpson and received a posthumous production in Dublin in 1973.

Belfast Agreement (1998), an agreement between the Irish and British governments and the main political organisations in Northern Ireland (with the exception of the DEMOCRATIC UNIONIST PARTY). Sometimes known as the Good Friday Agreement, it was signed on 10 April 1998 and was the outcome of multi-party talks extending over two years. Under the agreement, which replaced the ANGLO-IRISH AGREEMENT (1985), the 108-member Northern Ireland Assembly was elected by proportional representation (single transferable vote) from the existing British House of Commons constituencies to exercise executive and legislative authority subject to 'safeguards to protect the rights and interests of all sides of the community.' The Assembly was intended as the 'prime source of authority in respect of all devolved responsibilities.' All important decisions were to be taken 'on a cross-community basis,' i.e. with the agreement of all the main parties, not just a simple majority. The Assembly had a committee for each of the main executive functions, the chairs of the committees being allocated proportionately, using the d'Hondt system (which gives added weight to the larger parties), with membership of the committees 'in broad proportion to party strengths in the Assembly.'

Under the agreement a First Minister and Deputy First Minister were given executive authority, with up to ten ministers given departmental responsibilities and together constituting the Executive Committee. The Secretary of State for Northern Ireland (a member of the British government) continued to have a role under the agreement, and the powers of the British Parliament to make laws for Northern Ireland were not affected.

A North-South Ministerial Council was

established to bring together those with executive responsibilities in Northern Ireland and the Irish government for consultation on cross-border issues. A BRITISH-IRISH COUNCIL was also established 'to promote the harmonious and mutually beneficial development of the totality of relationships' among the people of Ireland and Britain. A British-Irish Intergovernmental Conference was also established to subsume 'both the Anglo-Irish Intergovernmental Council and the Intergovernmental Conference established under the 1985 Agreement.'

Under the Belfast Agreement the 'decommissioning' of arms in the possession of paramilitary organisations was left to the INDEPENDENT INTERNATIONAL COMMISSION ON DECOMMISSIONING, while the contentious issue of policing was delegated to the Patten Commission (see PATTEN REPORT).

The referendums on the agreement saw the electorate of both parts of Ireland exercise their franchise on the same issue for the first time since 1918. In Northern Ireland, 676,966 (71 per cent) voted for the agreement and 274,879 (29 per cent) voted against. The vote in the Republic was 1,442,583 (94 per cent) for and 85,748 (6 per cent) against. The composite vote for the country as a whole was therefore 2,119,549 (85 per cent) for and 360,627 (15 per cent) against.

The Northern Ireland Assembly was elected on 25 June 1998. The results were: Ulster Unionist Party 28, SDLP 24, DUP 20, Sinn Féin 18, Alliance Party 6, UK Unionist Party 5, Northern Ireland Women's Coalition 2, Progressive Unionist Party 2, Unionist 1, UU 1, and UUU 1. Sinn Féin was now entitled to two seats on the Executive.

On 1 July 1998 all the parties met in the same room for the first time. The leader of the Ulster Unionist Party, DAVID TRIMBLE, was elected First Minister and the deputy leader of the SDLP, Séamus Mallon, Deputy First Minister. Attempts to deny Sinn Féin its places because of the IRA's failure to decommission were unsuccessful but continued to be a source of anger for unionists. In an attempt to save the agreement and the institutions, the Executive and Assembly were suspended for the fourth time in October 2002.

Belfast Boycott, 1920–22, a boycott of goods produced and distributed from Belfast during the WAR OF INDEPENDENCE. During the summer of 1920 there was a reaction in the south of Ireland to anti-Catholic rioting in Belfast. A Belfast Boycott Committee, whose members included Bishop Joseph MacRory, SEÁN MACENTEE, and DENIS MCCULLOUGH, was established, August 1920. The boycott originated in Galway when shopkeepers refused to stock Belfast goods. It was opposed by ERNEST BLYTHE and CONSTANCE MARKIEVICZ. The second Dáil appointed Joseph McDonagh director of the Belfast Boycott, August 1921 to January 1922; from January to February 1922 it was directed by MICHAEL STAINES. The boycott ended with the signing of the CRAIG-COLLINS AGREEMENTS, January and March 1922.

Belfast Protestant Association, an anti-Catholic organisation founded by Arthur Trew and THOMAS H. SLOAN from Belfast lodges of the ORANGE ORDER, 1900. When Trew was imprisoned for twelve months for inciting a riot during a Corpus Christi procession, 1901, the association was taken over by Sloan. He was expelled from the Orange Order for making derogatory remarks about E. J. SAUNDERSON and used the association as the basis for the INDEPENDENT ORANGE ORDER.

Belfast Telegraph, a unionist-controlled daily newspaper founded in 1871 as the *Belfast Evening Telegraph,* becoming the *Belfast Telegraph* in 1918. In March 2000 the Belfast Telegraph Group and its titles were sold to Independent News and Media PLC, controlled by Dr Anthony O'Reilly.

Bell, The, a literary magazine founded by SEÁN Ó FAOLÁIN, 1940, becoming an influential literary journal and in time attracting contributions from leading writers of the day. Apart from fiction and poetry it published articles on national and international affairs, pioneered new views, and led the struggle of writers against censorship (see CENSORSHIP OF PUBLICATIONS ACTS). The magazine appeared regularly throughout the war years but ceased publication in April 1948; it appeared again in November 1950 and was published until 1955.

Bennett, Edward Halloran (1837–1907), surgeon; born in Cork, educated at TCD. He was the first to identify a fracture caused by a blow to the first metacarpal bone of the thumb, becoming known as Bennett's fracture, 1881. He was surgeon to Sir Patrick Dun's Hospital, Dublin, and professor of surgery at TCD, 1873–1906. President of the Pathological Society, 1880, and of the Royal College of Surgeons in Ireland, 1884–86, he was one of the earliest Irish surgeons to employ Listerian methods during surgical operations.

Bennett, Louie (1870–1956), trade unionist, suffragist, and pacifist; born in Dublin to a wealthy family, educated at Alexandra College and abroad. With her companion Helen Chenevix she founded and was first secretary of the IRISH WOMEN'S SUFFRAGE FEDERATION, 1911. She supported JAMES CONNOLLY during the DUBLIN LOCK-OUT (1913). On the outbreak of the First World War she joined the Women's International League for Peace and Freedom; as Ireland's executive member she was active in attempts to promote an end to the war. She was general secretary of the Irish Women Workers' Union for some forty years from 1917. She opposed the Labour Party's support for Fianna Fáil in 1927. In 1932 she was elected first woman president of the IRISH TRADE UNION CONGRESS and held the office again, 1946–47. As a member of the Administrative Council of the Labour Party, 1932, she opposed the Conditions of Employment Bill (1935). A member of the Commission on Youth Unemployment, 1951, she refused to endorse its report, which she believed infringed women's right to work. She contributed to the IRISH CITIZEN, published trade union pamphlets and articles, and wrote novels, the first of which, *The Proving of Priscilla,* was published in 1902.

Bennett Report (1979). A three-member committee chaired by Judge Harry Bennett of the English Crown Court was established in June 1978 by the Secretary of State for Northern Ireland, ROY MASON, to inquire into the interrogation procedures of the RUC and the machinery for dealing with complaints, following an inquiry by Amnesty International into allegations of ill-treatment at CASTLEREAGH INTERROGATION CENTRE, Belfast. The report noted that there had been cases where injuries in RUC custody were not self-inflicted; it was pointed out by a government minister, however, that of some 3,000 people detained, 1977–78, only fifteen fell into the category of injuries in police custody not self-inflicted. The Bennett Report recommended the installing of closed-circuit television in interview rooms, and that terrorist suspects should have access to a solicitor after forty-eight hours. The report was accepted by the British government.

Beresford, Lord John George (1773–1862), Archbishop of Armagh (Church of Ireland) and Primate of All Ireland, 1822–62; born in Dublin, a member of one of the wealthiest and most powerful families in Ireland, educated at the University of Oxford. He was Dean of Clogher, 1799, Bishop of Cork, 1806, Bishop of Raphoe, 1808, and Bishop of Clogher, 1819. He founded a Protestant weekly paper, the *Patriot.* It has been estimated that Beresford's various church offices yielded him a total of £887,900, and that his family benefited to the amount of £3 million. He spent £30,000 of his fortune restoring Armagh Cathedral, and donated £6,000 to St Columba's College, Rathfarnham, Co. Dublin. He opposed CATHOLIC EMANCIPATION, on the grounds that 'it would transfer from Protestants to Roman Catholics the ascendancy of Ireland.' Opposed to the anti-TITHES agitation, he financially supported clergymen whose income suffered during the tithes war. As Chancellor of Trinity College, Dublin, from 1851, he helped endow a chair of ecclesiastical history and contributed to its library and the erection of the famous campanile.

Bergin, Osborn (1873–1950), scholar; born in Cork, educated at Queen's College, Cork, and in Germany. Professor of Old Irish at UCD, 1908–40, he was first director of the School of Celtic Studies at the DUBLIN INSTITUTE FOR ADVANCED STUDIES, 1940, but resigned within a year. His many publications include *Maidin i mBéarra* (poems, 1918) and *Lebor na hUidre* (with R. I. BEST, 1929). He made several translations from Céitinn, translated Hans Christian Andersen's tales to Irish, 1912, and edited *Irish Grammatical Tracts,* which appeared as a supplement to *Ériu,* 1916–29.

Bernard, John Henry (1860–1927), scholar and Archbishop of Dublin (Church of Ireland), 1915–27; born in India, educated privately and at TCD. Ordained in 1886, he was chaplain to the Lord Lieutenant of Ireland until 1902, when he was appointed Dean of St Patrick's Cathedral, Dublin, and a lecturer in divinity at Trinity College. Commissioner of National Education, 1897–1903, and of Intermediate Education, 1915, he was Bishop of Ossory, Ferns and Leighlin, 1911–15. He was an influential unionist member of the IRISH CONVENTION (1917–18). His writings include *The Cathedral Church of St Patrick* (1903), *The Relationship between Swift and Stella* (1908), and *The Bernards of Kerry* (1922). He translated works by Kant and Eusebius and edited *The Works of Bishop Butler* (2 vols., 1900).

Berry, James (1842–1914), folklorist and SEANCHAÍ; born in Bunowen, Louisburgh, Co. Mayo, educated at HEDGE SCHOOLS and by his uncle, Father Edward O'Malley. In his youth he moved to Carna, Co. Galway, where he remained, working as a farm labourer. His collected and invented stories in the traditional idiom were published in the *Mayo News,* 1910–13. Many of his stories depicted life in the west during the GREAT FAMINE (1845–49).

Bessborough, John William Ponsonby, fourth Earl of (1781–1847), British politician (Whig); educated at the University of Oxford. Though he supported CATHOLIC EMANCIPATION, Bessborough was opposed by DANIEL O'CONNELL when he successfully contested the constituency of Kilkenny, 1826, where he owned extensive estates. He won O'Connell's friendship shortly afterwards and introduced him to the House of Commons, February 1830. He retained Kilkenny, 1831, when JAMES WARREN DOYLE, Bishop of Kildare and Leighlin, ordered his clergy not to oppose him. Appointed Home Secretary, 1834, by his brother-in-law, VISCOUNT MELBOURNE, he was Lord Privy Seal, 1835–39. In July 1846 he became the first resident Irish landlord for a generation to become Lord Lieutenant. His appointment was greeted with enthusiasm by O'Connell and the Irish people, as the country was in the throes of the GREAT FAMINE (1845–49); Bessborough, however, proved unable to influence government policy. He died in office.

Bessborough Commission, appointed under the chairmanship of the sixth Earl of Bessborough, 29 July 1880, to investigate the workings of the Landlord and Tenant (Ireland) Act (1870) (see LAND ACTS) and to recommend further amendments for the purpose of improving the relations between landlords and tenants and of facilitating the purchase of land by tenants. Other members of the Commission were Richard Dowse, CHARLES OWEN O'CONOR, ARTHUR MACMURROGH KAVANAGH, and WILLIAM SHAW. The commissioners held sixty sittings throughout Ireland and interviewed 700 witnesses, including 80 landlords, 70 land agents, and 500 tenant-farmers. The LAND LEAGUE opposed the commission, as tenants were not represented on it. The Bessborough Report, signed on 4 January 1881, found that the 1870 act had not succeeded in its aims and recommended that the 'THREE FS', the basic demand of the LAND LEAGUE, should be granted. Arthur Kavanagh did not support the latter recommendation. In his minority report, O'Conor stressed the need for absolute ownership of the land by the people who worked it. The commission's findings, supported later that month by the report of the RICHMOND COMMISSION, influenced the Land Bill that the Prime Minister, W. E. GLADSTONE, introduced in April 1881.

Best, R. I. [Richard Irvine] (1872–1959), scholar; born in Derry. A bank official in London, he later moved to Paris, where he studied Old Irish under Henri d'Arbois de Jubainville, whose book *Le Cycle Mythologique Irlandais et la Mythologie Celtique* (1884) he translated into English. He was a friend of J. M. SYNGE and JAMES JOYCE (who portrayed him unflatteringly in *Ulysses*). Assistant director of the National Library of Ireland, 1904–24, and director, 1924–40, he was senior professor of Celtic studies at the DUBLIN INSTITUTE FOR ADVANCED STUDIES, 1940–47, and chairman of the IRISH MANUSCRIPTS COMMISSION, 1948–56. An authority on Irish palaeography and philology, he made translations from French to Irish and English. His magnum opus, *Bibliography of Irish Philology and of Printed Irish Literature in the National Library* (1913), was an extension of his card index guide. Other works include *Bibliography of the Publications of Whitley Stokes* (1911), *Bibliography of the Publications of Kuno Meyer* (1923), *Gein Branduib ocus Aedain from the Yellow Book of Lecan* (1927), *Lebor na hUidre* (with Osborn Bergin, 1929), *Seanchas Már: The Ancient Laws of Ireland* (1931), and *Bibliography of Irish Philology and Manuscript Literature Publications, 1913–1941* (1942).

Bewley, Charles (1890–1969), lawyer and diplomat; born in Dublin to a Quaker family, educated at the University of Oxford, where he became a Catholic. After practising on the western circuit he established his own legal practice and also lectured in University College, Galway. Active in SINN FÉIN, he represented Ireland in Germany, 1921–23. The first envoy of the Irish Free State to the Vatican, 1929–33, he continued in the diplomatic service after Éamon de Valera came to power, 1932. Anti-communist, anti-Jewish, and anti-British, he represented Ireland in Berlin from 1933 until he was in effect forced to resign by 1939 because of embarrassment in the Department of External Affairs at his pro-Nazi positions. He continued to support the Nazis, working as a journalist and propagandist; under the alias 'Dreher' he received a salary of 1,000 marks per month from Berlin. He was transferred in 1943 to the jurisdiction of Göring, about whom he later wrote an uncritical biography, *Herman Goering and the Third Reich* (1952). He was briefly interned after the war and released on 18 December 1945. He published an autobiography, *Memoirs of a Wild Goose* (1989).

Bianconi, Charles (Carlo) (1785–1875), businessman and transport pioneer; born in Tregelo, Como, Italy, left school at fifteen. His travels brought him to Dublin, 1802, where he worked for a print-seller. He became a print-seller and opened a shop in Carrick-on-Suir, Co. Tipperary, 1807, then moved to Waterford, 1808, where he met EDMUND RICE, who taught him English. Following Napoléon Bonaparte's defeat at the Battle of Waterloo (1815) the demand for horses dropped, and Bianconi bought a horse and jaunting-car for less than £10. In Clonmel, Co. Tipperary, where he was called 'Brian Cooney', he organised the first of his coaches (which came to be known as 'bians'), Clonmel–Caher, 6 July 1815, carrying six passengers at a return fare of 2 pence. By 1816 he had larger cars, known as 'Finn McCools' and 'Master Dawsons' (after a popular landlord), covering some 226 miles per day in 1816, 1,170 miles by 1825, and 2,234 miles by 1836. Accommodating up to twenty passengers and drawn by two pairs of horses, by 1837 his sixty-seven cars and nine hundred horses were averaging 4,244 miles daily.

With the introduction of railways, 1838, Bianconi adapted his coaching business to provide feeder services between stations and also bought railway shares, becoming a director of the Waterford and Limerick Railway Company and of the National Bank. He was elected Mayor of Clonmel, 1844. He bought a building in St Stephen's Green, Dublin, to be used in the founding of the CATHOLIC UNIVERSITY OF IRELAND, 1854. Deputy Lieutenant of Co. Tipperary, 1863, he retired after disposing of his business to employees and agents, 1865. His last major benefaction was the erection of a shrine to house the heart of DANIEL O'CONNELL in the Irish College, Rome.

'Biblicals', a name given to the 'NEW REFORMERS', evangelical clergymen active among the Catholic population in the second decade of the nineteenth century. Proselytising, preaching, and distributing free Bibles, they were part of the 'SECOND REFORMATION'.

Biggar, Joseph Gillis (1828–1890), politician (nationalist); born in Belfast, educated at the RBAI. Raised as a Presbyterian, he became a Catholic in 1877 (allegedly to annoy his sister). He joined the HOME GOVERNMENT ASSOCIATION, 1870, and was member of Parliament for Co. Cavan, 1874–90. He inaugurated the 'OBSTRUCTIONISM' policy in the House of Commons, 1875. A member of the Supreme Council of the IRB, he was expelled for refusing to break with the constitutional approach in 1877. He was treasurer of the LAND LEAGUE and at one time a close associate of T. M. HEALY. He caused a sensation in the House of Commons when he forced the withdrawal of the Prince of Wales (Queen Victoria's son) with the traditional challenge 'I spy a stranger.' He conducted his own case before the Parnell Commission, 1889 (see 'PARNELLISM AND CRIME'). One of his last acts was to move the re-election of CHARLES STEWART PARNELL as chairman of the Irish Party, 11 February 1890. Because of his inelegant style of speech it was said that no member with such poor qualifications occupied so much of the Parliament's time; he once spoke for more than four hours on swine fever, and would have continued longer had his voice not failed him.

Bigger, Francis Joseph (1863–1926), scholar; born in Belfast, educated at the RBAI and King's Inns, Dublin. Qualified as a solicitor, 1888, he founded a law firm with George W. Strahan. A student of Irish and a piper, he was a member of the Royal Irish Academy and a fellow of the Royal Society of Antiquaries of Ireland. His home outside Belfast was the organisational centre for literary and cultural movements, and from his own resources he restored ruined castles and churches and re-erected ancient gravestones and crosses. His extensive library, with that of J. S. CRONE, formed the basis of Belfast Public Library's Irish collection. His works include *Vicinity of Belfast* (1894), *Gaelic Leaguers and Irish Industries* (1907), *Labourers' Cottages for Ireland* (1907), *Irish Penal Crosses, 1713–1781* (1909), *The Ulster Land War of 1770* (1910), *Relic of Penal Days* (1920), and several biographies. He also edited the *Ulster Journal of Archaeology* from 1894.

Birkenhead, F. E. [Frederick Edwin] Smith, first Earl of (1872–1930), lawyer and politician (Conservative); born in Birkenhead, Cheshire. A member of Parliament from 1906 and a leading Conservative spokesman for the unionist movement, he opposed the PARLIA-

MENT ACT (1911). He served in the ULSTER VOLUNTEER FORCE as EDWARD CARSON's *aide de camp* or 'galloper' and became known contemptuously as 'Galloper Smith'. As Attorney-General he led the prosecution at the trial of ROGER CASEMENT. As Lord Chancellor, 1919–22, he was a member of the British delegation that negotiated the ANGLO-IRISH TREATY in December 1921. He published legal and historical works, including *International Law* (1911), *Famous Trials of History* (1927), and *Turning Points in History* (1930).

Birmingham Six. On 21 November 1974 nineteen people died and 182 were injured in explosions at two pubs in Birmingham, the Mulberry Bush and Tavern in the Town. One Irishman was arrested in the city and five others were arrested as they were about to board the Heysham–Belfast ferry. The six men—Hugh Callaghan, Patrick Hill, Gerard Hunter, Richard McIlkenny, Billy Power, and John Walker, soon to be known as the 'Birmingham Six'—were sentenced to twenty-one terms of life imprisonment, though repeatedly claiming their innocence. Their case was taken up widely in Ireland and England. The six were released when the Director of Public Prosecutions announced in February 1991 that the scientific evidence against them was being dropped and it was found that the convictions secured by the West Midlands Police were 'unsafe'. (See also GUILDFORD FOUR.)

Birrell, Augustine (1850–1933), British politician (Liberal); born in Liverpool, educated at the University of Cambridge and called to the bar. A member of Parliament from 1889, he earned a wide reputation as an orator. His IRISH COUNCIL BILL was dropped, 3 June 1907, following nationalist opposition. As Chief Secretary for Ireland, 1907–16, his main achievements were the IRISH UNIVERSITIES ACT (1908) and the Irish Land Act (1909) (see LAND ACTS). His readings of the monthly reports of the RIC, he claimed, afforded him a real insight into the customs, habits and pastimes of every village in the country. The Royal Commission into the EASTER RISING (1916) held Birrell 'primarily responsible for the situation that was allowed to arise and the outbreak that occurred.' He resigned his post immediately after the rising and left politics in 1918.

Black and Tans. During the WAR OF INDEPENDENCE the RIC became the particular target of the Volunteers (later the IRA). There were mass resignations, and recruitment to the force was adversely affected. The British government, unwilling to acknowledge an armed rebellion in a Crown territory, decided to augment the RIC rather than use the British army. The new recruits on their arrival, 25 March 1920, were placed under the control of SIR NEVILLE MACREADY. Because of a shortage of uniforms they were issued with dark-green RIC tunics and khaki British army trousers; this combination reminded people in Munster of the Co. Limerick hunt known as the Scarteen Black-and-Tans. According to WINSTON CHURCHILL they were selected from 'a great press of applicants on account of their intelligence, their characters, and their records in the war'; in fact the great majority were from the ranks of the unemployed in the wake of the Great War. According to the guerrilla leader TOM BARRY, quite a number were 'rather decent men,' including one William Hill stationed in Mallow, who 'liked his pint, and never insulted anyone or did anything to anyone' (and who subsequently became a multi-millionaire bookmaker).

The Black and Tans were paid 10 shillings a day 'all found', in addition to a separation allowance. Their avowed intention, according to the *Dublin Police Journal,* was to 'make Ireland a hell for rebels to live in.' They were based principally in recognised trouble spots in Cos. Clare, Cork, Dublin, Galway, Kerry, Kilkenny, Limerick, Mayo, Meath, and Tipperary. Their notoriety stemmed from the ferocity of reprisals to IRA actions. They drove through towns and villages firing rifles indiscriminately while singing 'We are the boys of the RIC, as happy, happy as can be.' The incidents with which they were associated include the burning of Bruff (Co. Limerick), Kilmallock (Co. Limerick), Balbriggan (Co. Dublin), Cork, Milltown Malbay (Co. Clare), Lehinch (Co. Clare), Ennistimon (Co. Clare), Tubercurry (Co. Sligo), Midleton (Co. Cork), and Trim (Co. Meath). They were also responsible for the murders of TOMÁS MACCURTAIN and GEORGE CLANCY and the killings in Croke Park, Dublin, on BLOODY SUNDAY (1920).

Increasing concern among liberal opinion in Britain, the United States and the dominions influenced the Prime Minister, DAVID LLOYD GEORGE, to open negotiations with the Irish Republican government, culminating in the ANGLO-IRISH TREATY (1921).

Blair, Tony (born 1953), lawyer and politician (British Labour Party). Committed to 'unity by consent' when he became leader of the British Labour Party, 1994, he later stated that a British government should not push Northern Ireland one way or the other. He supported the Prime Minister, JOHN MAJOR, on the 'decommissioning' of paramilitary arms as a preliminary to admission to multi-party talks (the Northern Ireland Forum). He urged Sinn Féin to accept the Mitchell Principles (see GEORGE MITCHELL) and join the talks, April 1997. As Prime Minister from 1997, he appointed MARJORIE MOWLAM Secretary of State for Northern Ireland, 1997, and also authorised government officials to hold talks with SINN FÉIN, provided 'events on the ground did not make it impossible to do so.' He issued a statement, 1 June 1997, saying that British policy during the GREAT FAMINE (1845–49) had failed the people of Ireland.

Blair worked closely with the Taoiseach, BERTIE AHERN, on the PEACE PROCESS. With the Provisional IRA observing a ceasefire from July 1997, he became the first Prime Minister since 1921 to meet a Sinn Féin leader when he met GERRY ADAMS in October. He conceded a long-standing nationalist demand for a new inquiry into the events of BLOODY SUNDAY (1972) (see WIDGERY TRIBUNAL and SAVILLE INQUIRY). Blair and Ahern played central roles in bringing about the BELFAST AGREEMENT (1998) and subsequently holding the peace process and the Northern Ireland institutions together through periodic crises. Following the establishment of the INDEPENDENT INTERNATIONAL BODY ON DECOMMISSIONING they made a joint statement declaring that while decommissioning was not a 'precondition' for participation in the Executive it was an 'obligation'; there should be an act of reconciliation during which some arms would voluntarily be put beyond use, to be verified by General John de Chastelain, head of the decommissioning body. Reassuring unionists, Blair confirmed that there would be no change in the status of Northern Ireland without the consent of the people, and that decision-making should lie with a power-sharing Assembly; there must be fairness and accountability, paramilitary groups and their supporters would be excluded from government, and prisoners would not be released unless violence ended. (Prisoners were released, though sporadic violence and feuds continued over the next few years.)

Following the bomb explosion in Omagh, Co. Tyrone, 15 August 1998, Blair introduced new anti-terrorist legislation that permitted the state to imprison suspects on the word of a senior police officer (a policy that already existed in the Republic). He was the first British Prime Minister to address the Oireachtas, November 1998. He suspended the Northern Ireland Executive and Assembly and reintroduced direct rule from London on 14 October 2002.

Blaney, Neil T. (1922–1995), politician (Fianna Fáil and INDEPENDENT FIANNA FÁIL); born in Rossnakill, Fanad, Co. Donegal, educated at St Eunan's College, Letterkenny. He won his father's Dáil seat in December 1948 and held it until his death. As Minister for Posts and Telegraphs, March–December 1957, he initiated the plans for a national television service. As Minister for Local Government until November 1966 he was responsible for the introduction of a scheme to bring piped water to rural Ireland, the building of high-rise flats at BALLYMUN, Dublin, and the introduction of planning legislation. He was Minister for Agriculture and Fisheries in the first government headed by JACK LYNCH, 1966, and played a leading role in the organising of Fianna Fáil election campaigns.

Events in Northern Ireland from August 1969 brought Blaney into conflict with Lynch. He publicly challenged Lynch's leadership during a rally at Letterkenny, Co. Donegal, 8 December 1969; he refused Lynch's request for his resignation and was dismissed together with CHARLES HAUGHEY, 6 May. Arrested on 28 May with Haughey and others, he was charged with conspiracy to illegally import arms and ammunition; the charges against him were dropped by Dublin District Court, 2 July (see ARMS TRIALS). When he abstained on a motion of confidence in his former colleague James Gibbons he was expelled from the parliamentary party, November 1971, and from Fianna Fáil, June 1972. He was the sole member of Independent Fianna Fáil until joined by Patrick Keaveney, June 1976 to June 1977. He broke with the Dáil consensus on the HUNGER STRIKES and campaigned for BOBBY SANDS in Fermanagh-South Tyrone. Elected to the European Parliament for Connacht-Ulster in 1979, he lost the seat to Ray MacSharry, 1984, but regained it in 1989. Because of ill-health he did not stand in 1994. He was the last survivor of de Valera's last government (1957–59). Blaney's control of the Fianna Fáil organisation in Co. Donegal was the subject of a study, *The Donegal Mafia* (1976) by Paul Martin Sacks.

blanket protest, a protest that began on 15

September 1976 at the Maze Prison (known to republicans by its original name, Long Kesh), near Lisburn, Co. Antrim, when Kieran Nugent, refusing to wear prison uniform, protested by wearing only a blanket. Grievances among imprisoned members of paramilitary groups, who saw themselves as political prisoners, had been festering since the removal of privileges as SPECIAL CATEGORY prisoners earlier that year. The prisoners had five demands: the right not to wear prison uniform; the right not to perform prison work; the right to associate freely with other prisoners; the right to weekly visits, letters and parcels and to organise education and recreational pursuits; and the full restoration of remission lost through the protest. Within two years nearly three hundred prisoners were refusing to wear prison clothes, most of them in Block H5.

A new phase of the protest began in March 1978 when the prisoners refused to leave their cells to attend the showers and toilets, alleging harassment by prison officers. Starting as the 'no wash' protest, it was soon notorious as the 'dirty protest', during which the prisoners refused to wash or attend the toilets and soiled their cells. By 1980 five hundred prisoners were involved.

Blasket Islands, Co. Kerry, a small group of islands off the south-west coast of Co. Kerry, north of the entrance to Dingle Bay, the most westerly inhabited part of Europe (with Iceland) until November 1953, when the last inhabitants were taken to the mainland. The community and culture of the Great Blasket attracted the attention of numerous native and foreign scholars of Irish; noted foreign scholars included Robin Flower (1881–1946), Carl Marstrander (1883–1965), and George Thomson (1903–1987). Books derived from the Blasket community's way of life and rich oral tradition include works by Tomás Ó Criomhthainn: *Allagar na hInise* (1928), *An tOileánach* (edited by Pádraig Ó Siochfhradha, 1929), and *Seanchas ón Oileán Tiar* (1965); Peig Sayers (1873–1958): *Peig* (1936) and *Machnamh Seanmhná* (1939, translated by Séamus Ennis as *Reflections of an Old Woman,* 1962); Seán Ó Criomhthainn (1898–1975), son of Tomás: *Lá dár Saol* (1969, translated by Tim Enright as *A Day in Our Life,* 1992); Mícheál Ó Gaoithín (1904–1974), son of Peig Sayers and Patsy 'Flint' Ó Gaoithín and a noted and prolific poet: *Is Trua Ná Fanann an Óige* (1953, translated by Tim Enright as *A Pity Youth Does Not Last,* 1982), *Coinnle Corra* (1968), and *Beatha Pheig Sayers* (1970); and Muiris Ó Súileabháin (1904–1950): *Fiche Bliain ag Fás* (translated by Moya Llewelyn Davies and George Thomson as *Twenty Years a-Growing,* 1933).

Bloody Friday (1972). On 21 July 1972 some twenty Provisional IRA bomb explosions killed eleven people and injured 130 within little more than an hour in the centre of Belfast.

Bloody Sunday (1920). The threat posed by British agents under Ormond Winter (the 'CAIRO GANG') to smash his intelligence network forced MICHAEL COLLINS into a pre-emptive strike. A list of twenty agents was prepared for summary execution. On Sunday 21 November there was a co-ordinated swoop by the 'SQUAD' at several places, and fourteen British officers were shot dead: Lieutenant Peter Ashmunt Ames, Captain G. T. Bagally, Temporary Captain George Bennett, Major Dowling, Captain Fitzgerald, Captain H. B. Keenlyside, Lieutenant D. L. McLean (chief intelligence officer), Lieutenant McMahon (alias Angliss), Colonel Montgomery, Captain W. F. Newbury, Captain Leonard Price, T. H. Smith (a civilian agent), A. L. Wilde, and Colonel Woodcock. Four agents were wounded but survived, and two others were absent from their lodgings. Captain McCormack of the Royal Army Veterinary Corps, in Dublin from Egypt for the purchase of mules, was shot in error at the Gresham Hotel, the doorman pointing out room 22 instead of room 24. The only IRA casualty, Frank Teeling, was wounded in the leg; he escaped from Kilmainham Jail, where he was under sentence of death.

Later the same day two Republican prisoners, Peadar Clancy and Dick McKee, captured the previous evening, were shot at Dublin Castle together with Conor Clune 'while trying to escape.' Two IRA members, Paddy Moran and Tom Whelan, were hanged at Mountjoy Jail, Dublin, 21 March 1921, for alleged complicity in the shootings. Moran was so convinced of his innocence that he refused to join Teeling in his escape.

The killing of the agents provoked reprisal in the afternoon by BLACK AND TANS at Croke Park, Dublin, where a football match was being played in aid of the IRISH VOLUNTEERS DEPENDANTS' FUND. The soldiers, using machine-guns and rifles, fired into the crowd and onto the playing-field; twelve spectators were killed and some sixty wounded, while many more were injured in the resultant panic. One player, Michael Hogan of Co. Tipperary, was killed, as was a young Wexford man, Thomas Ryan, who was kneeling in prayer beside the dying Hogan. The casualties would undoubtedly have been higher had not officers of the AUXILIARIES ordered the Black and Tans to cease fire. A British regular army officer demanded the release of the Tipperary team from a number of Black and Tans who had surrounded them; having advised the players to don overcoats over their playing kit, he and his unit escorted them to their hotel. According to BRIGADIER-GENERAL FRANK CROZIER, who commanded the Auxiliaries (and who coined the name 'Bloody Sunday'), the intention of the soldiers had been to search for arms.

Bloody Sunday (1921), a name given by Catholics in Belfast to concerted attacks by factions of the Orange Order and RUC Special Constabulary on Catholic people and property on 10 July 1921. Fifteen people were killed and sixty-eight seriously injured, and 161 Catholic homes were razed. There was no material damage to Protestant-owned properties. The unprovoked assaults were believed in part to have been a Protestant reaction to the BELFAST BOYCOTT.

Bloody Sunday (1972). On 30 January 1972 thirteen people were shot dead and seventeen injured within thirty minutes by British soldiers of the Parachute Regiment in the Bogside area of Derry during an anti-internment rally organised by the Derry Civil Rights Association. Six of the dead were seventeen years old. Some twenty thousand people had participated in the march, which was illegal (as were many demonstrations at the time). To prevent the march from entering the city centre the British army diverted it into the Bogside, where civil rights leaders intended to rally at 'Free Derry Corner'. The role of the army, according to its commander, Lieutenant-General Harry Tuzo, was to be low-key and to avoid confrontation with demonstrators. Towards the end of the march some youths threw stones and other missiles at the soldiers, who, apparently believing they were under sniper attack, fired a total of 108 rounds. There was a general local rejection of claims that the soldiers had been fired on; both the Provisional IRA and Official IRA denied any involvement. The Taoiseach, JACK LYNCH, described it as 'an unwarranted attack on unarmed civilians,' and the government declared a national day of mourning. There were widespread anti-British demonstrations, notably in Dublin, where the British Embassy was burned down, 2 February.

The British government appointed the WIDGERY TRIBUNAL, which began sitting within a month. While exonerating the British army, Widgery found that

> none of the deceased or wounded is proved to have been shot while handling a firearm or bomb. Some are wholly acquitted of complicity in such action; but there is a strong suspicion that some others had been firing weapons or handling bombs in the course of the afternoon and that yet others had been closely supporting them.

On 21 August 1973 the Derry City Coroner, Major Hubert O'Neill, said that the soldiers had been guilty of 'sheer unadulterated murder.' Following more than two decades of agitation by relatives of the victims, the SAVILLE INQUIRY, authorised by the British government, opened at the Guildhall, Derry, on 27 March 2000.

Blowick, Joseph (1903–1970), farmer and politician (Clann na Talmhan); born in Belcarra, Co. Mayo, educated at national school. First elected to Dáil Éireann in 1943 for the Farmers' Union, he subsequently represented CLANN NA TALMHAN, of which he was leader, 1944–65. He was Minister for Lands and Fisheries, 1948–51 and 1954–57, in which capacity he was closely associated with re-afforestation schemes. Dissatisfaction with the party's electoral performance led to his replacement as leader by a committee of seven in 1958. He continued as party leader in Dáil Éireann but from 1961 was in effect an independent TD.

Blueshirts, the name given to an organisation originally known as the ARMY COMRADES' ASSOCIATION. Members adopted blue shirts as a uniform in April 1933. On 20 July the leadership was given to EOIN O'DUFFY, who renamed the organisation the NATIONAL GUARD. The philosophy of the movement came from the Papal encyclical *Quadragesimo Anno* and from Mussolini's theory of the corporate state; among its aims was the reunification of Ireland. Members had to be Irish or have Irish parents and to profess the Christian faith and were pledged to uphold Christian principles. Anti-Jewish and anti-communist, the organisation was opposed to alien control and influence in national affairs. The 'St Patrick's Cross' flag (a red diagonal cross on white) was adopted as its emblem. Early apologists for the movement included Dr Michael Tierney and Dr J. J. Hogan of UCD, both of whom contributed to UNITED IRELAND and to the movement's own paper, the *Blueshirt,* 1933–35.

The effect of the ECONOMIC WAR on agriculture gained support for the Blueshirts. O'Duffy attacked the IRA and the government of ÉAMON DE VALERA. The government, alarmed by the rhetoric of the movement and the public violence that resulted, moved against the Blueshirts, banning unauthorised firearms, including those held by former members of CUMANN NA NGAEDHEAL. O'Duffy announced that he would lead a march to Leinster Lawn on 13 March 1933 to hold a commemorative rally in honour of ARTHUR GRIFFITH, MICHAEL COLLINS, and KEVIN O'HIGGINS. The government, alarmed at the prospect of a clash between Blueshirt and IRA sympathisers, and viewing the march as O'Duffy's attempt to emulate his hero Mussolini's march on Rome, banned it, 12 August. The Military Tribunal established by W. T. COSGRAVE in 1931 was revived, and the National Guard was outlawed.

O'Duffy announced the establishment of the League of Ireland Association. Cumann na nGaedheal, disillusioned with Cosgrave's leadership in the wake of electoral failures, looked to O'Duffy to head a new party, which was formed in September 1933 from a merger of Cumann na nGaedheal, the NATIONAL CENTRE PARTY, and the Blueshirts. The new party, FINE GAEL, had O'Duffy as president and Cosgrave as a vice-president, and the National Guard became a youth movement within Fine Gael under the title of the YOUNG IRELAND ASSOCIATION. This was reorganised as the LEAGUE OF YOUTH, 14 December 1933. The first TD to appear in Dáil Éireann wearing his blue shirt was Captain Sidney Minch of Kildare on 27 September 1933; his example was followed the next day by some dozen TDs, including Thomas F. O'Higgins and DESMOND FITZGERALD.

When the Blueshirts called for the withholding of land annuities from the government, O'Duffy's leadership became a source of embarrassment. The government's bill to outlaw the wearing of unauthorised uniforms was defeated in the Seanad. Fine Gael became more disenchanted with the movement when the party failed to make an impact during the local government elections, 26 June 1934. It won a majority on eight out of twenty-four county councils (the rest were won by Fianna Fáil). The congress of 18–19 August 1934 called on farmers not to pay land annuities if the government insisted on collecting them during the agricultural depression (see ECONOMIC WAR) and unless the government set up an independent tribunal to examine the farmers' case. In August, J. J. Hogan resigned in protest at O'Duffy's behaviour, and within a brief period, under pressure from the Fine Gael leadership, O'Duffy resigned, 21 September 1934. When Ned Cronin defeated O'Duffy for leadership of the Blueshirts, O'Duffy founded the League of Greenshirts.

The Blueshirts' decline continued throughout 1935. Though the Fine Gael leadership disbanded the movement in October 1936, there was a brief revival when O'Duffy led a group to Spain to support Franco's forces in the SPANISH CIVIL WAR.

Blunt, Wilfrid Scawen (1840–1922), diplomat and author; born in Sussex, educated at Stonyhurst College, Lancashire. He entered the diplomatic service in 1858 and served in the principal European capitals until 1872, when he inherited valuable properties. His travels, particularly in India, made him a strong opponent of imperialism. He supported the IRISH PARTY and was imprisoned for two months in 1887 for advocating the PLAN OF CAMPAIGN. He acted as intermediary between his cousin GEORGE WYNDHAM and JOHN REDMOND in discussions leading to the introduction of the Irish Land Act (1903) (see LAND ACTS). In his will he stipulated that his body was to be wrapped in his old oriental travelling-rug and not placed in a coffin. Blunt's *Diaries* (2 vols., 1919–20) were published with a foreword by LADY AUGUSTA GREGORY, with whom he had a close relationship.

Blythe, Ernest (1889–1975), soldier, politician (Sinn Féin and Cumann na nGaedheal), and writer; born in Lisburn, Co. Antrim, educated at national school. A civil servant in the Department of Agriculture and Technical Instruction in Dublin from 1905, he joined the Gaelic League and Sinn Féin and was recruited to the IRB by SEÁN O'CASEY. He worked for the *North Down Herald* while organising the IRB in Ulster. Organiser for the Irish Volunteers in Munster and south Connacht, he was arrested before the Easter Rising (1916). Having represented Co. Monaghan in the first Dáil, he was successively Minister for Trade and Commerce, 1919–22, Minister for Local Government in the Provisional Government, August–

September 1922, Minister for Local Government and Public Health, September 1922 to September 1923, and Minister for Finance, 1923–32. In Finance he reduced the old-age pension from 10 shillings to 9 shillings, January 1924. He established AN GÚM, the publishing branch of the Department of Education, and encouraged the establishment of TAIBHDHEARC NA GAILLIMHE and of Coláiste Mhuire, the first Irish-medium secondary school in Dublin, and was responsible for the first direct grant to the ABBEY THEATRE. He was Vice-President of the Executive Council (deputy head of government), 1927–32. He reduced government expenditure from £42 million in 1923 to £24 million in 1926/27; income tax during the same period was reduced from 25 per cent to 15 per cent.

After losing his seat in the general election of 1933 he was a senator, 1934–36. Placed on the board of the Abbey Theatre by W. B. YEATS, he was managing director from 1941 until his retirement in 1967 but continued as a director until 1972. A charge sometimes laid against him at the Abbey was that a knowledge of Irish was more important than acting ability. De Valera appointed him president of Comhdháil Náisiúnta na Gaeilge, 1943. He produced a blueprint for a Gaeltacht Development Board, 1953, which led to the founding of the Department of the Gaeltacht, 1956, and Gaeltarra Éireann, 1957. He published *Briseadh na Teorann* ('the breaking of the border') in 1955.

Board of Erin (Ancient Order of Hibernians), the executive of the Irish branch of the AOH, created at the 1902 conference in an attempt to heal the breach between the Irish and American sections. A minority in Ireland (approximately 6,500) refused to accept the reconciliation and abrogated the authority of the board, which represented 60,000 members in 700 branches. The national president was JOSEPH DEVLIN, who used the AOH as his constituency machine in Belfast.

Bodenstown Sunday, the annual commemoration of Theobald Wolfe Tone, generally regarded as the father of Irish republicanism, who is buried at Bodenstown, near Sallins, Co. Kildare. Annual ceremonies are organised by the IRA, traditionally on the Sunday nearest 20 June, and also by Fianna Fáil. The 1913 ceremony was filmed by the newsreel cameraman and exhibitor J. T. Jameson of the Irish Animated Picture Company and shown several times nightly in Dublin; writing to JOHN DEVOY, THOMAS CLARKE commented: 'No pictures he has ever shown (and he has been fourteen years in the business) ever received such tremendous applause. The Old Room [in the Rotunda Rooms] appeared to shake . . .' In 1939 the Taoiseach, ÉAMON DE VALERA, in response to IRA outrages in Britain, banned its traditional Bodenstown commemoration.

Boland, F. H. [Frederick] (1904–1985), civil servant and diplomat; born in Dublin, educated at TCD and King's Inns. Awarded a Rockefeller Research Fellowship in social science, he studied at universities in the United States, 1926–28. He entered the Department of External Affairs in 1929, was first secretary at Paris, 1932–34, and head of section, 1934–36; he moved to the Department of Industry and Commerce, of which he was secretary, 1945–50. He had an uneasy relationship with the Minister for External Affairs, SEÁN MACBRIDE, with whom he worked on the LONG-TERM RECOVERY PROGRAMME. Ambassador to Britain, 1950–56, he was Ireland's first permanent representative at the United Nations, 1956–64, and president of the General Assembly, 1960–61. A member of the Royal Irish Academy, he was chancellor of Trinity College, Dublin, 1964–85. The poet Eavan Boland (born 1944) is his daughter.

Boland, Gerald (1885–1973), politician (Fianna Fáil); born in Manchester and raised in Dublin, educated at the O'Brien Institute, Fairview. He worked as a fitter with the Midland Great Western Railway of Ireland. Having fought at Jacob's factory, Bishop Street, Dublin, in the EASTER RISING (1916), he was later active in both Sinn Féin and the IRA. Opposed to the ANGLO-IRISH TREATY (1921), he fought against the Provisional Government during the CIVIL WAR. A founder-member of Fianna Fáil, he worked with SEÁN LEMASS to create the party's national constituency organisation, which made it the best-organised party in the country. As Minister for Justice, 1939–48, he was vilified in republican circles for the measures used against the IRA. He resigned from Fianna Fáil when his son, KEVIN BOLAND, broke with the organisation, 1970.

Boland, Harry (1887–1922), republican; born in Dublin, educated at Synge Street Christian Brothers' School and De La Salle College, Castletown, Co. Laois. A member of the IRB, he was a prominent member of the Irish

Volunteers. Imprisoned for his part in the Easter Rising (1916), on his release in 1917 he was secretary of Sinn Féin, working with his friend MICHAEL COLLINS in the reorganising of the Volunteers and the IRB. He assisted Collins in planning the escape of ÉAMON DE VALERA from Lincoln Jail, 3 February 1919. Member of the first Dáil for Co. Roscommon, he represented Dáil Éireann in the United States, May 1919, helping to organise de Valera's fund-raising trip. As his secretary he supported de Valera in the rift with JOHN DEVOY and CLAN NA GAEL. He rejected the ANGLO-IRISH TREATY (1921), claiming it was a betrayal of the republic established by the first Dáil. Influential in arranging the PACT ELECTION with Collins and de Valera, he was re-elected for Co. Roscommon, June 1922; a month later he was mortally wounded at a hotel in Skerries, Co. Dublin, during the CIVIL WAR.

Boland, John Pius (1870–1958), Olympic gold-medallist and politician (Home Rule Party); born in Dublin, educated at the Universities of Oxford, Bonn, and London. On 30 March 1896 he became the first Irish person to win an Olympic gold medal when he won the tennis singles in Athens; he also won the doubles. Called to the bar in London, where he was active in the Gaelic League, he was Nationalist MP for South Kerry, 1900–18, and party whip, 1906–18. Active in the campaign for the NATIONAL UNIVERSITY OF IRELAND and for a knowledge of Irish as a prerequisite to matriculation, he was a major influence in the library movement and in the founding of the Irish Rural Libraries Association; he also encouraged the establishment of Irish-language summer schools for teachers.

Boland, Kevin (1917–2001), politician (Fianna Fáil and Aontacht Éireann); born in Dublin, son of GERALD BOLAND, educated at St Joseph's Christian Brothers' School, Fairview. On his first day in Dáil Éireann, 1957, ÉAMON DE VALERA appointed him Minister for Defence, a portfolio he held until October 1961. He was Minister for Social Welfare, 1961–65, and Minister for Local Government under JACK LYNCH, November 1966. He worked closely with NEIL BLANEY in achieving important Fianna Fáil by-election successes, including Limerick East, where DESMOND O'MALLEY was returned, 1968. He resigned on 6 May 1970 in protest at the dismissal of NEIL BLANEY and CHARLES HAUGHEY (see ARMS TRIALS). He was expelled from Fianna Fáil by secret ballot (60 to 11) on 4 June 1970 and resigned from the National Executive, of which he was general secretary, 22 June. He resigned his Dáil seat on 4 November and in 1971 founded AONTACHT ÉIREANN; the party failed to make an impact and he resigned from the leadership and from active politics, 1976. He published *We Won't Stand (Idly) By* (1972) and *The Rise and Fall of Fianna Fáil* (1982).

Border Campaign (1956–62). Devised by Seán Cronin, 'Operation Harvest' was the code-name for the declaration of war by the IRA against the British presence in Northern Ireland. Launched on 12 December 1956, it resulted in the death of six members of the RUC and two IRA volunteers; seven others were killed in premature explosions before the end of the campaign. Early casualties included SEÁN SOUTH and Fergal O'Hanlon (the subjects of Dominic Behan's ballad 'The Patriot Game'). There were several hundred incidents causing some £1½ million worth of damage. The campaign received little support and was called off in 1962.

Boundary Commission. On 26 April 1924 the Irish Free State formally requested the British government to constitute the Boundary Commission provided for by article 12 of the ANGLO-IRISH TREATY (1921). The process was delayed until 10 May 1924, when the Prime Minister of Northern Ireland, Sir James Craig, refused to appoint a commissioner, and the British government introduced legislation empowering the appointment of a third member.

The commission consisted of J. R. Fisher (1855–1939), a unionist journalist; EOIN MACNEILL, Minister for Education of the Irish Free State; and Mr Justice Feetham (1874–1965), a South African judge, appointed chairman jointly by the British and Irish governments. Its brief was to 'determine in accordance with the wishes of the inhabitants, so far as may be compatible with economic and geographic conditions, the boundaries between Northern Ireland and the rest of Ireland.' The commission sat from 5 November 1924 to 2 July 1925, during which time it considered 130 submissions and examined 585 witnesses. The commissioners agreed not to publish or disclose their findings until they could agree on a joint report. On 7 November 1925 the *Morning Post* (London) broke the embargo to reveal that the commissioners would leave Cos. Antrim, Derry, Down, Fermanagh and Tyrone as they were, while an area of east Co. Donegal would become part of Northern Ireland and south Co. Armagh would become part of the Free State. In all, the commission proposed that 183,290 acres and 31,319 people, of whom 27,843 were Catholics, would transfer to the Free State, while Northern Ireland would receive 49,242 acres and 7,594 people, of whom 4,830 were Protestants. The effect of the changes would be to reduce the area of Northern Ireland by 3.7 per cent and its population by 1.8 per cent. The border would be shortened from 286 miles to 229 miles.

MacNeill resigned, accusing the chairman of having subordinated the wishes of border inhabitants to political influence; Feetham had in fact interpreted the commission's brief in accordance with the letter of article 12. On 3 December 1925 the three governments agreed that the border should remain as fixed by the ANGLO-IRISH TREATY and the GOVERNMENT OF IRELAND ACT (1920). The Irish Free State and Northern Ireland were relieved of their financial liabilities under the Treaty, and Northern Ireland was to retain powers conferred on it by the Government of Ireland Act. The Free State assumed the total cost of the damages incurred during the period 1919–22, and the payment of LAND ANNUITIES to the British government was to continue. The British government transferred its powers under the Council of Ireland to Northern Ireland. The report of the commission was published in 1969.

Bourke, Thomas Francis (born 1840), Fenian; born in Fethard, Co. Tipperary. Having emigrated to the United States, 1852, he trained as a house-painter and joined the FENIANS, 1865. He returned to Ireland in 1866 with the rank of general in the Fenian army and led a column in the rising of 1867. He was wounded and captured while making his escape at Ballyhurst, Co. Tipperary, following the rout of his inexperienced soldiers. He was sentenced to be hanged, drawn, and quartered, but the sentence was commuted to penal servitude for life. On release, 1873, he returned to the United States, where he was elected to the Council of the Fenians in New York, 27 January 1876.

Boycott, Captain Charles Cunningham (1832–1897), land agent; born in Burgh St Peter, Norfolk. Stationed in Ireland with the 39th Regiment of Foot, he sold his commission, 1853, married, and bought a short lease on a farm in Co. Tipperary. In 1855 he obtained a sub-lease on some 2,000 acres on Achill Island, Co. Mayo, from the IRISH CHURCH MISSIONS. Notoriously litigious, he was frequently at odds with his neighbours until moving to Lough Mask House, near Ballinrobe, Co. Mayo, 1873, where he took a 31-year lease on the house and its 300 acres from Lord Erne, for whom he was land agent. In August 1879 he refused a demand from the LAND LEAGUE for rent reductions. After he evicted three tenants who refused to pay rent he required police protection following a meeting of some twenty-five thousand people at Ballinrobe, where Rev. John O'Malley, parish priest at nearby Neale, addressed the crowd. Boycott was one of the earliest victims of the 'moral Coventry' called for by CHARLES STEWART PARNELL in a speech at Ennis, Co. Clare, 19 September 1880, against those who transgressed Land League policy.

On 23 September a mob rushed Lough Mask House, forcing Boycott's staff to leave. Shopkeepers in Ballinrobe refused his custom, but supplies were brought by boat from Cong. Vigilantes patrolled the roads to the estate, and post was delivered by the RIC. The *Daily Express, Daily Telegraph, Daily News* and *News Letter* (Belfast) raised £2,000 to save Boycott's crops from rotting in the ground, while the *Times* (London) called on the Chief Secretary for Ireland, W. E. FORSTER, to invoke constitutional powers. The crops were saved by a work force of fifty Orangemen, called 'EMERGENCY MEN', mostly from Co. Cavan. More than a thousand soldiers escorted the workers to and from their homes and remained at Lough Mask House during harvesting, 12–26 November. The 'Boycott Relief Expedition' cost the government an estimated £10,000, or, as Parnell put it, 'one shilling for every turnip dug from Boycott's land.'

On 12 October 1880, in *Inter-Ocean,* a Father O'Neill used the term 'boycott', which the *Daily Mail* carried in a banner headline, 13 December, to describe the new Land League weapon. Captain Boycott remained in Co. Mayo until February 1886, when he sold his interest at Lough Mask House and moved to England. He continued to holiday at his 95-acre farm and woods in Ireland, which he had bought in April 1879. In December 1888 he appeared as a witness before the parliamentary commission on 'PARNELLISM AND CRIME'.

Breen, Dan (1894–1969), republican soldier and politician (CLANN ÉIREANN and Fianna Fáil); born in Grange, Donohill, Co. Tipperary. While working as a linesman with the Great Southern Railway he was sworn in to the IRB by his friend SEÁN TREACY. He was present at the action at Solloheadbeg, Co. Tipperary, 21 January 1919, and his exploits with the 3rd Tipperary Brigade of the IRA during the War of Independence led to a bounty of £10,000 for his capture. After the TRUCE he went to the United States, but he returned at the request of LIAM LYNCH. Though opposed to the ANGLO-IRISH TREATY (1921), in an effort to avert civil war he met RICHARD MULCAHY and was a signatory of the UNITY PROPOSALS. Elected to Dáil Éireann for Co. Tipperary while imprisoned, he embarked on a series of hunger and thirst strikes until he was released. In April 1927 he became the first Republican to subscribe to the OATH OF ALLEGIANCE; the IRA paper *An Phoblacht* commented: 'Irishmen will regret that he should have overshadowed his other days by this crime.' Breen's bill to have the oath abolished was defeated (47 to 17). He was defeated as an independent candidate, June 1927, but headed the poll in Co. Tipperary for Fianna Fáil, 1932, and held the seat until 1965. His autobiography, *My Fight for Irish Freedom* (1924), is a colourful account of his life and times during the years 1913–23.

Brennan, Robert (1881–1964), journalist and diplomat; born in Wexford, educated locally. Active in the Gaelic League, Sinn Féin, and IRB, he led the Irish Volunteers in their occupation of Enniscorthy during the EASTER RISING (1916). Imprisoned in the aftermath, on his release he played a leading role in the reorganising of the Volunteers and Sinn Féin, working as a propagandist for both organisations. He was national director of elections for Sinn Féin in the general election of December 1918 and Under-Secretary of the Department of Foreign Affairs in the first Dáil, February 1921 to January 1922, in which capacity he organised the IRISH RACE CONVENTION (1922) in Paris. Rejecting the ANGLO-IRISH TREATY (1921), he worked as propagandist for the Republicans during the CIVIL WAR. On the establishment of the IRISH PRESS by Éamon de Valera, 1931, Brennan became general manager, a position he held until appointed secretary of the Irish Legation in Washington, 1934–38; he was acting *chargé d'affaires* in Washington from March to September 1938, when he became minister plenipotentiary and ambassador, a post he held from 1938 to 1947. He was director of broadcasting of Radio Éireann, May 1947 to August 1948. His autobiography, *Allegiance,* was published in 1950.

Brennan, Thomas (1842–1915), land agitator; born in Co. Mayo, educated locally. A member of the IRB, he was prominent in the AMNESTY ASSOCIATION. He resigned his Dublin employment to become full-time secretary of the LAND LEAGUE. During a speech at Balla, Co. Mayo, 22 November 1879, he called on the RIC to assist the Land League and for the implementation of the policy that later became known as the 'boycott': if a person took a farm from which another had been evicted, Brennan urged that he be treated

> as an unclean thing. Let none of you be found to buy with him or sell with him, and watch how the modern Iscariot will prosper.

This policy was adopted during the following year by CHARLES STEWART PARNELL. Imprisoned with Parnell and other Land League figures in October 1881, Brennan was a signatory of the 'NO-RENT MANIFESTO'. He opposed the extremism of the LADIES' LAND LEAGUE, believing (with Parnell) that their activities would bring ridicule on the movement. Emigrating to the United States following the 'KILMAINHAM TREATY', he adopted a radical position in Irish-American politics.

Breslin, John J. (c. 1836–1888), Fenian; born in Drogheda, educated locally. A member of the IRB, he was employed as a hospital steward at Richmond Prison, Dublin, during the imprisonment of JAMES STEPHENS. He secured an impression of the keys, enabling Stephens to escape, 24 November 1865. He became a prominent member of CLAN NA GAEL, and JOHN DEVOY appointed him to supervise the rescue of Fenian prisoners from Fremantle on the CATALPA, 17 April 1876. He was involved with JOHN P. HOLLAND on the *Fenian Ram* project and worked for Devoy as business manager of the *Irish Nation.*

British Association for the Relief of Extreme Distress in Ireland and Scotland, founded at a meeting organised by Stephen Spring Rice at the London offices of the Rothschild bank, 1 January 1847. It aimed to alleviate distress caused by the GREAT FAMINE (1845–47) and by famine in Scotland (where the potato crop was also ruined by blight). A committee of twenty-one was appointed under Thomas Baring as chairman (see BARING BROTHERS). The meeting approved the appointment of the Polish explorer PAUL EDMUNDE DE STRZELECKI to oversee the distribution of funds, five-sixths of which were allotted to Irish distress and one-sixth to aid impoverished crofters in the Scottish Highlands. Among early respondents to the appeal were Queen Victoria (£2,000), her husband, Prince Albert (£500), the Sultan of the Ottoman Empire (£1,000), Baron Lionel de Rothschild (£1,000), the Duke of Devonshire (£1,000), and CHARLES WOOD (£400). The Chancellor of the Exchequer, CHARLES TREVELYAN, wished the association's funds to be placed at the disposal of the POOR LAW unions; following a visit to the west of Ireland, Strzelecki witnessed such appalling hardship that he insisted that the money be used for feeding and clothing children. The fund distributed £13,000 per week; £12,000 was also distributed for the clothing of children. The total collected was £470,000. The association's overheads were minimal—£12,000, or 2 per cent—as many of those involved worked at their own expense.

British-Irish Council, established 2 December 1999 under the BELFAST AGREEMENT 'to promote the harmonious and mutually beneficial development of the totality of relationships among the people of these islands.' The inaugural meeting, on 17 December, was attended by the Taoiseach, BERTIE AHERN, three ministers and British government representatives, and representatives of the devolved institutions in Northern Ireland, Scotland, and Wales, as well as representatives from the Channel Islands and the Isle of Man. It was intended that the council should meet twice-yearly at summit level (heads of government and administrations) and also meet regularly in sectoral formats, with each government or administration represented by appropriate ministers.

British-Irish Interparliamentary Body, established to consider issues of common concern, including matters involving the European Union, a development from the ANGLO-IRISH INTERGOVERNMENTAL CONFERENCE (1982). The inaugural meeting, 26 February 1990, brought British and Irish parliamentarians together for the first time since 1918. The body consisted of twenty-five members of the British Parliament, twenty-five members of Dáil Éireann, and three members (two unionists and one nationalist) from the three British parliamentary constituencies for Northern Ireland. In the event, the Unionists refused their places, while Séamus Mallon represented the SDLP. The joint chairpersons were Peter Temple-Morris (Conservative, later Labour) and Jim Tunney (Fianna Fáil). They met at six-monthly intervals in London and Dublin. The body reported an improvement in relations between British and Irish representatives.

Broadcasting Act (1960), an act to set up an authority to administer the new television service, Telefís Éireann, later Raidió Teilifís Éireann (RTE), which was to derive its revenue from both commercial advertising and licence fees.

Broighter Hoard. While ploughing at Broighter, near Limavady, Co. Derry, February 1896, a farm worker, Tom Nicoll, unearthed a treasure described as 'the oldest, the rarest, the most beautiful ornaments ever discovered outside Ancient Egypt.' His employer, Joseph Gibson, sold the find to a jeweller in Derry for a reputed 'few sovereigns'; the British Museum later bought the treasure for £600. Following protracted litigation the Royal Irish Academy, which subsequently claimed the find as treasure trove, was awarded the treasure. The hoard contains the Broighter Collar, a classic example of the work of the La Tène period, dating from the first century AD. The collection is now on display in the National Museum of Ireland, Dublin, while replicas are on view at the Ulster Museum, Belfast.

Brooke, Sir Peter (born 1934), British politician (Conservative). As Secretary of State for Northern Ireland, 1989–92, Brooke arrived in office hoping to establish devolution at a time when Unionists favoured integration. Inheriting the 'talks about talks' initiated by TOM KING, he began the discussions at Stormont, April 1991, that led to the BROOKE-MAYHEW TALKS, a significant step in the PEACE PROCESS. Unionists were offended by his announcement that the British Government had no selfish or strategic interest in Northern Ireland. The Prime Minister, JOHN MAJOR, declined his offer to resign following Unionist outrage at his singing of 'My Darling Clementine' on the RTE television programme 'The Late Late Show' within hours of a Provisional IRA bomb that killed eight workers at Teebane, Co. Tyrone, 17 January 1992. Following the general election Brooke sat on the back benches before his appointment as Secretary of State for the National Heritage, September 1992.

Brooke-Mayhew talks, originating in 'talks about talks' organised between the Northern Ireland political parties by TOM KING and his successor, PETER BROOKE, 1988–91, and culminating in the BELFAST AGREEMENT (1998).

Involving the British and Irish governments, they were attended by the Ulster Unionist Party, Democratic Unionist Party, SDLP, and Alliance Party. Sir Ninian Stephen chaired the talks in Belfast, London, and Dublin, which identified three 'strands' or sets of relations: strand 1, relations within Northern Ireland; strand 2, relations between the north and south of Ireland; and strand 3, relations between Britain and Ireland. Nothing was to be agreed until everything was agreed. The process was halted on 3 July 1991 when the Unionists would not continue meetings in the shadow of a planned ANGLO-IRISH INTERGOVERNMENTAL CONFERENCE. Agreement was reached to resume after the general election of April 1992 when SIR PATRICK MAYHEW replaced Brooke and ALBERT REYNOLDS had succeeded CHARLES HAUGHEY as Taoiseach. Reynolds insisted that the GOVERNMENT OF IRELAND ACT (1920) must be on the table if the definition of the national territory contained in articles 2 and 3 of the Constitution of Ireland (1937) was. The Unionists were insisting on a referendum on the constitutional articles; the Republic would consider a referendum only in the event of a general agreement. Differences also emerged on the question of devolution. While the UUP, DUP and Alliance Party were in general agreement on a system of local rule based on an Assembly, the SDLP was not, and the talks collapsed temporarily. (See also PEACE PROCESS.)

Brookeborough, Basil Brooke, Viscount (1888–1974), politician (Ulster Unionist Party); born in Colebrook, Co. Fermanagh. Following the First World War he resigned his commission as a captain in the British army to manage his extensive estates. Founder and county commandant of the Fermanagh Special Constabulary, 1920–29, he was a member of the first Senate of Northern Ireland, 1921, and Unionist MP for Lisnaskea, 1929–68. He was assistant chief whip of the Unionist Party, 1930–33, Minister of Agriculture, 1933–41, and Minister of Commerce, 1941–43. He dismissed all Catholics from employment on his estates on becoming Minister of Agriculture, equating Catholicism with 'disloyalty' and anti-unionism, and exhorted others to follow his example. He replaced JOHN MILLER ANDREWS as Prime Minister, 28 April 1943, and held the position for twenty years, the longest term of any Prime Minister of Northern Ireland.

As Prime Minister and as a member of the ORANGE ORDER Brookeborough did little to resolve the sectarian tension that marked life in the Northern state. His government introduced internment to deal with the IRA and SAOR ULADH, 1956–62. In the depression of 1961–62, redundancies affected almost half of Harland and Wolff's 21,000 workers, while the aircraft manufacturing firm of Short Brothers cut its work force by 20 per cent. Brookeborough received no concessions when he led a delegation to London, March 1961, to seek help in alleviating the crisis. In August 1962 approximately twelve thousand workers marched to Belfast City Hall demanding aid for the beleaguered economy. In October there was an announcement of a further 620 redundancies in the shipyards, with an additional 'two to three thousand' to follow within three months. Increasing ill-health hastened Brookeborough's resignation, March 1963, when he was replaced by a more liberal Unionist, TERENCE O'NEILL.

Browne, Dr Noel C. (1915–1997), politician (Clann na Poblachta, independent, Fianna Fáil, National Progressive Democratic Party, Labour Party, and Socialist Labour Party); born in Waterford, educated at TCD, where he qualified as a doctor. After contracting tuberculosis he became a campaigner for the eradication of the disease, which had killed his parents. Elected for CLANN NA POBLACHTA, 1948, on his first day in Dáil Éireann he became Minister for Health in the first inter-party Government (1948–51). His campaign against tuberculosis led to the virtual eradication of the disease. His attempt to implement the MOTHER AND CHILD SCHEME led to a confrontation with the Catholic hierarchy and was a factor in the fall of the Government, 1951.

He continued to hold his Dublin seat as an independent from 1951 until, standing for Fianna Fáil, he was defeated, 1954. He regained the seat as an independent in 1957. He was a joint founder of the NATIONAL PROGRESSIVE DEMOCRATIC PARTY, for which he sat from 1958. He stood unsuccessfully for the Labour Party in 1965, then held the seat for Labour from 1969 until 1973, when he became a senator. Though nominated by a Labour Party convention to contest Artane (Dublin) in 1977, he failed to secure ratification from the Administrative Council but won the seat as 'Independent Labour' candidate. In 1981, in Dublin North-Central, he became the sole Dáil representative of the SOCIALIST LABOUR PARTY, until February 1982, when he retired. He spent his last years living in Connemara. His autobiography, *Against the Tide* (1986), became a best-seller.

Broy, Colonel Éamonn (1887–1972), soldier and Garda Commissioner; born in Ballinure, Co. Kildare, educated locally. He became a civil servant in DUBLIN CASTLE and supplied MICHAEL COLLINS with vital information during the WAR OF INDEPENDENCE; in April 1919 he brought Collins into the castle to see the intelligence unit at work, and he used his position to warn Collins of imminent raids. When his role was uncovered, February 1921, he was imprisoned, but Collins arranged for his release during the TRUCE. He accompanied Collins to London during the negotiations on the ANGLO-IRISH TREATY (1921). A supporter of ÉAMON DE VALERA, he rejected the Treaty but was later made adjutant of the Irish Air Service, with the rank of colonel. Secretary of the DUBLIN METROPOLITAN POLICE, 1923, and chief superintendent, 1925, he was briefly head of the Detective Division before his appointment as Commissioner of the Garda Síochána in succession to the dismissed EOIN O'DUFFY, 22 February 1933.

To deal with opposition by the BLUESHIRTS to the Fianna Fáil government, Broy recruited former IRA soldiers into the Gardaí as an auxiliary force; armed (unlike other Gardaí), they was popularly known as the 'Broy Harriers'. The force was disbanded when the Blueshirt movement disintegrated during 1935.

Bruce, William (1757–1841), Presbyterian minister; born in Dublin, educated at TCD. During his Belfast ministry, 1789–1831, he was principal of Belfast Academy, 1790–1822. Active in the Hibernian Bible Society and in the Volunteers, he was the last survivor of the Rotunda Convention (1783). He secured terms for the Presbyterian Church before the ACT OF UNION (1800). He established the Belfast Literary Society, 23 October 1801, and the Unitarian Society, 9 April 1831. He was a frequent contributor to the *Transactions of the Royal Irish Academy* and to DUBLIN UNIVERSITY MAGAZINE; his publications included *The State of Society in the Age of Homer* (1827) and *A Brief Commentary on the New Testament* (1836).

Brugha, Cathal (1874–1922), republican soldier and politician (Sinn Féin); born Charles Burgess in Dublin, educated at Belvedere College. He was joint founder of a candle manufacturing business, Lalor and Company, 1909. He was active in the Gaelic League, IRB, and Irish Volunteers; he was also a singer and all-round sportsman. During the EASTER RISING (1916) he was second in command (under ÉAMONN CEANNT) at the South Dublin Union, James's Street (St James's Hospital), where he was wounded and left permanently crippled. Chief of staff of the IRA, October 1917 to April 1919, when he developed deep reservations about the IRB, he was President of the first Dáil from January to April 1919, when he became Minister for National Defence, a position he also held in the second Dáil and throughout the WAR OF INDEPENDENCE. His proposal for an oath of allegiance to the Irish Republic and Dáil Éireann, 20 August 1919, was approved by the Dáil. As Minister for National Defence he disapproved of Volunteer action without the prior sanction of the Dáil.

Brugha had a poor relationship with MICHAEL COLLINS. He refused to participate in the negotiations for the ANGLO-IRISH TREATY, which he completely rejected. A highly personalised attack on Collins during the Treaty debates was perceived at the time as influencing several TDs to support the Treaty in the subsequent Dáil division. He was among those who occupied the FOUR COURTS at the start of the CIVIL WAR, April–June 1922; when the Four Courts fell he took up a position in the Hammam Hotel, O'Connell Street, and when this too came under heavy fire he ordered his men to surrender. After they did so he came out of the hotel in a final act of defiance, with guns blazing, and was mortally wounded, the first Republican minister to die during the Civil War.

Brunswick Clubs, Protestant clubs founded by the Duke of Brunswick, 1828, to oppose CATHOLIC EMANCIPATION. Its members, known as 'Brunswickers', were active in opposition to DANIEL O'CONNELL and the ORDER OF LIBERATORS, 1828–29. They ceased to function after the grant of emancipation, 1828.

Bruton, John (born 1947), politician (Fine Gael); born in Dublin, educated at UCD and King's Inns. Secretary of the Fine Gael Youth Group in the mid-1960s, in 1969 he was the youngest politician returned to Dáil Éireann (for Co. Meath). Spokesperson on agriculture, 1972, Parliamentary Secretary to the Minister for Education, 1973–77, and also Parliamentary Secretary to the Minister for Industry and Commerce, 1975–77, he became Minister for Finance in the coalition Government (Fine Gael and Labour Party) led by GARRETT FITZGERALD, 1981. His budget, 27 January 1982, led to the fall of the Government on the proposal to extend 18 per cent value-added tax to footwear (including children's shoes) and clothing. As Minister for Industry and Commerce, 1982–86, he clashed with FRANK CLUSKEY of the Labour Party over a proposal to nationalise Dublin Gas Company. He presided over the demise of the state-owned IRISH SHIPPING LTD and introduced emergency legislation to rescue the Insurance Company of Ireland, a subsidiary of Allied Irish Banks. In a reshuffle, January 1986, he was returned to the Department of Finance. He succeeded ALAN DUKES as leader of Fine Gael in 1990; two years later the party lost a fifth of its seats, its 19 per cent share of the vote its worst result ever. Following the collapse of the coalition Government (Fianna Fáil and Labour Party), November 1994, Bruton became the first leader of a Dáil opposition to become Taoiseach without a general election when he headed the 'rainbow coalition' (Fine Gael, Labour Party, and DEMOCRATIC LEFT), 14 December 1994. His Government inherited the biggest economic boom in Irish history, dubbed by journalists the 'Celtic Tiger', characterised by the highest growth rate in the world.

Seen as less accommodating than ALBERT REYNOLDS in relation to the republican movement, Bruton was insistent that he would not participate in talks unless IRA violence ended permanently. He launched the FRAMEWORK DOCUMENTS with the British Prime Minister, JOHN MAJOR, 22 February 1995. At the end of November he issued a joint communiqué with Major outlining a 'twin-track' process of negotiations and decommissioning. On 10 June 1996 he and Major opened multi-party talks, from which Sinn Féin was excluded. In November he compared the Provisional IRA to Nazis but a month later supported President Bill Clinton in accepting the early admission of Sinn Féin to talks if the Provisional IRA ceasefire was renewed. In 1997 he urged nationalists not to vote for Sinn Féin.

Despite the booming economy and a united front by the 'rainbow coalition' in the general election of June 1997, Bruton lost office to a minority Government (Fianna Fáil and Progressive Democrats) led by BERTIE AHERN, 26 June 1997. Following an opinion poll, 26 January 2001, showing a four-point drop in support for Fine Gael (to 20 per cent), with core support down two points to 15 per cent, a motion of no confidence was tabled by Jim Mitchell and MICHAEL NOONAN, who became Bruton's successor as leader of Fine Gael, 9 February 2001.

Bryan, Colonel Dan (1900–1985), army officer; born in Dunhill, Gowra, Co. Kilkenny, studied medicine for two years at UCD. Having served as intelligence officer for the Dublin No. 1 Brigade during the WAR OF INDEPENDENCE he joined the Free State army, 20 June 1922; he played a crucial role in army intelligence during the CIVIL WAR, 1922–23, and spent most of the 1920s in Military Intelligence. After returning from training courses in the United States, 1926–27, he was transferred to the Defence Planning Division in 1928 and worked in the office of the Chief of Staff, 1931–34, after which he returned to the Intelligence Branch. He served as assistant director of military intelligence until he took over as director from Liam Archer, June 1941, holding the office until March 1952. His role was pivotal during the years of the Second World War, when, as well as working against the IRA, he developed a close working relationship with British and US military intelligence. He was subsequently commandant of the Military College, 1952–55.

Bryce, James Bryce, first Viscount (1838–1922), politician (Liberal); born in Belfast. A member of Parliament from 1880, he was Under-Secretary for Foreign Affairs, 1886, and President of the Board of Trade, 1894, and Chief Secretary for Ireland, 1905–07. His experience in Ireland convinced him that some form of HOME RULE was inevitable, and he urged unionists to safeguard the interests of a Protestant Ulster. A prolific writer on Ireland and Irish affairs, he was a recipient of the Order of Merit and of honorary degrees from several universities. He was a keen mountaineer and president of the Alpine Club; Mount Bryce (11,506 ft) in British Columbia was named in his honour. He edited the *Handbook of Home Rule* (2nd edition, 1887) and wrote an introduction to *Two Centuries of Irish History* (1888).

Buckingham Palace Conference (21–24 July 1914), an attempt by KING GEORGE V to break the deadlock over the third HOME RULE BILL. Orange and Unionist movements were united in opposition to home rule. An amending bill passed a month earlier provided for the exclusion of either four or six of the Ulster counties (the fate of Cos. Fermanagh and Tyrone had not yet been decided). Leaders of the conference parties were H. H. ASQUITH and DAVID LLOYD GEORGE (Liberal), Lord Lansdowne and ANDREW BONAR LAW (Conservative), JOHN REDMOND and JOHN DILLON (Nationalist), and Sir

James Craig (VISCOUNT CRAIGAVON) and SIR EDWARD CARSON (Unionist). The conference was presided over by the Speaker of the House of Commons. The King met each delegation separately to measure progress during the conference. Carson, failing to obtain exclusion from the bill for the entire province of Ulster, sought a six-county exclusion, which Redmond vetoed. The lack of compromise, particularly on the vexed question of Co. Tyrone, provoked the Speaker to comment, 'When each of two people say they must have the whole, why not cut it in half?' Also rejected was a proposal by Asquith for the inclusion within the scope of the bill of all of Co. Antrim, north and mid Armagh, east, north and west Down, the whole of Derry, south Tyrone, and north Fermanagh.

The conference broke up inconclusively. The Government of Ireland Bill was passed and with it another bill postponing the implementation of home rule until the end of the Great War. The bills became law on 18 September 1914.

Buckley, Tim (1863–1945), storyteller; born in Kilgarvan, Co. Kerry. A tailor, he settled in Garrynapeaka, near Gougane Barra, Co. Cork, with his wife, Anastasia ('Ansty') (1872–1947). His tales and observations earned him the friendship of literary and artistic figures, including FRANK O'CONNOR, SEÁN Ó FAOLÁIN, and Séamus Murphy (1907–1975). He was the subject of *The Tailor and Ansty* (1942) by Eric Cross, which caused a furore on its appearance and incurred clerical condemnation; local clergymen forced Buckley to burn copies in his own fireplace, and it was banned until the 1960s. A collection of his lore in Irish, *Seanchas an Táilliúra,* collected in 1947 by Seán Ó Cróinín and edited by Aindrias Ó Muimhneacháin, was published in 1978.

Bunting, Edward (1773–1843), music-collector and organist; born in Co. Armagh. His brother trained him as an organist. He travelled throughout Ireland collecting material for *The Ancient Music of Ireland* (1797), which included sixty-six previously unpublished pieces, many of which were later used by Thomas Moore for his *Melodies.* His second collection, published in 1809, contained, in addition to a history of the Irish harp, seventy-seven pieces arranged for the piano, with words for twenty of them. Hampered by his lack of Irish, he was accompanied on several journeys by Patrick Lynch, a teacher. He was instrumental in staging the Belfast Harp Festival (1792). In 1813 he organised a music festival that featured organ and harp recitals and during which he also conducted the first performance in Belfast of Handel's *Messiah.* Following his marriage he moved to Dublin, 1820, where, at the urging of GEORGE PETRIE, he published his *General Collection of the Ancient Music of Ireland* (1840).

Burke, Ricard O'Sullivan (1838–1922), Fenian; born in Dunmanway, Co. Cork. He joined the Cork Militia, 1853; on the disbanding of his regiment he went to sea, learning several languages in voyages around the world. He organised Fenian circles in the Union Army during the American Civil War (1861–65). THOMAS J. KELLY recommended him to JAMES STEPHENS as a purchaser of arms for the FENIANS in Ireland. Using the pseudonym Edward C. Winslow, he built up contacts with the Birmingham Small Arms Company and imported Enfield rifles from the United States, until he had some two thousand stored in Liverpool. He organised the rescue of Kelly and TIMOTHY DEASY in Manchester, 18 September 1867 (see MANCHESTER MARTYRS). Betrayed by a spy, John J. Corydon, he was held in Clerkenwell House of Detention, London, from which a Fenian rescue party attempted to free him (see CLERKENWELL EXPLOSION). After he was sentenced to fifteen years' imprisonment he feigned insanity and was eventually moved to Broadmoor Asylum, Berkshire, from which he was released in 1872. He returned to the United States and, while engaged on various engineering projects, joined CLAN NA GAEL and continued his efforts in the Fenian cause.

Burke, Thomas Henry (1829–1882), Under-Secretary for Ireland, 1869–82; born in Knocknagur, Co. Galway. He worked as a clerk in the Chief Secretary's Office from 1847 and was private secretary to three Chief Secretaries before becoming Under-Secretary, 1869. Closely associated with the COERCION policy adopted during the LAND WAR (1879–82), he earned the hostility of extremists. He was murdered by the INVINCIBLES, 6 May 1882, while walking in the Phoenix Park, Dublin, with the newly arrived Chief Secretary, LORD FREDERICK CAVENDISH. (See PHOENIX PARK MURDERS.)

Burke, Father Thomas Nicholas Anthony (1830–1883), Dominican preacher; born in Galway. Ordained 1853, he returned from England to head the novitiate at Tallaght, Co. Dublin, 1855, where thousands flocked to hear him preach. Rector of the Irish College, Rome, from 1864, he returned to the Friary of St Saviour, Dominick Street, Dublin, 1867. When the remains of DANIEL O'CONNELL were re-interred in Glasnevin Cemetery, Dublin, 14 May 1869, Burke preached the panegyric to an estimated crowd of fifty thousand. He was theological adviser to the Bishop of Dromore at the First Vatican Council (1869–70), where he was opposed to the decree of Papal infallibility, fearing it would imperil Christian unity. In February 1872 he began a fund-raising tour of the United States, on which he undermined his health. His most popular theme in America was his rebuttal of the historian and lecturer James Anthony Froude (1818–1894), whose controversial views on Ireland were enunciated in *Essays on Ireland in the Eighteenth Century* (1871–74).

Butler, Thomas O'Brien (1861–1915), composer; born in Cahersiveen, Co. Kerry. He studied music in Rome and London. His opera *Muirgheis,* first performed on 20 April 1902, is believed to be the first in Irish. He was drowned when the LUSITANIA sank on 7 May 1915.

Butt, Isaac (1813–1879), barrister and politician; born in Glenfin, Co. Donegal, educated at TCD, where he had a brilliant academic career. Instrumental in founding DUBLIN UNIVERSITY MAGAZINE, 1833, he edited it from 1834 to 1838. He was the first professor of political economy at TCD, 1836–41. While he practised at the bar from 1838, his *Protestant Guardian* championed the unionist cause, in opposition to DANIEL O'CONNELL and the REPEAL ASSOCIATION.

Butt's political opinions underwent a change as a result of the GREAT FAMINE (1845–49). In *The Famine on the Land* (1847) he stated that the neglect of Irish grievances would lead to an anti-British coalition in Ireland. Irish property, he wrote, was expected to carry the burden of Irish poverty, a task that it was patently unequal to at that time. During the following year he defended members of YOUNG IRELAND, including WILLIAM SMITH O'BRIEN. He was member of Parliament (Liberal Conservative) for Harwich and later for Youghal, 1852–65. Debts, accumulated through extravagant living and gambling, forced him to give up his political career and resume practice at the bar, and he returned to Ireland in 1865. His defence of the leaders of the IRB, 1865–67, gave him a national reputation, which he consolidated by assuming the presidency of the AMNESTY ASSOCIATION. Elected MP for Limerick, 1871, he held the seat for the rest of his life.

The desire to wrest the initiative from the revolutionary FENIANS led Butt to propose a federal solution to the Irish demand for self-government; he envisaged a subordinate parliament in Ireland that would deal with Irish affairs. His proposal in the *Nation,* November 1869, for a united nationalist party led to the HOME GOVERNMENT ASSOCIATION, 1 September 1870. Three years later he replaced it with the HOME RULE LEAGUE but failed to offer consistent leadership. As a constitutionalist he disapproved of the policy of OBSTRUCTIONISM.

After losing the leadership of the Home Rule Confederation of Great Britain to CHARLES STEWART PARNELL in 1877, Butt attempted to bring his party behind the Conservative government, and he was attacked at the Home Rule Conference in Dublin, January 1878; this attack was renewed and strengthened at a meeting of the Home Rule League in February 1879. Butt died shortly afterwards. His writings include *Land Tenure in Ireland: A Plea for the Celtic Race* (1866), *The Power and the Land* (1867), and *Irish Federalism* (1870).

Byrne, Alfred 'Alfie' (1882–1956), publican and politician (Nationalist); born in Dublin, educated locally. He was member of Parliament for the Harbour division of Dublin, 1914–18, and independent TD for various Dublin constituencies, 1923–28 and 1931–56. He was a member of the Senate from 1928 until his resignation in 1931. Three of his sons were also at various times TDs. He was a candidate for the Presidency of Ireland in 1938 but withdrew to allow DR DOUGLAS HYDE become an agreed candidate. His record in local government was unique; ten times lord mayor of Dublin, 1930–39 and 1954–55, he was popularly believed to have shaken the hand of every man, woman and child in the city. He lost the mayoral election in 1955 by one vote to Denis Larkin (Labour Party).

Byrne, Edward (1847–1899), journalist; born in Tuam, Co. Galway, educated at St Jarlath's College. He worked on the *Tuam Herald* and the *Tuam News* before moving to Belfast, where he became editor of the *Morning News* at the age of twenty-five. From there he was recruited by EDMUND DWYER GRAY to the literary department of the FREEMAN'S JOURNAL, of which he was later editor. Under his editorship the paper supported CHARLES STEWART PARNELL, about whom he published a memoir in 1898. He published Parnell's manifesto 'To the People of Ireland' (29 November 1990). After the *Freeman's Journal* declared against Parnell on 24 September 1891, Byrne moved to become editor of Parnell's rival *Irish Daily Independent* until poor health forced his resignation, after which he lived in poverty.

C

'Cairo Gang'. Alarmed at the espionage network established by MICHAEL COLLINS during the War of Independence, GENERAL SIR HENRY WILSON proposed the formation of a special intelligence unit to operate in Ireland. Agents then working in Cairo were placed under the command of Lieutenant D. F. McLean, to work independently of DUBLIN CASTLE and with freedom to use any methods, including murder. It was described at the time as a classic confrontation between those above the law and those (the IRA) beyond the law. On 21 November 1920 (BLOODY SUNDAY) the 'SQUAD', controlled by Collins, assassinated fourteen members of the group, and it was then disbanded.

'cake', a traditional practice for helping a distressed family, whereby the family baked a large ornamental cake (some two or three stone in weight) and provided drink. The event normally took place on a Sunday or holiday and was attended by neighbours and friends; it could attract hundreds of people, who feasted and danced until dawn. The receipts from the sale of drinks went to the hosts to alleviate their distress.

Callan, Nicholas (1799–1864), priest and scientist; born in Darver, near Ardee, Co. Louth; educated at St Patrick's College, Maynooth (ordained 1823) and Sapienza University, Rome (doctor of divinity 1826), where he became acquainted with the work of Luigi Galvani and Alessandro Volta. He held the chair of natural philosophy (physics) at Maynooth, 1826–64. He invented the induction coil, 1836—forerunner of the modern step-up/step-down transformer—and built an induction machine that generated an unprecedented 60,000 volts, 1837. He also discovered the principle of the self-exciting dynamo, discovered an early form of galvanisation, constructed electric motors, and predicted electric light. He developed batteries using inexpensive cast iron in place of platinum and carbon, connecting 577 batteries together to make the world's largest battery (the 'Maynooth battery'), 1854, and the single-fluid cell, 1855. Callan's invention of the induction coil was formally recognised only in 1953; until then it had been attributed to the instrument-maker Heinrich Ruhmkorff (1803–1877).

Cameron Commission, appointed by the Northern Ireland Government, January 1969, to investigate disturbances following clashes between loyalists and supporters of the NORTHERN IRELAND CIVIL RIGHTS ASSOCIATION and PEOPLE'S DEMOCRACY. Its membership consisted of Lord Cameron (chairman), Sir John Biggart, and James Joseph Campbell; it sat in private under an assurance that no prosecutions would result from evidence submitted to it. BRIAN FAULKNER, Northern Ireland Minister of Commerce, resigned in protest at the inquiry.

The commission's report was published as *Disturbances in Northern Ireland,* 12 September 1969. Though critical of the NICRA, it found that civil rights protesters had right on their side with regard to housing, discrimination in local government appointments, the demand for one man one vote, and the existence of gerrymandering. It found that the Northern Ireland Government was 'hidebound' and 'complacent'. Rev. Ian Paisley's ULSTER CONSTITUTION DEFENCE COMMITTEE and ULSTER PROTESTANT VOLUNTEERS had helped create a climate that was 'readily translated into physical violence against civil rights demonstrations.' The report criticised loyalist agitators and found evidence that on 4–5 January 1969 members of the RUC had been guilty of misconduct that involved assault and battery and malicious damage to property in streets in the predominantly Catholic Bogside area of Derry. It also stated that 'subversive elements' had used civil rights activities to foment violence. (See also HUNT COMMITTEE.)

Campaign for Democracy in Ulster, founded in London, June 1965, by British Labour Party MPs, including Kevin McNamara, Stanley Orme, and Paul Rose. It opposed gerrymandering and discrimination against the Catholic population in Northern Ireland, sought a parliamentary inquiry into the Unionist government, sought to bring electoral law in Northern Ireland into line with that of Britain so as to provide fair representation for all sections of the community, and sought to have the Race Relations Act extended to Northern Ireland and amended to include religious discrimination and incitement. Sponsored by more than a hundred British Labour Party MPs and peers, the campaign received a boost through the election of GERRY FITT to the British House of Commons, 31 March 1966. It worked in close association with the CAMPAIGN FOR SOCIAL JUSTICE IN NORTHERN IRELAND. The campaign's conference in London in January 1968 called on MP supporters to use whatever methods were available to question the parliamentary convention that prevented the discussion of Northern Ireland affairs in the British House of Commons.

Campaign for Devolved Parliament, launched in March 1988 for 'a strong devolved parliament' to replace the ANGLO-IRISH AGREEMENT (1985). Its members, who included HARRY WEST, a former leader of the ULSTER UNIONIST PARTY, sought a Bill of Rights and legislative and administrative powers, together with a considerable degree of financial autonomy, and an Executive to be chosen either through proportional representation or by voluntary coalition.

Campaign for Equal Citizenship, a pressure group led by ROBERT MCCARTNEY that campaigned for the main British political parties to organise in Northern Ireland. Its members feared that devolved government under the ANGLO-IRISH AGREEMENT (1985) would lead to a united Ireland.

Campaign for Labour Representation, established in 1977 to promote British Labour Party organisation in Northern Ireland, for which it lobbied annual Labour Party conferences. It had a poor electoral record (in district council elections in 1993 only one of its thirteen endorsed candidates was elected) and was dissolved in September 1993.

Campaign for Social Justice in Northern Ireland, launched by Dr Conn McCluskey and Patricia McCluskey, 17 January 1964, having its genesis in the Homeless Citizens' League in Dungannon, Co. Tyrone, and influenced by the success of the civil rights movement in the United States. It sought to direct attention in Britain to social injustice in Northern Ireland, and to this end it accumulated data on discrimination in housing, employment, electoral practices, and public appointments. Over the next five years it conducted a strong campaign in Britain and other countries, working in association with the British Labour Party, the CAMPAIGN FOR DEMOCRACY IN ULSTER, and the British Council for Civil Liberties. The organisation helped to establish the NORTHERN IRELAND CIVIL RIGHTS ASSOCIATION, into which it was absorbed, 1967, and was also credited with helping to establish the CAMERON COMMISSION.

Campbell, Joseph (1879–44), poet and scholar; born in Belfast. Introduced to the Irish literary revival through his friend Pádraic Colum (1881–1972), he submitted articles and poetry to the IRISHMAN and *All-Ireland Review.* A founder-member and editor of the ULSTER LITERARY THEATRE, he was joint editor (with BULMER HOBSON) of two early editions of *Uladh.* In London from 1906 as a teacher, he was secretary to the IRISH LITERARY SOCIETY and an assistant to Eleanor Hull (1860–1935) in the IRISH TEXTS SOCIETY. In 1912 he settled in Co. Wicklow. He was an organiser for the Irish Volunteers and a stretcher-bearer during the Easter Rising (1916). Opposed to the Anglo-Irish Treaty (1921), he was imprisoned at the outbreak of the Civil War, following which he emigrated to the United States, where he lectured at Fordham University during his thirteen-year stay. He retired to Glencree, Co. Wicklow, 1939. Campbell's most enduring work, 'My Lagan Love', was adapted to one of the hundreds of traditional airs he had collected.

Campbell-Bannerman, Sir Henry (1836–1908), British politician (Liberal); born Henry Campbell in Glasgow. As member of Parliament for Stirling Burghs from 1868 he supported W. E. GLADSTONE on the DISESTABLISHMENT of the Church of Ireland and on granting TENANT RIGHT to Irish farmers (see LAND ACTS). In October 1884 he succeeded George Otto Trevelyan as Chief Secretary for Ireland, in which post he won the admiration of CHARLES STEWART PARNELL, who said of him, 'He left things alone—a sensible thing for an Irish secretary.' Campbell-Bannerman supported Gladstone on the latter's conversion to home rule for Ireland. He succeeded Sir William Harcourt as leader of the Liberal Party, 1899. Prime Minister from 1905, he supported home rule but when faced with opposition from within his own party sought to introduce a system of devolved government through the IRISH COUNCIL BILL. This measure failed because of Unionist and Nationalist opposition. He died on 11 April 1908, three days after being succeeded as leader of the party and Prime Minister by H. H. ASQUITH.

canting (from the Irish *ceant,* 'auction'), a system

common during the eighteenth century and persisting into the early decades of the nineteenth whereby a lease held by a tenant-farmer was auctioned to the highest bidder when it fell in, giving the former occupier no right to the property unless he could meet the highest bid. On Sir John Ben-Walsh's estate in Co. Kerry in 1857 a lease was offered to the son of a former occupier for £200, which he refused; the farm was then advertised and was let for £280, the highest of several bids received. The system was a source of great insecurity and hardship among poor tenants. It had largely ceased by the late nineteenth century, when landlords favoured tenants who had the capital to stock and enlarge holdings, rather than those who simply offered the highest bid on an auctioned lease.

Capital Investment Advisory Committee, a group of nine experts appointed to carry out research and to advise the Government on economic policy. Its first meeting was held on 14 December 1956. When the coalition Government (Fine Gael and Labour Party) fell shortly afterwards, the Fianna Fáil Government retained the committee.

Capuchin Annual (1930–77), published by the Capuchin Friary, Dublin. Under successive editors, Father Senan and Father Henry, it published articles on art, history and theology as well as fiction and verse and was renowned for its art and photographic work; the work of the stained-glass artist Richard King was a familiar feature from 1940. It reached sales of approximately 25,000 per volume. The distinctive cover of *St Francis and the Wolf*, designed by Seán O'Sullivan, did not change throughout the years. Certain issues, such as the 1946/47 volume, featuring a tribute to John McCormack, have become collectors' items because of the accompanying photographs (many previously unpublished) and the commissioned illustrations.

Caravats, a fighting faction originally known as the 'Moyle Rangers'; they owed their new name to an incident during the hanging of their leader Nicholas Hanley in Clonmel, 1805. Hanley had been sentenced for burning the house of a man who had occupied the lands of a dispossessed tenant. Paddy Car, leader of a rival faction, the SHANAVESTS, when asked to leave the scene of execution, exclaimed he would not do so until he had seen 'the cravat put around Hanley's neck.' This was reported to Hanley's relatives and friends, who pledged to support each other for a period of three years; as a result the group was known alternatively as the 'Three-Year-Olds'.

Carders, an agrarian secret society active in Connacht in the early nineteenth century; it took its name from the mutilation its members inflicted by dragging a card or hackle used for carding wool, with its long spikes, through their victims' flesh. (See also SECRET SOCIETIES.)

Carey, James (1845–1883), informer; born in Dublin, where he worked as a bricklayer. A leading member of the INVINCIBLES, he was involved in the PHOENIX PARK MURDERS. When arrested he turned Queen's evidence, leading to the execution of five of his associates. Offered resettlement in South Africa, he travelled under the name Power with his wife and family on the *Melrose Castle* but was shot dead off Cape Town by Padaí Mhichíl Airt Ó Dónaill, also called Patrick O'Donnell (born 1838 in Mín an Chladaigh, Co. Donegal), who was hanged at Newgate Prison, London, 17 December 1883.

Carlisle, George William Frederick Howard, seventh Earl of (1802–1864), British politician (Whig); born in London. A member of Parliament from 1826, he supported CATHOLIC EMANCIPATION. As Chief Secretary for Ireland (under his earlier title, Viscount Morpeth), he worked with the Lord Lieutenant, EARL MULGRAVE, and Under-Secretary, THOMAS DRUMMOND, to form one of the most constructive Irish administrations since the Union. He carried the Tithe Rentcharge (Ireland) Act (1838), which brought an end to the widespread agrarian discontent over the payment of tithes, the Irish Municipal Relief Act (see MUNICIPAL CORPORATIONS (IRELAND) ACT (1840)), and the Poor Relief (Ireland) Act (1838) (see POOR LAW). He was a member of the cabinet from February 1839 until the fall of Melbourne's government, July 1841, and was defeated in the Dublin by-election of 1842.

Carnarvon, Henry Howard Molyneux Herbert, fourth Earl of (1831–90), British politician (Conservative). He supported DISESTABLISHMENT of the Church of Ireland and the LAND ACTS of 1870 and 1881. Though committed in principle to a limited measure of self-government for Ireland, he was not, as CHARLES STEWART PARNELL appeared to believe, committed to home rule. Within a short time of his appointment as Lord Lieutenant of Ireland, 1885, the Conservatives introduced the

'Ashbourne Act' (see LAND ACTS) and a Labourers' Act. At a private meeting with Parnell on 1 August 1885 to exchange opinions on the 'Irish question', Lord Carnarvon made it clear that while he would support limited powers for an elective assembly he would not accept any measure that would interfere with the legislative union. Parnell left the meeting apparently satisfied that he had achieved unanimity with Carnarvon. During the debate on HOME RULE in June 1886, when Parnell claimed that Carnarvon had declared an acceptance of self-government for Ireland, Carnarvon rebutted Parnell's version of the meeting. In 1887, when the *Times* (London) published the series 'PARNELLISM AND CRIME', Carnarvon's proposal for a special parliamentary commission to investigate the allegations was granted in 1888.

Carnegie Libraries, also known as the Carnegie Free Libraries, built with funds disbursed by the Scottish-American philanthropist Andrew Carnegie (1835–1919) or by trusts established by him. Ireland was allocated $598,000 (out of $39,325,240 for 1,200 libraries in different countries); altogether some 2,500 were built. Between 1897 and 1913 Carnegie's bequest enabled sixty-six libraries to be built, providing a boost to the development of the library movement. The first grant of £100 went to Newtownards, Co. Down, 1897. In 1903 some £49,000 was granted. The Carnegie United Kingdom Trust took over disbursement of the fund in 1913.

Carney, Winifrid (1888–1943), trade unionist, socialist, and suffragist; born in Bangor, Co. Down. A member of the Gaelic League and Cumann na mBan, she was secretary of the Textile Workers' Union from 1912 and confidante of JAMES CONNOLLY while he was in Belfast. She was Connolly's adjutant in the GPO during the EASTER RISING (1916). Advocating a workers' republic, she unsuccessfully contested election to the first Dáil Éireann for the Victoria division of Belfast, securing 539 votes and losing to the Labour Unionist Donald Thompson. She opposed the ANGLO-IRISH TREATY (1921). Her marriage in 1928 to George Macbride, a former member of the Ulster Volunteer Force, alienated her from family and friends.

Carrick's Morning Post, a daily newspaper founded by Richard Lonergan, 1812. Though it derived the greater portion of its revenue from advertising, it managed to maintain an independent stance and gave a measure of support to CATHOLIC EMANCIPATION. Lonergan ran into difficulties with his staff in 1825, the first labour problems to affect an Irish newspaper, when he took on apprentices against the wishes of his unionised staff, who physically attacked him and the non-union employees. Following continuing losses in circulation the title was bought by the *Dublin Times,* 1832.

Carroll, Dr William (1835–1926), Fenian; born in Rathmullan, Co. Donegal. He emigrated to the United States, 1838, and became Surgeon-General to the Federal Army during the American Civil War (1861–65). He later settled in Philadelphia, where he practised medicine. Prominent in opposition to JAMES STEPHENS (whom he regarded as interested only in 'self-aggrandisement'), as chairman of CLAN NA GAEL, 1875–80, he proposed a 'Revolutionary Directory', which led to the establishment of the Revolutionary Council within the IRB. He withdrew his early support for the NEW DEPARTURE, having reservations about the motives of CHARLES STEWART PARNELL, but continued to support JOHN DEVOY and Clan na Gael policies.

Carson, Sir Edward, Baron Carson of Duncairn (1854–1935), lawyer and politician (Unionist); born in Dublin, educated at TCD and King's Inns. The youngest Queen's counsel in Ireland, 1889, he became Solicitor-General for Ireland, 1 July 1892, and a month later a Liberal Unionist MP (for University of Dublin). Noted for his vigorous prosecution against the PLAN OF CAMPAIGN, he moved to England when called to the English bar, 1893, and became a member of the Irish Privy Council, 1896. He was a prominent advocate in many famous trials of the era: he appeared for the Marquess of Queensberry against Oscar Wilde, 1895, when his devastating cross-examination destroyed Wilde's career. He was Solicitor-General of England, 1900–06. He supported the demand for a Catholic university and lent his support to the IRISH UNIVERSITIES ACT (1908). He was elected leader of the Unionist Party, 21 February 1910. He refused to contest the leadership of the Conservative Party when Balfour resigned, 8 November 1911. He believed that if Ulster resistance was effectively motivated, home rule would be impossible for any part of Ireland. In 1911 he told a gathering of 100,000 Unionists at

Craigavon, near Belfast, that should home rule become law they would resist it and establish their own government in Ulster. He accepted the Agar-Robartes Proposal for the exclusion of four Ulster counties (Antrim, Armagh, Derry and Down), though on 1 January 1913 he had looked for the exclusion of the entire province.

Appointed Attorney-General, 25 May 1915, he resigned, 19 October, in protest at the mishandling of the Great War, in particular the Gallipoli campaign. He accepted office again, this time as First Lord of the Admiralty, 7 December 1916, but resigned, 22 January 1918, ostensibly in protest at Irish policy (in fact because of the dismissal of his protégé Jellicoe). In December 1918 he was elected member of Parliament for the Duncairn division of Belfast. Carson suggested the establishment of a Council of Ireland, which he described as 'the biggest advance towards unity in Ireland.' In July 1920 he supported Craig (see VISCOUNT CRAIGAVON) in calling for the reorganising of the ULSTER VOLUNTEER FORCE. Welcoming the Government of Ireland Bill, 11 November 1920, he expressed the wish that it would eventually lead to Ireland's being 'one and undivided, loyal to this country [England], and loyal to the Empire.' Accepting a peerage, he resigned the leadership of the Unionist Party to become Lord of Appeal, 21 May 1921. His *Ireland and Home Rule* was published in 1919.

Casement, Roger (1864–1916), civil servant, nationalist, and humanitarian; born in Sandycove, Co. Dublin, raised in Co. Antrim. Entering the British foreign service, 1892, he earned a reputation as a humanitarian for his investigations into atrocities committed by European employers in the Belgian Congo and later in Putamayo, Peru. His service in the tropics undermined his health. Knighted, 1911, he retired from the service in 1913. During visits to Ireland he became interested in nationalist movements. He joined the Gaelic League, 1904, became a friend of BULMER HOBSON, and contributed to the nationalist press as 'Sean-Bhean Bhocht'. He joined the Irish Volunteers in 1913 and became a member of its Provisional Committee. Through influential friends in London he raised money for the purchase of arms.

During a visit to the United States in 1914 he made contact with the German embassy through JOHN DEVOY. In poor health, in October 1914 he travelled to Berlin, where he was unsuccessful in his efforts to raise an Irish Brigade from among Irish prisoners of war. He was joined in Germany by ROBERT MONTEITH. Feeling that the German grant of 20,000 guns was inadequate, he decided to return to Ireland to prevent the proposed EASTER RISING (1916). He sailed for Ireland aboard a German submarine and arrived with Monteith and Daniel Bailey (one of the fifty or so who had answered his call for an Irish Brigade) at Banna Strand, Co. Kerry, Friday 21 April. As 'Richard Morton' he was arrested at Mackenna's Fort and taken to Dublin and later to London, where he was being interrogated when the rising broke out.

In the only public trial of those involved in the rising, Casement was charged with high treason. His defence was organised by GEORGE GAVAN DUFFY, whose cousin, A. M. Sullivan, undertook the brief; F. E. Smith (later EARL OF BIRKENHEAD) led for the prosecution. Casement was sentenced to death on 29 June. During July, while attempts were being made to organise a reprieve, copies of sections of his diaries were circulated, with government knowledge; these 'Black Diaries', revealing the fact that Casement was homosexual, eroded public sympathy. He became a Catholic before his execution by hanging at Pentonville Jail, London, 3 August.

In 1965 the British Government under Harold Wilson allowed the return of Casement's remains to Ireland, and following a state funeral he was re-interred in Glasnevin Cemetery, Dublin.

'Castle Document', a document released on 19 April 1916, purporting to have been issued by DUBLIN CASTLE, giving instructions for the suppression of the IRISH VOLUNTEERS, ordering the occupation of areas suspected of harbouring sedition (including the residence of the Catholic Archbishop of Dublin, WILLIAM WALSH), and calling also for the arrest of certain individuals. The document was a forgery, the work of JOSEPH PLUNKETT and SEÁN MAC DIARMADA, with the intention of provoking more Volunteers to support the EASTER RISING (1916). It achieved its objective when moderate Volunteers, including EOIN MACNEILL, adopted a more belligerent position.

Castlereagh, Robert Stewart, Viscount (1769–1822), politician (Whig, Conservative); born in Dublin. Member of Parliament for Co. Down, 1790, and a liberal in his earlier years, Castlereagh supported the principles of the UNITED IRISHMEN but, appalled by the excesses of the French Revolution, became a noted Conservative. He supported the Relief Act

(1793). In March 1798 he became acting Chief Secretary for Ireland and the following November replaced Thomas Pelham in the post. The rising of the United Irishmen in the summer of 1798 convinced him, as it did WILLIAM PITT, of the need for a legislative union of Ireland and Britain (see UNION). Assisted by the EARL OF CLARE, he dispensed largesse, patronage, sinecures and titles on an unprecedented scale until he had turned the narrow majority against union (111 to 106 in January 1799) into a sizeable majority in favour (158 to 115 on 6 February 1800).

After the Union, Pitt retained Castlereagh in the post of Chief Secretary for Ireland. From 1802 he held a variety of posts, including minister plenipotentiary to the allied sovereigns after the defeat of Napoléon Bonaparte, 1814–15. He played a leading role in the restoration of the old order in Europe at the Congress of Vienna (1815). Following a nervous breakdown, attributed to overwork, he underwent bouts of acute depression until he took his own life, believing he was being blackmailed because of homosexuality.

Castlereagh RUC Barracks, Castlereagh, Co. Down, an RUC station outside Belfast that, together with Gough Barracks, Belfast, became notorious, 1976–77, as a holding centre where physical force was used to extract confessions for the DIPLOCK COURTS.

Catalpa, a whaling vessel, built in 1844, bought for $5,250 by CLAN NA GAEL for the rescue of six Fenians—Thomas Darragh, Martin Hogan, Michael Harrington, Thomas Hassett, Robert Cranston, and James Wilson—from Fremantle, Australia, 17 April 1876. The rescue was planned by JOHN DEVOY and his agents JOHN J. BRESLIN and Thomas Desmond. The organisation spent some $13,760 equipping the vessel for a whaling expedition. Only the captain, George S. Anthony, and one other member of the crew, Denis Duggan, a Fenian agent, knew the true purpose of the voyage. They met two members of the IRB, Denis Florence McCarthy and John Walsh, who were also in Fremantle with independent rescue plans; on learning of the *Catalpa's* purpose they agreed to co-operate with it.

On the morning of the rescue attempt the *Catalpa* hove to in international waters. Anthony took a whaling-boat from the ship, which was left to the command of the first mate, Samuel Smith (who had only recently become acquainted with the purpose of the voyage). The rescue was effected without difficulty, but on its return the *Catalpa* was challenged by a British naval cutter, the *Georgette,* which, however, abandoned a boarding attempt when the *Catalpa* ran up the American flag.

The rescue was intended as a self-financing venture, with the *Catalpa* scheduled to spend some time in the whaling-grounds before returning to New York, but this plan was cancelled when some of the escapers objected. The rescued Fenians were landed at New York harbour at 2 a.m. on 19 August 1876. Anthony received $3,166 (which included a $1,000 bonus), and Smith received $1,644 (including a bonus of $299); the Portuguese and African crew members each received a $200 bonus. The escapers received sums in the region of $2,500—half the amount originally intended, because of the vessel's failure to engage in whaling on its return journey. The rescue was a morale boost to nationalist organisations; in Ireland, torchlight processions greeted news of the mission's success.

'Cat and Mouse Act', popular name for the Prisoners (Temporary Discharge for Health) Act (1913), originally used as a tactic against the women's suffrage movement. Prisoners were released on parole but could be returned to prison at any time, usually when they had recovered from their hunger-strike ordeal. The act was later invoked against hunger-striking Irish republicans as an alternative to forcible feeding.

Catholic Association of Ireland, the last in a line of movements that sought to secure CATHOLIC EMANCIPATION, formed by DANIEL O'CONNELL and RICHARD LALOR SHEIL, 2 May 1823. Its aims included giving legal effect to the procurement of Catholic rights, the regulation of Orange marches, and the return of Catholic graveyards to Catholic control. The membership subscription was 1 guinea a year, though members of the clergy were admitted free; the association broke with the aristocratic leadership of the past when in 1824 O'Connell allowed associate membership at the rate of 1 penny per month to harness popular support. O'Connell turned the association into a mass movement, earning himself the title 'King of the Beggars'. The 'Catholic Rent', as the subscription came to be called, collected at church doors throughout the country, averaged £1,000 a month.

The Catholic Association was the first

organised mass movement in Irish history to use constitutional methods. The principle followed by O'Connell and Sheil was 'agitation', of which O'Connell's addresses to huge meetings were an integral part. When the association was suppressed, 1825, O'Connell resorted to a favourite device and renamed it the New Catholic Association. It won its first victory in Co. Waterford in 1826 when THOMAS WYSE and a local committee secured the election of VILLIERS STUART against the powerful LORD GEORGE BERESFORD. Further successes followed: the association returned a candidate in each of the by-elections in Cos. Louth, Monaghan, and Westmeath. The culmination of the struggle for emancipation was the Co. Clare by-election, in which O'Connell defeated the government candidate, WILLIAM VESEY-FITZGERALD (by 2,057 to 982). This latest victory showed that Catholic Emancipation could no longer be denied; and, as the DUKE OF WELLINGTON and SIR ROBERT PEEL set about this, the Catholic Association dissolved itself, 12 February 1829.

Catholic Association (Belfast). The Belfast Catholic Association was founded in 1896 by Bishop Henry Henry of Down and Connor as a local political machine. Bishop Henry's opposition to the UNITED IRISH LEAGUE lost him support among his own clergy; realising his failure, he consented to the disintegration of the association in 1905.

Catholic Association (Dublin). The Dublin Catholic Association was founded under the presidency of EDWARD MARTYN, November 1902, following the publication of an article in the *Irish Rosary.* Members included D. P. MORAN and T. M. HEALY, supporters of Catholic Action (which sought a federation of Catholic societies), and Father TOM FINLAY; it had the support of the *Irish Independent* and *Irish Catholic,* both owned by WILLIAM MARTIN MURPHY. Though individual members of the Catholic hierarchy supported it, the association lacked official approval. WILLIAM WALSH, Archbishop of Dublin, warned that the existence of the association could be counter-productive, in that it might lead to a Protestant boycott of Catholic businesses. The movement survived as the Catholic Defence Society and later became part of the KNIGHTS OF COLUMBANUS.

Catholic Board, established in 1812 to press for CATHOLIC EMANCIPATION following the suppression of the CATHOLIC COMMITTEE. The revival of the VETO issue, involving aristocratic and anti-veto populist elements, led by Lord Fingall and DANIEL O'CONNELL, respectively, plunged the board into early crisis. Intense government pressure prevented the O'Connellites from exploiting their victory over supporters of the veto, and the board was dissolved, June 1814. It was revived in effect in 1823 with the establishment of the CATHOLIC ASSOCIATION by O'Connell and RICHARD LALOR SHEIL.

Catholic Boy Scouts of Ireland, founded in Dublin, 1927, by Father Ernest Farrell and his brother Father Tom Farrell to promote and foster youth training through the application of Catholic principles. It is organised on a diocesan, regional and parish basis; its patrons are the members of the Catholic hierarchy. It was a member of the Federation of Irish Scout Associations, affiliated to the World Scout Conference. Renamed 'Scouting Ireland CSI' in 1997, on 11 May 2003 it voted for a merger with the rival Scouting Ireland SAI, over the objections of the Catholic bishops.

Catholic Committee. The first Catholic Committee to pursue religious rather than secular interests was founded in 1760; it was dissolved in 1793 following the passing of the Relief Act. Revived in 1805, the committee had a strong aristocratic flavour, being led by Lord Fingall and Lord Kenmare, who lost much of their influence, however, when they supported the VETO. The initiative then passed to the rising Catholic middle class, led by DANIEL O'CONNELL. In February 1811 the British Government, alarmed at the boldness of O'Connell's leadership, invoked the Convention Act (1793) to suppress the movement. Prominent committee members, including Lord Fingall, were imprisoned during 1812, and the committee dissolved, to be reconstituted as the CATHOLIC BOARD.

Catholic Emancipation (1829). Emancipation meant the right of Catholics to sit as members of the British Parliament without having to subscribe to the Oath of Supremacy. Catholics were also excluded from senior government office, the judiciary and the bar, the offices of High Sheriff or county sheriff, and the Privy Council; THOMAS WYSE calculated that out of a total of 2,062 offices connected with the administration of justice in Ireland in 1828, 2,023 were filled by Protestants and 39 by Catholics. Despite a widespread belief that emancipation would follow the UNION, King George III resisted it, believing that the removal of the Oath of Supremacy would violate his Coronation Oath to maintain the Protestant constitution.

An Emancipation Bill proposed by HENRY GRATTAN failed by two votes in 1819. This proposed permitting the Crown a veto over episcopal appointments. It was strenuously opposed by DANIEL O'CONNELL, who believed that appointees under the veto would be no more than government lackeys. In 1823 O'Connell and RICHARD LALOR SHEIL founded the CATHOLIC ASSOCIATION, which attracted a support unparalleled in Irish history. Its electoral defeat of the powerful Beresford family in Co. Waterford, 1826, was followed by a series of election victories in Cos. Waterford, Louth, Monaghan, Westmeath, and Clare. O'Connell's victory in Co. Clare in 1828, when he defeated the government (and pro-Emancipation) candidate WILLIAM VESEY-FITZGERALD, convinced the DUKE OF WELLINGTON and SIR ROBERT PEEL that Emancipation was inevitable, and they pressured KING GEORGE IV, who eventually conceded.

The Roman Catholic Relief Act (1829) became law on 13 April 1829. In addition to emancipation, which allowed O'Connell to take his seat, Peel curbed the power of the Catholic Association by disfranchising the FORTY-SHILLING FREEHOLDERS, who had been the mainstay of the movement, by raising the qualification for the franchise to possession of property with a rateable valuation of £10.

Catholic Emancipation Centenary (1929). To mark the centenary of CATHOLIC EMANCIPATION, 1929 was designated a year of national celebration. A 129-member committee was formed in Dublin to organise a week-long programme of events, culminating in Pontifical High Mass and a Solemn Eucharistic Procession at the Phoenix Park, Dublin, Sunday 23 June. Social events included a garden party at Blackrock College attended by four thousand people, 19 June, and nightly sessions of choral and community singing. Pope Pius XI was represented by Monsignor Pisani, Archbishop of Constantia. It was estimated that some 300,000 people, marshalled by 10,000 stewards, were present at the Mass in the Fifteen Acres in the Phoenix Park, where every parish in the country was represented. Ireland's first sound film, a record of the celebrations, was shown for the first time at the Capitol Cinema, Dublin, 1 July 1929.

Catholic University of Ireland, established under Papal authority in 1854 to provide higher education for Catholics. It opened in Dublin, 3 November 1854, with JOHN HENRY NEWMAN as first rector. Holders of academic posts included Gerard Manley Hopkins and EUGENE O'CURRY. CHARLES BIANCONI was a patron. Newman and ARCHBISHOP PAUL CULLEN differed on the concept of the new university: Newman wished to provide a liberal education, while Cullen sought a college that would provide the Catholic middle class with a Catholic education. The experiment ended in failure: the institution could not grant degrees and, deprived of state funds, was beset by chronic financial problems. The University Education (Ireland) Act (1879) attempted a solution by establishing an examining body, the ROYAL UNIVERSITY OF IRELAND, which was empowered to grant degrees to students possessing the requisite standard. Fellowships of the Royal University were distributed so as to provide an endowment in the region of £6,000 a year to the CATHOLIC UNIVERSITY OF IRELAND. While this did not wholly meet episcopal demands it did enable Catholic students to graduate without attending Trinity College, Dublin.

As University College, Dublin, from 1883, the university was administered by the Society of Jesus until it became a college of the NATIONAL UNIVERSITY OF IRELAND in 1908.

cattle-driving, the impounding of cattle owned by a tenant in arrears with rent. The cattle were driven to the nearest town, where they were held until the arrears were met.

cattle 'thatching'. Unable to afford buildings or shelters for their stock, poorer farmers resorted to 'thatching' or covering individual cattle with straw or rushes to protect them during inclement weather.

Cavendish, Lord Frederick (1836–82), British politician (Liberal); born in Eastbourne, Sussex, educated privately and at the University of Cambridge. Member of Parliament for the Northern division of Yorkshire West Riding, 1865–82, he was private secretary to W. E. GLADSTONE, 1872–73, who appointed him Chief Secretary for Ireland, May 1882, in succession to W. E. FORSTER. On arrival he accompanied the new Lord Lieutenant, Lord Spencer, in a ceremonial entry into Dublin, 6 May 1882. That evening Cavendish and the Under-Secretary, T. H. BURKE, were murdered by the INVINCIBLES in the Phoenix Park (see PHOENIX PARK MURDERS). It was widely believed that Burke, closely associated with draconian COERCION measures taken against the LAND LEAGUE, was the target and that Cavendish (in the words of ANNA PARNELL) was 'sacrificed to the accident of his being in Burke's company.'

Ceann Comhairle, chairperson of Dáil Éireann. The Ceann Comhairle of the first Dáil was SEÁN T. O'KELLY, 1919–20; he was succeeded by EOIN MACNEILL, who held the office during the Treaty debates. His successors in the office were MICHAEL HAYES, 1922–32, Frank Fahy, 1932–51, PATRICK HOGAN, 1951–67, Cormac Breslin, 1967–73, Seán Treacy, 1973–77, Joseph Brennan, 1977–80, Pádraig Faulkner, 1980–81, John O'Connell, 1981–82, Thomas Fitzpatrick, 1982–87, Seán Treacy, 1987–97, Séamus Pattison, 1997–2002, and Dr Rory O'Hanlon, 2002–. The Leas-Cheann Comhairle is the deputy chairperson.

Ceannt, Éamonn (1881–1916), republican soldier; born in Ballymore, near Glennamaddy, Co. Galway, son of an RIC man, educated at UCD. He worked as a clerk in the Treasury Department of Dublin Corporation. A piper, he founded the Dublin Pipers' Club and led Irish athletes in Rome. A member of the Gaelic League and Sinn Féin, he joined the IRB and became a member of its Supreme Council, 1915. A founder-member of the Irish Volunteers, as captain of A Company, 4th Battalion, Dublin Brigade he assisted in the HOWTH GUN-RUNNING. He was a member of the IRB Military Council that planned the EASTER RISING (1916). A signatory of the Proclamation of the Irish Republic, he commanded the South Dublin Union area (James's Street) during the fighting, with W. T. COSGRAVE as vice-commandant. On the eve of his execution, 7 May, he wrote from cell 88 in Kilmainham Jail, Dublin:

> I bear no ill-will towards those against whom I have fought. I have found the common soldiers and the higher officers human and companionable, even the English who were actually in the fight against us. Thank God soldiering for Ireland has opened my heart and made me see poor humanity where I expected to see only scorn and reproach . . .

Celtic Literary Society, founded by WILLIAM ROONEY (first chairman) and ARTHUR GRIFFITH from the Leinster Literary Society, October 1893, with the object of studying Irish language, history, literature, and music; its political policy was 'independent action.' The exclusively male membership included JOHN O'LEARY and FRANK HUGH O'DONNELL. The society held weekly meetings at which debates and readings were held and maintained a manuscript journal, *An Seanachie*. Branches of the society were later absorbed by CUMANN NA NGAEDHEAL, 1900.

Celtic Society, founded by WILLIAM ELIOT HUDSON, JAMES HARDIMAN and others, 1846, for the preservation and publication of early Irish manuscripts. Supported mainly by academics, it merged with the Irish Archaeological Society, 1840, to form the Irish Archaeological and Celtic Society, of which Prince Albert (husband of Queen Victoria) became patron. Hudson endowed much of the society's work, including publication of the writings of JOHN O'DONOVAN and Hardiman.

Censorship of Films Act (1923), one of the earliest pieces of legislation enacted by the Irish Free State, establishing a Censorship Board to examine films offered for commercial distribution. The act was amended in 1930 to allow for the censoring of sound films. John Ford's film of Liam O'Flaherty's *The Informer* (1935) was one of seventeen whose banning by the censor was reversed by the Censorship of Films Appeals Board, 1930–39. A Film Appeals Board was established in 1964.

Censorship of Publications Acts (1929–67). The Censorship Board, consisting of five members, was established on 13 February 1930 under the Censorship of Publications Act (1929), following the recommendations of the COMMITTEE ON EVIL LITERATURE. It was empowered to prohibit the sale and distribution of 'indecent and obscene' books. The August issue of the magazine *Health and Strength* was the first publication banned under the act, 29 August, for including material relating to contraceptives. Among early works banned by the board were Radclyffe Hall's *The Well of Loneliness* (1928), Aldous Huxley's *Point Counter Point* (1928), Bertrand Russell's *Marriage and Morals* (1929), and all the works of Marie Stopes up to 1930. The board banned books by nearly every major Irish writer of the first half of the twentieth century and works by most of the recipients of the Nobel Prize for Literature. Altogether, 1,200 books and 140 periodicals were banned between 1930 and 1939. Press censorship, which during the years of the Second World War produced duels between the censor and R. M. SMYLLIE, editor of the *Irish Times*, was terminated on 11 May 1944.

An amendment to the act, 1946, allowing

for appeals, also empowered customs officers to seize literature believed to infringe the act. A further amendment, 11 July 1967, led to reconsideration of previously banned works, some of which were removed from the list. Under this amendment a book remained banned for a maximum of twelve years.

Centenary Celebrations, 1898. The centenary of the rising of the UNITED IRISHMEN was marked by nationwide celebrations in 1898. Among the many clubs founded in honour of 1798 activists were the Wolfe Tone, Father Murphy, Oliver Bond, Lord Edward Fitzgerald, Napper Tandy and Sheares Brothers Clubs. Nationalists, moderates and republicans combined with literary and other figures in arranging the celebrations; among those involved were JOHN O'LEARY (president of the IRB committee formed to commemorate the occasion), FRED ALLAN, MAUD GONNE, JOHN MACBRIDE, JAMES CONNOLLY, and W. B. YEATS. The event, which was celebrated also by Irish people in the United States, Australia, and South Africa, helped to rejuvenate the republican movement.

Central Bank of Ireland, established under the Central Bank Act (1942), which became law on 4 November 1942, replacing the CURRENCY COMMISSION. The Central Bank became operative on 1 February 1943 under its first governor, Joseph Brennan, 1943–53.

Central Board, also called the Irish Board, suggested by JOSEPH CHAMBERLAIN (who also called it the National Council) as part of his strategy of opposition to HOME RULE. Negotiations with CHARLES STEWART PARNELL on the scheme were conducted through WILLIAM O'SHEA, who conveyed to Chamberlain the mistaken impression that the scheme was an acceptable compromise in Irish demands for self-government; in fact it was unacceptable to the Irish, as it offered only a small measure of local government in such areas as land, communications, and education. The Archbishop of Westminster, Cardinal Manning, assured Chamberlain that the board had the support of the Irish Catholic hierarchy. In May 1885 the cabinet vetoed the scheme, increasing Chamberlain's determination to destroy home rule.

Central Citizens' Defence Committee, formed in Belfast, 16 August 1969, by Jim Sullivan, second in command (under Billy McMillen) of the IRA in Belfast. It sought to organise the defence and welfare of Catholics engaged in erecting barricades in Belfast. Members included Canon Pádraig Murphy, PADDY DEVLIN (NILP), Paddy Kennedy (Republican Labour), and Tom Conaty. Members patrolled Catholic areas, published a newsletter, and organised broadcasts over the illegal Radio Belfast. They criticised the behaviour of the British army during the 34-hour curfew in July 1970, when five people died. Leaders claimed that violence could harm the cause of justice. They organised visits to Long Kesh (later the Maze Prison) after the introduction of internment in August 1971. They attempted to secure a Provisional IRA ceasefire in 1973. In the same year they issued a 'Black Paper' calling for the replacement of the RUC with an 'impartial police force', a demand rejected by the Secretary of State for Northern Ireland, WILLIAM WHITELAW.

'centre', the head of a 'circle' within the IRB. With the designated letter A and the rank of colonel, a centre had nominal command of 820 men. The first 'Head Centre' or chief organiser of the IRB was JAMES STEPHENS.

Chalk Sunday, the name given in rural Ireland to Quinquagesima Sunday, the last Sunday before Lent. As marriages were not contracted during Lent, it was customary on that day to make two chalk marks on the clothes of local bachelors to remind them that they had only two days remaining in which to get married.

Chamberlain, Joseph (1836–1914), British politician (Liberal and Liberal Unionist); born in Birmingham, educated at University College School. Opposed to COERCION, he was influential in the negotiations leading to the 'KILMAINHAM TREATY'. He worked out a 'CENTRAL BOARD' scheme for Ireland, 1884–85, being led by WILLIAM O'SHEA to believe that CHARLES STEWART PARNELL would consider it a settlement of Irish demands. He was a staunch imperialist and a leading social-imperialist and tariff reformer; his opposition to home rule for Ireland divided the Liberal Party, 1886, and led the Liberal Unionists against the Gladstonian Liberals and home rule. His negotiating skills were employed by successive British governments.

Chamberlain, (Arthur) Neville (1869–1940), British politician (Conservative); born in Birmingham, second son of JOSEPH CHAMBERLAIN. Succeeding STANLEY BALDWIN as Prime Minister, 1937, he negotiated with ÉAMON DE VALERA an end to the 'ECONOMIC WAR', March

1938. An element of their agreement, the return of the TREATY PORTS, was severely criticised by Chamberlain's successor, SIR WINSTON CHURCHILL.

changedale, a system of landholding under the RUNDALE system, allowing for a rotation of land portions held by individual tenants, ensuring that everyone shared both the good and the bad holdings.

Chester Beatty Library, Dublin, opened 6 September 1953 to house the priceless collection of Islamic and Oriental art and manuscripts bequeathed to Ireland by the mining magnate and philanthropist Sir Alfred Chester Beatty (1875–1968). The bequest included more than 13,000 volumes of Babylonian clay tablets dating from 2,500 BC, together with Greek and Egyptian papyri, miniatures, and outstanding examples of calligraphy. Born in New York, Beatty moved to Ireland in 1950 and in 1957 became the first honorary citizen of Ireland. He was a patron of the National Gallery of Ireland, to which he presented his collection of pictures, and a benefactor of Irish hospitals. Following his death in Monte Carlo he was accorded a state funeral and buried in Glasnevin Cemetery, Dublin, 20 January 1968.

Chichester-Clark, Major James Dawson, Lord Moyola (1923–2002), politician (Ulster Unionist Party); born in Castledawson, Co. Derry. After retiring from the British army in 1960 he was elected to the Stormont seat for South Derry vacated by his grandmother, Dehra Parker (1882–1963). He was assistant whip of the UUP, 1963, chief whip, 1963–69, and Minister of Agriculture, 1967–69. He resigned his agriculture portfolio, 23 April 1969, opposing the granting of universal suffrage in local government elections and precipitating the fall of the Prime Minister, his cousin TERENCE O'NEILL, whom he succeeded as Prime Minister, 1 May.

The British Government granted Chichester-Clark's request for soldiers on the street when violence erupted in Belfast, August 1969. On 20 August the Home Secretary, James Callaghan, failed to allay unionist fears by declaring that the status of Northern Ireland would remain unchanged without majority consent, and unrest continued in the face of continued demands by the NORTHERN IRELAND CIVIL RIGHTS ASSOCIATION for an end to discrimination. Tensions between Chichester-Clark and the Taoiseach, JACK LYNCH, surfaced when Lynch called for intervention by the United Nations, established army field hospitals in border areas, and arranged camps in the Republic for those fleeing the violence. Chichester-Clark was severely criticised by IAN PAISLEY, who demanded stronger action against the IRA. A television interview with the British Prime Minister, HAROLD WILSON, during which he intimated the phasing out of the B Special Constabulary, together with the loss of two by-elections to Paisley and Rev. William Beattie, further weakened Chichester-Clark's position. When his request for more soldiers was denied he resigned, 20 March, and was succeeded by BRIAN FAULKNER.

Chief Secretary for Ireland. Following the ACT OF UNION (1800), the Chief Secretary to the LORD LIEUTENANT OF IRELAND was the effective head of the executive in Ireland. With the Lord Lieutenant he was responsible for implementing cabinet policy in relation to Ireland; he defended Irish policy in Parliament and was responsible for the Irish civil service, which was supervised by the Under-Secretary. Though his office in Dublin Castle was the centre of British administration in Ireland, the Chief Secretary spent the parliamentary year in London, working through the Irish Office. Throughout the nineteenth century the Chief Secretary's office assumed an increasingly wide range of powers as the ceremonial role of the Lord Lieutenant increased. Patronage was generally at his pleasure; the increasing importance of his role was recognised when Lord Stanley (Chief Secretary 1830–33) was granted membership of the cabinet.

The following were the Chief Secretaries from 1800 to 1922:

1800 VISCOUNT CASTLEREAGH
1801 Charles Abbot
1802 William Wickham
1804 Sir Evan Nepean
1805 Sir Nicholas Vansittart
1805 Charles Lang
1806 William Elliot
1807 Arthur Wellesley (see DUKE OF WELLINGTON)
1809 WILLIAM WELLESLEY-POLE
1812 SIR ROBERT PEEL
1818 Charles Grant
1821 HENRY GOULBOURN
1827 William Lamb (see VISCOUNT MEBOURNE)

1828 Francis Leveson Gower
1830 Sir Henry Hardinge
1830 Lord Stanley (see EARL OF DERBY)
1833 Sir John Cam Hobhouse
1833 Edward John Littleton
1834 Sir Henry Hardinge
1835 Viscount Morpeth (see EARL OF CARLISLE)
1841 Lord Eliot (see EARL OF ST GEMANS)
1845 Baron Cottesloe
1846 Earl of Lincoln
1846 HENRY LABOUCHERE
1847 SIR WILLIAM SOMERVILLE
1852 Lord Naas (see EARL OF MAYO)
1853 Sir John Young
1855 Edward Horsman
1857 Henry A. Herbert
1858 Lord Naas
1859 Edward Cardwell
1861 Sir Robert Peel
1865 CHICHESTER FORTESCUE-PARKINSON
1866 Lord Naas
1868 Lord Winmarleigh
1868 Lord Carlingford
1870 Marquess of Hartington (see DUKE OF DEVONSHIRE)
1874 SIR MICHAEL F. HICKS BEACH
1878 JAMES LOWTHER
1880 W. E. FORSTER
1882 LORD FREDERICK CAVENDISH
1882 SIR G. O. TREVELYAN
1884 HENRY CAMPBELL-BANNERMAN
1885 Sir W. Hart Dyke
1886 W. H. Smith
1886 JOHN MORLEY
1886 Sir Michael F. Hicks Beach
1887 ARTHUR BALFOUR
1891 William Lawless Jackson
1892 John Morley
1895 Gerald W. Balfour
1900 GEORGE WYNDHAM
1905 WALTER HUME LONG
1905 JAMES BRYCE
1907 AUGUSTINE BIRRELL
1916 H. E. DUKE
1918 EDWARD SHORTT
1919 Ian Macpherson
1920 SIR HAMAR GREENWOOD

Childers, (Robert) Erskine (1870–1922), author and politician (Sinn Féin); born in London but raised at the maternal home, Glendalough House, Co. Wicklow, with his cousin ROBERT BARTON; educated at the University of Cambridge. He was wounded while serving with the British army during the Anglo-Boer War. He worked as Committee Clerk of the House of Commons, 1894–1910. On his marriage to Mary Ellen Osgood of Boston, 6 January 1904, he received a present of the yacht ASGARD from his wife's father, Dr Hamilton Osgood. A convert to home rule, he used the *Asgard* in July 1914 to ferry arms bought in Germany by DARRELL FIGGIS from the North Sea to Howth (see HOWTH GUN-RUNNING). During the First World War, serving with the Royal Auxiliary Naval Service, he was decorated and promoted to lieutenant-commander, and appointed to the secretariat of the IRISH CONVENTION, 1917–18.

Demobilised, March 1919, he moved his family to Ireland and espoused the Sinn Féin cause. Elected to Dáil Éireann for Kildare-Wicklow, he succeeded DESMOND FITZGERALD as Director of Publicity and editor of the IRISH BULLETIN. He was a member of the secretariat to the negotiating team during the discussions on the ANGLO-IRISH TREATY (1921). Opposed to the Treaty, he supported the Republicans during the CIVIL WAR, when he was Director of Publicity and editor of the *Republic of Ireland.* Arrested at Barton's home by Provisional Government soldiers, 11 November 1922, he was court-martialled for possession of a revolver (a present from MICHAEL COLLINS) and sentenced to death, 17 November. A writ of *habeas corpus* was refused, on the grounds that a state of war existed and the court could not 'for any purpose, or under any circumstance, control the military authority'—a ruling that ran contrary to the government's assertion that it was dealing with a revolt and not a war, and that captured insurgents therefore were not entitled to the restraints applying to prisoners-of war. Despite widespread pleas for clemency he was shot on 24 November, after shaking hands with each member of the firing squad, the first of a series of executions of Republican prisoners. Childers was the author of *The Riddle of the Sands* (1903), *The Framework of Home Rule* (1911), *Military Rule in Ireland* (1920), and *The Constructive Works of Dáil Éireann* (1921). His son, ERSKINE CHILDERS, was fourth President of Ireland, 1973–74.

Childers, Erskine Hamilton (1905–1975), politician (Fianna Fáil); born in London, son of (ROBERT) ERSKINE CHILDERS, educated at the University of Cambridge. European manager of an American travel agency, 1928–31, he became advertising manager of the IRISH PRESS, 1931–36, then secretary of the Federation of Irish Manufacturers, 1936–44. He was Parliamentary Secretary to the Minister for

Local Government, 1944–48, Minister for Posts and Telegraphs, 1951–54, for Lands, 1957–59, for Transport and Power, 1959–66, for Transport and Power and Posts and Telegraphs, 1966–69, and Tánaiste and Minister for Health, 1969–73. He defeated the Fine Gael candidate, T. F. O'Higgins (635,867 to 578,771) to succeed ÉAMON DE VALERA as President of Ireland, 1973. He sought to make the office more accessible by a round of visiting, speech-making and travelling throughout the country. On 16 November 1974, after delivering a lecture on drug abuse to the Royal College of Physicians in Ireland, he suffered a fatal heart attack.

Children's Land League, established in 1881 by the LAND LEAGUE and the LADIES' LAND LEAGUE. Members were taught the following 'Alphabet':

A is the army that covers the ground;
B is the buckshot we're getting all round;
C is the crowbar of cruellest fame;
D is our Davitt, a right glorious name;
E is the English who've robbed us of bread;
F is the famine they've left us instead;
G is for Gladstone, whose life is a lie;
H is the harvest we'll hold or we'll die;
I is the inspector, who when drunk is bold;
J is the jarvey, who'll not drive him for gold;
K is Kilmainham, where our true men abide;
L is the Land League, our hope and our pride;
M is the magistrate, who makes black of our white;
N is no rent, which will make our wrongs right;
O is Old Ireland, that yet shall be free'd;
P is the Peelers, who've sold her for greed;
Q is the Queen, whose use is not known;
R is the Rifles, which keep up her throne;
S is the sheriff, with woe in his train;
T is the toil that others may gain;
U is the Union that works bitter harm;
V is the villain that grabs up a farm;
W is the warrant for death or for chains;
X is the 'Express', all lies and no brains;
Y is 'Young Ireland', spreading the light;
Z is the zeal that will win the great fight.

Chotah, a yacht owned by the surgeon Sir Thomas Myles (1857–1937). It took a consignment of German arms bought by DARRELL FIGGIS on behalf of the Irish Volunteers from CONOR O'BRIEN's yacht, the *KELPIE*, near St Tudwall Roads, off the Welsh coast. It was planned to land them at Kilcoole, Co. Wicklow, on the same day (26 July) that the *ASGARD*, owned by ERSKINE CHILDERS, landed the rest of the consignment at Howth (see HOWTH GUN-RUNNING). The *Chotah*, however, crewed by Myles and James Creed Meredith, running foul of a gale, split its mainsail and did not deliver the cargo at Kilcoole until 1 August, to a detachment of Volunteers led by SEÁN T. O'KELLY and Seán Fitzgibbon.

Christus Rex, a Catholic clerical organisation founded by Dr Cornelius Lucey, professor of ethics at St Patrick's College, Maynooth (later Bishop of Cork), 1941, under the chairmanship of FATHER CAHAL DALY (later Archbishop of Armagh). Its purpose was to study social issues from a Catholic viewpoint.

Church Education Society, founded within the Church of Ireland, 1839, because of dissatisfaction with the system of national education established in 1831. It advocated free use of the Bible in class, and made no distinction between religious and literary training. On the establishment of the national school system, 1831, the society had 825 schools, with an enrolment of 43,627 pupils, 10,868 of whom were Catholics; enrolment reached a peak in 1848, with 120,202 pupils. After SIR ROBERT PEEL refused separate grants for the society in 1845, placing a considerable burden on the society's resources, the number of schools gradually fell, from 1,885 in 1851 to 1,202 in 1870, in which year the society was dissolved and its schools joined to the national education system.

Churchill, Lord Randolph Henry Spencer (1849–1895), British politician (Conservative); born in Woodstock, Oxfordshire. Member of Parliament for Woodstock from 1874, he frequently visited Ireland while his father was Lord Lieutenant, 1876–80. While urging a policy of conciliation, he opposed HOME RULE. He was instrumental in arranging the Tory-Nationalist entente, 1885, to secure the support of the Irish Party against the Liberals in return for dropping COERCION. With the announcement of W. E. GLADSTONE's conversion to support for home rule, 1885, Churchill moved against the measure. Having decided that 'the Orange card would be the one to play,' speaking at the Ulster Hall, Belfast, 22 February 1886, he declared: 'Ulster will fight, and Ulster will be right,' which became the watchword of Unionists. He saw the fight against home rule as a fight to defend the British Empire. When the Liberals failed to carry home rule, July 1886, and the

Conservatives returned to power, Churchill was Chancellor of the Exchequer and leader of the House of Commons, July 1886. He promised a general inquiry into affairs in Ireland, as a result of which certain reforms were granted, including smallholdings for agricultural labourers, land transfers, and land purchases. He resigned as Chancellor, 23 December 1886, on the passing of the army and navy estimates, which he considered excessive. He was the father of WINSTON SPENCER CHURCHILL.

Churchill, Sir Winston Spencer (1874–1965), British politician (Liberal and Conservative); born in Woodstock, Oxfordshire, eldest son of LORD RANDOLPH CHURCHILL. After a military career he entered politics as a Conservative, 1900–05, and then as a Liberal, 1906–08, Conservative Liberal, 1908–22, and Conservative, 1924–65. Supporting home rule for Ireland, he arrived in Belfast in 1912 but had to speak in a huge tent erected on the grounds of the Celtic Park Football Club, as hostile unionists denied him the use of the Ulster Hall. Held responsible for the Gallipoli disaster, 1915, he resigned and served in the trenches before accepting office as Minister for Munitions, 1917. As Secretary for the Colonies and chairman of the Cabinet Commission on Irish Affairs he played a leading role in the negotiations leading to the ANGLO-IRISH TREATY, October–December 1921. He was adamant that Britain should hold ports in Ireland for defence purposes (the TREATY PORTS). Later he defended the Treaty on the grounds that the reconquest of Ireland by force would involve a costly campaign and the extension of martial law to the entire Free State. In 1922 he was responsible for the transfer of services to the PROVISIONAL GOVERNMENT and the evacuation of Ireland by British forces. He organised the meetings between Sir James Craig (see VISCOUNT CRAIGAVON) and MICHAEL COLLINS, January–March 1922, that led to the CRAIG-COLLINS AGREEMENTS. He pressed Collins to move against Republicans holding the FOUR COURTS, which precipitated the CIVIL WAR. He steered the Irish Free State (Agreement) Bill, which ratified the Treaty, through the House of Commons, 1922. On 19 March 1926 he signed the ULTIMATE FINANCIAL AGREEMENT with the Free State Minister for Finance, ERNEST BLYTHE.

Out of office, 1929–39, Churchill unsuccessfully fought against the return of the Treaty ports to Ireland, 1938. He replaced NEVILLE CHAMBERLAIN as Prime Minister, 10 May 1940, heading the coalition cabinet until July 1945. His implied promise to recognise the principle of Irish unity when the war ended failed to persuade ÉAMON DE VALERA to abandon Ireland's neutrality. His carping reference to the neutrality policy in his victory speech provoked one of de Valera's most famous speeches; however, he later told his son Randolph:

> It was a speech which, perhaps, I should not have made, but it was made in the heat of the moment. We had just come through the war, and I had been looking around at our victories; the idea of Éire sitting at our feet without giving us a hand annoyed me.

Church Temporalities (Ireland) Act (1833), enacted on 14 August 1833 to rationalise the organisation of the Church of Ireland. It suppressed ten sees and reduced the revenues of the remaining twelve. Opposed by DANIEL O'CONNELL, it was a minor concession to those who sought the DISESTABLISHMENT of the Church of Ireland.

cinema. Dan Lowry's Star of Erin Theatre of Varieties, Dublin, was the venue for the first public showing of a film in Ireland, 20 April 1896. The first Irish company employed in the exhibition and distribution of films, the Irish Animated Picture Company, made the first Irish documentary, *Life on the Great Southern and Western Railway* (1904). When Ireland's first cinema, the Volta, opened at 45 Mary Street, Dublin, 20 December 1909, under the management of JAMES JOYCE, *Devilled Crab* (comedy), *Bewitched Castle* (fantasy), *The First Paris Orphanage, La Pourponnière* (documentary) and *The Tragic Story of Beatrice Ceni* (murder) shared the bill. In 1916 there were 149 cinemas and halls in Ireland showing films, a figure that reached 265 by 1930.

The DRUMCOLLOGHER CINEMA TRAGEDY led to the introduction of many safety features, both in the manufacture of the film and in the buildings in which they were being shown. The Irish-Canadian screenwriter and director Sidney Olcott (1873–1949) directed and starred in *The Lad from Old Ireland* (1910), often regarded as the first American film made outside the United States. The Film Company of Ireland, established March 1916, lost much of its early film during the EASTER RISING (1916). Its epic, an eight-reel version of Charles Kickham's novel *Knocknagow* (1917), was a popular success. 'Pathé Gazette' and 'Gaumont Graphic' provided newsreel coverage until the

General Film Supply Company established the 'Irish Events' newsreel, 1917–20. Its first release included film of members of the Irish Volunteers returning from English prisons, 18 June 1917. The centenary of CATHOLIC EMANCIPATION, 1929, provided material for the first sound film shot in Ireland for public screening, 1 July 1929. The tenor John McCormack featured and sang eleven songs in *Song o' My Heart* (1930), made in Dublin by Fox Film Productions.

The film censor banned three thousand films and made cuts in a further eight thousand during the years 1924–30. John Ford's *The Informer* (1935) was one of seventeen films whose banning under the CENSORSHIP OF FILMS ACT (1923) was later revoked by the Censorship of Films Appeal Board. Robert O'Flaherty spent some two years filming the award-winning semi-documentary *Man of Aran* (1934). Three years later Tom Cooper produced the first full-length indigenous Irish sound film, *The Dawn,* based on the War of Independence. EMMET DALTON was influential in the establishment of Ardmore Studios, 12 May 1958. GAEL-LINN filled the 36-year void in Irish newsreel production with its 'Amharc Éireann', 267 editions of which were produced, 1956–64. It also financed a series of documentary films, 1960–75, most of them directed by Louis Marcus; George Morrison directed *Mise Éire* (1959) and a sequel, *Saoirse?* (1961), both featuring the music of SEÁN Ó RIADA. Gael-Linn combined with Louis Marcus to produce *An Tine Bheo* (1966), marking the fiftieth anniversary of the Easter Rising.

In 1977 the Arts Council's Film Script Award provided a boost to film-makers. *Poitín* (1978), featuring Cyril Cusack, Niall Tóibín, and Dónal McCann, took the initial award. The Irish film industry earned an international reputation during the 1980s and 90s, mainly as a result of works by Neil Jordan—*Angel* (1982), *The Company of Wolves* (1984), *Mona Lisa* (1986), *The Crying Game* (1992), and *Michael Collins* (1996)—and Jim Sheridan—*My Left Foot* (1989), *The Field* (1990), and *In the Name of the Father* (1993).

Civic Guard, established on 22 February 1922 to replace the ROYAL IRISH CONSTABULARY. The first commissioner was MICHAEL STAINES. Because of the CIVIL WAR, members were armed for a time. On 24 April 1922 anti-Treaty members mutinied, seized the armoury and camp at Kildare, and ejected Staines and his followers. The mutiny led to a commission of inquiry, which found that the force should not have been armed, and that Staines should not have been appointed to such a senior post. The force was disbanded and replaced in September with the GARDA SÍOCHÁNA.

Civil War (1922–23). On 7 January 1922 Dáil Éireann voted (64 to 57) to accept the ANGLO-IRISH TREATY. In an unauthorised action, some anti-Treaty forces seized the FOUR COURTS, Dublin, 13 April 1922; responding to pressure from London, government forces, under EOIN O'DUFFY, moved against the occupants, precipitating the Civil War, 28 June. The opposing forces were:

> *Free State army:* MICHAEL COLLINS was Commander in Chief and EOIN O'DUFFY Chief of Staff of the Free State army, which was under the direction of the Minister for Defence, RICHARD MULCAHY. Its structure on the outbreak of hostilities was:
>
> 1st Western Division: Cos. Clare and south Galway; Commandant Michael Brennan
> 5th Northern Division: east Cavan, south Fermanagh, and Monaghan; Commandant Dan Hogan
> 1st Northern Division (four brigades): Co. Donegal; Commandant Joseph Sweeney
> North Wexford Brigade: north Wexford and south Wicklow; Commandant Joseph Cummin
> Carlow Brigade: Co. Carlow; Commandant Liam Stack
> Midland Division: Cos. Fermanagh, Leitrim, and Longford; Commandant SEÁN MAC EOIN
> 3rd Southern Division (five brigades): Cos. Laois, Offaly, and parts of Tipperary; Commandant Michael McCormack
>
> A War Council established by the Provisional Government, 12 July 1922, consisted of General Seán Mac Eoin (Western Command), General Eoin O'Duffy (Southern Command), General EMMET DALTON (Eastern Command), General John Prout (South-Eastern Command), and General J. J. O'CONNELL (Curragh Command).

The strength of the army at the outbreak of the war was estimated at 8,000 by the Adjutant-General, Seán MacMahon, 6,000 of whom were in arms. Khaki uniforms, bought in England, were dyed green; many soldiers wore part uniform and part civilian dress. In June 1922 the army's strength was increased to

15,000, while the number on the roll of the Volunteer Reserve was stated as 35,000.

The British Government, concerned at the lack of arms, supplied the Free State army with 79 Lewis machine-guns, 8 eighteen-pound artillery pieces, 11,900 rifles, 4,200 revolvers, and 3,504 grenades. By September 1922 it had supplied a further 167 Lewis guns, 15,500 rifles, 2,406 revolvers, and 5 Vickers machine-guns. An offer by Winston Churchill of aeroplanes, 'which you could paint green,' was not availed of.

In the early stages of the fighting the army was infrequently paid and rationed, a factor that led to large-scale commandeering. A Disciplinary Code was not introduced until 1923.

Anti-Treaty IRA ('Irregulars'): Anti-Treaty forces were under the command of LIAM LYNCH; LIAM MELLOWS was Quartermaster-General. Government sources placed their strength at approximately 12,900 and estimated that they had 6,780 rifles at their disposal.

2nd Northern Division (four brigades): Cos. Tyrone and Derry; Commandant Charles Daly
3rd Northern Division (three brigades): Co. Antrim, Belfast, north Down; Commandant-General Joseph McKelvey
Dublin No. 1 Brigade (independent); Commandant OSCAR TRAYNOR
South Dublin Brigade: south Co. Dublin; Commandant Andrew MacDonnell
2nd Western Division: north Galway, south and east Mayo, south Roscommon; Commandant-General Thomas Maguire
3rd Western Division: part of Co. Mayo, north Roscommon, and Sligo; Commandant Liam Pilkington
4th Western Division (ten brigades): parts of Co. Galway, north and west Mayo, and parts of Sligo; Commandant-General Michael Kilroy
1st Southern Division (ten brigades): Cos. Cork, Kerry, west Limerick, and Waterford; Commandant-General Liam Lynch
2nd Southern Division (five brigades): Cos. Kilkenny, Limerick, and part of Tipperary; Commandant ERNIE O'MALLEY
4th Northern Division (three brigades, neutral to 14 August, then anti-Treaty): Co. Armagh, south and west Down, north Louth; Commandant FRANK AIKEN

Major encounters and incidents of the Civil War

Boyle, Co. Roscommon, 5 April to July 1922. In early April, Commandant Martin Fallon surprised the Republican garrison and took the town. Acceding to the request of Republican officers to be placed under open arrest, Fallon and his men were later overcome by the prisoners. Fallon was temporarily relieved of command by his commanding officer, Seán Mac Eoin.

Republican soldiers attacked the workhouse, and in the ensuing engagement Brigadier-General Michael Dockery, officer commanding Government forces, was killed, 2 July. Fighting continued until the arrival of General Mac Eoin with the *Ballinalee* and an eighteen-pounder gun, 5 July. The Republicans withdrew, having destroyed a large quantity of stores and leaving the barracks partly in flames.

Dublin, 28 June to 5 July 1922. Following the evacuation of the Four Courts, Republican soldiers occupied some buildings, including the Hammam Hotel, O'Connell Street, Dublin, as headquarters, while Traynor's Dublin No. 1 Brigade operated from Barry's Hotel.

Government forces encircled the city, 2 July. Their superior firepower led to early advances, and on 5 July the Hammam Hotel, O'Connell Street, fell to government forces under Commandant O'Connor. In a last heroic gesture CATHAL BRUGHA, gun raised, rushed from the blazing building and was cut down. Republicans, having lost Dublin, fell back on Blessington, Co. Wicklow.

The fighting in Dublin cost sixty-five lives, including some civilians. The cost of damage was more than £3½ million, while the centre of the city was severely damaged by artillery.

Waterford, 28 June to 21 July 1922. With headquarters in the Grenville Hotel, Republicans under Patrick (Pax) Whelan, assisted by units from Cos. Cork and Tipperary, held the city. Crucially, however, they neglected to occupy Mount Mercy, overlooking the city and river. Approach roads were mined and the cantilever bridge over the River Suir raised. Government forces were commanded by Major-General John Prout. Commandant Patrick Paul, officer commanding the Waterford Brigade, through his local knowledge played a vital role in the attack, which opened at 6:45 a.m. on 18 July. On 20 July a hundred government soldiers in small boats crossed the river at Giles Quay and, surprising the Republican right flank, established a bridgehead and lowered the bridge. Prout's eighteen-pounder gun forced the evacuation of the Post Office. Following shelling, Ballybricken Jail was surrendered and several Republican prisoners taken, 21 July. With the arrival of reinforcements and a supply of arms on the HELGA, the Republicans abandoned their positions.

Looting was widespread in the city, described in a contemporary report as 'an erupting slag-heap.' Despite the intensity of the fighting there were only nine recorded deaths; one of the two civilian casualties was a nine-year-old girl.

Dundalk, Co. Louth, 28 June to 15 August 1922. The town was headquarters of the then neutral 4th Northern Division under Commandant Frank Aiken. The barrack gates were opened to Government soldiers, and Aiken and his men were taken prisoner, 16 July. Government forces released a number of imprisoned B Specials. Republican soldiers escaped when the barrack wall was breached with a mine, 27 July. In the early hours of 14 August, Aiken and his men retook the barracks with mines and machine-gun fire. Other Government posts in the town then surrendered, and a large haul of rifles, machine-guns and ammunition fell into Republican hands.

Commandant-General Dan Hogan and Colonel Hugo McNeill retook the barracks, 17 August, during an operation in which an aeroplane was used for the first time in the conflict. It flew over the barracks, strafing the defenders, leading to the withdrawal of Aiken's command.

Six lives were lost and forty-five people were wounded during the Dundalk operation, in which the town suffered little material damage.

Enniscorthy, Co. Wexford, 30 June to 7 July 1922. The town was occupied by opposing forces. Government forces, led by Captain Seán Gallagher, took possession of the police barracks in Abbey Street and of Enniscorthy Castle. Local Republicans under Adjutant Frank Carty occupied the Courthouse and adjoining dwellings and St Mary's (Protestant) Church, setting up a machine-gun emplacement in the belfry but temporarily vacating the post so that Sunday Service could be held. They were reinforced by units from South Tipperary. Gallagher refused a surrender ultimatum on Sunday 2 July. On 5 July, Republicans took possession of both the castle and the barracks, seizing a quantity of arms and a large supply of ammunition. Following the intervention of local clergy, Ernie O'Malley released all prisoners. Government reinforcements arrived from Dublin, and the Republicans, having fired the Courthouse, withdrew from the town, 7 July.

Sligo, 30 June 1922 to 11 January 1923. Republican soldiers under Brigadier Séamus Devins and Frank Carty occupied the Barracks and the Recreational Hall, while a smaller and poorly equipped Government force under Colonel Martin Fallon held the Jail, Courthouse, Williams's Garage, and other buildings. Republicans burned the barracks and left the town, 1 July. At an ambush at Rockwood, Government troops lost five men, including their commanding officer, Commandant Paddy Callaghan, 13 July. Guns and equipment, including the armoured car *Ballinalee,* fell into Republican hands.

Government forces under General Seán Mac Eoin later recaptured Sligo. On 14 July the *Ballinalee* entered the town and fired at Government-held positions. In a Republican incursion during curfew the Custom House was burned, 17 July. A large Government force arrived in Sligo, 21 July, and occupied strategic buildings. On 4 August, Republicans attacked Government-held buildings using the captured *Ballinalee* (shortly to be repossessed by Government forces). Having accepted the surrender of the garrison in the Ulster Bank, Republican soldiers mined the premises before retiring. On 11 January, Sligo Railway Station was burned and rolling stock destroyed. Government soldiers were severely criticised for their inaction, having failed to put in an appearance until an hour after the attack.

Blessington, Co. Wicklow, 2 to 7 July 1922. A force of 1,000 government soldiers under Commandants Bishop, Heaslip and McNulty attacked Blessington. Following an artillery barrage and some five hours of fighting, Republican positions were overrun and a large number of prisoners taken, together with supplies of arms. During the night Ernie O'Malley, leaving a token force of fifteen, withdrew his forces.

Limerick, 2 to 20 July 1922. Four hundred government soldiers under Commandant-Generals Ó hAnnagáin and Brennan held the city but were short of arms. Liam Lynch, from his headquarters in the New Barracks, commanded a well-armed Republican force of 800. Republicans also occupied the Strand, Castle and Ordnance Barracks. Both sides were reluctant to initiate combat, and a truce was arranged, 4 July. The agreement, however, did not receive the sanction of Free State army headquarters, and Commandant-General

Diarmuid MacManus informed both sides accordingly, 5 July. A further agreement was made, 7 July, which did not affect the military situation and called for a meeting of divisional commands with General Seán Mac Eoin. Brennan was reinforced by some 150 soldiers, 11 July. He contacted Lynch, informing him that the truce was at an end. Lynch left the city, moving his headquarters to Clonmel, Co. Tipperary. O'Duffy arrived with artillery and a large supply of arms and ammunition and established his headquarters at Killaloe, Co. Clare, 18 July. On 20 July sustained artillery fire breached the walls of the Strand Barracks, and during the night, having fired some barracks, the Republicans withdrew.

Deaths in the city were estimated at forty. Some damage was caused to city-centre property and to King John's Castle. The loss of the city, from such a strong initial position, dealt a serious blow to Republican morale.

Tipperary, 9 to 30 July 1922. Government forces under Commandant Jerry Ryan joined the Dublin Guards under Commandant Patrick O'Connor and the local brigade under Vice-Brigadier Patrick Dalton. Republicans held the Infantry Barracks and other large buildings. Cleeve's Creamery was in the hands of a 'workers' republic'. Shooting began on 29 July; after some twenty hours of fierce fighting, including hand-to-hand engagements, government forces took possession of the town. Before retreating to the Glen of Aherlow, Republicans burned the Infantry Barracks and caused considerable local resentment by setting Cleeve's Creamery ablaze.

Tuam, Co. Galway, 15 July 1922 to 11 April 1923. Republican soldiers occupied the RIC barracks in the town. Government forces entered the town without opposition and occupied the workhouse, 25 July. Members of the newly arrived Garda Síochána helped prevent confrontation between the factions. Republicans, in a series of raids, seized cigarettes, tobacco, bacon, and trench-coats, 22 November. Following an ambush at Headford, Co. Galway, two days previously in which there were two Government deaths, six Republican prisoners were shot at Tuam, 11 April.

Kilmallock, Co. Limerick, 21 July to 5 August 1922. Kilmallock, with Bruree 4 miles to the west and Bruff 6 miles to the north-east, formed the apex of a strong Republican triangle. Members of the Republican command in the town included Liam Lynch, Liam Deasy, SEÁN MOYLAN, and MAURICE TWOMEY. Republicans took several government prisoners and captured a large quantity of guns and equipment at Ballycullane Cross, near Kilmallock, 23 July. In a five-hour battle Major-General Humphrey Murphy and Commandant Flood, with artillery support, retook Bruree, 30 July. The retreat of the Republicans was covered by a herd of cattle that wandered in front of Government guns. The recapture of Patrickswell, Adare and Bruff enabled Government forces to concentrate on Kilmallock, which was attacked and retaken, 5 July.

There were eight deaths and a large number of wounded in the campaign, while many prisoners were taken on both sides.

Westport, Co. Mayo, 22 to 24 July 1922. Republican soldiers under Commandant-General Michael Kilroy and Commandant-General Tom Maguire held the town. A 400-strong heavily armed force under Colonel-Commandant Christopher O'Malley left Dublin for Westport aboard the *Arvonia,* 24 July. Rossmoney coastguard station was recaptured without a struggle and some forty prisoners released. Republicans evacuated the town, which was occupied by Government forces later on 24 July.

Cork, 26 July to 12 August 1922. Though the city was in turmoil, Cork Regatta was held as usual on 26 July. Republican forces controlled the city and occupied all barracks. Outlying defensive positions had also been adopted, with a general strategy directed at facing an attack by road from the north. Roads were cut, rail bridges were blown up, and the River Lee was blocked with sunken craft and mined as far as Passage West. By early August water rationing was introduced, and food supplies were low. On 7 August the *Arvonia,* with 456 Government soldiers, left Dublin for Cork. Two other vessels set sail for Union Hall and Youghal, carrying 180 and 200 men. The expedition was commanded by General Emmet Dalton, assisted by General Tom Ennis. Commander H. C. Somerville, head of British naval forces in Cork, provided Dalton with a chart affording a course through the Republican minefield to Passage West. The landing of Government forces was virtually unopposed at both Passage and Youghal, 8 August. Wishing to avoid civilian casualties, the Republican command, having ordered the destruction of all barracks in the city, ordered its men to return to their units and await instructions. By 9 August, Government forces were in possession of the city, and Dalton established his headquarters in the Imperial Hotel.

With the fall of Cork, Republican morale reached its lowest ebb. Commenting on his fellow-Republicans after its fall, SEÁN Ó FAOLÁIN wrote: 'There was nothing left for the majority of them to do but to scatter, go into hiding, slip back at night into the city like winter foxes.'

Carrick-on-Suir, Co. Tipperary, 28 July to 2 August 1922. Some 400 Republican soldiers under DENIS LACEY held the town. Having established their headquarters in the workhouse, they blew two bridges, mined and trenched roads, and sabotaged railway tracks and equipment. DAN BREEN held an outer defensive position at Ninemilehouse. Some 450 Government soldiers under Commandant Liam McCarthy, Colonel Tommy Ryan and Joseph Byrne led a three-pronged attack on Republican outposts. Ryan, in a ten-hour battle, forced Breen to withdraw. Reinforcements under General Prout began an artillery assault and captured the town after some hours' fighting, 2 August. Before abandoning their positions the Republicans burned the RIC barracks and Courthouse.

On 13 December 1922 TOM BARRY led a combined Cork and Tipperary Republican force in the recapture of the town, during which a large quantity of guns and equipment was seized.

Clonmel, Co. Tipperary, 8 to 10 August 1922. Republican soldiers under Séamus Robinson, Dan Breen and Dinny Lacey held the town, within which all transport and fuel had been commandeered, as had £20,000 from the Bank of Ireland. Government soldiers left Carrick-on-Suir and advanced by way of Ballyneill and Ballypatrick, 8 August, unaware that Clonmel had been partially vacated by the defenders. As midnight approached, the remaining Republicans withdrew under machine-gun cover. Only one death, a government soldier, was recorded from the fight, during which eleven Republican prisoners were taken.

Fermoy, Co. Cork, 11 August 1922. Having burned the barracks and other buildings lately garrisoned by them, the Republican commander in chief, Liam Lynch, led the evacuation of Fermoy, the last town in Republican hands.

Kenmare, Co. Kerry, 11 August to 9 September 1922. Early on 11 August, with Commandant-General Diarmuid MacManus in charge of the landing operation, the Government vessel *Margaret,* with the *Mermaid* in tow, left Limerick for Kenmare. Commandant-General Thomas 'Scarteen' O'Connor of Kerry No. 2 Brigade commanded the Government forces. Kenmare was occupied unchallenged.

On 9 September, Republican soldiers under Commandant J. J. Rice retook the town following a seven-hour exchange. Commandant O'Connor and his younger brother, John, were killed at their nearby home. Republicans took some 120 prisoners and more than a hundred rifles and 20,000 rounds of ammunition. The capture of Kenmare, following widespread defeats, was a tremendous boost to Republican morale. The town was retaken by Government forces without opposition in early December. It had been vacated by Republican forces following the adoption of a guerrilla policy.

Dublin, 12 August 1922. ARTHUR GRIFFITH, President of Dáil Éireann, died from a cerebral haemorrhage, the first Irish leader to die as head of state.

Bealnablagh, Co. Cork, 22 August 1922. Michael Collins, commander in chief of Government forces, was killed in an ambush. The official notice of his death, 23 August, stated:

> General Michael Collins, Commander-in-Chief of the Army, was killed in an ambush by irregulars at Beal-na-Blath, between Macroom and Bandon, on last night (Tuesday). Towards the close of the engagement, which lasted close upon an hour, the Commander-in-Chief was wounded in the head.

Ballina, Co. Mayo, 12 September 1922. While Government soldiers attended Mass, Republican soldiers under Commandant Luke Pilkington forced the surrender of the garrison in the Imperial Hotel and recaptured the town. More than a hundred rifles, 20,000 rounds of ammunition and some £25,000 were seized.

Dáil Éireann, 28 September 1922. Dáil Éireann approved the Emergency Powers Act (by 47 to 15), empowering military courts to impose the death penalty. W. T. Cosgrave declared: 'We are not going to treat rebels as prisoners of war.' On 14 November four Republican prisoners were shot at Kilmainham Jail, Dublin, the first of seventy-seven such executions.

Catholic hierarchy's pastoral letter, 22 October 1922. A pastoral letter from CARDINAL LOGUE and the hierarchy, denouncing Republican involvement in civil war, was read at all Masses. 'The guerrilla warfare now being carried on by the Irregulars is without moral sanction: and therefore the killing of National soldiers in the course of it is murder before God . . . All those who, in contravention of this teaching, participate in such crimes, are guilty of the gravest sins, and may not be absolved in Confession, nor admitted to Holy Communion, if they purpose to persevere in such evil courses . . .' The pastoral letter affected the morale of Republicans in the field, many of whom returned home, but served to harden the resolve of others, who interpreted it as an *imprimatur* for the Emergency Powers Act.

'Orders of Frightfulness', 30 November 1922. An order issued by Liam Lynch, as a response to the execution of Republican prisoners, listed fourteen classes of 'legitimate' targets for execution, including members of Dáil Éireann and the Senate, the judiciary, the press, and 'aggressive' Free State supporters.

Knocknagoshel, Co. Kerry, 6 March 1923. Five Government soldiers were killed and another seriously injured in a Republican booby-trap. The incident led to an instruction from Major-General Paddy Daly that Republican prisoners would henceforth be used to clear mined obstructions.

Ballyseedy Cross, Co. Kerry, 7 March 1923. Nine Republican soldiers were taken from Ballymullen Barracks, ostensibly to clear a mined obstruction. The prisoners were tied together by flex and rope, a mine was detonated under them and bombs thrown, followed by a discharge of rifle fire. One of the prisoners, Stephen Fuller, was blown over a ditch by the explosion but was otherwise unharmed.

There was a near-riot in Tralee when relatives of missing Republican soldiers insisted on opening the coffins.

Countess Bridge, Killarney, 7 to 8 March 1923. In an incident similar to that at Ballyseedy Cross, four Republican prisoners died and one, Tadhg Coffey, had a miraculous escape.

Garrane Mountains, Co. Kerry, 11 March 1923. Thirty-six Republican soldiers were surrounded in their mountain hide-out by several hundred Government soldiers. During a lengthy engagement the Government forces lost five men and had several wounded; the Republicans lost one and had six taken prisoner, while the remainder escaped. One of the prisoners was shot that evening by the captain of his escort party.

Cahersiveen, Co. Kerry, 12 March 1923. Five Republican prisoners removed from nearby Bahaghs Workhouse by a unit of the Dublin Guards were killed by an explosion and rifle fire. One of the Government soldiers, Lieutenant McCarthy, who resigned from the force, published a report condemning the incident.

Monsignor Luzio's meeting with Cardinal Logue, 21 March. In response to appeals from Republican interests for a Vatican peace initiative, Cardinal Luzio visited Cardinal Logue and later met leading Republicans, including Éamon de Valera, at the Shelbourne Hotel, Dublin. As the cardinal did not present credentials, his visit was treated as a private one by the Government of the Free State. Having received little co-operation from church or state, he was recalled by Rome, 5 April.

Crohan West, Knockmealdown Mountains, Co. Tipperary, 10 April 1923. Liam Lynch, commander in chief of Republican forces, was mortally wounded by Government soldiers.

Clashmealcon Caves, Co. Kerry, 15 to 25 April 1923. A group of Republican soldiers led by Timothy 'Aeroplane' Lyons was besieged in caves by Government forces. Two of them fell from the rocks while attempting to seek reinforcements. After three days, during which two Government soldiers were shot, Lyons surrendered. While he was being raised to the cliff-top the rope parted; Lyons, seriously injured, was killed by gunfire where he lay. Three of the four surviving Republicans were shot on 25 April.

Ennis, Co. Clare, 2 May 1923. The death sentence was carried out on Christopher Quinn and William Shaughnessy, the last of seventy-seven Republican prisoners shot while in custody during the Civil War.

'Cease Fire and Dump Arms', 24 May 1923. This order, issued by Frank Aiken, commander in chief, officially ended Republican involvement in the Civil War.

'Soldiers of the Republic, Legion of the Rearguard', 24 May 1923. This statement, addressed to Republican soldiers still in the field by Éamon de Valera, said:

> The Republic can no longer be successfully defended by your arms. Further sacrifice of life would now be vain and continuance of the struggle in arms unwise in the national interest and prejudicial to the future of our cause. Military victory must be allowed to rest for the moment with those who have destroyed the Republic. Other means must be sought to safeguard the nation's right . . .

Aftermath. The Civil War, begun without formal declaration, ended without a negotiated peace. Government casualties were estimated at eight hundred; Republican losses have never been confirmed, nor is there a definitive figure for civilian deaths. Material damage has been estimated at £30 million; Government expenditure in the prosecution of the war was £17 million. Additionally, the Government had to provide for more than 27,000 dependants' allowance claims, £1 million for Civic Guard salaries, compensation claims, and the expense of housing some twelve thousand Republican prisoners.

Difficulties were encountered in the collection of rates and taxes during and after the conflict, and Government sources later revealed that only a 'large contribution from the Bank of Ireland to the Exchequer at a crucial time, prevented bankruptcy.'

The legacy of bitterness left by the Civil War took decades to assuage. It led to the founding of the dominant parties in Irish politics for almost seventy years, FINE GAEL (pro-Treaty) and FIANNA FÁIL (anti-Treaty).

An Claidheamh Soluis ('the sword of light'), official organ of the GAELIC LEAGUE, first published on 17 March 1899 and weekly thereafter, in succession to *Fáinne an Lae.* A bilingual publication, edited by EOIN MACNEILL, it sought to foster the ideal of a distinctively Irish culture for a progressive readership. Under the editorship of PATRICK PEARSE, 1903–09, it became a medium for contemporary Irish writing as well as a platform for Pearse's increasing militarism. He enlarged the format, introduced illustrations, and returned the paper to profitability. It was reorganised again by its managing editor, MICHAEL O'RAHILLY, 1913. MacNeill's article 'The North began', 1 November 1913, led to the founding of the IRISH VOLUNTEERS. *An Claidheamh Soluis* was at the centre of many controversies over the role of Irish in the national independence movement.

Clancy, George (1881–1921), republican; born in Grange, Co. Limerick, to a family with a strong Fenian tradition, educated at UCD, where he joined the Gaelic League and was taught by Patrick Pearse. He formed a branch of the Gaelic League in the university and persuaded many of his friends to study Irish, including JAMES JOYCE (for whom he was the model for Davin in *A Portrait of the Artist as a Young Man*). He taught Irish at Clongowes Wood College before returning to Limerick, 1908, to continue teaching. He was an influential member of the Sinn Féin committee that helped to elect ÉAMON DE VALERA in East Clare, 1917. When his health was impaired by the flu epidemic of 1918 he was forced to retire from teaching. A superintendent with the Irish National Assurance Company, he was Mayor of Limerick when he was murdered at his home on the morning of 7 March, allegedly by members of the 'CAIRO GANG'.

Clan na Gael, a secret oath-bound organisation founded in New York, 20 June 1867, by Jerome Collins, meteorological and science editor of the *New York Herald.* Sometimes called the United Brotherhood, its Revolutionary Directorate consisted of seven members: three chosen by the Executive, three by the IRB, and one nominated by the six others. Members met in innocuously named lodges or 'camps', such as the Emmet Literary Association. Its earliest mission, 1869, was reorganising the IRB in Ireland and Britain. In 1878 it acted as host to MICHAEL DAVITT on his visit to the United States.

From its inception the Clan was infiltrated by British agents, notably HENRI LE CARON, who informed the Canadian authorities of the projected invasion of Canada; F. F. Millen, who had charge of the Clan's Military Board, was also in the pay of London. Despite such infiltration the Clan managed a spectacular success in 1876, when it organised the escape of six Fenians from Fremantle on the CATALPA.

The Clan attracted leading IRB members in America, including JEREMIAH O'DONOVAN ROSSA and JOHN DEVOY. The latter exerted a powerful influence on the organisation, making it a party to the NEW DEPARTURE. He opposed Rossa's SKIRMISHING FUND but supported the Clan in its granting of $60,000 to the *Holland II* and *Fenian Ram* submarine experiments of JOHN P. HOLLAND. In 1878 the Clan sent $17,000 to the IRB and a year later a further $25,000; it also provided $10,000 for the Skirmishing Fund and $2,000 for the LAND LEAGUE. From his arrival in the United States, 2 January 1880, CHARLES STEWART PARNELL was a guest of the Clan, which arranged a series of monster meetings at which he was rapturously received.

During the 1880s a section of Clan na Gael was dominated by the 'TRIANGLE' (Alexander Sullivan, Michael Boland, and Denis Feeley), whose policy of terrorism spawned the DYNAMITERS. Devoy and 'Red' Jim MacDermott—a spy—regained control of the movement from the Triangle by 1890. JOSEPH MCGARRITY in Philadelphia and JUDGE DANIEL COHALAN in

New York were leading members of the Clan in the 1890s.

Clan na Gael played an active part in the preparations for the EASTER RISING (1916). In 1907 THOMAS J. CLARKE returned to Dublin from New York and became an inspiration to the younger generation of republicans. Rossa died at New York, 29 June 1915, and his funeral in Dublin, organised by Devoy, Clarke, and THOMAS MACDONAGH, fired nationalist sentiment. ROGER CASEMENT received $8,000 from Clan funds to assist in his mission to Germany to secure arms for the rising. Shortly before the rising Clan na Gael founded the FRIENDS OF IRISH FREEDOM 'to encourage and assist any movement that will help to bring about the National independence of Ireland.' However, ÉAMON DE VALERA's visit to the United States during the WAR OF INDEPENDENCE led to a split, when Cohalan and McGarrity supported de Valera against Devoy over the lobbying of American presidential candidates on the question of American recognition for the Irish Republic. Devoy's faction of Clan na Gel accepted the ANGLO-IRISH TREATY (1921), while McGarrity, leading a reorganised body, rejected it; he supported the anti-Treatyites in the CIVIL WAR and continued to support the IRA after it was outlawed in June 1936. He helped finance the campaign against Northern Ireland and Britain in 1939, provoking de Valera into passing the OFFENCES AGAINST THE STATE ACT (1939). Clan na Gael ceased to be an active force after McGarrity's death in 1940.

Clann Éireann, a short-lived party founded in 1925 by WILLIAM MAGENNIS as a breakaway from CUMANN NA NGAEDHEAL in protest at the settlement that shelved the report of the BOUNDARY COMMISSION. It vanished from the political scene following the eclipse of its seven candidates in the 1927 general election; many of its members subsequently joined Fianna Fáil.

Clann na Poblachta, a political party founded at Barry's Hotel, Dublin, 6 July 1946, by SEÁN MACBRIDE, Noel Hartnett, JACK MCQUILLAN, and Michael Kelly, who became general secretary. Twenty-two of the twenty-seven members of the provisional Executive had been active in the IRA. With its structure modelled on that of Fianna Fáil, the party saw itself as a modernising force and attracted support from many who wished to see a wide range of social reforms. Victorious in two by-elections in 1947, MacBride and Patrick Kinnane in Co. Tipperary entered Dáil Éireann, 5 November. The party's victory prompted ÉAMON DE VALERA to call a general election.

On 4 February 1948 Clann na Poblachta put up ninety-three candidates, a tactical error that overextended its organisation and ran foul of recent constituency revisions. Winning ten seats, six of them in Dublin, it entered into coalition with Fine Gael, Clann na Talmhan, the Labour Party and National Labour to form the first inter-party Government, with JOHN A. COSTELLO as Taoiseach. Two ministerial portfolios went to Clann na Poblachta: External Affairs (MacBride) and Health (DR NOEL BROWNE). The party supported the passing of the REPUBLIC OF IRELAND ACT (1948). One prominent member, Peadar Cowan, was expelled from the party, 2 July 1948, for 'disloyalty to the organisation' when he objected to the acceptance by Ireland of MARSHALL AID, which he saw as an extension of US foreign policy and 'a surrender of certain of our national rights.' (He refused to resign his seat and continued to sit as an independent). Browne attempted to implement health reforms, including the eradication of tuberculosis, in which he was successful, but his attempt to introduce the MOTHER AND CHILD SCHEME brought him into conflict with the Catholic hierarchy and the Irish Medical Association, and the party leader did not support him. The split between the two ministers was echoed within the party, and Jack McQuillan resigned with Browne.

Their resignations, and the controversy over Browne's health plans, helped to precipitate a general election. In 1951 Clann na Poblachta returned with two out of the twenty-six seats contested. MacBride held Dublin South-West, and John Tully was elected in Co. Cavan. Of the ten elected in 1948 three who stood as independents were elected and one, Joseph Brennan, who joined the Labour Party, was defeated.

The party won three of the twenty seats it contested in the 1954 general election, and MacBride and his two colleagues gave external support to the second inter-party Government. The party put up eleven candidates in 1957, when only one, John Tully in Co. Cavan, was elected. Joseph Barron in Dublin South-Central was the only candidate elected in 1961. Tully, now essentially an independent, was the sole deputy elected again in 1965, when the party put up four candidates. At a special ard-fheis, 10 July 1965, the decision was taken to dissolve the party. The party's share of first-preference votes and seats was:

	First-preference votes	Seats
1948	13.3%	10
1952	4.1%	2
1954	3.1%	3
1957	1.7%	1
1961	1.1%	1
1965	0.8%	1

Clann na Talmhan, founded in July 1939 at Athenry, Co. Galway, by Michael Donnellan, the first completely new political party since the establishment of the state. It was established for the defence of western farmers; though it had links with the eastern National Agricultural Party, its strongholds were in Cos. Galway, Mayo, and Roscommon. Seeking state intervention in land reclamation and minimal agrarian taxes, following a merger with the Irish Farmers' Federation, January 1943, the party secured ten seats in the general election of 1943. Joseph Blowick became leader in 1944, when the party won eleven seats. Patrick Cogan, deputy leader, left in 1947 to found the National Agricultural Party. Clann na Talmhan secured seven seats in the 1948 election, when it joined the inter-party Government. Its sole minister was Blowick (Lands and Fisheries), while Donnellan was a parliamentary secretary. The party took six seats in 1951, five in 1954 (when it again joined an inter-party Government), three in 1957, and two in 1961. The last two were Donnellan (died 1964) and Blowick (who retired in 1965). The party's share of first-preference votes and seats was:

	First-preference votes	Seats
1943	9.8%	11
1944	10.1%	9
1948	5.5%	7
1951	2.9%	6
1954	3.8%	5
1957	2.4%	3
1961	1.5%	2

Clanricarde, Hubert George de Burgh-Canning, second Marquess and fifteenth Earl of (1832–1916), landlord and politician. One of the most notorious of absentee landlords and opposed to the LAND LEAGUE, he was member of Parliament (Conservative) for Co. Galway, 1867–70, but resigned his seat in protest at the first Land Act of W. E. GLADSTONE. Evictions on his 57,000-acre estate at Woodford, Co. Galway, led to a renewal of the LAND WAR through the PLAN OF CAMPAIGN; in 1885, 186 of his 1,159 tenants were evicted. In a letter to the *Times* (London) in 1889 T. W. RUSSELL wrote: 'Thank God there is but one Lord Clanricarde. If it were otherwise the country would be in a worse plight than it is.' Clanricarde refused to sell parts of his estate to tenants who wished to buy their holdings under the LAND ACTS. When the CONGESTED DISTRICTS BOARD was granted powers of compulsory purchase in 1909, it took four years for the Land Court to be enabled to transfer his estates to the board, at a cost of £238,000.

Clare, John Fitzgibbon, Earl of (1749–1802), lawyer and politician (Tory); born in Donnybrook, Dublin, educated at TCD and called to the bar. Possessor of a lucrative bar practice and member of Parliament for University of Dublin, 1778, he was a staunch government supporter and opposed to parliamentary reform, CATHOLIC EMANCIPATION, and the UNITED IRISHMEN. Created Baron Fitzgibbon, he was the first native Lord Chancellor for nearly a century, 1789; he was created Earl of Clare in 1795. He became the most powerful man in the country, sharing power only with LORD JOHN BERESFORD. He threw his support behind the proposal for the UNION of the Irish and British parliaments. During 1799 he assisted CASTLEREAGH in buying enough support for the government to ensure the passing of the Union, February–March 1800. He was universally unpopular among the poorer classes; a cheering mob showered his coffin with dead cats and debris.

Clarendon, George William Frederick Villiers, fourth Earl of (1800–1870); born in London. He arrived in Ireland, 1827, as adviser to the Lord Lieutenant, ANGLESEY, on the union of the Irish and English excise. He was an advocate of free trade, and was highly regarded by O'CONNELL. Lord Lieutenant of Ireland, 1847–52, appointed at the height of the GREAT FAMINE (1845–49), he was granted formidable COERCION powers to deal with the general unrest. He opposed YOUNG IRELAND, the IRISH CONFEDERATION, and the ORANGE ORDER. Following the DOLLY'S BRAE AFFRAY he ordered that EARL RODEN's name be struck from the roll of commissioners of the peace. Sympathetic to the plight of landlords deprived of their rents because of the famine, he lent his support to the ENCUMBERED ESTATES ACTS (1848 AND 1849).

Clarke, Kathleen, née Daly (1879–1972), republican; born in Co. Limerick, a niece of

JOHN DALY and sister of EDWARD DALY; educated locally. She operated a successful dressmaking business until her marriage to THOMAS J. CLARKE in New York, 1901. Returning to Ireland, November 1907, the couple opened tobacconists' shops in Amiens Street and Parnell Street, Dublin. Closely involved in her husband's work with the IRB, she played a leading role in CUMANN NA MBAN and supported Sinn Féin and the Irish Volunteers following her husband's execution for participation in the EASTER RISING (1916). She was a committee member of the IRISH VOLUNTEERS DEPENDANTS' FUND, a County Court judge in the DÁIL COURTS, and a committee member of the WHITE CROSS during the War of Independence. A member of Dáil Éireann from 1921, she opposed the ANGLO-IRISH TREATY (1921) and was briefly imprisoned during the Civil War. She lost her seat in 1922.

An early member of FIANNA FÁIL, she regained her Dáil seat in June 1927 but lost it the following September. She was defeated in a by-election in April 1928 and nominated to the Senate, where she continued to sit after 1937 as a Taoiseach's nominee. She was the first woman lord mayor of Dublin, June 1939; she refused to wear the mayoral chain, because it had been donated by King William III (a replacement was provided), and also had all portraits of British royalty withdrawn from the Mansion House, fuelling weeks of debate in the national newspapers. During her mayoralty she established the Irish Red Cross Society, presiding over its inaugural meeting in the Mansion House. She resigned from Fianna Fáil, May 1943, in protest at the treatment of republican prisoners (four of whom had been given a death sentence for murder). A founder-member of CLANN NA POBLACHTA, she was defeated when she stood for the party in 1948 in Dublin North-East. She was accorded a state funeral. Her autobiography, *My Fight for Ireland's Freedom,* was published in 1991.

Clarke, Thomas J. (1858–1916), Fenian; born in the Isle of Wight, where his father was serving in the British army. Following a period in South Africa the family moved to Dungannon, Co. Tyrone, 1867. In the United States, Clarke met DR THOMAS GALLAGHER on joining CLAN NA GAEL. Under the alias 'Wilson', Clarke was arrested with Gallagher on a dynamiting mission to England, 1883 (see DYNAMITERS), and imprisoned in Millbank, Chatham and Portland Prisons. Under the harsh regime reserved for treason-felons his health was permanently undermined (Gallagher and Alfred Whitehead were driven insane). He formed a friendship with JOHN DALY during his imprisonment; in the final years of his sentence he shared a prison wing with John Lee (the 'Man They Couldn't Hang').

Released, September 1898, he returned to the United States, where he married Daly's niece in 1901 (see KATHLEEN CLARKE) and resumed his Clan na Gael activities, working on the *Gaelic American* with JOHN DEVOY. He became a naturalised citizen of the United States, 1905, two years before be returned to Dublin, where he set up tobacconists' shops in Amiens Street and Parnell Street, which became centres of republican activity. Elected to the Supreme Council of the IRB, he urged the establishment of a Military Council to examine the feasibility of an armed insurrection. He established the Dublin Central Branch of the Wolfe Tone Clubs 'to propagate the principles of the United Irishmen and of the men of '98.' A mentor to a new generation of republicans, including BULMER HOBSON and DENIS MCCULLOUGH, he was instrumental in the establishment of IRISH FREEDOM, 1910. He organised the first BODENSTOWN SUNDAY and was a leading figure in organising the dispersal of arms following the HOWTH GUN-RUNNING, July 1914.

Aghast at the countermanding order issued by EOIN MACNEILL to the IRISH VOLUNTEERS, Clarke presided at the Easter Sunday meeting of the Supreme Council that ensured that the rising began the following day. In deference to his long service he was the first signatory of the Proclamation of the Irish Republic. Having fought in the GPO, he was court-martialled on 1 May and shot by firing squad at Kilmainham Jail two days later. In his will he left £3,100 to the IRISH VOLUNTEERS DEPENDANTS' FUND. His *Glimpses of a Prison Felon's Life* was published in 1922.

***Claudia*.** On 28 March 1973 the motor vessel *Claudia,* registered in Cyprus, was intercepted off Co. Waterford with a cargo of arms from Libya. Among those arrested on board was the IRA leader Joe Cahill, who was jailed for three years by the Special Criminal Court. The cargo included 250 rifles, 240 small arms, anti-tank guns, mines, and explosives.

Cleggan Disaster, 28 October 1927. Forty-four fishermen lost their lives during a freak storm while fishing for mackerel in Cleggan Bay, Co. Galway. Twenty-five were from

Cleggan and surrounding areas, including Rossadilisk and the neighbouring island, Inishbofin. Nine men from the Co. Mayo village of Lacken were lost, as were ten from the Inniskeas. One boat, the *True Light,* survived the storm after a terrifying twelve-hour ordeal. The men had set out at 5 p.m. on a calm Friday evening and were less than an hour at sea when a messenger arrived to alert them to the impending storm (a retired doctor, Dr Holberton, had heard the storm warning on his radio).

One of the bodies was found enmeshed in a net, leading to speculation that the men's efforts to retrieve their precious nets may have contributed to the large number of deaths. In response to an emotional appeal by the President of the Executive Council, W. T. Cosgrave, £36,719 was subscribed in less than four months. The calamity devastated the island communities, many of which abandoned fishing in its wake.

Clerkenwell Explosion, 13 December 1867. A purchaser of arms for the Fenians, RICARD O'SULLIVAN BURKE, was arrested on 27 November 1867 and lodged in the Clerkenwell House of Detention, London. Two other Fenians, John Murphy and Jeremiah Sullivan, attempted to effect his escape by placing a barrel of explosives on a cart against a section of the prison wall. They misjudged the power of the explosive, which not only blew down a section of the prison wall but also demolished a row of houses opposite; twelve people were killed and more than fifty injured.

The incident outraged public opinion. Queen Victoria urged that summary justice be dispensed to Irish suspects apprehended at the scene of such crimes, while BENJAMIN DISRAELI advocated the suspension of *habeas corpus.* Two men and a woman, Ann Justice, were charged with responsibility for the deaths and injuries but were discharged for lack of evidence. A known Fenian, MICHAEL BARRETT, arraigned on questionable evidence, was hanged for alleged involvement in the explosion, the last victim of a public hanging in England, 26 May 1868.

Clew Bay Disaster, 14 June 1894. Thirty-two migrant harvesters lost their lives when the 15-ton Achill hooker *Victory* overturned in Clew Bay, Co. Mayo. The vessel, skippered by John Healy, was conveying 110 passengers on the 20-mile journey to Westport for embarkation for Glasgow aboard the *Elm.* Approximately a mile off Westport the hooker, in full sail, caught by a sudden gust of wind, capsized, throwing all those aboard into the water. Many were struck by the rigging or trapped underneath the vessel. Rescue was effected by the *Elm* and boats from the shore. On 29 June 1894 a coroner's jury, while leaving the issue of prosecution aside, recorded that the ship had been improperly ballasted and was grossly overcrowded. No civil proceedings ensued.

closure (Irish *clabhsúr*), a celebration of the end of the harvest season, when refreshment and music were provided by the farm-owner for the workers. In some parts of the country it was customary to place a farm implement in the fire to signal that labour was at an end and a feast was demanded; the employer either pulled the implement out of the fire or, less frequently, let it burn to indicate refusal.

Clune, Conor (1893–1921), Irish-language activist, actor, and singer; born in Quin, Co. Clare, a nephew of Archbishop Joseph Clune, educated at St Flannan's College, Ennis. A member of the Gaelic League and the Irish Volunteers, he worked in Dublin in the Irish Bookshop. He returned to Co. Clare to work as a teacher of Irish at Raheen, near Scarriff. While on a visit to Dublin on 20 November 1920 he was arrested with Dick McKee and Peadar Clancy in Vaughan's Hotel, Parnell Square. They were shot the next day, 'BLOODY SUNDAY'.

Cluseret, General Gustave-Paul (1823–1900), soldier of fortune and briefly Fenian commander in chief; born in France. An officer in the French army, he served in several campaigns and was made a member of the Legion of Honour, 1855. Having supported Garibaldi, 1860, he was a brigadier-general in the Federal Army during the American Civil War (1861–65). He was introduced to JAMES STEPHENS by THOMAS KELLY in New York, 1866; he accepted Stephens's invitation to become commander in chief of the Fenian army on condition that the army would number ten thousand armed men in the field. Leaving New York, 11 January 1867, he used documents provided by the Fenians to inspect Woolwich Arsenal near London, naval dockyards, and Aldershot camp, Hampshire. He advised against a rising because of lack of arms. The premature rising in Co. Kerry, March 1867, curtailed his tour; rather than risk an ill-equipped army in the field, he resigned his position and returned to France, where he played a leading role in the Paris Commune (1871).

Cluskey, Frank (1930–1989), politician (Labour Party); born in Dublin, educated at Glasnevin Christian Brothers' School and Harvard University, Massachusetts. A butcher by trade, he was active in the WORKERS' UNION OF IRELAND and the Labour Party. A member of Dáil Éireann from 1965, chief whip of the Labour Party, 1969–73, and Parliamentary Secretary to the Minister for Social Welfare, 1973–77, he succeeded BRENDAN CORISH as leader of the Labour Party, 1 July 1977, but lost his seat in 1981. He was succeeded as leader of the party by MICHAEL O'LEARY. A member of the European Parliament, 1981–83, he regained his Dáil seat, February 1982, and became Minister for Trade, Communications, and Tourism. In this capacity he clashed with Government colleagues, in particular JOHN BRUTON (Fine Gael), over plans to refinance Dublin Gas Company, at a cost of £126 million. This led to his resignation, December 1983; his Labour Party fellow-ministers remained in office until 20 January 1987. He failed to win a seat in Dublin in the first direct election to the European Parliament, 14 June 1984.

Coal-Cattle Pact (3 January 1935), an agreement during the 'ECONOMIC WAR' whereby an increase of a third was allowed in the quota of Irish cattle allowed into Britain, in return for which Ireland agreed to import coal only from British sources.

coercion, special legislation giving the Irish administration emergency powers during what were considered times of severe public unrest. Under coercion policies the Lord Lieutenant of Ireland was empowered to suspend *habeas corpus,* suppress all public meetings, suspend newspapers, arrest without warrant and hold without trial, suspend jury trials, invest magistrates with summary powers to try criminal or political charges, and appoint any three judges to constitute a court to determine law and fact. There were fifty-two such acts from 1800 to May 1882 (when the PHOENIX PARK MURDERS took place) and a further fifty-three to December 1921. (See also PROTECTION OF PERSONS AND PROPERTY (IRELAND) ACT (1881).)

'coffin ships' or 'famine ships', cargo ships crudely adapted to ply the lucrative emigrant trade, especially during and in the aftermath of the GREAT FAMINE (1845–49). To comply with the Passenger Acts, many such vessels, few of which were registered at Lloyd's, underwent rudimentary alterations, with the fixing of additional berths or the addition of toilets; such temporary work rarely survived the rigours of the Atlantic crossing. American ships, subject to more stringent regulations, were generally superior to British vessels, but fares, as a consequence, were much higher. Steerage decks on non-American vessels were uncaulked, and many had temporary decks and could not be hosed, as cargoes were stowed in the orlop deck directly beneath. This had serious consequences when, during storms, hatches were battened down, denying steerage passengers access to the few available toilets, a situation exacerbated by regular outbreaks of cholera, dysentery, and 'ship fever' (typhus). Thousands of passengers died on board the ships, while many survivors carried disease to their port of entry. Only 2 per cent of British and Irish ships carried a medical officer.

Passengers were crowded together without regard to sex, four to a berth (some 6 feet square). The Passenger Act (1848) sought to end these conditions by legislating against the berthing together of single men and women; a further act, in 1852, required all single men to be berthed together in a separate part of the steerage. Stephen de Vere, a philanthropic Co. Limerick landlord, described a voyage on an emigrant ship (quoted in the first report of the Select Committee of the House of Lords on Colonisation from Ireland, 1847):

> Hundreds of poor people, men, women and children, of all ages, from the driveling idiot of ninety to the babe just born, huddled together without light, without air, wallowing in filth and breathing a fetid atmosphere . . . living without food or medicine, dying without the voice of spiritual consolation, and buried in the depths without the rites of the church.

Herman Melville, in *Redburn: His First Voyage* (1849), described a voyage from Liverpool to America:

> The bunks were rapidly knocked together and looked more like dog kennels than anything else. The emigrants talked soon of seeing America. The agent had told them that twenty days would be an unusually long voyage. Suddenly there was a cry of 'Land' and emigrants crowded on deck expecting America, but it was only Ireland which they had left three or four weeks before in a steam-boat for Liverpool . . . The steerage was like a crowded jail. From the rows of bunks hundreds of thin, dirty faces looked out. Scores of un-shaven men, seated on chests, smoked tea-leaves and created a suffocating vapour which was, still, better than the fetid air of the place.

Members of the crew generally exploited the passengers. VERE FOSTER recalled how, on a voyage on the *Washington,* he observed the surgeon hurl the chamber-pots of women passengers overboard and heard him order them to use the privies on deck, which were filthy (*Correspondence on the Treatment of the Passengers on Board the Emigrant Ship 'Washington',* 1851) . The doctor was overheard to say, 'There are a hundred cases of dysentery on the ship which will turn to cholera and I swear to God that I will not go amongst them; if they want medicines they must come to me.' On learning of this, one of the passengers collected money to placate him. The doctor then claimed that the steerage passengers had 'plenty of money and if they would not look after him, he would not look after them.' Some passengers immediately offered a shilling, provided it was used to buy a rope to hang the doctor.

As proper records were not kept, the exact number of lives lost directly from travelling on coffin ships cannot he estimated. In 1847 alone 17,465 documented deaths occurred as a result of either typhus or cholera on board; this is a sixth of all travellers on the ships concerned, and it does not include the countless dead who were simply cast overboard without record, nor does it include the many ships that foundered without trace on the voyage.

Some typical coffin ships were:

Elizabeth and Sarah, built 1763, capable of carrying a maximum of 155 adults. It sailed from Killala, Co. Mayo, 26 May 1846, listing 276 names on its manifest. Berths collapsed shortly after sailing, and the majority of steerage passengers spent the entire voyage on the ship's floor. Water putrefied in unclean casks. No food was provided for steerage passengers, and the vessel was devoid of sanitary conveniences. The master and some twenty passengers succumbed to fever.

Wandsworth, arrived at GROSSE ÎLE from Dublin, 19 May 1847, with fever on board, from which forty-five passengers and crew members had perished.

Virginius, carrying a large number of pauper-tenants from the estates of Major Denis Mahon at Strokestown, Co. Roscommon; arrived at Québec, 28 May 1847, having lost 149 of its 476 passengers and nine members of the crew en route. Nineteen more died while the ship was at anchor, and a further ninety died when removed to the fever sheds.

Erin's Queen, also chartered by Major Mahon of Strokestown; almost a third of its passengers died on the voyage. On arrival at Grosse Île the captain had to bribe the crew, at the rate of a sovereign per corpse, to remove 136 bodies from the hold.

Naomi, departed Liverpool, 15 June 1847, with 331 passengers aboard, 78 of whom died at sea. The Grosse Île medical superintendent, Dr George Douglas, commented that 'the filth and dirt in this vessel's hold create such an effluvium as to make it difficult to breathe.' This vessel also carried some of Major Mahon's tenants from Co. Roscommon.

Larch, lost 108 of its complement on its journey from Sligo to Québec, where it arrived with a large number of fever-ravaged emigrants aboard.

Eliza Liddel, one of nine that the Anglo-Irish peer and future British Prime Minister Lord Palmerston used for clearing some two thousand impoverished tenants off his Co. Sligo estates. When it dropped anchor off New Brunswick, July 1847, the Canadian authorities particularly condemned 'a serving Foreign Secretary of the Crown, who would unleash such a burden of human misery on another administration.'

Lady Sale, arrived off Partridge Island, St John, September 1847, with fever affecting 85 of its 340 passengers—tenants from the Co. Sligo estate of Sir Robert Gore-Booth. An inspecting medical officer, Dr W. S. Harding, complained to the Lieutenant-Governor of St John of the 'freight of paupers, chiefly widows and old people . . . all displayed the heartless character of the person sending them . . .'

Lord Ashburton, arrived at Québec, 30 October 1847, having lost 107 of its 477 passengers to fever and dysentery and with fever affecting 60 of its complement. Five passengers had to be recruited on the voyage to help sail the ship, which had been chartered on Lord Palmerston's behalf.

Aeolus, also carrying tenants of Lord Palmerston. Though well treated on the voyage, the women and children who formed the majority of its 428 passengers arrived at St John, 2 November 1847, in an emaciated and distressed condition. Their obvious poverty led the authorities to demand the lodging of a bond of £250 before emigrants were allowed ashore.

Sir Henry Pottinger, lost 96 passengers to fever on its voyage from Cork to Québec, where, according to the Colonial Land and Emigration Commissioner's annual report for 1848, it arrived with 112 fever cases aboard.

Blanche, lost 25 of its complement through

fever on the voyage from Liverpool, February 1851; a further 140 took sick, and at one point only four crew members were manning the ship. On arrival at New Orleans the vessel was found to have pigs and people lying together on deck 'in filth and feculent matter, presenting a spectacle such as humanity shudders to contemplate.' An inquiry found that the ship had 84 passengers more than in the manifest, and that cramped living conditions probably contributed to the rapid spread of fever. Mould was found on the ship's store of bread and biscuit.

George Canning, lost eighteen passengers en route to New York, August 1853. A girl of four, described as a 'perfect skeleton,' died of dysentery on arrival. In reporting the subsequent inquest the *New York Times* stated that a dollar was charged for the use of a fire on which emigrants cooked a meal. The cook made coffee for steerage passengers with sea water, reserving the ship's store of water for cabin passengers and crew. When the captain was informed that many of the steerage passengers were either sick or dying he expressed a wish that they might all die.

Fingal, left Liverpool for Québec, 3 September 1853, with 300 passengers and a cargo of 1,100 tons of railway iron. Because of falsification of the manifest the exact number of deaths was undetermined but was estimated at between 37 and 41. Asked why bodies had been thrown overboard without being covered, the captain replied: 'We are not bound to do it: it is only a courtesy.'

Cohalan, Daniel (1859–1952), bishop (Catholic); born in Kilmichael, Co. Cork. A curate at Kilbrittain, Co. Cork, 1883, he held a professorship at St Finbarr's Seminary and a chaplaincy to the military prison. He was professor of theology at St Patrick's College, Maynooth, from 1886 until his appointment as coadjutor at Cork and Ross, 1914. Bishop of Cork and Ross from 1916, he denounced the violence of the WAR OF INDEPENDENCE, condemning atrocities on both sides and the tactic of reprisal. In July 1920 he pronounced an interdict on the killers of an RIC sergeant shot in the church porch at Bandon, Co. Cork. He warned that anyone killing from ambush would face excommunication, following which he received a death threat from the IRA. In August 1920 he condemned the authorities following the death of TERENCE MACSWINEY on hunger strike. Strongly pro-government throughout the CIVIL WAR, he warned in a pastoral letter, 24 September 1922: 'According to the declaration of the Bishops of Ireland the killing of National soldiers is murder.' The statement, issued without reference to the killing of Republicans and at a time when six anti-Treaty soldiers in Co. Sligo had been shot after surrendering, further alienated Republican supporters in his dioceses.

Cohalan was a frequent contributor to the *Catholic Bulletin* and IRISH ECCLESIASTICAL RECORD. His publications included *Trinity College and the Trinity Commissions* (1908) and *Trinity College: Its Income and Its Value to the Nation* (1911).

Cohalan, Judge Daniel (1865–1946), Irish-American political leader; born in Middletown, New York, where he was influential in Democratic Party circles and was later prominent in the leadership of the Tammany Society, 1908–11. A judge of the Supreme Court of New York State, 1912, he was regarded as virtual resident counsel to CLAN NA GAEL. Close to JOHN DEVOY, he played an important role in New York in preparations for the EASTER RISING (1916), was chairman of the Irish Convention in Philadelphia, 22–23 February 1919, and was active in the FRIENDS OF IRISH FREEDOM. After he supported ÉAMON DE VALERA during his American tour, a bitter rift developed between the Cohalan-Devoy faction and the de Valera-MCGARRITY faction in late 1919.

Colbert, Con (1896–1916), republican soldier; born near Athea, Co. Limerick, educated at Christian Brothers' school. He was employed as a clerk at Limerick railway station and later in the office of Kennedy's bakery, Dublin. A member of FIANNA ÉIREANN, he was drill instructor at ST ENDA'S SCHOOL and later joined the Irish Volunteers in a similar capacity. In the weeks preceding the EASTER RISING (1916) he acted as bodyguard to THOMAS J. CLARKE. He fought at Watkins' Brewery, Jameson's Distillery and Marrowbone Lane during the rising and assumed the command on the surrender of his unit to save the life of his married superior officer. He was shot by firing squad in Kilmainham Jail, Dublin, on 8 May.

'Collar the King', a name given to the policy advocated by D. P. MORAN on the occasion of a visit by King Edward VII to Dublin in 1903. Moran maintained that if nationalists accepted autonomy within the British Empire they should be loyal to the Crown as a constitutional symbol, they should present a statement of grievances and offer their loyalty in return if these grievances were removed, and should recognise the Union Jack if it ceased to be a party flag for unionists. Moran's proposal was denounced by ARTHUR GRIFFITH and THOMAS KETTLE. After the Liberals returned to power in 1906, Moran claimed that the IRISH PARTY was in fact implementing his policy half-heartedly and without admitting it.

'Colleen Bawn' murder, the elopement and murder of Ellie Hanley, which resulted in one of the most sensational murder trials in Irish history. Raised by her maternal uncle John Connery following the death of her mother, Ellie Hanley eloped with Lieutenant John Scanlan, a Co. Limerick squire and neighbour, June 1819. The couple went through a form of marriage performed, unknown to her, by an actor. Within a month, having robbed her of £200 and valuables, Scanlan arranged for his servant, Stephen Sullivan, to murder her; Sullivan clubbed her to death and threw her body from a boat into the River Shannon. When the body later surfaced it was identified from rope that had been given by a boatman, John King, to Scanlan. The RIC also recovered the dead woman's clothing, which had been given to various women by Scanlan and Sullivan.

Scanlan was arrested, but Sullivan absconded. Following a trial in which he was defended by DANIEL O'CONNELL, Scanlan was hanged, 16 March 1820. Sullivan was arrested at Castleisland, Co. Kerry, May 1829, for uttering forged banknotes, and confessed to the murder on the scaffold, 27 July 1829, when he fully implicated his former employer.

The crime provided the plot for a novel, *The Collegians* (1829), by Gerald Griffin, a play, *The Colleen Bawn* (1860), by Dion Boucicault, and an opera, *The Lily of Killarney* (1862), by Julius Benedict. The most factual account of events leading to the trial was published in *The True History of the Colleen Bawn* (1869) by Rev. Richard Fitzgerald of Trinity College, Dublin, who was in the area at the time. Ellie Hanley is commemorated by a monument at Tarbert, Co. Kerry, on the River Shannon.

Collins, Michael (1890–1922), soldier and politician (Sinn Féin); born in Woodfield, Clonakilty, Co. Cork, educated at national school. He worked as a Post Office clerk in London, 1906–10, in a stockbroking firm, and in the London office of the Guaranty Trust Company of New York. Active in the IRB and Irish Volunteers, he returned to Ireland, January 1916, where he was employed in Dublin by Countess Plunkett, mother of JOSEPH PLUNKETT. Close to THOMAS J. CLARKE and SEÁN MAC DIARMADA, he was a staff captain and *aide de camp* to Plunkett during the EASTER RISING (1916), after which he was interned in England and Wales until December 1916. He was secretary of the IRISH NATIONAL AID and IRISH VOLUNTEERS DEPENDANTS' FUND. Secretary of the Supreme Council of the IRB, he was a member of the Provisional Committee of the Irish Volunteers, of which he became Adjutant-General, and was involved in the production and distribution of its organ, *An tÓglach,* to which he was also a contributor.

Elected to the first Dáil Éireann, he was Minister for Home Affairs and subsequently Minister for Finance, April 1919 to August 1922, in which capacity he organised the National Loan, which raised more than £350,000 (having had a target of £100,000). With HARRY BOLAND he organised the escape of ÉAMON DE VALERA, SEÁN MILROY and Seán McGarry from Lincoln Jail, 3 February 1919.

As president of the Supreme Council of the IRB, Collins held a unique position in the IRA—rivalling that of CATHAL BRUGHA, who was Minister for Defence during the WAR OF INDEPENDENCE. He resigned from the Executive of Sinn Féin to work with Boland on the formation of an intelligence system. Through a concentrated policy of attack on the smaller barracks of the RIC and against members of the force, he forced the closure of such posts, depriving government intelligence of vital local information and leading to mass resignations from the RIC. His intelligence sources included a woman in the service of Colonel Hill-Dillon, chief intelligence officer in Dublin Castle, another employed in the headquarters of the British army 6th Division, a major in F Company of the AUXILIARIES, and agents within Dublin Castle's G Division: ÉAMONN BROY, DAVID NELIGAN, Joe Kavanagh, and James McNamara.

Members of Collins's personal staff, known as the 'SQUAD', wiped out the British intelligence system, the 'CAIRO GANG', on BLOODY SUNDAY (21 November 1920); in the ensuing forty-eight hours more than a hundred agents and informants, many previously unknown to Collins, were observed contacting their Dublin 'handlers'. Though the master-builder Batt O'Connor ensured that Collins operated from houses specially adapted for concealment and escape, he showed little thought for personal safety, travelling openly throughout Dublin and on one occasion visiting DUBLIN CASTLE.

Collins reluctantly accepted nomination as a delegate to London for the negotiations that led to the ANGLO-IRISH TREATY (1921), a settlement he passionately defended during the Dáil debates, 14 December 1921 to 10 January 1922. He was Chairman of the Provisional Government.

The CRAIG-COLLINS AGREEMENTS were brought about through Collins's meetings with Sir James Craig (see VISCOUNT CRAIGAVON), January and March 1922, in an attempt to bring an end to the continued unrest in Northern Ireland, though Collins was in fact supporting the IRA in its war against the northern state. In an effort to prevent a widening gap between supporters and opponents of the Treaty he made a controversial election pact with de Valera (see COLLINS-DE VALERA PACT) but repudiated it two days before the election.

The assassination of SIR HENRY WILSON, 22 June 1922, of which British intelligence suspected Collins had prior knowledge, the continuing occupation of the FOUR COURTS, Dublin, by Republicans and their kidnapping of J. J. O'CONNELL, 26 June, in addition to pressure from London, forced Collins to move against the occupants of the Four Courts, thus precipitating the CIVIL WAR. He relinquished his post as Minister for Finance to become commander in chief of the Free State army. The unexpected death of ARTHUR GRIFFITH, 12 August, hardened Collins's resolve to bring an end to the conflict, and he left Dublin, Sunday 20 August, ostensibly for a tour of inspection of the south. His usual driver, Pat Swan, was arraigned on a minor misdemeanour, and M. B. Corry took his place. Collins left Cork for Macroom shortly after 6 a.m. on 22 August. He had private discussions with a number of neutral IRA officers, including FLORENCE O'DONOGHUE, who agreed to act as liaison officer between the warring sides.

Collins left for Bandon on his Leyland 8 transport by a circuitous route. At Bealnablagh, near Macroom, Co. Cork, their passage was obstructed by a mined cart, placed there earlier by a Republican ambush party. The majority of the ambushing party having dispersed, the remaining members were in the act of dismantling the barricade and the attached mine when the approach of a military cavalcade was signalled by a warning shot. The Collins cavalcade halted to return fire, and in the ensuing engagement Collins was mortally wounded. On its way to Cork the vehicle conveying Collins halted briefly at Cloughduv church, where the local curate blessed Collins's remains. Reaching Cork after midnight, and bypassing city hospitals, the body, under the direction of EMMET DALTON, was taken to the British Military Hospital at Shanakiel. The remains were later taken by sea aboard the *Classic* to the North Wall, Dublin. Oliver St John Gogarty's autopsy report was not published. General TOM BARRY, then a Republican prisoner in Kilmainham Jail, Dublin, related how almost a thousand fellow-prisoners reacted to news of the death of Collins by spontaneously reciting the Rosary.

An estimated 300,000 people lined the streets of Dublin as Collins's funeral procession wound its way to Glasnevin Cemetery, where the graveside oration was given by the commander in chief of the Free State army, RICHARD MULCAHY.

'collop' (Irish *colpa*), the amount of land considered capable of producing enough to support one family. The basis for the division of common land in the west of Ireland in the eighteenth and early part of the nineteenth century, it was known in Ulster and parts of Connacht as a 'sum'. As in the RUNDALE system, the collop was scattered over different fields, so that good and bad land was equally divided. The area allotted was decided by the number of animals likely to be grazed on it; in an equation that varied slightly between districts this was based on a unit that consisted of three horses, four sheep, eight goats, or twenty geese.

Colwyn Committee, established under Lord Colwyn, 1923, to examine the question of Northern Ireland's finances and the contributions to be made to the Imperial Fund. The committee suggested that the contribution made by Northern Ireland should be the residue after domestic expenditure had been met.

Combined Loyalist Military Command, an umbrella group for the ULSTER VOLUNTEER FORCE, Ulster Freedom Fighters and RED HAND COMMANDO that emerged in April 1991 to call a ceasefire to coincide with the beginning of inter-party talks at Stormont. The ceasefire ended together with the talks at midnight on 4 July. It was believed that the CLMC had a role in the resurgence of loyalist violence, 1991–92. During 1993 it refused to abandon its campaign unless the Provisional IRA called a total cessation of violence. In July 1994, when the Provisional IRA called off its campaign, the

CLMC was prepared to respond to allow 'magnanimous dialogue' but rejected any 'diminution' of the Union. It demanded assurances that the Provisional IRA ceasefire was permanent, that no secret deal had been made, and that the constitutional position of Northern Ireland was secure. The loyalist ceasefire statement on 13 October 1994 was read by the veteran loyalist paramilitary GUSTY SPENCE, who offered 'abject and true remorse' to 'innocent victims.'

On the first anniversary of the CLMC ceasefire, between 15,000 and 20,000 people attended a rally at Belfast City Hall, making a commitment to 'no first strike.' However, there was some criticism of the CLMC from dissidents in the Mid-Ulster UVF, who broke away to form what later became the LOYALIST VOLUNTEER FORCE, led by BILLY WRIGHT. In January 1998 Billy Hutchinson made an unsuccessful attempt to reconstitute the CLMC.

Comhairle na dTeachtaí, a political group formed in 1923 from among SINN FÉIN members of the second Dáil and other Sinn Féin members elected subsequently to the Dáil, members of which, led by ÉAMON DE VALERA, refused to take their seats in the Free State Dáil. Many were later subsumed into Fianna Fáil, 1926, and entered Dáil Éireann in 1927.

Comhairle na Poblachta, a political party founded in April 1929 from a number of social and republican organisations, its membership including SEÁN MACBRIDE, MAUD GONNE, MARY MACSWINEY, and FRANK RYAN. It issued a weekly paper, AN PHOBLACHT. Its hostility to the Cumann na nGaedheal government prompted a Garda report, 16 October 1931, that described the aims of the organisation as 'the overthrow of the State by force of arms.' Unable to combine its military and social aspirations, the organisation broke up in the early 1930s.

Comhaltas Ceoltóirí Éireann, founded in 1951 to promote traditional music, song, and dancing. It has branches throughout Ireland and in Britain, Continental Europe, Asia, Australia, Canada and the United States and is financed through state grants and voluntary subscriptions. Its activities include the organising of some forty annual fleánna ceoil, teaching traditional music and dancing, and promoting international concert tours by members. Its activities also extend to the fields of radio, television, and audio production, and it publishes a magazine, *Treoir.*

Comhdháil Náisiúnta na Gaeilge, founded in 1943 as a co-ordinating body of the movement to promote the use of Irish. In 1953 it became the patron of a new organisation, GAEL-LINN.

commanders of British forces in Ireland, 1801–1922

1801 General Sir William Meadows
1803 Lieutenant-General Henry Edward Fox
1803 General William Cathcart, Lord Cathcart
1806 General Charles Stanhope, Earl of Harrington
1812 General Sir J. Hope
1813 General Sir George Hewett
1816 General Sir George Beckwith
1820 General Sir David Baird
1822 Lieutenant-General Sir Samuel Auchmuty
1822 Field-Marshal Viscoun Cumbermere
1825 Lieutenant-General Sir George Murray
1828 Lieutenant-General Sir John Byng
1831 Lieutenant-General Sir R. Hussey Vivian
1836 Field-Marshal Sir Edward Blakeney
1855 Field-Marshal Lord Seaton
1860 General Sir George Brown
1865 General Lord Strathnairn
1870 General Lord Sandhurst
1875 General Sir John Michel
1880 General Sir Thomas M. Steele
1885 General Prince Edward of Saxe-Weimar
1890 Field-Marshal Viscount Wolseley
1895 Field-Marshal Earl Roberts
1900 Field-Marshal the Duke of Connaught
1904 Field-Marshal Lord Grenfall
1908 General Sir Neville Lyttleton
1912 LIEUTENANT-GENERAL SIR A. H. PAGET
1914 MAJOR-GENERAL L. BRANSBY FRIEND
1916 LIEUTENANT-GENERAL SIR J. G. MAXWELL
1918 Lieutenant-General Sir F. C. Shaw
1920 GENERAL SIR C. F. N. MACREADY

Commission on Higher Education, a Government commission appointed to investigate higher education. Its report, 1967, recommended that UCC, UCD and UCG should be reconstituted as independent universities, and that the constitution of TCD should be 'restated'. Other recommendations included making more finance available for students, the establishment of technological colleges rather than a new university, the establishment of an authority for technological training and research, and the appointment of a Commission for Higher Education.

The Higher Education Authority was established in September 1968 to advise the Minister for Education on proposals for the co-ordination and development of the higher education system generally. The National Science Council, which first met in January 1968, was established 'to advise the Government on science and technology, with particular reference to economic development, recognising the need to establish closer liaison between academic scientists and technologists, state research institutes and industrial firms.'

Regional technical colleges (RTCs) were established during the 1970s, with an emphasis on providing certificate, diploma and degree courses in engineering, science, commerce, catering, art, and design. Another development in line with the recommendations of the Commission on Higher Education was the establishment in 1972 of the National Institute for Higher Education (NIHE), Limerick, followed by one in Dublin, 1980, offering courses at diploma and degree level, to be validated by the NATIONAL COUNCIL FOR EDUCATIONAL AWARDS; the NIHEs became the University of Limerick and Dublin City University in 1989. The regional technical colleges were renamed institutes of technology during the 1990s. Under the Universities Act (1997) the constituent colleges of the NATIONAL UNIVERSITY OF IRELAND became the National University of Ireland, Cork (NUIC), National University of Ireland, Dublin (NUID), National University of Ireland, Galway (NUIG), and National University of Ireland, Maynooth.

Commission on the Revival of the Irish Language, established in July 1958 under its chairman, Rev. (later Cardinal) TOMÁS Ó FIAICH. It submitted an interim report, 20 March 1959, recommending that Irish be used in the control and administration of the proposed national television service, and that the majority of children's programming should be in Irish. The commission's report (July 1963) was the basis for a white paper on Irish, January 1965, drafted by the Department of Finance. In 1965 Ó Fiaich was chairman of the Consultative Commission on the Restoration of the Language.

Committee on Evil Literature, appointed 12 February 1926 to report 'whether it is necessary or advisable in the interest of the public morality to extend the existing powers of the State to prohibit or restrict the sale and circulation of printed matter.' The three laymen and two clergymen (one Catholic and one Church of Ireland) met from February to December 1926 to hear submissions from individuals, organisations, and various social and religious institutions. In its report, 28 December, the committee expressed dissatisfaction with the existing laws and urged that it was the duty of the state to take action to prevent the circulation of literature considered obscene and morally corrupting, and recommended the establishment of a Censorship Board.

commonage, a large tract of land held in common by small farmers, often dating from the Middle Ages. Owing its origin to the traditional Irish system of land tenure, the principle has survived chiefly in Cos. Donegal, Kerry, and Mayo. The right of commonage entitled holders to graze their animals on such lands free of charge; the seizure and enclosure of commonage was a source of agrarian unrest, giving rise to the activities of SECRET SOCIETIES.

Commonwealth Labour Party, a pro-unionist party founded by HARRY MIDGLEY after he broke with the NORTHERN IRELAND LABOUR PARTY, 1942. Midgley was the sole electoral success of the six candidates who contested the 1945 general election.

Communist Party of Ireland (CPI), founded in November 1921, with RODERIC CONNOLLY as first president and Walter Carpenter as secretary. It contained former members of the SOCIALIST PARTY OF IRELAND and was recognised as the Irish section of the Comintern. Opposed to the ANGLO-IRISH TREATY (1921), it put forward a republican-socialist programme. The party was supported by PEADAR O'DONNELL and LIAM O'FLAHERTY; O'Flaherty and Connolly jointly edited the CPI's paper, the WORKERS' REPUBLIC. Members of the party established the Munster Council of Action, December 1921, and organised twelve SOVIETS. The party dissolved in 1923 following the Comintern's transfer of recognition to the Irish Worker League, headed by JAMES LARKIN.

The party was re-established in June 1933 by the REVOLUTIONARY WORKERS' GROUPS. In July 1941 the southern section suspended its activities because of restrictions imposed by the government, while the northern section regrouped as the Communist Party of Northern Ireland. The Irish Workers' League was established in November 1948 and renamed Irish Workers' Party in 1962; it merged with the Communist Party of Northern Ireland, March 1970, to re-establish the Communist Party of Ireland. The general secretary of the new CPI was MICHAEL O'RIORDAN.

Compensation for Disturbance Bill (1880), introduced by the Chief Secretary for Ireland, W. E. FORSTER, 18 June 1880, as a temporary measure to deal with a deteriorating situation brought about by famine and LAND LEAGUE agitation. It sought to empower the courts to order a landlord to compensate a tenant for improvements made when evicted, even if the eviction was for non-payment of rent, provided the tenant could prove that inability to pay was due to two successive bad harvests. Applying to the south and west of the country, the legislation was to remain in force for eighteen months. Opposed by CHARLES STEWART PARNELL and the Irish Party, the bill passed the House of Commons, 26 July, but was rejected by the House of Lords, 3 August. The House of Lords had rarely been so crowded as during the debate on this bill, which deeply affected the landlord class. JOSEPH CHAMBERLAIN remarked: 'The bill is rejected: the civil war has begun.' The rejection of the bill was followed by an increase in violence in Ireland.

Compton Report (16 November 1971), issued following an investigation by Sir Edmund Compton, Edgar Kay QC and Dr Ronald Gibson into allegations that interned prisoners were treated with brutality. It dismissed charges of brutality and torture but found that there had been physical ill-treatment of detainees and accepted that there had been 'in-depth interrogation with hooding' and the use of 'white noise'. Only one detainee gave evidence: others refused on the grounds that, as the Compton Commission was sitting in private, there would be no opportunity to cross-examine official witnesses. The report was widely criticised. The British Government announced a new inquiry under Lord Parker to consider whether interrogation methods should be changed. Most of the cases before the Compton Commission eventually went to the European Court of Human rights. (See also PARKER REPORT.)

conacre, setting out a portion of land either for eleven months or for a season for the purpose of growing crops, in return for rent or labour. Those holding land under this system were generally the poorer cottier or landless agricultural labourer. Holding the land under conacre granted the tenant no legal right to the land. The system was most commonly found in Munster and Connacht; according to the report of the DEVON COMMISSION (1847), conacre in Leinster and Ulster was usually for a potato crop alone, while in Connacht and Munster the crops included oats, hay and flax as well as potatoes.

Rents varied between £6 and £14 per acre, depending on the quality and site of the land and whether the landlord had to manure the holding. In Macroom, Co. Cork, in 1840 Rev. Thomas Gollock, having to procure lime from a considerable distance, charged £8.40 per acre, but lands closer to the seashore could be had for £6 per acre, because of the ready supply of kelp. An average acre yielded six tons of potatoes, which sold for £15 in 1841. The failure of the potato crop, resulting in the GREAT FAMINE (1845–49), obliged many labourers to renegotiate the terms for conacre. Others refused to pay for a useless crop and were forced into public works or the workhouse. Many landlords as a consequence demanded rent in advance, thus making it impossible for a majority of labourers to rent land, while the poorest worked in lieu of cabin rent or simply for a few privileges.

The principal defect of the practice was its speculative nature: the labourer who took the land was frequently an indigent speculator who, depending on the weather, either made a profit or faced ruin. There were many cases of MIDDLEMEN renting the land and letting it out on conacre to desperate landless labourers or cottiers at a high profit.

The conacre system persisted into the 1930s. A 15 per cent fall in agricultural income between 1929 and 1933 led to a drop in conacre, which in Co. Limerick fell from £2 per acre in 1932 to just over £1 per acre in 1935. (See also RUNDALE and SPALPEEN.)

Concannon, Helena, née Walsh (1878–1952), historian, poet, Gaelic League activist, and politician (Fianna Fáil); born in Co. Derry. Following her marriage, 1906, she settled in Salthill, Galway. A prominent figure in the Gaelic League before becoming a member of Dáil Éireann, 1933–37, she became a senator in 1938. She promoted the Belgian concept of the rural domestic school, and defended the CONSTITUTION OF IRELAND (1937), which was attacked as anti-feminist by some leading women intellectuals: 'I sincerely hope that not a comma of this noble document will be altered.' Some of her works reflect the role of women in Irish history. She contributed to nationalist periodicals and journals and wrote religious articles for the *Irish Messenger.* Her works (published under the name Mrs Thomas Concannon) include *Makers of Irish History* (c. 1920), *Irish History for Junior Classes* (1921), *Daughters of Banba* (1922), *Irish Nuns in Penal Days* (1931), and *The Irish Sisters of Mercy in the Crimean War* (1950).

Conditions of Employment Act (1936), introduced by SEÁN LEMASS as Minister for Industry and Commerce to improve working conditions, with particular regard to juvenile labour. The act enabled wage agreements to be registered and made legally enforceable, limited the adult working week to forty-eight hours, restricted overtime, set the working day to end at 8 p.m. for the majority, and controlled the employment of women and young people. It aroused strong feminist opposition. Under section 16 the minister could prohibit female employment in an industry; where women were already employed, the number allowed was to be fixed in proportion to the number of men employed, and employers were forbidden to employ more women than men.

Condon, Edward O'Meagher (1835–1915), Fenian; born in Cork. Emigrating to the United States, where he joined the Fenians, he fought in the Federal Army during the American Civil War (1861–65). Returning to Ireland as a Fenian activist, he was a party to the rescue of T. J. KELLY and TIMOTHY DEASY in Manchester, where, under the alias 'Shore', he was tried for murder together with Allen, Larkin, and O'Brien, the MANCHESTER MARTYRS. His statement that 'I have nothing to regret, to retract, or to take home. I can only say "God save Ireland",' to which the other prisoners chorused 'God save Ireland,' provided T. D. SULLIVAN with the inspiration for the ballad of that name. Because of his American citizenship, Condon was reprieved; on his release from Portland Prison, 1878, he returned to America, where he supported the Allied cause during the First World War. His book *The Irish Race in America* was published in 1889. The honorary freedom of the city of Dublin was conferred on him, September 1909.

Congested Districts Board, established 5 August 1891 under the Purchase of Land (Ireland) Act (1891) (see LAND ACTS), introduced by the Chief Secretary for Ireland, ARTHUR J. BALFOUR, to dispense assistance to the 'congested districts' of Cos. Donegal, Clare, Cork, Galway, Kerry, Limerick, Leitrim, Roscommon and Sligo as part of the Conservative policy of 'constructive unionism' or 'killing home rule with kindness.' The board consisted of two Land Commissioners, five experts appointed by the Chief Secretary, with the Chief Secretary sitting as an *ex officio* member; the numbers were later increased to ten and then to fourteen. Temporary experts were added when necessary.

Regions under the board's authority were those in which the rateable valuation was less than £1.50; the total was about 3½ million acres, with a population (1901) of approximately 500,000. According to the Commissioners, the population could be divided into two classes, 'the poor and the destitute.' Funds came from the disestablished Church of Ireland, amounting initially to £41,000; by 1912 it had acquired other funds and had assets of £530,000. The sums at its disposal were spent on building harbours, encouraging a fishing industry, curing fish, supporting cottage industries, and attempting to modernise farming methods. Under the Irish Land Act (1903) (also called the Wyndham Act) the Congested Districts Board was authorised to buy extra land from large estates to enlarge the smallholdings. In 1909 it was granted powers of compulsory purchase, and it redistributed a thousand estates, totalling 2 million acres.

The board was dissolved by the government of the Irish Free State, 1923, and its functions handed over to the LAND COMMISSION. One legacy of the board was the CO-OPERATIVE MOVEMENT, founded by SIR HORACE PLUNKETT, who had been shocked by his experiences while working as a member of the first board.

Congress of Irish Unions, founded in 1945 when the IRISH TRANSPORT AND GENERAL WORKERS' UNION and fourteen other unions disaffiliated from the IRISH TRADE UNION CONGRESS and the LABOUR PARTY. The split was caused by the decision of the Executive of the ITUC to send delegates to the World Trades Union Congress in London, February 1945; WILLIAM O'BRIEN and his followers in the ITGWU claimed that the WTUC was dominated by communists. The CIU gained from the growth of the trade union movement during the 1950s and by 1958 had approximately

190,000 members in twenty-nine unions. It entered into negotiations with the ITUC in 1955 and four years later amalgamated with it to form the IRISH CONGRESS OF TRADE UNIONS.

Connaught Rangers Mutiny (28–30 June 1920), an incident involving members of B and C Companies, 1st Battalion, Connaught Rangers, quartered at Jullundur, Punjab. Joseph Hawes and a committee including Paddy Gogarty, Paddy Sweeney and Stephen Lally led the action. The men refused to soldier because of reports reaching them of atrocities being committed in Ireland by members of the BLACK AND TANS and AUXILIARIES. Their protest was supported two days later by a detachment of C Company at a hill station in Solon, led by James Daly, a member of the IRB. The men had surrendered their arms, retaining only bayonets, when rumours of a massacre of their comrades involved in the Jullundur protest prompted Daly to lead an attack on the magazine at Solon. Sears and Smith were killed in the attack, and a third man, John Egan, was wounded.

The first of three courts-martial opened at Dagshai on 23 August 1920 under Major-General Sir Sidney Lawson, at which the majority of the men represented themselves. Hawes, Daly and some others refused to recognise the court's jurisdiction. Of the seventy court-martialled, fourteen were sentenced to death and the remainder to varying terms of imprisonment. While awaiting trial the men were subjected to an extremely harsh regime, which resulted in the death of Private John Miranda. The ill-treatment continued for some time during their subsequent imprisonment. All the death sentences save that of James Daly were commuted to life imprisonment. On 1 November 1920, 22-year-old Daly was shot by a firing squad from the Royal Fusiliers. All the imprisoned men were released in 1923. The Connaught Rangers regiment, which had been raised in 1793 by the family of Lord Clanricarde, was disbanded in 1922.

Following prolonged representation on behalf of the mutineers the Irish Free State awarded a small pension to the survivors from 1936. On 1 November 1970 James Daly was re-interred in his native Tyrrellspass, Co. Westmeath.

Connolly, James (1868–1916), socialist and trade union organiser; born in Edinburgh of Irish parents. He worked in a succession of jobs from the age of eleven until he enlisted in the British army at the age of fourteen. He served most of his seven years in Ireland until he deserted in 1889 and returned to Edinburgh. Influenced by the Scottish socialist John Leslie, he became secretary of the Independent Labour Party in Edinburgh. When he was made redundant by Edinburgh Corporation, Leslie arranged for Connolly to be employed by the Dublin Socialist Society, 1896. He became a member of the United Labourers of Ireland, which he represented on Dublin Trades Council.

Connolly founded the IRISH REPUBLICAN SOCIALIST PARTY and the *Workers' Republic* (1898–99). After a successful American lecture tour, 1902, he moved his family to New York, 1903. He founded the Irish Socialist Federation and another paper, the *Harp,* and was also active in the Industrial Workers of the World.

Returning to Ireland, July 1910, he worked as an organiser for the IRISH TRANSPORT AND GENERAL WORKERS' UNION in Belfast. He was joint founder (with JAMES LARKIN) of the LABOUR PARTY, 1912. Returning to Dublin, he assisted Larkin in the DUBLIN LOCK-OUT (1913) and jointly founded the IRISH CITIZEN ARMY. He returned to Dublin permanently in October 1914 to lead the labour movement following Larkin's departure for the United States. He revived the *Workers' Republic* after the *Irish Worker* was suppressed, December 1914. He committed the labour movement against the Allies when war broke out in 1914 and criticised the IRISH VOLUNTEERS for their inactivity but pledged the Citizen Army to support the Volunteers in the EASTER RISING (1916). The Proclamation of the Irish Republic bears evidence of Connolly's influence:

> We declare the right of the people of Ireland to the ownership of Ireland, and to the unfettered control of Irish destinies . . . The Republic guarantees . . . equal rights and equal opportunities to all its citizens . . . cherishing all the children of the nation equally, and oblivious of the differences carefully fostered by an alien government, which have divided a minority from a majority in the past . . .

Connolly was severely wounded while serving as a commandant in the General Post Office, O'Connell Street, Dublin, during the fighting. He was shot by firing squad on 9 May. His writings include *Erin's Hope* (1897), *Labour in Irish History* (1910), *Labour, Nationality and Religion* (1910), and *The Re-Conquest of Ireland* (1915).

Connolly, Roderic (1901–1980), trade unionist and politician (Labour Party); born in

Dublin, son of JAMES CONNOLLY, educated locally. At the age of fifteen he fought alongside his father in the General Post Office, Dublin, during the EASTER RISING (1916), after which he was interned for eight days. While in Moscow to discuss the affiliation of the SOCIALIST PARTY OF IRELAND to the Comintern he met leading communist figures, including Lenin. Having organised the takeover of the SPI, September 1921, he secured the expulsion of WILLIAM O'BRIEN and CATHAL O'SHANNON, October, and renamed it the COMMUNIST PARTY OF IRELAND, for which he edited the *Workers' Republic*. The first CPI was short-lived, and Connolly later founded the equally short-lived WORKERS' PARTY OF IRELAND. Member of Dáil Éireann for Co. Louth, 1943–45, Connolly was financial secretary and later chairman of the Labour Party.

Connolly Column, part of the Abraham Lincoln Battalion, International Brigade, formed from among volunteers who accompanied FRANK RYAN to Spain, December 1936, to support the republican government in the SPANISH CIVIL WAR (1936–39). The column, numbering approximately eighty, included the poet Charlie Donnelly (born 1914) and Rev. R. M. Hilliard of Killarney, who were killed in the Battle of Jarama, where Ryan was also wounded. In all, 61 of the 161 Irish volunteers who served in the International Brigade were killed. MICHAEL O'RIORDAN, who served in the column, published a history, *Connolly Column* (1979).

Conolly, Lady Louise, née Lennox (1742–1821), philanthropist and model landlord, daughter of the third Duke of Richmond. Following the death of her husband, Thomas Conolly, 1803, she administered the magnificent Castletown estate at Celbridge, Co. Kildare. Anticipating the industrial school system, she established schools that offered education to her tenants' children and to the poorer children of the surrounding district.

conscription. The question of extending conscription to Ireland arose in 1916 following the heavy allied losses at Verdun (from February) and the Somme (from July). However, public unrest in Ireland after the EASTER RISING (1916) made it unlikely that conscription could be peacefully implemented. The Prime Minister, DAVID LLOYD GEORGE, told the House of Commons in February 1917 that if a Conscription Act were passed it would produce only 160,000 men, and

> you would get them at the point of the bayonet, and a conscientious objection clause would exempt by far the greater number. As it is, these men are producing food which we badly need.

Between March and April 1918 the British army lost more than 300,000 men on the Western Front. In March the Russians signed the Treaty of Brest-Litovsk with Germany. On 24 March the cabinet decided to raise the age limit for suitability from forty-two to fifty. Four days later the question of conscription for Ireland was once more discussed. Central to the discussions was a *quid pro quo* of home rule for conscription and the likelihood of British trade union opposition to the age extension unless provision was made for the introduction of conscription in Ireland. It was agreed to wait for the report of the IRISH CONVENTION, due to begin its final sitting on 4 April.

When the Conscription Bill was passed (301 to 103), 16 April 1918, the Irish members withdrew from the House of Commons and returned to Ireland, where they joined forces with SINN FÉIN. Soon they were joined by the Catholic hierarchy, trade unions, Labour Party, Irish Volunteers, and Cumann na mBan ('We will not have our men conscripted'). On 18 April the lord mayor of Dublin, Laurence O'Neill, brought political leaders together at the Mansion House. Among those present were JOHN DILLON, ÉAMON DE VALERA, T. M. HEALY, WILIAM O'BRIEN, and ARTHUR GRIFFITH. De Valera drafted a pledge to be taken all over Ireland on the following Sunday, 21 April:

> Denying the right of the British Government to enforce compulsory service in this country, we pledge ourselves solemnly to one another to resist conscription by the most effective means at our disposal.

Anti-conscription demonstrations were held throughout the country, Committees of Defence were established, and a National Defence Fund was launched. On Sunday 21 April almost two million people signed the anti-conscription pledge. The Irish Trade Union Congress organised a general strike, 23 April, observed everywhere except Belfast. Membership of the Irish Volunteers trebled. Clan na Gael organised a mass meeting in New York, 4 May, when leading Irish nationalists, including JOHN DEVOY, denounced conscription.

Conscription also faced opposition from Protestants. A leaflet entitled 'Protestant protest against conscription' was circulated.

We, the undersigned, wish to join our Roman Catholic fellow-countrymen in protesting in the strongest possible manner against the application of Conscription to Ireland. We believe that to force any people to act contrary to their will and conscience is a violation of the law of God, and cannot but be productive of the gravest and most disastrous moral, religious and material consequences.

At the beginning of May the Irish administration was changed, when Wimborne was replaced by EARL FRENCH, and Edward Shortt replaced H. E. DUKE. They immediately set about a recruiting campaign as the alternative to conscription. On 3 July 1918 the administration proclaimed as 'a growing menace' the various Sinn Féin organisations, the Irish Volunteers, and the Gaelic League. Another proclamation the next day prohibited all public meetings (and the playing of Gaelic games) without police authorisation. As a result, Sinn Féin went underground. By the time the war ended, 11 November 1918, more than 150,000 Irishmen had enlisted in the British army, 49,000 of whom were killed.

Constitutional Convention (1975), established by the British Government to consider 'what provision for the government of Northern Ireland is likely to command the most widespread acceptance throughout the community there.' The seventy-eight members were elected by proportional representation. The chairman was Sir Robert Lowry, with Dr John A. Oliver and Maurice Hayes. Forty-seven seats were held by supporters of the UNITED ULSTER UNIONIST COUNCIL, committed to a rejection of 'power-sharing' (multi-party government). The House of Commons refused to accept that this met the criteria of the white paper; by the time meetings ended, in March 1976, no satisfactory agreement had been reached.

Constitution (Amendment No. 17) Act (1931), introduced by the Cumann na nGaedheal government during a period of intense republican activity. It established a Military Tribunal empowered to impose the death penalty for political and other crimes, allowed the Garda Síochána extensive powers of arrest and detention, and facilitated the outlawing of associations and societies, including the IRA and SAOR ÉIRE.

Constitution of Ireland (1937). In May 1935 ÉAMON DE VALERA instructed the law officer of the Department of External Affairs, John J. Hearn, to prepare the heads of a constitution to replace the CONSTITUTION OF THE IRISH FREE STATE (1922). During 1936 de Valera and a team of civil servants studied the *Code Social: Esquisse d'une Synthèse Social Catholique* and recent Papal encyclicals; he also consulted academic, legal and religious leaders. The finished draft was published on 1 May and passed the first reading in Dáil Éireann by 69 votes to 43. Enacted by plebiscite (685,105 to 526,945) on 1 July 1937, it came into force on 29 December.

Though the Constitution was greeted with hostility by the British press, the British Government declared on 29 December that it did not affect Ireland's membership of the Commonwealth of Nations.

Under the Constitution (article 4) the title of the state is *Éire* (in Irish) or *Ireland* (in English). The Constitution affirmed the essential unity of the country, stating (article 2) that 'the national territory consists of the whole island of Ireland, its islands and the territorial seas' but also (article 3) that 'pending the re-integration of the national territory,' the laws enacted by Dáil Éireann under the Constitution would apply only to the twenty-six counties. Article 5 declares that Ireland is a 'sovereign, independent, democratic state.' Irish is given the status of first official language and English as second official language (article 8). The legislature is the Oireachtas, consisting of the President of Ireland, Dáil Éireann, and Seanad Éireann. Dáil Éireann is to be elected by universal franchise, and Seanad Éireann partly elected on a vocational basis (49 members) and partly nominated by the Taoiseach (11 members). The Government, to be selected by the Taoiseach and approved by the President and the Dáil, consists of no less than seven members and no more than fifteen.

Articles 34–44 grant certain fundamental rights. In an effort to protect the family as the basic social unit, divorce was prohibited (until the fifteenth amendment to the Constitution, 1995). Article 44.1 recognised the 'special position' of the Catholic Church as the church of the majority of the population, while also granting recognition and equal rights to all other religious denominations. The special position of the Catholic Church was removed by referendum, 1972.

The REPUBLIC OF IRELAND ACT (1948), introduced by the first inter-party Government and coming into effect on 18 April 1949, declared that the 'description' of the state was 'Republic of Ireland' and repealed the EXTERNAL RELATIONS ACT (1936), thus taking Ireland out of the British Commonwealth.

Articles 2 and 3 of the Constitution were replaced by 'aspiration' towards a united Ireland in accordance with the BELFAST AGREEMENT (1998).

Constitution of the Irish Free State (1922). A committee to draft a constitution for the Irish Free State was appointed under the chairmanship of MICHAEL COLLINS, February 1922; because of the CIVIL WAR, much of the work fell to the deputy chairman, DARRELL FIGGIS. Members included JAMES DOUGLAS, T. C. J. France, HUGH KENNEDY, JAMES MACNEILL, James Murnaghan, John O'Byrne, Prof. Alfred O'Rahilly, and Kevin O'Sheil; the secretariat consisted of R. J. P. MORTISHED, E. M. Stephens, and P. A. O'Toole. The committee met from February to May in room 112 (the 'Constitution Room') of the Shelbourne Hotel, St Stephen's Green, Dublin.

Having examined the constitutions of other countries, printed translations of which were supplied to the legislature, three drafts were submitted to the Ministry (government).

The Constitution consisted of seventy-nine articles, together with the ANGLO-IRISH TREATY (1921), to which it was subordinate. It was enshrined in British legislation by the Irish Free State Constitution Act (1922) and was published for the first time on 16 June 1922, the day of the general election, allowing the electorate little time for perusal. On 18 September the Constitution of the Irish Free State (Saorstát Éireann) Bill (1922) was steered through Dáil Éireann by KEVIN O'HIGGINS.

Article 1 declared that the Irish Free State was a co-equal member of the community of nations forming the British Commonwealth of Nations. The legislature was to be the Oireachtas, consisting of the King, Dáil Éireann, and Seanad Éireann (commonly called the Senate). Article 12 vested the 'sole and exclusive' power of making laws in the Oireachtas; executive authority was vested in the King. The state was to be governed by the Executive Council, responsible to the Dáil and consisting of ministers appointed by the representative of the Crown, the Governor-General.

The Irish Free State came into existence on 6 December 1922. By the time it was replaced by the CONSTITUTION OF IRELAND (1937), forty-one of the Free State constitution's original articles had been amended.

Constitution (Removal of Oath) Act (1933), legislation introduced in Dáil Éireann by EAMON DE VALERA, 20 April 1932, to amend the CONSTITUTION OF THE IRISH FREE STATE (1922) by removing the OATH OF ALLEGIANCE. The bill was passed by the Dáil without amendment, 19 May, but was rejected by the Senate, which sought to prevent its adoption unless a mutual agreement between the Free State and Britain abrogated article 4 of the Anglo-Irish Treaty (1921). De Valera refused, and following its suspension period the bill passed into law, 18 November. In the interim de Valera called a general election, and the act came into force on 3 May 1933.

Contemporary Club, founded to discuss 'the social, political and literary questions of the day.' It held its first meeting on 21 November 1885. Its membership, which reflected a cross-section of literary and artistic life and included both unionists and nationalists, included MICHAEL DAVITT, GEORGE RUSSELL, and JOHN O'LEARY. The club lasted until c. 1915.

'Continuity IRA', active in the 1990s and widely believed to be the military wing of REPUBLICAN SINN FÉIN. It consisted of members who broke with the Provisional IRA in 1986 after a vote to end abstention from Dáil Éireann. Two people believed to be members were captured by gardaí following the robbery of an oil depot in Co. Limerick, 1993. The organisation claimed responsibility for a bomb that destroyed the Killyhelvin Hotel in Enniskillen, Co Fermanagh, 1997. It exploded a huge car bomb outside Markethill RUC Station, Co. Armagh, 16 September 1997. During that year it was believed to have attracted support from members of the Provisional IRA unhappy with the ceasefire, and it opposed the BELFAST AGREEMENT (1998). In 2002 it was reported that the bomb explosion in Omagh, Co. Tyrone, on 15 August 1998 in which 28 people were killed and 310 injured was a joint operation between the 'Continuity IRA' and 'REAL IRA'.

Control of Manufactures Acts (1932 and 1934), introduced by SEÁN LEMASS as Minister for Industry and Commerce and becoming law from 29 October 1932. Their ostensible purpose was to retain as much manufacturing industry as possible in Irish hands, part of the Fianna Fáil government's aggressive protectionist economic policy.

Conway, Frederick William (1782–1853), journalist and publisher; born in Loughrea, Co. Galway. He was founder-editor of *Dublin*

Political Review, 1813, and *The Drama,* 1821. Though a supporter of CATHOLIC EMANCIPATION, he became estranged from DANIEL O'CONNELL, who nicknamed him 'Castle Conway', in reference to an alleged pension he received from DUBLIN CASTLE. On his death the sale of his extensive library took almost a month to complete; much of its contents were bought on behalf of Trinity College, the Royal College of Surgeons in Ireland, and the libraries of other Dublin institutions.

Conway, William (1913–1977), bishop (Catholic); born in Belfast, educated at QUB and St Patrick's College, Maynooth. Ordained in 1937; after teaching at St Malachy's College, Belfast, he became professor of moral theology at Maynooth, 1942; he also held the chair of canon law until appointed auxiliary to Cardinal D'Alton, 1958–63. He was a member of the Income Tax Commission, which recommended the introduction of pay-as-you-earn (PAYE) income tax, 1957. He attended the Second Vatican Council (1962–65) and was made a cardinal at its conclusion, 22 February 1965. Joint chairman of the first Synod of Bishops in Rome, 1967, he was a member of the Pontifical Commission for the Revision of Canon Law, which led to the establishment of the International Theological Commission, 1969, and a Papal direction on mixed marriages, 1970. Papal Envoy to India, 1972, he initiated the establishment of Trócaire, the Catholic development agency for the Third World, 1973. He was the author of *Problems of Canon Law* (1950) and contributed to the *Irish Ecclesiastical Record, Christus Rex, Furrow,* and *Irish Theological Quarterly* (of which he had been editor).

Cooke, Rev. Henry (1788–1868), clergyman (Presbyterian), leader of the ORANGE ORDER, and pamphleteer; born in Grillagh, Co. Derry, educated at Glasgow College (arts and divinity), Trinity College, Dublin, and Royal College of Surgeons. Ordained 10 November 1808, he held a variety of ministries in Ulster, where he was a noted opponent of Arianism; his personal triumphs at the synods of Strabane, Co. Down (1827), Cookstown, Co. Tyrone (1828) and Lurgan, Co. Armagh (1829), forced the Arians to secede from the Synod of Ulster. In 1829 he entered into spirited public debate with the champion of Arianism, REV. HENRY MONTGOMERY. Cooke's extremist views were enunciated in *Orthodox Presbyterians,* established December 1829. At a meeting at Hillsborough, Co. Down, 30 October 1834, attended by more than forty thousand people Cooke published the banns of a marriage between the established Church of Ireland and Presbyterian church that he said would help guard against the onslaught of Roman Catholicism. His opposition to the NATIONAL EDUCATION system (1831) led to the establishment of its own scheme by the Ulster Synod (recognised by the Education Board in 1840). DANIEL O'CONNELL declined a challenge from Cooke to debate the issue in Belfast, January 1841. At Cooke's urging the government endowed a theological college under the General Assembly, where he became professor of rhetoric, 1855, having been dean of residence at Queen's College, Belfast, since 1849. He retired from active ministry in 1867. In his later years Cooke was noted for his opposition to the DISESTABLISHMENT of the Church of Ireland. He published a *Family Bible and Concordance of Scripture.*

co-operative movement. A study group headed by Lord Monteagle sent R. A. ANDERSON to report on co-operative methods in Denmark and Sweden, 1890. The group was joined by FATHER THOMAS FINLAY and, after making contact with the British Co-Operative Union, formed an Irish section, under the chairmanship of SIR HORACE PLUNKETT. The first co-operative creamery was established in Drumcolliher, Co. Limerick, 1890. By 1891 there were seventeen such creameries, increasing to sixty by 1894. Agricultural societies were also established for the purchase of manure and seedlings. The IRISH AGRICULTURAL ORGANISATION SOCIETY was formed in Dublin in 1894 under the presidency of Plunkett. In 1895 the first agricultural credit society was opened at Doneraile, Co. Cork. The movement employed the IRISH HOMESTEAD, under the editorship of GEORGE RUSSELL, to spread co-operative ideals.

An Irish Co-operative Agricultural Agency Society was founded to purchase agricultural requisites for affiliated societies; this became the Irish Agricultural Wholesale Society in 1898, when it dropped agency methods to undertake general trading. Additional finance was provided in 1899 when the IAOS received a grant of £500 a year for five years from the Carnegie Trust. In 1900 the Department of Agriculture and Technical Instruction began to operate; it made grants available to creameries for the purchase of pasteurising plants (grants were also provided by county councils). In 1900 there were 171 central creameries, 65 auxiliaries, 106 agricultural societies, and 76 credit societies, with a total membership of 46,206 and a turnover of £796,528. The UNITED IRISHWOMEN assumed control of home industries and poultry societies, 1910.

The Great War (1914–18) presented the co-operative movement with a crisis when the state funds available from the Development Commission and the CONGESTED DISTRICTS BOARD were withdrawn. Following the ANGLO-IRISH TREATY, December 1921, the societies in Northern Ireland became a separate body as the Ulster Agricultural Organisation Society, while the Irish Free State made grants available to the IAOS. In 1923 the *Irish Homestead* was incorporated in Russell's IRISH STATESMAN.

The Agricultural Credit Corporation was established in 1927 to make funds available for expansion in agriculture, and the Dairy Disposal Company was founded by the state in 1928 to rationalise the dairy industry. Between 1930 and 1939 the number of creamery societies fell from 279 to 219, while membership increased from 52,000 to 54,000 and turnover on dairy produce rose from £4.4 million to £5.3 million. Non-creamery turnover rose from 11 per cent to 28 per cent.

During the years of the Second World War an increased demand for dairy produce was hampered by a shortage of farm supplies and machinery. Societies were forced to diversify into cereal milling, egg production, bacon-curing, the sale and hire of agricultural machinery, flax scutching, and the operation of hatcheries. Clover Meats was established, and Ballyclough and Mitchelstown Co-ops began the manufacture of chocolate crumb and, with Golden Vale (Charleville) and Dungarvan, began to manufacture milk powder. Mitchelstown and Golden Vale also began the production of cheese. The Ballyclough Creamery pioneered artificial insemination in cattle-breeding, 1946. A later development, the establishment of co-operative livestock marts, gradually replaced traditional fairs.

By 1961 the movement had 108,000 members, with a turnover of £65 million, rising to 222,0000 members and a turnover of £173 million by 1977. With Ireland's membership of the European Union a policy of rationalisation emerged: smaller co-ops were taken over by district co-operatives, which in turn were taken over by provincial groupings. The Kerry Group was one of a number of former co-ops that extended the scope of their operations to become commercial corporations. (See also PATRICK GALLAGHER and CANON JAMES MCDYER.)

Cope, Sir Alfred ('Andy') (1880–1954), civil servant and businessman. Following a career as a detective in the British Customs and Excise service and working at the Ministry of Pensions, 1919–20, he was Assistant Under-Secretary to SIR ROBERT ANDERSON at Dublin Castle during the WAR OF INDEPENDENCE. He worked closely with the Intelligence Unit in Dublin Castle while providing a constant stream of information on Irish affairs to the Prime Minister, DAVID LLOYD GEORGE, and the Colonial Office. He was closely involved in securing the TRUCE (July 1921) and was available to both delegations during the Treaty negotiations in London. After the ANGLO-IRISH TREATY (1921) he urged the Provisional Government to adopt an offensive strategy against the Republicans occupying the FOUR COURTS, Dublin. Following the assassination of GENERAL SIR HENRY WILSON, 22 June 1922, he secretly met ARTHUR GRIFFITH and EMMET DALTON; within days the Provisional Government forces attacked the Four Courts, marking the start of the CIVIL WAR. Cope helped oversee the dismantling of British institutions and the withdrawal of British forces from Ireland.

Córas na Poblachta, a radical republican party founded by members of the IRA, 21 February 1940. Members included Seán Dowling, Simon Donnelly, Seán Fitzpatrick, and Séamus Gibbons. Opposing measures pursued by the Fianna Fáil government against republican activists, it engaged in a crusade against the execution of Peter Barnes and James McCormack, suspected of involvement in the COVENTRY EXPLOSION. Failing to make an impact at a subsequent by-election, the party suffered a rapid decline; many members later joined the more widely based CLANN NA POBLACHTA in 1946.

Corish, Brendan (1918–1990), politician (Labour Party); born in Wexford, educated at the Christian Brothers' school. A clerk with Wexford County Council, in 1945 he succeeded his late father, Richard Corish, as a member of Dáil Éireann for Wexford. Labour Party whip, 1947–49, he was vice-chairman of the party, 1946–49, and chairman, 1949–53. Serving in both inter-party Governments, he was Parliamentary Secretary to the Minister for Local Government and to the Minister for Defence, 1948–51, and Minister for Social

Welfare, 1954–57. Succeeding WILLIAM NORTON as leader of the party, 1960, he made radical changes to its organisation, including affiliation to the Socialist International. Though previously opposed to the principle of coalition, he entered into a tactical arrangement before the 1973 general election when the National Coalition defeated Fianna Fáil. Corish was Tánaiste and Minister for Health and Minister for Social Welfare until 1977. Following the coalition's heavy defeat, June 1977, in which the Labour Party lost two seats, he resigned the leadership and was succeeded by FRANK CLUSKEY.

Cork Defence Union, formed 28 September 1885 at a meeting of landlords organised by A. H. SMITH-BARRY and Pasco Savage French. Smith-Barry, elected chairman, urged the attendance, which included Lord Doneraile and Lord Bandon, to 'stand shoulder to shoulder as the Land League did and . . . support each other when in trouble.' 'Non-sectarian and non-political,' the union was encouraged 'to unite together all friends of law and order of all classes in this country in a body for their mutual defence and protection.' The organisation became a legally constituted body on 25 October 1886 under its trustees Smith-Barry, French, James Penrose Fitzgerald, D. P. Sarsfield, and John H. Bainbridge. Opposed to home rule and the Irish National League and supported by the Chief Secretary for Ireland, ARTHUR J. BALFOUR, the union assisted materially and financially those landlords who became victims of either rent-strikers or boycotting and those whose estates were later involved in the PLAN OF CAMPAIGN.

Cork Examiner, a daily newspaper founded in 1841 by JOHN FRANCIS MAGUIRE and taken over by the Crosbie family during the 1870s. Its circulation was mainly confined to Munster. The publishers also issued the *Cork Evening Echo* and *Cork Weekly Examiner.* To help broaden its appeal it was renamed the *Examiner* in 1996 and *Irish Examiner* in 2000. Its Christmas Holly Bough supplement is especially popular with emigrants.

Cork Free Press, a newspaper founded as the *Cork Accent* by WILLIAM O'BRIEN, 1 January 1910, renamed *Cork Free Press* six months later. It was edited by FRANK GALLAGHER (later first editor of the IRISH PRESS). The paper went into decline when O'Brien endorsed the British war effort.

Cork Gunpowder Explosion, 3 November 1810. Twenty-two people lost their lives and more than forty were injured in an explosion at a labourer's home in Brandy Lane, Cork. Three houses were reduced to rubble and several others, badly damaged by the explosion, were demolished. An inquiry revealed that employees of the Ballincollig gunpowder works in the nine months preceding the accident had systematically stolen almost half a ton of gunpowder to sell to quarrymen. The illicit gunpowder had to be dried before resale; the inquiry revealed that the method chosen was to hold a lighted candle over it. On the night of the disaster at least one of the men involved in the operation was seen to be drinking heavily (he lost a leg in the explosion and subsequently died). A fund for the victims and their dependants received more than £12,000 in two weeks.

Corkery, Daniel (1878–1968), teacher and writer; born in Cork, educated at St Patrick's College, Dublin, where he trained as a national schoolteacher. Prominent in the Gaelic League and Sinn Féin, he taught at various schools in Co. Cork. He began his literary career by contributing to the LEADER, 1901. An active member of the Twenty Club, he was a founder-member of the Munster Fine Arts Society. With TERENCE MACSWINEY he founded the Cork Dramatic Society, 1908, for which he wrote plays. His pupils at St Patrick's School, 1912–21, included Michael O'Donovan (FRANK O'CONNOR) and Séamus Murphy (1907–1975).

Opposed to the ANGLO-IRISH TREATY (1921), he supported the anti-Treaty forces in the CIVIL WAR. From 1921 he taught art at various Cork schools and offered refresher courses in literature and drama to teachers. He was clerical assistant to the Co. Cork Inspector of Irish from 1923 until 1928. *The Hidden Ireland* (1924) was a seminal study of the fortunes of Irish culture in the eighteenth century. He was awarded an MA degree for his thesis on Synge and Anglo-Irish literature, 1931, appointed professor of English at UCC, 1931–47, and co-opted to the Arts Council, 1952. He was an accomplished artist whose work was exhibited by the Munster Fine Arts Society; his painting *The Fortunes of the Irish Language* was shown at the Victor Waddington Gallery, Dublin, 1954. His other publications include *A Munster Twilight* (short stories, 1916), *The Threshold of Quiet* (novel, 1917), *The Hounds of Banba* (short stories, 1920), and *The Wager and Other*

Stories (1950). Three of his plays were produced at the ABBEY THEATRE, Dublin: *The Labour Leader* (1919), *The Yellow Bittern* (1920), and *Fohnam the Sculptor* (1939).

Cornwallis, Charles, first Marquess and second Earl (1738–1805), soldier and politician; born in London. Following his surrender to Washington at Yorktown, Virginia, 19 October 1781, marking victory for the American rebels in the War of Independence, he became Governor-General of India and commander in chief of British forces there. He was appointed to Ireland as commander in chief and Lord Lieutenant to suppress the rising of the UNITED IRISHMEN, 1798. He crushed the rising and received the surrender of General Humbert in September. The British government conceded when he threatened to resign if pledges to supporters of the Union were not met. He left Ireland in May 1801, having joined WILLIAM PITT in resigning over the King's refusal to grant CATHOLIC EMANCIPATION.

Cosgrave, Liam (born 1920), politician (Fine Gael); born in Dublin, son of WILLIAM T. COSGRAVE, educated at Castleknock College and King's Inns. He served in the Defence Forces before his election to DÁIL ÉIREANN, 1943. Called to the bar, 1943, he became a senior counsel, 1958. Parliamentary Secretary to the Taoiseach and to the Minister for Industry and Commerce in the first inter-party Government, 1948–51, he was Minister for External Affairs in the second, 1954–57. Chairman of the Committee of Ministers of the Council of Europe, 1955, he was chairman of the first Irish delegation to the United Nations General Assembly, 1956.

Having lost to JAMES DILLON in the contest for leadership of Fine Gael in 1959, he succeeded him in 1965. He was chairman of the policy committee that produced the 'Just Society' policy in 1964. He played a crucial role in precipitating a crisis in Fianna Fáil in 1970 by informing the Taoiseach, JACK LYNCH, of plans to illegally import arms (see ARMS TRIALS). He was leader of the Irish parliamentary delegation to the Conference of the Inter-Parliamentary Union, Rome, and was elected vice-president of the IPU, 1972. He agreed a fourteen-point plan with the Labour Party, February 1973, as a basis for fighting the general election; crucial transfers between Fine Gael and the Labour Party brought them to power, despite an increase in the Fianna Fáil vote, and Cosgrave became Taoiseach, 1973–77.

Though he was a signatory of the SUNNINGDALE AGREEMENT (1973), Cosgrave opposed any changes to the Constitution of Ireland to facilitate relations with Northern Ireland. On 16 July 1974 he caused consternation when, without warning, he opposed the Contraception Bill introduced by his own Government.

Cosgrave's Government adopted a hard line with the IRA, and during this period there were widespread allegations of a 'HEAVY GANG' operating within the Garda Síochána. The Government suffered widespread condemnation when Cosgrave refused to accept an offer of resignation from the Minister for Defence, Patrick Donegan, who had criticised PRESIDENT CEARBHALL Ó DÁLAIGH (who resigned on 22 October 1976). Cosgrave's controversial speech to the Fine Gael ard-fheis, May 1977, with its reference to 'blow-ins' and 'mongrel foxes', with some of his targets sitting close to him, aroused deep resentment in the liberal wing of the party. When Fine Gael lost 11 of its 54 seats in the general election, 16 June 1977, Cosgrave resigned and was succeeded by DR GARRETT FITZGERALD.

Cosgrave, William T. (1880–1965), politician (Sinn Féin, Cumann na nGaedheal, and Fine Gael); born in Dublin, educated at Francis Street Christian Brothers' School and the O'Brien Institute. A Sinn Féin member of Dublin City Council, 1909, he was a member of the Irish Volunteers from 1913 and fought in the EASTER RISING (1916). His death sentence was commuted to penal servitude for life; he was released under general amnesty, December 1916. He was again interned in the 'GERMAN PLOT' arrests. Elected to the first Dáil Éireann, he was Minister for Local Government, April 1919 to September 1922. On 14 September 1921 he introduced a motion that ÉAMON DE VALERA lead the Irish delegation to London; he was later the only non-signatory in the Ministry (government) to accept the ANGLO-IRISH TREATY (1921).

Cosgrave succeeded ARTHUR GRIFFITH as President of the second Dáil Éireann and succeeded MICHAEL COLLINS as chairman of the Provisional Government. His home in Templeogue, Co. Dublin, was burned down by the anti-Treaty IRA, 13 January 1923, and valuable historical documents were destroyed. In 1923 he jointly founded the pro-Treaty party CUMANN NA NGAEDHEAL, of which he was leader until 1933. During the 1920s he led the government through several crises, including the ARMY MUTINY, the BOUNDARY COMMISSION, the resignations of three government ministers and eleven elected members of his party, and the assassination of his right-hand man, O'Higgins. His government restored law and order, stabilised the political process, and set about laying an industrial infrastructure and the extension of agriculture, particularly for the export market. In addition, Free State representatives made noteworthy contributions to the IMPERIAL CONFERENCES, particularly those of 1926 and 1931, when the STATUTE OF WESTMINSTER was secured. His governments dealt harshly with the IRA and also with radical social and political organisations. Attempts to deal with the depression in the wake of the Wall Street crash by reducing public expenditure were politically unpopular.

Cosgrave resisted urgings from militants within his party to compromise the handing over of power to the first Fianna Fáil government in 1932. Having presided over another defeat in 1933, he stood aside to allow EOIN O'DUFFY assume the presidency of Cumann na nGaedheal's successor, FINE GAEL, of which he became a joint vice-president; when O'Duffy fell from power, Cosgrave returned as leader in 1935. He held the office and was leader of the opposition to successive Fianna Fáil governments until his retirement in 1944. His son, LIAM COSGRAVE, was later leader of Fine Gael.

Costello, John A. (1891–1976), barrister and politician (Fine Gael); born in Dublin, educated at UCD and King's Inns and called to the bar. Involved in the DÁIL COURTS, 1919–21, assistant to the Law Officer of the Provisional Government, 1922, and to the Attorney-General, Hugh Kennedy, 1923–26, he was Attorney-General, 1926–32, in which capacity he was government adviser at the IMPERIAL CONFERENCES, 1926, 1928, and 1931, and in the League of Nations and advised the government in establishing legations in Washington, the Vatican, Berlin, and Paris. A leading counsel, 1932–48, he was elected to Dáil Éireann, 1933. He declared in the Dáil (2 February 1934) that the BLUESHIRTS would be victorious in Ireland, as the Blackshirts and Brownshirts were in Italy and Germany.

When Clann na Poblachta vetoed the appointment of the leader of Fine Gael, RICHARD MULCAHY, as Taoiseach, Costello became Taoiseach in the first inter-party Government, 1948–51. In a move that surprised national and international political circles he informed a press conference in Ottawa, 7 September 1948, that the EXTERNAL RELATIONS ACT (1936) would be repealed, bringing Ireland finally out of the British Commonwealth; this was done with the REPUBLIC OF IRELAND ACT (1949).

Costello was liberal in economic affairs: his government brought in the first capital budget in 1950, and he supported the Minister for Finance, PATRICK MCGILLIGAN, in adopting a Keynesian approach to public finances. Two controversial events dominated the government's term: the 'BATTLE OF BALTINGLASS' and the MOTHER AND CHILD SCHEME. As head of the second inter-party Government from 1954 he was faced with a renewal of IRA activity against Northern Ireland. His efforts to deal with the campaign provoked a motion of no confidence from the leader of Clann na Poblachta, SEÁN MACBRIDE, and Costello advised a dissolution of the Dáil, January 1957. He resumed his career at the bar and retired to the back benches in 1963. He supported his son, Declan Costello (born 1927), in the Fine Gael 'Just Society' policy, 1964. Elected to the Royal Irish Academy, 1948, he was the recipient of many honorary degrees. In March 1975, together with his old political adversary ÉAMON DE VALERA, he was made an honorary freeman of the city of Dublin.

Costello, Major-General M. J. [Michael Joseph] (1904–1986), soldier and businessman; born in Cloghjordan, Co. Tipperary; educated at Nenagh Christian Brothers' School. Following his father's internment during the War of Independence he joined the IRA. He supported the ANGLO-IRISH TREATY (1921) and joined the Free State army, receiving the rank of colonel during the CIVIL WAR and appointed Director of Intelligence, 1923. Following a military course in the United States he organised the Military College, 1926. He was later Assistant Chief of Staff and during the years of the Second World War was officer commanding the 1st Division. After retiring from the army, 1945, he became managing director of Comhlucht Siúcra Éireann, where he oversaw the introduction of worker participation, diversification into machinery and fertilisers, and experiments with food-growing on bogland. He was responsible for the establishment of Erin Foods Ltd, 1964. He bought a farm in Co. Roscommon and was vice-president of the MILITARY HISTORY SOCIETY OF IRELAND. His opposition to participation by the Defence

Forces in Remembrance Day celebrations organised by the British Legion led to the introduction of an annual National Day of Commemoration for all war dead.

Costello, Séamus (1939–1977), politician (Sinn Féin and Irish Republican Socialist Party); born in Bray, Co. Wicklow. Active in the IRA in south Derry during the 1950s, he was interned for two years at the Curragh Camp. He was elected to both Bray Urban District Council and Wicklow County Council, 1967. By 1968 his attempts to end Sinn Féin's traditional policy of abstention from Dáil Éireann had brought him into conflict with the IRA and Sinn Féin leadership. In a Co. Wicklow by-election, 1968, he secured 2,009 votes as an independent republican socialist. He remained within the Official IRA in the 1969–70 split, but his demand for continuation of the armed struggle in the North led to his expulsion from the Official IRA and Sinn Féin, 13 July 1974. He formed the Irish Republican Socialist Party, 8 December 1974, with a broad republican-socialist non-abstention policy; the IRISH NATIONAL LIBERATION ARMY (formerly called People's Liberation Army), of which he became chief of staff, became its military wing, April 1975. By January 1975 the Official IRA and Sinn Féin were believed to have lost about a third of their membership to Costello's party, leading to a bitter struggle between the organisations. Costello's failure to exert control over the Belfast IRSP led to divisions between the Dublin leadership and Belfast; his leadership of the INLA was successfully challenged by Belfast, and he was replaced by Eddy McNicholl. Murdered by an Official IRA gunman, Jimmy Flynn, on 5 October 1977, Costello was the first party leader in the history of the Republic to be murdered. His killer was subsequently murdered by INLA gunmen, 4 June 1982.

Cotter, Patrick (1760–1806), giant; born in Pallastown, near Kinsale, Co. Cork. He is believed to have been the tallest Irishman whose height was officially recorded, at 7 feet 11 inches (241 cm). A stonemason by trade, he worked on ceilings without a ladder, until in his early teens he was sold by his father to a showman for £50 and was exhibited in England under the name O'Brien. At the age of twenty-six he claimed a height of 8 feet 7¾ inches (264 cm). In his will he left £2,000 to his mother and a specific direction that his body not be used for medical research. When no hearse large enough to accommodate his coffin could be found, his remains were borne to the grave by relays of fourteen men. Following exhumation, Cotter, minus one arm (preserved in the Royal College of Surgeons, London), was later re-interred in the grounds of the Jesuit Chapel, Trenchard Street, Bristol.

cottier, a labourer whose rent for a cabin and small plot of land (between 1 and 1½ acres) was paid for in labour rather than money. The land was enough to maintain a family in potatoes and enabled the cottier to keep a cow, a pig, and some poultry. Additionally, he had the right to use COMMONAGE for the grazing of livestock and to cut turf from a neighbouring bog (see TURBARY RIGHT). The cottier existed at subsistence level, because of high rents driven by competition for land. Some of the more fortunate received a balance of money from the employer following the deduction of rent; others, in the absence of full-time employment, were forced to become migrant labourers (see SPALPEEN) to earn their rent.

An increase in population in the early decades of the nineteenth century exacerbated the cottier's position. The GREAT FAMINE (1845–49) devastated the cottier class, which had all but disappeared by the end of the century. The works of William Carleton, Arthur Young's *Tour in Ireland* (1777) and T. Campbell Foster's *Letters on the Condition of the People of Ireland* (1846) provide contemporary accounts of their lives. (See also CONACRE.)

Council of Europe. Ireland was one of the ten founding member-states of the Council of Europe, 5 May 1949, established

> to achieve a greater unity between its Members for the purpose of safeguarding and realising the ideals and principles which are their common heritage, and facilitating their economic and social progress . . . This aim shall be pursued through the organs of the Council by discussion of questions of common concern and by agreements and common action in economic, social, cultural, scientific, legal and administrative matters and in the maintenance and further realisation of human rights and fundamental freedoms.

Council of Ireland, provided for by the GOVERNMENT OF IRELAND ACT (1920) and intended as a forum for twenty representatives each from the northern and southern states to discuss matters of mutual concern. Nationalist and unionist interpretations of the council differed widely: nationalists viewed the forum as a mechanism leading to the eventual establishment of a united Irish state, while unionist perception was that of a united Ireland under the Crown. Following the agreement that shelved the BOUNDARY COMMISSION, December 1925, the powers of the council in relation to Northern Ireland were transferred to the Northern Ireland Government, and plans for the Council of Ireland were dropped. The idea was revived in the SUNNINGDALE AGREEMENT (1973) but discarded following widespread unionist opposition and the subsequent collapse of the power-sharing Executive led by BRIAN FAULKNER.

Council of State, established by the CONSTITUTION OF IRELAND (1937) 'to aid and counsel the President on all matters on which the President may consult the said Council in relation to the exercise and performance by him of such of his powers and functions as are by this Constitution expressed to be exercisable and performable after consultation with the Council of State . . .' The members *ex officio* are the TAOISEACH, TÁNAISTE, Chief Justice, President of the High Court, Ceann Comhairle, Cathaoirleach of Seanad Éireann, and Attorney-General; in addition it may also include any of those 'able and willing to act' who previously held the office of President, Taoiseach, or Chief Justice. The President may also appoint additional members, to a maximum of seven. Members of the Council of State hold office until the appointment of a new President. The President convenes meetings of the council 'at such times and places as he shall determine,' subject to article 32.

The Council of State met for the first time on 8 January 1940 at the request of PRESIDENT DOUGLAS HYDE, following which he referred the Offences Against the State (Amendment) Bill (1940) to the Supreme Court (which upheld its constitutionality).

Council of Three Hundred, first proposed by the NATION and later adopted by DANIEL O'CONNELL. He modelled the concept of a quasi-official legislature on existing English and Scottish procedures, which allowed the election to Parliament of specifically mandated delegates (300 had been the number of members of the Irish Parliament before the Union). The proposal was for the sixty Irish Party members of the British House of Commons to join with 240 others and form an independent Irish parliament under the Crown. The Prime Minister, LORD JOHN RUSSELL, warned the House of Commons, 28 July 1843, that O'Connell would succeed in evading the Convention Act (1793) and that the powers and functions of government would be wrested from the Lord Lieutenant of Ireland. The authorities responded by proscribing O'Connell's 'monster meeting' scheduled for Clontarf, Dublin, 8 October 1843, and imprisoning O'Connell and leading Young Irelanders for conspiracy. By the time of their release enthusiasm for the council had waned, and the proposal was not pursued. ARTHUR GRIFFITH received little support when he put forward a similar proposal.

Courts of Justice Act (1924). A Judiciary Committee under BARON GLENAVY was established by the Irish Free State to make recommendations on the transfer of the courts to Irish jurisdiction. Having studied the legal systems of Australia, New Zealand, Scotland and the United States and received submissions from a wide variety of legal, cultural, political and social interests, the committee submitted a report to the Executive Council (government), 17 May 1923. The resulting bill, moved in Dáil Éireann on 31 July 1923, was denied a second reading because of an intervening general election. It was moved in the new Dáil on 20 September but ran into difficulties in the Senate, which recommended forty-two amendments before passing it, 3 April 1923. The District Court, Circuit Court, High Court, Court of Criminal Appeal and Supreme Court replaced the County Court system; judges replaced justices of the peace and resident magistrates, and Petty Sessions were abolished. Each Circuit Court area comprised a population of approximately 400,000.

Coventry Explosion, 25 August 1939. The IRA, led by SEÁN RUSSELL, declared war on Britain, 16 January 1939. This took the form of a series of explosions, some 120 in all, during that year and culminated in the explosion at 2:30 p.m. at Astley's, Broadgate, Coventry, when a bomb placed on the carrier of a bicycle exploded, killing five people and injuring more than seventy. The incident caused outrage in both England and Ireland. The Fianna Fáil government, which had already introduced the TREASON ACT (1939) and OFFENCES AGAINST THE STATE ACT (1939), introduced the EMERGENCY POWERS (AMENDMENT) ACT (1940). On 24 July the Prevention of Violence (Temporary Provisions) Bill had its first reading in the House of Commons. Two men, Peter Barnes and James McCormack, alias Richards, were hanged in Birmingham Jail in connection with the explosion, 7 February 1940; while McCormack admitted guilt, Barnes strenuously protested his innocence, a stance that was widely supported, with ÉAMON DE VALERA making strong representations on the matter.

Cowper, Francis Thomas de Grey Cowper, seventh Earl (1834–1905), British politician (Liberal); born in London. Appointed Lord Lieutenant of Ireland, 1880, at the height of the LAND LEAGUE agitation, he had a difficult relationship with the Chief Secretary for Ireland, W. E. FORSTER, and considered resigning when he did not receive the full COERCION measures he felt the agitation warranted. Unhappy with the easy relationship between GLADSTONE and CHARLES STEWART PARNELL, Cowper resigned following the 'KILMAINHAM TREATY' and left Ireland on 4 May 1882. The killing of Lord Frederick Cavendish in the PHOENIX PARK MURDERS two days later led to the introduction of a tough coercion bill that he had drafted shortly before his resignation. Cowper later opposed home rule and was president of the Royal Commission on the LAND ACTS.

Cox, Pat (born 1952), academic, broadcaster, and politician (Progressive Democrats and independent); born in Dublin, educated at TCD. After working at the Institute of Public Administration and lecturing in the National Institute of Higher Education, Limerick, he was a reporter and presenter of the television current affairs series 'Prime Time', 1982–86. Originally a member of Fianna Fáil in Limerick, he left RTE to become first general secretary of the newly formed PROGRESSIVE DEMOCRATS, 1986–89. He headed the poll in elections to the European Parliament, 1989, and was elected to Dáil Éireann for Cork South-Central, 1992–94. Following the resignation of DESMOND O'MALLEY, 1993, Cox lost to MARY HARNEY as leader of the Progressive Democrats and was appointed deputy leader. However, the following year he refused to secede when O'Malley was nominated to contest the Munster seat in the European Parliament; he resigned, and retained the seat as an independent. In 1998 he became the first Irish person to lead a European political grouping when he was elected president of the European Liberal Democrats. He played a leading role in demanding accountability from the European Commission, presided over by Jacques Santer, whose presidency collapsed as a result of the campaign, and was elected President of the European Parliament, 15 January 2002.

Craig, William (born 1924), politician (Ulster Unionist Party and Vanguard). As a member of the Parliament of Northern Ireland he served under TERENCE O'NEILL as Minister of Home Affairs, Minister of Health, and Minister of Development. At Home Affairs he opposed concessions to the NORTHERN IRELAND CIVIL RIGHTS ASSOCIATION and restricted the demonstration in Derry on 5 October 1968; the violent scenes that ensued attracted world attention. Dismissed by O'Neill, 11 December 1968, he founded ULSTER VANGUARD, February 1972, and a year later its ineffectual political wing, the Vanguard Unionist Progressive Party. His leather-clad motorcycle escorts, open-top transport, mass rallies and emotive speeches led to charges of neo-fascism.

Craig was a member of the UNITED ULSTER UNIONIST COUNCIL and a leading figure in the loyalist strike that brought down the power-sharing Northern Ireland Executive, 1974. He caused a schism in the Vanguard movement when, supported by DAVID TRIMBLE, he suggested in 1975 that Unionists should enter a coalition with the SDLP to fill the post-Executive political vacuum. As a member of the Council of Europe, 1977, he was appointed to initiate research to update the European Convention on Human Rights. He lost his Belfast seat in 1979 and, following a poor showing in the 1982 Assembly elections, faded from the political scene.

Craigavon, James Craig, first Viscount (1871–1940), politician (Unionist); born in Strandstown, Belfast, son of a wealthy distiller. A stockbroker, he returned from England to establish his own firm, 1892, and was a founder-member of Belfast Stock Exchange. A captain in the British army during the Anglo-Boer War (1899–1902), he entered politics as Unionist MP for East Down, 1906, where he joined with a fellow-member of the Orange Order, SIR EDWARD CARSON, to oppose HOME RULE. A leader of the ULSTER UNIONIST COUNCIL from 1905 and ULSTER VOLUNTEER FORCE, 1913, he was a Unionist representative at the BUCKINGHAM PALACE CONFERENCE, July 1914. As Quartermaster-General of the 36th (Ulster) Division of the British army he saw action on the Western Front, 1914–15. Knighted in 1918, he served as Parliamentary Secretary to the Minister of Pensions, 1919–20, and Parliamentary and Financial Secretary to the Admiralty, 1920–21.

Having accepted the GOVERNMENT OF IRELAND ACT (1920) as the basis for the state of

Northern Ireland, on Carson's resignation he became leader of the Unionist Party and first Prime Minister of the new state, June 1921. A meeting with ÉAMON DE VALERA in Dublin, 5 May, demonstrated a lack of common ground. During the Treaty negotiations Craig insisted to the British Prime Minister, DAVID LLOYD GEORGE, that the position of Northern Ireland was not negotiable; Lloyd George kept Craig informed of all developments during the negotiations. To defuse continuing violence against Catholics in Northern Ireland, and to curb IRA actions against the new state and to end the BELFAST BOYCOTT, he twice met MICHAEL COLLINS in London (see CRAIG-COLLINS AGREEMENTS). He refused to nominate a Northern Ireland representative to the BOUNDARY COMMISSION, describing article 12 of the Treaty, under which it was established, as 'the root of all evil.' In December 1925 he attended a tripartite meeting that shelved the commission's report. He was created Viscount Craigavon in 1928.

To ensure that Northern Ireland would remain a unionist state, the abolition of proportional representation in 1929 established a Unionist majority in local government in areas where there was a Catholic majority. In 1932 Craig declared, 'Ours is a Protestant government and I am an Orangeman,' and 'I have always said that I am an Orangeman first and a politician and a member of this parliament afterwards.' He reacted to the adoption of the CONSTITUTION OF IRELAND (1937) by calling a snap election, 1938, in which partition was the main issue and which resulted in an overwhelming victory for the Unionists. Though opposed by Sir Basil Brooke (see VISCOUNT BROOKEBOROUGH) and JOHN MILLER ANDREWS, he supported the ANGLO-IRISH AGREEMENTS (1938), in return for which Northern Ireland was rewarded with armaments contracts. When de Valera suggested, October 1938, that the time had come to consider an all-Ireland parliament, to be elected by proportional representation, Craig replied, 'I can only reiterate the old battle-cry—"No surrender".' On retiring from office in 1940, Craigavon was succeeded by John Miller Andrews.

Craig-Collins Agreements (21 January and 30 March 1922), made between MICHAEL COLLINS, Chairman of the Provisional Government, and Sir James Craig (see VISCOUNT CRAIGAVON), Prime Minister of Northern Ireland. They met in response to demands to end pogroms directed against the Catholic population in the North, retaliatory attacks by the IRA, and the BELFAST BOYCOTT in the South. Through the offices of WINSTON CHURCHILL they met in London.

The first agreement (21 January 1922) promised the reinstatement of Catholics in their jobs (some ten thousand had been dismissed in the pogrom), in return for an end to the boycott and the appointment of a subcommittee to examine proposals for an agreement on the boundary between the two states. In the event, the agreement proved fruitless: Catholics were not restored to their jobs, and Craig stated, 28 March, that he would not accept the verdict of the Boundary Commission should it prove unfavourable to Northern Ireland. Militant republicans continued the Belfast Boycott.

The two leaders met again, with Churchill also present, as a result of which a more comprehensive agreement was signed, and counter-signed by the British Government, 30 March. It began by stating that 'Peace is to-day declared' and continued: 'From today, the two governments undertake to co-operate in every way in their power with a view to the restoration of peaceful conditions in the unsettled areas.' There was agreement on a Catholic-Protestant police force, and on a joint nationalist and loyalist committee to investigate charges of intimidation and outrage. The agreement called for a cessation of IRA activity in Northern Ireland (something over which Collins had very little control). There would be a further meeting between the signatories to establish whether a means could be devised of securing the unity of Ireland and, in the absence of such an agreement, whether the boundary question could be settled without recourse to the Boundary Commission. The Northern and Free State governments undertook to arrange the release of political prisoners imprisoned for acts committed before 31 March 1922. The agreement concluded: 'The two governments unite in appealing to all concerned to refrain from inflammatory speeches and to exercise restraint in the interests of peace.'

Both agreements remained inconclusive, as none of the main terms were implemented. Catholics in the Northern state remained victims of institutional discrimination, while IRA attacks on Northern Ireland, both from internal and cross-border bases, continued unabated.

Crawford, Lieutenant-Colonel Frederick (1861–1952), soldier and Unionist; born in Belfast, where his father owned a chemical factory; educated at University College, London.

While an apprentice engineer at Harland and Wolff's shipyard in Belfast he was awarded the Bronze Medal of the Royal Humane Society for his involvement in saving workers from drowning, December 1891. He founded YOUNG ULSTER, 1892, membership of which was conditional on the possession of a specified firearm. Holding a commission in the Mid-Ulster Artillery, 1894, and a captaincy in the Donegal Artillery, 1898, he was mentioned in despatches during the Anglo-Boer War (1899–1902).

Crawford's proposal to kidnap W. E. GLADSTONE (because of his sympathy for home rule) and hold him indefinitely on an isolated Pacific island was abandoned for want of £10,000 with which to finance the adventure. He was a founder-member of the ULSTER VOLUNTEER FORCE, 1913. In 1914 he was commissioned by the ULSTER UNIONIST COUNCIL to buy the guns for the LARNE GUN-RUNNING. When the state of Northern Ireland was formed, 1921, Crawford unsuccessfully sought legal status for the UVF. He was appointed commandant of the new Special Constabulary in South Belfast, 1921.

Crawford, Robert Lindsay (1868–1945), journalist; born in Lisburn, Co. Antrim; educated privately. A journalist in Dublin, he was founder-editor of the *Irish Protestant* (1901–06) and Grand Master of the INDEPENDENT ORANGE ORDER, through which he attempted to bridge the sectarian divide. In the 'MAGHERAMORNE MANIFESTO' (1905), an attempt to form a political party out of the Independent Orange Order, he attacked the ULSTER UNIONIST COUNCIL and called on Orangemen to befriend their fellow-countrymen, regardless of creed. This led to his expulsion in 1906. He supported home rule. Returning to Ulster, November 1906, he edited the *Ulster Guardian,* 1908, weekly organ of the Ulster Liberal Association, but was forced to resign after he attacked poor working conditions in the linen industry. In Canada from May 1910, he worked on the *Toronto Globe.* It returned him to Ireland in 1914.

After the Great War, Crawford founded his own journal, the *Statesman,* for Protestant supporters of Irish independence. He was president of the Self-Determination for Ireland Leagues of Canada and Newfoundland. An Irish-language enthusiast, he performed the opening ceremony of the Tipperary Feis at Nenagh, July 1909. Retiring from journalism in 1922, he became the Irish Free State trade representative in New York.

Crawford, William Sharman (1781–1861), politician (Liberal); born William Sharman in Co. Down, where, despite ownership of extensive estates, he supported TENANT RIGHT. In 1805 he added his wife's surname, Crawford, to his own. Member of Parliament for Dundalk, 1835, he supported CATHOLIC EMANCIPATION but differed with DANIEL O'CONNELL on TITHES and on Repeal (see REPEAL ASSOCIATION). He argued that O'Connell had compromised on the tithes issue to preserve his alliance with the Whigs. He supported a federal solution to Repeal, with an Irish parliament legislating exclusively on Irish affairs. Losing his Dundalk seat as a result of his opposition to Repeal, he was elected for Rochdale, Lancashire, 1841–52, and continued to support agrarian reform, forming the ULSTER TENANT RIGHT ASSOCIATION, 1846. He was defeated when he stood for Parliament in Co. Down, 1852, largely because of his identification with tenant right in the south of Ireland.

credit union movement. Based on the principles behind the nineteenth-century co-operative movement, the credit union movement in Ireland arose out of initiatives taken by Seán Forde, Nora Herlihy and Seán P. Mac Eoin in December 1953. A paper read by Mac Eoin led to the establishment of the Dublin Central Co-Op Society, 6 March 1954, which formed an investment bank. Mac Eoin, Herlihy and Forde established the Credit Union Extension Service in 1957 to examine the creation of a system of low-cost credit for urban and rural workers. In 1958 there were two credit unions, on the South Circular Road in Dublin and in Dún Laoghaire. The Credit Union League of Ireland (later renamed the Irish League of Credit Unions) was founded on 7 February 1960. Credit unions are now regulated by the Credit Union Act (1966). JOHN HUME, later second president of the league, played a leading role in establishing the movement in Northern Ireland. In 2002 there were 540 affiliates in Ireland, with a total membership of 2.2 million and deposits of €6.6 billion.

Crime and Outrage (Ireland) Act (1847), adopted on 20 December 1847 in an attempt to stem the tide of violent agrarian discontent (sixteen landlords had been killed in a period of twelve months). It gave widespread discretionary powers to the authorities, empowering the Lord Lieutenant to draft police into a district, the costs of which were immediately payable by the district concerned. Arms could be borne only by those already licensed or holding official positions, including justices of the peace and military officers; gamekeepers were allowed a weapon, and householders might keep firearms within the house for protection. Where a murder had been committed, all males between the ages of sixteen and sixty were liable to be called on to assist in finding the perpetrators; failure to assist was punishable by two years' imprisonment. To reinforce the legislation, thirty-three districts were proclaimed and five thousand soldiers deployed between Arklow, Clonmel, and Limerick. (See also AGRARIAN CRIME.)

Criminal Law Amendment Act (1935), an act to prohibit the importing or sale of 'any appliance, instrument, drug, preparation or thing, designed, prepared or intended to prevent pregnancy resulting from sexual intercourse between human beings.' (See MCGEE CASE.)

Croke, T. W. [Thomas William] (1824–1902), bishop (Catholic); born in Ballyclough, Co. Cork, educated at the Irish Colleges in Paris and Rome. Having ministered at Cloyne, Co. Cork, 1849–58, and taught at St Colman's College, Fermoy (where he was president, 1858–65), he was parish priest of Doneraile, Co. Cork, 1865–70. Theological adviser to the Bishop of Cloyne at the First Vatican Council (1870) while Bishop of Auckland, New Zealand, he was translated to the archdiocese of Cashel, 1875. He became a national figure, involving himself in land agitation, the LAND LEAGUE, the GAELIC ATHLETIC ASSOCIATION, and the GAELIC LEAGUE. When the Vatican condemned the PLAN OF CAMPAIGN he devised a formula that allowed it to continue. He was the author of the 'No Tax' Manifesto. A staunch supporter of home rule, he supported CHARLES STEWART PARNELL until the O'Shea divorce case, 1890, after which his influence was a significant factor in the replacement of Parnell by JUSTIN MCCARTHY as leader of the IRISH PARTY. A lifelong opponent of intemperance, he established temperance branches throughout his archdiocese. Widely known as 'Croke of Cashel' and first patron of the GAA, 1884, he is commemorated by Croke Park, Dublin, principal stadium and head office of the GAA.

Croker, T. Crofton (1798–1854), folklorist and antiquarian; born in Cork, educated locally to the age of fifteen, when he was apprenticed to a mercantile firm. As a teenager he walked around south Munster (though with little knowledge of Irish), sketching and absorbing the traditions of the countryside. He was an accomplished painter and illustrator, and his sketches enhance many of his works. Following the death of his father he moved to London to work as a clerk in the Admiralty, 1818–50. He made frequent visits to the south-west of Ireland, where he devoted himself to the collection of poetry and folklore, sometimes with his wife, Marianne (née Nicholson). Instrumental in the founding of the Camden Society, 1839, and Percy Society, 1840, he was also a founder-member of the British Archaeological Association, 1843. Yeats said of Croker's work that it was 'touched everywhere with beauty—a gentle Arcadian beauty.' His most popular work, *Fairy Legends and Traditions of the South of Ireland* (1825), was translated to German by the Brothers Grimm. He also edited *The Popular Songs of Ireland* (1839) and *The Historical Songs of Ireland* (1841).

Crone, John Smyth (1858–1945), physician and author; born in Belfast, educated at QUB, where he qualified as a doctor. He established a medical practice at Willesden, London, where he worked for forty years and was Deputy Coroner from 1917. Founder of the *Irish Book Lover,* 1909, he remained editor until 1924. A member of the Royal Irish Academy from 1917, he was president of the IRISH LITERARY SOCIETY, 1918–20. He was a lifelong friend of FRANCIS JOSEPH BIGGER, and their combined libraries were donated to Belfast Public Library; he wrote a biography of Bigger, *In Remembrance* (1927). *A Concise Dictionary of Irish Biography* (1928) remained a standard work until superseded by *A Dictionary of Irish Biography* (1978) by Henry Boylan.

Crowley, Peter O'Neill (1832–1867). Fenian; born in Ballymacoda, Co. Cork. A farmer, he led a successful raid on Knockadoon coastguard station during the Fenian rising in 1867. He was on the run for several weeks with Captain McClure and Edward Kelly. On Sunday 31 March soldiers surrounded their hiding place in Kilcloney Wood, Co. Tipperary. Concealment was difficult, as the woods had recently been thinned. Wounded in the engagement, Crowley died in Mitchelstown, Co. Cork, where his wounds were being attended to.

Crozier, Brigadier-General Frank Percy (1879–1937), British soldier. A veteran of the Anglo-Boer Wars, he retired in 1908. He trained the ULSTER VOLUNTEER FORCE and served during the First World War, becoming officer commanding the 40th Division in France, March–April 1919. He saw action in the Lithuanian army and the Polish army against Soviet Russia, 1919–20, before returning to Ireland as commandant of the AUXILIARIES, August 1920 to February 1921; he became a centre of controversy when he resigned the post in February 1921. Ignoring an instruction from MAJOR-GENERAL SIR HUGH TUDOR, Chief of Police in Ireland, not to dismiss Auxiliaries for indiscipline, he dismissed five and suspended twenty-one for looting in Trim, Co. Meath, and the murder of two young men in Drumcondra, Dublin. According to Crozier, those disciplined threatened to reveal the truth about the burning of Cork, 11 December 1920 (see WAR OF INDEPENDENCE), and were reinstated by Tudor. Crozier's resignation drew world attention to the indiscipline of the Auxiliaries and the BLACK AND TANS. He published *A Brass Hat in No Man's Land* (1930), *Impressions and Recollections* (1930), *Ireland for Ever* (1932), and *The Men I Killed* (1937).

Cruise O'Brien, Dr Conor (born 1917), civil servant, historian, writer, politician (Labour Party), and polemicist; born in Dublin, a grandson of DAVID SHEEHY, nephew of REV. EUGENE SHEEHY, and cousin of Owen Sheehy-Skeffington; educated at TCD. A civil servant in the Department of Finance, 1944, he moved to External Affairs, where he was managing editor of the IRISH NEWS AGENCY and formed a friendship with the Minister for External Affairs, SEÁN MACBRIDE. Posted to Paris as a counsellor in 1955, he returned a year later to head the new United Nations Section of the department, 1956. In 1960 he became Assistant Secretary and head of the Political Information Section. He represented the UN Secretary-General in Katanga (a breakaway province of the Belgian Congo) in 1961. Resigning from the United Nations and the Irish service, he was vice-chancellor of the University of Ghana, 1962–65. He was Albert Schweitzer professor of humanities at New York University, 1965–69, from which post he resigned to return to Ireland.

A member of a group of intellectuals who joined the Labour Party at the end of the 1960s, Cruise O'Brien was elected to Dáil Éireann in 1969. Appointed a member of the European Parliament, 1972, he resigned, 1 June 1973, to enter the Government as Minister for Posts and Telegraphs, 1973–77. During this period he was a leading critic of the IRA and of what he claimed was national ambiguity in relation to Northern Ireland. After losing his seat in 1977 he was a member of Seanad Éireann, 1977–79. He was editor in chief of the *Observer* (London), 1978–81. In the 1990s he declared himself a unionist, becoming a representative of the UNITED KINGDOM UNIONIST PARTY until resigning on 27 October 1998 'in the interests of the party and of my own freedom as a writer.' This followed the publication on 25 October 1998 of excerpts from his forthcoming *Memoir: My Life and Themes* in which he hypothesised that 'in certain future circumstances the preferred option [for Northern Unionists] might be a negotiated united Ireland.' Among his many publications are *Parnell and His Party* (1957), *To Katanga and Back* (1962), and *States of Ireland* (1972).

'Cuba Five', five Fenians released from imprisonment in England who arrived in New York, January 1871, aboard the steamship *Cuba*: JOHN DEVOY, John McClure, Henry Mulleda, CHARLES UNDERWOOD O'CONNELL, and JEREMIAH O'DONOVAN ROSSA. Greeted by a tumultuous reception from New York's Irish population, they were later joined by a further nine released Fenians, who arrived on board the *Russia*. Granted a resolution of welcome by the House of Representatives, the fourteen were presented to President Grant at the White House, 22 February.

Cullen, Paul (1803–1878), Archbishop of Dublin and the first Irish cardinal; born in Ballitore, Co. Kildare, educated at Quaker School (Ballitore), Carlow College, and Urban College of the Propaganda, Rome. Ordained in 1829; as rector of the Irish College, Rome, 1832–49, he represented the views of the Irish hierarchy and worked to counter British influence at the Vatican. Appointed Archbishop of Armagh, 1849, he convened the SYNOD OF THURLES (1850), the first national synod for eight hundred years. On translation to Dublin, 1852, he embarked on an ambitious church-building scheme and attempted to counter the interdenominational education provided by the QUEEN'S COLLEGES by establishing the CATHOLIC UNIVERSITY OF IRELAND under JOHN HENRY NEWMAN. Though he had helped FREDERICK LUCAS to win the Co. Meath seat, 1852, Cullen opposed the INDEPENDENT IRISH PARTY, ordering his clergy to abstain from partisan politics except where specific Catholic interests were involved. He promoted an Irish Brigade to defend the Papal States against Garibaldi, 1859. He founded Holy Cross College (Clonliffe Road) as the Dublin diocesan seminary, 1859. As opposed to the FENIANS as he had been to YOUNG IRELAND, in 1861 he forbade the use of the Pro-Cathedral, Dublin, for the lying in state of TERENCE BELLEW MCMANUS. He attempted to channel nationalism to his own ends by founding the NATIONAL ASSOCIATION, 1864, to secure DISESTABLISHMENT of the Church of Ireland; he also established the *Irish Ecclesiastical Record,* 1864. At the First Vatican Council, 1870, he was a leading figure in defining the dogma of Papal infallibility. He presided over the Synod of Maynooth (1875) and left an indelible mark on the organisational structures of the Catholic Church in Ireland. Cullen's nephew Patrick Francis Moran (1830–1911) was Bishop of Ossory, 1872–84, Archbishop of Sydney, 1884–1911, and also a cardinal.

Cumann Gaodhalach na hEaglaise, founded 1914 by Church of Ireland clergymen to give expression to 'all those aspirations for a more intense and real national character in the church.' Within four years it had 140 members, held services in Irish, sponsored lectures on Irish religious literature, and published a hymnal in Irish. In June 1916 it passed a resolution condemning the EASTER RISING (1916) and affirming loyalty to the King; the resolution was rescinded in 1918, following which the Executive founded Comhluadar Gaodhalach na Fiadhnuise, consisting of many former members of the association.

Cumann na mBan, launched in Wynne's Hotel, Dublin, April 1914; those present, under the chairmanship of Agnes O'Farrelly, included CONSTANCE MARKIEVICZ, KATHLEEN CLARKE, Áine Ceannt (widow of ÉAMONN CEANNT), Louise Duffy, Mrs Thomas Kettle, Mrs Eoin MacNeill, LILY O'BRENNAN, and Nannie O'Rahilly (widow of MICHAEL O'RAHILLY). Its first branch, the Central Branch, rented rooms from the Gaelic League in Parnell Square, Dublin. It lost some members in November 1914 when it declared support for the IRISH VOLUNTEERS. By 1916 it had forty-three affiliated branches. It supported the EASTER RISING (1916), during which members acted as nurses and despatch-carriers and in other supporting roles; Nurse Elizabeth O'Farrell delivered the surrender document issued by PATRICK PEARSE.

In its constitution following the rising the association declared itself 'an independent body of Irish women, pledged to work for the establishment of an Irish republic, by organising and training the women of Ireland to take their places by the side of those who are working for a free Ireland.' It continued to work for the republican movement during the WAR OF INDEPENDENCE. A majority of members rejected the ANGLO-IRISH TREATY (1921), and many were imprisoned during the CIVIL WAR. During the 1920s Cumann na mBan, led by MAUD GONNE, supported the IRA and was associated with some of the radical movements of the period.

Cumann na nGaedheal (1900–07), founded 30 September 1900 by ARTHUR GRIFFITH and WILLIAM ROONEY as a co-ordinating body for smaller societies whose aim was to oppose English influences in Ireland. Its aims, promulgated through Griffith's UNITED IRISHMAN, were to diffuse knowledge of Ireland's economic resources and culture and to encourage and support Irish industry. Griffith was elected president; vice-presidents included THOMAS J. CLARKE (then in the United States), JOHN DALY, MAUD GONNE, JOHN MACBRIDE, JOHN O'LEARY, and Rooney. Griffith urged the Cumann na nGaedheal convention in 1902 to demand the withdrawal of the IRISH PARTY from the British House of Commons. A year later the Executive constituted itself the NATIONAL COUNCIL to lead the protest against the visit of King Edward VII. Cumann na nGaedheal was later absorbed into SINN FÉIN. In 1923 WILLIAM T. COSGRAVE used the name for a new political party formed by those who accepted the ANGLO-IRISH TREATY (1921).

Cumann na nGaedheal (1923–33), a political party launched in April 1923 in the Mansion House, Dublin; it drew its members almost exclusively from supporters of the ANGLO-IRISH TREATY (1921). Identified with commercial and large farming interests, it was strongest in the midlands and east. Led by WILLIAM T. COSGRAVE, it enjoyed majority Catholic hierarchical support and received sympathetic coverage from the *Cork Examiner, Irish Independent,* and *Irish Times.* It won sixty-three seats in Dáil Éireann with 39 per cent of the vote in August 1923. As republicans did not enter Dáil Éireann until 1927, when FIANNA FÁIL broke with its policy of abstention, Cumann na nGaedheal formed the governments of the Irish Free State until 1932; in 1933 it merged with the NATIONAL CENTRE PARTY and the BLUESHIRTS to form FINE GAEL. The party's share of first-preference votes and seats was:

	First-preference votes	Seats
1923	38.5%	63
1927 (June)	39%	47
1927 (Sept.)	38.7%	62
1932	35.3%	57
1933	30.5%	48

For governments formed by the party see GOVERNMENTS; for details on the party in power see PUBLIC SAFETY ACTS; IRISH REPUBLICAN ARMY; CIVIL WAR; ARMY MUTINY; BOUNDARY COMMISSION; LAND ACTS; AGRICULTURAL CREDIT CORPORATION; KEVIN O'HIGGINS; ELECTORAL AMENDMENT ACT (1927); JINKS AFFAIR; SHANNON SCHEME; LAND ANNUITIES; ULTIMATE FINANCIAL AGREEMENT; ARMY COMRADES' ASSOCIATION; BLUESHIRTS.

Cumann na Poblachta, a political party founded by ÉAMON DE VALERA, March 1922, supported principally by opponents of the ANGLO-IRISH TREATY (1921). Following the defeat of the Republicans in the CIVIL WAR the party was absorbed into SINN FÉIN. A majority of former members joined de Valera in FIANNA FÁIL, May 1926.

Cumann Poblachta na hÉireann, founded by SEÁN MACBRIDE, 1936, to provide a political platform for republicans opposed to the REPUBLICAN CONGRESS. It received relatively little support from the IRA and disappeared following its first ard-fheis, November 1936.

Curragh Incident (1914), sometimes known as the Curragh Mutiny, an event that occurred in March 1914, before the enactment of the (third) Home Rule Bill, a measure strongly opposed by Ulster Unionists. The War Office instructed GENERAL SIR ARTHUR PAGET to prepare plans for the protection of arms depots in Ulster, 14 March 1914. He was informed that while officers who lived in Ulster would not be asked to act in the province, all others would be required to carry out their orders or face dismissal. BRIGADIER-GENERAL SIR HUBERT GOUGH, officer commanding the 3rd Cavalry Brigade, chaired a meeting of fifty-six officers at the Curragh Camp, 20 March. Their decision was telegraphed to the War Office, 21 March, by Paget:

> Officer commanding 5th Lancers states that all officers except two, and one doubtful, are resigning their commissions today. I fear same conditions in the 16th Lancers. Fear men will refuse to move.

Later that evening he reported:

> Regret to report Brigadier and fifty-seven Officers 3rd Cavalry Brigade, prefer to accept dismissal if ordered north.

Gough led a deputation to London, where they were sympathetically received by GENERAL SIR HENRY WILSON, Director of Military Operations. The British Government, faced with a situation tantamount to mutiny, prevaricated. Through the Army Council, Gough was authorised, 23 March, to inform the officers that the incident of the 'resignations' had been a misunderstanding. In an interview with the *Daily Telegraph* he stated that he had received a signed guarantee that in no circumstances would he or his officers be sent to enforce home rule in Ulster; if the issue had to be resolved in open conflict, he would rather fight for Ulster than against it.

The affair culminated in the resignation of the Chief of the Imperial Staff, FIELD-MARSHAL SIR JOHN FRENCH, the Adjutant-General, Sir Spencer Ewart, and the Secretary of State for War, Colonel John Seely.

Curran, Sarah (1782–1808), fiancée of ROBERT EMMET. Her father, the lawyer John Philpot Curran (1750–1817), was outraged at her engagement, and his behaviour led to her fleeing the family home in Dublin for Cork, where, with her sister, she lived with the Penrose family. Curran, who defended many of the insurgents of 1803, ignored her pleas for him to defend Emmet. Her marriage to Captain R. H. Sturgeon, a nephew of Lord Rockingham, 1805, failed to lift the melancholia from which she suffered following Emmet's execution, and she died shortly after taking up residence in Hythe, Kent, 5 May. In deference to her wishes her husband had her body returned for burial to the family seat in Newmarket, Co. Cork. A slab of Sicilian marble intended for her tombstone never reached its destination because of misdelivery to Newberry, Mallow. The citizens of Newmarket subscribed for the erection of a stone cross over her grave.

Sarah Curran's tragic romance features in Washington Irving's 'The Broken Heart' (1820) and in Thomas Moore's poem 'She Is Far from the Land' (1834).

Currency Commission, created in 1927 as a statutory non-political institution, in effect the central bank of the Irish Free State. (See also PARKER-WILLIS COMMISSION.)

Cusack, Michael (1847–1906), joint founder of the GAELIC ATHLETIC ASSOCIATION; born in

Carron, Co. Clare. A tutor to the family of Lord Gough, he spent some years in the United States and later taught at Newry and at Blackrock College and Clongowes Wood College. He prospered from the establishment of a grind school, the Civil Service Academy. Attached to the school was the Civil Service Academy Hurling Club, which led to his founding, with MAURICE DAVIN, the Gaelic Athletic Association, 1884. On his death the *Gaelic Journal* commented that he 'was the living embodiment of the GAA.' Cusack was the model for 'the Citizen' in James Joyce's *Ulysses* (1922).

Cushnahan, John (born 1948), politician (Alliance Party); born in Belfast; educated at St Joseph's College of Education and QUB. General secretary of the ALLIANCE PARTY, 1974–82, and chief whip, 1982–84, he became leader of the party in 1984, having been a member of Belfast City Council, 1977–85. He was a member and chairperson of the Education Committee of the Northern Ireland Assembly, 1982–86. Following the collapse of the Assembly he resigned the leadership of the Alliance Party and moved to the Republic, where he won a seat for Fine Gael in the European Parliament election, 1989, and was returned in the Munster constituency in subsequent elections.

Custom House, Dublin, designed by James Gandon (1742–1823). Its destruction during the WAR OF INDEPENDENCE was planned by OSCAR TRAYNOR, officer commanding the Dublin Brigade of the IRA, at the suggestion of ÉAMON DE VALERA. The plan was opposed by MICHAEL COLLINS, but de Valera contended that the loss of public records would seriously compromise the working of the civil service and concentrate international attention on the WAR OF INDEPENDENCE. Several hundred members of the IRA were engaged in the operation, during which the building was surrounded by the BLACK AND TANS. In the ensuing gun-battle five IRA volunteers were killed and some eighty wounded; casualties to Crown forces were not revealed. The interior of the building was gutted by a fire that burned for eight days. The Custom House was faithfully restored and later became the offices of the Department of Local Government (now Department of the Environment and Local Government).

D

Dáil Courts (often called 'Sinn Féin Courts'), established during the War of Independence to replace the existing courts of law. In June 1920 they came under the authority of the Minister for Home Affairs, AUSTIN STACK. The justice administered by the Dáil Courts was based on the law as it stood on 2 January 1919. Their decrees were enforced by police provided by the IRA.

There were four types of court: parish, district and circuit courts (special sessions of the district court held thrice yearly and presided over by a circuit judge), and a Supreme Court. Attempts to suppress the courts were unsuccessful, but they were forced to operate underground. In the immediate aftermath of the Truce (July 1921) the Dáil Courts operated less secretly.

On the establishment of the Irish Free State, 1922, a new courts system was established under the COURTS OF JUSTICE ACT (1924), in which Dáil court precedents were generally accepted.

Dáil Éireann (21 January 1919 to 5 December 1922). Dáil Éireann first assembled on 21 January 1919, attended by Sinn Féin representatives returned at the general election of December 1918. Twenty-seven Sinn Féin members were present; thirty-four had been imprisoned before the election, eight were unable to attend, and CATHAL BRUGHA deputised as President for the imprisoned ÉAMON DE VALERA. Members approved the Constitution of Dáil Éireann, the Declaration of Independence, the DEMOCRATIC PROGRAMME, and a Message to the Free Nations of the World. The Constitution of Dáil Éireann, as amended on 25 August 1921, was as follows:

The Constitution of Dáil Éireann

Article 1.
All legislative powers shall be vested in Dáil Éireann, composed of Deputies, elected by the Irish people from the existing parliamentary constituencies.

Article 2.
(*a*) All executive powers shall be vested in the members, for the time being, of the Ministry.
(*b*) The Ministry shall consist of a President of the Ministry, elected by Dáil Éireann, and four Executive Officers, viz: a Secretary of Finance, A Secretary of Home Affairs, A

Secretary of Foreign Affairs, A Secretary of National Defence, each of whom the President shall nominate and have power to dismiss.
(*c*) Every member of the Ministry shall be a member of Dáil Éireann, and shall at all times be responsible to the Dáil.
(*d*) At the first meeting of Dáil Éireann after their nomination by the President, the names of the Executive Officers shall be separately submitted to Dáil Éireann for approval.
(*e*) The appointment of the President shall date from his election, and the appointment of each Executive officer from the date of the approval by the Dáil of his nomination.
(*f*) The Ministry or any members, therefore, may at any time, be removed by the vote of the Dáil upon motion for that specific purpose, provided that at least seven days' notice in writing of that motion shall have been given.

Article 3.
A Chairman elected annually by the Dáil, or in his absence a Deputy Chairman so elected, shall preside at the meetings of Dáil Éireann. Only members of the Dáil shall be eligible for these offices. In the case of the absence of the Chairman and Deputy Chairman the Dáil shall fill the vacancies or elect a temporary Chairman.

Article 4.
All monies required by the Ministry shall be obtained on vote of the Dáil. The Ministry shall be responsible to the Dáil for all monies so obtained, and shall present properly audited accounts for the expenditure of same—twice yearly—in the months of May and November.

The Audit shall be conducted by an Auditor or Auditors appointed by the Dáil. No member of the Dáil shall be eligible for such appointment.

Article 5.
This Constitution is provisional and is liable to alteration upon seven days' notice of motion for that specific purpose.

The first Ministry consisted of Cathal Brugha (President), EOIN MACNEILL (Finance), MICHAEL COLLINS (Home Affairs), and COUNT PLUNKETT (National Defence).

The second session of the first Dáil was held on 1 April 1919, when de Valera was elected President. His Ministry was: Michael Collins (Finance), Cathal Brugha (Defence), ARTHUR GRIFFITH (Home Affairs), Count Plunkett (Foreign Affairs), WILLIAM T. COSGRAVE (Local Government), CONSTANCE MARKIEVICZ (Labour), Eoin MacNeill (Industries), ERNEST BLYTHE (Trades and Commerce), and SEÁN T. O'KELLY (Irish), from June 1920. Other ministers were Seán Etchingham (Fisheries), ROBERT BARTON (Agriculture), and LAWRENCE GINNELL (Publicity).

On 20 August, on the proposal of Brugha, seconded by TERENCE MACSWINEY, it was agreed that every deputy and officer, the clerk of the Dáil and every member of the Irish Volunteers should swear allegiance to the Dáil:

> I, [. . .], do solemnly swear (or affirm) that I do not and shall not yield a voluntary support to any pretended government authority or power within Ireland hostile and inimical thereto, and I do further swear (or affirm) that to the best of my knowledge and ability I will support and defend the Irish Republic and the Government of the Irish Republic, which is Dáil Éireann, against all enemies, foreign and domestic, and I will bear true faith and allegiance to the same, and that I take this obligation freely without any mental reservation or purpose of evasion, so help me God.

The oath made the Irish Volunteers the *de facto* army of the Irish Republic or, as it came to be called, the IRISH REPUBLICAN ARMY.

On 10 September 1919 Dáil Éireann was declared a dangerous association and prohibited. Thereafter its meetings were in secret. The first Dáil established ARBITRATION COURTS for resolving agrarian disputes. A Consular Service was also established, and funds were allocated for afforestation and fisheries. A National Commission of Inquiry into the Industrial Resources of Ireland was appointed; under the aegis of the Minister for Agriculture, Land Banks were established to advance funds to farmers. A committee was appointed to draft the Constitution and Rules of Court, resulting in the creation of a Supreme Court and a district and parish court system (see DÁIL COURTS).

The GOVERNMENT OF IRELAND ACT (1920) established two parliaments in Ireland, one for 'NORTHERN IRELAND' and one for 'SOUTHERN IRELAND'. Elections to the new parliament were held in May 1921, when Sinn Féin won 128 out of 132 seats in the twenty-six counties (four Unionists were elected for University of Dublin). Sitting as Dáil Éireann, they ignored the existence of Northern Ireland and denied the validity of the parliament of Southern Ireland, whose inaugural meeting, 28 June, was attended only by the four Unionist members and whose only other meeting, 14 January

1922, was for the purpose of transferring power to the PROVISIONAL GOVERNMENT.

The second Dáil Éireann met in the Mansion House, Dublin, 16 August 1921, to receive reports from de Valera on his meetings with the British Prime Minister, DAVID LLOYD GEORGE, embracing discussions on which a treaty might be fashioned to end the WAR OF INDEPENDENCE. De Valera rejected proposals offering dominion status, and the Dáil, in secret session, supported this rejection, 23 August 1921.

De Valera was elected President of the Irish Republic on 26 August. The new Ministry consisted of Michael Collins (Finance), AUSTIN STACK (Home Affairs), Arthur Griffith (Foreign Affairs), Cathal Brugha (National Defence), W. T. Cosgrave (Local Government), and Robert Barton (Economic Affairs). Other ministers were Constance Markievicz (Labour), Ernest Blythe (Trade and Commerce), Seán Etchingham (Fisheries), J. J. O'KELLY (Education), A. O'Connor (Agriculture), and DESMOND FITZGERALD (Publicity).

Plenipotentiaries to meet the British were appointed, 14 September, and negotiations began in London, 5 October. On 3 December, when the Ministry met to consider the proposed Articles of Agreement, opinion was divided: de Valera, favouring his 'EXTERNAL ASSOCIATION' proposal, would not accept the articles as presented. The delegates returned to London under instructions not to sign any document until the Ministry had first ratified it; but on 6 December, under threat from Lloyd George that the alternative was 'immediate and terrible war,' the delegates signed the document.

The Dáil debated the Treaty terms between 14 December 1921 and 10 January 1922. The debates were conducted in an atmosphere of increasing bitterness as division widened between those who stood for the republic of Easter 1916 and those who found the terms of the Treaty acceptable. The Dáil divided, 7 January, on the motion 'that Dáil Éireann approves the Treaty.' On a vote in favour (64 to 57), de Valera resigned the Presidency; on 9 January he was replaced by Arthur Griffith.

Griffith's Ministry (January–September 1922) consisted of Arthur Griffith (President), Michael Collins (Finance), ÉAMONN DUGGAN (Home Affairs), GEORGE GAVAN DUFFY (Foreign Affairs, July–August), MICHAEL HAYES (Foreign Affairs, August–September), RICHARD MULCAHY (National Defence), W. T. Cosgrave (Local Government), and KEVIN O'HIGGINS (Economic Affairs). Other ministers were JOSEPH MCGRATH (Labour), Ernest Blythe (Trade and Commerce), Michael Hayes (Education), PATRICK HOGAN (Agriculture), Desmond Fitzgerald (Publicity), and MICHAEL STAINES (Director of the BELFAST BOYCOTT).

On 8 June the Second Dáil adjourned; when it again met, 30 June, the CIVIL WAR had begun. The meeting of 30 June was for the express purpose of transferring power to the new Dáil, elected on 16 June; having completed its agenda, and having arranged a session for 1 July, it again adjourned. That meeting, because of the outbreak of the Civil War, did not take place, and Dáil Éireann was prorogued, 4 August.

When the new Dáil met, 9 September, Republican deputies refused to recognise its legitimacy, as membership required taking the OATH OF ALLEGIANCE. The sole Republican in attendance, LAURENCE GINNELL, held a watching brief for de Valera. While Republicans referred to it as the Provisional Dáil, its supporters regarded it as the third Dáil Éireann.

On 6 December 1922 the IRISH FREE STATE came into existence and assumed the powers of the Provisional Government.

Dallas, Rev. Alexander (1791–1869), English evangelical clergyman. He served with the IRISH CHURCH MISSIONS before his ordination, 1840, and was persuaded by influential Protestants, including Arthur Guinness, to remain in Ireland. He had a deep-rooted suspicion of Catholicism, in particular the doctrine of Papal authority. He established his first mission at Castlekerke, Co. Galway, where he also built a school. He regarded the GREAT FAMINE (1845–49) as an ideal opportunity to win converts from Catholicism; his missionary approach of spiritual rather than material assistance, while having the support of the Church of Ireland Archbishop of Tuam, THOMAS PLUNKET, alienated many of the more moderate Protestant clergy. With REV. HYACINTH D'ARCY he established seven mission centres in Co. Galway, twenty-five churches, eight parsonages, and thirty schools, despite the vigorous opposition of the Catholic Archbishop of Tuam, JOHN MACHALE, and FATHER PATRICK LAVELLE. MacHale countered the proselytising activities of the evangelicals by introducing the Third Order of St Francis to his diocese. Dallas was a prolific pamphleteer: his publications included *Popery in Ireland: A Warning to Protestants*

(1847), *Points of Hope in Ireland's Present Crisis* (1849), and *The Story of the Irish Church Missions* (1867). (See also SECOND REFORMATION.)

Dalton, (James) Emmet (1898–1978), soldier and film producer; born in Dublin. As a member of the British army during the First World War he distinguished himself at Ginchy and was decorated and promoted to commissioned rank; as *aide de camp* to SIR HENRY WILSON he retired with the rank of major. He became Assistant Director of Training in the IRA and was close to MICHAEL COLLINS. During the War of Independence he attempted to rescue SEÁN MAC EOIN from Mountjoy Jail, Dublin, 14 May 1921 (British state papers released in 1990 show that certain members of the prison staff were aware of the rescue attempt). He accompanied Collins to London during the Treaty negotiations, 1921, and supported the ANGLO-IRISH TREATY (though his younger brother, Charley, took the anti-Treaty side) and was Director of Military Operations in the Free State army during the CIVIL WAR. Commanding the attack on the FOUR COURTS, he personally manned an eighteen-pound artillery piece. Realising the vulnerability of Republicans to seaborne attack, he led 456 men on the *Arvonia* and took the crucial Republican stronghold of Cork, 9 August 1922. He was at Bealnablagh, Co. Cork, with Collins when he was killed, 22 August; shortly afterwards he prohibited the holding of an inquest within Co. Cork.

Following Collins's death, Dalton was appointed Clerk of the Senate. A keen sportsman, he played soccer with the Dublin club Bohemians during the 1920s. He moved to England, where he became a photographer, and was later a Hollywood film producer. Returning to England, he produced some films and met Louis Elliman, with whom he founded Ardmore Studios, Bray, Co. Wicklow, 1958.

Dalton, John (1792–1867), historian, antiquarian, and poet; born in Bessville, Co. Westmeath, educated at TCD and King's Inns and called to the bar. He achieved his first publishing success with *Dermid, or Erin in the Days of Boroimhe* (1814). In 1827 he was awarded the Cunningham Medal of the Royal Irish Academy for his essay 'The Social and Political State of Ireland from the First to the Twelfth Century'. He was appointed a Loan Fund Commissioner, 1835. He contributed to George Petrie's *Dublin Penny Journal* and the *Transactions of the Royal Irish Academy.* His works include *Memoirs of the Archbishops of Dublin* (1838), *History of the County of Dublin* (1838), *History of Drogheda* (2 vols., 1844), and *King James II's Irish Army List in 1689* (1855). He received a special award from the RIA for his *History of Ireland from the Earliest Period to 1245* (2 vols., 1845).

Daly, Cahal (born 1917), bishop (Catholic); born in Loughguile, Co. Antrim, educated at QUB and St Patrick's College, Maynooth. Following ordination, 1941, he studied philosophy at the Institut Catholique, Paris. He taught at St Malachy's College, Belfast, before lecturing in philosophy at Queen's University, Belfast, 1956–67. Theologian to CARDINAL WILLIAM CONWAY at the Second Vatican Council, he was Bishop of Ardagh and Clonmacnoise, 1967, Bishop of Down and Connor, 1983, and Archbishop of Armagh and Primate of All Ireland, 1990–96, the oldest incumbent for 170 years. A cardinal from 1991, he was a constant critic of paramilitary violence. His contribution to ecumenism was widely acknowledged. In 1984 he presented the hierarchy's submission to the NEW IRELAND FORUM. His support for the acceptance of SINN FÉIN at a round-table conference was conditional on the cessation of IRA violence. In January 1995 he became the first Catholic leader since the Reformation to address a congregation from the pulpit of Canterbury Cathedral, during a homily in which he asked the English people to forgive the wrongs and hurt inflicted on them by the Irish people. Never robust in health, he was succeeded at Armagh by Archbishop Seán Brady, 3 November 1996.

Daly, Edward 'Ned' (1891–1916), Fenian; born in Limerick. His father, Edward Daly, and paternal uncle JOHN DALY were prominent members of the IRB. His sister Kathleen married THOMAS J. CLARKE; while assisting her with her tobacconist business in Dublin he joined the Irish Volunteers. As captain of B Company, 1st Battalion, Dublin Brigade he played a leading role in the HOWTH GUN-RUNNING (1914). He commanded his company in the Four Courts area of Dublin during the EASTER RISING (1916). Following the surrender he was sentenced to death and was shot by firing squad, 4 May. With SEÁN HEUSTON he was the youngest of those executed during the rising.

Daly, James (1836–1916), journalist and land agitator; born in Castlebar, Co. Mayo, educated locally. As editor of the *Connaught Telegraph* he waged a tireless campaign for agrarian reform in his native county. His involvement in the land movement forged a bitter debate with FATHER PATRICK LAVELLE, who threatened him with libel action. The *Telegraph* was saved from closure, 1879, through a grant of £50 from the LAND LEAGUE. One of the founders of the Mayo Defence Association, 26 October 1878, Daly reminded tenants of their obligation to pay fair, but not excessive, rents. He was a central figure in the arrangements and proceedings of the agrarian meeting at IRISHTOWN, Co. Mayo, 20 April 1879. His evidence before the BESSBOROUGH COMMISSION influenced it in its recommendation for land reform.

Daly became estranged from the LAND LEAGUE and was later highly critical of its direction. He campaigned for an equitable distribution of grazing land among smallholders and the landless but opposed MICHAEL DAVITT in the demand for nationalisation of the land. Supporting CHARLES STEWART PARNELL in his demand for home rule, Daly defined the measure as 'unqualified control of Irish affairs by the Irish people.'

Daly, John (1845–1916), Fenian; born in Limerick, a paternal uncle of EDWARD DALY and KATHLEEN CLARKE. Active in the IRB, he went to the United States after the 1867 Rising. A friend of JOHN DEVOY, he returned to Ireland, where he played a leading role in achieving the electoral success of JOHN MITCHEL in Co. Tipperary in 1875 (Mitchel was later disqualified as a treason-felon). During the LAND WAR Daly, now a member of the Supreme Council of the IRB, became organiser for Connacht and Ulster. Later, while working in Birmingham, he was arrested and accused of involvement in a find of explosives in the garden of his landlord, James Egan. While in prison he formed a friendship with THOMAS J. CLARKE. His claim that he was being poisoned was investigated by a commission of inquiry, 1886; it was admitted by prison officials as an error by a warder. The head of the Birmingham police later made a deathbed confession that Daly had been convicted on perjured evidence.

Elected member of Parliament for Limerick, 1895, Daly was disqualified as a treason-felon. Released following a hunger strike, August 1896, he embarked on a lecture tour of England with MAUD GONNE and in 1897 on a financially rewarding American tour organised by Devoy. He founded a successful bakery business in Limerick and was three times mayor of the city, 1899–1901. A member of the NATIONAL COUNCIL, he jointly financed (with DR PATRICK MCCARTAN) *Irish Freedom*, 1910, but his offer of further financial assistance following the paper's suppression, 1914, was rejected by ARTHUR GRIFFITH. The reminiscences of 'John Daly of Limerick' appeared in *Irish Freedom*, 1912–13.

D'Arcy, Rev. Hyacinth Talbot (1806–1874), evangelical clergyman (Church of Ireland); born in Glen Ierne, Clifden, Co. Galway, educated at TCD. The eldest son of John D'Arcy, a model landlord who developed Clifden, he became an evangelical while convalescing after the amputation of a leg. On his father's death, 1839, he became an active missionary around Clifden, where be was popular, working in association with REV. ALEXANDER R. C. DALLAS, REV. EDWARD NANGLE, and the IRISH CHURCH MISSIONS. He helped to establish missions at Ballyconree, Errisconor, Claggan, Sellema, Moyruss, Roundstone, and Ballinahinch. When his estate was taken under the ENCUMBERED ESTATE ACTS in 1851 he was ordained by the evangelical Bishop of Tuam, THOMAS PLUNKET. He was respected for his philanthropic work during the GREAT FAMINE (1845–49).

Dargan, William (1799–1867), businessman; born in Carlow, educated in England. Under Thomas Telford (1757–1834) he worked on the Holyhead road project, 1820. As a contractor he built several arterial roads, including the Dublin–Howth road, before becoming a successful railway contractor. He constructed the first Irish railway, Dublin–Kingstown (Dún Laoghaire), which opened on 17 December 1838. He also built the Ulster Railway, opened August 1839, and the Great Southern and Western Railway, 1843–50. He was responsible for the construction of the Ulster Canal, 1841, at a cost of £231,000, which he subsequently leased for £400 a year. It was estimated that he had paid out £4 million in wages, 1845–50. QUEEN VICTORIA, impressed by his organising and financing of the DUBLIN EXHIBITION (1853), offered him a baronetcy, which he refused. In 1864 he made a donation towards the building of the NATIONAL GALLERY OF IRELAND of £5,000 from a testimonial he had received. He was employed in the initial construction of what became the Harland and Wolff shipbuilding complex; the area first named Dargan's Island, created by the dredging of a channel, later became Queen's Island. A riding accident in 1866 left him unable to supervise his business interests, and this, allied with ill-advised investment in the textile industry, brought him to financial ruin. His widow was awarded a pension of £100 a year.

Darlington Conference (25–27 September 1972), an unsuccessful attempt by WILLIAM WHITELAW to gain inter-party agreement for a government in Northern Ireland; those attending included representatives of the ULSTER UNIONIST PARTY and the ALLIANCE PARTY but it was boycotted by the SDLP and DEMOCRATIC UNIONIST PARTY. The participants failed to agree on a form of government, but a position paper, *The Future of Northern Ireland,* was published, 30 October. It affirmed the commitment of the British government to Northern Ireland (or the Union) for as long as the people of Northern Ireland wished it but also recognised, for the first time, what came to be called the 'Irish dimension', i.e. a role for the Irish government.

Davin, Maurice (1841–1927), athlete and joint founder of the GAELIC ATHLETIC ASSOCIATION; born in Carrick-on-Suir, Co. Tipperary, to a family celebrated for its athletic prowess, educated locally. During the 1880s he and his brothers Tom and Pat held more than half the world's records for running, jumping, hurdling, and weight-throwing. In 1881, as the oldest competitor at the British amateur athletic championships, Davin won both the shot and hammer events; he won the Irish All-Round Championships, 1888, when he was forty-seven. The athletic grounds at his home at Deerpark fostered Irish athletics, and he was a popular choice as first president of the GAA.

Davis, Thomas Osborne (1814–1845), poet, journalist, and Young Irelander; born in Mallow, Co. Cork, where his father, a surgeon in the British army, died before he was born. The family moved to Dublin, 1818, where, at Mongan's School, Davis was considered 'dim-witted and difficult.' Following an undistinguished career at TCD, having graduated in 1836, he was called to the bar, 1838, but never practised. An early contributor to the *Citizen* (later the *Dublin Monthly Magazine*), he also wrote for the *Public Morning Register.* With CHARLES GAVAN DUFFY and JOHN BLAKE DILLON he founded the NATION, 15 October 1842. The first of some fifty of his poems for the paper, 'My Grave', was published in its third issue over the signature 'A True Celt'.

Davis joined the REPEAL ASSOCIATION, April 1841, and was in effect the leader of YOUNG IRELAND, 1842–45. He became disenchanted with O'CONNELL and the apparent dilution of Repeal policies and O'Connell's intransigent opposition to the QUEEN'S COLLEGES and his pursuit of an alliance with the Whigs.

He died of scarlet fever, his dream of compiling a history of Ireland unfulfilled. His funeral to Mount Jerome Cemetery, Dublin, was witnessed by thousands, escorted by members of the Corporation of Dublin, Young Ireland, the EIGHTY-TWO CLUB, the Committee of the Repeal Association, and the antiquaries and scholars of the Royal Irish Academy. His fiancée, Annie Hutton, died 7 June 1853, aged twenty-eight, having, in the words of a friend, 'faded away from the hour of his death.' Davis's ballad poetry, including 'Lament for Owen Roe O'Neill', 'A Nation Once Again', and 'The West's Awake', have infused the national spirit for generations. His prose works were edited by T. W. Rolleston (1889). A *Life of Davis* (1896) was published by JAMES DUFFY, who also wrote a lengthy introduction to Davis's *The Patriot Parliament of 1689* (1893).

Davitt, Michael (1846–1906), agrarian agitator, politician (anti-Parnellite), and journalist; born in Straide, Co. Mayo. Evicted from their smallholding, 1850, the family settled in Haslingden, Lancashire, where Davitt lost his right arm while working in Stellfoxe's cotton mill, 8 May 1857. Having attended Poskett's School, he was employed in Haslingden post office, 1865–69. A 'CENTRE' in the IRB, he led an abortive raid on Chester Castle, 11 February 1867, was sentenced to fifteen years' imprisonment, 18 July 1870, and as a treason-felon was subjected to a harsh regime in Dartmoor Prison until released on ticket-of-leave, 19 December 1877. He discussed the NEW DEPARTURE with JOHN DEVOY in the United States, where he met Henry George (1839–1897), whose *Our Land and Land Policy* (1871) and *Progress and Poverty* (1877–79) deeply influenced him.

Returning to Co. Mayo, 1879, Davitt played a pivotal role in the organising of the mass meetings at IRISHTOWN in April and in Westport in June that led to the founding of the LAND LEAGUE OF MAYO. Working in close co-operation with CHARLES STEWART PARNELL on the land issue, Davitt, though he had ceased his active involvement in Fenianism, had his ticket-of-leave revoked for agrarian agitation and was imprisoned, 3 February 1881. Parnell's involvement in the 'KILMAINHAM TREATY' led to a breach with Davitt, who later commented, 'It was the vital turning point in Mr Parnell's career, and he unfortunately turned the wrong way.' Davitt was unseated by special writ of the House of Commons following his election for Co. Meath, 1882.

Though he had described the PLAN OF CAMPAIGN as being 'too moderate,' Davitt nonetheless lent his support to the agitation. He was in Bodyke, Co. Clare, May 1887, when thirty-two families on the estate of Colonel John O'Callaghan were evicted by a force of five hundred police and militia. Addressing the tenants following the evictions, he regretted that they 'did not have the weapons to teach the evictors a lesson they would never forget.' He founded a short-lived newspaper in London, the *Irish World*, 1890, which collapsed following his resignation.

Following the revelations of the O'Shea divorce case, Davitt became one of Parnell's most vociferous critics. Elected member of Parliament for North Meath, 1892, he was again unseated on petition. Returned for North-East Cork in 1893, in his first speech to the House of Commons he supported the second Home Rule Bill, but as a declared bankrupt he was forced to resign his seat later that year.

Keir Hardie's Independent Labour Party—which endorsed home rule—attracted Davitt, who, in deference to the Liberals' support for the measure, was circumspect in his dealings with Hardie, leading to a breach that was not healed until 1905. He represented East Kerry and South Mayo in the House of Commons, 1895–99. He was joint founder (with WILLIAM O'BRIEN) of the UNITED IRISH LEAGUE, during a period in which he sought to reconcile constitutional with revolutionary nationalism. He withdrew from Parliament, 1899, in protest at the Anglo-Boer War; his experiences as a war correspondent in South Africa, March–July 1900, inspired his *Boer Fight for Freedom* (1904).

Davitt's support for non-denominational education and his opposition to clerical interference in politics placed him at odds with the Catholic hierarchy, notably with WILLIAM WALSH, Archbishop of Dublin, and EDWARD THOMAS O'DWYER, Bishop of Limerick. He opposed the Irish Land Act (1903) (see LAND ACTS) and denounced the anti-Jewish sermons of the Limerick Redemptorist Father John Creagh. In 1904, as correspondent of the *New York American Journal*, he travelled to Russia and met leading revolutionaries, including Lev Tolstoy (1828–1910). In latter years he espoused socialism, which he perceived as a unifying force between the Irish and British working class, leading to ultimate Irish independence. His call for nationalisation of the land was generally misinterpreted.

Davitt died as a result of septicaemia following a tooth extraction. His writings include *The Prison Life of Michael Davitt* (1878), *Leaves from a Prison Diary* (2 vols., 1885), *Within the Pale* (1903), and *The Fall of Feudalism in Ireland* (1904).

daylight-saving time, commonly called 'summer time', introduced in Britain and Ireland (following the lead of Germany, Austria and the Netherlands) on 21 May 1916 as a fuel-saving measure; it lapsed after the Great War but was reintroduced in 1922. Previous to its adoption, Irish time was 25 minutes behind GMT.

Deasy, Timothy (1841–1880), Fenian; born in Clonakilty, Co. Cork. His family settled in Lawrence, Massachusetts, 1847. Together with his brother Connie, Deasy enlisted in the 9th Massachusetts Regiment (composed entirely of Irish emigrants) of the Union Army during the American Civil War (1861–65). He joined the IRB and became a member of its Supreme Council. He travelled to Ireland, 26 August 1865, but was arrested at Skibbereen, Co. Cork, and ordered to leave the country. Returning, he later helped THOMAS J. KELLY to organise the escape of JAMES STEPHENS from the Bridewell, Dublin, 24 November 1865. He returned to the United States, where he supported John O'Neill in his ill-fated invasion of Canada. As second in command to Kelly he oversaw preparations for the Fenian rising in Co. Cork. Leading the raid on Chester Castle, he evaded arrest (the authorities had been informed by the Fenian spy J. J. Corydon). The Manchester police, alerted by Corydon, arrested Deasy and Kelly, 11 September. As they were being conveyed with other prisoners from the courthouse to prison, the prison van was attacked by a number of Fenians; during the encounter Sergeant Charles Brett was fatally injured, and both Deasy and Kelly were rescued. (See MANCHESTER MARTYRS.)

Deasy returned to the United States, 1869, and ceased his open involvement with Fenianism. He became landlord of a saloon in Lawrence, Massachusetts, was elected to the city council, and served two terms in the House of Representatives.

Declaration of Independence (1919), drafted by a committee selected at a meeting of Sinn Féin representatives, 8 January 1919, the greater part of it by GEORGE GAVAN DUFFY. It was read out (in Irish, French and English) at the first meeting of Dáil Éireann, 21 January 1919.

Whereas the Irish people is by right a free people;

And whereas for seven hundred years the Irish people has never ceased to repudiate and has repeatedly protested in arms against foreign usurpation;

And whereas English rule in this country is, and always has been, based upon force and fraud and maintained by military occupation against the declared will of the people;

And whereas the Irish Republic was proclaimed in Dublin on Easter Monday, 1916, by the Irish Republican Army, acting on behalf of the Irish people;

And whereas the Irish people is resolved to secure and maintain its complete independence in order to promote the common weal, to re-establish justice, to provide for future defence, to ensure peace at home and good will with all nations, and to constitute a national policy based upon the people's will, with equal right and equal opportunity for every citizen;

And whereas at the threshold of a new era in history the Irish electorate has in the General Election of December 1918, seized the first occasion to declare by an overwhelming majority its firm allegiance to the Irish Republic;

Now, therefore, we, the elected Representatives of the ancient Irish people in National Parliament assembled do, in the name of the Irish Nation, ratify the establishment of the Irish Republic and pledge ourselves and our people to make this declaration effective by every means at our command.

We ordain that the elected Representatives of the Irish people alone have power to make laws binding on the people of Ireland, that the Irish Parliament is the only Parliament to which the people will give its allegiance;

We solemnly declare foreign government in Ireland to be an invasion of our national right which we will never tolerate, and we demand the evacuation of our country by the English Government;

We claim for our national independence the recognition and support of every free nation in the world, and we proclaim that independence to be a condition precedent to the international peace thereafter;

In the name of the Irish people we humbly commit our destiny to Almighty God who gave our fathers the courage and determination to persevere through long centuries of a ruthless tyranny, and strong in the justice of the cause which they have handed down to us, we ask His Divine blessing on this the last stage of the struggle we have pledged ourselves to carry through to freedom.

See also EASTER RISING (1916) and DEMOCRATIC PROGRAMME.

Deeny, Dr James (1906–1994), doctor and civil servant; born in Lurgan, Co. Armagh, educated at QUB. While working with his father in local practice he continued postgraduate studies for a science degree. From his practice in Lurgan, Co. Armagh, 1931–44, where he had conducted surveys on nutrition, infant mortality, and tuberculosis, he joined the Department of Local Government and Health as Chief Medical Adviser. Differences with the Minister for Health, DR NOEL BROWNE, led to Deeny's secondment to the Medical Research Council, where he conducted a National Tuberculosis Survey, 1950–53; he later directed projects on tuberculosis for the World Health Organisation in Ceylon (Sri Lanka), 1956.

Defence Forces. The army of the Irish Free State was established in January 1922 from members of the IRA who had supported the ANGLO-IRISH TREATY (1921). By June it was engaged in the CIVIL WAR, fighting the section of the IRA that had rejected the Treaty. Following the CIVIL WAR the army was reduced from approximately 60,000 to 30,000, a measure that provoked the ARMY MUTINY (1924). The policy of reduction continued during the 1920s. After his accession to power in 1932, ÉAMON DE VALERA recruited Volunteers from IRA veterans of the WAR OF INDEPENDENCE. Distinctively uniformed, they were recruited during December 1933. Another force, containing many former IRA men, was also established as the A and B Reserves.

The volunteer army reserve, An Fórsa Cosanta Áitiúil (FCA), was established in 1947 as a successor to the LOCAL DEFENCE FORCE.

Air Corps. The Irish Air Service was established in 1922 on the creation of the Irish Free

State. Its successor, the Air Corps, provides air co-operation for the army, fishery protection, a search-and-rescue and air ambulance service, aerial photography for the Ordnance Survey, and VIP flights.

Naval Service. The Coastal and Marine Service was established in May 1923 to prevent gun-running and to provide fishery protection. Commanded by General Joseph Vise, with headquarters at Portobello Barracks (Cathal Brugha Barracks), Dublin, its vessels included the *Muirchú* (formerly the HELGA), six Mersey-class trawlers, six Castle-class trawlers, two drifters, five river patrol boats (on the River Shannon and River Lee and in Waterford Harbour), three motor launches, and two steam launches. The service had a strength of 365 when it was disbanded in March 1924, its personnel either demobilised or transferred to the army. Coastal defence until 1938 was delegated to the South Irish Flotilla of the British navy, consisting of the *Tenedos* and the *Thracian.* Under the ANGLO-IRISH TREATY (1921), Britain retained mooring rights in the three 'TREATY PORTS' of Lough Swilly, Co. Donegal, Bearhaven, Co. Cork, and Queenstown (Cóbh), Co. Cork. The British navy withdrew from them, 11 July 1938, following the agreement that ended the 'ECONOMIC WAR'.

The outbreak of the Second World War created a problem of coastal defence and led to the creation of the Marine and Coastwatching Service, 5 September 1939, with three craft borrowed from the Air Corps. Commanded by Colonel T. A. Lawlor, it was augmented by a volunteer reserve, the Maritime Inscription, from September 1940; in 1941 the fleet was increased and a Minesweeping Section established. The Marine Service and Coastwatching Service were separated on 17 July 1942; the latter was disbanded on 19 November 1945.

In accordance with a Government decision of 15 March 1946, a new Marine Service was established. Commanded by H. J. A. Jerome, it was renamed the Naval Service in 1947, at which time it had a strength of 400. The first cadets, enlisted in December 1946, were trained at the Royal Naval College, Dartmouth. Three corvettes—*Macha* (1946–68), *Maev* (1946–69), and *Clíona* (1947–71)—performed fishery protection duties; they were replaced during 1970–71 by three former minesweepers, *Gráinne, Banba,* and *Fóla.* The service's first custom-built ship, *Deirdre,* built at Verolme Cork Dockyard, was commissioned on 19 June 1972.

The Naval Service undertook a hydrographic survey in 1963. Training courses for boy fishermen were carried out under Naval Service direction, 1964–68, and courses for merchant service officers from October 1966.

The volunteer naval reserve, An Slua Muirí, replaced the Maritime Inscription from 10 June 1947. From 1949 it has been organised in five companies, based in army barracks in Dublin, Cork, Limerick, and Waterford.

Defence of the Realm Act (1914), often called 'DORA', the first in a series of emergency laws passed by the British Parliament, 27 November 1914. Designed to prevent collaboration between Irish revolutionaries and Germany during the Great War, its scope was extended in May 1915 to cover the sale and supply of liquor. Giving the authorities sweeping powers of arrest, the act was used as the executing authority against the leaders of the EASTER RISING (1916) and to suppress revolutionary organisations in its wake and was cited when suspected persons and members of Sinn Féin were imprisoned, 1916–19. It was extended, August 1920, during the WAR OF INDEPENDENCE to include the RESTORATION OF ORDER IN IRELAND ACT (1920), under which the British military authorities operated. The act ceased to function on 31 August 1921.

Defenders, a Catholic secret society founded in Co. Armagh as a response to the PEEP O' DAY BOYS. Envisaged as purely defensive, it soon adopted an aggressive role and was party to the 'Battle of the Diamond' (21 September 1795). Unlike other nationalist secret societies, the Defenders had a regional and national structure, and its policies evolved beyond petty sectarianism. It was assimilated into the UNITED IRISHMEN, following whose defeat in 1798 it was reorganised as the 'RIBBONMEN'. (See SECRET SOCIETIES.)

Democratic Left, initially called New Agenda, a left-wing political party led by PROINSIAS DE ROSSA, founded following a split in the WORKERS' PARTY, February–March 1992. De Rossa had proposed at an extraordinary party congress that the Workers' Party be reconstituted as 'an independent democratic socialist party,' repudiating 'any vestiges of "democratic centralism" as a method of organisation and . . . "revolutionary tactics" as a means of addressing the party's aims.' When this motion failed to secure the necessary two-thirds majority, six of the seven Workers' Party TDs and a majority of the party's activists formed New Agenda; the name was changed to Democratic Left on 28 March 1992. The party won four seats in the November 1992 general election. After entering the 'rainbow coalition' with Fine Gael and the Labour Party in 1994, de Rossa was Minister for Social Welfare. The party failed to secure any seats in Northern Ireland; in the June 1997 election it retained its four Dáil seats. It amalgamated with the LABOUR PARTY in 1999.

Democratic Programme (1919), adopted by the first Dáil Éireann, drafted by THOMAS JOHNSON and edited by SEÁN T. O'KELLY, designed to enhance Ireland's claim to self-government when Johnson attended the International Socialist Conference in Bern, 1919. It was proposed to Dáil Éireann when it met for the first time on 21 January 1919; the version approved by the Dáil was:

> We declare in the words of the Irish Republican Proclamation the right of the people of Ireland to the ownership of Ireland, and to the unfettered control of Irish destinies to be indefeasible, and in the language of the first President, Pádraig MacPhiarais, we declare that the Nation's sovereignty extends not only to all men and women of the Nation, but to all its material possessions; the Nation's soil and all its resources, all the wealth and all the wealth-producing processes within the Nation, and with him we re-affirm that all rights to private property must be subordinated to the public right and welfare.
>
> We declare that we desire our country to be ruled in accordance with the principles of Liberty, Equality and Justice for all, which alone can secure permanence of Government in the willing adhesion of the people.
>
> We affirm the duty of every man and woman to give allegiance and service to the Commonwealth, and declare it is the duty of the Nation to assure that every citizen shall have opportunity to spend his or her strength and faculties in the service of the people. In return for willing service, we, in the name of the Republic, declare the right of every citizen to an adequate share of the produce of the Nation's labour.
>
> It shall be the first duty of the Government of the Republic to make provision for the physical, mental and spiritual well-being of the children, to secure that no child shall suffer hunger or cold from lack of food, clothing or shelter, but that all shall be provided with the means and facilities requisite for their proper education and training as Citizens of a Free and Gaelic Ireland.
>
> The Irish Republic fully realises the necessity of abolishing the present odious, degrading and foreign Poor Law System, substituting therefor a sympathetic native scheme for the care of the Nation's aged and infirm, who shall not be regarded as a burden but rather entitled to the Nation's gratitude and consideration. Likewise it shall be the duty of the Republic to take such measures as will safeguard the health of the people and ensure the physical as well as the moral well-being of the Nation.
>
> It shall be our duty to promote the development of the Nation's resources, to increase the productivity of its soil, to exploit its mineral deposits, peat bogs and fisheries, its waterways and harbours, in the interests and for the benefit of the Irish people.
>
> It shall be the duty of the Republic to adopt all measures necessary for the recreation and invigoration of our industries, and to ensure their being developed on the most beneficial and progressive co-operative and industrial lines. With the adoption of an extensive Irish Consular Service, trade with foreign Nations shall be revived on terms of mutual advantage and good will, and while undertaking the organisation of the Nation's trade, imports and exports, it shall be the duty of the Republic to prevent the shipment from Ireland of food and other necessaries until the wants of the Irish people are fully satisfied and the future provided for.
>
> It shall devolve upon the present government to seek co-operation of the governments of other countries in determining the standard of social and industrial legislation with a view to a general and lasting improvement in the conditions under which the working class live and labour.

Democratic Socialist Party, a left-wing political party founded in 1982 by JIM KEMMY (who had left the LABOUR PARTY in 1972) as an anti-nationalist socialist party; its support was mainly in Kemmy's Limerick East constituency. It supported the deletion of articles 2 and 3 of the Constitution of Ireland and sought the provision of contraceptive facilities. Kemmy led the party into a merger with the Labour Party, 1 May 1990; he became vice-chairman of the Labour Party, 1991, and was chairman at his death in September 1997.

Democratic Unionist Party, founded by REV. IAN PAISLEY and Desmond Boal, September 1971. Boal, a former member of the Parliament of Northern Ireland expelled from the ULSTER UNIONIST PARTY, was the party's first chairman. A replacement for Paisley's Protestant Unionist Party, it formed an opposition to the UUP. Seeking maintenance of the Union and closer integration with London, the party opposed power-sharing with the SDLP and was vocal in its opposition to the reformist policies of the Prime Minister, TERENCE O'NEILL.

Winning eight seats in the June 1973 elections to the Northern Ireland Assembly, the DUP opposed the power-sharing Executive led by BRIAN FAULKNER. Following the 1974 elections to the British House of Commons, in which it won three seats, the DUP, as a constituent of the UNITED ULSTER UNIONIST COUNCIL, played a pivotal role in the fall of the Executive. Having taken twelve seats in the Constitutional Convention, it won seventy-four seats in the 1977 district council elections. Paisley, as party leader, topped the poll in the 1979 elections to the European Parliament. With five candidates it won an extra two seats at the 1979 elections to the British House of Commons. It continued its successes in the 1981 district council elections, with 142 seats, and won twenty-one seats in the 1982 Assembly elections. However, it was reduced to three seats in the 1983 elections to the British House of Commons and lost forty-eight seats in the district councils in 1985.

The DUP supported the Ulster Unionist Party in opposing the ANGLO-IRISH AGREEMENT and worked closely with it during the 'talks about talks' with TOM KING and PETER BROOKE, 1988–91. Consistent in its rejection of power-sharing (multi-party government), it reacted bitterly when the UUP attended talks in Dublin Castle. It suffered further losses in the 1989 district council elections; its representation of 110 seats was a loss of 32 from its position in 1985.

The DUP's paper on Northern Ireland, *Breaking the Log-Jam,* was published in November 1993. Rejecting the DOWNING STREET DECLARATION (1993) as a 'sell-out', it organised a series of 'Save Ulster' rallies, beginning with Portadown, 17 January 1994. The only party to reject the INTERNATIONAL BODY ON DECOMMISSIONING, it dismissed the Mitchell Report (January 1996) as 'fudge and falsehood.' Having boycotted the 'proximity talks', March 1996, the party became the third-largest in the Northern Ireland Forum when it secured 24 out of 110 seats. In the 1997 district council elections it won 91 seats.

The DUP delegation walked out of multi-party talks, 16 July 1997, and withdrew from discussions five days later. Refusing an invitation in January 1998 to participate in talks, it rejected the BELFAST AGREEMENT on 10 April. It manifested its continuing disregard for consensus by rotating its two ministerial portfolios among its elected members in the Northern Ireland Executive.

The DUP secured five seats in the June 2001 elections to the British House of Commons, where Iris Robinson became the party's first woman MP and, with her husband, Peter Robinson, the first husband-and-wife team from Northern Ireland in the House of Commons. In the local elections the party gained forty seats, in contrast to the loss of thirty-one suffered by the UUP.

Denieffe, Joseph (1833–1910), Fenian; born in Co. Kilkenny. A tailor by trade and a member of YOUNG IRELAND and the IRISH CONFEDERATION, he settled in New York, 1851, where he carried on his trade and joined the EMMET MONUMENT ASSOCIATION. While visiting his ailing father, 1885, he attempted to establish the association in Ireland but had little success outside Co. Kilkenny; he did, however, make contact with Dublin activists through Peter Langan. Before his return to the United States he was contacted by JAMES STEPHENS, December 1857. On Stephens's behalf he raised £80 from members of the EMMET MONUMENT ASSOCIATION and returned to Ireland. He was present when Stephens used this fund to launch the IRISH REPUBLICAN BROTHERHOOD, 17 March 1858.

Following the failure of the Fenian rising in 1867, Denieffe returned to the United States, where he maintained close links with CLAN NA GAEL until his death in Chicago. His obituary in the *Gaelic American* acknowledged that he had remained 'true to the principles of Fenianism till the last.' His 'Recollections of the Irish Revolutionary Brotherhood', serialised in the *Gael* (New York) in 1904, was published in expanded form as *A Personal Narrative of the Irish Revolutionary Brotherhood* (1906).

Denvir, John (1834–1916), journalist and Fenian; born in Bushmills, Co. Antrim. In Liverpool as a youth he entered journalism and edited several papers, including the *Catholic Times* and the *Nationalist.* An arms smuggler for the IRB, he left the movement following the unsuccessful Fenian rising of 1867. He joined the home rule movement and was the first secretary of the HOME RULE CONFEDERATION OF GREAT BRITAIN. In 1870 he began the publication of 'Denvir's Penny Library', featuring Irish history, archaeology, and biography, and also published *Denvir's Monthly.* He was the author of *The Irish in Britain* (1892) and *The Life Story of an Old Rebel* (1910).

Derby, Edward Geoffrey Smith Stanley, fourteenth Earl of (1799–1869), British politician (Whig). As Chief Secretary for Ireland, 1830–33, and British Prime Minister, 1852, 1858–59, and 1866–68, his outstanding achievement in Ireland was the creation of the NATIONAL EDUCATION system, which he outlined in a letter to the Duke of Leinster (the 'Stanley Letter'). He sought a system, he said, 'from which would be banished for ever the suspicion of proselytism and which, admitting children of all religious persuasions, should not interfere with the peculiar tenets of any.' He held office during a period of acute agrarian unrest, compounded by the imposition of TITHES, which he attempted to address through the Tithe Composition Bill. While dedicated to the preservation of the established church, he supported the CHURCH TEMPORALITIES (IRELAND) ACT (1833) but without appropriation, as had been proposed by his rival, LORD JOHN RUSSELL, January 1832. Despite reservations on reform he introduced a Reform Bill for Ireland and proposed an increase in Irish representation in the British House of Commons. He established the Irish Board of Works and secured improvements in the Shannon Navigation Scheme. In 1833, following a bitter cabinet debate, he used COERCION to deal with the continuing unrest in Ireland; he resigned from the cabinet in protest at the conciliatory approach of his successor, E. J. LITTLETON, and Russell on the tithes issue.

de Rossa, Proinsias (born 1940), politician (Sinn Féin, Workers' Party, Democratic Left, and Labour Party); born in Dublin, educated at Capel Street and Kevin Street Technical Schools. A member of FIANNA ÉIREANN and later the IRA, at sixteen he was the youngest internee up to that time. He resigned from the IRA in 1960 but remained active in SINN FÉIN and its successor, the WORKERS' PARTY. A member of Dáil Éireann from 1982, in February–March 1982, having failed to secure a new constitution that would condemn political violence, he and five other members left the Workers' Party to found DEMOCRATIC LEFT. Following the collapse of the coalition Government (Fianna Fáil and Labour Party), 1994, he led Democratic Left into coalition with Fine Gael and the Labour Party in the 'rainbow coalition', in which he was Minister for Social Welfare. He retained his seat in the general election of 1997 and, having negotiated a merger with the Labour Party, was one of the few remaining holders of a dual mandate when elected a member of the European Parliament, 11 June 1999.

Derry Citizens' Action Committee, established 9 October 1968 by groups involved in organising the civil rights march in Derry four days earlier. The chairman of the committee was Ivan Cooper, with JOHN HUME as vice-chairman. On 19 October it staged a sit-down in the Diamond; on 2 November 1968 it sponsored a parade from the Waterside across Craigavon Bridge. It supported the PEOPLE'S DEMOCRACY march from Belfast to Derry, 1–4 January 1969, which was subjected to unprovoked violence by loyalists at Burntollet Bridge. It reacted to complaints regarding the behaviour of the RUC by organising patrols in the Bogside and petitioning the British Government for police reform. The committee was replaced by the more militant DERRY CITIZENS' DEFENCE COMMITTEE.

Derry Citizens' Defence Committee, established at the end of July 1969 by a group of veteran republicans led by Seán Keenan, a more militant group than the DERRY CITIZENS' ACTION COMMITTEE. During August 1969 it erected barricades around 'Free Derry', operated patrols, and provided first aid to casualties during CS gas attacks by the British army and the RUC during the 'Battle of the Bogside', 12–15 August 1969.

Derrynaflan Hoard, a hoard consisting of a chalice, strainer and paten dating from the eighth or ninth centuries, unearthed with the aid of metal-detectors by Michael Webb and his son Michael, 17 February 1980, while exploring the sixth-century monastic site of St Ruán of Lorrha at Derrynaflan, Killenaule, Co. Tipperary. The chalice, measuring 192 mm by 207 mm and of similar design to the ARDAGH CHALICE, is decorated with eighty-four gold filigree panels in amber settings. The strainer is of gilt bronze, its bowl divided by a central bronze plate. Considered the most significant find, the large circular paten is of complex construction, decorated with stamped gold or gilded panels bearing interlaced and spiral motifs. The find was cleaned by Hazel Newey, chief metals conservation officer of the British Museum, London, and put on display at the National Museum, Dublin, 13 July 1983.

Despard, Charlotte, née French (1844–1939), suffragist and socialist; born in Kent, elder sister of EARL FRENCH OF YPRES, future Lord Lieutenant of Ireland. Following the death of her husband, Maximilian Despard, 1890, she worked among the underprivileged in the East End of London and later settled in Ireland, dividing her time between Belfast and Dublin. A member of the Women's Freedom League, she advocated a boycott by women of the 1911 census. She was an ameliorating figure among families of those involved in the DUBLIN LOCK-OUT (1913). She supported Sinn Féin and the IRA during the WAR OF INDEPENDENCE and was a member of the British Labour Party committee of inquiry into conditions in Ireland, November 1920. A member of the Administrative Committee of the WHITE CROSS, she was first president of the WOMEN'S PRISONERS' DEFENCE LEAGUE, 1922. During the confrontation at the FOUR COURTS she was a member of a delegation that visited both sides in an effort to prevent civil war.

She was disowned by her brother because of her republican socialism; he refused to reconcile with her on his deathbed, 1925, even though she had expended much of her fortune in paying his debts. As a delegate of Friends of Soviet Russia she visited the Soviet Union, August 1931, with HANNA SHEEHY-SKEFFINGTON and studied the Soviet educational and penal systems. Following an attempt to burn her home in Dublin, used by the Irish Workers' College as well as the Friends of Soviet Russia, she left the house to her friend MAUD GONNE and moved to Belfast and later to Whitehead, Co. Antrim. As a Catholic, her association with socialism isolated her from her friends, and the clergy condemned her. Her finances exhausted through philanthropic endeavours, she was declared a bankrupt shortly before her death. In a graveside oration MAUD GONNE MACBRIDE described her as 'a white flame in the defence of prisoners and the oppressed.'

de Valera, Éamon (1882–1975), politician (Sinn Féin, Cumann na Poblachta, and Fianna Fáil); born in New York, raised in Bruree, Co. Limerick, by his maternal grandmother, Elisabeth Coll, educated at UCD. A mathematics teacher in a number of Dublin educational institutions, he was a member of the Gaelic League from 1908 and the IRISH VOLUNTEERS from 25 November 1913 and assisted at the HOWTH GUN-RUNNING (1914). Though sworn in to the IRB (by THOMAS MACDONAGH), he did not attend meetings. In the EASTER RISING (1916) he was commandant of the 3rd Battalion of the Dublin Brigade of the Irish Volunteers, which fought in Boland's Mills, Grand Canal Street, Dublin, and was the last commandant to surrender (to Captain E. J. Hitzen). His sentence of death was commuted to life imprisonment (as was that of his later *bête noire,* W. T. COSGRAVE) and he was released, 16 June 1917. Shortly afterwards he was elected Sinn Féin MP for East Clare, a constituency he represented until elected President of Ireland, 1959.

He became president of Sinn Féin, 25 October 1917, and two days later president of the Irish Volunteers. He drafted the anti-conscription pledge of 18 April 1918 (see CONSCRIPTION). After the 'GERMAN PLOT' arrests, 17 May 1918, he was held at Lincoln Prison, from which his escape was engineered by HARRY BOLAND and MICHAEL COLLINS, 3 February 1919. While imprisoned he had been elected to the first Dáil Éireann for four constituencies in the general election of December 1918, and he was elected president of the Ministry, 21 January 1919.

Against the wishes of the new government he went to the United States, June 1919, to float the Dáil Éireann External Loan, to secure recognition for the Irish Republic, and to channel American influence into securing recognition for the Republic by the League of Nations. Though he collected $5 million, some $3 million was retained in America when he returned in December 1920. The success of his American tour was marred when a rift developed between de Valera, JUDGE DANIEL COHALAN, and JOHN DEVOY. The quarrel split the FRIENDS OF IRISH FREEDOM, and de Valera founded the AMERICAN ASSOCIATION FOR THE RECOGNITION OF THE IRISH REPUBLIC, June 1920. Before leaving America he entered into negotiations with the government of Soviet Russia for recognition of the Irish Republic; draft terms included plans for training the IRA in Russia and for the interests of the Catholic Church in Russia to be entrusted to representatives of the Irish Republic. On behalf of the Republic de Valera made a loan of $25,000 to the Soviet government, through its consul in

New York, receiving as collateral a selection of the RUSSIAN CROWN JEWELS. (The loan was repaid in 1948.)

De Valera returned to Ireland in December 1920. He was not an active participant in peace initiatives to end the WAR OF INDEPENDENCE but had a fruitless meeting with Sir James Craig (see VISCOUNT CRAIGAVON) in Dublin, 5 May 1921, in an effort to secure cross-border détente. He was arrested on 22 June, the day on which King George V opened the Parliament of Northern Ireland. The British Government ordered his release, and two days later he received an invitation to peace talks from DAVID LLOYD GEORGE. His invitation to Ulster Unionists to attend preliminary discussions was rejected by Craig.

After the TRUCE, 11 July, de Valera travelled to London and had three meetings with Lloyd George. On 20 July he received British proposals, which he considered unacceptable as they offered only dominion status and did not recognise 'the indefeasible right of the Irish people to sovereignty and independence.' The British rejected his own proposals, which offered a formula of 'EXTERNAL ASSOCIATION' with the British Commonwealth. The talks ended when the Irish Ministry supported de Valera's stance. On 26 August 1921, accepting his new title of President of the Irish Republic, de Valera told members of Dáil Éireann: 'I am representing the nation and I shall represent the whole nation and I shall not be bound by any section of the nation whatever.'

At a Ministry meeting on 9 September the delegates for any future negotiations were selected. De Valera gave as his reasons for not wishing to be a delegate (*a*) that while he remained in Ireland he could act as reserve should the talks break down, (*b*) that there was a need for strong leadership at home to reconcile militant republicans to the concept of external association, (*c*) that ARTHUR GRIFFITH was a moderate, while his own ideas on certain crucial issues were well known, and (*d*) that while remaining in Dublin he could mould and give free expression to national feeling. While his decision did not meet with unanimous approval, the Dáil on 14 September ratified the choice of delegates. De Valera's correspondence with Lloyd George ended, 30 September, with agreement to a conference between Irish and British delegations to discuss the 'GAIRLOCH FORMULA'. Maintaining a close interest from Dublin in the negotiations for a treaty, he informed Griffith, 2 December, that the Articles of Agreement (see ANGLO-IRISH TREATY) as drafted in London were unacceptable. Together with the rest of the Ministry he understood that the plenipotentiaries would adhere to their written instructions, by which they were to refer any settlement to Dublin before signing. Only the plea of W. T. Cosgrave dissuaded him from dismissing Griffith, Collins and ROBERT BARTON from the Ministry when they arrived back with the signed document. (Years later de Valera said that the only regret of his political life was that he had not ordered the arrest of the delegates on their return from London.)

In a private session of Dáil Éireann, 15 December, de Valera produced a new draft of the Treaty, which became known as DOCUMENT NO. 2. In it he developed his idea of 'external association', but he refused to allow its public discussion. Following his defeat in the vote on the Treaty (64 to 57), 7 January 1922, he resigned the Presidency of Dáil Éireann when defeated by Griffith (60 to 58). Shortly afterwards he called a meeting of anti-Treaty members and formed CUMANN NA POBLACHTA. He reached an agreement with Griffith on 22 February 1922 that, in the interests of avoiding a split in Sinn Féin, a general election should be postponed for three months. Without recognising the authority of the PROVISIONAL GOVERNMENT, he continued to sit in the Dáil, recognising only the Ministry of the second Dáil, presided over by Griffith.

In the opening phase of the CIVIL WAR de Valera was in the Hammam Hotel, O'Connell Street, Dublin, which he vacated on orders from CATHAL BRUGHA, 3 July 1922. He was afterwards adjutant to SEÁN MOYLAN, Director of Operations in the anti-Treaty IRA. The IRA Executive authorised him, 24 March 1923, to negotiate peace terms with the Free State government. The government, however, demanded unconditional surrender as a prerequisite, and this was rejected. Following the death of LIAM LYNCH and the collapse of the Republican position, de Valera and FRANK AIKEN jointly signed an order suspending IRA activity, 24 May. Three days later his statement 'Cease Fire and Dump Arms' ended the Civil War. He was arrested by Free State soldiers in Ennis, 15 August, and held at Arbour Hill and Kilmainham Prisons, Dublin, until 16 July 1924. Though prohibited from entering Northern Ireland he did so and was arrested and held in solitary confinement in Belfast Jail, 1–29 November 1924.

From 1924 until 1927 de Valera led forty-four abstentionist TDs. They proclaimed their unalterable opposition to the partition of Ireland following the shelving of the report of the BOUNDARY COMMISSION, December 1925, when the Cosgrave government agreed to accept the *de facto* border. De Valera, by now committed to constitutional opposition, refused to enter Dáil Éireann as long as the OATH OF ALLEGIANCE was required. In an attempt to strengthen this position he proposed at the Sinn Féin ard-fheis, 11 March 1926, 'that once the admission oath of the twenty six county and six county assemblies is removed, it becomes a question not of principle, but of policy, whether or not republican representatives should attend these assemblies.' This motion was defeated (223 to 218).

Failing to overcome Sinn Féin's obdurate opposition, de Valera resigned the presidency and founded FIANNA FÁIL, of which he remained president until 1959. His forty-three deputies withdrew when they were not allowed to take their seats without taking the oath, 23 June 1927. However, their position changed following the introduction of the ELECTORAL AMENDMENT ACT (1927) in the wake of the assassination of KEVIN O'HIGGINS, July 1927. De Valera and his followers were now confronted with a dilemma: either take the oath or remain permanently outside Dáil Éireann. When he led his followers into the Dáil, 11 August, de Valera, having removed a copy of the Bible from the table and covered the wording of the oath with some papers, signed where indicated by the Clerk of the Dáil, Colm Ó Murchadha, saying,

> I am not prepared to take an oath. I am not going to take an oath. I am prepared to put my name down in this book in order to get permission to go into the Dáil, but it has no other significance.

The oath, he said, was 'an empty formula.' The Dáil was dissolved almost immediately and a general election called for 15 September, as a result of which Fianna Fáil returned with fifty-seven seats. For the next five years Fianna Fáil and the Labour Party provided the parliamentary opposition. De Valera opposed the payment of LAND ANNUITIES and the economic policies of the Cosgrave government. He founded a Fianna Fáil daily newspaper, the IRISH PRESS, 5 September 1931.

The general election of March 1932 returned Fianna Fáil with 72 seats, against 57 for Cumann na nGaedheal; supported by the Labour Party, de Valera formed his first government. He retained the External Affairs portfolio in all his governments until 1948. Invoking the STATUTE OF WESTMINSTER, he gradually dismantled elements of the Treaty repugnant to republican sensibilities: his government removed the oath of allegiance, 1933, and abolished *de facto* the office of GOVERNOR-GENERAL, 1932–36.

The withholding of the land annuities led to the 'ECONOMIC WAR' with Britain. In addition, the government was faced with the rise of the BLUESHIRTS; this threat from the right gained de Valera the temporary support of the Labour Party and the IRA. Endeavouring to consolidate his position, he called another election for January 1933 and gained five seats. He dismissed EOIN O'DUFFY from the Commissionership of the Garda Síochána and replaced him with ÉAMONN BROY. A new armed police auxiliary was recruited from among the IRA. The threat posed by the Blueshirts having receded, 1934–33, de Valera now concentrated on the IRA, which he outlawed in 1936.

Opening the thirteenth assembly of the LEAGUE OF NATIONS, 26 September 1932, as President of the Council of the League, de Valera called on the participating states to abide by the principles of the league, not to permit breaches of smaller countries' rights by aggressive countries, and to work for disarmament. He supported the admission of the Soviet Union, 1934, and favoured a policy of non-intervention in the SPANISH CIVIL WAR (1936–39). As President of the Assembly, 1938–39, he supported the policy of appeasement of Germany adopted by NEVILLE CHAMBERLAIN.

Throughout the years 1936–37 de Valera worked on a new constitution. He took advantage of the ABDICATION CRISIS of December 1936 to remove all references to the King and the Governor-General from the Constitution of the Irish Free State, retaining the King only for the purposes of external relations (see EXTERNAL RELATIONS ACT). The new CONSTITUTION OF IRELAND came into force on 29 December 1937. Despite radical changes in the position of the former Free State under de Valera's government, relations with Britain remained cordial. The COAL-CATTLE PACT had assuaged the difficulties of the 'ECONOMIC WAR', which ended in April 1938 with the ANGLO-IRISH AGREEMENTS and saw the return of the TREATY PORTS.

When war broke out in September 1939,

de Valera declared that 'the aim of government policy is to keep this country out of war.' JAMES DILLON raised the only dissenting voice to de Valera's policy of neutrality. To deal with a new IRA campaign, directed against Northern Ireland and England, he introduced the TREASON ACT (1939), OFFENCES AGAINST THE STATE ACT (1939), and EMERGENCY POWERS ACT (1939). During the war he enjoyed a good relationship with the British and German ambassadors but had a stormy one with the American ambassador, David Gray. He resisted considerable pressure from the United States and Britain to enter the war (see 'AMERICAN NOTE'): his rationale was that Ireland could not aid Britain while the country was partitioned, and he ignored Churchill's vague promise to examine the question of partition after the war. Britain heeded his protest against the extension of conscription to Northern Ireland when de Valera claimed that the nationalist minority would not tolerate it. On 2 May 1941, when a German air raid left Belfast in flames, he ordered Dundalk, Drogheda, Dublin and Dún Laoghaire Fire Brigades to Belfast.

Throughout the war de Valera presided over a benign neutrality favourable to the Allied cause. He took the opportunity afforded by the hardships of the period to describe his vision of Ireland; speaking in a radio broadcast on St Patrick's Day, 1943, he said:

> The Ireland which we have dreamed of would be the home of a people who valued material wealth only as the basis of right living, of a people who were satisfied with frugal comfort and devoted their leisure to the things of the spirit; a land whose countryside would be bright with cosy homesteads, whose fields and villages would be joyous with the sounds of industry, with the romping of sturdy children, the contests of athletic youths, the laughter of comely maidens; whose firesides would be forums for the wisdom of old age. It would, in a word, be the home of a people living the life that God desires men should live.

His visit to the German embassy, 30 April 1945, to offer his condolences on the death of Adolf Hitler earned him widespread unpopularity among the Allies (two weeks earlier he had visited the US embassy to offer condolences on the death of Franklin D. Roosevelt). However, he more than compensated at home when he made his celebrated reply to Churchill's attack on Ireland's neutrality. Speaking in a victory broadcast, 13 May 1945, Churchill had said:

> The approaches which the southern Irish ports and airfields could so easily have guarded were closed by the hostile aircraft and U-boats. This indeed was a deadly moment in our life, and if it had not been for the loyalty and friendship of Northern Ireland, we should have been forced to come to close quarters with Mr de Valera, or perish for ever from the earth. However, with a restraint and poise to which, I venture to say, history will find few parallels, His Majesty's Government never laid a violent hand upon them, though at times it would have been quite easy and quite natural, and we left the de Valera Government to frolic with the German and later with the Japanese representatives to their heart's content.

Four days later, in a broadcast on Radio Éireann, 17 May 1943, de Valera replied:

> Allowances can be made for Mr Churchill's statement, however unworthy, in the first flush of victory. No such excuse could be found for me in this quieter atmosphere. There are, however, some things it is essential to say. I shall try to say them as dispassionately as I can.
>
> Mr Churchill makes it clear that, in certain circumstances, he would have violated our neutrality and that he would justify his action by Britain's necessity. It seems strange to me that Mr Churchill does not see that this, if accepted, would mean that Britain's necessity would become a moral code and that when this necessity became sufficiently great, other people's rights were not to count . . .
>
> That is precisely why we have the disastrous succession of wars—World War No. 1 and World War No. 2—and shall it be World War No. 3?
>
> . . . Mr Churchill is proud of Britain's stand alone, after France had fallen and before America entered the war. Could he not find in his heart the generosity to acknowledge that there is a small nation that stood alone not for one year or two, but for several hundred years against aggression; that endured spoliations, famine, massacres, in endless succession; that was clubbed many times into insensibility, but each time on returning consciousness took up the fight anew; a small nation that could never he got to accept defeat and has never surrendered her soul?

De Valera's reply did much to restore flagging morale in the wake of Churchill's speech, which had been internationally reported. In an interview with FRANK GALLAGHER shortly afterwards, Churchill's son Randolph confided that his father 'didn't like it . . . and was very quiet for a long time after it was delivered.'

The economy had stagnated during the war years, and after sixteen years in power Fianna Fáil lost office in 1948, being succeeded by the first inter-party Government. Three years later de Valera returned to power, 13 June 1951, but in 1954 his Government, unable to solve mounting economic problems, again lost office to an inter-party Government. Fianna Fáil won the election of 1957 with seventy-eight seats, and de Valera returned to form his last Government. He retired from the office of Taoiseach, 17 June 1959, and was succeeded by his own choice, SEÁN LEMASS. He defeated SEÁN MAC EOIN in the election for President of Ireland, 1959, and Thomas F. O'Higgins, another Fine Gael candidate, in the election of 1966. Before his retirement in 1973 he was the oldest head of state in the world. His wife, Sinéad de Valera (née Flanagan), died, aged ninety-six, 7 January 1975. On 7 March 1975 de Valera and JOHN A. COSTELLO, who had led both inter-party Governments, were made honorary freemen of the city of Dublin.

Devlin, Joseph (1871–1934), politician (Irish Party and Nationalist Party of Northern Ireland); born in Belfast, educated at Christian Brothers' school. He left school at the age of eleven to work as a pot-boy in a public house. When he was fourteen he founded the Thomas Sexton Debating Society. He was a member of the staff of the IRISH NEWS, which sparked a life-long interest in politics, and later worked in the Belfast office of the FREEMAN'S JOURNAL. Elected member of Parliament for Kilkenny North and Belfast West, 1902, he chose the latter, which he represented until 1918, then sat for the Falls division of Belfast until 1922. A gifted public speaker once called the 'pocket Demosthenes', he was also assistant manager of a public house and secretary of the UNITED IRISH LEAGUE, 1903. A leading member of the ANCIENT ORDER OF HIBERNIANS, he used the BOARD OF ERIN from 1905 as a powerful political machine in opposition to the ORANGE ORDER.

Popularly known as 'Wee Joe', Devlin was the definitive voice of Northern nationalism for almost thirty years. He supported the strike call of JAMES LARKIN in Belfast, 1907, and aided nationalist acceptance of the HOME RULE BILL (1914). During the First World War he encouraged nationalists to join the British army (see CONSCRIPTION). Sitting with the IRISH PARTY in the British House of Commons, he declined the leadership of the party, 1918. Following the general election of 1918 (in which he defeated ÉAMON DE VALERA in the Falls division) he became the undisputed leader of Northern nationalists but continued to sit in the House of Commons when the GOVERNMENT OF IRELAND ACT (1920) created the six-county state of NORTHERN IRELAND. Before the general election of May 1921 he signed a pact with de Valera in which he agreed not to oppose SINN FÉIN candidates; the tactic resulted in Nationalist and Sinn Féin candidates sharing 12 of the 52 seats. Having campaigned on an abstention policy, he remained outside the British Parliament until April 1925, when he took his seat with his fellow-nationalist T. S. McAllister (Co. Antrim).

Opposing the abolition of proportional representation for the parliamentary elections of 1927, Devlin described its removal as a 'mean and contemptible thing.' He did not enter the Parliament of Northern Ireland until 1925. Following his death the Nationalist Party went into a decline that was not halted until the mid-1940s.

Devlin, Paddy (1925–1999), trade unionist and politician (Labour, SDLP, United Labour, and Labour Party of Northern Ireland); born in the Falls Road area, Belfast, educated at primary school. A member of the IRA, 1936–50, he was interned, 1942–45, after which he abandoned militant republicanism, became an implacable enemy of violence, and sought a solution to social problems. A member of the Irish Labour Party from 1950, he defeated GERRY FITT for a Belfast City Council seat in 1955. Three years later he joined the NORTHERN IRELAND LABOUR PARTY. Involved in the civil rights movement in the late 1960s, he won a seat in the Parliament of Northern Ireland for the Falls area in 1969 and a year later was a founder-member of the SOCIAL DEMOCRATIC AND LABOUR PARTY, though from its inception he was unhappy with the tension between nationalists and socialists in the party. Attacked for his outspoken criticism of the Provisional IRA, he nonetheless helped arrange the Cheyne Walk meeting in July 1972 between representatives of the British Government and the Provisional IRA.

He was Minister for Health and Social

Services in the short-lived power-sharing Executive, 1974. In 1977 he was expelled from the SDLP when he suggested that the 'nationalist agenda' was influencing the party's socialist programme. Joint founder of the United Labour Party, he was an unsuccessful candidate in the 1979 elections for the European Parliament. He was a member of the Housing Executive, 1983–86. In 1985 he failed to win a seat as a candidate for the new Labour Party of Northern Ireland, of which he was also joint founder. As chairman of LABOUR '87 in 1987 he campaigned in the United States against the MACBRIDE PRINCIPLES. In 1996 he was awarded an honorary degree by the University of Ulster and in 1999 was made a commander of the Order of the British Empire. His writings include *The Fall of the Northern Ireland Executive* (1975), *And Yes, We Have No Bananas: Outdoor Relief in Belfast, 1920–39* (1981), and his autobiography, *Straight Left* (1995).

devolution, the proposal for the granting of a limited form of devolved power to Ireland through an extension of LOCAL GOVERNMENT in 1904. Though supported by southern unionists, led by EARL DUNRAVEN, it provoked northern unionist hostility and led to the resignation of the Chief Secretary for Ireland, GEORGE WYNDHAM, and the formation of the ULSTER UNIONIST COUNCIL. Published by the IRISH REFORM ASSOCIATION, 1904, and supported by the architect of the scheme, SIR ANTONY MACDONNELL, Under-Secretary for Ireland, the proposal was renounced by Wyndham, who publicly admonished MacDonnell. Simmering unionist discontent, and MacDonnell's assertion that he acted with Wyndham's tacit approval, forced Wyndham's resignation. The proposal failed to achieve unanimous nationalist approval, as did its successor, the IRISH COUNCIL BILL (1907).

Devon Commission, a commission (the 175th since the Union to inquire into matters relating specifically to Ireland) appointed in 1843 by SIR ROBERT PEEL, under the chairmanship of Lord Devon. Its secretary, John Pitt Kennedy, was a landlord, as were all its members. DANIEL O'CONNELL, on being informed of its composition, declared: 'It is perfectly one-sided, all landlords and no tenants.'

The commission investigated relations between landlord and tenant, mode of land occupation, the need for improvement, and the conditions and habits of the labouring class. Having heard more than a thousand witnesses, it issued its report in 1847. Drawing attention to the extreme and widespread poverty of labourers and their families, it concluded:

> It will be seen in the Evidence, that in many districts their only food is the potato, their only beverage water, that their cabins are seldom a protection against the weather, that a bed or a blanket is a rare luxury, and that nearly in all, their pig and manure heap constitute their only property.

The rejection of the minor improvements recommended in the report was rendered immaterial by the onset of the GREAT FAMINE (1845–49).

Devonshire, Spencer Compton Cavendish, Marquess of Hartington and eighth Duke of (1833–1908); British politician (Liberal); born in Lancashire, elder brother of LORD FREDERICK CAVENDISH. He entered Parliament in 1857 and was created Marquess of Hartington in 1858. He supported W. E. GLADSTONE on the DISESTABLISHMENT of the Church of Ireland. Having refused the Viceroyalty of Ireland, 1869, he accepted office as Chief Secretary, 1870–74, and secured wide powers of COERCION to suppress the RIBBONMEN. His term of office saw the emergence of the campaign for home rule (of which he disapproved), led by ISAAC BUTT. He introduced the BALLOT ACT (1872), which established the secret ballot at Irish elections, enabling tenants to vote for candidates of their choice. He refused an invitation by QUEEN VICTORIA to form an administration on the fall of the Disraeli government, 1880, and served as Lord President of the Council in the Unionist government, 1895–1903.

Devoy, John (1842–1928), Fenian; born in Johnstown, Co. Kildare, educated in Marlborough Street and School Street, Dublin, where he became monitor at 10 shillings a week. Short-sighted from an early age, on leaving school he was employed with his father at Watkins' Brewery, Naas, Co. Kildare. He joined the IRB, 1861, and the Engineering Corps of the French Foreign Legion but saw little action in Algiers. Returning to Ireland, 1862, he became IRB organiser for the Naas area, with weekly expenses of £3. With PATRICK 'PAGAN' O'LEARY and JOHN BOYLE O'REILLY he recruited some fifteen thousand serving soldiers to Fenian ranks but was identified as a Fenian activist and *agent provocateur*. Following the arrest of Fenian leaders, 1865, he became chief organiser for the movement. Shortly after masterminding the escape of JAMES STEPHENS from Richmond

Prison he was arrested, 22 February 1866, and sentenced to fifteen years' penal servitude. In prison he met JEREMIAH O'DONOVAN ROSSA.

Released in 1871 on condition that he not re-enter the United Kingdom until his sentence had expired, Devoy went to the United States as one of the 'CUBA FIVE'. At first employed as a clerk with a New York sugar trader at $700 a year, he joined CLAN NA GAEL and had a brief flirtation with left-wing politics, 1871, when appointed Irish delegate to the North American Convention of the International Workingmens' Association. He worked on a variety of newspapers, including the *Chicago Evening Post, Chicago Herald, Evening Journal,* GAELIC AMERICAN (which he published and edited), and *New York Herald.* He masterminded the CATALPA expedition, 1876, to rescue Fenian prisoners from Fremantle, Australia. Having opposed the 'SKIRMISHING FUND', he supported the NEW DEPARTURE and financed the efforts of MICHAEL DAVITT and CHARLES STEWART PARNELL to bring the land question to a satisfactory conclusion. He founded the *Irish Nation,* 1881, with the incentive of a free rifle for every twenty subscriptions sold. He supported the PLAN OF CAMPAIGN but vehemently opposed the 'TRIANGLE' or terrorist wing of Clan na Gael, whose members he supplanted in the late 1880s.

In 1897 Devoy arranged a financially successful lecture tour of the United States for JOHN DALY and in 1901 was a guest at the wedding in New York of his lifelong friends THOMAS J. CLARKE and Kathleen Daly (John Daly's niece). In 1914, aided by JUDGE DANIEL COHALAN and JOSEPH MCGARRITY, he arranged a lecture tour for PATRICK PEARSE that realised £1,500 and saved ST ENDA'S SCHOOL from imminent closure.

Unsuccessful in his efforts to interest the German ambassador in Ireland's potential as an ally, Devoy arranged a contact between ROGER CASEMENT and the ambassador, 1914. Though troubled with deafness and increasingly poor vision, he attempted to involve himself in the EASTER RISING (1916)—in which his nephew Peadar fought—but was unable to obtain the necessary travel papers. In the aftermath of the rising he arranged a subscription to the widowed Kathleen Clarke. The commission that investigated the rising found it incomprehensible that a man so actively engaged in the Fenian movement of the 1860s could have been so deeply involved in the planning of a revolution almost fifty years later.

Devoy broke with ÉAMON DE VALERA and the IRB in 1920 on the question of de Valera's American tactics. He supported the ANGLO-IRISH TREATY (1921), which he viewed as a necessary precursor to statehood. He returned to Ireland, 26 July 1924, and during a six-week stay met the President of the Executive Council (head of the Free State government), W. T. COSGRAVE, visited Rossa's grave at Glasnevin, Dublin, met his one-time fiancée Elizabeth Kenny Kilmurry, and was a guest of honour at the Tailteann Games and a guest of the Distinguished Visitors' Committee at the invitation of its chairman, W. B. YEATS. He died on 29 September 1928, and his remains were returned to Ireland aboard the *President Harding.* Following a state funeral, 16 June 1929, he was interred in Glasnevin. Reporting the event, the *Times* (London) commented that Devoy was 'the most bitter and persistent, as well as the most dangerous, enemy of this country which Ireland has produced since Wolfe Tone.'

Dickson, Anne (born 1928), politician (Ulster Unionist Party and Unionist Party of Northern Ireland); born in London. As member for Carrick in the Parliament of Northern Ireland, 1969, she supported TERENCE O'NEILL. She was a member of the Northern Ireland Assembly from 1973 and succeeded BRIAN FAULKNER as leader of the UNIONIST PARTY OF NORTHERN IRELAND, 1976–81, the first woman leader of a Northern political party. Active in local politics, she was chairperson of the Northern Ireland Consumer Council, 1985–90.

Dillon, James (1902–1986), politician (independent and Fine Gael); born in Dublin, son of JOHN DILLON, educated at UCD. He studied business management in London and Chicago before his election as independent member of Dáil Éireann for Co. Donegal, 1932–37. With FRANK MCDERMOT he founded the NATIONAL CENTRE PARTY, 1932, which in 1933 joined with CUMANN NA NGAEDHEAL and the BLUESHIRTS to form the United Ireland Party, which shortly afterwards became known as FINE GAEL and of which he became vice-president. Representing Co. Monaghan from 1937 until his retirement in 1968, he opposed the Republicans in the SPANISH CIVIL WAR (1936–39), describing the core issue as 'God or no God'. During the years of the Second World War he challenged the Dáil consensus on neutrality and was disowned by his party when he suggested that Ireland should align itself with the United States; when the Fine Gael ard-fheis rejected his call to support the Allied cause he resigned from the party, February 1942, and sat on the independent benches. Throughout the war he remained close to the US ambassador, David Gray, and his British counterpart, Sir John Maffey, who described Dillon as possessing 'religious fanaticism of the purest kind I have met.'

Returned as an independent in the general elections of 1943, 1944, and 1948, Dillon accepted office as Minister for Agriculture in the first inter-party Government, 1948–51. He rejoined Fine Gael before the general election of 1951 and was again Minister for Agriculture, 1954–57. He was leader of Fine Gael from 1959 until his retirement to the back benches in 1965.

A colourful character with an orotund style of delivery, Dillon was widely regarded as the finest orator in Dáil Éireann. Possessor of a sardonic wit, he was also prone to the occasional bull, famously describing a deputy standing as an electoral 'stalking horse' as someone who had made 'a complete ass of himself.'

Dillon, John (1851–1927), land agitator and politician (Nationalist); born in Blackrock, Co. Dublin, son of JOHN BLAKE DILLON, educated privately and at the Catholic University. His father moved the family to the United States until 1855. After working briefly in Manchester for a cotton merchant Dillon returned to Dublin, where he qualified as a doctor in 1875, though he never practised. He assisted the campaign that secured the Co. Tipperary parliamentary seat for an ailing JOHN MITCHEL, 1875. Dillon, who supported the use of force in settlement of the land question, was a member of the HOME RULE LEAGUE and of the SOCIETY FOR THE PRESERVATION OF THE IRISH LANGUAGE (to which he introduced ISAAC BUTT). Impressed by the policy of obstructionism, he became increasingly disillusioned with Butt's leadership. In a letter to the *Freeman's Journal*, 23 December 1878, he asserted: 'No honest Irish nationalist can any longer continue to recognise Mr. Butt as leader.' He arrived in New York with CHARLES STEWART PARNELL, 2 January 1880, on a fund-raising tour that raised £70,000 for the LAND LEAGUE. As member of Parliament for Co. Tipperary he was a signatory of the 'NO-RENT MANIFESTO', October 1881; the campaign mirrored a policy he had advocated the previous year.

Following a break in America for reasons of health, 1883–85, Dillon returned to Ireland and was elected member of Parliament for Mayo East, which he represented until 1918. With WILLIAM O'BRIEN he oversaw the PLAN OF CAMPAIGN at the estate of the EARL OF CLANRICARDE at Woodford, Co. Mayo.

On 9 September 1887 Dillon appeared at Mitchelstown (O'Brien did not), where three people were killed and two wounded by the RIC in the 'MITCHELSTOWN MASSACRE'. He entered into a bitter controversy with BISHOP EDWARD THOMAS O'DWYER, who had denounced the Plan of Campaign on the O'Grady estate at Herbertstown, Co. Limerick, as 'highway robbery and plunder.' With ARCHBISHOP CROKE he devised a formula for circumventing the Papal decree of 1888 that condemned both the Plan of Campaign and the boycott weapon. He raised £33,000 for the Plan of Campaign in Australia and returned to Ireland, 20 April 1890. Due to stand trial for his activities, he and O'Brien skipped bail and went to America. They were abroad when the crisis broke over Parnell's leadership in the wake of the O'Shea divorce case. When attempts at compromise failed, Dillon and O'Brien became leaders of the anti-Parnell wing of the IRISH NATIONAL FEDERATION. As its chairman from February 1896, Dillon was a member of the ALL-IRELAND COMMITTEE (1897). He was at the launch of O'Brien's UNITED IRISH LEAGUE, 23 January 1898; a year later he resigned the leadership of the Irish National Federation to facilitate the reunification of the party under the auspices of the United Irish League and the leadership of JOHN REDMOND. Noted for his attacks on the Anglo-Boer War, he was acknowledged by the Boers as one of their strongest defenders.

Dillon was sceptical of O'Brien's enthusiasm for finding solutions through conference and conciliation, as evidenced in the LAND CONFERENCE (1902), which led to the Irish Land Act (1903) (see LAND ACTS). His condemnation of the act led to a permanent breach with O'Brien. He condemned plans to have Irish made an obligatory subject for matriculation to the National University of Ireland. He led opposition to the attempt to suppress the demand for home rule through a process of devolution in the IRISH COUNCIL BILL (1907). He supported the third HOME RULE BILL and was present at various meetings, including the BUCKINGHAM PALACE CONFERENCE, that endeavoured to settle the Ulster question.

Dillon and other moderates were alarmed by the rise of the IRISH VOLUNTEERS and the strong nationalist movement developing under the aegis of the IRB. Following the EASTER RISING (1916) he made representations to Britain in an effort to prevent the executions and distanced himself from Redmond's unequivocal condemnation of those involved. He was also deeply involved in attempts to keep the FREEMAN'S JOURNAL afloat after 1916. He succeeded Redmond as leader of the Irish Party in March 1918 and was a member of the MANSION HOUSE COMMITTEE (1918), which organised the campaign against CONSCRIPTION. He witnessed the emergence of SINN FÉIN as a political force and in December 1918 was defeated by the imprisoned ÉAMON DE VALERA (8,975 to 4,514). He retired from public life shortly afterwards.

Dillon, John Blake (1816–1866), lawyer and Young Irelander; born in Ballaghaderreen, Co. Roscommon, educated at St Patrick's College, Maynooth, and TCD, where he met THOMAS DAVIS. A member of the REPEAL ASSOCIATION, 1840, he was called to the bar, 1842. He was a member of YOUNG IRELAND and the IRISH CONFEDERATION. With Davis and CHARLES GAVAN DUFFY he founded the NATION in 1842. Though opposed to the extremism of JOHN MITCHEL he took part in the Rising of 1848 and commanded the insurgents at Killenaule, Co. Tipperary. Following the collapse of the rising he made his way to the United States, where he had a successful law practice with RICHARD O'GORMAN, 1826–95. In 1849 he advocated a federal republic for Britain and Ireland.

He returned to Ireland under amnesty, 1855, and was elected to Dublin Corporation and member of Parliament for Co. Tipperary, 1865–66. He was joint founder and first secretary of the NATIONAL ASSOCIATION, 1865, which he used to denounce the FENIANS. Following his death from cholera on 15 September, Mitchel said of him that he was all wrong on almost every question but was nevertheless better than most people who were right.

Dillon, Myles (1900–1972), Celtic scholar; born in Dublin, son of JOHN DILLON, educated at UCD and the Universities of Bonn, Heidelberg, and Paris. Reader in Sanskrit at Trinity College, Dublin, 1928–39, and comparative philology and Sanskrit at University College, Dublin, 1930–37, he was professor of Irish at Wisconsin University until 1946, when the American Office of War Information employed him in London. Following a brief period as professor of Celtic studies at the University of Edinburgh he joined the Dublin Institute of Advanced Studies as senior professor in the School of Celtic Studies, of which he was director, 1960–68. He lectured in several countries, including England, Australia, India, and the United States. His works include *The Cycle of the Kings* (1946), *Early Irish Literature* (1948), and *Lebor na gCert: The Book of Rights* (1962). He edited *Early Irish Society* (1954) and *Irish Sagas* (1959) for the Radio Éireann Thomas Davis Lecture Series.

Dinneen, Rev. Patrick (1860–1934), clergyman (Catholic), scholar, and lexicographer; born in Carn, Rathmore, Co. Kerry, educated at UCD, where he studied Latin under Gerald Manley Hopkins (1844–89). Following his ordination as a Jesuit, 1894, he taught English and mathematics at Mungret College, Limerick, and Clongowes Wood College, Co. Kildare. He left the Jesuit order in 1900. A prominent member of the Gaelic League, he devoted the remainder of his life to the study of Irish manuscripts in the National Library. One of the earliest professional journalists writing solely in Irish, he edited several poetical works, including those of Aogán Ó Raithile (1900), Eoghan Rua Ó Súileabháin (1901), Seán Clárach Mac Dónaill (1902), and Piaras Feirtéir (1903). His most celebrated work, *Foclóir Gaedhilge agus Béarla* (Irish–English dictionary), was published in 1904; it appeared again in 1927, completely rewritten because of the loss of the original plates in the EASTER RISING (1916). The new edition was underwritten by the IRISH TEXTS SOCIETY and a government grant of £1,000. Dinneen wrote school texts and edited Céitinn's history, *Foras Feasa ar Éirinn.* His translations into Irish include *A Christmas Carol* (1903) and the *Aeneid* (1931).

Diplock Courts, a name given to courts operating in Northern Ireland as a result of the Diplock Report, presented to the British House of Commons, 20 December 1972. The Diplock Commission sought a means of circumventing problems in the judicial system resulting from the intimidation of witnesses and juries. Condemned by republicans, the Diplock courts were presided over by one judge, without a jury, to try those accused of terrorist offences or violence, and had an easier admissibility of confession than normal courts.

Director of Public Prosecutions, an office established in 1974. Independent of all other legal and quasi-legal institutions, it has jealously guarded its independence. The first director,

1975–2000, was Éamon Barnes.

DIRT Inquiry (1999). The Comptroller and Auditor-General, John Purcell, published a report, 20 July 1999, giving evidence of bogus accounts operated by most of the country's financial institutions during the late 1980s and early 90s. The accounts were specifically intended to avoid the payment of deposit interest retention tax (DIRT), introduced in 1986. The report showed that tax evasion through the abuse of non-resident accounts was known to successive Governments, the Department of Finance, the Central Bank, and the Revenue Commissioners; their reluctance to deal with the abuse stemmed from a fear that investigation would lead to the flight of capital, undermining the Irish pound and affecting interest rates. In 1993 the Department of Finance estimated that £2 billion was lodged in such accounts. It also emerged that Allied Irish Banks believed that it had in effect a tax amnesty from the Revenue Commissioners in relation to taxes due since the 1980s.

The Dáil Committee of Public Accounts conducted a public inquiry into the evasion of tax through bogus non-resident accounts. The inquiry, conducted by Seán Ardagh, Seán Doherty and Denis Foley (Fianna Fáil), Bernard Durkan (Fine Gael), and PAT RABBITTE (Labour Party), under the chairmanship of Jim Mitchell (Fine Gael), made use of the Comptroller and Auditor-General's report. The inquiry had the constitutional and legal power to direct witnesses from financial institutions, the Revenue Commissioners, the Central Bank and the Department of Finance to appear. The hearings, which were televised live, were in two phases: the committee's own public hearings, and a section dealing with the Comptroller and Auditor-General's investigation. Following twenty-six days of hearings, involving 150,000 pages of evidence and 142 witnesses, the committee adjourned on 12 October 1999 to compile its report, which was published on 15 December.

Finding that tax evasion was 'an industry-wide phenomenon,' the report was critical of the Central Bank, Department of Finance, Revenue Commissioners, and senior management of all the principal financial institutions (Allied Irish Banks, Bank of Ireland, Ulster Bank, National Irish Bank, Agricultural Credit Corporation, Irish Life, and Irish Permanent). It found that the Revenue Commissioners in the 1980s and early 90s had not implemented the tax laws fairly and that there was an 'inappropriate relationship' between banks and the state and state agencies: the latter were 'perhaps too mindful of the concerns of the banks and too attentive to their pleas and lobbying.' It found that bogus non-resident accounts facilitated large-scale tax evasion.

In July 1986, following the introduction of DIRT, a 'temporary' instruction (SIM 263) prohibited Revenue inspectors from inspecting non-resident declaration forms maintained by the banks for each non-resident account. (The Committee of Public Accounts failed to identify the author of SIM 263, which was not rescinded until 1998, when the DIRT controversy entered the public arena.) It found that, contrary to the contention of Allied Irish Banks, there had been 'no deal, agreement or understanding' by the Revenue Commissioners with AIB for the writing off of DIRT (which left AIB liable for a £100 million claim for evaded tax).

The committee found that the Department of Finance 'did not fully inform Ministers during the relevant period [1986–98] in relation to problems of bogus non-resident accounts.' It also found that the Central Bank had taken no action, though bogus non-resident accounts were in breach of the exchange control regulations that existed up to 1992. 'There was insufficient concern with ethics and supervision other than from a standpoint of a tradition of narrow concern with prudential supervision in the Central Bank.' The Central Bank, Department of Finance and Revenue Commissioners were all aware 'before and after the introduction of DIRT of the existence of evasion.' The committee also found that the failure to tackle the DIRT problems was 'a contributing factor to the fiscal crisis of the time and delayed the process of restoring order to the public finances.' As a result of the committee's findings, financial institutions paid £100 million in settlements to the Revenue Commissioners.

On 27 January 2000 it was revealed that the deputy chairman of the Committee of Public Accounts, Denis Foley TD (Fianna Fáil), was the possessor of an Ansbacher account. He resigned from his position on the committee. (See ANSBACHER INQUIRY.)

disestablishment of the Church of Ireland (1869). The anomalous position of an established church, which represented 12½ per cent of the population, enjoying privileges denied to the Roman Catholic and Presbyterian churches was a contributing factor to simmering unrest in Ireland. The payment of TITHES by the adherents of one church for the upkeep of another provoked frequent outrage, culminating in the 'Tithe War' of the 1830s. The situation was exacerbated by the educational advantages and the patronage enjoyed by members of the established church.

The disestablishment of the Church of Ireland was a central plank in the electoral policy put forward by W. E. GLADSTONE in 1868. Despite opposition both in Ireland and in England, he introduced an act requiring that the Church of Ireland become a voluntary body from 1 January 1871. The Irish Church Act (1869), drafted by Hugh Lane Law (1818–1883), also provided for the disendowment of the church's considerable landholdings, property, and bequests (valued at £600,000 a year in 1867). Apart from the churches and churchyards in use, the Church of Ireland was to lose its holdings and property, to be vested in a body of Commissioners for the Irish Church Temporalities. Compensation paid under the act amounted to £16 million, representing approximately half the value of the confiscated properties. The remainder was to be used for the relief of poverty, endowments for higher education, and the encouragement of agriculture and fisheries (between 1871 and 1923, £1.3 million was paid out for these purposes). Some six thousand tenants availed of the offer to buy lands formerly owned by the Church of Ireland. Embodied in the act was a general disestablishment of all religion, under which the Maynooth Grant and the Presbyterian REGIUM DONUM were also abolished.

From January 1871 the Church of Ireland became a voluntary body, governed by the General Synod, while its financial affairs, including payments to clergy, were dealt with by the Representative Church Body.

Disraeli, Benjamin, first Earl of Beaconsfield (1804–1881), British politician (Conservative); born in London. Disraeli became member of Parliament for Maidstone in 1837 on his fifth attempt at election. His first speech in the House of Commons was greeted with such derision that only his closing words were audible: 'And though I sit down now, the time will come when you will hear me.' In 1844 he described the 'Irish question' as 'a starving population, an absentee aristocracy, an alien church, and . . . the weakest executive in the world.' He opposed the Maynooth grant, 1845, and led opposition to the repeal of the Corn Laws proposed by SIR ROBERT PEEL during the GREAT FAMINE (1845–49). As Chancellor of the Exchequer, 1858–59, he attempted to harmonise Irish and British tax regimes. Opposed to DISESTABLISHMENT OF THE CHURCH OF IRELAND, on his return to office he was responsible for two acts of consequence to Ireland: the first, 1878, provided grants to secondary schools based on results obtained in the Intermediate Board Examination; the second, 1879, did not fully respond to the demands of the Catholic hierarchy for an autonomous Catholic university but established the ROYAL UNIVERSITY OF IRELAND, with examinations open to all students.

Created Earl of Beaconsfield, 1876, Disraeli retired from politics following his electoral defeat in 1880 and was succeeded as Prime Minister by W. E. GLADSTONE. A successful novelist, his works included the trilogy *Coningsby* (1844), *Sybil* (1845), and *Tancred* (1847).

Document No. 2, an alternative proposal for a treaty between Ireland and Britain put forward at a private session of Dáil Éireann, 14 December 1921, by ÉAMON DE VALERA, who sought to avoid discussion on the document in the Dáil before the debate on the Treaty. He claimed, 4 January, that he was formally giving notice of intention to move the document as an amendment to the motion on the ANGLO-IRISH TREATY. Responding to a charge by ARTHUR GRIFFITH that six clauses had been omitted from the original draft, de Valera claimed it had been amended 'as I would have done with any other document.' MICHAEL COLLINS disparagingly referred to the proposal as 'Document No. 3'.

On his resignation as President of Dáil Éireann, 6 January, de Valera stated that if re-elected he would place the document before the new Ministry for submission to the Dáil. On the acceptance of the treaty (64 to 57) he resigned. Griffith stated on 7 January that London had absolutely rejected de Valera's proposals on EXTERNAL ASSOCIATION, and that Document No. 2 was a third attempt at presenting a twice-rejected concept.

In Document No. 2 de Valera had proposed:

> That inasmuch as the "Articles of Agreement for a Treaty between Great Britain and Ireland" signed in London on December 6th, 1921, do not reconcile Irish National aspirations and the Association of Ireland with the Community of Nations known as the British Commonwealth, and cannot be the basis of an enduring peace between the Irish and British peoples, Dáil Éireann, in the name of the Sovereign Irish Nation, makes to the Government of Great Britain, to the Governments of the other

> States of the British Commonwealth, and to the peoples of Great Britain and of those several States, the following proposal for a Treaty of Amity and Association which Dáil Éireann is convinced could be entered into by the Irish people with the sincerity of goodwill.

This alternative differed in important points from the Anglo-Irish Treaty, article 1 of which declared 'that the legislative, executive, and judicial authority of Ireland shall be derived solely from the people of Ireland.' De Valera's 'external association' model was asserted in article 2: 'That, for purposes of common concern, Ireland shall be associated with the States of the British Commonwealth, viz: the Kingdom of Great Britain, the Dominion of Canada, the Commonwealth of Australia, the Dominion of New Zealand, and the Union of South Africa.' Whereas the Treaty included an oath of allegiance that embraced the King, de Valera's document proposed (article 6) 'that, for purposes of the Association, Ireland shall recognise His Britannic Majesty as head of the Association.'

Having dealt with the terms of association (articles 2–6), Document No. 2 remained close to the Treaty. Articles 7–10 dealt with defence, giving a guarantee of good will to Britain in the event of war: 'That for five years, pending the establishment of Irish coastal defence forces, or for such other period as the Governments of the two countries may later agree upon, facilities for the coastal defence of Ireland shall be given to the British Government . . .' (article 8). An annex arising out of this article was identical to one contained in the Treaty.

As an alternative to articles 12–15 of the Treaty, Document No. 2 contained an addendum dealing with Northern Ireland; headed 'North-East Ulster', it submitted

> that whilst refusing to admit the right of any part of Ireland to be excluded from the supreme authority of the Parliament of Ireland, or that the relationship between the Parliament of Ireland and any subordinate legislature in Ireland can be a matter for treaty with a Government outside Ireland, nevertheless, in sincere regard for internal peace, and in order to make manifest our desire not to bring force or coercion to bear on any substantial part of the Province of Ulster, whose inhabitants may not be unwilling to accept the national authority, we are prepared to grant to that portion of Ulster which is defined as Northern Ireland in the British Government of Ireland Act 1920, privileges and safeguards not less substantial than those provided for in the "Articles of Agreement for a Treaty between Great Britain and Ireland" signed in London on December 6th, 1921.

Doheny, Michael (1805–1863), Young Irelander and poet; born in Brookhill, Fethard, Co. Tipperary. Largely self-educated, he worked on his father's smallholding and taught school on occasion. He entered Gray's Inn, London, 1834, and helped pay for his legal studies by working as a parliamentary reporter, then enjoyed a successful legal career. A member of the REPEAL ASSOCIATION, as 'Éreanach' he was a frequent contributor to the *Nation*. As a member of the IRISH CONFEDERATION he was influenced by the speeches and writings of THOMAS DAVIS and the agrarian reformist JAMES FINTAN LALOR, but he opposed the extremism of JOHN MITCHEL. Following the collapse of the 1848 Rising he went to the United States, where he continued his legal career and was a founder-member of the FENIANS. In a letter on the land question to WILLIAM SMITH O'BRIEN, 20 August 1858, he wrote: 'I favour the abolition of Irish landlordism, and I would put a limit on the amount of land one person can hold, so that the land would be brought within the reach of all.'

Doheny attended the funeral of the Fenian TERENCE BELLEW MCMANUS, November 1861. *In the Felon's Track, or History of the Attempted Outbreak in Ireland,* was published in 1847. His best-known poems are 'A Cushla Gal Mo Chree', 'The Shan Van Vocht', and 'The Outlaw's Wife'. His nephew Edward L. Doheny (1856–1935) amassed a fortune in the Californian and Mexican oil business and was selected by ÉAMON DE VALERA to lead the American Committee for Relief in Ireland, 1920.

Doherty, John (1783–1850), lawyer and politician (Conservative); born in Dublin, educated at TCD. From 1808 he practised on the Leinster Circuit and was member of Parliament for New Ross, 1824–26, and Kilkenny, 1826–30. He became Solicitor-General, 1827, and Lord Chief Justice of the Common Pleas, 1830. He led for the state in the DONERAILE CONSPIRACY when DANIEL O'CONNELL successfully represented a number of the accused. Doherty was a noted parliamentary orator and wit and played a leading role in debates on Irish affairs. He supported CATHOLIC EMANCIPATION (believed to have been the only time he was at one with O'Connell). He lost much of his fortune in railway speculation and was a depressive in his later years.

Dolly's Brae Affray (12 July 1849). Dolly's Brae, near Magheramayo, Co. Down, was the scene of a bloody confrontation between RIBBONMEN and members of an ORANGE ORDER rally. Ribbonmen confronted the Orangemen returning under police and military protection from a rally on the estate of the EARL OF RODEN at Tullymore as they passed through Magheramayo. Shots were fired during the three-hour engagement, and thirty Catholics were killed. The victory at Dolly's Brae entered the annals of Orange folklore. It also led to the enactment of the ineffectual Party Processions Act (1850). Roden was censured by a commission of inquiry and deprived of the office of peace commissioner.

Doneraile Conspiracy (1829). The area around Doneraile, Co. Cork, home of the St Leger family, was the scene of intense activity by the WHITEBOYS. Following an attack on a local Protestant, Dr John Norcott, and a belief that there was a conspiracy to murder three local landlords—Michael Creagh, Rear-Admiral Henry Evans, and George Bond Low—a campaign was organised by Bond Low, who was a magistrate, to end Whiteboy activity in the area. A fund was launched and a sum of £732 collected for information leading to the arrest of Whiteboys. Perjured evidence presented by Owen 'Cloumper' Daly, his cousin Patrick Daly, William Nowlan, David Sheehan and Thomas Murphy resulted in the appearance of twenty-one men in four stages before packed juries.

The trial opened under Judges Torrens and Pennefather, 23 October, with JOHN DOHERTY leading for the prosecution. Four prisoners—John Leary, James Roche, James McGrath, and William Shine—were sentenced to death. The following day, a Saturday, Timothy Barrett, Edmund Connors, Patrick Lynch and Michael Wallace were sentenced to death. The trial of the other accused was postponed until the following Monday.

William Burke of Ballyhea, a brother of one of the accused yet to be tried, rode to Derrynane, Co. Kerry, and procured the services of DANIEL O'CONNELL. Having rested, he returned to Cork on the same horse within thirty-eight hours, having covered some 180 miles. O'Connell, arriving in court during the Solicitor-General's speech, obtained permission to take breakfast. He then set out to undermine the prosecutor and, with a series of timely interruptions, succeeded in turning the spotlight entirely onto the case for the defence. During the evidence of Patrick Daly, Judge Pennefather drew O'Connell's attention to the fact that the oral evidence now presented by the witness was at variance with an earlier affidavit. O'Connell so hopelessly confused the other witnesses that the jury, though confined for up to forty-eight hours, failed to agree, and the trials were postponed. The sentence of death on the original four was commuted to transportation to New South Wales, and the remainder of the prisoners were acquitted.

The trial is the subject of the novel *Glenanaar* (1905) by Canon P. A. Sheehan

Donnellan, Michael (1900–1964), farmer and politician (Clann na Talmhan); born in Dunmore, Co. Galway, educated at St Jarlath's College, Tuam. He founded and was leader of CLANN NA TALMHAN, 1938–44, established to further the interests of the smaller farmers of the west of Ireland. He represented Galway West, 1943–48, Galway North, 1948–61, and Galway East, 1961–64, and was parliamentary secretary to the Minister for Finance in two inter-party Governments, 1948–51 and 1954–57.

Doolough Death March (30–31 March 1849). On Friday 30 March 1849 a large body of poorly clad and starving tenant-farmers gathered at Louisburgh, Co. Mayo, seeking either food or admission to Westport Workhouse. They had travelled over inhospitable terrain in appalling weather, carrying their children. The relieving officer, Carroll, and the Poor Law inspectors, Primrose and Hogrove, later instructed them to present themselves at Delphi Lodge, Bundorragha, 20 miles away, at seven o'clock the following morning for inspection. Hundreds waited at Delphi on Saturday 31 March while the officials finished their breakfast, after which they informed the starving applicants that neither relief nor tickets to the workhouse would be granted. Returning home in a blizzard, many collapsed from hunger and exhaustion or were drowned in Stroppabue Lake or the swollen Glankeen River. Others later died from their exertions. In an editorial the *Mayo Constitution* commented, 17 April 1849:

> Our blood curdles at the frightful history—to imagine that poor wretches, after dragging their enfeebled bodies and the emaciated persons of their children distances varying from five to seven miles to the town of Louisburgh, to await the ease of the Poor Law Guardians! are ordered to proceed further, without food or clothing, a distance of twenty miles to a locality where, if they had the means, they could not procure a morsel of food,

> nor shelter for a night . . . We also are of opinion that other officials, whose duty it was to hold inquests, have not discharged that duty in a proper manner. We refer to the Coroner [Bourke], who, we are told, held three inquests, without taking the trouble to examine witnesses to arrive at the truth of how or by what means the victims of cruelty came by their deaths, instead of which he merely examined persons who were strangers to the facts, and found the hasty verdict of "death by starvation;" and then, after doing the friendly turn, and holding a post mortem examination, he directs the bodies to be huddled back into the boghole from which they were dragged after having a few guineas earned by their inspection.

Many of those who died were buried where they fell; others were drowned. The deaths of entire families or of those living alone went largely unrecorded, and there were horrific tales of bodies being devoured by domestic or wild animals. The total number of deaths has been disputed: officially estimated at approximately twenty, some contemporary accounts put the figure at hundreds.

Douglas, James G. (1887–1954), politician; born in Dublin, educated at Friends' School, Lisburn. A lifelong activist in the Society of Friends, during the WAR OF INDEPENDENCE he was treasurer and a trustee of the WHITE CROSS. On the establishment of the Irish Free State he became a senator and was vice-chairman of the Senate, 1922–25, and also chairman of the Joint Committee of the Dáil and Senate on Standing Orders (Private Business). He was a member of he committee that drafted the CONSTITUTION OF THE IRISH FREE STATE (1922) and a member of Seanad Éireann, 1938–43 and 1944–54.

Downing Street Declaration (1969), issued as a result of a meeting between the Prime Minister of Northern Ireland, JAMES CHICHESTER-CLARK, and the British Prime Minister, HAROLD WILSON, 19 August 1969. It affirmed that 'every citizen of Northern Ireland is entitled to the same equality of treatment and freedom from discrimination as obtains in the rest of the United Kingdom irrespective of political views or religion,' and that 'Northern Ireland should not cease to be part of the United Kingdom without the consent of the people of Northern Ireland . . . The border is not an issue.'

Downing Street Declaration (1993), also known as the Joint Declaration, signed by the Taoiseach, ALBERT REYNOLDS, and the British Prime Minister, JOHN MAJOR, 15 December 1993. It reaffirmed Northern Ireland's constitutional guarantee and aimed to foster agreement and reconciliation leading to a new political framework within Ireland. It pledged to preserve the Union until a majority within Northern Ireland determined otherwise. The Irish Government accepted that 'the democratic right of self-determination by the people as a whole must be achieved and exercised with and subject to the agreement and consent of a majority of the people of Northern Ireland and must . . . respect the democratic dignity and the civil rights and religious liberties of both communities.'

Doyle, James Warren ('JKL') (1786–1834), bishop (Catholic); born near New Ross, Co. Wexford, educated at the Augustinian College, New Ross, and the University of Coimbra, Portugal. As a child he witnessed the rising of the UNITED IRISHMEN at New Ross in 1798. Having served with the Spanish army during the Peninsular War (1808–14), he worked as an interpreter with the British mission in Lisbon, 1808. After ordination, 1809, he taught logic at New Ross Friary for four years, held the chair of rhetoric at Carlow College, 1813, and was professor of theology, 1814–19. As Bishop of Kildare and Leighlin, 1819–34, he was close to the Archbishop of Dublin, DANIEL MURRAY. He founded public libraries for the poor with a borrowing fee of 1 penny and revived the practice of parish retreats; in 1820 he organised a mammoth retreat in which the majority of the hierarchy and more than a thousand priests participated.

Doyle was an influential witness together with DANIEL O'CONNELL and others before a select committee inquiring into conditions in Ireland, March 1825. He was questioned on topics including the sacraments, miracles, Papal authority, the VETO, and the payment of clergy. During a break in the proceedings the Duke of Wellington, asked if they were still examining Doyle, replied, 'No, but Doyle is examining us.'

Though he was the first well-known prelate to join the CATHOLIC ASSOCIATION, he did not support O'Connell on the issues of Repeal, disfranchisement of the forty-shilling freeholders, and the POOR LAW. He supported the NATIONAL EDUCATION system, 1831, and when the landlords of the area did not make land available for the building of schools he had schools built in graveyards. His best-known pamphlets, which he signed 'JKL' (for James of Kildare and Leighlin), include *A Vindication of the Religious and Civil Principles of the Irish Catholics* (1822), *Letters on the State of Ireland* (1824–25), and

On the Origin, Nature and Destination of Church Property (1831).

Druid Theatre, Galway, founded in 1975 by Gary Hynes (director), Mick Lally, and Máire Mullen, former members of UCG Drama Society; the original company also included Bríd Brennan, Maelíosa Stafford, Ray MacBride, and Seán McGinley. For a time it was the only professional theatre in the Republic outside Dublin. It opened with *The Playboy of the Western World* in the Jesuit Hall, Galway, 3 July 1975, directed by Gary Hynes and starring Mick Lally (Christy Mahon) and Máire Mullen (Pegeen Mike). It has had some outstanding successes, including Tom Murphy's *Conversations on a Homecoming,* which had a six-week run following its opening at the Druid Lane Theatre, Galway, 16 April 1985. Moving to the Gate Theatre, Dublin, in September, where it also had a successful run, it toured Ireland, February 1986, before playing to packed houses in New York, July 1987, and a month later appeared at the Belvoir Street Theatre, Sidney, Australia. Apart from works by Murphy the company has featured new works by Geraldine Aron (*Same Old Moon*), Marina Carr (*The Mai*), Vincent Woods (*At the Black Pig's Dyke*), and Martin McDonagh (the Leenane Trilogy, comprising *The Beauty Queen of Leenane, A Skull in Connemara,* and *The Lonesome West,* which opened in Galway in June 1997).

Drumcollogher Cinema Tragedy (5 September 1926). Forty-eight people died and many were injured as a result of a fire during a film show in Drumcollogher, Co. Limerick. The films on view (*The White Outlaw* and a supporting comedy, *Baby, Be Good*) had been showing at the Assembly Rooms, Cork, which closed on Sunday, allowing an arrangement between the projectionist, Patrick Downing, and the showman, William 'Baby' Forde, to show the films in Drumcollogher. Before travelling, Downing removed the reels of film from their protective metal cans. The venue for the film show was a two-storey shed in Church Street owned by Patrick Brennan. Access to the first floor was by means of a wooden ladder and handrail. An estimated two hundred people were in attendance when, during the showing of the main film, a candle upset near exposed celluloid reels caused a flash fire. The audience panicked as they rushed to safety. The venue had formerly been a meeting-place of the IRA, and iron bars on its two small windows had been sawn through as an emergency escape route, which now facilitated the escape of some people onto a hayrick underneath.

Almost every family in Drumcollogher and its environs was touched by the catastrophe, the victims of which were communally buried in the local graveyard. A fund of £16,000 was raised for dependants. Forde and Downing were charged with manslaughter but were discharged following a *nolle prosequi* by the state. Stringent safety precautions introduced in many countries as a result of the disaster included the development of a new type of film, which smouldered rather than flared if burned.

Drummond, Thomas (1797–1840), British politician; born in Scotland, educated at the University of Edinburgh. As a member of the British army he worked on the Ordnance Survey of Scotland, developed the 'Drummond limelight', and improved the heliostat. Serving in the ORDNANCE SURVEY OF IRELAND from 1824, he came into everyday contact with small tenant-farmers, an experience uniquely fitting him to understand the principal grievances of the Irish people, and his term of office as Under-Secretary for Ireland, 1835–40, was conspicuous for its tolerance and constructiveness. The Constabulary (Ireland) Act (1836) encouraged Catholics to join the Irish Constabulary (see ROYAL IRISH CONSTABULARY). He was also involved in the establishment of the Poor Law in Ireland. He had little sympathy for Irish landlords, among whom he was highly unpopular. He reminded them that 'property had its obligations as well as its rights; to the neglect of these duties in times past is mainly to be attributed that diseased state of society in which such crimes can take their rise.' STIPENDIARY MAGISTRATES, independent of the landlords, were appointed, and Drummond's handling of the unrest over TITHES resulted in a decrease in agrarian crime. The Tithe Rentcharge Act (1838) converted the hated tithes into a fixed rent, and soldiers were no longer to be used for its collection. Drummond died in office after a life of chronic ill-health.

'dry lodgings', a term used in the eighteenth century for houses offering accommodation to travellers in remote areas. Unlike post-houses, neither food nor drink was available at a dry lodging. Accommodation was announced by the presence of a cloth or other sign attached to a makeshift pole. Frequently the traveller had to share a room with the landlord and his family. (See also STRADOGUE.)

Dublin Castle. Built on the orders of King John, 30 August 1204, during the nineteenth century Dublin Castle housed some two dozen departments vital to the apparatus of British administration, headed by the CHIEF SECRETARY FOR IRELAND. Throughout its history Dublin Castle was remote from, and at variance with, the rest of Ireland. During the GREAT FAMINE (1845–49) the Viceregal court was maintained, and receptions, balls and levees continued uninterrupted. JOSEPH CHAMBERLAIN was prompted to comment in 1885: 'I say the time has come to reform altogether the absurd and irritating anachronism which is known as Dublin Castle.' KING GEORGE V and Queen Mary were the last members of the British royal family to stay in the castle when they performed the formal opening of the Dublin College of Science, 1911.

Following the ANGLO-IRISH TREATY (1921) the Lord Lieutenant, Lord Fitzalan of Derwent, formally handed over Dublin Castle to the PROVISIONAL GOVERNMENT, 16 January 1922. A press release stated: 'The members of Rialtas Sealadach na hÉireann (the Provisional Government of Ireland), received the surrender of Dublin Castle at 1.45 p.m. to-day. It is now in the hands of the Irish people.'

Dublin Castle now houses the offices of a number of state institutions, including the Revenue Commissioners, as well as the CHESTER BEATTY LIBRARY, and is used for the inauguration of the President of Ireland. It is normally open to the public. While Taoiseach, CHARLES HAUGHEY initiated an extensive renovation.

Dublin Drama League, founded in 1919 by W. B. YEATS, JAMES STEPHENS and Lennox Robinson to broaden the scope of drama offered by the ABBEY THEATRE, which had confined itself to plays by Irish authors. Each play was intended to run for two days (Sundays and Mondays) in the Abbey. The first play produced by the new company was *The Liberators* by Srgjan Tucic, 17 February 1919. Other authors whose works were presented included Chekhov, Chesterton, Cocteau, D'Annunzio, Lord Dunsany, Euripides, Eugene O'Neill, Pirandello, GEORGE BERNARD SHAW, and Strindberg. In 1928 the league was succeeded by the GATE THEATRE company, which, using the same personnel, extended the run of its presentations to at least one week.

Dublin Exhibition (1853), an exhibition of Irish industry and art on Leinster Lawn, opened by the Lord Lieutenant of Ireland, Lord St Germans, 12 May 1853. The Executive Committee included George Roe (chairman), WILLIAM DARGAN, Nathaniel Hone, SIR ROBERT KANE, and Sir C. P. Roney (secretary); a Fine Arts sub-committee consisted of Lord Talbot de Malahide (chairman), John Barton, Robert Harrison, Sir Kingston James, and John Lentaigne. Almost a million visitors attended the exhibition before it closed in October 1853. Dargan advanced £87,000 towards the exhibition's financial overrun and was virtually ruined by a shortfall of £27,000.

Dublin Hermetic Society, founded 16 June 1885; its membership included W. B. YEATS and Alaud Ali, professor of Persian, Arabic and Hindustani at Trinity College, Dublin. It became the Dublin Theosophical Society in April 1886 and attracted Mohini Chatterjee, by whom Yeats was deeply influenced.

Dublin Institute of Advanced Studies, founded by the Institute of Advanced Studies Act (1940) to provide facilities for the furtherance of advanced study and the conduct and publishing of research. Two constituent schools were simultaneously established: the School of Celtic Studies and the School of Theoretical Physics; a third, the School of Cosmic Physics, was established in 1947, with three sub-sections: Astronomy, Cosmic Ray Physics, and Geophysics. Each school is independently governed, and all contribute to its publications and to frequent articles in international journals.

Dublin Lock-Out (1913), the culmination of a protracted struggle between Dublin's organised labour, led by JAMES LARKIN, and the Dublin Employers' Federation, led by WILLIAM MARTIN MURPHY. It began when Larkin founded the IRISH TRANSPORT AND GENERAL WORKERS' UNION, January 1909, during a period of economic crisis for Dublin's labourers, who, with their families, numbered 100,000 or approximately a third of the population of the city. The tenements in which the majority of them lived were described by PATRICK PEARSE in *Irish Freedom* as 'so rotten that now and then they collapse, and if the inhabitants collect in the streets to discuss matters, the police baton them.' In 1913 unemployment was approximately 10 per cent, at a time when the average pay of unskilled labourers was £1 a week.

Since his arrival in Dublin, Larkin had been the bane of the employers, not least for his use of sympathetic strikes. He controlled the Dublin docks; in June 1913 he forced Co.

Dublin farmers to reach a settlement with the unionised agricultural workers. Murphy, who had organised nearly four hundred employers, had rejected Larkin's invitation to enter into talks since 1911. At midnight on 19 July he told some seven hundred employees of the Dublin United Tramway Company that while it had no objection to their forming a union, it did oppose the 'disreputable organisation' under an 'unscrupulous man' seeking to use the workers as 'tools to make him the labour dictator of Dublin.' The workers were informed that the Tramway Company had £100,000 or more with which to 'put down the terrorism which was being imported into the labour conditions of this city.' In August 1913 Murphy dismissed all workers who refused to give a written undertaking that they would not join Larkin's or any other union. He had assurances from the DUBLIN CASTLE authorities that in the event of a tramway strike the RIC and Dublin Metropolitan Police would be at his disposal.

At 9:40 a.m. on 26 August, as crowds were making their way to the Dublin Horse Show at Ballsbridge, up to two hundred drivers and conductors created chaos when, having donned their union badge, they abandoned their trams without warning on the line from College Green to the GPO, O'Connell Street. Larkin's call was answered by 700 out of 1,700 workers; but the DMP and non-striking tram workers restored the service. JAMES CONNOLLY, Larkin, WILLIAM O'BRIEN and other ITGWU leaders, charged the next day with 'seditious conspiracy', were released on bail. On 31 August the DMP baton-charged onlookers in O'Connell Street after Larkin was arrested, having succeeded in addressing a crowd from a window of the Imperial Hotel (owned by Murphy). Three hundred members of the public and fifty policemen were injured.

On 2 September Jacob's biscuit factory closed, and the coal merchants locked out their workers; on the same day two four-storey tenement houses collapsed, killing seven people and injuring many others. On 3 September the Employers' Federation locked out all their workers, between 20,000 and 25,000 of whom were affected by 22 September. On 27 September the *Hare,* organised through British trade union efforts, arrived with 340 tons of food for strikers and their dependants.

An inquiry into events in Dublin began under the direction of Sir George Askwith of the Board of Trade, 29 September. The employers were represented by T. M. HEALY, while Larkin spoke for the workers. British as well as Irish trade unionists gave evidence. The Askwith Report (6 October) condemned Larkin's use of the sympathetic strike while stating that employees had been asked to sign conditions that were 'contrary to individual liberty' and that 'no workman or body of workmen could reasonably be expected to accept.' The employers rejected the report, provoking a scathing denunciation from GEORGE RUSSELL, who wrote an open letter 'to the Masters of Dublin' (*Irish Times,* 7 October 1913):

> You were within the rights . . . when you locked out your men and insisted on the fixing of some principle to adjust your future relations with labour, when the policy of labour made it impossible for some of you to carry on your enterprises . . . you determined deliberately in cold blood to starve out one-third of the population of this city, to break the manhood of the men by the sight of the suffering of their wives and the hunger of their children . . . the men whose manhood you have broken will loathe you . . . The infant being moulded in the womb will have breathed into its starved body the vitality of hate . . . You are sounding the death knell of autocracy in industry.

The employers were also condemned by the *Times* (London). The workers were led by James Connolly following Larkin's imprisonment on 27 October. To protect the workers in the streets Connolly and JACK WHITE formed the IRISH CITIZEN ARMY, 23 November, ostensibly to keep unemployed workers occupied through drilling.

The situation of the workers' children caused grave concern, and with Larkin's approval in late October Dora Montefiore and Lucille Rand arrived in Dublin to arrange for the children to be taken to England. This proposal was attacked by the Archbishop of Dublin, WILLIAM WALSH, who accused the women of proselytising, 21 October. (Walsh was in Paris recovering from illness for most of the strike and was dependent on reports from the Dublin clergy, many of whom were biased in favour of the employers.) Children about to be taken to England were wrested from the arms of British philanthropists by priests or members of lay organisations, and the organisers were arrested on charges of kidnapping. The concentrated efforts of the clergy ensured that when Delia Larkin (James Larkin's sister) took over the project she was defeated. However, the clergy were now enjoined by the archbishop to oversee the distribution of relief in the tenements.

In November the workers' situation was desperate, with no end to the lock-out in sight. Connolly attacked the Liberal government, and DAVID LLOYD GEORGE attributed by-election reverses for the Liberals to Larkin. Connolly closed Dublin port, and Larkin, released from jail, embarked on the 'fiery cross' campaign to gain help in England, gathering food and clothing for the workers and their families and sailing shiploads of aid into the Liffey. His campaign in England ran into difficulties when he called on British unions to help the Irish dockers by closing the docks. This was rejected by the Trade Union Congress, sensitive to the perception of Larkin dictating to British unions. After Larkin had attacked the British union leaders J. H. Thomas and J. H. Wilson the only major British labour figure to remain friendly was Keir Hardie. The British unions helped to open negotiations with the Dublin employers, but these broke down, 20 December. Aid from England, the United States and the Continent dried up.

By the end of January 1914 many workers had applied for reinstatement, provided they did not have to sign an undertaking not to join the ITGWU. The end came when the British TUC announced the winding up of the Dublin Relief Fund, 11 February, by which time it had raised £150,000. By the end of that month the lock-out was over, but it left a legacy of bitterness that endured for a generation.

ITGWU membership was undermined, falling from an estimated maximum of 20,000 to 3,500 after the lock-out. Many hundreds of workers not offered re-employment had to seek assisted passage to England or Scotland. In October 1914 Larkin embarked on a fund-raising tour in the United States, which turned into a stay of nine years (three of them in jail). In contrast, Murphy was lauded by employers. A testimonial was presented and his portrait by William Orpen presented to him at the annual meeting of the Dublin Chamber of Commerce, 29 January 1915. With the painting was an inscribed address from

> noblemen and gentlemen of trade, commerce, and of the professions, not only in Dublin, but throughout the country . . . the stand taken by the companies which you presided over, and your services on the Employers' Executive Committee, saved the city from a peril that threatened to destroy the industrial enterprises of all the metropolis, as well as the rest of the country.

Dublin Metropolitan Police (DMP), an unarmed police force covering the city and county of Dublin and Co. Wicklow, established in 1786 in succession to the organising of night watchmen and private security police. By 1839 it was fully organised, distinct from the Irish Constabulary (see ROYAL IRISH CONSTABULARY), and operating under its own code of regulations (revised 1889 and 1909). The G Division of the DMP was responsible for intelligence-gathering. The DMP lost much of its popularity during the DUBLIN LOCK-OUT (1913) following the excessive zeal exercised by some of its members against the striking workers. The force was not involved in the WAR OF INDEPENDENCE. It became part of the GARDA SÍOCHÁNA under the Police Forces Amalgamation Act (1925).

Dublin Morning Register, a liberal newspaper founded in 1824 by MICHAEL STAUNTON. It supported DANIEL O'CONNELL in the struggle for CATHOLIC EMANCIPATION and differed from its contemporaries in that it concentrated on Irish events (most newspapers carried more foreign, particularly British, news) and employed a permanent staff of trained reporters, which in the 1830s included CHARLES GAVAN DUFFY, JOHN BLAKE DILLON, and THOMAS DAVIS. Sales rose to 800 in 1835 but had declined to 300 by 1841, having been damaged by industrial disputes. It ceased publication in 1843.

Dublin Morning Star, a newspaper founded by JOSEPH TIMOTHY HAYDN in February 1824. It was bitterly anti-Catholic but was also hostile to DUBLIN CASTLE and was noted for the libellous nature of its attacks. An article directed against the Castle in its first issue provoked a libel action, in which DANIEL O'CONNELL defended Haydn. The sensational nature of the paper's content led to a rapid increase in circulation and advertising income, but its demise in 1825 was hastened through a number of costly libel actions.

Dublin Opinion, a satirical magazine founded in March 1922 by Charles E. Kelly ('CEK'), Tom Collins, and its editor, Arthur Booth (died 1926). Collins and Kelly were joint editors, 1926–68. Kelly (died 1981) was a renowned cartoonist. Noted for the bite of its political satire and cartoons, at its peak it sold 70,000 copies. Gordon Clark was editor, 1968–70; Lelia Doolan and Jack Dowling were editors when the magazine ceased publication in 1972. Louis O'Sullivan, who bought the title, published it briefly as a Christmas annual, edited by James D. O'Donnell.

Dublin Times, founded 1832 with the active

support of DUBLIN CASTLE. The first Irish newspaper to be issued free of charge, it consisted almost entirely of advertising; its non-advertising sections were particularly virulent in their denunciation of DANIEL O'CONNELL and the Repeal movement but also of the Anglo-Irish Ascendancy. It enjoyed little success and ceased publication at the end of 1833.

Dublin University Magazine, a monthly literary journal founded in 1833 by ISAAC BUTT, who became the magazine's second editor in succession to Charles Villiers Stanford (1852–1924). Also on the editorial staff (all of whom were associated with Trinity College) were John Anster, SAMUEL FERGUSON, CAESAR OTWAY, and John Francis Waller. Loyalist and anti-liberal in tone, the magazine was, according to Butt, 'a monthly advocate of the Protestantism, the intelligence, and the respectability of Dublin.' It published a disparaging review of James Hardiman's *Irish Minstresly* (1834) and rejoiced in the arrest of DANIEL O'CONNELL in 1844. It was published by William Curry and Company to 1846, when the contract passed to James McGlashen (see M. H. GILL), who continued its printing until its demise in 1877.

Dublin University Review, founded in February 1885 by Charles Hubert Oldham and T. W. Rolleston, emulating Isaac Butt's DUBLIN UNIVERSITY MAGAZINE of the 1830s. Politically independent, it described itself as 'open to temperate discussion of certain political questions by representatives of the different parties or social movements in Ireland.'

Dublin Women's Suffrage Association, founded by Anne and Thomas Haslam, 1876, the first women's suffrage society in Dublin. Renamed the Irish Women's Suffrage and Local Government Association, 1901, it had 43 members in 1896 and 647 by 1911.

Duffy, James (1809–1871), publisher; born in Co. Monaghan, educated at a hedge-school. He moved to Dublin in early life as assistant to the publisher John Daly (1800–1873). In 1831 he launched his own publishing business with *Napoleon's Book of Fate,* a twopenny version of *Boney's Oraculum,* then popular on the Continent. Its financial success set him on a career spanning forty years, during which he was reputed never to have taken a regular holiday. A paternalist employer, Duffy presented each of his employees with Christmas bonuses ranging from £3 to £20.

Duffy's publications, though catering principally for the mass market, were nonetheless well produced. His green-covered books stamped with his device in gold (a harp encircled by a wreath of shamrock) were generally available in library and pocket editions. He published the majority of YOUNG IRELAND writers as well as the 'Library of Ireland' and 'Spirit of the Nation' series. According to CHARLES GAVAN DUFFY (no relation), 'the volumes projected by the Young Irelanders were nearly all published by James Duffy, whose enterprise and liberality ultimately created a trade extending to India, America and Australia.' Duffy published many of the leading Irish writers of the nineteenth century. On his death the company, run by his sons, maintained its nationalist tradition, publishing the work of ARTHUR GRIFFITH and D. P. MORAN. It continued in business to 1980.

Duggan, Edmund (Éamonn) (1874–1936), politician (Sinn Féin, Cumann na nGaedheal, and Fine Gael); born in Longwood, Co. Meath, educated locally and in Dublin, where he qualified as a solicitor. He fought in the GPO, Dublin, during the EASTER RISING (1916) and was interned; following his release he resumed activity in both the Irish Volunteers and Sinn Féin and represented the next of kin at the inquest on THOMAS ASHE, 1917. He became Director of Intelligence for the Volunteers, 1918. Representative for Meath South in the first Dáil Éireann, he was again imprisoned, 1920–21.

Involved in drafting details of the Truce, July 1921, Duggan was appointed to the team of plenipotentiaries to negotiate the treaty with Britain, October–December 1921. While acknowledging that he had not been present at the crucial conference in Downing Street, London, but had 'signed the Treaty in the quiet seclusion of 22 Hans Place,' he declared during the Treaty debate in the Dáil:

> I dislike the Treaty as much as any man or woman here, but that is not the point . . . I say under the terms of the treaty that if the Irish people cannot achieve their freedom it is the fault of the Irish people and not of the Treaty.

As Minister for Home Affairs in the Provisional Government he rescinded the courts of law and equity and criminal jurisdiction, 31 July 1922. He was Parliamentary Secretary to the Executive Council, September 1922 to September 1923, and Minister for Defence, 1927–32. Declining a nomination in the 1933 general election, he was elected to the

Senate and was the last member to take the oath of allegiance before its abolition.

Duisburg talks, secret talks held in Duisburg, Germany, 14–15 October 1988, attended by representatives of the main political parties in Northern Ireland: ULSTER UNIONIST PARTY (Jack Allen), SDLP (Austin Currie), DEMOCRATIC UNIONIST PARTY (Peter Robinson), and ALLIANCE PARTY (Gordon Mawhinney). The parties were attempting to accommodate the unionist demand for suspension of the ANGLO-IRISH AGREEMENT, a position unacceptable to the SDLP. The talks encouraged the Secretary of State for Northern Ireland, TOM KING, to arrange formal talks, which led to the BROOKE-MAYHEW TALKS.

Dukes, Alan (born 1945), politician (Fine Gael); born in Drimnagh, Dublin, educated at UCD. He was chief economist for the NATIONAL FARMERS' ASSOCIATION and IRISH FARMERS' ASSOCIATION, 1967–72. From January 1973 he headed the Brussels office of the IFA in its dealings with the European Economic Community (European Union). Later, working for the Irish member of the European Commission, Richard Burke, he became an authority on the Common Agricultural Policy. He resigned, March 1981, to successfully contest the June election in Co. Kildare. GARRETT FITZGERALD appointed him Minister for Agriculture, and he became Minister for Finance when Fine Gael returned to office, December 1982. His policy of fiscal rectitude brought him into conflict with Fine Gael's coalition partner, the Labour Party.

He opposed the 'pro-life' constitutional amendment in 1983, and in 1986 he supported the first (unsuccessful) constitutional amendment to allow divorce. He was moved to the Department of Justice in FitzGerald's controversial reshuffle, February 1986. Following the general election of February 1987 he replaced FitzGerald to become the party's youngest leader. In September 1987 he announced the 'Tallaght Strategy', whereby Fine Gael would in effect support the coalition Government of Fianna Fáil and Progressive Democrats in attempts to boost the economy. During 1988 Fine Gael supported the Government in forty-two votes and opposed it in twelve votes.

Following the general election of 15 June 1989 Dukes met CHARLES HAUGHEY, who rejected his demand for seven out of fifteen ministerial portfolios and a rotation of the office of Taoiseach. Following a poor performance by his party's candidate, Austin Currie, in the 1990 presidential election (he came third), Dukes was ousted by JOHN BRUTON, and he remained on the back benches when Bruton formed the 'rainbow coalition' Government in 1994 until appointed Minister for Transport, Energy and Communications (to succeed the disgraced Michael Lowry), November 1996. He lost his seat in the general election of 2002.

Dungannon Clubs, founded by BULMER HOBSON and DENIS MCCULLOUGH in commemoration of the 1782 Volunteer Convention at Dungannon, Co. Tyrone. They first met in Belfast, 8 March 1905. Republican and separatist, flourishing mainly in Ulster, they were described as 'semi-literary, semi-political and patriotic.' Pamphlets urging the wider use of Irish, non-cooperation with the British army, economic independence and self-sufficiency for Ireland were produced by the Executive. The Dungannon Clubs and CUMANN NA NGAEDHEAL became the Sinn Féin League, 21 April 1907, which joined the NATIONAL COUNCIL to become SINN FÉIN in September 1908.

Dungarvan Riots, 29 September 1846, during the GREAT FAMINE (1845–49), the result of an attempt by some five thousand starving unemployed men, led by 'Lame Pat' Power, to prevent the export of grain from the port. Failing to find food, the crowd became unruly and was charged by mounted soldiers. Fifty prisoners were taken, including Power. The crowd, seeking the release of Power, became hostile. When the police failed to restore order, a body of the 1st Royal Dragoons, commanded by Captain Sibthorp, was summoned; he ordered them to fire when the crowd refused to disperse after the warning prescribed by the Riot Act was read. Michael Fleming, a baggage carter for the military, was killed and several people were injured in the first volley. The Dungarvan riot was the first during the famine at which loss of life occurred. In its editorial, 3 October 1846, the *Waterford Freeman* commented:

> But above all things, the prohibition of exporting grain from the country is imperatively called for. When Indian corn and meal is purchased for our support, and carried half across the globe for our use, is it not a most unaccountable anomaly—a monstrous reality—that we are sending our wheat out of the country? The government should act boldly, promptly, and wisely, and lay an instantaneous embargo on the exportation of Irish food. If

they refuse to do this the consequences may be both melancholy and dangerous . . .

Dunraven and Mount Earl, Windham Thomas Wyndham-Quin, fourth Earl of (1841–1926), landowner and politician (Conservative); born in Adare, Co. Limerick, educated at Rome and the University of Oxford, which he left without graduating to become a junior officer in the British army. War correspondent for the *Daily Telegraph* in Abyssinia (Ethiopia) in 1867, he also covered the Franco-Prussian War and the Siege of Paris (1870–71). On a visit to the United States, 1871, he hunted around the Platte River with 'Buffalo Bill' Cody; after a further visit in 1874, when he explored the Yellowstone (where he is commemorated by the Dunraven Pass), he published *The Great Divide: The Upper Yellowstone* (1876). Strongly conservative, he was Under-Secretary for the Colonies, 1885–86 and 1886–87, and chairman of the Commission on Sweated Labour, 1888–90. A constructive unionist, he sought a peaceful solution to the Irish land question and the demand for home rule. His *Outlook in Ireland: The Case for Devolution and Conciliation* was published in 1897. He was chairman of the LAND CONFERENCE and president of the Irish Reform Association, 1904, and was appointed to the first Senate of the Irish Free State. He was regarded as a model landlord on his 39,000-acre estate at Adare, where he maintained a famous stud. His experiment with the growing of tobacco ended when his factory burned, 1916. His memoir, *Past Times and Pastimes,* was published in 1922.

Dunsink Observatory, Dunsink, Co. Dublin, founded in 1783 as the observatory of Trinity College, Dublin, under the will of Francis Andrews (died 1774), provost of the college, and completed in 1785. The architect was Graham Moyens. The first director was Rev. Dr Henry Usher, Andrews professor of astronomy; SIR WILLIAM ROWAN HAMILTON became director in 1827. The six-ton dome was added to house a new telescope in 1868. The observatory ceased to function on the creation of the Irish Free State, 1922, but was re-established by the de Valera government under the auspices of the DUBLIN INSTITUTE FOR ADVANCED STUDIES, 1947. Specialist investigations at Dunsink include measurement of the effects of the Sun on the Earth and the precision measurement of star brightness.

Durkan, Mark (born 1960), politician (SDLP); born in Derry, educated at St Columb's College, QUB, and Magee College. He was deputy president of the Union of Students in Ireland, 1982–84, and assistant and adviser to JOHN HUME, 1984–98. As chairperson of the SOCIAL DEMOCRATIC AND LABOUR PARTY, 1990–95, he championed the HUME-ADAMS TALKS. He was elected to the Northern Ireland Forum, 1996–98, and the Northern Ireland Assembly, 1998, after working closely with Hume on the negotiations that produced the BELFAST AGREEMENT (1998). Minister for Finance and Personnel in the Northern Ireland Executive from 29 November 1999, he became Deputy First Minister, 6 November 2001, and succeeded Hume as leader of the SDLP, 11 November 2001.

duty-services. Adding further clauses to tenancy agreements was a common practice among landlords in the eighteenth and early nineteenth centuries. Additional services required by such agreements, known as 'duty-services', included furnishing the landlord or his agent with labour or with horses for a specified number of days annually, spinning flax for the landlord's use, carting his fuel or LIME, and occasional gifts of poultry, eggs, and vegetables.

Dwyer, Michael (1771–c. 1826), United Irishman; born in the Glen of Imail, Co. Wicklow, educated privately. Dwyer was the maternal uncle of Anne Devlin (c. 1778–1851), Robert Emmet's faithful servant. Following the defeat of 1798 Dwyer fled with his followers into the Wicklow Mountains, from where they harassed the Yeomanry. He supported Emmet's abortive rising of 1803 but did not receive the signal to rise. In December 1803, lured by a promise of safe passage to America for his immediate family and those of his followers, he surrendered to Captain Hume. The promise was reneged on (by order of a higher authority), and Dwyer and his men were sentenced to transportation to Botany Bay. They arrived in Sydney on the *Tellicherry,* 15 February 1806. Accused by Governor William Bligh (of the *Bounty*) of 'treasonable practices,' he was sent to Norfolk Island for six months and from there to Van Diemen's Land (Tasmania) for some two years. He returned to Sydney, where he was granted 100 acres of land at Cabramatta and became district head constable. His wife, Mary, died there in 1861, aged ninety-three.

Dynamiters. A concerted dynamiting campaign, organised by a group within the FENIANS known as the 'TRIANGLE', was directed against Britain, 1881–85. Financed through the 'SKIRMISHING FUND' established by JEREMIAH O'DONOVAN ROSSA, the campaign did not have the approval of leading members of CLAN NA GAEL, including JOHN DEVOY. The principal events of the campaign were:

10 June 1881. An attempt to blow up Liverpool Town Hall caused little damage. James McKevitt and James McGrath were sentenced to penal servitude.

12 May 1882. A bomb with blasting powder left in the proximity of the Mansion House, London, was believed to be a hoax.

20 January 1883. Glasgow gasholder was destroyed in a massive explosion that also destroyed part of a railway siding. There were no reported injuries.

15 March 1883. A device left at the office of the *Times* (London) failed to explode, but an explosion that damaged government offices in Parliament Street was heard within a 50-mile radius. There were no reported injuries.

9 April 1883. The Explosive Substances Bill was rushed through Parliament.

30 October 1883. An explosion wrecked three rear coaches of a London Underground train, and more than seventy passengers were treated for shock. An explosion on a District Line train out of Charing Cross Station caused no injury to passengers and relatively little damage to the train.

26 February 1884. Three of the four explosive devices left at London main-line stations failed to explode; the fourth, at Victoria Station, exploded harmlessly.

30 May 1884. Three further explosions occurred in London, the most damaging of which, in a public toilet underneath Great Scotland Yard, caused severe damage to the building. The offices and record room of the Special Irish Branch bore the brunt of the explosion.

13 December 1884. WILLIAM MACKEY LOMASNEY, his brother Michael and John Fleming were killed by a device that exploded as they were attaching it to the arch of London Bridge. Little structural damage was caused to the bridge.

2 January 1885. An explosion on an underground train shortly after it left King's Cross Station caused no injuries to passengers though the train was extensively damaged.

24 January 1885. A bomb placed behind a gun carriage in the White Tower of the Tower of London injured four people. Further injuries and widespread damage were averted as the gun carriage absorbed the brunt of the explosion. James Cunningham was arrested in the vicinity of the Tower.

4 February 1885. Two US citizens, Thomas Callan and Michael Harkin, were sentenced to fifteen years' penal servitude for possession of explosives.

May 1885. The dynamiting campaign ended following life sentences imposed on two leading activists, Harry Burton and James Cunningham (convicted of the Tower of London explosion).

Dynamiters charged under the Treason-Felony Act were subjected to a particularly brutal prison regime. At least two, DR THOMAS GALLAGHER and Alfred Whithead, were driven insane as a result of their treatment. Another, JOHN DALY, forced an admission from prison authorities to a commission of inquiry that he had been 'accidentally poisoned' by prison staff. Agitation by the AMNESTY ASSOCIATION led to the early release of the Dynamiters, the last of whom, THOMAS J. CLARKE, was released in September 1898.

E

Early, Biddy (c. 1798–1874), reputed witch; born in Feakle, Co. Clare. Orphaned at sixteen, she spent some time in Ennis Workhouse. Her reputation as a woman having special powers arose from an accurate prediction of the death of a bailiff who had come to evict her from her smallholding. On the death of her elderly husband, O'Malley, she married her stepson; her last marriage—when she was in her seventies—was to a man fifty years her junior. He too predeceased her, believed to have died, as did her previous husbands, from excessive drinking of spirits provided by grateful or hopeful patients. Despite an unsubstantiated charge of witchcraft at Ennis court, 1865, and the opposition of local clergymen, she exercised her powers for more than sixty years at Carranroe and later at Kilbarron, near Feakle, where DANIEL O'CONNELL and the Prince of Wales were said to have consulted her. Before her death her famous 'dark bottle' was cast into Kilbarron Lake.

She is buried in an unmarked grave in Feakle. Her reconstructed cottage overlooking the lake is a tourist attraction.

Easter Rising (1916), planned by the Military Council of the IRB in January; the strategy was devised by JOSEPH PLUNKETT (Director of Operations). A series of mishaps prevented the rising from becoming the national insurrection envisaged by its planners. EOIN MACNEILL, chief of staff of the IRISH VOLUNTEERS, was not informed of it; on learning of the plan he confronted PATRICK PEARSE and SEÁN MAC DIARMADA, who convinced him that it would succeed. ROGER CASEMENT was captured when put ashore from a German submarine near Banna Strand, Co. Kerry, early on Friday 21 April. Later that day (some seventy-two hours earlier than expected) the AUD arrived off the Co. Kerry coast with its cargo of arms for the Volunteers; before its arrest by the British patrol vessel *Bluebell* its captain scuttled it.

On learning of these incidents, and now aware that the CASTLE DOCUMENT was a forgery, MacNeill countermanded Pearse's order for a full mobilisation of the Volunteers on Sunday 23 April—Easter Sunday—by placing a notice in the *Sunday Independent*: 'All orders given to Irish Volunteers for Easter Sunday are hereby rescinded and no parades, marches or other movements of Irish Volunteers will take place.' He also sent despatches to commanders of other units informing them of his decision. However, the leaders met at Liberty Hall on Sunday morning and decided to press ahead with their plans on the Monday. As a result of the confusion, the rising was confined almost exclusively to Dublin.

Monday 24 April. The General Post Office, in Sackville Street (O'Connell Street), was occupied at noon by Volunteers under Pearse and a detachment of the IRISH CITIZEN ARMY under JAMES CONNOLLY and became the insurgent headquarters. Pearse appeared in front of the GPO and read the Proclamation of the Irish Republic; copies were also posted in the area around the GPO.

POBLACHT NA H EIREANN

THE PROVISIONAL GOVERNMENT
OF THE
IRISH REPUBLIC
TO THE PEOPLE OF IRELAND

IRISHMEN AND IRISHWOMEN: In the name of God and of the dead generations from which she receives her old tradition of nationhood, Ireland, through us, summons her children to her flag and strikes for her freedom.

Having organised her manhood through her secret revolutionary organisation, the Irish Republican Brotherhood, and through her open military organisations, the Irish Volunteers and the Irish Citizen Army, having patiently perfected her discipline, having resolutely waited for the right moment to reveal itself, she now seizes that moment, and, supported by her exiled children in America and by gallant allies in Europe, but relying in the first on her own strength, she strikes in full confidence of victory.

We declare the right of the people of Ireland to the ownership of Ireland, and to the unfettered control of Irish destinies, to be sovereign and indefeasible. The long usurpation of that right by a foreign people and government has not extinguished the right, nor can it ever be extinguished except by the destruction of the Irish people. In every generation the Irish people have asserted their right to national freedom and sovereignty: six times during the past three hundred years they have asserted it in arms. Standing on that fundamental right and again asserting it in arms in the face of the world, we hereby proclaim the Irish Republic as a Sovereign Independent State, and we pledge our lives and the lives of our comrades-in-arms to the cause of its freedom, of its welfare, and of its exaltation among the nations.

The Irish Republic is entitled to, and hereby claims, the allegiance of every Irishman and Irishwoman. The Republic guarantees religious and civil liberty, equal rights and equal opportunities to all its citizens, and declares its resolve to pursue the happiness and prosperity of the whole nation and of all its parts, cherishing all the children of the nation equally, and oblivious of the differences carefully fostered by an alien government, which have divided a minority from the majority in the past.

Until our arms have brought the opportune moment for the establishment of a permanent National Government, representative of the whole people of Ireland and elected by the suffrages of all her men and women, the Provisional Government, hereby constituted, will administer the civil and military affairs of the Republic in trust for the people.

We place the cause of the Irish Republic under the protection of the Most High God, Whose blessing we invoke upon our arms, and we pray that no one who serves that cause will dishonour it by cowardice, inhumanity, or rapine. In this supreme hour the

Irish nation must, by its valour and discipline and by the readiness of its children to sacrifice themselves for the common good, prove itself worthy of the august destiny to which it is called.

Signed on Behalf of the Provisional Government,

THOMAS J. CLARKE,
SEAN Mac DIARMADA,
THOMAS MacDONAGH,
P. H. PEARSE
EAMONN CEANNT,
JAMES CONNOLLY
JOSEPH PLUNKETT

The deployment of the insurgents' forces was:

Irish Volunteers, Dublin Brigade, 1st Battalion (Commandant EDWARD DALY): Four Courts (Inns Quay), Mendicity Institute (Usher's Island), Jameson's Distillery (Bow Street), North King Street.

2nd Battalion (Commandant THOMAS MACDONAGH): Jacob's factory (Bishop Street).

3rd Battalion (Commandant ÉAMON DE VALERA): Boland's Mills (Grand Canal Street), Lansdowne Road, Westland Row Station (Pearse Station), Mount Street Bridge, Northumberland Road.

4th Battalion (Commandant ÉAMONN CEANNT, Vice-Commandant CATHAL BRUGHA): South Dublin Union (James's Street), Marrowbone Lane, Roe's Distillery (Watling Street), Ardee Street Bakery, Cork Street.

Irish Citizen Army (MICHAEL MALLIN, assisted by CONSTANCE MARKIEVICZ): St Stephen's Green, Royal College of Surgeons (St Stephen's Green, West). Members of the Citizen Army under Captain Seán Connolly (the first insurgent fatality of the rising) also took City Hall (Dame Street).

Communications between Ireland and Britain were severely hampered when the telephone line was cut by the insurgents; the cruiser *Adventure* in Kingstown (Dún Laoghaire) Harbour helped the authorities maintain a radio link.

Second Lieutenant Chalmers, 14th Royal Fusiliers, transacting business in the GPO, became the first prisoner of war. A troop of Lancers under Colonel B. A. Hammond escaped with only four fatalities when they ran the gauntlet of insurgent fire along Sackville Street (O'Connell Street).

Insurgents attacked Beggar's Bush Barracks, Haddington Road. 2,500 British reinforcements from the Curragh arrived and engaged insurgents in the Dublin Castle area and recovered City Hall. SEÁN HEUSTON's command at the Mendicity Institute also came under fire. During the British attack on the South Dublin Union, Nurse Keogh was killed by a stray bullet while leading patients to safety.

The operation of public trains was suspended from 24 April to 3 May by military order.

Tuesday 25 April. Brigadier-General W. H. M. Lowe assumed command of British forces in Dublin. From the Shelbourne Hotel (St Stephen's Green, North) British troops engaged the 178-strong unit of the Citizen Army, forcing them back on the College of Surgeons. Reinforcements from Belfast and Templemore (Co. Tipperary), with artillery support, enabled the military to tighten its cordon around Dublin.

Copies of *Irish War News,* a bulletin issued from within the GPO, went on sale, price 1 penny. Later that night martial law was proclaimed throughout Dublin City and County. Widespread looting was recorded; SEÁN O'CASEY remarked that the first shops looted were 'sweets and toy shops.'

Wednesday 26 April. At 8 a.m. the gunboat HELGA began shelling Liberty Hall (Beresford Place), which was empty save for the caretaker, Peter Ennis, who escaped; the fabric of the building escaped extensive damage. Boland's Mills were also shelled. Volunteers under Commandant Edward Daly burned Linenhall Barracks (captured on Monday). British forces took up positions in Sackville Street (O'Connell Street). Soldiers of the 178th Regiment (Sherwood Foresters) attacked insurgent positions at Lansdowne Road but were forced to retreat.

Intense fighting took place at Mount Street Bridge, commanded by Michael Malone (later killed), and at nearby Clanwilliam House, commanded by George Reynolds (killed during the action). The insurgents pinned down two battalions for more than five hours until, out of ammunition, they were forced to surrender. Volunteer losses were less than six, while the British, fighting from a largely open position, lost approximately two hundred (nearly half the casualties for the whole week). The Mendicity Institute fell as British forces advanced on the inner city.

Food was scarce. Supplies of bread and meat had been commandeered by the military; butter was selling at 6 shillings a pound. By military order, funerals were confined to a hearse and one mourner.

Thursday 27 April. Communications between insurgent outposts were cut. The military, now in control of Sackville Street (O'Connell Street), began an artillery barrage on the GPO. Other buildings damaged included the Hibernian Bank, Royal Hibernian Academy, Imperial Hotel (now Clery's department store), the Coliseum, Thom's (printers), and public houses, including the Ship and Mooney's. The O'Connell Monument remained largely unscathed during the intense bombardment.

Shelling of the Four Courts was begun, and Boland's Mills were subjected to further attack. Cathal Brugha was severely wounded in the fighting at the South Dublin Union (James's Street), from where British forces temporarily retreated.

Friday 28 April. GENERAL SIR JOHN MAXWELL, shortly after his arrival in Dublin to take over as supreme commander, declared: 'If necessary I shall not hesitate to destroy all buildings within any area occupied by the rebels.' Pearse was forced to abandon the burning GPO; MICHAEL O'RAHILLY was killed leading his men into Moore Street.

At Ashbourne, Co. Meath, THOMAS ASHE captured a number of RIC men with their arms and ammunition but failed to take the barracks. His force lost two men in an engagement with reinforcements from Navan, during which eight soldiers were killed and fifteen wounded.

Following bitter close-quarter engagements in the area, armoured cars entered North King Street, Dublin. The fighting here produced the only major recorded indiscipline by British soldiers: the bullet-riddled bodies of two unarmed civilians, Patrick Bealen and James Healy, shot while in military custody, were discovered buried in the cellar of O'Rourke's public house, 177 North King Street.

Saturday 29 April. Insurgent leaders, isolated with their command in Moore Street, decided to negotiate terms of surrender and sent Nurse Elizabeth O'Farrell as emissary to make preliminary arrangements. Brigadier-General Lowe accepted Pearse's sword at the junction of Sackville Street (O'Connell Street) and Great Britain Street (Parnell Street) at 3:30 p.m. Fifteen minutes later Pearse signed the surrender document at the British headquarters at Parkgate and signed orders for the other outposts:

> In order to prevent the further slaughter of Dublin citizens, and in the hope of saving the lives of our followers now surrounded and hopelessly outnumbered, the members of the Provisional Government present at Headquarters have agreed to an unconditional surrender, and the commandants of the various districts in the City and County will order their commands to lay down arms.

James Connolly and Thomas MacDonagh signed separate surrender documents on behalf of their commands.

On Monday 1 May the last major incident of the rising took place at Bawnard House, near Fermoy, Co. Cork, home of the Kent family. THOMAS KENT and his brothers, who had returned from being on the run during Easter Week, were surrounded in their home by the RIC. During the ensuing gun battle Head Constable Rowe was killed and several policemen were wounded; two of the Kent brothers were wounded, one (Richard) mortally. The family surrendered when they ran out of ammunition. Thomas Kent was shot by firing squad on 9 May.

Aftermath. Official casualty figures for the rising were 450 killed, 2,614 wounded, and 9 missing. British military: 116 killed, 368 wounded, 9 missing. RIC: 13 killed, 22 wounded. DMP: 3 killed, 7 wounded. Insurgents and civilians: 318 killed, 2,217 wounded.

Arrests. Of the 3,430 men and 79 women arrested for suspected complicity in the rising (according to British Parliamentary Archive papers), 1,424 men and 73 women were released without charge. Of the 170 men and 1 woman (Constance Markievicz) tried by court-martial, sixteen were put to death.

Executions. 3 May: Patrick Pearse, Thomas J. Clarke, Thomas MacDonagh. 4 May: Joseph Plunkett, Edward Daly, William Pearse, Michael O'Hanrahan. 5 May: John MacBride. 8 May: Éamonn Ceannt, Michael Mallin, Con Colbert, Seán Heuston. 9 May: Thomas Kent. 12 May: James Connolly, Seán Mac Diarmada. The executions were carried out at Kilmainham Jail, Dublin, with the exception of Thomas Kent (Cork Military Detention Barracks). Roger Casement was hanged in Pentonville Prison, London, 3 August, for his part in events preceding the rising.

Internment. 1,836 men and 5 women were sent to various prisons in Ireland and Britain and 11 men were acquitted. Following further investigation, 1,272 of those imprisoned were released. In the general amnesty of June, before the IRISH CONVENTION, all internees were released.

AUGUSTINE BIRRELL, Chief Secretary for Ireland, resigned following the rising. He was severely censured by the report of the Royal Commission on the Rebellion in Ireland (26 June 1916), which was also critical of the Under-Secretary, SIR MATTHEW NATHAN.

Economic and Social Research Institute, founded in 1960 as the Irish Economic and Social Research Institute, aided by a grant from the Ford Foundation, New York, as an independent, non-profit-making organisation limited by guarantee; its brief was later broadened to include social research. The ESRI is financed through a government grant in aid (covering some 35 per cent of expenditure) and from commissioned research projects, sales of publications, sponsorship, and membership subscriptions. It works with international bodies, including the European Commission, OECD, International Monetary Fund, and World Bank. Its research has been included in some five hundred published reports; it also publishes the influential *Quarterly Economic Commentary* and *Medium-Term Review*.

'Economic War' (1932–38), begun in 1932 when the Fianna Fáil government, in keeping with its election pledge, withheld the £5 million annual repayment of LAND ANNUITIES due to be paid to the British exchequer in July 1932. Many farmers were unable to meet such payments, while others were unwilling to do so. The British government asserted that the withholding of the annuities was a breach of the Financial Agreements of 1925–26; ÉAMON DE VALERA claimed that those agreements were in fact illegal, never having been ratified by Dáil Éireann. Expert legal opinion was divided.

Britain immediately imposed a special 20 per cent duty on cattle imported from Ireland; this was raised to 40 per cent, with a 30 per cent duty on other agricultural products, on the realisation that the original 20 per cent was not enough to recoup the outstanding £5 million. The Irish government responded by imposing special duties on British imports, including 5 shillings per ton on coke and coal, 20 per cent on cement, machinery, electrical goods, steel, and iron, and export bounties on certain agricultural exports to Britain. The value of exports to Britain fell from £43.5 million in 1929 to less than £18 million in 1935.

The decrease in the numbers of cattle exported was matched by a dramatic increase in smuggling to Northern Ireland. The *News Letter* (Belfast), 25 May 1933, published a report on the fair at Camlough, Co. Armagh, where a local farmer commented that he might as well have been at a fair in Ballina, Co. Mayo, as not 5 per cent of the cattle on sale were 'home-produced.'

There was considerable pressure to end the dispute. Senior civil servants in both countries disapproved of the measures, and Welsh mine-owners impressed on the British government their fears of losing the Irish market to other coal imports. The *Spectator* commented (5 April 1935): 'The economic war will exhaust neither side; it is more injurious to Ireland in times of peace and may be more injurious to England in times of war and rumours of war.' The position improved following the COAL-CATTLE PACT of 1935, and talks between de Valera and the British Premier, NEVILLE CHAMBERLAIN, in early 1938 led to the signing of the ANGLO-IRISH AGREEMENTS (1938), which ended the conflict.

The Irish government had sought to achieve a policy of self-sufficiency during the Economic War. Farmers responded to the appeal for an increase in wheat yield: the 1931 figure of 21,000 acres under wheat rose to 255,000 in 1936. SEÁN LEMASS, Minister for Industry and Commerce, encouraged industries to seek alternative export markets. The government also embarked on an ambitious building scheme of roads and rural cottages, costing more than £1 million. Dublin tenement families were resettled and the sugarbeet industry extended. Cement factories were established at Drogheda and Limerick and tentative mineral explorations begun. Between 1931 and 1938 there was a 44 per cent increase in industrial output, with a consequential increase in industrial employment from 110,000 to 166,000.

Edgar, Rev. John (1798–1866), clergyman (Presbyterian), philanthropist, and temperance crusader; born near Ballinahinch, Co. Down, educated in Belfast and Glasgow. Ordained in Belfast, 1820, he became professor of theology, 1826, and began his temperance crusade in 1829, which won support from prominent clergymen of all denominations. During the GREAT FAMINE (1845–49) he worked on famine relief in Connacht while pursuing his religious work. He founded industrial schools for the training of women in embroidery and established a house to assist in the reform of prostitutes in Great Brunswick Street (Pearse Street), Dublin, towards which he raised £6,000 during an American tour in 1859. He was the editor of several periodicals, and his *Select Works* was published in 1868.

Edgeworth, Maria (1767–1849), novelist; born in Black Bourton, Oxfordshire, educated at Derby and London. Attempts to increase her height included suspending her for periods by the neck. She not only ran the family estate at Edgeworthstown, Co. Longford, from 1782 but also looked after the twenty children from her father's four marriages. The family moved to Clifton, Westmorland, 1789, remaining until the autumn of 1793. Following the death of her father Maria divided her time between estate management and the preparation of her eighteen-volume collected works for publication. She formed friendships with Byron, Wordsworth, and Scott, visiting Scott in Edinburgh, 1823; he, with his daughter and biographer, returned the visit in 1825. (He acknowledged his debt to her in the general preface to the Waverley novels.) During the early years of the GREAT FAMINE (1845–49), at the age of eighty, she worked tirelessly on behalf of local famine victims, soliciting aid from all sources. A gift of 150 barrels of flour from Boston schoolchildren, addressed simply 'To Miss Edgeworth for her poor,' was delivered without undue delay.

She was a prolific writer: her educational and moral tales include *The Parent's Assistant, or Stories for Children* (2 vols., 1796), *Harry and Lucy . . . Being the First Part of Early Lessons* (1801), and *Moral Tales for Young People* (2 vols., 1801). Among her most enduring works are *Castle Rackrent* (1800), *Tales of Fashionable Life* (6 vols., 1809–12), and *The Absentee* (1812). Her last novel, *Helen,* was published in 1834. Her *Memorial of Richard Lovell Edgeworth* was published in 1820

Her father, Richard Lovell Edgeworth (1744–1817), was an educationalist, inventor, politician, and writer. He opposed the Act of Union, objecting to the widespread corruption employed to secure it. He proposed a plan for speeding 'telegraphic' (i.e. semaphore) communication between Dublin and Galway, 1804, to facilitate his reception of the racing results from Newmarket. He also invented a velocipede, spring suspension, and the road surfacing now called tarmacadam (named after a rival scheme). Among his papers submitted to the Royal Irish Academy was one that outlined a method of bog reclamation, 1810. Influenced by the writings of Jean-Jacques Rousseau (1712–1778), he had little success in attempts to raise his eldest son in accordance with the principles enunciated in *Émile* (1762).

education. During the nineteenth century separate education systems evolved at elementary, secondary and third (university) level. These were not brought under central control until after 1920. The Northern Ireland Ministry of Education assumed control of its entire education system in 1921; in the Irish Free State, control passed to the Department of Education in 1924.

For primary education see NATIONAL EDUCATION; for secondary education see SECONDARY EDUCATION, TECHNICAL EDUCATION, and VOCATIONAL EDUCATION; for university education see TRINITY COLLEGE, MAYNOOTH, QUEEN'S COLLEGES, CATHOLIC UNIVERSITY OF IRELAND, ROYAL UNIVERSITY OF IRELAND, and NATIONAL UNIVERSITY OF IRELAND.

Egan, Patrick (1841–1919), Fenian; born in Ballymahon, Co. Longford. A member of the Supreme Council of the IRB, as managing director of North City Milling Company, Dublin, he was in frequent contact with IRB members in the parent company and its branches. He was a founder-member and treasurer of the LAND LEAGUE and protected its funds by fleeing to Paris when it was outlawed, October 1881. Acting largely on his own initiative, in 1882 he acceded to a demand from A. M. SULLIVAN for $100,000 to be allotted to CLAN NA GAEL for a campaign against England. He was suspected of secretly financing the INVINCIBLES, the faction responsible for the PHOENIX PARK MURDERS.

With THOMAS BRENNAN he escaped to the United States, 1883, where he became a successful businessman and politician and founded the National League of America. He was US ambassador to Chile, 1888. He later supported JOHN REDMOND and the NATIONAL VOLUNTEERS. His antagonism towards JOHN DEVOY surfaced in 1916 when, in an interview with the *New York Times* following the executions of the leaders of the EASTER RISING (1916), he declared:

> Ninety-eight per cent of all Irishmen were not in sympathy with the revolt, and England had nothing to gain by shooting people after it is over . . . If anyone were shot it should have been John Devoy, who hatched the whole nefarious scheme here in New York and was personally responsible for it.

Eighty-Two Club, founded in 1845 in memory of the Volunteers of 1782 and the independent parliament of 1792. Guests at its inaugural banquet in Dublin, 16 April 1845, included THOMAS DAVIS (who designed its uniform), CHARLES GAVAN DUFFY, and DANIEL O'CONNELL. For a brief period the club raised hopes of an emulation of 1782 among its rather exclusive membership.

'Éire Nua' ('new Ireland'), the name adopted by SINN FÉIN, 25 October 1971, for a proposal to divide Ireland administratively into its four historical provinces, with a regional parliament for each under a federal government. It was designed by RUAIRÍ Ó BRÁDAIGH and DÁITHÍ Ó CONAILL, who believed it would be attractive to Ulster unionists, as it would provide a parliament for the nine-county province of Ulster (rather than the six counties heretofore). The plan proposed a new constitution, new government structures, and a programme for social and economic development through regional development councils. It had a strong left-wing bias in economic matters. The concept was removed from the constitution of Sinn Féin in 1982 following the party's success in the Northern Ireland Assembly elections.

Electoral Act (1963), legislation that allowed for party names to be printed on ballot papers for the first time to accompany the names of candidates. It also removed restrictions on campaign expenditure.

Electoral Amendment Act (1927), introduced by W. T. COSGRAVE following the assassination of KEVIN O'HIGGINS (10 July 1927). It stipulated that candidates for Dáil Éireann must sign an affidavit to the effect that if elected they would take their seat and subscribe to the OATH OF ALLEGIANCE within two months. The act ended Fianna Fáil's abstention policy.

Emerald Isle, a term first applied to Ireland by William Drennan (1754–1820) in his poem 'Erin':

> Nor one feeling of vengeance presume to defile
> The cause or the men of the Emerald Isle.

The island of Montserrat, to which Irish families fled during the Cromwellian period, is sometimes referred to as the 'Emerald Isle of the West Indies'.

'Emergency', a name once commonly used for the years of the SECOND WORLD WAR in Ireland, following the declaration of a state of emergency, September 1939 to August 1946.

'emergency men'. During the LAND WAR (1879–82) an Emergency Committee of the ORANGE ORDER was established 'for the purpose of protecting loyal subjects in Ireland' against the activities of the LAND LEAGUE. Financed by the committee, 'emergency men' took over farms from which tenants had been evicted and worked them in the landlord's interest. They also provided labour for landlords who had been boycotted. They generally required police protection while engaged in this work. One of the earliest beneficiaries of the scheme was CAPTAIN CHARLES BOYCOTT.

Emergency Powers Act (1940), introduced by the government of ÉAMON DE VALERA, January 1940, after MR JUSTICE GEORGE GAVAN DUFFY granted a *habeas corpus* application on behalf of a member of the IRA, on the grounds that his detention under the OFFENCES AGAINST THE STATE ACT (1939) was unconstitutional. As a result of the judgment an application by SEÁN MACBRIDE for the release of fifty-three IRA prisoners held under the legislation was also granted.

The new emergency legislation was not subject to judicial review. It supplemented the TREASON ACT (1939) and Offences Against the State Act (1939), both designed to deal with the IRA, which, since January 1939, had been engaged in a campaign against Northern Ireland and Britain. The act granted the Minister for Justice powers to intern known or suspected members of the IRA, or those who aided them, in the Curragh Camp, Co. Kildare.

The Emergency Powers (Amendment) Act (1940) was introduced to grant the Minister for Justice retrospective powers to intern known or suspected IRA sympathisers. The President, DR DOUGLAS HYDE, referred it to the Supreme Court, which upheld its constitutionality. A Dáil challenge by the Labour Party to the further strengthening of the act through the Emergency Powers Order (No. 139) was defeated (71 to 20), 29 January 1942. This order allowed the prosecution to introduce at the subsequent trial a statement voluntarily signed at the time of arrest, even if such statement was retracted before the trial. The legislation, first used at the trial of three IRA members for the murder of an IRA member, Michael Devereux, led to the execution of George Plant.

Emergency Powers Act (1976), introduced following the murder of the British ambassador, Christopher Ewart-Biggs, 23 July 1976. The government declared a new national emergency, 1 September, as a result of terrorist acts; it was opposed by FIANNA FÁIL, which claimed that existing legislation was sufficient to deal with the threat of the IRA. The act, passed on 16 September, extended the period for which suspects might be held; section 2 empowered the Garda Síochána to arrest without warrant and hold in custody for up to seven days persons arrested in connection with offences under the OFFENCES AGAINST THE STATE ACTS (1939 AND 1940). This section was to remain in force for one year from the date of enactment (16 October 1976). When Fianna Fáil returned to power, July 1977, section 2 was allowed to lapse in October.

The President, CEARBHALL Ó DÁLAIGH, referred the bill to the Supreme Court, which upheld its constitutionality. His action, publicly criticised by the Minister for Defence, Patrick Donegan, provoked a constitutional crisis when the Taoiseach, LIAM COSGRAVE, apparently failed to censure the minister. The President, believing his office had been denigrated, resigned on 22 October.

Emmet, Robert (1778–1803), United Irishman; born in Dublin, educated at TCD, where he befriended Thomas Moore. Emmet's connection with the UNITED IRISHMEN forced his departure from Trinity College, February 1798. In Paris he contacted exiled United men, and he was joined there by his brother Thomas Addis Emmet, 1802. Napoléon Bonaparte led him to believe that a French invasion of England was imminent. Following his return to Ireland, Emmet used a legacy to procure arms depots in Dublin. The outbreak of war between England and France, 1803, acted as stimulus to a rising, and Emmet began the manufacture of arms. An explosion at his ammunition factory in Patrick Street, Dublin, 16 July, led to a premature rising, 23 July, which collapsed when Thomas Russell (1767–1803) in Ulster and MICHAEL DWYER in Co. Wicklow failed to rise in unison. Emmet's force of approximately one hundred failed in their objective of taking Dublin Castle. An unruly mob that had joined them was responsible for the murder of the Chief Justice, Lord Kilwarden, and his nephew, Rev. Richard Wolfe.

Emmet refused safe passage to France until he had met his fiancée, SARAH CURRAN. He hid in Harold's Cross, Dublin, under the name Ellis, protected by his housekeeper, Anne Devlin. He was arrested, 25 August, by the town major (head of police), Henry Sirr. Letters from his fiancée betrayed his identity. Her father, John Philpot Curran (1750–1817), refused her plea to defend him.

Emmet was tried before the notorious EARL NORBURY. His speech from the dock became one of the most celebrated patriotic speeches of the century; he concluded:

> Let no man write my epitaph; for as no man who knows my motives dare now vindicate them, let not prejudice or ignorance asperse them. Let them rest in obscurity and peace: my memory be left in oblivion and my tomb remain uninscribed, until other times and other men can do justice to my character. When my country takes her place among the nations of the earth, then, and not till then, let my epitaph be written. I have done.

Emmet was hanged in Thomas Street, Dublin, on 20 September and his body buried in 'Bully's Acre' at the hospital fields, Kilmainham.

On 20 January 1968 a statue by Jerome O'Connor presented to the nation by an Irish-American group was unveiled by the Tánaiste and Minister for External Affairs, FRANK AIKEN, opposite Emmet's birthplace at St Stephen's Green, Dublin.

Emmet's older brother Thomas Addis Emmet (1764–1827) studied medicine at TCD and on the Continent but later turned to law. Essentially a constitutionalist, he supported electoral reform and CATHOLIC EMANCIPATION. Though he joined the United Irishmen, 1795, and became secretary of its Supreme Council, he opposed the rising of 1798. Following his arrest in early 1798 he was imprisoned in Scotland until 1802. He later settled in the United States, where he had a distinguished career at the American bar.

Emmet Monument Association, founded in New York by JOHN O'MAHONY and MICHAEL DOHENY, 1855, a precursor of the IRB. Its object was to achieve Irish independence with the assistance of an Irish-American army. JOSEPH DENIEFFE, given a brief to establish a similar organisation in Ireland, 1855, returned to New York in late 1857 with a request from JAMES STEPHENS to raise enough funds for the establishment of an underground movement. The initial capital raised, £80, was used by Stephens to found the IRISH REPUBLICAN BROTHERHOOD in Dublin, 17 March 1858. The Emmet Monument Association was absorbed by the FENIANS in 1859.

Employers' Federation, founded in Dublin, June 1911, modelled on the Cork Employers' Federation, which had helped defeat the IRISH TRANSPORT AND GENERAL WORKERS' UNION in Cork during 1909. In 1913 WILLIAM MARTIN MURPHY used the federation as his instrument in crushing strikers during the DUBLIN LOCK-OUT (1913).

Employment Equality Act (1977), legislation that prohibits discrimination on the grounds of sex or marital status in recruitment for employment, in training, in conditions of employment, and in the provision of opportunities for promotion. It also prohibits indirect discrimination. The Employment Equality Agency was established later the same year.

Encumbered Estates Acts (1848 and 1849), designed to facilitate the disposal of a number of Irish estates whose owners were unable to meet mortgage obligations because of the GREAT FAMINE (1845–49). Under the acts, from 28 July 1849 an Encumbered Estates Court was established with authority to sell estates on the application of the owner or encumbrancer. The first such court sat in Dublin on 24 October 1849. Money raised through the sale was distributed among creditors, and clear title was presented to the new owners, but existing tenants were not protected. Between 1849 and 1857 three thousand estates, totalling 5 million acres, were disposed of, many of which fell into the hands of speculators. Of the £21 million worth of land sold between 1848 and 1859, Irish people bought land worth £18 million (7,180 out of 7,489 purchasers). The functions of the Encumbered Estates Court were assumed by the Landed Estates Court in 1858.

Erin's Hope, originally the *Jacknell Packet*, a 200-ton brig bought by the Fenian Brotherhood in the United States to use for the landing of arms in Ireland. It sailed from New York, 20 April 1867, under the command of John F. Kavanagh, a former brigadier-general in the US Army and former congressman; General James J. Kerrigan was the military commander. Unable to effect a safe landing in Sligo Bay, 20 May, it proceeded south and arrived off Dungarvan, Co. Waterford, 1 June. Its cargo included five thousand breech-loading and repeating rifles, three unmounted cannon, revolvers, and more than a million rounds of ammunition. Put ashore at Cunnegar, close to Helvick Head, the twenty-eight Fenians (all of whom were former US army officers) were speedily captured.

One member of the expedition, Daniel J. Buckely, turned informer. The court disallowed claims by three defendants—Colonel John Warren, Lieutenant Augustine E. Costello, and Lieutenant William Halpin—that, as American citizens, they could not be tried by a foreign court for treason, and the Lord Chief Justice, WILLIAM NICHOLAS KEOGH, sentenced both Warren and Halpin to fifteen years' penal servitude and Costello to twelve. The remaining defendants were returned to the United States with their ship.

The trial had a sequel later the same year when the British House of Commons passed a law (the 'Warren and Costello Act') that allowed a British-born subject, in certain circumstances, to divest himself of birth allegiance and to adopt the citizenship of another country.

Ervine, David (born 1954), loyalist politician (Progressive Unionist Party); born in Belfast. He joined the ULSTER VOLUNTEER FORCE in 1972. On 2 November 1974 he was sentenced to eleven years' imprisonment (of which he served five) for possession of a gelignite bomb. He was influenced by GUSTY SPENCE in the Maze Prison, where he studied for a degree from the Open University. Following his release, 1980, he was active in loyalist politics, becoming chief spokesperson for the PROGRESSIVE UNIONIST PARTY, political wing of the UVF. He helped to organise the IRA and loyalist ceasefires of 1994, while maintaining that loyalist violence was a response to IRA violence. After the bomb explosion at Canary Wharf, London, 9 February 1996, he appealed for calm. Elected to Belfast City Council, June 1997, he was among the first to embrace the PEACE PROCESS but by the end of the year was warning that the PUP might withdraw from the Stormont peace talks early in 1998 if the 'endless flow of concessions' to republicans did not cease. He supported the BELFAST AGREEMENT (1998) and was a member of the Northern Ireland Assembly.

ether-drinking. Confined largely to the Ulster counties of Derry, Fermanagh, and Tyrone, ether-drinking, according to the *Times* (London), March 1891, accounted for an annual 17,000 gallons of alcohol consumption. Ether, a distillate of alcohol treated with sulphuric acid, was manufactured locally or smuggled from abroad. It requires an adulterate for it to be safely absorbed; in Ireland the adulterate was generally POITÍN. Ether occasionally rivalled whiskey in popularity.

The routine established by ether-drinkers began with the rinsing of the mouth with cold water; a little more water was then drunk and the nose held during the ingestion of the ether; a further draught of water was taken to reduce the burning effects of the ether. Vomiting was an occupational hazard. Chronic drinkers referred to sublime music experienced while tranquillised by the drink, a pint of which, according to Prof. K. H. Connell in *Irish Peasant Society* (1968), constituted a 'heroic debauch'.

Eucharistic Congress, 1932. The year 1932 was the 1,500th anniversary of the supposed year of St Patrick's mission to Ireland. (The true date is not known but was probably some time in the second half of the fifth century.) To celebrate the event, Dublin was chosen for the thirty-first International Eucharistic Congress, 22–26 June 1932. Under the patronage of the Archbishop of Dublin, Dr Byrne, the secretary was Rev. D. T. Moloney, the director of organisation was Frank O'Reilly, and the chief marshal was EOIN O'DUFFY, commissioner of the Garda Síochána.

Thousands of people arrived in Dublin for the occasion. The first overseas visitors arrived from Canada on the *Duchess of Bedford.* The congress was formally opened at St Mary's Pro-Cathedral, Dublin, by Cardinal Lorenso Lauri, the Papal legate, in the presence of nine cardinals, more than a hundred bishops, and a thousand priests and other religious. An altar was erected on O'Connell Bridge, where the cardinal legate imparted Benediction. The events of the congress were as follows:

Wednesday 22 June. Following Exposition, midnight Mass was celebrated at every church in Dublin.

Thursday 23 June. 'Men's Day'—more than 250,000 men attended Mass in the Phoenix Park.

Friday 24 June. 'Ladies' Day'—some 200,000 women attended Mass in the Phoenix Park.

Saturday 25 June. 'Children's Day'—100,000 children sang 'Missa de Angelis' at a special children's Mass in the Phoenix Park.

Sunday 26 June. An estimated million people attended the Pontifical High Mass in the Phoenix Park, where John McCormack sang 'Panis Angelicus'. Before the closing ceremonies a broadcast by Pope Plus XI, during which he imparted his apostolic blessing, was relayed to the vast congregation.

European Recovery Programme. Though neutral during the SECOND WORLD WAR, Ireland was a beneficiary of the European Recovery Programme, through which MARSHALL AID was distributed. Misgivings by the Department of Finance on debt repayment were overcome in June 1948 when Britain suspended Ireland's access to the sterling area dollar pool. The department's argument that loans should be used to offset import repayment were successfully resisted by the Minister for External Affairs, SEÁN MACBRIDE, and the money, to fulfil a major condition of the loan, was diverted to a long-term recovery programme. Altogether, $146.2 million, including $18 million by way of grant aid, was availed of and employed in projects designed to boost the economy. None of the government's aspirations was achieved, and the programme was abandoned when Fianna Fáil returned to office in 1951.

European Union. Ireland made its first application for membership of the European Economic Community on 31 July 1961, but it was withdrawn when President Charles de Gaulle of France opposed Britain's application. A later application led to the Taoiseach, JACK LYNCH, signing the Treaty of Accession, 22 January 1972. Membership was approved by referendum when 83 per cent of voters declared in favour, 10 May 1972. From January 1973 the first Irish member of the European Commission was DR PATRICK HILLERY, who became vice-president of the Commission with responsibility for social affairs; subsequent Irish commissioners were Richard Burke (tax, consumer affairs, transport, and relations with the European Parliament), 1977–80, Michael O'Kennedy, 1981–82, Richard Burke, 1982–85, Peter Sutherland (competition, social affairs, and education), 1985–89, Ray MacSharry (agriculture), 1889–93, Pádraig Flynn (employment, social affairs, and public health), 1993–99, and David Byrne (health and consumer protection), 1999–.

The first direct elections to the European Parliament were held on 7 June 1979. Those elected were:

Dublin	Ritchie Ryan (Fine Gael)
	John O'Connell (Labour Party)
	Síle de Valera (Fianna Fáil)
	MICHAEL O'LEARY (Labour Party)
Leinster	Mark Clinton (Fine Gael)
	Patrick Lalor (Fianna Fáil)
	Liam Kavanagh (Labour Party)
Connacht-Ulster	
	NEIL BLANEY (Independent)
	Joe McCartin (Fine Gael)
	Seán Flanagan (Fianna Fáil)
Munster	T. J. Maher (Independent)
	Eileen Desmond (Labour Party)

Tom O'Donnell (Fine Gael)
Jeremiah Cronin (Fianna Fáil)
Noel Davern (Fianna Fáil)

Northern Ireland

REV. IAN PAISLEY (Democratic Unionist Party)
JOHN HUME (SDLP)
John Taylor (Ulster Unionist Party)

The European Community became known as the European Union from 1 November 1993. Ireland endorsed the move towards greater economic integration at the end of the 1990s. Despite the unprecedented economic boom (sometimes called the 'Celtic Tiger'), Ireland in 2001 was the first member-state to incur a formal censure for its expansionary budgetary policy.

In a series of referendums the electorate endorsed subsequent changes to the European Union. However, the Treaty of Nice (to alter the weighting of votes in favour of larger countries, which had declared this to be a political requirement of expansion) was rejected on 7 June 2001. In the lowest poll of any of the referendums on the European Union (35 per cent), the Treaty was rejected (54 per cent to 46 per cent). The turn-out for a second referendum on the same treaty, 19 October 2002, was 1,446,588, and this time it was accepted (63 per cent to 37 per cent).

In 1998 PAT COX, member of the European Parliament for Munster, became the first Irish person to head a European political grouping when he was elected president of the European Liberal Democrats. He played a leading role in demanding accountability from the European Commission, presided over by Jacques Santer, whose presidency collapsed as a result of the campaign. Cox was subsequently elected president of the European Parliament, 15 January 2001.

Evening Herald (1805–14), a daily newspaper owned by John Magee junior. Its support for Catholic demands earned it the hostility of the Dublin Castle administration. It changed its name to the *Sentinel* in 1814 and altered its policy, but a decline in readership and advertising forced it to close in 1815.

Another paper of the same name established in 1891 as the evening edition of the *Irish Independent* is still published.

Evening Mail, a daily newspaper launched on 3 February 1823 as the *Dublin Evenning Mail*, changing to *Evening Mail* from 2 February 1928. It was Dublin's oldest newspaper when it last appeared on 19 July 1962.

Everett, James (1890–1967), trade unionist and politician (Labour Party and National Labour Party); born in Co. Wicklow, educated locally. A trade union official to 1918, as a member of Sinn Féin he was a judge of the DÁIL COURTS in Cos. Kildare and Wicklow during the War of Independence. He represented Kildare-Wicklow in Dáil Éireann, 1921–67. He was one of five members of the IRISH TRANSPORT AND GENERAL WORKERS' UNION to secede from the LABOUR PARTY, 1943, to form the NATIONAL LABOUR PARTY. He was a member of the first inter-party government (1948–51), in which he was Minister for Posts and Telegraphs and the centre of political controversy in 1950 through his involvement in the 'BATTLE OF BALTINGLASS'. The resulting allegations of political jobbery were considered a major factor in the defeat of the coalition government in the 1951 general election. Everett was Minister for Justice in the second inter-party government (1954–57).

Evicted Tenants (Ireland) Act (1907), introduced by the Chief Secretary for Ireland, AUGUSTINE BIRRELL, to extended the provisions of the Irish Land Act (1903) (see LAND ACTS). It facilitated the compulsory purchase and sale of untenanted land by the Land Commissioners for those tenants who (or whose predecessors) had been evicted from their holdings since 1878 and who had applied to the Commissioners before 1 May 1907. Up to 31 March 1911 there were 12,398 applications for holdings as evicted tenants. Of these, 6,276 were rejected following inquiry; 2,631 who applied were outside the time limit; 2,830 were reinstated in holdings; and the remaining 661 cases were unresolved.

Executive Council, the government of the Irish Free State, 6 December 1922 to 29 December 1937; the head of the government was known as President of the Executive Council. Under the CONSTITUTION OF IRELAND (1937) it became known as the Government, and its head as the Taoiseach. Presidents of the Executive Council were W. T. COSGRAVE, 1922–32, and ÉAMON DE VALERA, 1932–37.

external association. The concept of 'external association' was devised by ÉAMON DE VALERA in 1921 in an attempt to bridge the gap between the dominion status on offer from the British government and a completely independent republic demanded by hard-line republicans. Describing it as 'a certain treaty of free association with the British Commonwealth,' de Valera believed that such a formulation could satisfy Ulster unionists, 'to meet whose sentiments alone this step could be contemplated.' External association would not require an OATH OF ALLEGIANCE.

The British government rejected the idea when DAVID LLOYD GEORGE met de Valera, July 1921. The draft for a treaty that the Irish plenipotentiaries presented in London included the idea of external association, but it was rejected. The essence of his proposal, de Valera stated in a private session during the Treaty debates, 14 December, was that external association would recognise the King of England as head of the Commonwealth countries, 'with no reference to Ireland.' During the debates he produced a document headed 'Proposed Treaty of Association between Ireland and the British Commonwealth,' which again embodied external association. It declared (article 2)

> that, for the purposes of common concern, Ireland shall be associated with the States of the British Commonwealth, viz: The Kingdom of Great Britain, the Dominion of Canada, the Commonwealth of Australia, the Dominion of New Zealand, and the Union of South Africa.

This document, known as 'DOCUMENT NO. 2', was unacceptable to advocates of the Treaty, who felt that it differed very slightly from the one under discussion. However, it was also unacceptable to opponents of the Treaty. De Valera continued to press the principle of external association, which he eventually achieved through the EXTERNAL RELATIONS ACT (1936).

External Relations Act (1936), popular name for the Executive Authority (External Relations) Act (1936), introduced in Dáil Éireann by ÉAMON DE VALERA, 11 December 1936, during the ABDICATION CRISIS. He simultaneously introduced the CONSTITUTION (AMENDMENT NO. 27) BILL; both were under guillotine, 13 December. The External Relations Act delimited the functions of the British Crown with regard to the external relations of the Irish Free State, declaring that so long as Ireland was associated

> with the following nations, that is to say, Australia, Canada, Great Britain, New Zealand and South Africa, and so long as the King recognised by those nations as the symbol of their co-operation continues to act on behalf of each of those nations (on the advice of the several governments thereof), for the purpose of the appointment of diplomatic and consular representatives and the conclusion of international agreements, the King so recognised may, and is hereby authorised to, act on behalf of Saorstát Éireann for the like purpose as and when advised by the Executive Council to do so.

The act placed external relations firmly in the control of the government of the Irish Free State, while the link between Ireland and the British Commonwealth was maintained. The External Relations Act was repealed by the REPUBLIC OF IRELAND ACT (1948).

F

faction-fighting. Organised fights at FAIRS, PATTERNS and sporting events were common from the seventeenth century until the GREAT FAMINE (1845–49). Principally rural, factions included the CARAVATS and SHANAVESTS, Coffeys and Reaskawallaghs, Cooleens and Black Mulvihills, Bogboys and Tobbers. In Dublin the Ormond (Catholic) and Liberty Boys (Protestant) were two of the few groups in which religion was a factor. The practice was opposed by the clergy and by DANIEL O'CONNELL.

The principal weapon was a well-seasoned stick. Women were permitted to use stones; firearms were rarely used. Fights could involve several hundred people. Sylvester O'Halloran (1728–1807), a Limerick surgeon who became a celebrated specialist on head injuries through treating victims of faction fights, commented in 1793:

> Without doubt there is no part of the habitable globe which has afforded such an ample field for observation on injuries of the head—for our people soon catch fire; a slight offence is frequently followed by serious consequences and sticks, stones and every other species of offence next to hand, are dealt out with great liberality . . .

Until 1837 faction fights were listed as riots. THOMAS DRUMMOND used his newly formed Irish Constabulary in an effort to suppress the fighting. Co. Tipperary, the home of faction-fighting in the nineteenth century, witnessed the last recorded fight, at a fair in Cappawhite in 1887.

fairs. Dating from the early historical period, fairs were an important economic and social feature of Irish life, held at established times of the year at traditional venues. Goods, livestock and produce were available, as were the services of itinerant tradesmen. They attracted ballad-singers, musicians and other entertainers, stall-holders, and the occasional confidence-trickster.

Some of the more ancient surviving fairs are Ballinasloe [Co. Galway] Horse Fair (originally 5–9 October), Lammas Fair, Ballycastle, Co. Antrim (12 August), Cahirmee [Co. Cork] Horse Fair (now 12 July), and Spancel Hill [Co. Clare] Horse Fair (23 June). At Ireland's oldest fair, Puck Fair, in Killorglin, Co. Kerry (10–13 August), goats, horses and sheep are sold, while a wild goat selected as 'King Puck' presides over the event. One of the more infamous fairs, Donnybrook Fair, outside Dublin, suppressed in 1867, led to the coining of a new word in English, 'donnybrook', meaning a brawl. In 1850 the number of recorded fairs dropped by some 750 to approximately 1,300 and by 1900 to less than 790. (See also HIRING FAIRS.)

famine. Ireland experienced varying degrees of famine from earliest times. With the exception of the GREAT FAMINE (1845–49), adverse weather was a primary factor. There was famine, particularly along the western seaboard, in 1800, 1807, 1817, 1821–22, 1830–34, 1836, 1839, 1845–49, 1878–81, and several times during the 1890s. It was frequently accompanied by 'famine fever' (dropsy, typhus, and relapsing fever); in 1832 and 1849 there were outbreaks of cholera. Periods of famine also generated violent agrarian unrest (see AGRARIAN CRIME), and the harsh COERCION measures introduced to suppress such discontent generated a deep-seated hatred of the authorities.

Farmers' Party, a party representing the interests of the larger farmers, formed as the political wing of the Irish Farmers' Union. Made up largely of supporters of the ANGLO-IRISH TREATY (1921), it won seven seats in Dáil Éireann in the general election of June 1922; its greatest number (fifteen) was achieved in the election of 1923. It supported the CUMANN NA NGAEDHEAL governments. In the first general election of 1927 the party returned with eleven seats, but it suffered from the arrival of FIANNA FÁIL and held only six seats in the second general election of that year. The party leader, Denis Gorey, defected to Cumann na nGaedheal in 1927, as did his successor, M. R. Heffernan, and other leading members in 1932. The party secured four seats in the 1932 general election, and those members played a leading role in the founding of the NATIONAL CENTRE PARTY. In the months following the 1932 election the Farmers' Party was absorbed by Cumann na nGaedheal.

Faulkner, (Arthur) Brian, Baron Faulkner of Downpatrick (1921–1977), politician (Ulster Unionist Party and Unionist Party of Northern Ireland); born in Helen's Bay, Co. Down, educated at St Columba's College, Rathfarnham, Co. Dublin, and TCD. The youngest member of the Parliament of Northern Ireland when first elected, 1949, he was involved in the 'Long Stone Road Affair', 12 July 1955, when he led Orangemen, protected by 600 armed police, armoured cars and police dogs, through the (Catholic) Long Stone Road area of Co. Down. Following two days of tension, local people blew craters in sections of the road. As Minister of Home Affairs, 1959, he used internment to combat the campaign of the IRA. As Minister of Commerce in 1963 he ushered in a new era of prosperity when he encouraged transnational companies, including Du Pont, Ford, Goodyear, and ICI, to set up in Northern Ireland. He resigned in protest at reforming moves by TERENCE O'NEILL and in opposition to the appointment of the CAMERON COMMISSION, January 1969.

Serving under CHICHESTER-CLARK as Minister of Development from May 1969, he now declared he favoured a policy of reform. After becoming leader of the Unionist Party and Prime Minister, 23 March 1971, he retained the Home Affairs portfolio. His controversial announcement that any soldier could shoot to kill on suspicion provoked a storm of protest, 25 May 1971. He attempted to win the support of the SDLP in June with the announcement of committees on environmental, industrial and social affairs, two of which would be chaired by opposition MPs, and announced his commitment to reform by appointing Gerald Newe as a minister of state, the first Catholic to sit in a Stormont government.

On 9 August 1971 he introduced internment in response to the IRA's bombing campaign. At first directed against the Catholic population, the arrests sparked a nationalist reaction. Loyalists fled their homes in Ardoyne, Belfast, setting fire to them rather than allow them fall into Catholic hands. Some 2,500 Catholics fled the city for refugee camps set up by the Irish government. Over the following months Faulkner engaged in unproductive talks with the British Prime Minister, EDWARD HEATH, and the Taoiseach, JACK LYNCH. The British government published a green paper, *The Future of Northern Ireland: A Paper for Discussion,* in October, which implied the abolition of Stormont.

The events of BLOODY SUNDAY (30 January 1972) and the founding by party members of the right-wing ULSTER VANGUARD further exacerbated his position. Faulkner met Heath in London, where he refused to transfer responsibility for security and rejected the British government's power-sharing proposals, 22 March. Two days later the Parliament of Northern Ireland was prorogued, and direct rule from London was introduced. In 1973 Faulkner was a party to the SUNNINGDALE AGREEMENT, but the concept of power-sharing (multi-party government) and of a COUNCIL OF IRELAND led to the erosion of hard-line Unionist support.

Faulkner became Chief Executive of the Assembly of Northern Ireland in 1974. Following the collapse of the Executive as a result of the ULSTER WORKERS' COUNCIL strike, 14 May, he formed the UNIONIST PARTY OF NORTHERN IRELAND, which won five seats in the Convention. He announced his intention of retiring from active politics in 1975. In January 1977 he was created Lord Faulkner, but two days after his reception into the House of Lords he was killed in a hunting accident. His autobiography, *Memoirs of a Statesman,* was published in 1978.

Fay, Frank (1870–1931) and **William** (1872–1947), actor-producers; born in Dublin, educated at Belvedere College. William, an electrician by trade, toured Ireland with a number of 'fit-up' companies before making his Dublin debut at the Father Mathew Hall, 1891, under the name W. G. Ormonde. He taught elocution and stagecraft at the brothers' Dublin Dramatic School, where Sarah Allgood (1883–1950) was a pupil. Frank, whose stage name was originally Frank Evelyn, was a renowned speaker of verse (as acknowledged by W. B. Yeats in *The King's Threshold*) and is credited with endowing the ABBEY THEATRE with the clarity and diction of its performers. He is generally acknowledged as the first to advocate a national theatre for the production of native drama by Irish writers and its staging by Irish actors. He was also drama critic of the *United Irishman* (edited by ARTHUR GRIFFITH). William's production of *Casadh an tSúgáin* by Douglas Hyde at the Gaiety Theatre, Dublin, 1901—the first presentation of a play in Irish at a recognised theatre—was considered a remarkable feat for one with little Irish. The brothers also produced Yeats's *Cathleen ni Houlihan,* 2–4 April 1902, with MAUD GONNE in the lead, and GEORGE RUSSELL's *Deirdre,* 1907. They were instrumental in securing the financial support of Annie Horniman (1860–1937) for the Abbey Theatre project. William appeared in several Abbey productions, including his role as Christy Mahon in the first production of *The Playboy of the Western World* by JOHN MILLINGTON SYNGE, 1907, in which Frank played Shawn Keogh.

Following a dispute with the Abbey the brothers undertook a tour of the United States. William took up residence in England and appeared in a number of films, his last role being that of Father Tom in *Odd Man Out* (1947), while Frank returned to Dublin, where he became an elocution teacher. Their reminiscences were published in the same year: *Merely Players* (1935) and *The Joys of the Abbey Theatre* (1935) by Frank Fay and *The Fays of the Abbey Theatre: An Autobiographical Record* (1935) by William Fay.

federalism. In the yearly years of the nineteenth century the federal solution for self-government envisaged an Irish parliament sitting in Dublin legislating solely on Irish issues while imperial affairs were dealt with by the British Parliament in London. Such a solution was acceptable to the less extreme Orangemen led by WILLIAM SHARMAN CRAWFORD as an alternative to repeal of the Union. A committee of Whigs was set up to advise the government on the feasibility of the proposal. DANIEL O'CONNELL contemplated federalism but, having incurred the suspicions of YOUNG IRELAND, discarded it. ISAAC BUTT described his self-government proposals as federalist, while CHARLES STEWART PARNELL rejected it as a permanent solution. Federalism was less acceptable to militant nationalists such as the IRB, the majority of whom were absolute separatists.

Fenians, an oath-bound republican secret society established by JOHN O'MAHONY in New York, 17 March 1858, at the same time that JAMES STEPHENS founded the IRISH REPUBLICAN BROTHERHOOD in Dublin. O'Mahony named the organisation from the Fianna, the warrior bands of Irish mythology. The Fenians came to symbolise a dedication to physical force in pursuit of national independence and the establishment of an Irish republic. While the name was also used for the IRB, they were separate organisations, although, until their goal was achieved, the Fenians recognised the Supreme Council of the IRB as the provisional government of the Irish Republic.

While there were slight variants in the

Fenian oath, the one in general use was:

> I, [. . .], in the presence of Almighty God, do solemnly swear allegiance to the Irish Republic, now virtually established, and that I will do my utmost, at every risk, while life lasts, to defend its independence and integrity, and finally, that I will yield implicit obedience in all things not contrary to the laws of God, to the commands of my superior officers. So help me God! Amen.

The function of the Fenians, whose officers were elected, was to serve as an auxiliary to the IRB, supplying it with officers, volunteers, and arms. During the American Civil War (1861–65) the Fenians, many of whom fought on opposite sides, inducted hundreds of Irish-born soldiers or those of Irish descent into the organisation. O'Mahony organised a Fenian regiment, the 69th Regiment of the New York State Militia (National Guard), of which he was colonel.

Discontent with O'Mahony's leadership and with Stephens's unwillingness to lead the IRB in a rising led to a reorganisation, 1865. O'Mahony had his powers as 'head CENTRE' curbed by the creation of a Senate, which could exercise a veto over him. When he proceeded with a scheme to finance a rising in Ireland through the issue of bonds he was deposed, and replaced by W. R. Roberts. Further fragmentation occurred over proposals to launch raids on Canada. In 1866, as a consequence of these dissensions, there were three Fenian factions: the Fenian Brotherhood, led by O'Mahony, the Senate wing, led by Roberts, and a group known as the 'United Irishmen', who wished to attack Britain through Canada. When Stephens failed to call the anticipated rising during 1866, support for him evaporated, and he travelled to New York, accompanied by the prominent Fenian THOMAS J. KELLY, in a vain effort to unite the movement.

In an attempt to forestall the projected invasion of Canada by the Roberts faction, O'Mahony, against the advice of Stephens, launched an unsuccessful raid on the island of Campo Bello in the Bay of Fundy, between the United States and Canada. The capture of the island was intended to provoke a territorial dispute between Britain and the United States. O'Mahony was forced to abandon his plans when, on approaching the island, he faced six gunboats. He returned to New York, having expended $40,000 on the plan.

The Roberts wing proceeded with its attack on Canada, of which HENRI LE CARON had forewarned the authorities. In June 1866 John O'Neill (1834–1873) led his volunteer force in flat-bottomed boats across the Niagara River and, after occupying Fort Erie, advanced into Ontario. An estimated 300 of his force of 800 deserted en route, and the attackers, having suffered some fifty casualties at Ridgeway, retreated to Fort Erie. On the return journey they were arrested by the US patrol steamer *Michigan.*

In December 1866 the movement, weary of Stephens's procrastination, replaced him as leader with THOMAS J. KELLY.

The success of Fenian agents in recruiting serving British soldiers in Ireland had implications for the British army. Its commander in chief, Sir Hugh Ross, claimed that if there had been a rising before 1865, 'before Military Fenianism had been properly dealt with, something disagreeable might and would probably have occurred.' This 'something disagreeable' was dealt with in 1866 when more than 1,600 Fenian members of the British army in Ireland were arraigned before 150 courts-martial. All death sentences were commuted to life imprisonment, and ringleaders were flogged.

The Fenian organisation ran foul of the Irish Catholic hierarchy. The Archbishop of Dublin, PAUL CULLEN, who had refused the Pro-Cathedral, Dublin, for the lying in state of the Fenian TERENCE BELLEW MCMANUS, November 1861, described the movement in 1865 as 'a compound of folly and wickedness wearing the mask of patriotism.' Following the attempted rising in his diocese in 1867 the Bishop of Kerry, DAVID MORIARTY, called 'God's heaviest curse, his withering, blasting, blighting curse,' on the Fenians, for whose punishment 'eternity is not long enough, nor Hell hot enough.' The IRISH PEOPLE responded to the 'clerical calumniators.' CHARLES J. KICKHAM, who promoted a 'No priests in politics' campaign in his column, quoted the Franciscan scholar Luke Wadding (1588–1657): 'Time was when we had wooden chalices and golden priests but now we have golden chalices and wooden priests.' PATRICK 'PAGAN' O'LEARY and JAMES F. X. O'BRIEN supported Kickham in his denunciations. JOHN O'LEARY, in *Recollections of Fenians and Fenianism* (1896), declared, 'We meant to kill clerical dictation and we did kill it.'

In January 1867 Kelly, JOHN MACCAFFERTY and RICARD O'SULLIVAN BURKE sailed for Ireland. The commander in chief of the proposed rising, the French soldier of fortune GUSTAVE-PAUL CLUSERET, travelled to Ireland and, having assessed the situation, advised against a rising and returned to France. The same year saw Fenian involvement in England: the attempted rescue of prisoners in Manchester resulted in the death of a police sergeant and in the executions of Allen, Larkin, and O'Brien—the MANCHESTER MARTYRS. The CLERKENWELL EXPLOSION, which killed twelve people and injured more than fifty, was another attempt to rescue Fenian prisoners. Between 1881 and 1885 'the TRIANGLE', a group within the Fenians, organised the DYNAMITERS in their campaign against England.

The failure of the 1867 rising led to the founding of CLAN NA GAEL from among O'Mahony's Fenian Brotherhood and followers of the Senate wing. Assuming the same relationship to the IRB as the Fenians, Clan na Gael represented the essential element of republicanism destined to bring about Irish independence.

Ferguson, Harry George (1884–1960), inventor; born in Growell, Hillsborough, Co. Down, educated locally. With his elder brother Joe he established J. B. Ferguson and Company in Little Donegall Street, Belfast, 1903. A keen sportsman, he used his involvement in motorcycling and car racing to advance his business interests. He built his own aeroplane and flew it successfully for some 130 yards on the Downshire estate at Hillsborough, 31 December 1909—the first flight in Ireland by an aircraft constructed entirely in Ireland. He won the £100 prize offered for the first official three-mile flight in Ireland, 1910. In 1911 he established May Street Motors, which became Harry Ferguson Ltd a year later. In 1914 he was appointed agent for the American Overtime Tractor, in which year, as a supporter of the ULSTER VOLUNTEER FORCE, he participated in the LARNE GUN-RUNNING. His appointment by the Irish Board of Agriculture to give ploughing demonstrations led to the development of the Ferguson tractor, which, with his own prototype plough, made his fortune.

The only partner ever accepted by Henry Ford, Ferguson licensed Ford to produce the tractor in America, but the informal agreement was reneged on in 1947; in a celebrated court case, Ferguson was awarded $9 million for patent infringement and loss of business. He then entered into agreement with the Standard Motor Company to build a new tractor, and by 1956 more than half a million T20 Fergusons had been built. Soon afterwards he merged with Massey Hams of Toronto, and the Massey-Ferguson became an international success.

Ferguson, Sir Samuel (1810–1886), antiquarian and poet; born in Belfast, educated at RBAI and TCD and called to the bar, becoming a Queen's counsel in 1859. A unionist and pacifist in outlook, he identified with the ideals of his friends in YOUNG IRELAND. He had a particular rapport with THOMAS DAVIS, on whose early death he wrote the elegy 'Lament for Thomas Davis' (1845). Chronically ill, Ferguson was obliged to spend much of the year abroad. He founded the Protestant Repeal Association, 1848, but ceased his involvement following his marriage later that year. Retiring from the bar, 1867, he became Deputy Keeper of the Public Records of Ireland. Knighted for this work, 1878, he was president of the Royal Irish Academy, 1882. His published works include *Lays of the Western Gael and Other Poems* (1865), which includes his most enduring poem, 'The Burial of King Cormac'. *Ogham Inscriptions in Ireland, Scotland and Wales* and *Hibernian Nights' Entertainment* were posthumously published, 1887.

Fethard-on-Sea Boycott. Fethard, Co. Wexford, was the scene of a boycott of the local Protestant population in 1957. In 1949 Seán Cloney (1916–1999), a Catholic, married Sheila Kelly, a member of the Church of Ireland, in a register office in London. They subsequently married in a Catholic Church, when Sheila Cloney signed a document agreeing to bring up the children as Catholics, in accordance with the NE TEMERE decree. The couple had two children. In January 1957 the parish priest, William Stafford, informed Mrs Cloney that her eldest daughter, Eileen, was to attend the local Catholic school. Mrs Cloney objected to raising the children in the Catholic faith and took them from the family home, 27 April 1957. Three days later the Belfast lawyer Desmond Boal called on Seán Cloney with a list of 'settlement proposals', which required him to agree to the children being brought up in the Church of Ireland. It was also suggested that Cloney should consider changing his own religion, selling his farm, and emigrating with his wife and children. He rejected these proposals.

A boycott of the Protestant community in the area began on 13 May. Sheila Cloney's father was the first victim: a farmer, who enjoyed a good relationship with Seán Cloney, he was ruined as a result of the boycott. Cloney, supported by some local IRA veterans of the War of Independence, fought the boycott. In

Dáil Éireann the Taoiseach, ÉAMON DE VALERA, called the boycott 'ill-conceived, ill-considered and futile, unjust and cruel.' It came to an end after Mrs Cloney's father and a local TD issued a joint statement, and the parish priest bought a packet of cigarettes in the shop most affected by the boycott.

Cloney and his wife lived in England for a short time before returning home, where they educated their children themselves. Seán Cloney later established a reputation as a local historian. A film, *A Love Divided* (1999), was based on the Cloneys' story.

Fianna Éireann, a republican youth movement founded in Dublin, 16 August 1909, by CONSTANCE MARKIEVICZ and BULMER HOBSON, modelled on a similar organisation founded by Hobson in Belfast in 1902. Its uniformed members pledged to work for the independence of Ireland and never to join the British armed forces. The organisation's chief instructor, CON COLBERT, and secretary, Éamon Martin, were members of the IRB, for which the Fianna was a recruiting ground; patrons included ROGER CASEMENT, DR PATRICK MCCARTAN, and PATRICK PEARSE. Hobson resigned the presidency within a few months and was succeeded by Markievicz. LIAM MELLOWS joined in 1911 and became secretary of the Dublin District Council. By 1912 there were twenty-two branches. The Fianna actively supported the striking workers during the DUBLIN LOCK-OUT (1913), acted as stewards at the inaugural meeting of the IRISH VOLUNTEERS, and assisted at the HOWTH GUN-RUNNING (1914). They were involved in the EASTER RISING (1916) and in the WAR OF INDEPENDENCE.

Fianna Éireann later became the youth movement of the IRA and, after the split of 1969–70, of the Provisional IRA.

Fianna Fáil, a political party founded by ÉAMON DE VALERA. Its inaugural meeting was held in the La Scala Theatre, Dublin, 16 May 1926. At the suggestion of SEÁN LEMASS the party adopted the sub-title 'Republican Party'. The objectives of the party were the reunification of Ireland as an independent republic, the promotion of the use of Irish, the distribution of large farms among small farmers, and a policy of economic protection and self-sufficiency. The structure of the new party was based on SINN FÉIN and the old Parnellite party, consisting of a cumann or branch in each parish, a constituency organisation, and a National Executive.

The party broke with the Sinn Féin policy of abstention when members took their seats in Dáil Éireann, 1 August 1927. Its newspaper, the IRISH PRESS, controlled by the de Valera family, was founded in 1931. Fianna Fáil came to power in March 1932 and formed successive governments until February 1948. It formed a government, 1951–54 and again 1957–73. It returned in 1977 under JACK LYNCH, who was succeeded in December 1979 by CHARLES HAUGHEY. Under Haughey the party lost power in June 1981, regained it in February 1982, but lost it again in November of the same year. It returned to office in February 1987 when Haughey shed its long-standing tradition of single-party government and entered into a coalition with the PROGRESSIVE DEMOCRATS. Subsequent coalition governments led by ALBERT REYNOLDS and BERTIE AHERN had Fianna Fáil as the senior partner. The party's share of first-preference votes and seats was:

	First-preference votes	Seats
1927 (June)	26.1%	44
1927 (Sept.)	35.2%	57
1932	44.5%	72
1933	49.7%	77
1937	45.2%	69
1938	51.0%	77
1943	41.9%	67
1944	48.9%	76
1948	41.9%	68
1951	46.3%	69
1954	43.4%	65
1957	48.3%	78
1961	43.8%	70
1965	47.8%	72
1969	45.7%	75
1973	46.2%	69
1977	50.6%	84
1981	45.3%	78
1982 (Feb.)	47.3%	81
1982 (Nov.)	45.2%	72
1987	44.2%	81
1992	39.1%	68
1997	39.3%	77
2002	41.5%	81

Leaders of the party have been Éamon de Valera, 1926–59, Seán Lemass, 1959–66, John (Jack) Lynch, 1966–79, Charles Haughey, 1979–89, Albert Reynolds, 1989–94, and Bertie Ahern, 1994–.

For the members of the governments formed by Fianna Fáil see GOVERNMENTS. For details on the party in power see LAND ANNUITIES, 'ECONOMIC WAR', IRISH REPUBLICAN

ARMY, BLUESHIRTS, ABDICATION CRISIS, EXTERNAL RELATIONS ACT (1936), CONSTITUTION OF IRELAND (1937), ANGLO-IRISH AGREEMENT (1938), OFFENCES AGAINST THE STATE ACTS (1939 AND 1940), EMERGENCY POWERS ACT (1940), AND PROGRAMMES FOR ECONOMIC EXPANSION.

Fianna Uladh, the political wing of SAOR ULADH, founded in 1953 by followers of the imprisoned Liam Kelly of Pomeroy, Co. Tyrone, elected as Sinn Féin abstentionist MP shortly before his imprisonment. It aimed to 'develop an organisation of Republicans in occupied Ireland into a disciplined political movement and to use every legitimate means to bring about the re-unification of the territory of the Republic of Ireland.' In recognising the Irish government it breached traditional IRA policy, for which Kelly was expelled, October 1951. He was elected to Seanad Éireann with the help of CLANN NA POBLACHTA, 1954. Fianna Uladh was short-lived as a party; it was proscribed with SAOR ULADH and SINN FÉIN in 1956.

Figgis, Darrell (1882–1925), author, journalist, and politician (Sinn Féin); born in Rathmines, Dublin. He used experience gained on a tea plantation in Ceylon (Sri Lanka) to become a tea broker in Ireland and England, 1898–1910. He worked for the London publishers Dent and Sons, 1910–13. A supporter of the Gaelic League and Sinn Féin, he travelled to Hamburg, 8 May 1914, where he bought the arms for the Irish Volunteers that featured in the HOWTH GUN-RUNNING. After the guns were landed both he and THOMAS MACDONAGH managed to distract the police while the arms were spirited away by the Volunteers. Several times arrested for political activities, he was secretary of Sinn Féin, 1917–19, and editor of the *Republic* during its brief run before its suppression, September 1916. He represented Co. Dublin in the first Dáil Éireann, where he supported the ANGLO-IRISH TREATY (1921), and was acting chairman of the committee to draft the CONSTITUTION OF THE IRISH FREE STATE (1922). He was chairman of the Broadcasting Commission, which led to the founding of Radio Éireann. He took his own life a year after his wife's suicide.

Figgis's writings (some under the pseudonym Michael Ireland) include *Æ: George Russell: A Study of a Man and a Nation* (1915), *The Gaelic State in the Past and the Future* (1917), *The Sinn Féin Catechism* (1918), *The Economic Case for Irish Independence* (1920), *The Irish Constitution Explained* (1922), and *Recollections of the Irish War* (1927).

Fine Gael, originally called the United Ireland Party, founded on 2 September 1933 from a merger of CUMANN NA NGAEDHEAL, the NATIONAL GUARD, and the NATIONAL CENTRE PARTY. The first president of the party was EOIN O'DUFFY, then leader of the BLUESHIRTS; he was replaced by W. T. COSGRAVE, 1935. The traditional supporters of the party were industry, business, the professions, and substantial farmers. Fine Gael was the principal opposition to FIANNA FÁIL, 1933–48, 1951–54, 1957–73; it was the principal party in a number of coalition governments, 1948–51, 1954–57, 1973–77, 1982, 1982–1987, and 1994–97. It had a disastrous showing in the general election of 2002, when it lost 5 per cent of its first-preference vote (down to 22½ per cent) and lost twenty-three Dáil seats, including those of its deputy leader, Jim Mitchell, and former leader ALAN DUKES. The party's share of first-preference votes and seats was:

	First-preference votes	Seats
1933		59

Cumann na nGaedheal (48 seats) and the National Centre Party (11 seats) merged in September 1933, after the election.

1937	34.8%	48
1938	33.3%	45
1943	23.1%	32
1944	20.5%	30
1948	19.8%	31
1951	25.7%	40
1954	32.0%	50
1957	26.6%	40
1961	32.0%	47
1965	33.9%	47
1969	34.1%	50
1972	35.0%	54
1977	30.5%	43
1981	36.5%	65
1982 (Feb.)	37.3%	63
1982 (Nov.)	39.2%	70
1987	27.1%	51
1989	27.1%	55
1992	24.5%	45
1997	28.0%	54
2002	22.5%	31

The leaders of the party have been Eoin O'Duffy (who was not a member of Dáil Éireann), 1933–34, W. T. Cosgrave, 1935–44, RICHARD MULCAHY, 1944–59, JAMES DILLON,

1959–65, LIAM COSGRAVE, 1965–77, GARRET FITZGERALD, 1977–87, ALAN DUKEs, 1987–90, JOHN BRUTON, 1990–2001, MICHAEL NOONAN, 2001–02, and ENDA KENNY, 2002–.

For details on the party in power see INTER-PARTY GOVERNMENTS, REPUBLIC OF IRELAND ACT (1949), MARSHALL PLAN, EUROPEAN RECOVERY PROGRAMME, LONG-TERM RECOVERY PROGRAMME, INDUSTRIAL DEVELOPMENT AUTHORITY, LAND REHABILITATION PROJECT, MOTHER AND CHILD SCHEME, UNITED NATIONS AND IRELAND, NATIONAL COALITION, SUNNINGDALE AGREEMENT, and EMERGENCY POWERS ACT (1976).

Finlay, Thomas Aloysius (1848–1940), priest (Catholic) and political economist. Ordained at St Patrick's College, Maynooth, 1876, he was rector of Belvedere College, Dublin, 1882–87, and classics fellow of the Royal University of Ireland, 1882. With his brother Peter he was joint professor of mental and moral philosophy at University College, Dublin. Founder of the Lyceum Club, 1884, he was founder-editor of LYCEUM, 1887–94, and joint founder (with Father Matthew Russell) of the IRISH MONTHLY. A supporter of SIR HORACE PLUNKETT and the co-operative movement, he was a popular speaker at its meetings. He served on the formative committee of the IRISH AGRICULTURAL ORGANISATION SOCIETY and was a vice-president for more than forty years and editorial chairman of its journal, the IRISH HOMESTEAD. A member of the RECESS COMMITTEE, he was professor of political economy at the Royal University of Ireland, 1900, and at University College, Dublin, 1909–30. His articles and speeches appeared in a wide range of journals, including *New Ireland Review, Studies,* and *Economic Journal.*

Finlay Report (1997), the report of the Tribunal of Inquiry into the Blood Transfusion Service Board, chaired by Mr Justice T. A. Finlay. Its purpose was to investigate, among other matters, how some 1,600 women were infected with the hepatitis C virus from contaminated blood products. Using evidence from more than seventy witnesses, Mr Justice Finlay found that the primary source of the infection of the blood product anti-D serum was the use of plasma from a patient identified as Patient X and the subsequent use of that plasma to form pools from which the anti-D serum was manufactured. Patient X, who had herself been infected by an earlier transfusion from the BTSB, was unaware that her plasma was being used.

The tribunal found that there had been a series of failures within the Blood Transfusion Service, including a failure to report reactions to the anti-D serum, failure to investigate other possible causes of infection, and failure to recall contaminated batches of anti-D serum. With regard to Patient X the report found that the board acted unethically in using Patient X's plasma without her consent; this use was in breach of the board's own standards for donor selection, which prohibited the use of blood or plasma from a person with a history of jaundice or hepatitis and prohibited the use of blood from a person who had recently received a transfusion. It also found that the Department of Health was responsible for inadequate and inappropriate supervision of the BTSB. It was found that a further cause of infection of anti-D serum with hepatitis C was the use of plasma from Donor Y, who had been undergoing a course of therapeutic plasma exchange in 1989 and whose plasma was stored and then used in 1992, even though it had been tested for hepatitis C and found positive on four separate occasions. The Blood Transfusion Service Board was found to be 'inadequate' on a number of procedures and reactions. The tribunal also found that between 1975 and 1994 successive Ministers for Health and the Department of Health failed to adequately and appropriately supervise the National Drug Advisory Board and to provide it with enough resources to enable it to carry out the licensing and authorisation of products made by the BTSB.

The tribunal made a number of recommendations, all of which were accepted by the Minister for Health, MICHAEL NOONAN, who passed the report to the Director of Public Prosecutions. When the DPP announced, without explanation, 21 October 1997, that there would be no prosecutions arising out of the report he was condemned by Positive Action, the organisation established to look after the interests of women infected by the virus.

On 2 May 2000 the Tribunal of Inquiry into the Infection with HIV and Hepatitis C of Persons with Haemophilia and Related Matters, under Judge Alison Lindsay, began hearing oral evidence with a view to determining how some 260 haemophiliacs, of whom 73 had since died, had become infected with HIV and hepatitis C. (See LINDSAY REPORT.)

Fiscal Enquiry Committee (1923), established by the government to investigate the removal of tariffs (which had been introduced by the

British authorities to protect British industries). The report of the committee, whose members included the academic GEORGE O'BRIEN, argued that protection would raise the cost of living, increase agricultural wages, and push up costs and prices, and thereby diminish exports. Its underlying assumption that future prosperity must rely on the growth of agriculture influenced government policy at the time.

Fitt, Gerard (Gerry), Baron Fitt of Bell's Hill (born 1926), politician; born in Belfast, educated at Christian Brothers' School. A merchant seaman, 1941–53, he became a member of Belfast City Council and the Parliament of Northern Ireland for the REPUBLICAN LABOUR PARTY; he was also a member of the British House of Commons, 1966–83. He supported the NORTHERN IRELAND CIVIL RIGHTS ASSOCIATION during the 1960s and was injured in a demonstration in Derry, 5 October 1968. He was a founder-member of the SOCIAL DEMOCRATIC AND LABOUR PARTY and leader of the party, 1970–79. Though not consulted about the withdrawal of the SDLP from the Parliament of Northern Ireland during 1971, he reluctantly supported the tactic. He was Deputy Chief Executive under BRIAN FAULKNER in the power-sharing Executive of the Northern Ireland Assembly, July 1973 to May 1974. He also sat in the Convention, 8 May 1975 to 5 March 1976. In August 1976 he was forced to brandish a gun to disperse supporters of the Provisional IRA attacking his home in Belfast.

He resigned from the SDLP to sit in the British House of Commons as an independent socialist, 1979. He was generally supportive of the Labour Party, but his abstention on a vital division led to the defeat of the Callaghan government and ushered in the Thatcher era. After losing his seat to GERRY ADAMS (Sinn Féin) in 1983 he was created Lord Fitt, 1983. He was critical of the ANGLO-IRISH AGREEMENT (1985), claiming that it was a deal concocted between London and Dublin without consultation with Unionists. Severely critical of the SDLP over the years, he accused it of cowardice during the republican HUNGER STRIKES, 1980–81. He called on West Belfast voters to support the Workers' Party in 1987.

Fitzalan of Derwent, Edmund Bernard Fitzalan-Howard, first Viscount (1855–1947), British politician (Conservative). Lord Lieutenant of Ireland during the closing stages of the WAR OF INDEPENDENCE (1921–22), he was the first Catholic since the Union (1800) to hold the office. He was in close consultation with the cabinet during the period preceding the ANGLO-IRISH TREATY (1921). As the last Lord Lieutenant of Ireland his last major functions were the swearing in of the first government of Northern Ireland and the formal handing over of power to the representative of the Irish Free State, MICHAEL COLLINS, January 1922.

Fitzgerald, Desmond (c. 1888–1947), journalist and politician (Sinn Féin, Cumann na nGaedheal, and Fine Gael); born Thomas Fitzgerald in London of Kerry parents. He studied Irish at classes of the Gaelic League in London, where his literary friends included Ezra Pound. Having lived in France, Fitzgerald and his wife (Mabel McConnell) settled in Ventry, Co. Kerry, where he involved himself in nationalist movements. Joining the IRB and the IRISH VOLUNTEERS, he worked with ERNEST BLYTHE as a Volunteer organiser in Co. Kerry. During the EASTER RISING (1916) he fought in the GPO, Dublin, and was imprisoned in the aftermath. As Sinn Féin MP for Pembroke, Co. Dublin, 1918, he represented the party in the first Dáil Éireann. He was Substitute Director of Propaganda and editor of the *Irish Bulletin* during the WAR OF INDEPENDENCE. He supported the Treaty and was Minister for Foreign Affairs in both the Provisional Government and the Executive Council of the Irish Free State. During his tenure he secured Irish membership of the LEAGUE OF NATIONS and, over the objections of Britain, registered the ANGLO-IRISH TREATY as an international agreement. He was Minister for Defence, 1927–32, and a member of Seanad Éireann, 1938–43. A member of the Irish Academy of Letters, he also published poetry and drama. His interest in philosophy led to a visiting lectureship at the University of Notre Dame, Indiana. DR GARRET FITZGERALD was his son.

FitzGerald, Dr Garret (born 1926), politician (Fine Gael); born in Dublin, son of DESMOND FITZGERALD, educated at UCD and King's Inns. Having worked as research and schedules manager at Aer Lingus, 1947–58, he was a lecturer in the Department of Political Economy, UCD, 1959–73, and economics correspondent for the BBC, *Financial Times,* and *Economist.* While managing director of the Economist Intelligence Unit of Ireland he was retained as economic consultant by a variety of bodies. A senator from 1965, he was elected to Dáil Éireann for Dublin South-East, 1969, and was shadow spokesperson on education, 1969–72, and finance, 1972–73. As Minister for Foreign Affairs, 1973–77, he took part in negotiations leading to the SUNNINGDALE AGREEMENT and played an active role in Ireland's first presidency of the EEC, January–June 1975.

FitzGerald replaced LIAM COSGRAVE as leader of FINE GAEL, 1977, and set about re-organising the party by embarking on a tour of the constituencies. In the 1979 European Parliament elections Fine Gael won four of the fifteen seats (Fianna Fáil won five). In the 1981 general election Fine Gael won 65 seats (from 43 in 1977). FitzGerald became Taoiseach in a coalition government with the Labour Party, supported by three independents, 30 June 1981. His government introduced a supplementary budget, 21 July, to deal with the deteriorating economic situation. His 'constitutional crusade', announced on 27 September 1981, failed to galvanise support.

FitzGerald's meeting with MARGARET THATCHER and JIM PRIOR on 6 November resulted in the establishment of the Anglo-Irish Intergovernmental Council, 20 January 1982. A week later, when the budget introduced by JOHN BRUTON proposed the imposition of value-added tax on clothing, including children's shoes, the government fell. The general election led to the first television debate between CHARLES HAUGHEY and FitzGerald, 16 February 1982. The ensuing Fianna Fáil minority government fell on a Fine Gael motion of no confidence (82 to 80), 4 November. Following the second general election of that year, 24 November, FitzGerald again became Taoiseach in a coalition with the Labour Party.

During 1984 the government dealt with a number of contentious issues, not least of which was spiralling inflation. In March it controversially rescued a subsidiary of Allied Irish Banks, the Insurance Corporation of Ireland, which had encountered trading losses in the London market, removed half the food subsidies, and, in a universally unpopular move, liquidated IRISH SHIPPING LTD, the last Irish-owned shipping line, rendering some four hundred workers redundant and without adequate compensation.

Against the advice of the Attorney-General, Peter Sutherland, FitzGerald accepted the wording supplied by Fianna Fáil for his promised constitutional referendum to prevent the introduction of abortion. On 7 September 1983 the referendum was carried by a two-to-one majority, but this was to have serious ramifications (see X CASE).

FitzGerald launched the initiative that led to the NEW IRELAND FORUM. However, its three-strand report was stridently rejected by the British Prime Minister, Margaret Thatcher, while the 'unitary state' option was the only one acceptable to Fianna Fáil. The document served, however, as a basis for discussions that led to the ANGLO-IRISH AGREEMENT at Hillsborough, Co. Down, November 1985.

He suffered several serious reverses in 1986. A Government reshuffle ended in chaos and served to alienate some of his own party's ministers as well as those of his coalition partner. The erosion of confidence continued when his government's proposal to amend the constitutional ban on divorce was heavily defeated. The government's economic problems continued unabated: at the end of September there was an overrun of £180 million in government borrowing; a substantial sale of government stock followed, coupled with increased interest rates. FitzGerald's proposals for large-scale cuts in expenditure alarmed his Labour Party partners, but the government survived a motion of no confidence, 23 October. Implementing an EC edict to provide equality of treatment for women had the net effect of reducing the payments of some twenty thousand social welfare recipients. In a compromise motion the government was saved from defeat only through the casting vote of the Ceann Comhairle, 26 November. It fell on a proposal to embark on spending cuts of £350 million and to reduce the current spending deficit by 2 per cent. The general election of 17 February saw Fianna Fáil return to power. FitzGerald resigned on 11 March and was replaced as party leader by ALAN DUKES.

His political involvement continued, however. Though he refused a candidacy for the Presidency in 1990, he was destined to become a significant factor in its outcome. On a television programme, 23 October, FitzGerald produced a research student, Jim Duffy, who claimed that both Brian Lenihan (Fianna Fáil), the leading candidate for the Presidency, and Charles Haughey had phoned President Hillery on 27 January 1982 in an attempt to forestall FitzGerald's dissolution of the Dáil. In such circumstances Haughey, with the aid of independents, would have had the opportunity of forming a government without having an election. Lenihan denied the charge but was forced to recant when the *Irish Times* called a press conference, 25 October. Having had an eighteen-point lead in opinion polls until the controversy arose, Lenihan lost the Presidential election to MARY ROBINSON.

FitzGerald retired from Dáil Éireann in 1992. He was made a non-executive director of the ill-fated aircraft-leasing company Guinness Peat Aviation. He later wrote a weekly column for the *Irish Times.* In 1999, when there was considerable interest in Charles Haughey's personal finances (especially as Allied Irish Banks had written off nearly £1 million owed by Haughey), FitzGerald admitted that he had been unable to discharge all his indebtedness to AIB, from which he had borrowed heavily to buy shares in GPA; when the shares were declared worthless the bank had written off a considerable amount of his debt. His autobiography, *All in a Life,* was published in 1991.

Fitzgerald, G. F. [George Francis] (1851–1901); physicist; born in Dublin, educated at TCD, where he was Erasmus Smith professor of natural and experimental philosophy from 1881. He was the first to suggest that comets were not the continuous objects of common perception but that even their nuclei were stony aggregates. His hypothesis on the velocity of light, 1895, was expanded on by the Dutch physicist Hendrik Lorentz (1853–1928), becoming known as the Lorentz-Fitzgerald contraction, and formed an integral part of the theory of relativity advanced by Albert Einstein (1879–1955) in 1905.

Fitzmaurice, Colonel James (1898–1965), aviator; born in Dublin, educated at Rockwell College. As a member of the British army during the Great War he saw action at the Somme and Arras, was wounded and was decorated before his transfer to the Royal Flying Corps, 1917. Having flown a number of missions, including the first night mail crossing to Boulogne, 1919, he resigned and joined the newly formed Irish Air Service of the Free State army. During the Civil War he flew a number of missions and had his plane burned by Republicans in Mallow, Co. Cork, but was removed from operations following complaints from fellow-officers about his ill-treatment of prisoners. After the Civil War he became squadron commander and officer in command of training, 1 October 1924, was promoted acting commandant, 1 October 1925, commandant, 1 September 1927, and major (lieutenant-colonel), 13 April 1928.

With Captain R. H. Macintosh as co-pilot, Fitzmaurice unsuccessfully attempted the first east-west crossing of the Atlantic Ocean on the *Princess Zenia,* September 1927. In 1928 he joined Hermann Köhl as co-pilot and Günther von Hünefeld as observer on the 300-horsepower Junkers monoplane *Bremen* in a further attempt on the crossing. Leaving Baldonnel aerodrome, Co. Dublin, 12 April 1928, with car headlights illuminating its take-off, the plane, which did not carry a wireless, completed the 2,300-mile flight and landed on the frozen Greenly Lake, Labrador, more than thirty-six hours later. In recognition of their achievement all three were made honorary freemen of the city of Dublin.

Fitzmaurice resigned from the Air Corps, 16 February 1929, and spent some years in the United States before moving to London, 1939, where he operated a servicemen's club during the Second World War. He returned to Ireland in 1951. The *Bremen* is on display at the Ford Museum, Dearborn, Michigan.

Fitzpatrick, Patrick Vincent (1792–1865), Repealer; born in Dublin, educated at St Patrick's College, Maynooth. By profession a registrar of deeds, through his involvement in the CATHOLIC ASSOCIATION he came to the notice of DANIEL O'CONNELL, who appointed him treasurer. Fitzpatrick was responsible for the collection of the 'Catholic Rent', which, after 1829, became the 'O'Connell Tribute'. He was treasurer of the REPEAL ASSOCIATION from 1840. Following the death of O'Connell he obtained a government position and ceased his involvement in Irish affairs. His papers were edited by W. J. Fitzpatrick (1830–1895) as *The Correspondence of O'Connell* (1888).

Flags and Emblems (Display) Act (1954), enacted by the Parliament of Northern Ireland to give legal substance to displays of loyalty by the Unionist population. A provision of the act empowered the RUC to remove 'provocative emblems' likely to lead to disturbance; this was interpreted as banning the display of the TRICOLOUR.

Flood, John (1841–1909), Fenian; born in Dublin, educated at Clongowes Wood College. A journalist, he was a leading member of the IRB. Following the escape of JAMES STEPHENS from Richmond Prison he sailed the *Concord,* which took them to Scotland, 13 March 1866. He assisted CAPTAIN JOHN MACCAFFERTY in the raid on Chester Castle, 1867, and was arrested on his return to Dublin. He served five years of a fifteen-year prison sentence in Australia, following which he worked as a journalist in Queensland and founded the first branch of the LAND LEAGUE in Australia.

Flood, William Henry Grattan (1859–1928), musicologist and historian; born in Lismore, Co. Waterford, educated at Mount Melleray and Catholic University of Ireland. He became an organist in Belfast, 1879, and at Enniscorthy Cathedral, Co. Wexford, 1895. A knight of St Gregory, he was Irish correspondent of the *Tablet.* He published several works on music and history, including *History of Irish Music* (1905), *Story of the Harp* (1905), and *Story of the Bagpipes* (1911). His historical writings include *Diocese of Ferns* (1916) and *History of Enniscorthy* (1920).

Flood Tribunal, the Tribunal of Inquiry into Certain Planning Matters and Payments, chaired by Mr Justice Feargus Flood. It was established by Dáil Éireann, 4 November 1997, to investigate possible corruption in land rezoning and planning issues and in particular to investigate the circumstances surrounding a payment of £30,000 to the former Fianna Fáil minister Ray Burke by James Gogarty on behalf of a building firm, Joseph Murphy Structural Engineers Ltd, in June 1989.

The tribunal held its first public hearing in January 1999; its scope was later broadened to allow the investigation of all suspect payments to politicians and local authority officials. On 19 April 2000 the political lobbyist Frank Dunlop admitted that he had paid £112,000 to fifteen Dublin councillors before the vote on rezoning the Quarryvale site at Palmerston, Co. Dublin, for the Liffey Valley Shopping Centre, proposed by the building developer Owen Callaghan, just before the 1991 local elections. The amounts ranged from £1,000 to £48,000, the latter sum, according to Dunlop, paid to one 'powerful man'. He said he had worked 'hand in glove' with a number of councillors on rezoning the Quarryvale land, for which, he stated, he was reimbursed by O'Callaghan.

On 11 May 2000 the tribunal heard that the former Dublin city and county manager George Redmond had accumulated an estimated £1.05 million between 1971 and 1998, excluding his house in Castleknock, Co. Dublin (sold in April 2000 for £750,000). He told the tribunal that the accumulation of money for what he called his 'extramural activity' began about 1965. He eventually had thirty-eight bank accounts, including one in the Isle of Man, opened with £105,000 after deposit interest retention tax was introduced, 1986. Liam Lawlor TD (Fianna Fáil) became the first politician to be jailed as a result of a tribunal hearing; he served three separate prison terms for failure to co-operate with the tribunal during 2001.

The tribunal published its second interim report in September 2002. This covered what Mr Justice Flood called 'in effect three separate public inquiries' into what he termed the Brennan and McGowan module, the Century Radio module, and the Gogarty module. The subject of these inquiries, held between January 1999 and December 2001, during which 170 witnesses were heard, covered a period of more than thirty years and dealt with a number of issues, including land rezoning, radio broadcasting, and offshore trusts and corporations. Mr Justice Flood found that Ray Burke had taken illicit payments from builders and that his house had not been bought in the normal way but had been given to him by builders, including Tom Brennan, as corrupt payment; that offshore payments totalling £160,000 paid into five secret accounts were corrupt payments to Burke, mainly from the builders Tom Brennan and Joseph McGowan; that he received a corrupt payment of £35,000 from Oliver Barry of Century Radio, for whose benefit Burke had forced RTE to give it broadcasting facilities and, as minister, had put a cap on RTE's permitted income from advertising. Mr Justice Flood found that certain people, including Burke, Brennan, McGowan, Barry, and the former government press secretary P. J. Mara, 'chose not to co-operate with the Tribunal . . . and . . . having been duly sworn did not tell the truth.' He stated that he had sent a copy of the report to the Director of Public Prosecutions, and that he had been informed by the Revenue Commissioners and the Criminal Assets Bureau that more than €34.5 million had been paid to those bodies in connection with inquiries arising directly or indirectly from the tribunal.

Judge Mary Faherty and Judge Alan Mahon joined Mr Justice Flood on the tribunal on 29 October 2002; Judge Gerald Keys was appointed to sit as a reserve member. Mr Justice Flood resigned on 27 June 2003 and was succeeded by Judge Alan Mahon.

flying column. The feasibility of an active service unit continually in the field was first raised during the WAR OF INDEPENDENCE (1919–21) through the experience of a Co. Limerick group of the Irish Volunteers who had travelled more than 30 miles across country in daylight to rejoin their sections in the area of Bruree, Co. Limerick. The concept of a small mobile group of guerillas with intimate knowledge of their own terrain had obvious advantages: it allowed the maintenance of an independent standing force in the field, which, having completed an operation, could fly the scene and await the next engagement.

Only selected volunteers—generally unmarried—were accepted for service with the flying columns. The column commander had at his disposal the resources of all the units within the brigade area; he appointed section commanders, irrespective of the ranks previously held. Prominent leaders of flying columns were FRANK AIKEN (Co. Louth), TOM BARRY (west Cork), DAN BREEN (Co. Tipperary), SEÁN MAC EOIN (Co. Longford), and ERNIE O'MALLEY (Limerick-Tipperary).

Fogarty, Michael (1859–1955), bishop (Catholic); born in Kilcoleman, Nenagh, Co. Tipperary, educated at St Patrick's College, Maynooth. Professor of philosophy and canon law at Carlow College, 1886–89, he was professor of dogmatic and moral theology at Maynooth, 1889–1904. One of the few members of the Catholic hierarchy to voice nationalist sympathies, he supported SINN FÉIN during the 1917 by-election in Co. Clare and was a trustee of the Dáil Éireann Loan, June 1919. His support for Dáil Éireann led to an attempt by the AUXILIARIES to murder him, 3 December 1921. He participated in peace efforts during the WAR OF INDEPENDENCE and officiated at the funeral of ARTHUR GRIFFITH, August 1922. He became an archbishop, 1954, on appointment as assistant to the Pontifical Throne.

Foley, John Henry (1818–1874), sculptor; born in Dublin, studied at the Royal Dublin Society school of sculpture and, with his brother Edward, at the Royal Academy, London. He was a silver-medallist of the Royal Academy and a regular exhibitor there from 1839 and became a member in 1858. He worked with other Irish sculptors—JOHN LAWLOR, Samuel Ferris Lynn, and Patrick McDowell—on the Albert Memorial, London (he was responsible for the 'Asia' group). His Irish works include Lord Ardilaun (St Stephen's Green, Dublin), Burke, Goldsmith, and Grattan (Trinity College, Dublin), Sir Benjamin Lee Guinness (St Patrick's Cathedral, Dublin), and Father Theobald Mathew (Patrick Street, Cork). Following his death his assistant, Thomas Brock, completed the commission on the O'Connell Monument, Dublin.

Ford, David (born 1951), politician (Alliance Party); educated at Dulwich College (London), QUB, and Northern Ireland Polytechnic. Having worked in the Northern Ireland Department of Social Services from 1973, he became general secretary of the Alliance Party, 1990, a district councillor in Co. Antrim, 1993, and chief whip of the ALLIANCE PARTY, 1998–2001. Representing South Antrim in the Northern Ireland Assembly from 1998, he was party spokesperson on agriculture, rural development, and environmental issues. He become party leader on 6 October 2001.

Ford, Patrick (1837–1913), journalist; born in Galway. Brought to Boston, 1841, he completed his education there and was later apprenticed to a printer and was publisher and editor of the *Boston Sunday Times,* 1855–60. A veteran of the Union army in the American Civil War (1861–65), he edited the *Charleston Gazette,* 1864–66, and founded the IRISH WORLD, 1870, which he controlled until his death. He advocated support for the FENIANS and for the LAND LEAGUE, to which he donated $2,000, and helped to organise 2,500 of its branches in the United States. He supported JOHN REDMOND following the split in the IRISH PARTY and accepted the third Home Rule Bill (1912) as an answer to the Irish demand for self-government. He published *The Criminal History of the British Empire* (1881) and *The Irish Question and American Statesmen* (1885). The *Irish World* was edited by his nephew, Robert Ford, 1913–20.

Forster, W. E. [William Edward] (1819–1886), British politician (Liberal); born in Bradpole, Dorset. As a representative of the Society of Friends he visited Connemara on a relief mission during the GREAT FAMINE (1845–49). He was member of Parliament for Bradford from 1861. His Irish experience was a factor in his selection by W. E. GLADSTONE as Chief Secretary for Ireland, 1880–82, at the height of the LAND WAR. In the autumn of 1880 he mobilised police and soldiers in defence of Orange EMERGENCY MEN attempting to harvest the crops of CAPTAIN CHARLES CUNNINGHAM BOYCOTT. His request for COERCION to deal with the agitation was denied until 6 January 1881, and his efforts were further hindered through a poor relationship with the Lord Lieutenant of Ireland, EARL COWPER.

Foster's failure to secure the conviction of

CHARLES STEWART PARNELL and leading members of the LAND LEAGUE led to criticism by elements of the British press and Tory MPs. The eventual granting of coercion allowed him to arrest more than nine hundred members of the Land League. Following the issue of its 'NO-RENT MANIFESTO' the league was suppressed and Parnell, MICHAEL DAVITT, JOHN DILLON and WILLIAM O'BRIEN were imprisoned. Despite the soaring crime rate—much of it attributed to the imprisonment of Parnell—Forster travelled throughout the country in an effort to win acceptance for the Land Law (Ireland) Act (1881) (see LAND ACTS). By now a hated figure, widely known as 'Buckshot Forster', his humane gesture of replacing the dangerous ball-cartridge with buckshot was lost on demonstrators, as the police now opened fire more readily. Forster broke with Gladstone on the 'KILMAINHAM TREATY' and resigned, 4 May. His offer to temporarily resume the post following the assassination of his successor, LORD FREDERICK CAVENDISH, two days later was rejected by Gladstone. He played no further role in Irish affairs, apart from his accusation in 1883 that Parnell and others were conniving in criminal activities for political ends.

forty-shilling freeholders, the name given to life lessees holding property or a tract of land with a net annual value of 40 shillings (£2). Such tenants, enfranchised in 1793, were a potential source of power to a landlord, his electoral influence being in direct proportion to the number of voters on his land. The absence of a land tax encouraged landlords to sub-divide estates even further to enhance their electoral influence. With the passing of CATHOLIC EMANCIPATION in 1829, however, the qualification for the franchise was raised from £2 to £10, reducing the electorate from 230,000 to approximately 14,000.

Forum for Peace and Reconciliation, established in Dublin, 28 October 1994, by the Taoiseach, ALBERT REYNOLDS, in the wake of the Provisional IRA ceasefire of the previous August. Meeting in Dublin Castle, it heard submissions from southern and northern political parties (including the ULSTER UNIONIST PARTY, ALLIANCE PARTY, SDLP, and SINN FÉIN), commercial and trade union organisations, voluntary organisations, and prisoners' organisations and victims' groups. It also heard from two British MPs, Peter Temple-Morris and Roger Stott, and from F. W. de Klerk of South Africa. Widely differing interpretations of the fundamental problems in Northern Ireland emerged between the SDLP and Sinn Féin: the SDLP viewed the problem as a conflict between two 'identities' that lacked an acceptable structure to accommodate their differences; the Sinn Féin position was that, as the problems were created by the British government, the solution had to come from a radical change of policy by that government.

Following the Provisional IRA's return to violence, February 1996, the forum adjourned, 29 March, until a new ceasefire should be declared. A new plenary session opened in Dublin, 27 November 2002, the day before multi-party talks began at Stormont. Chaired by Senator Maurice Hayes, it was reactivated by the Taoiseach, Bertie Ahern, at the suggestion of MARK DURKAN (SDLP). No Unionists attended, and only four of the ten Northern Ireland Assembly parties were represented.

Foster, Vere Henry Lewis (1819–1900), philanthropist; born in Copenhagen, educated at the University of Oxford. After diplomatic postings at Rio de Janeiro, 1842–43, and Montevideo, 1845–47, he visited Ireland during the GREAT FAMINE (1845–49) and was touched by the poverty and misery he encountered. Devoting himself to social welfare, in particular that of emigrants, he made copies of his book *Work and Wages, or The Penny Emigrant's Guide to the United States and Canada, for Female Servants, Labourers, Mechanics, Farmers etc.* freely available to 250,000 emigrants. An account of his journey as a steerage passenger on COFFIN SHIPS was read before a British parliamentary committee of inquiry, 1851. He used his wealth to pay the fares of some 25,000 emigrants and, convinced that a good standard of education was vital to their needs, financed the building of schools. His 'Vere Foster Copy Books' sold more than a million copies in 1868. Claiming that copperplate handwriting was the most essential skill a child could learn, he designed copybooks with copperplate headlines such as 'More haste, less speed,' which remained in use in some schools up to the 1940s. In 1868 he founded and became first president of the Irish National Teachers' Association (later the IRISH NATIONAL TEACHERS' ORGANISATION).

In 1870 he moved to Belfast, where he spent the remainder of his life assisting the poor. With his fortune exhausted, he died in poverty; his death was noted in only two newspapers and his funeral attended by a handful of people. Among the educational aids he inspired were *Elementary Drawing Copybooks* (1868), *Copybooks* (1870), *Public School Copybooks* (1881), *Simple Lessons in Watercolour* (1883), and *Upright Writing Charts* (1897).

Four Courts, a complex of buildings at Inns Quay, Dublin, the centre of the Irish courts system. The buildings were seized in an unauthorised action by the 3rd Battalion, Dublin Brigade, IRA, on 14 April 1922; other buildings occupied at the same time included the Kildare Street Club and the Ballast Office (Westmorland Street). Over the next two months many prominent republicans joined the original garrison of 180. No attempt was made by the Provisional Government to oust them, though the President of Dáil Éireann, ARTHUR GRIFFITH, and the Chairman of the Provisional Government, MICHAEL COLLINS, were under considerable pressure from members of the Ministry and from the British government to move against them.

The general election of 16 June resulted in a victory for supporters of the ANGLO-IRISH TREATY and placed the Provisional Government in a strong position. On 22 June 1922 GENERAL SIR HENRY WILSON was assassinated at his home in London; the British government, attributing the murder to the IRA, demanded immediate action against the Four Courts. It issued an ultimatum on 25 June to the effect that it would consider the Treaty breached if the Provisional Government did not act. While the government was deliberating, the deputy chief of the Free State army, J. J. O'CONNELL, was kidnapped by Republicans and held in the Four Courts; this was a direct response to the arrest of the republican Leo Henderson, engaged in enforcing the BELFAST BOYCOTT, on which there had been tacit agreement between the sides.

At 3:40 a.m. on 28 June the garrison was called on to surrender. When the demand was ignored government forces began a bombardment of the Four Courts at 4:07 a.m., using two eighteen-pounder guns borrowed from the British army; the action marked the beginning of the CIVIL WAR. The same day, WINSTON CHURCHILL instructed the Under-Secretary for Ireland, ALFRED COPE, to 'tell Collins to ask for any assistance he requires and report to me any difficulty that has been raised by the Military.'

The following proclamation was issued by the Four Courts garrison:

Óglaigh na hÉireann
PROCLAMATION

Fellow citizens of the Irish Republic:

The fateful hour has come. At the dictation of our hereditary enemy our rightful cause is being treacherously assailed by recreant Irishmen. The crash of arms and the boom of artillery reverberate in this supreme test of the Nation's destiny.

Gallant soldiers of the Irish Republic stand rigorously firm in its defence and worthily uphold their noblest traditions. The sacred spirits of the Illustrious Dead are with us in this great struggle. "Death before Dishonour" being an unchanging principle of our national faith as it was of theirs, still inspires us to emulate their glorious effort.

We therefore appeal to all citizens who have withstood unflinchingly the oppression of the enemy during the past six years to rally to the support of the Republic and to recognise that the resistance now being offered is but the continuance of the struggle that was suspended by the truce with the British. We especially appeal to our former comrades of the Irish Republic to return that allegiance and thus guard the nation's honour from the infamous stigma that her sons aided her foes in retaining a hateful domination over her.

Confident of victory and of maintaining Ireland's Independence this appeal is issued by the Army Executive on behalf of the Irish Republican Army.

(Signed)
Commdt-Gen. Liam Mellows,
Commdt.-Gen. Rory O'Connor,
Commdt-Gen. Jos. McKelvey,
Commdt.-Gen. Earnán Ó Máille [Ernie O'Malley],
Commdt.-Gen. Séamus Robinson,
Commdt.-Gen Seán Moylan,
Commdt.-Gen. Michael Kilroy,
Commdt.-Gen. Frank Barrett,
Commdt.-Gen. Thomas Deerig [Derrig],
Commdt. Tom Barry,
Commdt. F. Ó Faoláin,
Brig. Gen. J. O'Connor,
Commdt. P. Ó Ruitléis [Patrick Ruttledge].

Following a 48-hour shelling of the building a government force of 2,000 attacked the Four Courts, overwhelming the garrison. Before the surrender, at 3:30 p.m. on 30 June, Republicans mined the Records Office, resulting in the destruction of documents dating from the twelfth century. Among those captured were LIAM MELLOWS, RORY O'CONNOR, and ERNIE O'MALLEY (who signed the surrender document); CATHAL BRUGHA and LIAM LYNCH were among those who escaped. The attack on the Four Courts resulted in sixty-five killed and 2,700 wounded and in the destruction of twenty-five buildings. (See also CIVIL WAR.)

'Four Horsemen', a term first used in the late 1970s to describe the Irish-American politicians Thomas 'Tip' O'Neill (Speaker of the US House of Representatives), Hugh Carey (Governor of the State of New York), Senator Edward Kennedy, and Senator Daniel Moynihan. Their aid was sought by JOHN HUME and Irish diplomatic sources to reflect concerns of constitutional nationalists at the prevailing unrest in Northern Ireland.

Foynes, Co. Limerick, site of the first transatlantic airport in Ireland. The Montreal Agreement (1935) between the governments of Canada, the Irish Free State, Britain and the United States specified that all transatlantic aircraft flying east or west would land at an Irish airport. In December 1935 Foynes, on the Shannon Estuary, was declared the European terminal for transatlantic services. A wireless station established at Ballygirreen, Co. Clare, sent experimental signals to Gander, Newfoundland, 28 October 1936, while a weather forecasting service was established at Rineanna, 16 February 1937. On 25 February 1937 the Imperial Airways plane *Cambria,* piloted by Captain Powell en route from Southampton, became the first flying-boat on a commercial flight to use the base. The Taoiseach, ÉAMON DE VALERA, was among the crowd that welcomed the first incoming flight from the United States, the Pan-American Airlines *Clipper III,* 6 July. Hundreds of sightseers witnessed the landing of the same airline's *Yankee Clipper* at Foynes, 11 April 1939, which on 28 June inaugurated the first regular commercial mail service from the United States.

During the SECOND WORLD WAR, Foynes became an important eastbound corridor in the movement of Allied diplomatic and military personnel. On 22 June 1942, with Captain Charles Blair at the controls, the American Export Airlines flying-boat VS44 completed the first non-stop commercial flight from Europe to New York; it docked in New York after a flight of twenty-five hours and forty minutes, with 95 gallons of fuel remaining in its reserve tank.

Later the same year an airport barman, Joe Sheridan, added a small amount of whiskey to coffee he was serving, thus inadvertently inventing 'Irish coffee', given this name in 1952 in the Buena Vista Café, San Francisco.

Framework Documents, published 22 February 1995, the culmination of a process that began with the DOWNING STREET DECLARATION (1993). The documents, launched by the British Prime Minister, JOHN MAJOR, and the Taoiseach, JOHN BRUTON, were *A New Framework for Agreement* (the joint work of the British and Irish governments) and *A Framework for Accountable Government in Northern Ireland* (authorised solely by the British government). The former dealt with north-south and British-Irish relations. Major emphasised that 'nothing in these Frameworks will be imposed . . . I cherish Northern Ireland as part of the UK and it will remain so for as long as this reflects the democratic wish of a greater number of its people.' The political objective was to secure a

> comprehensive political settlement which would return greater power, authority and responsibility to all the Northern Ireland people, on an agreed basis, and take fall account of Northern Ireland's wider relationship with the rest of the United Kingdom and the rest of the island of Ireland . . . such an overall agreement being secured by reference to the principles of the Joint Declaration.

The Ulster Unionist Party rejected the Frameworks, leading to the resignation of its leader, JAMES MOLYNEAUX, 28 August 1995, and his being succeeded by DAVID TRIMBLE.

Freedom of Information Act (1997), legislation granting a legal right to people to obtain access to information held by public bodies, to have official information relating to them amended where it is incomplete, incorrect, or misleading, and to obtain reasons for decisions affecting them.

Freeman's Journal, a newspaper founded in Dublin, 1763. By 1802 it was controlled by Philip Whitfield Harvey, who, being the recipient of a government pension of £200 a year, supported DUBLIN CASTLE. During the period 1809–12 it fell into dispute with the Chief Secretary for Ireland, WILLIAM WELLESLEY-POLE, and adopted an independent line. Prominent editors and owners included MICHAEL STAUNTON, SIR JOHN GRAY, and EDWARD DWYER GRAY. The paper supported CATHOLIC EMANCIPATION, the REPEAL ASSOCIATION, the LAND LEAGUE, and HOME RULE. In the early years of the twentieth century it supported moderate nationalism and the IRISH PARTY under JOHN REDMOND.

By 1916 the paper was in serious financial difficulties, and JOHN DILLON and other Irish Party leaders were involved in efforts to help it survive. It was bought by Martin Fitzgerald and Hamilton Edwards, October 1919, after it had been forced into liquidation. It was suppressed, 15 December 1919 to January 1920, and Fitzgerald, Edwards and the editor, Patrick J. Hooper, were imprisoned at Christmas 1920. The paper's support for the ANGLO-IRISH TREATY (1921) and the government of the IRISH FREE STATE led to the destruction of presses and the burning of its offices by the IRA, 29–30 March 1922, which was angered by the publication of an official report from Free State army headquarters on the IRA army convention. Dáil Éireann voted £2,600 in compensation to the paper, which appeared briefly in typed format. It reappeared in April as a 24-page newspaper but ceased publication the following year, being incorporated in the IRISH INDEPENDENT.

French, Sir John Denton Pinkstone, first Earl French of Ypres (1852–1925), soldier and politician; born in Ripple, Kent, of a Co. Roscommon family. An officer in the British army from 1874, he became a field-marshal in 1913 and commanded the British Expeditionary Force in France, 1914, until replaced by General Douglas Haig, December 1915. He was commander in chief of Home Forces, was made a viscount and awarded £50,000 for services to the Crown. During the crisis over CONSCRIPTION he claimed to the cabinet, 25 March 1918, that with a 'slight augmentation' of soldiers he could enforce conscription. He replaced VISCOUNT WIMBORNE as Lord Lieutenant of Ireland, 11 May 1918, and under the DEFENCE OF THE REALM ACT had the widest powers ever placed at the disposal of a Viceroy. Having assured DAVID LLOYD GEORGE that he would prevent 'any German intrigues,' he had supporters of Sinn Féin, the Irish Volunteers and other nationalist organisations arrested on charges of involvement in a 'GERMAN PLOT'.

Following the sweeping success of Sinn Féin in the general election of 1918 and the establishment of DÁIL ÉIREANN, French requested the release of those interned following the EASTER RISING (1916). Shortly after the start of the WAR OF INDEPENDENCE he induced his former subordinate GENERAL SIR NEVIL MACREADY to become commander in chief of British forces in Ireland. The arrival of the AUXILIARIES and BLACK AND TANS during 1920 led to an intensification of the war. Following the imposition of martial law in December, French became a target of the IRA; more than a dozen attempts were made on his life, and following a particularly narrow escape at Ashtown, Co. Dublin, he confined himself to the Viceregal Lodge in the Phoenix Park, Dublin. As efforts continued to end the war, French, in what was perceived as a conciliatory gesture, was replaced as Lord Lieutenant by VISCOUNT FITZALAN OF DERWENT, the first Catholic to hold the office. French's elder sister, CHARLOTTE DESPARD (whom he disowned), publicly supported Sinn Féin and the IRA.

Friend, Major-General Sir Lovick Bransby (1856–1944), British soldier; born in North Crag, Kent. Following commissioning as a lieutenant in the British army, 1873, he served in South Africa and Egypt. With the rank of major-general he was in charge of administration in Ireland, 1912–14, before being appointed commander of British forces in Ireland, 1914–16. In 1915 his advice that the IRISH VOLUNTEERS should be proscribed was rejected by the Chief Secretary for Ireland, AUGUSTINE BIRRELL. Following the start of the EASTER RISING (1916) he was replaced as commander of British forces in Ireland by GENERAL SIR JOHN MAXWELL but retained his administrative role. As military governor of Dublin, 1918, he was responsible for the issue of deportation orders.

Friends of Ireland, a group launched in Washington, 16 March 1981, by prominent Irish-Americans, including Senator Edward Kennedy and Thomas 'Tip' O'Neill (see FOUR HORSEMEN). It concentrated its attention on the ANGLO-IRISH AGREEMENT and the International Fund for Ireland. Later, through Congressman Brian Donnelly, it campaigned for additional US visas ('Donnelly visas') for emigrants from Ireland.

Friends of Ireland Group, a loose liaison group of left-wing British Labour Party MPs who in 1945 voiced opposition to the rule of the ULSTER UNIONIST PARTY in Northern Ireland. Led by Geoffrey Bing, an Ulsterman, the group attempted to influence the Labour Party government of Clement Attlee (1883–1967) into adopting a more positive role in Northern Ireland affairs. It ceased its activities following the fall of the first inter-party government, 1951.

Friends of Irish Freedom, an organisation founded at the first IRISH RACE CONVENTION, New York, 4–5 March 1916, attended by 2,500 prominent Irish-Americans. It was supported by the UNITED IRISH LEAGUE, ANCIENT ORDER OF HIBERNIANS and other Irish-American organisations but was dominated by CLAN NA GAEL, whose members held fifteen of the seventeen seats on its Executive. With the support of prominent American clergy, notably Cardinal William O'Connell, Archbishop of Boston, it aimed to 'encourage and assist any movement that will tend to bring about National Independence of Ireland.' Its first president was the Irish composer Victor Herbert (1859–1954), Thomas Hughes Kelly was treasurer, and John D. Moore was secretary until replaced by DIARMUID LYNCH, 1918–32.

The organisation supported the EASTER RISING (1916), in the aftermath of which it raised $350,000 to assist dependants. It organised the American lecture tour of HANNA SHEEHY-SKEFFINGTON, 1917. By 1920 its membership was over 100,000, with 484 associate branches having a membership of 175,000. During the WAR OF INDEPENDENCE the Friends of Irish Freedom, through the promotion of bond certificates for the newly declared Irish Republic, helped ÉAMON DE VALERA raise $5 million (of which he received only $3 million) during his extended American visit.

In October 1920 a rift developed, placing de Valera and the IRB in Ireland at odds with the Americans DANIEL COHALAN and JOHN DEVOY. In an effort to unite all strands of American-Irish interests, de Valera founded the AMERICAN ASSOCIATION FOR THE RECOGNITION OF THE IRISH REPUBLIC. Many members of the Friends of Irish Freedom were attracted to the new organisation. In 1932, following litigation concerning the $2 million outstanding since 1930 from the Irish Republic bond issue, the organisation was wound up and most of the money returned to the donors.

Friends of Religious Freedom and Equality, a short-lived organisation founded in October 1862, led by GEORGE HENRY MOORE and twenty-six Irish Liberal MPs. Supported by the Archbishop of Dublin, PAUL CULLEN, the group aimed to draw attention to leading religious issues of the day, including repeal of the Ecclesiastical Titles Act (1851) and DISESTABLISHMENT of the Church of Ireland. It called on Irish Liberals to oppose any British governments not prepared to accede to their demands.

Friends of the Union, an organisation established in June 1986 to increase knowledge and understanding of the need to maintain the union between Great Britain and Northern Ireland. Its patrons included Conservative supporters opposed to the ANGLO-IRISH AGREEMENT (1985). In 1988 they proposed to the British Prime Minister, MARGARET THATCHER, that the Anglo-Irish Intergovernmental Council (1981) should replace the ANGLO-IRISH AGREEMENT (1985).

funeral processions. Many traditions were formerly associated with funeral processions in Ireland. When a dead person had been waked (see WAKE) the priest sprinkled earth from the grave into the coffin or, alternatively, blessed earth for throwing onto the coffin at the burial; this was a survival of the Penal Laws of the eighteenth century, when Catholic priests were forbidden to officiate in Catholic graveyards. When the coffin was taken from the house it was placed on four chairs before being raised onto the shoulders of the bearers; the chairs were then knocked over. Four men bore the coffin in relays, in accordance with their degree of kinship or friendship with the deceased. In some areas it was customary for the bearers to place salt or some other charm in their pockets, in the belief that 'there is never a funeral but the Other People are at it too, walking along behind.'

A funeral procession always made its way to the graveyard by the longest route. The bearers were followed by the immediate family, then the extended family, then friends and neighbours, followed by the main procession in a variety of modes of transport. Houses along the funeral route had their doors closed and curtains drawn. The funeral stopped at traditional halting-places and at crossroads for brief prayers. Along the route a few stones were added to cairns from previous funerals. Anyone coming from the opposite direction was expected to join the procession and to take at least three steps with it.

When two funerals approached a cemetery at the same time, it was a matter of honour which entered first. Samuel Carter Hall and Anna Maria Hall noted to their astonishment that 'the funeral processions, at one moment reverently approaching the gate of the cemetery, were the next moment running at full speed in competition.' They commented that 'such encounters, become a contest of speed if not of blood.' At the cemetery, whiskey and tobacco were available to mourners; unused pipes were left at the graveside. When the priest had departed it was not uncommon for a lay person to offer some additional prayers.

Despite the advent of the motor-car and, later, the funeral parlour, some of the traditions associated with funeral processions are still observed, particularly in rural areas of the west.

Furrow, The, a theological journal founded in February 1950 by Canon James G. McGarry (died 1977), published at St Patrick's College, Maynooth. It established itself as the most important organ of its genre. Its advanced views, frequently at odds with those of the hierarchy, anticipated the findings of the Second Vatican Council (1962–65) and prompted social investigation. Through its exploration of Continental writing and opinion it had a profound influence on a younger generation of Irish theologians.

Future of Northern Ireland, a document issued by the Northern Ireland Office, 30 October 1972, that laid the basis for future British policy. It stated that the status of Northern Ireland would not be changed without the consent of the majority of the people there, and that any future arrangements must take account of Northern Ireland's relationship with the Republic.

G

Gael, a paper published by the GAELIC ATHLETIC ASSOCIATION in 1887. Contributors included JOHN O'LEARY and his sister Ellen O'Leary, DOUGLAS HYDE, and W. B. YEATS.

Gaelic American, a weekly paper published by JOHN DEVOY in New York from 13 September 1903 as a propaganda vehicle for CLAN NA GAEL. Its business agent and managing editor was THOMAS J. CLARKE; DR PATRICK MCCARTAN was a special correspondent. Its anti-British content led to its being banned from the US mails, January 1918. It supported the EASTER RISING (1916) and opposed the ANGLO-IRISH TREATY (1921). It ceased publication in 1927.

Gaelic Athletic Association (Cumann Lúthchleas Gael), an amateur sporting association founded by MICHAEL CUSACK and MAURICE DAVIN, 1 November 1884. The founding meeting, in the billiard room of the Hayes Hotel, Thurles, Co. Tipperary, was also attended by John Wyse Power, John McKay, J. K. Bracken (father of Brendan Bracken), P. J. Ryan, and St George McCarthy. Davin was elected president and Cusack, Wyse Power and McKay secretaries; T. W. CROKE, Archbishop of Cashel, was the first patron, 18 December 1884. MICHAEL DAVITT and CHARLES STEWART PARNELL, also patrons, were among prominent nationalists who identified with the association. Anti-British in outlook, the GAA imposed a ban (later rescinded) on members participating in or attending certain non-Gaelic games and a rule (also later rescinded) that excluded from membership those serving in Crown forces. Largely a rural movement, it originated and fostered county loyalties among its supporters. Its popularity attracted the attention of the IRB, which supported many of its ideals. Many GAA members were also active in the GAELIC LEAGUE, FIANNA ÉIREANN, and IRISH VOLUNTEERS.

Football (*peil*), hurling (*iománaíocht*), handball (*liathróid láimhe*) and camogie (*camógaíocht*) are the games fostered by the association. The all-Ireland hurling and football finals are played annually in September at Croke Park, Dublin. Exhibition games are played annually in the United States between the winners and unsuccessful finalists of the senior all-Ireland codes, while 'compromise rules' games are played biannually between an Irish team and an Australian Rules team. The association also sponsors the festivals Scór, Féile na nGael, and Scór na nÓg.

Gaelic League (Conradh na Gaeilge), founded in Dublin, 31 July 1893, by DR DOUGLAS HYDE, EOIN MACNEILL (who became its secretary), and Father Eugene O'Growney (who was absent in Scotland when the inaugural meeting took place); other founder-members were James Cogan, Charles P. Bushe, Father William Hayden, Patrick Hogan, Pádraig Ó Briain, Máirtín Ó Ceallaigh, and Thomas W. Ellerker. The league established the Oireachtas (now generally known as Oireachtas na Gaeilge), 1897, an annual festival of Irish culture. Hyde hoped that a non-political and non-sectarian organisation would offer common ground on which all sections of Irish political and religious opinion could meet for a cultural purpose.

The league published AN CLAIDHEAMH SOLUIS, organised competitions, and successfully campaigned to have St Patrick's Day accepted as a national holiday. *Timirí* (travelling teachers) journeyed to all parts of the country and encouraged the formation of language classes. Following the establishment of the first college for training teachers of Irish at Béal Átha an Ghaorthaidh (Ballingeary), Co. Cork, 1905, Irish appeared on the curriculum of primary and secondary schools. As a result of lobbying by the league, which now had more than nine hundred branches, Irish was accepted as an obligatory subject for matriculation to the new NATIONAL UNIVERSITY OF IRELAND, 1909. Hyde resigned the presidency when, under the influence of PATRICK PEARSE, the ard-fheis of 1915 resolved that the political independence of Ireland was a primary aim. In 1920 the league published an educational policy whereby Irish would be recognised as the principal language of Ireland and would become the medium of instruction in all schools within five years. This demand was acknowledged in principle in article 8 of the Constitution of Ireland (1937).

Prominent activists associated with the league have included:

Canon Ulick Bourke (1829–1887), who prepared books in Irish and had a special font cast for his publications in the *Tuam News* and *Celtic Educator.* His works included *The College Irish Grammar* (1856) and *Easy Lessons on Self-Instruction in Irish* (1874).

Mícheál Breathnach ('Cois Fhairrge') (1881–1908), who taught in Tuam, Co. Galway, and in the Irish College at Toormakeady, Co. Mayo. His most important work was his history of Ireland, *Stair na hÉireann* (1911–16).

Mary Lambert Butler (c. 1872–1920), who learnt Irish at Loreto College, Dublin, from Seán Hogan and in the Aran Islands.

David Comyn (1854–1907), born in Kilrush, Co. Clare, who was a clerk with the National Bank, Dublin, from 1875. A founder-member of the Society for the Preservation of the Irish Language, he contributed to the *Irishman, Shamrock, Young Ireland* and *Teacher's Journal* and was the first editor of *Gaelic Journal.* Ill-health forced him to abandon his translation of Céitinn's *Foras Feasa ar Éirinn,* having completed one volume for the Irish Texts Society, 1902. His collection of books was presented to the National Library as the Comyn Bequest, 1907.

Thomas Derrig (1897–1956), who, as Minister for Education, 1932–48, was an advocate of Irish as an obligatory school subject and provided financial assistance for children living in Irish-speaking districts.

Bernard Doyle (c. 1860–1933), a printer by occupation, who launched at his own expense *Fáinne an Lae,* the first Gaelic League paper, 8 January 1898, taken over by the league and re-issued as *An Claidheamh Soluis agus Fáinne an Lae,* 4 August 1900; he also designed a font of Irish type.

Rev. James Owen Hannay (1865–1950), a Church of Ireland clergyman and prolific author under the pen-name George Birmingham, who was an executive member of the league during his ministry at Westport, Co. Mayo.

Father Eugene O'Growney (1863–1899), editor of the *Gaelic Journal,* September 1891, and vice-president of the league from its foundation. Ill-health forced his resignation from the chair of Irish at Maynooth, 1896 (where he was succeeded by Father Michael O'Hickey). A collection of his popular articles for the *Gaelic Journal* and the *Weekly Freeman* was published as *Simple Lessons in Irish* (1894). His body was returned from Los Angeles for reburial in Maynooth, 1901.

Séamus Ó Grianna (1889–1969), known by his pen-name 'Máire', an itinerant teacher of Irish who edited *Fáinne an Lae,* 1926–29, and was a translator for An Gúm. The author of some twenty-seven books, he was an opponent of the use of the roman alphabet in place of Irish type for printing in Irish.

Father Michael O'Hickey (1860–1916), apologist for the league and vice-president, 1903. His support for Irish as an obligatory subject for matriculation at the National University of Ireland brought him into conflict with the hierarchy and led to his dismissal from the chair of Irish at Maynooth, 1909 (where he had succeeded Father Eugene O'Growney). He remained in Rome, February 1910 to April 1916, seeking restoration to his post; following the rejection of his appeal he returned home and died within a few months.

Pádraig Ó Siochfhradha (1883–1964), known by his pen-name 'An Seabhac' (the hawk), who worked for An Gúm and was active in the formation of Irish-medium schools. His two most popular books were *An Baile Seo 'Gainne* (1913) and *Jimín Mháire Thaidhg* (1921); he also edited (and chose the titles for) *Allagar na hInise* (1928) and *An tOileánach* (1929) by Tomás Ó Criomhthainn.

Thomas O'Neill Russell (1828–1908), an enthusiastic language activist and writer who spent some thirty years in the United States and returned to continue his work through the newly founded Gaelic League. His works included *Beauties and Antiquities of Ireland* (1897), *The Last Irish High King* (a play, 1904), *Red Hugh* (1905) and *Is Ireland a Dying Nation?* (1906) as well as works in Irish.

Gaelic Society (of Dublin), a short-lived scholarly society founded in 1807, devoted to the discovery, translation and publication of early manuscripts. Its first secretary was Theophilus O'Flanagan (died 1814); other early members included William Haliday, Rev. John Lanigan, William Neilson, Pádraig Ó Loinsigh (later secretary), and EDWARD O'REILLY. Some of its members independently published an Irish grammar, but the society itself published little. *Transactions of the Gaelic Society*, edited by O'Flanagan, was published in 1808.

Gaelic Union, founded in 1878 by Father John Nolan, Thomas O'Neill Russell, David Comyn and DOUGLAS HYDE following their break with the SOCIETY FOR THE PRESERVATION OF THE IRISH LANGUAGE. They had argued for the promotion of Modern Irish usage rather than the Old and Middle Irish favoured by the society. It produced the *Gaelic Journal* (*Irisleabhar na Gaeilge*), the first periodical printed in Irish, though available only through private subscription. The organisation was not successful as a medium for the promotion of Irish and was superseded in 1893 by the GAELIC LEAGUE, of which Hyde was also one of the founders.

Gael-Linn, a cultural organisation founded under the patronage of Comhdháil Náisiúnta na Gaeilge, May 1953, directed by its founder, DÓNALL Ó MÓRÁIN. At first financed by a donation of £100 from ERNEST BLYTHE, it received regular funds from a football pool. In addition to its principal aim of fostering the use of Irish and Irish culture it sought to provide a means of livelihood for people in Irish-speaking districts through investment in the fishing and oyster-farming industries. An early venture was the production of the newsreel 'Amharc Éireann', distributed throughout the country by the Rank Organisation until 1961. With the assistance of the film-makers George Morrison, Colm Ó Laoghaire and Louis Marcus it produced two documentaries on Irish history, *Miss Éire* (1959) and *Saoirse?* (1961), for which the music was composed by SEÁN Ó RIADA. It also made the films *Peil* and *Christy Ring*, produced recordings of traditional music, and from 1954 sponsored scholarships to enable young people to stay in Irish-speaking districts during school holidays. From 1984 to 1996 it published the weekly newspaper *Anois*.

Gaeltacht ('Irishness', 'Irish-speaking people'), a term used in English to mean an Irish-speaking district or all such districts collectively. They are sometimes divided into two types: *fíor-Ghaeltacht*, in which 80 per cent or more of the population speak Irish, and *breac-Ghaeltacht*, in which between 25 and 80 per cent speak Irish. The Gaeltacht Areas Order (1956) determined the boundaries of such districts in Cos. Clare, Cork, Donegal, Galway, Kerry, Mayo, and Waterford.

In 1835 it was estimated that 50 per cent of all Irish people spoke Irish. The census of 1851 put the figure at 1.5 million (30 per cent). Determined efforts were made during the second half of the nineteenth century to promote the use of Irish, though revival groups tended to be localised and to be patronised almost exclusively by scholars and academics; one group, the GAELIC LEAGUE, founded in 1893, did enjoy a large measure of success. Irish became an obligatory subject in primary schools in 1922; in 1923 it became an essential qualification for entry to the civil service. The CONSTITUTION OF THE IRISH FREE STATE (1922) declared Irish and English joint official languages; the Constitution of Ireland (1937) made Irish the first official language.

The following are the numbers of Irish-speakers recorded by the census of population between 1891 and 1946 (Irish-speaking in this context includes those speaking both Irish and English); the percentage refers to the population of the twenty-six counties that now constitute the Republic.

Year	Population	%
1891	664,387	19.2
1901	619,710	19.2
1911	533,717	17.6
1926	543,511	18.3
	Aged three and over	
1926	540,802	19.3
1936	666,601	23.7
	Gaeltacht area: population 426,685 of which 238,338 were Irish-speaking	
1946	588,725	21.2

The population of the Gaeltacht as defined in the Gaeltacht Areas Order (1956) was

1956	85,703
1961	78,524
1966	73,630
1971	70,568

By 1996, when the official population of Gaeltacht areas was 86,039, Irish was spoken daily by 20,813.

Gaiety Theatre, Dublin, opened in South King Street, 27 November 1871, by the brothers John and Michael Gunn. Designed by C. J. Phipps, the theatre was completed in twenty-six weeks from the laying of the first stone. Goldsmith's *She Stoops to Conquer* shared the opening billing with the burlesque *La Belle Sauvage* performed by Mrs John Wood's company.

'Gairloch Formula'. During the talks between ÉAMON DE VALERA, President of Dáil Éireann, and DAVID LLOYD GEORGE, the British Prime Minister, 14–21 July 1921, a deadlock was reached. De Valera sought an independent Irish republic, whereas Lloyd George would offer no more than dominion home rule. Lloyd George's 'formula' was a response to a letter dated 12 September 1921 from de Valera, delivered to Lloyd George while he was on holiday at Gairloch, Ross-shire. De Valera stated that Ireland had 'formally declared its independence and recognises itself as a sovereign state.' The formula Lloyd George then proposed was delivered on 29–30 September. It stated that the British government could not afford to recognise the independence and sovereignty of Ireland.

> The proposals which we have already made have been taken by the whole world as proof that our endeavours for reconciliation and settlement are no empty form, and we feel that conference not correspondence is the most practical and hopeful way to an understanding . . . We, therefore, send you herewith a fresh invitation to a conference in London on October 11th, where we can meet your delegates . . . with a view to ascertaining how the association of Ireland with the community of nations known as the British Empire may best be reconciled with Irish national aspirations.

This last sentence was the basis for the talks between an Irish delegation led by ARTHUR GRIFFITH and MICHAEL COLLINS and a British delegation led by LLOYD GEORGE in October 1921. As a result of these discussions the ANGLO-IRISH TREATY (1921) was signed on 6 December 1921.

gale, the twice-yearly payment of rent. The gale day (the day on which the rent fell due) assumed great importance for the rural tenant. Non-payment led to an increase in debt and could lead to eviction. A 'hanging gale' was an arrear of rent, of which Edward Wakefield observed in 1812:

> The hanging-gale is one of the greatest levers of oppression by which the lower classes are kept in a kind of perpetual bondage . . . this debt hangs over their heads like a load, and keeps them in a continuous state of anxiety and terror.

Gallagher, Frank (1893–1962), journalist and author, pen-name 'David Hogan'; born in Cork, educated locally. Having worked on the *Cork Free Press* he joined the IRISH VOLUNTEERS and assisted ERSKINE CHILDERS on the publicity staff of the first Dáil Éireann. Imprisoned during the WAR OF INDEPENDENCE, he embarked on a series of hunger strikes, varying from three days to forty-one days. He edited the IRISH BULLETIN, 1920–22, and was first editor of the IRISH PRESS, 1931; later that year he was imprisoned under emergency legislation introduced by the government of W. T. COSGRAVE. Until he became director of the Government Information Bureau, 1940, he worked as deputy director of Radio Éireann. From 1954 he was on the staff of the National Library. His works include a journal of his hunger strikes, *Days of Fear* (1928), *Four Glorious Years* (1953), an account of the War of Independence, and *Indivisible Island* (1957), a history of partition.

Gallagher, Patrick ('Paddy the Cope') (1873–1966), co-operative pioneer; born in the Rosses, Co. Donegal. From the age of nine he was in the employ of a Strabane farmer who paid him £3 for six months' work. He had his first experience of the co-operative system while potato-picking in Scotland, and on his return to Co. Donegal he established a co-operative in his native parish. While he had the support of the co-operative movement, he had to overcome intense resistance from 'MIDDLEMEN' in his own area. GEORGE RUSSELL supported his efforts. Gallagher launched the Templecrone Co-Op Society with a capital of £1.75 in 1906; it had a turnover in the first year of £490, which by 1975 had reached £1.17 million. Gallagher (whose nickname was a mispronunciation of 'co-op') was a justice of the peace from 1906 and was elected to Donegal County Council in 1911. His autobiography, *My Story*, was published in 1939.

Gallagher, Dr Thomas (1851–1925), Fenian dynamiter; born in Glasgow. He became a prominent member of the FENIANS in the United States, where he directed training for the DYNAMITERS. His students, who included THOMAS J. CLARKE, were instructed on Long Island beaches. Clarke accompanied him to

England in March 1883; their mission was betrayed, and they were arrested with others, 4 April. Gallagher was sentenced to life imprisonment as a 'treason-felon' and was treated so harshly under the special conditions for those in this category that he became deranged. Agitation over his treatment led to his release, 1896; he returned to the United States and died in a New York asylum without recovering his sanity.

Gallicanism, a tenet that favours the partial autonomy of a national Catholic Church through a church-state relationship. It found favour with a large section of the Irish hierarchy in the first half of the nineteenth century. It was first propagated in the writings of Dr Louis-Gilles Delahogue, professor of moral theology at St Patrick's College, Maynooth, from 1798; leading Gallicans included ARCHBISHOP JOHN MACHALE, Archbishop of Tuam, and FATHER PATRICK LAVELLE.

The leading ultramontanist (exponent of Papal authority) was ARCHBISHOP PAUL CULLEN. From the time of his arrival in Ireland as Archbishop of Armagh, 1849–52, he made strenuous efforts to combat Gallicanism in the hierarchy; he regarded St Patrick's College, Maynooth, with particular suspicion. Under his influence as Archbishop of Dublin, 1852–78, the complexion of the hierarchy changed, until only half the bishops had a Maynooth background, and ULTRAMONTANISM became a feature of the Irish hierarchy in the second part of the nineteenth century. A residue of Gallicanism remained, as was evident during the LAND WAR, when priests supported the LAND LEAGUE and the PLAN OF CAMPAIGN, particularly in Munster, where they took their lead from the Archbishop of Cashel, T. W. CROKE.

Ganly, Patrick (1809–1899), geologist; born in Dublin, educated at TCD. While he was employed on the Boundary Survey and General Valuation of Ireland his correspondence with SIR RICHARD GRIFFITH formed the basis for Griffith's revision of the Geological Map of Ireland. Three manuscript volumes of Ganly's letters were deposited in the Valuation Office, Dublin. In a paper read to the Geological Society of Dublin, 1856, he first put forward the method of current-bedding to determine the orientation of strata.

Garda Síochána, the national police force established in the autumn of 1922, originally under the title Civic Guard; on 31 July, on a motion by Cathal O'Shannon, the name was changed to Garda Síochána ('peace guard'). The first Commissioner was MICHAEL STAINES, who was succeeded by EOIN O'DUFFY, September 1922. The force had an initial strength of 4,000, increased by the Garda Síochána Act (1924) to 6,300, consisting of 1 Commissioner, 5 supervising officers, 27 chief superintendents, 150 superintendents and inspectors, 1,200 sergeants, and 4,918 gardaí. The Garda Síochána Act (1958) provided for the admission of women to the force, and by 1974 there were twenty women gardaí stationed in larger towns. Garda Headquarters is in the Phoenix Park, Dublin. The Training Depot (now the Garda Síochána College) is in Templemore, Co. Tipperary. The Technical Bureau oversees criminal records, fingerprinting, mapping, photographic work, and ballistics.

The Scott Medal for Bravery is awarded to members of the force. The first medal was awarded to Garda James Mulroy for bravery at O'Callaghan's Mills, Co. Clare. Garda Richard Fallon, killed by armed robbers during a bank raid in Dublin, 3 April 1970, was the first member of the force to be awarded the medal posthumously. Only one person has been awarded two Scott Medals: Detective-Garda Ben O'Sullivan of Henry Street, Limerick, was awarded his first medal for arresting a man carrying a loaded shotgun in Limerick, January 1991, and a second one, 6 July 2000, after he was the sole survivor when he and Garda Jerry McCabe were shot during an attempted armed raid at Adare, Co. Limerick, 7 June 1996. (Detective-Garda McCabe was awarded the Scott Medal posthumously.)

Gardiner Report (1975), the report of the committee of inquiry established under a former Lord Chancellor, Lord Gardiner, to examine measures taken to deal with terrorism in Northern Ireland in the context of civil liberties and human rights. Other members of the committee were Lord MacDermott, Alistair Buchan, J. P. Higgins, Kathleen Jones, Nicholas Morland, and John Whyte. The committee, which issued its report in January 1975, found that detention without trial was a short-term necessity and recommended that SPECIAL CATEGORY (or political-prisoner) status for convicted prisoners should end, initially for new prisoners; non-jury trials for terrorist offences should be continued for the time being; and there should be a new offence of 'terrorism'. The prison-building programme was to be speeded up, and an independent police complaints procedure should be introduced. The report noted that no political framework could endure without both communities sharing responsibility for administering Northern Ireland. An additional point—not accepted by Lord MacDermott, who claimed he could not understand it—called for the recognition of the different national inheritances of the two communities.

Gate Theatre, Dublin, founded in 1928 by Hilton Edwards and Micheál Mac Liammóir. Its policy, to provide Ireland with the best of international drama as well as 'non-peasant' drama by Irish writers, was similar to that of the DUBLIN DRAMA LEAGUE, which it replaced. Each play was to have a run of one week. The first production was Ibsen's *Peer Gynt,* 14 October 1928. The company played at the Peacock Theatre (attached to the ABBEY THEATRE) until 1930. The Concert Rooms of the Rotunda in Cavendish Row were leased in 1930 with funds provided by public subscription, and a limited company was formed, with Edwards as managing director. The first production at the new premises was Goethe's *Faust.* After Lord Longford (1902–1961) became a director in 1931, Longford Productions leased the premises for six months annually, from 1936.

Edwards and Mac Liammóir performed at the Gate as well as producing, directing, and (in Mac Liammóir's case) writing and designing. Among the actors who worked with the company were Coralie Carmichael, Geraldine Fitzgerald, James Mason, Gearóid Ó Lochlainn, and Orson Welles. Early productions included works by Aeschylus, Chekhov, Cocteau, Galsworthy, DENIS JOHNSTON, Eugene O'Neill, Shakespeare, GEORGE BERNARD SHAW, Sophocles, Gertrude Stein, Tolstoy, Oscar Wilde, W. B. YEATS, and Mac Liammóir. From 1983 the theatre has enjoyed international recognition under its artistic director, Michael Colgan.

Gavan Duffy, Sir Charles (1816–1903), Young Ireland journalist; born in Monaghan, educated at RBAI. A journalist with the *Northern Herald* and *Dublin Morning Register,* he became first editor of the biweekly *Belfast Vindicator* (established in 1839 to promote the interests of Ulster Catholics). He moved to Dublin and was called to the bar in 1841. With THOMAS DAVIS and JOHN BLAKE DILLON he founded and was first editor of the NATION, 15 October 1842. With other members of YOUNG IRELAND he supported DANIEL O'CONNELL and the REPEAL ASSOCIATION until 1846 and was among those tried for sedition with O'Connell; he was sentenced to imprisonment and then released by order of the House of Lords, 1844. In January 1847 he was a joint founder of the IRISH CONFEDERATION, and he prevailed on WILLIAM SMITH O'BRIEN to accept its leadership. For his involvement in the 1848 rising at BALLINGARRY he was imprisoned during a period in which he was tried and acquitted on four occasions.

He became leader of the TENANT LEAGUE with FREDERICK LUCAS, 1850, and two years later, as member of Parliament for New Ross, was instrumental in founding the INDEPENDENT IRISH PARTY. Disillusioned with the failure of the party, and suffering from chronic bronchitis, he left Ireland for Australia with £20 in his pocket, October 1855. He settled in Melbourne, 1856, and was elected for a constituency with a majority Irish population. He became Governor-General of Victoria, 1871–72, and was knighted in 1873. Speaker of the Assembly, 1876–80, he retired on a pension of £1,000 and settled in Nice in 1880. He died on 9 February 1903, survived by seven sons and four daughters from his three marriages. In response to appeals, his family agreed to his re-interment in Ireland, and he was buried in Glasnevin Cemetery, Dublin, 8 March 1903. His principal works were *The Ballad Poetry of Young Ireland* (1845), which ran to fifty editions, *Young Ireland: A Fragment of Irish History* (1880), *The League of North and South* (1886), *Thomas Davis: The Memoirs of a Patriot* (1892), *A Short Life of Thomas Davis* (1896), and *My Life in Two Hemispheres* (1898).

His daughter Louise Gavan Duffy (1884–1969) taught in the Education Department of University College, Dublin, and was joint founder of Scoil Bhríde, a secondary school for girls at 70 St Stephen's Green, opened on 1 September 1917, which was also the venue for meetings of the first DÁIL ÉIREANN.

Gavan Duffy, George (1882–1951), lawyer and politician (Sinn Féin); born in Cheshire, son of SIR CHARLES GAVAN DUFFY, educated at Nice and at Stonyhurst College, Lancashire. Having compromised his lucrative legal practice in London through his involvement in the defence of ROGER CASEMENT, May 1916, he returned to Ireland, where he was called to the bar in 1917. He became Sinn Féin MP for South Dublin, 1918, and was an influential figure in the drafting of the DECLARATION OF INDEPENDENCE. Assistant to SEÁN T. O'KELLY at the Paris Peace Conference (1919), he was ambassador to the Holy See a year later. Nominated by ÉAMON DE VALERA and MICHAEL COLLINS as a plenipotentiary in the negotiations that led to the ANGLO-IRISH TREATY (1921), he was the last delegate to sign. He succeeded ARTHUR GRIFFITH as Minister for Foreign Affairs in the second Dáil, July 1922, but resigned the following month in protest against the suppression of the Supreme Court, which he described as 'a desperate act of official lawlessness.' His suggestion that Irregulars (anti-Treaty soldiers) should be treated as prisoners of war was defeated, 27 September 1922.

Gavan Duffy criticised the CONSTITUTION OF THE IRISH FREE STATE (1922), the government's policy of detention without trial, and the execution of ERSKINE CHILDERS, whose case was the subject of a *habeas corpus* application to the High Court. A senior counsel from 1929, he was a judge of the High Court from 1936. On 1 December 1939 he ruled that a detention under the OFFENCES AGAINST THE STATE ACT (1939) was unconstitutional, following which the government was obliged to release fifty-three prisoners and then introduced the EMERGENCY POWERS ACT (1940). Gavan Duffy ended a distinguished legal career as president of the High Court from 1946.

George III (1738–1820), King of Great Britain and Ireland, 1760–1820. Shortly after his coronation he decreed that the Lord Lieutenant of Ireland should live continuously in Ireland. Towards the end of the eighteenth century the demand for CATHOLIC EMANCIPATION caused him great uneasiness because of its inconsistency with his coronation oath. He opposed Catholic relief measures. The insurrection of the UNITED IRISHMEN, 1798, convinced him (as well as the Prime Minister, WILLIAM PITT) of the necessity for a legislative union between Ireland and England, but he refused to assent to Pitt's proposition that it should be accompanied by Catholic Emancipation; his refusal led to Pitt's resignation, 5 February 1801.

Following the king's initial bout of insanity, February–March 1801, Pitt gave an undertaking that he would not again raise the question of Catholic relief. In 1810 he suffered a relapse and from 1811 was permanently incapacitated. His son, later KING GEORGE IV, was regent until becoming king in 1820.

George IV (1762–1830), King of Great Britain and Ireland, 1820–30, son of KING GEORGE III. In 1785 he and Maria Fitzherbert, a Catholic, had secretly married, contrary to English law. He became regent when his father was declared permanently insane in 1811. Though he had earlier supported CATHOLIC EMANCIPATION, he now urged the suppression of the CATHOLIC COMMITTEE and was as opposed to Catholic relief as his father had been. He influenced the defeat of the Catholic Relief Bill introduced by HENRY GRATTAN, 1819. After becoming king he visited Ireland, May–September 1821, when DANIEL O'CONNELL was among those who attended on him to demonstrate their loyalty. He resolutely refused the proposal for Catholic Emancipation put forward by the DUKE OF WELLINGTON and SIR ROBERT PEEL after O'Connell's victory in the Co. Clare by-election, 1828. There were fears that he might become insane under the pressure that the prospect of Catholic Emancipation appeared to place on him; however, in January 1829 he announced that a measure of Catholic relief would be introduced, and then on 1 March declared that he would rather abdicate than concede it. Three days later he informed Wellington and Peel that he had never understood that Catholic Emancipation would mean the repeal of the oath of supremacy, and so he could not agree to it. He consented when Wellington and Peel tendered their resignations. In deference to the king's wishes, O'Connell had to contest Co. Clare a second time before he could take his seat.

George V (1865–1936), King of Great Britain and Ireland. Concerned at the impasse on HOME RULE for Ireland, 1912–14, he persuaded ASQUITH to hold the BUCKINGHAM PALACE CONFERENCE. In September 1914 he signed the Government of Ireland Act, which was then suspended for the duration of the Great War. When formally opening the new Parliament of Northern Ireland he appealed for an end to the WAR OF INDEPENDENCE, 22 June 1921: 'I speak from a full heart when I pray that my coming to Ireland today may prove to be the first step towards an end of strife amongst her peoples . . .' This was followed immediately by an invitation from the British Prime Minister, DAVID LLOYD GEORGE, to ÉAMON DE VALERA to attend a conference. The TRUCE followed on 11 July.

German-Irish Society, a short-lived society founded in Berlin, January 1916. It contributed 50,000 marks to ROGER CASEMENT, then in Germany, for the purchase of arms for the IRISH VOLUNTEERS.

'German Plot'. On 8 May 1918 the *Times* (London) published a statement, attributed to SIR EDWARD CARSON, that the British government had evidence of an alliance between SINN FÉIN and Germany. On 18 May the newly arrived Lord Lieutenant of Ireland, EARL FRENCH, announced that evidence had been found that 'certain subjects . . . domiciled in Ireland' had entered into 'treasonable communication with the German enemy.' The announcement was followed by an extensive campaign against Sinn Féin in the British press. The revelation of the 'plot' came at the height of the campaign to resist CONSCRIPTION in Ireland. On 17–18 May almost the entire leadership of Sinn Féin was arrested.

No evidence of such a plot was ever found. Its apparent purpose was to discredit the leaders of the anti-conscription campaign and of Sinn Féin in the eyes of the American authorities. Speaking in the House of Lords, 20 June 1918, VISCOUNT WIMBOURNE, who had been recalled as Lord Lieutenant in favour of Lord French, stated that neither he nor any member of the Irish Executive had been aware of the plot until it was discovered by the British government.

Gifford, Grace (1888–1955), artist; born in Rathmines, Dublin. She studied under William Orpen at the Metropolitan School of Art, Dublin, and Slade School of Fine Art, London, 1907–08. Through CONSTANCE MARKIEVICZ she became a member of Sinn Féin and later of INGHINIDHE NA HÉIREANN. She was also active in the IRISH WOMEN'S FRANCHISE LEAGUE. She became engaged to be married to JOSEPH PLUNKETT, May 1915; after he was sentenced to death for his participation in the EASTER RISING (1916) they were married in his cell in Kilmainham Jail, Dublin, 4 May, and were allowed ten minutes together a few hours before he was shot by firing squad.

Following the rising she became a member of the Executive of Sinn Féin and produced banners, posters, and other publicity material. Active in the WOMEN'S PRISONERS' DEFENCE LEAGUE, she rejected the ANGLO-IRISH TREATY (1921) and was imprisoned during the CIVIL WAR, 1923. While in jail she painted the allegorical *Kilmainham Madonna* on the wall of her cell; a facsimile has now replaced the original. She was awarded a state pension by the de Valera government and was buried in Glasnevin Cemetery, Dublin, with military honours in the presence of President Seán T. O'Kelly.

Gilbert, Sir John Thomas (1829–1898), historian; born in Dublin, educated at Bective College and Prior Park College, Bath. He was librarian of the Royal Irish Academy for thirty-four years. Editor of *Contemporary History*, 1841–52, he was joint founder and joint secretary (with James Henthorn Todd, 1805–1869) of the Irish Celtic and Archaeological Society, 1855. His attack on the competence of the editors of the *Calendars of Patent and Close Rolls of Chancery in Ireland* (1863) was subsequently justified. He helped to establish the PUBLIC RECORD OFFICE and was its secretary, 1867–75. His works include *History of the City of Dublin* (3 vols., 1854–59), *Ancient Historical Manuscripts* (1861), and *History of the Viceroys of Ireland down to 1500* (1865). His unique collection of historical and archaeological works passed to Dublin Corporation following his death.

Gill, M. H. [Michael Henry] (1794–1879), printer and publisher; born in Co. Offaly. Apprenticed to Dublin University Press (part of the University of Dublin), he became sole lessee in 1842 and manager, 1842–75. He bought the stock, copyrights and premises of the Dublin printer James McGlashan, 1856, and founded the publishing house of McGlashan and Gill, which produced the monumental *Annals of the Four Masters* in seven volumes (1849–51, second edition 1856). The company became M. H. Gill and Son in 1876, part of the Macmillan group as Gill and Macmillan Ltd from 1968, and part of the Holtzbrinck group from 1995.

Gill, Thomas Patrick (1858–1931), politician (Nationalist) and civil servant; born in Ballygraigue, Nenagh, Co. Tipperary, educated at TCD. Having edited the *Catholic World* in New York and worked as associate editor of the *North American Review*, 1883–85, he represented South Louth for the Irish Party, 1885–92. After fund-raising with leading members of the party in America, when the crisis over PARNELL's leadership occurred, December 1890, he resigned when he was unable to heal the breach. Through his friendship with SIR HORACE PLUNKETT he was appointed secretary of the RECESS COMMITTEE, and he was later secretary of the Department of Agriculture and Technical Instruction, 1900–23. He was a member of the War Committee for Supply and Distribution, 1914–19, a member of the General Assembly of the Institute of Agriculture, Rome, president of the Grand Committee on Economic and Social Policy, 1920, chairman of the Free State Central Savings Committee, and president of the Irish Technical Education Association, 1925–29.

Gilmore, George (1898–1987), socialist republican; born in Belfast, educated locally and in Dublin, where his father was an evangelical Protestant. Trained as an accountant, he was a member of Fianna Éireann and later joined the IRA, as did his brothers Charlie and Harry. Opposed to the ANGLO-IRISH TREATY (1921), he was secretary to SEÁN LEMASS during the Civil War. As a member of the Army Council of the IRA he supported PEADAR O'DONNELL and FRANK RYAN in their efforts to fuse republicanism and socialism in movements such as SAOR ÉIRE and the REPUBLICAN CONGRESS. In 1926, dressed as a garda, he led a raid on Mountjoy Jail, Dublin, and released nineteen prisoners. He was sentenced to five years' imprisonment after the IRA was outlawed, 7 December 1931. During his imprisonment he and his brother Charlie led a campaign for political status. They were released on the accession of the FIANNA FÁIL government, March 1932. Later that year, 14 August, he was wounded by gardaí near Kilrush, Co. Clare. With FRANK RYAN and others he organised a short-lived Citizens' Army in opposition to the orthodox IRA. He organised support for the Spanish Republic in the SPANISH CIVIL WAR (1936–39). He finished bottom of the poll when he stood as a republican labour candidate for Co. Dublin in the 1938 general election.

Ginnell, Lawrence (1854–1923), politician (Nationalist) and writer; born in Co. Westmeath, largely self-educated. He was called to the Irish and English bar. As member of Parliament for Co. Westmeath, 1907–18, he was popularly known as the 'member for Ireland'. An impassioned orator, he was several times ejected from the House of Commons for his refusal to follow official procedure. After the EASTER RISING (1916) he became the first member of the IRISH PARTY to join Sinn Féin, of which he became treasurer. Following his election for Co. Westmeath to the first Dáil Éireann he became Director of Publicity, April 1919 to August 1921. At the request of ÉAMON DE VALERA he held a watching brief as the only anti-Treatyite to enter Dáil Éireann, August 1922; after demanding the credentials of the Dáil he was ejected. He became a member of the 'Council of State' formed by the 'government' led by de Valera from a remnant of the second Dáil, October 1922. He died in the United States. His writings include *The Brehon Laws* (1894), *The Doubtful Grant of Ireland* (1899), and *Land and Liberty* (1908).

'girlcotting', a term (derived from 'boycotting') sometimes used for the ostracising of women who, during the LAND WAR, breached a LAND LEAGUE edict by marrying or associating with boycotted farmers. In extreme cases women had their hair shorn or were tarred and feathered.

Gladstone, W. E. [William Ewart] (1809–1898), British politician (Liberal-Tory and Liberal); born in Liverpool. At first opposed to the Maynooth Grant (see MAYNOOTH), he supported it from the back benches. Returning to office as Colonial Secretary, he supported Peel's repeal of the Corn Laws. He took up the cause of Irish grievances in the 1860s. Despite the resolute opposition of BENJAMIN DISRAELI and the Conservatives, during his first ministry, 1868–74, he introduced the DISESTABLISHMENT of the Church of Ireland. Having stated that 'my mission is to pacify Ireland,' he introduced the Landlord and Tenant (Ireland) Act (1870) (see LAND ACTS). Though the act failed in its attempt to legalise the ULSTER CUSTOM, it introduced a policy that continued in Gladstone's second ministry, 1880–85. In 1873 he tackled the problem of suitable university education for Catholics, whose needs were not catered for either in the QUEEN'S COLLEGES or the CATHOLIC UNIVERSITY OF IRELAND. His proposal to abolish Queen's College, Galway, and amalgamate the other two Queen's Colleges (Cork and Belfast), Trinity College (Dublin), Magee College (Derry) and the Catholic University into one non-sectarian national university was opposed by all shades of Irish political and religious opinion and led to the fall of his ministry. During his period in opposition, 1874–80, his suggestion that the Lord Lieutenancy of Ireland be abolished and the eldest son of the monarch become the permanent Viceroy was rejected by QUEEN VICTORIA.

When Gladstone formed his second ministry, April 1880, Ireland was in the throes of a land agitation, led by the LAND LEAGUE. Though the Irish Executive was determined to resist the league, in 1881 Gladstone conceded the demand for tenant right and peasant proprietorship. CHARLES STEWART PARNELL was imprisoned in October, and unrest mounted until he and Gladstone came to an accommodation in the 'KILMAINHAM TREATY', which led to Parnell's release, 2 May 1882. The Representation of the People Act (1884) established universal male householder franchise; with the Redistribution of Seats Act (1885) it worked in Ireland to the distinct advantage of the IRISH PARTY. Gladstone's ministry was defeated on the budget, June 1885. When he refused to bargain with Parnell over home rule, the Irish Party gave its support to the Conservatives. However, Gladstone recovered Irish support when the 'HAWARDEN KITE', December 1885, revealed that he now favoured home rule; this lost him the support of the Whigs and of JOSEPH CHAMBERLAIN and the Radicals.

Following the defeat of the first Home Rule Bill he went to the country and lost, July 1886. On returning to office, 1892, he introduced the second Home Rule Bill, which was passed by the House of Commons but was defeated in the House of Lords, 1893. In 1894 Gladstone resigned office and the leadership of the Liberal Party and retired to pursue Bible studies.

Glenavy, James Henry Mussen Campbell, first Baron (1851–1933), lawyer and politician (Unionist); born in Terenure, Dublin, educated at TCD, where he was senior moderator and gold-medallist in classics, history, law, and political economy. He was called to the bar, 1878, and made a Queen's counsel, 1890. A member of Parliament, 1898–1916, he was Solicitor-General, 1901–05, Attorney-General, 1905–1916, Lord Chief Justice, 1916–18, and Lord Chancellor of Ireland, 1918–21. He was created Baron Glenavy in 1921. He was vice-chancellor of the University of Dublin, 1919–31, and first chairman of the Senate of the Irish Free State, 1922–28.

Godkin, James (1806–1879), writer; born in Gorey, Co. Wexford. A dissenting minister, he was sent as a missionary to Connacht by the Irish Evangelical Society, 1834, and contributed articles on religion and agrarian reform to various periodicals. He founded the *Christian Patriot* in Belfast, 1849, and was editor of the *Derry Standard* and Dublin correspondent for the *Times* (London). He was active on behalf of the TENANT LEAGUE, 1850, and his writings on agrarian and church reforms were very influential. He held a highly personalised view of the Reformation, which he expounded in *Land War in Ireland* (1870):

> The Reformation was in reality nothing but a special form of the land war. The Oath of Supremacy was simply a lever for evicting owners of the land. The process was simple. The king demanded spiritual allegiance; refusal was high treason; the punishment of high treason was forfeiture of estates, with death or banishments to the recusants . . . Hence Protestantism was detested, not as a religion so much as an instrument of spoliation.

As a special commissioner for the *Times* he travelled Ulster and the south of Ireland making observations on the system of landholding. His other works include *Ireland and Her Churches* (1867) and *Religious History of Ireland: Primitive, Papal and Protestant* (1873). He was awarded a pension by Queen Victoria for his *Illustrated History of England from 1820 to the Death of the Prince Consort.*

gombeen men (from Irish *gaimbín,* 'usury'), a derisive term reserved in rural Ireland for those who lent money at exorbitant rates of interest. Gombeen men, who were found in nearly every rural community, sold meat or potatoes at the highest price during times of scarcity and frequently lent money to those in desperate need. In his *Letters on the Condition of the People of Ireland* (1846) Thomas Campbell Foster recalled an instance of a gombeen man who made a loan of £1 with interest of 50 per cent per month, or 600 per cent per year. If a loan was not repaid, the gombeen man could bring ruin on his creditor by seizing his property. Many gombeen men also acted as landlords' agents or MIDDLEMEN.

Gonne MacBride, Maud (1866–1953), nationalist and suffragist; born near Aldershot, Hampshire, where her father, a colonel in the British army, was stationed, educated privately. She joined her father on his posting to DUBLIN CASTLE, 1882, and was left financially independent on his early death four years later. While recovering from illness in France she met Lucien Millevoye, whom she assisted with the publication of his book *La Patrie.* They had two children: Georges (who succumbed to meningitis at the age of eighteen months, 1891), and Iseult (1895–1954). JOHN O'LEARY introduced her to Fenianism, 1886, and to W. B. YEATS, 1889. Despite several refusals of his marriage proposals, she remained for Yeats the embodiment of Irish womanhood.

During the famine of the 1890s she led agitation in Cos. Donegal and Mayo and was successful in galvanising Boards of Governors in support of the rural poor. As a prominent member of the AMNESTY ASSOCIATION she organised counter-attractions to loyalist celebrations for the jubilee of QUEEN VICTORIA. A member of CUMANN NA NGAEDHEAL, the Irish Transvaal Committee (which organised support for the

Boers), and the NATIONAL COUNCIL, she jointly founded INGHINIDHE NA HÉIREANN, 1900. In 1902 she took the lead in Yeats's play *Cathleen ni Houlihan,* a role he had created for her.

Arthur Griffith introduced her to MAJOR JOHN MACBRIDE, 1900, whom she married in Paris, 1903. When the marriage failed within a few years she became unpopular in Ireland and took up residence in Paris while MacBride returned to Dublin. She edited *L'Irlande Libre* and contributed to BEAN NA HÉIREANN. Her writings advocated physical force as a method of achieving independence. Following MacBride's execution for his part in the EASTER RISING (1916) she returned to Ireland, 1917, and was active in the anti-conscription campaign. She was imprisoned in Holloway Prison, London, together with KATHLEEN CLARKE and CONSTANCE MARKIEVICZ following the 'GERMAN PLOT' but was released on grounds of ill-health. During the WAR OF INDEPENDENCE she worked for the WHITE CROSS and, having opposed the ANGLO-IRISH TREATY (1921), founded the WOMEN'S PRISONERS' DEFENCE LEAGUE, with CHARLOTTE DESPARD and HANNA SHEEHY-SKEFFINGTON, 1922. Imprisoned during the CIVIL WAR, she joined ninety others on hunger strike but was released after twenty days, January 1923. She supported her son, SEÁN MACBRIDE, in his attempts to establish CLANN NA POBLACHTA. Her autobiography, *A Servant of the Queen,* was published in 1938.

Goodman, Canon James (1829–1896), musician; born in Dingle, Co. Kerry, educated at TCD. Ordained in 1851, he was professor of Irish in Trinity College, Dublin, from 1879. Between 1884 and 1896 he collaborated with James Harnett Murphy in translating the Gospel of St Luke, and translated 'St Patrick's Breastplate' from Old Irish to Modern Irish. While a curate at Ardgroom, Castletown Bearhaven, Co. Cork, 1858–66, he was visited by the most famous of the Co. Kerry musicians, including the blind Dingle fiddler Thomas Kennedy. He collected more than a thousand tunes, which he sent in four volumes to P. W. JOYCE. Having heard him perform on the uilleann pipes, Dr Douglas Hyde described Goodman as 'the best piper I have ever heard.'

Görtz, Dr Hermann (1890–1947), German spy; born in Lübeck. After studying law at Heidelberg he was called to the bar but chose a military career. He was awarded the Iron Cross for bravery during the First World War, and in 1935 he joined the German air force. He was imprisoned in England for espionage, 1935–39; on his release he returned to Germany and was transferred to Military Intelligence, January 1940. Sent to Ireland, 5 May 1940, he was contacted shortly afterwards by the IRA. His Irish mission met with a reverse when the home of a contact at Templeogue, Co. Dublin, was raided by the Gardaí, 22 May, and plans for an airborne invasion of Ireland, details of military installations, maps showing harbours, bridges and roads, a radio transmitter and £20,000 were found. A code book found during the raid was passed to the Office of Strategic Services (forerunner of the Central Intelligence Agency), with which the Irish authorities worked in close collaboration.

Görtz had informed his superiors that the IRA would be of little practical use to Germany. Following his arrest, 27 November, he was interned in Athlone until September 1946. He was secretary of the Save the German Children fund until his re-arrest, together with former German prisoners, for deportation in accordance with an Allied request to Ireland, 12 April 1947. While awaiting deportation he died at the Aliens Registration Office, Dublin Castle, 23 May; a post-mortem examination revealed that he had ingested a quantity of potassium cyanide.

gossoon (Irish *garsún,* from French *garçon*), a servant-boy at the beck and call of the butler and cook. When serving as messenger-boys some of them are recorded to have covered more than 50 miles on foot in a surprisingly quick time.

Gough, General Sir Hubert de La Poer (1870–1963), British soldier; born in London, raised in India until he was seven. He joined the British army as a cadet, 1887, was commissioned as a second lieutenant, 1889, and served in India and South Africa, where he saw action at the relief of Ladysmith, 28 February 1900. He was the youngest brigadier-general in the British army while serving in Ireland. When GENERAL SIR ARTHUR PAGET was ordered to prepare to protect arms depots in Ulster, Gough led the revolt of officers in the CURRAGH INCIDENT, March 1914; he travelled to London. where, after a meeting with GENERAL SIR HENRY WILSON, he succeeded in having the order revoked. He later served on the Western Front in the Great War.

Goulburn, Henry (1784–1856), British politician (Conservative); born in London, educated at the University of Cambridge. His appointment as Chief Secretary for Ireland, 1821–27, under RICHARD COLLEY WELLESLEY was unpopular in Ireland because of his earlier opposition to the Catholic Disability Removal Bill. Within two years he was confronted by the national agitation for CATHOLIC EMANCIPATION. In 1823 he introduced the Irish Tithe Composition Act (see TITHES). His act of February 1825 to suppress unlawful societies ('Goulburn's Act') failed in its purpose, as DANIEL O'CONNELL simply changed the name of the CATHOLIC ASSOCIATION and continued the agitation. He supported the DUKE OF WELLINGTON and SIR ROBERT PEEL in their opposition to the granting of Catholic Emancipation. He was later Home Secretary under Peel, 1834–35, and Chancellor of the Exchequer, 1841–46.

Goulding, Cathal (1922–1998), IRA leader; born in Dublin, educated at national school. A painter and decorator by trade, he was a colleague of BRENDAN BEHAN, with whom he was a member of FIANNA ÉIREANN and of the IRA during the 1930s and 40s. He served a twelve-month prison sentence in 1946, and later oversaw IRA training camps in the Wicklow Mountains. In 1953 he was jailed for eight years, together with SEÁN MAC STIOFÁIN and Manus Canning, for stealing guns and ammunition from a British army training camp at Felstead, Essex. Following his release in 1959 he became quartermaster-general of the IRA and two years later chief of staff. Influenced by left-wing academics, he introduced Marxist socio-economic theories to the republican movement, which created tensions between the Marxist tendency and traditional physical-force republicanism that led to the split, 1969–70, and the founding of the Provisional IRA. He was acquitted on a charge of incitement to cause explosions or to shoot people following an oration in July 1971. His policies within the Official IRA and Sinn Féin were considered instrumental in the founding of the WORKERS' PARTY. In January 1994 he appealed for an end to violence, calling on the Provisional IRA to follow the path taken by the Official IRA.

Government Information Services, established in 1934 as the Government Information Bureau, attached to the Department of the President of the Executive Council. The first director was SHAN Ó CUÍV, who was succeeded by FRANK GALLAGHER. The function of the bureau was to facilitate communication between the Government, departments of state, and the public. It provided official documents to the media, arranged press conferences for ministers and officials, and briefed correspondents on official statements. The Government Information Services, as it became from 1973, was later attached to the Department of the Taoiseach. The title of director was later changed to that of head of the GIS.

Government of Ireland Act (1920). A Bill for the Better Government of Ireland, repealing the Home Rule Act (1914), came into force on 3 May 1921, during the WAR OF INDEPENDENCE. The act attempted to find a compromise solution to the question of Irish independence by granting a large measure of home rule while making the six north-eastern Ulster counties (Antrim, Armagh, Derry, Down, Fermanagh, and Tyrone) a separate state within the United Kingdom. A Parliament of Northern Ireland would sit in Belfast and a Parliament of Southern Ireland would legislate for the rest of the country. In addition, a COUNCIL OF IRELAND was to be established to consider questions of common concern. Forty-two Irish members would sit in the British House of Commons, where imperial matters would be dealt with.

Elections under the act were held on 24 May 1921. In the North, 40 of the 52 seats were won by the ULSTER UNIONIST PARTY, and on 22 June, King George V formally opened the Parliament of Northern Ireland. In the rest of the country SINN FÉIN (ignoring the Parliament of Southern Ireland) used the elections, 24 May, to return members to the republican DÁIL ÉIREANN. Four Unionists, representing the University of Dublin constituency, were elected to the Parliament of Southern Ireland; but as they were the only ones to attend, it was adjourned. It met once more to dissolve itself and hand its powers to the Provisional Government.

governments of Ireland. The governments of the state known successively as the Irish Free State (1922–37) and Ireland (1937–) have been:

***First Dáil** (21 January 1919 to 10 May 1921)*
Ceann Comhairle: Seán T. O'Kelly
Sinn Féin

The first (temporary) Ministry was appointed on 22 January 1919. Cathal Brugha was elected Príomh-Aire (President) *pro tem* in place of Éamon de Valera, who was imprisoned in England. The ministers held office until 1 April 1919.

Cathal Brugha
Eoin MacNeill (Finance)
Michael Collins (Home Affairs)
George Noble Plunkett (Foreign Affairs)
Richard Mulcahy (National Defence)

Éamon de Valera assumed the office of Príomh-Aire on 1 April 1919 and appointed the second Ministry the following day. Eight of the eleven members were in the Ministry until 17 June 1919, when Ernest Blythe, Minister for Trade and Commerce, became the ninth. The ministers held office until 26 August 1921.
Éamon de Valera
Arthur Griffith (Home Affairs; appointed Deputy President of the Dáil on 17 June while President de Valera was in the United States)
Michael Collins (Finance; acted as Deputy President from 1 December 1920 during the imprisonment of Griffith from 26 November)
Cathal Brugha (Defence)
William T. Cosgrave (Local Government)
George Noble Plunkett (Foreign Affairs)
Eoin MacNeill (Industries)
Constance Markievicz (Labour)
Ernest Blythe (Trade and Commerce; member of the Ministry from 17 June 1919)

Not members of the Ministry
Seán Etchingham (Fisheries, from 29 June 1920)
Robert C. Barton (Agriculture)
Laurence Ginnell (Publicity and Propaganda)

Second Dáil *(16 August 1921 to 8 June 1922)*
Ceann Comhairle: Eoin MacNeill

The ministers held office from 26 August 1921 to 9 January 1922. Though commonly called ministers, those who were members of the Ministry were officially called secretaries of state, while non-Ministry members were called secretaries.

Sinn Féin

Éamon de Valera (President)
Arthur Griffith (Foreign Affairs)
Michael Collins (Finance)
Cathal Brugha (Defence)
William T. Cosgrave (Local Government)
Austin Stack (Home Affairs)
Robert C. Barton (Economic Affairs)

Not members of the Ministry
Kevin O'Higgins (Assistant, Local Government)
Constance Markievicz (Labour)
Ernest Blythe (Trade and Commerce)
Seán Etchingham (Fisheries)
John J. O'Kelly ('Sceilg') (Education)
Desmond Fitzgerald (Publicity)
George Noble Plunkett (Fine Arts)
Art O'Connor (Agriculture; Deputy, Economic Affairs from 14 October 1921)

Following the vote on the Anglo-Irish Agreement (64 to 57), 7 January, President de Valera tendered his resignation, 9 January. Arthur Griffith succeeded him as President, 10 January. The members of the Ministry held office until 9 September 1922. Because of the outbreak of the CIVIL WAR, 29 June 1922, some ministers were seconded to the army and were replaced by substitute ministers.

Sinn Féin

Arthur Griffith (President; Foreign Affairs from 26 July to his death, 12 August 1922)
Michael Collins (Finance; Defence from 1 July; he was commander in chief of the army until his death in action, 22 August 1922; William T. Cosgrave replaced him as Chairman of the Provisional Government and Minister for Finance on 12 July)
George Gavan Duffy (Foreign Affairs until 25 July, when he resigned and was replaced by Michael Hayes, 12 August)
Éamonn Duggan (Home Affairs)
William T. Cosgrave (Local Government)
Kevin O'Higgins (Economic Affairs; became assistant adjutant-general of the army and replaced by Ernest Blythe on 17 July)
Richard Mulcahy (Defence, until he became commander in chief of the army, 1 July; replaced by Michael Collins)
Michael Hayes (a non-Ministry member as Minister for Education, assumed Foreign Affairs on 12 August)

Not members of the Ministry
Ernest Blythe (Trade)
Joseph McGrath (Labour)
Desmond Fitzgerald (Publicity)
Patrick Hogan (Agriculture)
Mícheál Staines (Director of BELFAST BOYCOTT, January–February)

For the purposes of transferring power to an Irish government, the British government would recognise only the authority of the Provisional Government. The ministers assumed office on 16 January 1922. There were now two governments: the one appointed by the second Dáil, and the 'Provisional Government of Southern Ireland', which was the only one recognised by the British government for the purpose of transferring power to the Irish Free State, due to come into existence on 6 December 1922. From 9 September the Provisional Government appointed by the third Dáil continued in existence as the sole government until 6 December 1922, when, under the Constitution of the Irish Free State, it was superseded by the Executive Council.

Provisional Government *(10 January 1921 to 22 August 1922)*

Sinn Féin

Michael Collins (Chairman and Minister for Finance until his death in action, 22 August 1922)
William T. Cosgrave (Local Government)
Joseph McGrath (Labour; Director of Intelligence during the Civil War, replaced by Patrick Hogan, 17 July, who was also Minister for Agriculture)
Kevin O'Higgins (Economic Affairs)
Fionán Lynch (Education; during the Civil War he was vice-commandant of the South-Western Division, with the rank of lieutenant-general; replaced by Michael Hayes, 17 July to 30 August)
Patrick Hogan (Agriculture)
James J. Walsh (Postmaster-General, from 22 April)
Eoin MacNeill (without portfolio)

Not a member of the Ministry
Hugh Kennedy (Law Officer)

Following Collins's death, William T. Cosgrave became Chairman on 25 August. The appointments were from 9 September to 6 December 1922.

William T. Cosgrave (Chairman; also President of Dáil Éireann, 9 September to 6 December 1922)
Desmond Fitzgerald (External Affairs)
Kevin O'Higgins (Home Affairs)
Richard Mulcahy (National Defence)
Ernest Blythe (Local Government)
Joseph McGrath (Labour, Industry and Commerce and Economic Affairs)
Eoin MacNeill (Education)
Patrick Hogan (Agriculture)
James J. Walsh (Postmaster-General)
Edmund Duggan (without portfolio)
Fionán Lynch (without portfolio)

Not a member of the Ministry
Hugh Kennedy (Law Officer)

The Provisional Government was suspended from 6 December 1922, when the First Executive Council of the Irish Free State came into existence.

Third Dáil *(9 September 1922 to 9 August 1923)*

Ceann Comhairle: Michael Hayes

Provisional Government (30 August to 6 December 1922); first Executive Council (6 December 1922 to 19 September 1923)

Cumann na nGaedheal

William T. Cosgrave (President and Minister for Finance)
Kevin O'Higgins (Vice-President and Minister for Home Affairs)
Eoin MacNeill (Education, until 3 October 1923)
Richard Mulcahy (Defence)
Joseph McGrath (Industry and Commerce)
Desmond Fitzgerald (External Affairs)
Ernest Blythe (Local Government, to 15 October 1923)
Éamon Duggan (without portfolio, to 14 December)

Not members of the Executive Council
J. J. Walsh (Postmaster-General)
Patrick Hogan (Agriculture)
Fionán Lynch (Fisheries, from 14 December)
Hugh Kennedy (Attorney-General)

Fourth Dáil *(19 September 1923 to 20 May 1927)*

Ceann Comhairle: Michael Hayes

Second Executive Council (19 September 1923 to 23 May 1927)

Cumann na nGaedheal

During the period in office of this Executive Council the nomenclature of some departments changed. Under the Ministers and Secretaries Act (1924) the following changes took effect from 2 June 1924: the title of Postmaster-General was changed to Minister for Posts and Telegraphs; Home Affairs became Justice; Local Government became Local Government and Public Health; and Agriculture became Lands and Agriculture (until 1928).

William T. Cosgrave (President and Minister for Defence from 20 March until 21 November 1924; Minister for Finance, 30 June to 28 August 1924; Minister for Industry and

Commerce, 30 June to 28 August; External Affairs, 30 June to 28 August 1924)
Kevin O'Higgins (Vice-President and Minister for Home Affairs, known as Justice from 2 June 1924)
Ernest Blythe (Finance)
Richard Mulcahy (Defence, until 19 March 1924)
Peter Hughes (Defence, from 21 November 1924)
Desmond Fitzgerald (External Affairs)
Joseph McGrath (Industry and Commerce, until 7 March 1924)
Eoin MacNeill (Education, until 24 November 1925)
John M. O'Sullivan (Education, from 28 January 1926)
Patrick McGilligan (Industry and Commerce, from 4 April)

Not members of the Executive Council
James J. Walsh (Posts and Telegraphs)
Patrick Hogan (Lands and Agriculture)
Fionán Lynch (Fisheries)
James A. Burke (Local Government and Public Health)
Hugh Kennedy (Attorney-General, until 5 June 1924)
J. O'Byrne (Attorney-General, 5 June 1924 to 9 January 1926)
John A. Costello (Attorney-General, from 9 January 1926)

Fifth Dáil *(3 June 1927 to 16 August 1927)*

Ceann Comhairle: Michael Hayes

Third Executive Council (23 June to 12 October 1927)

Cumann na nGaedheal

William T. Cosgrave (President and Minister for Justice from 10 July)
Kevin O'Higgins (Vice-President, Minister for Justice and for External Affairs until his assassination, 10 July)
Ernest Blythe (Finance; Vice-president from 10 July)
Desmond Fitzgerald (Defence)
Patrick McGilligan (Industry and Commerce)
Patrick Hogan (Lands and Agriculture)
J. J. Walsh (Posts and Telegraphs)
Fionán Lynch (Fisheries)
John M. O'Sullivan (Education)
Richard Mulcahy (Local Government and Public Health)

Not a member of the Executive Council
John A. Costello (Attorney-General from 24 June)

Sixth Dáil *(11 October 1927 to 17 December 1932)*

Ceann Comhairle: Michael Hayes

Fourth Executive Council (11 October 1927 to 3 April 1930)

Cumann na nGaedheal

Fisheries became Lands and Fisheries.

William T. Cosgrave (President)
Ernest Blythe (Vice-President and Minister for Finance and Posts and Telegraphs)
James Fitzgerald-Kenny (Justice)
Desmond Fitzgerald (Defence)
Patrick McGilligan (External Affairs and Industry and Commerce)
Patrick Hogan (Agriculture)
Fionán Lynch (Lands and Fisheries)
John M. O'Sullivan (Education)
Richard Mulcahy (Local Government and Public Health)

Not a member of the Executive Council
John A. Costello (Attorney-General)

Fifth Executive Council (3 April 1930 to 9 March 1932)

William T. Cosgrave (President until 9 March 1932)
Ernest Blythe (Vice-President, Minister for Finance and Minister for Posts and Telegraphs)
Desmond Fitzgerald (Defence)
Patrick Hogan (Agriculture)
Fionán Lynch (Lands and Fisheries)
Richard Mulcahy (Local Government and Public Health)
Patrick McGilligan (External Affairs; Industry and Commerce)
John M. O'Sullivan (Education)
James Fitzgerald-Kenney (Justice)
John A. Costello (Attorney-General)

Seventh Dáil *(9 March 1932 to 22 December 1932)*

Ceann Comhairle: Frank Fahy

Sixth Executive Council (9 March 1932 to 8 January 1933)

Fianna Fáil

Éamon de Valera (President and Minister for External Affairs)

Seán T. O'Kelly (Vice-President and Minister for Local Government and Public Health)
Seán MacEntee (Finance)
Seán F. Lemass (Industry and Commerce)
James Geoghegan (Justice)
Frank Aiken (Defence)
James Ryan (Agriculture)
Patrick J. Ruttledge (Lands and Fisheries)
Joseph Connolly (Posts and Telegraphs)
Thomas Derrig (Education)

Not a member of the Executive Council
Conor A. Maguire (Attorney-General)

Eighth Dáil *(8 February 1933 to 14 June 1937)*

Ceann Comhairle: Frank Fahy

Seventh Executive Council (8 February 1933 to 21 July 1937)

Fianna Fáil

In 1934 the Department of Lands and Fisheries became the Department of Lands.

Éamon de Valera (President and Minister for External Affairs)
Seán T. O'Kelly (Vice-President and Minister for Local Government and Public Health)
Seán MacEntee (Finance)
Seán Lemass (Industry and Commerce)
Patrick J. Ruttledge (Justice)
Frank Aiken (Defence; Lands from 29 June to 11 November 1936)
James Ryan (Agriculture)
Joseph Connolly (Land and Fisheries to 29 May 1936; Lands and Fisheries from 11 November 1936)
Thomas Derrig (Education)
Gerald Boland (Posts and Telegraphs to 11 November 1936, then Lands)
Oscar Traynor (Posts and Telegraphs from 11 November 1936)

Not members of the Executive Council
Conor A. Maguire (Attorney-General to 2 November 1936, when he became a judge of the High Court)
James Geoghegan (Attorney-General from 2 November to 22 December 1936, when he became a judge of the Supreme Court)
Patrick Lynch (Attorney-General from 22 December 1936)

Ninth Dáil *(21 July 1937 to 27 May 1938)*

Ceann Comhairle: Frank Fahy

This was the eighth and last Executive Council of the Irish Free State and the first Government of Ireland; the members received their formal appointments from the President of Ireland on 28 June 1938. Under the Constitution of Ireland (1937) the head of the Government is known as the Taoiseach and the deputy head of the Government as the Tánaiste.

Fianna Fáil

Éamon de Valera (President of the Executive Council, Taoiseach from 29 December 1937, also Minister for External Affairs)
Seán T. O'Kelly (Vice-President of the Executive Council, Tánaiste from 29 December 1937, also Minister for Local Government)
Seán MacEntee (Finance)
Patrick J. Ruttledge (Justice)
Frank Aiken (Defence)
Seán Lemass (Industry and Commerce)
James Ryan (Agriculture)
Thomas Derrig (Education)
Gerald Boland (Lands)
Oscar Traynor (Posts and Telegraphs)

Not a member of the Government
Patrick Lynch (Attorney General)

Tenth Dáil *(30 June 1938 to 26 May 1943)*

Ceann Comhairle: Frank Fahy

Second Government (30 June 1938 to 2 July 1943)

Fianna Fáil

During the years of the Second World War two new Government posts were created: Minister for Supplies and Minister for the Co-ordination of Defensive Measures.

Éamon de Valera (Taoiseach and Minister for External Affairs; Education, 27 September 1939 to 18 June 1940; Local Government and Public Health, 15–18 August 1941)
Seán T. O'Kelly (Tánaiste and Minister for Local Government and Public Health to 8 September 1939; Education, 8–27 September 1939; Finance from 16 September 1939)
Seán MacEntee (Finance until 16 September 1939; Industry and Commerce, 16 September 1939 to 18 August 1941; Local Government and Public Health from 18 August 1941)
Patrick J. Ruttledge (Justice until 8 September 1939; Local Government and Public Health, 8 September 1939 to 14 August 1941)
Frank Aiken (Defence until 8 September 1939, Minister for the Co-ordination of Defensive

Measures from 8 September 1939)
Seán Lemass (Industry and Commerce until 16 September 1939; Minister for Supplies from 16 September 1939; Industry and Commerce again from 18 August 1941)
James Ryan (Agriculture)
Thomas Derrig (Education until 8 September 1939; Lands from 8 September 1939; Posts and Telegraphs 8–27 September 1939; Education from 18 June 1940)
Gerald Boland (Lands until 8 September 1939, then Justice)
Oscar Traynor (Posts and Telegraphs until 8 September 1939, then Defence)
Patrick J. Little (Posts and Telegraphs from 27 September 1939)

Not a member of the Government
Patrick Lynch (Attorney-General until 1 March 1940)
Kevin Haugh (Attorney-General from 1 March 1940 to 10 October 1942, when he became a judge of the High Court)
Kevin Dixon (Attorney-General from 10 October 1942 to 1 July 1943)

***Eleventh Dáil** (1 July 1943 to 10 May 1944)*

Ceann Comhairle: Frank Fahy

Third Government (2 July 1943 to 9 June 1944)

Fianna Fáil

Éamon de Valera (Taoiseach and Minister for External Affairs)
Seán T. O'Kelly (Tánaiste and Minister for Finance)
Gerald Boland (Justice)
Seán MacEntee (Local Government and Public Health)
Seán Lemass (Industry and Commerce and Supplies)
Frank Aiken (Co-ordination of Defensive Measures)
Oscar Traynor (Defence)
James Ryan (Agriculture)
Thomas Derrig (Education)
Patrick J. Little (Posts and Telegraphs)
Seán Moylan (Lands)

Not a member of the Government
Kevin Dixon (Attorney-General)

***Twelfth Dáil** (9 June 1944 to 11 December 1948)*

Ceann Comhairle: Frank Fahy

Fourth Government (9 June 1944 to 18 February 1948)

Fianna Fáil

The Department of Supplies was terminated on 19 June 1945 and its functions transferred to the Department of Industry and Commerce, 31 July 1945. The Department of Local Government and Public Health was divided into the Department of Local Government and Department of Health, 22 January 1947. The Department of Social Welfare was created in 1947.

Éamon de Valera (Taoiseach and Minister for External Affairs)
Seán T. O'Kelly (Tánaiste and Minister for Finance to 16 June 1945, when he became President of Ireland)
Seán Lemass (Industry and Commerce; Supplies to 21 July 1945; Tánaiste from 14 June 1945)
Gerald Boland (Justice)
Frank Aiken (Co-ordination of Defensive Measures to 19 June 1945; Finance from 19 June 1945)
Oscar Traynor (Defence)
James Ryan (Agriculture to 21 January 1947, then Health and Social Welfare)
Thomas Derrig (Education)
Seán MacEntee (Local Government and Public Health; Local Government from 21 January 1947)
Patrick J. Little (Posts and Telegraphs)
Seán Moylan (Lands)
Patrick Smith (Agriculture from 21 January 1947)

Not members of the Government
Kevin Dixon (Attorney-General to 30 April 1946, when he became a judge of the High Court)
Cearbhall Ó Dálaigh (Attorney-General from 30 April 1946)

***Thirteenth Dáil** (18 February 1948 to 7 May 1951)*

Ceann Comhairle: Frank Fahy

Fifth Government (18 February 1948 to 13 June 1951)

First inter-party (coalition) Government (Fine Gael, Clann na Poblachta, Labour Party, National Labour, Clann na Talmhan)

John A. Costello (Taoiseach; Minister for Health from 11 April 1951)

William Norton (Tánaiste and Minister for Social Welfare; acting Minister for Local Government, 29 April to 11 May 1949)
Seán Mac Eoin (Justice to 7 March 1951; Defence from 7 March 1951)
Patrick J. McGilligan (Finance)
Seán MacBride (External Affairs)
Daniel Morrissey (Industry and Commerce to 7 March 1951; Justice from 7 March 1951)
Thomas F. O'Higgins (Defence to 7 March 1951; Industry and Commerce from 1 March 1951)
Noel C. Browne (Health to 11 April 1951, when he resigned)
James Dillon (Agriculture)
Richard Mulcahy (Education)
Joseph Blowick (Lands)
James Everett (Posts and Telegraphs)
Timothy J. Murphy (Local Government, to his death on 29 April 1949)
Michael C. Keyes (Local Government from 11 May 1949)

Not members of the Government
C. Lavery (Attorney-General to 21 April 1951)
C. F. Casey (Attorney-General from 21 April 1951)

Fourteenth Dáil *(13 June 1951 to 24 April 1954)*

Ceann Comhairle: Patrick Hogan

Sixth Government (13 June 1951 to 2 June 1954)

Fianna Fáil

Éamon de Valera (Taoiseach)
Seán Lemass (Tánaiste and Minister for Industry and Commerce)
Seán MacEntee (Finance)
Gerald Boland (Justice)
Oscar Traynor (Defence)
Frank Aiken (External Affairs)
James Ryan (Health; Social Welfare)
Thomas Derrig (Lands)
Patrick Smith (Local Government)
Seán Moylan (Education)
T. Walsh (Agriculture)
Erskine Childers (Posts and Telegraphs)

Not members of the Government
Cearbhall Ó Dálaigh (Attorney-General to 1 July 1953)
T. Teevan (Attorney-General from 11 July 1953)

Fifteenth Dáil *(2 June 1954 to 12 February 1957)*

Ceann Comhairle: Patrick Hogan

Seventh Government (2 June 1951 to 20 March 1957)

(Second) inter-party (coalition) Government (Fine Gael and Labour Party)

The Department of the Gaeltacht was created in July 1956.

John A. Costello (Taoiseach)
William Norton (Tánaiste and Minister for Industry and Commerce)
Seán Mac Eoin (Defence)
Gerard Sweetman (Finance)
James Everett (Justice)
Thomas F. O'Higgins (Health)
James M. Dillon (Agriculture)
Richard Mulcahy (Education; Gaeltacht, July to 24 October 1956)
Joseph Blowick (Lands)
Michael Keyes (Posts and Telegraphs)
Liam Cosgrave (External Affairs)
Brendan Corish (Social Welfare)
Patrick O'Donnell (Local Government)
Patrick J. Lindsay (Gaeltacht from 24 October 1956)

Not a member of the Government
Patrick McGilligan (Attorney-General)

Sixteenth Dáil *(20 March 1957 to 15 September 1961)*

Ceann Comhairle: Patrick Hogan

Eighth Government (20 March to 23/24 June 1959)

Fianna Fáil

Éamon de Valera (Taoiseach; resigned on 17 June 1959 but carried out the duties until Seán Lemass was appointed, 23 June 1959)
Seán Lemass (Tánaiste and Minister for Industry and Commerce; Taoiseach from 23 June 1959)
James Ryan (Finance)
Oscar Traynor (Justice)
Kevin Boland (Defence)
Frank Aiken (External Affairs; Agriculture to 16 May 1957)
Patrick Smith (Local Government and Social Welfare to 27 November 1957; Agriculture from 27 November 1957)
Seán MacEntee (Health; Social Welfare from 27

November 1957)
Seán Moylan (Agriculture, 16 May 1957 until his death on 16 November 1957)
Erskine Childers (Lands)
Jack Lynch (Education; Gaeltacht to 26 June 1957)
Neil Blaney (Posts and Telegraphs to 4 December 1957; Local Government from 27 November 1957)
Micheál Ó Móráin (Gaeltacht from 26 June 1957)
John Ormonde (Posts and Telegraphs from 4 December 1957)

Not a member of the Government
Aindreas Ó Caoimh (Attorney-General)

Seán Lemass became Taoiseach on 23 June 1959. The Department of Transport and Power was created on 27 July 1959.

Ninth Government (23/34 June 1959 to 11 October 1961)

Seán Lemass (Taoiseach)
Seán MacEntee (Tánaiste and Minister for Health and Social Welfare)
James Ryan (Finance)
Oscar Traynor (Justice)
Kevin Boland (Defence)
Frank Aiken (External Affairs)
Patrick Smith (Agriculture)
Erskine Childers (Lands to 23 July 1959; without portfolio, 24–26 July 1959; Transport and Power from 27 July 1959)
Jack Lynch (Industry and Commerce)
Neil Blaney (Local Government)
Micheál Ó Móráin (Gaeltacht to 23 July 1959; Lands from 23 July 1959
Patrick J. Hillery (Education)
Gerard Bartley (Gaeltacht from 23 July 1959)
Michael Hilliard (Posts and Telegraphs)

Not a member of the Government
Aindréas Ó Caoimh (Attorney-General)

Seventeenth Dáil *(11 October 1961 to 18 March 1965)*

Ceann Comhairle: Patrick Hogan

Tenth Government (11/12 October 1961 to 21 April 1965)

Fianna Fáil

Seán Lemass (Taoiseach; Minister for Justice, 8 October to 3 November 1964)
Seán MacEntee (Tánaiste and Minister for Health)
James Ryan (Finance)
Frank Aiken (External Affairs)
Patrick Smith (Agriculture to 8 October 1964)
Erskine Childers (Transport and Power)
Jack Lynch (Industry and Commerce)
Neil Blaney (Local Government)
Micheál Ó Móráin (Lands and the Gaeltacht)
Patrick J. Hillery (Education)
Michael Hilliard (Posts and Telegraphs)
Gerard Bartley (Defence)
Kevin Boland (Social Welfare)
Charles J. Haughey (Justice to 8 October 1964; Agriculture from 8 October 1964)
Brian Lenihan (Justice from 3 November 1964)

Not members of the Government
Aindréas Ó Caoimh (Attorney-General to 16 March 1965)
Colm Condon (Attorney-General from 16 March 1965)

Eighteenth Dáil *(21 April 1965 to 22 May 1969)*

Ceann Comhairle: Cormac Breslin

Eleventh Government (21 April 1965 to 10 November 1966)

Fianna Fáil

On 6 July 1965 the Department of Agriculture became the Department of Agriculture and Fisheries. The Department of Labour was established on 13 July 1966. Jack Lynch succeeded Lemass as Taoiseach on 10 November 1966.

Seán Lemass (Taoiseach)
Frank Aiken (Tánaiste and Minister for External Affairs)
Jack Lynch (Finance)
Brian Lenihan (Justice)
Michael Hilliard (Defence)
Erskine Childers (Transport and Power)
Charles J. Haughey (Agriculture; Agriculture and Fisheries from 6 July 1965)
Patrick J. Hillery (Industry and Commerce to 13 July 1966; Labour from 13 July 1966)
Neil Blaney (Local Government)
Kevin Boland (Social Welfare)
Micheál Ó Móráin (Lands and the Gaeltacht)
Joseph Brennan (Posts and Telegraphs)
George Colley (Education to 13 July 1966; Industry and Commerce from 13 July 1966)
Seán Flanagan (Health from 13 July 1966)
Donogh O'Malley (Health to 13 July 1966; Education from 13 July 1966)

Not a member of the Government
Colm Condon (Attorney-General)

Jack Lynch succeeded Seán Lemass as Taoiseach on 10 November 1966 and formed a new Government.

Twelfth Government (10 November 1966 to 2 July 1969)

Jack Lynch (Taoiseach; Minister for Education, 11–26 March 1968)
Frank Aiken (Tánaiste and Minister for External Affairs)
Charles J. Haughey (Finance)
Brian Lenihan (Justice to 26 March 1968, then Education)
Kevin Boland (Local Government)
Neil Blaney (Agriculture and Fisheries)
George Colley (Industry and Commerce)
Erskine Childers (Transport and Power, Posts and Telegraphs)
Micheál Ó Móráin (Lands and the Gaeltacht to 26 March 1968, then Justice)
Donogh O'Malley (Education to 1 March 1968)
Michael Hilliard (Defence)
Seán Flanagan (Health)
Joseph Brennan (Social Welfare)
Patrick J. Hillery (Labour)
Pádraig Faulkner (Lands and the Gaeltacht from 27 March 1968)

Not a member of the Government
Colm Condon (Attorney-General)

Nineteenth Dáil *(18 June 1969 to 5 February 1973)*

Ceann Comhairle: Cormac Breslin

Thirteenth Government (2 July 1969 to 13 March 1973)

Fianna Fáil

During the lifetime of this Government there was a crisis over policy on Northern Ireland. Two ministers, Charles Haughey and Neil Blaney, were dismissed, 7 May 1970, and two resigned: Micheál Ó Móráin, 5 May, and Kevin Boland, 7 May. The Department of External Affairs was renamed Department of Foreign Affairs on 3 March 1971.

Ireland joined the EEC, and Patrick Hillery became the first Irish member of the European Commission, 3 January 1973. The Department of Agriculture became the Department of Agriculture and Fisheries in 1969.

Jack Lynch (Taoiseach)
Erskine Childers (Tánaiste and Minister for Health)
Charles J. Haughey (Finance to 7 May 1970, when he was dismissed)
Micheál Ó Móráin (Justice to 4 May 1970, when he resigned)
Neil Blaney (Agriculture and Fisheries to 7 May 1970, when he was dismissed)
Kevin Boland (Local Government, and Social Welfare to 7 May 1970, when he resigned)
Patrick J. Hillery (External Affairs to 3 January 1973)
George Colley (Gaeltacht; Industry and Commerce to 9 May 1970, then Finance)
Brian Lenihan (Transport and Power to 3 January 1973, then Foreign Affairs)
Joseph Brennan (Labour to 9 May 1970, then Labour and Social Welfare)
Seán Flanagan (Lands)
Pádraig Faulkner (Education)
James Gibbons (Defence to 8 May 1970, then Agriculture and Fisheries)
P. J. Lalor (Posts and Telegraphs to 9 May 1970, then Industry and Commerce)
Robert Molloy (Local Government from 9 May 1970)
Desmond O'Malley (Justice from 7 May 1970)
Gerard Cronin (Defence from 9 May 1970)
Gerard Collins (Posts and Telegraphs from 9 May 1970)
Michael O'Kennedy (without portfolio, 18 December 1972 to 3 January 1973, then Transport and Power)

Not a member of the Government
Colm Condon (Attorney-General)

Twentieth Dáil *(14 March 1973 to 25 May 1977)*

Ceann Comhairle: Seán Treacy

Fourteenth Government (14 March 1973 to 5 July 1977)

National Coalition (Fine Gael and Labour Party)

On 1 November 1973 the Department of the Public Service was established under the Minister for Finance. The Department of the Gaeltacht became a separate department at the beginning of the Government's term. The Department of Lands became the Department of Fisheries in February 1977.

Liam Cosgrave (Taoiseach and Minister for Defence, 2–15 December 1976)
Brendan Corish (Tánaiste and Minister for

Health and Social Welfare)
Richie Ryan (Finance; Public Service from November 1973)
Patrick Cooney (Justice)
Patrick S. Donegan (Defence to 1 December 1976; Lands, 2 December 1976 to 7 February 1977; Fisheries from 8 February 1977)
Garret FitzGerald (Foreign Affairs)
James Tully (Local Government)
Mark Clinton (Agriculture and Fisheries to 7 February 1976, then Agriculture)
Michael O'Leary (Labour)
Justin Keating (Industry and Commerce)
Tom Fitzpatrick (Lands to 1 December 1976, then Transport and Power)
Conor Cruise O'Brien (Posts and Telegraphs)
Richard Burke (Education, until he resigned on 2 December 1976 when he became a member of the European Commission)
Peter Barry (Transport and Power to 2 December 1976, then Education)
Tom O'Donnell (Gaeltacht)
Oliver J. Flanagan (Defence from 16 December 1976)
Declan Costello (Attorney-General)

Twenty-first Dáil *(5 July 1977 to 21 May 1981)*

Ceann Comhairle: Joseph Brennan (died 13 July 1980); Pádraig Faulkner

Fifteenth Government (5 July 1977 to 11 December 1979)

Fianna Fáil

The Department of Economic Planning and Development was created on 8 September 1977. In addition, the titles of some departments changed: Local Government to Environment (16 August 1977); Transport and Power to Tourism and Transport (23 September 1977); Industry and Commerce to Industry, Commerce and Energy (23 September 1977); Fisheries to Fisheries and Forestry (15 July 1978). The office of minister of state, to replace that of parliamentary secretary, was created in November 1977. Ministers of state are not members of the Government.

Jack Lynch (Taoiseach)
George Colley (Tánaiste and Minister for Finance and the Public Service)
Gerard Collins (Justice)
Michael O'Kennedy (Foreign Affairs)
James Gibbons (Agriculture)
Desmond O'Malley (Industry and Commerce; Industry, Commerce and Energy from 23 September 1977)
Brian Lenihan (Fisheries; Fisheries and Forestry from 15 July 1978)
Charles J. Haughey (Health and Social Welfare)
Pádraig Faulkner (Post and Telegraphs; Transport and Power; Tourism and Transport from 23 September 1977)
Robert Molloy (Defence)
John Wilson (Education)
Gene Fitzgerald (Labour)
Denis Gallagher (Gaeltacht)
Martin O'Donoghue (without portfolio, 5–8 July 1977; Economic Planning and Development from 8 July 1977)
Sylvester Barrett (Local Government; Environment from 16 August 1977)

Not a member of the Government
A. J. Hederman (Attorney-General)

Jack Lynch resigned and was succeeded as Taoiseach by Charles J Haughey on 11 December 1979.

Sixteenth Government (11 December 1979 to 30 June 1981)

Haughey announced that he proposed to restore the economic planning functions of the Department of Economic Planning and Development to the Department of Finance, which would become the Department of Finance and Economic Planning. The Department of the Public Service and the Department of Labour were to be brought together under one minister. Tourism and Transport changed to Transport on 25 January 1980.

Charles J. Haughey (Taoiseach)
George Colley (Tánaiste and Minister for Tourism and Transport; Energy from 22 January 1980)
Brian Lenihan (Foreign Affairs)
Pádraig Faulkner (Defence until his resignation on 15 October 1980)
Desmond O'Malley (Industry, Commerce and Energy; Industry, Commerce and Tourism from 23 January 1980)
Gerard Collins (Justice)
Michael O'Kennedy (Finance to 16 December 1980, when he resigned to become a member of the European Commission; Minister for the Public Service to 24 March 1980; Economic Planning and Development to 21 January 1981; Energy, 21–22 January 1980)
Sylvester Barrett (Environment; Defence from

15 October 1980)
Gene Fitzgerald (Labour to 16 December 1980; Public Service, 24 March 1980 to 30 June 1981; Finance, 16 December 1980 to 30 June 1981)
John Wilson (Education)
Ray MacSharry (Agriculture)
Máire Geoghegan-Quinn (Gaeltacht)
Michael Woods (Health; Social Welfare)
Patrick Power (Fisheries and Forestry)
Albert Reynolds (Posts and Telegraphs; Transport from 25 January 1980)
Ray Burke (Environment, from 15 October 1980)
Tom Nolan (Labour, 16 December 1980 to 30 June 1981)

Not a member of the Government
A. J. Hederman (Attorney-General)

Twenty-second Dáil *(30 June 1981 to 22 January 1982)*

Ceann Comhairle: John O'Connell

Seventeenth Government (30 June 1981 to 9 March 1982)

Coalition (Fine Gael and Labour Party)

The Department of Energy became the Department of Industry and Energy, 21 August 1981; Industry, Commerce and Energy became Trade, Commerce and Tourism, 21 August 1981.

Dr Garret FitzGerald (Taoiseach)
Michael O'Leary (Tánaiste and Minister for Energy)
John Bruton (Finance)
James Dooge (Foreign Affairs from 21 October 1981)
Peter Barry (Environment)
James Tully (Defence)
Tom Fitzpatrick (Fisheries and Forestry)
Eileen Desmond (Health and Social Welfare)
Liam Kavanagh (Labour; Public Service)
Patrick Cooney (Transport; Posts and Telegraphs)
John Kelly (Industry, Commerce and Tourism; Trade, Commerce and Tourism from 21 August 1981; Foreign Affairs until Senator James Dooge took up the appointment on 21 October 1981)
John Boland (Education)
Patrick O'Toole (Gaeltacht)
Jim Mitchell (Justice)
Alan Dukes (Agriculture)

Twenty-third Dáil *(9 March 1982 to 14 November 1982)*

Ceann Comhairle: John O'Connell

Eighteenth Government (9 March to 14 December 1982

Fianna Fáil

Charles J Haughey (Taoiseach and Minister for Education, 6–27 October 1982)
Ray MacSharry (Tánaiste and Minister for Finance)
Patrick Power (Defence)
Seán Doherty (Justice)
Desmond O'Malley (Trade, Commerce and Tourism until he resigned on 6 October 1982)
Gerard Collins (Foreign Affairs)
Martin O'Donoghue (Education until he resigned on 6 October 1982)
Brendan Daly (Fisheries and Forestry)
Ray Burke (Environment)
Brian J. Lenihan (Agriculture)
Michael Woods (Health and Social Welfare)
Pádraig Flynn (Gaeltacht to 27 October 1982; Trade, Commerce and Tourism from 27 October 1982)
Albert Reynolds (Industry and Energy; Trade, Commerce and Tourism, 7–27 October 1982)
Gene Fitzgerald (Labour; Public Service)
John Wilson (Transport; Posts and Telegraphs)
Denis Gallagher (Gaeltacht from 27 October 1982)
Gerard Brady (Education from 27 October 1982)

Twenty-fourth Dáil *(14 December 1982 to 29 January 1987*

Ceann Comhairle: Thomas J. Fitzpatrick

Nineteenth Government (14 December 1982 to 10 March 1987)

Coalition (Fine Gael and Labour Party)

The Department of Industry and Energy became the Department of Energy, 17 December 1983. Trade, Commerce and Tourism became Industry, Trade, Commerce and Tourism, 17 December 1983, while the latter became Industry and Commerce from 17 February 1986. Communications was taken from the Department of Transport. The Department of Post and Telegraphs was abolished on 2 January 1984. Fisheries and Forestry became Tourism, Fisheries and Forestry on 19 February 1986. The Taoiseach reshuffled the Government on 13 December 1983, following the resignation of Frank Cluskey, and again on 14 February 1986. The Labour Party members of the Government resigned on 20 January 1987, when their portfolios were reassigned.

Garret FitzGerald (Taoiseach)
Dick Spring (Tánaiste; Minister for the Environment to 13 December 1983)
Peter Barry (Foreign Affairs)
John Bruton (Industry and Energy to 13 December 1983; Industry, Trade, Commerce and Tourism to 14 February 1986; Finance from 14 February 1986)
Liam Kavanagh (Labour to 13 December 1983; Environment to 14 February 1986; Tourism, Fisheries and Energy to 19 February, when it became Tourism, Fisheries and Forestry; resigned on 29 January 1987)
Patrick Mark Cooney (Defence to 14 February 1986; Education)
John Boland (Public Service to 14 February 1986; Environment; Health from 20 January 1987)
Patrick O'Toole (Fisheries and Forestry to 14 February 1986; Gaeltacht; Defence; Tourism, Fisheries and Forestry from 20 January 1987)
Jim Mitchell (Transport; Posts and Telegraphs; Communications from 2 January 1984)
Alan Dukes (Finance to 14 February 1986; Justice)
Frank Cluskey (Trade, Commerce and Tourism until his resignation on 8 December 1983)
Barry Desmond (Health to 20 January 1987; Social Welfare to 14 February 1986; Health until his resignation on 20 January 1987)
Austin Deasy (Agriculture)
Michael Noonan (Justice to 14 February 1986; Industry, Trade, Commerce and Tourism, known as Industry and Commerce from 19 February 1986; Energy from 20 January 1987)
Gemma Hussey (Education to 14 February 1986; Social Welfare; Labour from 20 January 1987)
Ruairí Quinn (Labour from 13 December 1983; Labour and the Public Service from 14 February 1986 until his resignation on 20 January 1987)

Twenty-fifth Dáil *(10 March 1987 to 21 May 1989)*

Ceann Comhairle: Seán Treacy

Twentieth Government (10 March 1987 to 12 July 1989)

The functions of the Department of the Public Service were transferred to the Department of Finance from 19 March 1987. The Department of the Public Service was transferred to the Department of Tourism and Transport from 20 March 1987. The Department of Tourism, Fisheries and Forestry became the Department of the Marine from 20 March 1987. The Department of Agriculture became the Department of Agriculture and Food from 31 March 1987.

Fianna Fáil

Following a tie (82 to 82) Charles Haughey was elected Taoiseach on the casting vote of the Ceann Comhairle (Seán Treacy).

Charles J. Haughey (Taoiseach)
Brian Lenihan (Tánaiste and Minister for Foreign Affairs)
Ray MacSharry (Finance to 24 November 1988, when he became a member of the European Commission; Public Service, 10–20 March 1987; Tourism and Transport, 20–31 March 1987)
Gerard Collins (Justice)
John Wilson (Communications, 10–31 March 1987; Tourism and Transport from 31 March)
Michael O'Kennedy (Agriculture; Agriculture and Food from 31 March 1987)
Michael Woods (Social Welfare)
Albert Reynolds (Industry and Commerce to 24 November 1988; Finance from 24 November 1988)
Ray Burke (Energy; Communications from 31 March 1987; Industry and Commerce from 24 November 1988)
Brendan Daly (Tourism, Fisheries and Forestry; Marine from 20 March 1987)
Pádraig Flynn (Environment)
Bertie Ahern (Labour)
Rory O'Hanlon (Health)
Michael J. Noonan (Defence)
Mary O'Rourke (Education)
Michael Smith (Energy from 24 November 1988)

Twenty-sixth Dáil *(12 July 1989 to 5 November 1992)*

Ceann Comhairle: Seán Treacy

Twenty-first Government (12 July 1989 to 11 February 1992)

Charles Haughey did not secure enough support to form a Government until 12 July, when he led Fianna Fáil into its first coalition, with the Progressive Democrats, who secured two ministerial portfolios, for Desmond O'Malley and Robert Molloy. Haughey resigned on 11 February 1992. The Department of Tourism and Transport changed to Tourism, Transport and Communications from 7 February 1991.

Coalition (Fianna Fáil and Progressive Democrats)

Charles J. Haughey (Taoiseach; Minister for the Gaeltacht until his resignation on 11 February 1992; acting Minister for Defence, 1 November 1990)
Brian Lenihan (Tánaiste and Minister for Defence until dismissed on 31 October 1990)
Gerard Collins (Foreign Affairs)
Albert Reynolds (Finance until dismissed on 7 November 1991)
John Wilson (Marine; Environment, 9–14 November 1991; Tánaiste from 13 November 1990)
Michael O'Kennedy (Agriculture and Food)
Desmond O'Malley (Industry and Commerce)
Bertie Ahern (Labour to 14 November 1991; Finance)
Robert Molloy (Energy)
Joe Walsh (Agriculture and Food)
Charlie McCreevy (Social Welfare)
Ray Burke (Justice; Communications to 6 February 1991)
Brian Cowen (Labour)
Michael Woods (Social Welfare to 14 November 1991; Labour from 14 November 1991; Agriculture and Food, 14 November 1991 to 11 February 1992)
Pádraig Flynn (Environment)
Mary O'Rourke (Education)
Séamus Brennan (Tourism and Transport to 6 February 1991; Tourism, Transport and Communications, 6 February 1991 to 11 February 1992; Health, 14 November 1991 to 11 February 1992)
Brendan Daly (Defence, 5 February to 14 November 1991; Social Welfare, 14 November 1991 to 11 February 1992)
Noel Davern (Education from 14 November 1991)
Vincent Brady (Defence from 14 November 1991)

Albert Reynolds succeeded Charles Haughey as Taoiseach on 11 February 1992. The coalition government of Fianna Fáil and the Progressive Democrats continued in office.

Twenty-second Government (11 February 1992 to 12 January 1993)

Albert Reynolds (Taoiseach)
John Wilson (Tánaiste and Minister for Defence; Gaeltacht; Energy, 4 November 1992 to 12 January 1993)
Bertie Ahern (Finance)
Michael Woods (Marine; Industry and Commerce, 4–12 January 1993)
Máire Geoghegan-Quinn (Tourism, Trade and Communications; Justice, 4–12 January 1993)
Desmond O'Malley (Industry and Commerce until his resignation on 4 November 1992)
Michael Smith (Environment)
Joe Walsh (Agriculture and Food)
Charlie McCreevy (Social Welfare)
Brian Cowen (Labour)
Pádraig Flynn (Justice until 4 January 1993, when he resigned to become a member of the European Commission; Industry and Commerce, 5 November 1992 to 4 January 1993)
Robert Molloy (Energy until he resigned on 4 November)
Séamus Brennan (Education)
Dr John O'Connell (Health)

Twenty-seventh Dáil *(14 December 1992 to 15 May 1997)*

Ceann Comhairle: Seán Treacy

Twenty-third Government (12 January 1993 to 15 December 1994)

The following changes took place from 21 January 1993: the Department of Agriculture and Food changed to Agriculture, Food and Forestry; Industry and Commerce changed to Enterprise and Employment; Labour became Equality and Law Reform; the Department of the Gaeltacht became the Department of Arts, Culture and the Gaeltacht. Energy changed to Tourism and Trade on 22 January 1993. The Labour Party ministers resigned on 17 November 1994; their portfolios were re-assigned.

Coalition (Fianna Fáil and Labour Party)

Albert Reynolds (Taoiseach)
Dick Spring (Tánaiste and Minister for Foreign Affairs until he resigned on 17 November 1994)
Bertie Ahern (Finance; Tánaiste from 19 November 1994)
Michael Woods (Social Welfare; Health from 18 November 1994)
Máire Geoghegan-Quinn (Justice; Equality and Law Reform, 18 November to 12 December 1994)

Michael Smith (Environment; Education from 18 November 1994)
Joe Walsh (Agriculture; Agriculture, Food and Forestry from 21 January 1993)
David Andrews (Defence and the Marine from 12 January 1993)
Charlie McCreevy (Tourism, Transport and Communications until 22 January 1993, then Tourism and Trade)
Brian Cowen (Energy until 22 January 1993, then Transport, Energy and Communications)
Ruairí Quinn (Industry and Commerce until 21 January 1993, then Enterprise and Employment until he resigned on 17 November 1994)
Brendan Howlin (Health until he resigned on 17 November 1994)
Niamh Bhreathnach (Education until she resigned on 17 November 1994)
Michael D. Higgins (Gaeltacht until 21 January 1993, then Arts, Culture and the Gaeltacht until he resigned on 17 November 1994)
Mervyn Taylor (Labour until 21 January 1993, then Equality and Law Reform until he resigned on 17 November 1994)

Albert Reynolds resigned on 17 November 1994 but remained as Taoiseach until 15 December.

Twenty-fourth Government (15 December to 15 May 1997)

The coalition Government of Fine Gael, the Labour Party and Democratic Left (known as the 'Rainbow Coalition') was the first change of parties forming the Government without a dissolution of the Dáil.

John Bruton (Taoiseach and Minister for Transport, Energy and Commerce, 30 November to 3 December 1996)
Dick Spring (Foreign Affairs)
Ruairí Quinn (Finance)
Michael Noonan (Health)
Mervyn Taylor (Equality and Law Reform)
Michael D. Higgins (Arts, Culture and the Gaeltacht)
Brendan Howlin (Environment)
Niamh Bhreathnach (Education)
Nora Owen (Justice)
Proinsias de Rossa (Social Welfare)
Enda Kenny (Tourism and Trade)
Richard Bruton (Enterprise and Employment)
Ivan Yates (Agriculture, Food and Forestry)
Michael Lowry (Transport, Energy and Communications until his resignation on 30 November 1996)
Hugh Coveney (Defence and the Marine until his resignation on 23 May 1995)
Alan Dukes (Transport, Energy and Communications from 30 November 1996)
Seán Barrett (Defence and the Marine from 23 May 1995)

Twenty-eighth Dáil *(26 June 1997 to May 2002*

Ceann Comhairle: Séamus Pattison

Twenty-fifth Government (26 June 1997 to 6 June 2002)

Fianna Fáil and Progressive Democrats

Bertie Ahern (Taoiseach)
Mary Harney (Tánaiste and Minister for Enterprise, Employment and Trade)
Charlie McCreevy (Finance)
Noel Dempsey (Environment and Rural Development)
Mícheál Martin (Education and Science, and Technology until 27 January, then Health and Children)
John O'Donoghue (Justice and Equality and Law Reform)
Brian Cowen (Health and Children until 27 January 2000, then Foreign Affairs)
Mary O'Rourke (Transport, Energy and Communications, and Public Enterprise)
Ray Burke (Foreign Affairs, until his resignation on 7 October 1997)
Dermot Ahern (Social Welfare, Social, Community and Family Affairs)
David Andrews (Defence; Defence and the Marine; Foreign Affairs from 7 October 1997 until he resigned on 27 January 2000)
Síle de Valera (Arts, Heritage, the Gaeltacht and the Islands)
James McDaid (Tourism, Sport and Recreation)
Michael Woods (Marine and Natural Resources until 27 January 2000)
Joe Walsh (Agriculture, Food and Forestry)
Frank Fahey (Marine and Natural Resources from 27 January 2000)
David Byrne (Attorney-General)

Twenty-ninth Dáil *(6 June 2002–)*

Having led the longest-serving Government since the 1940s, Bertie Ahern became the first Taoiseach to be re-elected since Jack Lynch in 1969. He was elected Taoiseach with the highest majority in the history of the state (93 to 68).

Twenty-sixth Government (6 June 2002)

Fianna Fáil and Progressive Democrats

Ceann Comhairle: Dr Rory O'Hanlon

Bertie Ahern (Taoiseach)
Mary Harney (Tánaiste and Minister for Enterprise, Trade and Employment)
Charlie McCreevy (Finance)
Joe Walsh (Agriculture)
Brian Cowen (Foreign Affairs)
Noel Dempsey (Education and Science)
Séamus Brennan (Transport)
Martin Cullen (Environment)
Éamon Ó Cuív (Community, Rural and Gaeltacht Affairs)
Mary Coughlan (Social and Family Affairs)
Dermot Ahern (Communications and Natural Resources)
Mícheál Martin (Health and Children)
Michael McDowell (Justice, Equality and Law Reform)
John O'Donoghue (Arts, Sport and Tourism)
Michael Smith (Defence)
Rory Brady (Attorney-General)

Governor-General of the Irish Free State. In accordance with article 3 of the ANGLO-IRISH TREATY (1921) the post of Governor-General of the Irish Free State was created in December 1922. He represented the Crown in Ireland and occupied the Viceregal Lodge (now Áras an Uachtaráin) in the Phoenix Park, Dublin. ÉAMON DE VALERA abolished the office with the passing of the EXTERNAL RELATIONS ACT (1936). Under the CONSTITUTION OF IRELAND (1937) the elected President of Ireland is the head of the Irish state. The three Governors-General were T. M. HEALY, 1922–28, James MacNeill, 1928–32, and DOMHNALL UA BUACHALLA, 1932–37.

Gralton, James (1886–1945), republican socialist; born in Effernagh, Drumsna, Co. Leitrim. After working on Liverpool docks and in the Welsh coalfields he emigrated to the United States, where he became an active communist. An American citizen from 1909, he returned to Co. Leitrim, 1921, joined the IRA, and played a leading role in land agitation. He built a community hall, the Pearse-Connolly Memorial Hall, at Gowel. His communism incurred the wrath of the Catholic clergy and political opposition, and he returned to the United States, 1922–32. On his return to Ireland he founded a Co. Leitrim branch of the REVOLUTIONARY WORKERS' GROUP and also joined Fianna Fáil. He reopened the Pearse-Connolly Memorial Hall, which became the focus of an attack by the local clergy during a campaign against dancing and dancehalls; the hall was burned down, 24 December 1932. Served with a deportation order, Gralton went on the run, March 1933. A Gralton Defence Committee was formed, supported by FRANK O'CONNOR, GEORGE GILMORE, and PEADAR O'DONNELL. Following his arrest, 10 August, Gralton became the first Irish citizen to be deported from Ireland. He died in New York.

grand jury. From the time of King Charles I (1625–1649) the grand jury, described as 'the gentlemen of most consequence in the county,' was the body responsible for the administration of a county. Members were generally the leading landowners (peers could not serve); in Ireland in the nineteenth century they were generally members of the Anglo-Irish ASCENDANCY. The upper limit was twenty-three members, and the position was honorary. The grand jury met at the assizes to assist the judges on circuit. Its chief function was to strike the 'cess' or rate for the county. It also discharged responsibilities connected with the provision of asylums and fever hospitals and had the right to demand forced labour for the maintenance of roads.

The Grand Jury Presentments, the printed abstracts of the presentments as passed by the grand jury of each county, form a record of local taxation from 1663 until 1898. Under the Local Government (Ireland) Act (1898) a new system of elected county and district councils came into operation and took over the grand juries' functions. (See also LOCAL GOVERNMENT.)

Grant, Charles, Baron Glenelg (1778–1866), British politician (Whig); born in Bengal, raised in England. A member of Parliament from 1811, he was Chief Secretary for Ireland, 1818–21. During his period of office he adopted measures to conciliate the Catholic population. He unsuccessfully attempted to suppress Orange demonstrations, to establish a system of national education, and to effect changes in the police and magistracy. He was so frequently at odds with the Lord Lieutenant of Ireland, Lord Talbot, that both were recalled to London in December 1821.

Grattan, Henry (1746–1820), politician and orator; born in Dublin, educated at TCD and called to the bar. When the Irish Parliament, of which he had been a member from 1775, achieved independence in 1782 it became popularly known as 'Grattan's Parliament', though he consistently refused office in it. During the life of the Parliament he sought CATHOLIC EMANCIPATION, introducing a bill that was defeated in 1794. The rising of the UNITED IRISHMEN, 1798, greatly distressed him. Strongly opposed to the union, he declared on the abolition of the Irish Parliament, 'I sat by its cradle and I followed the hearse.' Speaking in opposition to the measure, he was allowed, because of illness, the singular privilege of addressing the Parliament while sitting. Following the Union he lived in England and remained committed to Catholic Emancipation. He is buried in Westminster Abbey.

gravedigging. Among Irish people there were many customs and ceremonies associated with burial. A grave was usually dug on the morning of a funeral or the evening before, when digging-tools were placed across the open grave in the form of a cross. By tradition, graves were not dug on a Monday unless the first sod had been cut on Sunday evening. It was considered a privilege to dig a grave, and those asked were selected in accordance with closeness of friendship with the deceased. It was also customary for the chief mourner to provide whiskey to be drunk at the graveyard by the gravediggers and important mourners.

Graves, Alfred Percival (1846–1931), poet; born in Dublin, son of CHARLES GRAVES. He was best known for *Father O'Flynn and Other Lyrics* (1889). A leader of the Literary Revival, he edited several works of Irish interest, including *The Irish Fairy Book* (1909), *The Book of Irish Poetry* (1915), *A Treasury of Irish Prose and Verse* (1915), *A Celtic Psaltery* (1917), and *The Celtic Song Book* (1928). The poet Robert Graves (1895–1985) was his son. His last years were spent at Harlech, Wales, where he wrote his autobiography, *To Return to All That* (1930), a reply to Robert's *Good-bye to All That* (1929).

Graves, Charles (1812–1899), mathematician and bishop (Church of Ireland); born in Dublin, educated at Bristol and TCD. He became a fellow of Trinity College, Dublin, in 1836 and professor of mathematics from 1843 and was elected to the Royal Irish Academy in 1837. He became dean of the Castle Chapel, Dublin, 1860, and the following year was elected president of the RIA. He became Dean of Clonfert in 1864 and was made Bishop of Limerick, Ardfert and Aghadoe in 1866. His major published mathematical work was his translation of Charles's *On the General Properties of Cones of the Second Degree and of Spherical Cones* (1841), his notes in which aroused considerable interest. Much of his work was published in the *Proceedings* of the RIA. Several of his poems appeared in *Kattabos*, while many others were printed for private circulation. He worked on the interpretation of ogham stones and successfully urged the translation of the Brehon Laws into English, 1851.

Graves, Robert James (1796–1853), physician; born in Dublin, educated at TCD. After a stay on the Continent, when he travelled with the artist Turner in the Alps and Italy, he became physician to the Meath Hospital, Dublin, 1821–43, and founded Park Street School of Medicine. He held positions at the Adelaide Hospital from 1834 and Sir Patrick Dun's Hospital, 1829–41. He pioneered 'bedside teaching', during which students, under supervision, diagnosed patients' illnesses. He was among the earliest advocates of a disciplined feeding regime to replace the accepted routine of bleeding, purging and starvation in fever cases. He was clinical lecturer at the Irish College of Physicians and president, 1843–44. His identification of Graves' disease (exophthalmic goitre) and the publication of his *Clinical Lectures on the Practice of Medicine* (1843), translated into French, German, and Italian, gained him an international reputation. He edited the fifth and last volume of *Dublin Hospital Records* in 1830.

Gray, Edmund Dwyer (1845–1888), journalist and politician (Nationalist); born in Dublin, son of SIR JOHN GRAY, whom he succeeded as proprietor of the FREEMAN'S JOURNAL. A moderate within the IRISH PARTY, he became estranged from CHARLES STEWART PARNELL, 1879, following debate on a speech made by Parnell in Limerick. Parnell accused him of cowardice. They were eventually reconciled through the offices of ARCHBISHOP CROKE of Cashel, and Dwyer put the *Freeman's Journal* behind Parnell and the LAND LEAGUE. A member of Dublin Corporation, he became lord mayor, 1880, and high sheriff, 1882. He was imprisoned for six weeks, 1882, for criticising the composition of a jury. In the bitter controversy aroused by the selection of W. H. O'SHEA to contest the Galway by-election, 1886, Dwyer and his paper supported Parnell. Having represented Co. Tipperary, 1877–80, and Co. Carlow, 1880–85, in the British House of Commons, he sat for the St Stephen's Green division of Dublin from 1885 until his death.

Gray, Sir John (1816–1875), journalist and politician (Repeal); born in Claremorris, Co. Mayo. He was editor and part proprietor of the *Freeman's Journal,* of which he became sole owner in 1850. With DANIEL O'CONNELL and others he was tried during the state trials of 1843–44. He was instrumental in securing Dublin's first efficient water supply.

Great Famine (1845–49). The famine of 1845–49, caused by the failure of the potato crop through blight, was the worst catastrophe in modern Irish history. The crisis affected Ireland adversely because of the dependence of a third of the population on the potato as the sole article of diet. The poorest tenant-farmer rented some piece of land on which to grow potatoes for consumption (see CONACRE); other crops were used to pay the rent. More than £1 million worth of foodstuffs left Ireland between July 1845 and February 1846, for which armed escorts had to be provided at the ports (see DUNGARVAN RIOT). Many vessels passed incoming charter ships bringing the hated Indian corn, known colloquially as 'Peel's Brimstone', which was distributed for relief.

Four main varieties of potato were in general use during the 1840s: the apple, black, cup, and (the most common) lumper. One of the earliest to observe the arrival of the disease in Ireland was David Moore, curator of the RDS Gardens at Glasnevin, Dublin, who noted its symptoms on 20 August 1845. An English journal, the *Gardeners' Chronicle,* proclaimed (13 September 1845):

> We stop the Press, with very great regret to announce that the Potato Murrain has unequivocally declared itself in Ireland. The crops about Dublin are suddenly perishing . . .

The potato blight (*Phytophthora infestans*) appeared in 1845 as dark brownish spots on the leaf, which, under prevailing damp conditions, quickly infected the entire plant, leading to rapid decay and the release of an offensive odour. Heavy rainfall washed spores off diseased plants onto potatoes in the soil, which rotted when harvested. Infected seed potatoes incubated the disease and helped restart the cycle. As the disease had not manifested itself until August 1845, in what had otherwise been a bumper yield, the loss of crop for that year was estimated at between 40 and 50 per cent.

SIR ROBERT PEEL, who had finally carried repeal of the Corn Laws, was replaced in office by a ministry headed by LORD JOHN RUSSELL, whose antipathy towards the 'ungrateful Irish' was widely known. At a meeting of Dublin Corporation, 28 October 1845, DANIEL O'CONNELL proposed a series of measures for presenting to the Lord Lieutenant of Ireland, BARON HEYTESBURY, including the immediate stopping of distilling and brewing, a prohibition on the export of foodstuffs, the raising of a loan of £74,000 at 4 per cent on the proceeds of the woodlands and forests of Ireland, and the levying of a 50 per cent tax on absentee landlords and a 10 per cent tax on resident landlords. The deputation, which included Lord Cloncurry, HENRY GRATTAN, and O'Connell, were quickly 'bowed out' of the Viceregal Lodge by Heytesbury.

The first food depots for famine relief opened on 28 March 1846. Relief schemes were introduced at the same time, giving employment in the building of roads, piers and bridges to some 140,000 people. These schemes were inefficiently (and in some instances corruptly) administered. The Chancellor of the Exchequer, SIR CHARLES WOOD, and Assistant Secretary of the Treasury, CHARLES EDWARD TREVELYAN, both champions of *laissez-faire,* called for an end to relief, demanding that Ireland should bear the cost of the public works. As distress mounted, the numbers on relief schemes increased, from approximately 500,000 (December 1846) to 734,000 (March 1847). Trevelyan's LABOUR RATE ACT, designed to force local landlords to pay for relief, sought an end to government schemes by 15 August 1847.

Famine conditions throughout Europe led to speculation in corn prices. In Ireland, even if food was available to the rural poor, they could not afford to buy it. As much of the work was seasonal (and involved the potato), unemployment was rife, rents went unpaid, and tenants were evicted in increasing numbers. Starving people wandered the countryside, subsisting on berries, nettles, roots, and even grass. Many landlords allowed rent reductions, while some impoverished their estates in endeavours to assist their tenants. The Poor Law system—never intended to deal with a crisis of such magnitude—proved completely inadequate, and deaths from malnutrition became a feature of the workhouses. Government grain depots were opened in the west of Ireland in December, when grain was offered to the starving at market price plus 5 per cent.

Private relief organisations were established during 1846. The Society of Friends raised £198,326, the General Central Relief Committee raised £63,000, and the Irish Relief Association raised £42,000. The BRITISH ASSOCIATION FOR THE RELIEF OF EXTREME DISTRESS raised £391,667, including a donation of £2,000 from Queen Victoria. In addition, the Society of Friends provided soup kitchens in towns. Contributions flowed in from diverse sources: the people of Calcutta contributed £16,500, citizens of Bombay £3,000, the French Society of St Vincent de Paul 110,000 francs, the Jamaican House of Assembly £2,000, the island of Antigua £144, and the Choctaw nation $170. Students at the University of Oxford sent £50; their counterparts at Trinity College, Dublin, made regular payments to the parish priest of Skibbereen, Co. Cork.

The Temporary Relief of Destitute Persons (Ireland) Act—the 'Soup Kitchens Act'—making Ireland pay for Ireland's woes, became law in January 1847. Boards of Guardians resigned in protest, and many of the public works closed. Tens of thousands were thrown onto the workhouse system. Soup became the staple diet, but there were not enough soup kitchens to meet demand, and some of those in operation produced a broth of little nutritional value. In the west of Ireland many such food sources were treated with suspicion because of the involvement of evangelicals (see SOUPERISM).

From 1847 disease was an additional element. Medical resources were grossly inadequate, but the Board of Health worked to prevent the number of deaths from mounting: from February 1847 to August 1850, 473 extra doctors were made available to its 373 fever hospitals. 'Fever sheds' were set up to accommodate the overflow; deaths from fever and disease now exceeded those from hunger. The mortality rate was especially high among those attending the sick in the workhouse: during 1847, 191 doctors and medical students died, and there were numerous deaths also among orderlies, administrators, and members of the clergy and religious orders. The Irish Fever Act placed responsibility for the provision of facilities on Relief Committees, which could call on central funds.

During 1847 the numbers dependent on soup kitchens increased from 2¾ million in May to more than 3 million in July. In July the government, while announcing that the money that had financed relief and the soup kitchens would be forgiven, ordered the closure of the soup kitchens by October. There was a low yield from the 1847 potato harvest, and as tenants were again unable to pay rents, a majority of landlords seized corn in lieu. The new Lord Lieutenant of Ireland, the EARL OF CLARENDON, arrived in May 1847, during a period of credit restriction by the Bank of England. Wood rejected his appeal to the Treasury for extra funds. The Prime Minister, Russell, announced a suspension of relief until the Irish Poor Law rate of 5 shillings in the pound (25 per cent) was collected. Nearly £1 million was collected, frequently with the use of force.

As a consequence of the rising crime rate, much of it involving assault on rent and rate collectors, the CRIME AND OUTRAGE (IRELAND) ACT (1847) was introduced, 29 November, and 15,000 additional soldiers arrived to help administer martial law. Clarendon was threatened with assassination, and a number of landlords were murdered. Frightened property-owners fled the country. Extremists in YOUNG IRELAND, who had formed the IRISH CONFEDERATION in January 1847, became more violent in tone. WILLIAM SMITH O'BRIEN, THOMAS FRANCIS MEAGHER and JOHN MITCHEL were arrested in March 1848. The TREASON FELONY ACT (1848) was introduced to deal with revolutionaries. O'Brien and Meagher were acquitted in April, but Mitchel was sentenced to fourteen years' transportation. *Habeas corpus* was suspended in July; the Young Irelanders, alarmed, attempted an abortive insurrection. Few responded to O'Brien's call, and after an affray at BALLINGARRY, Co. Tipperary, the insurrectionists were either arrested or managed to escape.

When the potato crop again failed, the Treasury ignored appeals. Officials were ordered to collect the poor rates to finance the Poor Law unions, for which no more state money was being made available. Farms were abandoned as a new wave of emigration began from among the more prosperous tenant-farmers and small businessmen. High rates with no incoming rents were having an adverse effect on landlords, many of whom had mortgaged properties. The ENCUMBERED ESTATES ACT established courts to effect the sales of bankrupt estates. At the end of December there was an outbreak of Asiatic cholera, which continued until July 1849.

As conditions showed little sign of improving, the British government was forced into action. A 'rate in aid' was to be levied from the more prosperous Poor Law unions to support those in distress. The Treasury promised £100,000, £50,000 of it immediately, while an additional 6 pence in the pound (2½ per cent) was to be paid by every Poor Law union. Opposition by landlords was supported by Twistleton, Chief Constable for the Poor Law, who resigned, calling it 'a policy of extermination.' The numbers receiving outdoor relief rose to 768,902. The Society of Friends, having done 'all that was humanly possible,' announced that it was ceasing its relief operations.

Cholera, death and attempted revolution notwithstanding, it was announced that Queen Victoria would visit Ireland, and she arrived on 1 August 1849 at Cóbh, Co. Cork (which was renamed Queenstown in her honour).

The census of 1851 recorded a population of 6,554,074 (compared with 8,177,744 in 1841); the Census Commissioners claimed that had the population continued to increase at its normal rate it would have been 9,018,799. Marriage and birth rates had also declined. The number of deaths due to the famine could not be calculated, but it is generally accepted that approximately one million people died and that the remainder of the decline was due to emigration. Many also perished aboard COFFIN SHIPS. Not until 1880 did scientists discover an effective antidote to the potato blight, the application of a copper sulphate solution.

Diseases endemic during the famine were:

Cholera. An epidemic of Asiatic cholera, which reached Belfast from Britain in the winter of 1848, ended in June 1849. The Poor Law Commissioners attributed the high level of mortality to the lack of funds provided for the prevention and treatment of the disease.

Dysentery. Caused by exposure and lack of nutritional food and liquids, it particularly affected the young.

Typhus ('black fever'). Transmitted by lice, it had a very high mortality rate.

Relapsing fever. A variant of typhus, commonly known as *fiabhras buí* ('yellow fever'), from the jaundice induced by its severe liver and gastric problems. It was a highly contagious disease, transmitted by lice. Recurrence, rather than the virulence, was a factor in its high mortality rate.

Scurvy ('blackleg'). Previously unknown in Ireland, scurvy was fatal if untreated. The Commissioners of Health attributed its appearance to

> the want and variety of food, the potato being gone . . . the eating of 'potato flour' from rotten potatoes; it was not flour at all and did not contain the elements of the potato but consisted wholly of starch as foccula, [and] . . . the use of raw or badly cooked food.

They strongly recommended the provision of cooked food. Other sources cited the substitution of Indian meal (which lacks vitamin C) for the potato as the main cause of the spread of the disease.

Xerophthalmia. Caused by a lack of vitamin A, this disease was particularly common among children. It frequently led to blindness, typically of one eye. There were 13,812 cases in 1849 and 45,947 in 1851. By 1852 there was a reduction in incidence of the disease, as famine conditions considerably eased and dietary regimes improved.

See also COFFIN SHIPS, GROSSE ÎLE, POINTE SAINT-CHARLES, and WARD'S ISLAND.

Green, Alice Stopford (1847–1929), historian and nationalist; born Alice Stopford in Kells, Co. Meath, educated privately. She married Rev. John Richard Green, 1877, for whom she acted as research assistant; she also completed his works following his death, 1883. Her first independent work was *Henry II* (1888); *The Making of Ireland and Its Undoing* (1908) was received with hostility by English reviewers. Sympathetic to HOME RULE, at the urging of her friend ROGER CASEMENT she organised the 'London Committee' to raise £1,500 for the Irish Volunteers. The money was used to buy arms brought to Ireland on the ASGARD, though she subsequently disapproved of the EASTER RISING (1916). She returned to Dublin, where her house at 90 St Stephen's Green became a fashionable meeting-place. She supported the ANGLO-IRISH TREATY (1921) and was a founder-member of CUMANN NA NGAEDHEAL. She was nominated by W. T. COSGRAVE to the first Senate of the Irish Free State, where in 1925 she supported W. B. YEATS in efforts to retain the right to divorce. Other major works were *Irish Nationality* (1911), *Ourselves Alone and Ulster* (a pamphlet riposte to Carson's policies, 1918), and *A History of the Irish State to 1014* (1925).

Greene, David (1915–1981), scholar; born in Dublin, educated at St Andrew's College, where he fell under the influence of Seán Óg Caomhánach (Seán an Chóta) and TCD. He completed studies in Oslo under Marstrander, Somerfelt and Borgstrom and worked in the Celtic Department in Trinity College, Dublin. Assistant librarian at the National Library of

Ireland until 1948, he jointly founded *Comhar* in 1942. He was a professor at the Dublin Institute of Advanced Studies, 1953–55, before his appointment to the professorship of Irish at Trinity College, where he increased the size of the department and employed Máirtín Ó Cadhain (1906–1970). Editor of *Ériu* from 1969, he was a joint founder and chairman, 1975–78, of Cumann Merriman and president of the Royal Irish Academy, 1973–76. He contributed to *A Dictionary of the Irish Language* (1943, 1948) and edited *Fingal Rónáin and Other Stories* (1955), *The Irish Language* (1966), *A Golden Treasury of Irish Poetry, AD 600–1200* (with FRANK O'CONNOR, 1967), *Irish Bardic Poetry* (with Fergus Kelly, 1970), *Duanaire Mheig Uidhir* (1972), and *Writing in Irish Today* (1972).

'Green Knights', the contemptuous name used by members of the BRUNSWICK CLUBS when referring to the ORDER OF LIBERATORS, led by DANIEL O'CONNELL.

Green Party, founded as the Ecology Party of Ireland, 1981, becoming the Green Alliance (Comhaontas Glas), 1983. This group split in 1986 on the issue of whether to become a political party; those who supported this move formed the Green Party (Comhaontas Glas) in 1987. Roger Garland became its first member of Dáil Éireann, June 1989. Thirteen Green Party councillors were elected in the local elections of 1991. Garland lost his seat in Dublin South, 1992, while Trevor Sargent won Dublin North. The party won two seats in the European Parliament in 1994 (Patricia McKenna and Nuala Ahern), and retained both seats in 1999. John Gormley became the first Green Party lord mayor of Dublin, June 1994. After being governed by a collective leadership since its founding, the Green Party elected Trevor Sargent as its first leader, 6 October 2001.

The party's seven principles were: the impact of society on the environment should not be ecologically disruptive; the conservation of resources is vital to a sustainable society; all political, social and economic decisions should be taken at the lowest effective level; society should be guided by self-reliance and co-operation at all levels; as caretakers of the Earth we have the responsibility to pass it on in a fit and healthy state; the need for world peace overrides national and commercial interests; poverty can be solved with a redistribution of the world's resources.

In the general election of 17 May 2002 the party increased its Dáil representation from two to six seats, with 3.8 per cent of first-preference votes.

Greenwood, Sir Hamar, first Viscount (1870–1948), British politician (Conservative); born in Canada. A member of Parliament from 1906, he supported DAVID LLOYD GEORGE in the rigorous opposition to the WAR OF INDEPENDENCE after accepting appointment as Chief Secretary for Ireland at the peak of the fighting, 1920. At a time when coroners' inquests had returned more than twenty verdicts of murder against members of Crown forces, he admitted to knowledge of only one such charge. Speaking in the House of Commons, 20 October 1920, he said:

> I protest with all the vigour that I can command against the suggestion that these heroes of yesterday have become murderers today . . . Men who acquiesced in, connived at, condoned or supported the murders of policemen have no right to complain of reprisals.

During a debate following the burning of Cork, 11 December 1920, he informed the House of Commons that the citizens of Cork had burned their own city. He was a member of both the British team that negotiated the ANGLO-IRISH TREATY (1921) and the Truce Observance Sub-Committee.

Gregg, Rev. John (1798–1878), bishop (Church of Ireland) and evangelical; born in Cappa, Co. Clare, educated at TCD. Ordained in 1826, he was curate at the French Church, Portarlington, ministered in Killsallaghan, Co. Dublin, and Bethesda Chapel, Dublin, 1836, and was Archdeacon of Kildare, 1857. During his term as Bishop of Cork, Cloyne and Ross, 1862–78, he began the building of St Fin Barre's Cathedral, Cork. A celebrated evangelical, he was the author of *A Missionary Visit to Achill and Erris* (1850). His son Robert Samuel Gregg (1834–1896), who completed the building of St Fin Barre's, was Archbishop of Armagh. (See also SECOND REFORMATION.)

Gregg, Tresham Dames (c. 1800–1887), cleric; born in Dublin, educated at TCD, ordained 1826. His espousal of extreme Protestantism deprived him of official appointments by ARCHBISHOP RICHARD WHATELY. Chaplain of the suffragan parish of St Nicholas Within, Dublin, he was the author of *Protestant Ascendancy Vindicated* (1840) and *Free Thoughts on Protestant Matters* (1846) as well as tracts, pamphlets, and plays.

Gregory, Lady Augusta, née Persse (1852–1932), dramatist and folklorist; born in Loughrea, Co. Galway, to an Anglo-Irish Ascendancy family, educated privately. She married Sir William Gregory, 1880, by whom she had one child, Robert Gregory (1881–1918). She took up residence at Coole Park, Gort, Co. Galway, following the death of her husband, 1892. Apart from editing her father-in-law's papers and her husband's *Autobiography* (1894), her literary career did not begin until she was almost fifty. She met W. B. YEATS in London, 1894, and again two years later when visiting the home of their mutual friend EDWARD MARTYN at Ardrahan, Co. Galway. From 1897 Yeats spent holidays at her home, collecting folklore with her in the area around Kiltartan. She assisted Yeats and Martyn in the founding of the IRISH LITERARY THEATRE, 1898, and collaborated with Yeats on *The Pot of Broth* (1902).

She was fascinated and stimulated by the wealth of stories, myth and legend of a rural tenantry that spoke English while thinking in Irish, so producing a unique idiom. To express this language she wrote in the Kiltartan dialect or 'Kiltartanese'; this led to *Cuchulain of Muirthemne* (1902), *Poets and Dreamers* (1903), and *Gods and Fighting Men* (1904). A joint founder of the ABBEY THEATRE, 1904, she accompanied the cast on its American tour, 1911, during which she met President Theodore Roosevelt and dealt with riots in New York and Philadelphia during performances of *The Playboy of the Western World* by J. M. SYNGE. She remained an active director of the Abbey until 1928, when ill-health forced her to retire to Coole Park. Between 1901 and 1928 she wrote more than forty plays, most of which were produced at the Abbey. During her later years she campaigned for the return of the art collection of her nephew HUGH LANE from England. Her home at Coole Park was open to the leading figures of the Literary Revival and to visiting literati: the famous 'autograph tree' bears the initials of Yeats, Synge, GEORGE RUSSELL, George Moore, SEÁN O'CASEY, and GEORGE BERNARD SHAW.

Her published works include *Spreading the News* (1904), *The Workhouse Ward* (1908), *The Kiltartan Handbook* (1909), *The Kiltartan Wonder Book* (1910), *The Kiltartan Molière* (1910), *Our Irish Theatre* (1913), *The Kiltartan Poetry Book* (1918), *Visions and Beliefs in the West of Ireland* (1920), and *Hugh Lane's Life and Achievement* (1921). Her *Journals, 1916–30,* were edited by Lennox Robinson in 1946.

Griffith, Arthur (1871–1922), journalist and politician (Sinn Féin); born in Dublin, educated at Strand Street Christian Brothers' School. He worked as a printer with the *Irish Independent* and the *Nation*. Through the Eblana and Leinster Debating Societies he met WILLIAM ROONEY, by whom he was deeply influenced. A founder-member of the CELTIC LITERARY SOCIETY, he was also active in the Gaelic League and was a member of the IRB until 1910. He accepted an invitation to join JOHN MACBRIDE in South Africa, where he gave support to the Boers, and helped to organise the CENTENARY CELEBRATIONS of 1898. At Rooney's request he returned to Ireland to edit a new paper, the UNITED IRISHMAN. Having founded the Irish Transvaal Society to organise Irish support for the Boers, he assisted Rooney in his founding of CUMANN NA NGAEDHEAL, 30 September 1900. While in Paris to attend the International Exhibition in 1900 he introduced MAUD GONNE to MacBride.

The Resurrection of Hungary: A Parallel for Ireland sold more than 30,000 copies in 1904. Basing his concept on the *ausgleich* between Austria and Hungary in 1867, Griffith advocated a 'dual monarchy' for Ireland and Britain. Influenced by the German economist Friedrich List (1789–1846), he advocated protective tariffs to allow light industries to develop. His principle of economic self-sufficiency for a self-governing Ireland became part of the programme of Sinn Féin. His new paper, SINN FÉIN, replaced the *United Irishman* in 1906 and continued until it was suppressed in 1914.

Griffith's Sinn Féin policy incurred the hostility of the IRISH PARTY, while his constitutionalism failed to attract a younger generation of activists. Others, however, recognised the potential use of Sinn Féin to the IRB. Opposing the Home Rule Bill (1912), Griffith called on Redmond and the Irish Party to withdraw from the British House of Commons: 'If this is liberty, the lexicographers have deceived us,' he said; borrowing an idea from DANIEL O'CONNELL, he called for the establishment of a COUNCIL OF THREE HUNDRED to govern Ireland. He opposed JAMES LARKIN in the calling of strikes, which he believed not only impaired the economy but also affected national unity. Though he joined the IRISH VOLUNTEERS, 1913, he was not invited to become a member of the Provisional Committee, lest the new organisation should be too closely identified with Sinn Féin. He took part in the HOWTH GUN-RUNNING (1914).

After the suppression of another of his papers, *Éire,* 1914–15, Griffith published a short-lived compilation, *Scissors and Paste,* in which he reproduced headlines from British, Continental and American newspapers, giving an unofficial slant to the news. NATIONALITY, which he jointly edited (with Séamus O'Kelly), followed, 1915–19. He later acquired *Young Ireland,* a children's newspaper, which he transformed into a Sinn Féin vehicle.

Though he did not take part in the EASTER RISING (1916), Griffith was arrested and imprisoned, 3 May (as the authorities erroneously believed the rising to be the work of Sinn Féin). While in Reading Jail until February 1917 he organised chess and handball tournaments and edited a weekly manuscript journal, the *Outpost.* He stood aside to allow ÉAMON DE VALERA assume the presidency of Sinn Féin while he became a vice-president. He was a member of the MANSION HOUSE COMMITTEE, 1918, which organised resistance to CONSCRIPTION, and was arrested under the 'GERMAN PLOT'. While imprisoned he was elected to represent East Cavan for Sinn Féin.

Acting President of Dáil Éireann during de Valera's American tour, Griffith was again arrested in December 1920 and held until July 1921, when he was released under the terms of the TRUCE. Shortly afterwards he was appointed to head the Irish delegation in the negotiations for a treaty, October–December 1921. Outmanoeuvred by DAVID LLOYD GEORGE, he promised he would not break off the negotiations over Ulster if all other questions were satisfactorily concluded; Lloyd George held him to this promise and gave him to understand that partition would be temporary and that a BOUNDARY COMMISSION would in effect abolish it. Griffith defeated de Valera in the election for the Presidency of Dáil Éireann and appointed MICHAEL COLLINS to the post of chairman of the PROVISIONAL GOVERNMENT. Following the general election of 16 June 1922, which resulted in a victory for pro-Treaty candidates, he agreed, under pressure from Britain, to the bombardment of the FOUR COURTS, precipitating the CIVIL WAR. Together with Collins he prosecuted the war until his death from a cerebral haemorrhage, 12 August. Griffith was the first Irish leader to be buried as a head of state.

Griffith, Sir Richard John (1784–1878), geologist and civil engineer; born in Dublin, educated at the Universities of Dublin, London, and Edinburgh. He surveyed the coal-fields of Leinster, 1808, and made a topographical survey of south Roscommon before his appointment as engineer to the Commission on Irish Bogs, 1809–12. In 1825 he became civil engineer in charge of the new Boundary Department, Dublin, charged with ascertaining the 'reputed boundaries of parishes and townlands.' His Geological Map of Ireland, compiled during his survey, became a standard reference on its adoption by the Ordnance Board, 1855. He supervised the PRIMARY VALUATION of Ireland (popularly called the Griffith Valuation), which became highly controversial, as it was 'only a relative valuation of property to regulate the taxation of Ireland, and not for the purpose of fixing a letting value.' Griffith stated that the land had been valued 'from twenty-five to thirty per cent under its letting value . . . according to a scale of agricultural prices, not according to rents.' He was deputy chairman of the Board of Works, 1846, and chairman, 1850–64, and was retained in an unpaid advisory capacity on his resignation.

The LAND LEAGUE instructed tenants that payment of rents should be offered according to the Griffith Valuation only, and if this was not acceptable, rent should be withheld.

Grosse Île, an island in the St Lawrence River 30 miles downriver from Québec, one of the quarantine stations by which Irish emigrants entered Canada during the period of the GREAT FAMINE (1845–49); the others were at Partridge Island, St John (Newfoundland), POINTE SAINT-CHARLES, STATEN ISLAND, and WARD'S ISLAND. Later described as 'the most evocative Great Famine site outside of Ireland,' it was opened as a quarantine station in 1832. The *Syria,* with eighty-four fever victims on board, was the first of the COFFIN SHIPS to arrive at the island, 15 May 1847. Four-year-old Ellen Keane, from Kilmore, Co. Mayo, was the first recorded famine victim at Grosse Île. By May 1847 thirty-six ships lay at anchor, with 12,500 passengers awaiting the port inspectorate. Between 15 May and 17 July, 2,069 deaths were recorded, requiring six men working full time to dig trenches for the dead; Father Bernard O'Reilly reported that the dead were 'stacked, corded like firewood,' awaiting burial. By the end of August 1847 there were 3,950 deaths, many of which were unrecorded. Three doctors died of fever, including Dr John Benson from Castlecomer, Co. Kilkenny, who died within a week of landing from the *Wandsworth* in May 1847. During 1847 four Catholic priests, two Anglican ministers and thirty-four others employed at the site—carters, cooks, nurses, orderlies, policemen, servants, and stewards—also died.

A three-member select committee of doctors noted in their findings: 'At our inspection of many of the vessels, we witnessed some appalling instances of what we have now stated—corpses lying in the same beds with the sick and the dying, the healthy not taking the trouble to remove them.'

The 40 per cent death rate was dramatically reduced by the introduction of new regulations, doubling immigrant tax on ships, and demanding heavy bonds for passengers likely to become a charge on the public purse.

On 15 August 1909 a 46-foot granite cross, raised by the ANCIENT ORDER OF HIBERNIANS, was unveiled on the island's highest point, Telegraph Hill. It bears an inscription in Irish, French, and English:

> Sacred to the memory of thousands of Irish emigrants, who, to preserve the faith, suffered hunger and exile in 1847–48 and stricken with fever ended here their sorrowful pilgrimage.

Grubb, Thomas (1800–1878), optical manufacturer; born in Kilkenny. Originally an engraver with the family firm, he turned to the manufacturer of reflectors and refractors for observatories, including those of Armagh, DUNSINK, Glasgow, and Melbourne. He assisted the EARL OF ROSSE in the construction of the PARSONSTOWN TELESCOPE, 1845, and was the author of several papers on the comparative and defining powers of telescopes and optical instruments.

His son, Sir Howard Grubb (1844–1931), continued the family business, patented a new type of optical gun-sight, 1900, and was an influential figure in the development of the submarine periscope.

Guildford Four. Patrick Armstrong, Gerard Conlon, Paul Hill and Carole Richardson were found guilty of bomb explosions in two public houses in Guildford and Woolwich, England, on 5 October 1974. Four soldiers and one civilian were killed and fifty-four people were injured. Following a widespread campaign in Ireland and England, claiming that the police had manufactured the confessions, the four were released after their convictions were overturned in October 1989 when the Director of Public Prosecutions announced that it would be wrong for the Crown 'to seek to sustain' the convictions.

Guinness, Sir Benjamin Lee (1798–1868), brewer and philanthropist; born in Dublin, a grandson of Arthur Guinness (1725–1803). He assumed control of Arthur Guinness, Son and Company Ltd in 1855; under his guidance the company developed a considerable export trade, and he became the richest man in Ireland. He was lord mayor of Dublin, 1851. At a cost of £150,000 he restored St Patrick's Cathedral, Dublin, 1860–65, saving the building from almost certain ruin. In recognition of this and other philanthropic acts the citizens of Dublin and the dean and chapter of the cathedral presented him with an illuminated address.

His sons Sir Arthur Edward Guinness, fist Baron Ardilaun (1840–1915), and Edward Cecil Guinness, first Earl of Iveagh (1847–1927), also involved in the brewery and in Unionist politics, were noted for their philanthropy. They financed the Dublin Exhibition of Arts and Science, 1872. Sir Arthur Guinness restored Marsh's Library, built the Coombe Lying-In Hospital, financed the laying out of St Stephen's Green, and bore half the expense of the choir of St Patrick's Cathedral. In 1899 he bought the Muckross estate in Co. Kerry, to prevent it from falling into the hands of commercial interests. During his presidency of the ROYAL DUBLIN SOCIETY, 1897–1913, he financed the publication of the society's history. Edward Cecil Guinness, Earl of Iveagh, provided £250,000 for the clearing of some seven acres of Dublin slums, donated £250,000 for the building of housing for the Dublin and London poor (£50,000 for Dublin and £200,000 for London), and donated £250,000 to the Lister Institute of Tropical Medicine.

Gúm, An, the publishing agency of the Department of Education, established by ERNEST BLYTHE as Minister for Finance, 1926, for publishing texts in Irish. Between 1926 and 1964 it published 1,465 items, consisting of 1,108 general literary works, 230 pieces of music, and 127 textbooks.

Gwynn, Denis Rolleston (1893–1971), historian; son of Stephen Lucius Gwynn (1864–1950) and great-grandson of WILLIAM SMITH O'BRIEN. He worked at the British Ministry of Information during the First World War; he claimed later, in *The Life and Death of Roger Casement* (1930), that while employed there he learnt that a senior official of the ministry, G. H. Mair, had photographed Casement's 'Black Diaries' for distribution to embassies and journalists in 1916. Gwynn was research professor of modern history at

University College, Cork, 1946–63, a prolific writer, and frequent contributor to scholarly journals of the era. His works include *The Irish Free State, 1922–27* (1928), *A Hundred Years of Catholic Emancipation* (1929), *Daniel O'Connell* (1929), *The Life of John Redmond* (1932), *De Valera* (1933), *The O'Gorman-Mahon* (1934), *John Keogh* (1935), and *Young Ireland and 1848* (1949). He edited WALTER MACDONALD's *Reminiscences of a Maynooth Professor* (1925). His autobiography, *Experiences of a Literary Man,* was published in 1926.

H

habeas corpus. The Irish Habeas Corpus Act (1782) allowed for the suspension of *habeas corpus* in times of open rebellion: this was done in times of rebellion or violent agrarian unrest, 1798, 1848, 1881, and 1920. The act was notoriously suspended on 22 July 1848 when a bill to suspend it until March 1849 passed through all its stages in one day and was rushed through the House of Lords in similar fashion the following Monday. The PROVISIONAL GOVERNMENT suspended it in 1922 to allow the execution of ERSKINE CHILDERS while a *habeas corpus* application was pending in the High Court.

Hall, Anna Maria, née Fielding (1800–1871), author; born in Dublin. Having spent most of her childhood at Bannow, Co. Wexford, she moved to London, 1815, where in 1824 she married Samuel Carter Hall (1800–1889) and collaborated on several of his books. Her early writings were published in her husband's magazine *Amulet* and were published as *Sketches of Irish Character* (1829). Her studies of Irish rural life, including *Tales of the Irish Peasantry* (1840), are an invaluable contribution to the knowledge of pre-Famine Ireland. Individually and in collaboration the Halls produced more than five hundred works. They raised the statue to THOMAS MOORE in Bromham churchyard, Wiltshire.

Hamilton, Sir William Rowan (1805–1865), astronomer and mathematician; born in Dublin, educated privately and at TCD. A child prodigy, he spoke nine languages by the age of seven and a further five by the age of fourteen. Professor of astronomy at TCD, 1827, he became Astronomer-Royal for Ireland, 1828, and began a forty-year association with DUNSINK OBSERVATORY. Knighted in 1835, he was president of the Royal Irish Academy from 1837. His discovery of the fundamental formula for quaternion multiplication came as he crossed the Royal Canal at Broome Bridge, Dublin; having no other means of recording it, he scratched the formula on the masonry of the bridge with a penknife. He also worked in dynamics and optics. His writings include *Lectures on Quaternions* (1853) and *Elements of Quaternions* (1866).

Hanna, Rev. Hugh (1821–1892), clergyman (Presbyterian) and pamphleteer; born in Dromara, Co. Down, educated at Belfast. Shortly after ordination, 1852, he embarked on the building of St Enoch's Church, the largest of Belfast's Presbyterian churches. His virulent anti-Catholic sermons, which earned him the nickname 'Roaring Hanna', frequently incited riots. In 1857 his defiance of Belfast magistrates, who had banned preaching in the city centre to avoid violence, fuelled days of rioting. A statue of Hanna was blown up in 1970 during sectarian tensions in Belfast.

Hardebeck, Carl Gilbert (1869–1945), musician and collector of traditional music; born in London of German parents, educated at the Normal School for the Blind, London, where he trained as an organist, pianist, and music teacher. Moving to Belfast, 1893, he became a music teacher following the loss of his capital in an unsuccessful musical warehousing venture. His 'God of My Salvation' won first prize at the inaugural Feis Cheoil, 1897; he won first prize every year until 1908. He was organist at St Peter's Cathedral, Falls Road, Belfast, from 1904. Having studied traditional Irish music in Co. Donegal he invented a form of braille for Irish, later adopted by the National Institute for the Blind. The writings of PATRICK PEARSE influenced him to support nationalism. Master of Cork School of Music, 1919, he also held the chair of music at University College, Cork. He travelled in Cos. Donegal, Galway, Kerry and Mayo collecting traditional songs and airs, which he published at considerable personal expense. He published *The Red Hand of Ulster* (1898), but a textbook on Irish music, begun in 1926, remained unpublished. From 1932 he was employed by the state to continue his work as a collector. After he died, in poor circumstances, the editor of the CAPUCHIN ANNUAL established a Hardebeck Testimonial Fund to aid his widow.

Hardiman, James (1782–1855), antiquarian; born near Westport, Co. Mayo. The family moved to Galway in his childhood, where his father became a shopkeeper. He was intended for the priesthood, but he had only one eye, and prevailing rules excluded those with a physical disability from pursuing a vocation without Papal permission. By the time the dispensation arrived some nine years later Hardiman, who had meanwhile studied law, was pursuing a career at the PUBLIC RECORD OFFICE, where he employed JOHN O'DONOVAN as assistant, 1827–30. From 1827 he travelled through Cos. Longford and Roscommon gathering airs, traditional tales and verse and visiting the blind poet Antaine Ó Reachtaire ('Raiftearaí'). He refused the professorship of Irish at Queen's College, Galway, and was instrumental in the founding of the Irish Archaeological Society, 1840, of which he became librarian. He was an influential member of the Royal Irish Academy, for which he made a number of translations, including *Ancient Irish Deeds and Writings*. He was also instrumental in the founding of the CELTIC SOCIETY, 1845. His publications include *History of the Town and County of Galway* (1820), *Irish Minstrelsy, or Bardic Remains of Ireland, with English Poetical Translations* (2 vols., 1831), *The Statutes of Kilkenny* (1843), and an edition of O'Flaherty's *Iar-Connacht*, which he edited in 1846.

Hardwicke, Philip Yorke, third Earl of (1757–1834), British politician. As Lord Lieutenant of Ireland, 1801–06, he was the first post-Union Viceroy. Criticised by the parliamentary opposition for his leniency in dealing with the abortive rising of ROBERT EMMET (1803), he successfully argued that he had not required all available powers to effectively quell the insurrection. His insistence on the independence of the Irish Office in relation to the dispersion of patronage brought him into frequent conflict with the government; he engaged in a celebrated conflict with WILLIAM PITT when refusing to sanction a pension of £1,200 a year for the Prime Minister's nominee Isaac Corry (1755–1813), a Union supporter, who had been wounded in a duel with HENRY GRATTAN. He was sympathetic to Catholic grievances and on his return to London supported CATHOLIC EMANCIPATION.

Hardy, Philip Dixon (1793–1875), poet, printer, bookseller, and publisher; born in Dublin, educated at TCD. Hardy introduced steam printing into Ireland, 1833, and printed leading publications of the time, including the *Dublin Penny Journal* from its second edition. Beginning with *The Northern Tourist* (1830), he was one of the earliest Irish publishers to produce a comprehensive range of tourist guides. His poetry included *Bertha: A Tale of Erin* (1817) and *The Pleasure of Religion and Other Poems* (1869).

Harland, Sir Edward James (1831–1896), shipbuilder and politician (Conservative and Unionist); born in Scarborough, Yorkshire. Following apprenticeship with the shipbuilders Robert Stephens and Company of Newcastle upon Tyne he became manager of Robert Hickson's shipyards at Queen's Island, Belfast, 1854, and bought the company, 1858, for £5,000. After Gustav William Wolff (1834–1913), a native of Hamburg, became a partner, January 1862, they were joined in partnership by the chief draughtsman, WILLIAM JAMES PIRRIE, 1874. By 1914 Harland and Wolff had become Belfast's largest employer, with more than 12,000 employees. Under Pirrie's management the company built the *Iroquois* (1907), then the world's largest oil tanker, and the *Titanic* (1911), the world's largest liner. Harland, who was chief harbour commissioner of Belfast, 1875–87, was lord mayor, 1885 and 1886, and represented North Belfast in the British House of Commons from 1887 until his death.

Harney, Mary (born 1953), politician (Fianna Fáil and Progressive Democrats); born in Ballinasloe, Co. Galway, educated at TCD. At Trinity she was active in Ógra Fhianna Fáil and the first woman auditor of the Historical Society. Failing to secure a seat in Dáil Éireann in the 1977 general election, she became the youngest person appointed to Seanad Éireann as a nominee of the Taoiseach, JACK LYNCH. A member of Dublin County Council from 1979, she was elected to the Dáil for Dublin South-West in 1981. Expelled from Fianna Fáil for supporting the ANGLO-IRISH AGREEMENT (1985), she jointly founded the PROGRESSIVE DEMOCRATS (with DESMOND O'MALLEY), 21 December 1985. She was Minister for Environmental Protection in the coalition government of Fianna Fáil and the Progressive Democrats, 1989. On O'Malley's retirement from leadership of the Progressive Democrats she became the first woman to head a political party in the Republic, 12 October 1993. Though the party returned with only four seats following the general election of 1997, the Progressive Democrats were again in a coalition government with Fianna Fáil, in which Harney was Tánaiste and Minister for Trade and Employment. Her tenure, at a time of unprecedented economic boom, was marked by a number of inquiries that she instigated into the operation of financial institutions in the wake of revelations of irregular practices in the banking industry, 1998 (see ANSBACHER INQUIRY). She was embroiled in a number of controversies, notably her comment in 1999 that CHARLES HAUGHEY should be imprisoned, prompting Mr Justice Kevin Haugh to declare that a trial could not now be held, as the remarks were prejudicial to a fair trial. Her opposition to the proposed Stadium Ireland project promoted by the Taoiseach, BERTIE AHERN, led to a detailed cost analysis and subsequent scaling down of the project. In April 2001 she claimed she had not been consulted over his allocation of £60 million to the GAA. She was again Tánaiste and took the Industry, Trade and Employment portfolio in the coalition government that took office on 6 June 2002.

Harp Society (Belfast), founded in 1808 by Dr James MacDonnell and EDWARD BUNTING. The society aimed to present blind children with an opportunity to earn a living through playing the harp. Its president was Lord O'Neill; other members included Rev. James Bryson and Rev. John McCracken. It remained active until 1830, when many of its functions and much of its membership were absorbed by Ulster Gaelic Society.

Harrington, Timothy Charles (1851–1910), politician (Nationalist) and land agitator; born in Castletown Bearhaven, Co. Cork, educated at TCD. A teacher, he founded and edited the *Kerry Sentinel*, 1877, and used it to further land agitation. Member of Parliament for Co. Kerry, 1880, he became secretary of the LAND LEAGUE, 1882, and was twice imprisoned. While honorary secretary of the IRISH PARTY he was the architect of the PLAN OF CAMPAIGN. Called to the bar, 1887, he was counsel for CHARLES STEWART PARNELL during the sittings of the commission on 'PARNELLISM AND CRIME', 1888–89. He was in the United States, 1891, on a fund-raising mission when the split in the Irish Party occurred over the O'Shea divorce issue, after which he supported Parnell; on Parnell's death he supported JOHN REDMOND. He was lord mayor of Dublin, 1901–02, and continued to sit in the British House of Commons as a member of the Irish Party until his death.

Harris, Matthew (1825–1891), Fenian and politician (Nationalist); born in Ballinasloe, Co. Galway, educated at a hedge school. He became a successful building contractor and political activist and a supporter of YOUNG IRELAND, the TENANT LEAGUE, and DANIEL O'CONNELL. A member of the Supreme Council of the IRB, he was the movement's chief arms supplier for the Connacht circles. Following the abortive Fenian rising of 1867 he turned to constitutional politics. An influential figure in agrarian politics in the west, he founded Ballinasloe Tenants' Defence Association and forged a reputation as an orator. Elected member of Parliament for Galway East, 1880, he was critical of clerical interference in politics and was one of the first to condemn the Papal rescript (decree) of 1888.

Harrison, Henry (1867–1954), writer and politician (Irish Party); born in Holywood, Co. Down, educated at the University of Oxford, where he was secretary of the Oxford Union Home Rule Group. A lifelong supporter of CHARLES STEWART PARNELL, he represented Mid-Tipperary in Parliament, 1890–92. During the PLAN OF CAMPAIGN he was one of a group arrested, 17 April 1889, while delivering food to tenants on the Olphert estates in Co. Donegal. He was acquitted on all charges. Commissioned as an officer in the British army, 1915, he was later secretary to the IRISH DOMINION LEAGUE, Irish correspondent of the *Economist,* 1922–27, and editor of *Irish Truth,* 1924–27. In 1947 he challenged the *Times* (London) when its *History of the Times* distorted the facts concerning the Pigott forgeries in its series 'PARNELLISM AND CRIME'; the fourth volume of the history acknowledged the misrepresentation and included a corrigendum. Among Harrison's works were *Parnell Vindicated* (1931), *Ireland and the British Empire* (1937), *Parnell, Joseph Chamberlain and Mr. Garvin* (1938), *Ulster and the British Empire* (1939), and *The Nationality of Ireland* (1942). His last work, *Parnell, Joseph Chamberlain and the Times,* was published in 1953.

Haughey, Charles J. (born 1925), politician (Fianna Fáil); born in Castlebar, Co. Mayo, raised in Dublin, educated at UCD and King's Inns. A founder of the accountancy firm Haughey and Boland, 1950, and a son-in-law of SEÁN LEMASS, he was elected to Dáil Éireann, 1957, becoming Parliamentary Secretary to the Minister for Justice, 1960–61, Minister for Justice, 1961–64, and Minister for Agriculture and Fisheries, 1964–66. As Minister for Finance in JACK LYNCH's first government, 1966–70, he introduced schemes to aid weaker sections of the community, especially the elderly, and established Aosdána, aimed at supporting creative artists. He survived his dismissal from the Government, May 1970, amid allegations that attempts had been made to smuggle arms illegally into the Republic; following acquittal at the ARMS TRIALS he remained a member of Fianna Fáil and returned to office as Minister for Health and Social Welfare, 1977–79.

He became Taoiseach on 11 December 1979 (by a vote of 82 to 62). Though he identified serious economic problems facing the country and called for fiscal rectitude, his first budget ignored his own analysis. Having declared Northern Ireland a 'failed political entity,' 16 February 1980, he issued a joint communiqué with Margaret Thatcher, 21 May 1980, agreeing that 'any change in the constitutional status of Northern Ireland would only come about with the consent of the majority of the people of Northern Ireland.' The Fianna Fáil election campaign in 1981 was damaged by H BLOCKS candidates, two of whom were elected. In opposition, Haughey rejected the call of the Taoiseach, GARRET FITZGERALD, for a 'constitutional crusade', declared that articles 2 and 3 of the Constitution of Ireland asserted 'the belief that this island should be one political unit,' and denounced plans for an Anglo-Irish Intergovernmental Council. Before the 1982 general election Haughey and Fitzgerald met for the first televised debate between the two principal contestants, 16 February.

Fianna Fáil again failed to secure an overall majority. Having secured the support of the Workers' Party, NEIL BLANEY, and the independent TD Tony Gregory (in return for a deal that Gregory estimated would cost the government £150 million but that political analysts claimed fulfilled aspects of Fianna Fáil policy), Haughey returned as Taoiseach on 9 March (by a vote of 86 to 79). In an attempt to halt the decline in national finances his government announced plans, 30 July, to cut £120 million from public spending by the end of the year. He survived a motion of no confidence, 6 October (58 to 22). He called a general election, offering stringent measures to deal with the country's deteriorating economic plight. Fianna Fáil lost the election, and a coalition government of Fine Gael and the Labour Party was installed, with FitzGerald as Taoiseach, 14 December.

Amid allegations of the tapping of the phones of two journalists (Bruce Arnold and Geraldine Kennedy) and the recording of a conversation between the Minister for Finance, Ray MacSharry, and a former Fianna Fáil minister, Dr Martin O'Donoghue, 21 October 1982, speculation mounted that Haughey was about to resign the leadership of the party. The *Irish Press* published his political obituary, 27 January 1983; but a motion to force his resignation was defeated, 7 February (40 to 33). Haughey rejected FitzGerald's attempts to change the wording of an amendment to the Constitution of Ireland to prevent abortion. The amendment, carried by a two-to-one majority, later gave rise to constitutional issues (see X CASE).

Haughey participated in the deliberations of the NEW IRELAND FORUM but insisted that a unitary state with a new constitution was the only acceptable option of the three on offer. When DESMOND O'MALLEY criticised the lack of debate within the party, Haughey secured his expulsion from the parliamentary party (56 to 16). Fianna Fáil took eight of the fifteen seats in the elections to the European Parliament, 14 June 1984—the first overall majority in an election since he assumed the leadership. Following her expulsion from the party MARY HARNEY joined O'Malley in founding the PROGRESSIVE DEMOCRATS. Two other Fianna Fáil deputies (Bobby Molloy and Pierce Wyse) joined the new party in January 1986.

The fourteen seats won by the Progressive Democrats in the general election of 17 February 1987 denied Haughey a majority. Returning to government on the casting vote of the Ceann Comhairle, and committed to stringent fiscal rectitude, he appointed Ray MacSharry Minister for Finance. In tackling economic problems the new government benefited from the support of the leader of Fine Gael, ALAN DUKES, in the 'Tallaght Strategy'. Haughey enjoyed great popularity despite presiding over tough policies. Then, in 1989, with only half his term served, he called another general election, 15 June, and returned with four fewer seats. He led the party into its first coalition government, allocating the Progressive Democrats three ministerial posts. Opposition to his leadership centred on a group, mainly from Connacht (the 'western alliance'), who wished to replace him with ALBERT REYNOLDS.

While MacSharry took draconian measures in dealing with the economy, Haughey's last term in power was dogged by controversy. The party's links to the meat industry (see BEEF TRIBUNAL), a land deal that saw the chairman of Telecom Éireann, Michael Smurfit, 'stepping aside' from his role, and the sale of Carysfort Training College attracted widespread criticism. Having survived another motion of no confidence, 10 November 1991, following claims by Seán Doherty (a former Minister for Justice) that Haughey was aware of the tapping of journalists' phones and that he had supplied Haughey with transcripts, the Progressive Democrats made Haughey's resignation a matter of the government's survival. He resigned, to be succeeded by Reynolds on 10 February 1992.

By the time of Haughey's retirement there was some agreement that his achievements included work for the elderly, the arts, the redevelopment of the Temple Bar area of Dublin, and the establishment of the Irish Financial Services Centre and National Treasury Agency.

In 1997 the MCCRACKEN TRIBUNAL and later the MORIARTY TRIBUNAL investigated Haughey's finances; it emerged that, from the 1960s, a circle of wealthy patrons organised by DES TRAYNOR had financed his lavish life-style, estimated on occasion to have cost £25,000 per month.

'Hawarden Kite'. In an unauthorised disclosure on 16 December 1885, Herbert Gladstone, son of W. E. GLADSTONE, 'flew a kite' by informing Dawson Rogers of the National Press Agency that his father (whose home was at Hawarden Castle in Wales) now favoured HOME RULE as a solution to the 'Irish question'. The publication of the announcement the next day in the *Leeds Mercury* and the *Standard* alienated Conservative support for any measure of home rule. CHARLES STEWART PARNELL then entered into an alliance with Gladstone and the Liberals. When the Liberals returned to power, January 1886, their commitment to home rule was a factor in the division that followed within that party.

Hayden, Mary (1882–1942), scholar, historian, and social campaigner; born in Dublin, educated at the Royal University of Ireland. As a woman she was refused a professorship at the Royal University, 1902. She was joint founder and vice-president of the Irish Association of Women Graduates, 1903, and the only woman elected to the Senate of the National University of Ireland, 1909–24. Appointed first professor of modern Irish history at University College, Dublin, 1911, she held the post for twenty-seven years. A member of the Executive Council of the Gaelic League, she was close to PATRICK PEARSE but did not approve of the EASTER RISING (1916). With George A. Moonan she published *A Short History of the Irish People* (2 vols., 1920, revised 1921), which remained a standard text until the 1960s.

Haydn, J. T. [Joseph] (1786–1856), journalist and editor; born in Limerick. He edited the pro-establishment paper PATRIOT, 1812–22, founded the *Statesman,* 1828, and was editor of the *Dublin Evening Mail.* Returning to Limerick, he founded the *Limerick Star* and *Limerick Times.* He moved to London, 1839, where he continued his journalistic career. He edited Samuel Lewis's *Topographical Dictionary* (4 vols., 1849); his pioneering *Dictionary of Dates* (1841) ran to twenty-five editions before 1900.

Hayes, Rev. John (1887–1957), priest and social reformer; born in a LAND LEAGUE hut at Ballyvoreen, Co. Limerick, educated at Doon Classical School and Crescent College, Limerick. Ordained in 1913; following studies at St Patrick's College, Thurles, and the Irish College, Paris, he served at Kilbeg, Co. Meath, 1913–15, the House of Missions, Wexford, 1915, and Mount Carmel, Liverpool, 1915–23. In 1920 he participated in a protest outside Wormwood Scrubs Prison, London, to draw attention to the plight of republican hunger-strikers, who included his brother Mick. He was a curate at Ballybricken, Co. Limerick, 1923–27, and Castleiny, Co. Tipperary, 1927–34, and served in Tipperary before his appointment as parish priest of Bansha, Co. Tipperary, 1946–57. His concern to halt rural decline and to revitalise rural areas inspired him to found MUINTIR NA TÍRE.

Hayes, Michael (1889–1976), scholar and politician (Sinn Féin, Cumann na nGaedheal, and Fine Gael); born in Dublin, educated at UCD and called to the bar. Assistant in the French Department of University College, Dublin, 1912, he was a member of the Gaelic League and the Irish Volunteers and a supporter of James Larkin during the DUBLIN LOCK-OUT (1913). In the EASTER RISING (1916) he fought in Jacob's factory, Bishop Street, Dublin, under THOMAS MACDONAGH, after which he was imprisoned. Active in SINN FÉIN, he was imprisoned in Mountjoy and Arbour Hill prisons, Dublin. While imprisoned in Ballykinler, Co. Down, during the WAR OF

INDEPENDENCE he was director of education for the prisoners, organising classes in Irish, English, French, Spanish and history, and was elected to the second Dáil Éireann; he took his seat on his release, August 1921. He supported the ANGLO-IRISH TREATY (1921) and was Minister for Education, January to September 1922, and Minister for External Affairs, August to September. He was Ceann Comhairle of Dáil Éireann, 1922–32.

Having lost his seat in the general election of January 1933 he sat in Seanad Éireann, 1933–65, of which he was twice leader, 1948–51 and 1954–57. A lecturer in Modern Irish at UCD, 1933–51, and professor, 1951–60, he was a member of the Royal Irish Academy, the Governing Body of UCD, the Senate of the National University of Ireland, and the Royal Society of Antiquaries of Ireland. For a number of years he was a member of the National Council of Fine Gael.

Hayes, Dr Richard (1882–1958), scholar and politician (Sinn Féin); born in Bruree, Co. Limerick, educated locally, where he was influenced by REV. EUGENE SHEEHY; ÉAMON DE VALERA was a boyhood friend. Having obtained a medical position at Lusk, Co. Dublin, he joined the IRISH VOLUNTEERS and took part in the BATTLE OF ASHBOURNE (1916), for which he received a twenty-year prison sentence. Elected to the first Dáil Éireann for East Limerick, he supported the Anglo-Irish Treaty (1921), which he described as 'a compromise without dishonour.'

He withdrew from political life, 1924, to devote himself to his medical practice and to writing. His exhaustive study of the Wild Geese (Irish military emigrants) led to the publication of *Ireland and Irishmen in the French Revolution* (1932). The recipient of several awards, including membership of the Legion of Honour, he was a director of the ABBEY THEATRE from 1934 and vice-president of the Military History Society of Ireland. He was Film Censor, 1940–54. His other works include *Irish Swordsmen in France* (1934), *The German Colony in Co. Limerick* (1937), *The Last Invasion of Ireland* (1937), and *Biographical Dictionary of Irishmen in France* (1940).

Hayes, Richard J. (1902–1976), bibliographer; born in Abbeyfeale, Co. Limerick, educated at TCD (where he was believed to be the only person to take three simultaneous degrees—Celtic studies, modern languages, and philosophy; he was later awarded a doctorate in law). He worked at the National Library of Ireland from 1926 and was director from 1940 until his retirement in 1967. He published *Comparative Idiom* (1927), an introduction to the study of modern languages, and *Clár Litridheachta na Nua-Ghaedhilge, 1850–1936* (vol. 1, with Brighid Ní Dhonnchadha, 1938, vols. 2 and 3, 1938–40), a bibliography covering 1,000 books, 7,000 poems, and 18,000 essays. During the years of the SECOND WORLD WAR he was employed by Military Intelligence as a cryptologist and in the interrogation of German spies, including HERMAN GÖRTZ.

Significant events during his directorship of the National Library were the acquisition of the Lawrence Collection (see WILLIAM LAWRENCE) in 1942, the merger of the Genealogical Office with the National Library in 1943, and the procurement of manuscripts and first editions from GEORGE BERNARD SHAW in response to a personal letter to the writer. His magnum opus, the eleven-volume *Manuscript Sources for the History of Irish Civilisation* (1965), contains more than 300,000 entries from more than 1,300 archival sources in thirty countries. This was followed by *Sources for the History of Irish Civilisation: Articles and Periodicals* (1970), containing more than 270,000 entries from articles in more than 200 journals and periodicals published in Ireland between 1800 and 1967. Following his retirement from the National Library he became honorary librarian of the CHESTER BEATTY LIBRARY. He was a member of the ARTS COUNCIL, a director of the board of the ABBEY THEATRE, a member of the Cultural Experts Committee of the Council of Europe, and the recipient of numerous honorary degrees.

Hayes-McCoy, G. A. [Gerard Anthony] (1911–1975), historian; born in Galway, educated at UCG and the Universities of Edinburgh and London. He was an assistant keeper in the National Museum, 1939–58, and professor of history at University College, Galway, 1959–75. A member of the Royal Irish Academy and the Irish Manuscripts Commission, he was joint founder of the Military History Society of Ireland and editor of its journal, the *Irish Sword*, 1949–60. He was the author of *Scots Mercenary Forces in Ireland* (1939), *Irish Battles: A Military History of Ireland* (1969), *A History of Irish Flags* (1979) and three chapters of the *New History of Ireland, Vol. 3* (1976) and editor of *The Irish at War* (1964).

H blocks, special blocks established at the Maze Prison (then called Long Kesh), Lisburn, Co. Antrim, in 1976 for holding terrorist prisoners in accordance with recommendations of the GARDINER REPORT. The blocks were shaped like the letter H, with four wings to each block and each block holding 100 cells. Republican prisoners reacted to the abolition of SPECIAL CATEGORY status on 4 November 1975 by refusing to wear prison clothing from the spring of 1978, wearing blankets instead (see BLANKET PROTEST). The H blocks remained continually in the news with the HUNGER STRIKES of 1980–81. On 6 October 1981, three days after the hunger strikes had ended, the Secretary of State for Northern Ireland announced that all prisoners would be allowed wear their own clothes. On 25 September 1983 thirty-eight Provisional IRA prisoners staged the biggest break-out in Irish prison history (half were quickly recaptured). In 1991, when the H blocks contained some four hundred prisoners, the special category was abolished. The H blocks were closed in 1997.

Healy, John (1930–1991), journalist; born near Charlestown, Co. Mayo, educated at St Nathy's College, Ballaghaderreen. He began his journalistic career with the *Western People* in 1948 and worked with the short-lived *Sunday Review* (Dublin) before joining the *Irish Times* as a political journalist, where he established his 'Backbencher' column; inside information from impeccable sources ensured his position as the best-informed correspondent in the country and raised political journalism to a new level; he later wrote the 'Sounding Off' column for the *Irish Times.* He also worked on the *Western Journal.* A passionate man and a talented artist (with his wife he ran the Achill Art Gallery, Co. Mayo), he was concerned with the issue of rural depopulation in the west, not least his native Charlestown region, reflected in *Death of an Irish Town* (1967), based on a series of articles published in the *Irish Times,* and *Nineteen Acres* (1978).

Healy, T. M. [Timothy] (1855–1931), politician (Nationalist) and author; born in Bantry, Co. Cork, educated at Fermoy Christian Brothers' School. He left Lismore, Co. Waterford, at the age of thirteen to live with his aunt and her husband, T. D. SULLIVAN, in Dublin until March 1872, when he moved to Newcastle upon Tyne, where he worked as a railway clerk. At Sullivan's behest he moved to London, 1878, to contribute a political column to the *Nation*; in this capacity he reported the role played by the IRISH PARTY in the British House of Commons and the emergence of CHARLES STEWART PARNELL. He served as Parnell's secretary during the American tour of 1880; he was the first to refer to Parnell as the 'uncrowned king of Ireland' (during a triumphant reception in Montréal). Member of Parliament for Co. Wexford, 1880–83, Co. Monaghan, 1883–85, Longford North, 1887–92, Louth North, 1892–1910, and Cork North-East, 1911–18, he supported the policy of obstructionism in the House of Commons and came to be feared for the severity of his language and biting sarcasm. He was responsible for the incorporation of the 'Healy clause' in the Land Law (Ireland) Act (1881) (see LAND ACTS), ensuring that tenants' improvements did not result in rent increases.

Healy drafted the constitution for the Irish Party's new constituency organisation, the IRISH NATIONAL LEAGUE. Called to the bar, 1884, he became a leader in the PLAN OF CAMPAIGN, 1886–91, and was disappointed at Parnell's lack of support for the tactic. He was particularly insensitive during the crisis provoked by Parnell's involvement in the O'Shea divorce and in the ensuing leadership struggle: he referred to the ending of the alliance between the Irish Party and the Liberals as having 'perished in the stench of the divorce court'; during discussions on the leadership, when Parnell was referred to as 'master of the party,' Healy interjected: 'Who is mistress of the party?' This remark caused an emotional Parnell to refer to Healy as 'that cowardly little scoundrel there who dares, in an assembly of Irishmen, to insult a woman.'

Healy established the *National Press,* 7 March 1891. He was expelled from the Executive of the Irish National League of Great Britain, 7 November 1895, and from the Irish National Federation a week later; on 14 November he was voted off the Committee of the Irish Party. He was counsel for WILLIAM MARTIN MURPHY during the inquiry into the DUBLIN LOCK-OUT (1913) and also worked as counsel for suffragists. To the surprise of many he was chosen as first Governor-General of the Free State, 6 December 1922, and held the office until 1928, the last survivor of the old Irish Party to play a significant role in Irish politics. His writings include *A Record of Coercion* (1881), *There Is an Irish Land Question and an Irish Land League* (1881), *Loyalty plus Murder* (1884), *Key to the Land Law (Ireland) Act* (with his brother Maurice Healy MP, 1887), *Under*

Which Flag? or Is Parnell to Be Leader of the Irish People? (1890), *Why Ireland Is Not Free* (1898), and *Letters and Leaders of My Day* (2 vols., 1928).

Heaney, Seamus (born 1939), poet; born in Mossbawn, Co. Derry, educated at QUB. A secondary teacher and lecturer at Queen's University, 1966–72, he moved to Co. Wicklow, 1972, then to Co. Dublin, 1976, where he lectured at Carysfort Training College, Blackrock. Joint founder of Field Day, 1980, he became Boylston professor of poetry, rhetoric and oratory at Harvard University, Massachusetts, 1984, and professor of poetry at the University of Oxford, 1989. He was awarded the Nobel Prize in Literature, 1995, 'for an authorship filled with lyrical beauty and ethical depth which brings out the miracles of the ordinary day and the living past.' Following the publication of *Death of a Naturalist* in 1966, his works include *Door Into the Dark* (1969), *Wintering Out* (1972), *North* (1975), *Field Work* (1979), *New Selected Poems* (1966–87), *Preoccupations* (essays and lectures, 1980), *Sweeney Astray* (1983), *Station Island* (1984), *The Haw Lantern* (1987), and *The Spirit Level* (1997). *The Cure at Troy* (1990), his version of Sophocles' *Philoctetes,* was his first venture into theatre; *Ugolini* was his dramatic reworking of Dante. He jointly edited *The Rattle Bag* (with Ted Hughes, 1982); another collaboration, *The School Bag,* was published in 1999. His translation of *Beowulf* was a best-seller in 1999.

Heath, Edward (born 1916), British politician (Conservative). As British Prime Minister, 1970–74, Heath acknowledged in 1971 that the desire by Northern Catholics for a united Ireland 'by democratic and constitutional means' was 'legitimate,' but 'that was not what the majority [in Northern Ireland] want today.' He suspended the Northern Ireland government and introduced direct rule from London, March 1972, when the ULSTER UNIONIST PARTY refused to relinquish control of security. He secured agreement to 'power-sharing' (multi-party government) in the SUNNINGDALE AGREEMENT, December 1973.

Heath was cross-examined for a week during the SAVILLE INQUIRY, January 2003, when he rejected suggestions that he had authorised the British army to shoot into the crowd on BLOODY SUNDAY, 30 January 1972.

'Heavy Gang'. A series of articles in the *Irish Times* during 1976, by Joe Joyce and Don Buckley, claimed that a 'Heavy Gang' existed within the GARDA SÍOCHÁNA, allegedly specialising in mental, physical and verbal intimidation to extract confessions from republicans suspected of involvement in serious crime. The claim was supported by information from victims, lawyers, doctors, and some members of the force. Two gardaí approached GARRET FITZGERALD, Minister for Foreign Affairs in the Cosgrave government, with specific information, but it was not acted on. The 'gang', believed to have a floating membership based on a nucleus of detectives attached to the Special Investigation Unit, appeared to use methods similar to those used in Northern Ireland in the early 1970s, some of which had been condemned by the European Committee on Human Rights in a case instituted by Ireland against the British government. Having examined twenty-eight complaints in 1977, Amnesty International found that detectives who favoured the use of oppressive methods in extracting statements carried out maltreatment systematically. The EMERGENCY POWERS ACT (1976), under which the system largely operated, was allowed to lapse by the incoming Fianna Fáil government in 1977.

hedge schools, informal schools that became widespread during the eighteenth century to provide education for Catholics, who were prevented by the Penal Laws from attending schools either in Ireland or abroad. The historian W. E .H. Lecky wrote: 'The legislation on the subject of Catholic education may be briefly described, for it amounted to universal, unqualified, and unlimited proscription.' To avoid fines or imprisonment, teachers taught pupils secretly; they were often itinerant educators, establishing their schools where they could, sometimes in the open air.

The hedge-school curriculum included English, Irish, Latin, Greek, history, geography, arithmetic, bookkeeping, navigation, and surveying. Finding suitable texts was a perennial problem, and students were often taught from such works as Chesterfield's *Rules of Politeness, The Devil and Dr Faustus, Fair Rosamund and Jane Shore* (a story of two prostitutes), *The History of Witches and Apparitions, Irish Rogues and Rapparees, Moll Flanders,* Ovid's *Art of Love,* and the biography of Freney the highwayman. Payment to the schoolmaster depended on the size of the school, the standing of the teacher, and the need for education: it could be as little as £20 a year or as much as £50; one teacher lamented that he had taught school for 6 pence per quarter. But generally the teacher would also receive payment in kind, including butter, fowl, turf, or vegetables. He was a respected figure in the community and was frequently called to assist when letters had to be written; he was also consulted on the drawing up of wills and leases, the measuring of land, or arbitrating in disputes. According to T. CROFTON CROKER, writing of the celebrated Munster hedge schoolmasters, 'next to the lord of the manor, the parson, and the priest, he is the most important personage in the parish.'

Among the most famous poets of the eighteenth century there were several hedge-school masters, including Donncha Rua Mac Conmara (1715–1810), Eoghan Rua Ó Súileabháin (1748–1784), and Brian Merriman (1747–1805). Others included Philip Fitzgibbon, who died in Kilkenny in 1792 and is for ever enshrined in the annals of lexicography (he neglected to include the letter *S* in his Irish dictionary); Peter O'Connell from Co. Clare, who spent forty years in the compilation of an Irish dictionary, published, following his death in Kilrush, c. 1826, by JAMES HARDIMAN; Patrick Lynch, also from Co. Clare, who taught all over Ireland, published several textbooks, and became secretary of the GAELIC SOCIETY in 1815; and Amhlaoibh Ó Súileabháin (1783–1838), who taught with his father at Callan, Co. Kilkenny, and whose diary was published by the Irish Texts Society. David Mahony taught four-year-old DANIEL O'CONNELL the alphabet in less than two hours, while James Nash of Co. Waterford believed in flogging the boys every morning, 'to teach them to be Spartans.' Other well-known teachers were Richard McElligott, T. M. O'Brien (both of whom taught Gerald Griffin) and Eugene Cavanagh, Co. Limerick; Peter Daly and John Fitzgerald, Co. Cork; Richard Fitzgerald and James Fortune, Co. Wexford; Pat Frayne (who taught William Carleton), Co. Tyrone; Peter Galleghan (Co. Meath); Francis Grace (Co. Kilkenny); and Maurice Gorman and Peadar Ó Doirnín (Co. Armagh). Matt Tuohy, one of the last hedge-school masters, had a school in Killaloe, Co. Clare, where he charged half a crown a week for instruction in 'Latin, Greek, Irish, Sums and Dancing.' Hedge schools continued into the first part of the nineteenth century but were gradually supplanted by the schools established by the NATIONAL EDUCATION system, 1831.

Heeney, Patrick (Paddy) (1881–1911), musician; born in Dublin, educated at St Patrick's National School. Though not musically trained, he collaborated with PEADAR KEARNEY in composing the music (on his melodeon) for 'The Soldier's Song', which became a popular marching song of the Irish Volunteers and later the NATIONAL ANTHEM. Other songs for which he provided the music included 'Michael Dwyer Keeps His Word' and 'The Flag of Green'. Following Heeney's death, Kearney, then in London, arranged a collection for Heeney's impoverished mother; the contributors included MICHAEL COLLINS and SAM MAGUIRE. Kearney's 'Slán Libh', with musical arrangement by Seán Barlow, is dedicated to his friend Paddy Heeney.

Helga, a 323-ton, 156-foot fisheries protection vessel built in the Liffey Dockyard, 1908, which became an anti-submarine patrol ship during the First World War. During the EASTER RISING (1916) it was used against insurgent positions. It fired twenty-four rounds at Liberty Hall, Beresford Place, Dublin, headquarters of the IRISH CITIZEN ARMY, 26 April. Sixteen rounds were expended between Boland's Mills, Grand Canal Street, 25 April, and Ringsend Distillery, 27 April. Two Irish members of the crew refused to participate in the shelling.

Renamed *Muirchú,* the ship became the first fisheries protection vessel of the Coastal and Marine Service but was returned to the Department of Agriculture and Fisheries, 1924, being armed for its duties until 1927. It was recommissioned, 12 December 1939, shortly after the establishment of the Marine and Coastwatching Service. Sold as scrap to the Hammond Lane Foundry, Dublin, it was on its way to be broken up when it foundered off Tuskar Rock, Co. Wexford, 8 May 1947. The trawler *Ellesmere,* out of Milford Haven, picked up its delivery crew.

Henebry, Rev. Richard (1863–1916), scholar, musicologist, and violinist; born in Mount Barton, near Portlaw, Co. Waterford, educated at St Patrick's College, Maynooth, where he was an outstanding linguist, specialising in English, Hebrew, and Irish. Ordained in June 1892, he held a curacy at Salford, Manchester, 1892–96. He studied Old Irish under John Strachan and Whitley Stokes and engaged in a year's study of Celtic philology at the Universities of Freiburg (under Thurneysen) and Greifswald (under Zimmer). He was appointed to the chair of Irish at the University of Washington (endowed by the ANCIENT ORDER OF HIBERNIANS), 1900–03. While in the United States he made the acquaintance of FRANCIS O'NEILL, chief of police in Chicago and a well-known collector of Irish traditional music, and became president of the Gaelic League in America. Suffering from chronic ill-health, he spent a year in Colorado; on his return to the University of Washington he found that his post no longer existed. He obtained a post at Berkeley, California, 1903, but again his health failed and he returned to Ireland, 1908, as professor of Celtic studies at University College, Cork, where his class for Ancient Irish was one of the largest in the college. He was a contributor to leading journals of the day, including the *Leader* and *Irisleabhar na Gaedhilge*. His works include *The Sounds of Munster Irish* (1898), *Eachtra an Ghobáin Saoir* (1910), *Sgríbhne Ristéird de Hindeberg* (1924), and *A Handbook of Irish Music* (1928).

Hennessy, William Maunsell (1829–1889), linguist and scholar; born in Castlegregory, Co. Kerry. He worked for the NATION, 1853–56, on his return from the United States and was a member of YOUNG IRELAND. A member of the Royal Irish Academy, he became assistant deputy keeper of the PUBLIC RECORD OFFICE, 1868. He was acknowledged for his scholarship in Irish history and literature and in particular for his *Essays on MacPherson's Ossian and Ossianic Literature* (1871). His works included *Pedigree of the White Knight* (which he revised, 1856), *Annals of Loch Cé* (1858), *Chronicum Scotorum* (with glossary of the rarer words, 1866), *The Book of Fenagh* (1875), and *The Annals of Ulster* (1889). His translation of the Life of St Patrick with the Tripartite Life was published in 1870 and his *Poets and Poetry of Munster* (with Seán Ó Dálaigh) in 1883.

Henry, Dr Augustine (1857–1930), botanist; born in Tyanee, Co. Tyrone. He joined the Chinese Maritime Customs in 1882 and for the next eighteen years travelled extensively collecting specimens, many of which he sent to Kew Gardens, London. He also encouraged Christian missionaries in China to collect specimens on his behalf. Reader in forestry at the University of Cambridge, 1907, and professor of forestry at the Royal College of Science, Dublin, from 1913, he published papers and acted as adviser on diseases of Irish cultivated trees. He collaborated with Elwes on *Trees of Great Britain and Ireland* (7 vols., 1906–13). His unique collection of tree and plant specimens was donated to the NATIONAL BOTANIC GARDENS, where it was separately catalogued in 1957.

Heritage Council, established under the Heritage Act (1995) to provide policies for the identification, protection, preservation and enhancement of the national heritage. Its additional brief included the protection of archaeological objects, art and industrial works, botanical heritage, documents, fauna, flora, gardens, genealogical records, geology, landscapes, monuments, parks, inland waterways, seascapes, and wrecks.

Heuston, Seán (1891–1916), republican; born in Dublin, educated at Christian Brothers' School. He worked as a railway clerk in Limerick from 1908 and formed one of the largest branches of Fianna Éireann in the country in 1910, with 250 members. After returning to Dublin, 1913, he became a member of the Irish Volunteers and had a central involvement in the HOWTH GUN-RUNNING (1914). At the request of PATRICK PEARSE he assisted CON COLBERT in training the boys of ST ENDA'S SCHOOL in drill and musketry. A captain in the Volunteers, he was in command at the Mendicity Institute, Usher's Island, during the EASTER RISING (1916) and over three days prevented several hundred reinforcements from Kingsbridge Station (now Heuston Station) from reaching the centre of the city.

Heytesbury, William à Court, second Baron (1779–1860), British politician. As Lord Lieutenant of Ireland, 1844–46, he subscribed to the prevailing *laissez-faire* dictum of government and was unsympathetic to pleas from prominent leaders, including DANIEL O'CONNELL, for famine aid. Like his political contemporaries, he failed to realise the crucial role of the potato in the Irish economy. He was replaced in office by the EARL OF BESSBOROUGH.

Hibernia, a review of current affairs. Founded in 1937 by the KNIGHTS OF COLUMBANUS as a vehicle for their views, it subsequently passed out of their control and became one of the principal organs of debate in Ireland. It was a monthly to October 1968; having changed ownership it was then published fortnightly until September 1977, when it became a weekly. It ceased publication in 1980.

Hickey, Rev. William (1788–1875), clergyman (Church of Ireland), agriculturist, and author; born in Murragh, Co. Cork, educated at TCD and the University of Cambridge. He held various curacies from 1820 until he settled in Mulrankin, Co. Wexford. With Thomas Boyce he founded the South Wexford

Agricultural Society, the first in Ireland, 1820. Under the pseudonym 'Martin Doyle' he produced a series of books and pamphlets on practical husbandry, beginning with *Hints to Small Farmers* (1830). He contributed numerous articles to newspapers and journals on all aspects of agricultural life and on the need for a harmonious relationship between landlord and tenant. He also published prose and poetry in the *Dublin Penny Journal.* From 1834 to 1842 he assisted Edmund Murphy on the *Irish Farmers' and Gardeners' Magazine.* The Royal Literary Fund awarded him an annual pension for his services to agriculture. His works included *An Address to the Landlords of Ireland* (1831), *The Flower Garden* (1834), *Farm and Garden Produce* (1837), *A Cyclopaediia of Practical Husbandry* (1839), *The Labouring Classes in Ireland* (1846), and *Cottage Farming* (1870).

Hicks Beach, Sir Michael, first Earl of St Aldwyn (1837–1916), British politician (Conservative). A member of Parliament from 1864, he was Parliamentary Secretary to the Poor Law Board, 1868. As Chief Secretary for Ireland, 1874–78, he was the unwitting cause of alerting the IRB to the emergence of CHARLES STEWART PARNELL. On 30 June 1876 he referred during a parliamentary debate to 'the Manchester murderers'; Parnell, claiming that Hicks Beach was looking at him, declared: 'I do not believe, and never shall believe, that any murder was committed at Manchester.' Though sympathetic to reform, Hicks Beach opposed HOME RULE, on which he claimed the Irish Party itself held divergent views. On the fall of Gladstone's ministry, 1876, he became Chancellor for a second time. Returning to the Irish Office, 1886, he found the country in the throes of a new land agitation, the PLAN OF CAMPAIGN. He was succeeded by ARTHUR J. BALFOUR, 1887.

Hillery, Dr Patrick J. (born 1923), politician (Fianna Fáil); born in Milltown Malbay, Co. Clare, educated at UCD, qualifying as a doctor. As a member of Dáil Éireann for West Clare from 1951, he served in several governments: as Minister for Education, 1959–65, Industry and Commerce, 1965–66, and External Affairs, 1969–72. As Minister for Education in 1962 he established the committee under PATRICK LYNCH, professor of economics at University College, Dublin, that produced *Investment in Education* (1965).

While Minister for External Affairs, on 6 July 1970, without advance notice to the Northern Ireland or British governments, Hillery and a senior official, Éamon Gallagher of the Department of Foreign Affairs, examined the damage along the Falls Road, Belfast, resulting from the attempts to impose a curfew (3–5 July). Despite a hostile reaction from the British government, he informed the Secretary of State for Foreign Affairs two days later of the Irish government's fears that the harsh law-and-order regime was alienating the Catholic population. The British government in reply stated that it saw no reason to depart from its new policy of 'firm measures'. Hillery was responsible for the conduct of negotiations leading to Ireland's membership of the European Economic Community in 1973. He became a member of the European Commission and vice-president with responsibility for social affairs, 1973–76.

Following the resignation of CEARBHALL Ó DÁLAIGH, Hillery became the agreed candidate for President of Ireland, November 1976, and was re-elected unopposed for a second term in 1983.

hiring fairs, fairs at which prospective employees offered themselves to the more substantial farmers for the agricultural season. Such fairs were held biannually, the largest of them at Derry, Letterkenny, Omagh, and Strabane, and attracted hundreds of labourers and employers. While it was the prerogative of the hirer to bargain over wages, it was common for the one hiring himself to seek additional benefits in kind: bacon, potatoes, clothing, or footwear. A potential employee was known as a SPALPEEN (or, in Ulster, spulpin). In *Irish Folk Ways* (1957), E. Estyn Evans relates that when a bargain had been struck between employer and labourer, the employer handed over 'earnest money', and the servant in exchange handed over his bundle of clothing. An improvement in social welfare hastened the demise of the hiring fair, which had largely disappeared by the late 1930s.

Hobson, Bulmer (1883–1969), republican; born in Holywood, Co. Down, educated at Friends' School, Lisburn, Co. Antrim. A member of the Gaelic League, he founded the Protestant Nationalist Society and FIANNA ÉIREANN in Belfast, 1903. He was recruited into the IRB by DENIS MCCULLOUGH, 1904, and they jointly founded the DUNGANNON CLUBS, 1905. He resigned as secretary of the Antrim County GAA Board following its refusal to give priority to juvenile members. He was also a joint founder of the Ulster Literary Theatre, which produced his drama *Brian of Banba* (1905). He founded a journal, the *Republic,* 1906–07, and also worked on the *Peasant,* 1908, in Dublin following their merger. At his suggestion, IRISH FREEDOM was founded in 1910.

Once described by the British military authorities as 'the most dangerous man in Ireland,' Hobson was a member of the Supreme Council of the IRB and played a leading role in the establishment of the IRISH VOLUNTEERS. His support for JOHN REDMOND, who demanded half the seats on the Provisional Committee of the Volunteers for his nominees, June 1914, led to Hobson's forced resignation from the Supreme Council and from *Irish Freedom,* while JOHN DEVOY dismissed him from the GAELIC AMERICAN. He alerted EOIN MACNEILL to plans for the proposed EASTER RISING (1916) but was held prisoner by the IRB when he attempted to join MacNeill in efforts to prevent it.

He withdrew from public life following the rising and on the creation of the Irish Free State held a post in the philatelic division of the Department of Posts and Telegraphs. He retired to Roundstone, Co. Galway, 1946. A student of economics, he contributed to *Prosperity and Social Justice* during the 1930s. His publications include a history of the Irish Volunteers (1918), a life of Theobald Wolfe Tone (1919), *A National Forests Policy* (1923), and an autobiography, *Ireland Yesterday and Tomorrow* (1968).

Hogan, James J. (1898–1963), historian; born in Kilfrickle, Loughrea, Co. Galway, younger brother of PATRICK HOGAN, educated at UCD. A member of the 3rd Battalion, Dublin Brigade, Irish Volunteers, he was organiser for the Volunteers in the Loughrea district during the EASTER RISING (1916). He was intelligence officer of the 1st Western Division of the IRA and served in the East Clare Flying Column during the War of Independence. He presented his MA dissertation 'Ireland and the European System, 1550–57' while on active service. Accepting the ANGLO-IRISH TREATY (1921), he became adjutant-general of the Free State army, 1922, and, with the rank of major-general, was director of intelligence during the Civil War. On resigning from the army, 1923, he spent a year at the University of Paris before returning to take up the chair of history at University College, Cork, which he held until his death. A member of the Royal Irish Academy from 1927, he was a founder-member of the Irish Manuscripts Commission a year later and was joint editor and, from 1930, general editor of its journal, *Analecta Hibernica.* An apologist for the BLUESHIRTS, he supported its ideology of the corporate state and anti-communism as expounded in the Papal encyclical *Quadragesimo Anno* but resigned as vice-president of Fine Gael in 1934 in protest at the extremism of EOIN O'DUFFY. He was the author of the propagandist pamphlet *Could Ireland Become Communist?* (1935) and *Election and Representation* (1946) and was a regular contributor to *Studies* and *Proceedings of the Royal Irish Academy.*

Hogan, John (1800–1858), sculptor; born in Tallow, Co. Waterford. His family moved to Cork in 1814, where he worked as a solicitor's clerk and later as a draughtsman and woodcarver for the architect Thomas Deane. He received his first major commission from the Bishop of Cork, Dr Murphy, for twenty-seven statues in wood and bas-relief for the North Chapel. Under subscriptions organised by W. P. Carey and the patronage of Lord de Talbey he travelled to Rome, 1824. His first plaster model, *The Goat Herd,* brought him local recognition, and his work was seen by a visiting Irish priest, who commissioned *The Dead Christ* in marble for St Teresa's Church, Clarendon Street, Dublin. Apart from two working visits to Ireland, 1829 and 1840, he remained in Rome until 1849. Having earlier refused membership of the ROYAL HIBERNIAN ACADEMY, he was elected a member of the prestigious Virtuosi del Panteon in 1837, the first Irish person to be so honoured. He returned to Ireland, 1849, but found commissions difficult in a post-famine society. Bitterly disappointed at the rejection of his model for a statue of Thomas Moore (1855), he had a stroke within a week, from which he never fully recovered.

Hogan's best-known works in Ireland are *The Drunken Faun* (1826), now at the National University of Ireland, Dublin, *James Warren Doyle* (1840), Carlow Cathedral, *Daniel O'Connell* (1846), City Hall, Dublin, and also 1857, the Crescent Limerick, *Thomas Steele* (1851), *Thomas Davis* (1853), Mortuary Chapel, Mount Jerome Cemetery, Dublin, *Robert Graves* (1853), Royal College of Physicians, Dublin, and *Bishop Berkeley,* Cloyne Co. Cork. He was working on a statue of FATHER THEOBALD MATHEW to be erected in Patrick Street, Cork, when he died; the commission passed to JOHN HENRY FOLEY.

Hogan, Patrick J. (1891–1936), politician (Sinn Féin and Cumann na nGaedheal); born in Kilfrickle, Loughrea, Co. Galway, educated at UCD. A solicitor from 1915, he was a member of the Irish Volunteers and later of the IRA, for which he was interned at Ballykinler, Co. Down, 1919–21. Sinn Féin TD for Co. Galway from 1921, he was Minister for Agriculture in Cumann na nGaedheal governments, 1922–32. He introduced the Land Act (1923), sometimes called the Hogan Act (see LAND ACTS), and attempted to reform agriculture through his Dairy and Livestock Breeding Acts. He launched a campaign for increased agricultural output under the slogan 'One more cow, one more sow, one more acre under the plough.' His approach was challenged by the chief administrative officer of the Department of Economic Affairs, Gordon Campbell (BARON GLENAVY), who cautioned against an over-reliance on an agriculture-led economy. Considered close to the conservative element within Cumann na nGaedheal, Hogan, in opposition from 1932, distanced himself from EOIN O'DUFFY; he was particularly critical of his views on Northern Ireland and of his public eulogising of Adolf Hitler. He was killed in a car accident in July 1936.

Holland, John Philip (1841–1914), inventor of the submarine; born in Liscannor, Co. Clare, educated at Limerick Christian Brothers' School. Defective vision militated against his chosen seagoing career and he became a member of the Irish Christian Brothers. While teaching at various schools he worked on his submarine project, and at his last school, Dundalk, Co. Louth, demonstrated a model submarine. Released from his vows because of ill-health, 1872, he emigrated to the United States, 1873, and settled in Paterson, New Jersey, where he became a teacher and continued his experiments. Having dismissed a prototype as impracticable, the US Navy accepted a later version of Holland's invention. Meanwhile Holland, whose younger brother, Michael Holland, was a member of CLAN NA GAEL, offered his services to JOHN DEVOY, who provided $6,000 for further experiments. His third submarine, named the *Fenian Ram,* was successfully tested in the Hudson River, 1881. Armed with underwater cannon, it was intended for use against British ships. Later models were 31 feet long, driven by a petrol engine, with a surface speed of 10 miles an hour and provision for a crew of three. A pneumatic tube discharged a torpedo loaded with dynamite, capable of penetrating up to 50 feet.

In 1898 Holland's sixth submarine was launched in the Potomac River, where its trials impressed American naval observers. It had many features that later became standard: internal-combustion engine for surface cruising and an electric motor for submerged propulsion, hydroplanes and ballast tanks to regulate depth, torpedo tubes, and a retractable periscope. In 1901 Britain bought the first of several submarines from Holland's company. A 100-foot Holland submarine, which sank in 1913 as it was being towed to the breaker's yard, was recovered off Eddystone Lighthouse, 1 December 1982, and is now on display at the Royal Navy Museum, Gosport, Hampshire. The *Fenian Ram* is on display at the Paterson Museum, New Jersey.

Holloway, Joseph (1861–1944), diarist; born in Dublin. An architect, he retired in 1914 to devote himself to theatrical pursuits. He became a member of almost every theatrical society in the Dublin region, attending many first-night performances, including every first night, and many rehearsals, at the ABBEY THEATRE. His meticulous diaries, spanning forty-eight years of association with the theatre, provided material for a journal totalling twenty-eight million words. Occupying 221 volumes in the National Library of Ireland, it also records the writer's eye-witness accounts of the EASTER RISING (1916). An edited version, *Joseph Holloway's Abbey Theatre,* was published in 1967.

Holmes, Robert (1765–1859), lawyer; born in Dublin, educated at TCD and called to the bar. He resigned from the Lawyers' Corps of the Yeomanry during the rising of the UNITED IRISHMEN (1798) in protest at the atrocities committed by soldiers under General Edward Lake and published an appeal to the Irish Parliament to reject the union. He was imprisoned, 1803, on suspicion of having supported the rising led by his brother-in-law ROBERT EMMET. Known as 'Bitter Bob' for his resolute rejection of government advancement, he practised on the north-east circuit. He continued to practise at the bar into his eighties, representing the NATION, 1846, and JOHN MITCHEL, 1847. His support for the REPEAL ASSOCIATION was set out in *The Case of Ireland Stated* (1847).

Home Government Association (of Ireland), founded by ISAAC BUTT in Dublin, 19 May 1870. Its aim was the establishment of a federal system for the United Kingdom, which would grant Ireland a parliament responsible for national affairs. The association attracted all shades of political and religious opinion but failed to garner popular support and was succeeded by the HOME RULE LEAGUE, 1873.

home rule, a term first used in the 1860s, representing the aspirations of the majority of the people for an autonomous Irish parliament. It was variously interpreted. ISAAC BUTT saw it as part of a federal system for the United Kingdom, with a national parliament for Ireland while the imperial parliament in London would continue to have responsibility for imperial affairs. Republicans, represented by the FENIANS and the IRB, sought total separation from Britain and complete autonomy for Ireland but were prepared for a temporary accommodation with home-rulers. CHARLES STEWART PARNELL sought, as an interim measure, an Irish parliament with a limited amount of legislative power. ARTHUR GRIFFITH envisaged a 'dual monarchy', based on the Austro-Hungarian model. To unionists, and in particular to Ulster unionists and the ORANGE ORDER, home rule meant a diminution of the Union with Britain and a parliament in Dublin dominated by the Catholic Church.

The Liberal Party, under W. E. GLADSTONE, committed itself to home rule, while the Conservatives sought to divert attention from the demand by implementing a policy of moral force or constructive unionism ('killing home rule with kindness'). Butt's home rule motion was defeated (458 to 61) in the House of Commons, 2 July 1874. The first HOME RULE BILL, introduced by Gladstone, 8 April 1886, was defeated (343 to 311) in the House of Commons, 8 June. His second Home Rule Bill, introduced on 13 February 1893, was passed by the House of Commons, 2 September 1893, but was rejected by the House of Lords a week later.

The IRISH PARTY, split since 1890 over the Parnell-O'Shea affair, was reunited under JOHN REDMOND on 30 January 1900. Campbell-Bannerman's successor, H. H. ASQUITH, needed Redmond's support to secure the passing of the PARLIAMENT ACT (1911), in return for which he promised home rule for Ireland.

The third Home Rule Bill was introduced by Asquith, 11 April 1912. Opposition was led by SIR EDWARD CARSON and the Unionists. During the second reading a Liberal member, T. C. Agar-Robartes, raised for the first time the possibility of the partition of Ireland when he proposed, 2 May 1912, that Cos. Antrim, Armagh, Derry and Down be excluded from home rule. On the first day of the committee stage, 11 June, an amendment introduced by Agar-Robartes and Neil Primrose, making acceptance of the home rule parliament conditional on the exclusion of the four counties, failed to gain support from either Conservatives or Liberals. Partition, however, came to be regarded as the solution to the home rule question, with Cos. Fermanagh and Tyrone added to the four proposed by Agar-Robartes. The bill passed its third reading in the House of Commons on 16 January 1913. Following the outbreak of war in Europe, August 1914, Asquith secured from the Irish parties an agreement to the suspension of the act for the duration of the war; on 15 September it was suspended before being enacted and then signed into law by KING GEORGE V, 18 September. The Unionists were given to understand that the act would not come into force until some provision had been made for part of Ulster.

By 1919 the Irish political scene had dramatically altered: the conservative IRISH PARTY was annihilated by SINN FÉIN in the 1918 general election, and home rule as a consequence became an irrelevance. On 21 January 1919 Sinn Féin representatives constituted DÁIL ÉIREANN and declared the establishment of the Irish Republic. The British government attempted to settle the problem during the WAR OF INDEPENDENCE by passing the GOVERNMENT OF IRELAND ACT (1920). Home rule became a reality under the ANGLO-IRISH TREATY (1921) in 1922, when the IRISH FREE STATE was established, while the state of NORTHERN IRELAND, established under the Government of Ireland Act, continued in existence. The Treaty was to prove the prelude to the establishment of a 26-county Irish state, a republic in everything but name from 1922 and independent of the British Commonwealth from 1949.

Home Rule Bill (1886). The first Home Rule Bill, introduced by W. E. GLADSTONE on 8 April 1886, was defeated in the House of Commons, 8 June (343 to 311). The bill proposed an Irish legislature of two 'orders', one containing 103 members (of whom seventy-five were to be elected for a ten-year term, on a restricted franchise, and twenty-eight were to be peers), the second to consist of 204 members, elected for a five-year term on the existing franchise.

The legislative functions of the assembly would be restricted: it would not have the power to make laws dealing with the Crown, war or peace, defence, treaties, titles of honour, treason, alienage and naturalisation, navigation, trade, beacons and lighthouses, quarantine, coinage, weights, copyright, the undenominational nature of education, or the establishment or endowment of religion. Ireland would not be represented in the imperial parliament. The Irish executive would be the Crown, represented by the Lord Lieutenant of Ireland, who would have a power of veto and the aid and advice of the Executive Committee of the Irish Privy Council. Ireland would control its own taxes, with the exception of customs and excise. The revenue at the disposal of the Irish government would be the gross revenue collected in Ireland from Irish and imperial taxes and Crown lands; Ireland would bear the cost of collecting the revenue. The Irish contribution to the imperial exchequer was to be calculated at a fixed maximum, which could be diminished but could not be exceeded and was to be revised in thirty years. (The cost for 1886 would have been £3.242 million.) Judges were to be appointed by the Irish government. The DUBLIN METROPOLITAN POLICE was to remain under imperial control for two years, and the ROYAL IRISH CONSTABULARY was to be permanently under imperial control. However, it was envisaged that Ireland would ultimately create a new police force under the control of local authorities.

This form of limited self-government was accepted by CHARLES STEWART PARNELL, who believed that such a measure was a base for future advancement.

Home Rule Bill (1893). The second Home Rule Bill was introduced by W. E. GLADSTONE in January 1893. Strongly resisted in the House of Commons, it was forced through by the repeated use of closure. In September the House of Lords rejected it.

The bill again proposed that Ireland should have a two-tier legislature; there would be a Council of forty-eight members, elected for an eight-year term on a restricted franchise, and an Assembly of 103 members, elected for five years on the existing franchise. As in the 1886 bill, disagreements were to be settled by joint majority vote. The same restrictions applied as in the 1886 bill. Ireland would have eighty representatives in the imperial parliament in London. Certain powers relating to landlord-tenant relations and the purchase and letting of land were to be reserved to the imperial parliament. The executive was to be the same as in the 1886 bill, but a limit of six years was placed on the Lord Lieutenant's term of office. The system of taxation was to be the same as in the 1886 bill. Revenue was to be the true Irish revenue derived from imperial taxes, revenue from Irish taxes and Crown lands, and an imperial grant of one-third of the annual cost of the police forces (DUBLIN METROPOLITAN POLICE and ROYAL IRISH CONSTABULARY). Ireland's contribution to the imperial exchequer for six years would be one-third of the true revenue raised in Ireland (which in 1893 amounted to approximately one twenty-seventh of the total imperial expenditure); this scheme would be revised after six years. Judges would he appointed by the Irish government, but for six years judges of the Supreme Court would be appointed by the imperial parliament. The DMP and RIC were to be placed under permanent imperial control, but it was again envisaged that locally controlled police forces would gradually replace them.

Home Rule Bill (1912). The third Home Rule Bill was introduced by H. H. ASQUITH on 11 April 1912. It met with opposition in the House of Commons from Ulster Unionists and Conservatives, and the third reading was not carried until January 1913; it was then defeated in the House of Lords, which had the effect of delaying it for two years. It became law on 18 September 1914, but by agreement with the Ulster Unionists and the IRISH PARTY it was suspended for the duration of the Great War (1914–18), leaving the question of exclusion unresolved. However, by the time the war ended the EASTER RISING (1916) had altered public opinion in Ireland, and the act was not now acceptable to nationalists.

The bill provided for a parliament of two houses, a Senate of forty members, to be nominated by the Lord Lieutenant of Ireland in the first instance and thereafter elected for five-year terms under the existing franchise, and a House of Commons of 164 members, elected for five-year terms under the same franchise. Disagreements were to be resolved by joint majority. Restrictions on the legislature applied as in the 1886 and 1893 bills. It would not be able to enact laws on religious belief or ceremony as a condition of marriage. Ireland was to have forty-two representatives in the imperial parliament in London, which retained control of old-age pensions, national insurance, labour exchanges, the Post Office, savings banks and friendly societies for a minimum of ten years until a resolution of transfer had been passed by the Irish parliament. In addition, it reserved in perpetuity the collection of taxes and laws relating to the purchase of land. The executive, as in 1886 and 1893, was to be the Lord Lieutenant of Ireland, acting on behalf of the Crown and aided and advised by the Privy Council. The Irish parliament was to have the power to vary imperial taxes and to impose new taxes but not to vary the rate of income tax on incomes below £5,000 per annum. It would also have the power to impose customs duties on articles subject to imperial customs duty (including alcohol, tea, coffee, sugar, tobacco, and cocoa). Revenue was to be raised from sums transferred from the imperial treasury, consisting of the revenue derived from Irish taxes and a fixed annual grant from the imperial parliament (£500,000 for three years, to be reduced by £50,000 a year until it reached £200,000). The cost of reserved services was to be borne by the imperial parliament. Ireland's contribution to the imperial parliament was to be determined by a Joint Exchequer Board after total revenues had equalled total charges for three consecutive years; it would be based on an equitable contribution by Ireland to the common expenses of the United Kingdom. Judges were to be appointed as in the 1886 bill, and the police would be controlled by the Irish parliament, except for the ROYAL IRISH CONSTABULARY, which would be controlled by the imperial parliament for six years.

Home Rule Confederation of Great Britain, founded by ISAAC BUTT, 8 January 1873, to harness the support of Irish people in Britain for home rule. CHARLES STEWART PARNELL replaced Butt as president in 1877. Members of the IRB, recognising the potential of the movement to spread their influence among the large Irish population in British industrial centres, gradually infiltrated the confederation.

Home Rule League, founded at a conference in Dublin by ISAAC BUTT, 18–21 November 1873, to replace the HOME GOVERNMENT ASSOCIATION. Its principal aim was to obtain self-government for Ireland through a federal system for the United Kingdom. Under Butt's guidance the league was identified with the popular issues of the day: denominational education, land reform, and home rule. Despite insufficient time to organise for the 1874 general election—the first held under the Secret Ballot Act (1872)—the league secured fifty-nine seats, two of them in Ulster (Co. Cavan). The Home Rule League was the first positive step by Irish members towards a separate and distinct party in the British House of Commons, eventually realised by the IRISH PARTY.

Home Rule Union, organised by the Liberal Party in 1886. Two years later it had sixty affiliated Liberal Associations. It disseminated propagandist literature, much of it supplied by the IRISH PRESS AGENCY, in an attempt to foster support for HOME RULE. It provided lecturers (most of them Parnellite members of the IRISH PARTY) throughout Britain. It collapsed following the split in the party, 1890–91.

Horan, Monsignor James (1912–1986), priest and community activist; born in Partry, Co. Mayo, educated at St Patrick's College, Maynooth. Ordained in 1935, he was a curate in Scotland and later in Cos. Mayo and Galway. Concerned at the lack of recreational facilities in Toureen, Co. Mayo, he organised the building of a hall, before moving to Knock, Co. Mayo, 1963, where he became parish priest in 1967. There he established a hostel, care centre, social service centre and marriage bureau as well as overseeing the building of a basilica. His biggest project, an international airport, became embroiled in controversy when it secured financial aid from the government of CHARLES HAUGHEY. When funds were withdrawn by the succeeding coalition government (Fine Gael and Labour Party), Horan embarked on a fund-raising campaign in Britain and the United States. Knock International Airport was opened in 1986 by Haughey, then leader of the opposition.

houses. The Census Commissioners in the nineteenth century classified Irish houses into four main categories. In the fourth class were all mud cabins having only one room; the third class were also of mud but with two to four rooms and having windows; in the second class were good farmhouses with five to nine rooms, with windows; in the first class were all houses of a better description. The number of houses in these classes from 1841 to 1861 was as follows:

	1841	1851	1861
Class 1	40,080	50,164	55,416
Class 2	264,184	318,758	360,698
Class 3	533,297	541,712	489,668
Class 4	491,278	135,589	89,374

Howth Gun-Running (1914). The landing of guns at Howth, Co. Dublin, for the IRISH VOLUNTEERS on 26 July 1914 was organised by an *ad hoc* committee that included ROGER CASEMENT, ERSKINE CHILDERS, DARRELL FIGGIS, BULMER HOBSON, EOIN MACNEILL, MICHAEL O'RAHILLY, and Mary Spring Rice. The guns, bought in Germany by Figgis, were taken off the German ship *Gladiator* and taken aboard the ASGARD for transporting to Howth. Volunteers and members of FIANNA ÉIREANN collected the cargo at Howth. The successful landing was an emulation of the LARNE GUN-RUNNING (April 1914). Later the same evening there was a confrontation between British soldiers and sympathisers of the Volunteers at BACHELOR'S WALK, Dublin, resulting in three people being killed and more than thirty-eight injured in indiscriminate shooting by soldiers. The Volunteers holding the GPO in Sackville Street (O'Connell Street), Dublin, during the EASTER RISING (1916) used guns and ammunition from the gun-running. (See also CHOTAH and KELPIE.)

Hudson, William Elliot (1796–1853), lawyer; born in Dublin, educated at TCD and called to the bar. He practised on the Munster circuit and was a taxing master. A member of the REPEAL ASSOCIATION and a supporter of YOUNG IRELAND, he was a generous benefactor of the arts and culture. The CELTIC SOCIETY was founded in his house in 1840; he also helped to establish the Irish Archaeological Society, 1845, and the Ossianic Society, 1853. He subsidised the publication of *The Spirit of the Nation* and the 'Library of Ireland' series and contributed financially to the Irish dictionary sponsored by the Royal Irish Academy. He subsidised and edited the *Citizen,* a journal of politics and literature, 1839. Hudson composed the music for the ballad 'The Memory of the Dead' ('Who fears to speak of Ninety-Eight?') by John Kells Ingram, 'The Felons of Our Land', and other patriotic songs. He donated some eight hundred volumes and eighty manuscripts to the RIA. Most of his works remain unpublished.

Hume, John (born 1937), politician (SDLP); born in Derry, educated at St Patrick's College, Maynooth, and QUB. While a teacher in Derry he founded a housing association and played a leading role in launching the credit union movement and was president of the Irish League of Credit Unions, 1964–68. A pacifist, he was a member of the NORTHERN IRELAND CIVIL RIGHTS ASSOCIATION and was present at the riot that ensued when members were attacked by police in Derry, 5 October 1968. Four days later he was joint founder and vice-chairman of the DERRY CITIZENS' ACTION COMMITTEE. He was elected to the Parliament of Northern Ireland as an independent, 1969–73, winning the seat from the leader of the Nationalist Party, EDDIE MCATEER. A founder-member and deputy chairman of the SOCIAL DEMOCRATIC AND LABOUR PARTY, he emerged as its chief policy-maker and succeeded GERRY FITT as leader in 1979, the year in which he also became a member of the European Parliament. A member of the Northern Ireland Assembly, 1973, he became Minister of Commerce and was elected to the Northern Ireland Constitutional Convention, 1975. Having regained his seat lost in 1974, he became a member of the British House of Commons for the Foyle division of Derry in 1983.

Regarded by many as a principal architect of the NEW IRELAND FORUM (1983), Hume supported the ANGLO-IRISH AGREEMENT in 1985. His contacts with the Provisional IRA began in February 1985 but broke off precipitately when the IRA attempted to videotape the discussions. At the request of a third party (believed to have been the Belfast priest Father Alec Reid), Hume began talks with GERRY ADAMS, 11 January 1988. These talks (see HUME-ADAMS TALKS), precursor of the PEACE PROCESS, continued into the 1990s, culminating in the BELFAST AGREEMENT (1998). Throughout this period Hume ignored widespread criticism of his willingness to engage in the process with Adams. During the discussions he routinely briefed the Irish and British governments on progress. The Taoiseach, ALBERT REYNOLDS, became a party to the process in 1992.

Talks between Hume, Adams and Reynolds in 1993 were followed by the Provisional IRA ceasefire of August 1994, which lasted until February 1996. In 1998 Hume's role in the process was recognised when he shared the Nobel Prize for Peace with the Ulster Unionist Party leader DAVID TRIMBLE. He resigned the leadership of the SDLP in 2001.

Hume-Adams Talks, meetings between JOHN HUME, leader of the SDLP, and GERRY ADAMS, president of Sinn Féin, which began in secret in Belfast, January 1988. As an essential element of the PEACE PROCESS, Hume sought to persuade the IRA to abandon violence and seek a constitutional solution to the Northern problem. The two principals remained in communication after the talks were abandoned in September. Resumed in Derry in 1993, the talks became public knowledge on 25 April. Hume rejected criticism of his holding talks with republican representatives. Hume and Adams issued a joint statement in September, claiming that considerable progress had been made, though the talks were suspended. The Taoiseach, ALBERT REYNOLDS, and the British Prime Minister, JOHN MAJOR, considered the Hume-Adams position unbalanced (describing it as 'too green') and pursued their own discussions. The talks between Hume and Adams continued into the multi-party talks of the Northern Ireland Forum, which led to the BELFAST AGREEMENT (1998).

Humphries, Father David (1834–1930), clergyman (Catholic) and land agitator; born in Boher, Co. Tipperary, educated at St Patrick's College, Maynooth. A radical on the land question, he supported the LAND LEAGUE and played a leading role in organising the rent strike in Tipperary, where he was a curate, 1889–95. Replying to an article in the *Irish Times* that alleged that Catholic clergy in Co. Tipperary were totally opposed to boycotting, Humphries wrote, 9 May 1890:

> As one of the Catholic clergy of Tipperary, I protest against this libel on me. I am doing nothing to stop boycotting. I should be very much ashamed of myself if I were.

He formulated the plan for NEW TIPPERARY in the bitter campaign against A. H. SMITH-BARRY during the PLAN OF CAMPAIGN.

hunger strikes (1980–81). Protests by republican prisoners against the withdrawal of SPECIAL CATEGORY status (see BLANKET PROTEST) led to the 'dirty protest', when they refused to use toilet facilities and soiled the walls of their cells. This was followed four years later by the first of two hunger strikes for the restoration of the special category. The first, begun by Brendan Hughes and involving seven prisoners, ran from 27 October to 18 December 1980 and was directed by BOBBY SANDS. The hunger-strikers' five demands were: the right to wear their own clothing at all times, exemption from all forms of penal labour, free association at all hours, the right to organise their own recreation and education, and full restoration of remission.

The hunger strike was called off when the republican leaders believed they had won their demands. However, in January 1981, when the prison authorities refused to pass on clothing brought by relatives to those who had abandoned the protest, hunger strikes were resumed. The following hunger-strikers died:

5 May	Bobby Sands MP (66th day)
12 May	Francis Hughes (59th day)
21 May	Raymond McCreesh and Patsy O'Hare (61st day)
8 July	Joe McDonnell (61st day)
13 July	Martin Hurson (46th day)
1 August	Kevin Lynch (71st day)
3 August	Kieran Doherty TD (73rd day)
8 August	Thomas McElwee (65th day)
20 August	Michael Devine (66th day)

The families of the following prisoners sought medical intervention to end the hunger strike:

31 July	Pat Quinn (47 days)
21 August	Pat McGeown (42 days)
4 September	Matt Devlin (52 days)
6 September	Laurence McKeown (70 days)

The following seven prisoners abandoned their hunger strike on being informed that their families were about to intervene (a tactic believed to have been encouraged by Father Denis Faul):

27 September	Liam McCloskey (55 days)
3 October	Pat Sheehan (55 days), Jackie McMullan (48 days), Gerry Carville (34 days), John Pickering (27 days), Jim Devine (13 days), Gerald Hughes (20 days)

Two hunger-strikers ended their protest without apparent family intervention:

27 May	Brendan McLoughlin (13 days)
24 September	Bernard Fox (32 days)

Hunt, John (1900–1976), antiquarian; born near Newmarket-on-Fergus, Co. Clare. Having graduated from University College, Cork, with an MA in mediaeval sculpture, he lived in London for some twenty years. He returned to Ireland in 1940, and he and his wife, Gertrude Hunt, continued their collection of mediaeval artefacts. He worked on many of the principal excavations in Cos. Limerick and Clare, including Lough Gur, and supervised the restoration of Bunratty Castle, Co. Clare. In 1965 he bought and later restored Craggaunowen Castle, Co. Clare. He was a frequent contributor to specialist publications; his major work was *Irish Medieval Figure Sculpture, 1200–1500* (2 vols., 1974). He bequeathed his collection of antiquities to the National Institute of Higher Education, Limerick (now the University of Limerick); it was later transferred to the Hunt Museum in the renovated Custom House, Limerick.

Hunt Commission (1969), a commission of inquiry appointed by the British government in August 1969, under the chairmanship of Lord John Hunt, to examine the recruitment, organisation, structure and composition of the ROYAL ULSTER CONSTABULARY and the Special

Constabulary. The other members of the Commission were Sir James Robertson and Robert Mark. The commission's report, *Reorganisation of the Police in Northern Ireland,* published on 10 October, triggered two days of rioting in Belfast, during which members of the RUC were attacked with petrol bombs.

The report recommended that the RUC be relieved of all duties of a military nature and that its function be restricted to intelligence-gathering, the protection of important persons, and the enforcement of specified laws; it also recommended that the force be unarmed. It proposed a Police Authority for Northern Ireland, whose membership should reflect the proportions of the different religions in the community. The Special Constabulary should be disbanded and replaced with a locally recruited part-time force to operate under the authority of the commander in chief of British forces in Northern Ireland.

Despite objections from Ulster Unionists, the report was implemented. The Special Constabulary was disbanded, 1 April 1970, and the RUC lost its military powers. A new force, the ULSTER DEFENCE REGIMENT, was established for security duties. However, the government of Northern Ireland, headed by JAMES CHICHESTER-CLARK, granted the UDR many of the old powers of the B Specials, and many members of the Special Constabulary joined it. (See also CAMERON COMMISSION and PATTEN REPORT.)

Hyde, Dr Douglas (1860–1949), scholar; born in Castlerea, Co. Roscommon, educated at home by his father because of childhood illness and later at TCD. A member of the SOCIETY FOR THE PRESERVATION OF THE IRISH LANGUAGE while at Trinity College and later of the GAELIC UNION, with W. B. YEATS he founded the IRISH LITERARY SOCIETY in London, 1891, and the IRISH NATIONAL LITERARY SOCIETY in Dublin, May 1892. In November 1892 he delivered a manifesto to the National Literary Society under the title 'The Necessity for De-Anglicising Ireland', in which he urged the Irish people to assert their separate cultural identity. In July 1893 he became a joint founder of the GAELIC LEAGUE, of which he was president until 1915. During the 1890s he organised a successful campaign to have the Post Office accept letters and parcels addressed in Irish. As 'An Craoibhín Aoibhinn' he published poetry and drama in Irish. His play *Casadh an tSúgáin* (21 October 1901) was one of the first in Irish to be performed.

In 1897 Hyde became an assistant editor of the 'New Irish Library'. He was the editor of *Giolla an Fhiugha* (1901), published by the IRISH TEXTS SOCIETY, of which he was president. As a member of the Commission on Secondary Education he successfully fought J. P. MAHAFFY to have Irish included in the curriculum, 1901. In 1905 he embarked on a successful fund-raising tour on behalf of the Gaelic League. In 1906 he was a member of the Royal Commission on University Education and was successful in his efforts to have Irish included as an obligatory subject for matriculation.

He was professor of Modern Irish at the National University of Ireland, 1908–32, and dean of the Faculty of Celtic Studies and a member of the Senate of the NUI, 1909–19. He resigned from the presidency of the Gaelic League in 1915 when it altered its constitution to include political independence as a primary aim. He was chairman of the Irish Folklore Institute, 1930–34, and was awarded the Gregory Medal of the IRISH ACADEMY OF LETTERS, 1937. In 1938 he was the unopposed candidate for President of Ireland and was sworn in on 25 June. A stroke in 1940 left him a semi-invalid, and he retired from the Presidency in 1945.

Among his numerous works are *Amhráin Grádh Chúige Connacht* (1893), *The Story of Gaelic Literature* (1895), *The Story of Early Irish Literature* (1897), *A Literary History of Ireland* (1899), *Mediaeval Tales from the Irish* (1899), *Abhráin an Reachtabhraigh* (1903, enlarged edition 1933), *The Religious Songs of Connaught* (1906), *Legends, Saints and Sinners from the Irish* (1915), *The History of Charlemagne* (edited and translated from the Book of Lismore and other manuscripts, 1919), *Imeasg na nGaedheal ins an Oileán Úr* (1937), and *Sgéalta Thomáis Uí Chathasaigh* (1939). His autobiography, *Mise agus an Connradh,* was published in 1931.

I

IBEC Report, a report commissioned by the first inter-party government, 1948–51, from an American consultancy, IBEC Technical Services Corporation. Under the direction of Stacy May, the group presented its report, *Industrial Potential of Ireland: An Approach,* in December 1952. It opposed economic protection, supported the expansion of agriculture, and drew attention to the low levels of productivity in industry. It criticised what it saw as the government's timidity and urged an expansionist approach to free trade. The incoming Fianna Fáil government showed little enthusiasm for a report that in many ways ran counter to its traditional orthodoxies. T. K. WHITAKER, however, encompassed some of the features of the report in his paper *Economic Development.*

Iberno-Celtic Society, founded in Dublin, 18 January 1818, to preserve the 'venerable remains of Irish literature, by collecting, transcribing, illustrating and publishing the numerous fragments of the Law, History, Topography, Poetry, and Music of Ancient Ireland . . .' Members included JAMES HARDIMAN, the Duke of Leinster, GEORGE PETRIE, Lord Rosse, Lord Sligo, and Lord Talbot, the Lord Lieutenant. The society's only publication, *Chronological Account of Nearly Four Hundred Writers* (1820), was by another of its members, EDWARD O'REILLY.

Imperial Conferences, 1926–31. As a member of the British Commonwealth, the Irish Free State was represented at the Imperial Conferences at which the status of the member-countries was defined. At the early conferences KEVIN O'HIGGINS led a delegation that included DESMOND FITZGERALD and PATRICK MCGILLIGAN and the civil servants Diarmuid O'Hegarty, E. V. Oheland, and Joseph P. Walshe. The critical issue at the conferences of the 1920s was the exact status of the member-states of the Commonwealth in relation to the imperial parliament. A solution was arrived at in 1926 when ARTHUR JAMES BALFOUR defined that relationship as being between

> autonomous communities within the British Empire, equal in status, in no way subordinate one to another in any aspect of their domestic or external affairs, though united by common allegiance to the Crown and freely associated as members of the British Commonwealth of Nations.

The 'Balfour Definition', as it became known, led to the STATUTE OF WESTMINSTER (1931). By then O'Higgins's office had been filled by PATRICK MCGILLIGAN, who played a leading role in preparing the final draft of the statute, under which the parliaments of the member-states were free to repeal or reject the legislation of the imperial parliament.

indentured apprentices, apprentices bound to serve their master for a specified time. Under a malpractice promoted chiefly by American merchant ships touching at Irish ports, boys and young men were invited on board, where they were forced to sign agreements as indentured apprentices for a number of years; however, they were used only for the return voyage and then turned adrift. J. K. Trimmer, in *Further Observations on the Present State of Ireland* (1812), observed: 'This traffic in Irishmen has been of long continuance, and to a very great extent; as lately as last year I witnessed an American vessel freighted with nearly three hundred of these poor deluded self-sold men.' Robert Ross Rowan (1811–1864), an economist and member of the Irish Anti-Slavery Society, was also an outspoken opponent of the practice.

Independent International Commission on Decommissioning, appointed by the British and Irish governments on 24 September 1997, following the second IRA ceasefire, to oversee the decommissioning of arms by paramilitary groups. It was chaired by General John de Chastelain (Canada), who had formerly served with GEORGE MITCHELL on the INTERNATIONAL BODY ON DECOMMISSIONING OF ARMS; the other members were Brigadier Tauno Nieminen (Finland) and Donald C. Johnson (United States), who was replaced in 1999 by Andrew D. Sens. Under the Belfast Agreement (1998), 'all participants . . . reaffirm their commitment to the total disarmament of all paramilitary organisations . . . and to use any influence they may have, to achieve the decommissioning of all paramilitary arms within two years.' In a 'letter of reassurance' to the Northern Ireland First Minister, DAVID TRIMBLE, the British Prime Minister, TONY BLAIR, stated that if the provisions on decommissioning were shown to be ineffective the British government would support changes to ensure that people connected with paramilitary organisations that still held their weapons would not hold political office. He also confirmed that 'the process of decommissioning should begin straight away.'

In May 1998 General de Chastelain outlined some of the arrangements for decommissioning, including verifiable destruction of weapons by paramilitary organisations. By 1 July 1999 some loyalist weapons had been decommissioned (by the LOYALIST VOLUNTEER FORCE, 18 December 1998) but none by the Provisional IRA or any other republican body. The IRA did permit the inspection of weapons dumps by Martin Ahtisaari (Finland) and Cyril Ramaphosa (South Africa).

In a report dated 30 June 2001 the commission stated that, after meeting the IRA, the Ulster Freedom Fighters and the UVF it had no progress to report. By 23 October 2001 (after Trimble had led Unionist ministers out of the Executive), when the Provisional IRA announced that decommissioning was under way, Ulster Unionists declared that the level of decommissioning was negligible.

Independent Irish Party, founded in September 1852 from an alliance of the IRISH BRIGADE and the TENANT LEAGUE. It comprised some forty Irish MPs, led by CHARLES GAVAN DUFFY, GEORGE HENRY MOORE, and FREDERICK LUCAS. Members were pledged to be independent of and in opposition to all British governments that did not concede the demands of the Tenant League for land reform and repeal the Ecclesiastical Titles Act (1851). The party also sought the DISESTABLISHMENT of the Church of Ireland. The new Tory ministry in 1852 refused to consider the league's Land Reform Bill. The party helped to unseat the ministry, which was succeeded by a Liberal government in December.

Two members of the party, JOHN SADLEIR and WILLIAM KEOGH, accepted office from the government, breaking their pledge on independence; their example was followed by other members, and within a year the number of Irish independents had been reduced to twenty-six. Opposed to Archbishop Cullen's ordinance on clerical involvement in politics, Lucas took his case to Rome, December 1854 to May 1855, outraging both clerical and lay opinion in Ireland. Six members of the party sent a memorial to Rome, further alienating public opinion in their constituencies. The party lost its three leaders within a short time when Lucas died, 1855, Duffy emigrated, 1856, and Moore was unseated, 1857. The possibility of an independent Irish party did not arise again until 1873, with the emergence of the HOME RULE LEAGUE under ISAAC BUTT.

Independent Labour Party. A Belfast branch of the Independent Labour Party was formed in September 1892. A Dublin branch was launched at a meeting in the Rotunda Rooms, 10 November 1894; its members formed the Dublin Socialist Society, 1896, and invited JAMES CONNOLLY to become secretary. Under Connolly it became the IRISH SOCIALIST REPUBLICAN PARTY.

Independent Orange Order, a breakaway from the ORANGE ORDER, founded by T. H. SLOAN, 11 June 1903, after he was expelled from the Orange Order following a Belfast by-election in which he defeated the official Unionist candidate. Based on the militant BELFAST PROTESTANT ASSOCIATION, the institution had a predominantly working-class membership. It called on its members to 'hold out the right hand of fellowship to those who, while worshipping at other shrines, are yet our countrymen.' It co-operated with the ANCIENT ORDER OF HIBERNIANS and others in the general strike organised by JAMES LARKIN, 1907. ROBERT LINDSAY CRAWFORD, author of the 'MAGHERAMORNE MANIFESTO', provided much of its philosophy. Its 100 candidates fared poorly in the 1912 local elections, and the organisation was in decline from the 1920s.

The name was later associated with REV. IAN PAISLEY, who broke from the Orange Order in 1962. The order opposed the BELFAST AGREEMENT (1998). In July 1990 the Irish government permitted it access to the site of the Battle of the Boyne to celebrate the tercentenary of the battle, a privilege denied to the Orange Order.

Industrial Development Associations, established in various towns from 1903, representing small and medium-sized businesses, rather than the bigger, older businesses, which previously dominated Chambers of Commerce.

Industrial Development (Encouragement of External Investment) Act (1958), an act designed to encourage the inflow of foreign capital. SEÁN LEMASS intended it to remove many of the remaining restrictions imposed by his Control of Manufacturing Acts (1932 and 1934), which had impeded foreign investment. The legislation facilitated the PROGRAMMES FOR ECONOMIC EXPANSION in the 1960s.

informers. The system of using political informers in Northern Ireland between 1981 and 1986—referred to by sections of the media as 'supergrasses' (a journalistic variation on the underworld slang 'grass')—was an attempt to break the republican and loyalist paramilitary organisations. It enabled prosecutions to be made under a bill of indictment, avoiding the necessity for witnesses to give evidence at a preliminary hearing or at trial. Some of those who gave evidence were provided with immunity from prosecution as well as police protection; some were provided with the means to a new life outside Northern Ireland.

Between 1981 and 1983 the evidence provided by some thirty informers led to charges against approximately three hundred people. It is believed that up to thirteen informers retracted their evidence before the trial began. Provisional IRA informers included Christopher Black and Raymond Gilmour; from the INLA Harry Kirkpatrick and Jackie

Grimley; and from the UVF William 'Budgie' Allen and Joseph Bennett. Black, a member of the Provisional IRA in Belfast arrested on 21 November 1981, provided a list of thirty-eight names, all of whom were convicted on his testimony, 5 August 1983. (On 17 July 1986 the Northern Ireland Court of Appeal quashed 198 informer convictions.) Testimony by Gilmour of the Derry INLA and Provisional IRA led to thirty-five people being charged with 180 offences; thirty-five were later acquitted by Lord Chief Justice Lowry on the grounds that Gilmour had told so many lies that his evidence could not be accepted.

Inghinidhe na hÉireann ('daughters of Ireland'), a national movement founded by MAUD GONNE MACBRIDE (who became president), April 1900; its four vice-presidents were Annie Egan, Alice Furlong, Anna Johnston (the writer Ethna Carbery), and Jennie Wyse-Power; its joint secretaries were HELENA MOLONY and Máire Quinn. Other early members included the actor sisters Sarah Allgood and Máire O'Neill, Louise Gavan Duffy, GRACE GIFFORD, Sinéad Flanagan (later wife of ÉAMON DE VALERA), and the actor Máire Nic Shiúbhlaigh. The movement adopted St Brigid as its patron, and CONSTANCE MARKIEVICZ designed its banner.

The organisation opposed the IRISH PARTY; it supported separatism, the Irish-Ireland movement, women's' suffrage, and the provision of free school meals. It provided free classes in Irish history, language and music for children and organised a monthly céilí for adults. It was instrumental in preventing Dublin Corporation from presenting a 'loyal address' to King Edward, 1903, and organised opposition to the state visit of KING GEORGE V and Queen Mary to Dublin, 8 July 1911. It produced a magazine, *Bean na hÉireann* ('Irishwoman'), the first nationalist feminist journal in Ireland, from 1908. The organisation was absorbed into CUMANN NA MBAN, 1913, while some of its members joined the IRISH CITIZEN ARMY.

Institute of Public Administration, founded in 1957 by civil servants and employees of local government and state-sponsored bodies. Its first director was Dr T. J. Barrington, 1970–76. The institute's aims were to examine public administration with a view to its continuous improvement. It offered in-service degree courses, administrative training, research projects, and student exchange schemes. It publishes books and periodicals dealing with government as well as the annual *Administration Yearbook and Diary*.

International Body on Decommissioning of Arms (sometimes known as the Mitchell Commission, after its chairman, GEORGE MITCHELL), part of the 'twin-track' approach to finding peace in Northern Ireland. The other members were General John de Chastelain (Canada) and Harri Hokeri (Finland). From 15 December 1995 the commission accepted submissions from a wide variety of bodies and individuals. Its report, 24 January 1996, concluded that paramilitary groups would not disarm before talks and proposed that talks and decommissioning should occur simultaneously, with eventual total disarmament. It recommended the adoption of 'confidence-building measures', including action on the release of prisoners and the review of emergency laws. The commission was succeeded by the INDEPENDENT INTERNATIONAL COMMISSION ON DECOMMISSIONING, September 1997.

International Fund for Ireland, set up under an initiative taken in 1986 in the United States to support the policy of reconciliation in the ANGLO-IRISH AGREEMENT with economic measures for Northern Ireland and the border areas of the Republic. The US government would contribute $120 million over three years up to 1988; other contributions pledged were from Canada ($10 million over ten years), New Zealand ($1 million over ten years), and the European Commission (£9.75 million over three years). The Board of the fund was appointed by the British and Irish governments, while the donor countries appointed observers. A review after ten years found that the fund had succeeded in reaching all sections of the community in promoting economic activity and job creation (31,629 jobs in 4,700 projects to September 1997). It provided the model for the European Union's distribution of Peace and Reconciliation Funds.

By December 1999 the fund was $290 million, with another $20 million committed in 1998; Canada committed $10 million; New Zealand $900,000, Australia $7 million, and the European Union 5 million ECU.

internment. Following a 'declaration of war' against England by the IRA in 1939, the Government introduced the TREASON ACT (1939) and OFFENCES AGAINST THE STATE ACT (1939). A raid by the IRA on an army ordnance depot in the Magazine Fort, Phoenix Park, Dublin, December 1939, compelled the

Minister for Justice to seek additional powers under the Emergency Powers Act (1940). The special legislation enabled internment to be introduced, 4 January 1940, under which some five hundred IRA members were interned without trial. During the years of the Second World War six members of the IRA were given death sentences.

Following the IRA's BORDER CAMPAIGN against Northern Ireland beginning in 1956, internment was again introduced in the Republic and also in Northern Ireland (until 1961). Internment was reintroduced in Northern Ireland on 9 August 1971.

Investment in Education (1965), a report compiled by PROF. PATRICK LYNCH, sponsored by the OECD and the Department of Education, the first detailed scientific study of the education system. Against the background of the first of the PROGRAMMES FOR ECONOMIC EXPANSION, the study found that participation in post-primary education was significantly below the average for northern European countries; that working-class children lacked the opportunity to take advantage of second-level and further education; and that there was a shortage of qualified labour for expanding industry and an under-utilisation of resources. It identified inefficiency as well as organisational and structural weaknesses within the education system. By 1965, 20 per cent of secondary-school pupils completed the Leaving Certificate course, and only 11 per cent progressed to university level.

The survey identified two major problems: there were too many small rural primary schools, and post-primary education, most of it owned by private (generally religious) interests outside government control, was unequally distributed throughout the country. At that time professional and white-collar workers made up 20 per cent of the working population but their children occupied 65 per cent of university places, while manual workers made up 25 per cent of the working population but their children had 2 per cent of university places. The Minister for Education, George Colley, supported by the Taoiseach, SEÁN LEMASS, established a process of reform, proposing the amalgamation of smaller primary schools in larger population centres and the provision of free school transport for children in rural areas. Lemass gave priority to education, enabling Colley's successor, DONOGH O'MALLEY, to announce, 10 September 1966, the opportunity for free post-primary education for all families, up to completion of the Intermediate Certificate; this, and transport faculties, arrived in 1967. A grants scheme for third level was also introduced. Regional technical colleges (later renamed institutes of technology) were founded in the late 1960s, and two national institutes of higher education established, in Limerick (later the University of Limerick) and Dublin (later Dublin City University). Community colleges and schools replaced the more traditional secondary schools during the 1970s. The minimum age for school-leavers was raised to fifteen, and the national Council for Educational Awards was established in 1972. A Department of Labour was established to supervise labour needs in industry, 1966; in 1967 AnCO, the industrial training authority, was established to oversee the training required for new industries.

Invincibles. A breakaway group of the IRB, calling itself the Irish National Invincibles, was founded during the LAND LEAGUE agitation, December 1881. Many of the leaders, including John McCafferty, P. J. Tynan, and JAMES CAREY, had close connections with the Land League. They plotted the deaths of SUPERINTENDENT JOHN MALLON of G Division of the Dublin Metropolitan Police and W. E. FORSTER, Chief Secretary for Ireland, whose successor, LORD FREDERICK CAVENDISH, they assassinated together with the Under-Secretary, THOMAS HENRY BURKE, 6 May 1882 (see PHOENIX PARK MURDERS). Five members of the organisation were hanged for the murders; James Carey, who had turned informer and was granted a pardon and passage to South Africa in return, was shot dead before disembarking at Cape Town by Padaí Ó Dónaill (also called Patrick O'Donnell). The organisation was abhorred by orthodox Fenians and was condemned by CHARLES STEWART PARNELL. It had disappeared by the late 1880s.

Ireland Act (1949), introduced by the British Government, 2 June 1949, as a response to the REPUBLIC OF IRELAND ACT (1948). It acknowledged that the Irish state had ceased to be a member of the British Commonwealth and went on to affirm that 'in no event will Northern Ireland or any part thereof cease to be part of His Majesty's Dominions and of the United Kingdom without the consent of the Parliament of Northern Ireland.'

Ireland Funds, an initiative taken by the United States, Canada, France, Australia and Britain 'to promote peace, culture and charity in all of Ireland,' with 50 per cent to go to Northern Ireland. It derived from the Ireland Fund established in the United States in 1976 (which in 1986 merged with the Irish-American Foundation). The funds gave priority to innovative and self-help projects with community involvement. They were subsequently headed by DR ANTHONY O'REILLY, who made the largest donation—$5 million—in 1997.

Ireland's Own, an illustrated weekly magazine founded by Edward O'Cullen, editor of the *People* (Wexford), 27 November 1902. For ninety years it advertised itself as 'a journal of fiction, literature and general information.' Regular features included a four-page ballad supplement, 'Songs of your country', 'Land of saints', 'What's in your name?', ghost stories, a children's section, and readers' services.' Popular writers for the magazine included Annie M. P. Smithson, Mrs N. T. Pender, Victor O'D. Power (whose 'Kitty the Hare' stories continued to be reprinted long after the author died in the late 1920s), and Paul Vincent Carroll. The most frequently requested poem was John Locke's 'Morning on the Irish Coast'. The magazine continues to appear in special editions during the year and is especially popular with the Irish abroad.

Irish Academy of Letters, established by W. B. YEATS and GEORGE BERNARD SHAW at a meeting in the Peacock Theatre, Dublin, at which Lennox Robinson presided, 18 September 1932. Shaw and Yeats were elected president and vice-president, respectively, and F. R. Higgins became secretary. Other original academicians included GEORGE RUSSELL, Austin Clarke, Pádraic Colum, St John Ervine, Oliver St John Gogarty, Brinsley McNamara, T. C. Murray, FRANK O'CONNOR, PEADAR O'DONNELL, SEÁN Ó FAOLÁIN, LIAM O'FLAHERTY, Séamus O'Sullivan, Forrest Reid, Lennox Robinson, Edith Somerville, James Stephens, and Francis Stuart, while DANIEL CORKERY, DR DOUGLAS HYDE, Lord Dunsany, Stephen McKenna, JAMES JOYCE and SEÁN O'CASEY declined invitations to attend. (Dunsany latter joined.)

Irish Agricultural Labourers' Union, founded in 1873 by Joseph Arch (leader of the British agricultural workers), ISAAC BUTT, and W. C. Upton, a Limerick carpenter. Though some three thousand attended its inaugural meeting at Kanturk, Co. Cork, it collapsed within a few months. (See also IRISH FEDERATED TRADE AND LABOUR UNION.)

Irish Agricultural Organisation Society. The society had its genesis at a meeting presided over by SIR HORACE PLUNKETT, 18 April 1894, through a motion proposed by Lord Cloncurry and seconded by JAMES BYRNE. At its first ordinary general meeting, 10 May 1894, Plunkett was elected president, C. T. Redington vice-president, and R. A. Anderson secretary. The Committee (which had an even nationalist-unionist divide) included FATHER T. A. FINLAY, BARON MONTEAGLE, COUNT ARTHUR MOORE, Bishop Patrick O'Donnell of Raphoe, JOHN REDMOND, THOMAS SEXTON, and Christopher Digges La Touche (managing director of Guinness's brewery). The IAOS published the *Irish Homestead,* edited by GEORGE RUSSELL.

Irish Anti-War Crusade, an organisation of Quaker origin formed in 1938. COLONEL DAN BRYAN of Military Intelligence asserted that it had been 'infiltrated' by Communist Party activists by 1949, a charge that was never substantiated.

Irish Association for Cultural, Economic and Social Relations, an all-Ireland body established in 1938, prompted by Major-General Hugh Montgomery of Fivemiletown, Co. Tyrone, with the object of bringing together people of differing political and religious viewpoints. The first president was Lord Charlemont. During the late 1990s Prof. Paul Bew of Queen's University, Belfast, became president.

Irish Battalion of St Patrick, eight companies of soldiers raised in Ireland in 1860 to serve Pope Pius IX in his resistance to Italian nationalists who sought the unification of the country. They were recruited by Papal ambassadors with the help of the NATION. Despite a ban on recruiting, a force of 1,400 was raised. The volunteers were paid only 1½ pence per day but were enjoined to take consolation in the opportunities afforded them for martyrdom in the service of the Pope. In Italy the battalion was led by Major Myles O'Reilly (1825–1880), a former Militia officer. Living conditions experienced by the volunteers were appalling, particularly at Ancona and Spoleto. Under O'Reilly the Spoleto garrison defended the town with notable bravery before it was forced to surrender after a twelve-hour bombardment, 17 September 1860. By the end of the year many of the Irish had returned home, some with the Papal medal inscribed *Pro Petri Sede* ('For the Seat of Peter').

Irish Brigade. The original Irish Brigade consisted of the 'Wild Geese', soldiers who had left Ireland under Patrick Sarsfield following the second Siege of Limerick (1691) and formed an Irish unit in the service of France.

During the 1851 parliamentary session some twenty-four Liberal MPs, including WILLIAM KEOGH, GEORGE HENRY MOORE, and JOHN SADLEIR, who joined in opposition to the Ecclesiastical Titles Bill, became known as the 'Irish Brigade'. With the approval of Archbishop (later Cardinal) PAUL CULLEN they founded the Catholic Defence Association. The Brigade—also known facetiously as the Pope's Brass Band—entered into an alliance with the TENANT LEAGUE, August 1852, and formed the INDEPENDENT IRISH PARTY. The new alliance had immediate success at the polls when, in the 1852 general election, 40 of its 48 candidates were returned. The acceptance by Keogh and Sadleir of government office, despite a pledge of independence, led to the disappearance of the Brigade within a short period.

Irish Bulletin, a daily newssheet produced by the first DÁIL ÉIREANN as a response to a ban on all Republican newspapers and journals; it appeared from 11 November 1919 to 11 July 1921, when the Truce came into force. Using information obtained by agents in DUBLIN CASTLE and in the postal service, and through armed raids by the IRA on confidential mails, it rapidly established a reputation for accurate reportage. Contacts established by DESMOND FITZGERALD, substitute Minister for Propaganda, included M. Bourdet, London editor of the *Echo de Paris,* M. Valbert, London editor of Agence Havas, and representatives of *Le Journal, Le Matin, Le Journal des Débats,* and *Le Temps.* The *Bulletin* was circulated in Italy, Spain, Scandinavia, Egypt, South Africa, India, and the United States. The Dublin Castle authorities, embarrassed by its accounts of events in Ireland, made strenuous efforts to prevent its publication, including the capture of its equipment and the circulation of forged issues. Though obliged to change premises on twelve occasions, the staff, which also included ROBERT BRENNAN, ERSKINE CHILDERS, Anna Fitzsimons, FRANK GALLAGHER, ARTHUR GRIFFITH, and the typist and distribution manager Kathleen Napoli McKenna, ensured that production was not affected. ALFRED COPE subsequently acknowledged the significant part played by the *Bulletin* during the WAR OF INDEPENDENCE.

Irish Catholic, a paper established and edited by its part-owner, William F. Dennehy, May 1888, as a successor to *Sullivan's Weekly News* (established in 1860). Anti-liberal and anti-modernist in outlook, under Dennehy it combined a defence of Catholic interests with support for the Liberal-Nationalist alliance.

Irish Christian Brothers, a Catholic teaching order founded by EDMUND RICE in Waterford, where he opened his first schools in New Street, 1 June 1802, and at Mount Sion, May 1804. The community of four lived within the rules of the Presentation Order. On 15 August 1808, now with three communities, the Brothers (or 'monks', as they were popularly called) were given a religious habit and vows of poverty, chastity and obedience for one year; seven members took perpetual vows in 1809. Other schools were established in Clonmel (1806), Dungarvan (1806), Cork (1811), and Hannover Street, Dublin (1812). The Institute of the Religious Brothers of Christian Schools in Ireland was recognised by Pope Pius VII on 5 September 1820; Rice was elected superior-general, 20 January 1822, and occupied the position until his retirement in 1838. By then the order had seventeen schools, six of them in England, with 7,500 pupils.

The Christian Brothers concentrated on the provision of elementary education for those who could not otherwise afford any, and their schools remained outside the system of NATIONAL EDUCATION established in 1831. The order later provided education at post-primary level. It also established communities in England, Africa, India, Australia, North and South America, and New Zealand. Edmund Rice was beatified on 6 October 1996, by which time there were 1,862 Christian Brothers, 600 of them in Ireland. The Christian Brothers and Presentation Brothers were then operating 164 primary and secondary schools in Ireland.

By 2001 numbers had dramatically declined, and there were few brothers teaching in their own schools. The order was damaged in the 1990s by revelations of the sexual abuse of children in its care.

Irish Christian Front, a right-wing movement founded by Patrick Belton, 21 August 1935, to fight the 'menace of communism' in Ireland and to aid 'Christians in Spain in their fight against the new paganism.' It was closely associated with the BLUESHIRTS and had the tacit support of the Catholic hierarchy in its efforts to pressure the Fianna Fáil government into severing diplomatic relations with the

Republican government of Spain and to support Franco in his armed revolt against that government. The Front was opposed by the left wing of the IRA, led by PEADAR O'DONNELL and FRANK RYAN. During the SPANISH CIVIL WAR it collected some £40,000 for medical supplies for the Spanish rebels, but the movement failed through lack of continued support.

Irish Church Missions, popular name for the Society for Irish Church Missions to Roman Catholics, founded by REV. ALEXANDER R. C. DALLAS, 28 March 1849, for 'the great work of the enlightenment of large bodies of Roman Catholics in Ireland, by the affectionate preaching of an outspoken Gospel in antagonism to Roman dogma . . .' It concentrated on the west of Ireland, the area most affected by the Great Famine (1845–49). The missions, the first of which was founded at Castlekerke on Lough Corrib, came into conflict with the Catholic Archbishop of Tuam, JOHN MACHALE, but gained the support of the Protestant Bishop, THOMAS PLUNKET. In 1853 Dallas persuaded the less extreme IRISH SOCIETY to aid the Mission, but within three years the partnership was dissolved, as the society became alarmed at the mission's aggressiveness (see SECOND REFORMATION).

The mission had some success in its early years, but two factors eventually militated against it: the contempt in which the Catholics held one who changed his religion (see 'JUMPER', 'SOUPERISM', and 'PERVERTS'), and the waning of evangelical fervour in England during the late 1850s, depriving the mission of funds. While it had little support from the Church of Ireland, whose moderate members disapproved of evangelicalism, it strained relations between the Catholic Church and the Church of Ireland in many areas. It also prompted the appointment of the Ultramontanist PAUL CULLEN as Archbishop of Armagh. At its peak the society employed 697 people and in 1856 its total financial output exceeded £30,000. The organisation was wound up on the death of its founder in 1869.

Irish Citizen, jointly founded by James Cousins and FRANCIS SHEEHY-SKEFFINGTON, May 1912, as the journal of the Irish Women's Suffrage Movement. Edited by Cousins and his wife, Margaret Cousins, its motto was 'For men and women equally, the rights of citizenship; from men and women equally, the duties of citizenship.' LOUIE BENNETT was also closely identified with its production. The contributors were mainly women. After James and Margaret Cousins went to India, 1913, when its circulation was estimated at 3,000, Sheehy-Skeffington managed the paper, which was edited from 1916 by his widow, Hanna Sheehy-Skeffington. It ceased publication following the destruction of its presses by the British military during the WAR OF INDEPENDENCE.

Irish Citizen Army, regarded as the world's first workers' militia, founded as a workers' defence corps by JAMES CONNOLLY and JAMES LARKIN during the DUBLIN LOCK-OUT (1913). Its purpose, at the suggestion of its first drill-master, CAPTAIN J. R. WHITE, was to keep unemployed trade unionists occupied, but its immediate aim was to protect workers from attacks by the DUBLIN METROPOLITAN POLICE and the employers' hired bullies. The first members of the Army Council were Captain J. R. 'Jack' White (chairman), P. T. Daly, Thomas Foran, James Larkin, William Partridge, and FRANCIS SHEEHY-SKEFFINGTON (vice-chairmen), Richard Brannigan and CONSTANCE MARKIEVICZ (honorary treasurers), T. Blair, John Bohan, T. Burke, P. Coady, P. Fogarty, P. J. Fox, Thomas Healy, T. Kennedy, J. MacGowan, P. Morgan, F. Moss, Michael Mullin, P. O'Brien, C. Poole, and John Shelly.

Constitution of the Irish Citizen Army

1. That the first and last principle of the Irish Citizen Army is the avowal that the ownership of Ireland, moral and material, is vested in the people of Ireland.
2. That its principal objects shall be:
   a. To arm and train all Irishmen capable of bearing arms to enforce and defend its first principle.
   b. To sink all differences of birth, privilege and creed under the common name of the Irish People.
3. That the Citizen Army shall stand for the absolute unity of Irish Nationhood and recognition of the rights and liberties of the World's Democracies.
4. That the Citizen Army shall be open to all who are prepared to accept the principles of equal rights and opportunities for the People of Ireland and to work in harmony with organised Labour towards that end.
5. Every enrolled member must be, if possible, a member of a Trades Union recognized by the Irish Trade Union Congress.

The last clause was added at the specific request of Larkin.

Before the supply of their dark-green serge uniforms (which members paid for), Citizen Army men wore a light-blue linen armband; officers were distinguished by a band of crimson worn on the right arm. The army was divided into three battalions: 1st (City) Battalion, 2nd (North County) Battalion, and 3rd (South County) Battalion. Its headquarters was Liberty Hall, Beresford Place, Dublin, and it drilled twice weekly at Croydon Park, Fairview. It published a weekly paper, the *Irish Worker.*

While it was close to the IRISH VOLUNTEERS, the Citizen Army maintained a separate identity. After the lock-out ended, in the spring of 1914, the membership dwindled, and the remaining force of approximately two hundred was reorganised by Connolly. The secretary was SEÁN O'CASEY. Under Connolly's leadership the Citizen Army had twin aims: the ownership of the land of Ireland by the people of Ireland and the establishment of a workers' republic. In September 1914 it assisted in the recovery of the Irish Volunteers' headquarters from the National Volunteers (headed by JOHN REDMOND).

Connolly, impatient at the Volunteers' inactivity, considered using the army to rise in insurrection in Dublin to spark a national uprising. He was unaware that the Military Council of the IRB had decided to stage an insurrection during the coming year. After he was taken into its confidence, January 1916, he committed the Citizen Army to participation in the EASTER RISING (1916). He led his small band of about 200 onto the streets of Dublin on Monday 24 April. While he was in the General Post Office, Sackville Street (O'Connell Street), the Citizen Army was principally deployed in St Stephen's Green and the Royal College of Surgeons, under the command of MICHAEL MALLIN. A detachment also attacked DUBLIN CASTLE; they took five prisoners, after which they evacuated the castle, unaware that they had in fact taken it, as there was no other guard on duty that day. They retired to a position opposite the castle, where they were attacked that afternoon by the Dublin Fusiliers and Royal Irish Rifles. The Citizen Army force in St Stephen's Green held out for a time. Following the surrender, both Connolly and Mallin were shot by firing squad.

The Irish Citizen Army remained in existence after the rising, though numerically weak, and fought alongside the IRA during the WAR OF INDEPENDENCE. Influenced by Constance Markievicz in refusing to accept the ANGLO-IRISH TREATY (1921), members of the Citizen Army supported the Republicans during the CIVIL WAR. In June 1922 members were involved at the FOUR COURTS and took over Findlater's premises in Sackville Street and later the Hammam Hotel when the Four Courts fell. The Citizen Army had no further role after the Civil War ended, 1923, though a group of the same name was associated with the REPUBLICAN CONGRESS (1934).

Irish Confederation, founded 13 January 1847 by WILLIAM SMITH O'BRIEN of YOUNG IRELAND, who had seceded from the REPEAL ASSOCIATION. It promoted the establishment of Confederate Clubs throughout the country. The attendance at the inaugural meeting also included M. J. Barry, Dr Robert Cane, CHARLES GAVAN DUFFY, JOHN BLAKE DILLON, ROBERT HOLMES, FATHER JOHN KENYON, Denny Lane, THOMAS D'ARCY MCGEE, JOHN MARTIN, JOHN MITCHEL, THOMAS FRANCIS MEAGHER, Richard O'Gorman, and THOMAS DEVIN REILLY. At the first meeting of the Council, 19 January, O'Brien acknowledged Robert Holmes as the 'true leader' of the new movement. A subcommittee, which included Mitchel and Reilly, was instructed to draw up a petition for repeal of the Union. Proclaiming the right of Ireland to self-government and declaring the need for self-reliance, it disavowed the use of physical force and total separation from England. However, the radical views of JAMES FINTAN LALOR attracted the support of a minority led by Mitchel. Lalor insisted that there could be no support for the demand for self-government unless it was linked with land agitation. Mitchel, MICHAEL DOHENY and Thomas Devin Reilly broke away to found the UNITED IRISHMAN.

Following the outbreak of revolution in France, February 1848, the Repeal movement and the Confederate Clubs received a new impetus as the demand for repeal of the Union and the establishment of a national parliament was taken up throughout Ireland. Mitchel and Meagher, seeking an Irish republic, published a series of articles outlining military tactics for a proposed uprising. Smith O'Brien suggested that a National Guard be recruited. Confederates marched in England alongside the Chartists. A deputation in Paris met Lamartine but received little encouragement.

In March, O'Brien was arrested together

with Mitchel and Meagher and charged with sedition. O'Brien and Meagher were discharged, but Mitchel, tried in May under the TREASON FELONY ACT, was sentenced to fourteen years' transportation. Aided by Father John Kenyon, Duffy, Dillon and Reilly plotted insurrection. On 22 July the British Parliament suspended *habeas corpus*; Duffy, Meagher, Doheny and McGee were arrested; and membership of the Confederate Clubs was declared an offence. The suspension of *habeas corpus* provoked the Confederate leaders still at liberty into calling for an armed rebellion. Their attempts were unsuccessful: Smith O'Brien's tour of the south-east produced little support, and the 'Young Ireland Rising' ended with a brief skirmish, under O'Brien's leadership, at BALLINGARRY, Co. Tipperary. The Irish Confederation and Young Ireland collapsed. Two members of the movement, JAMES STEPHENS and JOHN O'MAHONY, later founded the IRISH REPUBLICAN BROTHERHOOD and the FENIANS.

Irish Congress of Trade Unions, formed from the amalgamation of the Irish Trade Union Congress and the Congress of Irish Unions. It held its inaugural meeting in September 1959, at which time there were ninety-three affiliated unions, with a membership of 438,000.

Irish Constabulary Act (1822), enacted on 1 August 1822 to set up county police forces and salaried magistrates. A further act, 20 May 1836, extended the centralised police force and salaried magistracy. (See POLICE and ROYAL IRISH CONSTABULARY.)

Irish Convention (1917–18), an attempt by DAVID LLOYD GEORGE to secure a final settlement of the demand for home rule. The ninety-five members, meeting from 25 July 1917 to 5 April 1918 in Trinity College, Dublin, under the chairmanship of SIR HORACE PLUNKETT, included representatives of the ULSTER UNIONIST PARTY, southern unionists, and the IRISH PARTY. A number of independents, including EDWARD MACLYSAGHT and GEORGE RUSSELL, also attended. SINN FÉIN and the LABOUR PARTY boycotted the proceedings.

The convention failed in its efforts to reconcile the nationalist demand for self-government with the unionist demand that Ireland remain within the United Kingdom. JOHN REDMOND alienated members of his own party when, in an attempt to form an alliance with southern unionists and so isolate the Ulster unionists, he suggested that a native parliament should waive its right to collect customs duties. The convention ended in failure, 5 April 1918, with a report recommending self-government signed by fewer than half the members. A minority report stated that it would be dangerous to extend CONSCRIPTION to Ireland. In the general election of December 1918 the Irish Party retained only six seats, while the abstentionist Sinn Féin won seventy-three.

Irish Council (1847), formed in an effort to alleviate famine distress; it was intended to be representative of all classes, political opinions, and religions, though the gentry, according to CHARLES GAVAN DUFFY, 'were but scantily represented.' Committees were established to deal with tenant right and the retaining of the harvest in the country (rather than exporting grain to meet rents), while JOHN MITCHEL chaired a sub-committee that circularised Poor Law boards requesting information on the projected availability of food supplies. As conditions deteriorated, chaos ensued, and the professional and landlord elements in the council sought COERCION. It adjourned for the duration of the general election of 1847; it reassembled briefly in its aftermath but achieved little of consequence.

Irish Council Bill (1907), also known as the Devolution Bill, largely drafted by the Under-Secretary for Ireland, SIR ANTONY MACDONNELL, an attempt by the Chief Secretary for Ireland, AUGUSTINE BIRRELL, to grant Ireland devolved powers of home government. The proposed council was a compromise between the HOME RULE and unionist positions: Ireland would receive control over eight out of forty-five government departments (including education, local government, and the CONGESTED DISTRICTS BOARD). There would be a chamber of 106 members, 82 of whom were to be nominated by the British Government. Though some nationalists, including PATRICK PEARSE, were prepared to accept it, the proposal was rejected by SINN FÉIN, the UNITED IRISH LEAGUE, and the IRISH PARTY.

Irish Council of the European Movement, established in 1954, following unsuccessful attempts during the 1940s. It was reconstituted by Denis Corboy in April 1959, when GARRET FITZGERALD became chairman; he issued a monthly *Bulletin on European Affairs.* Other members included Dónal O'Sullivan and Miriam Hederman.

Irish Countrywomen's Association (Bantracht na Tuaithe), formed in April 1935 from the UNITED IRISHWOMEN (founded 1911). Affiliated to the Associated Country Women of the World, the ICA is dedicated to the general improvement of rural life; it concentrates on instruction in home and farm management, handicrafts, and general cultural activities. It now has some nine hundred guilds or branches and publishes a monthly magazine, the *Irish Countrywoman.* In 1954 the association established An Grianán, a residential college at Termonfeckin, Co. Louth, where a horticultural college was opened in 1966 with aid from the Kellogg Foundation; in 1981 the foundation financed an extension comprising twenty bedrooms and additional classrooms. A self-catering complex was added in 1998 and a museum and exhibition area in 1999.

Irish Creamery Milk Suppliers' Association, founded in 1950 by John Feely to 'promote the interests of all engaged in agriculture and to advise, protect and regulate the agricultural industry in Ireland.' A member of the General Committee of International Catholic Rural Associations (Rome), the ICMSA is one of the leading pressure groups in the agriculture industry. Policies are decided by a National Council and an annually elected sixty-member Council.

'Irish crown jewels', a name sometimes given to the regalia of the Order of St Patrick, presented by King William IV in 1830 to its grand master, the Lord Lieutenant of Ireland. They consisted of an eight-pointed star of Brazilian diamonds, enclosing an emerald shamrock on a ruby cross. On Saturday 6 July 1907 the gems were stolen from a safe in the library of the Office of Arms, Dublin Castle. A locksmith confirmed that the lock had not been picked nor opened with a key made from a wax impression. The identity of the thieves was never established; suspicion fell on two officials of the Office of Arms, Pierce Gun Mahony and his friend Francis Richard Shackleton (brother of the explorer Henry Shackleton), and Lord Haddo (son of the Lord Lieutenant, the MARQUESS OF ABERDEEN), but charges were never preferred. The investigation was handled by Chief Inspector King of Scotland Yard, whose report, presented to the Chief Commissioner of the Dublin Metropolitan Police within a week, was not acted on. A commission of inquiry found that the head of the Office of Arms, Sir Arthur Vicars, was negligent in his role as keeper of the jewels, and he was removed from office.

On 4 July 1913 Vicars was awarded damages of £5,000 against the *Daily Mail* (London) and others for libellous allegations concerning the disappearance of the jewels. In 1927 the jewels were offered for sale to the government of the Irish Free State, but its procrastination on the issue led to the withdrawal of the offer.

Irish Democrat, a short-lived socialist paper published in Dublin, 1937–38, produced by PEADAR O'DONNELL to replace the *Republican Congress.* It is now the name of the monthly paper of the Connolly Association, published in London since 1944.

Irish Democratic Trade and Labour Federation, a short-lived organisation of rural and urban labourers, founded in Cork at a meeting presided over by MICHAEL DAVITT, 21 January 1890.

'Irish dimension', the recognition of a role for the Irish government in finding a solution to the conflict in Northern Ireland. It arose from the British government's white paper *Northern Ireland Constitutional Proposals* (20 March 1973). Proposing a power-sharing Executive, it anticipated a wider framework than hitherto when it stated that 'any new arrangement for Northern Ireland should . . . be so far as possible acceptable to and accepted by the Republic of Ireland.' The consequences of this announcement were far-reaching, including a split in the Ulster Unionist Party when WILLIAM CRAIG left and founded the VANGUARD PROGRESSIVE UNIONIST PARTY ten days later.

Irish Dominion League, founded on 27 June 1919 by SIR HORACE PLUNKETT, with HENRY HARRISON as secretary. The league sought self-government for Ireland within the British Empire and looked for an end to Irish representation in the British Parliament and the regulation of fiscal relations by treaty. The proposal had little appeal to the Ulster Unionists, and the organisation disappeared.

Irish Ecclesiastical Record, a monthly journal founded in March 1864 by the Catholic Archbishop of Dublin, PAUL CULLEN. Its purpose was to communicate encyclicals, decisions and instructions to the clergy as part his efforts at bringing the Catholic Church in Ireland more into line with Roman practice. The first editors were Rev. George Conroy and Rev. (later Cardinal) Patrick Moran (1839–1911), Archbishop Cullen's nephew.

Irish Education Act (1892), legislation designed to make primary education compulsory, with limited effectiveness. It abolished the payment of fees for all children between the ages of three and fifteen who were attending state-aided primary schools. A School Attendance Act followed in 1894, but local authorities were generally apathetic in its implementation.

Irish Family Planning Association. The first family planning clinic was established in Dublin in 1968; others were set up in 1974. The Dublin Well Woman Centre opened in 1978.

Irish Farmers' Association, formed on 1 January 1971 from an amalgamation of the NATIONAL FARMERS' ASSOCIATION, the Irish Sugar Beet and Vegetable Growers' Association, the Leinster Milk Producers, the Cork and District Milk Producers, and the Irish Commercial Horticultural Association. It is now the most influential farming lobby in the country. It is a member of the EU farmers' union, COPA. The first president was T. J. Maher.

Irish Federated Trade and Labour Union, founded in Cork in 1890 by MICHAEL DAVITT, a further effort to establish a trade union for the estimated 300,000 agricultural labourers in rural Ireland; a previous attempt had been made with the IRISH AGRICULTURAL LABOURERS' UNION. It sought universal suffrage, free education, land settlement, houses for workers, and reduced working hours. It was damaged as a result of the split in the IRISH PARTY, 1890–91, but a remnant persisted into the 1920s. A further attempt to organise agricultural workers was made with the IRISH LAND AND LABOUR NATIONAL ASSOCIATION.

Irish Fever Act (1847), introduced on 27 April 1847 to contain the widespread fever that accompanied the GREAT FAMINE (1845–49). It gave local bodies wide preventive powers, including the erection of temporary fever hospitals and proper burials for the dead. The legislation was responsible for the provision of additional accommodation for some 23,000 patients in extra hospitals and dispensaries. The total cost of the operation was covered by a grant by the government to the Poor Law unions. The act remained in force until August 1850.

Irish Folklore Commission (Coimisiún Béaloideasa Éireann), founded in 1927 as An Cumann le Béaloideas Éireann (Folklore of Ireland Society) for the purpose of collecting and preserving oral tradition. Aided by a government grant and the ROYAL IRISH ACADEMY, it established the Irish Folklore Institute for the systematic and scientific collection and examination of folklore and the publication of the preserved material. Reorganised as the Irish Folklore Commission under Dr James Hamilton Delargy from April 1935, it published valuable collections as well as the folklore periodical *Béaloideas* and maintained a library of manuscripts. The material is now housed in the Department of Irish Folklore at the National University of Ireland, Dublin.

Comhairle Bhéaloideas Éireann (the Folklore of Ireland Council) was established in 1972 to arrange the cataloguing, editing and publishing of material from the collections and to facilitate access to material in the archives under such headings as settlement and dwelling, livelihood and household support, communications and trade, the community, human life, nature, folk medicine, time, principles and rules of popular belief and practice, mythological tradition, historical tradition, religious tradition, popular 'oral literature', and sports and pastimes.

Irish Freedom, a paper published monthly from 15 November 1910 by members of the IRB, managed by SEÁN MAC DIARMADA, THOMAS J. CLARKE, JOHN DALY, and DR PATRICK MCCARTAN (who was briefly its editor). IRB members contributed 1 shilling a month towards its upkeep. BULMER HOBSON was editor for a time; SEÁN O'CASEY also worked for it. Under the control of the younger element within the IRB, and encouraged by Clarke and CLAN NA GAEL, the paper became a vehicle for radical republicanism and attracted contributions from PATRICK PEARSE and THOMAS MACDONAGH. As a result of its increasingly extreme and radical tone, and because it called on Irishmen to resist British imperialism and not to support Britain in the Great War, it was suppressed, December 1914. It was replaced by *Éire*, edited by ARTHUR GRIFFITH; when this too was suppressed, Griffith introduced SCISSORS AND PASTE.

Irish Freedom was also the name of a paper published by the republican movement in Dublin, 1939–44, and in Belfast in 1951.

Irish Free State, established on 6 December 1922 in accordance with the ANGLO-IRISH TREATY (1921) and consisting of twenty-six counties. It had a two-tier legislature, DÁIL ÉIREANN and SEANAD ÉIREANN, commonly called the Senate. It was governed by the EXECUTIVE COUNCIL under the CONSTITUTION OF THE IRISH FREE STATE (1922).

Irish Free State (Constitution) Act (1922), enacted by the British Parliament, incorporating the CONSTITUTION OF THE IRISH FREE STATE (1922) and affording it recognition in English law.

Irish Georgian Society, a society for the preservation and protection of buildings of architectural merit, founded in 1958 by Desmond and Marie-Gabrielle Guinness, Percy Le Clerk, and William Dillon. It is dedicated to the preservation of the finest examples of Georgian architecture in Ireland and also engages in research concerning furniture, silver, and the decorative arts. The society influenced the restoration of Castletown House, Co. Kildare, and the former home of the St Leger family at Doneraile, Co. Cork.

Irish Historical Studies, founded in 1958 as the joint journal of the Irish Historical Society and Ulster Society for Irish Historical Studies. The original joint editors were R. Dudley Edwards and T. W. Moody.

Irish Homestead, the weekly journal of the co-operative movement, founded in 1895 and edited by GEORGE RUSSELL with the financial support of SIR HORACE PLUNKETT. Under Russell it became an influential publication, campaigning against social injustice, including the DUBLIN LOCK-OUT (1913). Though consisting mainly of agricultural and political commentary, it also attracted contributions from Russell's many friends in the literary revival, including W. B. YEATS. It published a trilogy from *Dubliners* by JAMES JOYCE, who responded by referring to the journal as 'the pigs' paper'. Boycotted by commercial advertisers because of its co-operative ideals, the journal struggled financially until 1923, when it merged with the *Irish Statesman*, also edited by Russell.

Irish Hospitals Sweepstake, a private trust founded in 1930 by JOSEPH MCGRATH, with Richard Duggan and Spencer Freeman. It organised an annual lottery on three horse races, and large numbers of tickets were bought in Britain and the United States. The draw at the Sweepstake offices in Ballsbridge, Dublin, was traditionally performed by nurses in uniform and created huge national interest. Speculators frequently contacted those who had drawn favourite horses with an offer to buy the ticket. The first draw was held on the Manchester November Handicap, 1930; the prize money amounted to £409,233, and three Belfast men shared the first prize of £208,792.

Irish Hospitals Trust (1940) Ltd was founded to administer the Irish Hospitals Sweepstake under the provisions of the Public Hospitals Acts (1933–40). The 201 sweeps held in the years 1930–86 realised £134 million, which benefited more than four hundred hospitals and institutions. The Sweepstake closed in 1987 and Irish Hospitals Trust was placed in liquidation. Its office site in Ballsbridge was sold for £6.6 million in 1988.

Irish Independence Party, a short-lived party founded in Belfast in October 1977 by Frank McManus (Unity MP for Fermanagh and South Tyrone in the British House of Commons, 1970–74) and Fergus McAteer (son of EDDIE MCATEER, former leader of the Nationalist Party of Northern Ireland). It called for a British withdrawal as a prerequisite to negotiations on Northern Ireland's future status; its main tactic was to agree anti-Unionist candidates in elections for the British House of Commons. In May 1979 its four candidates obtained 3.3 per cent of the total vote. The party's highest vote-winner was Pat Fahy, with 12,055 votes in Mid-Ulster; in 1981 he became leader of the party, with McManus deputy leader and McAteer chairman. It won twenty-one seats with 3.9 per cent of the vote in the local government elections of May 1981 but did not nominate any candidates in the 1982 Assembly elections.

Irish Independent, founded as the *Irish Daily Independent* by CHARLES STEWART PARNELL following the split in the IRISH PARTY (December 1890 to January 1891) that lost him the support of the FREEMAN'S JOURNAL. The first issue, edited by Edward Byrne, appeared on 18 December 1891, two months after Parnell's death. A companion paper, the *Evening Herald*, was also published. The paper employed many members of the IRB, including the president of the Supreme Council, FRED ALLAN, and its offices became a rendezvous for Irish and foreign republicans.

JOHN REDMOND controlled the paper during the 1890s, when it lost readers to both the *Daily Nation* and the *Freeman's Journal*. It merged with the *Daily Nation*, controlled by the anti-Parnellite WILLIAM MARTIN MURPHY, to appear as the *Daily Independent and Nation*, 1 September 1900. Having founded Independent Newspapers in 1904, Murphy relaunched the paper as the *Irish Daily Independent*, 2 January 1905. A companion paper, the *Sunday Independent*, began publication in 1906.

The *Irish Independent* was identified during the 1920s with support for the ANGLO-IRISH TREATY and for the pro-Commonwealth position of CUMANN NA NGAEDHEAL; during the 1930s it gave support to FINE GAEL. It is now the leading publication of Independent News and Media PLC, controlled by Dr Anthony O'Reilly.

Irish Ireland, a name sometimes given to the forms of cultural nationalism that took shape during the 1890s and in the first decade of the twentieth century. Its most potent expressions were found in the GAELIC ATHLETIC ASSOCIATION, GAELIC LEAGUE, CUMANN NA NGAEDHEAL, and early SINN FÉIN movement. The idea was also promoted by the Irish literary movement and the ABBEY THEATRE. Irish-Irelanders sought cultural and economic independence for Ireland. In 1905 D. P. MORAN of the *Leader* published a collection of essays under the title 'A philosophy of Irish Ireland'; he identified what he saw as flaws in popular ideas of Irish culture, identity, and independence. In their enthusiasm, some Irish-Irelanders developed intolerance for Britain and all things British, regarding it as the source of all the influences that were, in their opinion, corrupting Irish national values.

Irish Labour Defence League, originally the Workers' Defence Corps, renamed after its first convention on 7 July 1931. It consisted of left-wing members of the IRA and Dublin trade unionists. Outlawed by the government together with eleven other radical organisations, 17 October 1931, it disappeared within a short time.

Irish Labour League, founded in 1891 by the Dublin Branch of the National Union of Gasworkers and General Labourers, seeking the nationalisation of transport. It failed within a short time through lack of support.

Irish Land and Labour Association, founded in Cork by Daniel Sheehan at the end of the nineteenth century as a successor to the Irish Democratic Labour Federation. It sought to organise agricultural labourers and small tenant-farmers; its platform included a demand for 'houses for the people, land for the people, work and wages for the people, education for the people, state pensions for old people,' and demanded that all local rates should be paid by the ground landlords. While it lacked widespread support, it attracted the attention of WILLIAM O'BRIEN of the UNITED IRISH LEAGUE, but it remained a local organisation. After the founding of the LABOUR PARTY, 1912, members were mainly absorbed into the new labour movement.

Irish Literary Society, jointly founded in London by T. W. Rolleston and W. B. YEATS from the SOUTHWARK LITERARY CLUB; its first meeting was held on 9 April 1892. Other founder-members included JOHN SMYTH CRONE, SIR CHARLES GAVAN DUFFY, DR DOUGLAS HYDE, MARTIN MCDERMOTT, and R. BARRY O'BRIEN. Its aim was to encourage and stimulate a new school of literature that would be thoroughly and distinctively Irish though written in English. The IRISH NATIONAL LITERARY SOCIETY was founded in Dublin a year later, with similar aims and involving many of the same people.

Irish Literary Theatre, founded at the end of 1898 by W. B. YEATS, after he broke with the IRISH NATIONAL LITERARY SOCIETY, with the support of LADY AUGUSTA GREGORY and EDWARD MARTYN. Early financial support was provided by Emily Lawless, W. E. H. LECKY, J. P. MAHAFFY, and Alice Milligan. The first productions were Yeats's *The Countess Cathleen* and Martyn's *The Heather Field*, 8 May 1899. Martyn's play was the popular success of the week-long run; the theme of Yeats's play—a woman selling her soul to feed the starving—was attacked by nationalists. One of the first plays in Irish, *Casadh an tSúgáin* by DOUGLAS HYDE, was produced by the Literary Theatre in 1901. *Diarmuid and Gráinne*, a collaboration between George Moore and Yeats, with music by Edward Elgar, was produced on 21 October 1901.

The aims of the theatre met with opposition from sections of 'IRISH IRELAND', led by ARTHUR GRIFFITH and D. P. MORAN, who denounced it as both false and offensive. The ILT joined with the National Dramatic Company of FRANK AND WILLIAM FAY in 1902 to form the IRISH NATIONAL THEATRE SOCIETY. One of the new company's first productions, *The Shadow of the Glen* by J. M. SYNGE in 1903, was also attacked by Griffith. The ABBEY THEATRE developed from the Irish Literary Theatre in 1904.

Irish Loyal and Patriotic Union, founded in Dublin on 1 May 1885 to organise resistance to HOME RULE. Members included Lord Castletown, Lord Longford, and Lord de Vesci. It fared poorly in the general election of November 1885, when only one of the five candidates was elected (for the University of Dublin). It achieved a degree of notoriety during the period 1887–88 when its secretary, Edward Houston, succeeded in bribing RICHARD PIGOTT to produce a forged letter attempting to link CHARLES STEWART PARNELL to the PHOENIX PARK MURDERS (see also 'PARNELLISM AND CRIME'). The organisation disseminated propaganda against home rule until 1891, when it was superseded by the IRISH UNIONIST ALLIANCE.

Irish Manuscripts Commission, established in 1928 under the chairmanship of EOIN MACNEILL. Its brief was to investigate and report on surviving manuscripts of literary, historical and general Irish interest and importance and to edit and publish such manuscripts. In March 1930 the commission began publication of the journal *Analecta Hibernica* to report on important manuscript collections and aspects of the work being undertaken.

Irish Monthly, a magazine of a religious and literary character founded in 1873 and edited until 1912 by Rev. Matthew Russell. It published leading writers of the era, including Alice Curtayne, Katherine Tynan, Denis Florence McCarthy, Francis MacManus, George Moore, T. D. SULLIVAN, Aubrey de Vere, Oscar Wilde, and W. B. YEATS. It ceased publication in 1954.

Irish Museum of Modern Art, opened in 1991 in the Royal Hospital, Kilmainham, Dublin. Its first director was Declan MacGonigal (until 2001).

Irish National Aid Association, founded after the EASTER RISING (1916) to raise funds for the dependants of deceased and imprisoned members of the IRISH VOLUNTEERS. Within a short time it amalgamated with the IRISH VOLUNTEERS DEPENDANTS' FUND.

Irish National Alliance, a republican organisation founded in 1894 by members of CLAN NA GAEL. Led by a militant, William Lyman, it was organised in Ireland and England by DR MARK RYAN. While it followed the rules and constitution of the IRB (except that it substituted a pledge for the oath), it was opposed to the IRB, which it attacked for its conservatism. The dispute between the two organisations emerged in the columns of various republican papers, including the INA's *Irish Republic*. It had a military wing, the Irish National Brotherhood. Through the activities of travelling organisers, such as James F. Egan, it became a force in the west of Ireland, but it failed to become a national movement, and by 1900 only two circles were left out of the original fourteen in Dublin.

Irish National Caucus, founded in the United States in the 1970s by Father Seán McManus to lobby support for nationalists and republicans in Northern Ireland. It won the support of the influential Congressman Mario Biaggi, who formed a committee from among congressmen and senators that influenced the US Congress into stopping the sale of arms to the RUC. It became an umbrella group for the GAA and the Ancient Order of Hibernians and local bodies throughout the United States. In Washington it urged a 'peace forum' on Northern Ireland. It met the Provisional IRA, UDA and others and sought the inclusion of paramilitary organisations in a solution to the Northern Ireland conflict. While the Taoiseach, JACK LYNCH, attacked its alleged support for the Provisional IRA, the INC claimed to have no connection with any organisation outside the United States.

Irish National Club, founded in London in January 1899, largely from among those who organised the CENTENARY CELEBRATIONS, 1898, including DR MARK RYAN. Its object was 'to promote a healthy spirit of nationality among London Irishmen and the study and encouragement of Irish history and literature.' It supported the GAA and the Gaelic League.

Irish National Federation, a constituency organisation formed in March 1891 by the anti-Parnell majority that seceded from the IRISH NATIONAL LEAGUE as a result of the split in the IRISH PARTY, 1890–91. It was led by JUSTIN MCCARTHY, JOHN DILLON, WILLIAM O'BRIEN, and T. M. HEALY (who was expelled in 1893). By December 1891 it had 83,000 members, and two years later it had 47,000 members. Dillon became leader in 1896. By 1898 there were 221 branches, compared with the National League's six. Disputes between branches of the party led to increasing disillusionment among the rising generation of nationalists. The rise of the UNITED IRISH LEAGUE, 1898, led to the National League and Irish National Federation reuniting in 1900.

Irish National Foresters, founded in Dublin in 1877 as a benefit society. Its leaders included members of the IRB and prominent nationalists, and the organisation was regarded with suspicion by DUBLIN CASTLE. To qualify for membership one had to be Irish by birth or descent. Officials were known by such names as high chief ranger and high sub-chief ranger, and each branch was led by a chief ranger and sub-chief ranger. The organisation still exists.

Irish Nationality and Citizenship Act (1935), introduced by the Fianna Fáil Government. Under the act, Irish nationals ceased to be British subjects.

Irish National League, inaugurated by CHARLES STEWART PARNELL on 17 October 1882, replacing the LAND LEAGUE. As the constituency organisation of the IRISH PARTY, it aimed to secure '(1) national self-government; (2) land law reform; (3) local self-government; (4) extension of the parliamentary and municipal franchise; (5) development and encouragement of the labour and industrial resources of Ireland.' Its structure was developed by TIMOTHY HARRINGTON, WILLIAM O'BRIEN, and T. M. HEALY (secretary), who drew up its constitution. The league had 1,261 branches by December 1885. In 1884 Parnell made Catholic priests *ex officio* delegates to the league's conventions but maintained the exclusion of women from its ranks by refusing the application of MAUD GONNE.

The Irish National League of America was established but came under the control of CLAN NA GAEL and was of limited use to the Irish organisation. The league's principal functions were the organising of county conventions and providing financial support for the parliamentary party, which, from 1884, gave financial assistance to its MPs. The constituency organisations played a vital role in the general election of November 1885, which saw the Parnellite party return with eighty-five seats in Ireland. The following year leading members of the league—Harrington, O'Brien, Healy, and JOHN DILLON—organised the PLAN OF CAMPAIGN. The amount of money raised increased from £11,616 (1884/85) to £47,275 (1885/86).

On 19 August 1887 the Chief Secretary for Ireland, A. J. BALFOUR, declared the league 'a dangerous association' and suppressed its 141 branches.

The league split during the years 1890–91 following the revelation of Parnell's relationship with KATHARINE O'SHEA. The Parnellites, led by JOHN REDMOND, controlled the league, while the anti-Parnellites established the IRISH NATIONAL FEDERATION. Membership of the league steadily decreased, from 13,108 in December 1891 to 6,500 in December 1893; by 1899 there were only six active branches. The rise of the UNITED IRISH LEAGUE brought about the reunification of the Irish Party in 1900, when the UIL replaced the Irish National League as its constituency organisation.

Irish National Liberation Army, formed in 1975 from a left-wing splinter group of the 'Official IRA', the 'People's Liberation Army'. It was controlled by SÉAMUS COSTELLO of the IRISH REPUBLICAN SOCIALIST PARTY and drew its main support from Belfast and south Derry. During its feud with the Official IRA in 1975 the INLA murdered the Official IRA commander in Belfast, Billy McMillen. 28 April 1975. The feud was ended through the efforts of Father Alec Reid of the Clonard monastery in Belfast. The INLA, which financed its operations through bank robberies in the South, sometimes used the cover name 'Catholic Reaction Force' in the North. It is believed to have carried out the murder of the Conservative spokesperson on Northern Ireland, Airey Neave, in London, 30 March 1979.

The INLA was declared illegal in Britain and Northern Ireland in July 1979 and in the Republic in January 1983. In 1981, now believed to be led by the former Provisional IRA member Dominic McGlinchey, it lost three of its members to a hunger strike in the Maze Prison. In 1982 it was responsible for the death of some thirty people, including those killed at the Droppin' Well at Ballykelly, Co. Derry, 6 December 1982. It was also responsible for the explosion at the radar station at Schull, Co. Cork, 20 September 1982. During this period some thirty members were arrested on the evidence of two INFORMERS, Harry Kirkpatrick and Jackie Grimley; they were released when their convictions were quashed on appeal, which led to another feud, December 1986 to March 1987. As the 'Catholic Reaction Force' the INLA was responsible for the Darkley massacre, 21 November 1983, when gunmen fired into a Pentecostal church during a service in Co. Armagh, killing three people. Mediation by the Belfast priests Father Gerry Reynolds and Father Alec Reid eventually led to a truce.

A year later the INLA was believed to have reorganised, its members now including Dessie

O'Hare (who was expelled in September 1987). The organisation was reactivated during the 1990s, when it claimed responsibility for a number of killings. In April 1995 it announced that it had been operating a ceasefire since July 1994, which it claimed was both 'tactical and permanent'.

The INLA chief of staff, Frank 'Gino' Gallagher, was killed in January 1996, and a new feud ensued. The ceasefire ended with the death of the former chief of staff Hugh Torney, 3 September 1996. The INLA rejected the Provisional IRA ceasefire of July 1997. INLA prisoners killed the LVF leader BILLY WRIGHT in the Maze Prison, 27 December 1997, sparking off sectarian attacks by the LVF, ULSTER FREEDOM FIGHTERS, and Provisional IRA. In January 1998 the INLA killed the UDA leader Jim Guiney and in June was responsible for a bomb in Manorhamilton, Co. Leitrim. In August the INLA announced a ceasefire and offered a 'sincere, heartfelt and genuine apology' for the deaths of so many innocent people; it also apologised for descending from a 'liberation army' to conducting 'sectarian and internecine warfare.'

Irish National Literary Society, founded by W. B. YEATS in 1892; its first president was DOUGLAS HYDE. The society was modelled on the IRISH LITERARY SOCIETY, founded in London the previous year. Hyde's inaugural address, 'The necessity for de-Anglicising Ireland', outlined the society's ideals. Yeats withdrew from the society in 1898 and founded the IRISH LITERARY THEATRE.

Irish National Society, founded in London in 1844 during the agitation for Repeal, designed to unite Irishmen, regardless of political or religious beliefs. Membership included MAURICE O'CONNELL, Lord Clanricarde, and Lord Castlereagh. It did not survive the break-up of the REPEAL ASSOCIATION.

Irish National Teachers' Organisation, the oldest and largest teachers' trade union in Ireland, founded in 1868 by VERE FOSTER as the National Teachers' Association for those employed in schools within the NATIONAL EDUCATION system.

Irish Nation League, founded in Ulster in September 1916. Membership was strongly representative of the legal profession. Opposed to partition, it was represented at the IRISH CONVENTION, July 1917 to April 1918, and merged with SINN FÉIN in 1917.

Irish Neutrality League, a short-lived nationalist body founded in 1914 with the aim of keeping Ireland from involvement on the side of Britain in the Great War (1914–18). It organised an intense anti-recruiting campaign. (See CONSCRIPTION.)

Irish News, a nationalist newspaper launched in Belfast by anti-Parnellites, 15 August 1891, later taken over by the Parnellite *Belfast Morning News* (which had been launched by the Read brothers, 2 July 1855, as the first penny newspaper). The *Irish News* has supported the SDLP throughout the conflict in Northern Ireland.

Irish News Agency, established in 1949 by the Minister for External Affairs, SEÁN MACBRIDE, to publicise Ireland abroad. Its first board of directors was appointed on 20 March 1950; the managing director was CONOR CRUISE O'BRIEN, who also edited *Éire-Ireland*. On Fianna Fáil's return to power in 1951 the agency was dismantled and its role assumed by the Department of External Affairs.

Irish Office, established in London in 1801 to facilitate the flow of correspondence between Dublin and London following the implementation of the ACT OF UNION. It was used by the Chief Secretary for Ireland to transact his business while in London for the parliamentary session. According to a report drawn up by Stafford Northcote and CHARLES EDWARD TREVELYAN, *The Organisation of the Permanent Civil Service* (1853), it was not entirely clear what the staff of the Irish Office did. The office was abolished following the ANGLO-IRISH TREATY (1921).

Irish Party, also known as the Irish Parliamentary Party, Home Rule Party, and Nationalist Party, developed from the Home Rule League, founded by ISAAC BUTT in 1873. The aim of the fifty-six Home Rulers returned in the general election of 1874 was to sustain and support each other in the manner 'best calculated to promote the grand object of national self-government which the Irish nation has committed to our cause.' Members also resolved to 'individually and collectively hold ourselves aloof from and independent of all party combinations.'

Butt failed to direct parliamentary attention on Irish affairs during the Conservatives' period in office, 1874–80. An avowed constitutionalist, he disapproved of the Fenian element in his party, which, led by JOSEPH BIGGAR, JOHN

O'CONNOR POWER, and FRANK HUGH O'DONNELL, adopted the policy of OBSTRUCTIONISM. Butt was succeeded as leader by WILLIAM SHAW, 1879. With his moderate followers he remained aloof from the LAND WAR, prosecuted under the leadership of CHARLES STEWART PARNELL. At the height of the Land War the general election of April 1880 returned sixty-nine Irish members styling themselves Home Rulers. Parnell was elected chairman of the party on 17 May (defeating Shaw by 23 to 18); his ascendancy over the party was confirmed when, in January 1881, a group of twelve led by Shaw, later known as 'nominal Home Rulers' or 'Whigs', seceded. Parnell and his followers drew attention to the plight of the tenant-farmers and supported the Land League in the House of Commons. He also established a party organ, UNITED IRELAND.

Agrarian and parliamentary agitation led to the Land Law (Ireland) Act (1881), introduced by W. E. GLADSTONE (see LAND ACTS). During the years 1882–85 Parnell built up a constituency organisation, the IRISH NATIONAL LEAGUE, financed by local collections, money from Irish business interests (in particular the drink trade), and money from America (where a branch of the Irish National League was also established). The Irish Party was the first modern parliamentary party in Europe: its members could draw salaries from National League finances, it operated under a whip (T. M. HEALY), and from August 1884 members were bound by a pledge (drawn up by TIMOTHY HARRINGTON), imposed at the Dungarvan Convention:

> I, [. . .], pledge myself that in the event of my election to parliament, I will sit, act and vote with the Irish Parliamentary Party and if at a meeting of the party convened upon due notice especially to consider the question, it be decided by a resolution supported by a majority of the entire parliamentary party that I have not fulfilled the above pledge I hereby undertake to resign my seat.

Home rule dominated Ireland during 1885. Gladstone's government fell in June 1885. Parnell had received little encouragement from the Liberals, and, believing that the Conservatives would introduce some measure of home rule, he placed the support of the party behind them. The Irish Party benefited from the Representation of the People Act (1884) and the Redistribution of Seats Act (1885). In addition it had clerical support. According to T. W. CROKE, the nationalist Archbishop of Cashel, June 1885,

> three years ago, the Irish Parliamentary Party was disliked, and distrusted by many of the best men in the land. Today the bishops, as a body, and the priests universally, thoroughly believe in their honour and honesty and have confided to them, accordingly, their most sacred interests.

In the 1885 general election the Home Rulers won eighty-six seats, the precise difference between the Liberals (335) and the Conservatives (249). The Conservatives contented themselves with the Purchase of Land (Ireland) Act (see LAND ACTS). In December the 'HAWARDEN KITE' revealed Gladstone's conversion to home rule for Ireland. When the Conservatives introduced COERCION in January 1886, Parnell switched the Irish Party's support to the Liberals. Gladstone formed his third ministry and introduced the first HOME RULE BILL, 8 April. Two months later it was defeated in the House of Commons. Gladstone lost the general election of July 1886, and the Home Rulers returned with eighty-five seats. Parnell and his party were committed to Gladstone and the Liberals in opposition.

Between 1887 and 1890 the party and its leader were the focus of constant public attention as a result of a libel action taken against the *Times* (London) following a series of articles entitled 'PARNELLISM AND CRIME'. A parliamentary commission investigated Parnell's role in the LAND WAR; the articles proved to be forgeries, and the commission cleared him after an exhaustive inquiry. However, the party was again plunged into crisis over Parnell's involvement in the *O'Shea v. O'Shea and Parnell* divorce case. The trial resulted in victory for W. H. O'SHEA, whose wife, Katharine, had been Parnell's lover since 1880. The revelations in the Divorce Court forced Gladstone to declare that the Liberals could not support home rule while Parnell led the Irish Party. With Parnell also condemned by the Catholic hierarchy, the party was now forced to choose between chief and cause. Having re-elected Parnell as chairman for the forthcoming parliamentary session, it now reconsidered its decision. A lengthy struggle took place, 1–6 December 1890, when Parnell refused to relinquish the leadership. Justin McCarthy, followed by a total of forty-five members, withdrew, leaving Parnell with twenty-eight followers.

Following Parnell's early death in October 1891 there were several factions in the parliamentary party fighting for home rule. McCarthy and others formed a new constituency organisation, the IRISH NATIONAL

FEDERATION, while Redmond retained control of the IRISH NATIONAL LEAGUE. In 1895 Healy left the INF and founded the clericalist PEOPLE'S RIGHTS ASSOCIATION. When McCarthy resigned from leadership of the anti-Parnellites, 1896, he was succeeded by JOHN DILLON.

The factions were forced to reunite by the swift success of a new organisation, the UNITED IRISH LEAGUE, founded by WILLIAM O'BRIEN in 1898. On 30 January 1900 the UIL was recognised as the new constituency organisation of the Irish Party, and Redmond was accepted as leader of the reunited party. The Redmondite party, however, lacked the solidarity of the old Parnellite party; Healy was a maverick, and Redmond had not got the unequivocal support of O'Brien and his followers. H. H. ASQUITH, who became Prime Minister in 1908, was not committed to home rule, and Redmond had to resist suggestions that he break the connection with the Liberals.

In the North Leitrim by-election of 1908 a former member of the party, C. J. Dolan, standing for SINN FÉIN, was defeated by a Redmondite. Before the general election of 1910, Asquith, seeking Irish support for his attempt to break the power of the House of Lords (a traditional enemy of home rule), promised in a speech in London, 10 December 1909, that Liberal policy, 'while explicitly safeguarding the supremacy and indefectible authority of the imperial parliament, will set upon Ireland a system of full self-government in regard to purely Irish affairs.'

The state of the parties after the general election of January 1910 was: 275 Liberals, 273 Conservatives and Unionists, 40 Labour, and 81 Home Rule (eleven of whom, as Independent Nationalists, were not subject to Redmond's whip). A second general election, December 1910, left Asquith in a sufficiently strong position to secure the passing of the PARLIAMENT ACT (1911). The removal of the House of Lords' veto ensured the eventual passing of the (third) Home Rule Bill. The Ulster Unionists and Conservatives fought to prevent the passing of the Home Rule Bill (introduced on 11 April 1912). Save for partition, the Irish Party was prepared to arrive at an accommodation of Unionists' interests. However, the rise of the ULSTER VOLUNTEER FORCE from January 1913 and the IRISH VOLUNTEERS from November 1913 led to government fears of civil war. In an attempt to resolve the deadlock between the Unionists and Nationalists, the BUCKINGHAM PALACE CONFERENCE was held, July 1914, but it ended in failure.

Unionists and nationalists agreed to the suspension of home rule, after it became law, for the duration of the Great War, leaving the position of Ulster unresolved. The Irish Party had accomplished the aim of Butt and Parnell; congratulatory messages poured in from Ireland and abroad. The EASTER RISING (1916) took the leaders of the Irish Party by surprise; Redmond denounced the organisers as traitors and pawns of Germany. The Irish Party, believing the rising might undermine its accomplishments, concentrated on the IRISH CONVENTION, 1917–18, which was boycotted by Sinn Féin. By the time it broke up inconclusively in the summer of 1918, Redmond was dead and JOHN DILLON was leader of the Irish Party. During 1918 the party won three by-elections. Its demise was aided by the British government's attempt to introduce CONSCRIPTION in Ireland, a move that united nationalists throughout the country in opposition. Though Dillon attended the MANSION HOUSE CONFERENCE (1918) to co-ordinate the anti-conscription campaign, the Irish Party suffered from past identification with British policy. Another series of arrests, triggered by the 'GERMAN PLOT', further alienated nationalist public opinion.

The final struggle between the Irish Party and Sinn Féin occurred during the bitterly fought general election of December 1918, which resulted in the virtual annihilation of the party. It retained only six seats, four of them in Ulster. Symbolically, Dillon lost his Co. Mayo seat to the imprisoned leader of Irish republicanism, ÉAMON DE VALERA. The party was vanquished, except for the Northern nationalist remnant led by JOSEPH DEVLIN, who sat in the British House of Commons until 1925. During the 1920s some supporters of the old Irish Party were absorbed by CUMANN NA NGAEDHEAL. On 21 January 1919 Sinn Féin representatives formed DÁIL ÉIREANN and declared the Irish Republic.

Irish Peasant, a paper founded in 1903 by James McCann, a Dublin stockbroker and Nationalist MP, but under the dynamic editorship of William Ryan it became of national importance. The paper played a leading role in the 'IRISH IRELAND' movement, promoting the philosophy of the GAELIC LEAGUE. It emphasised the negative attitude of the Catholic hierarchy towards Irish and Irish nationalism, provoking CARDINAL LOGUE to condemn it as 'a most pernicious anti-Catholic print.' The McCann family closed the paper in December

1906. Ryan, who recorded his experiences in *The Plough and the Cross* (1910), was unsuccessful in his attempt to continue the paper as the *Peasant*.

Irish People, a paper founded by JAMES STEPHENS as the organ of the IRB, 28 November 1863. The FENIANS published another paper of the same name in New York. Edited by JOHN O'LEARY, with CHARLES J. KICKHAM and THOMAS CLARKE LUBY as chief contributors and JEREMIAH O'DONOVAN ROSSA as business manager, the paper was outspoken in its republicanism. It was suppressed, 16 September 1865, and many of its staff arrested. The IRB published another paper, the *Flag of Ireland*, from 1868 to 1874.

Irish People, a weekly paper founded by WILLIAM O'BRIEN as the organ of the UNITED IRISH LEAGUE. The first issue, 16 September 1899, contained an article by CHARLES J. KICKHAM, 'Priests in politics'. Critical of the IRISH PARTY, from which O'Brien had seceded, it championed self-government for Ireland through conciliation and conference. O'Brien was succeeded as editor in 1907 by John Herlihy. Beset by financial difficulties, it ceased publication in 1908.

Irish People's Liberation Organisation, a republican paramilitary organisation, associated with a political group called the Republican Socialist Collective. During the period 1986–87 it sought the disbanding of the IRSP and INLA. A bitter three-month feud that cost twelve lives was ended through the intervention of two priests, Father Alec Reid and Father Gerry Reynolds. The IPLO, which also used the cover name 'Catholic Reaction Force', was believed to have been responsible for five deaths during 1991. A year later it was involved in an internal feud between the 'Army Council' and 'Belfast Brigade' factions. All factions were believed to have disbanded in 1992.

Irish Press, a daily newspaper launched by ÉAMON DE VALERA in 1931 as an organ of Fianna Fáil. Irish Press Ltd was incorporated on 4 September 1928; 200,000 ordinary shares were offered at £1 each. The first issue of the paper appeared on 5 September 1931. The first editor was FRANK GALLAGHER; the three controlling editors were, successively, Éamon de Valera, his son Vivion de Valera, and his grandson Éamon de Valera. The company also published the *Sunday Press* from 4 September 1949 and the *Evening Press* from September 1954. The group encountered serious financial difficulties during the 1980s, and the Irish Press titles ceased publication on 25 May 1995. Debts of £19 million resulted in the appointment of a liquidator, 8 September 1995.

Irish Press Agency, founded in October 1886 under the management of J. J. Clancy MP to disseminate information on Irish affairs in England. It issued pamphlets dealing with the land question, Ulster, and home rule. It was partly financed by the IRISH PARTY, which contributed £13,000 between 1886 and 1890; it also worked through the Home Rule Union. It collapsed following the split in the Irish Party, 1891.

Irish Race Congress, conceived by the Irish Republican Association of South Africa in February 1921 to secure international recognition for the Irish Republic and the withdrawal of British forces from Ireland. It was organised by ART Ó BRIAIN of the IRISH SELF-DETERMINATION LEAGUE OF GREAT BRITAIN and ROBERT BRENNAN, under-secretary of the Department of Foreign Affairs and intended as a showcase of the achievements of the Irish people; but by the time it opened in Paris, 21 January 1922, the Sinn Féin movement had been sundered by the ANGLO-IRISH TREATY. The ten-member Irish delegation included ÉAMON DE VALERA, EOIN MACNEILL, and DOUGLAS HYDE. The congress's cultural activities were overshadowed by the political tensions generated by the Treaty, which was rejected by a majority of the delegates. By the time it closed, 28 January 1922, a new organisation, Fine Ghaedheal, dominated by de Valera, had been established to express Irish unity; it achieved little of consequence and soon disappeared.

Irish Race Convention. The first Irish Race Convention, held in New York, 4–5 March 1916, under the auspices of CLAN NA GAEL, founded the FRIENDS OF IRISH FREEDOM. A second convention was organised by JOHN DEVOY and JUDGE DANIEL COHALAN in Philadelphia, 22–23 February 1919. It hoped to influence President Wilson in supporting the recognition of the Irish Republic at the Paris Peace Conference, 1919, but Wilson refused to see the Irish delegation.

Irish Reform Act (1832), enacted 7 August 1832 to increase the number of Irish seats in the British House of Commons from 100 to 105 and introduce the £10 franchise in boroughs.

Irish Reform Association, established on 26 August 1904 as a reconstitution of the LAND CONFERENCE. Its leading organiser was the EARL OF DUNRAVEN. The association sought the devolution of some power to an Irish body. It won the support of SIR ANTONY MCDONNELL, who, with Dunraven, issued a further proposal, September 1904, calling for a council for Ireland with powers to legislate and control finances. The proposal, attacked by Unionists and those opposed to home rule, led to the resignation of the Chief Secretary for Ireland, GEORGE WYNDHAM. (See also IRISH COUNCIL BILL.)

Irish Republican Army (IRA). The IRISH REPUBLICAN BROTHERHOOD secretly used the IRISH VOLUNTEERS as its army in planning the EASTER RISING (1916). The Irish Volunteers became the army of the Irish Republic during the WAR OF INDEPENDENCE (1919–21); thereafter, those who accepted the ANGLO-IRISH TREATY (December 1921) came to be known as the 'Old IRA', while those who rejected it were known during the CIVIL WAR as the 'New IRA' or 'Irregulars'. From their surrender in May 1923 the anti-Treaty faction remained implacably opposed to partition and refused recognition to the parliaments in Dublin and Belfast. They split again in 1925 following ÉAMON DE VALERA's decision to seek a gradual road to complete independence. Rejecting FIANNA FÁIL, a minority remained in the militant IRA and Sinn Féin. The IRA was outlawed in 1936.

In January 1933 the IRA 'declared war' on Northern Ireland and Britain. The Belfast and Dublin governments used emergency legislation to intern hundreds of IRA members; six members in the South received the death sentence. Released internees were among those who joined a new republican party, CLANN NA POBLACHTA. In December 1956 the IRA launched a new campaign against Northern Ireland; it received little support and was called off in 1962.

During the 1960s the republican movement moved leftwards, but with the rise of the NORTHERN IRELAND CIVIL RIGHTS ASSOCIATION differences in outlook led to another split. Attacks by loyalists on Catholic areas of Belfast caused alarm both in the Republic and in Britain. During the rioting in Belfast in August 1969 the Taoiseach, JACK LYNCH, announced that the Government would not stand by while innocent people were attacked because of their religion. Thousands of Northern nationalists fled to the Republic, where the Irish army provided field hospitals for shelter. At the end of 1969 guns and money from sympathisers in the Republic led to the creation of the militant 'Provisional' IRA. In December 1969 the Army Council split on the policy of parliamentary abstention; the dissident minority formed the 'Provisional Army Council', with SEÁN MAC STIOFÁIN as chief of staff; the majority, led by CATHAL GOULDING, became known as the 'Official' IRA. The split was mirrored at the SINN FÉIN ard-fheis of 11 January 1970, when a third of the delegates gave their allegiance to the 'Provisional' movement. It was primarily a Belfast-Dublin split, with the Provisionals mainly dominated by Belfast republicans and the Officials led from Dublin.

A smaller organisation than the Provisional IRA, the Official IRA was led by Goulding, while 'Official' Sinn Féin was led by TOMÁS MAC GIOLLA. Through the UNITED IRISHMAN the movement propounded a doctrine of socialist republicanism. Official Sinn Féin later changed its name to SINN FÉIN, THE WORKERS' PARTY. The Official IRA was involved in sporadic fighting with the Provisional IRA, the RUC, the British army, and the IRSP. However, in May 1972 outrage in Derry at the murder of a member of the British army home on leave in the Creggan estate forced the Official IRA into declaring a ceasefire, 29 May. Later, members working through the Republican Clubs in Northern Ireland co-operated with the Provisional IRA in anti-internment protests and in attempting to alleviate hardship in nationalist areas during the loyalist strikes in the 1970s.

The Provisional IRA published AN PHOBLACHT, through which it sought support for an end to the British presence in Ireland and the establishment of an all-Ireland republic. By mid-June it was estimated to have 1,500 active volunteers, of whom 800 were believed to be in Northern Ireland (600 in Belfast, 100 in Derry, and 100 in other areas). Initial support from the Republic was supplemented by arms and ammunition smuggled from Britain and the Continent, financed by Irish-American sympathisers through NORTHERN AID. The Provisional IRA also developed contacts with Libya and with the Basque paramilitary organisation ETA. Internment, introduced on 9 August 1971, failed to break the IRA (most volunteers had fled to the Republic in anticipation) but severely alienated the nationalist population and boosted Provisional IRA membership. The year 1972 was the bloodiest of the conflict, with a total of 496 deaths, of which republicans were responsible for 279. Support for the Provisional IRA grew after 'BLOODY SUNDAY', when British soldiers killed thirteen marchers during an anti-internment civil rights rally in Derry, 30 January 1972. Loyalist violence intensified following the introduction of direct rule from London, March 1972. The Secretary of State for Northern Ireland, WILLIAM WHITELAW, conceded SPECIAL CATEGORY status from 21 June 1972, in effect recognising paramilitary prisoners as prisoners of war, in return for a meeting with the Provisional leadership. He met Provisional IRA leaders in London in July but found it impossible to accept their demands.

Over the next three decades the Provisional IRA campaign was characterised by murder, atrocity, bank and post office robberies, kidnapping, kneecapping, racketeering, reprisal, and counter-reprisal. Targets included members of the RUC, UDR, British army, loyalist paramilitary groups, and alleged drug-dealers (dealt with under the cover name of Direct Action Against Drugs). The Provisional IRA extended its area of operations to England, the Netherlands, and Germany. Of the 3,569 deaths attributed by the authors of *Lost Lives* (1991 and 2001) to the Northern conflict, 2,108 (59 per cent) are attributed to the republican movement, and the majority of these to the Provisional IRA.

The campaign was periodically interrupted by ceasefires, most notably from December 1974 to September 1975, from August 1994 to February 1996, and continuously since July 1997. There were also a number of initiatives to secure a peace from 1972, leading eventually to the PEACE PROCESS. Responding to the Birmingham bomb explosions of 21 November 1974 (see BIRMINGHAM SIX), the British Government outlawed the IRA and introduced the Prevention of Terrorism (Temporary Provisions) Act to exclude people from any part of Ireland from entering England, Scotland, or Wales; the act also permitted the police to hold those suspected of terrorist acts without charge for forty-eight hours, or up to seven days on a higher authority. Non-jury courts were used in Northern Ireland and the Republic.

On 16 August 1975 the first of a series of articles appeared under the pen-name 'Brownie' (GERRY ADAMS) in the IRA paper *Republican News.* Analysing the republican position, he outlined what became the 'long war' strategy: the establishment of a political structure through Sinn Féin while simultaneously pursuing the military campaign. This became the basis of IRA and Sinn Féin strategy in the 1980s.

The annual number of deaths in the conflict fell to 113 in 1977, with republicans responsible for 74; in 1978 it fell to 88, of which republicans were responsible for 60. The reduction during 1977 and 1978 was due to the combined influences of the peace movement and an increasingly tough security policy inaugurated by the Secretary of State for Northern Ireland, ROY MASON. This forced a reorganisation within the IRA, led by Gerry Adams, Ivor Bell, and Martin McGuinness. The new system was based on a cell structure of three or four members, only one of whom was in contact with a higher level. Members were to be known only by pseudonyms, under the direction of an anonymous controller; information was distributed strictly on a 'need-to-know' basis. Crucially, Sinn Féin, now directly under Provisional IRA control, was directed towards involvement in community, social and economic issues, and useful organisations were to be infiltrated. The 'Green Book', a copy of which was given to each volunteer, outlined IRA strategy. British Military Intelligence responded by organising along similar lines and by activating its own secret undercover units.

Protests by imprisoned republicans in the Maze Prison at the withdrawal of SPECIAL CATEGORY status began with the BLANKET PROTEST, 14 September 1976, and were followed by the 'dirty protest', March 1978, when prisoners refused to wash or use the toilet facilities and soiled the walls of their cells. The H BLOCK protests developed into a hunger strike, during which ten hunger-strikers died in 1981. Each of the deaths aided recruitment to the IRA; but this was offset by the use by the RUC of INFORMERS, led by Christopher Black, who supplied thirty-eight names. The emergence of other informers prompted the Provisional IRA to offer an amnesty to informers who retracted their evidence, March 1982.

Adams and McGuinness took control of Sinn Féin on 13 November 1983 when they ousted RUAIRÍ Ó BRÁDAIGH and his followers. Three years later the IRA announced that it would support Sinn Féin members taking their seats in Dáil Éireann. At the Sinn Féin ard-fheis the following month delegates voted to end the policy of parliamentary abstention. Ó Brádaigh and some twenty supporters left to form REPUBLICAN SINN FÉIN and, allegedly, the 'Continuity IRA'.

Having reiterated its commitment to the 'armed struggle' in the early stages of the PEACE PROCESS in the 1990s, the IRA, while stating that the DOWNING STREET DECLARATION (1993) was not a solution, announced a 'complete cessation of military operations', 30 August 1994. Amid increasing demands that it 'decommission' its weapons to enable Sinn Féin to enter multi-party talks, the IRA ceasefire was terminated without warning, 9 February 1996, with a bomb explosion at Canary Wharf, London. Another ceasefire, from 20 July 1997, enabled Sinn Féin to enter the talks. Hard-liners in south Armagh and Co. Louth who rejected the ceasefire established the 32-County Sovereignty Committee and the 'REAL IRA'.

While Sinn Féin was a signatory of the BELFAST AGREEMENT (10 April 1998), the IRA stated that the agreement fell short of 'presenting a solid basis for a lasting settlement.' By the summer of 2001 the Provisional IRA had still not decommissioned its arms, though the ceasefire continued. On 6 August 2001, with the possibility of the institutions collapsing following Trimble's resignation, the Independent International Commission on Decommissioning stated that the IRA had 'proposed a method for putting IRA arms completely and verifiably beyond use.' Unionist scepticism led to the withdrawal of the proposal, 14 August. On the same day, newspapers reported that three members of the IRA had been detained in Colombia charged with falsifying documents and with terrorist activities (allegedly in aiding the Colombian guerrilla group FARC), reported to be part of a system of 'technology exchange'. Their trial was abandoned when key witnesses failed to appear, and a new trial was scheduled for 5 February 2003. The affair further damaged the IRA's reputation in Washington, already disappointed at the organisation's failure to put its arms beyond use.

On 23 October 2001 the Independent International Commission on Decommissioning announced that it had witnessed the IRA putting some of its weapons beyond use. This 'unprecedented move' was welcomed at home and abroad. The IRA announced that it had begun disposing of its weapons. An IRA statement apologising for civilian deaths during the 'armed struggle' was published in *An Phoblacht,* 16 July 2002.

In October 2002 the Provisional IRA announced that it had withdrawn its co-operation with the Independent International Commission on Decommissioning.

Irish Republican Brotherhood. The movement later known as the IRB was founded in Dublin by JAMES STEPHENS on 17 March 1858, using funds provided by JOHN O'MAHONY, who at the same time founded the FENIANS in New York. Though the American and Irish organisations were separate, the entire republican movement came to be popularly known as the Fenians. The Fenians were in fact an auxiliary of the IRB. In the beginning the Irish organisation was called the Irish Revolutionary Brotherhood. Known to members as 'the Society', 'the Organisation', and the 'Brotherhood', its aim was to overthrow British rule in Ireland and to create an Irish republic.

Stephens, as 'head centre', organised the IRB along lines he believed were best calculated to ensure secrecy. He divided the organisation into 'centres'. Under each centre, who was known as A or colonel, there were nine Bs or captains; each captain had nine Cs or sergeants, and under each sergeant were nine Ds or privates. Each member of the IRB had to swear an oath, of which there were several versions, one of which was:

> I, [. . .], in the presence of Almighty God, do solemnly swear allegiance to the Irish Republic now virtually established and that I will do my utmost, at every risk, while life lasts, to defend its independence and integrity; and finally that I will yield implicit obedience in all things, not contrary to the laws of God, to the commands of my superior officer. So help me God, Amen.

Leading recruiting agents for the IRB, together with Stephens, were JOHN DEVOY, PATRICK 'PAGAN' O'LEARY, and WILLIAM ROANTREE.

The IRB was denounced by the Catholic hierarchy in 1863. Two years later it was condemned by the Archbishop of Dublin, PAUL CULLEN, and after the rising of 1867 it was denounced by the Pope; nonetheless it gathered support among the lower orders of clergy. The movement published the IRISH PEOPLE, 1863–65, and the FLAG OF IRELAND (suppressed in 1874).

Stephens resisted pressure from America for a rising until, in December 1866, he lost the confidence of the Fenians, who replaced him with THOMAS J. KELLY. Kelly and his followers arrived in London in January 1867, where GENERAL GUSTAVE-PAUL CLUSERET was in charge of the military venture. The rising failed through a combination of bad planning and betrayal. The police and military speedily defeated Fenian forces at Glencullen, Stepaside, and Tallaght

(Co. Dublin), Ardagh and Kilmallock (Co. Limerick), Ballyhurst (Co. Tipperary), Ballyknockane and Knockadoon (Co. Cork), Drogheda (Co. Louth), and Drumcliff (Co. Sligo). As an acknowledgment of its role in suppressing the rising the Irish Constabulary was renamed the ROYAL IRISH CONSTABULARY. An attempt to rescue Kelly and others arrested in England resulted in the death of a police sergeant in Manchester, for which Allen, Larkin, and O'Brien—the MANCHESTER MARTYRS—were hanged. In December of that year an attempt to rescue RICARD O'SULLIVAN BURKE resulted in twelve civilian deaths in the CLERKENWELL EXPLOSION.

The rising and its aftermath caused widespread concern in England and drew attention to Irish affairs. Irish agitation was led by ISAAC BUTT, who defended leading Fenians. W. E. GLADSTONE formed his first government in 1868 with the words 'My mission is to pacify Ireland.'

In June 1867 a number of leading Fenians, including W. R. Roberts, leader of the 'Senate' wing of the American organisation, met in Paris, and an agreement was reached to set up an elected council to direct the movement in Ireland and Britain, to be known as the Supreme Council. The council met for the first time in Dublin, 13–14 February 1868; this was superseded in 1869 by a newly elected body, which issued an 'Address of the Supreme Council of the Irish Republic to the People of Ireland', 18 August 1869. Through its constitution, all authority was vested in the eleven-member Supreme Council: one from each of the four provinces of Ireland, one for Scotland, and one each for the North and South of England. The seven were empowered to co-opt an additional four members. Its executive consisted of a president, secretary, and treasurer. As an underground movement, the Supreme Council was frequently compelled to hold its meetings outside Ireland, either in London or in Paris, where many of its leaders had sought refuge. The new constitution stated that the Irish people should decide the opportune moment for a war against England.

Under the new constitution, IRB members were obliged to swear an oath undertaking to do their utmost to establish an independent Ireland, to be faithful to the Supreme Council and the government of the Irish Republic, and to obey their superior officers and the constitution of the IRB. Members recognised the president of the Supreme Council as president of the Irish Republic. Soldiers of the IRB were termed the Irish Republican Army. CLAN NA GAEL, founded in New York in 1867 in an attempt to heal the divisions within the Fenian movement there, was recognised as the American auxiliary of the IRB.

As an experiment in constitutionalism, some members, notably JOSEPH BIGGAR and JOHN O'CONNOR POWER, joined the HOME RULE LEAGUE and sat in the British House of Commons, where they adopted a policy of OBSTRUCTIONISM. The experiment ended when the Supreme Council withdrew support from the home rule movement, 20 August 1876, and members who remained in the Irish Party were expelled from the Supreme Council. Three years later, however, the rise of the LAND LEAGUE brought prominent IRB men back into the alliance known as the NEW DEPARTURE (rejected by the Supreme Council). Republicans were less prominent in the IRISH NATIONAL LEAGUE, the constitutional body that replaced the Land League in 1882. CHARLES STEWART PARNELL briefly recovered extremist support during the winter of 1890/91 when, following the split in the party, the 'hillside men' rallied to him, encouraged by the extremism of his language.

Numbers in the IRB declined during the 1890s (official sources estimated they had fallen from 11,000 to approximately 8,000). The IRB retained considerable influence through its policy of infiltrating nationalist organisations, from the founding of the GAA (1884) onwards. During the 1890s it engaged in a bitter struggle with the IRISH NATIONAL ALLIANCE, a splinter of Clan na Gael, which had a military wing, the IRISH NATIONAL BROTHERHOOD. The battle was fought out for the most part in the columns of various republican papers from 1895 until the turn of the century, when it ended in victory for the IRB, then led by FRED ALLAN. The IRB recovered support in 1898 when it took a leading role in the CENTENARY CELEBRATIONS to commemorate the rising of 1798. The nationalist political leader JOHN REDMOND shared a platform with Allan, ARTHUR GRIFFITH, MAUD GONNE, and JAMES CONNOLLY, which presented DUBLIN CASTLE with a dilemma in deciding who was, and who was not, a member of the IRB.

Despite an apparent resurgence in 1898, however, the IRB was losing support to constitutional organisations, such as Griffith's CUMANN NA NGAEDHEAL and the DUNGANNON CLUBS, organisations that would form the basis of SINN FÉIN. The revival of the IRB from 1904 was due to young men such as BULMER HOBSON and DENIS MCCULLOUGH. Inspired by THOMAS J. CLARKE, who arrived from New York in 1907 as an emissary from Devoy, most of them were involved in the early stages with the formation of SINN FÉIN. By 1912 the RIC had informed Dublin Castle that there was a revival of the IRB, but the authorities ignored the warning. The IRB at this time had 1,660 members in Ireland and 367 in Britain.

In November 1913 Hobson and SEÁN MAC DIARMADA played a leading role in the formation of the IRISH VOLUNTEERS, destined to become the IRISH REPUBLICAN ARMY. The EASTER RISING (1916) was planned by a small group in the IRB's Military Council, a secret cabal within a secret organisation, formed in 1915 under Clarke's guidance. The Military Council, also known as the Military Committee, planned to use the Irish Volunteers for an armed insurrection towards the end of the year. The original members—PATRICK PEARSE, JOSEPH PLUNKETT, and ÉAMONN CEANNT—were joined by Clarke and Mac Diarmada, September 1915. In January 1916 the council revealed its plans to JAMES CONNOLLY, who then became a member (though not a member of the IRB). The final member, THOMAS MACDONAGH, was recruited in April. These seven planned the rising and were the signatories of the Proclamation of the Irish Republic (1916). The secrecy attaching to the Military Council contributed to the confusion that surrounded the insurrection when the chief of staff of the Volunteers, EOIN MACNEILL, countermanded the Military Council's orders for a mobilisation on Sunday 23 April.

Following the defeat of the rising the IRB was reorganised under MICHAEL COLLINS and HARRY BOLAND. The Supreme Council was expanded to fifteen members (with four co-opted by the original eleven), and a subordinate Military Council was established. The president of the Supreme Council was THOMAS ASHE, who, following his arrest in August 1917, embarked on a hunger strike, as a result of which he died. Seán MacGarry replaced him as president, with Michael Collins as secretary. By the summer of 1918 there were 350 IRB circles, with a total membership of 3,000. As members of the local circle dominated each Irish Volunteers unit, the IRB had a significant influence. The Supreme Council chose many of the Sinn Féin candidates in the general election of December 1918. When Sinn Féin representatives met in Dublin on 21 January 1919 and declared DÁIL ÉIREANN the parliamentary assembly of the Irish Republic, it seemed that the IRB had achieved its central objective.

The IRB's influence declined during the WAR OF INDEPENDENCE as the authority of the IRA increased. Even where membership of the two organisations overlapped, the officers' loyalty to the Dáil took precedence over their oath to the IRB. The Supreme Council favoured the ANGLO-IRISH TREATY (1921), about which Collins had kept members informed during the negotiations that preceded it; the vote in the council, 11 December 1921, was 11 to 4 in favour. Outside the IRB there was a strong feeling among critics of the Treaty, in particular ÉAMON DE VALERA, that the Supreme Council was using its influence to win support for the Treaty. While supporting the IRISH FREE STATE, the IRB remained committed to severing the link with England; it financed a paper, the *Separatist* (February–September 1922), which expounded this theme.

During the CIVIL WAR the IRB split. Towards the end of 1922, Free State army officers reorganised and established circles within the army itself, under the leadership of Liam Tobin; they set up the Irish Republican Army Organisation, with the support of members of Dáil Éireann, including the Minister for Industry and Commerce, JOSEPH MCGRATH. The rejection by the government of the officers' demand for a guarantee that the Free State government was still working towards an Irish republic led to the ARMY MUTINY of 1924. Following the breaking of the mutiny by the government, the IRB dissolved itself later that year.

In 1964 surviving trustees of IRB funds handed £2,835 to KATHLEEN CLARKE, widow of Thomas J. Clarke. She had revived the Wolfe Tone Memorial Committee of 1898 to erect a statue to Theobald Wolfe Tone and the United Irishmen. This committee supplemented the IRB funds, and a statue at St Stephen's Green, Dublin, was unveiled by Éamon de Valera, President of Ireland, in November 1967.

Irish Republican Defence Association, founded in London in 1937 to organise support in Britain for the IRA and its aim of securing an all-Ireland republic. It supported the IRA's bombing campaign against Britain, 1939.

Irish Republican Socialist Party, founded in Belfast by SÉAMUS COSTELLO in December 1974. A breakaway from 'Official' SINN FÉIN, it was supported by BERNADETTE MCALISKEY (Bernadette Devlin) and some Provisional IRA dissidents. With a membership of approximately 1,000, it was registered as a political party in May 1975 and published a paper, the *Starry Plough*. From 1975 the IRSP, through its military wing, the People's Liberation Army (later the IRISH NATIONAL LIBERATION ARMY), engaged in a feud with the Official IRA, until a Belfast priest, Father Alec Reid, organised a ceasefire. Bernadette McAliskey left the party in 1975. Having survived one murder attempt, Costello was killed by an Official IRA gunman in Dublin, 5 October 1977. During the years 1983–86 INFORMERS implicated senior figures in the party.

At the end of 1986 another feud, resulting in the deaths of twelve people in three months, followed the release of those imprisoned on the evidence of the informer Harry Fitzpatrick. A new faction, calling itself the Irish People's Liberation Organisation, attempted to break up the IRSP-INLA movement. In 1995 the IRSP announced that it would not be recommending to the INLA that it make its ceasefire 'permanent' but that it hoped the INLA would not be responsible for any 'first strike'. The IRSP denied the existence of a feud, as alleged by the RUC, when the INLA chief of staff, Frank 'Gino' Gallagher, was murdered on the Falls Road, Belfast, 31 January 1996. The IRSP was excluded from the initial list of parties entitled to participate in the Forum elections. It criticised the declaration of a ceasefire by the Provisional IRA, July 1997, and did not contest the Assembly elections in June 1998.

Irish Self-Determination League of Great Britain, founded in London in March 1919 as a non-militant organisation to support SINN FÉIN and the first DÁIL ÉIREANN in pursuit of Irish independence. Its officers were P. J. Kelly (president), ART Ó BRIAIN (chairman and vice-president), and SEÁN MCGRATH (secretary). From 1921 it held classes in Irish language, music and dancing and distributed Sinn Féin literature through its three hundred branches. It was particularly active during the hunger strike of TERENCE MACSWINEY, August–October 1920. Though it was never proscribed, its offices were subjected to frequent police raids and its meetings banned or heavily policed. Many of its activists were deported from England in March 1923, but following a successful appeal to the House of Lords the ban was rescinded. However, members were re-arrested on their return to England and charged with conspiracy, receiving on average an eighteen-month prison sentence.

Irish Shipping Ltd, established in March 1941, charged by the Government with the task of supplying the country with vital foodstuffs and raw materials during the years of the Second World War. The first ship acquired, the Greek vessel *Vassilios Destoimis,* was renamed *Irish Poplar.* Nine other vessels were acquired in 1941. Two ships were lost during the war: the *Irish Pine* disappeared with all hands on a voyage to the United States, November 1942, and the *Irish Oak* was sunk in the North Atlantic, May 1943, but its entire crew was rescued by a sister-ship, the *Irish Plane.* The Irish merchant fleet lost 152 seamen from nineteen ships during the war.

In 1948 the *Irish Rose,* a vessel of 2,210 tons, became the first new ship to be built for Irish Shipping Ltd. During the late 1960s the company switched from its established North American cargo runs to international tramp shipping. Its tramp fleet later comprised a total of 159,467 tons: *Irish Rowan* (27,532 tons), *Irish Cedar* (27,572 tons), *Irish Pine* (26,091 tons), *Irish Maple* (26,091 tons), *Irish Oak* (26,061 tons), and *Irish Larch* (26,120 tons).

In April 1978 the *St Killian* (7,128 tons) joined the *St Patrick* (5,285 tons) on the Rosslare–Le Havre–Cherbourg service. By the early 1980s, however, the company was in financial crisis: it had chartered vessels at rates that became unsustainable when demand fell. Its debts were guaranteed by the government to the amount of £40 million; but when the coalition government (Fine Gael and Labour Party) discovered that long-term liabilities exceeded £140 million, November 1984, the company was put into liquidation. There was a public outcry when it was revealed that the staff of nearly four hundred would receive no compensation beyond the statutory minimum redundancy payment.

Irish Socialist Republican Party, founded in Dublin, 29 May 1896, by JAMES CONNOLLY as a successor to the Dublin Socialist Party. Connolly used its paper, the WORKERS' REPUBLIC, to further his social and nationalist policies. Five members unsuccessfully contested the Dublin municipal elections, 1899–1903. It was the first organisation to represent Irish socialism (with three delegates) at the fifth (Paris) congress of the Second International in September 1900. Following Connolly's resignation and departure for the United States, 1903, the party was reorganised by WILLIAM O'BRIEN as the Socialist Party of Ireland.

Irish Society for Promoting the Education of the Native Irish through the Medium of Their Own Language, generally known as the 'Irish Society', founded in 1818. Its leaders were members of the established churches of Ireland and England who wished to produce the Bible and the Book of Common Prayer in Irish; between 1836 and 1850 the society spent approximately £4,000 annually in pursuit of this ideal. Members also supported the campaign for a chair of Irish in Trinity College, Dublin (the chair was established in 1838). While directing its efforts at the poorer areas of Ireland, the society remained independent of the proselytising IRISH CHURCH MISSIONS established in 1849 by REV. ALEXANDER R. C. DALLAS. However, it came under such strong pressure from influential figures in the established church, both in Ireland and in England, that in 1853 it entered into an alliance with it. Within three years, alarmed at the 'aggressiveness' of Dallas and his movement, the society broke away. Its membership and influence were by now considerably reduced, and only the Dublin branch remained active for a short time.

Irish Statesman, a weekly review established in 1919 with the aid of SIR HORACE PLUNKETT, under the editorship of WARRE BRADLEY WELLS. It ceased publication temporarily in April 1920 because of the WAR OF INDEPENDENCE but was revived by Plunkett in September 1923. Following the takeover of the IRISH HOMESTEAD by the *Irish Statesman* it was edited by GEORGE RUSSELL. The last issue appeared on 12 April 1930 following the withdrawal of American financial support.

Irish Texts Society, founded in 1899 by Eleanor Hull (1860–1935), in association with David Comyn, Francis A. Fahy, DR DOUGLAS HYDE, Robin Flower, P. W. JOYCE and others for the purpose of publishing historic Irish texts. Among its most notable achievements was the promotion of Rev. PATRICK DINNEEN's revised Irish-English dictionary, *Foclóir Gaedhilge agus Béarla* (1927). Translations to English were undertaken under the editorship of STANDISH HAYES O'GRADY, Tomás Ó Máille, Douglas Hyde, EOIN MACNEILL, and David Comyn.

Irish Times, a newspaper founded in Dublin by Major Laurence E. Knox. The first issue appeared on 29 March 1859. Appearing on Tuesdays, Thursdays, and Saturdays, it became a daily on 8 June 1859. The unofficial organ of the Anglo-Irish ASCENDANCY for many years, it was bought by Sir John Arnott in 1873. The firm became a limited company in 1900 but continued to be controlled by the Arnott family until the middle of the century. Its most famous editor was R. M. SMYLLIE, 1934–54. From 21 April 1941 the paper featured news items, rather than small advertisements, on its front page. A trust to run the paper on independent lines was formed in 1974. The company encountered serious financial difficulties during the years 2001–02, resulting in the reduction by some 250 of its staff of 700. Geraldine Kennedy, the paper's political correspondent, became the first woman to edit an Irish daily newspaper, 11 October 2002.

Irishtown, Co. Mayo, site of a meeting organised by JAMES DALY and MICHAEL DAVITT and attended by more than ten thousand tenant-farmers, 20 April 1879, initiating the land agitation that led to the establishment of the LAND LEAGUE. The meeting was organised in protest at evictions ordered by a local landlord, Canon Geoffrey Bourke, the parish priest. The protest, which led to local landlords lowering rents by 25 per cent, was largely ignored by national newspapers. Following similar meetings in Westport, the LAND LEAGUE OF MAYO was founded in Castlebar, 16 August, and the Irish National Land League two months later.

Irish Trade and Labour Union, founded in 1890 in an attempt to form a general trade union. Supported by MICHAEL DAVITT, it failed within a short time through lack of support.

Irish Trade Union Congress, formed 27–28 April 1894 when 119 delegates of labour organisations met at the Trades Hall in Capel Street, Dublin. Largely apolitical in its early years, it adopted a political stance following the entry of JAMES LARKIN and JAMES CONNOLLY in 1910. In 1912 the congress passed a motion by Connolly calling for the formation of an Irish Labour Party, as a result of which the Irish Labour Party and Trade Union Congress was formed. The TUC also contained a large number of British unions that had branches in Ireland; this factor caused tensions within the congress with the growth of militant nationalism.

During the 1920s and 30s the congress was dominated by WILLIAM O'BRIEN of the ITGWU, whose quarrel with Larkin divided the trade union movement. In 1945 O'Brien split the congress and the Labour Party when the ITGWU's withdrawal was emulated by fourteen other unions; they formed the rival

CONGRESS OF IRISH UNIONS. The ITUC, with a large proportion of its 145,000 affiliated members in British unions, gave autonomy to members in Northern Ireland, who elected their own Northern Ireland Committee. During the 1950s there was a growth in trade union membership: in 1958 the ITUC had 250,000 members in 64 unions, while the CIU had approximately 190,000 members in 30 unions.

Following protracted negotiations from 1955 onwards, the congresses amalgamated in 1959 to form the IRISH CONGRESS OF TRADE UNIONS.

Irish Transport and General Workers' Union, founded on 29 December 1908 by JAMES LARKIN after he had broken with the National Union of Dock Labourers. Affiliated to the IRISH TRADE UNIONS CONGRESS from 1910, it had a membership of 5,000 within a year. Larkin was general secretary; other prominent members were Thomas Foran, P. T. Daly, and WILLIAM O'BRIEN. From June 1911 JAMES CONNOLLY was its Belfast organiser. Under Larkin, the union's campaign for members brought it into conflict with WILLIAM MARTIN MURPHY and the Dublin Employers' Federation, who sought to prevent their workers from joining; this led to the DUBLIN LOCK-OUT (1913). By the time the lock-out ended the ITGWU was in financial difficulties. Larkin went to the United States at the end of 1914 to raise money for the union and the LABOUR PARTY; during his absence the union was led by James Connolly.

Following the EASTER RISING (1916), after which Connolly was executed, the leadership devolved on O'Brien, Daly, and Foran, who brought the union to a position of strength, with 14,000 members in 40 branches; by 1919 this had risen to 100,000 members in 350 branches, making it the biggest union in the country. O'Brien's rise within the union was a source of concern to Daly and others, who sought to enlist the aid of Larkin, still in America. When Larkin returned, 1923, he attempted to resume control but was defeated by O'Brien and THOMAS JOHNSON. He then assumed control of the syndicalist WORKERS' UNION OF IRELAND, 1924 (founded during his absence in Russia by his brother Peter), and the membership of the ITGWU fell to 60,000.

The rivalry between the ITGWU and WUI was a source of tension within the labour movement throughout the 1930s and into the 40s. Following Larkin's return to the Labour Party and the WUI's affiliation to the ITUC, O'Brien and the ITGWU disaffiliated from the party and the congress in 1945. Five ITGWU parliamentary members formed the rival NATIONAL LABOUR PARTY, while O'Brien and the ITGWU formed the rival CONGRESS OF IRISH UNIONS. The breach remained until twelve years after Larkin's death, when the two congresses united to form the IRISH CONGRESS OF TRADE UNIONS, 1959. The ITGWU and Federated Workers' Union of Ireland united to form SIPTU in 1990.

Irish Unionist Alliance, founded in 1891 from the IRISH LOYAL AND PATRIOTIC UNION to resist HOME RULE. The alliance represented a small but influential number of unionists, who feared that self-government would jeopardise their social and commercial position. Though numerically weak, it had considerable influence among British Conservatives, where its chief spokesmen were Lord Midleton and Lord Lansdowne. As it included peers and their close associates, the alliance had considerable weight in the House of Lords, then overwhelmingly Conservative and opposed to home rule. However, it was more propagandist than political, as there was little prospect of Unionists winning seats in the south. During the debates on the second Home Rule Bill, 1892–93, and subsequently, the alliance used its resources to disseminate propaganda against home rule in Ireland and in Britain. It played a leading role in the Joint Committee of Unionist Associations, and during the debate on the third Home Rule Bill, 1912–14, it brought Conservative MPs to Ireland and sent Unionist spokesmen to Britain. When the act became law in September 1914, southern unionists were forced to come to terms with the immediate prospect of self-government, and following a split within the alliance they formed the Unionist Anti-Partition League. (See also UNIONIST PARTY and ULSTER UNIONIST PARTY.)

Irish Universities Act (1908), introduced by the Chief Secretary for Ireland, AUGUSTINE BIRRELL, as an attempt to solve the vexed question of acceptable higher education for Catholics. Under the act the ROYAL UNIVERSITY OF IRELAND was abolished and two new universities constituted: Queen's University, Belfast (see QUEEN'S COLLEGES), and the NATIONAL UNIVERSITY OF IRELAND, made up from the former Queen's Colleges of Galway and Cork together with University College, Dublin. The Catholic hierarchy was prominently represented on the Governing Body of the NUI, later declared to be a non-denominational university.

Irish Volunteers, founded on 25 November 1913 as the result of an article by EOIN MACNEILL in *An Claidheamh Soluis,* 1 November. In his article, headed 'The north began', MacNeill suggested that southern nationalists should form a volunteer movement on the lines of the ULSTER VOLUNTEER FORCE. A public meeting in the Rotunda Rooms was organised by BULMER HOBSON of the IRB, at which the new force was established. It attracted followers of SINN FÉIN and the GAELIC LEAGUE as well as members of the IRB, who envisaged a future role for the new force. CUMANN NA MBAN was established in November 1913 as a women's auxiliary to the Volunteers.

By May 1914 membership was approximately 80,000. Funds were collected through CLAN NA GAEL in the United States and by ROGER CASEMENT and Alice Stopford Green in England. In July 1914 DARRELL FIGGIS and ERSKINE CHILDERS arranged for the purchase of guns in Germany (see HOWTH GUN-RUNNING). There were now two armed volunteer armies in the country. The Ulster Volunteer Force had made clear its commitment to resisting home rule and was supported by ANDREW BONAR LAW and the Conservatives. JOHN REDMOND, fighting in the British House of Commons for home rule without partition, was concerned lest the Volunteers should prevent the passing of the third HOME RULE BILL. To ensure control of the Volunteers he demanded half the seats on the Provisional Committee for his nominees. As the alternative was to split the movement, his demands were conceded in June, much to the anger of IRB extremists.

By September, when the Home Rule Act was suspended for the duration of the Great War, membership numbered 180,000. The British government rejected an offer of the Volunteers as a defence force for Ireland. On 20 September, in the course of a speech at Woodenbridge, Co. Wicklow, Redmond urged Volunteers to support Britain in the war against Germany 'for the freedom of small nations.' His call was answered by a majority of the Volunteers, which became known as the National Volunteers, leaving some 11,000 Irish Volunteers, who opposed involvement in the war. This minority reorganised in October 1914; MacNeill became chief of staff, Hobson (no longer acceptable to the IRB) quartermaster, and MICHAEL O'RAHILLY director of arms. Three crucial posts were in the hands of the IRB: PATRICK PEARSE, director of military organisation, JOSEPH PLUNKETT, director of military operations, and THOMAS MACDONAGH, director of training. All three later became members of the secret IRB Military Council, which, under the influence of THOMAS J. CLARKE, organised the EASTER RISING (1916), for which the Volunteers provided a ready-made army. On 3 April 1916 the Volunteers were ordered to prepare for manoeuvres, which, unknown to the non-IRB leadership, was to be the insurrection set for Sunday 23 April. However, as a result of the confusion that ensued when Eoin MacNeill cancelled the order, the rising was rescheduled for the next day, Monday 24 April. The insurrection ended in surrender on the following Saturday.

Despite the failure of the military insurrection, the mass arrests and executions that followed led to a revitalisation of the Volunteer movement. On 21 January 1919 the first Dáil Éireann met and proclaimed the Irish Republic. In August 1920 the Volunteers took an oath to the Republic and became in effect the IRISH REPUBLICAN ARMY.

The Manifesto of the Irish Volunteers, read by MacNeill at the founding meeting in the Rotunda Rooms, 25 November 1913, declared in part:

> At a time when legislative proposals, universally confessed to be of vital concern for the future of Ireland, have been put forward, and are waiting decision, a plan has been deliberately adopted by one of the great English political parties, advocated by the leaders of that party and by its numerous organs in the press, brought systematically to bear on English public opinion, to make a display of military force and the menace of armed violence, the determining factor in the future relations between this country and Great Britain.
>
> The party which has thus substituted open force for the semblance of civil government is seeking by this means not merely to decide an immediately political issue of grave concern to this nation, but also to obtain for itself the future control of all our national affairs. It is plain to every man that the people of Ireland, if they acquiesce in this new policy by their action, will consent to the surrender not only of their rights as a nation, but of their civic rights as men. Are we to rest inactive in the hope that the course of politics in Great Britain may save us from the degradation openly threatened against us? British politics are controlled by British interests, and are complicated by problems of great importance to the people of Great Britain. In a crisis of this kind the duty of safeguarding our rights is our duty first and foremost. If we remain quiescent by what title can we expect the people of Great Britain to turn aside from their own pressing concerns to defend us? Will not such an attitude of itself mark us out as a

people unworthy of defence?

Such is the occasion, not altogether unfortunate, which has brought the inception of the Irish Volunteer movement. But the Volunteers, once they have been enrolled, will form a prominent element in the national life under a national government. The nation will maintain its Volunteer organisation as a guarantee of the liberties which the Irish people shall have secured . . .

The object proposed for the Irish Volunteers is to secure and maintain the rights and liberties common to all the people of Ireland. Their duties will be defensive and protective, and they will not contemplate either aggression or domination. Their ranks are open to all able-bodied Irishmen without distinction of creed, politics, or social grade. Means will be found whereby Irishmen unable to serve as ordinary Volunteers will be enabled to aid the Volunteer forces in various capacities. There will also be work for women to do, and there are signs that the women of Ireland, true to their records, are especially enthusiastic for the success of the Irish Volunteers.

We propose for the Volunteers' organisation the widest possible basis. Without any other association or classification the Volunteers will be enrolled according to the district in which they live. As soon as it is found feasible, the district sections will be called upon to join in making provision for the general administration and for united co-operation . . .

In the name of national unity, of national dignity, of national and individual liberty, of manly citizenship, we appeal to our countrymen to recognise and accept without hesitation the opportunity that has been granted them to join the ranks of the Irish Volunteers, and to make the movement now begun, not unworthy of the historic title which it has adopted.

Irish Volunteers Dependants' Fund, established in 1916 through the efforts of KATHLEEN CLARKE to aid the dependants of those who took part in the EASTER RISING (1916). Kathleen Clarke was president and Áine Ceannt (widow of ÉAMONN CEANNT) vice-president. The initial fund consisted of £3,000 in gold remaining from money sent by CLAN NA GAEL to finance the insurrection. The fund merged with the IRISH NATIONAL AID ASSOCIATION, August 1916. MICHAEL COLLINS became chief organiser and secretary of the fund and remained in the post until 1918. Dáil Éireann later assumed responsibility through the Ministry of Home Affairs. The Dublin v. Tipperary football match at Croke Park on BLOODY SUNDAY (21 November 1920) was arranged in aid of the fund.

Irish Women's Franchise League, founded in February 1911 in Dublin at the home of HANNA SHEEHY-SKEFFINGTON, who became its first secretary; other early members included Margaret (Gretta) Cousins (treasurer), CHARLOTTE DESPARD, Kathleen Houston, Marjorie Hasler, Maud Lloyd, Jane and Margaret Murphy, Margaret Palmer, and Hilda Webb. Men joined as associate members; these included Francis Cruise O'Brien, James Cousins, THOMAS MACDONAGH, and FRANCIS SHEEHY-SKEFFINGTON. Modelled on the Women's Social and Political Union (founded in Manchester, 1903), the movement grew from an initial membership of twelve to more than a thousand within a year to become the largest suffrage group in Ireland. It organised a boycott of the 1911 census by advising women to absent themselves from their home on the night of the census. In April 1912 it organised interruptions at a meeting in Belfast addressed by Winston Churchill. It received wide press coverage following its activities on 13 June 1912, when a number of members broke windows in government buildings; eight were arrested and sentenced to between two and six months' imprisonment, during which they demanded, and received, political status. The league abandoned its militant campaign in August 1914 on the outbreak of war. It opposed the ANGLO-IRISH TREATY and attempted to reconcile the rival factions before the outbreak of the CIVIL WAR.

Irish Women's Liberation Movement, founded in 1970. It received widespread publicity on 22 May 1971 when members held a protest against the law banning the importing of contraceptives: they travelled to Belfast by train and bought contraceptives, which they displayed on arrival at Connolly Station, Dublin. (See also MCGEE CASE.) The movement was to the fore in seeking equal pay for women, which was conceded by the Government, 31 July 1973.

Irish Women's Reform League, founded in Dublin in 1911 by LOUIE BENNETT. Actively involved in practical attempts to improve the lot of women, it campaigned for suffrage, school meals, and technical education for girls.

Irish Women's Suffrage Federation. The Dublin Women's Suffrage Association was founded by Anna and Thomas Haslam in 1876. As the scope of the society broadened it became the IRISH WOMEN'S SUFFRAGE AND LOCAL GOVERNMENT ASSOCIATION in 1901, three years after women had been enfranchised for local government elections by the Local Government (Ireland) Act (1898). On the initiative of LOUIE

BENNETT and Helen Chenevix the association and various local suffrage societies were absorbed into the Irish Women's Suffrage Federation, 21 August 1911, as an umbrella organisation for non-militant suffrage groups; it had twenty-six affiliated societies, with a membership of two to three hundred. Presidents of the federation included MARY HAYDEN; GEORGE RUSSELL was one of its vice-presidents. Under the Representation of the People Act (1918) women over the age of thirty received the vote. Among the first Irish women to exercise the franchise was Anna Haslam, a veteran suffragist, then aged eighty-nine, who had sown the seed of women's emancipation more than forty years earlier.

Irish Worker and People's Advocate, a weekly paper founded by JAMES LARKIN, May 1911, representing the trade union and labour movement (see IRISH TRANSPORT AND GENERAL WORKERS' UNION and LABOUR PARTY). It attacked capitalism, imperialism, employers, the bourgeoisie in general, and the IRISH PARTY. It sold an average of 20,000 copies per issue. During its first years it was sued for libel seven times as a result of Larkin's policy of denouncing individuals by name. It was suppressed by DUBLIN CASTLE for its anti-war sentiments, December 1914 to January 1915. After Larkin's departure for the United States in October 1914 JAMES CONNOLLY edited the paper until it was suppressed. It was revived by Larkin and edited by his son JAMES LARKIN JUNIOR from October 1930 until March 1932.

Irish Worker League, a militant socialist organisation founded by JAMES LARKIN in September 1923. It replaced the COMMUNIST PARTY OF IRELAND as the Irish section of the Comintern, and Larkin represented the league at the Moscow congresses of the Comintern, 1924 and 1928. It won one Dáil seat in September 1927, when Larkin was elected as an independent labour candidate in Dublin North, but he was subsequently disqualified.

Irish Workers' and Farmers' Republican Party, a radical movement founded in 1930. Its objectives were 'to break the connection with England' and 'to bring about the closest co-operation between workers in . . . rural districts . . . in cities . . . all victims of the same exploiting agencies.' As with other groups, including the WORKERS' REVOLUTIONARY PARTY and the IRISH WORKING FARMERS' COMMITTEE, it lacked popular support. It was outlawed on 17 October 1931.

Irish Working Farmers' Committee, a radical rural movement founded in the west of Ireland in the late 1920s by PEADAR O'DONNELL and Seán Hayes, with the support of the left wing of the IRA. It failed in its efforts to recruit the smaller farmer and the largely exploited agricultural worker, while its co-operative precepts were anathema to the conservative older farmer. In common with other radical and revolutionary movements, it was banned by the Free State government in October 1931.

Irish World, a paper founded by Patrick Ford in New York in 1870. Its radical position during the depression of the 1870s had an appeal beyond its immediate Irish constituency, and it enjoyed a circulation of 35,000. With JEREMIAH O'DONOVAN ROSSA as a columnist, it adopted a strong nationalist line on Irish affairs. It launched the 'SKIRMISHING FUND', March 1876, and played a significant role in the fund-raising efforts of the IRISH PARTY and the LAND LEAGUE. The paper was banned from the US mails, 21 January 1918, because of its extremist anti-British tone. During the 1920s it was engaged in a libel case with JOHN DEVOY, whose original award of $25,000 damages was reduced on appeal to 6 cents. Following Ford's death the paper, edited by his nephew Robert Ford, supported JOHN REDMOND.

J

Jacob, Arthur (1790–1874), oculist; born in Maryborough (Port Laoise), Co. Laois. Having studied surgery under his father he completed his studies in Edinburgh, London, and Paris. He returned to Dublin c. 1816, where he became established as an ophthalmologist. Joint founder of Park Street School of Medicine, he was instrumental in the founding of the City of Dublin Hospital, Baggot Street, 1832. He held professorships of anatomy and of physiology and surgery (into his seventieth year) at the Royal College of Surgeons in Ireland, of which he was president, 1837 and 1864. He was joint founder and joint editor (with Henry Maunsell) of the *Dublin Medical Press*, 9 January 1839. He discovered the layer of cone-shaped and rod-shaped cells in the retina that react to different kinds of light, and was the first to describe the condition known as Jacob's ulcer (basal cell carcinoma).

Jacob, Joshua (1805–1877), founder of the White Quakers; born in Clonmel, Co. Tipperary, educated at Newtown School,

Waterford. A successful grocer and tea merchant, he was a philanthropist whose generosity extended to bringing street urchins to dine at his home in Dublin. Disowned by the Society of Friends, 1838, for his extreme puritanical views, he formed the White Quaker movement. Members wore undyed clothing, were vegetarians, and spurned all manifestations of the contemporary world, including clocks and watches, mirrors, and newspapers. Jacob encouraged others to follow his lead in placing his property in a trust fund; this resulted in litigation regarding unauthorised use of orphans' funds for his society, and he received a two-year jail sentence for contempt of court. His wife, Sarah, left him; on his release he began a relationship with Abigail Beale, which scandalised his supporters, and the movement fragmented. The group established a community at Newlands, Co. Dublin, c. 1849, where they lived on the produce of their gardens and vineyards. Jacob's dictatorial behaviour led to the break-up of the movement, 1851. Following Sarah's death he married a Catholic, Catherine Divine, whom he occasionally accompanied to Mass. One of their descendants was DOMHNALL UA BUACHALLA, Governor-General of the Irish Free State, 1932–37.

Jamestown, an American naval sloop from the Charlestown Navy Yard, the most famous of the ships that brought American aid to Ireland during the GREAT FAMINE (1845–49). Following representation by prominent Bostonians, the vessel was released from the war with Mexico by act of Congress, 3 March 1846, to transport aid to Cork. A volunteer group of Irish members of the Boston Laborers' Aid Society loaded 800 tons of foodstuffs and clothing, a gift from the people of Massachusetts, and the vessel left Boston on 27 March. With a volunteer crew under Captain Robert Bennet Forbes, it arrived in Cork on 12 April. The operation was organised by the Society of Friends, under the chairmanship of Jacob Harvey. The British government paid the freight charges, and all canal and toll fees were waived on food marked *For Ireland*.

Jebb, John (1775–1833), bishop (Church of Ireland) and author; born in Drogheda, Co. Louth, educated at TCD. Ordained in 1799, he was successively curate at Mogarvane, Co. Tipperary, and rector of Abingdon, Co. Limerick, from 1809. As Archdeacon of Emly, Co. Tipperary, from 1820, he devoted himself to the welfare of the district. Immensely popular with his Catholic neighbours, he gave a sermon from the pulpit of the local Catholic church at the height of the famine of 1822. Following a stroke that left him paralysed, 1827, he retired from active duty and settled in England. His writings included *Sermons* (1815) and *Thirty Years of Correspondence between . . . Bishop Jebb . . . and Alexander Knox* (2 vols., 1836).

Jinks Affair (1927). Alderman John Jinks was a member of Dáil Éireann for Sligo-Leitrim in 1927, at a time when his NATIONAL LEAGUE PARTY and the Labour Party had entered into an alliance with Fianna Fáil to oust the Cumann na nGaedheal government. On 16 August the leader of the Labour Party, Thomas Johnson, put down a motion of no confidence. Jinks's absence led to a tie, and the government survived on the casting vote of the Ceann Comhairle, Michael Hayes. An independent deputy, Major Bryan Cooper, and the editor of the *Irish Times*, R. M. SMYLLIE, were suspected of intercepting Jinks on his way to the Dáil and liberally entertaining him, a belief given credence by the wry observation of CAPTAIN WILLIAM REDMOND that Jinks had been 'spirited away.' W. T. COSGRAVE dissolved the Dáil, 25 August, and won a comfortable majority in the ensuing election (in which Jinks was defeated).

When the name of a horse newly purchased by the National Stud was in question, 1928, Cosgrave suggested Mr Jinks. The horse won the 1929 English Two Thousand Guineas, at odds of 5 to 2.

Johnson, Thomas (1872–1963), trade unionist and politician (Labour Party); born in Liverpool. He worked in the fishing industry in Kinsale, Co. Cork, and Dunmore East, Co. Waterford, until 1901, when he was employed as a commercial traveller in Belfast. His experiences on the strike committee during the Belfast general strike of 1907, organised by JAMES LARKIN, led to his involvement in the founding of the Labour Party, 1912, of which he was executive vice-president, 1913, and president, 1916. A member of the MANSION HOUSE CONFERENCE (1918), his opposition to CONSCRIPTION led to the loss of his Belfast job. He moved to Dublin, where he became treasurer of the IRISH TRANSPORT AND GENERAL WORKERS' UNION. He supported the abstention of the Labour Party from the December 1918 election to maximise the Sinn Féin vote. He was joint author (with WILLIAM O'BRIEN) of the DEMOCRATIC PROGRAMME of the first Dáil Éireann, which he and CATHAL O'SHANNON presented to the conference of the Socialist International in Bern, 1919.

As a TD for Dublin from June 1922, Johnson opposed the election of W. T. COSGRAVE as President of the Executive Council. The return of Larkin from the United States, 1923, precipitated a power struggle within the labour movement as O'Brien and Johnson resisted Larkin's efforts to regain control of the ITGWU.

Johnson was critical of the government's economic programme and was especially virulent in his denunciation of the policy of executing imprisoned republicans. This, and his opposition to the payment of LAND ANNUITIES, led to a statement by Johnson during the 1927 election campaign that he would support Fianna Fáil in government provided it subscribed to the OATH OF ALLEGIANCE. On 16 August the government survived a motion of no confidence initiated by Johnson through the absence of John Jinks (see JINKS AFFAIR). Having lost his Dáil seat to JAMES LARKIN JUNIOR, Johnson resigned as secretary of the Labour Party, 1928, but continued to represent the party in the Senate until it was abolished by the government of Éamon de Valera, 1936. He was a member of the Labour Court from 1946 until his retirement in 1955.

Johnston, Francis (1760–1829), architect; born in Armagh, where he practised before moving to Dublin, 1793. As architect to the Board of Works from 1805 he designed the buildings of several institutions, including Richmond Jail, Dublin (1811), Armagh Asylum (1820), and Belfast Asylum (1826). He worked on the adaptation of the Parliament House, Dublin, for the Bank of Ireland (1802) and on the reconstruction of the Viceregal Lodge, now Áras an Uachtaráin (1815–16), and the General Post Office, Sackville Street (O'Connell Street), Dublin. Severely damaged during the EASTER RISING (1916), only the classical façade of the original GPO now remains. Popularly known as the Wren of Ireland, Johnston was a founder-member of the ROYAL HIBERNIAN ACADEMY and its president, 1824–29; he designed and paid for its premises in Ely Place, Dublin (also destroyed during the 1916 Rising). A campanologist, he erected a bell-tower in his garden that was later given to his local church, St George's, Drumcondra; the bells were tolled at his funeral on 16 March.

Johnston's other works include Townley Hall, Co. Louth (1794), Corbalton Hall, Co. Meath (1801), Charleville Forest, Co. Offaly (1801–12), Killeen Castle, Co. Meath (1802–03), St George's Church, Temple Street, Dublin (1802–17), and the Chapel Royal (now the Church of the Most Holy Trinity), Dublin Castle (1807–14).

Johnston, William (1829–1902), politician (Unionist); born in Ballykilbeg, Co. Down, educated at TCD. A leading member of the ORANGE ORDER from 1848, he was imprisoned under the Party Processions Act (1867); his intemperate speeches in opposition to the LAND LEAGUE led to dismissal from his post as a fisheries inspector. Implacably opposed to HOME RULE, he supported security of tenure for tenant-farmers and was a noted advocate of the temperance movement and of women's emancipation. The South Belfast parliamentary seat he held for seventeen years was won by T. H. SLOAN in 1902.

Joint Committee of Unionist Associations of Ireland, founded in 1907 to co-ordinate northern and southern opposition to home rule, its members coming from the ULSTER UNIONIST COUNCIL and the IRISH UNIONIST ALLIANCE. It was wound up following the passing of the third HOME RULE BILL (1914).

Joly, Rev. Jasper (1819–1892), clergyman (Church of Ireland) and bibliophile; born near Clonbulloge, Co. Offaly. He was called to the bar, 1857, but never practised. On taking holy orders he was appointed Vicar-General of the diocese of Tuam, Co. Galway, an office he held until it was abolished, 1869. He was also a member of the Council of the Royal Dublin Society. His collection of books, manuscripts and papers was presented to the National Library, 29 August 1900, under a deed of trust. The collection of 23,000 printed volumes includes rare works on Irish history and culture, an extensive collection of Irish and Scottish music, and a selection of invaluable material on the Napoleonic era.

Joyce, James (1882–1941), novelist; born in Dublin, educated at UCD, which he entered on a scholarship. He studied mathematics, philosophy, English, French, and Italian. His fellow-students, including GEORGE CLANCY and Oliver St John Gogarty, were models for some of his literary characters. Encouraged by Clancy, he attended Irish classes under the Gaelic League, but the hostile attitude to English on the part of his teacher, PATRICK PEARSE (whom he pilloried in his autobiographical *Stephen Hero,* 1944), led him to abandon them. He left Ireland after graduating from the Royal University, 1902; he returned in August 1903 to attend his mother's funeral. Leaving Ireland on 8 October 1904, he settled in Trieste, where he taught languages while working on his novels. He returned to Dublin, 1911, as partner in a cinema venture and opened Ireland's first cinema, the Volta, in Mary Street, Dublin, 20 December 1911; the venture failed, and Joyce settled in Zürich from 30 June 1915. Ezra Pound (1885–1972) helped him find a publisher for *A Portrait of the Artist as a Young Man* (1916) and introduced him to Harriet Weaver, later Joyce's patron.

Joyce's difficulties with censorship, encountered during the publication of his collection of short stories, *Dubliners* (1910), continued until his return to Paris, 8 July 1920, where he met the publisher Sylvia Beach, who published *Ulysses* (1922) under her imprint Shakespeare and Company. His health, never robust, was undermined by rheumatic fever and by bouts of heavy drinking. From 1917 his eyesight deteriorated. He returned to Zürich, 1940, where, with Nora Barnacle (1884–1951) and their two children, he remained until his death. His other works include *Chamber Music* (poems, 1907), *Exiles* (a play, 1918), and *Finnegans Wake* (1939). The martello tower at Sandycove, Co. Dublin, which features in the opening sequence of *Ulysses,* was opened as a Joyce Museum by Sylvia Beach, 16 June 1962.

Joyce, P. W. [Patrick Weston] (1827–1914), scholar, historian, musician, and linguist; born in Ballyorgan, Co. Limerick, educated at a hedge school and TCD. A teacher at eighteen, he was principal of the Model School, Clonmel, until 1856. Commissioner for National Education, 1856–74, he was a professor and later principal of Marlborough Street Training College, Dublin, 1874–93. A leading member of the SOCIETY FOR THE PRESERVATION OF THE IRISH LANGUAGE, he was elected to the Royal Irish Academy, 1863, and was president of the Royal Society of Antiquaries of Ireland, 1906–08. His *Ancient Irish Music* (1873) contains the air that became popular as 'Amhrán Dóchais'. *The Origin and History of Irish Names of Places* (3 vols., 1869–70) and *A Social History of Ancient Ireland* (1907) were considered standard reference works. His last major work, *Old Irish Folk Music and Songs* (1909), contains more than eight hundred previously unpublished airs.

Joyce's brother Robert Dwyer Joyce (1830–1883), physician, poet, and writer, was a Fenian. He enjoyed a successful medical practice in Boston and lectured at Harvard University, Massachusetts. His most popular poems were 'The Blacksmith of Limerick', 'The Boys of Wexford', 'The Leprachaun', and 'The Wind That Shakes the Barley'. His published works include *Ballads, Romances and Songs* (1861), *Legends of the Wars in Ireland* (1868), *Irish Fireside Tales* (1871), and *Ballads of Irish Chivalry* (1872).

Joyce, William ('Lord Haw-haw') (1906–1946), Nazi sympathiser and propagandist; born in New York of Irish parentage. The family moved to Ballinrobe, Co. Mayo, in 1909 and to Galway three years later, where Joyce received his education at St Ignatius' Jesuit College. In England from 1923, he joined the British Union of Fascists but was expelled in 1937 and founded the Brirish Nationalist Socialist League, which adopted Adolf Hitler as its figurehead.

Having obtained a British passport by falsely giving his place of birth as Galway, Joyce travelled to Germany before the outbreak of the Second World War and placed himself at Hitler's disposal. On 18 September 1939 he made his first propaganda broadcast from Radio Hamburg. His broadcasts, introduced by 'Germany calling, Germany calling,' had a wide audience throughout Europe and especially in Ireland and Britain. Nicknamed 'Lord Haw-haw' because of his contrived English upper-class accent, he became a naturalised German citizen in 1940. His last broadcast was transmitted by Radio Hamburg on 30 April 1945.

Despite elaborate plans by the German Minister for Propaganda, Joseph Goebbels, to facilitate Joyce's escape, he was captured at Flensburg by British officers, 28 May 1945. At his trial in London his British passport enabled the prosecution to have his plea of American birth rejected, and he was sentenced to death. Before he was hanged at Wandsworth Prison, London, 3 January 1946, Joyce warned the people of Britain against Soviet Russia and expressed a hope that the swastika might be 'raised from the dust.' His remains were returned to Galway for reburial in November 1976.

'jumper'. Among the Catholic Irish in the nineteenth century a person who changed religion for monetary or other gain was derisively referred to as a 'jumper' or a 'pervert'. Many such people were obliged to seek residence elsewhere because of the contempt in which they were held by the community; generations might pass before the insulting epithet was expunged from a family's record. (See also SOUPERISM.)

Juno, a Norwegian ship raided by Fenian sympathisers while at anchor in Cork Harbour, 11 August 1880. Forty cases of arms, containing an assortment of 960 weapons, were taken. Few of the arms were recovered, and the perpetrators were never apprehended.

Juries Protection Act (1929), introduced by the Cumann na nGaedheal government as a response to left-wing and republican agitation and the intimidation of jury members in political trials. Opposed by Fianna Fáil, the bill was passed under guillotine.

K

Kane, Sir Robert (1809–1890), scientist; born in Dublin, educated at TCD and Paris. First attracting attention with *Elements of Practical Pharmacy* (1831), he became a licentiate of the King's and Queen's College of Physicians, 1832, when he also founded the *Dublin Journal of Medical Science.* He was editor of the *Philosophical Magazine,* 1840, professor of natural philosophy at the RDS, 1841–47, secretary of the Council of the Royal Irish Academy, 1842, and a member of the Commission to Investigate Potato Blight in Ireland, 1845. At his suggestion, the Museum of Irish Industries was established, of which he became first director in 1846. First president of Queen's College, Cork, 1849–73, he was also president of the RIA, 1877, and vice-chancellor of the Royal University of Ireland, 1880. He published *Industrial Resources of Ireland* (the economic blueprint for YOUNG IRELAND, 1844), and *The Large and Small Farm Question Considered* (1844).

Kavanagh, Arthur MacMurrough (1831–1889), landlord, magistrate, and politician (Conservative); born in Borris, Co. Carlow. Born with rudimentary limbs, he became a proficient horseman and rode to hounds with a specially adapted saddle. He could draw and write and was an expert yachtsman and keen angler (in a single day, fishing from horseback, he landed eight salmon, including one of 36 pounds). He travelled extensively on the Continent and in the East with his brothers, all of whom predeceased him. From 1835 he rebuilt the famine-ravaged estate, on which he was considered a generous and humane landlord. He financed the rebuilding of Borris and introduced cottage industries, including lacemaking. He opposed the DISESTABLISHMENT of the Church of Ireland but supported the Landlord and Tenant (Ireland) Act (1870) (see LAND ACTS). He was member of Parliament for Co. Wexford, 1866–68, and Co. Carlow, 1868–80, until, in a bitter blow, he lost his seat in the general election to EDMUND DWYER GRAY. Replying to a sympathiser, he wrote: 'But to feel that almost every one of my own men who met me with kind expressions and cheerful promises were traitors, is the hard part of the burden and the poison of the sting.' His outstanding career, in which he completely overcame his disabilities, made him the subject of a number of stories and books.

Kavanagh, Patrick (1904–1967), poet; born in Inishkeen, Co. Monaghan, educated locally. His early poems were published in the *Irish Weekly Independent* before he attracted the attention of GEORGE RUSSELL, who published 'The Intangible', 29 October 1928, and 'Ploughman' and 'Dreamer', 15 February 1930, in the *Irish Statesman.* Poems also appeared in the *Dublin Magazine* and the *Spectator* (London). 'Ploughman' was published in *Best Poems* (1930). Kavanagh was befriended by SEÁN Ó FAOLÁIN and FRANK O'CONNOR. Having worked as a small farmer and cobbler and published his first collection, *Ploughman and Other Poems* (1936), he moved to Dublin, 1939. *Kavanagh's Weekly,* 'a journal of literature and politics', 12 April to 5 July 1952, edited by himself and his brother Peter (born 1916), who also financed it, enlivened Dublin's intellectual life with biting attacks on a wide variety of targets during its thirteen issues. Kavanagh's friendship with John Betjeman led to work with the BBC. He was film critic for the *Irish Press,* 1942–44, and the *Standard,* 1946–49; he also wrote for the *Irish Farmer's Journal,* 1958–63, and *RTV Guide,* 1964–66. His hand-to-mouth existence was often leavened by the generosity of JOHN CHARLES MCQUAID.

Kavanagh's later years were dogged by ill-health. He married his long-time friend Katherine Barry Moloney, 1967. He published *The Great Hunger* (1942), *A Soul for Sale* (1947), and *Come Dance with Kitty Stobling and Other Poems* (1960). He also published two semi-autobiographical novels, *The Green Fool* (1938) and *Tarry Flynn* (1948). His *Collected*

Poems appeared in 1964 and *Collected Prose* in 1967. Kavanagh's grave in Inishkeen bears the inscription *Pray for him who walked apart on the hills loving life's miracles.*

Kearney, Peadar (1883–1942), ballad-writer; born in Dublin, educated at Model School and Marino Christian Brothers' School. He worked as a messenger-boy before turning to house-painting. WILLIAM ROONEY, whose lecture on the MANCHESTER MARTYRS he had attended, awakened his national consciousness. A teacher in the Gaelic League (where his students included SEÁN O'CASEY), he joined the IRB, 1903, and became a member of the Supreme Council. Keenly interested in the theatre, he worked for some time without pay at the early ABBEY THEATRE before being employed as a props man, 1910. He met PATRICK HEENEY in 1903, and four years later they collaborated on 'The Soldier's Song', for which Kearney wrote the words; the air (largely the work of Heeney) later became the NATIONAL ANTHEM. Kearney's early poetry was published in *St Patrick's,* edited by WILLIAM O'BRIEN. A founder-member of the Irish Volunteers, he took part in the HOWTH GUN-RUNNING (1914). He returned from an Abbey Theatre tour in England to take part in the EASTER RISING (1916) and fought in Jacob's factory, Bishop Street, Dublin, after which he avoided capture. A friend of MICHAEL COLLINS, he was interned at Ballykinler, Co. Down, 1920–21, during the War of Independence. Apart from 'The Soldier's Song' his best-known ballads are 'The Tri-Coloured Ribbon', 'Down by the Glenside', and 'Whack Fol the Diddle'. BRENDAN BEHAN was his nephew.

Keating, Seán (1889–1977), artist; born in Limerick, educated at St Munchin's College and the Metropolitan School of Art, Dublin. A protégé of William Orpen (1878–1931), under whom he worked in London, he modelled for Orpen's *The Holy Well* (1915). Returning from London, 1916, he visited the Aran Islands, and they remained a source of artistic inspiration for the rest of his life. First exhibited at the Royal Hibernian Academy, of which he was a member from 1919 and president, 1948–62, his work featured there for more than sixty years. He was commissioned to produce works illustrating progress on the SHANNON SCHEME in the 1920s. A teacher from 1918 and later professor at the Metropolitan School of Art, later the National College of Art and Design, he was an honorary member of the Royal Academy (London) and Royal Scottish Academy (Edinburgh). He was made an honorary freeman of the city of Limerick, 1948. His works include a canvas 72 feet by 24 feet for the New York World's Fair, 1939, and a mural 24 feet by 12 feet for the head office of the International Labour Organisation in Geneva. His best-known work, *Men of the West,* is in the Hugh Lane Municipal Gallery of Modern Art, Dublin.

keen (Irish *caoineadh,* 'crying'), lamenting over the body of a deceased person, a widespread practice in ancient times. Virgil records it among the Phoenicians: 'They shake the roof with their female crying and lamentation.' In Ireland, keening began when the body had been laid out for the WAKE, when all danger had passed of awakening the 'Devil's dogs' (who, it was believed, fed on passing souls). Relatives then gathered around the body and began a ritual crying. When their grief had subsided they were led from the room. The wailing began again when the body was taken from the house; the final keen was reserved for the graveyard.

Professional keeners, usually older women, were often hired for their talent of dramatic and anguished crying over the body. They received up to 5 shillings for their services as well as being liberally plied with food and drink; it was sometimes remarked that the volume, quality and sense of grief projected by professional keeners was in direct proportion to the hospitality on offer. The traditional form of keen had the refrain 'Ochón! ochón! olagón-ó,' with lines addressed to the body asking why he or she had gone away, leaving grieving relatives, and listing the virtues of the departed.

Keening was regularly condemned by the Catholic Church. In 1800 Thomas Bray, Archbishop of Cashel, issued a pastoral letter that roundly condemned the practice: 'We also condemn and reprobate, in the strongest terms, all unnatural screams and shrieks and fictitious tuneful cries and elegies at wakes, together with the savage custom of howling and bawling at funerals.' The custom lingered in some areas up to the early part of the twentieth century.

Kelly, Thomas J. (1833–1908), Fenian; born in Mount Bellew, Co. Galway. A printer by trade, in 1851 he was in Nashville, Tennessee, where he became a newspaper proprietor, 1857. He served in the 10th Ohio Regiment during the American Civil War (1861–65). A member of the FENIANS with the rank of colonel in the Army of the Irish Republic, he was sent to Ireland to assess the situation there, March 1865, and to urge JAMES STEPHENS to call for an insurrection. As chief of staff of the IRB he took part in the rescue of Stephens from Richmond Jail, Dublin, 24 November 1865. He escaped to England with Stephens following the arrest of JOHN DEVOY, February 1866. Kelly replaced Stephens as head organiser for Ireland and England, with the title of acting chief executive of the Irish Republic, December 1866.

In January 1867 he returned to England from America accompanied by Fenian officers. Establishing headquarters in London, where he was aided by GENERAL GUSTAVE-PAUL CLUSERET, RICARD O'SULLIVAN BURKE, and GODFREY MASSEY, he planned the rising for 11 February. When the plan for a raid on Chester Castle misfired, the rising was postponed. After Massey's arrest had led to the failure of the rising, Kelly was arrested together with TIMOTHY DEASY in Manchester, 11 September 1867. Their rescue from a police van a week later by Fenians led to the death of a police sergeant, for which three were hanged (see MANCHESTER MARTYRS). Kelly escaped to the United States and had no further role in Irish nationalism.

Kelpie, a yacht owned by CONOR O'BRIEN used, together with the ASGARD and the CHOTAH, in the HOWTH GUN-RUNNING (1914). It sailed from Dublin, 2 July, to rendezvous in the North Sea with DARRELL FIGGIS, who had bought arms in Hamburg. Because the owner and his yacht were so well known to the authorities, the *Kelpie's* cargo of arms was transferred to the *Chotah* for landing at Kilcoole, Co. Wexford.

Kemmy, Jim (1936–1997), historian and politician (Labour Party and Democratic Socialist Party); born in Limerick, educated at Sexton Street Christian Brothers' School and Municipal Technical Institute. A stonemason, he was an active trade unionist in both Limerick and London. He broke with the Labour Party, 1972, and formed his own organisation, later the Democratic Socialist Party. A member of Limerick City Council from 1974, he was twice mayor of the city and donated his salary for 1991 to community projects. He was a member of Dáil Éireann for Limerick East, 1981 (when his vote against the imposition of VAT on children's shoes helped bring about the fall of the government), and held the seat from 1987 until his death. His Democratic Socialist Party merged with the Labour Party, 1 May 1990, of which he was subsequently chairman. A prolific writer, he was founder and editor of the *Limerick Socialist* and joint founder of the *Old Limerick Journal,* 1979. His best-selling *Limerick Anthology* was published in 1996; its sequel, *The Limerick Compendium,* was posthumously published in 1997.

Kennedy, Hugh (1879–1936), lawyer and judge; born in Dublin, educated at UCD. As editor of the college magazine, *St Stephen's,* he rejected an article by JAMES JOYCE that was hostile to the works of George Moore (1852–1933) and W. B. YEATS. He was Law Officer to the PROVISIONAL GOVERNMENT, January–December 1922, first Attorney-General of the Irish Free State, 1922–24, and first Chief Justice, 1924–36.

Kennedy, John Pitt (1796–1879), soldier, engineer, and agriculturalist; born in Carndonagh, Co. Donegal, educated at Foyle College, Derry. Commissioned in the Corps of Engineers of the British army, after working abroad he returned to Ireland, 1831, and settled in Co. Tyrone, where he interested himself in progressive farming. As an estate manager at Lough Ash and Clogher he operated model farms, placing the emphasis on land reclamation. He was inspector-general to the Board of National Education, 1837–39, where he emphasised agricultural instruction, but resigned because of lack of official support. Following a period in Australia and India he returned to Ireland as secretary of the DEVON COMMISSION. During the GREAT FAMINE (1845–49) he was secretary of the Famine Relief Committee and superintendent of relief works in west Limerick, 1846, where he was also agent for Lord Devon's estates. He commanded the defence of Dublin during the 1848 YOUNG IRELAND rising, when he distributed arms to Orange Order volunteers.

Kenny, Enda (born 1951), politician (Fine Gael); born in Castlebar, Co. Mayo, educated at St Patrick's Training College, Drumcondra, Dublin. He was a national teacher before winning his late father's Dáil seat in a by-election, 1975. He was Fine Gael spokesperson on youth affairs and sport, 1977–80, on western development, 1982, and the Gaeltacht, 1987–88, and later arts, heritage, the Gaeltacht and the islands, and minister of state in the Department of Education and Department of Labour, with special responsibility for youth affairs, 1986–87. A member of the British-Irish Interparliamentary Body, 1991–92, and Fine Gael chief whip, 1992–94, he was Minister for Tourism and Trade, 1994–97. In 2000 he failed in his challenge to succeed JOHN BRUTON as leader of Fine Gael but succeeded MICHAEL NOONAN when the latter resigned following the party's disastrous showing in the general election of May 2002.

Kent, Thomas (1865–1916), land agitator and republican; born in Fermoy, Co. Cork, to a noted republican family. Joining the Irish Volunteers, he organised the disruption of British army recruitment in Ireland. A leading member of the Provisional Committee of the Volunteers, in which his brothers Richard, David and William also figured prominently, he was on the run during the EASTER RISING (1916). On his return home, 1 May, a party of soldiers and RIC men, seeking to arrest the entire family, surrounded the house. Following an engagement that resulted in the death of Head Constable William Rowe and several casualties to the military and during which David Kent was wounded, the family was forced to surrender. Richard Kent attempted to escape and was shot dead. The remainder of the family, including their eighty-year-old mother, were arrested. Following a court-martial Thomas Kent requested that no Irishman should be included in the firing party at his execution by firing squad, 9 May. His brother William Kent was acquitted, and David's death sentence was commuted to five years' penal servitude.

Kenyon, Rev. John (1812–1869), clergyman (Catholic) and revolutionary; born in Limerick, educated at St Patrick's College, Maynooth. After ordination he served in Templederry, Co. Tipperary, where he was later parish priest. A supporter of YOUNG IRELAND, he contributed to the *Nation*. Disapproving of the moral force argument of DANIEL O'CONNELL, he supported JOHN MITCHEL in the demand for a militant policy. He supported the Young Irelanders when they seceded from the REPEAL ASSOCIATION, July 1846, and established the IRISH CONFEDERATION, January 1848. Suspended by his bishop, Dr Kennedy, in April 1848 for incitement to violence, he did not support WILLIAM SMITH O'BRIEN and the insurrection of 1848 (see BALLINGARRY), as he believed the GREAT FAMINE (1845–49) had sapped the energies of the people. He was reinstated in his parish. He subsequently accompanied JOHN MARTIN to Paris, 1866, to meet Mitchel for the last time; during the visit he persuaded Mitchel to visit the Irish College, where they received a standing ovation from the clerical students. Kenyon again incurred episcopal displeasure when, contrary to the wishes of Archbishop Paul Cullen of Dublin, he participated in the funeral rites of TERENCE BELLEW MCMANUS.

Keogh, William Nicholas (1817–1878), politician (Independent Irish Party and Conservative) and judge; born in Galway, educated at TCD and called to the bar. He practised on the Connacht circuit, where he built up a lucrative practice and a considerable reputation as an advocate, though his knowledge of law was not considered profound. A member of Parliament from 1847, he was the only Irish Catholic Conservative in the House of Commons. A joint founder of the CATHOLIC DEFENCE ASSOCIATION (with JOHN SADLEIR and GEORGE HENRY MOORE), he became a member of the INDEPENDENT IRISH PARTY in 1852 and seconded the Tenant Right Bill introduced by WILLIAM SHARMAN CRAWFORD. He supported his party in bringing down Lord Derby's ministry, 1852, but then helped to destroy it when he accepted office as Solicitor-General, contrary to the party pledge not to accept government office. Three years later he became Attorney-General and in 1857 a judge of the Court of Common Pleas. He was special commissioner at the trials of the FENIANS in 1865, when he was noted for his intemperate remarks during sentencing. As judge during the Galway county election petition of 1872, when the nationalist John P. Nolan (2,823 votes) was unseated in favour of the Conservative candidate, Captain Le Poer Trench (658 votes), Keogh's remarks and scathing attack on Catholic clergy led to questions in the House of Commons; a petition by ISAAC BUTT to have him removed from the bench was defeated.

From 1856, when he had been embarrassed by the revelations of fraud and embezzlement surrounding his close associate John Sadleir, Keogh showed symptoms of mental instability. While visiting Germany he died, reportedly by committing suicide. His works included *A Treatise on the Practice of the High Court of Chancery in Ireland* (with M. J. Barry, 1840), *Ireland under Lord Grey* (1844), *Ireland Imperialised* (1863), and *An Essay on Milton's Prose Writings* (1863).

Kettle, Andrew (1833–1916), land agitator; born in Dublin. As a child of six he had an extraordinary escape when a neighbour snatched him from the air as he was about to be swept away during the NIGHT OF THE BIG WIND (6/7 January 1839). A tenant-farmer with properties in Co. Dublin, he and his father were members of the REPEAL ASSOCIATION. As a member of the TENANT LEAGUE in the 1850s he was influenced by the policies of ISAAC BUTT following the latter's publication of *Plea for the Celtic Race* (1866). He later supported MICHAEL DAVITT and was instrumental in persuading CHARLES STEWART PARNELL to support the land agitation in the late 1870s. He presided at the first meeting of the LAND LEAGUE, at which he became honorary secretary and Parnell president, October 1879. Kettle proposed in February 1881 that the answer to the British government's COERCION policy was that 'the whole Irish Party should rise and leave the house, and cross to Ireland and carry out a no-rent campaign.' This policy of 'concentration', though opposed by Parnell, was adopted in modified form. Kettle was imprisoned for organising resistance to coercion. He was a signatory of the NO-RENT MANIFESTO.

Following the 'KILMAINHAM TREATY' he retired from active politics to work his farms but continued to give passive support to Parnell's policies and supported him after the split (see IRISH PARTY). *Material for Victory: The Memoirs of Andrew J. Kettle* was published in 1958.

Kettle, Thomas (1880–1916), poet and politician (Nationalist); born in Dublin, son of ANDREW KETTLE, educated at Clongowes Wood College, Co. Kildare, and UCD. Though called to the bar, he never practised. President of the Young Ireland Branch of the UNITED IRISH LEAGUE, he edited the controversial but short-lived *Nationalist* with FRANCIS SHEEHY-SKEFFINGTON. Member of Parliament for East Tyrone, 1906–10, he supported HOME RULE, and became an authority on the economic implications of self-government. He became the first professor of economics at UCD, 1908. He supported the IRISH VOLUNTEERS, for whom he bought weapons in Belgium in 1914.

Following the outbreak of the Great War in 1914 he acted as war correspondent of the *Daily News.* In November 1914 he joined the British army and toured Ireland as a recruiting officer. Following the murder of Sheehy-Skeffington during the EASTER RISING (1916) he volunteered for active service and was sent to the western front, where he was killed at Givenchy during the Battle of the Somme. His writings include *The Open Secret of Ireland* (1912), *Poems and Parodies* (1916), and two posthumous publications, *The Ways of War* (1917) and *The Day's Burden* (1918).

Kickham, Charles J. (1828–1882), writer and Fenian; born near Mullinahone, Co. Tipperary, a cousin of JOHN O'MAHONY; his education ended at the age of thirteen, when gunpowder exploded in his face, leaving him with hearing and sight impairment. A supporter of the REPEAL ASSOCIATION and YOUNG IRELAND, he contributed verse to the *Nation,* the *Celt,* and the *Irishman.* Having founded a branch of the IRISH CONFEDERATION in Mullinahone in 1848, he was forced into hiding after the unsuccessful rising at BALLINGARRY, Co. Tipperary (1848). After joining the IRB in 1860, he visited the United States in 1863. He was on the editorial staff of the IRISH PEOPLE, of which he became joint editor. Following his arrest, 1865, he was tried before JUDGE WILLIAM KEOGH and sentenced to fourteen years' imprisonment, after which he returned to Mullinahone with his health severely impaired, 1869.

Following the annulment of the election of JEREMIAH O'DONOVAN ROSSA as member of Parliament for Co. Tipperary, Kickham stood and polled even higher (1,664 votes) but was defeated by four votes. He became a member of the Supreme Council of the IRB, 1872, of which he was president until his death. He opposed the NEW DEPARTURE. A national collection to alleviate his hardship was taken up in 1878. His death was hastened by an accident in Blackrock, Co. Dublin, when he was knocked down by a jaunting-car. His funeral was followed to Kingsbridge Station (Heuston Station) by more than ten thousand mourners, but the church of his native parish was closed to him, and he was buried without the presence of local clergymen.

Kickham's first novel, *Sally Cavanagh,* was published in 1869. He published *Poems, Sketches and Narratives, Illustrative of Irish Life* in 1870 and in 1873 published his most famous work, *Knocknagow, or The Homes of Tipperary* (first popular edition in 1879, originally serialised in the *Emerald* from 16 April 1870). His last work, *For the Old Land* (1886), was completed by WILLIAM O'BRIEN. Kickham's ballads include 'Patrick Sheehan' (which prompted the government to award a pension to a veteran of the Crimean War), 'Rory of the Hill', 'The Maid of Slievenamon', and 'The Irish Peasant Girl'.

Kildare Place Society, popular name for the Society for the Education of the Poor in Ireland, founded in 1811, having its head office in Kildare Place, Dublin. It was unique among societies of the era: a Protestant organisation aimed at providing non-denominational education without any attempt at proselytising. Its teachers, when reading the Scriptures, were forbidden to make any comment that would reflect the doctrine of a specific religion. The society was awarded a state grant of £7,000 in 1817, which rose to £30,000 in 1831, by which time 137,639 pupils were attending its 1,621 schools. However, when it became evident that the society was providing funds to proselytising agencies, the Catholic Church and prominent laymen, including DANIEL O'CONNELL, withdrew support.

Kildare Street Club, a popular meeting-place for members of 'Grattan's Parliament' (1782–1800) and members of the Anglo-Irish ASCENDANCY, founded in 1782 by Burton Conyngham. At its peak, membership was in the region of eight hundred. Famed for its oysters, delivered daily from its own oyster beds in Co. Galway, the club also had a reputation for the quality of its champagne. There was also a Masonic lodge drawn exclusively from the club's members. Catholics never numbered more than 4 per cent of the establishment, the number being regulated by a system that allowed for the blackballing of any application by a single member; rather than risk the embarrassing social consequences of refusal, Catholics tended to become members of the St Stephen's Green Club.

The premises of the club in Kildare Street, Dublin, were occupied by anti-Treaty forces during the CIVIL WAR. The club merged with the University Club in 1975.

Kilkenny Design Workshops, set up by Córas Tráchtála in 1963 as a result of the critical report *Design in Ireland*. The workshops, covering a range of crafts, were established in the former coach-house of Kilkenny Castle, restored by Niall Montgomery and officially opened in November 1965.

'Kilmainham Treaty', an understanding between CHARLES STEWART PARNELL and W. E. GLADSTONE, April 1882, following the imprisonment of Parnell and leading members of his party under COERCION, October 1881, for opposing Gladstone's Land Law (Ireland) Act (1881) (see LAND ACTS). There was considerable pressure on Gladstone to resolve the deteriorating situation in Ireland, exacerbated by the imprisonments and the NO-RENT MANIFESTO, while Parnell was anxious to leave prison for political and private reasons. In April 1882 he sent a letter to Gladstone stating that if tenants in arrears and leaseholders were brought within the scope of the 1881 act the IRISH PARTY would 'co-operate cordially for the future with the Liberal Party in forwarding Liberal principles and measures of general reform.'

By the terms of the 'treaty' it was agreed that the 130,000 tenants in arrears and some 150,000 leaseholders would be allowed the benefits of the act, and that coercion would be dropped. Parnell agreed to use his influence to counter the violence and to end the land agitation by accepting the amended act as a settlement of the land question, while collaborating with the Liberals on Gladstone's Irish policy. Parnell and his associates were released, 2 May; but the PHOENIX PARK MURDERS four days later provoked Gladstone into introducing further coercive measures and seriously endangered the alliance of the Irish Party and the Liberals. The 'treaty' was received without enthusiasm by MICHAEL DAVITT and other radicals but was described by T. M. HEALY as 'one of the most sagacious arrangements that ever enabled a hard pressed general to secure terms for his forces.'

King, Tom (born 1933), British politician (Conservative). King's tenure as Secretary of State for Northern Ireland, 1985–89, began amid Unionist anger at the signing of the ANGLO-IRISH AGREEMENT, November 1985. His attempts to allay loyalist fears made little impression, and he dissolved the Assembly of Northern Ireland, June 1986. During the period 1987–88 he was at odds on security issues with the Irish government, now headed by CHARLES HAUGHEY. The Ulster Unionist Party entered into 'talks about talks' with King; when these failed because he would not overturn the Anglo-Irish Agreement, he began talks with the SDLP. In October 1988 three people from the Republic were convicted of conspiracy to murder him; the conviction was overturned when the Court of Appeal held that King had prejudiced their right to a fair trial by remarking on alleged abuse of the right to silence.

Attempts to revive talks with the constitutional parties in Northern Ireland were resumed by King's successor, PETER BROOKE.

King's County, the name given by English planters to the territory of Co. Offaly, in honour of King Philip II of Spain, husband of Queen Mary, 1553–58, during the Plantation of Laois and Offaly. It was used officially until the establishment of the Irish Free State, 1922, when it was replaced by *Offaly* (Irish *Uíbh Fhailí*). The county town, Philipstown (after King Philip), was renamed Daingean.

King's Inns Library, Dublin, founded in 1787 and maintained by the Benchers (governing body) of the King's Inns. The building was designed by Frederick Darley, 1827. The library holds a unique collection of country house histories, rare books, manuscripts, and almost 10,000 pamphlets.

'king's shilling' (or 'queen's shilling'), popular name for the bounty paid to a recruit on enlisting in the British army. The shilling—a not insignificant sum in late nineteenth and early twentieth-century Ireland—was a factor in the decision of many to enlist. They were then contemptuously referred to as having 'taken the shilling.'

Kinnear, Rev. John (1824–1909), clergyman (Presbyterian) and politician (Liberal); born in Clonaneese, Co. Tyrone, educated at Belfast. Ordained in Co. Donegal, 1848, he spent his ministry in Letterkenny. He was sympathetic to the tenant right movement and was elected member of Parliament for Co. Donegal, 1880–85, during the LAND WAR, the first clergyman who had a congregation to sit in the House of Commons. He bequeathed his extensive library to Presbyterian College, Belfast.

Kirk, Thomas (1781–1845), sculptor; born in Cork. Trained at the RDS schools, he was a founder-member of the ROYAL HIBERNIAN ACADEMY, at which he was a regular exhibitor. His most famous work was the figure of Nelson for NELSON'S PILLAR, Dublin (demolished by explosion on 8 March 1966). Other works include *Thomas Spring Rice* (People's Park, Limerick), the *Metal Man* (Great Newton Head, Tramore, Co. Waterford), and another *Metal Man* at Perch Rock, Sligo. Examples of his work in Dublin can be seen at Trinity College, the College of Surgeons, and the Royal Dublin Society.

Kirkintilloch Bothy Disaster (1937). Ten tattie-hokers (potato-pickers) out of a party of twenty-six, newly arrived from Achill Island, Co. Mayo, were burned to death in a bothy (farm building) at Kirkintilloch, Dunbartonshire, 23 September 1937. The 'gaffer', Pat Dougan, and his son, occupying an adjoining room, raised the alarm, facilitating the escape of the twelve women members of the party, who were sleeping in a separate area. The prophetic words of the seventeenth-century Co. Mayo writer Brian Rua Ó Cearbháin, that 'carriages on iron wheels, emitting smoke and fire,' would carry coffins to Achill both at the beginning and the end of a new era of transport were recalled when the newly opened Achill line brought the bodies of victims of the CLEW BAY DISASTER (1894) from Westport and the same line—closed a fortnight earlier—was reopened in 1937 to allow the Kirkintilloch victims to be conveyed to Kildownet churchyard. PEADAR O'DONNELL described the commission that investigated the disaster as nothing more than a 'scratching-post' for alleviating public disquiet.

Knights of Columbanus. The Order of Knights of St Columbanus was founded in Belfast in 1915 by Canon James O'Neill, its aim being to cherish 'fraternal charity and to develop practical Christianity among its members.' An extension of the Catholic Defence Society and the CATHOLIC ASSOCIATION of 1902 and opposed to Orange ascendancy and 'British socialism', it is structured on Masonic lines. Branches were founded in Dublin in 1917 and in Cork two years later. An earlier group, the Columban Knights, merged with it in 1922. By 1935 it had six thousand members, drawn for the most part from the professional and business class. Its activities are cloaked in secrecy, which has earned it the suspicion of outsiders. The order, which is headed by a 'supreme knight', received formal recognition from the Catholic Church, 1934, and was a founder-member of the International Alliance of Catholic Knights. It is also affiliated to the International Council for Men (Unum Omnes). In recent times the organisation, which publishes a quarterly journal, *Columbanus,* was involved in the field of emigrants' welfare.

Knock, Co. Mayo, scene of a reported apparition by the Virgin Mary at approximately 8 p.m. on Thursday 21 August 1879. Dominic Beirne (aged 28), Dominic Beirne (20), Margaret Beirne (70), Margaret Beirne (10), Mary Beirne (26), Patrick Beirne (16), Judith Campbell (40), John Curry (6), John Durkan (11), Mrs Hugh Flatley (68), Patrick Hill (13), Mary McLoughlin (26), Catherine Murray (8), Bridget Trench (75) and Patrick Walsh (65) claimed that the Virgin Mary, accompanied by St Joseph and St John the Evangelist, appeared on the southern gable of Knock Church. They described an altar to the right of the gable, on which a cross and a lamb with angels were visible. Though it was raining heavily at the time, the witnesses, who were extremely wet, stated that there was no rain in the area of the apparition.

An ecclesiastical commission examined the witnesses in 1879. A second commission, 1936, took a further deposition from the last survivor of the witnesses, Mrs Mary O'Connell, who added to her testimony: 'I make this statement on my deathbed, knowing that I am about to go to my God.' As a result of the report, Knock became a centre of pilgrimage. The first reported cure at the site occurred on 31 August 1879, when twelve-year-old Delia Gordon was apparently cured of chronic deafness. The Knock Shrine Society was founded in 1935 by Justice Liam D. Coyne. An Irish Folk Museum was opened at Knock, 1 August 1973, to demonstrate the social and economic background in Ireland at the time of the apparition (see LAND WAR). The village was the focal point of the visit to Ireland by Pope John Paul II; after celebrating Mass there on 30 September 1979 he presented a golden rose to the parish priest, MONSIGNOR JAMES HORAN. *The Light of Other Days* (1974) by Thomas Neary, with photographs by Séamus Malee, shows the contents of the museum.

Knox, Rev. Robert (1815–1883), clergyman (Presbyterian); born in Clady, Urney, Co. Tyrone, educated at the University of Glasgow and Belfast College. Ordained in 1840, he played a prominent role in promoting the union between the Synod of Ulster and the secessionists, a unity that led to the General Assembly of the Presbyterian Church in Ireland, 1840. He was a Presbyterian missionary in the south of Ireland until his appointment as minister of the Linen Hall Church, Belfast, 1842. A prolific builder of churches and schools, he founded and edited the monthly *Irish Protestant* and was also joint founder of the Sabbath School Society. He engaged in a celebrated controversy with Rev. Theophilus Campbell on the subject of baptismal regeneration. He died while organising an initial conference of the International Presbyterian Alliance, towards which he had worked for many years.

Knox, Robert Bent (1808–1893), bishop (Church of Ireland); born in Dungannon, Co. Tyrone, educated at TCD. Ordained in 1832, he became chancellor of Ardfert, 1834, prebendary of St Munchin's, Limerick, 1841, and Bishop of Down, Connor and Dromore, 1848, in succession to Bishop Richard Mant. Convinced that the DISESTABLISHMENT of the Church of Ireland was inevitable, he set about the reorganising of his diocese; he founded the Belfast Church Christian Society, 1862, and also the Diocesan Board of Missions. During the years 1867–68 he proposed a reduction in the hierarchy to one archbishopric and five bishoprics. He succeeded Marcus Gervais Beresford as Archbishop of Armagh and Primate of All Ireland, 1885–93. His *Ecclesiastical Index* was published in 1830.

L

Labouchere, Henry, Baron Taunton (1798–1869), British politician (Whig). A member of Parliament from 1826, he held various offices before his appointment by LORD JOHN RUSSELL as Chief Secretary for Ireland, 1846–47, taking office during the GREAT FAMINE (1845–49). He issued what became known as the 'Labouchere Letter', virtually repealing the LABOUR RATE ACT (1846) in an attempt to have the money for relief work spent 'usefully' rather than in 'the execution of works comparatively unproductive.' His proposal was opposed by landowners unwilling to meet the cost of the scheme, and by the head of the Treasury, CHARLES EDWARD TREVELYAN. Labouchere proved sanguine in the face of a fever epidemic during the winter of 1846/47; he informed the House of Commons that it was not necessary to introduce extra powers for the health authorities, in spite of the fact that the Central Board of Health had not yet been re-established and the Poor Law system was patently unable to cope. This contrasted with his view in a letter to the Prime Minister, Russell (11 December 1846):

> The workhouses are full and the people turned away to perish. It is impossible to allow the state of things to continue without making some effectual effort to relieve it. The mortality in the workhouse is rapidly increasing, both from the crowded state of the unions and the exhausted state in which the applicants are received.

Though he had reports from doctors, ministers and magistrates calling attention to the extent of the outbreak, he told the House of Commons, 25 January 1847, that 'accounts given . . . were, to a great extent, undoubtedly inaccurate.' He confirmed the *laissez-faire* approach of the British government when, replying to an accusation from Lord George Bentinck that many of the deaths in Ireland were directly attributable to government neglect, he stated, 2 March 1847, that everyday experience had convinced him that 'the government had pursued a wise policy in not interfering with the supply of food to Ireland in any way which could compete with the efforts of private traders.' He was succeeded in office by Sir William Somerville.

Labour Court, created by the Industrial Relations Act (1946) and granted revised powers under the Industrial Relations Acts (1969 and 1975) to provide industrial relations officers for preventing or settling disputes. Its first chairman was R. J. P. MORTISHED. The court originally consisted of an employers' representative nominated by the Federated Union of Employers, a workers' representative nominated by the Irish Congress of Trade Unions, a neutral chairman, and two deputy chairmen appointed by the Minister for Labour. It was later expanded to include a chairman, two deputy chairmen (nominated by the Minister for Labour), and three members each from employers' and workers' organisations.

Under the Industrial Relations Act (1990) the Labour Relations Commission assumed certain functions of the Labour Court. Employment regulation orders issued by the court are based on proposals submitted to it by joint labour committees. Under the provisions of the Industrial Relations Acts the court also registers agreements on wages and working conditions and provides chairpersons and secretarial assistance to the Joint Industrial Council. The court's equality officers investigate and make recommendations on claims arising from alleged discrimination in pay and employment, whose recommendations may be returned to the court on appeal. Its ancillary services are available to management and unions free of charge.

Labour '87, a group established in March 1987, with members drawn from the Northern Ireland Labour Party, LABOUR PARTY OF NORTHERN IRELAND, Ulster Labour Party, and Newtown Abbey Labour Party. Its first chairman was PADDY DEVLIN. In 1989 the group proposed a two-chamber assembly for Northern Ireland. It won one seat (for Newtown Abbey) in the local elections.

Labour Party, founded in 1914 as a result of a resolution of the Irish Trade Union Congress, 1912. Its first leaders were JAMES CONNOLLY and JAMES LARKIN. From 1918 it was known as the Irish Labour Party and Trade Union Congress; in 1930 the IRISH TRADE UNION CONGRESS became a separate body. The party sought to provide a political platform for workers to achieve Connolly's ideal of a workers' republic. It supported the nationalist cause between 1916 and 1921; under pressure from Sinn Féin it abstained from the general election of December 1918, to avoid a split in the nationalist vote. It played no direct role in the establishment of Dáil Éireann, though its leader, THOMAS JOHNSON, wrote the draft of the DEMOCRATIC PROGRAMME. It also took no official position on the ANGLO-IRISH TREATY (1921), but party members elected in the general election of June 1922 were obliged to take their seats in the Dáil.

The Labour Party was the main opposition party to Cumann na nGaedheal governments, 1922–27, and it supported Fianna Fáil in 1932. It dropped its declared aim of a workers' republic and the nationalisation of the means of production in 1930, adopted it again in 1936, dropped it again in 1939 under pressure from the Catholic hierarchy, and adopted the aim of nationalisation again in 1969. It was a minority party in several coalition governments (1948–51, 1954–57, 1973–77, 1981, 1982–87, 1992–94, 1994–97). The leaders of the Labour Party have been James Larkin, 1912–14, James Connolly, 1914–16, Thomas Johnson, 1916–27, THOMAS J. O'CONNELL, 1927–32, WILLIAM NORTON, 1932–60, BRENDAN CORISH, 1960–77, FRANK CLUSKEY, 1977–81, MICHAEL O'LEARY, 1981–82 (resigned to join Fine Gael), DICK SPRING, 1982–97, RUAIRÍ QUINN, 1997–2002, and PAT RABBITTE, 2002–.

For the Labour Party in government see GOVERNMENTS.

The party's share of first-preference votes and seats was:

	First-preference votes	Seats
1922	21.3%	17
1923	10.6%	14
1927 (June)	12.6%	22
1927 (Sep.)	9.1%	13
1932	7.7%	7
1933	5.7%	8
1937	10.3%	13
1938	10.0%	9
1943	15.7%	17
1944	8.8%	8
1951	11.4%	16
1954	12.1%	19
1957	9.1%	12

1961	11.4%	16
1965	15.4%	22
1969	17.0%	18
1973	13.7%	19
1977	11.6%	17
1981	9.9%	15
1982 (Feb.)	9.1%	15
1982 (Nov.)	9.4%	16
1987	6.4%	12
1989	9.5%	15
1992	19.3%	33
1997	10.4%	17
2002	10.8%	21

Labour Party of Northern Ireland, a short-lived group jointly founded by PADDY DEVLIN in 1984, later a partner in LABOUR '87.

Labour Rate Act (1846), introduced by LORD JOHN RUSSELL during the GREAT FAMINE (1845–49). It required that the district in which public works were being carried out would in future bear the total expense of such works; it also ruled that works were to be approved and executed by the Board of Works, the cost to be met by a treasury advance, repaid within ten years at 3½ per cent, the money for repayment to be raised by a rate levied on all those locally who paid Poor Law rates. The whole burden and expense of supplying food to the famine-stricken during the remainder of 1846 and for 1847 was thus made a local charge, the government no longer bearing half the cost of public works. The act, rushed through Parliament in August 1846, was repealed almost in its entirety some six weeks later. (See HENRY LABOUCHERE.)

Labour World, a weekly paper founded in London, September 1890, by MICHAEL DAVITT, intended as a 'journal of progress for the masses.' The paper, which was circulated in Ireland, had an initial print run of 60,000 copies, but under-capitalisation forced its closure after eight months.

Lacey, Denis 'Dinny' (1890–1923), republican soldier; born in Attybrack, Co. Tipperary; educated at national school. He assisted SEÁN TREACY and DAN BREEN in the reorganising of the Irish Volunteers and Sinn Féin in Co. Tipperary after the Easter Rising (1916). He became commandant of the 3rd Tipperary Brigade of the IRA during the WAR OF INDEPENDENCE. Rejecting the ANGLO-IRISH TREATY (1921), he commanded Irregulars during the CIVIL WAR. He led a raid on Clonmel Barracks, February 1922, in which his unit captured 300 rifles, 7 machine-guns, 200,000 rounds of ammunition, several hundred boxes of bombs, twelve armoured cars, ten Lancia cars and Crossley tenders, and two armoured Lancias. After holding the region around Carrick-on-Suir for a short time, in December he was forced into the hills and was killed in the Glen of Aherlow, 18 February 1923.

Ladies' Land League, popular name for the Central Land League of the Ladies of Ireland, launched by ANNA PARNELL (sister of CHARLES STEWART PARNELL), with the support of MICHAEL DAVITT, 31 January 1881, to aid the LAND LEAGUE. Its officers were Mrs Dean (aunt of JOHN DILLON), president, Mrs Moloney and Ellen O'Leary (sister of JOHN O'LEARY), treasurers, and Anna Parnell, Miss Stritch, and Miss Lynch, secretaries; other members of the Committee included Katharine Tynan and Mrs A. M. Sullivan. A reserve list of twenty-one was drawn up to provide substitutes for imprisoned members. The women compiled a book jocosely called the 'Book of Kells', providing information on every estate, including the number of tenants, rents paid, government valuation, financial situation of the tenants and their attitude towards the Land League, number of evictions carried out or pending, and details of landlords, agents, and the constabulary. It was an invaluable aid to planning Land League strategy. When Davitt, Charles Stewart Parnell and other leaders in the land movement were imprisoned, the women took over the organising of the movement and oversaw the underground publication of UNITED IRELAND.

The first radical movement in Ireland organised by women, the league was denounced by ARCHBISHOP JOHN MACHALE of Tuam and Archbishop Edward MacCabe of Dublin. The Chief Secretary for Ireland, W. E. FORSTER, who attempted to suppress it under statutes designed to curb prostitution, merely enhanced the women's stature. Parnell was alarmed by the militancy of the women, and on his release from prison, May 1882, he set about dismantling the organisation, which was dissolved in August of that year.

'Lady Betty', nickname of Betty Sugrue, public executioner for Connacht in the eighteenth century; born in Co. Kerry. Left destitute on the death of her husband, she took to the roads with her three children and took possession of a near-derelict cabin in Co. Roscommon, where she kept DRY LODGINGS following the departure of her eldest son for America. Some years later she stabbed a lodger to death, unaware that he was her son. Overcome with remorse, she surrendered to the authorities and was sentenced to death. When the hangman failed to turn up on the day she and her fellow-prisoners were to be put to death, she volunteered to perform the job in return for her freedom. She then accepted the post of official executioner. Despised throughout the province, she had quarters within the prison walls until granted a free pardon, 1802.

Lady Clares, an agrarian secret society in Connacht and west Munster during the early decades of the nineteenth century. (See SECRET SOCIETIES.)

Lalor, James Fintan (1807–1849), land agitator; born in Tinakill, Co. Laois, son of Patrick Lalor, radical member of Parliament for the county, 1832–35; educated at Carlow Lay College. A congenital spinal disease, complicated by deafness and poor vision, forced him to abandon his education. Influenced by local land reformers, led by William Conners, he broke with his father, who supported DANIEL O'CONNELL in the view that land reform would follow repeal of the Corn Laws. He wrote to SIR ROBERT PEEL, 1843, outlining his view of the land question; Peel afterwards established a commission of inquiry into the land issue, but to Lalor's disappointment there were no concrete results.

He divided his time between Belfast and Dublin until 1846, when he was reconciled with his father. He supported YOUNG IRELAND on its break with O'Connell, 1846. 'A secure and independent agricultural peasantry is the only base on which a people rises or ever can be raised; or, on which a nation can safely rest,' he said. His view that only those who work on the land could own it, expressed in the *Nation* during 1847, attracted the attention of militant Young Irelanders, including JOHN MITCHEL and MICHAEL DOHENY. During the GREAT FAMINE (1845–49) he suggested that tenants should withhold rents. With JOHN MARTIN he jointly edited Mitchel's paper, the IRISH FELON.

Following the attempted insurrection by WILLIAM SMITH O'BRIEN at BALLINGARRY, Co. Tipperary, 1848, Lalor was arrested in Templederry but was released from prison on health grounds. By now he was close to THOMAS CLARKE LUBY, with whom he became involved in a secret organisation in Cos. Waterford and Tipperary whose members included JOHN O'LEARY and CHARLES J. KICKHAM. His plans for an insurrection in Co. Tipperary failed, 16 September, through lack of support. He died in Dublin two days later.

Lalor's doctrine that 'the entire ownership of Ireland, moral and material . . . is vested of right in the people of Ireland' appealed to MICHAEL DAVITT and the LAND LEAGUE and later to JAMES CONNOLLY, ARTHUR GRIFFITH, and PATRICK PEARSE.

His younger brother, Peter Lalor (1823–1889), led insurgent miners in a licence dispute with the Australian government. At Eureka Stockade, Ballarat, 3 December 1854, twenty miners and two policemen were killed, and Lalor lost an arm. Lalor subsequently represented the miners as member of Parliament for Ballarat; he became Postmaster-General and was speaker of the Australian Parliament, 1880–88.

Land Acts (1860–1933). Between 1860 and 1923 a series of Land Acts transformed the landholding system in Ireland. In 1870 there were some 19,288 landlords, of whom many were absentees; 302 had estates of more than 10,000 acres. Of 538,833 tenants, fewer than a third (135,000) had a lease, while the remainder held land by verbal agreement, subject to six months' notice of eviction.

Within a generation, following the passing of the Irish Land Act (1903) (the 'Wyndham Act'), power on the land had shifted to a new class of peasant proprietors, now holding more than half the holdings. The 1870 act, introduced by W. E. GLADSTONE, sought to redress the injustices of the system. His next act, that of 1881, was a response to the sustained agitation prosecuted by the LAND LEAGUE against landlordism. Other major acts were introduced by Conservative governments. The act of 1923 was the first introduced by an Irish government.

Landlord and Tenant Law (Amendment) Act (Ireland) (1860)

Popularly known as Deasy's Act, after its sponsor (the Attorney-General, Richard Deasy), it strengthened the position of the landlord. The relationship between landlord and tenant was now 'deemed to be founded on the express or implied contract of the parties and not upon tenure or service.' It permitted the landlord to recover the landholding at the termination of a lease or yearly letting. As the tenant was frequently in a vulnerable position, the act enabled the landlord to set terms. This act was overturned in essence by the act of 1870.

Landlord and Tenant (Ireland) Act (1870)
Gladstone attempted to give legal status to the ULSTER CUSTOM, but it proved difficult in practice. The act failed in its endeavour to compensate for disturbance in occupancy. Its 'Bright Clause' made provision for the purchase of the holding by the tenant, who could borrow up to two-thirds of the price, to be repaid at 5 per cent over thirty-five years. The average price was 23½ years' rent. Altogether, 877 tenants availed of the act to purchase their holdings.

Land Law (Ireland) Act (1881)
Framing his second act in the midst of the Land War, Gladstone referred to the Richmond and Bessborough Commissions, both of which had recommended legislating for the Ulster custom. The act established the principle of dual ownership by landlord and tenant, gave legal status to the Ulster custom throughout the country, provided for compensation for improvements and disturbance, and established a LAND COMMISSION and a Land Court. The intention, in Gladstone's words, was not to destroy landlordism but to make it impossible. It was a complicated piece of legislation (more than 14,000 speeches were made during the debates, 2,000 points of order, and some 800 amendments proposed and rejected). It also provided for land purchase, with three-quarters of the money to be advanced by the Land Commission, to be repaid over thirty-five years at 5 per cent. Tenants were enabled to have their rents reviewed by the Land Court under the 'fair rent' clause (reductions were typically between 15 and 20 per cent). The act benefited 731 tenants who bought under its provisions, while excluding almost 280,000 tenants who were either leaseholders or were in arrears.

Settled Land Act (1882)
Introduced as a result of the 'KILMAINHAM TREATY', this act empowered the Land Commission to cancel arrears of rent of less than £30. Tenants were obliged to pay the 1881 rent, and the tenant and the state had to pay equal amounts, but not more than a total of two years' rent. The money was drawn from the Church Surplus Fund. It was estimated that £2 million was written off.

Purchase of Land (Ireland) Act (1885)
Known as 'LORD ASHBOURNE's Act' or the 'Ashbourne Act', after its proposer, this act permitted a tenant to borrow the full amount of the purchase price, to be repaid over forty-nine years at 4 per cent. £5 million was made immediately available, and this was supplemented in 1888. Between 1885 and 1888 some 25,400 tenants bought their holdings, many of them in Ulster. A total of 942,000 acres was bought, making an average holding of 37 acres at a purchase price of 17½ years' rent.

Land Law (Ireland) Act (1887)
The first Land Act introduced by ARTHUR J. BALFOUR, this was an amendment to the 1881 act, extending the terms of the act to leaseholders.

Land Purchase Act (1888)
Also introduced by Balfour, this provided a further £5 million to the amount granted for purchase by the Ashbourne Act.

Purchase of Land (Ireland) Act (1891)
Balfour's major Land Act came at the end of the land agitation known as the PLAN OF CAMPAIGN. It substituted peasant proprietorship for dual ownership as the principle of land tenure. At the same time Balfour created the CONGESTED DISTRICTS BOARD to deal with distress in the economically backward areas of the west. The intricacies of its clauses discouraged purchase, to the extent that only £13.5 million of the £33 million available was taken up until the act was amended in 1896.

Land Law (Ireland) Act (1896)
Introduced by GERALD BALFOUR, this amended the 1891 act, increasing the amount available for purchase while removing the unattractive clauses of the earlier act. It empowered the Land Court to sell 1,500 bankrupt estates to tenants. Altogether, 47,000 holdings were bought out during the years 1891–96.

Irish Land Act (1903)
Introduced by GEORGE WYNDHAM and popularly known as the Wyndham Act, this was based largely on recommendations of the LAND CONFERENCE (1902). It offered landlords a 12 per cent bonus in addition to the selling price as an incentive towards the disposal of entire estates. Individual purchase was not permissible. It encouraged landlords to sell large areas, including non-tenanted and tenanted land. Additionally, the landlord could sell his demesne lands to the Estate Commissioners and buy them back on the same annuity terms as the tenants. Money was raised by the issue of 2.67 per cent guaranteed land stock. Prices for the holdings ranged from the equivalent of 18½ to 24½ years' rent on rents fixed by the Land Courts under the 1881 act, or 21½ to 27 years

on rents fixed in or after 1896, the whole sum to be advanced at 3¼ per cent, to be repaid over 68½ years. Sub-division or mortgaging was forbidden. Perceived as pro-landlord, this act was opposed by leading agrarian agitators, including MICHAEL DAVITT and JOHN DILLON, and the *Freeman's Journal.* The act brought about significant changes in the Irish landholding system: more than 1,500 evicted tenants were reinstated under its provisions, and by 1908 £28 million had been advanced, and arrears of sales equalled some £56 million. The average price was approximately £12 per acre. By 1909 approximately one million acres remained to be disposed of.

Evicted Tenants (Ireland) Act (1907)
Introduced by AUGUSTINE BIRRELL, this act enabled 735 tenants to be reinstated, at a cost of £390,000.

Irish Land Act (1909)
This act was also introduced by Birrell. An issue of £33 million worth of land stock had fallen in value; the difficulty of financing the remaining £56 million led to the introduction of the act. Under the act, landlords were to be paid 3 per cent stock as a bonus (varying from 3 per cent to 18 per cent, according to the purchase price). If the price was less than sixteen years' rent, the bonus would be 3 per cent. An element of compulsory purchase was included: the landlord had to sell if the majority of his tenants sought purchase. From the time of the act of 1903 to this act, 256,000 holdings were bought, for £82 million.

On the establishment of the IRISH FREE STATE in 1922, 316,00 holdings, amounting to 11 million acres, had been bought; 35,000 beneficiaries, mostly in areas under the supervision of the Congested Districts Board, had been allotted 750,000 acres. Approximately 100,000 holdings remained to be dealt with, amounting to 3 million acres.

Land Law (Commission) Act (1923)
This act abolished the Congested Districts Board and the Estates Commission and reconstituted the Land Commission.

Land Act (1923)
Sometimes called the Hogan Act, this was introduced in Dáil Éireann by the Minister for Agriculture, PATRICK HOGAN. It enabled the compulsory purchase of all land not yet dealt with. Rents fixed before 1911 were reduced by 35 per cent and those fixed later by 30 per cent. Annuities were calculated at 4 per cent over sixty-six years. The seller was to receive the equivalent of approximately fourteen years' rent as originally paid, in addition to which the state paid 10 per cent to the seller and paid legal and other expenses. In tackling arrears, the act stipulated that all arrears due up to 1920 were written off (few rents were paid during the WAR OF INDEPENDENCE and the CIVIL WAR, 1919–23); arrears subsequent to 1920 were reduced by 25 per cent. Sub-tenants illegally on lands were recognised as tenants, but the further sub-letting or sub-division of land was again prohibited.

Land Act (1927)
Also introduced by Hogan, this was provoked by an accumulation of arrears arising from a general laxity in the collection of debts caused by the post-war economic depression. Under the act, arrears were funded and added to the annuities. Sub-tenants illegally in possession were confirmed, and sub-letting was again prohibited.

Land Act (1933)
Accumulated arrears had now reached £4,611,381. FIANNA FÁIL, in power since March 1932, had promised that land annuities would no longer be paid to the British exchequer; they would, however, continue to be collected, but many of the new owners were withholding. The 1933 act, introduced by the Minister for Agriculture, JAMES RYAN, cleared all arrears from before 1930 and funded subsequent arrears. Annuity repayments were reduced by 50 per cent because of the 'ECONOMIC WAR'. The Land Commission was empowered to compulsorily acquire land for the landless or for those who needed more. The commissioners were also enabled to demand the return of land they themselves had vested in the tenants. Fixity of tenure was also abolished.

Between 1870 and 1933, tenants in the 26-county area bought 450,000 holdings—a total of 15 million acres out of 17 million, at a total cost of £130 million or an average price of £8.67 per acre.

land annuities, devised as a system for the repayment of loans made by the British exchequer to Irish tenants who bought their holdings under a series of LAND ACTS from 1870. Following the creation of the IRISH FREE STATE, 1922, the amounts were collected by the Irish exchequer on behalf of the Crown.

Representing some 3 per cent of national

income, the unpopular annuities proved difficult to collect. A series of measures were taken by Dáil Éireann to deal with the arrears that had arisen between 1916 and 1923. During the 1920s PEADAR O'DONNELL and MAURICE MOORE spearheaded a campaign to retain the amounts in Ireland. FIANNA FÁIL promised during the 1932 general election campaign that it would withhold the annuities from the British exchequer. On assuming office, March 1932, ÉAMON DE VALERA withheld payment, and refused an offer of Commonwealth mediation on the issue. He claimed that the payments were illegal, as neither the ANGLO-IRISH FINANCIAL AGREEMENT (1923) nor the ULTIMATE FINANCIAL AGREEMENT (1926) had been ratified by the Dáil. The 'ECONOMIC WAR' between the Free State and Britain ensued, 1932–38.

Following his re-election, January 1932, de Valera announced that annuities would be collected but would be reduced by half. A campaign of non-payment was organised by the BLUESHIRTS, to which the government reacted by seizing cattle and goods in lieu of payment. Payment to the Free State exchequer was resumed within a short time. As part of the agreement ending the Economic War in 1938, the government paid the British government £10 million as full and final settlement of all outstanding claims (which totalled £104 million).

Land Commission, established under the Land Law (Ireland) Act (1881) (see LAND ACTS). Its main purpose was to adjudicate on 'fair rents' within the terms of the act; it also had responsibility for overseeing the land purchase schemes introduced under later acts. Under the Land Law (Commission) Act (1923) the commission assumed the control of estates where landlord and tenant had a dual interest and arranged for such land to be passed to the tenant under the stipulated land annuities. In 1923 the Land Commission absorbed the functions of the CONGESTED DISTRICTS BOARD. It later redistributed land.

Land Conference (1902). Captain John Shawe-Taylor, in a letter to the press, September 1902, proposed a conference as a means of achieving a final settlement of the land question. He proposed that the DUKE OF ABERCORN, A. H. SMITH-BARRY, CHARLES OWEN O'CONOR and E. J. SAUNDERSON represent landlords and suggested JOHN REDMOND, WILLIAM O'BRIEN, TIMOTHY HARRINGTON and T. W. RUSSELL as tenants' representatives. The proposal was supported by the Chief Secretary for Ireland, GEORGE WYNDHAM, and the Under-Secretary, SIR ANTONY MACDONNELL, but was rejected by the nominated Unionists, who were replaced by the EARL OF DUNRAVEN, Lord Mayo, Colonel W. H. Hutcheson-Poe, and Colonel Nugent Everard. The tenants' representatives were as proposed.

Dunraven chaired the two-week conference, which opened in the Mansion House, Dublin, on 20 December 1902. The main recommendations were that the government should embark on a comprehensive and equitable land purchase scheme; that such a scheme be voluntary; that landlords receive the market price for the sale of their estates; and that repayments be by means of land annuities, spread over 68½ years (in the interests of the tenant-purchaser). These proposals were almost totally incorporated in the Irish Land Act (1903) (see LAND ACTS). The conference further suggested that the CONGESTED DISTRICTS BOARD be restructured; that the question of evicted tenants be re-addressed; and that an improvement be made in the quality of housing provided for labourers.

Members of the conference, in particular William O'Brien, hoped that the methods employed to reach agreement on the land issue might offer a framework for resolving the home rule issue. The members remained as the Land Committee throughout the years 1903–04, during which time they reconstituted themselves as the IRISH REFORM ASSOCIATION to examine the question of self-government.

Land Court, established under the Land Law (Ireland) Act (1881) (see LAND ACTS) to arbitrate in landlord-tenant rent disputes, improvements, and compensation. It was also empowered to annul any existing unfair clause or condition.

Landed Estates Court, established in 1858 from what had been the Encumbered Estates Court. It sought to guarantee the title of estates being sold as a result of the bankruptcy of their owners, either before or during the Great Famine (1845–49). Its functions were taken over by the Land Judges in Chancery, 1877. (See ENCUMBERED ESTATES ACTS.)

Landed Property Improvement (Ireland) Act (1847). Administered by the Commissioners of Public Works, the act was designed to advance money for agricultural use. £350,000 was advanced in 1848 and 1849 and £250,000 in

1850. Much of the money was used for drainage schemes.

Land League, popular name for the Irish National Land League, founded on 21 October 1879 at a meeting in the Imperial Hotel, Dublin, presided over by ANDREW KETTLE and attended by MICHAEL DAVITT and CHARLES STEWART PARNELL, who was elected president; Davitt and Kettle were elected secretaries and JOSEPH BIGGAR, PATRICK EGAN and W. H. O'Sullivan MP treasurers. Modelled on the LAND LEAGUE OF MAYO (founded 16 August 1879), the Land League was a reaction to the worsening conditions experienced by tenant-farmers during the agricultural depression of the late 1870s and was a significant development in what became known as the LAND WAR.

The radical nature of the Land League was demonstrated in its constitution. Echoing JAMES FINTAN LALOR, the Declaration of Principles stated:

> The land of Ireland belongs to the people of Ireland, to be held and cultivated for the sustenance of those whom God decreed to be the inhabitants thereof . . . Those who cultivate it . . . have a higher claim to its absolute possession than those who make it an article of barter to be used or disposed of for purposes of profit or pleasure. The end for which the land of a country is created requires an equitable distribution of the same among the people who are to live upon the fruits of their labour in its cultivation.

The league was supported by members of the IRB, the IRISH PARTY, and the American Fenians; this linking of the revolutionary, constitutional and agrarian elements came to be known as the NEW DEPARTURE. A total of £192,256 was subscribed through CLAN NA GAEL during the years 1879–83. The league's aims, protecting the tenantry and abolishing landlordism, were to be achieved by 'every means compatible with justice, morality, and right reason.' It was also intended to 'expose the injustice, wrong or injury which may be inflicted upon any farmer . . . either by rack-renting, eviction, or other arbitrary exercise of power which the existing laws enable the landlords to exercise over their tenantry.' The economic depression of the 1870s caused widespread hardship among tenant-farmers. The primary aim of the small tenant-farmer was the procurement of tenant right or the ULSTER CUSTOM, popularly known as the three Fs (fair rent, free sale, and fixity of tenure). Others sought to destroy landlordism and to establish peasant proprietorship.

The Land League united the country outside the north-eastern part of Ulster. The first truly democratic organisation in modern Irish history, it brought together those of different classes, political persuasions, and religions. Members of the clergy, many of them from the tenant-farmer class, were ceaseless organisers at local level. The league was also supported by ARCHBISHOP T. W. CROKE and by BISHOP THOMAS NULTY of Meath, the first member of the hierarchy to give support. Most of the hierarchy, however, remained aloof from the agitation.

The slogans of the Land League became the catchcries of the people: *Down with landlordism, The land for the people, Keep a firm grip upon your lands,* and *Pay no rent.* The conservative press denounced the new movement as 'communistic', but it won the support of the *Nation,* the *Irishman,* and the *Flag of Ireland* (the latter two owned by RICHARD PIGOTT), the *Freeman's Journal* (after 1880), and the *Irish World.* Parnell bought two of Pigott's papers and founded UNITED IRELAND, which, under the editorship of WILLIAM O'BRIEN, was the most outspoken organ of the league.

Incessant rain throughout 1879 destroyed the potato and grain crops, and near-famine conditions prevailed. The number of evictions, at 1,098, was almost treble that of 1877. The Catholic hierarchy, at a meeting in Dublin, 24 October, approved an appeal to the British Parliament for aid for the starving. On 5 November seventy Irish MPs signed a declaration addressed to the Prime Minister, BENJAMIN DISRAELI, asking him to urgently address the 'distressful situation', which was likely to result in famine. The government failed to respond.

On 19 September 1880 the Land League unsheathed the most feared weapon in its armoury: the boycott. Parnell, speaking at Ennis, Co. Clare, called for the public shunning of anyone involved in any way with the land or property of an evicted tenant.

> You must show him on the roadside when you meet him, you must show him in the streets of the town, you must show him at the shop-counter . . . and even in the house of worship, by leaving him severely alone, by putting him into moral Coventry . . .

The policy was put into effect on an estate in Co. Mayo managed by CAPTAIN CHARLES BOYCOTT. On Land League platforms throughout the country, attended by the largest crowds since the monster meetings of Daniel O'Connell, Parnell tinged agrarian aggression with respect for the law.

American support for the league remained constant throughout the Land War. Parnell addressed the House of Representatives, 2 February 1880, during his American tour with Davitt and Dillon. In the autumn of 1880, despite opposition from the ORANGE ORDER, branches of the league were formed in Cos. Armagh, Derry, Down, Fermanagh, and Tyrone. Following the defeat of his COMPENSATION FOR DISTURBANCE BILL in the House of Lords there was mounting pressure on the Chief Secretary for Ireland, W. E. FORSTER, to adopt a more aggressive policy towards the league. He responded by arresting activists, including Davitt, JAMES DALY, and MATTHEW HARRIS, on charges of criminal conspiracy, 19 November. The 'state trial' collapsed when the jury disagreed, January 1881. In the same month the BESSBOROUGH COMMISSION recommended the reform of the land law and the implementation of the long-sought three Fs.

The queen's speech on the opening of Parliament, January 1881, revealed that, together with a Land Bill, COERCION would be introduced. From 31 January, Irish members, using OBSTRUCTIONISM for the last time, forced the House of Commons into a record 41-hour sitting during the debate on the Protection of Persons and Property (Ireland) Bill. On 3 February, Davitt was arrested and thirty-six protesting Irish members were expelled from the House of Commons. The act became law, 2 March, and *habeas corpus* was suspended. W. E. GLADSTONE introduced his Land Law (Ireland) Bill on 7 April 1881 (see LAND ACTS); it became law on 22 August, granting the three Fs but excluding from its compass leaseholders and those in arrears. While twenty-six members of his party supported the bill, Parnell opposed it but urged the convention of the Land League, 15 September, to test the new act in the courts. He continued to oppose Gladstone and the act until he was lodged in Kilmainham Jail, Dublin, with some of his principal associates, 13 October 1881. He signed the NO-RENT MANIFESTO, 19 October (to which the names of Michael Davitt and Patrick Egan had been appended without their knowledge). The document was condemned by moderate opinion, including Archbishop Croke. The British government responded by suppressing the Land League the next day, but the vacuum was filled by the LADIES' LAND LEAGUE.

Parnell's imprisonment was perceived as contributing to the rising crime rate during the winter of 1881/82. Through WILLIAM O'SHEA, Parnell maintained contact with the British government, and he was released after reaching an understanding with Gladstone in the 'KILMAINHAM TREATY', 2 May 1882. Four days later the PHOENIX PARK MURDERS plunged the country into crisis. The murders were the work of a hitherto unknown group, the INVINCIBLES, some of whom were proved to have links with prominent figures in the Land League (see 'PARNELLISM AND CRIME').

The Land League had united the Irish tenantry in an unprecedented demonstration of solidarity. It began a process that resulted in the erosion and ultimate collapse of the privileged landholders, and catapulted Parnell to national prominence and leadership of the Irish Party. Gladstone later admitted that without the Land League there would not have been a Land Act in 1881.

Land League of Mayo, founded by JAMES DALY and MICHAEL DAVITT following meetings in IRISHTOWN and Westport, Co. Mayo, 16 August 1879. Its first president was the barrister and landholder J. J. Louden. The league, which sought the legalisation of the ULSTER CUSTOM, was supported by CHARLES STEWART PARNELL and led to a national organisation, the Irish National Land League (see LAND LEAGUE), which modelled itself on the constitution of the Land League of Mayo.

Land Rehabilitation Project (1949), introduced by the Minister for Agriculture, JAMES DILLON, and financed through MARSHALL AID. The scheme, considered a major achievement of the first inter-party government (1948–51), aimed to reclaim more than a million acres over a period of ten years.

Land War, the name given to the campaign of agrarian unrest during the years 1879–82. It arose during a period of severe economic depression that led to a fall in agricultural incomes, provoking a demand by tenants for rent abatements. Many landlords, affected by the depression, strenuously resisted tenants' demands.

The 'war' may be divided into three phases: 1879–82, a violent struggle between landlords and tenants led by the LAND LEAGUE; 1886–91, the PLAN OF CAMPAIGN, mainly confined to Munster; and 1891–1903, a more conciliatory phase, when the transfer of landholdings to tenants was effected through a series of LAND ACTS introduced by ARTHUR J. BALFOUR, Gerald

Balfour, and GEORGE WYNDHAM. In the strictest sense, the term 'Land War' refers to the first phase.

Lane, Sir Hugh (1873–1915), art dealer and collector; born in Blackrock, Co. Cork, son of a rector and maternal nephew of LADY AUGUSTA GREGORY; educated privately because of ill-health. After visiting Continental art galleries with his mother he moved to London, where he worked for the art dealers Colnaghi, 1893–97, before establishing his own successful business, 1898. A visit to a joint exhibition of the works of Nathaniel Hone and JOHN BUTLER YEATS in Dublin, 1901, awakened his interest in Irish art. During a trip to Paris, 1903, he began his valuable collection of modern works.

When Dublin Corporation opened its temporary Municipal Gallery site in Harcourt Street, 1908, Lane offered his impressionist and modern collection, including works by Renoir, Pissarro, Monet, Manet, Degas, and Corot, with the proviso that a permanent site be established for their exhibition. Lane's concept, to a design by Sir Edward Lutyens, was of a gallery built on a new bridge over the River Liffey (in place of the Ha'penny Bridge) and linked to the National Gallery, but it was rejected by Dublin Corporation, on grounds of cost. The controversy prompted W. B. YEATS to write 'To a Wealthy Man Who Promised a Second Subscription to the Dublin Municipal Gallery If It Were Proved the People Wanted Pictures'. Lane withdrew his offer and instead bequeathed his collection to the National Gallery, London. In an unwitnessed codicil, called the 'Codicil of Forgiveness', February 1915, he donated thirty-nine paintings to Dublin. He died in the sinking of the LUSITANIA, 7 May 1915, and the unwitnessed and unsigned codicil gave rise to bitter litigation concerning the future of the collection. Under an agreement in 1959 between the Municipal Gallery and the National Gallery, London, the paintings, divided into two groups, rotate between London and Dublin every five years.

Lane, Timothy O'Neill (1852–1915), lexicographer; born in Templeglantine, Co. Limerick. Successful in a civil service examination, he failed the medical inspection, then trained as a teacher and worked in his home area from 1852 until he moved to London, 1877, where he worked as a clerk. After some time as a newspaper correspondent in London and Paris he returned to Ireland. The work of producing and publishing his *English–Irish Dictionary* (1904) cost him many years of research and almost £3,000. Enlarged editions were published in 1915 and 1922.

Language Freedom Movement, an organisation founded in 1956 and active during the 1960s to campaign against Irish as an obligatory school subject. It was bitterly opposed by Irish-language activists. The writer John B. Keane (1928–2002) was a leading spokesperson in the 1960s.

Lansdowne, Henry Petty-Fitzmaurice, third Marquess of (1780–1863), British politician (Whig); born in London, educated at the Universities of Edinburgh and Cambridge. A landowner in Cos. Kerry and Limerick, he was noted in the House of Commons, 1803–07, for contributions on economic issues; his support for CATHOLIC EMANCIPATION lost him his seat, 1807. Succeeding to the title in 1809, in the House of Lords he supported liberal causes but opposed Emancipation. President of the Council, November 1830 and 1835–41, he opposed DANIEL O'CONNELL and the REPEAL ASSOCIATION, though he sought justice for Ireland. He supported SIR ROBERT PEEL on the repeal of the Corn Laws. He spoke on distress in Ireland during the GREAT FAMINE, 15 February 1847, and expressed himself filled with 'horror and dread' at the attempt by LORD JOHN RUSSELL to place the burden of financing relief on landowners. Generally regarded as a good landlord on his Irish estates, he was a patron of THOMAS MOORE.

Laochra Uladh ('warriors of Ulster'), a republican splinter group founded by Brendan O'Boyle that used American aid for his one-man bombing campaign. A mysterious figure, O'Boyle was killed and his wife injured, July 1955, in a premature explosion outside the Stormont telephone exchange, Belfast.

Larcom, Sir Thomas (1801–1879), soldier and civil servant. After working on the Ordnance Survey in England, 1824–26, he became director of the ORDNANCE SURVEY OF IRELAND, where he employed, among others, JOHN O'DONOVAN, GEORGE PETRIE, and EUGENE O'CURRY. As Census Commissioner, 1841, he introduced large-scale changes, including a systematic classification of occupation and the collection of statistics on the general conditions of the population. He sat on various public bodies, including the commission to investigate the reform of Dublin Corporation, 1849. After a period as deputy chairman of the Board of

Works, 1850–53, he became the first permanent Under-Secretary for Ireland at Dublin Castle, 1853–68, when he had to deal with the FENIANS, adopting what was regarded as a firm but fair approach. He sought to have the law dispensed in Ireland on the same principles as obtained in Britain. Following sectarian rioting in Belfast, 1864, Larcom received reports of police participation and complicity in the rioting. He suggested banning 'all processions of magnitude' and abolishing all ORANGE ORDER societies to prevent future rioting; he also recommended that Belfast be placed under police magistrates and that a government police force, similar to the Dublin model, be considered for the city.

Larkin, James (Jim) (1874–1947), trade unionist, socialist, and politician (Labour Party); born in Liverpool of Irish parents, 28 January 1874. Following his father's early death from tuberculosis, Larkin went to work from the age of eleven as a labourer and a sailor. He later became a supervisor on Liverpool docks, 1894, but lost the position when he joined striking workers under his supervision. After reorganising the Scottish ports as an organiser for the National Union of Dock Labourers, he was sent to Belfast, 1907, where he organised a number of strikes (including one by the RIC, which had been sent in to quell strikers). Calling on workers to join the NUDL, 'not as Catholics or Protestants, as nationalists or unionists, but as Belfast men and workers,' he succeeded briefly in bridging the sectarian, political and cultural divides.

His activities in Belfast alienated the NUDL leadership, which transferred him to Dublin, where he formally launched the NUDL, 11 August 1907. He re-formed the Irish branch of the INDEPENDENT LABOUR PARTY and organised Dublin's casual and unskilled workers. Within a year he had called three strikes and had been suspended by the NUDL, which refused to finance his industrial action. He then founded the IRISH TRANSPORT AND GENERAL WORKERS' UNION, December 1908 to January 1909. He called strikes on the docks, organised a temperance campaign, and succeeded in ending the system whereby casual labourers were paid in public houses. His strike tactics alienated employers and the leaders of the IRISH TRADE UNION CONGRESS, leading to his expulsion in 1909; his union was not re-affiliated until 1911, shortly after which he became president of the Congress. In June 1910 he was sentenced to a year's imprisonment on a charge of misappropriating Cork dockers' money while working for the NUDL. He was released, 1 October 1910, following a petition from the Dublin Trades Council to the MARQUESS OF ABERDEEN. From 1911 he attacked the Dublin employers in his paper, the IRISH WORKER.

His organising of Co. Dublin agricultural workers and his leadership of a series of strikes involving carters, dockers, railwaymen and tramworkers unified the Dublin employers, determined to resist Larkin's demand for employer-labour discussions on wages, hours, and general conditions. They formed the 400-member Employers' Federation, led by WILLIAM MARTIN MURPHY. From January to August 1913 there were some thirty strikes, with accompanying disorder. Murphy's dismissal of suspected Larkinites led to the DUBLIN LOCK-OUT (1913). Larkin organised assistance from England and the United States to feed the workers in his 'fiery cross' campaign. By the end of January 1914, however, with the workers defeated, Larkin's union was depleted, both numerically and financially. The tone of the *Irish Worker* became increasingly bitter, and in August it was suppressed.

In October 1914 Larkin went on a fund-raising lecture tour of the United States, leaving the union organisation to JAMES CONNOLLY and WILLIAM O'BRIEN. His visit became a nine-year stay, during which he was involved in the American socialist and labour movement. Arrested for membership of the Communist Labor Party, 7–8 November 1919, he was sentenced to five to ten years' imprisonment, 3 May 1920. From his prison cell he denounced the ANGLO-IRISH TREATY (1921). Granted a free pardon by Governor Al Smith of New York, 17 January 1923, and deported at his own request, he returned to Ireland, 30 April, to a tumultuous reception in Dublin. His attempts to regain control of the ITGWU were resisted by O'Brien and THOMAS JOHNSON, who engineered his expulsion; he lost a court case for control of the union and was declared a bankrupt. With his brother, Peter Larkin (1880–1931), and his son James Larkin (Junior) he formed the WORKERS' UNION OF IRELAND, 1923, which won support from Dublin ITGWU members. His IRISH WORKER LEAGUE secured recognition from the Comintern, and he was invited to attend its fifth congress in Moscow, where he addressed the delegates, June 1923. He returned to the

Soviet Union in 1928 to address the sixth congress of the International.

From 1927 to 1944 Larkin had an erratic parliamentary career. Elected to Dáil Éireann as an independent labour candidate, September 1927, he was disqualified as an undischarged bankrupt. He sought re-election in the by-election caused by his own disqualification but lost, 3 April 1928; he was again defeated in 1932 and 1933. Elected as an independent labour candidate, 1 July 1937, he lost the seat on 17 June 1938. He returned to the Labour Party, having played a prominent role in securing amendments to the Trade Union Act (1941) and in opposing the WAGES STANDSTILL ORDER (1941). He won a seat in Dublin North-East in June 1943, only to lose it again in May 1944. His return to the Labour Party, however, precipitated another bitter fight, which ended in 1945 with the ITGWU disaffiliating from the Irish Trade Union Congress and five members of the Labour parliamentary party forming the NATIONAL LABOUR PARTY. In the same year, following ten years of applications, the WUI affiliated to the ITUC. During his last two years Larkin led a fight against rising prices.

A statue by Oisín Kelly (1915–1981) in O'Connell Street, Dublin, shows Larkin in typical pose. His eldest son, James Larkin junior (1904–1969), trade unionist and politician (Labour Party), was a member of Dáil Éireann, 1927, when he took the Dublin seat of THOMAS JOHNSON. A member of Dublin City Council, 1930, he was chairman of the COMMUNIST PARTY OF IRELAND, 1933, and joint founder of the WORKERS' UNION OF IRELAND, 1923, of which he became general secretary, 1947. He was the first trade unionist to present a case at the LABOUR COURT, 1947. His fourteen-year effort to heal the divide in the trade union movement ended with the establishment of the IRISH CONGRESS OF TRADE UNIONS, 1959, of which he was twice president.

Larkin's second son, Denis Larkin (1908–1987), also a trade unionist and politician, returned from London to assist his father and brother in the Workers' Union of Ireland, 1923–27. A member of the Executive of the Irish Trade Union Congress from 1949, as president of the ICTU, 1974–75, he presided over the Employer-Labour Conference, which negotiated the 1974 national pay agreement. During his thirty-year year membership of Dublin City Council he was lord mayor, 1955 and 1959, and chairman of the Housing Committee. A member of Dáil Éireann for Dublin North-East, 1954–57 and 1965–69, he was a member of the Executive of the European Trade Union Conference and the European Social Fund Committee and the sole trade unionist on the European Special Commission to Combat Poverty.

Larne Gun-Running (1914). The purchase and landing of German arms for the UVF was planned by a secret committee—RICHARD DAWSON BATES, Sir George Clark (partner in the Belfast shipbuilding firm Workman Clark), Richard Cowzer (of the Belfast stockbrokers Josias Cunningham and Company), Sir James Craig (later VISCOUNT CRAIGAVON), FREDERICK CRAWFORD, James Cunningham (head of Josias Cunningham and Company), Captain Frank Hall (member of the Ulster Unionist Council), Sir Samuel Kelly (a Belfast coal importer), Alexander McDowell (a Belfast businessman), Colonel William Hacket Pain, and CAPTAIN WILFRID SPENDER—which reported to SIR EDWARD CARSON. William Chaine (chairman of Larne Harbour Board), Lieutenant-General Sir George Richardson (officer commanding the UVF), Lord Massereene and Major Robert McCalmont were involved with the logistics of the operation, which took place on 24–25 April.

Belfast was first chosen as the landing site, but security considerations forced a change to Larne. The weapons, brought from Germany on the *Fanny* and *Clyde Valley*, were transferred to the *Roma* for landing at Belfast and to the *Innishmurray* bound for Donaghadee, Co. Down. Motor cars assembled on the quayside at Larne were loaded with eighty tons of rifles and ammunition for local dispersal. Security was provided by some 2,500 members of the UVF. The operation landed some 35,000 rifles and an estimated five million rounds of ammunition. The guns were taken over by GENERAL SIR WILLIAM ADAIR, assisted by Spender. In the south the IRISH VOLUNTEERS responded to events at Larne with the HOWTH GUN-RUNNING in July.

On 14 December 1968 the *Clyde Valley* returned to Larne to participate in commemoration ceremonies organised by members of the ORANGE ORDER.

Lartigue Railway, a monorail, invented by Francis Marie-Theresa Lartigue, linking Listowel and Ballybunnion, Co. Kerry, a distance of 8 miles. Lartigue had conceived the idea in Algeria after observing a caravan of camels with their loads distributed on panniers.

His design allowed for a steam locomotive with carriages to balance on a single central track; care had to be taken when loading to ensure an even distribution of passengers on each side. The only monorail operated in Ireland, it was opened on 29 February 1888. Its first official run, on 5 March, set the standard time of one hour. The highest recorded number of passengers carried was on 11 August 1911, between 10:30 a.m. and 2 p.m., when 1,500 people were conveyed from Listowel for a PATTERN in Ballybunnion. After the machinery and rolling stock were damaged during the CIVIL WAR, the line was closed, 14 October 1924.

Lavelle, Rev. Patrick (1825–1886), clergyman (Catholic) and nationalist; born at Louisburgh, Co. Mayo; educated at a hedge school, St Patrick's College, Maynooth, and the Irish College, Paris, where he was an outstanding student and also later taught. He was forced to resign his professorship in Paris following a dispute with the rector, REV. THOMAS MILEY, which led not only to Lavelle's expulsion from France, 1858, but to the closure of the college. Appointed administrator of Toormakeady, and later parish priest, 1858–69, Lavelle, with the encouragement of ARCHBISHOP JOHN MACHALE, played a leading role in combating the evangelical new reformers, championed by the Church of Ireland Bishop of Tuam, THOMAS PLUNKET. His attack on Bishop Plunket over the treatment of tenants at Tourmakeady led to an editorial in the *Times* (London) and questions in the House of Commons.

Vice-president of the National Brotherhood of St Patrick and a supporter of the IRB, Lavelle came into conflict with PAUL CULLEN, Archbishop of Dublin, leading to his eventual suspension by Rome (lifted in June 1856 following representations by MacHale and Bishop Derry of Clonfert). After delivering the funeral oration at the grave of TERENCE BELLEW MCMANUS, 10 November 1861, Lavelle was supported by Archbishop MacHale when Archbishop Cullen again attempted to have him suspended. He lectured on 'The Catholic doctrine of the right of revolution' in 1862. During the 1860s he exhorted tenants not to pay rent increases (which averaged 44 per cent) and not to yield to notices to quit, on peril of being barred from the church; he did in fact close church doors on the few who paid.

His own litigation ruined him financially. JOHN 'AMNESTY' NOLAN launched a Lavelle Indemnity Fund, which brought temporary financial respite. Lavelle travelled to England and Scotland to address meetings attacking landlordism. He was appointed parish priest of Cong, Co. Mayo, in 1869. He served on the central committees of the HOME GOVERNMENT ASSOCIATION and HOME RULE LEAGUE. He galvanised members of the Co. Galway clergy into supporting JOHN P. NOLAN in the Co. Galway election, 1872; during a celebrated court case (for clerical intimidation) he was denounced by JUDGE WILLIAM KEOGH.

After he lost the good will of Archbishop MacHale for opposing the candidacy of JOHN O'CONNOR POWER in the 1874 Co. Mayo election, his influence declined. He supported CHARLES STEWART PARNELL, OBSTRUCTIONISM, and the NEW DEPARTURE. His main publication was *The Irish Landlords since the Revolution* (1870).

Lavery, Lady Hazel, née Martyn (1881–1935), society hostess and noted beauty; born in Chicago. She accompanied her mother to Europe and remained to study art. She married SIR JOHN LAVERY (her second husband) in London, 1910; among her friends there were GEORGE BERNARD SHAW, the EARL OF BIRKENHEAD, and SIR WINSTON CHURCHILL. Lavery was commissioned by the Free State government to paint a portrait of his wife as an idealised image of Ireland, 1927, which was used as a central feature of banknotes from 1928 until 1977 and also as the watermark until 2001. Through her husband's interest in Irish politics Lady Lavery formed a friendship with MICHAEL COLLINS during the Treaty negotiations, October–December 1921. In 1927 KEVIN O'HIGGINS suggested that Lavery be appointed Governor-General of the Irish Free State so as to give her an opportunity to display her talent as a hostess, but the idea was dropped after O'Higgins's death, July 1927. Her best-known paintings are of her husband and of Shaw.

Lavery, Sir John (1856–1941), artist; born in Belfast, studied art in Glasgow, where he was a member of the 'Glasgow School'. He built a reputation as a portraitist, in particular for his portraits of women. His best-known works include *Hazel Lavery* (Hugh Lane Municipal Gallery of Modern Art, Dublin), *Polymnia* (National Gallery, Rome), *A Lady in Black* (National Gallery, Berlin), *Spring* (the Luxembourg, Paris), *Game of Tennis* (New Pinelothek, Munich), and *Cardinal Logue* (Belfast Gallery).

Law, (Andrew) Bonar (1858–1923), British politician (Conservative-Unionist); born in

Kingstown, New Brunswick, of Ulster descent. A Glasgow iron merchant when elected to the British Parliament, 1900, he supported JOSEPH CHAMBERLAIN on tariff reform and in opposition to HOME RULE. He denounced the 'people's budget' introduced by DAVID LLOYD GEORGE, 1909, describing it as 'pure and unadulterated socialism.' On 13 November 1911 he succeeded ARTHUR J. BALFOUR as leader of the Conservative Party, and he supported the 'No surrender' stance adopted by the ULSTER UNIONIST COUNCIL. He assured the Ulster Unionists, July 1912: 'I can imagine no length of resistance to which Ulster will go which I shall not be ready to support.' He supported the formation of the ULSTER VOLUNTEER FORCE, January 1913, and was present at the BUCKINGHAM PALACE CONFERENCE, July 1914, which attempted to break the deadlock on home rule. When home rule was passed (and suspended in September) he claimed it was a breach of faith with Ulster Unionists.

As Chancellor of the Exchequer in the coalition 'war cabinet' he was responsible for the raising of war loans. He unsuccessfully urged the extension of CONSCRIPTION to Ireland, and while a member of the cabinet he reached an understanding with the Prime Minister, Lloyd George, on the position of Ulster in relation to home rule. After the failure of the IRISH CONVENTION he issued a joint letter with the Prime Minister on the eve of the general election of December 1918, stating that Ireland could not leave the British Empire, nor would the six north-eastern counties be forced against their will into home rule. He supported the GOVERNMENT OF IRELAND ACT (1920).

Briefly Prime Minister, October 1922 to May 1923, his career ended in seven months through ill-health, and he died five months later.

Law Adviser, an official of the Irish executive in DUBLIN CASTLE who advised the executive and magistracy on points of law. Magistrates based their judgments on his advice; such a close connection between the executive and the judiciary was considered injurious in practice, as the course of 'law and order' was interpreted according to the prevailing political climate. The last such official was John Naish in 1880.

Law Reform Commission. Established by the Law Reform Commission Act (1975), it came into existence in 1977, with Mr Justice Brian Walsh as first president.

Lawrence, William (1841–1932), photographer; born in Dublin, educated locally. He was a toy-maker in Upper Sackville Street (O'Connell Street), Dublin; during the 1870s the photographic department in his shop was so successful that he closed the toy-making business to concentrate on photography. His chief photographer, Robert French, travelled the country, amassing a huge collection of photographic plates of people and places. The National Library bought the Lawrence Collection, consisting of 40,000 plates, in 1942. An important source of photographic material for Irish history between 1880 and 1910, the material has been used in books and documentary films.

Leader (1900–71), a weekly paper founded and edited by D. P. MORAN as a vehicle for his trenchantly expressed IRISH-IRELAND views. The first issue appeared on 1 September 1900. Its offices were destroyed during the EASTER RISING (1916). The paper was suppressed in August 1919 but reappeared as the *New Leader*, with Joseph Dolan as nominal proprietor, and resumed its original title in 1920. During the 1940s it became a fortnightly, and in the 1950s it was revived under the influence of the historian T. Desmond. Williams (1921–1987). After becoming a monthly in the 1960s, it ceased publication in 1971.

League of Nations. The Irish Free State became a member of the League of Nations on 10 September 1923, having registered the ANGLO-IRISH TREATY (1921) with the league, though the registration of the Treaty and Ireland's admission to membership were opposed by Britain, which claimed the right to represent its dominions. The Free State was unsuccessful when it stood for election to the Council of the League, 1926, but was later elected with the support of other Commonwealth countries, 1930. The Irish permanent delegate to the league was SEÁN LESTER, 1929–34, who was replaced by Francis T. Cremins.

When ÉAMON DE VALERA formed his first government in 1932 he held also the post of Minister for External Affairs, and he was elected president of the Council, September 1932. His suggestion that the smaller countries form an independent bloc met with a subdued response among member-states but was praised in the international press. De Valera supported the league's policy during the Ethiopian crisis (1935) and its non-intervention during the

SPANISH CIVIL WAR (1936–39). As president of the Assembly, 1938–39, he supported the appeasement policy of NEVILLE CHAMBERLAIN towards Hitler. Seán Lester was the last secretary-general of the league, 1940–45. (See also UNITED NATIONS.)

League of Women Delegates, a coalition of feminist nationalists, led by Áine Ceannt (widow of ÉAMONN CEANNT), HANNA SHEEHY-SKEFFINGTON, KATHLEEN CLARKE, and others. It sought representation on the Executive of SINN FÉIN in 1918, on the grounds that women took risks equally with men to secure an Irish republic. The name of the organisation was later changed to Cumann na dTeachtaí, which secured four seats on the 24-member Executive of Sinn Féin. Many women were co-opted to various organisations set up by Sinn Féin and were elected to county councils and Poor Law boards of guardians. The league expressed disappointment when only two women were nominated to contest the 1918 general election (WINIFRED CARNEY was unsuccessful in Belfast, while CONSTANCE MARKIEVICZ won a seat in Dublin.).

League of Youth, the name adopted in 1934 by the YOUNG IRELAND ASSOCIATION, popularly known as the BLUESHIRTS.

Le Caron, Henri, pseudonym of Thomas Miller Beach (1841–1894), British spy and informer; born in Colchester. An apprentice draper, he went to the United States, 1861, enlisted in the 8th Pennsylvanian Reserves using the title 'major' and the name 'Le Caron', and in 1865 became Assistant Adjutant-General. During the American Civil War (1861–65) he joined the FENIANS. He settled in Nashville, Tennessee, where he studied medicine.

His career as an informer began in 1866 when he notified the authorities of a Fenian raid to be undertaken on Canada by JOHN O'NEILL, whose confidence he had won. (The raid was defeated by the Canadian authorities on 1 June 1866.) When he visited England the following year he made contact with ROBERT ANDERSON of the Home Office, to whom he relayed extensive information on Fenianism in Ireland, England, and America. Between 1868 and 1870 he earned £2,000 from the Home Office for information, and frustrated a second raid on Canada. A founder-member of CLAN NA GAEL, he was privy to information on the NEW DEPARTURE and formed a friendship with both ALEXANDER SULLIVAN of the terrorist 'TRIANGLE' wing and JOHN DEVOY. Devoy commissioned him to take packets for JOHN O'LEARY and PATRICK EGAN to Paris in 1881; while passing through London he gave Anderson an opportunity to study the packets. Egan accompanied him to London on the return journey from Paris and introduced him to CHARLES STEWART PARNELL, who commissioned him to bring about an understanding between the constitutionalists and the Fenians in America.

After returning to the United States he was denounced for his Fenianism when he stood for election to the House of Representatives, 1885. Returning to England permanently, December 1888, he was questioned in February 1889 during the hearings of the Special Commission on 'PARNELLISM AND CRIME'. He was paid £10,000 to smear Parnell; his testimony did not damage Parnell but revealed his own extraordinary career as double agent and the fact that he was one of five British agents who had infiltrated Clan na Gael. In his autobiography, *Twenty-Five Years in the Secret Service* (1892), he claimed that his spying had been motivated by patriotism and not by money.

Lecky, W. E. H. [William Edward Hartpole] (1838–1903), historian and politician (Liberal-Unionist); born in Blackrock, Co. Dublin; educated at TCD. A landlord of considerable means, he was widely travelled. Declining the chair of history at the University of Oxford, he became member of Parliament for the University of Dublin, 1895. He opposed HOME RULE, supported SIR HORACE PLUNKETT and the co-operative movement and the establishment of a CATHOLIC UNIVERSITY, and called for the release of DYNAMITERS. He became a Privy Councillor in 1897. Lecky's works include *Leaders of Public Opinion in Ireland* (1862)—essays on Swift, Flood, GRATTAN, and O'CONNELL; *The History of England in the Eighteenth Century* (1878–90)—written to counteract Froude's *History of Ireland*; *Democracy and Liberty* (1896); *The Map of Life* (1899); and *A History of Ireland in the Eighteenth Century* (1892)—culled from a twelve-volume history of England.

Legion of Mary, a Catholic lay organisation, founded in Dublin as the Association of Our Lady of Mercy, 7 September 1921, by a group of seventeen people including Frank Duff, Father Michael Toher, and Elizabeth Kirwan; it was renamed the Legion of Mary on 15 November 1925. Guided by Duff's *Legion of*

Mary Handbook, members directed their activities towards charitable works, including the reform of prostitutes. It opened its first branch outside Dublin in Waterford, 1927, and the first branch outside Ireland in Glasgow, April 1928.

Leinster, a passenger ship of the City of Dublin Steam Packet Company also used as a British troop transport, sunk by torpedo during the First World War. On 10 October 1918, shortly after leaving Kingstown (Dún Laoghaire) for Holyhead, the *Leinster* was struck by two torpedoes from the German submarine *U123,* resulting in the loss of 501 lives, including that of Captain W. Birch (who died during the rescue). The British ships *Lively, Mallard* and *Seal,* assisted by a flotilla of small craft, rescued 270 passengers and crew. Of the 771 aboard the *Leinster,* 489 were British and Allied military, many of whom are buried in the military cemetery at Blackhorse Road, Dublin.

Leinster, Augustus Frederick Fitzgerald, third Duke of (1791–1874), landowner and politician (Whig); educated at the University of Oxford. An extensive landowner at Carton, Co. Kildare, he succeeded to the title while a boy. He supported CATHOLIC EMANCIPATION and parliamentary reform. He received a letter from Edward Stanley (see EARL OF DERBY), outlining a proposal for a system of national education in Ireland; this letter, the 'Stanley Letter', was the basis for a non-denominational system of primary education. The Duke of Leinster was the first chairman of the Board of Commissioners until his resignation in 1850. He was also grand master of the Freemasons in Ireland.

Leinster House, Kildare Street, Dublin, the seat of Dáil Éireann and Seanad Éireann. It was built as Kildare House (1745) to the design of Richard Cassels as the town house of Lord Kildare, heir to the DUKE OF LEINSTER. It was sold in 1815 to the Dublin Society (see ROYAL DUBLIN SOCIETY), which developed the institutions that became the NATIONAL GALLERY, NATIONAL LIBRARY, National College of Art, and NATIONAL MUSEUM. Dáil Éireann occupies the former RDS lecture theatre, while the Seanad sits in the former saloon in the North Wing.

Leitrim, William Sydney Clements, third Earl of (1806–1878), landowner and politician (Conservative); born in Dublin. After a career in the British army, where he reached the rank of lieutenant-colonel, he became member of Parliament for Co. Leitrim, 1839–47, and in 1854 succeeded to the title and to estates in Cos. Leitrim and Donegal. He sat in the House of Lords as Lord Clements, was a magistrate for Cos. Donegal, Galway, and Leitrim, and was colonel of the Leitrim Militia. Notoriously litigious, he prosecuted more than 180 of the 3,000 tenants on his 57,000-acre estate at Milford, Co. Donegal. His relentless litigation (going as far as the House of Lords) seriously reduced his annual income. He refused to allow the ULSTER CUSTOM to his tenants after the passing of the Landlord and Tenant (Ireland) Act (1870). His tenants claimed that he used his position as landlord to seduce young women on his estates. He was murdered at Woodquarter, near Mulroy Bay, Co. Donegal, together with his driver and clerk, 2 April 1878. His funeral turned into a near-riot when Dublin crowds attempted to drag his coffin from the hearse. As recorded in the *Freeman's Journal,*

> the crowd closed round the hearse as it approached the graveyard . . . The police sought in vain to clear a path for the coffin . . . over a quarter of an hour elapsed before it could be finally removed . . . The mob hooted and groaned, and voices from the worst of them saying, "Out with the old b—," "Lug him out," "Dance on him."

Despite widespread arrests and large rewards, his assassins were never apprehended. A cross was erected in 1960 at the scene of the murders, commemorating Michael Hegarty, Michael McElwee, and Neil Sheilds, *'who, by their heroism at Cratlagh Wood on 2nd April 1878, ended the tyranny of landlordism in Ireland.'*

Lemass, Seán (1899–1971), politician (Fianna Fáil); born John Lemass in Dublin, educated at Christian Brothers' school. A member of the Irish Volunteers, he fought in the GPO, Dublin, during the EASTER RISING (1916) and was later active in the IRA during the WAR OF INDEPENDENCE. In December 1920 he was arrested and interned at Ballykinler, Co. Down. Opposing the ANGLO-IRISH TREATY (1921), he was a member of the FOUR COURTS garrison. Elected to Dáil Éireann, June 1922, he did not take his seat and was a member of the alternative Republican government formed by ÉAMON DE VALERA. During the CIVIL WAR he served with the headquarters staff of the Eastern Command of the IRA. He was interned in the Curragh from 28 November 1922 until released in October 1923 on compassionate grounds after the discovery of the body of his brother, Noel Lemass, who had been tortured and killed by Free State soldiers. On 27 November 1925 Lemass and GEORGE GILMORE were responsible for the escape of nineteen Republican prisoners from Mountjoy Jail, Dublin.

A founder-member of Fianna Fáil, 1926, with GERALD BOLAND he created the party's constituency organisation, through which it developed into the largest party in the country. After the party entered the Dáil, 1927, he played a leading role in opposition to the Cumann na nGaedheal government. In March 1928 he famously described Fianna Fáil as a 'slightly constitutional party.' He propounded a doctrine of self-sufficiency, advocating protection for industry. As Minister for Industry and Commerce in de Valera's first government, 1932, and its youngest member, he described himself as a 'pragmatic protectionist'. Giving priority to employment and creating and protecting native industry, he played a crucial role in the government's Economic Committee. He made Industry and Commerce a central department in fostering economic recovery during the 1930s. Foreign investment was encouraged only where it filled a need that could not be met by native industry. Two cement factories were built (Drogheda and Limerick) and funds provided for mineral exploration. He introduced the CONTROL OF MANUFACTURES ACTS (1932 AND 1934) to protect against foreign ownership of Irish companies. A series of Conditions of Employment Acts oversaw a gradual improvement in working conditions. Funds were also provided for industry and businesses to help them find new markets for manufactured products. The Industrial Credit Company was established in 1933, and, in an effort to fill the labour vacuum, Lemass urged the Department of Education to establish factory courses for industrial apprentices. He established bodies to investigate the expansion of the turf industry and the possibility of increasing electricity output. The sugarbeet industry was expanded, and he extended the role of the state by widening the range of state-sponsored bodies, creating a managerial class within the protected industries.

The Control of Prices Act (1937) was viewed as a response to the high prices sought by Irish manufacturers protected from external competition. Net industrial output rose from £25.6 million in 1931 to £36 million in 1938. Employment in manufacturing industry rose from 110,000 to 166,000 during the same period, though this had to be offset against losses in agricultural employment. In 1939 he legislated for a week's paid holiday for all workers. He also oversaw the establishment of Aer Lingus, 1936, Aer Rianta, 1937, the Irish Tourist Board, 1939, and Irish Life Assurance, 1939.

During the years of the Second World War he was appointed Minister for Supplies, with responsibility for rationing. In this capacity he controlled the distribution of raw materials and fuel resources to industry. His experiences during this period provided him with an insight into the need for strategic planning. Fianna Fáil was out of office, 1948–51; when Lemass returned to Industry and Commerce he was faced with an ailing economy, with inflation, unemployment and high emigration among the main problems. He tried unsuccessfully to prevent SEÁN MACENTEE from becoming Minister for Finance. Unable to solve the economic crisis, Fianna Fáil was defeated in the 1954 general election.

During Lemass's period in opposition he began an intensive study of economics. He made what became known as his '100,000 jobs speech' in Clery's Ballroom, Dublin, 16 October 1955, in which, influenced by the Italian Vanoni Plan of the 1950s, he outlined a programme costing some £67 million. Holding Industry and Commerce again in de Valera's last government, March 1957 to June 1959, Lemass organised the creation of a sub-committee on 22 July 1958 to supervise the drafting of the white paper *Programme for Economic Expansion* (based on *Economic Development,* supervised by T. K. WHITAKER). Implementing the programmes became a priority when Lemass succeeded de Valera as Taoiseach, 23 June 1959. Among other measures, foreign companies were offered tax 'holidays', and new bodies were established while existing bodies were streamlined and intensive efforts were made to boost export industries.

Output increased by almost a quarter between 1958 and 1963. Ireland became a party to the General Agreement on Tariffs and Trade (GATT) in 1960. Unemployment fell by a third, and there was a sharp decrease in emigration (a reduction of 40 per cent during the years 1961–66 compared with 1956–61). Citing Ireland's application for membership of the Common Market as his reason, he called a snap election for 4 October 1961. He returned with three seats short of an overall majority but was sustained by independents. He responded to de Gaulle's veto on Ireland's application for membership of the EEC, 1963, with a series of unilateral tariff cuts. Relaxation of the Control of Manufactures Act (1964) led to a significant increase in foreign investment. The Second Programme for Economic Expansion covered the period 1964–70; for some, the 1960s became the 'best of decades'.

In October 1959 Lemass made a significant speech to the Oxford Union. Accepting that the position of Northern Ireland could be changed only by the parliamentary will of its people, he proposed a qualified federal solution to the problem of partition. He called on the British government to allow difficulties to be resolved through dialogue between North and South, and categorically assured Unionists that the definition of the national territory in the Constitution of Ireland would be revised. These changes in attitude were strongly confirmed by one of Lemass's last public acts when he travelled to Belfast in 1965 to have tea with the Prime Minister of Northern Ireland, TERENCE O'NEILL.

From 1961 to 1965 Lemass led a minority government, with Fianna Fáil holding seventy seats, compared with a combined opposition of seventy-four. In the general election of 1965 Fianna Fáil gained two seats, to equal the combined opposition of seventy-two. On 10 November 1966 he informed the Dáil, 'I have resigned.' He was succeeded by JACK LYNCH, who in turn was succeeded by Lemass's son-in-law, CHARLES HAUGHEY.

Lester, Seán (1888–1959), journalist and diplomat; born in Carrickfergus, Co. Antrim, educated at Methodist College, Belfast. He had experience on Republican journals and newspapers when he joined the *North Down Herald.* He worked on the *Connacht Tribune* before moving to Dublin, 1913, where he became news editor of the *Freeman's Journal.* He worked in the Department of External Affairs from 1923 until he was appointed permanent representative of the Irish Free State to the LEAGUE OF NATIONS in 1929. He served on the Council of the league and presided over arbitration on the Peru-Colombia and Bolivia-Paraguay disputes. He left the Irish service to take up a position as High Commissioner in Danzig (Gdańsk), 1934–37. An outspoken critic of Nazism and of the Italian invasion of Abyssinia (Ethiopia), he was deputy secretary-general of the league, 1937–40, and last secretary-general, 1940–46.

Leydon, John (1895–1979), civil servant; born in Arigna, Co. Roscommon; educated at St Patrick's College, Maynooth, which he left after two years. He entered the British civil service in London, 1915, where he was active in the Gaelic League and the Irish Self-Determination League of Great Britain. He moved to Dublin, 1923, to assist in the establishment of the civil service of the Irish Free State. In the Department of Finance he worked on claims for compensation for damage incurred during the War of Independence. He was secretary of the De-Rating Commission, 1926–31. A critic of state intervention, he turned down the office of secretary of the Department of Industry and Commerce when it was offered by W. T. COSGRAVE but in 1932 accepted it from SEÁN LEMASS, with whom he was closely associated in efforts to secure industrial expansion. He was involved in the establishment of Aer Lingus, of which he became chairman, 1936, and also Aer Rianta, 1937–49, and Bord na Móna, 1946. During the years of the Second World War he followed Lemass to the Department of Supplies, where he helped establish IRISH SHIPPING LTD. His influence waned after Fianna Fáil lost power in 1948.

Lia Fáil, a movement founded in 1957 by Father John Fahy to agitate against the purchase of land by foreigners (taking its name from the ancient inauguration stone at the Hill of Tara, Co. Meath). It failed to achieve popular support.

Liberty Clubs, founded in 1917 within the Liberty League by COUNT PLUNKETT, which he hoped would replace both SINN FÉIN and the Irish Nation League. A Council of Nine was formed; although it included one woman (Countess Plunkett), prominent feminists organised the LEAGUE OF WOMEN DELEGATES to achieve a wider influence within Sinn Féin, which absorbed the Liberty Clubs.

Lichfield House Compact, an informal agreement (named from the London home of Lord Lichfield) between DANIEL O'CONNELL and VISCOUNT MELBOURNE, 18 February 1835, to secure the fall of the Tory ministry headed by SIR ROBERT PEEL. In return for his support, O'Connell was given to understand that a Melbourne administration would provide a settlement of the tithes question and a measure of municipal reform that would help Catholics in local government. Melbourne formed a new ministry when Peel's fell, 11 April. The tithes question was satisfactorily settled, and the

MUNICIPAL CORPORATIONS (IRELAND) ACT (1840) was introduced. A new Irish executive, headed by the EARL OF CARLISLE, with THOMAS DRUMMOND as Under-Secretary, increased the number of Catholics under executive appointment and ensured a more equitable enforcement of the law. The compact lasted until the end of the Melbourne ministry, 1841.

lighthouse service. Lighthouses were originally operated by private individuals. In 1660 King Charles II granted letters patent to Sir Richard Reading to erect six lighthouses on the coast of Ireland: two at Howth, Co. Dublin, one at the Old Head of Kinsale, Co. Cork, one at Barry Óg's Castle, near Kinsale, one at Hook Tower, Co. Wexford, and the last at Island Magee, near Carrickfergus, Co. Antrim. Control of the lighthouses was vested in commissioners in 1704. In 1786 an act was passed setting up the Corporation for Preserving and Improving the Port of Dublin; this body divided in 1854 to form the Dublin Port and Docks Board and the Port of Dublin Corporation, which in 1867 became the Commissioners of Irish Lights. The twenty-one honorary commissioners, elected for life under a rotating chairman, fulfilled a statutory duty to inspect all lighthouses and navigational aids around the coast.

Some of the best-known lighthouses (all now automatic) are: Bailey (1814), Black Rock (1864), Blacksod (1866), Dunmore East (1825), Fastnet Rock (1854), Hook Head (the oldest in Ireland, re-established c. 1666), Howth Harbour (1818), Kish Bank (1965), Loop Head (1854), Mine Head (1851, Ireland's highest, at 285 feet), Mizen Head (1959), Old Head of Kinsale (1814), Rathlin East (1856), Sceilg Mhichíl (1826), Tory Island (1832), Tuskar Rock (1815), and Valencia Island (1841). Two lightvessel stations—Coninbeg, off Co. Wexford, and South Rock, off Co. Down—were also maintained by the commissioners, who inspected the entire lighthouse network annually.

limekiln. The practice of manufacturing lime for use as an agricultural fertiliser was common from the seventeenth to the early twentieth century. On larger farms where limestone was readily available, a purpose-built limekiln was constructed. Such buildings were approximately 20 feet wide and 18 feet high, with a 6-foot frontal opening. The base was a mixture of rubble and clay, with a stone or brick-lined interior. A hole at the base in front facilitated the escape of smoke. Wood and turf and, less frequently, a mixture of anthracite and coal were used to achieve the temperature of 1,000° required to reduce the broken limestone to ash. When cooled, the lime was withdrawn through a slanted rear opening. Because of its corrosive qualities, great care needed to be exercised when dealing with the product. The lime was also used as a whitewash on farm buildings and walls, and as a pest-repellent in gardens. With the availability of commercially produced fertiliser from the 1940s, limekilns fell into disuse, and relatively few survive in their entirety.

Limerick Chronicle, the oldest newspaper in the Republic, founded in 1766 by the Scotsman John Ferrar. Andrew Watson, also a Scot, was the first editor of the paper, which appeared twice weekly until 1862, when it appeared thrice weekly. With the exception of an enforced stoppage during the general strike (the Limerick 'Soviet') of 1919 and a ten-day suspension during the Civil War, the paper, now published on Tuesdays, has appeared continuously. It covered the American War of Independence (1776–81), the French Revolution (1789), the 1798 Rising, the trial of ROBERT EMMET (1803), and the Fenian Rising (1867). Its files, much sought after by researchers, form an invaluable historical record.

Limerick Declaration, made in 1868 by 1,600 priests, organised by the Dean of Limerick, Dr O'Brien. It stated in effect that repeal of the UNION was the only logical final solution to the 'Irish question'. The declaration was symptomatic of an increasing nationalism, which culminated in the founding of the HOME RULE LEAGUE, 1873.

Lindsay Report (2002), the report of the Tribunal of Inquiry into the Infection with HIV and Hepatitis C of Persons with Haemophilia and Related Matters, its sole member Judge Alison Lindsay. The tribunal, appointed by the Oireachtas, 2 June 1999, was the second to examine these matters (the first, conducted during the period 1995–96 by Mr Justice Finlay (see FINLAY REPORT), was rejected by haemophiliacs, who were dissatisfied with the terms of reference). Judge Lindsay was directed to examine how contaminated blood products were supplied to haemophiliacs from the mid-1970s to the later 1980s, the adequacy of screening procedures applied by the Blood Transfusion Service Board in relation to the selection, screening and testing of donors, the treatment of blood products, and the adequacy of the board's decision-making process. She also inquired into the actions of the BTSB and into the adequacy of the response of the Minister for Health and the Department of Health to the dangers of infection.

After sitting for 196 days, from 27 September 1999, and hearing oral evidence from 2 May 2000 from 146 people, including haemophiliacs and members of their families, the inquiry closed on 28 November 2001.

The report criticised the Blood Transfusion Service Board, the Department of Health and Children, and certain doctors. Judge Lindsay found it 'inexplicable' that the BTSB failed to pursue an agreement with a centre in Scotland to supply safer blood products for haemophiliacs, which she regarded as a missed opportunity that could have reduced the risk of hepatitis infections. While the report was critical of Professor Ian Temperley, it praised his work for the National Haemophilia Treatment Centre, of which he was medical director for the period covered by the inquiry (he was also a member of the BTSB, 1987–99). The NHTC provided a 'high standard' of medical care, but inadequacies in facilities and resources created problems for members of the staff.

At least 252 of the 400 haemophiliacs in Ireland contracted either the AIDS virus (HIV) or hepatitis C while receiving treatment from the BTSB. In all, 260 were infected with HIV or hepatitis C (or both) over a period of twenty years up to the late 1980s; seventy-two had died.

Judge Lindsay made eight recommendations relating to the treatment of haemophiliacs but recommended against the referral of her findings to the Director of Public Prosecutions. The successor to the BTSB, the Irish Blood Transfusion Service, apologised 'unreservedly' to haemophiliacs for 'all deaths and injury' caused by the products supplied by the BTSB.

The Irish Haemophilia Society welcomed the Lindsay Report but later expressed disappointment that the inquiry did not find that the BTSB had compromised safety in the interests of profit.

Linen Hall Library, Belfast, an independent and charitable body founded in 1788, the oldest library in Belfast and the last subscribing library in Ireland. The first librarian was the United Irishman Thomas Russell (1763–1803). The library has the largest archive dealing with the Northern Ireland conflict since 1968, comprising 250,000 items; other collections include Irish and local studies, early Belfast, and Ulster printed books.

Little, P. J. [Patrick John] (1884–1963), politician (Fianna Fáil). He was a member of Dáil Éireann for Dublin (Rathmines), 1918, and later for Waterford, 1927–54, parliamentary secretary to ÉAMON DE VALERA, 1933–39, and Minister for Posts and Telegraphs, 1939–48. He failed in his campaign to secure support for a national concert hall in the 1940s. His vision for an ARTS COUNCIL was not shared by de Valera but was adopted by JOHN A. COSTELLO, following a report from Thomas Bodkin. The inter-party government fell before the Arts Council could be set up; de Valera, on assuming office, established the council, using Little's scheme and appointing him director. Though frustrated by chronic lack of finance, he established local advisory committees in Athlone, Cork, Dublin, Galway, Killarney, Limerick, Sligo, Tralee, Waterford, and Wexford. There were five panels: music, drama, architecture, painting, and literature in Irish; all were disbanded within a short time, and Little's far-reaching plans for the arts failed through lack of financial support.

Little Christmas, also known as Women's Christmas (from the Irish *Nollaig na mBan*), 6 January, the Feast of the Epiphany. As the last day of the 'twelve days of Christmas' it is the time when holly is traditionally taken down and burned. In some areas, twelve candles were lit in honour of the Apostles. A belief persisted that the first candle to burn out presaged that the family member who lit it would be the first member of the family to die.

Littleton, Edward John, first Baron Hatherton (1791–1863), British politician (Whig); born Edward John Walhouse in Wolverhampton (he changed his name to benefit from a granduncle's will), educated at the University of Oxford and Lincoln's Inn, London. Entering politics in 1812, he supported CATHOLIC EMANCIPATION. As Chief Secretary for Ireland, 1833–34, he introduced an Irish Tithes Arrears Act, which advanced £1 million to tithe-owners; he also introduced a bill to commute tithes into a land tax to be paid to the government, 20 February 1823. His opposition to the aims of the REPEAL ASSOCIATION led to conflict with DANIEL O'CONNELL, who opposed the commutation of tithes. Littleton was prepared to accept a minimum of COERCION if O'Connell would support the Tithes Bill, an exchange acceptable to O'Connell; but following Littleton's failure to secure the support of the cabinet for a reduction in coercion, O'Connell charged him with duplicity.

The revelation of Littleton's dealings with O'Connell damaged the British government. Though Lord Grey refused to accept Littleton's offer of resignation, the government fell after the Tithe Rentcharge (Ireland) Bill was rejected by the House of Lords. Littleton became Baron Hatherton in 1835.

Lloyd George, David, first Earl (1863–1945), British politician (Liberal); born in Manchester of Welsh parents and raised by an uncle in Caernarvonshire. A member of Parliament from 1890, he was Prime Minister, 1916–22. His 'people's budget' provoked such opposition from the House of Lords that H. H. ASQUITH was forced to seek the support of JOHN REDMOND in breaking the veto power of the House of Lords through the PARLIAMENT ACT (1911). In return, the Irish Party received the (third) HOME RULE BILL. In May 1917 he offered Redmond immediate home rule, with six Ulster counties excluded for five years. Following Redmond's rejection he established the IRISH CONVENTION (1917–18). Efforts to introduce CONSCRIPTION triggered nationalist resistance, increased support for SINN FÉIN, and destroyed Redmond's party.

Rejecting the legitimacy of DÁIL ÉIREANN, throughout the WAR OF INDEPENDENCE he sought a solution that would retain Ireland within the British Empire. His GOVERNMENT OF IRELAND ACT (1920) established the state of Northern Ireland but was ignored in the south. The activities of the AUXILIARIES and BLACK AND TANS, sent to defeat the IRA, provoked international hostility. Failure to subdue the IRA forced Lloyd George into contact with Sinn Féin leaders, but ÉAMON DE VALERA refused to treat with him through intermediaries, while Lloyd George was not prepared to treat with MICHAEL COLLINS, whom he regarded as the leader of a band of assassins. He helped to draft the conciliatory speech made by King George V at the opening of the Parliament of Northern Ireland, 22 June 1921; two days later he invited de Valera to attend a conference in London, reluctantly agreeing to a truce (beginning on 11 July). His meetings with de Valera in July proved fruitless when he presented him with a proposal for dominion home rule within the British Empire, and he rejected de Valera's formula of 'EXTERNAL ASSOCIATION'. On 29 September he telegraphed the 'GAIRLOCH FORMULA' as the basis for discussions, which began in London on 11 October.

During negotiations leading to the ANGLO-IRISH TREATY (1921), Lloyd George used a combination of charm, cunning, intrigue, and bullying. On 24 October he met ARTHUR GRIFFITH and Collins alone, ostensibly to reduce the numbers involved in discussion. He raised the question of the Crown, and the Irish presented de Valera's formula of external association (which Lloyd George had rejected in July). It was agreed to leave the question of the Crown as the last item of discussion.

Lloyd George now broached the question of Ulster. From the beginning, the Prime Minister of Northern Ireland, Sir James Craig (VISCOUNT CRAIGAVON) had made it clear that the position of Northern Ireland was not negotiable. Griffith received the impression on 3 November that if Ulster proved intractable, the British ministers involved would resign their posts rather than force the new state into submission. Griffith accepted Lloyd George's offer of a BOUNDARY COMMISSION as a diplomatic solution to the impasse, and allowed him to use this acquiescence as an assurance that if Northern Ireland was presented with the alternatives of an all-Ireland parliament or a boundary commission, Griffith would not break off negotiations. Lloyd George then triumphed at the Liverpool Unionist Conference, where opponents intended to condemn his government for negotiating with Sinn Féin.

On 28 November the Irish were offered an opportunity to insert in the Treaty 'any phrase they liked' to ensure that the position of the Crown in Ireland would be no more than it was in relation to Canada or any other dominion. Lloyd George met Griffith, Collins and Éamon Duggan, 29 November, and offered them a form of the OATH OF ALLEGIANCE different from the one subscribed to by other dominion parliaments, which the Irish rejected. Griffith brought the Treaty proposals to Dublin, 2 December, while Lloyd George met Collins and ERSKINE CHILDERS to discuss the financial arrangements on Ulster. After rejecting counter-proposals from the Irish Ministry, Lloyd George met Collins, 5 December. He offered Ireland full financial autonomy, and stated that there would be no further concessions. Without warning, the Irish delegates were presented with an ultimatum. Holding up two letters, one containing the Articles of Agreement for a Treaty, the other containing the news that Sinn Féin had refused terms, Lloyd George demanded to know which one he should send to Craig. Was it to be war or peace? He demanded that they sign the Treaty immediately, without consultation with Dublin, or both sides would be free to resume war within three days. This ultimatum was considered a significant factor in persuading the delegates to sign.

Lloyd George's role in the negotiations earned him a legendary reputation in Irish history for unparalleled deceit. After his government fell, November 1922, he spent the rest of his career on the back benches.

Local Appointments Commission, established in 1926 by the Cumann na nGaedheal government to undertake recruitment to the senior administrative and professional posts in local authorities. The commission was involved in a celebrated controversy in 1930 when it recommended Letitia Dunbar-Harrison (a Protestant) for the post of Mayo County Librarian. The Library Committee refused to endorse the appointment to the county council, citing as their reason the applicant's inadequate knowledge of Irish; the county council upheld the committee's decision and refused to sanction the appointment. The government dissolved the county council, replacing it with a commissioner. Other committees of the council refused to co-operate with the commissioner. In December 1931, Dunbar-Harrison was appointed to the library of the Department of Defence in Dublin. Vacancies within local government were subsequently advertised and filled by competition under the auspices of the commissioners in Dublin.

Local Defence Force, formed in September 1940 under the Defence Forces (Temporary Provisions) Act (1940), which created a new type of soldier, the emergency durationist. Recruited from the A Group of the Local Security Force, the LDF, which soon numbered some 100,000 volunteers, served as an armed auxiliary to the regular army. Under the command of the chief of staff and a local defence directorate, the LDF was intended to be the first line of defence in the event of an invasion. After the war the LDF was replaced by An Fórsa Cosanta Áitiúil (FCA). (See DEFENCE FORCES.)

local government. The territorial division known as the county was introduced into Ireland after the twelfth-century Anglo-Norman conquest. The counties were later subdivided along English lines into baronies (of which there are now 324), then further divided into boroughs. Local government during the nineteenth century was based on the county, each governed by a GRAND JURY, solely representing the Anglo-Irish ASCENDANCY class. The grand jury financed local expenditure by raising a 'cess' or levy on the occupiers of the land within its jurisdiction.

Borough corporations were reformed and reconstituted under the MUNICIPAL CORPORATIONS (IRELAND) ACT (1840). Some town commissioners were established in 1828, but most came into existence under the Towns Improvement (Ireland) Act (1854). Commissioners were responsible for the provision of lighting, cleaning services and water supply in all towns with a population of more than 1,500. The Local Government Board established central control from 1872 but allowed a large measure of local autonomy. The provision of health facilities was vested in the boards of guardians for each Poor Law union, established under the Poor Relief (Ireland) Act (1851). The boards divided the unions into dispensary districts, each with a salaried medical officer.

The Public Health (Ireland) Acts (1874 and 1878) granted borough corporations and town commissioners considerable powers with regard to the provision of health facilities and housing services. Additional boards administered lunatic asylums, county infirmaries, and fever hospitals. From 1883 boards of guardians provided rural housing.

The Local Government (Ireland) Act (1898) rationalised the web of authorities and boards, one of the most sweeping measures introduced during the century. Destroying in effect the power of the Ascendancy, it transferred the administrative responsibilities of grand juries to elected borough and county councils, while the functions of the Poor Law boards became the responsibility of elected rural district councils, urban district councils, and borough corporations. The act led to nationalist control of local government. It also granted limited female suffrage: women could become members of rural district councils and urban district councils, though not of county councils. Larger towns continued to be governed by town commissioners.

The Local Government (Ireland) Act (1919) extended the system of proportional representation to twenty-six town councils and urban district councils and two hundred other local authorities. Further administrative changes occurred after the creation of the Irish Free State, 6 December 1922. Boards of guardians were replaced by boards of health (later boards of health and public assistance), while a new system of home assistance granted to 'any poor person who is unable by his own industry or other lawful means to provide for himself or his dependants the necessaries of life or necessary medical or surgical treatment.' The Local Government Act (1925) abolished the rural district councils, whose functions were assumed by the boards of health, now additionally responsible for sanitation, housing, drainage, water supplies, and general public health services. Between 1922 and 1942 a series of reforms to secure maximum efficiency in local government were introduced; as part of these reforms the LOCAL APPOINTMENTS COMMISSION was established to select qualified personnel for a wide range of administrative and professional posts in local government.

The chief executive in local government, the county or city manager, is a salaried official who can be removed from office only by the Minister for the Environment and Local Government. The management system, first introduced in Cork, 1929, was extended to Dublin, 1930, Limerick, 1934, Waterford, 1939, and the remaining counties in 1942. The functions of local authorities are divided into two classes: 'reserved functions', the prerogative of the elected members, and 'executive functions', which devolve on the manager, who must, however, act in conformity with general policy as laid down by the members.

The general functions of the local authorities relate to housing, planning, roads, water supply and sewerage, development incentives and controls, environmental protection (including rivers, lakes, air, and noise), recreation facilities and amenities, agriculture, education, health, and welfare. Health services have been the responsibility of regional health boards since 1 April 1971. Rates (property tax) on private dwellings were abolished from 1 January 1978; local authorities received finance from central funds for the loss of this revenue.

Galway, previously a borough, became a county borough (city) under the Local Government (Reorganisation) Act (1985). From 1 January 1994 Dublin County Council was abolished and its functions divided between three new county councils: Fingal (north Co. Dublin), Dún Laoghaire and Rathdown, and South Dublin.

The Local Government Act (2001) simplified structures, introduced a range of reforms, and repealed some nineteenth-century law and terminology. With effect from January 2002, county boroughs are simply called cities, and urban districts and towns with town commissioners became simply towns.

Local Government Board, established in 1872 to assume responsibilities formerly vested in the Poor Law Commissioners. It supervised the dispensary system, adjudicated between local authorities, administered hospitals and the Housing and Public Health Acts, and took responsibility for public hygiene and distressed areas. From 1908 it was responsible for the administration of OLD-AGE PENSIONS.

Local Option Party, a party founded by the Presbyterian minister Rev. A. Wylie Blue in Belfast in 1929, advocating the prohibition of alcohol. It contested the general election of that year; reflecting the strong prohibitionist lobby in Northern Ireland, it proposed that the population of a local authority area should be enabled to vote to prohibit the sale of alcoholic drink, as the Licensing Act (Northern Ireland) (1923) had failed to provide a compromise between publicans and temperance bodies. Having unsuccessfully contested three seats against Unionist candidates in the general election, the party faded from the political scene.

Local Security Force, a non-military auxiliary to the regular army, formed in May 1940. It was divided into A and B Groups, both of which were trained by the GARDA SÍOCHÁNA, the A Group considered suitable for certain military duties, the B Group to perform auxiliary police duties. The force was reorganised under the Defence Forces (Temporary Provisions) Act (1940), whereby the A Group became the LOCAL DEFENCE FORCE and the B Group remained the Local Security Force, under Garda control.

Locke's Distillery Tribunal. In 1947 Locke's Distillery in Kilbeggan, Co. Westmeath (founded 1757), was sold to foreign interests. The sale became an embarrassment for the government when it was alleged that the Department of Industry and Commerce (where SEÁN LEMASS was minister) had been approached before the sale about the enlargement of the company's export quota. There was further embarrassment when it was alleged that President SEÁN T. O'KELLY had entertained some of the foreign interests, including those with a criminal past, at Áras an Uachtaráin. Oliver J. Flanagan claimed in Dáil Éireann, 22, 29 and 30 October, that the Taoiseach, Éamon de Valera, his son Éamon, Seán Lemass and GERALD BOLAND had used influence on behalf of their political and personal friends in granting licences to trading concerns. After sitting for eighteen days, a tribunal of inquiry reported, 19 December 1947, that the charges were without foundation and accused Flanagan of 'complete irresponsibility'.

Lockwood Report on Higher Education, established 'to review the facilities for university and higher technical education in Northern Ireland, having regard to the report of the Robbins Committee, and to make recommendations.' The commission reported in February 1965. It proposed Coleraine as the site for a new university; the acceptance of this proposal caused resentment in Derry, where nationalists had expected the new university would be established.

Logue, Michael (1840–1924), bishop (Catholic); born in Carrigart, Co. Donegal, educated at hedge schools, privately, and at St Patrick's College, Maynooth, ordained 1866. Professor of dogmatic theology at the Irish College, Paris, 1866–74, he was later dean of St Patrick's College, Maynooth, professor of Irish, 1876–78, and professor of theology, 1878. As Bishop of Raphoe, 1879–87, he distributed large amounts to famine-stricken tenant-farmers, having collected £30,000 on one visit to the United States. He undertook an ambitious afforestation scheme, planting some 25,000 trees around Glenswilly, Co. Donegal, where he was a curate, 1874–76. A supporter of the total abstinence movement, he preached widely on the abuses of POITÍN. He became Archbishop of Armagh and Primate of All Ireland in December 1887 and raised more than £50,000 towards the cost of St Patrick's Cathedral, Armagh. He considered the PLAN OF CAMPAIGN a tactical mistake. He opposed CHARLES STEWART PARNELL as leader of the IRISH PARTY after the divorce scandal broke in 1890. A patron of the Gaelic League, he criticised the Board of Intermediate Education for its failure to promote Irish.

A cardinal from 1893, in 1918 he supported the anti-conscription coalition (see CONSCRIPTION). He supported Sinn Féin until it became a physical force movement, denounced British forces and the British government for the policy of official reprisals during the WAR OF INDEPENDENCE, and was involved in peace initiatives with the Under-Secretary for Ireland, A. W. COPE. He supported the Anglo-Irish Treaty (1921) but opposed partition. Through a pastoral letter, 22 October 1922, he condemned Republican actions in the CIVIL WAR:

> They have wrecked Ireland from end to end—they have caused more damage to Ireland in three months than could be laid to the charge of British rule in so many decades . . . All those who . . . participate in such crimes . . . may not be absolved in Confession, nor admitted to Holy Communion.

Unsuccessful in his attempts to sponsor peace, he exhorted the Free State government, 18 November 1923, to release all Republican prisoners not guilty of crime, and called on imprisoned members of the IRA to abandon the weapon of the hunger strike.

Lomasney, William Francis Mackey (1841–1884), Fenian; born in Cincinnati, Ohio, of Cork parents (his father was a Fenian). Better known by his alias of Captain Mackey, he was a veteran of the American Civil War (1861–65). Betrayed by HENRI LE CARON, he was arrested while in Ireland to make contact with JAMES STEPHENS and the IRB but was allowed to leave the country. Before the 1867 IRB rising he travelled to France to withdraw funds from the Fenian treasury. He took part in the ill-fated rising, after which he held out until captured, 8 February 1868, having taken Ballyknockane RIC Barracks, April 1867, and made sorties against barracks and gunsmiths. He was sentenced to twelve years' imprisonment. As a result of agitation by ISAAC BUTT and the AMNESTY ASSOCIATION he was released, 1871, and later established a bookselling business in Detroit. He supported the LAND LEAGUE and later joined the DYNAMITERS. He was killed, together with his brother Michael and John Fleming, while attempting to blow up London Bridge, 12 December 1884.

Londonderry, Charles Stewart Vane-Tempest-Stewart, sixth Marquess of (1852–1915), landowner and politician (Unionist); born in London, educated at the University of Oxford. He was a member of Parliament for Co. Down, 1878–84, and Lord Lieutenant of Ireland, 1886–89. During his term as Lord Lieutenant the Irish executive had to contend with the renewal of the LAND WAR in the form of the PLAN OF CAMPAIGN. He gave total support to the Chief Secretary for Ireland, ARTHUR J. BALFOUR, with whom he formed a lifelong friendship. He opposed home rule. The

LONDONDERRY HOUSE AGREEMENT was reached at his home, 6 April 1911. He helped to organise the ULSTER SOLEMN LEAGUE AND COVENANT (1912) and the LARNE GUN-RUNNING (1914).

Londonderry, Charles Stewart Vane-Tempest-Stewart, seventh Marquess of (1878–1949), politician (Ulster Unionist) and landowner; born in London. Member of Parliament for Maidstone, 1906–15, and second in command of the Home Guard during the First World War, he was a well-known air enthusiast and served as Under-Secretary for Air, 1920–21. He was active in the ULSTER UNIONIST PARTY, and his 50,000-acre estate was the scene of frequent Unionist meetings and events. As first Minister of Education in Northern Ireland, 1921, he was unsuccessful in his attempt to establish a system of education that would not be segregated on religious lines. Leader of the Northern Ireland Senate, 1921–26, Secretary of State for Air, 1931–35, and Lord Privy Seal and leader of the House of Lords, 1935, he was the author of *Ourselves and Germany* (1938) and *Wings of Destiny* (1943).

Londonderry House Agreement, reached at the London home of the MARQUESS OF LONDONDERRY, 6 April 1911, between the UNION DEFENCE LEAGUE and the JOINT COMMITTEE OF UNIONIST ASSOCIATIONS OF IRELAND. Its aim was to collect funds for the Unionist cause and to disseminate propaganda against home rule in Britain.

London Tavern Committee, established in 1822 by philanthropic English businessmen to provide relief from distress in Ireland, particularly in the west. It raised £311,000, which was used to provide public works, cheap food, and seed potatoes. It also provided aid during the crisis of 1831.

Long, Walter Hume, first Viscount Long of Wraxall (1854–1924), British politician (Conservative, Unionist). A member of Parliament from 1880, he succeeded GEORGE WYNDHAM as Chief Secretary for Ireland, March–December 1905. Member of Parliament for South Co. Dublin, 1906–10, he succeeded E. J. SAUNDERSON as leader of the Unionist Party and was a founder of the UNION DEFENCE LEAGUE, 1907. He was president of the Budget Protection League, established to oppose the 'people's budget' introduced by DAVID LLOYD GEORGE, 1909. Winning a London seat in 1910, he was succeeded as leader of the UUP by SIR EDWARD CARSON. He withdrew his challenge for leadership of the Conservative Party in favour of ANDREW BONAR LAW. He introduced the Franchise Bill (1917), which granted the franchise to women over the age of thirty. Before the adoption of the GOVERNMENT OF IRELAND ACT (1920) he was in Ulster on behalf of the British government, gauging Unionist reaction to alternative proposals on home rule. He published *My Memories* in 1923.

Long-Term Recovery Programme, adopted following the publication of a white paper by the first inter-party government, January 1949, as part of Ireland's qualification for MARSHALL AID. A plan for the economy from 1949 to 1953, it was drawn up by the Minister for External Affairs, SEÁN MACBRIDE, and the secretary of the department, F. H. BOLAND. The use of 1947, climatically the worst in history, as the base for projections failed to impress the plan's American supervisors, who sought additional information in respect of both investment and internal consumption projections. Its main achievement was the land rehabilitation project undertaken by the Minister for Agriculture, JAMES DILLON. It marked the beginning of economic planning that bore fruit a decade later in the PROGRAMMES FOR ECONOMIC EXPANSION. Benefits of the Long-Term Recovery Programme included the establishment of the Central Statistics Office, Córas Tráchtála, and the Industrial Development Authority.

Lord Lieutenant or Viceroy, officially 'Lord Lieutenant-General and Governor-General of Ireland', the senior representative of the Crown and head of its Irish executive in Dublin. His office was in DUBLIN CASTLE and his home the Viceregal Lodge (now Áras an Uachtaráin) in the Phoenix Park. Lord Townshend, 1767–72, was the first holder of the office to establish permanent residence in Ireland: previous office-holders had come to Ireland biennially to attend sittings of the Irish Parliament. Though the Lord Lieutenant was responsible for the civilian government of Ireland and also controlled the military forces of the Crown, actual power was vested in the Chief Secretary for Ireland, who was a member of Parliament and sometimes of the cabinet. The function of the Viceroy was largely ceremonial. Alexis de Tocqueville (*Journey in Ireland, July–August 1835*) remarked: 'The political tendency . . . is to leave the Lord Lieutenant only the appearance of authority and to concentrate the real power in the hands of the Minister in London,' while R. BARRY O'BRIEN commented that the Lord Lieutenant wore the insignia of command and signed the log, but the Chief Secretary was the captain of the ship.

A Lord Lieutenant's popularity was often determined by the generosity of his entertainment. As political power had shifted from Dublin after the Union, much of the glitter of a capital city disappeared, and the Viceregal ceremonials offered rare glimpses of pomp and circumstance. Only one Lord Lieutenant, Lord Fitzalan of Derwent, the last person to hold the office, was a Catholic.

The following is a list of Lords Lieutenant, 1800–1922. Those marked with an asterisk were either born in, or owned land in, Ireland.

1800	MARQUESS CORNWALLIS
1801	EARL OF HARDWICKE
1806	Earl of Bedford
1807	Duke of Richmond
1813	Viscount Whitworth
1817	Earl Talbot of Hensol
1821	RICHARD COLLEY WELLESLEY*
1828	MARQUESS OF ANGLESEY
1829	Duke of Northumberland
1830	Marquess of Anglesey
1833	Richard Colley Wellesley
1834	Earl of Haddington
1835	Earl of Mulgrave
1839	CHICHESTER-FORTESCUE PARKINSON, Baron Carlingford*
1841	Earl de Grey
1844	Baron Heytesbury
1846	EARL OF BESSBOROUGH*
1847	Earl of Clarendon
1852	Earl of Eglinton
1853	Earl of St Germans
1855	Earl of Carlisle
1858	Earl of Eglinton
1859	Earl of Carlisle
1864	Earl of Kimberley
1866	DUKE OF ABERCORN*
1868	Earl Spencer
1874	Duke of Abercorn
1876	Duke of Marlborough
1880	EARL COWPER
1882	Earl Spencer
1885	Earl of Carnarvon
1886	Marquess of Aberdeen
1886	MARQUESS OF LONDONDERRY*
1889	Earl of Zetland
1892	Marquess of Crewe
1895	Earl of Cadogan
1902	Earl of Dudley
1905	MARQUESS OF ABERDEEN
1915	Baron Wimborne
1918	EARL FRENCH OF YPRES
1921	VISCOUNT FITZALAN OF DERWENT

Loyalist Association of Workers, founded in Belfast in 1971 by Billy Hull. Membership was drawn from his Workers' Committee for the Defence of the Constitution at the Harland and Wolff shipyard, Mackie's foundry, and Gallaher's tobacco factory. Claiming an initial membership of 100,000, it developed close links with loyalist paramilitary organisations. As a constituent of the Ulster Loyalist Central Co-ordinating Committee it organised a series of lightning one-day strikes to draw attention to demands for the establishment of a pan-unionist programme to 'fight for democracy in Northern Ireland.' It played a leading role in the Ulster Workers' Council's general strike, 1974, which precipitated the collapse of the power-sharing Executive of the Northern Ireland Assembly. Falling membership, coupled with strategic and other differences, led to Hull's isolation within the paramilitary organisations, culminating in his being wounded in an apparent loyalist attack on the Crumlin Road, Belfast, 9 November 1974.

Loyalist Volunteer Force, founded by dissident members of the Mid-Ulster UVF, led by BILLY WRIGHT, following the confrontation resulting from the Drumcree Orange march at Portadown, July 1996, which led to their expulsion from the UVF. The group was considered responsible for a number of murders during the following year. Attracting support from former members of the UDA as well as the UVF, it was proscribed, June 1997. Wright was killed by the INLA in the Maze Prison, 27 December 1997, leading to retaliatory sectarian killings by the LVF. Rejecting the loyalist ceasefire, stating that it was not in the interests of the Protestant people, the LVF declared its own ceasefire, May 1998, while urging a 'no' vote in the referendum on the BELFAST AGREEMENT. After declaring in August that 'our war is over,' in December it handed over some guns and ammunition, pipe bombs and detonators to the INDEPENDENT INTERNATIONAL BODY ON DECOMMISSIONING. Members of the LVF were still believed to be active in 2001.

Luby, Thomas Clarke (1821–1901), revolutionary; born in Dublin, son of a Church of Ireland clergyman, educated at TCD. Abandoning a proposed clerical career, he supported the REPEAL ASSOCIATION, joined YOUNG IRELAND, and was a contributor to the *Nation*. After the breach with DANIEL O'CONNELL he joined the IRISH CONFEDERATION and befriended JAMES FINTAN LALOR, by whom he was deeply influenced. Following the collapse of the 1848 rising (see BALLINGARRY) he attempted to revive the fighting by working with the secret Irish Democratic Association, to which Lalor also belonged. He was transported to Australia.

Back in Ireland, during the years 1856–58 he accompanied JAMES STEPHENS on an organising tour to establish the IRISH REPUBLICAN BROTHERHOOD, whose oath he formulated, 1858. Joint editor of the IRISH PEOPLE, 1863–65, he was among those arrested, 1865, when he was sentenced to twenty years' imprisonment, of which he served six before his release, 1871, as a result of agitation by the AMNESTY ASSOCIATION. He moved to the United States, where he joined CLAN NA GAEL. A supporter of JEREMIAH O'DONOVAN ROSSA, he was a trustee of the SKIRMISHING FUND, which was used to finance the DYNAMITERS. Suspicious of the Irish Party, he opposed the NEW DEPARTURE and the LAND LEAGUE. John O'Leary's *Recollections* are dedicated to him in acknowledgment of his assistance in their composition. Luby published *A Life of Daniel O'Connell* (1872) and *The Lives and Times of Illustrious and Representative Irishmen* (1878).

Lucas, Frederick (1812–1855), journalist and politician (Independent Irish Party); born in England, educated at the Quaker School, Darlington. A convert to Catholicism, 1839, he founded the *Tablet,* 1840, which became an influential weekly organ of English Catholicism. A keen student of Irish affairs, he moved to Ireland with his newspaper in 1850. In the aftermath of the Great Famine (1845–49) he became involved with CHARLES GAVAN DUFFY in the TENANT LEAGUE, 1850. When the 'IRISH BRIGADE' was established in 1851 to fight the Ecclesiastical Titles Bill, Lucas successfully advocated that the Tenant League join with it to form the INDEPENDENT IRISH PARTY. He was elected member of Parliament for Co. Meath with the help of ARCHBISHOP PAUL CULLEN, 1852. Over the next few years relations between Cullen and the party deteriorated, and the Tenant League attributed the loss of the Co. Louth by-election to his intervention, February 1854; the league and the Independent Irish Party suffered from clerical and lay reaction when Lucas, supported by ARCHBISHOP JOHN MACHALE of Tuam, complained to Rome about Cullen's behaviour.

lunacy. No organised provision for the mentally ill existed in Ireland up to the eighteenth century. In 1711 cells for holding mentally disturbed soldiers were built at the Royal Hospital, Kilmainham, Dublin; apart from additional cells in 1803, they remained in their original condition for 140 years. Foundling children took precedence over the insane, and from 1730 Dublin was left without a mental institution until Jonathan Swift's bequest led to the eventual opening of St Patrick's Hospital, Dublin, 26 September 1857. For many years this fifty-bed unit was the only specialised hospital for the mentally ill in Ireland. The House of Industry, North Brunswick Street, Dublin, served as part-hospital and part-asylum from 1773; it housed ten mental patients in 1776, a number that increased to seventy-six within twenty-five years. In the period 1799–1802 its mortality rate averaged three per day.

From the early nineteenth century small private asylums were opened throughout the country; the most celebrated of which was Cittadella, near Cork, run by Dr William Saunders Halloran. His records, 1798–1818, show that of 1,431 patients treated, 429 died, 751 were cured, and the remaining 251 remained in the asylum. Treatment included bathing with various additives, bleeding, blistering, camphor, emetics, mercury, opium, and purgatives. In addition, Dr Halloran used a device immediately after the administration of an emetic or purgative that was designed to stimulate the effects of the medicine. It rotated the patient at 100 revolutions per minute and apparently was most successful. As an alternative, the patient was placed in a hammock, which was then shaken violently until the desired effect was achieved.

Under the Lunacy (Ireland) Act (1821) the Lord Lieutenant was empowered to build mental hospitals and to set up the necessary control mechanisms. Twenty-three asylums were built under the act, catering for 6,200 patients. Under the Local Government (Ireland) Act (1898), county councils were given the responsibility of providing for the insane poor.

Before the establishment of institutions, the household, particularly in rural areas, had to support its own afflicted. A witness appearing before the Poor Law Commission (1817) stated:

> When a strong man gets the complaint the only way they have to manage is by making a hole in the floor of the cabin, not high enough for a person to stand up in, with a crib over it to prevent his getting up. The hole is about four feet deep, and they

give this wretched being his food there, and there he generally dies. Of all human calamities I know of, none are equal to this in the country parts of Ireland I am acquainted with.

The Mental Treatment Act (1945) regulated admission and discharge procedures. Temporary admissions were also legislated for, and out-patient clinics established. Psychiatric clinics were opened in the 1950s, and private psychiatric hospitals now also play a role in the general treatment of mental health.

Lusitania, a 32,000-ton Cunard liner torpedoed off the Old Head of Kinsale, Co. Cork, by the German submarine *U20,* 7 May 1915. Returning from New York to Liverpool with 1,959 passengers and crew, the liner was also carrying a cargo of 173 tons of rifle ammunition and shells, which exploded shortly after the torpedo's impact; 1,198 passengers and crew, including 128 Americans, were lost. The possible presence of a German submarine pack in the area hindered the arrival of Admiralty vessels from nearby Kinsale and Queenstown (Cóbh), and local fisherman rescued the majority of the survivors. President Woodrow Wilson described the sinking as an 'illegal and inhuman' act. American anger was mollified in February 1916 when, though the German government did not concede the illegality of the sinking, it offered an apology and indemnity. However, the German declaration that it would sink on sight all ships, belligerent and neutral, helped bring the United States into the Great War in 1917.

In 1983 the *Archimedes* recovered the ship's bell, which is now on display at the Imperial War Museum, London. One of the tackier aspects of modern entrepreneurship emerged in 1990 when 3,500 golf clubs, fashioned from the propellers of the *Lusitania,* went on sale, at $9,000 a set.

Lyceum, a literary review founded in 1887 by FATHER THOMAS A. FINLAY, attached to University College, Dublin. Edited by PROF. WILLIAM MAGENNIS, it attracted a wide range of contributors on matters of literary, topical, political and cultural interest, including DR DOUGLAS HYDE, THOMAS KETTLE, EOIN MACNEILL, SIR HORACE PLUNKETT, DR GEORGE SIGERSON, and W. B. YEATS. It was replaced by the *New Ireland Review* in 1893.

Lynch, Diarmuid (1878–1950), republican soldier; born Jeremiah Lynch in Tracton, Co. Cork, educated locally. After working as a Post Office clerk in Cork and later in the British civil service he went to the United States, 1896, where he joined the Gaelic League and the New York Philo-Celtic Society. Returning to Ireland, 1907, he joined the IRB and became a member of its Supreme Council, 1911–16. He raised £2,000 with THOMAS ASHE in the United States on a fund-raising tour for the Gaelic League and the Irish Volunteers. In September 1915, detailed by PATRICK PEARSE to find a suitable landing-place for an arms ship before the proposed rising, he selected Fenit, Co. Kerry, as the landing-place for the AUD. After fighting in the GPO, Dublin, he was imprisoned in England until June 1917. As Sinn Féin controller of food he ordered the seizure of pigs being exported to England and had them slaughtered for home consumption; arrested, he served two months in Dundalk Jail.

Deported, he went once more to the United States, where he became national secretary of the FRIENDS OF IRISH FREEDOM, 1918–32. He assisted ÉAMON DE VALERA on his fund-raising mission, 1920, and opposed the Anglo-Irish Treaty (1921). He returned to Ireland in 1932. Between 1936 and 1940 he collected material from survivors of the rising in an attempt to produce a factual account of events; this appeared in *The IRB and the 1916 Insurrection* (1957), edited by Florence O'Donoghue. He returned to his native Tracton in 1939.

Lynch, Fionán (1889–1966), soldier and politician (Sinn Féin, Cumann na nGaedheal, Fine Gael); born in Cahersiveen, Co. Kerry, educated at UCD. A teacher and later a barrister, he took part in the EASTER RISING (1916), for which he was imprisoned. Twice on hunger strike, May and November 1917, following his release he was jailed under the 'GERMAN PLOT' arrests, 1918. As a Sinn Féin member of Dáil Éireann for South Kerry, December 1918 and May 1921, he represented the constituency later for both Cumann na nGaedheal and Fine Gael until 1944, when he resigned from politics. He was assistant secretary to the Treaty delegation, 1921. Appointed Minister for Education in the Provisional Government, 1922, he was a brigadier in the Free State army during the CIVIL WAR, commanding in Co. Kerry. He was Minister for Fisheries, 1923–27, and Minister for Lands and Fisheries, 1927–32, and a supporter of the BLUESHIRTS. He was made a judge following his retirement from politics, 1944.

Lynch, John (Jack) (1917–1999), politician (Fianna Fáil); born in Cork, educated at UCC and King's Inns. After working in the Department of Justice from 1936 he was called to the bar, 1945, and practised on the Munster circuit. An outstanding sportsman with the GAA, he had the unique distinction of winning six consecutive all-Ireland senior medals for hurling (1941–44 and 1946) and football (1945). He was elected to Dáil Éireann for Cork in 1948, becoming Parliamentary Secretary to the Government and the Minister for Lands, 1951–54, Minister for the Gaeltacht, March–June 1957, Minister for Education, 1957–59, Minister for Industry and Commerce, 1959–65, and Minister for Finance, 1965–66. He defeated George Colley (by 52 to 19) to succeed SEÁN LEMASS as leader of Fianna Fáil and Taoiseach, 10 November 1966. Under his leadership the party gained three seats in 1969 (from seventy-two in 1965).

Almost immediately he had to face a crisis as the civil rights movement in Northern Ireland provoked loyalist reactions (see NORTHERN IRELAND CIVIL RIGHTS ASSOCIATION). In dealing with the situation he was advised by DR T. K. WHITAKER. On 13 August 1969 he promised that the government would not stand by while the Catholic minority in the North was subjected to harassment by Protestant paramilitary groups. Calling for intervention by the United Nations, he resisted pressure for intervention by the Irish army, making it clear that there could be no resort to the use of force. Army units were moved to border areas, where field hospitals and camps were set up to accommodate those fleeing across the border from the violence. His policy was criticised by NEIL BLANEY.

In December 1969 the IRA split into two factions, to become known as Provisionals and Officials, followed by a corresponding split in SINN FÉIN, January 1970. Speaking at the Fianna Fáil ard-fheis, 16–18 January, Lynch admitted that 'the plain truth—the naked reality—is that we do not possess the capacity to impose a solution by force' on Northern Ireland.

The leader of Fine Gael, LIAM COSGRAVE, alleged in April that members of Lynch's government were providing arms for the Provisional IRA. On 6 May, Lynch dismissed Blaney and CHARLES HAUGHEY (see ARMS TRIAL); two other members of the Government, KEVIN BOLAND and Mícheál Ó Móráin, resigned. Then and subsequently Lynch declared that a united Ireland could come about only through consent, and not through violence.

The government moved against the IRA by introducing the Offences Against the State (Amendment) Act (1972). When the events of BLOODY SUNDAY, 30 January 1972, aroused public anger, which resulted in the burning of the British Embassy in Dublin, Lynch continued to state that only consensus from within could solve the Northern problem. He met EDWARD HEATH and BRIAN FAULKNER for an unproductive meeting in England; within a few weeks Heath introduced direct rule of Northern Ireland from London.

Before his defeat in the 1973 general election Lynch fulfilled Lemass's dream of leading the Republic into the European Economic Community. During the general election campaign he claimed success for his government's policy on the North and on security. While in opposition, 1973–77, he appointed Haughey to the front bench. An extravagant election manifesto resulted in Lynch returning to power with eighty-four seats, giving him the largest single-party majority in the history of the state. He appointed Haughey Minister for Health. He broke the link with sterling, 1978, to enter the European monetary mechanism. The economy suffered from the price turmoil in the world oil market. The atmosphere of industrial and agrarian unrest was reflected in the dismal performance by Fianna Fáil in elections for the European Parliament, when it won five of the fifteen seats instead of the eight anticipated, 7 June 1979. There was a postal strike, petrol shortages, and a 20 per cent increase in electricity charges, June 1979. By the time he left on a visit to the United States, 7 November, Lynch had decided to resign following Ireland's presidency of the EEC, June–December 1979. In his absence, opposition to his leadership grew. His hold on the leadership was weakened when Fianna Fáil lost two by-elections, 7 November, both in his native county (Cork City and Cork North-East). Believing that George Colley would succeed him, he unexpectedly resigned, 5 December 1979; two days later Haughey defeated Colley (44 to 38) and became Taoiseach on 11 December. Lynch retired from politics in 1981. The encomium at his funeral was delivered by his former protégé DESMOND O'MALLEY (founder of the PROGRESSIVE DEMOCRATS). Lynch is commemorated by the Jack Lynch Tunnel under the River Lee in Cork, opened in May 1999.

Lynch, Liam (1890–1923), republican soldier; born in Anglesborough, Ballylanders, Co. Limerick, educated locally. Trained for the hardware business, he worked in Mitchelstown and Fermoy, Co. Cork. A member of the Supreme Council of the IRB and of the ANCIENT ORDER OF HIBERNIANS, he was active in the reorganising of the IRISH VOLUNTEERS in Co. Cork, 1917, and played a prominent role in the opposition to CONSCRIPTION. He commanded Cork No. 2 Brigade of the IRA during the WAR OF INDEPENDENCE. His unit captured and burned the RIC Barracks at Araglin, Co. Cork, April 1919; in September his column surrounded and disarmed a party of British soldiers following an ambush in which he was winged by his own forces. He was among those captured by British soldiers, 12 August, who failed to recognise him and released all but TERENCE MACSWINEY.

Throughout the early months of 1922, as the nationalist movement split on the Treaty, Lynch attempted to avoid confrontation in order to preserve the Republic. This did not prove possible, and the country moved towards civil war. When a convention of the IRA resolved, 26 March 1922, to reaffirm allegiance to the Republic, Lynch was appointed chief of staff. Establishing an Army Executive, the convention abrogated the authority of the Minister for Defence. Within a short time Lynch resigned when the Executive split over tactics. He disapproved of the seizure of the FOUR COURTS in April but on 27 June joined the garrison, just before the Provisional Government attacked. He subsequently made his escape to the south, where he assumed command of the 1st Southern Division of the IRA, its largest command, with a quarter of the total force. He announced, 30 June, that he was chief of staff of the IRA, with military command of the south and west. He now appeared to hope that hostilities might be confined to Dublin, and that if Republicans could control the rest of the country the Provisional Government would recognise its hopeless position and allow the Republic to function.

Moving to Co. Limerick at the beginning of July, in command of a quarter of the total republican forces, Lynch attempted to avoid clashes between pro-Treaty and anti-Treaty forces and to hold what became known as the 'Munster Republic' (south of a line from Limerick to Waterford). Fighting broke out in Limerick on 7 July, and a week later he abandoned the city to pro-Treaty forces. He established new headquarters in Clonmel, Co. Tipperary, before moving to Fermoy, Co. Cork, the last town held by the Irregulars before he abandoned it on 11 August. He directed that IRA units should divide into small 'active service units' or 'FLYING COLUMNS', in order to operate more effectively against Provisional Government forces. From then until May 1923 the Republicans were under increasing pressure.

Lynch was a member of the Army Council that hoped to negotiate peace terms that would 'not bring this country within the Empire.' He revealed some of his desperation when, on 27 November, he sent a letter to the Ceann Comhairle of Dáil Éireann, stating that 'as the illegal body over which you preside has declared war on the soldiers of the Republic and suppressed the legitimate parliament of the Irish People [the second Dáil Éireann], we therefore give you and each member of your body due notice that unless your army recognises the rules of warfare in future we shall adopt very drastic measures to protect our forces.' Three days later he issued the 'orders of frightfulness', listing for all battalion commanders fourteen categories of persons who were to be shot on sight. The killing on 7 December 1922 of a member of Dáil Éireann, Seán Hales, and the wounding of another, Pádraic Ó Máille, provoked the government into executing imprisoned republicans. Thereafter, property rather than persons became Republican targets.

On 9 February 1923 Lynch rejected a plea from the captured republican Liam Deasy that they should unconditionally surrender within nine days. Lynch called on republicans not to surrender, but over the next two months more of his battalion commanders were captured. Despite the hopelessness of his position, he attempted to continue the fight. A meeting of the Army Executive was called to consider the new situation, as by now both ÉAMON DE VALERA and FRANK AIKEN favoured coming to terms with the Free State government. Accompanied by Aiken, Lynch travelled to Cork to attend the meeting, stopping en route at a hideout in Co. Tipperary. On 10 April, the day of the meeting, he was shot by a party of Free State soldiers in the Knockmealdown Mountains and died in Mitchelstown.

Lynch, Patrick (1917–2001), economist; born in Dublin, educated at UCD and the University of Cambridge. Joining the Department of Finance, 1941, he became private secretary to the Taoiseach, JOHN A. COSTELLO, whom Lynch persuaded to adopt a Keynesian approach to economic policy, 1948–51. He left the civil service to become a lecturer in political economy at University

College, Dublin, where he was subsequently associate professor, 1966, and then professor, 1975–80. He advised Charles Murray and T. K. WHITAKER on *Economic Development* and the PROGRAMMES FOR ECONOMIC EXPANSION. He was chairman of Aer Lingus and Aer Rianta, 1954–75, a director of the Provincial Bank of Ireland, 1959, a director of Allied Irish Banks, 1970, vice-chairman of the AIB Group, 1975, and the first Irish member of the Club of Rome, 1973. He led the survey team that produced the seminal report *Investment in Education* (1962–65). He was chairman of the Institute of Public Administration and treasurer of the Royal Irish Academy, a member of the Senate of the National University of Ireland, 1972, and a life member of the Royal Dublin Society. A prolific writer on economic, educational and social questions, he was considered a major influence in the development of the public and private sectors from the 1950s until his death.

Lynn, Kathleen (1874–1955), doctor, suffragist, and humanitarian; born in Cong, Co. Mayo, daughter of a Church of Ireland rector, educated at Alexandra College. Qualifying as a doctor, 1899, she established a practice in Rathmines, Dublin. She was chief medical officer to the IRISH CITIZEN ARMY during the Easter Rising (1916). With her lifelong companion Madeleine Ffrench-Mullen she founded St Ultan's Hospital for Children at 37 Charlemont Street, Dublin, in 1918, to combat the flu and TUBERCULOSIS epidemics. The hospital was the first built specifically to care for infants. A member of Sinn Féin, she was a member of the LEAGUE OF WOMEN DELEGATES, 1918. She was elected to the fourth Dáil Éireann as a republican for Co. Dublin, 1923, until defeated in June 1927, after which she was defeated as a Sinn Féin candidate in the August by-election occasioned by the murder of KEVIN O'HIGGINS.

Lyons, John Charles (1792–1874), antiquarian; born in Ledeston, Co. Westmeath, educated at the University of Oxford. A self-taught mechanic, he built his own printing press, and under the imprint of the Ledeston Press he printed and published, among other works, *The Book of Surveys and Distribution of the Estates of the County of Westmeath . . .* (1852) and *The Grand Juries of the County of Westmeath from the Year 1727 to the Year 1853* (2 vols., 1853), now regarded as valuable antiquarian and genealogical material. He was Seneschal of Mullingar and High Sheriff of Co. Westmeath, 1816. He was also an authority on orchids, and his *Remarks on the Management of Orchidaceous Plants* (1843) was one of the earliest standard works on the subject.

M

'Maamtrasna Massacre' (18 August 1882), the murder of five members of the Joyce family, who occupied boycotted land at Maamtrasna, near Headford, Co. Galway. Before he died the sole survivor, Patrick Joyce, the youngest son of the family, gave evidence that led to the arrest of ten men, who were subsequently charged with the murders. Two of them—Anthony Philbin and Thomas Casey—became witnesses for the Crown. Patrick Casey, Patrick Joyce and Myles Joyce were hanged at Galway, 15 December 1882. The remaining five accused—Michael Casey, Patrick Joyce, Thomas Joyce, John Casey, and Martin Joyce—who pleaded guilty on the advice of their priest, Father Michael McHugh, had their death sentences commuted to life imprisonment. Michael Casey died in Maryborough (Port Laoise) Jail, 22 August 1895, and John Casey in Mountjoy Jail, Dublin, 27 February 1900. The remaining three were freed, October 1902, following appeals by their wives to the Lord Lieutenant, Lord Dudley.

Philbin and Casey subsequently admitted to perjury; Philbin admitted that he had not been present at the murders. The matter was twice raised in the House of Commons, on the second occasion by CHARLES STEWART PARNELL, 17 July 1885, and there were numerous appeals to the Irish executive. It is now generally accepted that Myles Joyce was innocent, and that the imprisoned five had no connection with the murders. Father McHugh, when parish priest of Carna, wrote to the Lord Lieutenant, Lord Crewe, 22 June 1894:

> You will ask at once why did I induce them to plead guilty, if I believed them to be innocent. Well, I was not at the time as satisfied of their innocence as I am now . . . on the other hand it was represented by the Crown that their sentence would be commuted if they entered a plea of guilty.

McAleese, Mary, née Leneghan (born 1951), lawyer, academic, journalist, and politician; born in Belfast, educated at QUB and called to the bar. She practised law for a year before moving to Trinity College, Dublin, where she succeeded MARY ROBINSON as Reid professor of criminal law. She left Trinity College to work in current affairs at RTE, 1979–81, as reporter and presenter on the programmes 'Frontline' and 'Today Tonight', before returning to Trinity College. She was a member of the Catholic Church delegation to the NEW IRELAND FORUM (1984). Active in the campaign for homosexual law reform, she supported the call for women priests in the Catholic Church. In 1987 she was defeated when she stood as a Fianna Fáil candidate for Dáil Éireann in Dublin South-East. In the same year she was chairperson of the Constitution Rights Committee, which lobbied against the Single European Act (perceived as a threat to the constitutional right to life of the unborn and to Irish neutrality). In 1987 she returned to Belfast as director of the Institute of Professional Legal Studies at Queen's University, where, after receiving a professorial chair, she became one of three pro-vice-chancellors, 1994, the first woman and the first Catholic to be appointed to the office.

Having defeated the former Taoiseach ALBERT REYNOLDS to secure the Fianna Fáil nomination for President of Ireland, September 1997, she defeated four other candidates to succeed Mary Robinson, becoming the first Northern nationalist to become head of state of the Republic, and was inaugurated on 11 November 1997.

McAliskey, Bernadette, née Devlin (born 1947), republican socialist; born in Cookstown, Co. Tyrone, educated at QUB. A member of the NORTHERN IRELAND CIVIL RIGHTS ASSOCIATION and PEOPLE'S DEMOCRACY, she took part in the first civil rights march from Coalisland to Dungannon, 24 August 1968. She was in Derry on 5 October 1968 when the RUC baton-charged the demonstrators, and was among the People's Democracy marchers attacked at Burntollet Bridge en route to Derry, January 1969. On 24 February 1969 she contested the Londonderry South seat in the Parliament of Northern Ireland against JAMES CHICHESTER-CLARK, receiving 5,812 votes to his 9,195. She then stood as unity candidate for the Mid-Ulster seat in the British House of Commons, 17 April 1969, receiving 33,648 votes, to enter Parliament on 22 April as its youngest member for fifty years and the youngest woman ever elected. She was sentenced to six months' imprisonment for incitement to riot during the 'Battle of the Bogside', Derry, 12–15 August 1969. She retained her seat in the general election of 18 June 1970 but lost it when she later stood as an independent, 28 February 1974.

Joint founder (with SÉAMUS COSTELLO) of the IRISH REPUBLICAN SOCIALIST PARTY, 1974, she broke with Costello on tactics, 1975. She and her husband, Michael McAliskey, were seriously wounded in front of their children at their home at Derrylaughan, near Coalisland, Co. Tyrone, by UFF gunmen, 16 January 1981. She stood unsuccessfully for Dáil Éireann in February and November 1982. In the 1992 general election she stood unsuccessfully for Sinn Féin in Fermanagh-South Tyrone. She was later chairperson of the Independent Socialist Party. Her autobiography, *The Price of My Soul*, was published in 1969.

Her daughter Róisín successfully fought attempts by the German government to have her extradited from Britain to answer terrorist charges, 1996–97.

Macalister, R. A. S. [Robert Alexander Stewart] (1870–1950), archaeologist and musician; born in Dublin, educated at TCD, in Germany, and at the University of Cambridge. A member of the Royal Society of Antiquaries of Ireland, he edited its *Journal*, 1910–18, and was president, 1924–28. First professor of Celtic archaeology at University College, Dublin, 1909–43, he was president of the Royal Irish Academy and chairman of the National Monuments Advisory Council, 1926–31. He was organist and choirmaster at the Adelaide Road Church, Dublin, and composed a suite in D minor for piano and organ. His works include *Studies in Irish Epigraphy* (3 vols., 1897–1907), *Leabhar Gabhála: The Book of Conquests of Ireland* (with EOIN MACNEILL, 1916), *The History of Antiquities at Inis Cealtra* (1916), *Life of Ciarán of Clonmacnoise* (1921), *Ireland in Pre-Celtic Times* (1921), *The Archaeology of Ireland* (1927), *The Excavations of Uisneach* (with Robert Lloyd Praeger, 1929), *Tara, Ancient Pagan Sanctuary of Ireland* (1931), *Ancient Ireland* (1935), *The Secret Language of Ireland* (about Travellers' language, 1937), and *Corpus Inscriptionum Insularum Celticarum* (1945). He also published more than fifty volumes covering his work as director of excavations for the Palestine Exploration Fund, 1900–09.

Macardle, Dorothy (1899–1958), historian and dramatist; born in Dublin, a member of the Dundalk brewing family, educated at UCD. A teacher of English at Alexandra College, she was influenced by MAUD GONNE and was active in the Gaelic League and Sinn Féin. She supported the EASTER RISING (1916), went on hunger strike when imprisoned, and on her release returned to her teaching post. A follower of ÉAMON DE VALERA, she rejected the Anglo-Irish Treaty (1921) and supported the Irregulars during the Civil War. She was a founder-member of the WOMEN'S PRISONERS' DEFENCE LEAGUE and a member of the first Executive of Fianna Fáil, 16 May 1926. At de Valera's suggestion she wrote *The Irish Republic* (1937), which became a standard history of the events leading up to the establishment of the Irish Free State. For a time she was drama critic of the *Irish Press.* During the Second World War she worked for refugee children, about whom she wrote *Children of Europe* (1949), and she was president of the Irish Council for Civil Liberties, 1951. Her works include biography, plays, and short stories. *Tragedies of Kerry* (1946) is a record of events in Co. Kerry during the CIVIL WAR.

McAteer, Eddie (1914–1986), politician (Nationalist Party of Northern Ireland); born in Coatbridge, Lanarkshire, son of a Donegal labourer. In 1916 his family moved to Derry, where he was educated at St Columb's College. He was a civil servant, 1930–44, before setting up an accountancy practice. Through his brother, Hugh McAteer (died 1970), a former chief of staff of the IRA, he had close connections with the republican movement, but he opposed a military solution to partition. As a Nationalist member of the Parliament of Northern Ireland from 1945 he was involved in the Anti-Partition League, which had close connections with Fianna Fáil. As leader of the reorganised Nationalist Party from 2 June 1964 he led the official opposition at Stormont from 2 February 1965 until 1969, when he lost his British House of Commons seat to JOHN HUME. He was an unsuccessful candidate in the elections for the Assembly of Northern Ireland, 1973. In 1977 he gave his support to the IRISH INDEPENDENCE PARTY.

McAuley, Catherine (1778–1841), founder of the Order of Mercy; born in Dublin. Orphaned in her teens, she was adopted by a Dublin Quaker family. She returned to the Catholic faith through ARCHBISHOP DANIEL MURRAY; her adoptive family also became Catholics, and from them she inherited £27,000, an income of £600 a year, and Coolock House, Dublin. Keenly interested in the education of the poor, she visited France to study Catholic methods of education. She also studied the methods used by the KILDARE PLACE SOCIETY. Encouraged by Archbishop Murray, she opened a school, 24 September 1827, and a small orphanage shortly afterwards. With two companions, Mary Ann Doyle and Elizabeth Hanley, she was professed a nun, 12 December 1831, and returned to Baggot Street, Dublin, as superior of the new Order of Mercy, which received Papal approval in 1835 and operated under rules modified from those of the Presentation Order, with an additional vow of service to the underprivileged. By 1887 there were 175 houses of the order in Ireland, and it later spread throughout the world.

MacBride, Major John (1865–1916), republican soldier; born in Westport, Co. Mayo, to a prominent business family. He joined the IRB in the 1880s when he was befriended by MICHAEL CUSACK but later became disillusioned, describing it as 'older men . . . sitting on their backsides and criticising and abusing one another.' A member of the CELTIC LITERARY SOCIETY, he was influenced by ARTHUR GRIFFITH. Shortly after returning from an IRB mission to the United States he emigrated to South Africa, where he was an assayer for the Rand Mining Corporation. He persuaded Griffith to join him in South Africa, 1897, where they organised the CENTENARY CELEBRATIONS. Their sympathies were with the Boers, for whom MacBride and Arthur Lynch (1864–1934) organised an Irish Brigade.

Returning to Ireland, he was unsuccessful in his bid for the South Mayo parliamentary seat. Griffith introduced him to MAUD GONNE, who converted to Catholicism to marry him, 21 February 1903. They had one son, SEÁN MACBRIDE, but the marriage ended in a judicial separation, September 1905, and he returned to Dublin while his wife and son remained in Paris until 1917. He eventually secured a permanent position with Dublin Corporation. He was vice-president of CUMANN NA NGAEDHEAL and a member of the NATIONAL COUNCIL and Sinn Féin. He sat on the Supreme Council of the revitalised IRB; in the EASTER RISING (1916) he fought under THOMAS MACDONAGH at Jacob's factory, Bishop Street, Dublin, for which he was shot by firing squad, 5 May.

MacBride, Seán (1904–1988), lawyer and politician (Clann na Poblachta); born in Paris, son of MAUD GONNE and MAJOR JOHN MACBRIDE, educated in Paris and at UCD. A member of the IRB from his teens, he fought in the WAR OF INDEPENDENCE. He was in London as bodyguard to MICHAEL COLLINS during the negotiations leading to the ANGLO-IRISH TREATY

(1921), which he rejected, and he was imprisoned for a short time during the CIVIL WAR. After working as a journalist in Paris and London he returned to Ireland, where he worked as a sub-editor on the *Irish Press,* 1931. He became a leading member of the short-lived COMHAIRLE NA POBLACHTA and organised the first convention of SAOR ÉIRE, 1931; he succeeded MAURICE 'MOSS' TWOMEY as chief of staff of the IRA, 1936–38, but his call for the creation of a republican political party was rejected by the Army Council, from which he was ousted by SEÁN RUSSELL.

Following the adoption of the Constitution of Ireland (1937), in the same year that he was called to the bar, MacBride saw no further use for the IRA, and he severed his connection in protest at the bombing campaign in England launched by Russell in 1939. Called to the inner bar, 1943, he won a reputation during the 1940s for his defence of republicans charged under emergency legislation; his challenge to the constitutionality of the OFFENCES AGAINST THE STATE ACT (1939) led to the release of fifty-three internees, 1 December 1939.

Joint founder of CLANN NA POBLACHTA, 1946, he led the party in the first inter-party government, 1948–51, in which he was Minister for External Affairs. He drafted the white paper that formed the basis for the LONG-TERM RECOVERY PROGRAMME (1949). He was vice-president of the Convention for European Economic Co-operation in Paris, 1948, and was involved in the establishment of the Council of Europe, 1949, the Geneva Convention for the Protection of War Victims, 1949, and the European Convention on Human Rights, 1950. When the MOTHER AND CHILD SCHEME, introduced by the Minister for Health, DR NOEL BROWNE, proved unacceptable to the Catholic bishops and the Irish Medical Association, MacBride asked for Browne's resignation. The government fell shortly afterwards.

While he did not participate in the second inter-party government, 1954–57, MacBride agreed not to oppose it. However, when a new IRA campaign in 1956 prompted harsh government measures, including internment, his motion of no confidence, supported by Fianna Fáil, brought down the government, January 1957. He lost his seat in the ensuing general election and failed again in 1958, 1959, and 1961. On behalf of Gerard Lawless he challenged the constitutionality of internment in November 1957; the European Court of Human Rights ruled in 1959 that while the government had the right to intern people, the European Court could decide for itself whether conditions existed in a state to justify it. He acted in the fluoridation case of *Ryan v. Attorney-General* (1965) and in the MCGEE CASE, which established the right to import contraceptives.

As chairman of the Irish branch of the IRISH NATIONAL CAUCUS he led the campaign in 1983 against the award of contracts by the US Air Force to Short Brothers, Belfast, because of the company's reputation for discrimination against Catholics. In November 1984 he put forward a set of principles designed to end discrimination in Northern Ireland, which became known as the MACBRIDE PRINCIPLES. He was secretary-general of the International Commission of Jurists from 1963 until 1970, when he resigned after discovering that it was indirectly financed by the CIA. A founder-member and chairman of Amnesty International, 1961, he was Irish representative in the Assembly of the Council of Europe and UN commissioner in Namibia, 1973, and a joint author of the UN Declaration of Human Rights. He was the first Irish person to receive the Nobel Peace Prize (shared with the Prime Minister of Japan, Eisaku Sato), 1974, and was also awarded the Lenin Peace Prize, 1977, and the Dag Hammarskjöld Award for International Solidarity, 1981. He published *Civil Liberty* (1948) and *Our People—Our Money* (1951).

MacBride Principles, a name given to a set of nine principles put forward in November 1984 by SEÁN MACBRIDE, designed to end discrimination against Catholics in employment by making their adoption a condition of American investment in Northern Ireland. They sought increased Catholic representation in the work force (including managerial and administrative posts), security for Catholics at work and travelling to and from work, and training schemes for employees from the Catholic population. Approved by the American Federation of Labor and Congress of Industrial Organizations (AFL-CIO) and the US National Council of Churches, they were adopted by some sixteen states of the United States. In May 1995 the International Relations Committee of the US Congress voted to link aid to Northern Ireland with the MacBride Principles.

Mac Cába, Alasdair (1886–1972), teacher, politician (Sinn Féin), and businessman; born in Keash, Co. Sligo, educated at St Patrick's College, Dublin. Principal teacher at

Drumnagranchy National School, Co. Sligo, he joined the IRB, 1913, and represented Connacht on the Supreme Council, 1915–16. He was arrested for possession of explosives, 1915; though acquitted, he was dismissed from his teaching post. During the EASTER RISING (1916) he was responsible for creating diversions in Cos. Cavan, Longford, and Sligo, following which he was on the run. He assisted COUNT PLUNKETT during the Co. Roscommon by-election of 1917, after which he was arrested but released following a thirty-day hunger strike. He endured further terms of imprisonment in England and the Curragh. As a Sinn Féin member of Dáil Éireann for Sligo-Mayo, 1918–21, he was close to MICHAEL COLLINS during the WAR OF INDEPENDENCE and supported the ANGLO-IRISH TREATY (1921). Representing Leitrim-Sligo, 1923–24, he became a member of CUMANN NA NGAEDHEAL but resigned during the ARMY MUTINY and retired from politics to resume his teaching career. He jointly founded the Educational Building Society, 1935, and retained his teaching post until 1941, when he became the company's managing director.

McCafferty, Captain John (1838–?), Fenian; born in Sandusky, Ohio, of Irish parentage. After service with 'Morgan's Guerillas' in the Confederate Army during the American Civil War (1861–65), with a reputation for bravery and as a skilled tactician, he joined the FENIANS. He travelled to Ireland in 1865 but was arrested in Dungarvan, together with WILLIAM MACKEY LOMASNEY; they were freed on condition that they return to the United States. Returning to Ireland, he was introduced by JOHN DEVOY to leading Dublin republicans as a leader for the proposed rising. When the rising failed to materialise, McCafferty and John Flood organised the raid on Chester Castle, 11 March 1867, which was betrayed by John J. Corydon. Arrested aboard the *New Draper* in Dublin Bay, he was sentenced to death, 1 May, later commuted to life imprisonment, and deported, June 1871. His scheme for kidnapping the Prince of Wales was rejected both by CLAN NA GAEL and the IRB. He was again in Ireland during the Co. Mayo by-election of 1874, when he challenged the IRB candidate, JOHN O'CONNOR POWER, to a duel. A prominent member of the INVINCIBLES, he fled Ireland after the PHOENIX PARK MURDERS. He was quoted by the *Irishman* as saying in Paris, 'Terrorism is the lawful weapon of the weak against the strong.'

McCartan, Dr Patrick (1878–1966), politician (Sinn Féin); born in Carrickmore, Co. Tyrone, educated at St Patrick's College, Armagh, and St Malachy's, Belfast. After moving to the United States, 1905, he worked as a barman in Philadelphia, joined CLAN NA GAEL, and became a close associate of JOSEPH MCGARRITY. Returning to Ireland, 1905, he qualified as a doctor and practised medicine in Co. Tyrone. He maintained a close association with the IRB on behalf of McGarrity and for a time edited IRISH FREEDOM. A member of the first Dáil Éireann, 1918, as an envoy of the Irish Republic he travelled to the United States but was refused an audience with President Wilson. He unsuccessfully attempted to resolve the differences between ÉAMON DE VALERA, JUDGE DANIEL COHALAN, and JOHN DEVOY. Visiting Soviet Russia, December 1921, he secured a Treaty of Recognition between Russia and the Irish Republic, but it was never signed. He brought part of the RUSSIAN CROWN JEWELS to America as collateral for a loan of $25,000 advanced by de Valera to Russian representatives in Washington. British intelligence described him as a 'very dangerous man'. He voted for the ANGLO-IRISH TREATY (1921), though he did not agree with it, and left politics to resume his medical practice. He came third as independent republican in the election for President of Ireland, 1945, and was a member of Seanad Éireann, 1948–51. He published *With de Valera in America* (1935).

McCarthy, Justin (1830–1912), writer, historian, and politician (Irish Party); born in Cork. He left school at fifteen to work in a solicitor's office before joining the *Cork Examiner*, 1847. He covered the trials of the Young Ireland leaders WILLIAM SMITH O'BRIEN and THOMAS FRANCIS MEAGHER, whose cause he espoused. Moving to England, he worked on the *Northern Daily News* (Liverpool), 1853–60, and *Morning Star* (London), 1860–64, of which he became editor, 1864–68. A leader-writer for the *Daily News* from 1870, he taught himself to read German, Italian, French, and Spanish.

At the invitation of CHARLES STEWART PARNELL he successfully contested the Co. Longford seat in the British House of Commons, 1880, after which he became the first vice-chairman of the IRISH PARTY, 27 December 1880, and one of Parnell's chief lieutenants. At the end of the 41-hour sitting of the House of Commons on the Protection of Persons and Property (Ireland) Bill on 2 February 1881 (which ended OBSTRUCTIONISM when the speaker put the question under a motion of closure) he led his colleagues from the chamber. On 3 February 1881 he was among thirty-six members suspended when protesting at the arrest of MICHAEL DAVITT. He became first president of the National Land League of Great Britain in March 1881. During the crisis caused by the verdict in the *O'Shea v. O'Shea and Parnell* divorce case he was delegated by the Liberal leader W. E. GLADSTONE to inform Parnell that he could not support home rule if Parnell remained leader of the Irish Party. When this became public after the publication of Gladstone's letter to Morley, Parnell refused to resign the chairmanship of the party. After the split in the party McCarthy became reluctant chairman of the majority anti-Parnellite faction, the IRISH NATIONAL LEAGUE, December 1890 to 3 February 1896, though he remained on friendly terms with Parnell. His followers won seventy-two seats in the general election of 1892, when he lost his Derry seat but regained Longford. Ill-health and failing eyesight led to his resignation from the chairmanship of the party, 1896, when JOHN DILLON succeeded him.

Apart from fiction and biographical works he published *A History of Our Own Times* (5 vols., 1877–1901), *The Story of Mr Gladstone* (1898), *Modern England* (1898), *Reminiscences* (1899), *The Story of an Irishman* (1904), and *Irish Recollections* (1911).

His son, Justin Huntly McCarthy (1861–1936), was also a member of the Irish Party (a Parnellite until he followed his father in rejecting Parnell's leadership), translator, and prolific author.

McCartney, Robert (born 1936), lawyer and politician (Ulster Unionist Party and United Kingdom Unionist Party); born in Belfast, educated at QUB and called to the bar. He led a delegation of Northern lawyers and businessmen to talks with the Taoiseach, DR GARRET FITZGERALD, on FitzGerald's proposed 'constitutional crusade'. Leader of the Campaign for Equal Citizenship, he was expelled from the Unionist Party, 1987, for defying an agreement that sitting Unionists would not be opposed in the general election. Having described Northern Ireland as a 'political wasteland', he was critical of the DOWNING STREET DECLARATION (1993). Winning the North Down seat in the British House of Commons in a by-election, May 1995, on 15 November 1995 he stood alongside REV. IAN PAISLEY (whom he had described in 1981 as a 'fascist') and DAVID TRIMBLE to denounce the ten-year-old ANGLO-IRISH AGREEMENT. He formed the UNITED KINGDOM UNIONIST PARTY in 1996. When difficulties arose over the decommissioning of IRA arms before talks, he led his party out of the Northern Ireland Forum, 16 July 1997, in protest at the participation of Sinn Féin in talks. He opposed the BELFAST AGREEMENT (1998), saying it would produce more violence. His party split in December 1998 over an exit strategy from the Northern Ireland Assembly if Sinn Féin took seats in the Executive. He denounced the PATTEN REPORT (1999) and lost his House of Commons seat to Lady Sylvia Hermon (UUP) in June 2001.

McCormick, Liam (1916–1996), architect; born in Derry, educated at St Columb's College. After studying architecture at the University of Liverpool he practised in Derry from 1947, when he won a competition for a new church in Ennistimon, Co. Clare. He designed St Aengus's Church, Burt, Co. Donegal ('my pagan building'), inspired by and aligned on the hill-fort of the Grianán of Aileach. In 1968 he was awarded the Triennial Gold Medal of the Royal Institute of the Architects of Ireland for St Aengus's Church; he also won an award from the Royal Institute of British Architects for a church at Steelstown, Derry. Regarded as the foremost church architect in the country, he designed some twenty-seven new churches and church reconstructions in Ireland and England.

McCracken Tribunal, the Tribunal of Inquiry into Alleged Payments by Dunne's Stores, chaired by Mr Justice Brian McCracken. The report of the tribunal, published on 25 August 1997, found that the former leader of Fianna Fáil and former Taoiseach CHARLES HAUGHEY had received £1.3 million from Ben Dunne, one of the owners of Dunne's Stores. Having found Haughey's evidence either 'unacceptable' or 'unbelievable' on eleven different points, McCracken forwarded papers in the case to the Director of Public Prosecutions for consideration in relation to Haughey's evidence under oath, but attempts to prosecute him were unsuccessful. Other findings were that Michael Lowry, a former Fine Gael minister and sitting member of Dáil Éireann, had entered into arrangements with Ben Dunne to facilitate tax evasion. The findings of the tribunal led the Oireachtas to establish the MORIARTY TRIBUNAL to investigate the financial affairs of Haughey and Lowry; it also led to the inquiry into the activities of Haughey's financial adviser, DES

TRAYNOR, the creator of offshore tax-avoidance accounts (see ANSBACHER INQUIRY).

McCullough, Denis (1883–1968), republican; born in Belfast, the son of a Fenian, educated at Christian Brothers' school. A piano-tuner by trade, he established a business in Belfast, 1909, later moving it to Dublin, 1919, where he traded under the name McCullough's Ltd, becoming McCullough-Piggott Ltd from 1968. After joining the IRB, 1901, he became disillusioned with its lack of discipline and its deep-seated traditionalism. He recruited younger men, including BULMER HOBSON, with whom he founded the DUNGANNON CLUBS, to give new impetus to the organisation. Co-opted to the IRB Supreme Council, 1906, he was director of the IRB in Ulster. He played a leading role, together with Hobson and THOMAS J. CLARKE, in moving the IRB along more militant lines after the founding of the IRISH VOLUNTEERS. He supported the EASTER RISING (1916), though he was not informed of the final details. He was detailed to bring 132 volunteers from Belfast to Coalisland, Co. Tyrone, to meet DR PATRICK MCCARTAN and travel south to Co. Fermanagh to join LIAM MELLOWS in Connacht, but because of the general confusion surrounding the rising he returned with his men to Belfast on Sunday evening and so had no direct involvement. He was arrested the following Friday. His account of events was published in the *Capuchin Annual*, 1966.

MacCurtain, Tomás (1884–1920), politician (Sinn Féin); born in Ballyknockane, Co. Cork, educated at North Monastery Christian Brothers' School, Cork. Secretary of the Blackpool [Cork] Branch of the Gaelic League, he left his employment in the City of Cork Steam Packet Company to become a Gaelic League teacher. Returning to Cork to work at a local mill, 1907, he joined Sinn Féin and was inducted into the IRB. When Fianna Éireann was established in Cork he was treasurer and Irish-teacher, 1911–14. With TERENCE MACSWINEY he joined the Irish Volunteers on its formation in Cork, 14 December 1913. He led protests against the application of economic conscription by local employers to persuade Irish Volunteers to support the British war effort.

The entire Volunteer movement in Cork had been mobilised in preparation for the EASTER RISING (1916), with orders to meet at Crookstown. On learning of the countermanding order, MacCurtain allowed units to proceed as arranged to Crookstown, where exercises took place. Remaining in the area until the following night, he was astonished to learn that a rising had taken place. Awaiting a confirmatory despatch from Dublin, he ordered that Cork Volunteers were to act only in a defensive capacity. During the week of fighting in Dublin, BISHOP DANIEL COHALAN and the lord mayor, T. C. Butterfield, arranged with Captain Dickie of the British army that there would be no arrests of Volunteers in Cork in return for the surrender of arms. Guarantees made on the British side were not honoured, and MacCurtain and ten other Volunteers were arrested, 2 May. He served varying terms of imprisonment.

During the WAR OF INDEPENDENCE, MacCurtain was active in the organising of an efficient despatch system between county and city brigades, in drilling, discipline, and the capture of arms. He was elected lord mayor of Cork, 30 January 1920, the first republican to hold the office. At 1:12 a.m. on Saturday 20 March he was murdered at his home. The verdict of the coroner's court, 17 April, was that 'the murder was organised and carried out by the Royal Irish Constabulary.' District Inspector Oswald Swanzy, one of those charged with the murder by the coroner's court, was shot dead in Lisburn, Co. Antrim, 22 August 1920.

MacDermot, Frank (1886–1975), soldier, barrister, politician (National Centre Party and Fine Gael), and author; born in Coolavin, Co. Sligo, educated at the University of Oxford and called to the bar. After serving in the British army during the First World War he worked in a merchant bank in New York. Returning to Ireland in the late 1920s, he was elected as an independent member of Dáil Éireann for Co. Roscommon, 1932. Later that year, with JAMES DILLON, he founded the NATIONAL CENTRE PARTY, which secured eleven seats in the general election of January 1933. Its opposition to the Fianna Fáil government brought the party close to CUMANN NA NGAEDHEAL and the BLUESHIRTS, and MacDermot was instrumental in bringing about a merger of the parties as FINE GAEL, September 1933, of which he was vice-president. Unhappy with the leadership of EOIN O'DUFFY and his support for Mussolini's invasion of Ethiopia, MacDermot resigned as vice-president of Fine Gael, 1936, and sat as an independent for the remainder of the term. Nominated to Seanad Éireann by Éamon de Valera, 1937, he jointly sponsored a motion for a commission of inquiry into vocational education. He left politics to become American correspondent of the *Sunday Times,* 1942, and was later its Paris correspondent. His historical study, *Theobald Wolfe Tone,* was published in 1939.

MacDermott, Martin (1823–1905), author and poet. While training as an architect he was one of the earliest contributors of poetry to the *Nation* and the *Irish Felon.* A member of YOUNG IRELAND, he was later a founder-member of the SOUTHWARK LITERARY CLUB and the IRISH LITERARY SOCIETY. His best-known poem is 'The Cúilin'. He edited several volumes of poetry, including *Songs and Ballads of Young Ireland* (1896), and was the last surviving poet of the *Nation.*

Mac Diarmada, Seán (1884–1916), republican soldier; born in Scregg, Kiltyclogher, Co. Leitrim, educated at Corracloona National School and evening classes at Tullynamoyle, Dowra, Co. Cavan, where he studied Irish and bookkeeping. He worked in Glasgow at a variety of jobs, returning to Ireland in 1905. Working in Belfast, he was for a time a member of the Ancient Order of Hibernians. BULMER HOBSON and DENIS MCCULLOUGH employed him as an organiser for the DUNGANNON CLUBS and inducted him into the IRB, 1906. He organised the unsuccessful Sinn Féin campaign for C. J. Dolan in the North Leitrim by-election, 1908.

Recruited by THOMAS J. CLARKE, he moved to Dublin as a full-time organiser for the IRB, 1908. He was joint founder and editor of IRISH FREEDOM, 1910. An attack of polio in 1912 left him disabled, but he continued to work for the IRB; as secretary of the Supreme Council he was closely involved in the founding of the IRISH VOLUNTEERS, 25 November 1913. He was estranged from Hobson when the latter agreed to the virtual take-over of the Volunteers by JOHN REDMOND, July 1914. He was sentenced to four months' imprisonment with hard labour under the DEFENCE OF THE REALM ACT for making anti-recruiting speeches, 9 June 1915; his election to the executive committee of the Gaelic League led to the resignation of DR DOUGLAS HYDE. On his release, 20 September, he was co-opted onto the Military Council of the IRB, at Clarke's suggestion; at its last meeting before the EASTER RISING (1916) it adopted his motion 'to fight at the earliest date possible.'

Mac Diarmada was joint author (with JOSEPH PLUNKETT) of the CASTLE DOCUMENT, which was intended to produce a favourable climate for the rising among the Volunteers. When the plans for the rising were discovered by Hobson and EOIN MACNEILL on Thursday 20 April, Mac Diarmada persuaded MacNeill that the arrival of the *Aud* would mean the success of the rising. However, when news of the scuttling of the *Aud* and of the capture of ROGER CASEMENT reached MacNeill, who countermanded orders for an insurrection, Mac Diarmada and his colleagues changed the date to the following Monday, 24 April. A member of the Provisional Government of the Irish Republic, he remained in the GPO until the building was burned. He was court-martialled and shot by firing squad, 12 May 1916.

MacDonagh, Thomas (1878–1916), revolutionary and poet; born in Cloughjordan, Co. Tipperary, educated at UCD. He taught in St Kieran's College, Kilkenny, 1901–03, where he joined the Gaelic League. After moving to St Colman's College, Fermoy, Co. Cork, 1903–08, he was a founder-member of the Association of Secondary Teachers, Ireland (ASTI). He met PATRICK PEARSE while on holiday in the Aran Islands and was invited to teach at ST ENDA'S SCHOOL while studying for his MA degree, 1911, after which he became a lecturer in the English Department of University College, Dublin. He was joint editor (with JOSEPH PLUNKETT) of the *Irish Review,* 1911, and joint founder (with Plunkett and EDWARD MARTYN) of the Irish Theatre, 1914, which produced his play *Pagans* (1915).

A founder-member of the IRISH VOLUNTEERS, 25 November 1913, for which he was director of training, he organised the collection of weapons in the HOWTH GUN-RUNNING (1914) and the parade that accompanied the remains of JEREMIAH O'DONOVAN ROSSA to Glasnevin Cemetery, Dublin, 1 August 1915. A member of the IRB from September 1915, he was co-opted in April 1916 to the secret Military Council that planned the EASTER RISING (1916). Commandant of the 2nd Battalion of the Dublin Brigade at Jacob's factory, Bishop Street, during the rising, he was shot by firing squad on 3 May. He was married to Muriel Gifford, whose sister, GRACE GIFFORD, was married to Plunkett in his prison cell the day before his execution.

MacDonagh's works include *Through the Ivory Gate* (poems, 1902), *When Dawn is Come* (produced at the Abbey Theatre, 1908), *Songs of Myself* (poems, 1910), *Metempsychosis, or A Mad World* (play, 1912), and *Lyrical Poems* (1913). His PhD thesis, *Literature in Ireland,* was published after his death in 1916. *The Poetical Works of Thomas MacDonagh* (1916) was edited by JAMES STEPHENS.

His younger brother, Joseph MacDonagh (1883–1922), also a member of the republican movement, taught at St Enda's School. A member of Dáil Éireann and director of the BELFAST BOYCOTT, he was arrested at the beginning of the Civil War and died shortly after his release in November 1922.

Thomas MacDonagh's son, Donagh MacDonagh (1912–1958), was a district justice and an author. Joint editor (with Lennox Robinson) of *The Oxford Book of Irish Verse* (1956), he was a student of folklore, a radio broadcaster, and a collector of Dublin slang.

MacDonald, Dr Walter (1854–1920), clergyman (Catholic) and author; born in Mooncoin, Co. Kilkenny, educated at St Patrick's College, Maynooth, ordained in 1876. After teaching in St Kieran's College, Kilkenny, he returned to Maynooth, 1881, where he was professor of dogmatic theology and professor of canon law. His first major work, *Motion, Its Origin and Conservation* (1898), in which he examined the relationship between theology and science, was placed on the Index of Prohibited Books for being in conflict with the doctrine of free will, but in deference to his piety the decree was not published; subsequent theological works were refused an *imprimatur*.

During his career at Maynooth he was involved in a number of other controversies. He pressed for the appointment of professors by open competition and for security of tenure. He also supported CHARLES STEWART PARNELL after the split in the Irish Party. He championed the cause of Father Michael O'Hickey (see GAELIC LEAGUE), who had been dismissed by the bishops, and supported JAMES LARKIN. His circle of friends included SEÁN O'CASEY. He was again in conflict with the bishops when he pressed for reforms in the managerial system of national education and for supporting the right of Catholic students to attend Trinity College, Dublin.

His published works include *Ethical Questions of Peace and War, with Special Reference to Ireland* (1919), which caused controversy, *Some Ethical Aspects of the Social Question: Suggestions for Priests* (1920), and *A History of the Parish of Mooncoin* (1960). *Reminiscences of a Maynooth Professor* was published in 1925, edited by DENIS R. GWYNN.

Macdonnell, Sir Antony (1844–1925), civil servant; born in Shragh, Co. Mayo, educated at Queen's College, Galway, where he took the Peel Gold Medal, 1864. After entering the Indian civil service in the 1860s he became an expert on the organising of famine relief. He accepted the post of Under-Secretary for Ireland, 1902, from the Chief Secretary, GEORGE WYNDHAM, with the proviso that he be granted additional powers; he also sought educational and economic reforms. Sympathetic to the Liberal Party (his brother was a member of the Irish Party), to Unionists he appeared to be a home-ruler, while to home-rulers he appeared a renegade. In his efforts to expedite a solution to the land question he supported the LAND CONFERENCE, which influenced Wyndham's Irish Land Act (1903) (see LAND ACTS).

Following Wyndham's departure, hastened by the controversy over devolution, MacDonnell served under WALTER LONG, JAMES BRYCE, and AUGUSTINE BIRRELL. His IRISH COUNCIL BILL (1907), proposing the establishment of an Irish Central Council exercising local autonomy, was denounced from all sides. When he failed to secure support for suppressing disorder he resigned, 1908. Sitting in the House of Lords as Baron Shragh of Swinford, he served as chairman of the Royal Commission on the Civil Service, 1912–14, and attended the IRISH CONVENTION (1917–18). He urged EARL FRENCH in October 1918 to abandon plans for introducing CONSCRIPTION. He declined a seat in the Senate of the Irish Free State, December 1922.

McDyer, Canon James (1911–1987), clergyman (Catholic) and social reformer; born in Kilraine, Glenties, Co. Donegal, educated at St Patrick's College, Maynooth, ordained in 1937. He ministered in England until appointed curate on Tory Island, 1947–51. As curate at Gleann Cholm Cille from 1951 and parish priest from 6 March 1961, appalled at the high level of emigration and the inexorable decline of the community, he set about its regeneration and studied rural development on the Continent and in the United States. He founded Glencolumbkille Co-Operative Society, 1962, which fostered and encouraged local hand-knitters. His Errigal Co-Op, 1962, a vegetable-growing and processing project, grew from an initial work force of 30 to 153; aided by Comhlucht Siúcra Éireann and Gaeltarra Éireann, and under Father McDyer's chairmanship, the new co-op achieved early profitability; when fish-processing replaced vegetables in 1973 it became Earagail Éisc Tta, 1975.

Following the opening of a holiday village, 1968, he founded a development association, 1970. A craft shop was opened in Anne Street, Dublin, 1970, and the Glenbeigh Hotel, Malin Beg, Co. Donegal, was bought in 1971, in which year he became parish priest of Carrick and Gleann Cholm Cille. The development association was wound up in 1980. His pet project was the folk village, which spanned three centuries of Co. Donegal life and included among its novel features a century-old schoolhouse and a SHEBEEN, complete with still. He published *The Glencolumbkille Story* (1962) and his autobiography, *Father McDyer of Glencolumbkille* (1982).

McElligott, James J. (1893–1974), civil servant; born in Tralee, Co. Kerry, educated at UCD. He entered the civil service in 1913 and served in the Local Government Board. A member of the Irish Volunteers, he served in the GPO, Dublin, during the EASTER RISING (1916), for which he was imprisoned. He was a freelance financial journalist and later managing editor of the *Statist* (London). In 1923 he was invited to help establish the Department of Finance, of which he became secretary and *de facto* head of the civil service, 1927–53, in succession to JOSEPH BRENNAN. Considered one of the most influential civil servants of his era, he served on the Banking Commission (1926), when he expressed the opinion in his minority report that there were too many banks in the country; he was chairman of the TARIFF COMMISSION (1926–30). A conservative, he advocated economic orthodoxy and retrenchment of public finances, a policy supported by the Minister for Finance, ERNEST BLYTHE, during the depression that followed the Wall Street Crash, 1929. Essentially anti-Keynesian, he favoured a *laissez-faire* approach. From 1932 he served under SEÁN MACENTEE, over whom he exercised influence. He opposed the slum clearance policy of the 1930s and the payment of the children's allowance, 1944, and disapproved of Keynesian attempts to expand the economy, 1948–51. He was much happier with the deflationary approach taken by MacEntee, 1951–54. In 1950 he supported a proposal by T. K. WHITAKER for the creation of the post of deputy assistant secretary of the department (which was given to Whitaker). He was governor of the CENTRAL BANK, 1953–60.

McElligott, Thomas J. (1888–1961), policeman and republican; born in Duagh, Co. Kerry, educated at national school. A member of the RIC, 1907, in which he became a sergeant, he realised, as did JEREMIAH MEE, the pressures to which nationally minded policemen would be subjected, and supported republican causes. He established the Irish Branch of the National Union of Police and Prison Officers, of which he became chairman, April 1918. His support for Sinn Féin, for the anti-CONSCRIPTION campaign and for the Labour Party (using the pen-name 'Pro Patria') forced his resignation from the RIC, May 1919. He was a friend of THOMAS JOHNSON, and he provided MICHAEL COLLINS with valuable intelligence on the *modus operandi* of the RIC. An inspector with the WHITE CROSS, he established the Resigned and Dismissed Members of the RIC and DMP, 1916–21. Though he opposed the ANGLO-IRISH TREATY (1921), he was nominated by Collins and ARTHUR GRIFFITH to advise on the police force of the Irish Free State (see CIVIC GUARD). The government accepted his recommendation for an unarmed force. While imprisoned during the CIVIL WAR he went on a 35-day hunger strike.

A supporter of FIANNA FÁIL, he negotiated with ÉAMON DE VALERA on behalf of the Resigned and Dismissed Members of the RIC and DMP. He was critical of the financial agreement made between de Valera and the British government in 1938 that ended the 'ECONOMIC WAR'. He published pamphlets on economic and social theory, including *National Monetary Policy and National Agricultural Policy* (1943). Breaking with Fianna Fáil, he worked for the welfare of republican prisoners during the 1930s and later supported CLANN NA POBLACHTA.

MacEntee, Seán (1889–1984), politician (Sinn Féin and Fianna Fáil); born in Belfast, educated at St Malachy's College and Belfast Municipal Institute of Technology, where he qualified as an engineer. A member the Socialist Party of Ireland in Belfast, he joined the Irish Volunteers and fought in the EASTER RISING (1916). Released under the general amnesty, 17 June 1917, he opposed the ANGLO-IRISH TREATY (1921). After supporting the Republicans in the CIVIL WAR he became national treasurer of Sinn Féin, 1924. A founder-member of Fianna Fáil, 1926, he was joint treasurer until 1932, a member of the National Executive from 1926, and national vice-president, 1933–65.

He was Minister for Finance, 1932–39, Minister for Industry and Commerce, 1939–41, Minister for Local Government and Health, 1941–48, Minister for Finance,

1931–34, and Minister for Health, 1937–65. As Minister for Local Government and Public Health he opposed the non-means-tested children's allowance (but failed to prevent its introduction in 1944) and unemployment assistance. He was again Minister for Finance in 1951 (against SEÁN LEMASS's warnings). Repeatedly at odds with Lemass in the Department of Industry and Commerce over the demarcation between their departments, his deflationary policies were blamed for Fianna Fáil's poor showing in the 1954 general election. When it returned to power in 1957 Lemass prevented MacEntee's return to the Department of Finance; instead he was given Health and then Social Welfare. He was a member of the Council of State from 1948 and Tánaiste, 1939–65.

After retiring from active politics in 1969 he resumed his engineering consultancy. He published *Poems* (1918) and *Episode at Easter* (1966). His daughter is the poet Máire Mhac an tSaoi (born 1922).

Mac Eoin, General Seán (1894–1973), soldier and politician (Cumann na nGaedheal and Fine Gael); born in Bunlahy, Co. Longford, where he became a blacksmith. As a company commander in the Irish Volunteers, 1914, and later commandant of the 1st Battalion, Longford Brigade, during the WAR OF INDEPENDENCE he was noted for his fair treatment of prisoners. He led the IRA in one of the most celebrated events of the war when, anticipating an attack by BLACK AND TANS on Ballinalee, he routed them after an all-night battle, 3 November 1920, earning himself the nickname 'Blacksmith of Ballinalee'. Having defeated a force of AUXILIARIES, 2 February, he was captured at Mullingar Railway Station and severely wounded in an attempted escape, 21 March 1921. He was court-martialled and sentenced to death for the murder of District Inspector McGrath; a rescue attempt, planned by MICHAEL COLLINS and executed by EMMET DALTON, failed, but ÉAMON DE VALERA made his release one of the conditions for a truce.

Mac Eoin nominated de Valera for the position of President of the Irish Republic, August 1921. He accepted the ANGLO-IRISH TREATY (1921), saying, 'As long as the armed forces of Britain are gone and the armed forces of Ireland remain we can develop our own nation in our own way.' He took possession of Longford Barracks from the British garrison, January 1922, and during the CIVIL WAR was officer commanding the Western Command of the Free State army, of which he was later chief of staff, 1923. Resigning his command, he was elected to Dáil Éireann for Sligo, 1929–63. He jointly founded the National Defence Association, 1929, and supported the BLUESHIRTS during the early 1930s. He served in the two inter-party governments, as Minister for Justice, 1948–51, and Minister for Defence, March–June 1951 and 1954–57. He was an unsuccessful candidate in two elections for President of Ireland, losing to SEÁN T. O'KELLY in 1945 and to de Valera in 1959. He retired from political life in 1965.

Mac Eoin, Lieutenant-General Seán (1910–1998), soldier; born in Cooley, Co. Louth. Commissioned in 1931, during the emergency years of the Second World War he was officer commanding the 12th Infantry Battalion, which won the title of Premier Unit, 1944. He became chief of staff of the Defence Forces, January 1960, the first graduate of the Military College to do so. He was commander of the 20,000-strong multinational UN force in Congo, 1961–62, for which he earned international acclaim. He resumed his position as chief of staff in 1962 and retired in 1971.

McFadden, Canon James (1842–1917), clergyman (Catholic) and land agitator; born in Carrigart, Co. Donegal, educated at St Patrick's College, Maynooth. As parish priest of Gaoth Dobhair (Gweedore) from 1875 he was active in the defence of smallholders against rackrenting and evictions and wrote several pamphlets on the land question for the LAND LEAGUE. During the PLAN OF CAMPAIGN he was imprisoned, 1888, for inciting parishioners to withhold rents. While he was being arrested at Doirí Beaga (Derrybeg) chapel for a repetition of the offence, a fracas developed between local people and the RIC, in which District Inspector William Martin died after striking his head off a stone when he fell to the ground, 3 February 1889. McFadden and twelve others were charged with manslaughter. Their defence counsel, T. M. HEALY, made a plea bargain whereby the death penalty would not be imposed. McFadden was bound to the peace for two years, while the others received sentences of up to thirty years' imprisonment. He subsequently played little part in the national agitation and finished his clerical career as parish priest of Inishkeel, Glenties, Co. Donegal, 1901–17. Known locally as An Sagart Mór ('the big priest') for the uncompromising manner in which he managed his parish and parishioners, he visited the United States, 1898–99 and 1900–02, to raise money for the building of St Eunan's Cathedral, Letterkenny.

McGarrity, Joseph (1874–1940), republican; born in Carrickmore, Co. Tyrone, educated at national school. He emigrated to America and settled in Philadelphia, where he worked at a variety of jobs until he bought a tavern and liquor business (which he lost in 1919). He was a prominent member of CLAN NA GAEL from 1893; his support for Irish causes over the course of his life was said to have cost him $100,000. He encouraged the DUNGANNON CLUBS, the Gaelic League, Sinn Féin and the Irish Volunteers and was president of the American Volunteers' Aid Association. He was responsible for the prosecution in Philadelphia of the ABBEY THEATRE players for performing an 'immoral play' (*The Playboy of the Western World*), September 1911.

Throughout the WAR OF INDEPENDENCE he supported Dáil Éireann through the FRIENDS OF IRISH FREEDOM. The *Irish Press* (Philadelphia), which he founded, ran from 23 March 1918 to 6 May 1922, at a cost of $60,000. He managed Éamon de Valera's American tour, 1919–20, and supported de Valera in the dispute with JOHN DEVOY and JUDGE DANIEL COHALAN that split the Friends of Irish Freedom, 1920. He led the AMERICAN ASSOCIATION FOR THE RECOGNITION OF THE IRISH REPUBLIC on de Valera's behalf.

Opposed to the ANGLO-IRISH TREATY (1921), following the defeat of the republican cause in the CIVIL WAR he continued his support for the IRA. As leader of the extremists in CLAN NA GAEL he described de Valera's entry into Dáil Éireann in 1927 as an 'act of treason'. Temporarily reconciled, he broke completely with him when de Valera's government moved against the IRA in 1936. One of his last acts was to support SEÁN RUSSELL in the demand for an IRA 'war' against Britain, but he could drum up only token financial support in America for the venture. He was expelled from Ireland while on holiday in 1939 and returned to the United States by way of Germany, where he unsuccessfully sought aid for the IRA from Hermann Göring.

McGarrity's library of ten thousand books, many of them rare, passed to Villanova University, Pennsylvania, when Clan na Gael was unable to house them in accordance with his will. His poetry, *Celtic Moods and Memories* (1942), with a foreword by Pádraic Colum, was published in New York. IRA communiqués were signed in his name (*J. J. McGarrity*) up to the end of the twentieth century.

McGee, Thomas D'Arcy (1825–1868), journalist and Young Irelander; born in Carlingford, Co. Louth, educated at Wexford. Emigrating to the United States, 1842, he worked as a clerk for the *Pilot* (Boston), which he later edited. He returned to Europe as parliamentary correspondent of the *Freeman's Journal* and subsequently of the *Nation*, in which he published patriotic verse under a variety of pen-names ('Amergin', 'Montanus', 'Sarsfield', and 'Gilla-Patrick'). As secretary of the IRISH CONFEDERATION he was sent to Scotland on an unsuccessful recruiting mission before the attempted insurrection of 1848; following its collapse he escaped to the United States.

After founding the *New York Nation*, he moved to Boston, where he founded the *American Celt*, 1850, which, initially republican, became moderate and constitutional. He moved to Buffalo and then returned to New York, where he was attacked by THOMAS DEVIN REILLY and other influential figures. Settling in Montréal, 1857, he founded the *New Era* and entered Canadian politics. He played a prominent role in guiding Canada towards dominion home rule and was president of the Council of the Legislative Assembly, 1862 and 1864, and Minister of Agriculture and Emigration, 1867. Following his denunciation of Fenian raids on Canada he was murdered outside his home in Ottawa, 7 April 1868.

His works include *The Life of Art MacMurrough* (1847), *Irish Writers of the Seventeenth Century* (1847), *History of Irish Settlers in North America* (1852), and *A Popular History of Ireland* (3 vols., 1862–69).

McGee Case. Mary McGee, married since 1968, lived in a mobile home with her husband and four children. Because her pregnancies had been accompanied by serious complications, medical advice suggested that another pregnancy might result in paralysis or death. As a form of birth control her doctor prescribed spermicidal jelly, which was not available in Ireland. Mrs McGee's attempts to import it were frustrated by the Customs authorities when a parcel was seized under the CRIMINAL LAW AMENDMENT ACT (1935). Aided by the IRISH FAMILY PLANNING ASSOCIATION, Mrs McGee sought legal redress. Her case was dismissed in the High Court but upheld on appeal to the Supreme Court, which ruled by a majority decision, 19

December 1973, that it was unconstitutional to prohibit the importing of contraceptives. The landmark decision legalised the importing of contraceptives for married couples. In 1974 a bill proposing the removal of restrictions on the importing of contraceptives was defeated when the Taoiseach, LIAM COSGRAVE, one of his ministers, Richard Burke, and five other Fine Gael TDs voted against their own motion. Four years later CHARLES HAUGHEY introduced legislation that legalised the sale of contraceptives with a doctor's prescription for medical reasons or for 'bona fide' family planning purposes, which he famously described as 'an Irish solution to an Irish problem.'

McGilligan, Patrick (1889–1979), politician (Cumann na nGaedheal and Fine Gael); born in Coleraine, Co. Derry, educated at UCD. Having worked as a secondary teacher in Cork and at St Patrick's Academy, Armagh, he was an assistant lecturer in classics at University College, Dublin, 1918, where he also studied law. Called to the bar, 1921, and the inner bar, 1946, he was professor of constitutional law, international law, criminal law and legal procedure from 1934. He was secretary to KEVIN O'HIGGINS, Minister for Home Affairs in the first Dáil Éireann, and a member of Dáil Éireann, 1923–65. As secretary to the Irish High Commissioner in London (James MacNeill) he deputised for EOIN MACNEILL at the Imperial Conference of 1923. He succeeded JOSEPH MCGRATH as Minister for Industry and Commerce, 1924–32, launched the first national loan, and was a member of the Irish delegation that negotiated the tripartite agreement of December 1925, shelving the report of the BOUNDARY COMMISSION. As minister he persuaded sceptical colleagues to support the SHANNON SCHEME. Following the murder of O'Higgins, July 1927, he assumed the External Affairs portfolio, 1927–32, and, as leader of the Irish delegation to the Imperial Conferences, drafted the final version of the STATUTE OF WESTMINSTER.

As Minister for Finance, 1948–51, and by now a convinced Keynesian, McGilligan introduced the first capital budget, 1950. He took part in the negotiations leading to the repeal of the EXTERNAL RELATIONS ACT (1936). Because of ill-health he declined a ministerial portfolio in the second inter-party government, 1954–57, accepting instead the office of Attorney-General. He was highly critical of the government's deflationary measures during this period. He supported the 'Just Society' tendency within Fine Gael, 1964. Defeated in the 1965 general election, he was the last survivor of the first Free State government.

Mac Giolla, Tomás (born 1924), socialist-republican and politician (Sinn Féin, Sinn Féin the Workers' Party, and Workers' Party); born in Nenagh, Co. Tipperary, educated at UCD. He was interned in the 1950s. As president of Sinn Féin, 1962–70, he supported the leftward tendency, becoming president of 'Official' Sinn Féin after the split, January 1970. In 1972 he was acquitted of a charge of membership of the IRA; in the same year he was twice deported from England. He stood unsuccessfully for Sinn Féin the Workers' Party in the elections for the European Parliament, 1979. Following six unsuccessful attempts he won a seat in Dáil Éireann for Dublin West, November 1982. He was president of Sinn Féin, renamed Sinn Féin the Workers' Party and then the Workers' Party, until 1988. When the Workers' Party split in 1992 Mac Giolla was the only TD among the party's seven not to join DEMOCRATIC LEFT. He lost his seat in November of that year, and was lord mayor of Dublin in 1993.

McGrath, Joseph (1888–1966), politician (Sinn Féin and Cumann na nGaedheal) and businessman; born in Dublin, educated at Christian Brothers' school. Leaving school at the age of fourteen to work at various jobs, he was a founder-member of the Irish Volunteers and fought in the EASTER RISING (1916), for which he was imprisoned. A member of the first Dáil Éireann, 21 January 1919, he replaced CONSTANCE MARKIEVICZ as Minister for Labour following her arrest, September 1920. He supported the ANGLO-IRISH TREATY (1921) and was Minister for Labour in the second Dáil and in the Provisional Government. He was also Minister for Industry and Commerce and Economic Affairs until September 1922. A founder-member of CUMANN NA NGAEDHEAL, he was Minister for Industry and Commerce until 7 March 1924, when he resigned (together with eight other TDs) over the government's handling of the ARMY MUTINY; his sympathies were with the IRA element within the Free State army. As a private citizen he attempted to act as an intermediary between army officers and the government.

He left politics to pursue a business career and helped to promote the SHANNON SCHEME, for which he was director of labour. Founder of Waterford Glass and Donegal Carpets, he was joint founder of the IRISH HOSPITALS SWEEPSTAKE, 1930. He was an authority on bloodstock and horse-racing; his horses won all the Irish classics, the English Derby, 1951, and the English Cambridgeshire, 1965.

McGrath, Seán (1882–1954), republican; born in Ballymahon, Co. Longford, educated locally. Working as a railway clerk in London, 1908, he joined the Gaelic League and the IRB and was active in the Irish Volunteers, for which he bought arms. Having served with the London Corps of the Volunteers in the GPO, Dublin, during the Easter Rising (1916), he was interned in Fron-Goch in Wales with MICHAEL COLLINS until December 1916. Again arrested in March 1918, he was imprisoned for a year. He was joint founder and general secretary until 1924 of the IRISH SELF-DETERMINATION LEAGUE OF GREAT BRITAIN. He opposed the ANGLO-IRISH TREATY (1921) and remained in England during the CIVIL WAR. He was among the Irish republican activists who were deported in March 1923 but returned to London when the House of Lords ruled that the deportations were illegal. He was then charged with conspiracy, for which he served one year of a two-year jail sentence.

MacHale, John (1791–1881), bishop (Catholic); born in Tobbernavine, Co. Mayo, educated at a hedge school and at St Patrick's College, Maynooth. Ordained in 1814, he was a lecturer, 1814–20, and later professor of theology, 1820–25, at Maynooth. His early writings attacking the system of religious education in schools, under the pen name 'Hierophilus', 1820, attracted the attention of DANIEL O'CONNELL, with whom he formed a friendship. When appointed Coadjutor Bishop of Killala, 1825, he was the first Irish bishop since the sixteenth century to complete his education entirely in Ireland. He was the only member of the hierarchy to show concern for the survival of Irish. In 1826 he supported BISHOP JAMES WARREN DOYLE in his condemnation of the proselytising activities of the KILDARE PLACE SOCIETY. He supported O'Connell in the struggle for CATHOLIC EMANCIPATION, for which O'Connell dubbed him the 'Lion of the Tribe of Judah', causing his critics to deride him as 'Lion of the Tribe of Dan'. He travelled to London on an unsuccessful mission to secure government aid for his starving flock following a partial famine, 1830.

After spending more than a year in Rome as a remedy for ill-health, he was appointed Archbishop of Tuam, despite attempts by the British government to block the appointment, 1834. He refused to allow the new system of NATIONAL EDUCATION into his archdiocese. He supported the REPEAL ASSOCIATION, O'Connell's denunciation of the Charitable Donations and Bequests (Ireland) Act (1844), and the establishment of the QUEEN'S COLLEGES (which he called 'Godless colleges'). To oppose the proselytising activities of REV. EDWARD NANGLE and the New Reformers he increased the number of priests and established the Franciscan monks of the Third Order of St Francis on Achill Island, 1834.

During the GREAT FAMINE (1845–49) he worked tirelessly to aid the starving, inundating the British press and the Prime Minister, LORD JOHN RUSSELL, with appeals for help. He personally acknowledged every donation sent to aid the starving. He was deeply affected by the death of O'Connell, 1847. He opposed YOUNG IRELAND, particularly its acceptance of mixed religious education. Though he had proposed PAUL CULLEN for the Archdiocese of Armagh, they were frequently opposed on important issues, including the concept of a Catholic university. He refused to discipline FATHER PATRICK LAVELLE following Lavelle's defiance of Cullen's ban on the attendance of priests at the funeral of TERENCE BELLEW MCMANUS, 10 November 1861.

A constitutional nationalist, MacHale condemned the methods while he sympathised with the aims of the FENIANS (though in 1864 he sent three autographed pictures of himself to be auctioned at a Fenian fair in Chicago). He called for the release of the imprisoned Manchester Fenians (see MANCHESTER MARTYRS) and supported the aims of the AMNESTY ASSOCIATION. He attended the First Vatican Council in 1870 and spoke and voted against the dogma of Papal infallibility. While he had supported the call for TENANT RIGHT in the 1850s, he opposed the LAND LEAGUE OF MAYO. His denunciation of the Westport meeting, following the success of that at Irishtown, intimidated many political figures, with the notable exception of CHARLES STEWART PARNELL. His last major public appearance was in Dublin in August 1879 when he unveiled a statue to his friend SIR JOHN GRAY.

MacHale was the author of a Catechism in Irish, 1840, which remained in use in Connacht for nearly a century. His Irish translation of Moore's *Melodies,* 1841, was said to have 'greatly pleased the poet.' He translated the

Iliad into Irish verse, 1844–71, and also translated the Pentateuch as part of an Irish translation of the Bible, 1861. *Turas na Croiche* (1834) was his rendering into Irish of *The Way of the Cross* by St Alfonso Liguori.

MacLysaght, Edward (1887–1986), scholar and genealogist; born Edgeworth Anthony Edward Lysaght in Somerset, raised in Raheen, Co. Clare, educated at the University of Oxford and UCC. Having worked on the family farm, which became a horticultural nursery in 1913, he joined the publishers Maunsell in Dublin, 1916, where he came into contact with leading literary figures of the period. A member of the IRISH CONVENTION (1917–18), he was identified with the nationalist cause and was imprisoned during the WAR OF INDEPENDENCE. A member of the Senate of the Irish Free State, 1922–25, he worked as a journalist in South Africa, 1932–38, before returning to Ireland. As an inspector with the IRISH MANUSCRIPTS COMMISSION he travelled the country on bicycle collecting material. On the staff of the National Library, he was head of the Genealogical Office, 1943–55, and keeper of manuscripts from 1949. He retired from the chairmanship of the Irish Manuscripts Commission in 1973.

His writings include *Cúrsaí Thomáis* (a novel, 1927), *Irish Life in the Seventeenth Century* (1939) *An Afraic Theas* (1947), *Irish Families: Their Names, Arms and Origins* (4 vols., 1957–65), *More Irish Families* (1960), *Supplement to Irish Families* (1964), and *Guide to Irish Surnames* (1964). His autobiography, *Changing Times: Ireland since 1898,* was published in 1978.

McManus, Terence Bellew (1823–1860), Young Irelander and Fenian; born in Tempo, Co. Fermanagh. He established a successful shipping agency in Liverpool before returning to Ireland, 1848, where he joined the REPEAL ASSOCIATION and YOUNG IRELAND. He was sentenced to death for his part in the attempted insurrection at BALLINGARRY, Co. Tipperary; the sentence was commuted to transportation to Van Diemen's Land (Tasmania), from where he escaped to the United States with THOMAS FRANCIS MEAGHER, 1852. He died impoverished following the collapse of his business interests.

Believing that his funeral would become a propaganda coup for the Fenians, ARCHBISHOP PAUL CULLEN refused permission for a lying in state at the Pro-Cathedral, Dublin, and instead he lay in state in the Mechanics' Institute, Abbey Street. An estimated 150,000 people lined the streets as the funeral procession made its way to Glasnevin Cemetery. Eight priests, all from dioceses other than Dublin, were in attendance. Graveside orations were delivered by one of the principals in the funeral arrangements, FATHER PATRICK LAVELLE, and an American, Colonel M. D. Smith. The funeral gained national attention for the IRB.

McMichael, Gary (born 1969), loyalist and politician (Ulster Democratic Party); born in Lisburn, son of John McMichael (a UDA spokesperson killed by the Provisional IRA), educated locally. He took over the leadership of the UDP when Raymond Smallwoods was killed, 11 July 1994. At the end of 1994 he said it was unrealistic to expect paramilitary groups to hand over weapons at that stage. Having called for the release of prisoners if the ceasefire held in 1995, he addressed a fringe meeting at the British Liberal Democratic conference, also attended by Mitchel McLaughlin of Sinn Féin, 1995. He accused the unionist parties of trying to exclude fringe loyalists from the talks process, and was UDP representative at the Northern Ireland Forum, 1996–98. Having failed to persuade UDA prisoners in the Maze Prison to embrace the talks process, January 1998, he led the UDP team in the negotiations that produced the BELFAST AGREEMENT (1998).

MacNeill, Eoin (1867–1945), historian and politician (Sinn Féin and Cumann na nGaedheal); born in Glenarm, Co. Antrim, educated privately and at St Malachy's College, Belfast. Through research in the library of the Royal Irish Academy he became an authority on Old Irish. One of the founders of the GAELIC LEAGUE, 1893, of which he was vice-president, he edited *Irisleabhar na Gaedhilge,* 1894, and was a joint founder of the Feis Cheoil. He edited AN CLAIDHEAMH SOLUIS from 1899. He was the first professor of early and mediaeval Irish history at University College, Dublin, 1908. The publication of his article 'The north began' in *An Claidheamh Soluis,* 1 November 1913, led to the founding of the IRISH VOLUNTEERS, of which he became chief of staff. He helped to plan the HOWTH GUN-RUNNING (1914) and opposed JOHN REDMOND in his call for members of the Volunteers to join the British army.

MacNeill was unaware that the Military Council of the IRB was planning the EASTER RISING (1916). When he learnt of the proposed rising he confronted SEÁN MAC DIARMADA and THOMAS MACDONAGH, who assured him that arms from Germany would guarantee its success. However, learning that the *Aud* had been scuttled and Casement arrested, and told by PATRICK PEARSE that 'we have used your name and influence, for what they are worth, but we have done with you now,' MacNeill countermanded the orders issued to the Volunteers for Sunday 23 April. This led to confusion and the abandoning of plans for that day; as a result, the rising, which began the next day, was confined mainly to Dublin.

Shortly before their execution MacDonagh and Pearse exonerated MacNeill from all blame. Though widely blamed for having virtually destroyed the rising, he was interned in England with thousands of other Volunteers and members of Sinn Féin. ÉAMON DE VALERA, the only surviving commandant from the rising, ordered the internees to salute MacNeill when he entered the prison, and he was rehabilitated within the national movement. Released under the general amnesty, he was a signatory of the Message to the President and Congress of the United States (June 1917).

Elected to the first Dáil Éireann, 21 January 1919, MacNeill was Minister for Finance, January–April 1919, until replaced by MICHAEL COLLINS. He was Minister for Industries, 1919–21, supported the ANGLO-IRISH TREATY (1921), and was Ceann Comhairle during the Treaty debate. He was a minister without portfolio in the PROVISIONAL GOVERNMENT, January–August 1922, and Minister for Education, August–December 1922. He was also Minister for Education in the first Executive Council of the Irish Free State, December 1922 to November 1925.

A member of Dáil Éireann for Co. Clare, 1923–27, MacNeill was the Free State representative on the BOUNDARY COMMISSION. At the conclusion of their sittings the three members agreed that their report should not be published until its findings were unanimously acceptable. MacNeill believed that the findings would favour the Free State; but a leak to the *Morning Post* (London), 7 November 1925, revealed that there would be no significant change to the border. He resigned from the commission, 20 November, and refused to accept its report. Widely criticised for failing to protect Free State interests on the commission, he resigned from the government. Losing his seat in the subsequent election, 1927, he withdrew from politics.

First chairman of the IRISH MANUSCRIPTS COMMISSION, 1927–45, he was a joint founder of IRISH HISTORICAL STUDIES, 1936, and president of the Royal Irish Academy, 1940–43. His works include *Phases of Irish History* (1919), *Celtic Ireland* (1921), *Ancient Irish Law* (1923, written while he was imprisoned in 1921), and *Early Irish Laws and Institutions* (1935).

MacNeill's son, Brian MacNeill, who opposed the Treaty, was killed in action in Co. Sligo during the CIVIL WAR, 1922. His brother, James MacNeill (1869–1938), a civil servant, was a member of the committee that drafted the Constitution of the Irish Free State (1922). High Commissioner of the Irish Free State in London, 1922–28, he succeeded T. M. HEALY as Governor-General. The office was slighted when ÉAMON DE VALERA formed the first Fianna Fáil government in 1932. Following an exchange of letters, MacNeill was dismissed for publishing correspondence concerning his office.

McQuaid, John Charles (1895–1973), bishop (Catholic); born in Cootehill, Co. Cavan, educated at UCD. Ordained in the Holy Ghost Fathers, 1924, following a doctorate in theology from the Gregorian University, Rome, he was dean of studies, 1928–31, and president, 1931–39, of Blackrock College, Co. Dublin. He was among those consulted by ÉAMON DE VALERA while the CONSTITUTION OF IRELAND (1937) was being drafted. Noted for his interest in educational and social matters, he established the Advisory Commission on Secondary Schools and encouraged the Society of Jesus to open the Catholic Workers' College, Dublin, 1948. His concern for the impoverished led to the founding of the Catholic Social Service Conference, 1941, while the Catholic Social Welfare Bureau, 1942, aided Irish emigrants. During the 1940s he mediated in industrial disputes, often alongside JAMES LARKIN, whose deathbed he attended. De Valera was unhappy with his support for the striking national teachers in Dublin, 1946–47.

His opposition to the MOTHER AND CHILD SCHEME led de Valera to shelve contentious aspects of the Health Bill (1947). When DR NOEL BROWNE revived the scheme in 1950, McQuaid successfully led episcopal opposition to its enactment. In 1959 he helped to finance an extension to the Irish Centre in London. A conservative man, he assured his flock after his return from a session of the Second Vatican Council that 'no changes will worry the tranquillity of your Christian lives.' He defended the encyclical *Humanae Vitae* (1968). A minimalist in correspondence, his two-sentence letters were legendary: replying to a request from Father Joe Dunne of the Radharc film team to visit east Africa, where he looked forward to seeing 'lions and tigers,' McQuaid replied, 'Dear Fr. Dunne, You have permission to film in East Africa. There are no tigers in Africa.' Towards the end of his career he financed a unit at St Anthony's Hospital, Dublin, to aid young drug addicts. Suspicious of the media, he did little to explain the reasoning behind his decisions, which the creation of a diocesan media liaison office did little to alleviate.

A talented administrator, McQuaid built thirty-four churches and established twenty-six new parishes in the Archdiocese of Dublin between 1940 and 1965. The number of clergy rose from 370 to more than 600 and the number of religious from 500 to 800. The increase in population during the same period led to the building of additional schools, which he encouraged religious orders to administer. He retired in January 1972 (thought to be under pressure from the Vatican). After his death it was revealed that he had retained £20,000 a year from diocesan funds for donations to charities and for making bequests. From private donations he endowed his favourite domestic and international charities.

Macra na Feirme ('farm youth'), a voluntary organisation founded in 1944 by Stephen Cullinan, a rural science teacher, to provide rural youth with farming skills, to encourage leadership skills, to improve relations between farming and non-farming communities, and to provide a medium of social contact between young people in rural Ireland. Activities for some eight thousand members in three hundred clubs include sports and social events, travel, competitions, arts and culture, farming, rural development, education, and leadership training. The organisation founded the *Irish Farmer's Journal,* Foróige, the NATIONAL FARMERS' ASSOCIATION, and the IRISH CREAMERY MILK SUPPLIERS' ASSOCIATION, and it jointly sponsors community enterprise awards to encourage community groups to develop local resources.

Macready, General Sir (Cecil Frederick) Nevil (1862–1945), British soldier. Commissioner of London Metropolitan Police, 1918–20, he was appointed commander in chief of British forces in Ireland, 1920–23, arriving during the WAR OF INDEPENDENCE as the AUXILIARIES and BLACK AND TANS stepped up the campaign against the IRA. Disapproving of the tactics for which these irregular forces became notorious, he threatened in December 1920 that he would 'break any officer who was mixed up in reprisals.' At the same time he admitted that the police had a difficult job and that they had no clear code under which to operate. He failed to support BRIGADIER-GENERAL FRANK CROZIER, commandant of the Auxiliaries, when Crozier was forced to resign over serious indiscipline in his command, February 1921.

Macready had a fruitless meeting with the captured GENERAL SEÁN MAC EOIN, March 1921, in an attempt to negotiate with the IRA. The Prime Minister, DAVID LLOYD GEORGE, did not welcome Macready's view that the IRA would not negotiate if they first had to lay down arms. He negotiated a truce with the IRA from 11 July 1921 and was adviser to the British government during the negotiations leading to the ANGLO-IRISH TREATY (1921), attending meetings of the cabinet. He oversaw the withdrawal of British forces from Ireland, January 1922. Present at the start of the CIVIL WAR, he retired from active service in 1923 and published *Annals of an Active Life* in 1942.

Macrory Report (1970). The review body chaired by Sir Patrick Macrory (1911–1993) examined proposals for local government reform in Northern Ireland. The proposals were accepted by the NORTHERN IRELAND CIVIL RIGHTS ASSOCIATION but were not acceptable to the majority of traditional unionists, as the majority of members of the new boards of education and library and health boards would be nominated by the government and not elected. The government of SIR JAMES CHICHESTER-CLARK accepted the report. Twenty-six district councils, first elected in 1973, replaced the six county councils. However, the top tier of local government disappeared with the Assembly of Northern Ireland (sometimes known as the 'Macrory gap').

Mac Stiofáin, Seán (1928–2001), republican; born John Stephenson in London (his mother, who died when he was ten, was from Belfast). Working with Irish building workers stimulated an interest in Irish history and the Irish language. After national service he joined the IRA. In 1953, together with CATHAL GOULDING and Manus Canning, he was sentenced to eight years' imprisonment for stealing arms from the armoury at Felstead School, Essex. Following his release, 1959, he came to Ireland. He became director of intelligence of the IRA and chief of staff of the Provisional IRA following the 1969 split. Sentenced to six months' imprisonment for membership of the Provisional IRA, 25 November 1972, he embarked on a hunger and thirst strike but ended the thirst strike when faced with imminent death; his hunger strike ended in January 1973, after fifty-seven days, on the orders of the IRA leadership. He never recovered his authority in the Provisional IRA and resigned in the 1980s over the abandonment of the ÉIRE NUA policy. His autobiography, *Revolutionary in Ireland,* was published in 1974.

MacSwiney, Mary (1872–1942), republican; born in Surrey, educated at Ursuline Convent, Cork. Having trained and become a teacher in England, she returned to Cork to teach at St Angela's Ursuline School. Influenced by her brother, TERENCE MACSWINEY, she became involved in the Irish Volunteers, 1913, and joined Cumann na mBan, 1914. Following imprisonment after the Easter Rising (1916) she opened St Ita's School, a school for girls modelled on ST ENDA'S SCHOOL, assisted by her brother, TERENCE MACSWINEY, and their sister Eithne (died 1954). Involved in the reorganising of SINN FÉIN and the anti-CONSCRIPTION movement, she was with Terence and his wife, Muriel, when he died on hunger strike, after which she accompanied her sister-in-law to New York on a speaking tour, December 1920 to August 1921. She opposed the ANGLO-IRISH TREATY (1921) as 'the one unforgivable crime that has ever been committed by the representatives of the people of Ireland.'

Imprisoned during the Civil War, she was on hunger strike twice while in Mountjoy Jail, Dublin, 1922–23. She opposed ÉAMON DE VALERA when he circumvented the OATH OF ALLEGIANCE to enter Dáil Éireann. Increasingly isolated from Sinn Féin, she opposed the Marxist tendency of the 1930s. Her refusal to recognise the government of the Irish Free State meant that her school did not receive state grants or endowments; she resigned from Sinn Féin, 1934, when it supported FATHER MICHAEL O'FLANAGAN, who had accepted a salaried position from the government. She opposed the CONSTITUTION OF IRELAND (1937)—'all treason, since it is not the Republic'—and supported the IRA 'declaration of war' against England, January 1939.

MacSwiney, Terence (1879–1920), politician (Sinn Féin); born in Cork, younger brother of MARY MACSWINEY, educated at the RUI. He became a technical instructor in Cork, where he was a member of the Gaelic League and joint founder (with DANIEL CORKERY) of the Cork Dramatic Society, 1908, for which he wrote four plays in English. He was a joint founder of the IRISH VOLUNTEERS in Cork, December 1913, and resigned his teaching post to become a full-time organiser, 1915. He and his assistant TOMÁS MACCURTAIN mobilised local volunteers in anticipation of the EASTER RISING (1916) but obeyed Eoin MacNeill's countermanding order. Imprisoned during the period 1916–17, on his release he was active in the reorganised Volunteers and Sinn Féin, represented Mid-Cork in the first Dáil Éireann, and helped to establish the Dáil's arbitration courts.

He succeeded the murdered TOMÁS MACCURTAIN as lord mayor of Cork, 30 March 1920. Sentenced to two years' imprisonment, 16 August 1920, he embarked on a hunger strike in Brixton Prison, London, which captured international attention; he died after fasting for seventy-four days. A guard of honour of Volunteers in prohibited uniform accompanied his funeral procession through the streets of London, watched by thousands of Irish exiles. GENERAL SIR HENRY WILSON prevented funeral demonstrations in Dublin by having the body sent directly to Cork, where it lay in state in the City Hall.

MacSwiney was the author of several works, including *The Revolutionist* (1914) and *Battle Cries* (poems, 1918). Articles for *Irish Freedom* were posthumously published in New York as *Principles of Freedom* (1921).

MacWhite, Michael (1883–1958), diplomat; born in Co. Cork. After serving in the British army during the First World War (several times wounded and awarded the Croix de Guerre) he went to the United States with the French military mission, 1918. Recruited by SEÁN T. O'KELLY, he was secretary of the Dáil Éireann delegation to the Paris Peace Conference (1920–21). Head of the Irish Bureau in Geneva, 1921–22, on the establishment of the Irish Free State, December 1922, he was appointed permanent delegate to the League of Nations, 1923–29. He was vice-president of the International Labour Conference at Geneva, 1928, and held diplomatic postings as Irish envoy extraordinary and minister plenipotentiary to the United States, 1929–38, and to Italy, 1938–50. In the latter posting he was close to the Italian regent (later King Umberto II), who frequently sought his advice during the Second World War.

Madden, R. R. [Richard Robert] (1798–1886), historian; born in Dublin. A member of the Royal College of Surgeons, he was a magistrate in Jamaica and Colonial Secretary in Western Australia, where he investigated the plight of the aboriginal population. After returning to Dublin he was secretary of the Dublin Fund Board, 1850–80. On discovering Anne Devlin, former housekeeper of ROBERT EMMET, living in poverty in Dublin in 1843, he arranged for her support. She died during one of his absences abroad, 1851, and was buried in a pauper's grave; on his return he arranged for her re-interment in a plot beside the grave of DANIEL O'CONNELL in Glasnevin Cemetery. He also arranged support for the widow of the writer Michael Banim and for Jemmy Hope. His many publications include *The United Irishmen: Their Lives and Times* (7 vols., 1842–46), *The Life and Times of Robert Emmet* (1847), *The Literary Life and Correspondence of the Countess of Blessington* (3 vols., 1855), and *Historical Notice of the Penal Laws Against Roman Catholics* (1865).

Magee College, Derry, financed by Mariah Martha Magee and opened in 1865 by the General Assembly of the Presbyterian Church for students of arts and divinity. It was the first college to grant equal status to men and women students. As it had no university charter for granting degrees, divinity studies had to be completed in other institutions. Later known as McCrea-Magee Presbyterian College, it was incorporated in the New University of Ulster, 1968, and became a constituent college of the UNIVERSITY OF ULSTER, 1984.

Magennis, Prof. William (1869–1946), academic and politician (Cumann na nGaedheal and Clann Éireann); born in Belfast, educated at UCD. A fellow of the Royal University of Ireland, he was editor of LYCEUM, 1890–92, and its successor, NEW IRELAND REVIEW, 1893. Professor of philosophy at Carysfort Training College, Blackrock, Co. Dublin, and professor of metaphysics at University College, Dublin, he was a member of Dáil Éireann for the NUI constituency, 1922–36. In 1925 he founded CLANN ÉIREANN after breaking with Cumann na nGaedheal on the BOUNDARY COMMISSION issue. His appointment by ÉAMON DE VALERA to the board of the ABBEY THEATRE, 27 February 1933, was vetoed by W. B. YEATS: 'We refuse to admit Professor Magennis to our Board as we consider him entirely unfitted to be a Director of the Abbey Theatre . . .' He was a member of Seanad Éireann from 1937.

'Magheramorne Manifesto', a declaration prepared by ROBERT LINDSAY CRAWFORD for the INDEPENDENT ORANGE ORDER, ratified at a meeting of the members at Magheramorne, near Larne, Co. Antrim, 13 July 1905. It called on all Orangemen, whether in the grand lodges or in the independent institutions, to

> hold out the hand of friendship to those who, while worshipping at other shrines, are yet our countrymen . . . Hatred of their Roman Catholic countrymen is not the creed of Orangeism. We are taught as Orangemen to regard our Roman Catholic neighbours as our brethren.

The manifesto called for compulsory land purchase and a national university of Ireland and attacked the ULSTER UNIONIST COUNCIL. Crawford's views led to his expulsion from the Independent Orange Order, 1908.

Magill, a current affairs magazine launched on 27 September 1977 by Noel Pearson, Mary Holland, and Vincent Browne. Browne was first editor, 1977–83 and 1988–91; other editors were Colm Tóibín, 1983–85, Fintan O'Toole, 1985–86, Brian Trench, January–December 1987, and John Waters, January–October 1988. The magazine, noted for the quality of its investigative journalism, was relaunched on 28 August 1997; from then until the autumn of 1998 it was first to publish some of the biggest stories of the day, dealing with political and financial scandals. Browne sold the magazine to Mike Hogan, owner of a number of magazines, 12 October 1998, after which it saw many editorial changes.

Maguire, John Francis (1815–1872), newspaper proprietor, author, and politician (Repeal); born in Cork, educated locally. While a law student in Cork he was a supporter of DANIEL O'CONNELL. A frequent contributor to newspapers and periodicals, he founded the CORK EXAMINER, 1841, using it to publicise agrarian and social injustice. Called to the bar, 1843, he rarely practised, because of his literary and political commitments. He was member of Parliament for Dungarvan, Co. Waterford, 1852–65, and for Cork, 1865–72. Several times lord mayor of Cork, 1853, 1862–1864, he was a powerful advocate of FATHER THEOBALD MATHEW, whose temperance crusade received extensive coverage in his newspaper. On each of his three visits to Rome he received an audience with Pope Pius IX, who made him a knight commander of the Order of St Gregory; on his return from Rome in 1856 he published a work on the pontificate of Pius IX.

He supported TENANT RIGHT, DISESTABLISHMENT of the Church of Ireland, and land reform. An early advocate of a system of technical instruction for the young, he supported women's emancipation and was active in the promotion of local industry. As chairman of the Cork Gas Company he was instrumental in breaking the monopoly previously enjoyed by British ships by using Irish vessels to carry coal from Cardiff. He went to the United States to gain first-hand experience of the conditions under which Irish emigrants lived and worked; his book *The Irish in America* (1868) is one of the earliest such studies. His other writings include *The Industrial Movement in Ireland* (1852) and *Life of Father Mathew* (1862). He made a gift of his home, Ardmannagh, overlooking Cork Harbour, to the people of Cork.

Maguire, Sam (1879–1927), republican; born in Dunmanway, Co. Cork, educated locally. A clerk in the General Post Office in London, he was a member of the IRB, Gaelic League, and Irish Volunteers. As chief intelligence officer of the IRB in Britain he recruited MICHAEL COLLINS into the organisation, 1909. British intelligence vainly sought 'S.M.', designated the 'most wanted man in England,' unaware of his name or the fact that he was employed by the government. For his role in supplying arms to the Irish Volunteers during the WAR OF INDEPENDENCE he was imprisoned and dismissed from his civil service post. On the creation of the Irish Free State he returned to Ireland, 1923, and worked for a short time in the civil service before ill-health forced his retirement to his native Dunmanway, 1924.

A keen sportsman, Maguire captained the London GAA teams that contested the all-Ireland football finals of 1903, 1905, and 1906. The all-Ireland football trophy, the Sam Maguire Cup, with a design based on the ARDAGH CHALICE, was presented to the GAA as a memorial to his work for the cause of Irish independence. The original was replaced by a duplicate in 1988.

Maguire, Father Thomas (Tom) (1792–1847), clergyman (Catholic); born in Co. Cavan. A noted debater, he engaged Rev. Richard Pope, an evangelical preacher, in an open doctrinal debate at the Dublin Institute in Sackville Street (O'Connell Street), 19–25 April 1827. The debate was jointly chaired by Admiral Robert Oliver and DANIEL O'CONNELL. Each side claimed victory; Maguire was presented with £1,000 worth of silver plate by prominent Dublin Catholics. An animated preacher, he perspired freely during sermons, following which he habitually took a large glass of mulled whiskey.

On 13 December 1827 he was defendant in a celebrated legal action when he was arraigned on charges of debauchery and seduction involving Anne McGarrahan, a 23-year-old Protestant, at whose inn in Drumkeerin, Co. Leitrim, he had lodged and who had been delivered of a stillborn infant, 2 July 1825. O'Connell led Maguire's defence, while John Henry North appeared for Miss McGarrahan. Several witnesses attested to having had sexual intercourse with McGarrahan. O'Connell elicited the fact that her father was an undeclared bankrupt; he also produced witnesses who attested that the plaintiff had confided that Maguire was innocent of the charge. The jury found for Maguire and awarded him damages of 6 pence. Two leading members of the SECOND REFORMATION, John Duckworth and Charles Cox, were suspected of complicity in the affair.

Foul play was suspected when Father Maguire died suddenly, 2 December 1847. When his body and that of his brother and sister-in-law, who had lived with him, were exhumed it was found that they had died from arsenic poisoning. Though his housekeeper was suspected locally, no-one was charged with the murders.

Mahaffy, Sir John Pentland (1839–1919), scholar and clergyman (Church of Ireland); born in Vevey, Switzerland, educated privately and at TCD, where he had a brilliant academic career and was ordained. He was made a fellow, 1864, senior fellow, 1899, and professor of ancient history, 1869. He was widely expected to become provost, but the post went instead to Dr Anthony Trail (1838–1914). His most famous pupil was Oscar Wilde, with whom he visited Greece and Italy. Generally hostile towards nationalism, he opposed the efforts of DOUGLAS HYDE and the Gaelic League to have Irish placed on the curriculum for secondary schools; he claimed it was impossible to find a text in Irish that was not 'either religious, silly, or indecent.' As provost of Trinity College, 1914–19, he denied the use of the college to 'a man called Pearse' to address a meeting at which W. B. YEATS was also a speaker, November 1914. A delegate to the IRISH CONVENTION

(1917–18), he proposed a federalist solution, along Swiss lines, to the home rule impasse. His receipt of a knighthood, 1918, set a precedent for clergymen.

Mahaffy was much in demand as a dinner guest for his brilliant conversation, which blunted the edge of his legendary snobbery. His description of JAMES JOYCE as a 'living argument' was answered in *Finnegans Wake,* where Mahaffy is 'that stern chuckler Mayhappy Mayhapnot.' He published works on Kant's philosophy, Irish history, poetry, Egyptian papyri and Trinity plate as well as on the art of speaking.

Mahon, Charles James Patrick, styling himself 'the O'Gorman Mahon' (1800–1891), adventurer and politician; born in Ennis, Co. Clare, educated privately and at TCD. He was a member of the CATHOLIC ASSOCIATION and persuaded DANIEL O'CONNELL to contest the Co. Clare parliamentary constituency in 1828. Mahon himself was elected for Co. Clare, 1830, but was unseated following charges of bribery and was succeeded by O'Connell's son, Maurice O'Connell. He travelled widely before returning to Ireland in 1846. Having represented Ennis in the British Parliament, 1847–52, following his defeat in 1853 he resumed his foreign travels and served in various armies, including the Union Army during the American Civil War (1861–65). Returning to Ireland, 1871, he was a delegate to the Home Rule Convention of 1873, supported CHARLES STEWART PARNELL, and in 1879 and 1880 won the Co. Clare seat. He won the Co. Carlow seat, 1887–91, and was an anti-Parnellite following the split in the IRISH PARTY, 1890–91. A noted duellist, he fought on thirteen occasions, later confiding to W. E. GLADSTONE that on every occasion he had been the aggressor.

Major, John (born 1943), British politician (Conservative). As Prime Minister in succession to MARGARET THATCHER, 1990–97, he supported the ANGLO-IRISH AGREEMENT (1985) and showed a willingness to deal directly with Northern politicians and with Irish governments. His meeting in London with the four Northern party leaders, February 1992, was the first in sixteen years and helped to restart the PEACE PROCESS. He re-established regular Anglo-Irish summit meetings (which had been dropped by Thatcher). Under his presidency of the European Community, Northern Ireland retained objective 1 priority in funding, 1992. He guaranteed that the people of Northern Ireland would determine its constitutional future and that no party would be permitted to veto progress. He also declared that he would respond to a 'cessation of violence.' He welcomed the Provisional IRA ceasefire, August 1994, but called on Sinn Féin to establish its permanence. He announced in mid-November that talks would be opened with 'loyalist political representatives'. Talks with Sinn Féin and loyalists began in December. It was envisaged that a new Northern Ireland Assembly would control only 'local government matters' and that 'huge progress' would have to be made towards the destruction of Provisional IRA weapons before formal talks could begin. He was joined by the Taoiseach, JOHN BRUTON, for the launch of the FRAMEWORK DOCUMENTS in Belfast, 22 February 1995. On 28 November a joint communiqué outlined a 'twin-track' process, with talks and decommissioning dealt with separately. Major said that the precondition of arms decommissioning before talks could be negotiated if the Provisional IRA promised a 'permanent and certain' end to violence.

Following the end of the Provisional IRA ceasefire, 9 February, he vowed to continue the peace process but declared that Sinn Féin could not take part in multi-party talks until the Provisional IRA ceasefire was renewed. Sinn Féin was not included in the talks, which opened with the former US senator GEORGE MITCHELL in the chair, 10 June. All parties would have to adhere to the Mitchell Principles of non-violence. Following the summer recess Major stated that it would take more than a renewed ceasefire for Sinn Féin to be admitted to the Stormont talks. The impasse continued into 1997. He resigned the leadership of the Conservative Party following a defeat in the general election of May 1997, when TONY BLAIR led the Labour Party to a resounding victory.

Mallin, Michael (1880–1916), republican; born in Inchicore, Dublin, educated locally. Having served with the British army in India, he returned to Ireland and, as secretary of the Silk Weavers' Union, met JAMES CONNOLLY and joined the IRISH CITIZEN ARMY. He published articles on military tactics in the *Workers' Republic* and instructed the Citizen Army in the use of guerrilla tactics. He was an accomplished musician and was active in the Workingmen's Temperance Committee. Appointed chief of staff of the Citizen Army before the EASTER RISING (1916), he suggested the General Post Office in Sackville Street (O'Connell Street),

Dublin, as headquarters for the rising. He commanded the Citizen Army at the St Stephen's Green outpost, where CONSTANCE MARKIEVICZ was his second in command. Following a court-martial he was shot by firing squad, 8 May. Markievicz later stated that Mallin's bearing, courage and example were instrumental in her decision to become a Catholic.

Mallon, John (1839–?), policeman; born in Meigh, Co. Armagh, educated at Newry Model School. After working as an apprentice to a draper in Newry he joined the DUBLIN METROPOLITAN POLICE and won rapid promotion, becoming director of G Division (the intelligence branch) at DUBLIN CASTLE, where he was responsible for investigating underground movements, including the IRB, CLAN NA GAEL, and the INVINCIBLES, and of other nationalist societies and organisations, including the Gaelic League. He investigated the activities of the LAND LEAGUE and the PLAN OF CAMPAIGN as well as the DYNAMITERS. He arrested CHARLES STEWART PARNELL at Morrison's Hotel, Dawson Street, Dublin, 12 October 1881 (Parnell refused to leave until he had received his customary 10 per cent off the bill). Exchange Court Clerk to Dublin Castle, 1892–94, he had reached the rank of assistant commissioner when he retired in 1901.

Manchester Martyrs. On 18 September 1867 a prison wagon conveying the Fenian leaders THOMAS J. KELLY and TIMOTHY DEASY was attacked by a party of FENIANS at Hyde Road, Manchester. The attackers were in the act of shooting out the lock when Sergeant Charles Brett, peering through the keyhole, was shot through the eye and died instantly. A prisoner passed the keys through an opening, and the handcuffed Fenians escaped. Some of the rescuers were quickly apprehended, and later that night approximately sixty Irishmen were arrested.

In the weeks before the trial, inflammatory press coverage fuelled anti-Irish hysteria. The verdict at the inquest on Sergeant Brett was 'wilful murder against Allen and others unknown.' On 28 October twenty-six prisoners were arraigned before a 'special commission'. The Attorney-General prosecuted the five 'principal offenders': William Philip Allen, Michael Larkin, Michael O'Brien, EDWARD O'MEAGHER CONDON, and Thomas Maguire. There was disquiet at the nature of the evidence sworn by some of the witnesses, one of whom, Frances Armstrong, had forty-three convictions for drunkenness. Found guilty of murder, the five were sentenced to death, 1 November. Condon concluded his speech from the dock, 'I have nothing to regret, or to retract, or take back. I can only say, "God save Ireland".' His companions repeated 'God save Ireland,' and the phrase became the title of a ballad by T. D. SULLIVAN, which became the marching song of the IRB and subsequently an unofficial national anthem.

Doubts regarding Maguire's conviction were widely expressed, and he was granted a free pardon; Condon's sentence was commuted on the intervention of the American government (as he was an American citizen). It was generally believed that the other three would also have their sentences reviewed, as they were convicted on the evidence of witnesses whose obvious perjury had led to the release of Maguire; but the sentences were not revoked. Allen, Larkin and O'Brien were hanged at Salford Prison, Manchester, at 8 a.m. on 23 November 1867. Their deaths aroused widespread indignation in Ireland and abroad. In Cork, tens of thousands marched to the beat of muffled drums behind a symbolic hearse and coffin, 1 October, and there were similar large demonstrations in towns throughout the south-west. On 8 December an estimated 60,000 people marched along a four-mile route in Dublin preceded by bands playing the Dead March and watched by a crowd of more than 150,000.

The issue was rekindled in the British House of Commons on 30 June 1876 when CHARLES STEWERT PARNELL brought MPs to their feet by declaring, 'I wish to say as publicly and as directly as I can that I do not believe, and never shall believe, that any murder was committed at Manchester.' Edward O'Meagher Condon stated in 1908 that one Peter Rice was the person who discharged the shot that killed Sergeant Brett.

Mandeville, John (1849–1888), agrarian agitator and politician (Irish Party); born in Mitchelstown, Co. Cork. Active in the PLAN OF CAMPAIGN, he was closely associated with WILIAM O'BRIEN in the organising of tenants' resistance on the Kingston estate near Mitchelstown. This led to a summons to trial, the occasion of the MITCHELSTOWN MASSACRE. The Crown prosecutor, EDWARD CARSON, secured three-month and two-month sentences for O'Brien and Mandeville, respectively. Imprisoned in Tullamore Jail, Mandeville, like many others involved in the plan, refused to wear prison uniform. Under orders from the

Chief Secretary for Ireland, ARTHUR J. BALFOUR, the prisoners were not allowed to wear their own clothing; as a result, Mandeville was kept naked in his cell, November 1887. Released on Christmas Eve, he died in July 1888. His death, attributed to ill-treatment in prison, aroused great indignation in Ireland and England. The inquest recorded that death had resulted from 'brutal and unjustifiable' treatment. The prison doctor, Dr George Ridley, who had certified Mandeville fit to bear the prison regime, committed suicide at the time of the inquest.

Mangan, James Clarence (1803–1849), poet and linguist, born James Mangan in Dublin (he added Clarence from one of his pseudonyms), educated at Saul's School. Because of his family's impoverished circumstances he left school at fifteen to find employment in a scrivener's office and later with various attorneys. A professional writer at twenty-five, he contributed to the periodicals and journals of the day, including the first and subsequent editions of the NATION, and various almanacs. Eccentric in habit and dress, even in the warmest weather he relinquished neither his voluminous cloak nor his two umbrellas. He led a solitary life and became increasingly dependent on alcohol and opium. He rarely sought the assistance of his friends, though GEORGE PETRIE found him employment in the ORDNANCE SURVEy. A skilful translator, he published works of Arabic, Spanish and German origin. The most popular of his poems, 'Dark Rosaleen', was, according to the poet, originally entitled 'Róisín Dubh' and written in the reign of Queen Elizabeth I by a bard of the O'Donnells. He died of malnutrition and cholera at the Meath Hospital, Dublin. Sir William Burton (1816–1900) made one of the few drawings of the poet to survive (now in the National Gallery).

Mannix, Daniel (1864–1963), bishop (Catholic); born in Charleville, Co. Cork, educated at St Patrick's College, Maynooth. The first priest ordained in the new chapel at Maynooth, 8 June 1890, he was professor of philosophy, 1891, professor of theology, 1894, vice-president, 1903, and president, 1903–12. During a visit to the college by King Edward and Queen Alexandra he found a compromise between his nationalist principles and the deference due to his guests by not flying the Union Jack but decorating the buildings in the king's racing colours. He became Archbishop of Melbourne in 1917. He condemned the proposed extension of CONSCRIPTION to Ireland and was particularly virulent in his denunciation of the excesses committed by the BLACK AND TANS and AUXILIARIES. En route to Ireland from the United States he was arrested, 8 August 1920, and taken to Penzance, Cornwall, to prevent him from addressing meetings in Ireland or in British centres of Irish population. Despite attempts to prevent him speaking at Liverpool, Manchester and Glasgow he succeeded in addressing huge torchlight gatherings throughout England and Scotland. He was made an honorary freeman of the city of Cork, 17 August 1922. An outspoken critic of war, he denounced the American bombing of Hiroshima, 1945, and in 1953 cabled President Eisenhower to seek clemency for the condemned American communists Ethel and Julius Rosenberg.

Mansion House Committee (1918), established as a central board to co-ordinate the activities of the various nationalist movements. Its members included ARTHUR GRIFFITH, COUNT PLUNKETT, and, later in the year, W. T. COSGRAVE and ÉAMON DE VALERA.

Mansion House Conference (1918), called by the lord mayor of Dublin, Laurence O'Neill, to discuss the British government's proposal to introduce CONSCRIPTION in Ireland, 18 April 1918. Conference delegates, representing all shades of nationalist opinion, supported an anti-conscription pledge, drafted by ÉAMON DE VALERA, to be taken at church doors throughout Ireland on Sunday 21 April. The delegates unanimously condemned the Conscription Bill as 'a direct violation of the rights of small nationalities to self-determination' and affirmed the right of all Irishmen to resist the bill by the 'most effective means at their disposal.'

Maria Duce ('under the leadership of Mary'), a right-wing Catholic movement founded in 1942 by Father Denis Fahy (1883–1954), a Holy Ghost Father in Dublin. A small movement, it sought to amend article 44 of the Constitution of Ireland, claiming it was not strong enough in defence of the Catholic Church. The organisation published the paper *Fiat*. After the death of its founder the movement, now known as An Fhírinne ('the truth'), lost its public focus and disappeared in the 1960s.

Marian Year (1954), centenary commemoration of the proclamation of the dogma of the Immaculate Conception by Pope Pius IX in 1854. On 16 May thirty thousand people marched in procession through the streets of Dublin in the largest parade since the EUCHARISTIC CONGRESS (1932). A record number of pilgrims attended the shrine at KNOCK, Co. Mayo, hundreds of wayside shrines and grottoes were erected, and many girls born in that year were given the name Marian.

Markievicz, Constance, née Gore-booth (1868–1927), revolutionary and politician (Sinn Féin); born in London, raised at Lissadell House, Drumcliff, Co. Sligo, educated privately. She was noted for her beauty, as a horsewoman, and as an excellent shot. Having studied at the Slade School of Fine Art, London, she continued her studies in Paris, where in 1900 she married Kazimierz Markiewicz, a Polish-Ukrainian landowner who called himself Count Markiewicz; she subsequently styled herself Countess Markievicz. When the marriage failed, their daughter Maeve, born 1901, was raised by her grandmother at Drumcliff. While living in London she was attracted to SINN FÉIN through reading the *United Irishman,* though she disagreed with the pacifism of ARTHUR GRIFFITH. At the suggestion of BULMER HOBSON (with whom she lived for some time in a commune at Raheny, Dublin), she founded FIANNA ÉIREANN, 1909. A leading suffragist, she joined INGHINIDHE NA HÉIREANN, for which she wrote a pamphlet, *A Call to the Women of Ireland* (1909); she also contributed to *Bean na hÉireann* and *United Irishman.* During the DUBLIN LOCK-OUT (1913) she organised soup kitchens in the slums and became an officer in the IRISH CITIZEN ARMY. During the EASTER RISING (1916) she was second in command to MICHAEL MALLIN at St Stephen's Green. Her death sentence was commuted; she became a Catholic shortly afterwards, inspired, she said, by the executed Mallin.

In the general election of 1918 she was the first woman elected to the British House of Commons (for the St Patrick's division of Dublin), but as a member of Sinn Féin she did not take her seat. She was a member of the first DÁIL ÉIREANN and was made Minister for Labour, 1919–21, though she spent much of this period in prison. She was again Minister for Labour in the second Dáil.

She denounced the ANGLO-IRISH TREATY (1921): 'It is the capitalist interests in England and Ireland that are pushing this treaty to block the march of the working people in England and Ireland . . .' An implacable opponent of the Irish Free State, she supported the Irregulars during the CIVIL WAR and was imprisoned, 1923–24. She was elected as Sinn Féin abstentionist TD for Dublin City South, 1923. She died in a general ward in Sir Patrick Dun's Hospital, Dublin, attended by family and friends, having rejected better accommodation on the grounds that if a public ward was good enough for ordinary Dubliners it was good enough for her. An estimated 100,000 people filed past her body in the Rotunda Rooms (the government refused the use of both City Hall and the Mansion House). ÉAMON DE VALERA was a pall-bearer.

Her sister, Eva Gore-Booth (1870–1926), poet, trade unionist, suffragist, and pacifist, moved to Manchester in the 1890s. She edited *Women's Labour News* and contributed poetry to the IRISH HOMESTEAD and *New Ireland Review.* Though she disapproved of Constance's militancy the sisters were close; the letters they exchanged while Constance was in prison were published as *Prison Letters* (1934). *The Poems of Eva Gore-Booth,* edited by her lifelong friend and fellow-suffragist Esther Roper, appeared in 1929.

Marlborough, John Winston Spencer Churchill, eighth Duke of (1822–1883), British politician (Conservative); born in Norfolk, educated at the University of Oxford. A member of Parliament, he succeeded to the dukedom in 1857. After rejecting an offer of the Lord Lieutenancy of Ireland from BENJAMIN DISRAELI in 1874, he accepted the office two years later; his son, LORD RANDOLPH CHURCHILL, was his private secretary. He was popular during his term of office, when nationalist aims were articulated by ISAAC BUTT. During the 1870s, a period of severe agricultural depression followed by famine, particularly in the west, Marlborough and his wife administered famine relief, setting up a fund that collected £12,484. He left office on the fall of the Disraeli ministry, 1880.

marriage. The pattern of marriage in Ireland changed considerably in the wake of the GREAT FAMINE (1845–49). Before the famine, early marriage was the custom; the historian K. H. Connell considers this to have been a significant factor in the population increase that was a marked feature of the period between 1780 and the famine. Contemporary observers noted the incidence of early marriage; Thomas Campbell Foster commented in 1845: 'A lad is no sooner sixteen or seventeen years of age, than he marries some girl of fifteen or sixteen . . . he has a family growing up about him before he is a man.' The principal cause of early marriages, according to contemporary accounts, was the reckless sub-division of land, which made it possible for a newly wedded couple to earn their subsistence.

Late marriages became a feature of rural life after the famine. In the period 1845–46 the average marrying age of southern farmers was thirty-nine, while that of the wife was thirty. One in four men on marriage was over sixty-five. Census returns show a pattern of late marriages and a declining birth rate. Marriage across social and religious divides was a rarity, while elopements and abductions, once a common feature of Irish life, were virtually unheard of by the turn of the century.

Contemporaries paid tribute to the chastity of Irish women and noted the low rate of pre-marital and extra-marital sexual activity. Lord Radnor told Alexis de Tocqueville in 1833 that he had heard it said that morals in Ireland and Scotland were better than in England. Monsignor Nolan of Carlow told de Tocqueville, 20 July 1835, 'Their morals, in the narrow sense of the word, are very chaste.' The Bishop of Kilkenny told him, 24 July 1835,

> Their morals are pure . . . Twenty years of confession have taught me [that] for a girl to fall is very rare, and for a married woman practically unknown . . . A woman suspected is lost for her whole life. I am sure that there are not twenty illegitimate children a year among the Catholic population of [County] Kilkenny, which numbers 26,000.

The MATCHMAKER was an influential member of the rural community. For a fee, he arranged marriages between couples introduced to him by their parents. It was important that the woman have a dowry, whether of cattle, money, or land, and it was important that she not be matched with one who was considered a social inferior. Landless sons were thrown on their wits and strove to find a mate within the landowning community. Marriage in rural Ireland after the famine and into the twentieth century was often decided on predominantly mercenary grounds.

Many customs and superstitions attached to the marriage ceremony. Until the 1850s marriages were performed in the house where the couple intended to live—generally the home of the husband's parents. Those attending the ceremony marched in procession from the home of the bride's parents to that of the groom—on foot, in traps, or on horseback. Drink, usually whiskey and wine, was provided at both houses. Feasting began as soon as the procession arrived at the house. If those responsible for the entertainment were poor, neighbours would provide for the merrymaking. The wedding service was usually performed in the kitchen, and as many people as wished could be registered as witnesses. The officiating priest was expected to remain for the duration of the festivities. Neither bride nor groom was allowed to sing at the wedding. At midnight, strawboys—young male singers and musicians dressed in straw and wearing masks—arrived to request admittance, which usually gave the party a fresh impetus. The entertainment normally continued into the early hours of the morning.

It was considered lucky to get married on a sunny day and unlucky to be married on a wet day; it was good luck to hear a cuckoo on the morning of the wedding or to see three magpies as the bridal party proceeded to the ceremony. It was unlucky to marry on a Saturday, or to meet a funeral on the way (in this case the party either turned back or went to the place of marriage by an alternative route). If anyone knotted a piece of string or a handkerchief during the ceremony the marriage was sure to be troubled until the knot was loosed.

Marshall Aid. In May 1948 Ireland was offered the first instalment of a £47 million loan under the American 'Plan for the Reconstruction of Europe'. Many in the Department of Finance, including T. K. WHITAKER, opposed the acceptance of the loan, while the Minister for External Affairs, SEÁN MACBRIDE, failed in his attempts to have the US government convert the loan to a grant. The inter-party government of 1948–51 decided not to accept the loan immediately but to continue borrowing from the sterling area dollar pool. After Britain barred Ireland from access to the pool, June 1948, the government then signed an agreement with the United States, accepting a loan of £47 million, conditional on the government's drawing up a programme outlining the country's import requirements for the next three years. The LONG-TERM RECOVERY PROGRAMME was drawn up by MacBride. Ireland also had to join the Organisation for European Economic Development (now the OECD). With the recovery of the sterling area, Marshall Aid to Ireland was suspended, May 1950, by which time Ireland's allocation from the plan totalled $146.2 million, of which $18 million was in grants. While it did not solve the main problems—emigration, rising prices, low wages, and unemployment—it was used to benefit agriculture (see LAND REHABILITATION PROJECT), a housing programme, and a restructuring of the social welfare system.

Martin, John (1812–1875), Young Irelander, journalist, and politician (Nationalist); born in Loughorne, Co. Down, educated at Newry (where he was a schoolfellow of JOHN MITCHEL) and TCD. An asthmatic, he used his independent means to travel extensively. A member of the REPEAL ASSOCIATION, he was also active in YOUNG IRELAND. He supported JAMES FINTAN LALOR on the land question, was joint editor with him of the *Irish Felon,* and assisted Mitchel on the UNITED IRISHMAN. He was arrested for membership of the IRISH CONFEDERATION; found guilty of treason-felony, he was transported to Van Diemen's Land (Tasmania), 1849–54, returning to Ireland in 1856. A supporter of TENANT RIGHT during the 1850s and 60s, he opposed the extremism of the IRB. He served on the Executive Committee of the AMNESTY ASSOCIATION and delivered the oration for the MANCHESTER MARTYRS, 1867. He made a successful lecture tour of the United States, 1869–70. A founder-member of the HOME GOVERNMENT ASSOCIATION, he was member of Parliament for Co. Meath, 1871. He died nine days after Mitchel's funeral. CHARLES STEWART PARNELL won his Meath seat.

Martin, Richard (1754–1834), landowner and politician; born in Dublin, educated at the University of Cambridge. Called to the bar, 1781, he practised on the Connacht circuit. His estate of 200,000 acres in Connemara was the largest in Ireland. He was a member of the Irish House of Commons, 1776–83 and 1798–1800, supported the ACT OF UNION, and held a seat in the British House of Commons until 1826. Losing his seat on a petition by James Staunton Lambert, 11 April 1827, he retired to Boulogne.

Martin's love of duelling earned him the nickname 'Hairtrigger Dick' (given to him by his friend the Prince of Wales, later KING GEORGE IV); he was reputed to have engaged in more than a hundred duels. His concern for animals earned him the popular name 'Humanity Dick'. He tabled a private member's bill in 1822 'to prevent the cruel and improper treatment of cattle' and was a founder-member of the Royal Society for the Prevention of Cruelty to Animals, 1824. Asked how he reconciled his love of animals with his penchant for duelling, he replied, 'Sir, an ox cannot hold a pistol.' A popular landlord, he was widely respected for his defence of the oppressed. During his period in Parliament he supported CATHOLIC EMANCIPATION.

His granddaughter Mary Letitia Martin (1814–1850), known as the 'Princess of Connemara', continued his philanthropic tradition. Her charity during the GREAT FAMINE (1845–49) bankrupted the estate, and she turned to writing to support her family. Her best-known novel, *Julia Howard* (1850), vividly portrays life in the famine-ravaged west of Ireland.

Martyn, Edward (1859–1923), dramatist and patron of the arts; born at Tullira Castle, Ardrahan, Co. Galway, educated at Belvedere College, Dublin, and the University of Oxford. A wealthy man, he travelled widely on the Continent before taking up residence at Tullira. A generous patron of the Irish cultural revival of the 1890s, he supported the GAELIC LEAGUE. With his neighbour LADY AUGUSTA GREGORY and W. B. YEATS he founded the IRISH LITERARY THEATRE, 1899, for which he wrote *The Heather Field,* and the ABBEY THEATRE, 1904. He established the Palestrina Choir (which became the Schola Cantorum of the Archdiocese of Dublin), 1903, and was instrumental in founding the Feis Cheoil. He played a leading role in the reform of church architecture and in the stained-glass revival. A fervent Catholic, he was so distressed when Yeats's play *The Countess Cathleen* was criticised on moral grounds that he threatened to break with the theatre.

With Lady Gregory and Yeats he was a member of the first board of directors of the Abbey Theatre but later, dissatisfied with its policy of peasant drama, severed his connection. With JOSEPH PLUNKETT and THOMAS MACDONAGH he engaged in a short-lived experiment, the Irish Theatre, in Hardwicke Street, Dublin, 1914, which featured plays in Irish, translations of European masterpieces, and works reflecting contemporary Irish life. He supported the NATIONAL COUNCIL and SINN FÉIN (of which he was president, 1905–08). In deteriorating health, he lived his remaining years as a recluse on his estate. His will directed that his body be given over for dissection and that he be buried in a pauper's grave.

His works include *Margante the Lesser* (a satirical novel, 1890) and the plays *Maeve* (1899), *The Bending of the Bough* (with George A. Moore, 1900), *The Placehunters* (1902), *The Enchanted Sea* (1902), *Romulus and Remus*

(1907), *Grangecolman* (1912), *The Dream Physician* (1914), and *The Privilege of Place* (1915).

Marwood, William (1820–1883), hangman; born in Horncastle, Lincolnshire. A cobbler by trade, he was so appalled by the victims' suffering during hangings that he suggested a more humane method: the descent of the body into a pit beneath the scaffold, which would cause instant death because of the dislocation of the vertebrae. He accepted the post of executioner, his first engagement being at Lincoln Jail, 1871. At Kilmainham Jail, Dublin, he hanged five members of the INVINCIBLES, May and June 1883, for the PHOENIX PARK MURDERS.

Mason, Roy (born 1924), British politician (Labour Party). As Secretary of State for Northern Ireland, 1976–79, he introduced the SAS Regiment into the intensely republican district of south Armagh, after which it soon operated throughout Northern Ireland. He was criticised by the media when he attempted to introduce the 'D notice' system (designed to prevent the publication of information considered harmful to national security). He was critical of the BBC and ITV for transmitting news and interviews dealing with allegations of the ill-treatment of suspects by the RUC. While his language suggested that the Provisional IRA was being defeated, by the end of 1977 it had mounted a new bombing campaign. Mason encouraged a policy known locally as 'Ulsterisation'—extending the role of the RUC and the UDR to enable the British army to withdraw from policing. He stood firm against the loyalist strike in 1977, and introduced legislation on divorce and homosexuality to bring Northern Ireland into line with Britain.

Massey, Godfrey, Fenian; born in Castleconnell, Co. Limerick, raised in the United States by his mother under the name Patrick Condon (as he was 'illegitimate'). Having worked in New Orleans, he served in the British army during the Crimean War (1854–56). Inspired by JAMES STEPHENS, he joined the FENIANS in New York, c. 1860. He reached the rank of colonel in the Confederate Army during the American Civil War (1861–65). Appointed a general in the Fenian army, he was sent to Ireland in January 1867 with funds for the IRISH REPUBLICAN BROTHERHOOD but was arrested as he alighted from a train at Limerick Junction, 4 March. Aware that the plans for the proposed rising were already known to DUBLIN CASTLE, he co-operated with the authorities.

matchmaker, a person in rural Ireland who undertook to arrange marriages. A highly regarded member of the community, he was often a knowledgeable elderly person well versed in the arts of rural diplomacy. Part of his function was to pair people according to social background, an important consideration in a community where wealth was judged according to farm size and the amount of livestock possessed. The matchmaker traditionally met the couple, with their parents, at his own home. After speaking to all parties individually he would meet both sides to confirm the settlement or to debate outstanding issues. When agreement was reached he brought the couple together for some words of advice, after which they were free to begin 'walking out' and, after a suitable period, to marry. The matchmaker was paid for his services, generally by both parties, and was frequently an important guest at the wedding he had helped to arrange.

Mathew, Rev. Theobald (1790–1856), Capuchin priest and temperance crusader; born in Thomastown Castle, Cashel, Co. Tipperary, educated at St Patrick's College, Maynooth, ordained in 1814. Following a ministry in Kilkenny he moved to Cork, where he worked among the poor. He bought the site of the old botanic gardens of the Royal Cork Institute to provide the city with a Catholic graveyard and was celebrated for his work during the cholera epidemic of 1832. Contemporary accounts suggest that excessive drinking was a serious social problem. Alexis de Tocqueville was told of the rural poor that 'when the chance of a drunken orgy offers, they do not know how to resist it. They become turbulent and often violent and disorderly . . . ' In August 1835 a judge of the Assizes in Galway told de Tocqueville that drinking was the chief cause of FACTION-FIGHTING. Encouraged by Protestant philanthropists, Father Mathew began a temperance crusade, 10 April 1838; thirteen years later his campaign embraced some five million people.

His first mission outside Cork was to Limerick, where in four days in December 1839, 150,000 people took the pledge. The income from the consumption of alcohol plummeted from £1.435 million in 1839 to £352,000 in 1844; some 20,000 publicans were reputed to have become bankrupt, but crime and lawlessness reached their lowest point ever. DANIEL O'CONNELL said he would have been unable to hold his monster Repeal meetings if Father Mathew had not first converted the population to sobriety. When he took his campaign to the United States, 1849, he was met by a deputation of New York City Council, addressed the US Senate, 19 December, and dined with President Taylor. Hundreds of thousands took the pledge. His crusade in Britain, aided by the work of the United Kingdom Alliance, was equally successful.

His latter days were dogged by ill-health and mounting debt caused by the costs of medals and stationery. A public subscription was raised to alleviate his financial distress. Ill-health led him to decline the offer of the Bishopric of Cork. He suffered a stroke, 1 February 1852, from which he never fully recovered, and resigned as provincial of the Irish Order of Capuchins. He spent from October 1854 to August 1855 convalescing in Madeira but on his return to Cork suffered a further stroke and died at Queenstown (Cóbh), 8 December. A statue by JOHN HENRY FOLEY was unveiled in Patrick Street, Cork, 10 October 1864 (the delay was occasioned by the death of JOHN HOGAN, who was executing the original commission).

Maxwell, Constantia Elizabeth (1886–1962), historian; born in Dublin, educated at TCD and Bedford College, London. A lecturer in history at Trinity College, Dublin, 1909–39, she was professor of economic history, 1939–45 (the first woman professor there), and professor of modern history, 1945–51. Her writings include *Short History of Ireland* (1914), *Irish History from Contemporary Sources* (1923), *Dublin under the Georges* (1936), *Country and Town in Ireland under the Georges* (1940), *A History of Trinity College* (1946), and *The Stranger in Ireland from the Reign of Elizabeth to the Great Famine* (1954). She also edited *Arthur Young's Tour of Ireland* (1925).

Maxwell, General Sir John Grenfell (1859–1929), British soldier; born in Liverpool. Commissioned in 1879, he was chief staff officer to the Duke of Connaught in Ireland, 1902–04, and commander of British forces in Egypt, 1909–12. Retired on half pay, he was recalled on the outbreak of the Great War. Attached to French headquarters as head of the British military mission until after the Battle of the Marne, he commanded in Egypt until 1916.

He accepted command in Ireland during the EASTER RISING (1916), arriving at 2 a.m. on 28 April. He isolated 'infected patches' of rebels in Dublin, and within two days the rising was over. He had fifteen of the leaders shot, and arrested thousands of suspected activists and sympathisers. His handling of the situation was widely criticised. His request to the Catholic hierarchy to condemn the rising was generally acceded to, with the exception of the Bishop of Limerick, EDWARD THOMAS O'DWYER, whose riposte was published by the international press, 17 May 1916. The next day, in an interview with the *Daily Mail* (London), Maxwell defended his soldiers against allegations of indiscriminate killing and wanton destruction of property.

> Possibly unfortunate incidents, which we should regret now, may have occurred. It did not perhaps always follow that if there were shots fired from a particular house the inmates were always necessarily aware of it or guilty, but how were the soldiers to discriminate? They saw their comrades killed beside them by hidden and treacherous assailants, and it is even possible that under the horrors of this particular attack some of them "saw red" . . .

Maxwell was defended by the Prime Minister, H. H. ASQUITH.

Mayhew, Sir Patrick (1929), British lawyer and politician (Conservative). Having served as Solicitor-General, 1983–87, and Attorney-General, 1987–92, he was appointed Secretary of State for Northern Ireland, April 1992 to May 1997. Succeeding PETER BROOKE, he took over the talks process begun by his predecessor (see BROOKE-MAYHEW TALKS). His first year in office saw an increase in Provisional IRA activity, with bomb explosions in London and Manchester, while loyalist paramilitary activity was also at a high level. While restating the guarantee of the constitutional status of Northern Ireland, he implied that SINN FÉIN could be brought into political talks if its renunciation of violence was real. Replying to the Hume-Adams statement, 25 September 1993, he stated that he was not prepared to contemplate 'any change to the status of Northern Ireland that does not represent self-determination of the people living in Northern Ireland.' After the Provisional IRA ceasefire, August 1996, he said that Provisional IRA arms would feature in any discussion with Sinn Féin. As the 'decommissioning' of arms became an issue, while speaking in Washington he enunciated a three-point policy, the third point of which (to become known as 'Washington 3') was that there must be decommissioning of some arms as a confidence-building measure before the republican movement could be admitted to talks.

In mid-April 1996 he invited the four main constitutional parties to attend bilateral talks. He met GERRY ADAMS at a Washington investment conference. In October he concurred with the 'twin-track' approach—separating political talks from the arms issue by means of an international committee to oversee decommissioning of arms; but the bomb explosion at Canary Wharf, London, 9 February 1997, marked the end of the Provisional IRA ceasefire. As the attempt to further the PEACE PROCESS continued, he accepted that GEORGE MITCHELL should have a central role in the forthcoming multi-party talks, which led to the BELFAST AGREEMENT (1998). He did not contest the May 1997 election, which saw his party routed by the Labour Party.

Maynooth. The Roman Catholic College of St Patrick was established at Maynooth, Co. Kildare, in 1795 by the Irish Parliament, at the prompting of WILLIAM PITT, as a seminary for clerical students and as a place of higher education for lay students. The lay college was discontinued in 1817. Maynooth students were generally intended to become priests in their own diocese; diocesan seminaries, producing the students who went on to Maynooth, were established throughout the country during the nineteenth century. The Maynooth grant—an annual government payment—rose from £9,000 to £26,000 in 1845; SIR ROBERT PEEL also included a £30,000 grant for capital expenditure. A source of resentment to nonconformist groups, the grant was discontinued in 1871 as part of the general disendowment of religion in Ireland (see DISESTABLISHMENT OF THE CHURCH OF IRELAND) and replaced by a capital sum of £369,000.

In 1910 St Patrick's College, Maynooth, became a recognised college of the NATIONAL UNIVERSITY OF IRELAND. It now consists of a seminary, a pontifical university (since 1899), and a lay college (since 1966). Its trustees are the Catholic bishops.

Meagher, Thomas Francis (1823–1867), Young Irelander, orator, and soldier; born in Waterford, son of a wealthy businessman, educated at Clongowes Wood College, Co. Kildare, and Stonyhurst College, Lancashire, where he won prizes for English poetry and in the Academic Debating Society. A friend of WILLIAM SMITH O'BRIEN and JOHN MITCHEL, he was the immediate cause of the break between YOUNG IRELAND and the REPEAL ASSOCIATION: in a speech at Conciliation Hall, Dublin, he angered DANIEL O'CONNELL when, refusing to 'stigmatise the sword,' he made a speech in which he used the word 'sword' eight times, earning from the novelist W. M. Thackeray the title 'Meagher of the Sword'.

A founder-member of the IRISH CONFEDERATION, he visited France in the wake of the revolution of February 1848 as an emissary from Young Ireland. For his role in the rising at BALLINGARRY he was defended by ISAAC BUTT; he was found guilty, but the jury added a rider asking for mercy, and he was transported to Van Diemen's Land (Tasmania), where he joined Mitchel. After informing the authorities that he was retracting his parole, he escaped, June 1852, and after four days in an open rowing-boat he was picked up by an American whaler and taken to the United States, where he became a popular lecturer on Irish affairs and entered American politics.

Called to the New York bar, he jointly founded (with Mitchel) the *Citizen,* 1854, and founded the *Irish News,* 1856. He also explored the Rocky Mountains and Central America. On the outbreak of the Civil War (1861–65) he served in the New York Irish Brigade, of which he was later brigadier-general. Becoming known as 'Meagher's Brigade', with flags displaying the Irish harp on a field of emerald green, it was distinguished for bravery in action at Bull Run, August–September 1862, Antietum, September 1862, Fredericksburg, December 1862, and Chancellorsville, May 1863; it was virtually annihilated during the last two battles but was re-formed and saw action at Gettysburg, July 1863, and Bristole's Station, October 1863.

Retiring with the rank of lieutenant-general, Meagher was appointed secretary of Montana Territory by President Johnson, in effect acting governor, 1865–66. While on his second expedition to the Northern Territory he mysteriously disappeared off the paddle steamer *J. S. Thompson,* 1 July 1867. He is commemorated by a statue in Helena, Montana.

Mee, Jeremiah (1889–1953), policeman; born in Knickanes, Glenamaddy, Co. Galway, educated at national school. Joining the RIC, 1910, he was transferred to Listowel, Co. Kerry, July 1919. He supported THOMAS MCELLIGOTT in the Irish Branch of the National Union of Police and Prison Officers, April 1918. Mee and fellow-members refused orders to hand over Listowel Barracks to military control and accept the more dangerous assignments to outlying barracks, 16 June 1920. Addressing the mutineers, Lieutenant-Colonel G. B. Smyth, divisional commander of the RIC for Munster, pointed out that the RIC were to go on the offensive against the IRA:

> You may make mistakes occasionally and innocent persons may be shot, but that cannot be helped, and you are bound to get the right parties some time. The more you shoot, the better I will like you . . .

Rather than co-operate with the BLACK AND TANS, Mee and some of his colleagues at Listowel resigned, 6 July. Unemployed, he worked as an agent for MICHAEL COLLINS, in February 1922 secured a job with the WHITE CROSS, and after internment during the CIVIL WAR, 12 August to 13 September 1922, was employed by British Petroleum Ltd but was dismissed when he organised a strike against the company's policy of discriminating against Catholics. Later employed by Russian Oil Products Ltd, 1926–32, he joined the Department of Local Government and Public Health and worked in Longford, Mullingar, and Dublin.

His *Memoirs,* written during the years 1951–52, appeared in *Reynolds News,* 25 November 1951 to 6 January 1952, and the *Leitrim Leader,* 15 March to 26 April 1952. Extensively rewritten, they were published in book form, edited by J. Anthony Gaughan, 1975.

meitheal, a group of workers, especially those who provide free labour to neighbouring farmers at times of turf-cutting and harvesting. The workers were provided with food and drink; music, dancing, singing and storytelling often followed the completion of the work. The person who received this communal assistance would in turn join other *meithleacha,* thus ensuring the preservation of the spirit of co-operation in rural communities.

Melbourne, William Lamb, second Viscount (1779–1848), British politician (Whig). As a member of Parliament from 1805, he was appointed Chief Secretary for Ireland, April 1827. While he was known to favour CATHOLIC EMANCIPATION, he disapproved of the agitation led by DANIEL O'CONNELL but cultivated his friendship. Melbourne's wish to open public offices to Catholics was strongly opposed by the Anglo-Irish ASCENDANCY and the ORANGE ORDER. When Wellington's ministry fell in the wake of emancipation, Melbourne became Secretary for Home Affairs in Lord Grey's ministry, 1830–34, in which office he continued his involvement in Irish affairs. He encouraged the implementation of the NATIONAL EDUCATION system, in the hope that constructive measures might win the Irish away from Repeal. However, there was widespread discontent during the cholera outbreak of 1830–31. Melbourne agreed with the principle of the POOR LAW but felt that the time was not opportune for its establishment. In 1832 the government attempted to put an end to the long-standing grievance of the tithes, when the system was adjusted and there was a redistribution of the Church of Ireland's income. An attempt to reform the Church of Ireland was made in 1833.

Melbourne became Prime Minister for the first time in July 1834 but by the end of the year was replaced by SIR ROBERT PEEL, whose ministry fell three months later. Melbourne's second ministry lasted until 1841. During a period of continuing reform in Ireland, the LICHFIELD HOUSE COMPACT gained the support of O'Connell and English radicals for Melbourne's ministry. In 1840 it introduced the MUNICIPAL CORPORATIONS (IRELAND) ACT (1840). When his ministry fell, Peel returned to office, 1841.

Mellows, Liam (1892–1922), republican; born in Ashton-under-Lyne, Lancashire, raised by his grandparents near Inch, Co. Wexford, educated at Cork, Portobello, and the Royal Hibernian Military School. Following his father's retirement from the British army the family moved to Dublin, where, against his father's wishes, Mellows chose not to pursue a military career but worked as a clerk. He became a nationalist under the influence of IRISH FREEDOM, joining FIANNA ÉIREANN and the IRB, 7 April 1912. As a Fianna organiser, April 1913, he worked closely with CONSTANCE MARKIEVICZ, building up the movement while travelling the country as a republican propagandist. He was also influenced by JAMES CONNOLLY. On the founding of the IRISH VOLUNTEERS, November 1913, he became a member of the Provisional Committee. He was sent to Galway as Volunteer organiser for south Connacht, where he was twice arrested and on the second occasion deported to England. Connolly arranged for his return (disguised as a priest) for the EASTER RISING (1916), after which he went on the run in Co. Clare until arrangements were made for his escape (sometimes disguised as a nun). He was smuggled to England and from there to the United States, where he worked for

JOHN DEVOY on the *Gaelic American.*

He was arrested in New York, November 1917, for using false papers and released on bail for two years. Maintaining contact with the reorganised Volunteers and Sinn Féin, he was an advance agent for the visit of ÉAMON DE VALERA, 1920, and supported him in the dispute with JUDGE DANIEL COHALAN and Devoy. He returned to Ireland to work in the IRA, October 1920, for which he was appointed director of purchases during the WAR OF INDEPENDENCE. Representing Co. Galway in the first Dáil Éireann, he rejected the ANGLO-IRISH TREATY, calling it 'the betrayal of the Republic.' Briefly editor of POBLACHT NA HÉIREANN, he was a member of the FOUR COURTS garrison when the Civil War broke out. He was arrested and imprisoned in Mountjoy Jail, Dublin, from which his 'Notes from Mountjoy' appeared in the *Irish Independent,* 21 September 1922, calling for the defence of the Republic and the re-establishment of a civilian republican government to counter the Provisional Government. He was shot by the Provisional Government (together with three other prisoners) on 8 December 1922 in reprisal for the assassination of Seán Hales the previous day.

middlemen, speculators who leased land from a landlord—often an absentee—and then sub-let it at an inflated rent. Considered one of the more blatant evils of a landholding system noted for its uneconomic and inefficient nature, it ensured a landlord's profit without the responsibilities attached to letting land. Generally there were layers of middlemen involved, as the sub-tenant, instead of working the land, might further sub-let it and thus become a middleman to one tenant while being a sub-tenant of another. The resultant pyramid was supported at the base by the unfortunate tenants, who had little means of redress. Contemporary sources denounced middlemen as 'land sharks' and 'bloodsuckers'. It was not unusual for the 'head middleman' to be an absentee, like the head landlord. Another source of profit for middlemen was the auction of lands, either when a lease fell due or when a tenant was unable to pay the rent. Here the middleman had an opportunity not only to raise the rent on the affected smallholding but also to split it into smaller units to gain additional rents.

An example brought before a House of Lords select committee, 1825, showed that rents on a smallholding in Connacht exceeded the total yield from the land. The tenant, having planted his potatoes, went to labour for the season in England, leaving his wife and family to exist as best they could. He then 'comes back to dig his potatoes; with the wages of his English labour in his pocket, he is able to pay a larger sum in rent than he could have extracted from the soil.'

While contemporary accounts generally portray the middlemen as a rapacious class, there were middlemen who attempted to assist the tenants. However, as long as there was an expanding population, placing continual pressure on land and food resources, there were few who could envisage an end to the system. The worst abuses were eliminated by the GREAT FAMINE (1845–49), when many middlemen became bankrupt through paying the POOR LAW rate. Many remaining middlemen became landlords through purchase under the ENCUMBERED ESTATES ACTS. (See also CONACRE, COTTIER, and GOMBEEN MEN.)

Midgley, Harry (1892–1957), trade unionist and politician (Labour and Ulster Unionist Party); born in Belfast. An apprentice joiner at the Workman Clark shipyard, he became a carpenter and later a trade union official and a member of the Independent Labour Party. Though sympathetic to the aims of JAMES CONNOLLY, he did not join the SOCIALIST PARTY OF IRELAND. He served in the British army in France during the Great War until 1919. He represented the Independent Labour Party at its conference in Glasgow in April 1920, when delegates voted to recognise the Irish Republic. A full-time union official, he was defeated when he contested the first general election in Northern Ireland as an anti-partitionist, 1921. A joint founder of the NORTHERN IRELAND LABOUR PARTY, 1924, he was elected to Belfast City Council, 1925 and 1929. Chairman of the NILP in 1932, he was elected to the Parliament of Northern Ireland for the Belfast Dock constituency, 1933–38.

By 1937, disillusioned with the social conservatism of the Irish Free State and the power of the Catholic Church, he declared that the future of Northern Ireland lay within the British Commonwealth. The following year, having lost nationalist support, he failed to hold his Stormont seat. He was re-elected for the NILP in a by-election, 3 December 1941, defeating a Unionist. He broke with the NILP over partition, 1942, to form the pro-unionist Commonwealth Labour Party; as Minister of Public Security, 1943–45, he was the first non-Unionist to become a member of the Northern

Ireland government. As member of the ULSTER UNIONIST PARTY from 1947, he was Minister of Labour, 1949–52, and Minister of Education, 1952–57. He was also a prominent member of the ORANGE ORDER.

milesmen, part-time constables engaged in night patrols of the roads during the early years of the nineteenth century.

Miley, Rev. John (1805–1861), clergyman (Catholic); born in Co. Kildare, educated at St Patrick's College, Maynooth, and at Rome. Returning to Ireland, 1835, he supported DANIEL O'CONNELL, to whom he became private chaplain. He accompanied O'Connell to the Continent, 1847, and attended him on his deathbed. In deference to his wishes he took the casket containing O'Connell's heart from Genoa to Rome, conveyed the body to Ireland, and preached the panegyric in the Pro-Cathedral, Dublin. As rector of the Irish College, Paris, 1849–59, he was constantly beset by financial problems. He opposed the appointment of FATHER PATRICK LAVELLE as professor of Irish, 1856, on financial grounds; the resultant feud, which involved Miley's archbishop, PAUL CULLEN, and Lavelle's archbishop, JOHN MACHALE, led to the closure of the Irish College, October 1858. Lavelle was parish priest of Bray, Co. Wicklow, from 1859. He published works on educational reform and *History of the Papal States* (1852).

Military History Society of Ireland, founded in January 1949 to promote the study of military history, especially the history of warfare in Ireland and of Irishmen at war. As the Irish Commission for Military History it is affiliated to the International Commission of Military History. The society produces a biannual journal, the *Irish Sword.*

Military Service (No. 2) Act (1918), introduced by the government of DAVID LLOYD GEORGE, 16 April 1918, to raise the age limit in England and provide for the extension of CONSCRIPTION to Ireland. Opponents of the bill in Ireland included some loyalists; nationalist politicians left the House of Commons in protest at the passing of the bill. Alarmed at the extent of the opposition, the government abandoned plans to extend conscription to Ireland.

Military Service Pensions Act (1934), introduced by the Fianna Fáil government to provide pensions for members of the IRA who had supported the Republican cause in the CIVIL WAR, 1922–23. The pensions drew support from the IRA, AS ÉAMON DE VALERA intended. Figures provided by the Minister for Finance, 10 November 1937, showed that £457 was paid out in 1934/35, £54,305 in 1935/36, and £164,845 in 1936/37.

Milroy, Seán (1877–1946), journalist and politician (Sinn Féin and Cumann na nGaedheal); born in Maryport, Cumberland. He came to Ireland to work in the nationalist cause, befriended ARTHUR GRIFFITH, and joined SINN FÉIN. A member of the Irish Volunteers, he fought in the EASTER RISING (1916), after which he was imprisoned. He was elected to the Executive of the Volunteers, 19 November 1917, and to Dublin City Council. Arrested under the 'GERMAN PLOT' arrests, he escaped from Lincoln Jail with ÉAMON DE VALERA and Seán McGarry, 3 February 1919. He assisted with the establishment of the IRISH SELF-DETERMINATION LEAGUE OF GREAT BRITAIN. An abstentionist member of the first Parliament of Northern Ireland for Fermanagh-Tyrone, 24 May 1921, he was a member of Dáil Éireann for Co. Cavan, 16 August 1921, and secretary of the Dáil Sub-Committee on Ulster and spokesman on Northern affairs. He supported the ANGLO-IRISH TREATY (1921), was re-elected to Dáil Éireann in 1923, but resigned his seat in 1924 following the ARMY MUTINY and broke with Cumann na nGaedheal following the shelving of the report of the BOUNDARY COMMISSION (1925). He was a member of the Senate, 1928–36, taking the Cumann na nGaedheal whip. He published a pamphlet, *The Case of Ulster* (1922).

Ministers and Secretaries Act (1924), legislation designed to streamline the administrative system by uniting the various government bodies under eleven departments: President of the Executive Council, Finance, Justice, Local Government and Public Health, Lands and Agriculture, Industry and Commerce, Fisheries, Posts and Telegraphs, Education, Defence, and External Affairs. The titles of some departments changed many times over the years.

Mitchel, John (1815–1875), revolutionary; born in Dungiven, Co. Derry, son of a Presbyterian minister and former member of the UNITED IRISHMEN, educated at Derry until his family moved to Newry, 1822, where he met JOHN MARTIN. Taking a law degree at TCD, 1834, he worked in a law office in Banbridge, Co. Down, where his outspoken nationalism brought him into conflict with the ORANGE ORDER. A member of the REPEAL ASSOCIATION, 1843, he joined YOUNG IRELAND and contributed to the NATION; following the death of THOMAS DAVIS he became principal contributor, and moved with his family to Dublin. The militancy of his articles in the *Nation* alienated many, and when CHARLES GAVAN DUFFY refused to publish two of his articles, he resigned. Following the breach between YOUNG IRELAND and DANIEL O'CONNELL he became a leading member of the militant IRISH CONFEDERATION, 1847. Under the influence of JAMES FINTAN LALOR he advocated an extreme policy to defend tenant-farmers during the GREAT FAMINE (1845–49). A member of the IRISH COUNCIL, he became disillusioned with its failure and, breaking with the IRISH CONFEDERATION in January 1848, established his own paper, the UNITED IRISHMAN, in which he advocated 'holy war' to eliminate English influence in Ireland.

Between February and March 1848 he proposed that starving tenant-farmers should withhold the harvest, not pay rent or rates, resist distraint and eviction, ostracise all who would not co-operate, and arm themselves. The *United Irishman* provided advice on the organising of barricades and pointed out that railway tracks could be turned into pikes and that vitriol (sulphuric acid) could be used against soldiers. This militant tone led to his arrest and the suppression of the paper in May. Mitchel became the first person tried under the TREASON FELONY ACT (1848), before a packed jury, and was sentenced to twenty years' transportation, 27 May 1848. The *United Irishman* was suppressed and Mitchel's property forfeit to the Crown. A collection for his wife and family raised £1,800. Having spent some time at Spike Island in Cork Harbour he was transported by the convict ship *Scourge,* 1 June 1848, to Van Diemen's Land (Tasmania). The secretary of the Admiralty had ordered that he should not be treated with undue harshness or anything that could be taken as 'vindictive cruelty', as a result of which he dined at the captain's table.

He was joined in Van Diemen's Land by his friend THOMAS FRANCIS MEAGHER, with whom he gave parole to the governor not to escape. After withdrawing his parole he escaped, 8 June 1853, and made his way to the United States, where he worked as a journalist in New York before turning to farming in Tennessee. During the Civil War (1861–65), in which he lost two sons, he supported the Confederacy (for which he was imprisoned by the victorious North). He consistently denounced the FENIANS during his time in America. Returning to Ireland, 1874, he was elected member of Parliament for North Tipperary, 16 February 1875, but was unseated by petition as an undischarged felon. A second election again returned him, 11 March 1875, but he died as his victory was being celebrated.

Mitchel's writings included *The Life and Times of Aodh O'Neill, Prince of Ulster* (1845), *History of Ireland from the Treaty of Limerick* (1858), and *The Last Conquest of Ireland (Perhaps)* (1876). He also edited the works of JAMES CLARENCE MANGAN (1859) and Thomas Davis (1868). His most famous work, *Jail Journal,* which first appeared in 1854 in his New York newspaper, the *Citizen,* details his prison experiences and philosophy; acclaimed as a classic of its genre, it influenced generations of nationalists. On reading Mitchel's *History of Ireland* DR DOUGLAS HYDE noted in his diary, 1881, 'He would make a rebel out of me if I weren't one already.'

Mitchell, George (born 1933), American lawyer and politician, member of the US Senate, 1980–95, and Senate Majority Leader, 1988–95. Appointed economic adviser on Ireland by President Clinton, December 1994, he addressed the FORUM FOR PEACE AND RECONCILIATION in Dublin, February 1995. As part of the 'twin-track' process (designed to separate the 'decommissioning' of arms from multi-party talks), he became chairman of the INTERNATIONAL BODY ON DECOMMISSIONING OF ARMS. His subsequent report, 24 January 1996, containing the 'Mitchell Principles' on non-violence as a precondition for admission to the talks, was widely welcomed. The six principles were that those involved must be committed

a. To democratic and exclusively peaceful means of resolving political issues;
b. To the total disarmament of all paramilitary organisations;
c. To agree that such disarmament must be verifiable to the satisfaction of an independent commission;
d. To renounce for themselves, and to oppose any effort by others, to use force, or threaten to use force, to influence the course or the outcome of all-party negotiations;
e. To agree to abide by the terms of any agreement reached in all-party negotiations and to resort to democratic and exclusively peaceful methods in trying to alter any aspect of that

outcome with which they may disagree; and,
f. To urge that "punishment" killings and beatings stop and to take effective steps to prevent such actions.

When talks continued after the end of the Provisional IRA ceasefire, 9 February 1996, Mitchell became chairman of the talks, which opened on 10 June, and also headed a sub-committee on decommissioning. He steered the talks to the BELFAST AGREEMENT, 10 April 1998. He published *Making Peace* (1999).

'Mitchelstown Massacre' (9 September 1887). During the PLAN OF CAMPAIGN, WILLIAM O'BRIEN and JOHN MANDEVILLE were ordered to appear before magistrates at Mitchelstown, Co. Cork, for using seditious language. They announced their intention not to appear; when the case proceeded, the Crown prosecutor, EDWARD CARSON, applied for a bench warrant for their arrest. Some eight thousand people from Cos. Cork, Limerick, Tipperary and Waterford arrived for a mass meeting to coincide with the court proceedings. The RIC attempted to clear a path to the platform, on which the speakers included JOHN DILLON, HENRY LABOUCHERE, and local clergymen. When the police used batons, horsemen surrounding the platform used whips and sticks. A riot ensued when the crowd attacked the police, who retreated to the barracks in Upper Cork Street. Gunfire from the barracks killed three members of the crowd: John Casey, Michael Lonergan, and John Shinnock. Fifty policemen and more civilians were injured.

The event received international press coverage because of the presence of Frederick Higginbotham of the Press Association. The Chief Secretary for Ireland, A. J. BALFOUR (henceforth known to nationalists as 'Bloody Balfour') informed Parliament, 12 September 1887, that the police had fired 'absolutely in self-defence' and that their action was 'absolutely justifiable.' The action was also defended by the Lord Lieutenant, the MARQUESS OF LONDONDERRY. As a result of an official investigation two officers, Captain H. Segrave and County Inspector Brownrigg, were held responsible and the latter forced to resign. The slogan 'Remember Mitchelstown' became a rallying cry for the IRISH NATIONAL LEAGUE and was used by opponents in Parliament to taunt the government.

Mná na Poblachta ('women of the republic'), founded in December 1933 by Nollaig Ní Bhrugha and Eibhlín Ní Thobraide, former members of CUMANN NA MBAN, to promote the cause of the Irish Republic. Its aim was

> organising and training the women and girls of Ireland for the purpose of breaking the connection with England by every right means in our power, helping the government of the Republic in the exercise of its functions as the lawful government of All Ireland and securing for the Republic international recognition.

model schools, established in 1846 as part of the training system for teachers. The schools, of which twenty-eight were opened between 1848 and 1867, were administered directly by the Commissioners for National Education. Selected trainees were supervised in their teaching of a hundred pupils for six months in each district model school. Each school was intended to produce six male and two female teachers annually, who would then take a two-year training course. Following an examination the trainees completed their training in the Central Model School, Dublin.

The Catholic hierarchy denounced the schools, because—unlike the national schools, which were under their management where the Catholic population warranted it—model schools were directly controlled by the Commissioners. The bishops objected to their religiously mixed boarding character; they ordered that no priest was to send any person from the schools under his control to be trained in a district model school, nor was any priest to employ teachers who had been trained in one. They also ordered that Catholic children be withdrawn from the model schools, and repeated this in 1866. Further criticism levelled at the model school system was its failure to meet the annual requirement of nine hundred trainee teachers, its average complement being less than 45 per cent of requirement. The model schools were abolished by the Powis Commission (1868–70), which also recommended a reduction in the number and proposed the centralisation of the agricultural model school system (introduced in the 1830s).

Molly Maguires, a Catholic agrarian secret society, 1835–55, the name derived from their custom of adopting women's clothing when committing their outrages. Their campaign of terror was directed against bailiffs, process-servers, landlords, and their agents. The movement spread to the anthracite mines of Pennsylvania as an offshoot of the ANCIENT ORDER OF HIBERNIANS. Membership was boosted by an influx of veterans of the American Civil War (1861–65).

In 1875 the Molly Maguires organised a strike at the Philadelphia and Reading Coal and Iron Company, whose president, Franklin B. Gowen, engaged the Pinkerton Detective Agency. A Pinkerton agent, James McParlan, infiltrated the Molly Maguires and won the confidence of its leaders. His evidence, 1876–77, resulted in leading figures in the organisation being hanged and many others being imprisoned. The society was disbanded in the United States in 1877.

In January 1979, signing a posthumous pardon to John Kehoe, who had been hanged for membership of the Molly Maguires, Governor Milton Shapp of Pennsylvania said:

> We can be proud of the men known as the Molly Maguires, because they defiantly faced allegations to make trade unionism a criminal conspiracy. These men gave their lives on behalf of the labour struggle.

(See also SECRET SOCIETIES.)

Molony, Helena (1884–1967), trade unionist, suffragist, and actor. Inspired by MAUD GONNE, she joined INGHINIDHE NA HÉIREANN, 1903, was editor of *Bean na hÉireann,* 1908, and assisted CONSTANCE MARKIEVICZ in the founding of FIANNA ÉIREANN, 1909. She was a member of the ABBEY THEATRE players, 1909–20, a member of the Irish Citizen Army, and secretary of the Irish Women Workers' Union from 1915. Imprisoned for participation in the attack on Dublin Castle at the start of the EASTER RISING (1916), she opposed the ANGLO-IRISH TREATY (1921). She was president of the Irish Trade Union Congress, 1922–23, and a member of the Executive of SAOR ÉIRE, 1931.

Molyneaux, James (born 1920), politician (Ulster Unionist Party); born in Seacash, Killead, Co. Antrim, educated at Aldergrove School. Having served in the Royal Air Force, 1941–46, he entered politics, holding office in Unionist Associations before election to the British House of Commons, 1970–97. He was whip and secretary of the Unionist Coalition MPs, March–October 1974, and lost to HARRY WEST for leadership of the Unionist Coalition, January 1974, but won it the following October, when West lost his seat. Vice-president of the ULSTER UNIONIST COUNCIL, he was imperial grand master of the ORANGE ORDER and sovereign Commonwealth grand master of the Royal Black Institution. He played a leading role in persuading the British Prime Minister, James Callaghan, to increase the number of Northern Ireland MPs.

Determined to uphold the Union, Molyneaux announced the establishment of a Council for the Union to 'defeat the drift towards a united Ireland, as indicated by the Anglo-Irish talks,' 1981. His party beat the DUP by five seats in the Assembly elections; he polled 19,978, the highest first-preference vote of the election, 1982. A year later the party took eleven of the seventeen British House of Commons seats, and his personal vote rose to 24,017 in the new Lagan Valley constituency (more than 17,000 ahead of his DUP rival, Rev. William Beattie). Molyneaux and REV. IAN PAISLEY of the DUP united to oppose the ANGLO-IRISH AGREEMENT (1985); their 'Ulster says no' campaign was launched with a rally of 150,000 people in Belfast City Hall. All fifteen Unionist MPs resigned their seats to provoke by-elections, 23 January 1986, but unionist jubilation was tempered by the loss of Newry-Armagh to Séamus Mallon of the SDLP.

In the 1987 elections to the British House of Commons the total UUP vote dropped. Molyneaux entered 'talks about talks' with the Secretary of State for Northern Ireland, TOM KING, but would not accept full power-sharing with nationalists, which he called a 'shotgun marriage', though he would be prepared to offer a role to the SDLP in government. During the BROOKE-MAYHEW TALKS (1991–92) he maintained a close political relationship with Paisley. During 1992 he found common ground with the DUP and the Alliance Party on a committee-based system of government at Stormont but on condition that the Republic drop the definition of the national territory in articles 2 and 3 of the Constitution of Ireland. In a warning to the British government, Unionist opposition to the Treaty of Maastricht, 1992, cut the government's majority to three. Molyneaux's statement that he and the British Prime Minister, JOHN MAJOR, did 'understand each other' led to nationalist fears of a sell-out by the British government. Unlike Paisley, Molyneaux travelled to Dublin to meet Irish government ministers. In August 1992 he told Orangemen in New York that the unionist people of Northern Ireland were 'victims of ethnic cleansing.' In October 1993, condemning the HUME-ADAMS TALKS, which he described as a 'recipe for bloodshed,' he insisted that there would have to be a lengthy period before SINN FÉIN could be admitted to talks. Following the DOWNING STREET DECLARATION (1993) he secured assurances from Major about the non-Irish character of the agreement.

By February 1994, when the Provisional IRA had not made a response, Molyneaux described the declaration as 'dead' and unveiled his party's 'Blueprint for Stability'. It rejected the three-strand talks process and called on Major to 'restore accountable democracy.' Following the publication of the joint British-Irish discussion documents FRAMEWORKS FOR THE FUTURE, February 1995, he told Orangemen that the North-South institutions with executive powers would be a 'stepping-stone to Irish unity.' He rejected an invitation to the FORUM FOR PEACE AND RECONCILIATION in Dublin. His followers became increasingly disillusioned with his leadership during 1995, and he stood down on his seventy-fifth birthday, 28 August 1995. He was knighted in 1996 and in July 1997 was made Lord Molyneaux of Killead. He was an adviser to Jeffrey Donaldson in opposing DAVID TRIMBLE's leadership of the UUP after the BELFAST AGREEMENT.

Monetary Reform, a maverick one-man political party founded by Oliver J. Flanagan (1920–1987), a Dáil candidate in Laois-Offaly in the general election of 1943. The party's programme was to print more money. Flanagan secured his seat, the party faded away, and he became a prominent member of FINE GAEL.

Monteagle of Brandon, Thomas Spring Rice, first Baron (1790–1866), landowner and politician (Conservative); born in Limerick, educated at the University of Cambridge. Member of Parliament for Co. Limerick, 1820–32, he was chairman of a commission on the education of the poor, 1828, which recommended the creation of a system of 'mixed' education under a governing body to protect children from interference with their religious beliefs. Other recommendations were that the governing board should superintend the MODEL SCHOOLS and that it should print books for literary and religious teaching. While Spring Rice was bitterly disappointed at the British government's lack of response, the recommendations were noted by E. G. Stanley (see EARL OF DERBY) when he established the system of NATIONAL EDUCATION, 1831.

Spring Rice opposed the extension of the Poor Law to Ireland. He was Chancellor of the Exchequer, 1835–39. Regarded as a good landlord on his estate at Mount Trenchard, Foynes, Co. Limerick, he favoured assisted emigration, supported by an Irish land tax; in 1847 he secured the establishment of the House of Lords Select Committee on Colonisation (i.e. emigration). During the GREAT FAMINE (1845–49) he paid the fares for large numbers of tenants from his estate, telling Lord Grey that what was formerly looked upon as 'banishment' was now regarded as a 'release'. Feeling that the timing was inopportune, and that the money lavished on preparations could have been more usefully expended, he refused to attend a banquet in honour of Queen Victoria's visit to Ireland, May 1849.

His granddaughter Mary Ellen Spring Rice was a member of the crew of the ASGARD in the HOWTH GUN-RUNNING (1914).

Monteith, Robert (1880–1956), nationalist; born in Newtown Mount Kennedy, Co. Wicklow, educated at Kilquade National School. Having served in the British army in India and in the Anglo-Boer War (1899–1902), he returned to Ireland to work in the Ordnance Survey but lost his position when he joined the IRISH VOLUNTEERS. His military experience made him a valuable asset, and he was appointed an instructor. He was sent to Germany to assist ROGER CASEMENT in recruiting an Irish Brigade from among Irish prisoners of war; on being informed that no German soldiers were available but that 20,000 rifles would be shipped to Ireland for the Easter Rising (1916), Monteith, considering this inadequate, accompanied Casement to Ireland to prevent the rising. Together with Casement and Sergeant Daniel Bailey of the 'Irish Brigade' he was put ashore at Banna Strand, near Fenit, Co. Kerry, where Casement was found to be too ill to travel. Leaving Casement hidden, Monteith (using the name Murray) and Bailey (using the name Mulcahy) travelled to Tralee, where Bailey was arrested.

Suffering from malaria, Monteith made his way to Cork, where he was hidden by Capuchin monks until he escaped to New York. ÉAMON DE VALERA appointed him organiser of the AMERICAN ASSOCIATION FOR THE RECOGNITION OF THE IRISH REPUBLIC, 1920–22. He later settled in Detroit, where he worked in the Ford car plant.

Montgomery, Henry (1788–1865), clergyman (Presbyterian); born in Killead, Co. Antrim, educated privately and at Glasgow College. Ordained in 1809, he held the living of Dunmurry, Co. Antrim, until his death while also working as headmaster of the English school in Royal Belfast Academical Institution from 1817. He vehemently rebutted the assertions of REV. HENRY COOKE, who had denounced the institution to the Royal Commission on Education in January 1824 as 'a seminary of Arianism'; Montgomery later defeated Cooke in the latter's efforts to exclude Arians from professorships at the institution, April 1841. He led the Arian secessionists from the Synod of Ulster and engaged in spirited public debate with Cooke thereafter. The new Remonstrant Synod, consisting of three presbyteries and seventeen congregations, held its first meeting on 25 May 1830. A supporter of religious liberty, Montgomery advocated CATHOLIC EMANCIPATION but opposed repeal of the Union and supported the NATIONAL EDUCATION system. A prolific pamphleteer, he edited *Bible Christians* for many years.

Montgomery, Hugh de Fellenburg (1844–1924), landowner and politician (Ulster Unionist); educated at the University of Oxford. From his home in Blessingbourne, Co. Tyrone, he oversaw the running of his 12,500-acre estate in Cos. Fermanagh and Tyrone, where he was a popular landlord. He granted rent reductions during the crisis of 1879–82 but opposed the LAND ACTS (1881–1903) and condemned compulsory purchase as destructive of the Union. Critical of the ORANGE ORDER, he was reconciled to it by the threat of home rule. He was suspicious of SIR EDWARD CARSON, whose commitment to unionism, he believed, could lead to the neglect of Ulster Unionists. A member of the Executive of the IRISH LOYAL AND PATRIOTIC UNION, he published propaganda opposing HOME RULE, was a member of the Advisory Committee of the Ulster Unionist Council, and helped to draft the ULSTER SOLEMN LEAGUE AND COVENANT, September 1912. He reluctantly accepted the idea of the exclusion of six counties from home rule and was 'Father' of the Senate of Northern Ireland, 1921–24. He founded the Irish Association for Cultural, Economic and Social Relations, 1938, to help bridge the gulf between the two communities in Ireland.

Moore, George Henry (1811–1870), landlord and politician; born at Ballyglass, Co. Mayo, educated at the University of Cambridge. Member of Parliament for Co. Mayo from 1847, he was considered an excellent landlord and supported TENANT RIGHT. Founder of the CATHOLIC DEFENCE ASSOCIATION, he was leader of the 'IRISH BRIGADE' and prominent in the formation of the INDEPENDENT IRISH PARTY. He lost his parliamentary seat in 1857 following charges of clerical interference in his election. Though critical of the FENIANS, he was appalled at their treatment in prison. Responding to a letter from JEREMIAH O'DONOVAN ROSSA, smuggled from Millbank Prison and published in the press, he successfully petitioned W. E. GLADSTONE for an inquiry, which confirmed Rossa's allegations and led to the release of more than thirty Fenians. Re-elected in 1868, he held the seat until his death. He was the father of the novelist George Moore (1852–1933) and COLONEL MAURICE MOORE.

Moore, Colonel Maurice George (1854–1939), soldier; born in Ballyglass, Co. Mayo, son of GEORGE HENRY MOORE and younger brother of the novelist George Moore (1852–1933), educated at St Mary's College, Birmingham. Commissioned in the British army, 1875, he fought in the Kaffir and Zulu Wars (1877–79) and in Natal. He commanded the 1st Battalion of the Connaught Rangers, 1900–06, forming a cavalry corps that distinguished itself during the Anglo-Boer War. After settling in Ireland he supported the IRISH PARTY in the struggle for HOME RULE. An instructor in the Irish Volunteers, he took part in the HOWTH GUN-RUNNING (1914), in the aftermath of which he succeeded in having guns that were seized in the struggle with police returned. Following the establishment of the Irish Free State he campaigned for the withholding of LAND ANNUITIES; referring to the financial agreement of 19 March 1926 between the Free State and the British government, he said, 'We have been burgled, and we have bribed the burglar.' With serving Irish officers and former officers of the British army he organised a campaign to free the sixty men serving prison sentences for participation in the CONNAUGHT RANGERS MUTINY (1920). He supported the NATIONAL LEAGUE PARTY, was a founder-member of FIANNA FÁIL in 1926, and was later a member of the Senate. He published *An Irish Gentleman: George Henry Moore* (an account of his father, 1913) and *The Rise of the Volunteers, 1913–17* (1938).

Moran, D. P. [David Patrick] (1869–1936), journalist and polemicist; born in Waterford, educated at Christian Brothers' school and Castleknock College. Secretary of a London branch of the IRISH NATIONAL LEAGUE, he was active in the Gaelic League and the Irish Literary Society. He took two extension courses in economics from the University of London and returned to Ireland in 1898 to edit *New Ireland Review*, in which he published the articles later collected as *The Philosophy of Irish Ireland* (1905). Inventor of the term 'IRISH IRELAND', he called for a thorough political, cultural and economic nationalism whereby Ireland would be a self-governing country 'living, moving and having its being in its own language, self-reliant . . . developing its own manners and customs, creating its own literature out of its own distinctive consciousness.'

He founded the LEADER, 1900–73, in which he criticised virtually every part of the national movement, including the GAELIC LEAGUE, W. B. YEATS and the LITERARY REVIVAL ('one of the most glaring frauds that the credulous Irish people ever swallowed'), SINN FÉIN (the 'Green Hungarian Band'), the IRB, and the IRISH PARTY ('West Britons' and 'shoneens'). Though perceived as bigoted and sectarian, he used Protestant printers and Protestant contributors, while campaigning against anti-Catholic discrimination in employment. He reserved some of his most vitriolic language for *The Playboy of the Western World* (1907), condemning its attitude towards Irish women. He organised a Buy Irish campaign and the 'Collar the King' policy (see EDWARD VII) and served on the Provisional Committee of the IRISH VOLUNTEERS, 1913.

Following the Easter Rising (1916), during which the offices of the *Leader* were destroyed, he ceased to have any significant influence. He became a supporter of Sinn Féin after the Co. Clare by-election in 1917. The *Leader* was suppressed during 1919; a year later he brought it out as the *New Leader,* before reverting to the original title later in the year. He supported the Anglo-Irish Treaty (1921). Having supported Fianna Fáil (sympathising with its protectionist economic policy), he switched to Cumann na nGaedheal, 1930, over Fianna Fáil's ambivalence on the constitutional status of the Irish Free State. He supported EOIN O'DUFFY during the 1930s. His daughter Nuala Moran succeeded him as editor of the *Leader.* He published a novel, *Tom Kelly* (1905).

***Moresby* Tragedy** (24 December 1895). The *Moresby,* a three-masted schooner, left Cardiff on 21 December 1895 with a cargo of coal for South America. It was captained by 35-year-old Charles Comber (whose wife and four-year-old daughter were on board), with a crew of twenty-two. Two days at sea, to avoid gales that had already damaged his sails, Comber put into Dungarvan Bay, Co. Waterford, dropping anchor at the harbour entrance. Deciding he and his crew were now safe, he declined the assistance of a lifeboat from Ballynacourty. The next day—Christmas Eve—the anchor chains snapped and the ship struck the Whitehouse Sandbank. A volunteer crew from Dungarvan, under Captain John Veale, set about the rescue; but by the time the lifeboat reached the vessel many of its crew had abandoned ship and drowned, including the captain and his family. Seven of the twenty-five were rescued, two of whom died shortly afterwards.

Moriarty, David (1814–1877), bishop (Catholic); born in Kilcarragh, Co. Kerry, educated at Boulogne-sur-Mer and St Patrick's College, Maynooth. Ordained in 1839, he was vice-president of the Irish College, Paris, and president of All Hallows' College, Drumcondra, Dublin, 1847–54, before becoming Bishop of Kerry, 1856. Following the IRB rising of 1867 in Co. Kerry he became notorious for the vehemence of his condemnation, calling down on the FENIANS 'God's heaviest curse, his withering, blasting, blighting curse,' while informing his public that 'Hell is not hot enough and eternity not long enough to punish these miscreants.' Opposed to HOME RULE, he put forward his own anti-home-rule candidate in Co. Kerry in the 1872 by-election, who was beaten by a Protestant home-ruler, R. P. Blennerhassett. Attending the First Vatican Council in 1870, he disapproved of the definition of Papal infallibility, claiming that the time was not opportune for its promulgation.

Moriarty Tribunal, the Tribunal of Inquiry into Payments to Messrs Charles Haughey and Michael Lowry, its sole member Mr Justice Michael Moriarty. The tribunal was established on 26 September 1997 to investigate payments made directly and indirectly to the former Taoiseach CHARLES HAUGHEY during any period in public office from January 1979 to December 1996. It was to build on the revelations uncovered by the MCCRACKEN TRIBUNAL. Its terms of reference included an examination of the source of money held in the Ansbacher accounts (see ANSBACHER INQUIRY) and to examine payments to Michael Lowry TD or any company associated with him. Public hearings began on 31 October 1997; the tribunal was still sitting in 2003.

Morley, John, first Viscount (1838–1923), British journalist and politician (Liberal). As editor of the *Fortnightly Review* he was one of the most influential political and intellectual forces in England. He edited the *Pall Mall*

Gazette, 1880–83. His integrity and sympathetic approach to HOME RULE made him an ideal intermediary for CHARLES STEWART PARNELL and W. E. GLADSTONE. He defended the LAND LEAGUE. After his election as member of Parliament for Newcastle upon Tyne, 1883, he supported JOSEPH CHAMBERLAIN until they broke over home rule (1886), when he made the celebrated accusation that Chamberlain had played Casca to Gladstone's Caesar. As Chief Secretary for Ireland, February–July 1886 and 1892–95, he was consulted by Gladstone on the (first) HOME RULE BILL, which was defeated in July 1886. He supported CHARLES STEWART PARNELL when the *Times* (London) published the series 'PARNELLISM AND CRIME' but discouraged him from taking action against the paper. He was closely involved with Parnell and Gladstone after the *O'Shea v. O'Shea and Parnell* divorce decision, November 1890. Gladstone wrote him a letter on 24 November to be shown to JUSTIN MCCARTHY, who was to make known its contents to Parnell: that if Parnell remained at the head of the Irish Party it would render Gladstone's leadership of the Liberals 'a nullity.' When Parnell was re-elected chairman of the party, 25 November, Gladstone published the letter.

Morley was noted for his caution during his second term as Chief Secretary. He assisted Gladstone in carrying the second Home Rule Bill (1893) and attacked the privileges of the Anglo-Irish ASCENDANCY, removing some of the more intransigent magistrates. His published works include *The Struggle for National Education* (1873), *On Compromises* (1874), *Burke* (1879), *The Life of Richard Cobden* (1881), *Life of Gladstone* (3 vols., 1903), and *Recollections* (1917).

Morrissey, Daniel (1895–1981), politician (Labour Party, independent, and Fine Gael); born in Nenagh, Co. Tipperary, educated at Christian Brothers' school. A labourer with the Great Southern Railway, he later became an insurance agent and from 1916 an official with the Irish Transport and General Workers' Union. A member of Dáil Éireann, 1922–57, he was chief whip of the Labour Party, 1923–28, and Leas-Cheann Comhairle, 1928–32. Close to CUMANN NA NGAEDHEAL, he and Richard Anthony defied the Labour Party whip to support Cosgrave's government in the establishment of the Military Tribunal, 1931; he was expelled from the Labour Party and was re-elected as independent labour candidate in 1932 before joining Fine Gael in 1933. He took part in talks between Fine Gael and the Labour Party that led to the first inter-party government (1948–51), in which he was Minister for Industry and Commerce, 1948–51, and Minister for Justice, 1951. During his time in the Department of Industry and Commerce he established the Industrial Development Authority and nationalised the railways and bus companies. He also took part in the negotiations leading to the ANGLO-IRISH TRADE AGREEMENT in 1948.

Mortished, R. J. P. [Ronald James Patrick] (1891–1957), labour leader; born in London of a Co. Limerick father, educated at London School of Economics. He entered the British civil service, 1908, and later became a member of the WHITE CROSS and the Reconstruction Committee, 1921. He was secretary of the committee that drafted the CONSTITUTION OF THE IRISH FREE STATE (1922). Assistant secretary of the Labour Party and of the IRISH TRADE UNION CONGRESS, 1922–30, he served in the International Labour Organisation, 1930–46, and was chairman of the LABOUR COURT 1946–52. He published *The World Parliament of Labour* (an account of the ILO, 1946).

Mossop, William Stephen (1788–1827), medallist; born in Dublin, educated at Samuel White's Academy, Dublin. He took over the family engraving business on the death of his father, 1805. He produced a series of medals on the prominent figures of his time, including the first one of DANIEL O'CONNELL, 1816; it failed commercially, as did his medal of HENRY GRATTAN. He enjoyed commercial success with his medal to mark the visit of KING GEORGE IV and a medal of Rev. George Walker, hero of the Siege of Derry, commissioned by the APPRENTICE BOYS' CLUB. He designed seals for most of the public bodies in Ireland. He became deranged as a result of worry and overwork and died in Richmond Asylum, Dublin. A selection of his original steel dies can be seen in the Royal Irish Academy, Dublin.

Mother and Child Scheme, originally part of the Health Act (1947); when the terms of the scheme were unacceptable to the Catholic hierarchy it was shelved on the direction of the Taoiseach, ÉAMON DE VALERA. Fianna Fáil lost office to the first inter-party government, 1948–51, and two years later the scheme was revived by the Minister for Health, DR NOEL BROWNE. Following consultations with the Child Health Scheme (consisting of medical specialists) and representatives of local authorities and of the Departments of Health, Education, and Social Welfare, a draft of the scheme was prepared, June 1950.

Browne's proposed scheme, which was not compulsory, included education 'in respect of motherhood' for all mothers, covered all mothers and children up to the age of sixteen, and had no means test. The Irish Medical Association objected to the concept of 'socialised medicine'. Browne received the support of the Government when he informed Dáil Éireann that he would not agree to a means test. Considering the scheme during October, the bishops expressed disquiet at clauses that they had already rejected in the 1947 draft (the lack of a means test, and granting patients a choice of doctor). An episcopal commission, consisting of JOHN CHARLES MCQUAID, BISHOP MICHAEL BROWNE of Galway and Bishop Staunton of Ferns, was established. Following a meeting with the bishops, 11 October 1950, Browne was under the impression that he had answered their objections. He again rejected a means test, 24 October, when the IMA pointed out the lack of resources at the disposal of the state. The bishops made it clear to the Government that they considered there was an important issue of 'faith and morals': the family, they stated, was the final arbiter with regard to sex education; they also objected to non-Catholic doctors treating Catholic mothers-to-be or offering them sex education.

The debate continued until March 1951, during which time the relationship between Browne and the leader of his party, SEÁN MACBRIDE, deteriorated, while he was also at odds with the head of the Government, JOHN A. COSTELLO, and his other colleagues, who wished to concede to the bishops and to the medical profession in their demand for a means test.

Browne published details of the scheme, 6 March, having refused his colleagues' request for the inclusion of a means test. It was rejected by the bishops, on the grounds that none of their objections had been met. Browne met Archbishop McQuaid, 24 March, and agreed that the bishops had the right to decide issues of 'faith and morals'. The bishops rejected the scheme as 'opposed to Catholic social teaching,' 4 April 1951; the Government, conceding to the bishops, refused to support Browne and abandoned the scheme. MacBride demanded Browne's resignation, 11 April. After resigning, Browne published his correspondence with the hierarchy. The government fell, June 1951; the incoming Fianna Fáil government introduced a public health scheme with a means test.

Mowlam, Dr Marjorie ('Mo') (born 1949), British politician (Labour Party). As British Labour Party spokesperson on Northern Ireland from October 1994 she pledged to extend the life of the Northern Ireland Forum if the Labour Party won the general election of May 1997 (the Forum had been suspended until the resumption of talks at Stormont scheduled for June 1997) and announced that a Provisional IRA ceasefire could enable SINN FÉIN to take part in talks. On her appointment as Secretary of State for Northern Ireland, May 1997, she stated that her priority was for a Provisional IRA ceasefire and then talks; 'decommissioning' was secondary to the talks. When the ceasefire arrived, 19 July, she said that contact with Sinn Féin would resume immediately. The British and Irish governments agreed on a new international body to oversee decommissioning. Mowlam worked to get the talks process off the ground but was downgraded by TONY BLAIR in the period leading up to the BELFAST AGREEMENT (1998). In July 1999 she declared the Provisional IRA, UDA and UVF inactive, thus enabling their imprisoned members to benefit from the early release scheme. Her popularity with Sinn Féin and the IRA was not mirrored among unionist politicians or loyalist organisations.

Moylan, Seán (1888–1957), politician (Fianna Fáil); born in Cork, educated at national school. He was active in the Irish Volunteers and the IRA during the WAR OF INDEPENDENCE. He assisted LIAM LYNCH in the capture of General Lucas and was a successful brigade commandant, notably at Clonbanin, Co. Cork, 5 March 1921, where British casualties included Colonel H. R. Cumming. Opposed to the ANGLO-IRISH TREATY (1921), he was director of operations in the new IRA during the CIVIL WAR, when his assistant was ÉAMON DE VALERA. He continued to support Sinn Féin until de Valera founded FIANNA FÁIL, 1926. He was Minister for Education in de Valera's government, 1951–54. Having lost his seat in the 1957 general election, he was nominated to Seanad Éireann by de Valera, and was one of very few senators to hold ministerial office (Minister for Agriculture, March–November 1957). He died within a few hours of handing in his resignation.

Muintir na Tíre ('people of the country'), a community development association founded by CANON JOHN HAYES, parish priest of Bansha,

Co. Tipperary, 17 May 1931. He adopted as his model the Belgian organisation Boerenbond Belge (fl. 1890); the Irish movement stated as its aim 'to unite the rural communities of Ireland . . . to unite in one body the rural workers of the country . . . to give the agricultural workers in Ireland their due and proper position in the life of the nation.' The organisation introduced informal 'fireside chats', rural weekends, and a national conference, and published the *Landmark* and *Rural Ireland*, sold at church gates on Sundays, later replaced by a monthly bulletin. It played a significant role in securing the rapid extension of rural electrification, local industries, the erection and extension of leisure facilities (mostly accomplished by voluntary labour), the establishment of group water schemes, and the provision of free school meals, or hot drinks, to children in many rural schools.

Mulcahy, General Richard (1886–1971), soldier and politician (Sinn Féin, Cumann na nGaedheal, and Fine Gael); born in Waterford, educated at Mount Sion and Thurles Christian Brothers' Schools. An engineer in the Post Office in 1902, he joined the IRB, the Gaelic League, and the Irish Volunteers. He was second in command to THOMAS ASHE at the BATTLE OF ASHBOURNE during the Easter Rising (1916). Interned in Knutsford and Fron-Goch, on his release, November 1916, he became deputy chief of staff of the Volunteers, working closely with MICHAEL COLLINS. Chief of staff of the IRA, he was elected to the first Dáil Éireann, becoming Minister for Defence and then assistant to CATHAL BRUGHA, April 1919. He was largely responsible with Collins for directing the military struggle against Crown forces during the WAR OF INDEPENDENCE.

Supporting the ANGLO-IRISH TREATY (1921), he became Minister for National Defence in the Provisional Government while also chief of staff of the Free State army. In these capacities he retained contact with that section of the IRA that had rejected the Treaty, and he was a signatory of the army document that attempted, in the interests of national unity, to secure a compromise between supporters and opponents of the Treaty. Following Collins's death, 22 August 1922, he was responsible for prosecuting the fight against the Republicans during the CIVIL WAR, during which he met ÉAMON DE VALERA in an unsuccessful attempt to end hostilities, 6 September. On 10 October he was granted emergency powers in the war against the Republicans, with a virtual *carte blanche* to expedite their defeat.

He remained Minister for Defence in the Free State government until March 1924, when he resigned during the ARMY MUTINY, becoming Minister for Local Government, 1927–32. A prominent member of the BLUESHIRTS, he was a founder-member of FINE GAEL, for which he was a Dáil representative throughout his political career, succeeding W. T. COSGRAVE as leader in 1944. When he was unacceptable as Taoiseach to CLANN NA POBLACHTA in 1948 he stood aside to allow JOHN A. COSTELLO become Taoiseach in the first inter-party government. He was Minister for Education, 1948–51, and held the post again as well as being Minister for the Gaeltacht, July–October 1956, when Clann na Poblachta again vetoed his appointment as Taoiseach. He retired from the Dáil in 1961. His papers were donated to the National University of Ireland, Dublin, where they are held in the Richard Mulcahy Trust.

Mulgrave, Constantine Henry Phipps, second Earl (1797–1863), British politician (Whig), educated at the University of Cambridge. He was a member of Parliament from 1822 until succeeding to the title in 1831. He supported CATHOLIC EMANCIPATION and parliamentary reform. His appointment as Lord Lieutenant of Ireland, 1835, was greeted with enthusiasm by DANIEL O'CONNELL and his Irish following. He headed one of the most constructive Irish administrations of the century, working with the Chief Secretary for Ireland, Lord Morpeth, and Under-Secretary, THOMAS DRUMMOND. He was widely criticised for his attempts to win Ireland to the Union through concessions. He supported Drummond in removing anti-Catholic officials from office and denounced the influence of the ORANGE ORDER. He incurred further hostility for consulting the Catholic hierarchy on important issues. He several times exercised the Viceregal prerogative to commute death sentences. Created Marquess of Normanby in 1839, he retired from Ireland to become Secretary of State for War and the Colonies, 1839.

Mulholland, Andrew (1791–1866), cotton and linen industrialist; born in Belfast. He rebuilt his mill after a fire, 1828, and within two years was producing some of the earliest flax yarn to be machine-spun in Ireland; previously flax had to be sent to Manchester to be spun and later re-imported as yarn. He was lord mayor of Belfast, 1845, and donated the great organ to the Ulster Hall. Other offices included justice of the peace and deputy lieutenant and high sheriff for Cos. Antrim and Down. He retired from public life in 1860.

Mullins, Thomas (1903–1978), politician (Fianna Fáil); born in New Rochelle, New York, educated in New York until he came to Ireland, 1914, and continued his education at ST ENDA'S SCHOOL. A member of Fianna Éireann, Sinn Féin, and the Irish Volunteers, he was a member of the IRA during the WAR OF INDEPENDENCE. Imprisoned on Spike Island, Co. Cork, in Wormwood Scrubs Prison, London (where he went on hunger strike), and in Ballykinler Camp, Co. Down, 1920–21, he rejected the Anglo-Irish Treaty (1921) and supported the Irregulars during the CIVIL WAR, when he was captured and sentenced to death. During his imprisonment in Mountjoy Jail, Dublin, he went on a 41-day hunger strike. He built up the FIANNA FÁIL organisation in west Cork and was a member of Dáil Éireann for the area from 1927. Close to leading radicals in the IRA, he supported SAOR ÉIRE and was prominent in opposition to the BLUESHIRTS. He organised public relations for the Fianna Fáil government when it took office in 1932. Having lost his seat, he contested Co. Dublin in the 1947 by-election, when he lost to SEÁN MACBRIDE. Organiser of the Fianna Fáil victory of 1957, he became a member of Seanad Éireann and was general secretary of Fianna Fáil until 1973.

Municipal Corporations (Ireland) Act (1840), introduced by the Whig government during its period of alliance with DANIEL O'CONNELL, whose support was vital to its survival. Under the act, fifty-eight corporations were dissolved and the ten remaining reconstituted with selective town councils (Belfast, Clonmel, Cork, Drogheda, Dublin, Kilkenny, Limerick, Derry, Sligo, and Waterford). Towns with valuations of less than £100 were administered by Poor Law guardians. The act differed from its English counterpart in that the municipal franchise was a £10 valuation, while control of the police was centrally vested in Dublin Castle. The act marked a further extension of the reform of LOCAL GOVERNMENT.

Murphy, Gerard (1901–1959), scholar; born in Clones, Co. Monaghan, educated at UCD, graduating in Celtic studies. He worked in the National Library under R. I. BEST and spent four years in Switzerland before returning to become lecturer in bardic poetry and Early Irish literature at University College, Dublin, 1930, then professor of the history of Celtic literature, 1948. Over a period of twenty years, 1933–53, he translated parts 2 and 3 of Duanaire Finn (the poem-book of Fionn) for the IRISH TEXTS SOCIETY. A frequent contributor to *Studies* and *Ériu*, he edited *Éigse* (the journal of Modern Irish studies) from 1938. Other works include *Glimpses of Gaelic Ireland* (1948), *Ossianic Lore and Romantic Tales of Mediaeval Ireland* (1955), *Saga and Myth in Ancient Ireland* (1955), *Early Irish Lyrics* (1956), and *Early Irish Metrics* (1961).

Murphy, John (1771–1847), bishop (Catholic); born in Cork, educated at Lisbon. He was the owner of the largest private library of his time in Ireland. Following ordination he returned to Cork, where he became bishop, 1814–47. He was an early patron of the sculptor JOHN HOGAN. He bequeathed more than 120 Irish volumes to St Patrick's College, Maynooth; the remainder of his library was divided into three lots for disposal in London.

Murphy, Patrick (1834–1862), giant; born in Kilbroney, Co. Down. Exhibited widely on the Continent as the tallest known living man, he was reputed to be 8 feet 1 inch (246 cm) in height. Following his death in Marseille, in deference to his frequently expressed wish his embalmed body was returned to his native parish for burial.

Murphy, William Martin (1844–1919), businessman and politician; born in Bantry, Co. Cork, educated at Belvedere College, Dublin. He took over the family contracting business when he was nineteen and in 1870 married the daughter of James F. Lombard, who had made a fortune in the drapery business and was one of the first promoters of tramways in Dublin. Having constructed railways in Britain and financed similar undertakings in the Gold Coast (Ghana) and South America, he returned to Ireland, where he built railways and tramways and bought newspapers, including the *Irish Catholic, Irish Independent,* and *Sunday Independent,* and other businesses. A member of Parliament, 1885–92, he was closely associated with T. M. HEALY. A supporter of the CENTENARY CELEBRATIONS, 1898, he was the chief promoter and chairman of the committee of the Irish International Exhibition (1907), following which he declined a knighthood. He was a director of the Great Southern Railway and Midland Great Western Railway and president of the Dublin Chamber of Commerce,

1912–13.

Though he was not, according to himself, 'in principle' opposed to workers joining unions, he was determined to oppose the militancy of JAMES LARKIN ('an unscrupulous man who claims the right to give you the word of command and issue his orders to you and to use you as tools to make him labour dictator of Dublin') and the IRISH TRANSPORT AND GENERAL WORKERS' UNION ('a disreputable organisation'). To combat 'Larkinism' he formed an Employers' Federation, of which he was president. In August 1913 he demanded that his employees give a written undertaking not to join the ITGWU. When he sacked a hundred workers who had joined the union, 21 August 1913, Larkin retaliated by calling out the tramway workers, 26 August. In September the Employers' Federation locked out the workers in a vicious confrontation that became the DUBLIN LOCK-OUT (1913).

During the Great War, Murphy recruited for the British army; he convened a meeting of employers in November at which he proposed sacking able-bodied men to force them to enlist. He chaired the inaugural meeting of the Fire and General Losses Association, 9 May 1916. He was chairman of the Finance and General Purposes Committee of Dublin Corporation. He left a personal estate of £264,005, allowing for bequests to charities and individual employees. His book *The Home Rule Act, 1914, Exposed* (1917) advocated colonial status for Ireland.

Murray, Charles (born 1917), civil servant and economist; born in Dublin, educated at the University of London. He served with the Revenue Commissioners and in the Department of Agriculture before moving to the Department of the Taoiseach. Having been an adviser to JOHN A. COSTELLO, 1948–51 and 1954–57, when SEÁN LEMASS succeeded ÉAMON DE VALERA he moved to the Department of Finance, where he was assistant secretary, 1959–69, and secretary from 1969. He worked closely with T. K. WHITAKER during the 1950s. He was responsible for a guideline memo in January 1957 that linked economic planning with events on the Continent; he believed that the future of Ireland's economy lay either in a European free trade area or with the EEC, which came into existence a few months later under the Treaty of Rome. Murray's and Whitaker's work led to the PROGRAMMES FOR ECONOMIC EXPANSION. Murray was a founder-member, chairman and later president of the Institute of Public Administration, governor of the Central Bank, 1976–81, and deputy chairman of Co-operation North. In 2000 he gave evidence before the MORIARTY TRIBUNAL.

Murray, Daniel (1768–1852), bishop (Catholic); born in Redcross, Co. Wicklow, educated at the Irish College, Salamanca, ordained in 1790. As a curate in Arklow he witnessed the Battle of Arklow during the rising of the UNITED IRISHMEN (1798). His aged parish priest having been murdered in his bed, Murray fled to Dublin, where he held various curacies before becoming a reluctant coadjutor to ARCHBISHOP TROY, 30 November 1809. He twice travelled to Rome to impress on Pope Pius VII the opposition of the Irish hierarchy to the VETO, 1908. He successfully represented the Irish church in Paris, January 1810, seeking the restitution of the property of religious houses confiscated during the Reformation. President of St Patrick's College, Maynooth, June 1812 to November 1813, he assisted MARY AIKENHEAD in founding the Irish Sisters of Charity, presenting her with a £4,000 bequest. He also encouraged EDMUND RICE to bring the Christian Brothers to Dublin.

His policy of détente with the British government was frequently criticised by nationalists; his acceptance of the NATIONAL EDUCATION system led to a prolonged quarrel with ARCHBISHOP JOHN MACHALE. He accepted a position on the Board of Education as one of the two Catholic members (the other was A. R. Blake), with the support of Rome and the majority of Irish bishops. Criticised for his frequent appearances at DUBLIN CASTLE functions, he contended that his appearance demonstrated an end to the ostracism of Catholics and that it 'helped check the sectarian animosity that unhappily pervades society.' Accepting the Charitable Donations and Bequests (Ireland) Act (1844) over the objections of DANIEL O'CONNELL and MacHale, he was at one with them in their denunciation of the QUEEN'S COLLEGES as an answer to the demand for a Catholic university. He declined the offer of a Privy Councillorship from LORD JOHN RUSSELL. He built ninety-seven new churches in the archdiocese of Dublin. With the exception of £100 towards the work of the Irish Sisters of Charity, the poor and sick were the sole beneficiaries of his will.

Myles, Sir Thomas (1857–1937), surgeon and nationalist; born in Limerick, educated at TCD. He entered Dr Steevens' Hospital,

Dublin, 1881, and was a surgeon at Richmond Hospital. Secretary of the Dublin Hospitals Committee, 1885, he was professor of pathology at the Royal College of Surgeons in Ireland, 1889–97, and later president, 1900–02, and Honorary Surgeon to the King in Ireland. His yacht, CHOTAH, was used to transport German guns for the Irish Volunteers in the HOWTH GUN-RUNNING (1914). On the outbreak of the Great War, with the rank of lieutenant-colonel, he became consulting surgeon to the British forces and in this capacity attended to members of the Irish Volunteers wounded during the EASTER RISING (1916). He published several papers on surgical matters, many of them advocating Listerian practices, which he had adopted.

N

Nally, Patrick W. (1857–1891), republican; born in Balla, Co. Mayo, educated locally. A member of the IRB, he was chief organiser in Connacht and delegate to the Supreme Council, 1879, and a founder-member and secretary of the LAND LEAGUE. He suggested to MICHAEL CUSACK the idea for what became the GAELIC ATHLETIC ASSOCIATION. Sentenced to ten years' imprisonment for the 'Crossmolina Conspiracy' (1881), he was subjected to harsh treatment in Mountjoy Jail, Dublin, and died shortly after his release. DR MARK RYAN unveiled a monument to Nally in Balla in 1900.

Nangle, Rev. Edward (1799–1883), evangelical clergyman (Church of Ireland); born in Kildalkey, Co. Meath, educated at TCD. He ministered at Athboy, Co. Meath, and at Arvagh, Co. Cavan, until his health broke. He was secretary of the Sunday School Society of Ireland and also agent for a Dublin firm that produced religious tracts. He arrived in Achill Island, Co. Mayo, in 1831 with famine relief and stayed to found a Protestant missionary colony that included a church, hospital, and school. He attacked the 'superstition and idolatry of the Church of Rome' in the *Achill Missionary Herald and Western Witness*. ARCHBISHOP JOHN MACHALE reacted by increasing the number of priests and introducing friars of the Third Order of St Francis to the island. During the GREAT FAMINE (1845–49) Nangle incurred the hostility of both Catholic and Protestant clergy when it appeared that his proselytising activities were directed to the starving on the 'food for conversion' principle. He bought the estate of his former landlord, Sir Richard O'Donnell, for £17,500. He published a popular *Introduction to the Irish Language* (1854) in an attempt to win native converts to his church. His colony was almost defunct by 1879, and Nangle spent his remaining years in opposing the LAND LEAGUE.

Napier, Oliver (born 1935), solicitor and politician (Alliance Party). He was prominent in the NEW ULSTER MOVEMENT before founding the ALLIANCE PARTY. He was head of the Office of Law Reform in the power-sharing Executive of the Northern Ireland Assembly, 1973–74, and represented the party at the conference that produced the SUNNINGDALE AGREEMENT (1973). A member of Belfast City Council, 1977–89, he was also elected to the Constitutional Convention (1975–76). He was a member for East Belfast in the Assembly, 1982–86. Having failed to win a seat in the 1983 election for the British House of Commons he resigned the leadership of the Alliance Party, 1984. Knighted in 1985, he represented Co. Down in the Northern Ireland Forum (1996–98) and was chairman of the Northern Ireland Standing Committee on Human Rights, 1988–92.

Nathan, Sir Matthew (1852–1939), British politician. As Under-Secretary for Ireland from September 1914 his *sang-froid* in the face of nationalist hostility and crisis, once considered a virtue, became a distinct liability. Birrell dubbed him 'Nathan the Unwise' when, in the face of overwhelming evidence of imminent action by the Irish Volunteers before the EASTER RISING (1916), he refused to take positive action. He believed there were not enough arms in the country to support an insurrection and that in any case 'revolutions never happen after noon.' He was trapped in Dublin Castle (shortly after noon) during the rising. He resigned on 3 May. A royal commission under Lord Hardinge concluded that while Nathan carried out his responsibilities

> with the utmost loyalty . . . we consider that he did not sufficiently impress upon the Chief Secretary during the latter's prolonged absences from Dublin the necessity for more active measures to remedy the situation in Ireland, which on December 18th last, in a letter to the Chief Secretary, he described as "most serious and menacing."

Nation, The (1842–91), a weekly paper founded by CHARLES GAVAN DUFFY, THOMAS DAVIS, and JOHN BLAKE DILLON; its motto, suggested by Davis, was 'To create and foster public opinion in Ireland, and make it racy of the soil.' Gavan Duffy, who financed the venture, became first editor. Davis, who edited it for some five months in 1844, hoped it would realise 'a nationality of the spirit as well as the letter . . . which would embrace Protestant, Catholic, and Dissenter—Milesian and Cromwellian—the Irishman of a hundred generations and the stranger within our gates.'

The first issue, differing in shape, size and layout from its contemporaries, went on sale on 15 October 1842 at a price of 6 pence and had sold out by noon. By 31 December 1843 sales had risen to 10,730, giving it the highest circulation of Dublin newspapers (next highest was the *Weekly Freeman,* at 7,150 copies). A number of articles were reproduced abroad, particularly in Paris, where *La National* was founded with similar ideals; it was also quoted in America and in the British colonies. Its poetry was published as *The Spirit of the Nation.* The British government was concerned at its growing influence and support for YOUNG IRELAND. The Recorder (law officer) of Dublin, Frederick Shaw, read a sample of its prose and poetry into the record of the House of Commons. The *Warder,* an influential pro-establishment publication, commented: 'We regard . . . the *Nation* as the most ominous and formidable phenomenon of these strange menacing times.'

On the death of Davis, September 1845, JOHN MITCHEL became manager and chief writer but in 1847 resigned in protest at Gavan Duffy's perceived policy of moderation. With the latter's departure for Australia, 1855, ownership passed to A. M. SULLIVAN. Following the secession of YOUNG IRELAND from the REPEAL ASSOCIATION, the subsequent banning of the *Nation* from Repeal reading-rooms, and the antipathy of the Catholic clergy towards any opposition to DANIEL O'CONNELL, the paper suffered a decline in readership. It later supported ISAAC BUTT and CHARLES STEWART PARNELL (but was anti-Parnellite following the split in the Irish Party).

The *Nation* ceased publication in 1891. Acquired by WILLIAM MARTIN MURPHY, it appeared as the WEEKLY NATION from 12 June 1897; he amalgamated it with the *Independent,* August 1900. The first issue of the *Daily Independent and Nation* appeared on 1 September 1900, relaunched as the *Irish Daily Independent* on 2 January 1905, edited by W. P. Dennehy. (See IRISH INDEPENDENT.)

National Agricultural Labourers' Union, a British union that extended its activities to Ireland in 1873 in an attempt to prevent Irish immigrant labourers strike-breaking in England. The Irish leader was P. F. Johnson of Kanturk, Co. Cork, in which area some Labourers' Clubs were formed. The union took on a pro-home-rule complexion when ISAAC BUTT and P. J. Smyth became president and vice-president, respectively. It faded after 1877.

national anthem. 'The Soldier's Song', written in 1907 by PEADAR KEARNEY, with music by PATRICK HEENEY, was first sung by Seán Kavanagh in Dublin. The words were published in *Irish Freedom* in 1912, and over the next two years it replaced Patrick Pearse's 'Óró 'Sé Do Bheatha 'Bhaile!' as the marching song of the IRISH VOLUNTEERS. Following the EASTER RISING (1916) it was adopted by interned Volunteers, supplanting 'God Save Ireland' as *de facto* national anthem. The chorus of 'The Soldier's Song' was informally adopted as the national anthem of the Irish Free State in 1924 and officially adopted in 1926, replacing 'God Save the King'. It is now better known in its Irish translation as 'Amhrán na bhFiann'.

National Archives, established on 1 June 1988 from an amalgamation of the State Paper Office (founded 1702) and the PUBLIC RECORD OFFICE OF IRELAND (founded 1867). Material held includes records of government departments relating mainly to the period 1922–70; archives of the Chief Secretary's Office and its associated offices, 1790–1922, and other state agencies for the last two centuries but including some from the seventeenth and eighteenth centuries; court and probate registries for the last two centuries but including some items dating from the fourteenth century; and archives acquired from other sources, including business firms, charities, Church of Ireland parishes, estate offices, harbour boards, health boards, hospitals, schools, solicitors' offices, trade unions, and private individuals. Responsibility for the National Archives was transferred on 20 January 1993 from the Department of the Taoiseach to the new Department of Arts, Culture and the Gaeltacht (renamed in 1997 the Department of Arts, Heritage, Gaeltacht and the Islands). The National Archives moved from the Four Courts to Bishop Street, Dublin, in September 1992.

National Association, inaugurated on 29 December 1864 under the influence of ARCHBISHOP PAUL CULLEN; its first secretary was JOHN

BLAKE DILLON. Its programme included TENANT RIGHT, DISESTABLISHMENT of the Church of Ireland, and educational freedom. Supporters included SIR JOHN GRAY, W. J. O'NEILL DAUNT, and the Catholic hierarchy, with the exception of JOHN MACHALE, Archbishop of Tuam, and THOMAS NULTY, Bishop of Meath. The movement failed through poor organisation, diffuse aims, insufficient finances, and internal differences; many supporters were absorbed into the HOME GOVERNMENT ASSOCIATION, 1870.

National Botanic Gardens, Glasnevin, Dublin, established by the ROYAL DUBLIN SOCIETY under the direction of Dr Walter Wade, 1795, on a site that had been a favourite meeting-place of eighteenth-century literati. The purchase of the initial 16-acre site, 25 March 1795, was aided by a grant from the Irish Parliament. John Underwood, appointed head gardener in 1798, collaborated over the next twenty-five years with Dr Wade in establishing the gardens. Ninian Nivan, 1834–38, and Dr David Moore, 1848–79, enlarged its range and extended its exotic collection. Under Moore the garden specialised in orchid experimentation, gaining international recognition when it became the first garden to successfully achieve the germination of orchid seedlings to flowering stage, 1844–49. Moore's son Frederick Moore expanded the orchid house and was responsible for building the Great Palm House, 1884. The conservatories were the work of the architect Frederick Darley (fl.1820–30).

Known as the Royal Botanic Gardens when coming under state control, 1878, it became the National Botanic Gardens with the establishment of the Irish Free State, 1922. John Beasant, 1922–44, Thomas Walsh, 1944–68, and Aidan Brady, 1968–1993, were long-serving keepers at the gardens, which are administered by the Department of Agriculture.

National Brotherhood of St Patrick, founded by Thomas Nelson Underwood, Denis Holland and Thomas Ryan at the Rotunda Rooms, Dublin, in May 1861. It was identified with the FENIANS, for whom it became a political front. On 4 August 1863 the Catholic hierarchy condemned the organisation.

National Centre Party, founded from the NATIONAL FARMERS' AND RATEPAYERS' LEAGUE on 4 January 1933; its principal aims were monetary reform, tariff protection, the abolition of rates on agricultural land, a reduction in legal fees, and wage stability. It was also critical of the 'ECONOMIC WAR' pursued by the Fianna Fáil government. Ideologically close to CUMANN NA NGAEDHEAL, it won eleven of the twenty-six seats it contested in the 1933 general election and in 1933 merged with FINE GAEL.

National Concert Hall. On 9 May 1974 the Government announced that the Aula Maxima of University College at Earlsfort Terrace, Dublin, was to become a national concert hall, with 900 seats. Adapted over the next few years by the Office of Public Works, it opened on 9 September 1981.

National Corporate Party, founded by EOIN O'DUFFY and inaugurated at a convention on 8 June 1935, inspired by Benito Mussolini (1883–1945) and the Italian Fascist Party. Its aims were the abolition of party politics, the establishment of a united Irish corporate state, and the protection of liberties against capitalism, communism, and dictatorships. Its full-time secretary was Thomas Gunning, later speech-writer to WILLIAM JOYCE ('Lord Haw-haw'). The party was supported by a number of former BLUESHIRTS but failed within a brief period for lack of support.

National Council, formed by members of the Executive of CUMANN NA NGAEDHEAL to protest against the proposed visit to Ireland of King Edward VII in 1903. Its chairman was EDWARD MARTYN; other members included ARTHUR GRIFFITH, MAUD GONNE, MAJOR JOHN MACBRIDE, and JOHN O'LEARY. It also attracted the support of the IRB. The organisation later merged with SINN FÉIN.

National Council of Women of Ireland, founded in 1924 to 'promote co-operation among women all over Ireland interested in social welfare.' (See NATIONAL WOMEN'S COUNCIL.)

National Day of Commemoration, established on 13 July 1986 with the unveiling of a plaque by President Hillery in the Garden of Remembrance, Dublin. It is intended to commemorate all Irish people who lost their lives as a result of armed conflict.

National Democratic Party, a short-lived party founded in 1965, arising from NATIONAL UNITY, confined mainly to the Belfast area. Members believed that the reunification of Ireland could be achieved only through majority support in Northern Ireland; they later joined the SDLP. (See also NATIONAL POLITICAL FRONT.)

national education. The national education system was established in 1831 under the direction of the Chief Secretary for Ireland, E. G. Stanley (see EARL OF DERBY). His concept of a non-denominational system was outlined in a letter to the Duke of Leinster. No material peculiar to any denomination was to be used in schools, and ministers and priests were excluded from teaching posts. The system was attacked by the principal religious denominations as well as by the ORANGE ORDER. Opposition from the Presbyterian Church, headed by DR HENRY COOKE, led to a protracted series of negotiations, until a formula was devised in 1840 that allowed for Presbyterian participation in the system without religious scruple. The Church of Ireland established its own CHURCH EDUCATION SOCIETY, 1839, whose schools (including Catholics on the rolls), being denied a grant by SIR ROBERT PEEL, ran into financial difficulties and entered the national system in 1870.

The Catholic Church largely accepted the system from its introduction, and ARCHBISHOP DANIEL MURRAY was a member of the Board. In 1835, 941 members of the Catholic clergy applied for grants. In 1836 the IRISH CHRISTIAN BROTHERS withdrew from the system. A significant opponent of the system was the influential Archbishop of Tuam, JOHN MACHALE, who did not allow national schools in his archdiocese. The death of Archbishop Murray and the succession of PAUL CULLEN to the Archdiocese of Dublin led to a change in the church's attitude, particularly after the SYNOD OF THURLES (1850).

The national schools were built with the aid of the Board of Commissioners of National Education and local trustees. Local parents were responsible for providing the site, which then became the responsibility of the trustees, who were frequently landlords or local clergymen. The patron was usually the bishop of the diocese, who appointed a manager (who was a minister or parish priest). Managers had virtually unlimited powers of hiring and firing and normally employed only teachers of their own denomination.

A second category of national school, the non-vested school, emerged during the 1830s. These establishments operated a unique set of rules, approved by the board. Some of these rules were restrictive: clergymen whose faith differed from that of the manager were forbidden to give religious instruction on school premises, while religious instruction became a managerial prerogative. The proportion of non-vested schools, 68 per cent in 1850, rose to 75 per cent in 1880 but fell to 66 per cent in 1900. The number of 'mixed' or interdenominational schools declined steadily in the second half of the century: in 1862 they accounted for 53 per cent, which had become 35 per cent by the turn of the century.

The efforts of the Board of Commissioners to control all future schools built with their aid was successfully opposed by the Catholic bishops. The Board of Commissioners was also responsible for producing textbooks. The system alienated nationalists: Irish was not included in the curriculum, and little Irish history was taught. In 1879 a controversial 'payment by results' system, already operating in England, was introduced; it was abolished in 1897 when a new pay scale came into operation.

The system of training teachers for the national schools had been considered generally unsatisfactory from its introduction in the mid-1840s. MODEL SCHOOLS were not generally welcomed by the Catholic hierarchy and failed to produce the required number of teachers, which led to many untrained teachers working in the schools. In 1874 there were 2,640 trained and 5,000 untrained teachers operating in Catholic schools, compared with 426 trained and 380 untrained teachers in Church of Ireland schools. Teacher-training schools were established in 1883, when St Patrick's College, Drumcondra, Dublin, opened to Catholic men and Our Lady of Mercy College, Carysfort Avenue, Blackrock, Co. Dublin, opened to Catholic women. Church of Ireland trainees attended the Kildare Place Training College. In the last quarter of the nineteenth century a number of schools with residences attached were constructed under the National Teachers' Residences (Ireland) Act (1875). There were 1,970 applications for loans and 83 applications for grants, all of which were approved. By the end of 1919, 2,200 schools had residences attached.

The parliamentary grant for the national schools rose from £125,000 in 1850 to £1,145,721 in 1900. The Board of Commissioners was dissolved when the Irish Free State was established, and in 1924 the national schools, together with the secondary and third-level colleges, came under the jurisdiction of the newly created Department of Education.

National Farmers' and Ratepayers' League, established at a meeting presided over by FRANK MACDERMOT, 6 October 1932. Its principal aims were the promotion of agriculture, a stronger representation of farmers in Dáil Éireann, and an end to the 'ECONOMIC WAR'. Members called for an end to Civil War divisions and for a solution to partition. A short time after JAMES DILLON joined, the league became the NATIONAL CENTRE PARTY.

National Farmers' Association, founded in Dublin on 6 January 1955 by Dr Juan Greene, its first president. Rickard Deasy succeeded him as president, 1961–67. The association, which tended to be representative of larger farmers, aimed to establish direct negotiations with the Government and purchasers of farm produce, the right to a fair tax system, reform of the system of rates on land, and the promotion of better farming. Deasy led the NFA in a bitter struggle to secure price increases for agricultural producers, resulting in the 'farmers' rights' march in 1966, several demonstrations, and a commodity strike and rates strike, 1967. This agitation continued under Deasy's successor, T. J. Maher, 1967, re-elected 1970. The NFA was affiliated to the International Federation of Agricultural Producers. It merged with other organisations to form the IRISH FARMERS' ASSOCIATION, 1 January 1971.

National Gallery of Ireland, Merrion Square (West), Dublin, opened in 1854. The building was designed by Francis Fowke, based on the plans of Charles Lanyon. The gallery's first director was George Mulvany (1806–1869). Early financial assistance was provided by WILLIAM DARGAN, from a testimonial of £5,000 he received in acknowledgment of his services to the DUBLIN EXHIBITION (1853). More than 1,300 paintings and sculptures and approximately 600 watercolours and drawings are on display. Gifts and bequests to the gallery have been made by the Countess of Milltown, SIR HUGH LANE, GEORGE BERNARD SHAW, Sir Alfred Chester Beatty, and the Friends of the National Collections. An extension designed by Frank du Berry of the Office of Public Works was completed in May 1968, and the Millennium Gallery was added in 2002.

National Guard, a title assumed by the ARMY COMRADES' ASSOCIATION when EOIN O'DUFFY became leader, July 1933; members were popularly known as BLUESHIRTS. Declared illegal, 21 August 1933, the organisation was renamed the YOUNG IRELAND ASSOCIATION. It merged with CUMANN NA NGAEDHEAL and the NATIONAL CENTRE PARTY in September 1933 to form the United Ireland Party, since known as FINE GAEL.

National Insurance Act (1911), legislation introduced by the Liberal government in 1911 to insure manual workers against ill-health and unemployment. It applied to workers earning less than £160 a year and was administered through 'approved societies'. It offered benefits for illness, maternity, and medical needs. Contributions were made by the insured person, the employer, and the government.

Nationalist Party of Northern Ireland, formerly the northern section of the IRISH PARTY. Led by JOSEPH DEVLIN, its six MPs abstained from the Parliament of Northern Ireland when it was opened, June 1921; three years later two of its ten MPs, Devlin and T. G. McAllister, took their seats. The domination of the Parliament by the ULSTER UNIONIST PARTY rendered the small Nationalist Party ineffective, and it refused to accept the title of official opposition.

Under a new constituency organisation, the NATIONAL LEAGUE OF THE NORTH, the party won eleven seats in the general election of 1929, the first election held after the abolition of proportional representation. Three years later Devlin led the members out of the chamber in protest at the actions of the Unionist government, and they did not return until October 1933. After Devlin's death, 1934, the National League lost direction and began to disintegrate through abstentionism and internal wrangling. The party was reorganised in preparation for the general election of 1945 and adopted a new title, the Anti-Partition League, reflecting its principal aim. It gained ten seats but was largely ignored by the government. Four years later it had nine seats, but its ineffectual leadership lost it ground to the IRA.

In 1959 the party was opposed by NATIONAL UNITY for its lack of leadership, policy, and relevance to the Catholic population. The Nationalists, led by EDDIE MCATEER from 2 June 1964, again reorganised. It produced a 39-point programme, seeking an end to unemployment, the public ownership of essential industries, and the establishment of industrial training schemes. A year later, following the meeting between SEÁN LEMASS and TERENCE O'NEILL, the party agreed to become the official opposition, 2 February 1965.

Following the establishment of the NORTHERN IRELAND CIVIL RIGHTS ASSOCIATION, 1967, and the loss of McAteer's seat in Derry to JOHN

HUME, 1969, the party gave way to the SOCIAL DEMOCRATIC AND LABOUR PARTY, 1970.

The Nationalist Party's parliamentary representation from 1921 to 1969 was:

	Seats
1921	6
1925	10
1929	11
1933	9
1938	8
1949	9
1953	7
1958	8
1962	9
1965	9
1969	6

Nationality, a journal published by ARTHUR GRIFFITH and edited by Griffith and Séamus O'Kelly, 1915–19. It sought Irish independence and advocated the rejection of partition as a solution to the 'Irish question'. It did not survive long in the turmoil of the period.

National Labour Party, founded in 1943 by five members of the LABOUR PARTY after the IRISH TRANSPORT AND GENERAL WORKERS' UNION disaffiliated from the party. Members secured four Dáil seats in the general election of 1944 and one more in 1948. The party joined the first inter-party government, 1948–51, in which one member, JAMES EVERETT, was Minister for Posts and Telegraphs. The National Labour Party and the Labour Party were reunited in June 1950.

National Land League, an organisation for small farmers founded by the Ballinagall Land Club, Co. Westmeath, in 1965, under the chairmanship of Dan McCarthy, with the support of PEADAR O'DONNELL. Opposed to Ireland's joining the European Economic Community and to the purchase of Irish land by foreigners, it sought the redistribution of large holdings among smaller farmers.

National League of the North, a political party founded in 1928 by JOSEPH DEVLIN (its first president) and Cahir Healy, supported by former adherents of the IRISH NATIONAL LEAGUE. It sought the reunification of Ireland while recognising the state of Northern Ireland. Devlin led his handful of followers in the Parliament of Northern Ireland as an ineffectual opposition to the governing Ulster Unionist Party. It disappeared after the death of its founder, 1934. (See also NATIONALIST PARTY OF NORTHERN IRELAND.)

National League Party, a political party founded in September 1926 by WILLIAM ARCHER REDMOND. It offered a programme of co-operation with Northern Ireland and Britain and sought to break established political patterns in the Irish Free State. Candidates won eight seats in the general election of June 1927; Redmond entered a pact with Fianna Fáil and the Labour Party in an attempt to oust the Cumann na nGaedheal government. Before a crucial vote one member, Vincent Rice, joined the government party and another, John Jinks, failed to appear (see JINKS AFFAIR). This ensured the government's survival; but the party was reduced to two in the next election and merged with Cumann na nGaedheal, 1931–32.

National Library of Ireland, Kildare Street, Dublin, established under the Dublin Science and Art Museum Act (1877). The building, designed by Thomas Deane (1828–1899), was officially opened on 29 August 1890. The nucleus of the library's collection consisted of 30,000 books from the ROYAL DUBLIN SOCIETY and 23,000 books held by the RDS in trust under the will of REV. JASPER JOLY. The Joly Bequest included a large collection of Irish and Scottish song music and a section of Napoleonic literature. Its first director was William Archer, 1877–95; other directors have included Thomas W. Lyster, 1895–1920, ROBERT LLOYD PRAEGER, 1920–22, R. I. BEST, 1924–40, and RICHARD J. HAYES, 1940–67. Under the Copyright Act the library receives a copy of all books published in Ireland. It is administered by the Department of Education through a board of trustees, four of whom are nominated by the Minister for Education and eight by the RDS.

National Literary Society, founded in Dublin, 9 June 1892, by John T. Kelly, W. B. YEATS, and DOUGLAS HYDE, modelled on their IRISH LITERARY SOCIETY (London). It was dedicated to the revival and preservation of Irish customs and culture and to combating foreign influences through the development of Anglo-Irish literature. Hyde delivered an address to the society, 'The necessity for de-Anglicising Ireland', 25 November 1892, and Yeats delivered 'Nationality and literature', 19 May 1893. They differed on the aims of the society, from which Yeats withdrew to found the IRISH NATIONAL LITERARY SOCIETY.

National Lottery. Established by An Post, the National Lottery held its first draw on 11 April 1988; the first mid-week draw took place on 30

May 1990. By 2002 it had paid out more than €1.3 billion, creating more than 180 millionaires. The biggest jackpot was £7,486,025, split between two people, on 2 November 1996. The biggest single amount, £6,216,084, was won in Cork on 21 May 1997.

National Museum of Ireland, Kildare Street, Dublin, established under the Dublin Science and Art Museum Act (1877), following investigations by a select committee, 1862 and 1864, into scientific institutions in Dublin and opened to the public on 29 August 1890. Its collection is spread over four divisions: Natural Science, Art and Industrial (endowed by the RDS), Irish Antiquities (formed from a gift of the Royal Irish Academy in 1890), and Irish Folk Life (formed in 1974). Treasures housed in the museum, which is administered by the Department of Education, include the Broighter Collar (first century), St Patrick's Bell (fifth century), the Tara Brooch (c. AD 700), the ARDAGH CHALICE (eighth century), the Lismore Crosier (c. 1110), and the Cross of Cong (1123). The museum acquired the scientific and mathematical Egersdorff Collection in 1995. The Art and Industrial Division moved to the former Collins Barracks, Benburb Street, Dublin, in 1997.

National Party, a political party founded in 1924, led by JOSEPH MCGRATH, as a result of the crisis over the ARMY MUTINY. Members came almost exclusively from CUMANN NA NGAEDHEAL. It failed to achieve its principal aim, the reinstatement of the leaders of the mutiny. In July, supported by the Labour Party, it unsuccessfully challenged the government on the appropriations of the Executive Council. After members resigned their seats in the autumn, the government party won the resulting by-elections, 11 March 1925.

The same name was used by a party launched in Dublin on 12 February 1996 by Nora Bennis of Limerick (who had polled 18,500 first-preference votes in the Munster constituency in the 1994 elections to the European Parliament). Described as 'pro-family,' it sought to promote 'community and nation' and opposed the 'liberal agenda.' It also sought lower taxes, a strict system of accountability and performance for the civil service, lower state spending, the restoration of child tax allowances, and job creation. Its candidates secured 1.1 per cent of the national vote in the general election of June 1997.

National Petition Movement, founded at the offices of the NATION, 1859, at the urging of J. P. Leonard, who wrote in a letter to the paper that Ireland should 'take England at her word.' He was referring to the support given by LORD JOHN RUSSELL and the *Times* (London) to the right of self-determination (with reference to Italy). The petition, directed by T. D. SULLIVAN, collected 500,000 signatures at church gates throughout the country and was presented to Parliament by DANIEL O'DONOGHUE. JOHN DEVOY claimed in his *Recollections* that the National Petition 'gave Fenianism its first real start in Dublin,' and that the local branches of the movement were sworn in to the IRB.

National Political Front, formed at a conference in Maghera, Co. Down, 18 April 1964, attended by supporters and representatives of NATIONAL UNITY, rural nationalists, and Belfast representatives, including Harry Diamond and GERRY FITT. Within a few months a split arose over lack of consultation on the issue of contesting a parliamentary seat in Fermanagh-South Tyrone, leading to the establishment of the NATIONAL DEMOCRATIC PARTY, 1965.

National Political Union, an organisation founded and controlled by DANIEL O'CONNELL as the political machine of the Repeal Party (see REPEAL ASSOCIATION) in 1832. It originally contained Whigs but became completely nationalist within a short period.

National Press, a newspaper launched on 7 March 1891 by T. M. HEALY, with financial support from WILLIAM MARTIN MURPHY, to counteract the FREEMAN'S JOURNAL, then edited by the Parnellite Edward Byrne. The last issue appeared on 26 March 1892, after which the paper was absorbed by the *Freeman's Journal.*

National Progressive Democratic Party, a left-wing party founded in 1957 by DR NOEL BROWNE and Jack McQuillan. It won two Dáil seats in the general election of 1961 (Browne and McQuillan, both of whom were already members) but was dissolved in 1963 when the founders joined the LABOUR PARTY.

National Theatre Society, formed in January 1903 from the Irish National Dramatic Society. W. B. YEATS was president.

National Unity, a movement founded in Belfast, December 1959, by a group of Catholic graduates who supported a united Ireland while recognising the constitution of Northern Ireland. The chairman was James Scott and the secretary Michael McKeown. It produced a magazine, *New Nation.* Opposed to the new campaign of violence by the IRA, members placed their expertise at the disposal of the NATIONALIST PARTY OF NORTHERN IRELAND but, disillusioned with that party's lack of policy and leadership, attacked it in 1964. National Unity founded the NATIONAL DEMOCRATIC PARTY, 1965.

National University of Ireland, established under the Irish Universities Act (1908) to placate the Catholic hierarchy, which had been demanding a Catholic system of university education. The move incurred the hostility of Ulster unionists. The university comprised the existing Queen's Colleges of Cork and Galway together with University College, Dublin. The Catholic hierarchy was given a central role in the governing body of each of the three constituent colleges. Theoretically non-denominational, the university was forbidden by charter to have chairs of theology or sacred scripture. St Patrick's College, Maynooth, was a 'recognised college' of the NUI from 1910 until 1967, when it became a full constituent college. Three colleges of education—St Patrick's College, Dublin (until 1995), Our Lady of Mercy College, Blackrock, Co. Dublin (until 1988), and Mary Immaculate College, Limerick (until 1994)—became recognised colleges in 1975. The National Institute of Higher Education, Limerick, was a recognised college from 11 March 1976 to 15 December 1977, as was Thomond College of Education, Limerick, 9 December 1976 to 15 December 1977. The Royal College of Surgeons in Ireland, 1977, St Angela's College of Education, Sligo, 1978, and the National College of Art and Design, Dublin, 1996, also became recognised colleges.

The Universities Act (1997) gave considerable independence to the constituent colleges, which became 'constituent universities' of the National University of Ireland from 16 June 1997 as National University of Ireland, Cork, National University of Ireland, Dublin, National University of Ireland, Galway, and National University of Ireland, Maynooth.

National Volunteers. In September 1914 JOHN REDMOND called on the IRISH VOLUNTEERS to help the British war effort. His plea split the Volunteer movement when the separatists seceded from it, retaining the title Irish Volunteers. Redmond's following, known as the National Volunteers, numbered approximately 170,000, accounting for the great majority of the original membership. Some 35,000 joined the British army and served on the Western Front; unlike the ULSTER VOLUNTEER FORCE, they were not permitted officers from within their own ranks and were denied an identifying badge denoting national identity. Irish casualties at Mons (August 1914) and the Dardanelles (1915–16) were exceedingly high, while the achievements of two regiments, the Munster Fusiliers and Dublin Fusiliers, which bore the brunt of the fighting, were not mentioned in despatches—the only regiments so omitted.

The minority Irish Volunteers, some 12,000, formed the basis of the force that fought in the EASTER RISING (1916).

National Women's Council of Ireland, 1995, originally the Council for the Status of Women, established in 1973. The national representative organisation for women and women's groups, by 2001 it had some 150 affiliated organisations and groups. The council, which seeks to empower women while publicising inequalities and injustices experienced by women, consists of four panels, covering social affairs, education, work, and health.

Neeson, Seán (born 1946), politician (Alliance Party). A member of Carrickfergus District Council from 1977, he was chairman of the ALLIANCE PARTY, 1982–83, a member of the Assembly for North Antrim, 1982–86, and a member of the Northern Ireland Forum, 1996. He was elected for Co. Antrim to the Northern Ireland Assembly, 1998. He was the first Catholic mayor of Carrickfergus, 1993–94. In July 1998 he succeeded DR JOHN ALDERDICE as leader of the Alliance Party but three years later stepped down, to be succeeded by DAVID FORD.

Neligan, David (1899–1983), soldier; born in Templeglantine, Co. Limerick. Having joined the Dublin Metropolitan Police, he became a detective in G Division, the intelligence branch. From within DUBLIN CASTLE, together with ÉAMONN BROY and James McNamara, he operated as a spy for MICHAEL COLLINS during the War of Independence. In May 1921 Neligan ('Agent 68') was promised £10,000 by his superior, Major Poges, if he should succeed in apprehending Collins. With the arrest of Broy and McNamara, Neligan was apparently Collins's last informant in the division.

Having accepted the ANGLO-IRISH TREATY (1921), as a colonel in the Free State army he operated with the Dublin Guards in Co. Kerry during the CIVIL WAR and was director of intelligence, 1922–23. A chief superintendent in the Detective Division of the DMP, he became head of the Crime Branch of the GARDA SÍOCHÁNA when the two forces were merged in 1925. From 1925 he commanded the armed Detective Branch and established the S Branch (strategic units to deal with threats to the state). He was suspended in 1932 for authorising a collection for detectives dismissed for ill-treating prisoners at Kilrush, Co. Clare. On the accession of the Fianna Fáil government in 1932 he was relegated to a relatively minor position in the Land Commission and replaced in office by Broy. He published an autobiography, *The Spy in the Castle* (1968).

Nelson's Pillar. The foundation stone of the former Dublin landmark was laid in Sackville Street (O'Connell Street) on 21 October 1809, the fourth anniversary of the death of Nelson at Trafalgar. It was designed by William Wilkins; the consulting architect was FRANCIS JOHNSTON. The cost of construction was raised by public and private subscription. The 168 steps leading to the doric abacus, 111 feet above the ground, offered a panoramic view of the city. Debate on its aesthetic merits ended at 1:32 a.m. on 8 March 1966, when, as its contribution to the commemoration of the fiftieth anniversary of the EASTER RISING (1916), a splinter group of the IRA blew the top off the pillar. The remainder of the column was officially blown up on 11 March 1966.

The SPIRE OF DUBLIN was erected on the site of Nelson's Pillar, January 2003.

Ne Temere (1908), a Papal edict stating that a non-Catholic partner in a marriage to a Catholic had to agree that the children of the marriage be raised as Catholics. It was widely considered as offensive to Protestants as well as contributing to the dramatic decline in the Protestant population of the Republic. (See FETHARD BOYCOTT.)

Neutral IRA, founded in December 1922 by MAJOR FLORENCE O'DONOGHUE and Seán Hegarty to seek a peaceful solution to the CIVIL WAR. Though it claimed a membership of 20,000, it was wound up in March 1923 when O'Donoghue admitted that its purpose could not be fulfilled.

New Catholic Association, the title adopted by DANIEL O'CONNELL in 1825 when the British government proscribed the CATHOLIC ASSOCIATION. The failure to suppress the organisation left it free to organise O'Connell's election victory in Co. Clare, 1828, which was followed by the conceding of CATHOLIC EMANCIPATION.

New Consensus Group, formed in 1989 to urge a form of democratic devolved government for Northern Ireland, integrated education, and a bill of rights. It argued that a solution to the Northern Ireland conflict lay in an integrated approach to bringing together people of differing ideological backgrounds. The first chairman was Michael Nugent. Prof. John A. Murphy of Cork and the Trinity College academic David Norris were among those who travelled north for talks with Northern politicians in 1989.

'New Departure'. Described as 'an open participation in a public movement by extreme men,' and named the 'New Departure' by JOHN DEVOY, it was an attempt to weld constitutional nationalism, agrarianism and extremism into a cohesive force in what became known as the LAND WAR. Outlining its programme, 26 October 1878, Devoy explained it as both a policy of co-operation that could be undertaken on the basis of a 'general declaration in favour of self-government instead of simple federal Home Rule' and 'a vigorous agitation of the land question on the basis of a peasant proprietary, while accepting concessions tending to abolish arbitrary eviction.' The concept was developed by CHARLES STEWART PARNELL during a four-day conference of the IRB at the Hôtel des Missions Éstrangères, Paris, from 29 January 1879. Though opposed by the president of the Supreme Council of the IRB, CHARLES J. KICKHAM, it was understood that individual FENIANS might participate.

In June 1879 Parnell accepted an invitation from MICHAEL DAVITT to attend a meeting of tenant-farmers at Westport, Co. Mayo, where Fenians and ex-Fenians joined land agitators and nationalist politicians on the platform. With the founding of the LAND LEAGUE OF MAYO, and later the Irish National Land League, the New Departure had produced its first fruits. It operated pragmatically: the Fenians in America provided the money for the Land League and Parnell; the Land League mounted a national campaign to secure land reform; and Parnell (as leader of the Irish Party from May 1880) represented these aims in the British House of Commons. The Land Law (Ireland) Act (1881) (see LAND ACTS) was seen as a response to the New Departure.

In October 1881 the Land League was suppressed, but American aid continued for the IRISH NATIONAL LEAGUE and later for the PLAN OF CAMPAIGN.

New Ireland Forum, popular name for the Forum for a New Ireland, a multi-party conference called at the suggestion of JOHN HUME 'to contribute to the achievement of lasting peace and stability in a new Ireland.' It opened in St Patrick's Hall, Dublin Castle, 30 May 1983, under the chairmanship of Prof. Colm Ó hEocha. The Fine Gael delegation was led by the Taoiseach, DR GARRET FITZGERALD, Fianna Fáil by CHARLES HAUGHEY, the Labour Party by DICK SPRING, and the SDLP by Hume. As participants had to denounce violence, SINN FÉIN was not represented. The forum was ignored by unionist parties.

Over a year the twenty-seven members or their substitutes met in twenty-eight private and thirteen public sessions, while the party leaders met on fifty-six occasions. There were 317 written submissions from home and abroad. Discussions with groups from all the principal parties were held in London, 23–24 January 1984.

The report of the forum, 2 May 1984, put forward three options: (*a*) a unitary all-Ireland state, to be achieved by agreement and consent; (*b*) a federal arrangement; and (*c*) joint authority, with the Irish and British governments sharing responsibility for the government of Northern Ireland. It went on to state that its work had been

> of historic importance in bringing together, for the first time since the division of Ireland in 1920, elected nationalist representatives from North and South to deliberate on the shape of a new Ireland in which people of differing identities would live together in peace and harmony and in which all traditions would find an honoured place and have equal validity.

All three options were rejected by the British Prime Minister, MARGARET THATCHER. The forum led to the ANGLO-IRISH AGREEMENT (Hillsborough agreement), 1985.

New Ireland Review, a journal published by the staff of University College, Dublin, from 1893, developing from LYCEUM. It appeared for the last time in February 1911 and was replaced by STUDIES in March 1912.

New Irish Library, a series of books published by SIR CHARLES GAVAN DUFFY after he settled in London in 1880. In 1897 DOUGLAS HYDE became assistant editor. Titles in the series included Duffy's *Four Years of Irish History* (1883), *A Short Life of Thomas Davis* (1896), and *My Life in Two Hemispheres* (1898); others included *The Patriot Parliament* (1893) by THOMAS DAVIS, *The Bog of Stars* (1893) by Standish James O'Grady, *The New Spirit of the Nation* (1894) and *The Irish Song Book* (1894), edited by ALFRED PERCEVAL GRAVES, and *The Story of Gaelic Literature* (1895) by Douglas Hyde.

Newman, John Henry (1801–1890), English clergyman (Church of England and Catholic). Ordained in the Church of England in 1824, he moved from Low to High Church, became a leader of the Oxford Movement, and was one of the best known of the Tractarians. He became a Roman Catholic in 1845, was ordained in 1847, and founded the Oratorian Congregation at Edgbaston, Birmingham. He was created a cardinal in 1879. PAUL CULLEN, Archbishop of Armagh, consulted Newman during the period 1850–51 on the establishment of a Catholic university. Newman was formally appointed to head the new university, 12 November 1851, three years before its founding. The *Discourses* that he delivered in the presence of Archbishop Cullen and other members of the hierarchy at the Rotunda Rooms, Dublin, 10 May to 7 June 1852, were the basis for *The Idea of a University Defined* (1873). His insistence that English professors should be among those appointed, while supported by Cullen, was opposed by JOHN MACHALE and some of the more nationalist bishops. Newman did not enjoy the degree of autonomy he had expected, and the university was in chronic financial difficulties and had no power to award degrees. In addition, his desire to return to his order in Birmingham led to his resignation, 12 November 1858.

'New Reformers', evangelical clergymen, sometimes known as 'Biblicals', active between 1822 and 1860. They were encouraged by the Church of Ireland Archbishop of Dublin, William Magee, who said, 1825, 'In Ireland the Reformation may . . . be truly said only now to have begun.' The 'New Reformation' was also called the SECOND REFORMATION.

News Letter (Belfast), the oldest newspaper in Ireland, founded on 1 September 1737 by Francis Joy (1697–1790). At first published weekly, with an early readership of approximately 1,000, it was published thrice weekly from 1851 and became a daily in 1855. The file in the LINEN HALL LIBRARY, Belfast, dates from 1738 (the earliest known surviving copy being that of 9 January 1738) and forms a unique source for Irish history. The *News Letter* of 27 August 1776 was almost certainly the first newspaper on this side of the Atlantic to publish the full text of the American Declaration of

Independence, under the headline 'Birth of the United States'. A pro-unionist paper, it was taken over by the Mirror Newspaper Group in June 1996.

New Theatre Group, a socialist theatre established in Dublin, 1937–45, with premises in Charlemont Road. It concentrated on works by such dramatists as Maxim Gorky, Ernst Toller, and Eugene O'Neill.

New Tipperary, a town established by REV. DAVID HUMPHRIES and WILLIAM O'BRIEN when A. H. SMITH-BARRY evicted 146 tenants during the PLAN OF CAMPAIGN. It was opened under the auspices of the TENANTS' DEFENCE ASSOCIATION, 12 April 1890, when the attendance included MICHAEL DAVITT and 'thirty distinguished English gentlemen,' including six MPs. Three of the streets were named after O'Brien, Davitt, and CHARLES STEWART PARNELL. Some forty local shopkeepers established businesses in the town, which became a tourist attraction for a short time, but local magistrates refused to grant liquor licences. Smith-Barry failed in his efforts to have T. W. CROKE, Archbishop of Cashel, condemn the project, but it collapsed within a few years, having cost the organisers £50,000. The land reverted to Smith-Barry, who had the town levelled.

New Ulster Movement, established in 1969 in support of moderation and non-sectarianism in politics. It sought reforms, a community relations commission, a centralised housing executive, and the abolition of the Special Constabulary. Its first chairman was Brian Walker, who was succeeded by Dr Stanley Worrall. It claimed a membership of 7,000 in 1969. Many of its members became active in the ALLIANCE PARTY.

New Ulster Political Research Group, established 1978 by Andie Tyrie, John McMichael and Glen Barr as a political research group for the UDA. It published *Beyond the Religious Divide* by McMichael and Tyrie.

New University of Ulster, opened at Coleraine, Co. Derry, 25 October 1968, following the recommendations of the LOCKWOOD REPORT, incorporating MAGEE COLLEGE, Derry. The siting of the university in Coleraine was a source of resentment to nationalists, who expected it to be established in Derry. The NUU was incorporated in the UNIVERSITY OF ULSTER, 1984.

Night of the Big Wind (6/7 January 1839). The storm that struck Ireland in 1839 was unparalleled in the documented history of the country, and its sustained ferocity and erratic behaviour passed into legend. A heavy snowfall during the night of Saturday 5 January gave way to sunshine by noon on Sunday. An eerie stillness prevailed. Shortly after noon thick, dark clouds blanketed the sun. Temperatures rose to 10°F between 3 and 9 p.m., resulting in flash flooding as the heavy snows suddenly melted. At about 9 p.m. a light westerly breeze increased in force until, accompanied in many places by lightning storms, it reached hurricane force.

The storm, reaching its peak between 2 and 5 a.m. on the Monday, passed as suddenly as it had arrived. Ulster, the west and the midlands bore the brunt. The estimated number of deaths in the country and off the coast was 219. Thousands of animals, particularly sheep, were lost; one Co. Clare farmer had 170 of his flock killed by a shower of rock blown from a nearby hill. The Dublin Police Commissioner reported two deaths and sixteen injuries, 38 houses demolished, 119 severely damaged, 243 completely unroofed, 4,846 chimneys blown down, 2,534 trees uprooted, and 150 walls levelled. Damage to property in the countryside (where buildings were generally inferior) was proportionately higher. Estates were denuded of timber, while hundreds of buildings were damaged. Factories, mills and other places of industry were demolished, causing widespread unemployment. Farmhouses, barns and outhouses were destroyed, and stored grain and hay from farms was scattered in heaps or deposited in rivers to such a depth as to make them fordable. Fish were discovered miles from shore; salt was caked on walls more than 40 miles inland, and seaweed was found in profusion on hilltops. *Saunders' News Letter*, 17 January 1839, reported that the hens of Kells gorged themselves on a store of whiskey-impregnated currants to such an extent that 'after an hour or so, every hen in Kells was on the spree.'

In the wake of the storm a shortage of grain ensued, and prices spiralled. Tradesmen were much in demand to repair the ravages of the wind; the more unscrupulous among them inflated their prices by up to 40 per cent. The forty insurance companies operating in Ireland were left virtually unscathed by the event, as property in general was insured for fire only, and in any case the great majority of those affected could not afford insurance. The number of people rendered homeless was estimated to exceed those displaced in all evictions between 1850 and 1880.

The ghost of the Big Wind was conjured up in 1909 with the introduction of OLD-AGE PENSIONS. Because of the lack of documented proof of age before the universal registration of births, claimants were asked, 'What do you remember about the Night of the Big Wind?' The number of applicants blessed with perfect memory resulted in the number of pensions exceeding the expected figure by almost 30 per cent.

Nineteen-Thirteen Club, founded by David Thornley in 1957 to commemorate JAMES CONNOLLY, JAMES LARKIN, and the DUBLIN LOCK-OUT (1913). The small movement was absorbed by the NATIONAL PROGRESSIVE DEMOCRATIC PARTY, from which Thornley withdrew. His pamphlet *Ireland: The End of an Era?* (1965) reflected the ideological argument he had hoped to pursue through the club.

Nobel Prizes. Endowed by the Swedish industrialist Alfred Nobel (1833–1896), the inventor of dynamite, the Nobel Prize has been awarded since 1901 for outstanding achievement in the categories of chemistry, physics, literature, and the promotion of world peace; further prizes in economics and physiology were created in 1969. A committee of Swedish academics deliberates on each of the categories, except for the peace prize, which is awarded by the Norwegian parliament. The Irish recipients of Nobel Prizes have been W. B. YEATS (literature prize, 1923), GEORGE BERNARD SHAW (literature prize, 1925), ERNEST WALTON (physics prize, jointly with Ernest Cockcroft, 1951), SAMUEL BECKETT (literature prize, 1969), SEÁN MACBRIDE (peace prize, jointly with Eisaku Sato, 1974), Mairéad Corrigan and Betty Williams (peace prize, 1976), SÉAMUS HEANEY (literature prize, 1995), and JOHN HUME and DAVID TRIMBLE (peace prize, 1998).

Nolan, John 'Amnesty' (died 1887), republican. A member of the IRB, he worked in a Dublin drapery shop. He earned the nickname 'Amnesty' for his work as secretary of the AMNESTY ASSOCIATION in securing the release of Fenians imprisoned during the 1860s. He settled in New York, 1877, where he died impoverished. A fund raised by PATRICK FORD to aid Nolan in his last months was employed to raise a memorial to him in Calvary Cemetery, New York. MICHAEL DAVITT later paid for a monument to be erected to him in Glasnevin Cemetery, Dublin. He is sometimes confused with John 'Jackie' Nolan, another Fenian, who died in 1920 after spending fifteen years in a Canadian prison.

Nolan, Colonel John Phillip (1838–1912), soldier and politician (Irish Party); born in Ballinderry, Co. Galway, educated at TCD. As an officer in the British army he served in the Abyssinian campaign. After his election to Parliament for Co. Galway, 1871, he was unseated on the grounds of clerical intimidation. This led to a court action, during which JUDGE WILLIAM KEOGH made a savage attack on the Catholic clergy for their role in the election. The case involved 111 witnesses and lasted forty-seven days; all Nolan's costs were raised through public subscription. He subsequently held the seat from 1874 to 1896 and introduced CHARLES STEWART PARNELL to the House of Commons in 1875. After seconding Parnell's nomination as chairman of the Irish Party, November 1890, when W. E. GLADSTONE had withdrawn support, he continued to urge Parnell to remain as chairman. On 1 December he put forward an amendment to a proposal by John Barry in an attempt to gain a breathing-space for Parnell: the amendment, which was defeated, proposed that the meeting be postponed until party members could meet their constituents and then hold a meeting in Dublin. Defeated in 1895 and 1896, Nolan regained his Co. Galway seat in 1900 as a supporter of JOHN REDMOND.

Noonan, Michael (born 1943), politician (Fine Gael); born in Foynes, Co. Limerick, educated at St Patrick's College, Drumcondra, Dublin. A member of Dáil Éireann from June 1981, he was Fine Gael spokesperson on education before becoming Minister for Justice, 1982–87. One of his first acts was to reveal that the phones of two journalists, Bruce Arnold and Geraldine Kennedy, had been tapped by the Garda Síochána on the orders of the Haughey government. His Criminal Justice Bill (1983) raised much opposition, even within his own party. He was Minister for Industry, Commerce and Trade, 1986–87, and Minister for Energy, January–February 1987. Party spokesperson on finance, 1987–93, and transport, communications and energy, 1993–94, he was Minister for Health, 1994–97, during the controversy surrounding the treatment of haemophiliacs by the Blood Transfusion Board (see LINDSAY REPORT). He was widely criticised for a letter sent to a woman dying as a result of receiving infected blood products, threatening that her compensation claim would be compromised if she persisted with legal action.

Noonan replaced JOHN BRUTON as leader of Fine Gael, 9 February 2001. He announced that the party would no longer accept corporate donations; shortly afterwards it was revealed that it had received $50,000 from Telenor, a major shareholder in Esat Digifone, soon after the latter company received the lucrative second mobile phone licence from the Government. The money had come to Fine Gael through a circuitous route involving an overseas account. It also emerged that an account of the transaction had not been submitted to the MORIARTY TRIBUNAL, then investigating the affairs of Michael Lowry, Minister for Communications when Esat Digifone secured the licence. Noonan ordered all correspondence in the matter to be handed over to the tribunal, amid calls for an investigation into Fine Gael's own accounts; the party, believed to have an accumulated deficit of £1.4 million by 1994 (when it came to power for the first time since 1987), had virtually wiped out the deficit three years later and now had an income of some £1.2 million.

Noonan resigned after the party's disastrous result in the general election of May 2002, when it lost twenty-three seats, and was succeeded by ENDA KENNY.

Norbury, John Toler, first Earl (1745–1831), lawyer and politician (Conservative); born in Beechwood, Co. Tipperary, educated at TCD and called to the bar. Toler is reputed to have begun his legal career with £50 and a brace of duelling pistols; his poor knowledge of the law was notorious. A member of Parliament from 1776, he led opposition to CATHOLIC EMANCIPATION and political reform. As Attorney-General in 1798 he prosecuted leading UNITED IRISHMEN, and he was appointed Chief Justice and a baronet as a reward for supporting the ACT OF UNION (1800). He ran his court like a circus, attracting large numbers of loungers to the free entertainment; he frequently entertained the court with impromptu recitals from his voluminous knowledge of Shakespeare and Milton. He displayed a complete indifference to the feelings of those in the dock: having acquitted a manifestly guilty defendant, he informed an astonished prosecution that he was attempting to compensate for having sentenced six innocent men to death at an earlier sitting. Despite attempts to have him removed, he remained on the bench until he was eighty-two, sometimes disturbing proceedings with his loud snoring. His most famous case was in 1803, when he presided at the trial of ROBERT EMMET. A popular social companion, he enjoyed a good reputation as a landlord.

No-Rent Manifesto, drawn up by WILLIAM O'BRIEN and issued from Kilmainham Jail, Dublin, by the leaders of the IRISH PARTY, CHARLES STEWART PARNELL and JOHN DILLON (who also added the names of MICHAEL DAVITT and PATRICK EGAN to the document), 18 October 1881, calling on supporters of the LAND LEAGUE to withhold the payment of rent. The leaders of the league objected to the exclusion from the Land Law (Ireland) Act (1881) (see LAND ACTS) of leaseholders and tenants in arrears with rent—a total of some 280,000—and hoped to bring pressure on the British government by organising a rent strike.

Parnell signed the document reluctantly, as a gesture to the extremist element within his movement. Davitt, who was imprisoned in England, denounced it, feeling it would lead to a revival of agrarian violence. (There was a dramatic increase in agrarian crime, but this was principally attributed to the fact that the league was for a long time without the moderating influence of its imprisoned leaders.) Condemned by the *Freeman's Journal* and deprecated by the *Nation,* the manifesto alienated influential members of the Catholic hierarchy, in particular ARCHBISHOP T. W. CROKE. It was also received with hostility by many members of the Land League, who stood to benefit under the new Land Act. On 20 October the British government reacted to the manifesto by declaring the Land League an illegal organisation.

The text of the Manifesto was:

> Mr. Gladstone has by a series of furious and wanton acts of despotism driven the Irish tenant farmers to choose between their own organisation and the mercy of his lawyers. You have to choose between all-powerful unity and unpopular disorganisation; between the lands for the landlord and the land for the people. We cannot doubt your choice. Every tenant farmer in Ireland is today the standard-bearer of the flag unfurled at Irishtown and can bear it to glorious victory. Stand together in the face of the brutal and cowardly enemies of your race. PAY NO RENT UNDER ANY PRETEXT. STAND PASSIVELY, FIRMLY, FEARLESSLY BY while the armies of England may be engaged in their hopeless struggle against a spirit which their weapons cannot touch . . .
>
> If you are evicted you shall not suffer. The landlord who evicts will be a ruined pauper, and the government who supports him with its bayo-

nets will learn in a single winter how powerless its armed force is against the will of a united and determined and self-reliant nation.
Charles Stewart Parnell, Kilmainham Jail
Andrew Kettle
Michael Davitt, Hon. Sec., Portland Jail
Thomas Sexton, Head Organiser, Kilmainham Jail
Patrick Egan, Treasurer, Paris.

Northern Aid. The Irish Northern Aid Committee (also called Noraid) was founded by Michael Flannery and others in the United States following the sectarian unrest in Northern Ireland, August 1969. Organised in Boston, New York, Philadelphia, and Chicago, it claimed to provide aid for republican families deprived of wage-earners because of the continuing conflict. By 1987 it was believed to have provided some $5 million in aid, to be distributed by SINN FÉIN; opponents claimed that some of the money went for the purchase of arms for the Provisional IRA. In 1977 the organisation was forced by the Foreign Agents Registration Act (1938 and 1966) to register as an agent of the Provisional IRA. Its director of publicity, Martin Galvin, was active on behalf of the Provisional IRA during the 1980s and 90s.

In November 1989 Northern Aid split when the Friends of Irish Freedom was established to adhere to the original principles of the organisation, according to its former leader, Michael Hurley. In August 1991 the Speaker of the US House of Representatives, Tom Foley, described Northern Aid as a 'disgusting charade'. In 1992 the organisation supported Bill Clinton in the presidential election. There was an apparent breach in the relationship between Northern Aid and Sinn Féin over the Provisional IRA ceasefire of 1994. In June 1995 two of the organisation's branches in New York dropped 'Irish Northern Aid' from the title to become independent bodies. The gap widened with the founding of the Friends of Sinn Féin. In September 1998 the US Department of Justice threatened to move against those raising money in the United States to oppose the PEACE PROCESS.

Northern Ireland, established under the GOVERNMENT OF IRELAND ACT (1920) in the six Ulster counties of Antrim, Armagh, Derry, Down, Fermanagh, and Tyrone. Its 5,238 square miles are approximately one-sixth of the land area of Ireland; its population of 1.257 million in 1926 was about one-third of the population of Ireland. The principal religious denominations were Roman Catholic (34 per cent), Presbyterian (31 per cent), and Church of Ireland (27 per cent).

The Parliament of Northern Ireland was opened by KING GEORGE V on 22 June 1921. It had sovereign powers, but numerous areas were reserved to the British Parliament, including matters concerning the Crown, peace and war, treaties, armed forces, dignities and titles, treason, naturalisation, domicile, trade outside Northern Ireland, cables and wireless, air and navigation, lighthouses, coinage, weights and measures, trade marks, copyright, patents, the Supreme Court, the postal service, savings banks, the imposition and collection of customs duties, income tax, purchase tax, and profits tax. It was also prohibited from passing any law discriminating against or endowing any religion. It could not repeal any act passed by the British Parliament nor pass any act repugnant to the statutes of the United Kingdom.

The legislature consisted of a House of Commons (52 members) and a Senate (26 members, 24 of whom were elected by the House of Commons). The first general election, 24 May 1921, was the first in Ireland or Britain to use proportional representation; it returned forty members of the ULSTER UNIONIST PARTY, the remaining twelve seats being divided among the NATIONALIST PARTY OF NORTHERN IRELAND, SINN FÉIN (neither of which recognised the new state), and the NORTHERN IRELAND LABOUR PARTY. The UUP formed all governments of Northern Ireland until 1972. The first Prime Minister was Sir James Craig (see VISCOUNT CRAIGAVON). The government departments were Finance, Home Affairs, Labour, Education, Commerce, and Agriculture; a Ministry of Health and Local Government was created in 1944, there was a Ministry of Public Security during the Second World War, and a Ministry of Community Relations was established in 1971. Under the terms of the ANGLO-IRISH TREATY (1921) Northern Ireland could opt out of the IRISH FREE STATE, in which case a BOUNDARY COMMISSION would be established; by the end of 1925 the commission and its report were a dead letter, and the arbitrary boundary, chosen to create a Unionist majority, remained permanently fixed.

The IRA was a constant threat to Northern Ireland. An additional problem was widespread unemployment, which created severe social discontent. To protect itself from the IRA the state had at its disposal the SPECIAL POWERS ACT, under which the Minister of Home Affairs had unlimited powers of arrest and detention; the act was made permanent on 9 May 1933. Action was also taken to lessen the influence of the Catholic population, which was assumed to be sympathetic to the IRA and the reunification of Ireland. Though proportional representation was ordained to be the method of election, it was abolished for local government elections from 11 September 1922 and abolished for central government elections in 1929. Local government elections were held on a rate-paying franchise, with business firms having multiple votes. Gerrymandering of constituencies for local government elections also helped to ensure permanent Unionist majorities: this system worked so successfully that Derry City Council, Armagh Urban District Council and Fermanagh County Council, all areas with a nationalist majority, had majority Unionist representation. Protestant employers were encouraged not to employ Catholics, and local authorities adopted the same policy. The allocation of public housing favoured Protestant applicants. While there were Catholics in the ROYAL ULSTER CONSTABULARY, an auxiliary, the Special Constabulary, was wholly Protestant. Many Unionist politicians, including most members of the government and all the Prime Ministers, maintained very close contact with the ORANGE ORDER, of which most were members.

Until the Second World War the economy was depressed. The unemployment rate was 23 per cent in 1923 and 25 per cent during the 1930s. Hospitals were inadequate, and the WORKHOUSE system was still being used in the 1940s. Between 1919 and 1936 some 50,000 of the 150,000 houses required were built. Approximately 85 per cent of rural dwellings had no running water as late as 1939. TUBERCULOSIS was responsible for almost 50 per cent of deaths in the 15–25 age group. As the southern state was neutral during the war, the ports of Northern Ireland, giving access to Atlantic sea lanes, were important to the Allied war effort. War materials were also produced: 550 tanks, 150 ships (totalling 500,000 tons) and 1,000 bombers were built in Northern Ireland. Within a short time unemployment fell to 5 per cent. Employment at the shipyards rose from 7,300 in 1938 to 20,600 by 1945; in the engineering works employment rose from 14,000 to 26,000 and in the aircraft industry from 5,800 to 23,000. Total employment in industry rose from 27,000 to 70,000. In addition, some 60,000 people emigrated to England. Agriculture benefited from increased demand, and the area under tillage increased from 400,000 to 800,000 acres. Between 1939 and 1948 wages almost doubled. Belfast, Derry and Larne became important naval bases; Derry was chosen as a depot for American destroyers as early as March 1941 and was later a base for escort groups for convoy protection. From January 1942 Northern Ireland provided training bases for US and Canadian forces, and in 1943 it was designated a strategic base for American aircraft carriers. Belfast became the assembly point for American ships that sailed for Normandy on 3 June 1944. The German air force made four raids on Belfast during April and May 1941, resulting in extensive damage and more than a thousand deaths (on two occasions units of Dublin Fire Brigade were despatched to Belfast).

Changes continued after the war. In accordance with the 'step-by-step' policy, which sought to ensure that citizens of Northern Ireland enjoyed parity of services with Britain, the welfare services were established; this was achieved at the expense of financial autonomy, as the Treasury in London gained more control over the area's finances. The New Industries (Development) Act (1945) assisted businesses in adjusting to post-war conditions. Grants were offered towards industrial services. By the end of 1955, 143 firms had taken advantage of the act and were employing 21,000 people. The New Industries Branch of the Ministry of Commerce also helped fifty firms to add a total of 4,900 employees to their payroll.

Advances made after the war were used by Unionists to justify the existence of partition. Anti-partition propaganda antagonised the Unionists, as did the REPUBLIC OF IRELAND ACT (1948), which led to the British Parliament's IRELAND ACT (1949), reiterating the position of Northern Ireland within the United Kingdom. A further source of resentment for nationalists was the FLAGS AND EMBLEMS (DISPLAY) ACT (1954), which in effect prohibited the display of the TRICOLOUR.

After 1956 there was a renewal of activity by the IRA when it attacked military and police targets in the North in its BORDER CAMPAIGN. Both the northern and southern governments reacted by introducing internment, but the IRA had received no support among the nationalist population in the North and called off the campaign in 1962. A year later the traditionalist Prime Minister, VISCOUNT BROOKEBOROUGH, resigned and was succeeded by TERENCE O'NEILL, who broke with the Unionist policy of ignoring the Republic. He invited the Taoiseach, SEÁN LEMASS, to visit him at Stormont in February 1965 and returned the visit later in the year. His actions were criticised by extreme loyalists, led by REV. IAN PAISLEY.

As the fiftieth anniversary of the Easter Rising (1916) approached, traditional unionists were outraged when O'Neill allowed commemorations in Northern Ireland. Demands for civil rights from a new generation of Catholics followed within a year. The NORTHERN IRELAND CIVIL RIGHTS ASSOCIATION, launched in February 1967, attracted all shades of political and religious opinion though its support was predominantly Catholic; it demanded reforms in local government, a new system for allocating local-authority housing, and equal civil rights for all. It organised protest marches, the first of which was held in Dungannon to protest against housing policy, 24 August 1968. Shortly afterwards a more strident organisation, PEOPLE'S DEMOCRACY, was established by students at Queen's University, Belfast.

Following an attack on the People's Democracy marchers at Burntollet Bridge, near Derry, January 1969, and the misbehaviour of the police in Derry afterwards, the RUC became a discredited force among Catholics (the report of the CAMERON COMMISSION, September 1969, would find that some police had been involved in the rioting). BRIAN FAULKNER resigned from the government in protest at the police investigation. O'Neill called a general election for 24 February 1969; he received only 47 per cent of the vote in his own constituency of Bannside, where Paisley polled 6,331 votes. The Unionist parliamentary party was now split into 24 pro-O'Neill and 12 anti-O'Neill members. The election also heralded the end of the old Nationalist Party of Northern Ireland, whose leader, EDDIE MCATEER, lost his seat to JOHN HUME, who had taken part in the civil rights campaign. Under pressure from London, O'Neill announced the introduction of 'one man, one vote' for local elections but resigned, 28 April 1969. His successor, JAMES CHICHESTER-CLARK, proved unable to prevent clashes between the two communities. On 13 August 1969 the (Catholic) Bogside area of Derry was in effect under siege. The Taoiseach, JACK LYNCH, announced that he was requesting intervention by the United Nations. Following rioting in Derry and Belfast, 14–15 August 1969, the British government, having rejected Lynch's appeal for a UN peace-keeping force, sent the first British soldiers to be deployed on the streets of the North to Derry. At the same time the British government promised reforms, 19 August, including a reform of the RUC; local government reforms would continue, an independent housing authority would be established, discrimination against Catholics in public employment would be abolished, and an ombudsman would be appointed. The report of the HUNT COMMISSION, 10 October 1969, recommended that the RUC be disarmed and that the Special Constabulary be abolished; the latter reform was carried out when the B Specials were disbanded on 30 April 1970 and from 18 December replaced with the ULSTER DEFENCE REGIMENT.

The British army was by now keeping the peace in Northern Ireland. However, it soon lost the support of the nationalist population as searches for arms and military actions became identified with hostility towards and harassment of Catholic areas of Belfast and Derry. In January 1970 the IRA split into 'Provisional' and 'Official' factions, and clashes between the IRA and loyalist paramilitary organisations continued.

Two new political parties, both aimed at the centre, appeared during 1970: the SOCIAL DEMOCRATIC AND LABOUR PARTY and the ALLIANCE PARTY. Brian Faulkner succeeded Chichester-Clark in March 1971; as a gesture of good will he appointed David Bleakley (Northern Ireland Labour Party) Minister of Community Relations and brought a Catholic, Dr Gerard Newe, into the government in October as a temporary junior minister. SDLP members walked out of the Parliament of Northern Ireland in July 1971 and remained abstentionists for the rest of the session.

Faulkner introduced internment on 9 August 1971. At first it was used exclusively against the Catholic population. The operation was mishandled: many IRA leaders escaped, while some of those arrested were victims of mistaken identity. Internment also led to an upsurge in support for the IRA. The level of violence increased considerably: there were twice as many bomb explosions from August to December 1971 as there had been from January to July. There were 17,262 house searches during 1971.

Following the events of BLOODY SUNDAY (30 January 1972) Faulkner was summoned to London by the Prime Minister, EDWARD HEATH, and informed that security would now become the responsibility of the British government, and that if violence did not cease the Parliament of Northern Ireland would be suspended and replaced with direct rule from London. He was also told that internment would have to be phased out, with London assuming complete responsibility for law and order. When the Stormont government rejected this proposal, Heath announced its suspension on 24 March and the introduction of direct rule. WILLIAM WHITELAW became the first Secretary of State for Northern Ireland. There were more than 21,000 British soldiers in Northern Ireland by July 1972.

Faulkner was head of the power-sharing Executive of the Northern Ireland Assembly, elected on 28 June 1973. The 78 members elected consisted of 52 pro-Assembly members and 26 anti-Assembly. Pro-Assembly members included Faulknerite Unionists (24), SDLP (19), Alliance Party (8), and NILP (1); anti-Assembly members were made up of 'anti-white -paper Unionists' (8), DUP (8), Vanguard (7), and other loyalists (3). The eleven-member Executive was made up of six Unionists, four SDLP, and one Alliance member. The Deputy Chief Executive was Gerry Fitt (SDLP). The anti-white-paper Unionists formed the UNITED ULSTER UNIONIST COUNCIL (also called the Loyalist Coalition).

The Executive was represented at the talks that led to the SUNNINGDALE AGREEMENT (6–9 December 1973); however, when the Executive took office, 5 January 1974, the Unionist Party rejected the agreement. Later that month (23 January) the 'Official' (anti-Faulkner) Unionists, DUP and Vanguard withdrew from the Assembly. In the British House of Commons, 11 of the 12 Northern Ireland members elected in the February general election supported the Loyalist Coalition; they also supported the strike organised by the ULSTER WORKERS' COUNCIL, 14 May. This brought the state to a standstill on 28 May; the Executive collapsed, and direct rule from London was resumed. Faulkner established the UNIONIST PARTY OF NORTHERN IRELAND, 24 June 1974. Until 1998 Northern Ireland was governed under the provisions of the Northern Ireland Act (1974): the British Parliament approved all laws, and the Northern Ireland government departments were placed under the control of the Secretary of State for Northern Ireland, a member of the British government.

Another white paper was published, 4 July, announcing a 78-member Constitutional Convention, to be elected on 1 May 1975. The Loyalist Coalition secured 47 of the 78 seats, divided among Official Unionists (19), DUP (12), Vanguard (14), and other loyalists (2). Those supporting power-sharing had 31 seats: SDLP (17), Alliance Party (8), UPNI (5), and NILP (1). The Convention, which was to produce a report by 7 November 1975, met on 8 May under the chairmanship of the Lord Chief Justice, Sir Robert Lowry, 'to consider what provision for the Government of Northern Ireland is likely to command the most widespread acceptance throughout the whole community.'

The parties in the Convention submitted five different reports for consideration. The UUUC sought in effect a return to the old Unionist-dominated Stormont; the SDLP continued to seek 'power-sharing' (multi-party government), with government offices for Catholics; the smaller parties advocated positions between these two poles. The Convention was unable to produce an acceptable unanimous draft for the British government, and the UUUC report was adopted (by 42 to 31). In the hope of breaking the deadlock, the British government extended the life of the Convention by another six months, to 7 May 1976, and referred the report back for consideration, 14 January 1976. Negotiations between the parties produced similar responses and demands, and the Constitutional Convention was dissolved in March.

Over the next two decades the republican and loyalist paramilitary campaigns were pursued with unrelenting ferocity. By the end of the century more than 3,000 people had been killed and more than 36,000 injured, including more than 900 members of the police and army.

The four main parties were invited to another Constitutional Conference in 1980. The UUP declined, while the SDLP, DUP and Alliance Party met privately under the chairmanship of the Secretary of State for Northern Ireland. The parties agreed to devolved government, but the SDLP and Alliance Party favoured power-sharing, while the DUP demanded 'majority rule' (i.e. no power-sharing), a view also held by the UUP outside the talks. A failure to reach agreement also on local government reform led the British government to abandon the conference, but it continued to look for a framework for restoring devolved government. The Northern Ireland Act (1982) provided for the resumption of legislative and executive functions by an elected Northern Ireland Assembly if agreement could be reached on how these powers should be exercised. The arrangements would have to command widespread acceptance throughout the community and be acceptable to the British Parliament.

The 78-member Assembly elected under the single transferable vote system of proportional representation sat from 1982 to 1986. The SDLP and Sinn Féin did not take their seats. The ANGLO-IRISH AGREEMENT (15 November 1985) was acceptable to nationalists but rejected by unionists, who suspended their monitoring work at the Assembly in protest. The Alliance Party then withdrew. The Assembly decided in March 1986 not to fulfil its statutory functions, and it was dissolved by the British government in June 1986.

The Anglo-Irish Agreement came into force on 29 November 1985; never acceptable to unionists, it stood until the adoption of the BELFAST AGREEMENT (1998). It affirmed that any change in the status of Northern Ireland would come about only with the consent of a majority of the people there, and recognised that at present a majority for such a change did not exist. Under the agreement an Intergovernmental Conference, to meet regularly in London, Belfast and Dublin at ministerial or official level, was also established. The INTERNATIONAL FUND FOR IRELAND came into existence in December 1986. Between 1987 and 1990 the UUP, SDLP, DUP and Alliance Party had meetings with the British government; the Irish government was also included in round-table talks during 1991 and 1992. An agreement emerged that any future settlement would have to deal with three 'strands' of relationships: those within Northern Ireland, those between Northern Ireland and the Republic, and those between the British and Irish governments. The talks ended in November 1992 with a measure of consensus; the British government continued discussions with the Northern Ireland parties and separately with the Irish government.

The PEACE PROCESS, which began in the late 1980s, was gaining momentum as a result of the HUME-ADAMS TALKS and BROOKE-MAYHEW TALKS. The DOWNING STREET DECLARATION (1993) reaffirmed that majority consent was necessary for any change in the constitutional status of Northern Ireland; parties committed to peace could participate in the democratic process to find a way forward. This was followed on 31 August 1994 by the Provisional IRA ceasefire, which in turn was followed on 13 October 1994 by the announcement of a ceasefire from the Combined Loyalist Military Command. With republican and loyalist ceasefires operating, the British government entered into talks with Sinn Féin and with the ULSTER DEMOCRATIC PARTY and PROGRESSIVE UNIONIST PARTY, parties linked with the UDA and UVF, respectively. The talks process continued with the publication of the FRAMEWORKS DOCUMENTS (February 1995). The governments launched a 'twin-track' initiative, 28 November 1995, dealing with the crucial question of illegal weapons by establishing the INTERNATIONAL BODY ON DECOMMISSIONING while simultaneously examining an inclusive basis for all-party negotiations. Chaired by GEORGE MITCHELL, the international body issued its seminal report on 24 January 1996, setting out six principles of democracy and non-violence to which all parties must adhere. However, when the Provisional IRA ceasefire ended with the bomb explosion at Canary Wharf, London, 9 February 1996, the British government excluded Sinn Féin from the talks until there was an unequivocal restoration of the ceasefire.

The elections to the Northern Ireland Forum, based on the list system of proportional representation, were held on 30 May 1996 and resulted in a forum comprising representatives of the Ulster Unionist Party (30), SDLP (27), DUP (24), Sinn Féin (17), Alliance Party (7), UK Unionist Party (3), PUP (2), UDP (2), Northern Ireland Women's Coalition (2), and Labour and 'No Going Back' (2). The Forum opened at the Interpoint Centre, Belfast, without the Sinn Féin representatives, 10 June. All parties were required to guarantee their total and absolute commitment to the Mitchell Principles and to 'address' the proposals on decommissioning. Sinn Féin was enabled to enter the talks following the Provisional IRA ceasefire of 19 July 1997; its participation in the talks from 9 September 1997 led to the withdrawal of the DUP and UKUP. After debating the Belfast Agreement (10 April 1998), the Northern Ireland Forum held its final session on 24 April 1998.

The agreement led to a new 108-member Assembly and a power-sharing Executive, with DAVID TRIMBLE (UUP) as First Minister and Séamus Mallon (SDLP) as Deputy First Minister. A referendum on the Belfast Agreement in both jurisdictions in Ireland was held on 22 May 1998; 71 per cent in Northern Ireland voted in favour and 94 per cent in the

Republic. A new Northern Ireland Act, giving effect to provisions of the agreement, was enacted in November 1998. Northern Ireland appeared to have embraced political normality. On 15 February 1999 the Northern Ireland Assembly approved the decision to have the following ten government departments after devolution: Agriculture and Rural Development; Environment; Regional Development; Social Development; Education; Higher and Further Education, Training and Employment; Enterprise, Trade and Investment; Culture, Arts and Leisure; Health, Social Services and Public Safety; and Finance and Personnel. There was also agreement on the six North-South implementation bodies, to be responsible for the all-Ireland administration of inland waterways, food safety, trade and business development, special EU schemes, language, and aquaculture and marine matters; these bodies were to operate within policy agreed by the North-South Ministerial Council and to be accountable to the Northern Ireland Assembly and Dáil Éireann. Power was devolved to the new Northern Ireland Assembly on 2 December 1999.

The general election for the British Parliament on 7 June 2001 was also interpreted as a referendum on the Belfast Agreement and the peace process. One-third of the seats changed hands, with losses for the Ulster Unionist Party and SDLP and gains for the DUP and Sinn Féin: Unionist Party 6 (–3), DUP 5 (+2), Sinn Féin 4 (+2), SDLP 3. This election saw the return of the first woman from Northern Ireland to the British Parliament since Bernadette Devlin in 1969, Lady Sylvia Hermon, who also became the first woman elected as a UUP member. Two other women were also elected: Iris Robinson (DUP), who joined her husband, Peter Robinson (the first husband and wife to represent Northern Ireland), and Michelle Gildernew, elected in Fermanagh-South Tyrone for Sinn Féin with a margin of fifty-four votes.

The Assembly and Executive were suspended from midnight on 14 October 2002.

The result of the local elections, to fill 582 city, borough and district council seats, was:

UUP	154	(–31)
DUP	131	(+40)
SDLP	117	(–3)
Sinn Féin	108	(+34)
Alliance Party	28	(–13)
Others	44	(–71)

Population of Northern Ireland, 1926–2001

1926	1.257 million
1937	1.280 million
1951	1.370 million
1961	1.425 million
1971	1.536 million
1981	1.482 million*
1991	1.578 million
2001	1.685 million

*A nationalist boycott of the census leaves the figure under-estimated.

Governor-General of Northern Ireland

Duke of Abercorn	1922–45
Lord Granville	1945–52
Lord Wakehurst	1952–64
Lord Erskine	1964–68
Lord Grey	1968–73

Distribution of seats in general elections, 1921–74

	24/5 1921	28/4 1925	22/5 1929	30/1 1933	9/2 1938	14/6 1945	10/2 1949	22/10 1953	20/3 1958	31/5 1962	25/11 1965	24/2 1969
Unionists	40	32	37	36	39	33	37	38	37	34	36	36
Independent Unionists	–	4	3	2	3	2	2	1	–	–	–	3
Liberals	–	–	–	–	–	–	–	–	–	1	1	–
Labour	–	3	1	2	1	2	–	–	4	4	2	2
Nationalists	6	10	11	9	8	9	9	7	8	9	9	6
Sinn Féin (abstentionist)	6	2	–	2	–	–	–	2	–	–	–	–
Republicans, Republican Labour, Socialist Republican, Independent Labour	–	–	–	–	1	3	2	3	2	3	2	2
Independents and others	–	1	–	1	–	3	2	1	1	1	2	3

Assembly, 28/6/1973

'Anti-white-paper' Unionists	DUP	Vanguard	Faulknerite Unionists
8	8	7	24
Alliance Party	SDLP	NILP	Other loyalists
8	19	1	3

Convention, 1/5/1975

Official Unionists	DUP	Vanguard	UPNI
19	12	14	5
Alliance Party	SDLP	NILP	Other loyalists
8	17	1	2

Government of Northern Ireland, 1921–72

Prime Minister

Sir James Craig (Lord Craigavon)	June 1921 to November 1940
John Miller Andrews	November 1940 to May 1943
Sir Basil Brooke (Lord Brookeborough)	May 1943 to March 1963
Terence O'Neill	March 1963 to April 1969
James Dawson Chichester-Clark	May 1969 to March 1971
Brian Faulkner	March 1971 to March 1972

Minister of Finance

H. M. Pollock	1921–37
J. M. Andrews	1937–41
J. M. Barbour	1941–43
J. M. Sinclair	1943–53
W. B. Maginess	1953–56
G. B. Hanna	1956
T. O'Neill	1956–63
J. L. O. Andrews	1963–65
H. V. Kirk	1965–72

Minister of Home Affairs

Richard Dawson Bates	1921–43
W. Lowry	1943–44
J. E. Warnock	1944–45
W. B. Maginess	1945–53
G. B. Hanna	1953–56
T. O'Neill	1956
W. W. B. Topping	1956–59
Brian Faulkner	1959–63
William Craig	1963–64
R. W. McConnell	1964–66
William Craig	1966–68
W. J. Long	1968–69
R. W. Porter	1969–72

Minister of Labour

J. M. Andrews	1921–37
O. G. Shillington	1937–39
J. F. Gordon	1939–43
W. Grant	1943–45
W. B. Maginess	1945–49
Harry Midgley	1949–51
Ivor Neill	1951–62
H. V. Kirk	1962–64
W. J. Morgan	1964–72

Minister of Agriculture (known as Agriculture and Commerce until 1925)

E. M. Archdale	1921–33
Sir Basil Brooke	1933–41
Lord Glentoran	1941–43
R. Moore	1943–60
Harry West	1960–67
James Chichester-Clark	1967–69
P. R. H. O'Neill	1969–72

Minister of Commerce

J. M. Barbour	1925–41
Sir Basil Brooke	1941–43
Sir R. I. Nugent	1943–49
W. V. McCleery	1949–53
I. L. O. Andrews	1961–63
Brian Faulkner	1963–69
P. R. H. O'Neill	1969
Roy Bradford	1969–71
R. L. Bailie	1971–72

Minister of Education

Lord Londonderry	1921–27
Lord Charlemont	1927–33
L. H. Robb	1933–43
Rev. R. Corkey	1943–44
S. H. Hall-Thompson	1944–52
Harry Midgley	1952–57
W. M. May	1957–62
Ivor Neill	1962–64
H. V. Kirk	1964–66
W. J. Long	1966–68
W. K. Fitzsimmons	1968–69
P. R. H. O'Neill	1969
W. J. Long	1969–72

Minister of Health

W. Grant	1944–49
Dame Dehra Parker	1949–57
I. L. O. Andrews	1957–61

W. I. Morgan	1961–64
William Craig	1964–65
W. I. Morgan	1965–69
R. W. Porter	1969
W. K. Fitzsimmons	1969–72

Minister of Public Security

W. Grant	1941–42
Harry Midgley	1942–45

Minister of Development

William Craig	1965–66
W. K. Fitzsimmons	1966–68
Ivor Neill	1968–69
W. I. Long	1969
Brian Faulkner	1969–71
Roy Bradford	1971–72

Minister of Community Relations

David Bleakley	1971
W. B. McIvor	1971

Executive of Northern Ireland (5 January to 28 May 1974)

Chief Executive	Brian Faulkner
Deputy Chief Executive	Gerry Fitt
Minister of Finance	H. V. Kirk
Minister of Agriculture	L. Morrell
Minister of Commerce	John Hume
Minister of Education	W. B. McIvor
Minister of Health and Social Services	Paddy Devlin
Minister of Manpower Services	R. Cooper
Minister of Environment	Roy Bradford
Minister of Community Relations	Ivan Cooper*
Minister of Local Government, Housing and Planning	Austin Currie
Minister of Planning and Co-ordination	Eddie McGrady*
Minister of Law Reform	Oliver Napier
Minister of Information	I. Baxter

*Holders of ministerial offices outside the Executive

Executive of the Northern Ireland Assembly, 2 December 1999–

First Minister	David Trimble (UUP)
Deputy First Minister	Séamus Mallon (SDLP)
Minister for Enterprise, Trade and Investment	Reg Empey (UUP)
Minister for Finance and Personnel	Mark Durkan (SDLP)
Minister for Regional Development	Peter Robinson (DUP)
Minister for Education	Martin McGuinness (SF)
Minister for the Environment	Sam Foster (UUP)
Minister for Higher and Further Education, Training and Employment	Seán Farren (SDLP)
Minister for Development	Nigel Dodds (DUP)
Minister for Culture, Arts and Leisure	Michael McGimpsey (UUP)
Minister for Health, Social Services and Public Safety	Bairbre de Brún (SF)
Minister for Agriculture and Rural Development	Bríd Rodgers (SDLP)

To show its objection to the new institutions, the DUP rotated its ministries among its members.

Secretary of State for Northern Ireland

William Whitelaw	1972–73
Francis Pym	1973–74
Merlyn Rees	1974–77
Roy Mason	1977–79
Humphrey Atkins	1979–81
Jim Prior	1981–83
Douglas Hurd	1983–85
Tom King	1985–89
Peter Brooke	1989–92
Sir Patrick Mayhew	1992–97
Dr Marjorie (Mo) Mowlam	1997–99
Peter Mandelson	1999–2001
Dr John Reid	2001–02
Paul Murphy	2002–

Northern Ireland Civil Rights Association, founded in Belfast, 29 January 1967; the first committee included Noel Harris (trade unionist and Communist Party), chairman, Dr Con McCluskey (CAMPAIGN FOR SOCIAL JUSTICE), vice-chairman, Fred Heatley, treasurer, Jack Bennett (Wolfe Tone Society), Betty Sinclair (Belfast Trades Council and Communist Party), Joe Sherry and Kevin Agnew (Republican Labour Party), Paddy Devlin (Northern Ireland Labour Party), John Quinn (Ulster Liberal Party), Michael Dolley (Queen's University), Robin Cole (Queen's University Young Unionist Group), Ken Banks (trade unionist), and Terence O'Brien. The association was concerned with the lack of civil rights in the Northern state and particularly with discrimination in the allocation of public authority housing. Based on the CAMPAIGN FOR SOCIAL JUSTICE IN NORTHERN IRELAND, it was modelled on the National Council for Civil Liberties in Britain, to which it was affiliated. It included among its aims 'one person, one vote' in local elections, the removal of gerrymandered electoral boundaries and discriminatory practices within local government authorities, the establishment of machinery to investigate complaints against local authorities, the allocation of public housing on a points system, the repeal of the Special Powers Act, and the disbanding of the B Specials (see SPECIAL CONSTABULARY).

The association's first major public involvement was on 24 August 1968, when, at the suggestion of the Nationalist MP Austin Currie, it organised a march from Coalisland to Dungannon in protest at anti-Catholic discrimination by local authorities. Dungannon was an appropriate focus for agitation: despite its 53 per cent Catholic population, local elections returned only seven Catholics and twice as many Protestants. The march attracted more than three thousand participants.

Another march was called for 5 October in Derry. Banned by the Minister of Home Affairs, WILLIAM CRAIG, it led to violent clashes between the marchers (seventy-seven of whom were injured) and the RUC (who suffered eleven casualties). Prominent politicians, including GERRY FITT and EDDIE MCATEER, were involved in clashes with the RUC. The violence in Derry, shown live on television, drew world attention to the deteriorating situation. The Wilson government reacted by calling on the Prime Minister, TERENCE O'NEILL, to introduce reforms to satisfy nationalist demands. Civil rights agitation spread throughout the North, provoking counter-demonstrations from Unionist traditionalists, led by REV. IAN PAISLEY. Both Paisley and Craig regarded the NICRA as a front for the IRA and other subversives. Students supporting the NICRA and protesting against the events in Derry founded PEOPLE'S DEMOCRACY in Belfast, 5 October. Terence O'Neill's reformist efforts were strongly opposed within his own party and by the powerful ORANGE ORDER.

As the NICRA gained only minor concessions, the situation continued to deteriorate. The British army was called on to maintain order when the RUC and B Specials were no longer able to contain the situation, August 1969. Caught in a maelstrom of terrorism and reprisal, the NICRA saw its role become less effective. In June 1977 it declared that the RUC was an unacceptable police force.

Northern Ireland Labour Party, a social-democratic party founded in 1923–24, drawing its membership mainly from Belfast trade unionists. It contained Catholics and Protestants, but because of the primacy of constitutional issues in Northern Ireland it was unable to muster sufficient support to make an impact. Unable to maintain a neutral position on partition during the period 1948–49, it gave its support to the Unionist government; the opponents of this policy formed the REPUBLICAN LABOUR PARTY. Following the enactment of the IRELAND ACT (1949) the NILP stated that it 'accepts the constitutional position of Northern Ireland, the close association with Britain and the Commonwealth . . . We are not seeking a mandate to change.' During the civil unrest of the 1960s the party supported the agitation for civil rights but lost ground to the newly established SDLP and ALLIANCE PARTY. It failed to win representation in the British House of Commons. Its strength in the Parliament of Northern Ireland was:

1925	3
1929	1
1933	2
1938	1
1945	2
1949	0
1953	0
1958	4
1962	4
1965	2
1969	2

At the 1970 British Labour Party conference the NILP unsuccessfully sought a merger with its British counterpart. It supported power-sharing (multi-party government) in the 1973 Assembly but had only one representative (David Bleakley) in the 1975–76 Convention. It took one seat in the 1977 and 1981 council elections. It did not contest the 1982 Assembly elections and was absorbed by LABOUR '87.

Northern Ireland Unionist Party, formed on 5 January 1999 by four former elected members of the UNITED KINGDOM UNIONIST PARTY, who alleged a lack of consultation by ROBERT MCCARTNEY. They insisted on their right to hold their seats in the Northern Ireland Assembly, which they had won as members of the UKUP.

Northern Ireland Women's Coalition, founded by women involved in various peace groups and occupying a centrist position in relation to the Northern conflict. Two members—Monica McWilliams (South Belfast) and Jane Morrice (North Down)—were elected to the Northern Ireland Forum, 1996, through the 'top-up' system, participated in the talks that produced the

BELFAST AGREEMENT (1998), and were elected to the post-agreement Assembly. One member temporarily redesignated herself 'unionist', 6 November 2001, to enable DAVID TRIMBLE and MARK DURKAN to be elected First Minister and Deputy First Minister, respectively, of the Northern Ireland Executive.

Northern Resistance Movement, founded in 1971 after the introduction of internment to bring republicans and radicals together in opposition to the government's policies. It included members of PEOPLE'S DEMOCRACY and the PROVISIONAL IRA. During the period 1971–72 it organised protests but in July 1972 was considerably weakened when the Provisional IRA made a truce with the British government.

North-South Ministerial Council, established under the BELFAST AGREEMENT (1998). Its inaugural meeting, held on 13 December 1999 at its offices in the former palace of the Church of Ireland Primate in Armagh, was attended by the entire Irish Government and eight of the ten members of the new Executive of the Northern Ireland Assembly.

North-West Loyalist Registration and Electoral Association, formed by the DUKE OF ABERCORN in 1886 in the struggle against HOME RULE. Its purpose was to organise the Unionist vote in Cos. Donegal, Tyrone and Derry in order to prevent a clash of interests at the polls between loyalist groups. Such an occurrence in Londonderry South in 1885 had allowed the election of a nationalist (T. M. HEALY). The association had only limited success, as the Liberal Unionists, concerned with a possible loss of identity to the Ulster Unionists, formed their own Liberal Unionist Association.

Norton, William (1900–1963), politician (Labour Party); born in Co. Kildare, educated locally. A Post Office clerk from 1918, he was elected in 1920 to the National Executive of the Post Office Workers' Union, for which he was honorary organising secretary, 1922–23, honorary general secretary, 1923–24, and full-time secretary, 1924–57. He was president of the Executive Council of the Postal, Telegraph and Telephone International, 1926–60. Elected to Dáil Éireann, 1926, he lost his seat the following year but returned in 1932 as leader of the Labour Party. It supported the Fianna Fáil opposition to the BLUESHIRTS, whom Norton denounced as 'Hitlerite'. He criticised the government's handling of the LAND ANNUITIES and during the 'ECONOMIC WAR' said that tariffs were not the answer to Ireland's economic problems. However, he supported the government's position during the war. He succeeded in having a motion on public ownership incorporated in the Labour Party constitution in 1936 but secured the removal of the aim of a workers' republic, which had been criticised by the Catholic hierarchy. In the general election of 1943 the Labour Party increased its representation from nine to seventeen seats, but the ITGWU disaffiliated from the party, and the union's members in the parliamentary Labour Party established the NATIONAL LABOUR PARTY. Following the general election of 1944 the parliamentary Labour Party consisted of only eight deputies. Four years later it secured fourteen seats and joined the first inter-party government, 1948–51, in which Norton held the posts of Tánaiste and Minister for Social Welfare. The party returned with nineteen seats and Norton was again Tánaiste in the second inter-party government, 1954–57, and Minister for Industry and Commerce. It lost seven seats in the general election of 1957. Norton resigned the leadership three years later and was succeeded by BRENDAN CORISH.

Notes from Ireland, a Conservative-Unionist bulletin that first appeared on 23 September 1886, following the defeat of the (first) HOME RULE BILL. It reported the efforts of the IRISH PARTY to secure support for home rule and provided facts on Ireland for the British Parliament, the press, and the public. It appeared until 1914, when the (third) HOME RULE BILL became law.

Nulty, Thomas (1818–1898), bishop (Catholic); born in Oldcastle, Co. Meath, educated at St Patrick's College, Maynooth, ordained in 1846. Among the earliest members of the Catholic hierarchy to take an active interest in the land question, he supported the NEW DEPARTURE and the LAND LEAGUE and issued a pastoral letter on the land question in 1881. He supported the IRISH PARTY, initiating a church-door collection to defray the election expenses of CHARLES STEWART PARNELL, member of Parliament for Co. Meath, 1880. Following the NO-RENT MANIFESTO he expressed surprise at the condemnation issued by T. W. CROKE, Archbishop of Cashel. After the split in the Irish Party over Parnell's involvement in the O'Shea divorce case, Nulty's denunciation of Parnellism was as forthright as his earlier support had been: 'Parnellites are anti-Catholic,' he stated in January 1892; in July he described Parnellism as

'Paganism . . . it impedes, obstructs and cripples the fruitfulness and the preaching of the Gospel . . .' Following a pastoral letter during the general election of 1892, the Meath South result (in which the anti-Parnellite Fulham defeated his Parnellite opponent by thirteen votes) was annulled on the grounds of clerical intimidation; the subsequent by-election was again won by an anti-Parnellite candidate.

O

Oath of Allegiance, laid down in article 4 of the ANGLO-IRISH TREATY (1921) and article 17 of the CONSTITUTION OF THE IRISH FREE STATE (1922). Its text, drafted by Crompton Llewelyn Davies at the request of MICHAEL COLLINS, was:

> I do solemnly swear true faith and allegiance to the Constitution of the Irish Free State as by law established and that I will be faithful to H.M. King George V, his heirs and successors by law, in virtue of the common citizenship of Ireland with Great Britain and her adherence to and membership of the group of nations forming the British Commonwealth of Nations.

The oath was rejected by some republicans, who, led by ÉAMON DE VALERA, refused to take their seats in Dáil Éireann. Their abstentionist policy was brought to an end by the ELECTORAL AMENDMENT ACT (1927). On 11 August 1927 de Valera and other elected members of FIANNA FÁIL, having removed the Bible from their immediate proximity, signed their names in the book containing the oath while declaring that they were not taking the oath but repeating an 'empty formula'. During the general election of March 1932 de Valera stated that Fianna Fáil in government would abolish the oath. On 2 March 1933 Dáil Éireann voted (71 to 38) to remove the oath, a decision given effect from 3 May 1933 in the CONSTITUTION (REMOVAL OF OATH) ACT (1933).

Ó Brádaigh, Ruairí (born 1932), republican; born in Co. Longford, educated at UCD. Having trained as a teacher, he joined Sinn Féin and later the IRA, of which he was chief of staff in the 1950s and again during the 1960s. Active in the BORDER CAMPAIGN from 1956, he was elected a member of Dáil Éireann for Longford-Westmeath, 1957, while imprisoned in Mountjoy Jail, Dublin; he lost the seat in the election of 1961. He was president of Provisional Sinn Féin, 1969–83, active in the development of the ÉIRE NUA policy, 1971, and influential in establishing contact with revolutionary groups in other countries. He was the first person imprisoned under the OFFENCES AGAINST THE STATE ACT (1972) when given a six-month sentence for membership of the Provisional IRA, 1973. He was party to the talks at Feakle, Co. Clare, with representatives of the main Protestant churches in Northern Ireland, December 1974. Having lost the presidency of Sinn Féin to GERRY ADAMS, 1983, Ó Brádaigh suffered another defeat in 1986 when the Sinn Féin ard-fheis supported Adams's proposal to abandon the policy of abstention from Dáil Éireann. Joint founder of REPUBLICAN SINN FÉIN, he opposed the BROOKE-MAYHEW TALKS, 1991–92, and the Provisional IRA ceasefires of 1994 and 1997. He said in 1997 that Republican Sinn Féin 'offered a home to Sinn Féin dissidents.' Opposed to the BELFAST AGREEMENT (1998), he condemned Sinn Féin's decision to take seats in the Northern Ireland Assembly and its acceptance of two ministerial offices in the Executive.

O'Brennan, Elizabeth (Lily) (1878–1948), republican; born in Dublin, educated at Dominican Convent, Eccles Street. A sister-in-law of ÉAMONN CEANNT, she was a vice-president and secretary of CUMANN NA MBAN. Following her participation with the IRISH CITIZEN ARMY in the Easter Rising (1916) she was an influential member of the IRISH NATIONAL AID ASSOCIATION and a member of Sinn Féin. An employee of the Department of Labour in the first Dáil Éireann, she assisted with the organising of the BELFAST BOYCOTT. Typist to ARTHUR GRIFFITH as President of Dáil Éireann, she later pursued a career in the civil service.

Ó Briain, Art (1872–1949), republican; born in London, educated at St Charles' College, London, where he qualified as a civil engineer. He was president of the London Gaelic League, 1914–35, a member of the Irish Volunteers, president of the Sinn Féin Council of Great Britain, 1916–23, and joint founder, vice-president, 1919–22, and president, 1922–24, of the IRISH SELF-DETERMINATION LEAGUE OF GREAT BRITAIN. He was removed from his position as official SINN FÉIN spokesman, June 1922, after opposing the ANGLO-IRISH TREATY (1921). He was among those deported from England, March 1923, but returned after a declaration by the House of Lords that the deportations were illegal. On return he was charged with conspiracy with a number of others and was imprisoned until July 1924. The republican movement in England split over accusations that he had revealed important information at his trial and that an excessive amount of money had been spent on his defence. He was managing editor of the *Music Trades Review*, 1924–33, and Irish minister plenipotentiary to France and Belgium from 1935. He retired in October 1939, settled in Ireland, and became deputy chairman of Mianraí Tta.

Ó Briain, Liam (1888–1974), scholar and republican; born in Dublin, educated at UCD, where he became an assistant in the French Department, 1910–11. A travelling scholarship in Celtic studies led to his working in Berlin under Kuno Meyer and at Bonn under Rudolf Thurneysen, returning to work again in the French Department, 1914–15. A member of the Irish Volunteers, he fought in the EASTER RISING (1916), after which he was interned. He was again imprisoned during the WAR OF INDEPENDENCE, following which he accepted the ANGLO-IRISH TREATY (1921). A member of the Executive Committee of the Gaelic League, 1915–27, he was professor of Romance languages at University College, Galway, 1917–58. Influential in the founding of TAIBHDHEARC NA GAILLIMHE, he was its secretary, 1928–38, and also a frequent performer. Dean of the Faculty of Arts in Galway for twenty years, he also served on the Censorship Appeals Board and the board of the Abbey Theatre, Dublin. He was a member of the MILITARY HISTORY SOCIETY OF IRELAND and a frequent contributor to its journal, the *Irish Sword.*

O'Brien, (Edward) Conor (1880–1952), architect, yachtsman, and author; born in Co. Limerick, a grandson of WILLIAM SMITH O'BRIEN and half-brother of the artist Dermod O'Brien, educated at TCD and the University of Oxford. A member of the Royal Society of Antiquaries of Ireland and of Sinn Féin, he was a noted mountaineer (climbing in his bare feet) and yachtsman. He used his yacht KELPIE to collect arms for the IRISH VOLUNTEERS for transfer to Sir Thomas Myles's yacht CHOTAH in the HOWTH GUN-RUNNING (1914). During the First World War he served as an officer in the British navy; returning to Ireland, he had the ketch *Saoirse* built to his own design at Baltimore, Co. Cork. Leaving Dún Laoghaire, Co. Dublin, 20 June 1923, he became the first Irish person to sail around the world in his own yacht, arriving at Dún Laoghaire exactly two years later on 20 June 1925. *Across Three Oceans* (1926) is his account of the voyage. He lived on the *Saoirse* until he sold it in 1940. During the Second World War he served in the Small Vessels Pool, sailing small craft across the Atlantic from America to Britain.

O'Brien, George (1892–1973), economist; born in Dublin, educated at UCD and King's Inns and called to the bar. He practised law until 1926, when he was appointed professor of national economics at University College, Dublin, 1926. Professor of political economy, 1930–61, he was a member of the Banking Commission, 1934–38. His works include *Economic History of Ireland* (3 vols., 1918–21), *An Essay on the Economic Effects of the Reformation* (1923), *Agricultural Economics* (1929), and *Four Green Fields* (a study of partition, 1936). He was a government appointee to the board of the ABBEY THEATRE.

O'Brien, James Francis Xavier (1828–1905), republican and politician (Nationalist). He studied medicine in Paris and subsequently travelled to South America, where he fought in the war in Nicaragua, 1856. He later joined the FENIANS and became a member of the Supreme Council. He contributed to the *Irish People* under the pseudonym 'De L'Abbaye'. An assistant surgeon in the American Civil War (1861–65), he returned to Ireland to take part in the rising of 1867. Leading an attack on Ballyknockane Barracks, Co. Cork, he was captured and sentenced to death. Released in 1869, he took little further part in the movement, devoting himself instead to his merchant business in Dublin. He supported CHARLES STEWART PARNELL and was treasurer of the NATIONAL LEAGUE. He was member of Parliament for Co. Mayo, 1885–95, and for Co. Cork, 1895–1905. He became an anti-Parnellite following the split in the IRISH PARTY.

O'Brien, Peter, Lord (1842–1914), lawyer; born in Ballynalacken, Co. Clare, educated at TCD and called to the bar, becoming a Queen's counsel in 1880. As Crown counsel at Green Street Courthouse, Dublin, during the trials of prominent LAND LEAGUE members, 1881–82, he was noted for his hostility towards the defendants and for his packing of juries, leading to his nickname 'Peter the Packer'. Solicitor-General, 1887, he was created Lord Chief Justice, 1889, awarded a baronetcy, 1891, and created Baron O'Brien, 1900. His *Reminiscences* appeared in 1916.

O'Brien, R. Barry (1847–1918), historian; born in Kilrush, Co. Clare, educated privately and at the Catholic University and called to the bar. As a journalist in London he edited the *Speaker* and was a member of the HOME RULE CONFEDERATION OF GREAT BRITAIN and of the Gaelic League. Following the split in the IRISH PARTY, 1890–91, he remained loyal to CHARLES STEWART PARNELL and for a period acted as his unofficial private secretary. His two-volume *Life of Charles Stewart Parnell* was published in 1898. His other works include *The Irish Land Question and English Public Opinion* (1879), *The Parliamentary History of the Irish Land Question* (1880), *Fifty Years of Concessions to Ireland* (1883), *Fifty Years of Irish History* (2 vols., 1883–85), *England's Title in Ireland* (1905), *Studies in Irish History* (second series, 1906), and *Dublin Castle and the Irish People* (1909); he also edited *Two Centuries of Irish History* (1888), *The Autobiography of Wolfe Tone* (1893), and *Speeches of John Redmond* (1910).

O'Brien, William (1852–1928), politician (Nationalist), journalist, and land agitator; born in Mallow, Co. Cork, educated at Queen's College, Cork, where he won a law scholarship but was unable to continue his studies because of ill-health. He worked on the *Cork Daily Herald,* 1868–76, and *Freeman's Journal,* 1876–81. A supporter of the LAND LEAGUE, he accepted the invitation from CHARLES STEWART PARNELL to edit *United Ireland,* 1881–90. Describing the paper as 'an insurrection in print,' he was one of the most influential journalists in the country, leading to his imprisonment with Parnell in October 1881. He was the author of the 'NO-RENT MANIFESTO'. After his release in April 1882 he became organiser of the NATIONAL LEAGUE and was a member of a delegation that secured the support of CLAN NA GAEL for the IRISH PARTY, August 1886. He was a leading figure in the PLAN OF CAMPAIGN.

Member of Parliament for North-East Cork from 1887, he organised a rent strike on the Kingston estate near Mitchelstown, which led to a magistrate's order for a court appearance in the town, 9 September, together with JOHN MANDEVILLE. Though they did not appear, a large crowd gathered, and in the resulting disorder three people were killed in what became known as the 'MITCHELSTOWN MASSACRE'. They were imprisoned, 2 November 1887; refusing to wear prison clothing, they suffered hardship, which resulted in Mandeville's death shortly after his release early in 1888. In an effort to centralise agrarian activities O'Brien launched the TENANTS' DEFENCE ASSOCIATION, November 1889. Imprisoned September–December 1890, on his release he gave his support to the NEW TIPPERARY project, which had a devastating financial effect on the Plan of Campaign.

In America with other Irish Party members when the crisis developed following the O'Shea divorce revelations, O'Brien at first supported Parnell. However, he joined with other members in repudiating him following his publication of the 'Manifesto to the Irish People', 29 November. At the request of the American delegates O'Brien travelled to France to meet Parnell at Boulogne, 30 December, when he declined his proposal that he (O'Brien) should replace JUSTIN MCCARTHY as chairman of the party. Following the termination of the talks in February, O'Brien and JOHN DILLON were imprisoned on their arrival in England, then transferred to Galway Jail, from which they were released on 30 July.

Though elected to Parliament for Cork in 1892, O'Brien took up residence in Co. Mayo and played only a peripheral role in politics during the early 1890s. Horrified by famine in Co. Mayo, he founded the UNITED IRISH LEAGUE, 28 January 1898, which became a national movement, leading to the reunification of the Irish Party under JOHN REDMOND, 1900. Though a member of the party, O'Brien continued to express his personal views through the IRISH PEOPLE, 1899–1908. By 1900 he was convinced that no solution to the demand for self-government or to the land question could come about without bringing together unionists and nationalists, landowners and tenants. His emphasis was on 'conference' and 'conciliation', and he was one of the most enthusiastic members of the LAND CONFERENCE, 1902–03, which led to the Irish Land Act (1903) (see LAND ACTS). Though he had reservations about the act, he believed the conference had been successful, and he broke with the party, November 1903, when it refused to accept that the conference system could be successfully applied to the question of self-government. He was a member of the IRISH REFORM ASSOCIATION. His attempts to negotiate with SINN FÉIN were a failure. Having rejoined the Irish Party in January 1908, he immediately clashed with party leaders when he opposed the British government's attempts to dilute the Irish Land Act (1903) (see LAND ACTS). Suffering from ill-health and fatigue, he resigned his seat in April 1909.

Within two years he was back in politics, with the *Cork Accent* and his seat for Cork regained, January 1910. Still seeking 'conference' and 'conciliation', he founded the ALL-FOR-IRELAND LEAGUE. Opposed to partition, he voted against the (third) HOME RULE BILL, 25 May 1914. He lost much support in Cork when he spoke on recruiting platforms, 1914–15. Following the EASTER RISING (1916) he recognised that the country was moving towards SINN FÉIN and did not contest the general election of December 1918, in which the Irish Party was annihilated. Earlier that year he had been a member of the MANSION HOUSE CONFERENCE to oppose CONSCRIPTION. On the founding of the Irish Free State he declined a nomination to the Senate and also refused a Fianna Fáil nomination in 1927.

His published works include 'Christmas on the Galtees', an account of tenants' conditions which was published in the *Freeman's Journal* during the winter of 1877/78, *When We Were Boys* (1890), *Recollections* (1905), *The Downfall of Parliamentarianism* (1918), *The Responsibility for Partition* (1921), *The Irish Revolution* (1921), *The Parnell of Real Life* (1926), and *Irish Fireside Hours* (1927).

O'Brien, William (1881–1968), trade unionist; born in Ballygurteen, Clonakilty, Co. Cork, educated at Dungarvan Christian Brothers' school and in Carrick-on-Suir. In Dublin from 1896, he was influenced by JAMES CONNOLLY and joined the IRISH SOCIALIST REPUBLICAN PARTY, of which he became financial secretary and treasurer. A tailor by trade, he was a founder-member of the United Socialist Party and a delegate to the Dublin Trades Council from 1908, becoming vice-president, 1913, and president, 1914. He was a founder-member of the IRISH TRANSPORT AND GENERAL WORKERS' UNION, to which he devoted the rest of his life. He influenced Connolly's return from the United States in 1910 and had him appointed Belfast organiser of the ITGWU. As a member of the Executive of the IRISH TRADE UNION CONGRESS he masterminded a takeover by the Larkinites and was secretary of the committee that organised the strike preceding the DUBLIN LOCK-OUT (1913), for which he was imprisoned. He was also a member of the IRISH NEUTRALITY LEAGUE during the First World War and sat on the Anti-Conscription Committee, 1915.

Through his involvement with Connolly and the IRISH CITIZEN ARMY he was interned after the EASTER RISING (1916). After his release, August 1916, he worked for the National Aid and Volunteers' Dependants' Fund, 1916–18. During this period also he played a leading role in the reorganising of the ITGWU, which by 1920 had 100,000 members. As general secretary and a member of the Executive of the LABOUR PARTY he assisted THOMAS JOHNSON in drafting the DEMOCRATIC PROGRAMME of Dáil Éireann, 1919. During the WAR OF INDEPENDENCE he supported the IRA and was imprisoned in Wormwood Scrubs Prison, London, 1920.

O'Brien had a brief parliamentary career. He was elected for the Labour Party during the session of 1922/23 and then lost his seat. Re-elected in the general election of June 1927, he lost his seat in the second election of that year in August. After this he concentrated on union activities as general secretary of the ITGWU. He was financial secretary of the Labour Party, 1931–39, and chairman of the Administrative Council, 1939–41. He resisted Larkin's attempts to regain control of the union in 1923; when Larkin forcibly took over the union's head office, O'Brien successfully took the case to court. Larkin's rival union, the WORKERS' UNION OF IRELAND, took Dublin support away from the ITGWU and reduced O'Brien's membership to approximately 60,000. The battle was resumed in 1943 when Larkin and his son James Larkin junior were admitted to the Labour Party. Having failed to exclude them, O'Brien led the ITGWU in disaffiliating from the Labour Party and forming the rival CONGRESS OF IRISH UNIONS. He retired from the ITGWU in 1946 but was retained in an advisory capacity. His autobiography, *Forth the Banners Go,* was published in 1969.

O'Brien, William Smith (1803–1864), politician (Repeal); born in Dromoland Castle, Ennis, Co. Clare, educated at the University of Cambridge. He entered Parliament as a Tory Emancipationist MP for Ennis, 1828–31, and for Co. Limerick, 1835–49; adjudged guilty of high treason, he was disqualified from membership. A member of the Committee of the CATHOLIC ASSOCIATION, he had an uneasy relationship with its leader, DANIEL O'CONNELL. He supported the struggle against the tithes, advocated peasant proprietorship of reclaimed land, and supported the use of Irish. He resigned his position as a commissioner of the peace after the dismissal in 1843 of pro-Repeal magistrates. A critical supporter of the REPEAL ASSOCIATION, he proposed the Repeal Pledge, November 1844. He was highly regarded by the *Nation* group within YOUNG IRELAND; perceived as bridging the gap between Young Ireland and what O'Connell called 'Old Ireland', O'Brien jocularly called himself 'Middle-Aged Ireland'.

A contentious issue within the association was O'Brien's (and Young Ireland's) support for the QUEEN'S COLLEGES, described as the 'godless colleges' by O'Connell and the Archbishop of Tuam, JOHN MACHALE. The breach between O'Brien and O'Connell was widened in December 1845 when O'Connell supported the repeal of the Corn Laws to assist Ireland, already in the throes of the Great Famine (1845–49). O'Brien also objected to O'Connell's alliance with the Whigs, which ran counter to O'Brien's concept of an Irish party.

In July 1846 Young Ireland withdrew from the Repeal Association. Though he did not agree with the Young Ireland extremists—led by JAMES FINTAN LALOR, JOHN MITCHEL, and THOMAS FRANCIS MEAGHER—O'Brien accepted the position of official spokesman in the House of Commons. In January 1847 he was persuaded by CHARLES GAVAN DUFFY to become leader of the IRISH CONFEDERATION. By this time the famine was widespread throughout the country. The British government reacted to unrest with the TREASON FELONY ACT (1848) and the suspension of *habeas corpus.* In March 1848, when O'Brien, Mitchel and Meagher were placed on trial, the charges failed, but Mitchel was retried in May under the new law and sentenced to twenty years' transportation.

By the summer of 1848, the Confederation having been outlawed from 26 July, O'Brien believed there was no alternative to an insurrection. His attempt to raise support along the Tipperary-Kilkenny border was not greeted with enthusiasm. The rising, for the most part centred on BALLINGARRY, Co. Tipperary, was a failure, and within days the leaders had either been captured or had surrendered. Of the small number who made their escape one was O'Brien's *aide de camp,* JAMES STEPHENS, who later founded the IRB. O'Brien was captured and condemned to death, commuted to transportation to Van Diemen's Land (Tasmania), where he remained until his release in 1854. He visited Poland and the United States, where he received a warm reception from his former colleagues and admirers. Following an unconditional pardon in 1856 he retired from politics and played little further part in public affairs. *Principles of Government, or Meditation in Exile* was published in 1856.

O'Brien's daughter Charlotte Grace O'Brien (1845–1909), who was with him when he died in Bangor, Wales, was a respected botanist and a noted philanthropist in the cause of emigrants' travel conditions.

obstructionism, the tactic of obstructing the business of the House of Commons through a series of questions, supplementary questions, lengthy speeches, amendments, motions of adjournment, and points of order, initiated by JOSEPH GILLIS BIGGAR, 22 April 1875. In an attempt to frustrate the passing of an Irish COERCION bill, Biggar once spoke for four hours in a rambling speech that included a discourse on the difficulties encountered by a Co. Kerry farmer in bringing his cow to market on the LARTIGUE RAILWAY. The tactic was subsequently adopted to great effect by CHARLES STEWART PARNELL and some other members of the IRISH PARTY, leading the House of Commons into marathon sittings. The policy ended when W. E. GLADSTONE proposed, 3 February 1881, that should a motion declaring the business 'urgent' be supported by forty members rising in their place, the motion should be put forthwith, without debate, and if carried by a majority of not less than three -to-one the regulation of the business for the time being should remain in the hands of the Speaker. This motion was accepted, with the amendment that there should be at least three hundred members present before 'urgency' could be moved. Before obstructionism was defeated the House of Commons had to sit through a record 41-hour session, and almost the entire membership of the Irish Party was suspended. Though supporting government moves to end the tactic, the English parliamentarian John Bright (1811–1889) agreed with the obstructionist approach, arguing in a speech to the House of Commons on 26 June 1879 that the Irish Party, being a minority group, was left with little alternative in publicising injustice.

O'Callaghan, John Cornelius (1805–1883), historian; born in Dublin, educated at Clongowes Wood College, Co. Kildare, and Blanchardstown, Co. Dublin. Called to the bar in 1829, he did not practise. He contributed to the NATION and was a member of the REPEAL ASSOCIATION. He was a supporter of DANIEL O'CONNELL; together with the sculptor JOHN HOGAN he placed a crown on O'Connell's head at a monster meeting at the Hill of Tara. He edited Charles O'Kelly's *Macariae Excidium* (1846), an account of the Williamite campaign in Ireland. His monumental *History of the Irish Brigades in the Service of France* took twenty-five years to complete, but he was not able to find a publisher in Ireland; it was published in Glasgow in eight volumes in 1890.

O'Casey, Seán (1880–1964), dramatist; born John Casey in Dublin. Though he attended school at St Dominic's and St Barnabas' schools, poor eyesight inhibited his formal education, and he was largely self-educated. He joined the Gaelic League (for which he later taught classes) while working as a labourer, and adopted a modified form of his name. He worked for a time as a clerk in Eason's bookshop and then for the Great Northern Railway. He was inducted into the IRB but never became an active member. Influenced by JAMES CONNOLLY and JAMES LARKIN, he joined the IRISH TRANSPORT AND GENERAL WORKERS' UNION in 1911 and the IRISH CITIZEN ARMY, of which he became secretary, 1913; under the name P. Ó Cathasaigh he wrote a highly coloured account of the movement, *The Story of the Irish Citizen Army* (1919). He was secretary of the first Strikers' Relief Committee during the DUBLIN LOCK-OUT (1913). He resigned from the Citizen Army in protest at its association with CONSTANCE MARKIEVICZ. He also published *The Story of Thomas Ashe* (1918), *Songs of the Wren, 1 and 2* (1918), and *More Songs of the Wren* (1918). His trilogy of plays dealing with aspects of the struggle for independence between 1913 and 1922, *The Shadow of a Gunman* (1923), *Juno and the Paycock* (1924), and *The Plough and the Stars* (1926), were produced at the ABBEY THEATRE, Dublin, where *The Plough and the Stars* was accompanied by rioting. He was deeply wounded by the Abbey's rejection of *The Silver Tassie* (1928) and moved to England in 1931. His six-volume *Autobiographies* appeared between 1939 and 1954.

Ó Conaill, Dáithí (1937–1991), republican; born in Cork. Wounded during the IRA's BORDER CAMPAIGN in 1956, he later escaped from the Curragh Internment Camp. He became a building and woodwork teacher in Ballyshannon vocational school, Co. Donegal. In 1960 he was sentenced to eight years' imprisonment (of which he served three years) for carrying a gun and ammunition with intent to endanger life. Credited by some with the invention of the car bomb, he was believed to be chief of staff of the Provisional IRA in April 1973. As vice-president of SINN FÉIN he was present at the meeting with Northern Protestant clergymen in Feakle, Co. Clare, 10 December 1974. In 1975 he received a twelve-month prison sentence for membership of the Provisional IRA. He is believed to have been an influential strategist in the Provisional IRA campaign into the 1980s. Refusing to accept an end to the Sinn Féin policy of parliamentary abstentionism in 1986, he and RUAIRÍ Ó BRÁDAIGH broke away and founded REPUBLICAN SINN FÉIN.

O'Connell, Daniel (1775–1847), lawyer and politician (Repeal); born in Carhan, near Cahersiveen, Co. Kerry, fostered at a herdsman's hut at Tiermoile, educated at a hedge school and at Redington, near Cóbh, Co. Cork. He was taken under the patronage of his uncle, Maurice 'Hunting Cap' O'Connell (1727–1825); his later education, and that of his brother, Morgan O'Connell, was at Saint-Omer, France, 1791–92, and at Douai, 1792–93. After studying law at Lincoln's Inn, London, 1794–96, he continued his studies in Dublin until called to the bar in 1798. He approved of the principles of the UNITED IRISHMEN but disagreed with the insurrection (1798). A member of the Lawyers' Corps of Artillery in the Volunteers, 1797, he returned to Co. Kerry during the rising.

His first public speech, in opposition to the Union, was made to the Catholic citizens of Dublin at the Royal Exchange (now City Hall), 13 January 1800. Popularly known as 'the Counsellor', O'Connell opposed the VETO and protested at Papal interference in Irish affairs. Having derided the 'beggarly Corporation of Dublin', he was challenged to a duel by a member, Norcot d'Esterre. The duel ended in the death of d'Esterre, whose widow refused O'Connell's offer of a pension, but he arranged an annuity for her daughter. He issued an Address to the Catholics of Ireland, 1 January 1821, calling for united action by all religious denominations to secure repeal of the ACT OF UNION. The CATHOLIC ASSOCIATION, 1823, became a mass movement when O'Connell created associate membership, which enabled people to become involved in its affairs for 1 penny per month. Known as the 'Catholic Rent', this became a central fighting fund of tens of thousands of pounds. An outstanding orator, O'Connell toured the country, and when the government suppressed the Catholic Association he renamed it the New Catholic Association to continue the campaign.

The first test of his organisation came in Waterford in 1826, when its candidate, HENRY VILLIERS STUART, defeated Lord George Thomas

Beresford (1,357 to 527). This was followed by other victories until, in 1828, O'Connell was himself elected for Co. Clare. His bitterest critic, SIR ROBERT PEEL, and the Prime Minister, the DUKE OF WELLINGTON, conceded defeat. At the King's insistence, O'Connell was not allowed to take his seat until he had been re-elected, 4 February 1830; he then became the first Catholic in modern history to sit in the House of Commons.

After the DONERAILE CONSPIRACY, October 1829, O'Connell retired from the bar to become a full-time politician. For the remainder of his life he was supported by the 'O'Connell Tribute', a public collection out of which he paid all his expenses. He was the leader of a party—'O'Connell's Tail', as it was sometimes called—that included a number of his relatives, all committed to the cause of repeal. He supported the Reform Act (1832), which increased the electorate. In the first election held under the act he was returned for Dublin; his 'household brigade' of three sons, two sons-in-law and one brother-in-law were also returned. He was now leading approximately forty members.

During this period Ireland was in turmoil, as the grievances of poor tenant-farmers concentrated on the TITHES. In 1834 O'Connell introduced a motion to reduce tithes by two-thirds. He rejected an offer of the posts of Attorney-General and Master of the Rolls for Ireland in the new ministry formed by VISCOUNT MELBOURNE, who was shortly succeeded by Peel; he became party to the LICHFIELD HOUSE COMPACT, which pledged his support to the Whigs on their return to office. Shortly afterwards Melbourne replaced Peel, and O'Connell's influence was apparent when his enemies were removed from office and replaced by those with whom he had a good relationship. The new Irish executive under EARL MULGRAVE, Lord Morpeth (see EARL OF CARLISLE) and THOMAS DRUMMOND was one of the most constructive of the century.

The years of Whig alliance were not personally happy ones. O'Connell's wife—a cousin, whom he had married against his family's wishes—died; the 'O'Connell Tribute' was in decline; and he became involved in a series of unlucky business ventures. On the political front he had some successes. In September 1836 he founded the General Association, with the aims of securing household suffrage, triennial parliamentary elections, one-member electoral districts, free trade, and the abolition of the property qualification for members of Parliament. Described by O'Connell as the Catholic Association on a 'broader basis', it was a prototype for the REPEAL ASSOCIATION. It was dissolved after the 1837 election, which returned forty-six Repeal candidates, and the following year O'Connell founded the PRECURSOR SOCIETY, with Repeal as its aim. The Tithe Rentcharge (Ireland) Act (1838) brought an end to the 'Tithe War'. O'Connell took part in the debates on the provision of relief for the indigent and sick in Ireland but unsuccessfully opposed the POOR LAW. He met with further success when his demand for reforms in municipal government became law through the MUNICIPAL CORPORATIONS (IRELAND) ACT (1840). One of its first consequences was that O'Connell became lord mayor of Dublin, 1841–42.

The National Association of Ireland for Full and Prompt Justice and Repeal, popularly called the REPEAL ASSOCIATION, was launched on 15 April 1840. O'Connell's chief lieutenant was his favourite son, John O'Connell (1810–1858). During these early years O'Connell attracted the support of YOUNG IRELAND, which, under THOMAS DAVIS and his colleagues at the *Nation,* gave Repeal a new platform, while other press support came from the PILOT.

O'Connell announced that 1843 would be the Year of Repeal. The agitation entered a new phase as he organised what the *Times* (London) called 'monster meetings' at historic sites, where hundreds of thousands came to listen to his impassioned oratory and then dispersed peacefully. The ageing Liberator addressed an estimated 100,000 people at Trim, Co. Meath, 19 March, Limerick, 19 April (120,000), Mullingar, Co. Westmeath, 9 May (100,000), Charleville, Co. Cork, 19 May (200,000), Cork, 21 May (500,000), Cashel, Co. Tipperary, 23 May (300,000), Nenagh, Co. Tipperary, 24 May (500,000), Longford, 28 May (100,000), Kilkenny, 8 June (300,000), Mallow, Co. Cork, 11 June (300,000), Ennis, Co. Clare, 15 June (500,000), Skibbereen, Co. Cork, 22 June (500,000), Donnybrook, Dublin, 3 July (200,000), Waterford, 9 July (500,000), Enniscorthy, Co. Wexford, 20 July (400,000), Tuam, Co. Galway, 23 July (200,000), Castlebar, Co. Mayo, 30 July (400,000), Hill of Tara, Co. Meath, 15 August (900,000), Loughrea, Co. Galway, 10 September (150,000), Lismore, Co. Waterford, 24 September (150,000) and Mullaghmast, Co. Kildare, 1 October (250,000). He called his last meeting for Clontarf, Dublin, 8 October 1843, confident that the government, overwhelmed by the weight of public opinion, would have to concede Repeal. When Peel, determined to oppose the agitation, proscribed the meeting, O'Connell, to the dismay of his followers, obeyed the law and called it off, while hundreds of thousands made their way to the meeting-place. He now adopted a new tactic, calling for the establishment of arbitration courts to take over from the government's courts of justice. A COUNCIL OF THREE HUNDRED would come together to form a national representative assembly. The government responded by arraigning O'Connell, together with his son John and other leaders of the Repeal movement, on charges of conspiracy.

The state trial of O'Connell for 'intimidation and demonstration of great physical force,' before a packed jury, resulted in a guilty verdict. He was sentenced to a year's imprisonment, fined £2,000, and ordered to give securities of £5,000 for seven years' good behaviour. Before entering prison, 30 May 1844. O'Connell went to the House of Commons, where he was cheered by the opposition, made a brief speech, and returned to Dublin to be lodged in the Richmond bridewell. On 4 September the House of Lords condemned his trial for its injustices and ordered his release. He emerged from prison physically and mentally weakened, already suffering from the encephalitis that eventually killed him. He no longer believed that Repeal could be won and in October 1844 divided the Repeal Party when he gave as his opinion that a federal system, in which Ireland would continue to be represented, was preferable to simple repeal of the Union. He was denounced by the *Nation* and Young Ireland, and he withdrew his support for federalism. He resumed his seat in Parliament, from where he joined his friend JOHN MACHALE, Archbishop of Tuam, in opposition to the Charitable Donations and Bequests (Ireland) Act (1844). He reluctantly supported Peel's endowment of St Patrick's College, Maynooth. However, his opposition to the QUEEN'S COLLEGES led to friction with Young Ireland in 1845, and within a year they were spilt irreconcilably.

O'Connell's control over the Repeal Association had by now passed to his son John. Young Ireland militants, led by THOMAS FRANCIS MEAGHER, forced O'Connell's hand. The old man denounced talk of militant action: 'It is, no doubt, a very fine thing to die for one's country, but believe me, one living patriot is worth a whole churchyard full of dead ones.' The O'Connells, fearful that talk of rebellion would lead to the suppression of the Repeal Association, demanded that all members subscribe to peace resolutions. Young Ireland seceded from the association, 28 July 1846, on the issue of physical force.

Ireland was by now in the throes of the GREAT FAMINE (1845–49). O'Connell supported the Whig ministry of LORD JOHN RUSSELL and, helplessly watching the situation deteriorate, provided what assistance he could on his own estate.

During his parliamentary career, 1830–47, O'Connell was associated with a wide variety of issues. He opposed slavery in the West Indies and in America (where his stand aroused considerable ill-feeling), the monopoly enjoyed by the East India Company, disabilities imposed on Jews, the blasphemy law, and flogging in the army; among the causes he espoused were free trade, a reduction in the national debt, male suffrage, parliamentary reform, and the liberal movements in Belgium, Poland, and Spain. He spoke in the House of Commons for the last time on 8 February 1847. Barely audible, he pleaded for aid for his starving country.

> Ireland is in your hands . . . She is in your power . . . If you do not save her she can't save herself. And I solemnly call on you to recollect that I predict with the sincerest conviction that one quarter of her population will perish unless you come to the relief.

In March, acting on the advice of his doctor, he set out for Italy; his journey to Rome was attended by receptions, addresses, and adulation. Following his death in Genoa on 15 May, his heart was buried in Rome, where CHARLES BIANCONI arranged for a monument enshrining it in the Irish College. His body was returned to Ireland, accompanied by his private chaplain, REV. JOHN MILEY, on board the *Duchess of Kent,* and he was buried in Glasnevin Cemetery, Dublin.

O'Connell, Lieutenant-General J. J. ('Ginger') (1887–1944), soldier; born in Co. Mayo, educated at UCD. Following service in the US army, 1912–14, he returned to Ireland and joined the Irish Volunteers. EOIN MACNEILL, attempting to prevent the EASTER RISING (1916), despatched him to Cork to take command of the Volunteers. He was interned after the collapse of the rising and attached to the headquarters staff of the IRA during the WAR OF INDEPENDENCE as assistant to the chief of staff, RICHARD MULCAHY. Supporting the ANGLO-

IRISH TREATY (1921), he became deputy chief of staff of the Free State army. He was kidnapped by ERNIE O'MALLEY, 26 June 1922, and lodged with the Four Courts garrison as a reprisal for the arrest of Leo Henderson, an anti-Treaty officer. His kidnapping was a precipitating factor in the formal outbreak of the CIVIL WAR, when the Provisional Government attacked the Four Courts two days later. O'Connell was assistant to EOIN O'DUFFY and Mulcahy during the Civil War, after which he was chief lecturer at the Army School of Instruction, 1924–29, director of No. 2 Bureau (intelligence branch), 1929–32, quartermaster-general, 1932–34, and director of military archives, 1934–44.

O'Connell, Peter (1775–1826), lexicographer; born in Carron, Co. Clare, educated at a hedge school. He spent practically his entire life preparing a comprehensive dictionary of Irish. His researches took him to the Hebrides, the Scottish Highlands, Wales, and all over Ireland. Basing himself in Limerick from 1812, he was aided by Dr Ó Ríordáin, who supported the Society for the Revival of Ancient Irish Literature in its project to publish a dictionary. Leaving Limerick on the death of his patron, he returned to Carron, where he lived with his brother, Pádraig. He had difficulty in finding a publisher for the completed work. He worked for periods at Trinity College, Dublin, and the Royal Irish Academy. When DANIEL O'CONNELL was asked to assist he is reported to have said, 'The man was a fool to waste his life on such a useless labour.' The manuscript was one of several later sold for 5 shillings to the British Museum by JAMES HARDIMAN; there are copies in the NATIONAL LIBRARY and the RIA. O'Connell is popularly believed to have been buried in the same grave as Ellie Hanley, victim of the 'COLLEEN BAWN' MURDER.

O'Connell, Thomas J. (1882–1969), trade unionist and politician (Labour Party); born in Bekan, near Claremorris, Co. Mayo, educated at St Patrick's College, Dublin, where he qualified as a teacher. General secretary of the IRISH NATIONAL TEACHERS' ORGANISATION, 1916–48, he was a Labour Party member of Dáil Éireann for Co. Galway, 1922–27, and for South Mayo, 1927–32. He succeeded THOMAS JOHNSON as leader of the parliamentary party in 1927. He followed a policy of co-operation with Fianna Fáil in opposition to Cumann na nGaedheal. In the 1932 general election the Labour Party lost six seats, including O'Connell's. He was a member of Seanad Éireann, 1941–44, 1948–51, and 1954–57, and served on the Youth Unemployment Commission, 1943–51. He was a member of the Central Council of the Irish Red Cross Society, 1927–40, director of the World Federation of Educational Associations, 1927–40, and later a director of the Educational Building Society. He was the author of *Story of the Irish National Teachers' Organisation, 1868–1968* (1968).

O'Connor, Frank (1903–1966), writer, born Michael O'Donovan in Cork, educated at Christian Brothers' school. Together with his friend SEÁN Ó FAOLÁIN he was deeply influenced by DANIEL CORKERY, supported the Republicans during the WAR OF INDEPENDENCE, and was interned during the CIVIL WAR. He was a librarian in Cork, 1925–28, and in Ballsbridge, Dublin, 1928–38, and a founder-member of the IRISH ACADEMY OF LETTERS. He was a regular contributor to the BELL and its first poetry editor. Widely read in Irish literature and culture, he lectured at Harvard University, Massachusetts, 1952 and 1954, and the University of Chicago, 1953. W. B. YEATS compared O'Connor as a short-story writer to Chekhov. A prolific writer, his works include *Guests of the Nation* (1931), *The Wild Bird's Nest* (1932), *The Big Fellow* (a study of MICHAEL COLLINS, 1937), *The Midnight Court* (a translation of Brian Merriman's *Cúirt an Mheán Oíche,* 1945), *Towards an Appreciation of Literature* (1945), *Art and the Theatre* (1947), *The Book of Ireland* (1958), *Kings, Lords and Commons* (translations from Irish poetry, 1960), *The Lonely Voice* (a study of the short story, 1963), and *The Backward Look* (a study of Irish literature, 1966). He had a long association with the ABBEY THEATRE, Dublin. His autobiography was published as *An Only Child* (1961) and *My Father's Son* (1968).

O'Connor, John (1850–1928), politician (Nationalist); born in Mallow, Co. Cork, educated locally. He worked as a commercial traveller and a van-driver. Known as 'Long John', he was a member of the IRB and secretary of the Supreme Council and was imprisoned five times under COERCION acts. He was a skilled interpreter of the deaf alphabet, which he taught to JOHN DEVOY. He met CHARLES STEWART PARNELL and others in March 1878 for the discussions that led to the NEW DEPARTURE. Though Parnell and the Archbishop of Cashel, T. W. CROKE, supported him for the Co. Tipperary parliamentary seat in

1885, the county convention of the NATIONAL LEAGUE refused his nomination; he received it only when Parnell called a second convention and personally piloted it through. O'Connor's continued loyalty to Parnell lost him Co. Tipperary and Co. Kilkenny, for which he was also standing in the 1892 election. Called to the bar in 1893, he became member of Parliament for North Kildare in 1905 and held the seat until defeated by SINN FÉIN, 1918.

O'Connor, Rory (1883–1922), republican; born in Dublin, educated at UCD, where he qualified as an engineer. He worked in Canada as a railway engineer, 1911–15; returning at the request of the IRB, he became an engineer with Dublin Corporation. He was wounded in the Easter Rising (1916) and, following a period of internment, left the IRB. Close to MICHAEL COLLINS, he was director of engineering of the IRA during the WAR OF INDEPENDENCE. Rejecting the ANGLO-IRISH TREATY (1921), he became chairman of the Army Council and repudiated the authority of Dáil Éireann when, during a press conference, 22 March 1922, he suggested a military dictatorship as a possible and even desirable outcome. He played a leading part in the establishment of a republican garrison in the FOUR COURTS in April 1922 and rejected the election pact between Collins and de Valera. While he disapproved of attempts to find a compromise formula to prevent outright civil war, he accepted the truce of May, which did not require the IRA to evacuate the Four Courts. Following the government's attack on the garrison, 28 June, he was captured; on 8 December he was one of the four prisoners shot in reprisal for the shooting of Seán Hales TD. The executions were authorised by the Minister for Home Affairs, KEVIN O'HIGGINS, at whose wedding a year earlier O'Connor had been best man.

O'Connor, T. P. [Timothy Power] (1848–1929), journalist and politician (Irish Party); born in Athlone, Co. Westmeath, educated at Queen's College, Galway. Moving to England, 1870, where he became a popular journalist, he formed close contacts with the Liberal Party. Widely known as Tay Pay (from his initials), he worked on *Saunders' Newsletter* and the *Daily Telegraph* and in the London office of the *New York Herald.* A supporter of the HOME RULE CONFEDERATION OF GREAT BRITAIN, he was the only member of the IRISH PARTY to sit for an English constituency (the Scotland division of Liverpool, 1880–1929). An important link between the Irish Party and leading Liberals, he supported the LAND LEAGUE and CHARLES STEWART PARNELL. Describing himself as 'an advanced radical', he advocated the extension of the Irish land legislation to the British working class. He toured the United States in 1881 and again in 1909 on fund-raising missions. He helped to draw up the Manifesto to the Irish in England, November 1885, before the general election, when Parnell called on Irish voters to oppose Liberals. He was elected for two constituencies, Liverpool and Co. Galway; when he opted to sit for Liverpool, Parnell's nomination of CAPTAIN W. H. O'SHEA for the Co. Galway seat led to a crisis in the party.

O'Connor opposed Parnell during the leadership crisis provoked by the divorce case, 1890. 'Father of the House of Commons' in his later years, he was Official Film Censor from 1917. A leading representative of the 'new journalism' (radicalism with the 'common touch'), he founded and edited the *Star,* 1887, where his reviewers included GEORGE BERNARD SHAW. He established the *Sun* in 1893 and his most popular paper, *T.P.'s Weekly,* in 1902, where he turned down an application for a job from JAMES JOYCE. His works included *The Parnell Movement* (1886), *Life of Charles Stewart Parnell* (1891), and *Memoirs of an Old Parliamentarian* (1929). He was also responsible for the publication of Charles Reade's *Cabinet of Irish Literature* (1880), editing the fourth and final volume.

O'Conor, Charles Owen, styling himself 'the O'Conor Don' (1838–1906), politician (Conservative) and author; born in Dublin, educated at the University of London. As member of Parliament for Co. Roscommon, 1860–80, he supported agrarian, taxation and educational reforms, about which he published pamphlets, including *Irish Land Tenure, Taxation of Ireland,* and *Freedom of Education.* High sheriff of Sligo, 1863, he sat on several royal commissions, including those on penal servitude, 1863, factories and workshops, 1875, and the registration of deeds, 1878. He was a member of the BESSBOROUGH COMMISSION, 1880, when he issued a minority report, and the Reformatories and Industrial Schools Commission, 1896. He played a prominent role in the passing of the Sale of Liquors on Sunday (Ireland) Act (1878). He was president of the Royal Irish Academy and of the SOCIETY FOR THE PRESERVATION OF THE IRISH LANGUAGE. His best-known work, *The O'Conors of Connaught,* was published in 1891.

Ó Cuív, Shán (1875–1940), journalist and educationalist; born Seán Ó Caoimh in Macroom, Co. Cork, educated at Dunmanway Model School. He invented and used a simplified spelling of Irish, which he applied to his own name. A journalist from 1898, he worked on several papers, including the *Cork Herald, Evening Telegraph* (chief sub-editor), and *Freeman's Journal.* He also edited *Glór na Ly,* 1911–12, and *Irish Opinion,* 1916. Active in the Gaelic League, he taught Irish at the Dublin College of Modem Irish and was active in the founding of Coláiste na Mumhan, 1904. He was Irish-language editor of the IRISH INDEPENDENT from 1931 and first director of the Government Information Bureau, 1934. He was the author of many textbooks; his works include *Fiche Duan* (1917), *Cúirt na Dála* (1918), *The Sounds of Irish* (1921), *Fuaimeanna agus Blas na Gaedhilge* (1922), *Sgéalta ón Radio* (1931), *An Eochair chun Labhartha na Gaedhilge* (1932), and *Prós na hAoise Seo* (1933).

O'Curry, Eugene (1796–1862), scholar; born at Carrigaholt, Co. Clare. He taught himself Irish from a collection of manuscripts kept by his father (a hawker, poet, and storyteller). After working at various occupations, including farming, teaching, inn-keeping, and keeper at the Limerick Lunatic Asylum, he moved to Dublin, where he was employed by GEORGE PETRIE as a researcher in the Historical Department of the Ordnance Survey, 1835–42. In this capacity, with JOHN O'DONOVAN, he pioneered a scholarly assessment of Irish manuscripts in the Royal Irish Academy, Trinity College, Dublin, and English institutions (the British Museum and the Bodleian Library), tabulating, translating and cataloguing some four hundred manuscripts. His work on Irish manuscripts in the British Museum, London, 1849 and 1855, was completed by Robin Flower in the twentieth century. O'Curry and O'Donovan were associated with their friend JAMES HENTHORN TODD in his founding of the Irish Archaeological Society, 1840. O'Curry was appointed professor of archaeology and Irish history by JOHN HENRY NEWMAN at the Catholic University. His lectures, delivered during the period 1854–56, were published as *Lectures on the Manuscript Materials of Ancient Irish History* (1860) and his second series as *On the Manners and Customs of the Ancient Irish* (3 vols., 1873). He made facsimiles of *The Genealogical Manuscript of Duald Mac Fhirbhis* (1836), *The Book of Lismore* (1839), *The Book of Lecan,* and other manuscripts. A member of the Celtic Society, 1853, for which he also made translations, he published *Manuscript Material of Ancient Irish History* (1861). Neither O'Curry nor O'Donovan lived to see the publication of the Seanchas Mór, a project to which they had both contributed.

Ó Dálaigh, Cearbhall (1911–1978), lawyer and politician; born in Bray, Co. Wicklow, educated at UCD (where he was taught by DOUGLAS HYDE). He was Irish-language editor of the *Irish Press,* 1931–40. Called to the bar in 1934 and a senior counsel from 1945, he was twice Attorney-General, 1946–48 and 1951–53. He unsuccessfully contested elections for Fianna Fáil in 1948 and 1951. A member of the Supreme Court from 1953, he was Chief Justice, 1961–73. When Ireland joined the European Economic Community, 1973, he became Irish representative at the European Court of Justice and in 1974 president of the First Chamber.

An agreed candidate to succeed ERSKINE CHILDERS as President of Ireland, he was inaugurated on 19 December 1974. In 1976 he referred two bills, the Criminal Law (Jurisdiction) Bill and the Emergency Powers Bill, to the Supreme Court (which upheld their constitutionality, 15 October). Three days later the Minister for Defence, Patrick Donegan (Fine Gael), provoked an unprecedented controversy when, speaking to army officers at Columb Barracks, Mullingar, he attacked Ó Dálaigh's action in referring the bill to the Supreme Court, describing it, according to newspaper reports, as 'a thundering disgrace.' The minister's offer to resign was refused by the Taoiseach, LIAM COSGRAVE. President Ó Dálaigh was not available when Donegan sought a meeting to offer an apology. Believing the office to have been slighted, he became the first president to resign, 22 October 1974. He was succeeded by DR PATRICK HILLERY.

O'Doherty, Kevin Izod (1823–1905), doctor and Young Irelander; born in Dublin, educated at Cecilia Street School of Medicine. A member of the REPEAL ASSOCIATION and YOUNG IRELAND and a contributor to the *Nation,* he supported the IRISH CONFEDERATION and was joint founder (with RICHARD DALTON WILLIAMS) of the *Irish Tribune,* which replaced the *United Irishman* after the transportation of his friend JOHN MITCHEL. Together with THOMAS FRANCIS MEAGHER he was transported for his role in the 1848 rising. He worked as a doctor in St Mary's

Hospital, Hobart, Australia, during his period of transportation, periodically meeting Mitchel, whose escape he organised (in *Jail Journal* Mitchel calls him 'St Kevin'). On his release in 1855 he returned to Europe. A fellow of the Royal College of Surgeons in Ireland, 1857, he studied medicine in Paris before settling in Brisbane, where he built up a considerable practice. He entered politics, becoming a member of both houses of the Australian legislature. On his return to Ireland he was elected member of Parliament for North Meath, 1885, and was made an honorary freeman of the city of Dublin. He returned to Australia, 1888, where he failed to re-establish his practice and died in poor circumstances. A collection was taken up for his widow in her last years.

O'Donnell, Frank Hugh (1848–1916), politician (Nationalist) and author; born in Co. Donegal, educated at Queen's College, Galway. A member of the IRB for a short time, he worked as a journalist with the *Morning Post* (London), specialising in foreign affairs. Following his election as member of Parliament for Co. Galway, 1874, he was unseated on the grounds of clerical intimidation and for libelling his opponent but three years later won Dungarvan, which he held until 1885. He was a distinguished speaker and a supporter of OBSTRUCTIONISM. A vain man, he made no secret of his feelings of intellectual superiority over most of his colleagues, to whom he was known as 'Crank Hugh' (a nickname first given to him by T. M. HEALY). He hoped for the chairmanship of the IRISH PARTY in succession to ISAAC BUTT but lost to CHARLES STEWART PARNELL, May 1880, whose leadership he refused to accept (referring to Parnell once as 'my runaway errand boy'). Refusing to support the LAND LEAGUE, he broke with the Parnellite wing of the party in 1881, resigned his seat four years later, and concentrated on journalism. He sued the *Times* (London) over its publication of the series 'PARNELLISM AND CRIME', 1887–88, but lost, because his counsel would not call Parnell as a witness. During the trial Parnell secured evidence that RICHARD PIGOTT was the author of forged letters on which the *Times* rested much of its case. O'Donnell's principal works include *How Home Rule Was Wrecked* (1895) and his *History of the Parliamentary Party* (2 vols., 1910), which is regarded as a less than forthright account.

O'Donnell, Peadar (1893–1986), socialist republican and writer; born in Meenmore, Dungloe, Co. Donegal, educated at St Patrick's College, Dublin. He taught on Árainn Mhór, Co. Donegal, before leaving for Scotland to aid migrant workers from Donegal in their strike for better pay and conditions. An organiser for the IRISH TRANSPORT AND GENERAL WORKERS' UNION, 1917, he was commandant of the Donegal Brigade of the IRA during the WAR OF INDEPENDENCE, 1919–21. Rejecting the ANGLO-IRISH TREATY (1921), he supported the occupation of the Rotunda Rooms, Dublin, in January 1922 and was also a member of the IRA garrison that occupied the FOUR COURTS in April; after the collapse of the garrison he was imprisoned and embarked on a 41-day hunger strike (called off by Republican leaders). After escaping in 1924 he resumed his career in the IRA and was elected to Dáil Éireann. A founder-member of SAOR ÉIRE, 1931, for which he edited *An Phoblacht,* he was a member of the Executive and Army Council of the IRA from 1924 until his expulsion in 1934. He was the first politician to oppose the payment of LAND ANNUITIES to the British government, for which he was imprisoned, 1927. He later persuaded COLONEL MAURICE MOORE to gain support from FIANNA FÁIL on the issue.

During the years 1928–30 he founded a number of short-lived revolutionary groups, including the IRISH WORKING FARMERS' COMMITTEE and the WORKERS' REVOLUTIONARY PARTY, for which he edited the *Workers' Voice.* During the 1930s he played a leading role in the struggle against the BLUESHIRTS and helped to establish the REPUBLICAN CONGRESS (1934), whose paper, *Republican Congress,* he edited. He supported the Republicans in the SPANISH CIVIL WAR and on his return helped to organise the CONNOLLY COLUMN. He later led the campaign to save FRANK RYAN, who was captured and imprisoned by the Franco government, 1939. He contributed articles and short stories to a wide variety of magazines and journals and was a managing editor and editor of the BELL.

His books include *Storm* (1925), *Islanders* (1928), *The Knife* (1930), *Edge of the Stream* (1934), *Muintir an Oileáin* (1935), *The Big Window* (1955), and *Proud Island* (1975). He published two autobiographical volumes, *The Gates Flew Open* (1932) and *There Will Be Another Day* (1963).

O'Donoghue, Daniel, styling himself 'the O'Donoghue' (1833–1889), politician (Whig); born in Co. Kerry, educated at Stonyhurst College, Lancashire. He supported the CATHOLIC UNIVERSITY OF IRELAND and the TEN-

ANT LEAGUE. He succeeded JOHN SADLEIR as member of Parliament for Co. Tipperary, March 1857, and held the seat at the ensuing general election, after which he sat for Tralee, 1865–85. Of fiery disposition, he was expelled from the House of Commons; SIR ROBERT PEEL referred to him as a 'mannikin traitor'. He was declared a bankrupt in 1870. A supporter of CHARLES STEWART PARNELL, he appealed to the electorate in the general election of 1880 to return him as, 'at the end of so many years in Parliament I should be sorry to lose my seat.' His plea had the desired effect: he topped the poll. He retired in 1885.

O'Donoghue, Florence (Florrie) (1894–1967), republican and author; born in Rathmore, Co. Kerry. He spent most of his life in Co. Cork, where he joined the Irish Volunteers in 1917 and was brigade adjutant and later intelligence officer of the FLYING COLUMN of Cork No. 1 Brigade. Active in peace initiatives during the CIVIL WAR, he and his friend Seán Hegarty met MICHAEL COLLINS in Cork a few hours before Collins met his death at Bealnablagh, near Macroom, 22 August 1922. During the years of the Second World War he was assistant intelligence officer, Southern Command, 1940–43, and 1st (Southern) Division, 1943–45. During this period he also edited the Defence Forces journal, *An Cosantóir.* Retiring with the rank of major (lieutenant-colonel), he spent some years expanding the reference library of the Bureau of Military History. Apart from contributions to a wide range of journals and newspapers, his writings include *No Other Law* (a biography of LIAM LYNCH, 1954), *The IRB and the Rising* (from DIARMUID LYNCH's papers, 1956), and *The Mystery of the Casement Ship* (1965). He was a pall-bearer at the funeral of his friend TOMÁS MACCURTAIN, whose biography he published in 1955.

O'Donovan, John (1806–1861), antiquarian and scholar; born in Atateemore, Co. Kilkenny, educated at a HEDGE SCHOOL and Hunt's Academy, Waterford. On the death of his father, 1817, he moved to Dublin, where he completed his education and was imbued by his uncle Patrick with a love of Irish culture. Having worked under JAMES HARDIMAN in the Irish Record Office, 1827–30, in 1830 he was appointed by THOMAS LARCOM to fill the vacancy created by the death of EDWARD O'REILLY in the Ordnance Survey and worked under GEORGE PETRIE in the Historical Department, alongside EUGENE O'CURRY. He listed 62,000 Irish place-names and fostered an Anglicised orthography that has largely survived. From 1836 he was also employed in the cataloguing of Irish manuscripts in the library of Trinity College, Dublin. With O'Curry he assisted JAMES HENTHORN TODD in founding the Irish Archaeological Society, 1840, and was retained on an annuity of £100 by the society until 1847. Called to the bar, 1847, he was appointed to the chair of Celtic languages in Queen's College, Belfast, August 1849, and appointed examiner in Celtic language and literature, 1852. O'Donovan and O'Curry were employed as joint editors by the Commission for the Publication of the Ancient Laws of Ireland to translate the Seanchas Mór, but both died before its publication.

He published an edition of the Irish dictionary by PETER O'CONNELL (1828), *The Banquet of Dún na nGedh and the Battle of Magh Rath* (1842), *Tracts Relating to Ireland* (1843), *The Tribes and Customs of Hy-Many, Commonly Called O'Kelly's Country* (1843), *Tribes and Customs of Hy-Fiachrach, Commonly Called O'Dowda's Country* (1844), *Grammar of the Irish Language* (1845), *The Annals of Ireland* (1846), *Leabhar na gCeart* (1847), *Annála Ríoghachta Éireann* (Annals of the Four Masters, 7 vols., 1848–56), *Three Fragments of Irish Annals* (1860), and *The Martyrology of Donegal* (1863). His Letters were edited in fifty volumes by Father MICHAEL O'FLANAGAN (1924–32).

O'Donovan Rossa, Jeremiah (1831–1915), republican; born in Ross Carbery, Co. Cork, educated locally. He worked distributing relief during the GREAT FAMINE (1845–49), during which he lost his father. He married the first of his three wives in 1853. After establishing a grocery business in Skibbereen he founded the PHOENIX NATIONAL AND LITERARY SOCIETIES, 1856, which were assimilated into the IRB in 1858. Rossa, as he was called (after his birthplace), became a leading organiser in the new movement, to the detriment of his business. Financial difficulties forced him to emigrate to the United States, where he remained until 1863, when he returned to become business manager of the IRISH PEOPLE. He was arrested together with other IRB leaders in 1865 and tried before JUDGE WILLIAM KEOGH, who sentenced him to life imprisonment after Rossa attacked him in a speech lasting eight hours. As a treason-felon he was treated with great harshness. The AMNESTY ASSOCIATION publicised letters from Rossa in which he claimed he had been handcuffed for thirty-five days and forced to lap his food; the allegation led to questions in the House of Commons, 4 June 1869, in reply to which the Home Secretary pointed out that Rossa had in fact been handcuffed for 'only twenty-eight days.'

While imprisoned he was elected to Parliament for Co. Tipperary, 1869. Continued agitation by the Amnesty Association through GEORGE HENRY MOORE led to the establishment of a commission to examine the conditions of Rossa's confinement, and he was released in 1871.

He accompanied JOHN DEVOY to New York, with other released FENIANS, to receive an address of welcome from the House of Representatives (see CUBA FIVE). Purchasing a low-grade hotel in New York, he called it the Chatham, after his English prison. He contributed to the *Irishman,* whose owner, RICHARD PIGOTT, financed the education of his sons at St Jarlath's College, Tuam. Rossa became head centre of the Fenians in 1877, by which time the movement was in disarray. He organised a SKIRMISHING FUND for a dynamiting campaign in England (see DYNAMITERS). When his plan to prosecute a war against Britain was opposed by Devoy, he broke with CLAN NA GAEL in 1880, and Devoy obtained control of the Skirmishing Fund, which had reached $23,000.

Through *United Ireland* he attacked British imperialism, lecturing throughout America on the theme. He returned to Ireland for a short visit in 1894 and for two years in 1904. Heavy drinking and attacks on former colleagues alienated him from the republican movement. He died in New York, and his remains were returned to Ireland, where, for a rising generation of republicans, he remained a symbol of the spirit of Fenianism. His burial at Glasnevin Cemetery, Dublin, 1 August 1915, was the occasion for an oration by PATRICK PEARSE, who, extolling O'Donovan Rossa's undying spirit, proclaimed:

> Life springs from death; and from the graves of patriot men and women spring living nations. The Defenders of this Realm . . . think that they have pacified Ireland . . . but the fools, the fools, the fools!—they have left us our Fenian dead, and while Ireland holds these graves, Ireland unfree shall never be at peace.

O'Donovan Rossa's Prison Life, published in New York in 1874, was reprinted as *Irish Rebels in English Prisons* (1882 and 1899) and later abridged as *My Years in English Jails* (1967). His autobiography, *Rossa's Recollections, 1838–1898,* was published in 1898.

O'Duffy, General Eoin (1892–1944), soldier and politician; born in Castleblayney, Co. Monaghan, educated locally. Following a period of apprenticeship in Co. Wexford he returned to Co. Monaghan, where he worked as an engineer and architect and later became an auctioneer. During the WAR OF INDEPENDENCE he was attached to the headquarters staff of the IRA, of which he was director of organisation, 1921. He supported the ANGLO-IRISH TREATY (1921) in Dáil Éireann and became assistant chief of staff of the Free State army, January 1922. During the Civil War he was officer commanding South-Western Command. Though commanding the Garda Síochána from September 1922, he became officer commanding the forces of the Free State on 10 March 1924, during the ARMY MUTINY. He showed great energy as Garda Commissioner. Closely identified with CUMANN NA NGAEDHEAL and the ARMY COMRADES' ASSOCIATION, he incurred the suspicion of ÉAMON DE VALERA when Fianna Fáil assumed office in March 1932. Declaring that he lacked 'full confidence' in him, de Valera dismissed him, 22 February 1933. O'Duffy rejected an offer of the office of Controller of Prices but accepted an annual pension of £520.

Following his dismissal he took command of the Army Comrades' Association, 20 July 1933. Changing the name of the organisation to the NATIONAL GUARD, commonly called the 'BLUESHIRTS', he introduced fascist-style marches, flags, and salutes. He admired Mussolini's concept of the corporate state. His proposed march to Leinster Lawn in Dublin on 13 August 1933 was banned by the government, and the organisation was declared illegal. When the Blueshirts merged with Cumann na nGaedheal to form FINE GAEL, September 1933, O'Duffy became president of the party. His increasing stridency as leader of the Blueshirts embarrassed the new party. He attacked the government and 'communist' IRA. His widely reported comment that Hitler had 'done more for Germany than any other leader in the world had done for his country' was ascribed by colleagues rather more to O'Duffy's drinking problem than to his political philosophy. He urged that farmers suffering from the effects of the 'ECONOMIC WAR' should withhold the payment of LAND ANNUITIES and rates.

Blueshirt candidates did poorly in the local government elections of 1934. O'Duffy attended the conference of European Fascists at

Montreux, December 1934, and later had talks with Mussolini in Rome. In an attempt to attract more members he issued a new programme, republican and anti-British in tone, calling for an end to partition. Opposition within Fine Gael led to his resignation from the presidency of the party. He attempted to retain the leadership of the Blueshirts but was ousted when he was opposed by the former leader of the Army Comrades' Association, Commandant Ned Cronin, and O'Duffy founded the short-lived NATIONAL CORPORATE PARTY on 8 June 1935.

In 1936 O'Duffy's small following had a temporary revival when he called for support for Franco in the revolt against the Spanish government (see SPANISH CIVIL WAR). Supported by the Catholic Church and right-wing newspapers, he led approximately six hundred followers to Spain. He had impressed Franco when he informed him that he had once controlled a million men; much later Franco learnt that O'Duffy had been referring to his role in the organising of the EUCHARISTIC CONGRESS. The volunteers returned in the summer of 1937, having seen little action. *Crusade in Spain,* O'Duffy's account of the campaign, was published in London in 1938.

O'Dwyer, Edward Thomas (1842–1917), bishop (Catholic); born in Co. Tipperary, educated at St Patrick's College, Maynooth, ordained 1867. As Bishop of Limerick he was hostile to the land agitation and the PLAN OF CAMPAIGN; he accepted the Papal rescript (decree) of 1887 as binding on priests and laity, withdrawing from priests in his diocese the power of giving absolution to anyone supporting the plan. He refused to sign the Catholic bishops' condemnation of CHARLES STEWART PARNELL, 4 December 1890. During the Great War he urged that Ireland remain neutral and criticised the pro-British policy of JOHN REDMOND. When Irish emigrant workers were attacked in Liverpool, November 1915, O'Dwyer wrote to the press, saying, 'Their crime is that they are not ready to die for England . . . Win or lose, Ireland will go on, in our old round of misgovernment intensified by a grinding poverty which will make life intolerable.' His letter was issued as a pamphlet by nationalists and also published as a postcard.

He again achieved national prominence when he became the first member of the hierarchy to defend the leaders of the EASTER RISING (1916). In reply to a request from GENERAL MAXWELL that he discipline two of his priests, O'Dwyer stated:

> You took care that no plea of mercy should interpose on behalf of the poor young fellows who surrendered to you in Dublin . . . Personally, I regard your action with horror, and I believe it has outraged the conscience of the country . . . Altogether your regime has been one of the worst and blackest chapters in the history of the misgovernment of the country.

This stand, in marked contrast to that of his fellow-bishops, earned him the respect of nationalists, and his picture was placed in shop windows throughout the country; SINN FÉIN had the letter reprinted in pamphlet form, while local bodies all over the country sent him resolutions of support. He was made an honorary freeman of the city of Limerick, 14 September 1916.

Ó Faoláin, Seán (1900–1991), writer; born John Whelan in Cork, educated at UCC. Influenced by DANIEL CORKERY, he became interested in Irish language and literature and joined the IRA (while at university) during the War of Independence. After rejecting the ANGLO-IRISH TREATY (1921) he was a bomb-maker for the IRA during the CIVIL WAR (1922–23), working also as acting director of publicity in Cork and Dublin. After teaching in Ennis Christian Brothers' School he returned to University College, Cork, and later went to Harvard University, Massachusetts, where he was a Commonwealth fellow, 1926–29. Having taught in England at Strawberry Hill College, London, 1929–33, he returned to Ireland in 1933 and was a founder-member of the IRISH ACADEMY OF LETTERS. The BELL, which he founded and edited, 1940–46, was the leading literary magazine of its time. He was director of the ARTS COUNCIL, 1956–59. A prolific writer, his works include biography, short stories, novels, criticism, translations, and an autobiography, *Vive Moi!* (1964).

Offences Against the State Act (1939 and 1940), introduced by the FIANNA FÁIL government, June 1939, in response to the campaign by the IRA, providing for the establishment of military tribunals and internment without trial. On 8 January 1940 the President of Ireland, DR DOUGLAS HYDE, acting on the advice of the Council of State, referred the Offences Against the State (Amendment) Act (1940) to the Supreme Court, the first such referral; on 9 February 1940 the court upheld its constitutionality. The act was again brought into force in 1957 to deal with the BORDER CAMPAIGN, during which 100 members of the IRA were interned.

Offences Against the State (Amendment) Act (1972), introduced on 22 November 1972 by the FIANNA FÁIL government in an attempt to curb the activities of the IRA; it sought to secure conviction on the testimony of a senior Garda officer that he believed a person was a member of an illegal organisation. The Labour Party and Fine Gael opposed the bill, and the Government seemed likely to lose the vote on 1 December. However, when two bombs exploded in Beresford Place and Sackville Place, Dublin, killing two people and injuring 127 others, Fine Gael withdrew its amendment and abstained in the vote. The Government won the division (69 to 22), and the bill was signed by the President on 2 December.

Office of Public Works, established in the eighteenth century as the Barrack Board, reconstituted under the name Board of Works in 1831 as a government department with responsibility for administering public money for relief works to ease hardship caused by unemployment. During the first half of the nineteenth century it assumed responsibility for the upkeep of public buildings, drainage, waterways and canals and played a prominent role as administrator of relief works during the GREAT FAMINE (1845–49). Its functions were extended in the later part of the century to include grants for improvement to land, building labourers' cottages and working-class housing in towns. It also researched projects for the construction of railway and tramlines.

The OPW is now responsible for the provision and maintenance of buildings and property used by Government departments, the design and supervision of the construction of new buildings, the design and execution of arterial drainage and flood relief schemes, and also the purchasing of supplies and services in common use in Government departments. It also advises the Government in relation to Dublin Zoo, the management of the state art collection, and the operation of the Dublin Castle Conference Centre.

Ó Fiaich, Tomás (1923–1990), clergyman (Catholic) and historian; born in Cullyhanna, Co. Armagh, educated at St Patrick's College, Maynooth, St Peter's College, Wexford, UCD, and the University of Louvain. A specialist in early and mediaeval Irish history, he was an authority on the contribution of early Irish monks to European Christianisation. He was professor of modern Irish history at Maynooth, 1959–74, and subsequently president of the college. He was chairman of the Commission on the Restoration of the Irish Language, 1959–63, and the Irish Language Advisory Council, 1965–68. He became Archbishop of Armagh and Primate of All Ireland, October 1977, and was made a cardinal, 30 June 1979. A committed nationalist and passionate advocate of a united Ireland, he was severely criticised in Britain for his protests at the treatment of republican prisoners, while his constant appeals to the Provisional IRA for a cessation of violence were rarely acknowledged. He died in Toulouse while leading a pilgrimage to Lourdes. His works include *Irish Cultural Influence in Europe* (1966), *Imeacht na nIarlaí* (1972), *Art Mac Cúmhaí—Dánta* (1973), and *St Oliver Plunkett* (1975).

O'Flaherty, Liam (1896–1984), writer and socialist; born in Gort na gCapall on the Aran Islands, educated at Holy Cross College, Dublin, and briefly at UCD. A member of the Irish Volunteers, on the outbreak of the Great War he enlisted in the British army under a false name and was in action on the Western Front, where he was wounded. After the war he joined a number of socialist organisations in London. He supported the IRA during the WAR OF INDEPENDENCE, worked as a seaman, and travelled to Rio de Janeiro, where he taught Greek, and to the United States, where he lectured and worked as a labourer and an oyster fisherman. Opposed to the ANGLO-IRISH TREATY (1921), he was a founder-member of the COMMUNIST PARTY OF IRELAND and sales manager for the *Workers' Republic*. While party leaders were on a visit to Russia he led the seizure of the Rotunda Rooms in Dublin, over which he raised the Red Flag, 18 January 1922; having proclaimed an Irish Soviet Workers' Republic, he surrendered after a four-day siege. Widely travelled, he twice suffered breakdowns, attributed to his experiences in the trenches. He supported the socialist wing of the IRA, which, under FRANK RYAN, saw action in the SPANISH CIVIL WAR. He was a founder-member of the IRISH ACADEMY OF LETTERS.

A prolific writer, his first novel, *Thy Neighbour's Wife*, was published in 1923. *The Informer* (1925) was made into a successful film by John Ford. Other novels include *The Assassin* (1928), *Famine* (1937), and *Insurrection* (1950). His three autobiographical books include *I Went to Russia* (1931). His short-story collections include *Dúil* (1953), *The Stories of*

Liam O'Flaherty (1956), and *The Wounded Cormorant and Other Stories* (1973). The writer and broadcaster Breandán Ó hEithir (1930–1990) was his nephew.

O'Flanagan, Michael (1876–1942), clergyman (Catholic), scholar, republican, land agitator, and inventor; born near Castlerea, Co. Roscommon, educated at St Patrick's College, Maynooth, ordained in 1900. A Gaelic League activist, when sent to the United States on a fund-raising mission for his bishop, 1904–10, he brought with him thirty-two sods of turf, one for each county, and charged Irish-Americans one dollar to 'tread once more their native sod.' As a curate in Co. Roscommon, 1912–14, he was deeply involved in land agitation, demanding 'land for the people' and leading a campaign against the CONGESTED DISTRICTS BOARD over turbary right. A noted public speaker, he delivered an oration over the body of JEREMIAH O'DONOVAN ROSSA in the City Hall, Dublin, 28 July 1915. During the North Roscommon by-election of 1917 he campaigned for COUNT PLUNKETT. Vice-president of SINN FÉIN, 25 October 1917, he was prominent in the anti-CONSCRIPTION campaign. His republicanism and his attempt to recruit other priests led to his suspension by his bishop, June 1918.

During the WAR OF INDEPENDENCE, Father O'Flanagan, known as 'the Sinn Féin priest', supported the IRA and served as a judge in the DÁIL COURTS. Having rejected the Anglo-Irish Treaty (1921), he visited the United States, 1921–26, as a Sinn Féin propagandist. On his return, 1926, he opposed the proposal by ÉAMON DE VALERA that if the OATH OF ALLEGIANCE was removed it would be a matter of policy rather than principle for republicans to take their seats in the Dáil; the motion was defeated (223 to 218). After de Valera formed FIANNA FÁIL, O'Flanagan blamed him for splitting the republican movement.

Though he resigned from Sinn Féin in 1927, he continued to support it and was later president, 1933–35. He was again silenced by his bishop, 1932. He supported republican volunteers led by FRANK RYAN in the Spanish Civil War (1936–39) and visited Canada and the United States, 1937, on behalf of the Friends of the Irish Republic and the North American Commission to Aid Spanish Democracy. On his return he settled in Dublin and devoted himself to the study of Irish literature. He edited fifty volumes of the letters of JOHN O'DONOVAN (1924–32). From 1932, at the request of the Minister for Education, Thomas Derrig, he wrote a history of the Irish counties; he spent nine years at the task, writing in English at the National Library while his assistants worked on the Irish versions. His name does not appear as author of the five published works (Cos. Roscommon, Monaghan, Carlow, Kerry, and Sligo); unpublished histories of Cos. Cork, Dublin, Donegal, Mayo and Wexford were among his papers left to the National Library. Other works include *Irish Phonetics* (1904) and *The Strength of Sinn Féin* (1934). He also submitted specifications to the Patent Office for what he called 'rón-súil'—spectacles for use under water.

An tÓglach, a paper published by the IRISH VOLUNTEERS, successor to the *Irish Volunteer*. The first issue, edited by PIARAS BÉASLAÍ, appeared on 15 August 1918. After it was declared illegal, those found in possession of a copy might be charged under the DEFENCE OF THE REALM ACT (1914). Sixteen issues appeared between 15 August 1918 and 15 December 1918, and a further seventeen between 15 January 1920 and the following October. It appeared intermittently during 1921 and 1922 and ceased publication after the Civil War. Its editors included ERNEST BLYTHE. The IRA published a paper of the same name in July 1951.

O'Grady, Standish Hayes (1832–1915), antiquarian; born in Castleconnell, Co. Limerick, educated at TCD. Though qualified as a civil engineer, he worked under the guidance of EUGENE O'CURRY and JOHN O'DONOVAN in copying manuscripts. After working for some thirty years in the United States as an engineer he returned to Ireland and began work on *A Catalogue of Irish Manuscripts in the British Museum,* on which O'Curry had worked and which was completed by Robin Flower and published in 1926. His major work was *Silva Gadelica* (tales from ancient Irish manuscripts, 2 vols., 1892).

O'Grady, Standish James (1846–1928), writer; born in Castletown Bearhaven, Co. Cork, educated at TCD, where he had an outstanding academic career and excelled also as a debater and as a sportsman. Called to the bar, 1872, he practised little, turning instead, under the influence of the works of JOHN O'DONOVAN and EUGENE O'CURRY, to a study of Irish myths and legends, though he knew little Irish. He edited and wrote much of the *All-Ireland Review,* 1900–07, in the cause of 'constructive unionism'. His works, which influenced the literary revival of the 1890s, include *History of Ireland—Heroic Period* (2 vols., 1878–81), *Early Bardic Literature of Ireland* (1879), *Finn and His Companions* (1892), *The Bog of Stars and Other Stories* (1893), *The Flight of the Eagle* (1897), and *The Triumph and Passing of Cuchulain* (1919).

O'Hagan, Thomas, Lord (1812–1885), lawyer and politician (Liberal); born in Belfast, educated at RBAI and called to the bar. He edited the *Newry Examiner,* 1836–40, before practising law. He defended CHARLES GAVAN DUFFY in a libel case, 1842, and in the state trials of 1843–44. As member of Parliament for Tralee, 1863–65, he supported a federal solution to the Irish demand for self-government. He defended many members of YOUNG IRELAND and was Solicitor-General and Attorney-General, 1861–62, before becoming a judge in 1865. On appointment as Lord Chancellor in 1868 he became the first Catholic to hold the office in modern times. Created a peer, 1870, he was reappointed Chancellor ten years later but resigned within a year. He took part in the O'Connell Centenary Celebrations of 1875. His *Speeches and Papers* were published in 1885–86.

O'Hanrahan, Michael (1877–1916), republican; born in New Ross, Co. Wexford, to a family of Fenian tradition, educated at St Patrick's College, Carlow. A member of the Gaelic League and of Sinn Féin, he was a founder-member of the IRISH VOLUNTEERS, of which he became quartermaster-general. He was second in command to THOMAS MACDONAGH at Jacob's factory, Bishop Street, Dublin, during the EASTER RISING (1916), after which he was shot by firing squad in Kilmainham Jail, 4 May. His brother Henry O'Hanrahan was also sentenced to death but the sentence was commuted to life imprisonment. His published works were *A Swordsman of the Brigade* (1915), *When the Normans Came* (1919), and *Irish Heroines* (1919).

O'Hart, John (1824–1902), genealogist; born in Crossmolina, Co. Mayo. He had little formal education and joined the Irish Constabulary, serving in Ballinrobe, Co. Mayo, and Oughterard, Co. Galway, resigning in 1845 to become a schoolteacher. As a teacher in Dublin in 1856 he began his genealogical researches. A fellow of the Royal Historical and Archaeological Association of Ireland and a member of the Harleian Society, he was the author of *Irish Pedigrees* (2 vols., 1876) and its supplement, *The Irish and Anglo-Irish Gentry when Cromwell Came to Ireland* (1884).

O'Hegarty, Patrick Sarsfield (1879–1955), republican, historian, and bibliographer; born in Cork, educated at North Monastery Christian Brothers' School. Largely self-educated, he was active in the Gaelic League and the IRB. After living in England, 1902–18, working in the postal service, he returned to Dublin, where he had a bookshop in Dawson Street. He contributed to many nationalist publications, including IRISH FREEDOM, 1911–14, *An tÉireannach,* 1913, the *Irish World,* 1915–19, and the *Separatist,* 1922. Following his acceptance of the ANGLO-IRISH TREATY (1921) he became head of the Free State postal service, in which position he had responsibility for 2RN (later Radio Éireann) after 1926. Despite a poor relationship with ÉAMON DE VALERA, he continued in his position following Fianna Fáil's accession to power in 1932 until his retirement in 1945. His published works include *John Mitchel* (1917), *Sinn Féin: An Illumination* (1919), *Ulster: A Brief Statement of Fact* (1919), *A Short Memoir of Terence MacSwiney* (1922), *The Victory of Sinn Féin* (1924), and *A History of Ireland Under the Union, 1801–1922* (1952). He also published biographies of leading nationalists.

His son, Seán Sáirséal Ó hÉigeartaigh (1917–1967), founded the publishing house of Sáirséal agus Dill.

O'Higgins, Kevin (1892–1927), politician (Sinn Féin and Cumann na nGaedheal); born in Stradbally, Co. Laois, educated at Clongowes Wood College, Co. Kildare (from which he was expelled for smoking), Carlow Seminary (from which he was expelled for drinking), and UCD and called to the bar. A member of the Irish Volunteers, while still a law student he was elected for Laois-Offaly to the first Dáil Éireann. He was assistant to the Minister for Local Government, W. T. COSGRAVE, January 1919 to January 1922. Defending the ANGLO-IRISH TREATY (1921), he said on 19 December 1921 that 'it represents such a broad measure of liberty for the Irish people and it acknowledges such a large proportion of its rights, you are not entitled to reject it without being able to show that you have a reasonable prospect of achieving more.'

After working as assistant to MICHAEL COLLINS in the Department of Finance he became Minister for Economic Affairs, January 1922, and held a similar position in the

Provisional Government. He recommended road and house-building schemes as well as drainage schemes to deal with high unemployment (130,000–150,000 in March 1922). Condemning republicans who took arms against the Provisional Government, he said in May 1922 that

> if civil war occurs in Ireland it will not be for the Treaty. It will be for a Free State versus anything else. It will be for a vital fundamental principle—for the right of the people of Ireland to decide any issue, great or small, that arises in the politics of this country.

He supervised the withdrawal of British forces from Ireland and played a leading role in drafting the CONSTITUTION OF THE IRISH FREE STATE (1922). He was Minister for Home Affairs, 1922–27, working closely with Cosgrave, on whose behalf he handled the ARMY MUTINY (1924). As Minister for Home Affairs (Justice after 1924) he was responsible for suppressing civilian disorder and for supervising the prison system. He was party to the decision that four republican prisoners, including RORY O'CONNOR, who had been best man at his wedding, should be shot as a reprisal for the assassination of Seán Hales TD on 7 December. WINSTON CHURCHILL admired O'Higgins, whom he described as 'a figure from antiquity cast in bronze.'

Following the murder of his father by republicans in front of his family, 11 February 1923, O'Higgins was identified with the implementation of the unpopular PUBLIC SAFETY ACTS, designed to destroy the IRA. His Intoxicating Liquor Act (1927) was also highly unpopular. He represented the Free State at the League of Nations and attended the annual Imperial Conferences, which shaped the evolution of the British Empire into the Commonwealth of Nations, made up of sovereign states, a concept that he had outlined during the Treaty debates.

O'Higgins was murdered on 10 July 1927 near his home at Booterstown, Co. Dublin, while on his way to Mass by a group of republicans acting independently of the IRA (which disapproved of the killing). This prompted a new Public Safety Act and the Electoral (Amendment) Act (1927).

Oireachtas, the legislature of the Republic, consisting of two chambers, DÁIL ÉIREANN (chamber of deputies), and SEANAD ÉIREANN (senate). The office of President of Ireland is also part of the Oireachtas, but the President may not be a member of either chamber.

Oireachtas Companion, a series of five volumes published between 1928 and 1945 by a member of the Oireachtas staff, William J. Flynn. Its purpose was to 'set out, in short compass and in attractive form, a budget of valuable information for ready reference.' It dealt with the political system and the functions of the Dáil and Seanad and gave background information on electoral results.

O'Kelly, James J. (1845–1916), politician (IRB and Irish Party); born in Dublin, educated locally. After joining the IRB, 1860, he joined the French Foreign Legion, 1863, leaving it within a short time at the request of JOHN DEVOY. He fought in the Mexican War (1864) and on his return became a member of the Supreme Council of the IRB, 1867. Opposed to the rising of 1867, he later played a central role in developing the IRB organisation in England and worked with MICHAEL DAVITT as a purchaser of arms. Under commission from the *New York Herald* (for which Devoy worked) he was a war correspondent in Cuba, where he was arrested and court-martialled by the Spanish authorities. He also served as a war correspondent for the *Daily News* in Egypt, where his contact with followers of the Mahdi convinced him that CLAN NA GAEL should provide 20,000 soldiers for the war in Sudan against Britain, a scheme rejected by the Clan in March 1879. While visiting France to meet JOHN O'LEARY he was introduced to CHARLES STEWART PARNELL, August 1877, and played a role in bringing about the NEW DEPARTURE. He was sent to Ireland with $10,000 for the purchase of arms in 1879, but funds were withdrawn when the Supreme Council rejected proposals by Clan na Gael designed to streamline the IRB.

Active in the LAND LEAGUE, he was elected as Parnellite member of Parliament for North Roscommon, 1880. In May 1881 he introduced Parnell to HENRI LE CARON. In October the same year he was imprisoned for his league activities. He continued to support Parnell after the split in the IRISH PARTY, 1890–91, and supported JOHN REDMOND after Parnell's death.

O'Kelly, John J. (1872–1957), republican and author, widely known by his pen-name, Sceilg; born in Valencia Island, Co. Kerry, educated locally. Domiciled in Dublin, he joined the Gaelic League and was president, 1919–23. He was elected for Sinn Féin to the first Dáil Éireann, in which he was Leas-Cheann Comhairle, 21 January 1919 to August 1921, and Minister for Irish; he was subsequently

Minister for Education, 26 August 1921 to January 1922. Opposed to the ANGLO-IRISH TREATY (1921), he followed a policy of abstention after 1922 and succeeded to the presidency of Sinn Féin when ÉAMON DE VALERA left in 1926 to form FIANNA FÁIL. He was editor of *Banba,* the *Catholic Bulletin,* and *An Camán.* His publications include *Beatha an Athair Tiobóid Maitiú* (a life of FATHER MATHEW, 1907), *Ireland: Elements of Her Early Story from the Coming of Caesar to the Anglo-Norman Invasion* (1921), *The Oath of Allegiance and All That It Implies* (1925), *Partition* (1940), *Cathal Brugha* (1942), *Éigse Éireann* (1942), and *O'Connell Calling, or The Liberator's Place in the World.*

O'Kelly, Seán T. (1882–1966), politician (Sinn Féin and Fianna Fáil); born in Dublin, educated at North Richmond Street Christian Brothers' School. Employed as a junior assistant in the National Library, he joined the Gaelic League in 1898, becoming manager of AN CLAIDHEAMH SOLUIS and general secretary in 1915. A founder-member of Sinn Féin and of the Irish Volunteers, he was a staff captain in the GPO, Dublin, during the EASTER RISING (1916), after which he was interned. He led the delegation that unsuccessfully sought a hearing for Ireland at the Paris Peace Conference, 7 January 1919. Elected for Dublin to the first Dáil Éireann, where he became Ceann Comhairle, 1 January 1919, he rejected the ANGLO-IRISH TREATY (1921) and supported the Republicans during the CIVIL WAR. Sinn Féin envoy to the United States, 1924–26, he was a founder-member of FIANNA FÁIL and became Vice-President of the Executive Council (deputy head of government) of the Irish Free State when ÉAMON DE VALERA took office in 1932. He was Minister for Local Government and Public Health, 1932–39, Tánaiste, 1937–45, and Minister for Finance, 1939–45. He succeeded DR DOUGLAS HYDE as President of Ireland, inaugurated on 25 June 1945.

old-age pensions. The Old Age Pensions Act (1908) established the principle of relief for the elderly poor. Those over the age of seventy whose income did not exceed £31 10s a year received a non-contributory pension of 5 shillings a week. Ireland, with its large population of indigent elderly, benefited considerably from the pension, which was administered by the Local Government Board. In the absence of documentary evidence of age, pensions were frequently awarded on the word of a clergyman; on 22 September 1909, following a court hearing at Magherafelt, Co. Derry, 150 pensioners had their allowance cancelled when census returns contradicted the statements of clergy who had believed the applicants were all over seventy. An alternative qualifying method chosen by officials was the question 'What do you remember about the NIGHT OF THE BIG WIND?' In 1910, £2.4 million was dispensed in old-age pensions in Ireland.

O'Leary, John (1830–1907), republican; born in Tipperary, educated at Queen's College, Cork and Galway, and TCD, where he studied medicine but did not graduate. Influenced by the *Nation* and YOUNG IRELAND, he took part in the rising of 1848 (see BALLINGARRY), for which he was arrested and imprisoned. On his release he supported JAMES FINTAN LALOR in 1849. He accepted a commission from JAMES STEPHENS to go to the United States to inform JOHN O'MAHONY of developments. In 1863 he became editor of the IRISH PEOPLE, where the staff included his sister Ellen O'Leary, CHARLES J. KICKHAM, and THOMAS CLARK LUBY. Following the suppression of the paper in 1865 he was sentenced to twenty years' imprisonment; after serving nine years in English prisons he was released, 1874, on condition that he go into exile until the period of his sentence had expired. A member of the IRB, he was president of the Supreme Council from 1885 until his death. While living in Paris he was visited by CHARLES STEWART PARNELL and JOHN DEVOY, who discussed with him the principles involved in the NEW DEPARTURE.

Following his return to Dublin, 1885, his hostility towards the IRISH PARTY and the National League made him unpopular, as did his continuing support for Parnell following the O'Shea divorce case. Within a short time of settling in Ireland he attracted many of the young generation, to whom he was a symbol of militant nationalism. W. B. YEATS sought his advice while editing *Folk Tales of the Irish Peasantry* (1888) and researched much of his writing in O'Leary's 10,000-volume library. O'Leary published works by Yeats and others of his generation in the literary section of the *Gael.* He also helped to finance *Poems and Ballads of Young Ireland* (which was dedicated to him, 1888). He was president of the IRB committee established to organise the CENTENARY CELEBRATIONS in 1898 and of the Young Ireland Society. In 1900 he became the first president of CUMANN NA NGAEDHEAL. His works include

Young Ireland, the Old and the New (1885), *What Irishmen Should Know, How Irishmen Should Feel* (1886), and *Recollections* (2 vols., 1896).

His sister Ellen O'Leary (1831–1889) contributed verse to the *Irish People,* 1863–65, and to the *Nation, Irish Fireside, Irishman,* and *Pilot* (Boston). She mortgaged her property to provide £200 for the escape of JAMES STEPHENS from Richmond Prison, Dublin, November 1865. She was a founder-member, joint treasurer and a militant activist of the LADIES' LAND LEAGUE. A volume of her verse, *Lays of Country, Homes and Fireside,* was published in 1891.

O'Leary, Michael (born 1936), politician (Labour Party and Fine Gael); born in Cork, educated at UCC, where he engaged in student politics and edited a student paper. He was international vice-president and later deputy president of the Union of Students in Ireland. An official in the Irish Transport and General Workers' Union, he spent a year on a scholarship at Columbia University, New York, and worked as education officer of the Irish Congress of Trade Unions. Elected to Dáil Éireann, 1965; as Minister for Labour, 1973–77, he introduced reforming legislation on women's rights and industrial relations and helped negotiate the 1976 national wage agreement. Having lost the election for leadership of the Labour Party to FRANK CLUSKEY, 1 July 1977, he succeeded him on 17 June 1981. He resigned from the European Parliament on 1 July 1981. In 1982, after failing to gain support for a pre-election pact with FINE GAEL, he resigned the leadership, 28 October, and joined Fine Gael. He was succeeded as leader of the Labour Party by DICK SPRING. A Fine Gael TD for Dublin South-West, 1982–87, he was called to the bar and was later appointed a District Court judge.

O'Leary, Patrick 'Pagan' (1825–?), republican; born in Macroom, Co. Cork. After running away from home as a youth he went to the United States, where he studied for the priesthood. He abandoned his studies to fight in the Mexican War (1846–48), during which he was wounded in the head. His nickname 'Pagan' came from his rejection of Christianity: he held that the worst thing that had happened to the Irish was their conversion to Christianity, which had taught them to love their enemies. The principal targets of his abuse were England, Rome, QUEEN VICTORIA ('Mrs Brown'), and the Pope ('the Boss'). After returning to Ireland he was a recruiting agent for the IRB and was believed to have recruited several thousand into the organisation. After his arrest in Athlone while he was administering the Fenian oath to a soldier, 1867, he was sentenced to several years' imprisonment. Following his release he again went to America, where he faded into obscurity.

O'Mahony, John (1815–1877), republican; born possibly in Kilbeheny, Co. Limerick, educated at TCD. A supporter of the REPEAL ASSOCIATION, he later joined YOUNG IRELAND and supported WILLIAM SMITH O'BRIEN during the rising of 1848. After its collapse he unsuccessfully attempted to organise another one. He escaped to France, where he made a precarious living teaching English and Irish at the Irish College. In Paris he met JAMES STEPHENS, 1851, and later in New York joined the EMMET MONUMENT ASSOCIATION. He supported himself by making a distinguished translation of Seathrún Céitinn's *Foras Feasa ar Éirinn* (*The History of Ireland,* 1857). After resuming contact with Stephens he raised $400, which enabled Stephens to establish the IRB in 1858. Simultaneously, O'Mahony founded the FENIANS. During the American Civil War (1861–65) he organised a Fenian regiment, the 69th Regiment of the New York State Militia (National Guard), in which he held the rank of colonel.

As head centre of the Fenians, O'Mahony's secretary was 'Red Jim' MacDermott, who was a spy for the British government; despite warnings from Stephens and others, O'Mahony defended MacDermott even after his treachery had been unmasked. When the Fenians were reorganised in 1865 O'Mahony lost his position as head centre to Colonel W. E. Roberts, leader of the 'Senate' faction, which advocated an attack on Britain through Canada. O'Mahony disapproved and urged Stephens to call the long-awaited rising in Ireland; instead, Stephens arrived in New York, attempting unsuccessfully to heal the breach between O'Mahony and Roberts. Stephens himself was deposed and replaced by THOMAS J. KELLY. Attempting to recover his own position, O'Mahony tried to capture the island of Campo Bello in the Bay of Fundy, between the United States and Canada, but was betrayed by MacDermott and others. After the collapse of Kelly's Irish venture in 1867, O'Mahony lost his remnant of the American movement, much of which was absorbed into CLAN NA GAEL in 1867. His last years were spent in poverty. His remains were brought back to

Ireland in a re-enactment of the funeral of his fellow-Fenian TERENCE BELLEW MCMANUS.

O'Malley, Desmond (born 1939), politician (Fianna Fáil and Progressive Democrats); born in Limerick, educated at UCD and the Incorporated Law Society. A solicitor in the family practice, on 22 May 1968 he won the Limerick East seat for Fianna Fáil in a by-election caused by the death of his uncle, DONOGH O'MALLEY, defeating the latter's widow, Hilda O'Malley, who stood as an independent. Chief whip and later Minister for Justice following the resignation of Mícheál Ó Móráin (during the Arms Crisis), May 1970, he steered the OFFENCES AGAINST THE STATE (AMENDMENT) ACT (1972) through the Dáil, which allowed for the transfer of political prisoners from civil to military custody and the setting up the Special Criminal Court for trying terrorist offences. He was Minister for Industry and Commerce, 1977–79, Minister for Industry, Commerce and Tourism, 1979–81, and Minister for Trade, Commerce and Tourism, 1982. He challenged CHARLES HAUGHEY for the leadership of Fianna Fáil but withdrew on the day of the meeting, 25 February 1982, and in October resigned from the Government. His support for the coalition government's Family Planning Bill, 20 February 1985, led to his expulsion from Fianna Fáil, 26 February.

He founded the Progressive Democrats, 21 December 1985, which had fourteen members elected in the general election of 1987. Following the 1989 general election, when the PDs (now reduced to six seats) entered a coalition government with Fianna Fáil under Haughey, O'Malley became Minister for Industry and Commerce, 1989–92. His party continued in coalition with Fianna Fáil when ALBERT REYNOLDS succeeded Haughey as Taoiseach, 6 February 1992, but tensions between O'Malley and Reynolds, exacerbated by their testimony before the BEEF TRIBUNAL, led to the collapse of the government. After resigning the leadership of the PDs in October 1993 he was defeated in the Munster constituency for a seat in the European Parliament, losing to PAT COX, who had left the PDs to stand as an independent. O'Malley became chairperson of the Joint Committee on Foreign Affairs, November 1997. On 29 April 2001 RTE began the transmission of a four-part television series, 'Des O'Malley: A Public Life', an unprecedented series on a living politician, widely criticised for allowing him to present an unchallenged version of the events surrounding the ARMS TRIALS. He retired from Dáil Éireann in 2002.

O'Malley, Donogh (1921–1968), politician (Fianna Fáil); born in Limerick, educated at UCG, where he qualified as an engineer. Head of the Fianna Fáil organisation in Limerick (of which he was mayor, 1961, the third of his family to hold the office), he was elected to Dáil Éireann for Limerick East, 1961–68. SEÁN LEMASS appointed him to the Office of Public Works as Parliamentary Secretary to the Minister for Finance. He was Minister for Health, April 1965 to August 1966. As Minister for Education, August 1966 until his death, he tackled several aspects of education: he established free primary and second-level education for all, closed small rural schools, introduced free bus travel to school for children in rural areas, and introduced Intermediate and Leaving Certificate courses in the vocational system. He was an uncle of DESMOND O'MALLEY.

O'Malley, Ernest (Ernie) (1898–1957), republican and writer; born in Castlebar, Co. Mayo. His family moved to Dublin, 1906, where he was educated at UCD. A member of the Irish Volunteers, he joined the insurgents on the fourth day of the EASTER RISING (1916), after which he was interned. As a staff captain he held a roving commission as an organiser for MICHAEL COLLINS during the War of Independence. At the request of SEÁN TREACY he was attached to the 3rd Tipperary Brigade, with which he took part in the attack on Hollyford Barracks, 10–11 May 1920, and was wounded during the attack on Rear Cross Barracks, 11 July. While serving in Co. Kilkenny later in the year he was captured and imprisoned for three months under the alias Bernard Stewart, refusing to reveal his identity even under torture. After escaping in February 1921 he took command of the 2nd Southern Division in March.

The first divisional commander to reject the ANGLO-IRISH TREATY (1921), he raided Clonmel Barracks, 26 February 1922, provoking a protest from the British government to the Provisional Government. As officer commanding the headquarters section of the garrison at the FOUR COURTS, Dublin, he remained in the building after the Provisional Government began its bombardment on 28 June; before leaving he triggered the explosion that destroyed the PUBLIC RECORD OFFICE. He was captured but almost immediately escaped and, as the CIVIL WAR spread, went to Co. Wexford, where he took part in the raid on Enniscorthy Castle. As a member of the IRA Executive and officer commanding the Northern and Eastern Areas, he was appointed to the Army Council, 16 October 1922, and became assistant chief of staff of the anti-Treaty IRA. He was severely wounded and captured by the Free State army, 4 November 1922, following a gun-fight at the Humphreys' home in Aylesbury Road, Dublin, during which a pro-Treaty soldier was killed and a guest in the house accidentally wounded by O'Malley. He spent five months in prison hospital, then went on a forty-day hunger strike. He remained under sentence of death until July 1924. He was elected a Sinn Féin member of Dáil Éireann for North Dublin in the general election of 1923. Under medical opinion that he would not walk again, he was released in 1924. He refused to take his Dáil seat while the OATH OF ALLEGIANCE was mandatory.

He recovered and left Ireland for Spain and the Basque Country, where he spent two years in the mountains and was in contact with the Basque separatist movement. On his return to Ireland in 1927 he decided against resuming his medical studies and travelled to the United States, where he helped to raise money for the IRISH PRESS. He travelled widely, working in a variety of jobs. Having settled for a time in Taos, New Mexico, where he lived with an American family, he wrote poetry and drafted early versions of his books *On Another Man's Wound* and *The Singing Flame.* He was Irish representative at the Chicago World's Fair (1933). Returning to Ireland in 1935, he divided his time between homes in Co. Mayo and Dublin. He was elected to the Irish Academy of Letters in 1947. *On Another Man's Wound,* his account of the period from 1916 to the end of the War of Independence, was serialised in the *Irish Press* and published in London in 1936. A sequel, *The Singing Flame,* dealing with the Civil War period, was published in 1978, edited by Frances-Mary Blake from the manuscript in the library of UCD.

O'Mara, James (1873–1948), politician (Nationalist and Sinn Féin); born in Limerick, educated locally. On leaving school he entered the extensive family business. Briefly a member of the Irish Party (resigning in 1907), he supported the Irish Volunteers and Sinn Féin, in which he was active after the Easter Rising (1916). A Sinn Féin member of Dáil Éireann, he spent most of his time raising funds in the United States. When ÉAMON DE VALERA toured the United States, O'Mara acted as a trustee for the Dáil Éireann fund, paying his own expenses. Following policy disagreements with de Valera, May 1921, he resigned from the Dáil and resumed his business interests.

His younger brother, Stephen O'Mara (1885–1926), was mayor of Limerick following the murder of GEORGE CLANCY, March 1921. Succeeding his brother as trustee of the Dáil Éireann funds, May 1921, he worked for a time in the United States.

Ó Móráin, Dónall (1923–2001), language activist; born in Dublin, raised in Waterville, Co. Kerry, returning at the age of twelve to Dublin to live with his aunt and educated at UCD and King's Inns. He worked for the Creation publishing group. Founder of GAEL-LINN, 1953, he supported the establishment of Irish-medium schools and of Raidió na Gaeltachta (on whose governing body he served for five years). As chairman of the RTE Authority from 1970 he was involved in controversy over the Government ban on broadcasting interviews with representatives of illegal organisations. The Authority was dismissed in 1972 over a radio interview with SEÁN MAC STIOFÁIN, a leading member of the Provisional IRA. He was reappointed chairman of the Authority in 1973, and resigned in 1976. He was managing editor of the weekly paper *Anois* (1984–96), published by Gael-Linn.

O'Neill, Francis (1848–1936), collector of traditional music; born in Tralibane, Bantry, Co. Cork, educated at national school. He joined the Chicago Police Department, July 1873. During an encounter with a gunman the following month he was shot in the back (the bullet was never extracted), and he was promoted for his bravery. He later became Chief of Police, 1901–05. His interest in traditional music was shared by Sergeant James O'Neill (no relation), who transcribed the tunes that O'Neill collected. He bequeathed his extensive library and papers to the University of Notre Dame, Indiana. His published works include *The Music of Ireland* (1,050 pieces, 1903), *The Dance Music of Ireland* (1,001 pieces, 1907), *O'Neill's Irish Music* (1908), *Irish Folk Music* (1910), *Irish Minstrels and Musicians* (1913), and *Waifs and Strays of Gaelic Melody* (1916).

O'Neill, Captain Terence, Lord O'Neill of the Maine (1914–1990), politician (Ulster Unionist); born in London, educated at Eton College. A captain in the British army in the

Second World War (in which he lost his two brothers), he was elected to the Parliament of Northern Ireland in 1946, becoming Parliamentary Secretary to the Minister of Health, 1948–52, Deputy Speaker, 1953–56, and Minister of Home Affairs, 1956. As Minister of Finance, 1956–63, he was successful in attracting foreign investment to Northern Ireland. He succeeded VISCOUNT BROOKEBOROUGH as leader of the Unionist Party and Prime Minister, 1963; his policy of rapprochement with the Republic was condemned by hardliners, who were further alienated during 1966 when he allowed the holding of commemorations of the Easter Rising (1916).

There was an increasing demand from the Catholic population for an end to the discrimination that characterised the Northern state at local government level. O'Neill agreed to the abolition of the business vote but he rejected other demands. There was a revival of the ULSTER VOLUNTEER FORCE to 'protect the loyalist heritage,' and REV. IAN PAISLEY founded the ULSTER CONSTITUTION DEFENCE COMMITTEE, with its militant wing, the ULSTER PROTESTANT VOLUNTEERS. O'Neill proscribed the UVF, 28 June 1966, for its role in the murders at Watson's Bar, Malvern Street, Belfast. Following demands by the NORTHERN IRELAND CIVIL RIGHTS ASSOCIATION he announced a five-point programme of civil rights, November 1968.

The division within the government over his concessions became public in December when he dismissed WILLIAM CRAIG, Minister of Home Affairs. The disturbances that accompanied a PEOPLE'S DEMOCRACY march in January 1969 received widespread publicity and criticism of Paisleyites and the RUC. Under pressure from London, O'Neill announced the establishment of the CAMERON COMMISSION, leading to the resignation of BRIAN FAULKNER, 23 January.

Challenged for leadership of the party, O'Neill called a general election (the 'Crossroads Election') for 24 February. In his own constituency he was opposed by Paisley, who polled 6,331 votes to O'Neill's 7,741. He secured 23 votes in the leadership contest, with Faulkner opposing him, Craig abstaining, and 10 withdrawing. As unrest continued he commented, 5 March:

> We are all sick of marchers and counter-marchers. Unless these warring minorities rapidly return to their senses, we will have to consider a further reinforcement of the regular police duties . . . Enough is enough. We have heard sufficient for now about civil rights, let us hear a little about civic responsibilities.

His position continued to be eroded, and when MAJOR JAMES CHICHESTER-CLARK, Minister of Agriculture and O'Neill's cousin, resigned, 23 April, O'Neill's moral authority within the party was shattered. He resigned, 28 April, and was succeeded by Faulkner; following his retirement in January 1970 his seat was won by Paisley. Shortly afterwards O'Neill was made Lord O'Neill of the Maine. His *Autobiography* was published in 1972.

Operation Demetrius, the code name for the British army operation to round up hundreds of republicans for internment, 9 August 1971, under section 12 of the SPECIAL POWERS ACT. In fact most republicans, anticipating internment, had gone to ground. Internment further radicalised the nationalist community. The last internees were released on 5 December 1975.

Operation Dove, the code name for the plan by German military intelligence to return the republicans SEÁN RUSSELL and FRANK RYAN to Ireland. A submarine commanded by Korvettenkapitän Hans-Gerrit von Stockhausen left Germany on 8 August 1941. Following Russell's death at sea, he overrode Ryan's request to be put ashore and returned to Germany.

Operation Motorman, the code name for the operation under which the British army cleared barricades in 'no-go' areas in Derry and Belfast, 31 July 1972. It involved 21,000 soldiers, with 9,000 mobilised UDR and 6,000 RUC men, supported by tanks, armoured cars, and helicopters. 1,500 soldiers entered the Bogside and Creggan areas of Derry, where they met with little resistance: in anticipation of such an operation the IRA had already vacated the 'no-go' areas.

Opsahl Report, sometimes referred to as Initiative '92, the result of an independent inquiry under the chairmanship of the Norwegian academic Torkel Opsahl into attitudes in Northern Ireland. Sitting from January 1993, the body received some five hundred submissions from three thousand people. *A Citizens' Inquiry: The Opsahl Report on Northern Ireland* was published on 9 June 1993. Recommendations included the creation of a devolved administration with equal membership from the unionist and nationalist communities with a mutual right of veto, formal legal recognition of the nationalist aspiration to a united Ireland, the opening of informal channels of communication with the Provisional IRA and Sinn Féin, the introduction of a bill of rights, and reform of the RUC under a decentralised structure. Opsahl also found that people on both sides of the divide would accept the inclusion of SINN FÉIN in political talks following a cessation of nationalist violence.

O'Rahilly, Michael Joseph, styling himself 'the O'Rahilly' (1875–1916), nationalist and journalist; born in Ballylongford, Co. Kerry, educated at UCD. His legal studies were terminated on the death of his father. Because of ill-health from 1898 he spent some time in the United States, where he married and worked for his wife's family in Philadelphia, 1905–09. Returning to Dublin, he became active in Sinn Féin. A member of the Gaelic League, he was assistant editor and circulation manager of *An Claidheamh Soluis* until 1914 and spent much of his income on league activities. His request for an article from EOIN MACNEILL led to the publication of 'The north began', which attracted the attention of the IRB and led to the founding of the Irish Volunteers, 11 November 1913. He was chairman of its sub-committee on arms, which organised the HOWTH GUN-RUNNING (July 1914), and personally pledged the surety necessary for the purchase of the arms. He opposed JOHN REDMOND in calling for Volunteers to assist the British war effort, and supported MacNeill's attempt to retain the Irish Volunteers as a pressure group until after the Great War.

Like MacNeill, he was unaware that the Military Council of the IRB planned to use the Volunteers in the EASTER RISING (1916). When MacNeill's attempt to call off the rising failed, O'Rahilly joined the insurgents in the GPO garrison. He was killed while leading a charge against a British barricade in Moore Street on the Friday of the week of fighting, leaving a widow and five children.

Orange Order, a Protestant organisation, originally known as the Orange Society, founded after a battle between the Catholic DEFENDERS and Protestant PEEP O' DAY BOYS at the Diamond, Armagh, 21 September 1795. Members inaugurated a campaign of violence against Catholic tenant-farmers, forcing thousands to seek refuge outside Ulster. The first Orange lodge was in Dyan, Co. Tyrone, and the first grand master was James Sloan of Loughgall, at whose inn the victory of the Peep o' Day Boys had been celebrated. Another Protestant organisation, the ROYAL BLACK PRECEPTORY, 1796, maintained strong links with the Orange movement. The founding of the Orange Order, modelled on the Freemasons, mirrored Protestant reaction to the Relief Act (1793), which precipitated fears that increasing reforms, leading to CATHOLIC EMANCIPATION, would give Catholics control over economic and political life. Orangemen were required to swear an oath:

> I, [. . .], do solemnly swear that I will, to the utmost of my power, support and defend the King and his heirs as long as he or they support the Protestant ascendancy.

The order has three principal aims: protection of Protestants from Catholics, support for the Protestant religion, and the maintenance of the English monarchy and constitution. It celebrates the victory of King William of Orange over James II at the Battle of the Boyne (1690). Following the ACT OF UNION (1800) the Orange Order viewed itself as guarantor of the Protestant supremacy in Ireland.

MARQUESS CORNWALLIS and VISCOUNT CASTLEREAGH attempted without success to suppress the order. Membership, always strongest in the north-east, declined during the early decades of the nineteenth century, and its ruling body, the Grand Orange Lodge of Ireland, was dissolved in 1825. Under the direction of the Duke of Cumberland (the King's brother) the order was reorganised to fight DANIEL O'CONNELL and the CATHOLIC ASSOCIATION. The Grand Orange Lodge was reconstituted in 1828, as O'Connell's drive proved inexorable, and members formed BRUNSWICK CLUBS to lobby against emancipation. The order opposed O'Connell's new movement for 'Repeal of the Union', O'Connell's battle cry during the 1830s. At Hillsborough, Co. Down, a call by DR HENRY COOKE for a united Protestant front to combat the effects of emancipation, 30 October 1834, precipitated serious sectarian rioting. When the government became alarmed, the Duke of Cumberland dissolved the Grand Orange Lodge again in 1836. It was again reconstituted in 1845.

The Orange Order was involved with Catholic RIBBONMEN in the DOLLY'S BRAE AFFRAY, 12 July 1849, when thirty Catholics were killed. It opposed the TENANT LEAGUE of the 1850s, supported the Ecclesiastical Titles Act (1851), and drew attention to the dangers of the IRB during the 1860s. It suffered a serious defeat in 1869 when W. E. GLADSTONE carried the DISESTABLISHMENT of the Church of Ireland. It had more success in combating the effects of the LAND LEAGUE in Ulster and organised a force of harvesters for CAPTAIN CHARLES BOYCOTT when he was ostracised by the league in Co. Mayo during the winter of 1880.

The imminent threat of HOME RULE in 1886 led to a revival of the order. The origins of the ULSTER UNIONIST PARTY lie in a meeting of seven members of Parliament who were also members of the order in London, January 1886. Later that year Conservative politicians, led by LORD RANDOLPH CHURCHILL, wooed the Orange lodges by 'playing the Orange card.' The influx of employers, businessmen and professionals led to tension within the movement once the immediate threat of home rule had vanished, 1893. A working-class element, led by T. H. SLOAN, broke away, 1902, to form the INDEPENDENT ORANGE ORDER, 1902, which in 1907 co-operated with the ANCIENT ORDER OF HIBERNIANS (traditional enemy of the order) and the DUNGANNON CLUBS to take part in the general strike organised by JAMES LARKIN.

When the public discussions on devolution, 1903–04, and the fall of the Conservative government in 1905 led to fears of self-government for Ireland, the Orange Order played a leading role in the formation of the Ulster Unionist Council, its members holding 122 of the 760 seats on the council as well as eighteen on the 300-strong Standing Committee. When the PARLIAMENT ACT (1911) made home rule inevitable within a few years, Orange leaders organised the ULSTER SOLEMN LEAGUE AND COVENANT and the ULSTER VOLUNTEER FORCE.

The Orange Order played a prominent role in the new state of Northern Ireland from 1921. Most Ulster Unionists were members of Orange lodges, as were all Prime Ministers. The British government did not seriously question discriminatory legislation directed against the Catholic population until the agitation by the NORTHERN IRELAND CIVIL RIGHTS ASSOCIATION in the 1960s. The Orange Order condemned this organisation for being republican and communist-inspired; it opposed the introduction of direct rule from London, 1972, as well as attempts to resolve the Northern conflict through 'power-sharing' (multi-party government). It condemned the ANGLO-IRISH AGREEMENT (1985).

During the 1990s, as the PEACE PROCESS showed signs of fostering a new relationship between the communities, the Orange Order in Portadown, Co. Armagh, became the centre of attention over its traditional march from Drumcree Church down the (Catholic) Garvaghy Road from 1995. The use of the British army to police (and sometimes prevent) the marches in Portadown and along the Lower Ormeau Road in Belfast incensed many Orangemen and other loyalists, while attempts by the RUC and British army to permit marches to take place provoked widespread nationalist unrest.

The Orange Order, which is open only to men, is associated with the APPRENTICE BOYS OF DERRY (often with overlapping membership) and also has women's and junior branches.

Orange Volunteers, a loyalist paramilitary organisation formed in 1972 from among members of the ORANGE ORDER and ex-servicemen. It provided stewards at rallies of ULSTER VANGUARD addressed by WILLIAM CRAIG and was reported to have some three thousand members by 1974, when they were involved in setting up roadblocks during the loyalist strike, 1977. After this it was believed to be defunct, but an organisation using the name reappeared in the 1990s, when the police believed that it worked closely with the RED HAND DEFENDERS. During 1999 there was speculation that the two organisations had united to form the Military Alliance.

Order of Liberators, founded by DANIEL O'CONNELL in 1824 to promote the struggle for CATHOLIC EMANCIPATION. Its aim was to protect the FORTY-SHILLING FREEHOLDERS who voted against their landlords. Members of the order wore a green ribbon and a medal. O'Connell was popularly known as the Liberator for his work to secure Catholic Emancipation, which was achieved in 1829.

'Orders of Frightfulness', instructions issued by LIAM LYNCH to the anti-Treaty section of the IRA during the CIVIL WAR, 30 November 1922. The orders listed fourteen categories of persons to be regarded as legitimate targets for shooting on sight and having their property destroyed, including members of Dáil Éireann who had voted for the emergency powers granted to the Minister for Defence of the Provisional Government, senators, unionists, hostile journalists, High Court judges, businessmen, and 'aggressive Free State supporters'. On 7 December, on the day after the Free State officially came into existence, a government

TD, Seán Hales, was killed. The government shot four republican prisoners in reprisal, and over the next few months a total of seventy-seven republican prisoners were similarly executed. The policy outlined in the 'Orders of Frightfulness' was later abandoned.

Ordnance Survey of Ireland. A select committee of the British Parliament chaired by Thomas Spring Rice (see MONTEAGLE OF BRANDON, FIRST BARON) presented a report on the state of the Ordnance Survey in Ireland, 22 March 1824, recommending that a survey of the country at 6 inches to 1 mile (1:10,560) be undertaken immediately. Preliminary work began in 1825, and by 1826 eighty-seven military engineers and fifty-three labourers were engaged on the project, under Colonel Thomas Colby of the Royal Engineers, assisted by LIEUTENANT THOMAS LARCOM. The antiquarians EDWARD O'REILLY and GEORGE PETRIE were employed on the survey; in 1830, following O'Reilly's death, JOHN O'DONOVAN was also employed, as were THOMAS DRUMMOND, JAMES CLARENCE MANGAN, and EUGENE O'CURRY. William Wakeman (1822–1900), together with Petrie, provided antiquarian notes and sketches for the team. The principal engraver was James Duncan. The head office was established at Mountjoy House in the Phoenix Park, Dublin, where it remains.

The surveyors were given various headings under which to list their material, each one broken down into sub-headings, as follows:

Natural topography: hills, bogs, woods, climate. Further information was added by the surveyor to include types of crop, sowing, and harvest times.

Ancient topography: ecclesiastical, pagan, military, and miscellaneous. Information under this heading included lists of ruined churches, graveyards, holy wells, prehistoric monuments, standing stones, and giants' graves. A sketch of local folk life and tradition appeared under the Miscellaneous heading.

Modern topography: towns, machinery, communications, general appearance and scenery, and social economy. Information compiled under this heading included the number of houses in a town, frequently with an entry on the occupation of the inhabitants, the machinery of the district, road widths and notes on construction, and the destinations and fares of mail-coaches. The 'General appearance and scenery' section depended to a great extent on the scenic taste of the compiler.

Social economy: habits of the people, their food and drink, dress, amusement, dialects, and customs. One researcher noted that the men 'were prone to whiskey while the women squander all their money on tea.' For amusement, dancing and tea parties were listed as being most popular; the violin and the highland pipe were the most common musical instruments. A subsidiary heading, 'Obstructions to improvements', listed SHEBEENS as a social ill.

The survey produced its first map (Co. Derry) in 1837 and its last (Co. Kerry) in 1846. The booksellers Hodges and Smith secured the initial right to publish the maps, and 119,000 had been sold by 1846. The first report was published in 1839, but in 1842 the government abandoned the survey on the grounds of expense.

O'Reilly, Edward (c. 1770–1829), lexicographer and antiquarian; born probably in Co. Cavan. After moving to Dublin c. 1790 he began the study of Irish. He was assistant secretary to the IBERNO-CELTIC SOCIETY and worked in the library of Trinity College, preparing catalogues of manuscripts. At the time of his death he was working on place-names for the ORDNANCE SURVEY under GEORGE PETRIE. He published an Irish–English Dictionary, 'containing upwards of 20,000 words that never appeared in any former Irish lexicon' (1817, reprinted 1821 and 1864). His *Chronological Account of Nearly 400 Irish Writers,* financed by the Iberno-Celtic Society, was published in 1820.

O'Reilly, John Boyle (1844–1890), Fenian and writer; born in Dowth, Co. Meath, educated privately. Apprenticed to a newspaper compositor in 1855, he went to England in 1858 and settled in Preston, returning to Ireland in 1863. He joined the IRB and, at the suggestion of JOHN DEVOY, enlisted in the British army at Drogheda, 1864, for the purpose of recruiting soldiers to the IRB. Arrested, he was sentenced to death, 9 July 1866, but the sentence was commuted to twenty years' penal servitude. After transportation to Western Australia in 1868 he escaped to the United States, 1869, where he worked on the staff of the *Pilot* (Boston), 1870–76, later becoming owner and editor, 1876–90. An influential voice on Irish affairs, the paper attracted contributions from leading Irish writers of the era. He edited the first edition of *The Poetry and Songs of Ireland* (1889). A keen sportsman and athlete, he also edited *Ethics of Boxing and Manly Sports* (1888).

Ó Riada, Seán (1931–1971), musician and composer; born in Cork, raised in Adare, Co. Limerick, where his father (a Garda sergeant) and mother were lovers of traditional music, educated at UCC. While taking his degree he played in a dance band and worked as a jazz pianist. After working as director of music at Radio Éireann he lived in France for a period before returning to work as director of music at the ABBEY THEATRE, composing music for plays. He achieved acclaim for his score for the film documentaries *Mise Éire* (1959) and *Saoirse?* (1961). In 1961 he formed Ceoltóirí Chualann, whose members subsequently formed the Chieftains. Following his appointment as a lecturer in Irish music at University College, Cork, he lived in Cúil Aodha, Co. Cork, where he formed Cór Chúil Aodha. A versatile musician, his compositions include twenty works for Radio Éireann, orchestral works, including *Overture—Olynthiac* (1955), *The Banks of Sullane* (1956), *Hercules Dux Ferrariae* (1957), and *Nomos No. 2,* film scores for *The Playboy of the Western World* (1961), *Young Cassidy* (1965), and *An Tine Bheo* (1966), and two Masses, one of which was first heard at his funeral.

Oriel House, 33–34 Westland Row, Dublin, headquarters of the Criminal Investigation Division, a special police unit set up by MICHAEL COLLINS during the Civil War (1922–23). The name gained a sinister reputation because of allegations of serious mistreatment of prisoners.

Ó Ríordáin, Seán P. (1905–1957), archaeologist; born in Cork, educated locally and trained as a primary teacher. He was professor of archaeology at University College, Cork, and later at University College, Dublin. His publications include *Excavation of a Cairn in the Townland of Curraghbinny* (1933), *Recent Acquisitions from Co. Donegal in the National Museum* (1935), *Lissard, Co. Limerick, and Other Sites in the Locality* (1936), *Fulacht Fiadha Discovery at Kilnagleary, Co. Cork* (1937), *Excavations at Cush, Co. Limerick* (1940), *Antiquities of the Irish Countryside* (1942), and his account of the 1939 excavations at Lough Gur, Co. Limerick, in *Proceedings of the Royal Irish Academy,* 1951. *Tara: The Monument on the Hill* was published in 1954 and *Newgrange and the Bend of the Boyne* (with Dr Glyn Daniel) in 1964.

O'Riordan, Michael (born 1917), trade unionist and communist; born in Cork, educated at Christian Brothers' school. A member of the IRA, he was influenced by the writings of JAMES CONNOLLY. He fought in the International Brigade in the SPANISH CIVIL WAR. Interned at the Curragh during the Second World War, he was converted to communism. On his release in 1943 he worked as a bus conductor in Cork and joined the Labour Party, from which he was expelled, 1945. He founded the Cork Socialist Party before moving to Dublin in 1947, where he worked again as a bus conductor and joined the Irish Workers' League, later the Irish Workers' Party, for which he contested the general election of 1951, when he ran foul of the Catholic hierarchy. He was secretary of the Irish Workers' Party from 1965, and when it merged with the Communist Party of Northern Ireland to re-establish the COMMUNIST PARTY OF IRELAND, 1970, he was its first general secretary. *Connolly Column* (1979) is an account of his experiences in the Spanish Civil War.

O'Shannon, Cathal (1889–1969), socialist and journalist; born in Randalstown, Co. Antrim, educated at St Columb's College, Derry. A member of the Gaelic League, IRB, and Irish Volunteers, he worked with JAMES CONNOLLY as an organiser for the IRISH TRANSPORT AND GENERAL WORKERS' UNION in Belfast as well as assisting on the *Workers' Republic.* Prominent in the Labour Party and the IRISH TRADE UNION CONGRESS, he was active in the anti-CONSCRIPTION campaign during 1918. He was close to the leaders of Sinn Féin and worked with THOMAS JOHNSON on early drafts of the DEMOCRATIC PROGRAMME of Dáil Éireann. A Labour Party delegate to the conference of the Socialist International in Bern, 1919, he and Johnson presented the Irish case for self-determination, published as *Ireland at Berne.* Editor of the *Voice of Labour,* 1918–19, and *Watchword of Labour,* 1919–20, he was arrested in March 1920 during a swoop on union officials. He was a founder-member of the SOCIALIST PARTY OF IRELAND, from which he was expelled, together with WILLIAM O'BRIEN, following its takeover by RODERIC CONNOLLY, 1921. He headed the poll in Louth-Meath in the general election of 16 June 1922 and was deputy chairman of the Labour parliamentary party until he lost his seat a year later. He worked for the ICTU and the CONGRESS OF IRISH UNIONS. On the establishment of the LABOUR COURT, 1946, he was the first workers' representative, holding the position until his retirement in 1969. He edited *Fifty Years of Liberty Hall* (a history of the ITGWU, 1969).

O'Shea, Katharine, née Wood (1845–1921), wife of CHARLES STEWART PARNELL; born in Rivenhall, Essex. She married CAPTAIN W. H. O'SHEA in 1867, but financial circumstances forced her and her children to live with her aunt, Mrs Benjamin Wood, at Eltham, Surrey. She supported her husband's political career after he was returned as a nominal Home Ruler for Co. Clare in 1880 and acted as hostess at his dinners. She engineered a meeting with Parnell, leader of the IRISH PARTY, July 1880, and within a short time was having a love affair with him, in which her husband appears to have acquiesced, using it to further his career. Following a divorce trial initiated by her husband, December 1889 to November 1890, she married Parnell, June 1891, and settled in Brighton, where he died the following October. She published *Charles Stewart Parnell: His Love Story and Political Life* (1914); much of her memoir was rebutted by HENRY HARRISON in *Parnell Vindicated* (1931).

O'Shea, Captain W. H. [William Henry] (1840–1905), politician (Home Rule); born in Dublin, educated at TCD. A junior officer in the British army, 1858, he was a spendthrift, living off his wits and his father, a Dublin solicitor. An absentee landlord, he received little income from his small Irish property. Unsuccessful business transactions in Spain, where he had small mining interests, rendered his financial position precarious. His marriage to Katharine Wood was not successful; shortage of money and general neglect led to his wife's moving with their children to live at Eltham, Surrey, where her aunt, Mrs Benjamin Wood, possessed an estate. With the assistance of CHARLES MAHON he was returned as nominal Home Ruler for Co. Clare in 1880, having promised to meet Mahon's election expenses (which, in the event, were borne by Mrs Wood). He supported CHARLES STEWART PARNELL for the leadership of the IRISH PARTY.

His wife's love affair with Parnell began shortly afterwards, and while O'Shea apparently ignored it, he occasionally used it to his advantage. He challenged Parnell to a duel, which did not take place. During the spring of 1882 he acted as intermediary between Parnell and JOSEPH CHAMBERLAIN in the negotiations leading to the 'KILMAINHAM TREATY', during which Katharine was in communication with W. E. GLADSTONE. O'Shea exulted in his role within the Irish Party, on one occasion telling Chamberlain, 'Eighteen months ago he [Parnell] used every effort to induce me to take over the leadership of the party.' In May 1882 O'Shea delivered Parnell's offer of resignation to Gladstone after the PHOENIX PARK MURDERS.

His relations with Parnell deteriorated between 1882 and 1885. Two girls, recognised within the family as Parnell's, were born in 1883 and 1884. Sensitive to the possibility of a scandal, O'Shea urged discretion on his wife; in fact most members of the Liberal government and of the Irish Party were aware of the relationship. In 1884 he founded the Irish Land Purchase and Settlement Company with Parnell; it failed shortly afterwards. His political career also suffered through his neglect and lack of interest; the Co. Clare Branch of the NATIONAL LEAGUE passed a motion of no confidence in him in June 1884, and the following October, when he rejected the party pledge, it became obvious that he would not hold the seat. During 1885 he placed increasing pressure on his wife and Parnell to secure a seat for him in the general election. Parnell supported him for the Exchange division of Liverpool, after failing to have him nominated for Mid-Armagh. Having lost the election, he insisted in 1886 that he should be put forward for the Co. Galway seat in the February by-election. This compromised Parnell, as influential members of the party believed that O'Shea was blackmailing him. A revolt was suppressed only when Parnell made the Galway election a test of his leadership. O'Shea won, but then resigned the seat in June.

When Parnell went to live with Mrs O'Shea at Eltham, O'Shea's hatred of him intensified. He was suspected of forging the letters to the *Times* (London) that formed the basis for the series 'PARNELLISM AND CRIME' (in fact the work of RICHARD PIGOTT). He appeared as a witness before the Special Commission on 31 October 1888 'to refute the slanders which have been circulated about me by Mr Parnell and his friends . . .' By this time he had published an unflattering portrait of Parnell in the *Times*, 2 August 1888. He informed the commission that he believed that Parnell's signatures on the letters were genuine. Immediately afterwards he went to Spain on a business trip, and he was in Madrid when Pigott committed suicide, 28 February 1889.

Mrs Wood's death, May 1889, led to a crisis. The only reason O'Shea had refrained from suing for divorce was that a scandal would have deprived his wife of her aunt's fortune. When he discovered that he could not benefit from his wife's inheritance, he sued for divorce, 24

December 1889, citing Parnell as co-respondent. (Mrs O'Shea afterwards alleged that O'Shea had had a love affair with her sister, Anna Steele.) The courtroom revelations destroyed Parnell's reputation in England and led to a split in the Irish Party when Gladstone repudiated Parnell's continuing leadership. O'Shea was granted a *decree nisi,* 18 November 1890, obtaining custody of the children under sixteen (including Parnell's two daughters). For the remainder of his life he lived off the money he received in a court settlement of Mrs Wood's will. He took up residence in Brighton, where his former wife and Parnell spent their brief married life.

Otway, Rev. Caesar (1780–1842), evangelical clergyman (Church of Ireland) and writer; born in Templederry, Co. Tipperary, educated at TCD. After taking orders he held rural curacies until his appointment as assistant chaplain to the Magdalen Chapel, Leeson Street, Dublin, and to a minor post in St Patrick's Cathedral. A noted preacher, he was joint founder (with Dr Joseph Henderson Singer) of the *Christian Examiner,* 1825, the first religious magazine published in Ireland associated with the established church. He wrote extensively on the imaginary sexual practices of nuns and priests; he toured Ireland, collecting stories of 'beastly rites', generally involving priests, and visited Lough Derg and other places of Catholic pilgrimage. His tour provided him with material for his *Sketches in Ireland* (1827), published under the initials O.C. In 1832 he jointly founded (with DR GEORGE PETRIE) the *Dublin Penny Journal,* on which *Dublin University Magazine* commented: 'Without containing one line that would mark the religious or political partialities of the writers, it contains more matter illustrative of the history and antiquities of Ireland than any previous publications.' He also published *A Tour of Connaught* (1839) and *Sketches in Erris and Tyrawley* (1841).

P

'Pact Election', the general election of 16 June 1922, held in effect on the issue of the ANGLO-IRISH TREATY (1921). The pact was an attempt by MICHAEL COLLINS (pro-Treaty) and ÉAMON DE VALERA (anti-Treaty) to ensure that the election would be held in an atmosphere of calm rather than of hostility between supporters and opponents of the Treaty. Agreed on 20 May, it was criticised by both sides and by the British government, which demanded a meeting with Irish representatives; on his return from London, Collins repudiated the pact.

The short text of the Pact was:

> We are agreed:
> (1) That a National Coalition panel for this Third Dáil, representing both parties in the Dáil and in the Sinn Féin organisation, be sent forward, on the ground that the national position requires the entrusting of the government of the country into the joint hands of those who have been the strength of the national situation during the last few years, without prejudice to their present respective positions.
> (2) That this coalition panel be sent forward as from the Sinn Féin organisation, the number from each party being their present strength in the Dáil.
> (3) That the candidates be nominated through each of the existing party Executives.
> (4) That every and any interest is free to go up and contest the election equally with the National-Sinn Féin panel.
> (5) That constituencies where an election is not held shall continue to be represented by then-present deputies.
> (6) That after the election the Executive shall consist of the President, elected as formerly; the Minister for Defence, representing the Army; and nine other ministers—five from the majority party and four from the minority, each party to choose its own nominees. The allocation will be in the hands of the President.
> (7) That in the event of the coalition government finding it necessary to dissolve, a general election will be held as soon as possible on adult suffrage.

In the ensuing election, pro-Treaty candidates received 239,193 votes, anti-Treatyites 133,864. Labour Party and non-aligned candidates received 247,276 votes. (See also DÁIL ÉIREANN; ANGLO-IRISH TREATY.)

Paget, Major-General Sir Arthur (1851–1928), British soldier. Shortly after his posting as commander in chief of British forces in Ireland, 1911–17, he was ordered to prepare plans for the protection of arms depots in Ulster, 14 March 1914. He went to London on 18 March to query the position should any officer be unwilling to serve in Ulster and was informed that officers who lived in Ulster would be exempt but that the remainder would have to carry out their orders or be dismissed. Returning to Ireland two days later, Paget informed his senior officers of the position. MAJOR-GENERAL SIR HUBERT GOUGH and fifty-seven other officers stated that they would accept dismissal rather than serve against Ulster, thus initiating the CURRAGH INCIDENT. After the EASTER RISING (1916), Paget was replaced by GENERAL SIR JOHN MAXWELL.

Paisley, Rev. Ian Richard Kyle (born 1926), clergyman (Free Presbyterian) and politician (Democratic Unionist Party); born in Armagh, raised in Ballymena, Co. Antrim, where he attended the Model School and Technical High School. Following studies at South Wales Bible College and the Theological Hall of the Reformed Presbyterian Church, Belfast, he was ordained by his father, 1946. Joint founder and moderator of the Free Presbyterian Church of Ulster, 11 March 1951, he built his own Martyrs' Memorial Church in Belfast and was awarded an honorary doctorate in divinity by the Bob Jones University of South Carolina. Joint founder of the ULSTER CONSTITUTION DEFENCE COMMITTEE and the ULSTER PROTESTANT VOLUNTEERS, 1966, he opposed Catholicism, ecumenism, the civil rights movement, republicanism, and reformist trends in the Unionist Party. Returned for every elected body for which he stood from 1971, he was vehemently critical of direct rule from London, March 1972, and opposed power-sharing (multi-party government) as 'undemocratic'. He was influential in the strike organised by the ULSTER WORKERS' COUNCIL, which brought about the collapse of the Northern Ireland Executive, May 1974. He consistently topped the poll in Northern Ireland elections for the European Parliament from 1979.

A leading voice of loyalism, Paisley opposed any role for the Irish government in Northern Ireland affairs, JAMES PRIOR's 'rolling devolution', the ANGLO-IRISH AGREEMENT (1985), the Anglo-Irish Intergovernmental Conference (from 1986), the HUME-ADAMS TALKS and joint statement (1993), the DOWNING STREET DECLARATION (1993), all-Ireland executive bodies, the Parades Commission, the PEACE PROCESS ('a hoax'), 'proximity talks', and the BELFAST AGREEMENT (1998). In these endeavours he forged temporary alliances with the Ulster Unionist Party under JAMES MOLYNEAUX and DAVID TRIMBLE and with ROBERT MCCARTNEY of the United Kingdom Unionist Party. He has controlled the PROTESTANT TELEGRAPH from its founding in 1966 and also edited the *Revivalist.* Other publications include *History of the 1859 Revival* (1959), *Christian Foundation* (1960), *Ravenhill Pulpit* (vols. 1 and 2, 1966–67), and *Billy Graham and the Church of Rome* (1970).

Pan-Celtic Society, founded as a nationalist and literary forum, 1 March 1888, later absorbed by the IRISH NATIONAL LITERARY SOCIETY. Its members, who included W. B. YEATS, T. W. Rolleston, and DOUGLAS HYDE, published *Poems and Ballads of Young Ireland* (1888), dedicated to JOHN O'LEARY, and *Lays and Lyrics of the Pan-Celtic Society* (1889). Membership was restricted to those who had published a story, essay, poem or sketch in a recognised Irish magazine or newspaper.

Parades Commission, established in March 1997 following a report by Dr Peter North into disturbances associated with contentious marches organised by the ORANGE ORDER, in particular when the local Orange lodge in Portadown, Co. Armagh, attempted to march from Drumcree Church down the (Catholic) Garvaghy Road. The commission, chaired by Alistair Graham, failed to reach an acceptable agreement for the 1997 Drumcree parade. Over the years there were many resignations from among members of the commission.

Parker Report (November 1972). The Parker Commission, established in the wake of the widely criticised COMPTON REPORT on the methods used in interrogating detainees in NORTHERN IRELAND during the early days of INTERNMENT, was concerned with the 'five techniques' used at Castlereagh RUC Station, Belfast (hooding, deprivation of food, deprivation of sleep, noise and forced standing against a wall). Both Lord Parker and John Boyd-Carpenter held that such methods could be justified in exceptional circumstances (subject to certain safeguards), while Lord Gardiner did not accept that such methods were ever morally justified, even against a ruthless enemy. The Prime Minister, EDWARD HEATH, promised that the five techniques would not be used again. These methods were later held by the European Court of Human Rights to amount to inhuman and degrading treatment, but not torture.

Parker-Willis Commission (1926–27), established under the chairmanship of the American economist Henry Parker-Willis to examine the Irish banking system. It found that there was no need for an Irish central bank, because of the soundness of Irish financial institutions. It also ruled out an independent Irish monetary policy, because of the lack of a domestic money or capital market. The sole dissenting voice was

Andrew Jameson (representing the Bank of Ireland). The commission's findings led to the creation of the CURRENCY COMMISSION (1927–42), replaced by the CENTRAL BANK OF IRELAND in 1942.

Parkinson-Fortescue, Chichester, Baron Carlingford (1823–1898), politician (Liberal); born Chichester Fortescue in Co. Louth, educated at the University of Oxford. As member of Parliament for Co. Louth, 1847–74, he opposed the Ecclesiastical Titles Bill (1851). In 1852 he assumed the additional surname Parkinson to comply with the will of Parkinson Ruxton of Ardee. He left the Colonial Office in November 1865 on appointment as Chief Secretary for Ireland, 1865–66. During his second term, 1868–70, he assisted W. E. GLADSTONE in his draft proposals for the DISESTABLISHMENT of the Church of Ireland and with the Landlord and Tenant (Ireland) Act (1870) (see LAND ACTS). Granted a Peace Preservation Act, which he had sought to deal with rising land agitation from 1870, he failed to convince the cabinet of his ability to handle the unrest and was replaced as Chief Secretary by the DUKE OF DEVONSHIRE. Having lost his seat, 1874, he was made Baron Carlingford. He wrote a minority report as a member of the RICHMOND COMMISSION, 1879.

Parliament Act (1911), introduced by the Liberal government of H. H. ASQUITH to remove the power of veto from the House of Lords and replace it with the power to delay a bill for two years. The act was prompted by the House of Lords' rejection of the 'people's budget' introduced in 1909 by DAVID LLOYD GEORGE. Asquith's dependence on JOHN REDMOND and the IRISH PARTY resulted in the (third) HOME RULE BILL (1912), now assured of passing, as the House of Lords' veto had been the principal Unionist guarantee of stopping it.

Parnell, Anna Catherine (1852–1911), painter, poet, and land agitator; born in Rathdrum, Co. Wicklow, a sister of CHARLES STEWART PARNELL. Rejecting a socialite existence, she studied at the Metropolitan School of Art, Dublin. She organised a Famine Relief Fund during the depression of the late 1870s and visited the United States, 1879–80, for fund-raising and to organise her brother's American visit. While she supported the LAND LEAGUE, she was disappointed at its lack of aggressiveness and was critical of the Land Law (Ireland) Act (1881) (see LAND ACTS). Prompted by her sister, FRANCES (FANNY) PARNELL, she established the LADIES' LAND LEAGUE and spoke at its first public meeting, at Claremorris, Co. Mayo, 31 January 1881. Her extremism was denounced by the Archbishop of Tuam, JOHN MACHALE, and the Archbishop of Dublin, EDWARD MCCABE, both of whom objected to women in public life. Much admired by MICHAEL DAVITT, she is regarded as the first outstanding woman agitator in modern Irish history.

She became permanently estranged from her brother following his decision to cut off funds to the Ladies' Land League, May 1882. Following her sister's death she moved to Cornwall, where she lived as a virtual recluse under an assumed name and in poor circumstances until her death in a drowning accident at Ilfracombe, Devon. She was the author of *The Tale of a Great Sham,* an attack on the Land League written in 1904, which lay in the National Library until published in Dublin in 1986, edited by Dana Hearne.

Parnell, Charles Stewart (1846–1891), politician (Irish Party); born in Rathdrum, Co. Wicklow. He had a fitful education before entering the University of Cambridge, from which he was expelled in 1869. He travelled on the Continent, 1871, and visited the United States, where his brother, John Howard Parnell, had a ranch in Alabama. Appointed high sheriff of Co. Wicklow, 1873, he unsuccessfully contested a Dublin parliamentary seat for the HOME RULE LEAGUE, 1874. After winning the Co. Meath seat (previously held by JOHN MARTIN), April 1875, he joined the obstructionist wing of the Irish Party. After his first speech in Parliament, 26 April 1875, he came to the attention of the IRB when, during an exchange with MICHAEL HICKS BEACH, 30 June 1876, he stated: 'I wish to say as publicly and directly as I can that I do not believe, and never shall believe, that any murder was committed at Manchester' (see MANCHESTER MARTYRS). He succeeded ISAAC BUTT as leader of the HOME RULE CONFEDERATION OF GREAT BRITAIN, 28 August 1877.

In December, at a reception for MICHAEL DAVITT, he met DR WILLIAM CARROLL of CLAN NA GAEL, who assured him that the movement could be relied on as an ally in the struggle for Irish self-government. This led to a meeting between influential constitutionalist Fenians in March 1878, followed on 25 October by a telegram from JOHN DEVOY, who proposed a policy of co-operation between constitutionalists and separatists to pursue home rule and the land agitation. Within a year Parnell had become the leader of the NEW DEPARTURE, holding the position of president of the LAND LEAGUE. Throughout the autumn of 1879 he repeated his message that tenants should keep a 'firm grip on their homesteads.' He left for America, 21 December, to secure support for home rule and to raise money for famine relief; he addressed the House of Representatives, 2 February 1880, and in March moved to Canada, where he was so well received in Toronto that T. M. HEALY dubbed him 'the uncrowned king of Ireland'.

Parnell's party collected £70,000 for famine relief and the Land League before returning to Ireland to fight the general election in April, when sixty-one Home Rulers were returned, including CAPTAIN W. H. O'SHEA, with whose wife, KATHARINE O'SHEA, Parnell began a love affair later in the year. At a meeting of the new parliamentary party attended by forty-one members, Parnell was elected chairman, defeating WILLIAM SHAW (23 to 18), 17 May 1881.

The Chief Secretary for Ireland, W. E. FORSTER, introduced the COMPENSATION FOR DISTURBANCE BILL, which was rejected by the House of Lords, 3 August. Violence in Ireland increased. When Parliament was prorogued, 7 September, Parnell returned to Ireland and continued the land agitation. He made his 'moral Coventry' speech in Ennis, Co. Clare, 19 September; its first target was CAPTAIN CHARLES CUNNINGHAM BOYCOTT. In an attempt to break the Land League, Forster prosecuted the leaders, but the trial collapsed, 23 January 1881. The government promised COERCION together with land reform; Parnell's policy was to fight coercion and secure suitable amendments in the land legislation (see LAND ACTS). He was suspended from the House of Commons, 1 August, and returned to Ireland.

Parnell's attack on the Land Law (Ireland) Bill was aided by *United Ireland,* edited by WILLIAM O'BRIEN. Rejecting a demand for a 'no-rent campaign' at this time, he waited to test the act in the Land Court. However, on 13 October he was arrested following his description of W. E. GLADSTONE as

> this masquerading knight errant, the pretending champion of the rights of every other nation except those of the Irish nation . . . the man who, by his own utterances, is prepared to carry fire and sword into your homesteads, unless you humbly abase yourselves before him and before the landlords of the country . . .

He was joined in Kilmainham Jail, Dublin, by many of his colleagues. He agreed to the NO-RENT MANIFESTO on 18 October. The Land League was suppressed immediately, but the agitation was taken over by the LADIES' LAND LEAGUE, led by his sister ANNA PARNELL.

Negotiations with Gladstone led to Parnell's release under the 'KILMAINHAM TREATY', 2 May 1882. Deeply shocked by the PHOENIX PARK MURDERS, he considered resigning the leadership of the Irish Party. Gladstone now came under attack for his deal with Parnell. Parnell, also under attack, led the obstruction of the new coercion measure, which became law in July. He also suppressed the Ladies' Land League. The land agitation was halted, at least temporarily, when the Settled Land Act (1882) became law on 18 August.

Parnell founded the NATIONAL LEAGUE in Dublin, 17 October 1882. His increasing popularity was reflected in the Parnell Tribute, which, despite condemnation by the Catholic hierarchy, raised £37,000 in 1883, when it became known that his own estate of Avondale at Rathdrum, Co. Wicklow, was in financial difficulties. He also won over the Catholic bishops, who, led by T. W. CROKE of Cashel and THOMAS NULTY of Meath, made the Irish Party the guardian of Catholic educational interests, 1884.

By 1885 Parnell was leading a party poised for a general election. His statements on home rule were designed to secure the widest possible support, as when he said in Cork, 21 January 1885,

> We cannot ask for less than the restitution of Grattan's Parliament . . . We cannot under the British constitution ask for *more* than the restitution of Grattan's Parliament. But no man has a right to fix the boundary to the march of a nation. No man has a right to say to his country, "Thus far shalt thou go and no farther," and we never attempted to fix the *ne plus ultra* to the progress of Ireland's nationhood, and we never shall.

When Gladstone's ministry fell, June 1885, Lord Salisbury formed a Conservative caretaker government. Now in a bargaining position, Parnell made contact with two prominent Conservatives, LORD RANDOLPH CHURCHILL and the EARL OF CARNARVON, the new Lord Lieutenant of Ireland. While Churchill appeared to believe that Parnell had committed the Irish Party to the Conservatives for the forthcoming general election, Carnarvon believed that Parnell had stated that he would not seek to break the Union in pursuit of home rule and that he would be prepared to accept something akin to the CENTRAL BOARD outlined by JOSEPH CHAMBERLAIN. Parnell was also in contact with Gladstone, who was not prepared to bargain.

Parnell issued a Manifesto to the Irish in Great Britain, 21 November, calling on them to support Conservative rather than Liberal or Radical candidates. The election gave the Liberals 335 seats, Conservatives 249, and Irish Party 86. Parnell, now holding the balance of power, supported Salisbury's Conservative ministry. Following Herbert Gladstone's revelation in the 'HAWARDEN KITE', 7 December 1885, that his father now favoured home rule for Ireland, the Conservatives moved away from any consideration.

Parnell refrained from becoming involved in the PLAN OF CAMPAIGN during 1886, despite the involvement of his chief lieutenants. The government responded to the plan with a new measure of coercion, January 1886. Parnell switched support to the Liberals, the Conservatives fell, and Gladstone took office, committed to home rule. Parnell's leadership was immediately tested, however, when, under pressure from Katharine O'Shea, he forced Captain O'Shea's candidature for the Co. Galway seat in the by-election of February 1886. He succeeded in having O'Shea elected, but only by placing his leadership of the party at stake.

Gladstone introduced the (first) HOME RULE BILL on 8 April 1886. During the debate on the second reading, Parnell was reminded that he had said that Ireland would not rest until the final link was broken. Now, to a direct question whether he accepted the bill 'as a final settlement of the [Irish] question,' he answered, 'Yes.' Unionist opposition in Ireland was increasing, particularly among Ulster Unionists, who were in alliance with Churchill, while Chamberlain was leading Liberal-Unionists in opposition. On the second reading, 7 June, the bill was defeated (341 to 311). Parliament was dissolved, 25 June, and home rule became the central issue of the ensuing election. The Irish Party campaigned throughout Britain, seeking support for the Liberals. The result was a defeat: a total of 394 anti-Home Rulers to 191 Liberals, giving the Conservatives a majority of 118 over the combined Liberal and Irish members. The Conservatives returned to office.

When Parnell moved to Eltham, Surrey, to take up residence with Katharine O'Shea in the summer of 1886, Captain O'Shea broke with the Irish Party and placed himself at the disposal of Parnell's opponents. Parnell appeared infrequently in the House of Commons and was virtually inaccessible to his colleagues. He became the centre of public attention over the series 'PARNELLISM AND CRIME' that began in the *Times* (London) on 7 March 1887. The articles were based on forged letters provided by RICHARD PIGOTT. On 18 April 1887 the paper published a facsimile of a letter linking Parnell with the PHOENIX PARK MURDERS. While Parnell took no action against the paper, his former supporter FRANK HUGH O'DONNELL did, and lost. During the O'Donnell action Parnell noticed evidence that would show that the letters were forgeries, and he demanded the appointment of a select committee of the House of Commons to investigate the charges. While this was rejected, it did establish a special parliamentary commission to examine not only the *Times* letters but also Parnell's career during and subsequent to the LAND WAR.

Parnell's counsel during the sitting of the special commission, 17 September 1888 to 22 November 1889, was SIR CHARLES RUSSELL, assisted by H. H. ASQUITH. Among those who gave evidence were O'Shea and HENRI LE CARON, a British spy within the Fenians. Pigott gave evidence over two days, 20–22 February, and, despite his shifty appearance in the witness box, emerged relatively unscathed until, in a moment of high drama, Russell demonstrated that Pigott spelt 'hesitancy' as 'hesitency', as it appeared in the letters. When Parnell, who had not impressed while giving evidence on his own behalf, appeared in the House of Commons on 1 March, Gladstone led the Liberals in a standing ovation. The report of the special commission was published in February 1890, clearing Parnell of all charges (though finding that he had supported boycotting).

On 24 December 1889 Captain O'Shea sued for divorce, citing Parnell as co-respondent. The case was not listed until 15 November 1890; meanwhile Parnell assured the Irish Party that there was no need to fear the verdict, as he would be completely exonerated. During January 1890 resolutions of confidence in his leadership were passed throughout the country. He did not contest the case in November, and O'Shea's action was unopposed, apart from a watching brief for Mrs O'Shea held by Frank Lockwood. Parnell's two children, Claire (1883–1909) and Katharine (1884–1947), were placed in O'Shea's custody.

Despite the unfavourable verdict, resolutions of confidence in Parnell continued; but a reaction had already set in. Michael Davitt's call for Parnell's resignation in *Labour World,* 20 November, was supported by members of the Liberal Party, the Irish Party, and the Catholic hierarchy. However, Parnell was re-elected chairman, 25 November, when the members were unaware that Gladstone had informed JUSTIN MCCARTHY that so long as Parnell remained leader there could be no alliance with the Liberals. The next day Gladstone published his position in a letter to JOHN MORLEY. The storm broke when Parnell refused a request that he reconsider the chairmanship.

On 28 November the Catholic hierarchy announced a meeting for 3 December. Parnell published a Manifesto to the Irish People, 29 November, in which he attacked Gladstone, the Liberals, and a section of his own party. This alienated members of the party who were fund-raising in the United States, including JOHN DILLON and William O'Brien. Before the party met for its fateful meeting on 1 December, the Catholic Archbishop of Dublin, WILLIAM WALSH, called on the members to 'act manfully.'

Seventy-three members were present at the meeting in Committee Room 15 of the House of Commons. Attempts at compromise proved ineffectual, and Parnell refused to make concessions. The parliamentary party split on 6 December when Justin McCarthy led 44 members out, leaving Parnell with 27. Parnell survived the split by less than a year. He broke with the cautious constitutionalism of the past, winning support from the Fenians. His blatant appeal to the underground tradition shocked former adherents, who clashed physically with his supporters as he campaigned around the country. In the North Kilkenny by-election, December 1890, his candidate was beaten by almost two to one. Another by-election, in North Sligo, produced a less resounding defeat, but here the clergy were not united, and Parnell's candidate lost by 2,493 votes to 3,261.

Parnell married Katharine O'Shea in Brighton, 25 June 1891, where they took up residence. He returned to fight the third and last by-election in Co. Carlow. By now the hierarchy, worried by the number of priests who had supported him in North Sligo, had issued a condemnation (on the day of his wedding). In part, it stated that Parnell 'by his public misconduct, has utterly disqualified himself to be . . . leader.' Only one bishop, EDWARD O'DWYER of Limerick, refrained from signing. Parnell lost in Co. Carlow and also now lost the support of the *Freeman's Journal.*

His health had been deteriorating during the year. He travelled in September to Creggs, Co. Galway, and spoke in pouring rain. After resting in a local hotel he travelled to Dublin and from there to Brighton, where he died on 6 October. His funeral to Glasnevin Cemetery, Dublin, 11 October 1891, was attended by more than 200,000 people.

The Parnell Monument in Sackville Street (O'Connell Street), Dublin, was erected close to Costigan's Hotel, from where he had made his last public speech. The monument, by the Irish-American sculptor Augustus Saint-Gaudens (1848–1907), was paid for through public subscription. Dublin Corporation, which had earlier arranged the rerouting of tram tracks to facilitate the siting of the monument, adopted a resolution that changed the name of nearby Great Britain Street to Parnell Street.

Parnell, Frances (Fanny) (1849–1882), poet and land agitator; born in Rathdrum, Co. Wicklow, a sister of CHARLES STEWART PARNELL, educated privately. A Fenian sympathiser, while still a teenager she contributed patriotic verse to the *Irish People.* While visiting the United States with her mother in 1874 her health failed, and she remained there. She wrote for the *Pilot* (Boston) and the *Nation,* 1879. She organised famine relief for Ireland and became a friend of MICHAEL DAVITT, at whose suggestion she founded the LADIES' LAND LEAGUE in America; it was then established in Ireland by her sister, ANNA PARNELL. Many of her poems urging support for the Land League appeared in *United Ireland*; her most famous poem was 'Hold the Harvest'. She also published a pamphlet, *Novels of Ireland* (1880). As her health deteriorated her themes became increasingly morbid.

'Parnellism and crime', a series of articles in the *Times* (London), 1887. Designed to damage the reputation of CHARLES STEWART PARNELL and other leading members of the IRISH PARTY, it accused them of criminal conspiracy and murder during the LAND WAR.

The first article appeared on 7 March 1887, with further articles on 10 and 14 March. On 18 April the paper printed a facsimile of what purported to be a letter written by Parnell in which he gave implicit approval to the PHOENIX PARK MURDERS:

> Dear Sir,
>
> I am not surprised at your friend's anger but he and you should have known that to denounce the murders was the only course

> open to us. To do that promptly was plainly our best policy. But you can tell him and all others concerned that though I regret the accident of Lord Cavendish's death, I cannot refuse to admit that Burke got no more than his deserts. You are at liberty to show him this, and others whom you can trust also, but let not my address be known. He can write to the House of Commons.
>
> Yours very truly,
> Chas. S. Parnell.

The *Times* commented that

> Parnell must understand the gravity of the questions raised by the accusations we have formulated and supported with evidence, but he cannot expect that his simple repudiation of the letter we publish this morning will have any weight with public opinion. He must be prepared with some more solid proofs, if he is to annul the effect of a disclosure which reduces the passionate denials with which his party encounter unpleasant truths.

Parnell was prevented from replying to the House of Commons until one o'clock the following morning. Having dealt with all aspects of the letter, he referred to the signature:

> Of course, this is not the time, as I have said, to enter into full details and minutiae as to comparisons of handwriting, but if the house could see my signature and the forged, fabricated signature they would see that, except as regards two letters, the whole signature bears no resemblance to mine.

But the *Times* continued the series, which resulted in an unsuccessful action for libel by FRANK HUGH O'DONNELL. During the case the Attorney-General, Sir Robert Webster, reiterated the charges levelled at Parnell and his colleagues. Forced to take action, Parnell demanded that a House of Commons select committee be appointed to investigate the charges. Its terms of reference were expanded to allow the committee not only to investigate the alleged forged letter but to address all indictable material relating to Parnell and his colleagues that featured in the series.

During the hearing, RICHARD PIGOTT was called as a witness. He was asked by Parnell's counsel, SIR CHARLES RUSSELL, to write a number of words, including 'hesitancy'. Pigott spelt it 'hesitency', as it had been written in letters in the possession of PATRICK EGAN. Numerous inconsistencies appeared in his testimony, and he was booed and catcalled as he left the stand. Reporting on 13 February 1890, the commission acquitted Parnell and others of the charge of insincerity in their denunciation of the Phoenix Park murders and concluded that the facsimile letter was a forgery. While it found that 'the respondents did not directly incite persons to the commission of crime,' it did find that 'they did incite to intimidation,' leading to 'crime and outrage.' Parnell subsequently received £5,000 in libel damages. The case cost the *Times* an estimated £200,000; it lost circulation, and its reputation was irretrievably damaged. It was later discovered that the Chief Secretary for Ireland, A. J. BALFOUR, had encouraged the *Times* in publishing the series and that Edward Houston, a former *Times* reporter and secretary of the IRISH LOYAL AND PATRIOTIC UNION, had paid Pigott for the forged letters. Pigott later allegedly committed suicide in a Madrid hotel.

Parsonstown Telescope, the 'Leviathan of Parsonstown', erected in the grounds of Birr Castle at Parsonstown (Birr), Co. Offaly, 1845 by William Parsons, THIRD EARL OF ROSSE (1800–1867), following a series of experiments that began in 1827. In 1839 he successfully cast a 3-foot mirror using custom-made tools and equipment. Dissatisfied with the telescope's penetration, he began the construction of a larger model, enlisting the aid of the optical firm of THOMAS GRUBB of Dublin for the more specialised work. After several failures, two mirrors, each 6 feet in diameter, 4 tons in weight and of 54-foot focus were cast in 1843. The tube of the telescope was 58 feet long and 7 feet in diameter. Slung on chains between two piers of masonry 50 feet high, 70 feet long and 23 feet apart, the mirror was supported in its tube by an intricate system of cast-iron platforms, triangles, and levers. The telescope's limited horizontal movement was compensated for by its 110° vertical range.

The first official observations with what was recognised as the biggest and finest telescope in the world, by Dr Romney Robinson of Armagh Observatory and the English astronomer Sir James South, took place on 15 February 1845. The results, including the discovery of binary and triple stars, were laid before the Royal Society, London, of which Parsons was president, 19 June 1850. The telescope was neglected following the death of Parsons' son, Laurence Parson, fourth Earl of Rosse, 1908, by which time new technology had rendered it obsolete (though it remained the largest telescope in the world until the opening of the Mount Wilson Observatory at Pasadena, California, 1917). Most of the iron castings and metal parts were melted down to aid the war effort, 1914–18; one of the original mirrors was put on display in the Science Museum, London. A reconstruction of the telescope at Birr Castle was completed in 1987.

Patrician Brothers, also called the Brothers of St Patrick, a Catholic educational organisation under simple vows, founded at Tullow, Co. Carlow, 1808, by the Bishop of Kildare and Leighlin, Daniel Delany.

Patriot, a paper founded by William Corbet in 1810 with the encouragement of the Chief Secretary for Ireland, WILLIAM WELLESLEY-POLE. It supported the British government and the Anglo-Irish ASCENDANCY. It was a financial failure; its circulation rarely rose above 700 until the editorship of J. T. HAYDN. It later supported CATHOLIC EMANCIPATION and lost government support. The title was changed to the *Statesman and Patriot,* 1828, but it failed to recover its readership and ceased publication a year later.

Patten Report (1999), report of the Independent Commission on Policing in Northern Ireland, chaired by Chris Patten, established under the BELFAST AGREEMENT (1998) to make recommendations for policing in Northern Ireland, including 'means of encouraging widespread community support for these arrangements.' The commission received more than a thousand submissions. Its recommendations, published on 9 September 1999, were largely adopted by the British government, 19 January 2000. The ROYAL ULSTER CONSTABULARY, to be renamed POLICE SERVICE OF NORTHERN IRELAND, would be reduced in numbers from 13,000 to 7,500. There would be a new badge and symbols, 'entirely free from any association with either the British or Irish states.' Membership would be made up equally of Catholics and Protestants (the RUC was then 90 per cent Protestant). Authority would be devolved to local commanders; District Policing Partnership Boards would be established, as would a new Policing Board. An Oversight Commissioner would monitor the implementation of changes agreed by the government. Those who at first welcomed the report criticised later attempts to dilute the proposals to embrace some of the Unionist objections.

pattern (a corruption of 'patron'), a communal visit to a holy well associated with the patron saint of a district. The community prayed beside the well or in the surrounding area, while offerings of medals, coins, pieces of cloth and flowers were left at the well as thanksgiving for favours received or expected. Because many of the wells were believed to have curative powers, the waters were drunk or applied to affected areas of the body. Bottles of water were taken by pilgrims for use during the ensuing year. At the end of prayers the community joined in dancing, singing, and storytelling. As the event usually took place on a holy day and no work was done, drink was provided for the occasion, and it was not uncommon for the evening to end in fighting (see FACTION-FIGHTING). Increasing disorder at patterns led to condemnation by the Church and the authorities. DANIEL O'CONNELL used his influence against them. Not many survived the GREAT FAMINE (1845–49), but some still take place.

Peace People, founded in Belfast in August 1976 by Mairéad Corrigan and Betty Williams to mobilise public opinion against violence after three children were killed when a getaway car mounted the pavement, its driver having been shot dead by British soldiers; Mairéad Corrigan was the children's aunt. The two women were later joined by the journalist Ciarán McKeown. The movement spread throughout Ireland and to Britain and the Continent. In 1976 the founders were given a Peace Foundation Award and in 1977 the Nobel Prize for Peace 'for acting out of a sense of conviction that individuals can make a contribution to peace.'

By February 1980 internal tensions in the leadership began to affect the movement. Williams resigned and moved to the United States, 1982, while McKeown returned to journalism, writing extensively on peace issues. Corrigan continued with the movement. In 1989 it opposed the broadcasting ban on spokespersons for republican paramilitary organisations and proposals to end the 'right to silence' for accused persons. It opposed the Gulf War, 1991, and financed holiday camps in Norway for young people as well as holidays in Britain and on the Continent for religiously mixed groups. It provided aid to the families of paramilitary prisoners and also supported the Peace '93 movement in Dublin.

peace process. Following the suspension of the Parliament of Northern Ireland and the introduction of direct rule from London, March

1972, an early initiative occurred when the Provisional IRA called a ceasefire, June 1972, to accommodate a meeting between republican leaders and the Secretary of State for Northern Ireland, WILLIAM WHITELAW, in London, 7 July. There was another initiative when Provisional IRA leaders met for secret talks with Northern Protestant clergymen in Feakle, Co. Clare, 10 December 1974. Meanwhile, working independently, Michael Oatley of the Secret Intelligence Service (commonly called MI6) secured a Provisional IRA ceasefire, December 1974, which lasted until the following September. Though officially denied, contacts between republicans and officials of the Northern Ireland Office took place over the next two decades. Further, unsuccessful efforts at ending the violence took place during the republican HUNGER STRIKES of 1980–81.

The British government's white paper *Northern Ireland: A Framework for Devolution* (1982) led to the establishment of the Northern Ireland Assembly, 1982–86. Before the Assembly ended, 23 June 1986, the ANGLO-IRISH AGREEMENT (1985) had outraged unionists at the consultative role granted to the Irish government; the British government, however, had received Irish recognition of the 'consent principle'—that the consent of a majority in Northern Ireland was necessary for any change in its constitutional status. There was also improved co-operation on security in the wake of the agreement.

Father Alec Reid of Belfast arranged secret contacts between GERRY ADAMS and CARDINAL TOMÁS Ó FIAICH; he was unsuccessful in attempts to persuade the Taoiseach, CHARLES HAUGHEY, to meet Adams but did set up private meetings between Adams and Haughey's adviser, Dr Martin Mansergh, and a Fianna Fáil TD for Co. Louth, Dermot Ahern. Reid's approach to JOHN HUME led to a meeting with Adams in 1987. The HUME-ADAMS TALKS, beginning in January 1988, ended on 5 September, after which both leaders remained in contact. Meanwhile TOM KING organised 'talks about talks' with local parties in Northern Ireland, forming the basis of the BROOKE-MAYHEW TALKS. At the same time, officials of the Northern Ireland Office retained a private channel of communication with the republican movement.

The Brooke-Mayhew Talks identified three 'strands' or sets of relationships: strand 1, relations within Northern Ireland, strand 2, relations between North and South, and strand 3, relations between the British and Irish governments. The principle that 'nothing was to be agreed until everything was agreed' remained the tenet of later initiatives.

Succeeding Haughey as Taoiseach, February 1992, ALBERT REYNOLDS maintained the Irish government's line, and an agenda gradually emerged. Reynolds insisted that the GOVERNMENT OF IRELAND ACT (1920) must also be on the table if articles 2 and 3 of the Constitution of Ireland, defining the national territory, were negotiable; the Unionists' insistence on a referendum on these articles would be considered only in the event of a general agreement. The SDLP and the ULSTER UNIONIST PARTY, DUP and ALLIANCE PARTY, while in general agreement on a system of local rule based on an Assembly, were at odds on the issue of an executive role for the Irish government.

The talks ended late in 1992 with no general settlement, but the parties had identified the principal elements that would constitute an eventual settlement. President Bill Clinton played an important role from 1992; his special adviser, GEORGE MITCHELL, appointed on 2 October 1994, played a central role in the peace process over the next six years. Despite the continuation of Provisional IRA violence, the British government met the IRA and SINN FÉIN in secret talks, during which the British passed a position paper to the IRA, 19 March 1993. The resumed Hume-Adams Talks produced a statement in April that excluded an internal settlement and asserted the right to 'national self-determination', in effect rejecting devolution as a solution to the conflict. Considering the Hume-Adams position unbalanced (too 'green' to be sold to unionists), the two governments sought to reassure both communities through the DOWNING STREET DECLARATION (1993).

The Provisional IRA ceasefire of 31 August 1994 was contingent on progress in all-party talks. When in November the British government and Unionists sought the 'decommissioning' of arms, the IRA rejected any handing over of weapons until a final settlement was reached. A loyalist ceasefire followed, 13 October; a week later Martin McGuinness led a Sinn Féin delegation into its first official meeting with government officials.

The peace process continued during 1995, a year that saw the first single-digit number of deaths (nine) since 1969 (five). The British and Irish governments published the FRAMEWORK DOCUMENTS on 22 February. On 7 March

1995, speaking in Washington, SIR PATRICK MAYHEW outlined three conditions before Sinn Féin could be permitted to take part in all-party talks: the Provisional IRA must be willing in principle 'to disarm progressively,' must agree how decommissioning would in practice be carried out, and must decommission some of its weapons at the start of talks as a 'tangible, confidence-building measure' (the last point became known as 'Washington 3'). In an effort to get around the continuing decommissioning impasse, the Taoiseach, JOHN BRUTON, and Prime Minister, JOHN MAJOR, agreed a 'twin-track' approach to resolving the decommissioning crisis, 28 November: George Mitchell would head an international body to study the problem, while attempts to find an agreeable agenda for peace talks continued. The Mitchell Report (24 January 1996) laid down what became known as the Mitchell Principles—a commitment to democratic and exclusively peaceful means of resolving political issues, the total disarmament of all paramilitary organisations, a renunciation of the use of force to influence the outcome of all-party talks, and an end to punishment killings and shootings. While Adams welcomed the report, the British government still viewed the decommissioning of arms as a precondition for Sinn Féin's admission to multi-party talks.

The Provisional IRA ceasefire ended with the bomb explosion at Canary Wharf, London, 9 February 1996. On 28 February a joint British-Irish communiqué set June 1996 as the date for all-party talks. Sinn Féin could participate only if the IRA ceasefire was restored, and all parties must adhere to the Mitchell Principles. When the talks opened in Stormont Castle, Belfast, 10 June 1996, Sinn Féin was excluded. Chaired by Mitchell, the talks continued until the signing of the BELFAST AGREEMENT on 10 April 1998.

Sinn Féin emerged as the third-largest party in Northern Ireland following the general election of May 1997, which also brought TONY BLAIR to power in London. Sinn Féin also made gains in the local elections, 21 May. The IRA announced 'a complete cessation of military operations from 12 midday, Sunday, 20 July 1997.' Though the ceasefire was generally welcomed, there were demands that decommissioning should precede Sinn Féin's admission to the talks scheduled for 15 September. Sinn Féin moved into office accommodation at Stormont. In an attempt to circumvent the decommissioning impasse and to reassure unionists, BERTIE AHERN (Taoiseach from 26 June 1997) and Blair announced the establishment of the INDEPENDENT INTERNATIONAL COMMISSION ON DECOMMISSIONING, to be headed by General John de Chastelain of Canada, to oversee the decommissioning of paramilitary weapons.

The Belfast Agreement (1998) replaced the Anglo-Irish Agreement of 1985. The referendums on the agreement, 22 May 1998, were the first occasion since 1918 on which the electorate of the entire country exercised its franchise at the same time. In Northern Ireland 676,966 (71 per cent) voted in favour and 274,879 (29 per cent) against; the vote in the Republic was 1,442,583 (94 per cent) in favour and 85,748 (6 per cent) against; the aggregate vote for the country as a whole was 2,119,549 (85 per cent) for and 360,627 (15 per cent) against.

The Northern Ireland Assembly met on 1 July, when, for the first time, all the political parties in Northern Ireland occupied the same room. The UUP leader DAVID TRIMBLE was elected First Minister designate, and the deputy leader of the SDLP, Séamus Mallon, Deputy First Minister.

Blair, Ahern and Mitchell intervened on several occasions to save the power-sharing Executive of the Assembly, dogged by decommissioning, demilitarisation and policing issues. Following a number of crises, including the temporary suspension of the Executive and Assembly, they were again suspended on 14 October 2002 and direct rule from London reintroduced.

Pearse, Patrick Henry (1879–1916), republican and writer; born in Dublin, educated at RUI, called to the bar but did not practise. He believed the desire for Irish independence could be fired only through the cultivation and promotion of Irish; after a study of bilingual systems abroad he founded ST ENDA'S SCHOOL in Ranelagh, Dublin, 8 September 1908, where he attempted to put his ideas into practice, aided by his brother, WILLIAM PEARSE and his friends THOMAS MACDONAGH and CON COLBERT.

Prominent in the Gaelic League from 1896, Pearse edited AN CLAIDHEAMH SOLUIS, 1903–09. He also supported SINN FÉIN and contributed to the *United Irishman.* He contributed to *Irish Freedom,* in which his series 'From a hermitage', June 1913 to February 1914, attracted the attention of the IRB. A founder-member of the IRISH VOLUNTEERS,

November 1913, he was inducted into the IRB in December. He visited the United States in February 1914 to raise money for his school and for the Volunteers and met JOHN DEVOY and JOSEPH MCGARRITY. When the Volunteers split in September, Pearse was a leader of the minority Irish Volunteers, holding the position of director of military organisation. He informed McGarrity, 24 September 1914, 'If at any time we seem to be too quiet, it is because we are awaiting a favourable moment for decisive action as regards the Volunteers.'

Pearse was a member of the Military Council of the IRB, which planned the EASTER RISING (1916). Despite the loss of the arms shipment on the AUD and the countermanding order issued to the Volunteers by EOIN MACNEILL, whom Pearse had not kept informed, he determined to press ahead with the rising the following day, Monday 24 April. As chairman of the Provisional Government he read the Proclamation of the Irish Republic from outside the GPO, Sackville Street (O'Connell Street). Following a week of fighting he surrendered to Brigadier-General W. H. M. Lowe in Parnell Street, 9 April. Following a court-martial he was shot by firing squad, 3 May. His brother, William Pearse, was shot the following day.

Pearse's works were collected and edited from 1917 to 1922 by his former pupil DESMOND RYAN. They include *Three Lectures on Gaelic Topics* (1898), *Íosagán agus Sgéalta Eile* (1907), *Íosagán* (a play, 1910), *The Murder Machine* (1912), *An Sgoil: A Direct Method Course in Irish* (1913), *Songs of the Irish Rebels* (1914), *The Master* (a play, 1915), *An Mháthair agus Sgéalta Eile* (1916), and the pamphlets *The Separatist Idea* (1916), *The Spiritual Nation* (1916), and *The Sovereign People* (1916).

His sister, Margaret Pearse (1878–1968), was a teacher at St Enda's and later a member of FIANNA FÁIL. Following the execution of her brothers she and her mother ran the school until 1935. A member of Dáil Éireann for Co. Dublin, 1933, she was a member of Seanad Éireann from 1938 until her death, when she was accorded a state funeral.

Pearse, William (1881–1916), sculptor and republican; born in Dublin, brother of PATRICK PEARSE, educated at Westland Row Christian Brothers' School. He studied art in Dublin and Paris. A keen actor, he appeared at a number of Dublin venues, including the Abbey Theatre. He worked for some time as a sculptor in the family business before joining his brother at ST ENDA'S SCHOOL as an art teacher. A member of the executive committee that organised the CENTENARY CELEBRATIONS of the United Irishmen, 1898, he followed his brother into the IRISH VOLUNTEERS. A headquarters staff officer, he was *aide de camp* to his brother in the GPO during the EASTER RISING (1916) and was the only one of those executed who entered a 'guilty' plea.

Peel, Sir Robert (1788–1850), British politician (Tory and Liberal Conservative). Following a period as Under-Secretary for War and the Colonies he was appointed Chief Secretary for Ireland, 1812–18, where his six-year term was the longest of the century. From the moment he took up office he became the particular target of DANIEL O'CONNELL, who, identifying him as an opponent of CATHOLIC EMANCIPATION, dubbed him 'Orange Peel' and referred to him as 'a raw youth, squeezed out of I know not what factory in England.' Peel suppressed the CATHOLIC BOARD and revised sections of the Insurrection Act (1807). In 1814 he introduced a COERCION bill under which he created the Peace Preservation Force, whose members became known as 'Peelers' (see POLICE). In 1815 he established a state subsidy for primary education by making a grant to the KILDARE PLACE SOCIETY. One of his most important acts before leaving Ireland in May 1818 was the provision of £250,000 for relief works during the famine of 1817.

Having resigned from the Home Office, 1827, he served in the ministry formed by the DUKE OF WELLINGTON and helped to introduce Catholic Emancipation. He opposed the reforms introduced by the Whig ministry of Lord Grey but supported the Reform Acts (1832 and 1833). As Prime Minister, 1834, he dissolved Parliament and returned with 100 extra supporters. However, when his ministry suffered defeat on the Irish and English Tithes Bills and on five other occasions, he resigned, and was succeeded by VISCOUNT MELBOURNE. As Prime Minister for a second term, 1841–46, his Irish policy was characterised by both firmness and concession. He defeated O'Connell's Repeal campaign in 1843, granted an annual endowment of £26,000 to St Patrick's College, Maynooth, in the face of widespread opposition, 1845, and established the QUEEN'S COLLEGES in an attempt to end the vexed question of university education for Catholics. He also introduced the Charitable Donations and Bequests (Ireland) Act (1844).

Peel had been considering the need for the repeal of the Corn Laws, and the outbreak of famine in Ireland, September 1845, presented him with an opportunity to introduce the necessary legislation. However, defeated by the landed interest in the House of Commons, he resigned, 9 December. When LORD JOHN RUSSELL failed to form a Whig ministry, Peel returned and immediately set about the repeal of the Corn Laws. Famine conditions in Ireland had produced discontent, and he proposed a new Coercion Act. This provided his opponents with an opportunity to attack him, and on the same night on which his Repeal Bill was carried in the House of Lords, 29 June 1846, he was defeated on coercion. Before he left office he had set in train relief measures for Ireland. He had arranged for £100,000 worth of Indian meal (which became known as 'Peel's brimstone') to be brought from the United States and stored in Ireland, intending that it be used only as a stabilising agent in the market. The political risks inherent in this act were considerable, as he lacked cabinet approval. Out of office he gave independent support to the Russell ministry, to whose free-trade principles he was now a convert.

Peep o' Day Boys, a Protestant agrarian secret society, operating in Ulster during the 1780s and 90s, so called because they attacked Catholic homes at daybreak. Following the 'Battle of the Diamond' (1795), when the Peep o' Day Boys defeated the DEFENDERS, they established a new society, which they later called the ORANGE ORDER. (See also SECRET SOCIETIES.)

People's Democracy, a leftist student organisation founded at Queen's University, Belfast, 9 October 1968, as a reaction to events in Derry on 5 October, when the NORTHERN IRELAND CIVIL RIGHTS ASSOCIATION was involved in a violent confrontation with the RUC. Its founders included Kevin Boyle, Michael Farrell, Bernadette Devlin (BERNADETTE MCALISKEY), and Éamonn McCann. It demanded an impartial inquiry into the events in Derry, equality of civil rights throughout Northern Ireland, and an end to discrimination against the Catholic population. Through the *Free Citizen* it demanded 'one man one vote' and an end to repressive legislation, in particular the Special Powers Act. It organised a march from Belfast to Derry, to begin on 1 January 1969. From the outset the 75-mile march was harried by militant loyalists, led by Major Ronald Bunting (died 1984). The marchers contended with mobs armed with bottles and studded batons. The most serious encounter occurred a few miles outside Derry at Burntollet Bridge, 4 January, when the unarmed marchers were subjected to violence while the police took little action to protect them. Further violence, triggered by the arrival of the marchers in Derry, spread to other Catholic areas in the North.

People's Democracy was denounced by the Prime Minister, TERENCE O'NEILL, who called the supporters of the march 'mere hooligans' and praised the RUC, 'who handled this most difficult situation as fairly and as firmly as they could.' However, the report of the CAMERON COMMISSION stated that

> our investigations had led us to the unhesitating conclusion that on the night of 4th/5th January a number of policemen were guilty of misconduct which involved assault and battery, malicious damage to property in streets in the predominantly Catholic Bogside area . . . For such conduct among members of a disciplined and well-led force there can be no acceptable justification or excuse.

A few months afterwards, Bernadette Devlin was elected to the British Parliament as member for Mid-Ulster, having defeated the widow of the former member, April 1969. In 1972 People's Democracy sought the dissolution of the two states in Ireland, the creation of a secular all-Ireland republic, and the disbanding of the RUC and Ulster Defence Regiment. The group won two seats on Belfast City Council in 1981 and opposed 'rolling devolution' in 1982.

People's National Party, founded early in 1940, one of a number of small fascist-inspired movements, none of which was widely supported. Its members included EOIN O'DUFFY and Liam Walshe. It produced two issues of its paper, *Penapa*, notable for its anti-Jewish sentiments.

People's Rights Association, founded by T. M. HEALY in January 1897 after he had broken with the IRISH NATIONAL FEDERATION. It was supported by Catholic clergy and financed by the People's Rights Fund. Healy rejoined the IRISH PARTY when it was reunited under JOHN REDMOND, January 1900; however, when he refused to disband the People's Rights Association he was expelled from the parliamentary party and sat as an independent. At that time a liberal estimate put the number of branches at twenty, while the constabulary estimated that it had a total of 228 members, mostly in Belfast.

Perpetual Coercion Act, popular name for the Criminal Law (Amendment) Act (1887), introduced in July 1887. It granted new powers to the Irish executive to fight the PLAN OF CAMPAIGN: the Lord Lieutenant could proclaim any association illegal and forbid the press to publish reports of meetings of any association so proclaimed. The act was variously interpreted: a boy was charged in court with looking at a policeman 'with a humbugging sort of a smile'; an Italian organ-grinder who had taught his monkey to draw a toy pistol and fire it in the air found himself and the monkey arrested and the pistol confiscated; a boy was summoned for whistling a popular tune, 'Harvey Duff', in the street 'with such a threatening air as to intimidate a magistrate.' One of the earliest organisations to be proclaimed under the act was the NATIONAL LEAGUE, 19 August. Between 19 July and 31 December 1887, 373 agrarian agitators were imprisoned under the act.

Persico, Monsignor Ignazio (1823–1895), an Italian Capuchin priest in the Vatican diplomatic service, on whose behalf he arrived in Ireland, 7 July 1887, together with the under-secretary of the Congregatio de Propaganda Fide, Enrico Gualdi, to investigate the PLAN OF CAMPAIGN. He began by visiting the Archbishop of Armagh, MICHAEL LOGUE, and then the hierarchy's foremost supporter of the plan, T. W. CROKE, Archbishop of Cashel, in Thurles, 29 August. He sympathised with the demand for home rule and was also sympathetic to the cause of tenant-farmers; however, like the Vatican, he was worried about clerical involvement in a movement that advocated reprisal, including boycotting. He enjoined priests to avoid activities that might make them victims of coercion by the Chief Secretary for Ireland, A. J. BALFOUR (see PERPETUAL COERCION ACT).

Persico's report to Rome showed sympathy for the tenants' grievances but not for the form their action was taking. While he was in Ireland, British government representatives were seeking a condemnation of the plan from the Vatican. Persico was taken aback by the Papal rescript (decree) of 20 April 1888 that denounced the plan and condemned boycotting, of which he had no prior notice. The rescript caused a strong anti-Vatican reaction among nationalists; the Pope, in correspondence with the Irish hierarchy, sought to cushion its impact. Most Irish bishops blamed Persico for the rescript, and he was hurt by the condemnation he received in Ireland. He was later an archbishop, a cardinal, and Secretary of Propaganda.

'pervert', a contemptuous epithet used in rural Ireland to denote those who, induced by the offer of food, clothing, or money, changed from the Catholic to the Protestant religion, especially during the GREAT FAMINE (1845–49). (See also 'JUMPER' and 'SOUPERISM'.)

Petrie, George (1789–1866), artist, antiquarian, and music collector; born in Dublin, educated at Samuel Whyte's School, Dublin, and trained at the Dublin Society schools. His career as an antiquarian began in 1808 when he travelled throughout Cos. Dublin and Wicklow collecting music and sketching ancient ecclesiastical architecture. He was a constant exhibitor at the Royal Hibernian Academy, 1826–58, of which he became a member in 1828 and president in 1857; his best-known painting was *Gougane Barra.* Elected a member of the Advisory Council of the Royal Irish Academy, 1830, he became a superintendent in the Topographical Section of the ORDNANCE SURVEY, responsible for a staff of eleven, including JOHN O'DONOVAN and EUGENE O'CURRY. He designed the typeface for O'Donovan's edition of the Annals of the Four Masters, was founder and first editor of the *Dublin Penny Journal,* 30 June 1832, and was awarded a Civil List pension of £300 in 1849.

Petrie made an immense contribution to the preservation of traditional music. He was president of the Society for the Publication of Irish Melodies (founded 1851) and supplied EDWARD BUNTING and THOMAS MOORE with material for their collections. His first collection, *Ancient Music of Ireland* (1853), contained 'Péarla an Bhrollaigh Bháin' ('The Snowy-Breasted Pearl') and the air later known as 'The Derry Air'. The second collection, *Music of Ireland,* was published in 1882.

Apart from contributions to scholarly and popular journals on art and antiquities, Petrie published *Essay on the Round Towers of Ireland* (1833) and *On the History and Antiquities of Tara Hill* (1839), for which he received gold medals from the RIA. Sir Charles Villiers Stanford (1852–1924) issued *The Complete Collection of Irish Music as Noted by George Petrie* (1905). Part of Petrie's archaeological collection, including the Iron Age 'Petrie Crown', is on display at the National Museum, Dublin.

An Phoblacht, a paper published by the IRA, edited by PEADAR O'DONNELL; the first issue appeared on 20 June 1925. Contributors included FRANK GALLAGHER and FRANK RYAN,who also served as editor. Critical of the CUMANN NA NGAEDHEAL government, the paper was also associated with SAOR ÉIRE. It supported FIANNA FÁIL in the call for withholding LAND ANNUITIES, and was active in opposition to the BLUESHIRTS. It ceased publication in 1937.

The Provisional IRA resurrected the title in May 1970 for its paper, published in Dublin. It also produced *Republican News* in Belfast; the two papers merged in February 1979.

Phoenix National and Literary Societies, republican societies founded in 1856 in Skibbereen, Co. Cork, by JEREMIAH O'DONOVAN ROSSA. They were ostensibly literary and debating societies but, under the motto 'Ireland for the Irish,' were patently revolutionary. JAMES STEPHENS, during his tour of Ireland preparatory to establishing the IRB, recruited them in 1858. On 26 October 1858 a leading article in the *Nation* incorporated a letter from WILLIAM SMITH O'BRIEN in which he denounced secret societies, such as the Phoenix. The Phoenix Societies were raided in December 1858 and more than thirty members, including the leaders, were arrested, but they were soon released for lack of evidence. By 1859, almost fully integrated into the IRB, the Phoenix Societies were dissolved.

Phoenix Park Murders (6 May 1882). Four days after the resignation of the Chief Secretary for Ireland, W. E. FORSTER, and the release of CHARLES STEWART PARNELL under the terms of the 'KILMAINHAM TREATY', the new Chief Secretary, LORD FREDERICK CAVENDISH, and the Under-Secretary, THOMAS HENRY BURKE, were murdered outside the Viceregal Lodge in the Phoenix Park, Dublin. The killings were the work of a Fenian splinter group, the INVINCIBLES, using surgical knives smuggled from London. The murders shocked public opinion in Ireland and Britain. Parnell issued a manifesto signed by a number of Irish members of Parliament appealing to the Irish people to 'show by every manner of expression possible, that amidst the universal feeling of horror which the assassination has excited, no people are so intense in their detestation of this atrocity, or entertain so deep a sympathy for those whose hearts must be seared by it . . .' Leaders of the IRB also denounced the killings. Parnell, who believed his work would be undone by the killings, considered resigning, but the Prime Minister, W. E. GLADSTONE (whose wife was related to Cavendish), persuaded him to remain as leader of the IRISH PARTY. Sixteen of the Invincibles were arrested, 13 January 1883. JAMES CAREY turned state's evidence, which led to the hanging of five of the principals; eight others were sentenced to long terms of imprisonment.

Pigot, John Edward (1822–1871), Young Irelander, musician, music collector, and poet; born in Kilworth, Co. Cork, educated at TCD and called to the bar. Under the pen-name 'Fermoy' he contributed articles and poems to the *Nation,* where he served on the editorial board; he later added music to some of the songs in *The Spirit of the Nation.* A member of the REPEAL ASSOCIATION, he was also active in the IRISH CONFEDERATION. He was a member of the defence team during the state trials of JOHN MITCHEL and WILLIAM SMITH O'BRIEN, 1848. Closely associated with several cultural bodies, he was joint honorary secretary of the Society for the Preservation and Publication of the Melodies of Ireland, 1851, in which capacity he travelled throughout the country collecting old airs, which were used by GEORGE PETRIE and P. W. JOYCE in their published collections. Pigot's manuscripts in the Royal Irish Academy include some two thousand airs (Breandán Breathnach credited him with collecting some three thousand). He also worked on the RIA's *Dictionary of the Irish Language,* assisted EUGENE O'CURRY in the preparation of his lectures at the Catholic University, and helped JOHN O'DALY with *The Poets and Poetry of Munster* (1849).

Pigott, Richard (1828–1889), journalist and forger; born in Ratoath, Co. Meath, educated locally. A supporter of nationalist causes for a period, he was imprisoned for sedition. At various times a pornographer and a blackmailer, he appeared to support the HOME RULE LEAGUE and was the owner of three ailing newspapers (the *Irishman, Flag of Ireland,* and *Shamrock*), which he sold to the IRISH PARTY in 1881; they formed the basis for *United Ireland,* controlled by CHARLES STEWART PARNELL. During this transaction Pigott acquired documents bearing Parnell's signature, which he subsequently forged. In 1885 he was again in financial difficulties, and he contacted Lord Richard Grosvenor, the Liberal chief whip, with a scheme for publicising material that would damage Parnell and the Irish Party. Through Grosvenor he met a former reporter for the *Times* (London), Edward Houston, then secretary of the IRISH LOYAL AND PATRIOTIC UNION, who retained him to seek information implicating the Parnellites in crime. Pigott failed to find any such information in his travels to France, Switzerland, and the United States; in despair of losing his income from Houston, he forged letters while in Paris.

Houston was persuaded that the letters were genuine and sold them to the *Times,* which used them as the basis for a series of articles headed 'PARNELLISM AND CRIME' from 7 March 1887. When Pigott was a witness before a House of Commons special commission on the accusations against Parnell, his forgery was exposed, 20–22 February 1888, when he misspelt 'hesitancy' as 'hesitency' (as it appeared in some of the letters). Further cross-examination revealed numerous inconsistencies in his testimony. In particular, he denied he had prior knowledge of the nature of the *Times* series, whereas letters he had written to the Catholic Archbishop of Dublin, WILLIAM WALSH, clearly showed that he had.

He failed to make his appearance in court on 26 February and, having signed a confession—which he almost immediately retracted—fled to Paris. From Paris he travelled to Madrid, where he registered as Ronald Ponsonby at the Hotel Embajadores, 28 February. Confronted by British policemen who wished to question him, he allegedly shot himself the next day.

Pike Theatre, Dublin, a fringe theatre, seating approximately sixty people, founded in 1953 by the husband-and-wife team Alan Simpson (1920–1980) and Carolyn Swift (1923–2002) to produce international drama. It presented the first Irish production of works by BRENDAN BEHAN (world première of *The Quare Fellow,* 19 November 1954) and SAMUEL BECKETT (Irish première of *Waiting for Godot,* October 1955).

During the first Dublin Theatre Festival, 1957, the Pike became the centre of a controversy over the European première of Tennessee Williams's *The Rose Tattoo.* Opening on 12 May, the production was a huge success, with Anna Manahan and Pat Nolan in the leading roles. On 21 May the Garda Síochána demanded that Simpson take the production off, on the grounds that it contained 'objectionable passages'. When gardaí refused to state what these were, or who was the source of the complaint against the production, Simpson went ahead with the performance, was arrested under a nineteenth-century law for producing 'an indecent and profane play for gain,' and was imprisoned, 23 May. Though he was supported by Behan, FRANK O'CONNOR, and others, neither the Dublin Theatre Festival nor the GATE THEATRE, where Simpson had entered into a contract with Lord Longford, provided support. During the hearing in the Dublin District Court, 4 July, when the garda giving evidence again refused to disclose the source of the complaint, or to say what the 'objectionable passages' were, District Justice Cathal Lynch refused to return the case for trial. While the state won on appeal to the High Court, the Supreme Court later ruled that it was a matter for the district justice to decide.

The critic Harold Hobson of the *Sunday Times* (London) later claimed that his enthusiastic review of the production, during which he implied that a contraceptive had been dropped on stage, was responsible for the Garda action; in fact during the performance the requirement that Alvaro drop a condom and kick it under a sofa was mimed by the actor, Pat Nolan. Simpson, Swift and the Pike incurred debts of some £200 as a result of the legal actions. The theatre closed in 1960.

Pillar of Fire Society, founded by Frank Duff and Leon Ó Broin, both members of the LEGION OF MARY, in 1942, 'to promote dialogue with Ireland's Jewish community.'

Pilot, a thrice-weekly paper founded and edited by Richard Barrett in 1828 to provide support for DANIEL O'CONNELL, the CATHOLIC ASSOCIATION, and the struggle for CATHOLIC EMANCIPATION; it later supported the REPEAL ASSOCIATION. It was viewed with hostility by the Irish executive, and Barrett was several times prosecuted and imprisoned. Material consisted almost exclusively of O'Connell's speeches and public letters. The paper was often involved in controversy with anti-O'Connell papers. In 1834 DUBLIN CASTLE withdrew its stamp, and the paper appeared under the name *Morning Register.* This persecution prompted its defence by the *Times* (London) and led to questions in the House of Commons, so that it shortly reappeared under its own name. It ceased publication in 1849, two years after O'Connell's death.

Pirrie, William James, first Viscount (1847–1924), shipbuilder; born in Québec, of Ulster parents, raised in Co. Down. Having entered the Harland and Wolff shipyard as an apprentice draughtsman, 1862, he proved so adept that he was co-opted to the board of directors, 1874; as chairman from 1904 he was in sole control of the company. Under his direction the shipyard built the biggest ships of the time, including the *Teutonic* (10,000 tons, 1889), *Oceanic* (17,000 tons, 1899), and *Titanic* (76,500 tons, 1911). Pirrie, who conceived the liners as 'floating hotels', recognised that oil was the fuel of the future and concluded a deal in 1912 by which he became a manufacturer of diesel engines in Glasgow. A supporter of the INDEPENDENT ORANGE ORDER, he was a Privy Councillor from 1897 and made Viscount Pirrie in 1906.

His wife, Margaret Pirrie, née Carlisle (1857–1935), was a noted philanthropist who was active in many charitable organisations. She was the first woman justice of the peace and the first woman to be made an honorary freeman of the city of Belfast.

pishogue (Irish *piseog*, also *pisreog*), a charm or spell that people believed could be visited on a person by a form of sympathetic magic; it was defined by ANNA MARIA HALL as a 'wise saw, a rural incantation, a charm, a sign, a cabalistic word.' Pishogues were generally directed towards obtaining cures for people or animals or increasing milk and butter yields. A belief in pishogues still persists in some areas.

There were four principal kinds:

(1) protective (for example from witchcraft): fire was not allowed to leave a house in which butter was being churned, nor was a person allowed to 'redden' his pipe in the house;

(2) seeking an increase in yield: an instance of this sort of pishogue was the placing of a cow's afterbirth under the milk-keelers to produce cream;

(3) love charms: the object of these pishogues was to gain the affection of a loved one or to determine the identity of a future spouse or lover. Mrs Hall, quoting from an encounter with a woman known as 'Poll the Pishogue' at Newbridge (Droichead Nua), Co. Kildare, relates that 'herbs used in love potions had to be gathered fasting in the bames [beams] of a full moon.' To ascertain the identity of a future spouse or lover one had to visit the local abbey churchyard on May Eve and put the right garter round the left knee and vice versa. The thumbs should be tied in the form of a cross with a peeled bark of rowan. The third snail found under the ivy was brought home between two plates and left with the twist of rowan until the morning. The following morning, when the plates were opened, the snail's trail on the rowan would contain the name of the future spouse;

(4*a*) warding off and curing disease: for example, a reduction in milk yield was prevented by placing a live cinder under the churn, or driving iron nails in a circle about it; or

(4*b*) inflicting injury on others: it was believed that hiding eggs or raw meat in a neighbour's field would cause his harvest to be adversely affected, or that if a cloth was dragged across a field wet by dew on May Eve the butter and milk produce of that farm would be destroyed.

Pitt, William (1759–1806), English politician (Tory). Entering politics in 1781, he became Prime Minister in 1783; he supported the Relief Act (1793), which conceded some rights to Catholics. A supporter of CATHOLIC EMANCIPATION, he intended that this should follow the Union, which became his prime objective following the rising of the UNITED IRISHMEN, 1798. The promise of emancipation won support for the Union from the Catholic hierarchy, but Pitt met with strong opposition from the EARL OF CLARE and from KING GEORGE III. When the Union was secure and Pitt became first Prime Minister of the United Kingdom of Great Britain and Ireland, 22 January 1801, he pressed for Emancipation. He met the King's resistance by announcing his resignation, 3 February, but postponed it when the King appeared to become deranged. On his recovery, Pitt resigned, 14 March 1801, and was out of office until 1804. Approached by the King to form another ministry, he laid down two conditions: that Charles James Fox be a member of the ministry, and that Catholic Emancipation be conceded. The King refused to include Fox, and extracted from Pitt a promise that he would not again raise the question of Emancipation. Fearful for the King's sanity, Pitt formed a new ministry, 1804–06, but his final years as Prime Minister witnessed the rapid deterioration of his health. He died heavily in debt; his parliamentary colleagues raised £40,000 to satisfy his creditors.

Plan Kathleen, the code name for a German invasion of Ireland proposed by the IRA during the Second World War. The plan (known to German military intelligence as the Artus Plan) proposed that invading forces would aid the IRA in overthrowing the government of Northern Ireland and bringing about the reunification of Ireland. However, the German agent HERMANN GÖRTZ reported unfavourably on the strength and potential of the IRA. On 3 December 1940, at a meeting of the Armed Forces Planning Staff with Adolf Hitler, Grossadmiral Erich Raeder expressed the opinion that the landing of a German expeditionary force in Ireland was virtually impossible, because of Britain's naval supremacy; subsequent logistical difficulties in providing supplies to such a force made the plan an unjustifiable risk. Hitler accepted the argument, and the plan was abandoned.

Plan of Campaign, a stratagem employed by tenant-farmers against landlords between 1886 and 1891, prompted by the depression in the price of dairy produce and cattle in the mid-1880s, which left many tenants in arrears with rent. On 4 August 1886 the IRISH PARTY passed a resolution warning the British government that the payment of judicial rents would be impossible. The Plan of Campaign, conceived by T. M. HEALY, was organised by TIM HARRINGTON, WILLIAM O'BRIEN and JOHN DILLON and was outlined in 'A plan of campaign' (written by Harrington), *United Ireland,* 23 October 1886.

The purpose of the plan was to secure a reduction in rent; if a landlord refused to accept a reduced rent, the tenant was to pay no rent at all. Rents were collected by campaigners, who banked them in the name of a committee of trustees and used them to assist evicted tenants. The plan was first implemented on the O'Grady estate in Co. Limerick, November 1886, and then applied by Dillon and O'Brien on the estate of Lord Clanricarde at Portumna, Co. Galway (where, in December 1885, three hundred Woodford tenants, led by Father Coen, had petitioned Lord Clanricarde for a 25 per cent reduction in rent). It spread to other estates, including the Lansdowne estate at Luggacurran, Co. Kerry, the Vandeleur estate at Kilrush, Co. Clare, the Ponsonby estate at Youghal, Co. Cork, the Smith-Barry estate in Co. Tipperary, the de Freyne estate in Co. Roscommon, the O'Callaghan estate at Bodyke, Co. Clare, the Dillon estate in Co. Mayo, the Kingston estate at Mitchelstown, Co. Cork, and the Massareene estate in Co. Louth. On all the estates a member of the Irish Party or its constituency organisation, the NATIONAL LEAGUE, led the plan. Some twenty thousand tenants were involved.

The plan was not supported by CHARLES STEWART PARNELL, chairman of the Irish Party, but he was unable to prevent it. In December 1886, when the British government declared it 'an unlawful and criminal conspiracy,' Parnell persuaded O'Brien to confine it to the 116 estates on which it was operating at that time. On the other hand, the campaigners had support from Archbishop WILLIAM WALSH and Archbishop T. W. CROKE. Many other bishops supported it, while opposition was led by the Bishop of Limerick, EDWARD O'DWYER.

The renewal of the LAND WAR, in the form of the Plan of Campaign, was a matter of concern to Lord Salisbury's government, and, determined to crush it, he appointed his nephew ARTHUR J. BALFOUR (fresh from his attack on the Highland Land League) as Chief Secretary for Ireland. Balfour secured a PERPETUAL COERCION ACT in the Criminal Law Amendment Act (1887). Dillon and O'Brien were arrested; when their supporters raised a public defence fund, Croke issued a 'no-tax manifesto'. Two priests, FATHER MATTHEW RYAN and Father Daniel Keller, both in Croke's archdiocese, were imprisoned. In the House of Commons, Balfour defended the instruction of a divisional magistrate, Thomas Plunkett, to the police, 'Do not hesitate to shoot,' which induced O'Brien to dub him 'Bloody Balfour'. Nationalists were horrified at the 'MITCHELSTOWN MASSACRE' later that year.

Boycotting became widespread, and the rising rate of AGRARIAN CRIME and general unrest forced the British government to seek the assistance of the Vatican in suppressing the clergymen involved in the plan. MONSIGNOR IGNAZIO PERSICO was despatched to Ireland, and a Papal rescript (decree) was issued, 20 April 1888, condemning the Plan of Campaign, boycotting, and clerical involvement, but it was ignored by Archbishop Croke and nationalists. A general resentment at the Vatican's intrusion in Irish affairs helped to win some support for the plan, by now in financial difficulties. The organisers looked unavailingly to Parnell for help. Fearing it would harm his alliance with the Liberals, Parnell made a speech to the Eighty Club, a Liberal group, in which he virtually renounced his association with the plan. The organisers were forced to seek financial assistance, and Dillon embarked on a fund-raising drive in Australia and New Zealand, May 1889 to April 1890, which raised some £33,000; but this was not enough for their needs.

Balfour encouraged the landlords in 1889 to form an anti-tenant combination, under the direction of the Co. Tipperary landlord A. H. SMITH-BARRY. As the landlords' agent, Smith-Barry was authorised to acquire estates threatened by the plan. This brought him into conflict with his own tenants in Tipperary; when they were evicted, they moved outside the town boundaries and built NEW TIPPERARY, under the direction of FATHER DAVID HUMPHRIES and O'Brien, but the project proved too costly for the plan's leaders.

By this time Parnell had been induced to

give some support, which helped in the formation of a tenants' defence association in Co. Tipperary, and this, together with Dillon's money, enabled the plan to continue. The organisers had £84,000 in 1890, but this had shrunk to £48,000 within a year, by which time almost 1,500 tenants were receiving grants from the funds. By 1893 the campaign was over.

A total of £234,000 was subscribed in support of the plan, £129,000 of which was raised in Ireland. Documented results available for 141 out of 203 estates show that settlements were achieved in approximately 88 per cent of cases, 5 per cent had settled on the landlords' terms, while 7 per cent had reached no settlement. The last landlord to settle was the absentee LORD CLANRICARDE; in 1913 he was compelled to sell his estate to the CONGESTED DISTRICTS BOARD for £238,000.

Plunket, Thomas Plunket, second Baron (1792–1866), evangelical bishop (Church of Ireland); born in Dublin, son of WILLIAM CONYNGHAM PLUNKET, FIRST BARON PLUNKET, educated at TCD. He was Dean of Down before being appointed Bishop of Tuam, Killala and Achonry, 1839–66. Within a few years he became one of the best-known evangelicals in the country. His support for the IRISH CHURCH MISSIONS and REV. EDWARD NANGLE led to a religious war in Connacht between himself and the Catholic Archbishop of Tuam, JOHN MACHALE. A highlight of the struggle was the so-called 'War in Partry', which led to questions in the House of Commons (see SECOND REFORMATION). Plunket was denounced in November 1860 by the *Times* (London) for evicting Catholic tenants from his estate at Tourmakeady, Co. Mayo, where his sister, Catherine Plunket, ran an evangelical school. He was the author of *Convert Confirmations: A Discourse Delivered to the Converts from Romanism in West Galway* (1851).

Plunket, William Conyngham Plunket, first Baron (1764–1854), lawyer and politician (Conservative); born in Enniskillen, Co. Fermanagh, educated at TCD and called to the bar. He defended members of the UNITED IRISHMEN, 1797–98. A member of Parliament from 1798, he opposed the ACT OF UNION but accepted office as Solicitor-General, 1803, and was chief prosecutor at the trial of ROBERT EMMET, 1803. As member of Parliament for Midhurst, Sussex, 1807–12, he supported CATHOLIC EMANCIPATION, leading the struggle after the death of HENRY GRATTAN. He was member of Parliament for the University of Dublin from 1812; his bill to secure Catholic relief was successfully opposed by the Duke of York in the House of Lords, 1821. Attorney-General in 1822, he supported the Catholic Relief Bill introduced by Sir Francis Burdett in 1825, which was also vetoed in the House of Lords. He was appointed Chief Justice of the Court of Common Pleas in Ireland, 1827, and Lord Chancellor from 1830 until his resignation in 1841.

Plunket, William Conyngham Plunket, fourth Baron (1828–1897), bishop (Church of Ireland); born in Dublin, educated at TCD. Following ordination in 1857 he was chaplain and private secretary to his uncle, THOMAS PLUNKET, evangelical Bishop of Tuam, Killala and Achonry. He gave support in the west of Ireland to the IRISH CHURCH MISSIONS. After his marriage to a daughter of SIR BENJAMIN LEE GUINNESS he was appointed to St Patrick's Cathedral, Dublin (then being restored by his father-in-law). He was Bishop of Meath from 1876 to 1884, when he was translated to Dublin. As Archbishop of Dublin he sought the unification of the Protestant churches and reorganised the KILDARE PLACE SOCIETY to establish the Church of Ireland Training College. He supported the Protestant movement in Spain and was president of the Italian Reform Society, 1886. His writings include *Short Visit to the Connemara Missions* (1863) and *The Missionary Character and Responsibility of Our Church in This Land* (1865).

Plunkett, George Noble Plunkett, Count (1851–1948), antiquarian and politician (Sinn Féin); born in Dublin, educated at TCD. His title was a Papal award. Active in a number of cultural societies, he was president of the SOCIETY FOR THE PRESERVATION OF THE IRISH LANGUAGE, vice-president of the IRISH NATIONAL LITERARY SOCIETY, and founder and editor of HIBERNIA, 1882–83. Called to the bar, 1886, he supported CHARLES STEWART PARNELL following the split in the IRISH PARTY and was defeated as a Parnellite Nationalist for Mid-Tyrone, 1892, and St Stephen's Green, Dublin, 1895. He was director of the National Museum, 1907–16, vice-president of the Royal Irish Academy, 1908–09 and 1911–14 (which he represented on the Nobel Committee for Literature), and president of the Royal Society of Antiquaries of Ireland.

Following the execution of his son JOSEPH PLUNKETT for his role in the EASTER RISING

(1916), Plunkett became a political figure and was imprisoned. Assisted by SINN FÉIN, he was elected for North Roscommon as an abstentionist independent, 5 February 1917. He held the seat in subsequent elections and was a member of the first Dáil Éireann, holding the position of Minister for Foreign Affairs, January 1919 to August 1921. He attended the Paris Peace Conference, 1919, and accompanied ÉAMON DE VALERA to London for discussions with DAVID LLOYD GEORGE, July 1921. Minister for the Fine Arts, 9 August 1921 to January 1922, he opposed the ANGLO-IRISH TREATY (1921). He did not take his seat in the Dáil when elected for Co. Roscommon, 1922–27, and continued to support Sinn Féin after de Valera broke from it to form FIANNA FÁIL.

He was joint editor of *The Jacobite War in Ireland* (1894) and edited WHITLEY STOKES's *Early Christian Art in Ireland* (1911–15). His works include *The Architecture of Dublin* (1908), *Arrows* (poems, 1921), *Echoes* (poems, 1928), and *Introduction to Church Symbolism* (1932).

Plunkett, Sir Horace Curzon (1854–1932), agriculturist and politician (Unionist); born in Gloucestershire, educated at the University of Oxford. Afflicted with pulmonary tuberculosis, he spent some ten years as a rancher in Wyoming; on moving to Ireland, 1888, he applied American techniques to his management of the family's estate in Co. Meath. He assisted the EARL OF DUNRAVEN AND MOUNT EARL and FATHER THOMAS FINLAY in their efforts to launch the CO-OPERATIVE MOVEMENT, 1889, and was instrumental in founding the IRISH AGRICULTURAL ORGANISATION SOCIETY, 1894. Member of Parliament for South Co. Dublin, 1892–1900, he organised the RECESS COMMITTEE, which succeeded in securing the establishment of the DEPARTMENT OF AGRICULTURE AND TECHNICAL INSTRUCTION, of which he was vice-president until his resignation in 1907. After 1908 he lent his support to the campaign for HOME RULE.

He was a man of tremendous energy but little tact. His work in agriculture and as a politician exposed him to attacks from virtually all sections of opinion: his unionism incurred the wrath of nationalists, his Protestantism made him suspect to Catholics, and his desire to eliminate the middleman from agriculture made him the *bête noire* of rural shopkeepers.

At the height of the debate on the (third) HOME RULE BILL he issued 'An Appeal to Ulster Not to Desert Ireland', 1914. Saddened by the blood sacrifice of the EASTER RISING (1916), he counselled restraint in the aftermath. He was chairman of the IRISH CONVENTION, 1917–18, and was bitterly disappointed at its failure. Seeking self-government for Ireland within the British Empire, 1919, he founded the IRISH DOMINION LEAGUE, a futile effort, as the WAR OF INDEPENDENCE had already begun. A member of the first Senate of the Irish Free State, 1922, he left Ireland permanently following the burning of his home at Foxrock, Co. Dublin, by republicans during the CIVIL WAR.

He published *Ireland in the New Century* (1904), which provoked a riposte from Father Michael O'Riordan under the title *Catholicity and Progress in Ireland* (1905). His autobiographical *Noblesse Oblige* was published in 1908.

Plunkett, Joseph Mary (1887–1916), poet and republican; born in Dublin, son of George Noble Plunkett (COUNT PLUNKETT), educated privately and at Stonyhurst College, Lancashire. Suffering from pulmonary tuberculosis, he spent much of his youth in Algeria, Malta, and Sicily. Widely read in the writings of Catholic mystics, he published his first volume of verse, *The Circle and Sword,* in 1911. He became editor of the *Irish Review,* 1913–14; his editorial line led to its suppression, November 1914. He was a member of the IRB and the IRISH VOLUNTEERS, in which he became director of operations, and a member of the Military Council of the IRB, which organised the EASTER RISING (1916).

He went to Germany, April 1915, to assist ROGER CASEMENT in securing aid for the rising from Germany. Casement—who felt that Plunkett's presence was an embarrassment—introduced him to members of the German General Staff, who rejected his request for guns. Some arms were sent on the AUD, April 1916.

As director of operations of the Volunteers, Plunkett displayed considerable tactical ability. He was joint author (with SEÁN MAC DIARMADA) of the 'CASTLE DOCUMENT', which was intended to prompt moderates into supporting the rising. Shortly before the rising he underwent throat surgery, and he was dying when he left the convalescent home to take his place in the GPO, Dublin (where his *aide de camp* was MICHAEL COLLINS). He was a member of the Provisional Government formed by PATRICK PEARSE and a signatory of the Proclamation of the Irish Republic. Following the collapse of the rising he was court-martialled and sentenced to death. On the eve of his execution he married his fiancée, GRACE GIFFORD, in Kilmainham Jail, Dublin. *The Poems of Joseph Mary Plunkett* were published posthumously in 1916.

Poblacht na hÉireann ('the Irish Republic'), a Republican news-sheet founded by ERSKINE CHILDERS, FRANK GALLAGHER, and LIAM MELLOWS, first published on 3 January 1922, edited by Childers from February until his execution in November. The editorial team also included CATHAL BRUGHA and MARY MACSWINEY. Reflecting the policies of ÉAMON DE VALERA, it was the only significant publication opposed to the ANGLO-IRISH TREATY (1921). It ceased publication after the CIVIL WAR.

Pointe Saint-Charles, a landing and quarantine station outside Montréal, erected in 1847 to replace immigrant sheds in use since 1832. As at GROSSE ÎLE, several thousand fever-ravaged Irish immigrants died either on board ship while awaiting medical inspection or in hospital sheds. One estimate put the number of deaths within the sheds at 3,144, while the number of deaths aboard ship is unknown. (See COFFIN SHIPS.)

During preparatory work for the Victoria Bridge over the St Lawrence River, 1859, sites of mass burials were disturbed. The predominantly Irish work force refused to continue working until the area had been restored and the last resting-place of the Irish immigrants acknowledged. A block of stone dredged from the St Lawrence was inscribed:

> To preserve from desecration the remains of 6,000 emigrants who died from ship fever A.D. 1847–48 this stone is erected by the workmen of Messrs. Peto, Brassey and Betts employed in the construction of the Victoria Bridge A.D. 1859.

(See also STATEN ISLAND and WARD'S ISLAND.)

poitín, the traditional illicit drink of rural Ireland after the British Parliament levied tax on Irish whiskey. The duty was 4 pence per gallon in 1661, when excise was reintroduced, and had reached 6 shillings per gallon by 1815—when whiskey was selling at 10 shillings per gallon. The drink 'that has never seen the face of a gauger [exciseman]' was openly consumed at weddings, fairs and funerals or sold in SHEBEENS, where it was coloured with 'parliament whiskey' or 'government whiskey'. Early in the nineteenth century poitín was made from malt barley, but as this was an inconvenient method, with an increased risk of detection, other materials were pressed into service, including sugar, porter, potatoes, apples, and rhubarb. Copper vessels were first used, but as copper became expensive, tin vessels were employed. To maintain secrecy, repairs to the equipment were usually carried out by travelling tinsmiths or 'tinkers'.

Poitín was most commonly made west of a line from Co. Clare to Co. Derry, but Cos. Cavan, Monaghan and Tyrone in southern Ulster were also areas of manufacture. In many instances the recipe was handed down from generation to generation. The price of the spirit varied according to the method used and the extent of the operation: between 1815 and 1850 it varied between 7 and 8 shillings per gallon; during the First World War it rose to approximately 8 shillings per pint. Prices of £3–£6 per bottle were being sought in parts of Ulster, Connacht and Munster in the early years of the twenty-first century.

A commercially made poitín launched in the late 1970s failed to displace the illicit product in popularity.

police. The first attempt to provide a police force for Ireland was by an act of 1787, which established a barony police. Known as 'Barnies', they were inadequate for the suppression of disturbances. Constables, who were exclusively Protestant, did not wear uniforms and were untrained and undisciplined.

Another attempt was made in 1814 with the creation of the Peace Preservation Force by SIR ROBERT PEEL, whose members came to be known as 'Peelers'. This force was at the disposal of the Lord Lieutenant of Ireland for use in any district that had been 'proclaimed' as a disturbed area. During a period of intense agitation, as a result of hunger or general discontent, this force also proved inadequate, and in 1822 the County Constabulary was established. There were now two police forces: the Peace Preservation Force, working independently in proclaimed districts, and the County Constabulary, preserving law and order throughout the country. To supervise the County Constabulary, four provincial inspectors were appointed, each with complete responsibility within his area; sixteen constables were appointed to each barony. In all, there were 313 chief constables and 5,008 constables. The constables were frequently used in attempts to suppress FACTION-FIGHTING.

Under the reforming Irish executive of 1835–41, THOMAS DRUMMOND, Under-Secretary for Ireland, remodelled the system under an act of 1836, and the existing police forces were absorbed into a new body, the Irish Constabulary, under an Inspector-General in Dublin. The power to appoint constables was removed from magistrates, who were now to be appointed by the Lord Lieutenant, and a new code of discipline was introduced. By 1840 there were 8,500 constables stationed throughout the country. In 1867, as a reward for their role in suppressing the rising of the IRB, the force was renamed the ROYAL IRISH CONSTABULARY. By this time there were 11,000 constables and officers stationed in 1,600 barracks. (See also DUBLIN METROPOLITAN POLICE and GARDA SÍOCHÁNA.)

Police Service of Northern Ireland. Following the recommendations of the PATTEN REPORT (1999), the ROYAL ULSTER CONSTABULARY was replaced by the Police Service of Northern Ireland from 4 November 2001, with a directive to recruit half its members from the Catholic community. By the time Hugh Orde became first full-time Chief Constable, 1 September 2002, Catholic recruitment was believed to be considerably below expectations, owing to republican hostility towards the new force. SINN FÉIN opposed participation in the force, while the SDLP supported participation and sat on the Police Board. The Chief Constable's announcement that, as the force was already under strength (at 6,846), he could not implement the recommendation of the Patten Report that the full-time reserve be phased out, was greeted with anger by nationalists.

Poor Law. A Commission of Inquiry into the Poor Law in Ireland was established in 1833. The members included RICHARD WHATELY, DANIEL MURRAY, Richard More O'Ferrall, William Nassau senior, A. R. Blake, and J. F. Richeno; the secretary was John Revans. In their report they found that 2.385 million people were in want or distressed for thirty weeks of the year. The Commission also noted that agricultural wages varied from 6 pence to 1 shilling per day and were available only for a short part of the year. The poor depended on private charity, estimated at some £2 million annually.

The Commissioners did not recommend the simple extension of the English Poor Law system; instead they suggested a scheme of 'enactments calculated to promote the improvement of the country, and to extend the demand for free and profitable labour.' Their principal recommendations included subsidised and organised emigration, a Board of Improvement to supervise the reclamation of land, the drainage and fencing of waste lands, the establishment of agricultural MODEL SCHOOLS, and a scheme of public works, to be administered by the Board of Works and the county boards.

When GEORGE NICHOLLS came to Ireland to investigate conditions in 1836 he had instructions that implied that he could ignore the Commission's recommendations, and he set about establishing a system on the English model. In his first report he stated:

> Ireland is now suffering under a circle of evils, producing and reproducing one another. Want of capital produces want of employment; want of employment, turbulence and misery; turbulence and misery, insecurity; insecurity prevents the introduction and accumulation of capital and so on. Until this circle is broken, the evils must continue and probably increase.

After a month in Ireland he recommended to the Irish executive that the English Poor Law system he extended to Ireland. Over the protests of Whately and the Commissioners, the Chief Secretary for Ireland, Lord Morpeth (see EARL OF CARLISLE), accepted the recommendation. The Poor Relief (Ireland) Bill was opposed by DANIEL O'CONNELL but was welcomed generally by the Catholic clergy and became law on 31 July 1838. Ireland was divided into 130 Poor Law unions (i.e. unions of parishes), each centred on a market town, where a WORKHOUSE was built for the relief of the distressed. Indoor relief only was to be administered: no relief was to be granted to anyone who remained outside the workhouse. Each union was sub-divided into district electoral divisions, of which in 1847 there were 2,049.

Work proceeded swiftly. Twenty-two unions were declared by the end of March 1839 and 104 a year later. Relief was financed by a rate collected under the POOR LAW VALUATION. The thirty-three unions in Leinster had an average population of 58,602, the thirty-five in Munster had 69,581, the nineteen in Connacht had 75,943, and the forty-three in Ulster had 54,933. Each workhouse was to be administered by a board of guardians, consisting of representative ratepayers. Each union was rated for the number of poor it sent to the workhouse; half was to be repaid by the tenants and half by the landlords. When the burden of paying the rate became too heavy for tenant-farmers, an amendment exempted those rated at £4 or less.

By the time the last workhouse was built,

Ireland was in the throes of the GREAT FAMINE (1845–49). Indoor relief was hopelessly inadequate, but outdoor relief was granted, on condition that the recipient not have a quarter of an acre or more of land (see QUARTER-ACRE CLAUSE). The workhouses were overcrowded, and it became impossible to collect the poor rate with which to finance relief.

The Poor Law Extension Act (1847) separated the Irish Poor Law from the British and increased the number of unions from 130 to 162. Inefficient boards of guardians were abolished and replaced by paid guardians. A total of 610,463 people received indoor relief in 1848, while 1,433,042 were granted outdoor relief; a year later the figures were 932,284 and 1,210,182. As the collection of rates became impossible, workhouses became bankrupt, and the Treasury ordered that a poor rate of 5 shillings in the pound (25 per cent) should be collected. Despite widespread protest from those involved in Irish relief, the Treasury order remained in force, and the old, sick and young were turned out to make room for able-bodied people who could be put to work.

After the Great Famine the Poor Law and the workhouses remained detested symbols of poverty. On the establishment of the IRISH FREE STATE they were abolished, and the county replaced the Poor Law union for the purpose of administering relief. (See also LOCAL GOVERNMENT.)

Poor Law Valuation, the valuation of property for the purpose of assessing the rates to finance Poor Law unions from 1838. Each district electoral division within the Poor Law union was charged with a proportion of the total cost in respect of the number of people from that division who had received relief in the workhouse. As some of the original valuations were made by tenant-farmers and others by surveyors, there was a wide variation in findings. A more scientific survey was undertaken by RICHARD GRIFFITH between 1848 and 1865; officially known as the PRIMARY VALUATION and also as the Griffith Valuation, this became the recognised system of assessing the rates for official purposes.

Pope John Paul II in Ireland. Pope John Paul II paid a pastoral visit to Ireland from Saturday 29 September to Monday 1 October 1979. He concelebrated Mass in the Phoenix Park, Dublin, before a congregation of more than 1¼ million. He travelled to Killineer, near Drogheda, Co. Louth, where, addressing a crowd of more than 250,000, he appealed for peace in Northern Ireland. Returning to Dublin, he gave audiences to journalists and the diplomatic corps and was received at Áras an Uachtaráin by President Hillery. On Sunday 30 September the Papal party travelled to Ballybrit Racecourse, Galway, to concelebrate a Mass for Youth before 200,000 people. En route he visited the monastic site at Clonmacnoise, Co. Offaly, where he briefly addressed 20,000 people. From Galway he was flown to KNOCK, Co. Mayo, scene of a reported apparition by the Virgin Mary, 1879, where he spoke to a crowd of 400,000. On the next day he addressed seminarians at St Patrick's College, Maynooth, and then travelled to Greenpark Racecourse, Limerick, where he delivered a homily on the theme of the family to 400,000 people. The Papal party then travelled to the United States from Shannon Airport.

population. The following table gives the population of Ireland from the first census until partition.

1821	6.802 million
1831	7.767 million
1841	8.175 million
1851	6.552 million
1861	5.799 million
1871	5.412 million
1881	5.175 million
1891	4.705 million
1901	4.459 million
1911	4.390 million

The following table gives the population of the twenty-six counties that constituted the Irish Free State, later the Republic. (Figures for the remaining six counties can be found under NORTHERN IRELAND.)

1926	2.972 million
1936	2.968 million
1946	2.955 million
1951	2.961 million
1956	2.898 million
1961	2.818 million
1966	2.884 million
1971	2.978 million
1981	3.443 million
1986	3.541 million
1991	3.526 million
1996	3.626 million
2002	3.917 million

(The 2001 census was deferred because of the outbreak of foot-and-mouth disease.)

Post Office. The Irish Post Office came into existence in 1631. The penny post was introduced to Dublin on 10 October 1773, and the first secretary of the Irish Post Office was John Lees, appointed in 1784. The Duke of Richmond became the first Postmaster-General of the united services when the British and Irish Post Offices were amalgamated in 1831. The first transatlantic cable was laid in August 1858 but failed; it was not successful until eight years later, when the cable was completed between Newfoundland and Valencia Island, Co. Kerry.

The first telephone exchange was opened by the United Telephone Company on the top floor of Commercial Buildings, Dame Street, Dublin, in 1880. Ireland's first telephone connection to Britain—from Donaghadee, Co. Down, to Portpatrick, Wigtownshire—was laid in 1893; in 1913 a cable was laid from the martello tower in Howth, Co. Dublin, to Nefyn in Wales. The General Post Office was established in Sackville Street (O'Connell Street), Dublin; largely destroyed during the EASTER RISING (1916), during which it was the headquarters of the Provisional Government of the Irish Republic, it was reconstructed under the supervision of Robert Cochrane and reopened in 1929.

The air mail service was inaugurated at 7:15 a.m. on 26 August 1929 at Oranmore Airfield, Co. Galway, when Colonel Charles Russell flew via Dublin and Chester to Croydon, Surrey, arriving at 11:36. Air mail was first transported officially to the Continent on 22 October 1932, when the second leg of a Galway–Berlin mail flight was flown by Russell.

In October 1979 two interim boards, for posts and telecommunications, were appointed as a preliminary to the Post Office becoming a state-sponsored corporation, later renamed An Post.

pound, an enclosure in which cattle were kept in the eighteenth and early nineteenth centuries when they had been seized by a bailiff for non-payment of 'parish cess', church and other rates. The cattle were returned to their owners when the sums due were fully paid. 'Hibernicus', writing in 1800, commented:

> There is no public establishment so much used in Ireland as the Pound; and the fees paid to the bailiffs in charge of these for indulgences, or dues arbitrarily imposed, are comparatively considerable. In consequence of ill-treatment in those places of confinement, it happens not only generally, but almost universally, that the cattle are much injured, often depreciated a third or more in value, whereby the poor peasant is made a serious sufferer.

Power, John O'Connor (1848–1919), Fenian and politician (Nationalist); born in Ballinasloe, Co. Galway, educated locally. After emigrating to England, 1861, be worked as a painter in Rochdale, Lancashire, and established a small business. A member of the IRB, he took part in the raid on Chester Castle, 1867. Following his release from prison he entered St Jarlath's College, Tuam, where he studied for the priesthood and was an assistant teacher. When he joined the HOME RULE LEAGUE, 1873, his lead was followed by other Fenians, who agreed to give the constitutional approach a trial for four years. Member of Parliament for Co. Mayo, 1874–80, he was a prominent exponent of OBSTRUCTIONISM. While in the United States, 1876, he did not enjoy the confidence of JOHN DEVOY or CLAN NA GAEL, because of his parliamentary career. His decision to remain in Parliament after the IRB ordered an end to the experiment led to his expulsion from the Supreme Council, 1877.

Though his Fenian background was viewed with suspicion within the IRISH PARTY, Power was considered a candidate for the leadership in succession to ISAAC BUTT. In a letter to a newspaper, 6 December 1878, he accused Butt of being 'a traitor to the cause.' He claimed to have anticipated the NEW DEPARTURE by some ten years, saying it failed because of the death of GEORGE HENRY MOORE.

Power became the first member of Parliament to offer public support to the tenant-farmers' meeting at IRISHTOWN, Co. Mayo, 20 April 1879, and was shortly afterwards the first to join the LAND LEAGUE OF MAYO. His ambition to lead the Irish Party was shattered when PARNELL, who he described as a 'mediocrity', was chosen instead, May 1880. Following the 'KILMAINHAM TREATY' he moved closer to the Liberal Party; standing as a Liberal in the general election of 1885 (when Parnell called on Irish voters in Britain to support the Conservatives), he lost his seat. Defeated as an independent nationalist in Mayo West in 1892, he retired from politics.

Power, Patrick (1862–1951), clergyman (Catholic) and archaeologist; born in Callaghane, near Waterford, educated at Catholic University School and St John's College, Waterford. After his ordination, 1885, he ministered in Liverpool and in Australia. He was later attached to Waterford Cathedral, where he was diocesan inspector of schools, lecturer in archaeology at St Patrick's College, Maynooth, 1910–31, and professor of archaeology at University College, Cork, 1931–34. His publications include *Place Names of Decies* (1907), *Parochial History of Waterford and Lismore* (1912), *Place Names and Antiquities of South-East Cork* (1917), *A Short History of County Waterford* (1933), and *Waterford and Lismore* (1937). He also edited nineteen volumes of the *Journal of the Waterford and South-East of Ireland Archaeological Society.*

Powis Commission, the Royal Commission of Inquiry into Primary Education in Ireland, under the chairmanship of Lord Powis. It met from February 1868 to May 1870 and consisted of seven Catholic, five Church of Ireland and two Presbyterian representatives. Together with ten assistant commissioners, they examined the system of NATIONAL EDUCATION, producing eight volumes of evidence and conclusions. The commission's recommendations included payment by results and compulsory attendance; it also recommended that local contributions be made towards primary schooling, and that varying textbooks should be allowed. An important recommendation was that where average daily attendance was less than twenty-five pupils a school should be allowed to become denominational in effect; this enabled schools owned by Catholic religious orders to become part of the national education system. The commission also recommended the virtual abolition of the MODEL SCHOOLS.

Nearly all the commission's recommendations were gradually implemented, including payment by results, though this differed from the system in England in that only a portion of the teachers' salaries was dependent on results.

Praeger, R. L. [Robert Lloyd] (1865–1953), naturalist; born in Holywood, Co. Down, son a Dutch businessman, educated at QUB. He was engaged on harbour and water engineering works, 1886–92, and was then appointed assistant librarian of Trinity College, Dublin, 1893, librarian of the ROYAL IRISH ACADEMY, 1903, and librarian of the NATIONAL LIBRARY, 1920–24. He was president of the National Trust of Ireland from 1928 and president of the RIA, 1931–34. A self-taught botanist, his research mostly carried out at weekends, he was active in the founding of the *Irish Naturalist,* of which he became editor, and was instrumental in setting up the Fauna and Flora Committee of the RIA. He was chairman of the RIA Committee for Quaternary Research in Ireland (whose field assistants, appointed by Professor Knud Jessen, included Frank Mitchell). He discovered the Neolithic tombs at Carrowkeel, Co. Sligo. His works include *Irish Topographical Botany* (1901), *The Way That I Went* (1937), *Some Irish Naturalists* (1950), and *Natural History of Ireland* (1951).

'praties and point', a fanciful 'dish' among the rural poor of the eighteenth and nineteenth centuries: when only a small portion of salt remained, the potato, instead of being dipped in the salt, was, 'as a sort of indulgence to the fancy,' pointed at it instead. A variation was to keep a portion of meat either on or hanging above the table; the potato was rubbed against the meat to give it a flavour.

Pre-Cursor Society, founded by DANIEL O'CONNELL in 1838 to seek reforming legislation for Ireland with the implied threat that, if not granted, a full demand for Repeal would be made. (Many of O'Connell's followers were under the misapprehension that the title meant that the society would engage in cursing the government.) At this point O'Connell and the Repeal Party had been in an alliance with the Whigs for three years (see LICHFIELD HOUSE COMPACT), and the weakness of the Whig ministry led by VISCOUNT MELBOURNE made it opportune for O'Connell's demands. He believed that reforms would precede Repeal. (See also REPEAL ASSOCIATION.)

Presentation Sisters, an order of nuns founded in 1776 by Honoria (Nano) Nagle (1728–1784). Primarily a teaching order, they were instructed by the founder to devote themselves to the education and care of the poor. The order later spread around the world.

Presidents of Ireland. (1) *President of Dáil Éireann* (1919–22). This was the title given to ÉAMON DE VALERA by the first DÁIL ÉIREANN, April 1919, though the office was in fact that of prime minister. During de Valera's visit to the United States, 1919–20, he was called President of the Irish Republic, an office to which his followers elected him after they had rejected the Anglo-Irish Treaty (1921), January 1922. De Valera resigned the Presidency of Dáil Éireann on 9 January 1921 and lost the election the same day to ARTHUR GRIFFITH (60 to 58), who held the office until his death in August 1922. Griffith was succeeded by W. T. COSGRAVE, who was also chairman of the PROVISIONAL GOVERNMENT.

When the Irish Free State came into existence, December 1922, the head of government was called President of the Executive Council (1922–37). Cosgrave held the post from

December 1922 to March 1932, when de Valera succeeded him. During this period the head of state was the GOVERNOR-GENERAL OF THE IRISH FREE STATE.

(2) *President of Ireland* (1937–). The title President of Ireland designates the head of state under the Constitution of Ireland (1937). The President is a member of the OIREACHTAS and appoints the Taoiseach (on conditions laid down by the Constitution). On the Taoiseach's advice, the President accepts or terminates the appointment of members of the Government and summons and dissolves Dáil Éireann.

The President's primary function is to act as guardian of the Constitution (in consultation with the COUNCIL OF STATE), to sign bills into law, and to perform the symbolic duties of head of state. The President is nominal head of the Defence Forces, and officers hold their commission from him or her. A number of additional powers are given to the President under the Constitution, including the power to refer any bill to the Supreme Court (with the exception of money bills and bills proposing to amend the Constitution) and to call a referendum on a bill at the request of a majority of Seanad Éireann and not less than one-third of Dáil Éireann if they instruct the President not to approve it on the grounds that it 'contains a proposal of such national importance that the will of the people thereon ought to be ascertained.' The President has 'absolute discretion' in refusing dissolution of the Dáil to a Taoiseach who has lost a majority or who chooses to interpret a defeat as a loss of confidence. Impeachment of the President requires a vote by a two-thirds majority of the Oireachtas. The Presidents of Ireland have been DR DOUGLAS HYDE, 1938–45, SEÁN T. O'KELLY, 1945–59, ÉAMON DE VALERA, 1959–73, ERSKINE CHILDERS, 1973–74, CEARBHALL Ó DÁLAIGH, 1974–76, PATRICK HILLERY, 1976–90, MARY ROBINSON, 1990–97, and MARY MCALEESE, 1997–. De Valera was the only person to hold all the offices of President of Dáil Éireann, President of the Executive Council, and President of Ireland.

Primary Valuation, popularly known as the Griffith Valuation, carried out between 1852 and 1865 under the Valuation (Ireland) Act (1852), directed by RICHARD GRIFFITH. This valuation placed the assessment of rates for the administration of the Poor Law on a uniform basis for the whole country, replacing the unsatisfactory POOR LAW VALUATION. Rates paid under the Primary Valuation were a substantial source of revenue for local government.

For the Primary Valuation a distinction was made between tenements (holdings) that consisted of land only and those on which houses or other buildings had been erected; land and buildings were valued separately. The net annual valuation of a tenement was defined as 'the rent for which, one year with another,' the holding might 'in its actual state be reasonably expected to let from year to year with cost of repairs, insurance, maintenance, rates, taxes and all other public charges except the tithe rent being paid by the tenement.' Land values were calculated on the basis of current prices, taking into account the fertility of the soil (and not according to the prices of 1850). Pastureland was to be valued at the price per acre proportionate to the number of cattle and sheep it might be capable of grazing during a year, according to the price per head prevailing in the district for grazing. In addition, the quality of the 'herbage' and of permanent improvements (roads, drainage, and fences) was noted. Other considerations, such as 'peculiar local circumstances,' climate, elevation, and shelter favourable to agriculture, would lead to an increase in valuation; where the 'peculiar local circumstances' were unfavourable there was to be a reduction.

The Valuation Act became the basic legislation for valuation. Only two comprehensive revaluations have been undertaken, by the cities of Dublin, 1908–15, and Waterford, 1924–26. Private dwellings were no longer liable for rates after 1 January 1978, when that source of finance became a charge on central funds. (See also LOCAL GOVERNMENT.)

Príomh-Aire, the title given to ÉAMON DE VALERA by the first DÁIL ÉIREANN, January 1919. Though literally meaning 'prime minister', the title in English was President of Dáil Éireann. Following the creation of the Irish Free State, December 1922, the head of government was called President of the Executive Council.

Prior, James (Jim) (born 1927), British politician (Conservative). As Secretary of State for Northern Ireland, 1981–84, Prior assumed office towards the end of the HUNGER STRIKES. He conceded the right of paramilitary prisoners to wear their own clothes. The killing of a member of Parliament, Rev. Robert Bradford (Ulster Unionist Party), led to loyalist demands for tougher security measures and provoked the rise of the 'Third Force', led by REV. IAN PAISLEY. Prior's principal initiative was 'rolling devolution': this envisaged an elected Assembly that would at first have a consultative and scrutiny role, later extended to the devolution of one or more local departments, all to depend on 'cross-community support'. While the DUP was prepared to accept this, the ULSTER UNIONIST PARTY and SDLP were hostile, and the Irish government, and even Prior's own government, were critical. In the event, Sinn Féin, contesting its first Stormont election, won five seats, with 10 per cent of the vote, and then boycotted the Assembly, as did the SDLP. The Assembly was dissolved in 1986 by Prior's successor, TOM KING.

Prison Bars, a paper published by the WOMEN'S PRISONERS' DEFENCE LEAGUE, 1937–38. It attempted to attract support for the release of republicans imprisoned by the de Valera government in 1936 and later.

Programmes for Economic Expansion (1958–72). The three Programmes for Economic Expansion were for the periods 1958–63, 1963–68, and 1969–72. The catalyst was the document *Economic Development*, written by the secretary of the Department of Finance, T. K. WHITAKER. This led to a white paper of the same name, written by CHARLES MURRAY of the Department of Finance, 11 November 1958.

Designed to 'accelerate progress by strengthening public confidence after the stagnation of the 1950s, indicating the opportunities for development and encouraging a progressive and expansionist outlook,' the First Programme for Economic Expansion (1958–63) was adopted at an opportune moment to make maximum use of renewed world economic activity. During this period national income rose by 2 per cent, compared with 0.5 per cent between 1952 and 1958. Real incomes rose by 4 per cent. This new-found prosperity was due to a rise in net agricultural output, which increased by 9 per cent during the 1960s, and to manufacturing industry, where the value of output rose by 82 per cent in the period 1959–68. The value of exports in 1960 was the highest for thirty years.

The Second Programme for Economic Expansion (1963–68), drawn up by Whitaker and SEÁN LEMASS, capitalised on the economic growth achieved during the period of the first programme. It set out to 'achieve the maximum sustainable rate of growth' to provide the rising standards made possible by the first programme. One significant accompaniment of the second programme was the reorganising of the education system by the Minister for Education, DONOGH O'MALLEY, prompted by the report INVESTMENT IN EDUCATION, written by PATRICK LYNCH.

The Third Programme for Economic Expansion (1969–72), published as *Economic and Social Development* (1969), introduced by JACK LYNCH, sought to take account of the social changes that had accompanied the revitalisation of the economy. Drawn up against the background of the National Industrial Economic Council's *Report on Full Employment,* which sought a growth rate of 17 per cent for the three-year period, the programme projected an increase of 16,000 in employment and a reduction of emigration to an annual level of 12,000–13,000. A population of more than 3 million for the 26 counties was projected for 1972 (the 1971 census revealed a population of 2.978 million). The third programme collapsed in the face of an international depression. In 1973 the FIANNA FÁIL government lost office to a coalition that did not attempt expansionist programmes in the prevailing adverse economic conditions.

Progressive Democrats, a political party founded on 21 December 1985 by DESMOND O'MALLEY and MARY HARNEY, both former members of FIANNA FÁIL. While largely a reaction to the founders' disenchantment with CHARLES HAUGHEY, the party's policies—substantial tax reductions, privatisation, fiscal rectitude, and cuts in public expenditure—attracted the more conservative elements in FINE GAEL; the PDs soon had twice as many former members of Fine Gael as of Fianna Fáil. The party's fourteen seats following the 1987 general election made it the third-largest party in Dáil Éireann (with two more seats than the LABOUR PARTY) and denied Haughey a majority. On 13 January 1988 the party announced that it would drop the definition of the national territory in articles 2 and 3 of the Constitution of Ireland in its draft version of a constitution for a 'new republic', replacing it with an 'aspiration' towards a united Ireland; it also proposed dropping references in the Constitution to God (but later restored this).

The party was reduced to six seats after the general election of 1989, once more denying power to Haughey. For the first time in the history of his party, Haughey conceded the principle of coalition, forming a government with the PDs, 12 July 1989. The smaller party received two full ministerial portfolios (O'Malley as Minister for Industry and

Commerce and Bobby Molloy as Minister for Energy), a junior portfolio (Mary Harney at the Department of the Environment and Local Government), and seats in Seanad Éireann.

Forcing Haughey's resignation, January 1992, the PDs entered a short-lived coalition with his successor, ALBERT REYNOLDS; this government fell, 5 November 1992, after O'Malley and two colleagues withdrew following an allegation by Reynolds, 27 October, that O'Malley was 'dishonest' in his evidence to the BEEF TRIBUNAL.

The PDs secured ten seats in the ensuing election. O'Malley announced his retirement from leadership of the party, 5 October 1993, and a week later was succeeded by Mary Harney, who, defeating PAT COX (7 to 3), became the first woman to head a political party in the South.

In the 1997 general election the party was reduced to four seats. Harney led it into coalition with BERTIE AHERN, who appointed her Tánaiste and Minister for Enterprise, Trade and Employment, together with two ministers of state, Bobby Molloy (Housing) and Liz O'Donnell (Foreign Affairs). Buoyed by the 'Celtic Tiger' economy, the December 1998 budget implemented the PDs' tax credit policy. In the local government elections of June 1999 the party had thirty-two councillors elected.

The PDs won eight seats in the general election of 17 May 2002 and re-entered coalition with Fianna Fáil.

The party's share of first-preference votes and seats was:

	First-preference votes	Seats
1987	11.8%	14
1989	5.5%	6
1992	4.7%	10
1997	4.7%	4
2002	4.0%	8

Progressive Unionist Party, a party founded in Belfast by W. J. Stewart to contest the general election of 1938. It was non-sectarian and, offering a radical housing programme and demanding an end to the high rate of unemployment, hoped to attract the Catholic (Nationalist) vote but was unable to break the hold of the ULSTER UNIONIST PARTY.

The second party of this name was formed in 1979 from the Independent Unionist Group (mainly in the Shankill Road area of Belfast) by DAVID ERVINE and GUSTY SPENCE as the political wing of the ULSTER VOLUNTEER FORCE. In June 1994 Hugh Smyth became the first PUP lord mayor of Belfast. The party called on loyalists to 'give peace a chance' after the Provisional IRA ceasefire, 31 August 1994. In October 1994 PUP leaders entered the Maze Prison to meet loyalist paramilitary prisoners to discuss a possible loyalist ceasefire after the Combined Loyalist Military Command announced a ceasefire on 13 October. In November the PUP advised people to discuss their problems with the RUC rather than with paramilitary groups. The party held meetings with government officials over reform of the RUC and the repeal of emergency legislation. It rejected DAVID TRIMBLE's suggestion that loyalists should put moral pressure on the Provisional IRA by handing in weapons.

After the bomb explosion at Canary Wharf, London, 9 February 1996, marking the end of the Provisional IRA ceasefire, the PUP advised loyalists to stay calm. It remained active in the peace talks that produced the BELFAST AGREEMENT (1998), calling for a yes vote in the referendum in May to ratify the agreement. In the elections in June for the new Assembly two members of the PUP were elected, for North Belfast and East Belfast, and supported David Trimble as (acting) First Minister.

Property Defence Association, founded in December 1880 to oppose the LAND LEAGUE, under the chairmanship of Lord Courtown. Its object was to 'uphold the rights of property against organised combinations to defraud and to maintain freedom of contract and liberty of actions.' Other leading members were Lord Castletown, Lord Dunraven and Mount Earl, Lord Rossmore, Colonel Nugent Everard, and A. H. SMITH-BARRY. The association served writs on tenants, provided caretakers on cleared holdings, combated boycotting, and employed a reserve force to help with evictions. It was reactivated under Smith-Barry to fight the PLAN OF CAMPAIGN when it opened a special shop at Mitchelstown, Co. Cork, to supply boycotted farms with provisions.

proportional representation. The Proportional Representation Society of Ireland was established in April 1911, with ARTHUR GRIFFITH among the founder-members. The first experiment with the system was made in Co. Sligo in 1919, and it was used officially for the first time in the local government elections of January 1920. Its first use in a general election was for the new Parliament of Northern Ireland, May 1921. However, it was abandoned in the North in 1929 and the constituencies reorganised under the straight-vote system. PR was chosen for elections in the South during negotiations leading to the ANGLO-IRISH TREATY, December 1921: the representatives of DÁIL ÉIREANN, in particular Griffith, the leader of the delegation, and representatives of the British government favoured the system as best suited to providing representation for minorities (in this case Unionists).

As used in the Republic, the PR system operates by means of the single transferable vote in multi-member constituencies. Each constituency elects at least three deputies, and all constituencies have approximately the same ratio of voters to seats. Voters indicate their choice by writing numbers, in order of preference, against the names on the ballot paper. Having marked their first preference with '1', they may then vote for as many more candidates as they wish by marking them '2', '3', etc. (Any paper that does not contain a '1' against a candidate's name is invalid.) A quota for election is set according to the Droop formula:

$$\frac{\textit{number of valid votes}}{\textit{number of seats} + 1} + 1$$

If no-one is elected on the first count, votes are transferred according to the preferences expressed, until all the seats are filled. A candidate's surplus votes when the quota is reached are distributed proportionately to the next available preferences indicated; when there are no surpluses to be distributed and seats remain to be filled, the candidate with the lowest number of votes is eliminated and that candidate's votes redistributed in accordance with the preferences indicated. This process continues until all the seats are filled. It is possible, therefore, for a candidate to be elected without reaching the quota.

There have been two unsuccessful attempts by FIANNA FÁIL governments to abolish PR and replace it with the single non-transferable vote in single-member constituencies. In the referendum of 1959 (held on the same day as the presidential election, won by the Fianna Fáil candidate ÉAMON DE VALERA), the result was 48 per cent in favour of change and 52 per cent against. In the second referendum, 1968, the result was 39 per cent in favour of change and 61 per cent against.

Protection of Persons and Property (Ireland) Act (1881), COERCION legislation introduced by W. E. FORSTER to deal with the LAND LEAGUE (see AGRARIAN CRIME). From its introduction, on 24 January 1881, the bill was opposed by the IRISH PARTY, because it proposed to suspend the law in selected 'proclaimed' districts. On 25 January the Irish members obstructed the bill on its first reading and forced the House of Commons into a 22-hour sitting; on 31 January they forced the house into a marathon 41-hour sitting, the second-longest on record. The Liberal government reacted with a motion of closure and guillotined the debate, 2 February. Within a few days the first reading was passed, and the Irish members had demonstrated the classic use of OBSTRUCTIONISM for the last time. The bill became law in March.

Protestant and Catholic Encounter, an organisation established in 1968 to bring together people of differing religious and political affiliations to promote harmony and good will. More than thirty groups throughout Northern Ireland were involved between 1973 and 1976, but by 1999 this had fallen to four: Newcastle, Portadown, Lisburn, and Belfast.

Protestant Colonisation Society, formed in 1830 when emigration was threatening the Protestant ASCENDANCY in Ulster. The society, which originated on the lands of Sir Edmund Hayes in Co. Donegal, sought to ensure that lands vacated through emigration or other causes would continue to be occupied by Protestants. Its members included landed proprietors, parsons, members of the military, and fellows of Trinity College. Among its rules were the following:

> 4th: Every tenant distinctly understands and agrees, that no Roman Catholic, under any pretence what ever, shall be allowed to reside or be employed in any Colony of the Society.
>
> 5th: Every colonist who shall marry a Roman Catholic shall, after due notice, retire from the colony, he being permitted to dispose of or carry away his private property.

Seven Scottish families were invited to settle and had slated dwellings erected for them. The foundations of a Protestant church were laid out and arrangements made to increase the number of settlers, but the scheme was abandoned after a few years, and the original families returned to Scotland impoverished. Several similar organisations were founded over the next decade, most notably the Protestant Tenantry Society, 1841.

Protestant Home Rule Association, founded by CHARLES HUBERT OLDHAM and Edward Perceval Wright in 1886 to bring together Protestant supporters of the (first) HOME RULE BILL, introduced by W. E. GLADSTONE. At an early meeting in Ballymoney, Co. Antrim, speakers proclaimed that the self-constituted Provisional Government of Ulster was not wholly representative of Protestant opinion. The association failed to gather popular support and soon disappeared.

Protestant Nationalist Party, founded in Ulster to fight the general election of 1892. It secured nine seats (in Co. Fermanagh, North Tyrone, North Antrim, and North Derry), at the expense of the IRISH PARTY. Led by Rev. McAuley Brown, the party attracted Protestant liberals who were anti-Tory and anti-landlord. It looked for the 'expropriation of the landlords,' who should be forced to sell out to their tenants. It was not successful in securing a sizeable Catholic vote and was unable to combat Unionist-Conservative influence in Ulster, and it disappeared at the turn of the century.

Protestant Task Force, a small paramilitary group established in the 1970s, suspected of involvement in the murder of republicans. In November 1974 a spokesperson claimed that the organisation had killed twenty-eight people in a couple of months. Claiming to be restricted to ex-servicemen, it denied involvement with any of the prominent paramilitary groups.

Protestant Telegraph, a propagandist paper founded by Noel Doherty and REV. IAN PAISLEY, 13 February 1966. It attacked the Church of Ireland, Catholicism, TERENCE O'NEILL, and the governments of Northern Ireland.

Protestant Unionist Party, established in the 1960s and led by REV. IAN PAISLEY until it was absorbed into his DEMOCRATIC UNIONIST PARTY. On 24 February 1969 five candidates designated Protestant Unionist, including Paisley and Rev. William Beattie, stood unsuccessfully in the election for the Parliament of Northern Ireland. Both were successful as Protestant Unionists in by-elections on 16 April 1970 (Paisley in Bannside in the by-election caused by the resignation of the Prime Minister, TERENCE O'NEILL, and Beattie in Antrim South). Standing as a Protestant Unionist, Paisley won the British House of Commons seat for Antrim North on 18 June 1970.

Provisional Government of Southern Ireland, 16 January to 6 December 1922, established under article 17 of the ANGLO-IRISH TREATY (1921) for the administration of the 26-county area pending the formal establishment of the IRISH FREE STATE. It was granted

> the powers and machinery requisite for the discharge of its duties, provided that every member of such Provisional Government shall have signified in writing his or her acceptance of this instrument [the Treaty]. But this arrangement shall not continue in force beyond the expiration of twelve months from the date hereof [6 December 1921].

The government, formed on 14 January 1922 under the chairmanship of MICHAEL COLLINS, formally received its authority from the Lord Lieutenant of Ireland, VISCOUNT FITZALAN OF DERWENT, on 16 January and held full power from 1 April.

Membership of the Provisional Government overlapped with membership of the Ministry (government) of DÁIL ÉIREANN, which was not recognised by Britain. The Provisional Government did not answer to the Dáil; and because every member of the Provisional Government had undertaken to uphold the Treaty, its authority was not recognised by republicans, led by ÉAMON DE VALERA. This led to some confusion, as the republicans addressed their queries to members of the Provisional Government only in their capacity as ministers in the Dáil government and not as ministers of the Provisional Government.

The first Provisional Government was as follows, with the office held in the Dáil government in brackets:

Michael Collins, Chairman and Finance [Finance]
Éamonn Duggan, Home Affairs [Home Affairs]
W. T. Cosgrave, Local Government [Local Government]
Joseph McGrath, Industries [Industries]
Kevin O'Higgins, Economic Affairs [Economic Affairs]
Fionán Lynch, Education
Patrick Hogan, Agriculture [Agriculture]
J. J. Walsh, Postmaster-General (from April 1922)
Eoin MacNeill, minister without portfolio
Hugh Kennedy, Law Officer

Two loans (£1 million from the Bank of Ireland and £500,000 from the British exchequer) helped finance government administration. In addition to its financial problems, the Provisional Government had to finance the new army in the CIVIL WAR that broke out in June 1922.

Before the Civil War the Provisional Government had responsibility for drafting the CONSTITUTION OF THE IRISH FREE STATE (1922) and for arranging the general election of that year (held on 16 June). In May an agreement on the 'PACT ELECTION' was reached between Collins and de Valera; however, the Constitution was not published until the day of the election, and two days before the election Collins repudiated the pact. The election resulted in a victory for the Provisional Government.

Following the deaths of Griffith (12 August) and Collins (22 August), WILLIAM T. COSGRAVE assumed office as President of Dáil Éireann and Chairman of the Provisional Government. This government, which took office in September, also became the government of the third Dáil. It was:

W. T. Cosgrave, Chairman and Finance
Kevin O'Higgins, Home Affairs
Desmond Fitzgerald, Foreign Affairs
Richard Mulcahy, National Defence
Ernest Blythe, Local Government
Joseph McGrath, Labour, Industry and Commerce, Economic Affairs
Eoin MacNeill, Education
Patrick Hogan, Agriculture
J. J. Walsh, Postmaster-General
Hugh Kennedy, Law Officer

When the Irish Free State came into existence, 6 December 1922, the Provisional Government became its first government, known as the Executive Council. (See also GOVERNMENTS OF IRELAND.)

Public Record Office of Ireland, established in 1867 under the historian JOHN T. GILBERT and housed in the FOUR COURTS, Dublin, containing records relating to life in Ireland since 1210. Most of the material was destroyed in the burning of the Four Courts in 1922. The surviving material, gathered from central and local government offices and, to a lesser extent, from private sources, is available in a variety of forms, ranging from parchment rolls to microfilm. The office was incorporated in the NATIONAL ARCHIVES in 1986.

Public Safety Acts, a series of acts introduced by the CUMANN NA NGAEDHEAL government from 1923 until 1927 in response to the unsettled conditions in the country resulting from the activities of the IRA. The Public Safety (Emergency Powers) Act (1923), Public Safety (Emergency Powers) (No. 2) Act (1923), Public Safety (Punishment of Offences) Temporary Act (1924) and Public Safety (Emergency Powers) Act (1926) were introduced by KEVIN O'HIGGINS, Minister for Home Affairs (Minister for Justice after 1924). The Public Safety Act (1927) was introduced following O'Higgins's assassination.

Though the anti-Treaty section of the IRA had surrendered in May 1923, bringing the CIVIL WAR to an end, O'Higgins considered it necessary to introduce a Public Safety Act later in the year (27 September). The act, which came into force on 15 October, authorised the minister to continue INTERNMENT and also granted powers to arrest and detain anyone considered a danger to public safety. *Habeas corpus* had been suspended during the Civil War, but when the Appeal Court granted an application of *habeas corpus,* the government did not consider that the state of the country warranted the full restoration of legal rights. Under the act, which became law on 1 August, *habeas corpus* was again suspended and applications for the release of internees refused.

The general state of lawlessness during the WAR OF INDEPENDENCE and Civil War continued during 1924; between August 1923 and February 1924 there were 738 cases of arson and armed robbery. The 1924 act renewed the minister's powers of detention and arrest and renewed the penalty of flogging, together with imprisonment, for arson and armed robbery. O'Higgins was also concerned at the increase in other forms of law-breaking. Some seven thousand decrees for debt remained to be enforced, as the payment of rents, taxes and other debts had virtually ceased during the struggle for independence. The new act gave increased powers to sheriffs engaged in the recovery of debts. By the end of the year it was felt that the acts of 1923 and 1924 had led to an improvement in conditions, and towards the end of this period some 12,000 republican prisoners had been released from internment.

Towards the end of 1925 there was an upsurge in republican activity in protest at the shelving of the report of the BOUNDARY COMMISSION. Republicans who had anticipated the ending of partition were bitterly disappointed when a financial agreement between the Free State and the British and Northern Ireland governments ensured the permanence of the border. In 1926 twelve Garda barracks were attacked and two unarmed gardaí killed. The government reacted with another Public Safety Act, which again suspended *habeas corpus* and gave the minister new powers of detention. Following O'Higgins's assassination by republicans in July 1927 the government introduced a new Public Safety Act, which outlawed any organisation dedicated to the overthrow of the state or to the use of arms. Severe penalties for membership of such organisations were laid down, and the authorities were granted extensive powers of search and detention. A Special Court could impose the death penalty or life imprisonment for the unlawful possession of arms. This act remained in force until December 1928.

The CONSTITUTION (AMENDMENT NO. 17) ACT (1931) authorised the establishment of a Military Tribunal and the proscription of approximately a dozen organisations. While ÉAMON DE VALERA opposed the legislation when he was in opposition and suspended it on coming to power, March 1932, he revived it for use against the IRA and the BLUESHIRTS.

Q

Quakers' Central Relief Committee, founded in Dublin on behalf of the Society of Friends by JAMES HACK TUKE and Marcus Goodbody, 13 November 1846; the secretary and joint treasurer was Joseph Bewley. The 24-member committee organised collections in Britain and America and oversaw the distribution and storing of food and clothing for victims of the GREAT FAMINE (1845–49). It arranged the building and equipping of a fishing station, the establishment of a model farm and agricultural school at Colmanstown, Co. Galway, the provision of grants to industrial schools, and the promotion of alternative forms of agriculture. Branches of the Society of Friends undertook other forms of famine relief, including the installation and operation of soup kitchens. The Central Relief Committee, having expended £198,326, disbanded in June 1849.

Quarter-Acre Clause (also called the 'Gregory Clause'), a clause inserted in section 10 of the Poor Law Extension Act (1847) through the efforts of Sir William Gregory. Stating that holders of more than a quarter of an acre could not be deemed destitute and were therefore ineligible for outdoor or indoor relief, it became a source of acute distress during the GREAT FAMINE (1845–49). Despite an opinion from the Attorney-General, Jonathan Henn, that the wife and children and, in cases of destitution, the leaseholder himself could obtain such relief, in practice they were generally refused. In spite of starvation, many small tenant-farmers remained on their holdings, aware that should they vacate them to pursue relief the landlord would level their cabins. The legislation resulted in cases of husbands abandoning their families and even of parents abandoning their children. The prohibition relating to workhouse relief was repealed by the Poor Relief (Ireland) Act (1862), while that relating to outdoor relief remained in force until 1921.

Queen's Colleges, established under the Provincial Colleges Act (1845) in an attempt to meet the demand for a system of higher education for Catholics within the broader demands of the REPEAL ASSOCIATION. In 1850, with a capital grant of £100,000 and an annual endow ment of £30,000, the three non-residential colleges at Cork, Belfast and Galway formed the Queen's University. The colleges were not permitted to have a theological faculty, but there was provision for private endowment of a chair of theology. A Senate and a Visitorial Board administered each college, and students' religious beliefs were protected from tutorial interference.

From their inception, the colleges were embroiled in controversy. Their non-denominational character earned them the label 'godless colleges', for which they were denounced by DANIEL O'CONNELL and the Catholic Archbishop of Tuam, JOHN MACHALE, but they had the support of YOUNG IRELAND and some members of the Catholic hierarchy, including Archbishop Crolly of Armagh and Archbishop DANIEL MURRAY of Dublin. Following a visit by MacHale to Rome, 1847, the colleges were condemned as a 'grave danger to faith and morals' and in papal rescripts (decrees) of 1847 and 1848 as 'dangerous to faith and morals.' The death within a short period of both Crolly and Murray resulted in the growth of opposition to the colleges, which were condemned by the SYNOD OF THURLES (1850) and further denounced by Rome in 1851. The more extreme element within the hierarchy refused the sacraments to parents who allowed their children to attend the colleges. Despite such formidable opposition, the Cork and Galway colleges survived to be incorporated in the NATIONAL UNIVERSITY OF IRELAND, 1908, while Queen's College, Belfast, became Queen's University.

Queen's County, the name given by English planters to the territory of Co. Laois, in honour of Queen Mary, 1553–58, during the Plantation of Laois and Offaly. It was used officially until the establishment of the Irish Free State, 1922, when it was replaced by Laois. The county town, Maryborough (after Queen Mary), was renamed Port Laoise.

Quinn, Ruairí (born 1946), architect and politician (Labour Party); born in Dublin, educated at UCD (architecture) and at Athens. A lecturer in architecture at University College, Dublin, 1971–82, he worked in a number of architectural practices before establishing Ruairí Quinn and Associates, 1987–93. A member of Dublin City Council, 1974–77, he was a member of Seanad Éireann as a Taoiseach's nominee, 1976–77 and 1981–82. A member of Dáil Éireann from 1977, he was Minister of State at the Department of the Environment with special responsibility for urban affairs and housing, 1982–83, Minister for Labour, 1983–84, Minister for the Public Service, 1986–87, Minister for Enterprise and Employment, 1993–94, and Minister for Finance, 1994–97. He was director of elections for MARY ROBINSON's successful presidential campaign, 1990, and for the Labour Party in the local government elections that year. He succeeded DICK SPRING as leader of the Labour Party, 1997, resigning after the general election of 2002 (when the party retained its twenty-one seats), being succeeded by PAT RABBITTE.

R

Rabbitte, Pat (born 1949), politician (Workers' Party, Democratic Left, Labour Party); born in Ballindine, Co. Mayo, educated at UCG. He was president of the Union of Students in Ireland and an official of the ITGWU before entering full-time politics as a member of the Labour Party and later of the Workers' Party. Elected to Dublin County Council, 1985–91, and South Dublin County Council, 1991, he was elected to Dáil Éireann (Workers' Party), 1989. A founder-member of Democratic Left, he was a noted Dáil debater. He was Minister of State at the Department of Enterprise, Trade and Employment, 1994–97, with special responsibility for commerce, science, and technology, and chief whip of Democratic Left. He played a leading role in questioning representatives of financial institutions during the inquiry by the Public Accounts Committee into bogus non-resident bank accounts (see DIRT INQUIRY). He succeeded RUAIRÍ QUINN as leader of the Labour Party, October 2002.

Radio Telefís Éireann (RTE). The national broadcasting service began transmission under the radio call-sign 2RN (based on a phonetic rendering of the last words of the line 'Come back to Erin'). The station was opened by DR DOUGLAS HYDE at 7:45 p.m. on 1 January 1926. The first director was Séamus Clandillon (1878–1944), who held the post until 1935, being succeeded by Dr T. J. Kiernan; the first announcer was Séamus Hughes, and the first director of music was Dr Vincent O'Brien. The radio orchestra, which began with four members in 1926, had increased to sixty-two by 1948; by 2001 the music division would encompass the National Symphony Orchestra, RTE Concert Orchestra, RTE Philharmonic Choir, RTE Vanbrugh String Quartet, and Cór na nÓg. The Radio Éireann Players, a repertory company established by Roibeard Ó Faracháin in 1947, gave their first stage performance as a company in October 1978.

An order by the Revenue Commissioners on 23 November 1925 decreed that 'wireless telegraphic sets assembled in cases or cabinets and composed wholly or partly of wood are liable to duty as furniture at a rate of thirty-three and one-third per cent,' a decision based on the principle that sets could be removed from cabinets, 'which cabinets would then become splendid articles of furniture.' Five thousand radio licences were issued in 1926, though official estimates claimed there were five times as many receivers.

The name of the service was changed to Radio Éireann in 1932. The same year the radio station moved to the General Post Office, Henry Street, Dublin, where it remained until 1974, when it moved to the new radio centre in Donnybrook, Dublin. The first RTE Authority, set up under the Broadcasting Authority Act (1960), assumed the functions of its predecessor, Comhairle Radio Éireann. The members of the first Authority were Éamonn Andrews (chairman), ERNEST BLYTHE, Áine Ní Cheannain, George Crosbie, James Fanning, Fintan Kennedy, Edward B. MacManus, and T. W. Moody.

The national television service was inaugurated on New Year's Eve, 1961, from the studios at Donnybrook. The title of the joint radio and television service was changed to Radio Telefís Éireann by the Broadcasting Authority (Amendment) Act (1966). Radio and television channels are financed by licence fees and advertising revenue. The Irish-language radio station, Raidió na Gaeltachta, began transmissions on 2 April 1972. Radio 2, later known as 2FM, began transmission on 31 May 1979. FM3 Classical Radio was replaced by Lyric FM, broadcasting from Limerick, on 1 May 1999. Radio One World was launched in March 2001; broadcasting from Cork, it caters for refugees, asylum-seekers, and other communities. A second television channel, Network 2, later renamed RTE2, began transmission on 2 November 1978. The Irish-language channel, Teilifís na Gaeilge, later renamed TG4, based in Baile na hAbhann, Co. Galway, opened on 31 October 1996.

railways. Ireland's first railway, the six-mile Dublin and Kingstown [Dún Laoghaire] Railway, was opened in 1834. The first sections of the Ulster Railway followed in 1839, and the Dublin and Drogheda in 1844. The railway speculation of the 1840s produced the principal trunk routes in the country. Dublin was linked with Cork in 1849, Galway in 1851, and Belfast in 1853. By 1900 the main railway companies were the Great Southern and Western Railway, Midland Great Western Railway of Ireland, Great Northern Railway (GNR), Dublin and South-Eastern Railway, Belfast and Northern Counties Railway, and Belfast and County Down Railway. In 1922, when the railway system was at its greatest extent, there were 3,454 route-miles, of which 2,896 miles were built to the Irish standard gauge of 5 feet 3 inches (1.6 m).

Following partition, southern railways amalgamated to form the Great Southern Railway (GSR), 1925. The GNR, whose lines straddled the border, continued its independent existence, as did the railway companies in Northern Ireland. In 1946 railways in the Republic were nationalised and amalgamated as part of Córas Iompair Éireann (CIE). In the late 1940s sections of the Belfast and Northern Counties Railway and Belfast and County Down Railway were taken over to form part of the Ulster Transport Authority (UTA). By the early 1950s the GNR was in financial difficulties. From 1952 to 1958 it was managed by a board with nominees from both governments; in 1958 this arrangement was ended and the company's assets were shared equally between the UTA and CIE.

Competition from road transport affected the traffic and profitability of railways from the 1920s. Despite a revival during the Second World War, falling business resulted in widespread closures in the 1950s and 60s. The 1970s saw a revival of interest, and the authorities north and south provided investment in rolling-stock, track, and facilities.

In addition to standard-gauge railways, Ireland possessed an extensive network of narrow-gauge railways, mainly in rural areas. The principal narrow-gauge systems were in Cos. Donegal, Antrim, Cavan, Leitrim, Cork, and Clare. The most celebrated narrow-gauge company was the West and South Clare Railway, serving Ennis, Milltown Malbay, Kilrush, and Kilkee, with a total of 53 miles of track. The railway was the subject of a popular song, 'Are ye right there, Michael?' (1902) which led the company to take a libel action against the writer, Percy French. Most narrow-gauge lines, built to a gauge of 3 feet (0.914 m) in the late nineteenth and early twentieth centuries, were early victims of road competition; all had closed by 1961. (See also LARTIGUE RAILWAY.)

Ralahine Agricultural and Manufacturing Co-operative Association, a co-operative society founded in 1831 by John Scott Vandeleur on his estate at Ralahine, Kilrush, Co. Clare, in the hope of weaning his tenants away from agrarian SECRET SOCIETIES. Influenced by the social reformer Robert Owen, he brought Thomas Craig from England to advise on the establishment of a commune similar to the one established by Owen at New Lanark, Scotland. The co-operative came into existence on 7 November 1831; its purpose was the acquisition of common capital and the mutual assurance of members 'against the evils of poverty, sickness, infirmity and old age, the attainment of a greater share of the comforts of life than the working class now possess, the mental and moral improvement of its adult members and the education of their children.'

The commune, consisting of seven married couples, twenty-one single men, five single women, four orphan boys, three orphan girls, and five infants under the age of nine—a total of fifty-two people—operated an estate of 618 acres, governed by a committee of nine, elected twice a year. Under an agreement between Vandeleur and the commune the estate and property were to remain his, at a rent of £700 per year, until the co-operative acquired the capital to purchase it. The commune also paid £200 per year for stock and equipment.

The co-operative lasted only two years, collapsing as a result of Vandeleur's reckless life; a noted gambler, he fled the country to avoid his creditors, who seized the estate. *The Irish Land and Labour Question: Illustrated in the History of Ralahine and Co-operative Farming* (1882) by Edward Thomas Craig was translated into several languages.

'Real IRA', an IRA splinter group, believed to be associated with the 32-County Sovereignty Committee, which was founded on 7 December 1997 after SINN FÉIN joined all-party talks in September. The group regarded the Provisional IRA as having 'sold out' by taking part in the PEACE PROCESS. Opposed to the BELFAST AGREEMENT, it is believed to have been responsible for the bomb explosion at Omagh, Co. Tyrone, 15 August 1998, that killed 29 people and injured a further 310. Widespread condemnation forced the group into declaring a 'complete cessation of all military activity' in September; this left the 'CONTINUITY IRA' as the only republican paramilitary organisation on continued offensive. The British police, however, believed that members of the 'Real IRA' remained active in Britain during the period 2000–01 and were responsible for three bomb explosions in London: an explosion at Hammersmith Bridge, June 2000, a taxi bomb outside the head office of the BBC, March 2001, and an explosion at a postal sorting office, 14 April 2001. On 3 October 2000, Liam Campbell, a 39-year-old farmer from Co. Louth, the first person convicted of membership of the 'Real IRA', was sentenced to five years' imprisonment.

Recess Committee, established in 1895, on the proposal of SIR HORACE PLUNKETT, to consider the means by which Irish farmers could best be served and the manner in which suitable legislation could assist them; its meetings were held during the parliamentary recess. Members included the Unionist peers Lord Mayo and Lord Monteagle, THOMAS ANDREWS, FATHER THOMAS FINLAY, THOMAS P. GILL (secretary), TIMOTHY HARRINGTON, and JOHN REDMOND. The leader of the anti-Parnellites, JUSTIN MCCARTHY, declined to attend, as did the leader of the Ulster Unionists, E. J. SAUNDERSON. The committee's report favoured assistance for agriculture and recommended fostering a climate of self-sufficiency. Its recommendations led to the establishment of the Department of Agriculture and Technical Instruction, 1899.

Red Hand Commando, a shadowy loyalist paramilitary group launched in 1972, believed to have been involved in sectarian assassinations. Declared illegal in 1973, the following year it threatened to kill five Catholics for every Protestant killed in border areas. When members of loyalist paramilitary groups met the Secretary of State for Northern Ireland, MERLYN REES, 7 August 1974, delegates of the ULSTER VOLUNTEER FORCE claimed to speak on behalf of the Red Hand Commando, which announced a qualified ceasefire within a few days. Four years later it was still closely identified with the UVF. In 1991 it was thought that another obscure group, the Loyalist Retaliation and Defence Group, which threatened in September 1992 to renew its murder campaign if the Provisional IRA killed or wounded any more Protestant workers, had links to the Red Hand Commando, which claimed responsibility for the death of an alleged informer in east Belfast and was also held responsible for additional shootings. It was reported to be included in the COMBINED LOYALIST MILITARY COMMAND ceasefire during the early stages of the BROOKE-MAYHEW TALKS, 1991–92.

Red Hand Defenders, a dissident loyalist group believed to have been formed by members of the LOYALIST VOLUNTEER FORCE who rejected the LVF's 1998 ceasefire and token decommissioning of arms. Its main strength was in mid-Ulster (where the LVF had been formed by BILLY WRIGHT). It claimed responsibility for killing a member of the RUC with a blast bomb during the 'Right to March' parade in Portadown, September 1998, and for killing a Catholic in north Belfast the following month. The group admitted in March 1999 to killing the solicitor Rosemary Nelson, who had been legal adviser to the Garvaghy Road Residents' Association, involved in the protests against the march by the ORANGE ORDER from Drumcree Church in Portadown. Opposed to the BELFAST AGREEMENT (1988), the group declared that, from 14 February 1999, 'we withdraw completely our consent to be governed . . . the authority of the Assembly has been cancelled,' and urged republican paramilitary groups to begin decommissioning before further implementation of the agreement.

Redmond, John (1856–1918), politician (Irish Party); born at Kilrane, Co. Wexford, son of a Home Rule MP, educated at TCD. He was appointed to a clerkship in the House of Commons, London, until he was elected for New Ross, 1881. An able speaker, he established himself within the Irish Party and the NATIONAL LEAGUE as principal lieutenant of CHARLES STEWART PARNELL. During the period 1883–84 he toured Australia and the United States with his brother, WILLIAM H. K. REDMOND, collecting £30,000. Though called to the bar, he never practised. He supported Parnell during the split in 1890 and was leading only nine members by January 1892. He sat on the RECESS COMMITTEE and retained contact with influential Irish-Americans through visits to the United States, 1895 and 1899.

When the rise of the UNITED IRISH LEAGUE led to the reunification of the Irish Party, Redmond was accepted as leader, 1900. He sought concessions for Ireland until the opportunity to press for home rule arose in 1910, when H. H. ASQUITH needed Irish support to secure the PARLIAMENT ACT (1911). Redmond's support was assured in return for the (third) HOME RULE BILL.

Opposition to home rule from the ULSTER UNIONIST PARTY, led by SIR EDWARD CARSON, constituted a serious threat. Redmond rejected partition, as did the Unionists. While they were prepared finally to accept a measure of permanent exclusion from home rule, Redmond would concede nothing more than temporary exclusion. By the summer of 1914, with home rule to become law in September, Redmond was worried that any action by the IRISH VOLUNTEERS might lead to increased tension. He confronted Volunteer leaders in June 1914 with a demand for the right to nominate half the members of the Provisional Committee of the Volunteers, which was conceded.

Redmond and his chief lieutenant, JOHN DILLON, represented the Irish Party at the BUCKINGHAM PALACE CONFERENCE, July 1914. The Unionists were now prepared to settle for the exclusion of the six north-eastern counties from home rule, but Redmond rejected partition. The situation was unresolved when war broke out in August. In September, before its adoption, Asquith passed two emergency provisos: that home rule not come into operation until Parliament had an opportunity to make special provision for Ulster, and that the act be suspended for the duration of the war.

Redmond, having apparently secured home rule, was inundated with congratulatory messages from Ireland and abroad. He offered the services of the Irish Volunteers for internal defence, which was rejected by Asquith; in September, speaking at Woodenbridge, Co. Wicklow, he called on the Volunteers to assist Britain by joining the British army. The great majority—some 170,000—answered his call; the minority, dominated by the IRB, retained the title Irish Volunteers, while Redmond's followers became known as the NATIONAL VOLUNTEERS. In May 1915 Redmond declined a seat in the war cabinet, in which Carson became Attorney-General.

Redmond described the EASTER RISING (1916) as a 'German intrigue'. He had little sympathy with the leaders but added his plea to that of Dillon for leniency in the aftermath. The Prime Minister, DAVID LLOYD GEORGE, accepted Redmond's suggestion for the IRISH CONVENTION (1917–18) to resolve the problem of home rule. Redmond died during the convention, March 1918, at which he had represented the Irish Party. Later that year the party was annihilated at the polls by a rejuvenated SINN FÉIN under ÉAMON DE VALERA.

Redmond, William Archer (1886–1932), soldier and politician (Nationalist); born in Waterford, eldest son of JOHN REDMOND, educated at TCD and called to the bar. Member of Parliament for Co. Tyrone, 1910–18, during the First World War he served in the British army and was decorated for bravery, 1917. Member of Parliament for Co. Waterford from 1918 until 1922, when he was elected to Dáil Éireann as an independent, he founded the NATIONAL LEAGUE, 1926, which secured eight seats in the general election of June 1927, after which he committed the party's support to FIANNA FÁIL and the LABOUR PARTY in a motion of no confidence in the Cosgrave government. The motion was defeated, because of the absence of Redmond's supporter Alderman John Jinks (see JINKS AFFAIR). The National League was reduced to two seats after the general election of September 1927, and Redmond joined CUMANN NA NGAEDHEAL in 1931.

Redmond, William H. K. (1861–1917), politician (Irish Party); born in Kilrane, Co. Wexford, younger brother of JOHN REDMOND, educated at Clongowes Wood College, Co. Kildare. A member of Parliament, 1883–1917, he assisted his brother in several fund-raising trips on behalf of the IRISH PARTY, including a visit to Australia and the United States, 1883, during which they raised £30,000. He supported CHARLES STEWART PARNELL after the split in the Irish Party, 1890. He accompanied JOSEPH DEVLIN to the United States, February–June 1902, when they met President Theodore Roosevelt. Having established two hundred branches of the UNITED IRISH LEAGUE in America, he returned in 1905, when he also visited Australia. In June 1917 he was fatally wounded while leading the 5th Battalion of the Royal Irish Regiment in the taking of Messines Ridge, France. A collection of articles contributed to the *News Chronicle* (London) was posthumously published as *Trench Pictures from France* (1917).

Rees, Merlyn (born 1920), British politician (Labour Party). As Secretary of State for Northern Ireland, 1974–76, Rees arrived in office just after the UNITED ULSTER UNIONIST COALITION had won eleven of the twelve Northern Ireland seats in the British House of Commons, vindicating, as they saw it, their rejection of the power-sharing Executive of the Northern Ireland Assembly. Rees rejected the UUUC's demand for new elections. As the Provisional IRA intensified its bombing campaign, the ULSTER WORKERS' COUNCIL organised a general strike, which paralysed Northern Ireland. While Rees would not negotiate with the strikers (supported by paramilitary groups), neither would he use the British army to keep industry operating. When the strike brought down the Executive and the power-sharing experiment, Rees reintroduced direct rule from London.

He announced a Constitutional Convention to seek a political settlement during the following year. He piloted the Northern Ireland portions of the Prevention of Terrorism Act through the House of Commons in the wake of the Birmingham bomb explosions, 21 November 1974, under which people could now be deported from Britain to the Republic or Northern Ireland, or from Northern Ireland to the Republic. A pause in Provisional IRA activity over Christmas 1974 was a prelude to a ceasefire from 10 February 1975 until the following September. During this period, while Rees rejected an approach from the Provisional IRA through Northern Protestant clergymen who had met the military leadership at Feakle, Co. Clare, before Christmas, officials of the Northern Ireland Office did meet SINN FÉIN and IRA personnel, who co-operated in setting up 'incident centres' to liaise with government officials. His hope that the Provisional IRA would be 'politicised' by these contacts was ill-founded. The UUUC won a majority of seats in the Convention, which collapsed in 1976, ruining any prospect of power-sharing (multi-party government). Though the ceasefire ended in September, Rees released the last of the republican internees. He was a member of the British-Irish Intergovernmental Body, 1989. Rees, who was succeeded by ROY MASON, later admitted that he was concerned about British army undercover units operating in Northern Ireland during his period in office.

Registrar-General, an office created in 1845. The duties were extended by an act of 1863 to include (*a*) the registration of births, deaths, marriages, and successful vaccinations, (*b*) the compiling of emigration statistics and an annual report on the criminal and judicial statistics, and (*c*) the superintending of the ten-yearly census of population, for which a special commission was appointed under the Registrar-General as chairman.

Regium Donum ('Kings' gift'), an annual payment to the Presbyterian Church in Ireland, introduced during the reign of King Charles II in the amount of £600 per year, increased to £1,200 per year by King William III. It was discontinued for a short time and then renewed in 1718 at the rate of £2,000 per year. Under the ACT OF UNION (1800) it became a charge on the British exchequer, and in 1802 it was paid directly to Presbyterian ministers, at the rate of between £50 and £100 each per year. On the DISESTABLISHMENT of the Church of Ireland it was abolished, and the Presbyterian Church received a capital sum of £770,000 as compensation.

Reilly, Thomas Devin (1824–1854), Young Irelander and journalist; born in Monaghan, educated at TCD. Influenced by CHARLES GAVAN DUFFY, he contributed to the *Nation* and was a prominent member of YOUNG IRELAND. He supported the extremist policy of JOHN MITCHEL, for whom he worked on the *United Irishman.* Following Mitchel's transportation he jointly founded the IRISH FELON with JOHN MARTIN. He skipped bail in May 1848 and went to the United States, where he worked as a journalist and edited the *Democratic Review.*

Repeal Association. The National Association of Ireland for Full and Prompt Justice and Repeal was founded by DANIEL O'CONNELL, 15 April 1840, to centralise his campaign for repeal of the ACT OF UNION (1800) and to establish a separate legislature in Dublin; the cumbersome title was changed to Loyal National Repeal Association in January 1841. From 1835 O'Connell led Repeal MPs in an alliance with the Liberals but achieved only moderate reform. By 1840, anticipating VISCOUNT MELBOURNE's losing office, he withdrew from the House of Commons to carry the struggle for Repeal to the country, on the lines of his earlier CATHOLIC ASSOCIATION, which had achieved CATHOLIC EMANCIPATION, 1829, through popular agitation.

The organising of the association was overseen by his son John O'Connell (1819–1858), PATRICK VINCENT FITZPATRICK, and THOMAS STEELE. Membership was divided into three classes: volunteers, who were life members for a subscription of £10, ordinary members, who paid £1 per year, and associates, who paid 1 shilling per year. O'Connell called for a 'Repeal Rent' to finance the agitation. 'Repeal Reading-Rooms' were opened to allow the free reading of books published by JAMES DUFFY on Irish history and culture. The agitation was also supported by the *Pilot,* YOUNG IRELAND, and the *Nation.* Within two years the popularity of the Repeal agitation was reflected in its revenues: by 1843 a total of £48,000 had been subscribed, and in that year the 'O'Connell Tribute' yielded £20,000. The staff at the association's offices in Conciliation Hall, Burgh Quay, Dublin, increased from seven clerks in 1841 to forty-eight in 1843. Throughout the country, thousands of voluntary workers, including many priests, worked for the cause and organised the monster meetings, usually held on historic sites, where O'Connell addressed his followers.

The Repeal agitation, unlike the struggle for Emancipation, did not enjoy the unanimous approval of the Catholic hierarchy, nor had it the support in England that Emancipation had obtained. In Ireland, Emancipation had been supported by Protestants, but they did not support Repeal.

Now advanced in years, O'Connell was increasingly distrusted by the extremist elements of Young Ireland, led by JOHN MITCHEL and THOMAS FRANCIS MEAGHER. However, the British government's reaction—to remove from office anyone sympathetic to Repeal—helped to secure temporary support for O'Connell from moderates, led by WILLIAM SMITH O'BRIEN.

O'Connell staked everything on 1843 being the 'Year of Repeal'. The size of his audiences increased as his followers became convinced that Repeal was imminent. For his final meeting of the year, on 8 October, he chose Clontarf, outside Dublin. The government proscribed the meeting, and threatened to use gunboats if it proceeded. At the last moment, with thousands making their way to Clontarf, O'Connell cancelled it. Shortly afterwards, when he had called for delegates to attend the COUNCIL OF THREE HUNDRED in Dublin, he was put on trial for conspiracy. By the time he was released from prison, by order of the House of Lords, 1844, he was weakened both mentally and physically, and control of the association fell to his son John, a man with little talent for leadership.

By 1845 O'Connell was in dispute with Young Ireland over the QUEEN'S COLLEGES; at the same time the country was devastated by the GREAT FAMINE (1845–49). The breach between Young Ireland and the O'Connellites was completed in 1846, when John O'Connell, on his father's behalf, proposed a motion demanding a declaration that physical force could never be justified; Mitchel, Meagher and O'Brien broke with the association.

O'Connell died in 1847. His son quickly alienated even some of the association's staunchest supporters, and it was soon dissolved. The legacy of Repeal remained, to be resurrected in the 1870s in the form of the HOME RULE agitation.

Representative Church Body of the Church of Ireland, set up following DISESTABLISHMENT, which came into force in January 1871. Its purpose was to take over the churches and burial grounds in actual use and to oversee the distribution of the finances available to the Church of Ireland as a result of the disendowment that accompanied disestablishment.

Republican Congress, a socialist-republican movement founded at Athlone, Co. Westmeath, 8 April 1934, from SAOR ÉIRE, following a split in the IRA in March. It was led by PEADAR O'DONNELL, GEORGE GILMORE, and FRANK RYAN. The 186 delegates at the inaugural meeting were representative of the COMMUNIST PARTY OF IRELAND, the IRISH CITIZEN ARMY, tenants' leagues, trade unions, the Unemployed Workers' Movement, and Working Farmers' Committees. They sought an ending to 'ranch' farmers and the establishment of a workers' republic on the lines advocated by JAMES CONNOLLY. In the 'Athlone Manifesto' the congress declared: 'We believe that a Republic or a united Ireland will never be achieved except through a struggle which uproots capitalism on its way . . .' The three leaders edited the publication *Republican Congress.*

The congress, which faced strong opposition from the orthodox IRA, was short-lived. When it attempted to participate in the Wolfe Tone commemoration at Bodenstown, Co. Kildare (see BODENSTOWN SUNDAY), 17 June 1934, there was a confrontation between the two groups. The congress was itself divided between those who sought the immediate establishment of a workers' republic and those who wished to establish a left-wing anti-de Valera popular front. Following a split on 29 September 1934 it was dissolved in 1935.

Republican Labour Party, founded in 1953 as

a splinter of the Labour Party by Harry Diamond, member of the Parliament of Northern Ireland for the Falls Road division of Belfast. A small party, jointly led by Diamond and GERRY FITT, it opposed partition and supported non-violent republicanism. In the 1960s members were active in the NORTHERN IRELAND CIVIL RIGHTS ASSOCIATION. Its electoral successes were in local government, with members elected to Belfast Corporation, and in having Diamond and Paddy Kennedy elected to the Parliament of Northern Ireland and Fitt elected to both the Northern Parliament and the British House of Commons. Strongest in the Belfast region, the party had five candidates in the 1969 Stormont general election, when it secured 2½ per cent of the total vote; Diamond lost his seat to PADDY DEVLIN (NILP), and Fitt and Kennedy won in Belfast (Dock) and Belfast Central, respectively. The party fragmented in 1970 following Fitt's election as leader of the SOCIAL DEMOCRATIC AND LABOUR PARTY. Kennedy withdrew from Stormont in 1971, and the party withdrew its six councillors from Belfast Corporation. They were active in the civil disobedience campaign in protest at internment. Kennedy failed to secure a seat in the Assembly elections in Belfast West, 28 June 1973.

Republican News, organ of the Provisional IRA, established in Belfast by Jimmy Steele and Hugh McAteer, February 1970. In February 1979 it merged with AN PHOBLACHT (Dublin). Under its joint editors, Danny Morrison and Tom Hartley, the paper was closely associated with initiatives taken by GERRY ADAMS in the 1980s.

Republican Sinn Féin, formed on 2 November 1986 when RUAIRÍ Ó BRÁDAIGH and DÁITHÍ Ó CONAILL led approximately a hundred delegates from the Sinn Féin ard-fheis, at which delegates had voted (429 to 16) to drop the traditional policy of parliamentary abstention. The group supported 'an armed struggle to re-establish the democratic socialist republic.' During the 1990s the 'CONTINUITY IRA' was believed to be its military wing. Membership of Republican Sinn Féin was based mainly in Derry, the border counties, and Dublin. It opposed the HUME-ADAMS TALKS, the PEACE PROCESS and the Provisional IRA ceasefires of 1994 and 1997 and rejected the BELFAST AGREEMENT (1998). Through its organ, *Saoirse,* it condemned decommissioning by the Provisional IRA as 'national treachery'.

Republic of Ireland Act (1948), adopted 21 December 1948, coming into effect on 18 April 1949. It repealed the EXTERNAL RELATIONS ACT (1936) and declared that the Irish state ceased to be part of the British Commonwealth from 18 April 1949. The British government reacted by passing the IRELAND ACT (1949).

Much confusion has been caused by the provision of the 1948 act that the 'description' of the state is 'Republic of Ireland', as the name of the state, in accordance with the CONSTITUTION OF IRELAND (1937), is 'Ireland'. In a Supreme Court judgment, 5 December 1989, Mr Justice Brian Walsh declared that 'the name of the State is as provided for in Article 4 of the Constitution' and that the Republic of Ireland Act 'does not purport to change the name of the State, nor could the Oireachtas do so even if it so wished.'

resident magistrates, an institution owing its origin to the perceived failure of county justices to maintain law and order during widespread periods of unrest in the early nineteenth century. The first resident magistrates were appointed under an act of 1814. The position was open to barristers of at least six years' standing. Each resident magistrate had at his disposal a chief constable and fifty sub-constables for deployment in any area 'proclaimed' by the Lord Lieutenant of Ireland. Following the enactment of the Constabulary (Ireland) Act (1836), when the reorganising of the police system was undertaken by THOMAS DRUMMOND, the Lord Lieutenant was empowered to appoint resident magistrates (replacing stipendiary magistrates) at his discretion; by 1860 the number of such appointments had risen from 42 to 72. Appointments in each administrative district were generally made in accordance with legal or administrative experience in the police or British army.

The resident magistrates' reports formed a vital part of the intelligence network that kept DUBLIN CASTLE informed of the mood in the country. During periods of emergency, such as the LAND WAR (1879–82), 'special' resident magistrates were appointed for the duration of the disturbance. During the WAR OF INDEPENDENCE, resident magistrates were harassed by the IRA. In August 1920 more than 140 resigned in protest at the substitution of military for civil law or as a consequence of reprisals by Crown forces.

Following the ANGLO-IRISH TREATY (1921) the office of resident magistrate was abolished and the thirty-eight remaining magistrates were placed on permanent, pensionable leave of absence by the government of the Irish Free State.

Resistance, a loyalist paramilitary group, believed to be active in the COMBINED LOYALIST MILITARY COMMAND in the 1980s and reported to contain former members of ULSTER RESISTANCE. The SDLP called for the group to be banned. In 1993 there was speculation that it may have supplied weapons to the ULSTER VOLUNTEER FORCE and ULSTER FREEDOM FIGHTERS.

Restoration of Order in Ireland Act (1920), emergency legislation introduced during the WAR OF INDEPENDENCE, becoming law on 9 August 1920. In extending the terms of the DEFENCE OF THE REALM ACT (1914) it empowered the commander of British forces in Ireland (GENERAL SIR NEVIL MACREADY) to arrest and hold without trial anyone suspected of membership of Sinn Féin or the IRA. Suspects could be tried by secret court-martial, and only a lawyer appointed by the Crown could be present for a charge that involved the death penalty. Under the act, coroners' inquests were suppressed (thirty-three coroners' inquests had already indicted either the military or the police for murder). The act led to increased activity by the AUXILIARIES and BLACK AND TANS.

Resurgence, a paper published by an IRA splinter group from June 1946. It opposed the admission of CLANN NA POBLACHTA and republicans to orthodox politics. It had disappeared by the end of the year.

'The resurrection of Hungary', a series of twenty-seven articles by ARTHUR GRIFFITH in the UNITED IRISHMAN, 1904, published later that year in book form as *The Resurrection of Hungary: A Parallel for Ireland.* Griffith first put forward the parallel between Ireland and Hungary at a convention of CUMANN NA NGAEDHEAL, 26 November 1902. He suggested that Irish members of Parliament should withdraw and, together with representatives of local authorities, form a legislative assembly in Dublin, to be known as the COUNCIL OF THREE HUNDRED. The idea was borrowed from Lajos Kossuth (1802–1894) and the Hungarian nationalists who withdrew from the Austrian parliament to form their own assembly in Budapest under the *Ausgleich* (compromise) of 1867, creating the 'dual monarchy' of Austria-Hungary. Griffith's concept of a dual monarchy for Ireland and Britain had some support in Sinn Féin but was opposed by the IRB.

Revolutionary Workers' Groups, Marxist groups founded in Dublin and Belfast during the economic depression of 1929–30. James Larkin Junior edited the movement's paper, the *Worker's Voice,* from August 1930. The groups were among a number of organisations, including SAOR ÉIRE, outlawed by the government, 17 October 1931. Larkin was elected for the RWG to Dublin City Council but failed to gain a Dáil seat in the general election of 1932. The Belfast branches of the RWG brought Catholic and Protestant workers together during 1932 under the leadership of Tommy Geehan. Dublin members were attacked by Catholic groups (see SIEGE OF GREAT STRAND STREET) and the BLUESHIRTS. At a convention in June 1932 the groups adopted a manifesto, 'Ireland's Path to Freedom'. A year later they helped to re-establish the COMMUNIST PARTY OF IRELAND.

Reynolds, Albert (born 1932), businessman and politician (Fianna Fáil); born in Rooskey, Co. Roscommon, educated at Summerhill College, Sligo. A successful businessman, he was elected to Dáil Éireann in 1977. He was Minister for Posts and Telegraphs and Minister for Transport, 1979–81, Minister for Industry and Energy, 1982, Minister for Industry and Commerce, 1987–88, and Minister for Finance, 1988–91. He was dropped from the government by CHARLES HAUGHEY, 7 November 1991, for supporting a move against his leadership. Following Haughey's resignation he became leader of FIANNA FÁIL and Taoiseach, 11 February 1992. On forming his government he sacked eight of the twelve outgoing ministers. The coalition with the PROGRESSIVE DEMOCRATS continued until November 1992, when the PDs resigned from the government (as a result of Reynolds's questioning of DESMOND O'MALLEY's evidence to the BEEF TRIBUNAL). In the resulting election Fianna Fáil fell to below 40 per cent of the first-preference vote (its lowest vote since 1927) and lost nine seats. Reynolds entered into an agreement with DICK SPRING whereby a coalition government with the LABOUR PARTY was formed, 12 January 1993.

Reynolds's involvement in the PEACE PROCESS was aided by a good relationship with the British Prime Minister, JOHN MAJOR. He insisted that the GOVERNMENT OF IRELAND ACT (1920) should be on the table to counterbalance Unionist objections to the definition of the national territory in articles 2 and 3 of the Constitution of Ireland, which he said were 'not for sale.' He supported the HUME-ADAMS TALKS during 1993. With Major he drafted the DOWNING STREET DECLARATION (1993). When the Provisional IRA ceasefire came, 31 August 1994, he accepted that its campaign was over 'for good.' He issued the invitations to the FORUM FOR PEACE AND RECONCILIATION, 28 October 1994. While the ULSTER UNIONIST PARTY would not attend, loyalist parties sent representatives.

There were tensions within the government: Reynolds had a tense relationship with his coalition partner Dick Spring, while the publication of the Hamilton Report on the Beef Tribunal spelt difficulty for Reynolds himself. The government fell following unresolved issues regarding the extradition of two priests accused of child abuse and on the appointment of the then Attorney-General, Harry Whelehan (whose office was widely blamed for delays in bringing the accused priests to justice) as President of the High Court; Whelehan was not the Labour Party's choice for the position. Reynolds resigned, 15 December 1994, remarking that while you can deal with the big things, 'it's the little things that bring you down.' He was succeeded by BERTIE AHERN. In 1997, when Reynolds appeared to be the favourite to become the Fianna Fáil candidate for President of Ireland in succession to Mary Robinson, the party selected Mary McAleese.

He was involved in a libel case against the *Sunday Times* (London) in 1996 and won the case but was awarded only 1 penny damages. After he lodged an appeal the issue was settled on undisclosed terms, amid reports that the paper would cover the costs, estimated at more than £1 million.

Ribbonmen, members of an agrarian secret society that emerged in 1826, so named from their identifying green ribbon. They attempted to prevent the exploitation of tenant-farmers and protested at the price of conacre, tithes, and dues to the Catholic clergy, using intimidation, the maiming of cattle, the burning of crops, and murder. Ribbonism was strongest in Cos. Dublin, Kilkenny, Limerick, Monaghan, Laois, Roscommon, and Tipperary. The societies were most active during winter. The following is a typical 'Ribbon notice', 23 May 1851:

> To Landlords, Agents, Bailiffs, Grippers, process-servers, and usurpers, or underminers who wish to step into the evicted tenants' property, and to all others concerned in Tyranny and Oppression of the Poor on the Bath Estate.
>
> TAKE NOTICE
>
> That you are hereby (under pain of a certain punishment which will inevitably occur), prohibited from evicting tenants, executing decrees, serving process, distraining for rent, or going into another's land, or to assist any tyrant Landlord or Agent in his insatiable desire for depopulation. Recollect the fate of Mauleverer, on this his anniversary.

The passing of ameliorative LAND ACTS from 1860 deprived the movement of its *raison d'être,* and Ribbonism gradually declined. (See also SECRET SOCIETIES.)

Rice, Edmund (1762–1844), educationalist and philanthropist, founder of the IRISH CHRISTIAN BROTHERS; born in Callan, Co. Kilkenny, educated at hedge school and boarding school. His wife was killed when she was thrown from a horse when seven months pregnant; their child was born severely retarded. He amassed a fortune after he took control of his uncle's business in Waterford. Prompted by the example of Nano Nagle, founder of the PRESENTATION SISTERS, he devoted himself to the education of the poor. He spent much of his fortune on the sick and indigent, paying the debts of imprisoned debtors to secure their release. He established his first school in New Street, Waterford, 1 June 1802, and opened another at Mount Sion, 1 May 1804. He befriended CHARLES BIANCONI, to whom he taught English. Having taken religious vows, together with eight others, in 1808, he secured Papal recognition for the Institute of the Religious Brothers of Christian Schools in Ireland from Pope Pius VII, 5 September 1820. He was elected superior-general, 20 January 1822, and occupied the position until his retirement in 1838. The case for his beatification was launched in 1963. In 1993 Pope John Paul II declared him 'venerable', and he was beatified on 6 October 1996.

Richmond, Charles Lennox, fourth Duke of (1754–1819), British aristocrat and politician. A lover of women and claret, he was described by his friends as 'irresistibly convivial' and by his detractors as 'a drunkard'. He was described by the Prime Minister, Spencer Perceval, as 'liberal, accommodating and friendly to the greatest degree.' As Lord Lieutenant of Ireland, 1807–13, his disbursement of patronage was hailed as innovative, but he failed to deal with the wider issues of tithes and ecclesiastical reform. He opposed the appointment of his successor, Lord Whitworth, because of his lower rank.

Richmond Commission, appointed by BENJAMIN DISRAELI, August 1879, under the chairmanship of the Duke of Richmond, to investigate agricultural conditions in Britain and Ireland during the depression of the late 1870s. Like the BESSBOROUGH COMMISSION, which issued its report a few weeks before, the Richmond Report suggested that the Landlord and Tenant (Ireland) Act (1870) had been a failure (see LAND ACTS). It found that Irish tenant-farmers were in great misery, and as a consequence there was widespread unrest throughout the country. The commission isolated what it considered the causes of the LAND WAR (1879–82), including the inclemency of the seasons and the consequent failure of the potato crop, foreign competition, and excessive competition for land, which led to an arbitrary increase in rents, overcrowding in some areas, and the sub-division of land. It recommended migration and emigration as solutions. A minority report by Lord Carlingford (see CHICHESTER PARKINSON-FORTESCUE) recommended the legalisation of the THREE FS or ULSTER CUSTOM, stating that there was no other solution to the problem.

Roantree, William Francis (1829–1918), republican; born in Leixlip, Co. Kildare. He joined the US Navy and later served in the army in Nicaragua. Returning to Ireland, 1861, he became a principal organiser in the IRB. His centre (branch) around Leixlip became one of the biggest in Ireland, with two thousand members. He replaced PATRICK 'PAGAN' O'LEARY as a Fenian recruiter until he was arrested, September 1865, and sentenced to ten years' imprisonment. As a result of agitation by the AMNESTY ASSOCIATION he was released, and he settled in the United States, where he became a commercial traveller in Philadelphia. He returned to Ireland in 1900 and worked for Dublin Corporation.

Robinson, Mary (born 1944), lawyer and politician; born in Ballina, Co. Mayo, educated at TCD and King's Inns. Following post-graduate studies at Harvard University, Massachusetts, she was a lecturer in law and Reid professor of law at Trinity College, Dublin. She joined the LABOUR PARTY in 1976. Elected to Seanad Éireann for the University of Dublin, 1969–89, she was active on feminist issues and minority rights. She resigned from the Labour Party (reportedly in protest at the ANGLO-IRISH AGREEMENT).

Nominated for the Presidency of Ireland by the Labour Party, she defeated the FIANNA FÁIL nominee, Brian Lenihan, on the second count and was sworn in on 9 November 1990. She paid her first official visit to Belfast in February 1992, when she met various women's groups. In July 1992 she addressed the houses of the Oireachtas. She visited Queen Elizabeth in London, 27 May, the first such meeting between the heads of state of the two countries. In November 1993 she was the first President of Ireland to attend an ecumenical service at St Patrick's Cathedral, Dublin, to commemorate those who died in the First World War. The Irish national anthem was played at Buckingham Palace for the first time when she met Queen Elizabeth for an informal lunch in 1996.

President Robinson announced in March 1996 that she was not seeking a second term. She took up the office of United Nations High Commissioner for Human Rights on 15 September 1997; early in 2002 she announced that she would not be seeking to continue in office when her current term ended.

Roden, Robert Jocelyn, third Earl (1788–1880), landowner and politician (Conservative). Owner of an extensive estate at Tullymore Park, Castlewellan, Co. Down, he was member of Parliament for Dundalk, 1810–20. A prominent supporter of Protestant organisations, including the Hibernian Bible Society, Sunday School Society, Evangelical Alliance, and Protestant Orphans' Society, he was active in the ORANGE ORDER, of which he was grand master. The violent DOLLY'S BRAE AFFRAY, 12 July 1849, occurred when Orangemen were returning from his home. Following censure by a commission of inquiry, he was deprived of his office as a commissioner of the peace.

Rooney, William (1873–1901), journalist and language activist; born in Dublin, educated at the O'Connell School. He worked in a lawyer's office before obtaining a clerical post in the Midland Great Western Railway. He was a joint founder of the Irish Fireside Club, a literary and debating society, where he met ARTHUR GRIFFITH, 1888. With other Parnellites he founded the CELTIC LITERARY SOCIETY, 3 February 1893, and he was a teacher in the Gaelic League. He influenced Griffith, with whom he founded the *United Irishman* (for which he wrote 'Irish Ireland Notes'), and CUMANN NA NGAEDHEAL. He attacked HOME RULE as not being enough to make Ireland a nation. Griffith edited *Poems* *and Ballads of William Rooney* (1901).

Rosse, William Parsons, third Earl of (1800–1867), scientist and politician (Conservative); born in York, educated at TCD and the University of Oxford. Member of Parliament for King's County (Co. Offaly), 1821–35, he was a member of the Royal Astronomical Society, 1824, and of the Royal Society, 1831. On retirement from politics he devoted himself to scientific research, with a particular interest in the improvement of the reflecting telescope. His work led to the construction of the PARSONSTOWN TELESCOPE and to his discovery of the nebula Messier 51 in 1845—the first recorded observation of a spiral galaxy. Appointed to the House of Lords as a representative Irish peer, 1845, he opposed the repeal of the Corn Laws and was an outspoken critic of secret societies. During the GREAT FAMINE (1845–49) he spent a considerable amount of his fortune on famine relief. President of the Royal Society (London), 1849–54, he was chancellor of the University of Dublin in 1862. His publications on Irish affairs include *Letters on the State of Ireland* (1847) and *A Few Words on the Relation of Landlord and Tenant* (1867).

Royal Black Preceptory, popular name for the Imperial Grand Black Chapter of the British Commonwealth, also called the Royal Black Institution, a Protestant organisation founded in Loughgall, Co. Armagh, 1796. It is closely associated with the ORANGE ORDER, of which it was for long a rival. Its parade is traditionally held on the last Saturday in August. Members, popularly known as 'Black men', are dedicated to the 'maintenance of pure evangelical truth as contained in the written Word of God, as well as the dissemination of strict moral ethics.' The organisation sponsors the annual sham fight at Scarva, Co. Down, 13 July, a mock battle between King William and King James. The Ulster Unionist Party leader JAMES MOLYNEAUX was grand master for nearly thirty years.

Royal Dublin Society (RDS). The Dublin Society for Improving Husbandry, Manufactures, and Other Useful Arts, popularly known as the Dublin Society, was established on 25 June 1731; it became the Royal Dublin Society in June 1820 when KING GEORGE IV became its patron. The RDS was responsible for the founding of Ireland's most important cultural institutions, including the NATIONAL LIBRARY, NATIONAL MUSEUM, NATIONAL GALLERY, and NATIONAL BOTANIC GARDENS; it also established the first substantial school of art, developing into the Metropolitan School of Art, now the National College of Art and Design.

The RDS maintained a keen interest in scientific matters, giving grants for research, the acquisition of scientific collections, and the purchase of scientific equipment. It published a series of *Statistical Surveys* of the counties (author and date in parentheses):
Antrim (Dubourdieu, 1812), Armagh (1804), Cavan (1802), Clare (Dutton, 1808), Cork (Townsend, 1810), Derry (1802), Donegal (McParlan, 1802), Down (Dubourdieu, 1802), Dublin (Archer, 1801), Galway (Dutton, 1824), Kildare (Rawson, 1807), Kilkenny (Tighe, 1802), Laois (Coote, 1801), Leitrim (Coote, 1802), Mayo (McParlan, 1802), Monaghan (1801), Offaly (Coote, 1801), Roscommon (Weld, 1832), Sligo (McParlan, 1802), Tyrone (McEvoy, 1802), Wexford (Fraser, 1807), and Wicklow (Fraser, 1801). The unpublished Survey of Co. Tipperary is in the National Library.

The RDS possesses one of the most valuable libraries in Ireland, including complete sets of the proceedings and transactions of learned societies in many parts of the world. It has published its own *Proceedings* since 1764. Part of the RDS collection formed the nucleus of the National Library (see REV. JASPER JOLY). Its grounds and buildings at Ballsbridge, Dublin (since 1881), are the venue for many exhibitions, performances, and other events. The Dublin Horse Show was first held in 1868, and international showjumping has been staged at the grounds since August 1926.

Royal Hibernian Academy of Arts, incorporated by charter in 1823 for the purpose of encouraging artists by offering them an annual opportunity of exhibiting their works. The first president was William Ashford (1746–1824). The academy was reorganised under a new charter in 1861. During the EASTER RISING (1916) its premises in Lower Abbey Street, Dublin, were extensively damaged and valuable records destroyed; its gallery and offices are now at 15 Ely Place. The academy has a president, twenty-three full members, ten associates, and ten honorary members, all of whom are elected. Its refusal to hang the pictures of Louis Le Brocquy was a factor in the establishment of the Irish Exhibition of Living Art, 1943.

Royal Irish Academy, founded in 1785 by

Lord Charlemont to 'advance the studies of science, polite literature, and antiquities.' Originally housed in Navigation House, Grafton Street, Dublin, it moved to its new premises at 19 Dawson Street in 1852. The academy was responsible for much of the historical and antiquarian research undertaken during the nineteenth century. Members, elected on the basis of scholarship, number approximately 240, with some 60 honorary members. The RIA was first to acquire many of the nation's treasures now housed in the NATIONAL MUSEUM, including the ARDAGH CHALICE, Cross of Cong, and Tara Brooch. The academy has published its *Transactions* (1786–1907) and its *Proceedings* (1830–).

Royal Irish Academy of Music, founded in 1834 by Joseph Robinson (1815–1898), evolving from the Antient Concerts Society. It was reorganised in 1856 as a state-subsidised charitable educational institution and received the title 'Royal' in 1872. Financed in part by the Department of Education, the RIAM oversees the annual examination of some twenty thousand students in varying musical disciplines.

Royal Irish Constabulary (RIC), an armed police force formed by THOMAS DRUMMOND in 1836 as the Irish Constabulary, granted the prefix 'Royal' for its role in the suppression of the IRB rising in 1867. Members of the force were recruited from among the tenant-farmer class, and it had barracks in likely trouble-spots. The RIC was unpopular in many areas because it assisted at evictions and because it filled a semi-military role. It supplied DUBLIN CASTLE with most of its intelligence. Members were poorly paid and subject to supervision by a variety of officials, most of whom were out of sympathy with the needs of those in the service. There were no recognised off-duty periods, days of rest, or annual leave, and constables were confined to barracks at night. A constable could marry only after seven years' service, and then his proposed wife had to receive official approval. Promotion was slow, and opportunities for promotion were unequally distributed throughout the country. Constables could not vote in elections.

Members were also subject to irksome regulations. Each had to keep a kit and horse (a condition enforced long after the RIC had ceased to fill a military role). Members also had to undergo military training, even when it was not relevant, and attend sessions of target practice.

The strength of the force by 1870 was approximately twelve thousand. Until a reorganisation in 1881 it was commanded by inspectors. The country was then divided into five divisions outside the DUBLIN METROPOLITAN POLICE area (Cos. Dublin and Wicklow). Each division had a divisional magistrate, with full powers over the entire force and complete responsibility for law and order. By 1885 the reorganisation was complete and divisional magistrates were operating in the Western, South-Western, South-Eastern, Midland and Northern Divisions.

Before the outbreak of the Great War, recruitment to the RIC had fallen, mainly because of the unpopular nature of the job and the poor financial reward. There were also increasing numbers of resignations because of the belief that there would be no future within the service after HOME RULE. Morale was low, particularly when Assistant Commissioner David Harrell was dismissed following the HOWTH GUN-RUNNING (July 1914). Falling numbers presented the authorities with a problem during the war: the Police (Emergency Provisions) Act (1915) forbade resignation or retirement except for enlistment in the armed forces.

Following the EASTER RISING (1916) nationalists and members of the IRISH VOLUNTEERS regarded members of the RIC with even greater hostility. In the early stages of the WAR OF INDEPENDENCE the RIC was the primary target of the IRA. It was not equipped to fight a guerrilla war and had to deal with sinking morale in the face of hostility and the risk of attack to members' families. To compensate for the shortage in numbers as recruiting declined and resignations increased, the British government recruited as reinforcements the AUXILIARIES and the BLACK AND TANS. The brutality with which these auxiliary forces set about the task of destroying the IRA created unrest within the RIC, many of whose members refused to be associated with their extremes. This led to an incident at Listowel Barracks in 1920 when CONSTABLE JEREMIAH MEE spoke for nationalist-minded policemen, for which they were dismissed.

There was no negotiating body within the RIC until 1919, when T. J. MCELLIGOTT established an Irish branch of the National Union of Police and Prison Officers, following which he was dismissed from the force. The Resigned and Dismissed Members of the RIC and DMP was founded by McElligott, with the approval of

MICHAEL COLLINS, to protect the interests of members who had been dismissed because of nationalist sympathies. They received little from the Irish Free State: they were praised for their nationalism by republicans but were left without adequate means of support.

Following the ANGLO-IRISH TREATY (1921) the RIC was disbanded, March 1922, and a new police force, the Civic Guard, was established (see GARDA SÍOCHÁNA). On 17 August 1922 a detachment of 380 members of the new force took possession of Dublin Castle within hours of its being vacated by the RIC. In Northern Ireland the new ROYAL ULSTER CONSTABULARY absorbed members of the RIC. (See also POLICE.)

Royal Irish Rangers, a regiment of the British army formed on 1 July 1968 from a merger of the Royal Ulster Rifles and Royal Ulster Fusiliers. Its members served abroad as well as in Northern Ireland. On 1 July 1992 it was merged with the ULSTER DEFENCE REGIMENT to form the ROYAL IRISH REGIMENT.

Royal Irish Regiment, a regiment of the British army formed on 1 July 1992 from a merger of the ROYAL IRISH RANGERS and ULSTER DEFENCE REGIMENT. It supported the RUC and PSNI in the fight against terrorism, mainly in Cos. Down, Armagh, and Tyrone.

Royal Society of Antiquaries of Ireland, established from the Kilkenny Archaeological Society in 1849 by Rev. James Graves 'to preserve, examine and illustrate the ancient monuments of the history, language, arts, manners and customs of the past as connected with Ireland.' The society sponsors scholarly publications, provides a library service, organises lectures, and publishes the annual *Journal of the Royal Society of Antiquaries of Ireland.*

Royal Ulster Constabulary (RUC), a police force established in Northern Ireland from among the ROYAL IRISH CONSTABULARY, 1 June 1922. Charles Wickham was inspector-general of the new force, which had its headquarters in Waring Street, Belfast. Supported by the ULSTER SPECIAL CONSTABULARY and acting under the SPECIAL POWERS ACT, the RUC was responsible for dealing not only with crime but also with the IRA. It was partially disarmed in April 1970, in line with the recommendations of the HUNT COMMISSION. From 1968 it was in the front line of increasing violence, which continued over the next three decades, during which 303 members of the RUC and RUC Reserve were killed. The force lacked support within the nationalist community. Following the recommendations of the PATTEN REPORT it became the POLICE SERVICE OF NORTHERN IRELAND on 4 November 2001, with a directive that half its members were to come from the Catholic community.

Royal University of Ireland, an examining body established by BENJAMIN DISRAELI under the University Education (Ireland) Act (1879) in an attempt to solve the complex problems of higher education in Ireland. The QUEEN'S COLLEGES and Trinity College, Dublin, were unacceptable to the Catholic hierarchy, while the CATHOLIC UNIVERSITY had been restricted by lack of state support and its lack of power to award degrees. Disraeli's solution was to establish the Royal University of Ireland, in effect a university with a staff but no student body: students from other institutions were free to sit for the examinations set by the Royal. The compromise proved acceptable, and the RUI lasted until the NATIONAL UNIVERSITY OF IRELAND and Queen's University, Belfast, were established in 1908.

Royal Zoological Society of Ireland, founded in 1830 for the study and display of natural history. The society is also responsible for the zoological gardens in the Phoenix Park, Dublin, opened to the public in September 1831.

rundale, a system of landholding common in Ireland before the Great Famine (1845–49), mainly found in the western parts of the country, also known as 'runrig'. The land was held in common and apportioned among tenant-farmers, so that everyone received a share of both good and bad land. In practice the system often meant that a tenant could have his individual strips scattered over many different fields; in *Irish Folk Ways* (1957) E. Estyn Evans tells of a tenant who had his holding scattered in thirty-two different places and also cites the case of a rundale cluster in Rathlackan, Co. Mayo, in 1918 where fifty-six families occupied 1,500 units, many of which were little more than a dozen square yards. An attempt was generally made to ensure a fair distribution of the good, middling and bad land; but as the system did not make use of fences, there were frequent disputes over the precise delineation of the plots. According to T. Campbell Foster in *Letters on the Condition of the People of Ireland* (1846), 'fights, trespasses, confusion, disputes and assaults, were the natural and unavoidable consequence of this system.' (See also CHANGEDALE.)

Russell, Charles, first Baron Russell of Killowen (1832–1900), lawyer and politician (Liberal); born in Killane, Co. Down, educated at TCD and called to the bar. A Queen's counsel from 1872 and member of Parliament for Dundalk, 1868–85, he served as Attorney-General, 1886 and 1892–94. CHARLES STEWART PARNELL retained him in 1888 during the special commission on 'PARNELLISM AND CRIME', having earlier dissuaded him from suing the paper for libel. Russell's cross-examination of RICHARD PIGOTT uncovered him as the forger of the letters. Russell was later counsel for KATHARINE O'SHEA when her aunt's will was contested. Regarded as the outstanding courtroom orator of his time, Russell became Lord of Appeal in Ordinary, 1894, and Lord Chief Justice of England, the first Catholic to hold the office since the Reformation.

Russell, George W. (1867–1935), artist, economist, mystic, and poet, widely known as 'AE', from his pen-name, Æ; born in Lurgan, Co. Armagh, educated at Rathmines School. He studied at the Metropolitan School of Art, Dublin, and worked as an assistant in Pim's drapery. He began to contribute to the *Irish Theosophist* in 1892, using the signature Æ (from Æon, the gnostic term for the first created beings). Two years later he published his first volume of verse, *Homeward: Songs by the Way.* He joined the IRISH AGRICULTURAL ORGANISATION SOCIETY, the central body of the co-operative movement, of which he became assistant secretary. As editor of the co-operative journal, *Irish Homestead,* he attracted contributions from the leading writers of the day, including his friend W. B. YEATS. He was later editor of the IRISH STATESMAN, 1923–30.

Russell, whose *Co-operation and Nationality* (1912) enhanced his international reputation as an agronomist, was generous in his encouragement of literary talent. He introduced JAMES JOYCE to a wide circle of influential literati and later helped launch the career of PATRICK KAVANAGH. As a polemicist he had a scathing style, demonstrated in his attack on the Dublin employers, 'the masters of Dublin,' as he called them in an open letter during the DUBLIN LOCK-OUT (1913). This experience of employer-worker relations prompted *The National Well-Being* (1916). He was invited to the United States by Franklin D. Roosevelt in 1935 to elaborate on the idea of employing young people on public works for two years. The heavy lecture tour undermined his health, and he died shortly afterwards in England.

Russell's works include *Literary Ideals of Ireland* (1899), *By Still Waters* (1906), *Deirdre* (1907), *Collected Poems* (1913), *Gods of War* (1915), *Song and Its Foundations* (1932), and *The Aviators* (1933).

Russell, Lord John (1792–1878), British politician (Whig). He visited Ireland in 1806 during the brief term of his father, the Earl of Bedford, as Lord Lieutenant. As a member of Parliament from 1813, his bills for repeal of the Test Act and Corporations Act enabled Catholics and dissenters to become members of corporations from 1823. He supported DANIEL O'CONNELL on CATHOLIC EMANCIPATION and put forward liberal views on TITHES, seeking an appropriations clause to convert the surplus to social ends. He supported various Irish reforms (see POLICE, POOR LAW, and MUNICIPAL CORPORATIONS (IRELAND) ACT (1840)). During the period 1837–41 he was Colonial Secretary. He supported the MAYNOOTH GRANT and the repeal of the Corn Laws. He was appointed Prime Minister in 1846, while Ireland was in the throes of the GREAT FAMINE (1845–49). He was handicapped in dealing with the crisis through heading a minority ministry and because, like his colleagues, he was committed to free trade and *laissez-faire*: in October 1846 he pointed out that, though the potato crop had again failed, 'it must be thoroughly understood that we cannot feed the people.' Irish relief would have to be provided from Irish resources; food was not to be sold below the market price, so as not to interfere with normal trade. Russell allowed the distribution of free soup but ordered the closing of public works, January 1847. He warned that no food would be imported from abroad and, against radical opposition, introduced COERCION to deal with unrest.

He claimed during the period 1847–48 that the financial crisis in England made it impossible to provide aid for Ireland. The case for Irish relief suffered in his eyes by the attempted rebellion of WILLIAM SMITH O'BRIEN and the IRISH CONFEDERATION in the summer of 1848. His policy on the application of the Poor Law rate was expressed on 11 September 1848: 'It is better that some should sink than they should drag others down to sink with them.' To deal with the impoverishment of Irish landlords he introduced two ENCUMBERED ESTATES ACTS, in 1848 and 1849, by which time the famine had run its course.

Russell, Seán (1893–1940), republican; born in Dublin, educated at Christian Brothers' school. He fought in the EASTER RISING (1916). On his release from internment he was a member of SINN FÉIN and the reorganised IRISH VOLUNTEERS. During the WAR OF INDEPENDENCE he was director of munitions of the IRA. Rejecting the ANGLO-IRISH TREATY (1921), he fought in the CIVIL WAR; following the Republican surrender, May 1923, he remained active in the IRA. He visited the Soviet Union with GERALD BOLAND in 1926 in an attempt to secure arms. On his return he broke with ÉAMON DE VALERA and the constitutional republicans who founded Fianna Fáil.

Russell opposed the left wing of the IRA, led by PEADAR O'DONNELL and FRANK RYAN, which founded SAOR ÉIRE, 1931. He refused to halt IRA drilling and parading in public unless Fianna Fáil would guarantee an all-Ireland republic within five years. By 1936, when de Valera outlawed the IRA, Russell, then quartermaster-general, demanded an all-out war against Britain. When this was opposed by MAURICE TWOMEY and SEÁN MACBRIDE, Russell left for the United States to win support from JOSEPH MCGARRITY and CLAN NA GAEL. This led to an IRA court-martial and a charge of misappropriation of funds. Suspended from IRA office, he returned to the United States, but at the IRA convention of April 1938 he secured a seat on the Army Council and became chief of staff. Despite a split on the issue, Russell pressed ahead with his plans for a 'war' against England, which started on 16 January 1939 and culminated in the COVENTRY EXPLOSION, 25 August. He was fund-raising in the United States on the outbreak of war in Europe, which prevented his return to Ireland, but he made his way to Germany, where he hoped German military intelligence would arrange his repatriation. There he met his old adversary Frank Ryan. Admiral Wilhelm Canaris arranged for their transport by submarine to Ireland on 8 August. Russell died en route and was buried at sea a hundred miles out of Galway. Ryan was returned to Germany.

Russell, Thomas Wallace, first Earl (1841–1920), politician (Liberal); born in Cupar, Fifeshire, educated locally. After settling in Ireland, 1859, he worked as a draper's assistant in Donaghmore, Co. Tyrone. Active in the cause of temperance, he was secretary of the Dublin Temperance Association, 1864, and played a prominent role in securing the Sale of Liquors on Sunday (Ireland) Act (1878). As a member of Parliament for Preston, Lancashire, 1885, he opposed HOME RULE for Ireland. In 1886 he defeated WILLIAM O'BRIEN for the South Tyrone seat. He promoted the Land Acts Commission of 1894 and a year later became under-secretary of the Local Government Board. He founded the New Land Movement in Ulster, advocating compulsory purchase (introduced in 1909). His support for HOME RULE lost him both government office and his South Tyrone seat in 1910, but he was elected for North Tyrone, 1911–18. After serving as vice-president of the Department of Agriculture and Technical Instruction, Dublin, 1907–18, he withdrew from public life. He published *England and the Empire* (1901) and *The Irish Land Question Up to Date* (1902).

Russian Crown Jewels. In August 1920 ÉAMON DE VALERA instructed DR PATRICK MCCARTAN to negotiate an interest-free loan of $25,000 to the Soviet Union. Ludvig Martens and Santeri Nuorteva, who acted as agents during the negotiations, offered part of the Crown Jewels of Imperial Russia as collateral. A draft treaty accompanying the agreement provided for the training of Irish officers and the provision of arms to the Irish Republic by Russia; it also provided 'to the accredited representatives of the Republic of Ireland in Russia' a guarantee that 'the interests of the Roman Catholic Church within the territory of the Russian Federal Soviet Republic' would be safeguarded. The deal did not, however, prevent the Soviet government from rejecting a proposed trade agreement between Ireland and the Soviet Union when McCartan visited the country. HARRY BOLAND brought the jewels to Ireland. Following the ANGLO-IRISH TREATY (1921) he entrusted the jewels to his family, with instructions that they be given to de Valera when he came to power. De Valera formed the first Fianna Fáil government in 1932, and the jewels lay in the office of a government department until they were discovered by PATRICK MCGILLIGAN, Minister for Finance in the first inter-party government, 1948–51. They were then returned to the Soviet Union, which repaid the loan in full.

'Ruthless warfare', an anonymous article, written by ERNEST BLYTHE, in *An tÓglach,* organ of the IRISH VOLUNTEERS, September 1918, during the anti-CONSCRIPTION campaign. It called on the Volunteers to regard any attempt to introduce conscription as an act of war, which must be resisted by war: 'We must recognise that anyone, civilian or soldier, who assists directly or by connivance in this crime against Ireland merits no more consideration than a wild beast, and should be killed without mercy or hesitation as opportunity offers.'

Ryan, Desmond (1893–1964), journalist, socialist, and historian; born in London, son of the journalist and writer William P. Ryan (1867–1842), educated at ST ENDA'S SCHOOL. While studying later at University College, Dublin, he lived in St Enda's, where he was secretary to PATRICK PEARSE. A member of the Irish Volunteers, he fought in the GPO, Dublin, during the EASTER RISING (1916), after which he was interned. Following his release he worked on the *Freeman's Journal.* He supported the ANGLO-IRISH TREATY (1921) and, disillusioned by the CIVIL WAR, moved to London to work as a journalist, later returning to Ireland to run a poultry farm near Swords, Co. Dublin. Influenced by the life and writings of JAMES CONNOLLY, he was an acknowledged authority on the IRB and on leading nationalists.

His works include *The Man Called Pearse* (1919), *The Invisible Army* (1932), *Unique Dictator* (a study of ÉAMON DE VALERA, 1936), *The Phoenix Flame: A Study of Fenianism and John Devoy* (1937), *The Sword of Light: From the Four Masters to Douglas Hyde* (1939), *The Rising: The Complete Story of Easter Week* (1948), and *The Fenian Chief* (1967).

Ryan, Frank (1902–1944), socialist republican; born in Elton, Co. Limerick, educated at UCD. He organised Republican Clubs at university, where his studies were interrupted by membership of the IRA during the WAR OF INDEPENDENCE. Rejecting the ANGLO-IRISH TREATY (1921), he was imprisoned during the CIVIL WAR, after which he resumed his work in Celtic studies. A teacher of Irish from 1925, he remained in the IRA, was adjutant of the Dublin Brigade from 1926 and a founder-member of COMHAIRLE NA POBLACHTA and SAOR ÉIRE. Joint editor of AN PHOBLACHT (though he was deaf, it was said he could always hear an offer of money for the paper), he was also editor of *Republican File,* 1929–33. Imprisoned for membership of SAOR ÉIRE, 8 December 1931, he was released with others on the accession of FIANNA FÁIL, 1932. A leading opponent of the BLUESHIRTS, he coined the slogan 'No free speech for traitors.' He was a founder-member of the REPUBLICAN CONGRESS, 1934, and jointly edited the paper of the same name.

Ryan organised IRA volunteers and others in support of the Spanish government during the SPANISH CIVIL WAR (1936–39), during which he was wounded at the battle of Jarama, February 1937. Following recuperation in Dublin he was appointed adjutant to General José Miaja. Captured at Calaceite on 1 April 1938, he was held at Miranda del Ebro detention camp and sentenced to death, which was commuted to thirty years' imprisonment following representations by de Valera and the Apostolic Delegate to Ireland. An international campaign for his release and the intervention of Helmut Clissmann and Jupp Hoven—members of German counter-intelligence who had known Ryan while they were exchange students in Dublin—led to his release into German custody, 1940. Arriving in Berlin, where he was known as Frank Richards, he was united with SEÁN RUSSELL, who arranged their transport to Ireland by submarine. Russell died during the voyage, 14 August, and Ryan was returned to Germany. In failing health, he remained there, living with Clissmann. He was buried in Loschwitz cemetery, near Dresden; his remains were returned to Ireland for re-interment in Glasnevin Cemetery, Dublin, 21 June 1979.

Ryan, Dr James (1891–1970), politician (Sinn Féin and Fianna Fáil); born in Tomcool, Co. Wexford, educated at UCD. While a student, as a member of the Irish Volunteers he led the medical unit in the GPO, Dublin, during the EASTER RISING (1916), after which he was imprisoned. On his release he was active in the reorganised Volunteers and was a member of Dáil Éireann for Wexford, 1918. Rejecting the ANGLO-IRISH TREATY (1921), he was a member of the FOUR COURTS garrison, April–June 1921, and following his arrest embarked on a hunger strike. A founder-member of FIANNA FÁIL, he represented Wexford from 1921 until his retirement in 1965. He was Minister for Agriculture, 1932–47, and the first Minister for Social Welfare (then combined with Health), 1947–48. He was Minister for Finance, 1951–54 and 1957–65, and later a member of Seanad Éireann.

Ryan, Dr Mark (1844–1940), Fenian; born in Kilconly, Tuam, Co. Galway, educated at a hedge school. Following eviction from their smallholding, the family moved to Lancashire. Ryan, sworn in to the IRB by MICHAEL DAVITT, returned to Ireland to resume his education at

St Jarlath's College, Tuam. While studying medicine at Queen's College, Galway, and in Dublin, he was an organiser for the IRB. After qualifying he moved to England, where he became a member of the IRB Supreme Council. He belonged to the extreme wing and after 1895 was leader of the IRISH NATIONAL ALLIANCE. A founder-member of the Gaelic League, he also helped to found the IRISH LITERARY SOCIETY. His autobiography, *Fenian Memories,* was published in 1945.

Ryan, Matthew (1844–1937), clergyman (Catholic) and land agitator, known as 'the General'; born in Kilduff, Pallasgreen, Co. Limerick, educated at the Irish College, Paris, where he was ordained, 1871, and taught physics for a short time. On his return to the Archdiocese of Cashel he was appointed fund-raiser for the cathedral in Thurles. As a curate in Lattin, Co. Tipperary, 1876–86, he was active in the LAND LEAGUE. A curate in Hospital, Co. Limerick, 1886–90, he played a leading role in the PLAN OF CAMPAIGN on the Herbertstown estate, where he earned his nickname. He held the money for the tenants, and in March 1887 he was charged by the state with bankruptcy. At his trial in April he was sentenced to two months' imprisonment for contempt of court when he refused to divulge details of the money. On appeal he was released, 24 May. He was again imprisoned, December 1887 to January 1888, when he resisted attempts to have him wear prison uniform instead of clerical clothing. He was later curate in Solloheadbeg, Co. Tipperary, 1890–97, and parish priest in Knockavella and Donaskeagh, Co. Tipperary, 1897–1937. A vice-president of the Gaelic League for many years, he supported Sinn Féin after the Easter Rising (1916) and rejected the ANGLO-IRISH TREATY (1921).

S

Sadleir, John (1815–1856), businessman and politician (Nationalist); born in Shronell, Co. Tipperary, educated at Clongowes Wood College, Co. Kildare. He entered the family banking business, becoming a director, 1845. Member of Parliament for Co. Carlow, 1847–53, he was a leading member of the 'IRISH BRIGADE' and of the CATHOLIC DEFENCE ASSOCIATION. He established the Irish Land Company to purchase estates under the ENCUMBERED ESTATES ACTS and founded the Tipperary Joint-Stock Bank to buy the Kingston estate in Mitchelstown, Co. Cork, on which the Land Company held a mortgage. This led to his becoming chairman of the London and County Joint-Stock Company. As a member of the INDEPENDENT IRISH PARTY he took the pledge not to accept government office, but he and WILLIAM KEOGH broke their pledge, and Sadleir accepted office as Lord of the Treasury, 17 December 1852. Having speculated in America, when his investments failed he embezzled £1¼ million from the Tipperary Joint-Stock Bank. His financial affairs in ruins, and fearing discovery, he committed suicide at a pub, Jack Straw's Castle, on Hampstead Heath, London. His career provided Charles Dickens and Charles Lever with material for their fiction.

St Enda's School (Scoil Éanna), opened by PATRICK PEARSE in Cullenswood House, Ranelagh, Dublin, 8 September 1908. A bilingual school catering for both boarders and day pupils, it attracted an initial complement of ninety boys; girls were taught by Pearse's sister, MARGARET PEARSE, at an attached preparatory school, St Ita's. The original teaching staff included Pearse, Pádraic Colum, Patrick Doody, Richard J. Feely, THOMAS MACDONAGH, Frank P. Nolan, Éamonn O'Toole, WILLIAM PEARSE, and Michael Smithwick; later teachers included DR DOUGLAS HYDE, EDWARD MARTYN, Joseph MacDonagh (brother of Thomas MacDonagh), EOIN MACNEILL, and W. B. YEATS. Pearse, who attacked the prevailing education system in his pamphlet *The Murder Machine,* imbued in his pupils a sense of nobility through Ireland's heroic past.

Though the school in its second year attracted 130 pupils, it encountered financial difficulties as the number of pupils declined because of Pearse's political reputation. Its move to a 50-acre site at Rathfarnham, Co. Dublin, 1910, proved a constant drain; it was saved through money from the United States, lecture tours, and the direct intervention of THOMAS J. CLARKE, who provided the £200 necessary to prevent imminent closure, January 1910.

Preparations for the EASTER RISING (1916) took place in the basement of the school, where bombs were assembled. Following the rising, St Enda's was kept open by Pearse's sister and mother, assisted by the headmaster, Joseph MacDonagh. On the death of their mother, 1932, the house and grounds passed to Margaret Pearse. The school was closed in 1935. On Margaret Pearse's death, 1969, the house and grounds were presented to the state as a memorial to her brothers; the house is now the Pearse Museum, and the grounds are a public park.

St John Ambulance Brigade of Ireland, founded in 1903 by Dr John Lumsden, who formed the first unit from among employees of the Guinness brewery, Dublin, where he was chief medical officer.

Sallins Train Robbery. The Dublin mail train was robbed of £221,000 near Sallins, Co. Kildare, at 3 a.m. on 31 March 1976. Sixteen members of the IRISH REPUBLICAN SOCIALIST PARTY were arrested. There was disquiet at the alleged manner in which confessions had been extracted from the accused. Six were eventually charged, but the state lost the case because of the delay in providing the book of evidence. Four of the six—Osgur Breatnach, Nicky Kelly, Brian McNally, and Michael Plunkett—appeared in the Special Criminal Court, 19 January 1978. The presiding judge was Mr Justice James McMahon of the High Court, with Judge John O'Connor of the Circuit Court and Judge John Garavan of Castlebar District Court. During the trial, observers noted that Judge O'Connor (who was under heavy medication) appeared to be asleep on a number of occasions. The court rejected defence submissions that he could not follow the trial, and the High Court and Supreme Court rejected applications to prohibit the Special Criminal Court from continuing with it. On 6 June 1978, the sixty-sixth day of the trial—by now the longest in Irish history—it was announced that Judge O'Connor had died of a heart attack.

A new trial opened on 10 October 1978 before Mr Justice Liam Hamilton of the High Court, Judge Gerard Clarken of the Circuit Court, and Judge Cathal O'Flinn of the District Court. On the second day the charges against Plunkett were dropped. The court eventually ruled that the three statements put forward by the prosecution should be allowed to stand. Under cross-examination, gardaí denied they had inflicted violence on any of the accused (see 'HEAVY GANG'); thirty-three days were taken up exclusively with the issue of whether or not statements made in the Bridewell were made and signed voluntarily. On 9 December 1978 Nicky Kelly went into hiding, and the court directed that the trial continue in his absence. Following a trial of forty-four days, the accused were found guilty, 13 December. Kelly and Breatnach were sentenced to twelve years' penal servitude and McNally to nine. The Special Criminal Court, under two separate sets of judges, had spent 108 days hearing evidence, submissions, and arguments; two years and nine months had elapsed since the robbery.

In April 1980, before the Court of Criminal Appeal was to hear applications for leave to appeal, 12 May 1980, the Provisional IRA announced that it was responsible for the Sallins train robbery. The appeal lasted six days; on 22 May the convictions of MacNally and Breatnach were set aside, but not that of Kelly, who had fled to New York. On returning to Ireland, 4 June 1980, he was taken into custody and ordered to serve his twelve-year sentence. He lost appeals to the Court of Criminal Appeal, 15–18 May 1982, and the Supreme Court, 13 July 1982. Amnesty International and the Irish Council for Civil Liberties supported a national campaign for his release. His appeal to the European Commission on Human Rights failed on a technicality (the appeal had not been lodged within six months of the Supreme Court verdict). By now his release was supported by the Minister for Justice, Michael Noonan. Released on 17 July 1984, he received a presidential pardon from MARY ROBINSON, a former member of his legal team.

Sands, Bobby (1954–1981), republican; born in Belfast, educated at Stella Maris School. Sectarian intimidation led to the family leaving its home in Rathcoole, Belfast, and settling in the Twinbrook area in west Belfast, where Sands became an apprentice coachbuilder and officer commanding the local IRA unit. A member of the Provisional IRA, he was imprisoned on arms charges, 1973–76, when, with other paramilitary prisoners, he had SPECIAL CATEGORY status in the Maze Prison. Re-arrested in 1977, he was imprisoned for fourteen years for being in a car containing weapons. In the H BLOCKS he took part in the 'blanket protest' and joined the 'dirty protest' against the removal of special category status.

As a senior Provisional IRA member he directed the first hunger strike, 27 October to 18 December 1980. When the concessions that ended the strike did not produce the restoration of special category status, he led the second hunger strike, 1 March 1981. Having attracted widespread attention to the prisoners' demands, on the sixty-sixth day of his hunger strike he was the first of ten prisoners to die, 5 May. On 9 April he had been elected member of the British Parliament for Fermanagh-South Tyrone, with 30,493 votes, a significant propaganda victory and a boost to republican morale. His death provoked rioting; his funeral at Milltown Cemetery, Belfast, was attended by more than 100,000 people.

Saor Éire, a socialist-republican IRA splinter group, founded by PEADAR O'DONNELL, FRANK RYAN, and GEORGE GILMORE, September 1931. Its first congress, 26–27 September, was attended by some 150 delegates. The organisation, which sought support from workers and working farmers, had the support of *An Phoblacht.* The first national convention, organised by SEÁN MACBRIDE, was held on 28 September, when Seán Hayes was elected chairman. Resolutions favouring control of land and the public ownership of transport were passed, and a National Executive, including members of CUMANN NA MBAN, the IRA, and left-wing members of the Labour Party, was elected.

The government outlawed Saor Éire and a number of other radical organisations, 17 October 1931. In a joint pastoral letter, 18 October, the Catholic hierarchy condemned it as communist, stating that Saor Éire and the IRA were 'sinful and irreligious' and that Catholics could not belong to them. The movement collapsed shortly afterwards; many of the leaders were associated later with the REPUBLICAN CONGRESS.

An organisation calling itself the Saor Éire Action Group appeared in the 1960s and was suspected of several bank robberies in the Republic. It was held responsible for the killing of Garda Richard Fallon during a bank robbery in Dublin, 3 April 1970, the first member of the force killed in the new eruption of violence.

Saor Uladh, an IRA splinter group founded as the military wing of FIANNA ULADH in Co. Tyrone by Liam Kelly in 1954. It was largely confined to east Tyrone but made occasional forays into Co. Fermanagh throughout the late 1950s. The group's recognition of the legitimacy of Dáil Éireann was unique within armed republicanism. During its brief existence it attacked RUC barracks and destroyed a number of custom posts and bridges, losing two members during the campaign, which coincided with the IRA's BORDER CAMPAIGN, 1956–62.

Saunderson, Colonel E. J. [Edward James] (1837–1906), landowner and politician (Unionist); born in Ballinamallard, Co. Fermanagh, raised and educated in Nice. He returned to Ireland to manage the estate on which his considerable wealth was based, 1858. An officer in the Cavan Militia, he was elected Liberal member of Parliament for Co. Cavan, 1865. Shortly afterwards he broke with W. E. GLADSTONE over the DISESTABLISHMENT of the Church of Ireland and became a Conservative. Fearing for the future of the Protestant religion under HOME RULE, he joined the ORANGE ORDER, 1882, and two years later became deputy grand master. He published *Two Irelands, or Loyalty versus Treason* (1884). As a Conservative member from 1885 he was a popular speaker in the House of Commons, where he was held in high regard for his wit and his swashbuckling manner.

During the period 1885–86 he organised Ulster Unionists to resist home rule and brought LORD RANDOLPH CHURCHILL to Belfast. He informed an anti-home-rule meeting in Belfast, May 1886, that 'rather than submit to such a Romish and rebel despotism the minority would take the field and defend their rights at the point of the sword.' By 1888 he was the recognised leader of the parliamentary Unionists. A leading member of the ULSTER LOYALIST ANTI-REPEAL UNION and later of the IRISH UNIONIST ALLIANCE, he rejected an invitation to sit on the RECESS COMMITTEE (1895) but was a member of the All-Ireland Committee (1897).

Saurin, William (1757–1839), lawyer and politician (Conservative); born in Belfast, educated at TCD and called to the bar. He opposed parliamentary reform and Catholic relief in the Irish Parliament. A member of the ORANGE ORDER, he prosecuted prominent UNITED IRISHMEN, 1798, and was a leader of the Irish bar in opposition to the ACT OF UNION, though he accepted office as Solicitor-General, 1807–22, in which he was said to have enjoyed more power than the Lord Lieutenant. Mortified at his removal from office at the insistence of the incoming Lord Lieutenant, RICHARD COLLEY WELLESLEY, 1822, he rejected a peerage and the post of Lord Chief Justice to return to his law practice. He continued to oppose O'Connell and CATHOLIC EMANCIPATION.

Savage, John (1828–1888), Young Irelander and Fenian; born in Dublin, where he trained as an artist. A member of YOUNG IRELAND and the IRISH CONFEDERATION, he was joint founder (with JOHN MARTIN) of the IRISH FELON. His paper, the *Patriot,* was suppressed on its appearance, 1848. Following the collapse of the Young Ireland rising at BALLINGARRY, Co. Tipperary, he escaped to the United States, November 1848, where he aided JOHN O'MAHONY in the attempt to renew the rising. He contributed to the *Citizen,* published by JOHN MITCHEL. A leading member of the FENIANS, he joined the 69th Regiment of the US Army, led by THOMAS FRANCIS MEAGHER, during the American Civil War (1861–65) and was a captain on General Corcoran's staff. After the war he sought a rising in Ireland and was involved in the attempt to land arms on the ERIN'S HOPE. When O'Mahony was deposed, 1867, Savage led the O'Mahony faction. He published *'98 and '48* (1856) and *Fenian Heroes and Martyrs* (1868). His best-known poem was 'Shane's Head'.

Saville Inquiry ('the tribunal for inquiring into the events on Sunday 30 January 1972 which led to loss of life in connection with the procession in Londonderry on that day, taking account of any new information relevant to events on that day'), chaired by Lord Saville of Newdigate, accompanied by Mr Justice William Hoyt (New Zealand) and Sir Edward Somers (Canada), set up as a consequence of the failure of the WIDGERY TRIBUNAL to satisfy public disquiet about the events of BLOODY SUNDAY (1972). The inquiry opened in the Guildhall, Derry, on 27 March 2000. It received 900 signed statements before opening and was awaiting another 400. Ninety-seven per cent of the 2,100 witnesses it desired to examine had been traced, as had the great majority of the British soldiers present on the day, including all but two who had given evidence to the Widgery Tribunal. Edward Heath, Prime Minister at the time, was questioned for a week in January 2003.

scalp (Irish *scailp*), also scalpeen, a makeshift hut built within the ruins of a cabin from which a family had been recently evicted. The Radical MP George Poulett Scrope, champion of the poor during the GREAT FAMINE (1845–49), described how they 'framed some temporary shelter out of the materials of their old homes against a broken wall, or behind a ditch or fence, or in a boghole . . . places unfit for human habitation.' Evicted tenants were often driven from these also, with the landlord being aided by the police and military.

Scarman Tribunal, the Tribunal of Inquiry into Violence and Civil Disturbances in Northern Ireland in 1969, chaired by Mr Justice (later Lord) Scarman, assisted by two businessmen, William Marshall and George Lavery. The tribunal heard some 400 witnesses at 170 sittings.

The Scarman Report (April 1972) found that there had been neither a plot to overthrow the government of Northern Ireland nor a plot to mount an armed insurrection: the riots had been communal disturbances arising from a complex political, social and economic situation, but that while there had not been a conspiracy, teenage hooligans had been exploited by those seeking to discredit the Stormont government. The tribunal found that the courage of RUC members was beyond praise in a situation beyond their control. It cleared the RUC of being partisan in its handling of Protestant mobs attacking Catholics but found that the burning of Catholic homes in west Belfast, 14 August, led to complete loss of confidence in the police among the Catholic community. It found that the ULSTER SPECIAL CONSTABULARY lacked the training and equipment for riot duty and lacked discipline with firearms in Dungannon and Armagh, and that there had been a lack of firm direction in handling disturbances in Derry, 12 August. The use by the RUC of machine-guns in Belfast, 14–15 August, had been a bad decision. The report found that there was no justification for the firing of a tracer bullet by the RUC from a machine-gun mounted on an armoured car, which killed nine-year-old Patrick Rooney as he lay in bed in Divis Tower.

The report cleared politicians opposed to the Northern Ireland government of being implicated in the violence but stated that they had added to the tension. It also found that the Protestant and Catholic communities had the same fears, the same forms of self-help, and the same distrust of lawful authority.

School Attendance Act (1926), legislation that made it compulsory for children between the ages of six and fourteen to attend national school; it also gave the Minister for Education power to extend the school-leaving age to sixteen. Previously attendance at school was governed by the Irish Education Act (1892), which left supervision to the discretion of the local authorities. Because this authority was not exercised to any significant degree, attendance at school until the 1920s rarely rose above 50 per cent.

scollop (Irish *scolb*), a rod of willow, hazel, briar or bog-fir used to pin down thatch. The system varied according to the area; the method in general use was to thrust the rods in vertically at each end or, bent like huge hairpins, to secure the tips of horizontal rods. In some areas scollop-making was a distinct trade, with coppices of hazel or willow being specially cultivated; in other parts of the country the thatcher himself made scallops during periods of inclement weather.

Scott, Michael (1905–1989), architect; born in Drogheda, Co. Louth, educated at Belvedere College, Dublin. Apprenticed to the architects Jones and Kelly, 1923–26, he studied art at the Metropolitan School of Art and later worked for a short time with Charles C. Dunlop and the Office of Public Works before opening his own practice in 1928. Trained as an actor with the ABBEY THEATRE, he also worked as a professional actor in the 1920s. He entered partnership with Norman Good, 1931; during the 1930s he specialised in hospital design and was also responsible for the art deco designs for the Theatre Royal and the Regal Cinema, Hawkins Street, Dublin. He attracted attention early with his design for his own home, 'Geragh', at Sandycove, Co. Dublin (1938). His Shamrock Building for the Irish Pavilion at the New York World's Fair (1939) was named best building of the fair, for which he was awarded a silver medal and honorary citizenship of New York.

Consultant architects to CIE from 1945, his firm worked on the Inchicore Chassis Works, Donnybrook Bus Garage, and Áras Mhic Dhiarmada (1944–51), Store Street, Dublin, the ground floor of which is the central bus station, Busáras; controversial for its cost, it was the first building in Dublin of any significance for a century and earned Scott the Gold Medal of the Royal Institute of the Architects of Ireland. He later became the first Irish architect to win the Gold Medal of the Royal Institute of British Architects, 1975. He designed the new studios and offices for RTE at Donnybrook, Dublin. His design for the new Abbey Theatre, opened in 1966, in association with Pierre Sonrel, was also controversial (his original design was not followed through, for lack of finance). Michael Scott and Partners, established in 1958, became Scott Tallon Walker in 1975, from which time he was less directly involved in projects. A member of the Arts Council, 1959–73 and 1978–83, he was for many years chairman of Dublin Theatre Festival and was the inspiration behind the art festival Rosc.

scouting. The Scouting Association of Ireland was founded in 1908 on the principles laid down by Robert Baden-Powell. Though multi-denominational, it was predominantly Protestant. Fears that it would prove anti-nationalist led BULMER HOBSON and CONSTANCE MARKIEVICZ to form FIANNA ÉIREANN. The CATHOLIC BOY SCOUTS OF IRELAND was founded in Dublin in 1927 by Father Ernest Farrell. Renamed Scouting Ireland CSI in 1997, it entered into consultations with its rival, now known as Scouting Ireland SAI. Despite the opposition of the Catholic bishops, the all-Ireland Scouting Ireland CSI (with 22,500 members) voted by the necessary two-thirds majority for a merger with Scouting Ireland SAI (8,000 members in the Republic) on 11 May 2003. There is a separate Protestant scouting organisation in Northern Ireland.

scraw or scragh (Irish *scraith*), a roofing-sod for poor dwellings. Some 2–3 feet wide and 2–3 inches thick, they were rolled onto a stick and conveyed to the thatcher, who laid them grass side upwards on the roof-frame to serve as insulation and as a hold for the SCOLLOP. A contemporary observer noted that they were used as bed-covering by the poverty-stricken before the Great Famine (1845–49).

scullogue (Irish *scológ*), a farmer who had saved money and was in a position to give loans. The loans were repaid after the harvest season or when the debtor returned from a period working as a migrant labourer in Ireland or in England.

Seahorse, a three-deck troopship wrecked less than a mile off Tramore, Co. Waterford, 31 January 1816, Ireland's worst shipwreck. The vessel, out of Ramsgate for Cork, was carrying 393 people, including 38 children. Caught in an easterly storm, the ship, having lost its masts and rudder, dragged its anchor and sank in sight of shore. Only thirty people, including the captain, managed to reach shore.

The troopship *Boadicea,* returning with approximately 250 soldiers from the Battle of Waterloo to garrison duty in Cork, was a victim of the same storm and was lost off the Old Head of Kinsale, with no survivors.

Seanad Éireann, the senate or secondary house of the OIREACHTAS. Despite de Valera's reservations about the efficacy of a second chamber and the abolition of the first Seanad Éireann (see SENATE OF THE IRISH FREE STATE), under the Constitution of Ireland (1937) Seanad Éireann was re-established. More firmly under the control of the Government, it still had sixty members, forty-three elected by vocational panels, three each for the University of Dublin and National University of Ireland, and eleven nominated by the Taoiseach. The Seanad can delay bills passed by Dáil Éireann only for ninety days (except for money bills, which can be delayed for only twenty-one days).

The new Seanad, which met for the first time in November 1938, became a second chamber for the political parties rather than a chamber of specialist knowledge: it became a haven for potential and defeated Dáil deputies and for those who had retired from the Dáil. The proliferation of Dáil committees in recent years has led to an increased use of senators on such committees.

The office of Cathaoirleach (Chairman) of the Seanad has been held by the following:

Seán Gibbons (1938–43)
Seán Goulding (1943–48)
Timothy J. O'Donovan (1948–51)
Liam Ó Buachalla (1951–54)
Patrick F. Baxter (1954–57)
Liam Ó Buachalla (1957–69)
Michael Yeats (1969–73)
Michael C. Cranitch (3 January to 1 June 1973)
James Dooge (1973–77)
Séamus Dolan (1977–81)
Charles McDonald (1981–82)
Treas Honan (1982–83)
Patrick J. Reynolds (1983–87)
Treas Honan (1987–89)
Seán Doherty (1989–92)
Seán Fallon (1992–95)
Liam Naughten (12 July 1995 to 16 November 1996)
Liam T. Cosgrave (27 November 1996 to 1997)
Brian Mullooly (1997–2002)
Rory Kiely (2002–)

seanchaí, a traditional storyteller who inherited the function of the *bard* (genealogist, local historian, and guardian of the community's history). The seanchaí was normally a member of a particular family, the repository of stories, myths, legends, and local and national history. Generally supported by the community, the seanchaí made a round of the houses, telling stories in a different house each night. (See also JAMES BERRY.) Much of his lore was unique and jealously guarded by the possessor, being handed on to a chosen successor but never written down. With the growth of the mass media in the early years of the twentieth century the seanchaí became obsolete as a younger generation turned to other forms of entertainment. The stories of several seanchaithe were recorded by the IRISH FOLKLORE COMMISSION and other bodies concerned with the preservation of native lore.

secondary education. Education for those who had completed primary education was generally known as 'intermediate education' during the nineteenth century. Such education was largely denominational. Between 1783 and 1870 some forty-seven Catholic intermediate schools were opened. By 1871 there were 587 intermediate schools, of which 265 were for boys, 162 for girls, and 160 mixed. Instruction was based on the humanities. Those schools providing foreign languages were known as 'superior' schools.

Intermediate education was not organised until the passing of the Intermediate Education (Ireland) Act (1878), which established the Intermediate Education Board for Ireland. The board's division into junior, middle and senior classes obtained until 1924. Its role included the organising of a system of public examinations, the provision of certificates, prizes, and exhibitions, and the allocation of finance to managers according to results. This system of 'payment by results', the main source of income for school managers, lasted until 1924.

When the examinations were first held, 1879, there were 3,954 candidates in the three grades. By 1880 the figure had risen to 5,561; it showed little increase until 1896, when there were 9,000 candidates. By 1907 there were 11,000. This figure did not change until 1924, when the system was reorganised.

An inquiry in 1899 recommended that more emphasis be placed on science and that payment by results be abolished. The Intermediate Education Act (1900) attempted to implement some of the recommendations. The newly created Department of Agriculture and Technical Instruction began to operate in 1899. The Technical Instructions Branch worked in close co-operation with the Intermediate Board.

There were now two separate secondary systems: the intermediate system catered for the middle and lower middle classes, preparing pupils for a wide range of commercial and civil service posts and those who wished to undertake higher studies, while the technical system catered for those in agriculture and allied fields, attempted to raise the standard of farming, and prepared pupils for the trades. The two systems operated separately until reorganised under the centralised control of the Department of Education in 1924.

From 1913 the Intermediate Board paid fees to managers according to inspections rather than solely on results. A commission of inquiry was established in 1918 to inquire 'as to any improvement which may appear desirable to be made in the conditions of service and on the method of remuneration of teachers in Intermediate Schools.' Its report, March 1919, recommended pension schemes and the abolition of payment by results; it also recommended that a capitation grant be paid for each pupil. The most important recommendation was that the division into Junior, Middle and Senior Grade be replaced by an Intermediate Certificate and Leaving Certificate. The first Department of Education of the Irish Free State, 1922, adopted the recommendations. The Intermediate Board was taken over by the Department of Education in 1923 and a new programme for secondary schools adopted, August 1924. Secondary education was divided into two cycles, Intermediate Certificate and Leaving Certificate. The Intermediate Certificate could be taken at about the age of sixteen by those who had followed a prescribed course for three or four years and the Leaving Certificate by those who had followed a prescribed course for a further two years. Irish and mathematics were made obligatory subjects for the Intermediate Certificate and Irish also for the Leaving Certificate. It was necessary to pass five subjects. A total of 11,841 pupils followed the first Intermediate Certificate course and the Leaving Certificate.

Access to secondary education was limited until the 1960s. Then, in the wake of the PROGRAMMES FOR ECONOMIC EXPANSION, a series of reforms led to the extension of access, until secondary education became universal in the 1970s. In addition to the voluntary (private) secondary schools there were now comprehensive schools, community colleges, and community schools.

Second Reformation, an evangelical campaign organised by fundamentalists in the Church of Ireland and Church of England in the 1820s; evangelical clergymen were known as 'Biblicals' or 'New Reformers'. The Second Reformation was most zealously prosecuted in Connacht, where it was encouraged by THOMAS PLUNKET, Bishop of Tuam; among the most active evangelicals were REV. ALEXANDER R. C. DALLAS, REV. EDWARD NANGLE, and REV. HYACINTH D'ARCY. Opposition in the west was led by the Catholic Archbishop of Tuam, JOHN MACHALE, who resented their proselytising campaign during the Great Famine (1845–49); he was assisted later by REV. PATRICK LAVELLE. The Second Reformation was also opposed by moderates within the Church of Ireland; it petered out during the 1860s, leaving a legacy of bitterness in its wake.

Second World War. On the outbreak of the Second World War, September 1939, the Taoiseach (and Minister for External Affairs), ÉAMON DE VALERA, announced a policy of neutrality. Speaking in Dáil Éireann, he said: 'I have stated in this house, and I have stated in the country, that the aim of government policy is to keep this country out of the war, and nobody, either here or elsewhere, has any right to assume anything else.' This position was widely supported; the sole dissenter in Dáil Éireann was JAMES DILLON, who resigned from FINE GAEL in protest. The policy was generally resented in England, despite the support of the Secretary of State for Foreign Affairs, Lord Halifax, who commented: 'British safety is not decreased but immeasurably increased, by a free and friendly Ireland.' Some British defence experts argued that Irish neutrality was opportune—provided Germany respected it—as British coastal defences were stretched to the limit. The *Times* (London) commented, 9 September 1939: 'It is more than probable that Éire's neutrality is the best policy that Mr. De Valera's government could have adopted.'The period was generally referred to as 'the Emergency' in Ireland (because of the declaration of a state of national emergency). Aspects of the Emergency were:

Diplomacy. Relations with the British representative in Ireland, Sir John Maffey, remained cordial during the war. Maffey was aware of the benevolent attitude towards British incursions into Irish air space and of the spurious distinction between 'operational' and 'non-operational' personnel that allowed for the swift repatriation of the 550 or so British and Allied air crews that landed or crashed in Ireland. The activities of British and American intelligence agents operating through the ports, Shannon Airport and the transatlantic flying-boat station at FOYNES, Co. Limerick, though monitored, went largely uninterrupted.

On the other hand, de Valera had an uneasy relationship with the American ambassador, David Gray (see 'AMERICAN NOTE').

Dr Edouard Hempel, the German ambassador, maintained a good working relationship with de Valera. At the onset of war he assured de Valera that Germany would respect Ireland's neutrality if Ireland strictly adhered to it. As the conflict progressed, he became aware of Irish sympathies with the Allied cause. In contrast to the treatment of Allied personnel, all Axis air crews and agents were interned for the duration of the war. By December 1944, 223 German and three Japanese prisoners were held at the Curragh Military Camp. Attempts by the IRA to establish contact with Germany were summarily dealt with.

Agriculture. A compulsory tillage policy, 1940–48, specified that three-eighths of all arable holdings over ten acres had to be under tillage. The increase in tillage—from 1.5 million acres in 1938 to 2.6 million acres in 1945—was effected through an over-utilisation and under-fertilisation of the soil; agricultural output, as a consequence, declined in efficiency. The cattle trade was severely affected by an outbreak of foot-and-mouth disease, 1941–42.

Defence. Defence was under the control of the Minister for the Co-ordination of Defensive Measures, FRANK AIKEN. An All-Party Consultative Defence Council was established to co-ordinate defence policy.

In 1938 the strength of the regular army, at 5,915, was less than 65 per cent of establishment. Successive recruiting campaigns to 1940 brought the total strength of volunteers and reservists to 54,502 under the new chief of staff, Lieutenant-General Dan McKenna, who had replaced General Michael Brennan in January. As the threat of invasion receded, numbers continued to decline to 1944, when the total was 36,211. In addition to the regular forces, auxiliary forces were recruited for the duration: the LOCAL SECURITY FORCE was established in May 1940 and the LOCAL DEFENCE FORCE the following September. The LDF at its maximum numbered some 100,000.

Air Corps strength in 1938 stood at 736, with fifty-four aircraft, later augmented to seventy-three. The service was also responsible for the recovery of crashed aircraft, of which there were 160 during this period: 39 American, 105 British, and 16 German; 223 crew members of the 830 involved in crash landings were killed.

The Coastwatching Service operated from eighty-eight look-out posts around the coast. Duties included the monitoring of all aircraft and shipping movements and the finding of drifting mines. The service also logged sightings of lifeboats and in many instances assisted survivors. At the request of the US Air Force, as a navigational aid to its aircraft, each post had the sign *EIRE* and a reference number displayed in 30-foot letters in its proximity.

The duties of the Construction Corps included the building of roads, the construction and repair of barracks, and the reclaiming of scrub and boglands.

The Maritime Inscription was a reserve formed from among fishermen, yachtsmen and others with seagoing experience. With a strength of 1,143, it was divided in 1942 into fourteen companies and separated from the Marine Service.

A Minefield Section was established in 1941 to lay mines in strategic waters. Casings were manufactured by Thompson's Foundry in Carlow and the Great Southern Railway and the mines were completed by the Ordnance Corps. The Royal Navy steamer *Shark* laid the mines. The Royal Navy later supplied mines of a more advanced design and planted an estimated five thousand on southern approaches to Irish territorial waters. On 10 May 1943, at Ballymanus, Co. Donegal, seventeen young men were killed and seven seriously injured when a mine at which they were throwing stones exploded. After the war a minesweeping flotilla of the Royal Navy was based at Cóbh; it swept or destroyed some four thousand mines during the period 1946–47.

Under article 6 of the ANGLO-IRISH TREATY (1921), Ireland was precluded from forming a navy for defensive purposes until the signing of the ANGLO-IRISH AGREEMENTS (1938). The Marine and Coastwatching Service was established on 5 September 1939. Two light tenders were transferred from port control duties to join the *Muirchú* (formerly HELGA), *Fort Rannoch*, and the training ship *Isaalt.* The *Muirchú* and *Fort Rannoch* were equipped with two twelve-pound guns, two light machine-guns, and depth charges. A small flotilla of motor torpedo boats carried two 18-inch torpedoes, a heavy machine-gun, and a hydrophone for detecting submarine activity. In January 1940 the service was placed under the command of Colonel Tony Lawlor.

Merchant shipping. IRISH SHIPPING LTD was established by the government in March 1941 to help maintain essential supplies of food and raw materials. During the war years it supplied the country with 712,000 tons of wheat, 178,000 tons of coal, 63,000 tons of phosphates, 24,000 tons of tobacco, 19,000 tons of newsprint, and some 10,000 tons of timber. All Irish merchant ships bore large neutral markings.

Losses incurred by these fleets during the war included:

City of Limerick (15 July 1940). Out of Cartagena, Spain, with a cargo of fruit for Liverpool, it lost two crew members when bombed and strafed in the Bay of Biscay. The ship was abandoned and the survivors landed at Penzance, Cornwall, by a Belgian trawler.

Ardmore (11/12 November 1940). Struck a mine off the Saltee Islands, Co. Wexford, en route from Fishguard to Cork with a cargo of livestock; all twenty-five on board were lost.

Isolda (19 December 1940). The Irish Lights vessel *Isolda* was ferrying a relief crew to the Coninbeg Lighthouse, Co. Wexford, when a German bomber attacked it. Though it was clearly identifiable as part of the Lighthouse Service, the bomber made two passes over the vessel before releasing a stick of bombs on its third run. Six of the crew were killed and seven injured. The remainder of the crew took to the lifeboats from the burning ship and landed at Kilmore Quay.

Innisfallen (21 December 1940). En route to Dublin from Liverpool with 157 passengers and a crew of 63, the *Innisfallen* struck a magnetic mine in the Mersey. Four members of the crew were killed. The vessel sank within twenty minutes; the remaining passengers and crew were rescued.

Kerry Head (22 October 1940). Horrified islanders watched the collier Kerry Head with its crew of twelve sink within minutes of being attacked by a German bomber off Cape Clear, Co. Cork.

St Fintan (22 March 1941). The collier *St Fintan,* en route from Drogheda, Co. Louth, to Cardiff, was attacked by two German bombers and sunk with its crew of nine off the coast of Pembrokeshire.

Clonlara (22 August 1941). The *Clonlara* was sunk in an Atlantic convoy by the German submarine *U564,* with the loss of eleven of its complement. It was carrying a cargo of coal from Cardiff to Lisbon.

City of Waterford (19 September 1941). The ship was sailing in convoy from Cardiff (via Milford Haven) to Lisbon with a cargo of coal when it was struck by the Dutch tug *Thames.* Its crew, picked up by the *Deptford,* was transferred to the convoy rescue ship *Walmer Castle.* On Sunday 21 September, some 700 miles off Ushant, the *Walmer Castle* was itself attacked by a German plane. The engine-room suffered a direct hit, and the ship sank with heavy loss of life; five of the previously rescued crew of the *City of Waterford* were among the fatalities.

Irish Pine (15 November 1942). The ship was en route to Boston for repairs to its fuel tanks before picking up its cargo of phosphates at Tampa, Florida, for Dublin when it was torpedoed in the North Atlantic. The log of the German submarine *U608* recorded that the vessel sank in approximately three minutes, with all thirty-three of its crew.

Kyle Clare (23 February 1943). Having discharged its cargo of coal at Lisbon, the *Kyle Clare* was making for its home port of Limerick when attacked in the Atlantic by the German submarine *U456.* The collier, with its crew of eighteen, sank immediately.

Cymric (February 1944). The ship, with its cargo of coal from Ardrossan, Ayrshire, to Lisbon and a crew of eleven, was last sighted off Co. Dublin on 24 February. No trace of it was ever found.

Fishing fleet losses included the trawler *Leukos* (9 March 1940), sunk by gunfire from the German submarine *U38* while fishing off Tory Island, Co. Donegal, with the loss of its crew of eleven, and the *Naomh Garbhán* (2 May 1945), whose crew of three were lost when a mine entangled in its nets exploded as it fished off Dungarvan, Co. Waterford.

Bombings. Wardens were recruited for air-raid duties. There were several bombing attacks by the German air force.

26 August 1940. Three women lost their lives when a bomb struck Campile creamery, Co. Wexford. (The German government subsequently apologised and offered £9,000 compensation.)

2 January 1941. Three members of a family at Knockroe, Co. Carlow, were killed when their farmhouse was struck by a bomb. Bombs also fell at Drogheda, Co. Louth, and in Cos. Kildare, Wexford, and Wicklow, without loss of life.

15–16 April 1941. Belfast: About 180 aircraft participated in an attack that resulted in approximately 750 deaths, with 1,511 more injured. Thirteen Fire Brigade units from the South spent two days in the city helping to deal with the fires.

4–5 May 1941. Belfast: 204 German aircraft dropped 96,000 incendiary bombs and an estimated 200 tons of explosives, killing more than 150 people and seriously disrupting the city's commercial life. The harbour area and shipyards were severely damaged; the aircraft manufacturers Short and Harland took a direct hit, affecting production for some six months.

5–6 May 1941. Belfast: Twelve people were killed when the city was bombed. Fire Brigade units from the South again assisted local brigades.

30–31 May 1941. Dublin: Thirty-four people died and at least 90 were injured when bombs struck the city. A 250-pound high-explosive bomb fell in North Richmond Street at 1:30 a.m., followed by a second at Rutland Place. A third in the Phoenix Park damaged the American ambassador's residence and Áras an Uachtaráin. A fourth, falling on North Strand and believed to be either a 500-pound bomb or a land mine, caused most of the death and destruction.

13 June 1941. Twenty-three people were killed when the Rosslare–Fishguard ferry *Patrick* was dive-bombed and sunk by German aircraft a few miles off Fishguard.

In 1958 the government, which had paid £344,000 in compensation to the bereaved and injured, accepted a compensation payment of £327,000 from West Germany in respect of the bombings.

Intelligence. Military Intelligence was headed by Colonel Liam Archer until 1941, when he was succeeded by COLONEL DAN BRYAN. Working in close co-operation with the Garda Síochána, it was supported by the Supplementary Intelligence Service, a secret adjunct of the Local Defence Force. A meeting between the secretary of the Department of Defence, J. P. Walshe, and Sir Harry Hinsley of MI5 (the British domestic intelligence service, now the Security Service) during the early period of the war established a collaboration between the two services. Communication was also established between Irish and American services. While Military Intelligence concentrated on the activities of Axis agents and sympathisers (including the IRA), it also monitored the movements of American and British agents and sympathisers.

Irish Republican Army. The government responded to the IRA's 'declaration of war' against Britain by introducing the TREASON ACT, 30 May 1939, and OFFENCES AGAINST THE STATE ACT, 14 June. Following further IRA activity, the passing of the EMERGENCY POWERS ACT, January 1940, resulted in the imprisonment or internment of large numbers of IRA members. Six members, including the chief of staff, Charles Kerins, were shot by firing squad following the killing of a Garda sergeant. Three IRA members died on hunger strike between 1940 and 1946. PLAN KATHLEEN, an IRA proposal for a German invasion of Ireland, was never seriously considered by Berlin, which held the organisation in little esteem.

Emigration. The numbers emigrating during the war were:

1940	25,964
1941	35,131
1942	51,711
1943	48,324
1944	13,613
1945	23,794

The low figure for 1944 may be explained by travel restrictions occasioned by the outbreak of foot-and-mouth disease. It has been suggested that as many as 30,000 of those who emigrated joined the British armed forces.

Rationing. Severe rationing restrictions were imposed by the Department of Supplies. Bread, clothing, gas, petrol, sugar and tea were among the items rationed; to prevent profiteering, the government issued an order fixing prices for essential foodstuffs. Coal supplies were soon exhausted, and the large-scale use of bogs, woodland and forests was undertaken. In 1942 the tea ration was reduced from 1 ounce to half an ounce per week. White bread was virtually unobtainable; a coarse, dark substitute known as 'one-way' was in general use, prompting a parody on the popular wartime song 'Bless 'Em All':

> God bless de Valera and Seán MacEntee
> For their loaf of brown bread and their half-ounce of tea.

Shortages became acute as the Allies attempted to force Ireland into joining the war by a further tightening of shipping and import restrictions. A thriving black market operated, particularly in border areas, with tea, cigarettes and tobacco among the most sought-after items.

13 September 1939. Petrol rationing was introduced; motorists were allowed between 8 and 16 gallons over six weeks, depending on horsepower.

30 March 1942. Buses were recommended to operate at reduced speeds to conserve fuel and help preserve tyres.

6 May 1942. Three million ration books were issued. Each booklet contained 52 differently coloured coupons.

2 June 1942. A speed limit was reinforced by government order: cars and motorcycles were restricted to 30 m.p.h., double-deck buses to 20 m.p.h., and single-deck buses to 25 m.p.h.

15 January 1948. Clothes rationing ended; gas, rationed from March 1942, was restored to full supply.

24 March 1949. Petrol rations for private cars and motorcycles were doubled, and restrictions on the distribution of diesel, fuel oils and paraffin were lifted.

Aftermath. Speaking on Radio Éireann, 16 May 1945, the Taoiseach, Éamon de Valera said:

> I know you all feel with me the deep debt of gratitude we owe to all those who, at heavy personal sacrifice, joined the army, including the Marine Service, and the various auxiliary defence organisations and helped to guard us against the most serious of all the dangers that threatened. The officers, non-commissioned officers and men of the regular army already in service at the beginning of the war formed, with the Reserve and the Volunteer Force, a well-trained nucleus around which it was possible, in an incredibly short time, to build up an efficient fighting force. Many tens of thousands of young men responded to the appeal of the Government, and of the leaders of all the political parties in the Defence Conference, to join the army. Without regard to their own personal interests, these young men left their employment or the studies which they had been pursuing in preparation for professional careers. To all of these, to the many other voluntary bodies who helped in the national effort and to the men of our merchant marine, who faced all the perils of the ocean to bring us essential supplies, the nation is proudly thankful.

The national emergency declared in 1939 formally ended on 31 August 1946.

secret societies. Agrarian secret societies were a feature of rural life in the eighteenth and nineteenth centuries. Many came into existence in response to oppression by landlords, rising rents, the price of CONACRE and labour duties, and the exactions of Protestant and Catholic TITHES, dues, and offerings. The first widespread secret society was that of the WHITEBOYS, 1761, whose activities continued into the nineteenth century.

Secret societies, recruited in the main from the tenant-farmer class, were usually organised for an immediate purpose. They included the Blackfeet, CARDERS, DEFENDERS, Hearts of Oak (or Oakboys), Hearts of Steel (or Steelboys), LADY CLARES, PEEP O' DAY BOYS, RIBBONMEN, Right Boys, Terry Alts, THRASHERS, and Whitefeet. Elements of the secret societies were also found among those who engaged in FACTION-FIGHTING. The societies were led by individuals using such pseudonyms as Captain Moonlight, Captain Rock, Captain Right, and Captain Starlight. The principal weapons were murder and intimidation, cattle-maiming, and crop-burning.

In the second part of the nineteenth century a new kind of secret society appeared: the IRISH REPUBLICAN BROTHERHOOD. It diverged from agrarian secret society traditions in that its membership was principally from towns and cities, it had a long-term objective (to destroy British rule in Ireland), and it had a rigid central organisation. The LAND LEAGUE (1879–81), which to some extent subsumed elements of the agrarian secret societies, was aimed at the economic betterment of tenant-farmers and the destruction of the landlord system, and many of its members resorted to violence.

In the twentieth century the IRISH REPUBLICAN ARMY, because of its outlawed position, took on some of the characteristics and rhetoric of the old secret societies.

Senate of the Irish Free State, popular name for the first Seanad Éireann, created by the CONSTITUTION OF THE IRISH FREE STATE (1922). It was intended to represent minority (i.e. Unionist) interests in the new state and to include people with specialist knowledge or experience or a record of public service. There were sixty seats, half filled by election and half on the appointment of the President of the Executive Council. Candidates for election had to be thirty-five years of age. The Senate's functions and powers were partly modelled on those of the British House of Lords. It could initiate legislation, amend it, and also suspend it for 270 days; if legislation was presented to it again at the end of 270 days and rejected again, it was deemed to be passed. The Senate was granted twenty-one days in which to consider money bills, which could not be suspended.

Among the first members of the Senate, which met for the first time on 11 December 1922, were W. B. YEATS, Oliver St John Gogarty, Lord Granard, Lord Kerry, Lord Mayo, and Lord Wicklow, all nominated by the President of the Executive Council, W. T. COSGRAVE. SENATOR ALICE STOPFORD GREEN presented the

Chairman, BARON GLENAVY, with a casket and scroll of the names of the first senators. Between 1922 and its abolition in 1936 the Senate initiated twenty-five bills, twelve of which were accepted by Dáil Éireann. It considered 489 bills (other than money bills) and proposed 1,831 amendments to 182 bills, most of which were accepted by the Dáil. It exercised suspension on nine bills, two of which the Dáil did not attempt to pass into law. Cosgrave's successor, ÉAMON DE VALERA, had a less than favourable view of the institution: 'We think that the proper thing to do is to end the Senate and not attempt to mend it. It is costly, and we do not see any useful function that it really serves' (February 1928). A joint commission, of which De Valera was a member, examined the efficiency of the Senate and recommended that its composition be changed.

The CONSTITUTION (REMOVAL OF OATH) ACT (1933), one of de Valera's first pieces of legislation, had a stormy passage through the Senate. He accused the senators of being hostile to his government while having favoured that of his predecessor. After it had been delayed by the Senate, the OATH OF ALLEGIANCE was removed in 1933. During the general election of January 1933 de Valera promised to abolish the Senate 'as at present constituted.' Later, his Wearing of Uniform (Restriction) Bill, designed to embarrass the BLUESHIRTS, was rejected in the Senate, where he was accused of allowing the IRA to act as a police force and harass the Blueshirts. The legislation to abolish the Senate, the Constitution (Amendment No. 24) Bill, came to the Senate on 30 May 1934. The Chairman, Thomas Westropp-Bennett, rejected de Valera's accusation that the Senate had been partisan and accused him of attempting to establish a dictatorship. After the bill was rejected (35 to 15) the period of suspension expired on 24 November 1935. The final sitting of the Senate was on 19 May 1936. The bill was carried in the Dáil (74 to 52) on 28 May.

The office of Cathaoirleach (Chairman) of the Senate was held by Lord Glenavy (1922–28) and Thomas Westropp-Bennett (1928–36).

Separatist, a paper edited by P. S. O'HEGARTY from February to September 1922. Though not formally an organ of the IRB, it was supported by the Supreme Council, which contributed £1,000 towards it. The paper accepted the ANGLO-IRISH TREATY (1921) while looking for a complete break with Britain in the future.

Services, Industrial, Professional and Technical Union (SIPTU), the largest trade union in Ireland, with more than 200,000 members in 2001. It was established in 1990 from an amalgamation of the IRISH TRANSPORT AND GENERAL WORKERS' UNION and the Federated Workers' Union of Ireland (formerly the WORKERS' UNION OF IRELAND).

Sexton, Thomas (1848–1932), politician (Irish Party); born in Co. Waterford, educated locally. A member of Parliament, 1880–96, he was high sheriff of Dublin, 1887, and lord mayor, 1888–89. He played a prominent role in the LAND LEAGUE and later in the PLAN OF CAMPAIGN. The Irish Party's chief spokesman on finance, he was a brilliant public speaker and was called 'silver-tongued Sexton'. Imprisoned together with CHARLES STEWART PARNELL in Kilmainham Jail, Dublin, October 1881, he was a signatory of the 'NO-RENT MANIFESTO' but was released shortly afterwards when his health deteriorated. He played a leading role in the NATIONAL LEAGUE and represented Parnell at the inaugural meeting of the TENANTS' DEFENCE ASSOCIATION, 1889. During the crisis over Parnell's leadership after the O'Shea divorce case he proposed Parnell for the chairmanship of the party but withdrew his support when it became clear that Parnell's continuation in office could be at the expense of home rule. He was chairman of the *Freeman's Journal*, 1892–1912.

Shanahan's Stamp Auctions Ltd. Dr Paul Singer, a native of Slovakia, settled in Ireland with his wife, Irma Singer, and family in 1954 and in February, with the aid of the auctioneering firm of Desmond and Diana Shanahan of Dún Laoghaire, Co. Dublin, launched the Shanahan Stamp Auction scheme. Thousands of small investors, attracted through newspaper advertisements, invested in the scheme—£5 million in 1959 alone. Following the theft of an uninsured collection of stamps valued at between £250,000 and £500,000, the company collapsed, 25 May 1959, with liabilities of almost £2 million, resulting in nine thousand claims from creditors and investors. About £30,000 worth of stolen stamps were later recovered.

The collapse of the business precipitated one of the most complex cases tried in an Irish court. Desmond Shanahan received a fifteen-mouth jail sentence. A *nolle prosequi* was entered by the state in the cases against Diana Shanahan and Irma Singer. The litigation involving Singer, during which he frequently represented himself and was occasionally represented by SEÁN MACBRIDE, was the lengthiest trial up to that time. He was acquitted at a retrial that began at Green Street Courthouse, Dublin, on 7 November 1961.

'Shanavests', a fighting faction, originally known as 'Padeen Car's Party', originating in Clonmel, Co. Tipperary, 1805, and spreading to Cos. Waterford, Limerick, and Kerry (see FACTION-FIGHTING). The faction owed its name to an old waistcoat (Irish *sean-veist*) worn by its founder, Paddy Car. His comment during the hanging of Nicholas Hanley that he wouldn't leave the place of execution until 'I have seen the cravat about Hanley's neck' was reported to Hanley's relatives and friends, who formed a rival faction, known as the CARAVATS. In 1818 the Shanavests vowed to support each other for a period of four years and became known as the Four-Year-Olds, while the Caravats took a vow for three years and became known as the Three-Year-Olds.

Shankill Butchers. Using butchers' knives, members of the UVF in the Shankill Road area of Belfast were responsible for the torture and killing of some twenty people, mostly Catholics, between November 1975 and March 1977. The leader of the gang, Hugh Leonard 'Lenny' Murphy, under whom they became independent of the UVF, initiated the campaign of torture followed by killing by throat-cutting that characterised their actions. Other members included Robert 'Basher' Bates and William Moore, whose taxi was used to transport the victims; he and others continued to terrorise the area after Murphy was arrested, 13 March 1976, and sentenced to twelve years' imprisonment for possession of firearms, of which he served six years (he was never tried for the murders). At least six victims were members of a rival loyalist faction. Part of the Lower Antrim Road where the gang operated became known as the 'Murder Mile'.

Eleven members of the 'Butchers', including Moore (who pleaded guilty to eleven murders) and Bates (who pleaded guilty to ten murders), were convicted, 20 February 1979, of 112 offences, including nineteen murders, attempted murders, kidnappings, and bomb explosions. They received a total of forty-two life sentences and other sentences, totalling nearly two thousand years. They were believed to have been captured on information supplied by Gerard McLaverty, who had been beaten up and left for dead, 10 May 1977. Murphy was shot by the Provisional IRA, 16 November 1982; thousands of loyalists attended his funeral. Bates was killed by a loyalist gunman, 11 June 1977.

Shankill Defence Association, a loyalist vigilante group established in the Shankill Road area of Belfast in the summer of 1969. Its chairman was John McKeague, an associate of REV. IAN PAISLEY (who denied any connection with the group). Members took part in clashes in the areas adjoining the (Catholic) Falls Road. The SCARMAN TRIBUNAL accepted that the organisation had played a role in intimidating Catholics to move out of Protestant areas. It was also involved in petrol-bombing and rioting at Unity Flats, Belfast, August 1969. It was believed that members of the ULSTER SPECIAL CONSTABULARY were active in the group, which called for the resignation of the Prime Minister of Northern Ireland, JAMES CHICHESTER-CLARK, when the HUNT REPORT recommended disbanding the Special Constabulary.

In November 1969 McKeague was cleared of a charge of conspiracy to cause explosions at the Silent Valley reservoir, Co. Down, and elsewhere, part of a series of explosions that, erroneously attributed to the IRA, played a role in forcing TERENCE O'NEILL out of office. McKeague's mother was killed in a petrol-bomb attack on his shop, 9 May 1971, believed to be the work of rival loyalists. One of the first loyalists to be interned, 1973, McKeague was subsequently connected with the UDA and the UVF and was founder of the RED HAND COMMANDO. He was killed by the INLA, 29 January 1982.

Shannon Scheme. The scheme for the electrification of Ireland was the brainchild of THOMAS A. MCLAUGHLIN, an engineer who, overcoming political and commercial opposition, persuaded the government to raise £5 million and to employ the German company Siemens, by which he was employed. Work on the scheme, the biggest hydro-electric project in the world at the time, began in August 1925 and was completed in 1929. Before the work began at Ardnacrusha, Co. Clare, there was a protracted strike in protest at the low wages on offer (32 shillings per week).

Siemens laid 60 miles of temporary railway, and eighty-seven steamers carried some 30,000 tons of equipment into Limerick for the project (one ship, the *Arabia,* sank with the loss of nineteen crew while en route from Germany).

At its peak the scheme employed 4,000 Irish and 1,000 German workers. There was tension between the Irish and foreign workers, who were better paid; a Limerick man, John Cox, was sentenced to death for the murder of a German. There was criticism also of the living conditions of the Irish workers. Specially constructed huts could accommodate less than 720 of the Irish work force, many of whom lived in barns, hen houses, stables, and even pigsties.

The Ardnacrusha power station is at the end of a 7½-mile headrace, which takes the water from a weir near O'Briens Bridge on the River Shannon; a tailrace of 1½ miles returns the water to the Shannon at Parteen, outside Limerick. The headrace is 300 feet wide at water level and some 35 feet deep.

The Shannon Scheme was for a time the model of international large-scale electrification projects. The Electricity (Supply) Act (1927) established the Electricity Supply Board for the distribution of electricity. During the 1930s, electricity supply increased fourfold. SEÁN KEATING spent some time at the site; his *Night's Candles Are Burnt Out* is one of several canvases on the subject.

On 29 July 2002, on the seventy-fifth anniversary of the scheme, the Shannon Scheme received two international awards: the Milestone Award of the Institute of Electrical and Electronic Engineers, which recognised it as an engineering feat that made a significant contribution to society, and the Landmark Award of the American Society of Civil Engineers, previous winners of which include the Eiffel Tower, the Forth Bridge, and the Panama Canal.

Shan Van Vocht, a separatist periodical founded in Belfast by its joint editors, ALICE MILLIGAN and Ethna Carbery (Anna Johnston), 1896. During its three years' existence it reflected nationalist ideals and published prose and poetry from leading nationalists of the era. It was taken over by ARTHUR GRIFFITH and the *United Irishman.*

Shaw, George Bernard (1856–1950), dramatist and critic; born in Dublin, educated at Central Model School and Wesley College. In London from 1876, he did not achieve success as a dramatist until *John Bull's Other Island* was banned in 1904. The ban did not apply to Ireland, and the play was produced later at the ABBEY THEATRE, Dublin. Shaw's penchant for controversy continued with the production of *O'Flaherty VC* in 1915 and his stand on the EASTER RISING (1916); he protested against the executions of the leaders, saying that 'an Irishman resorting to arms to achieve the independence of his country is doing only what Englishmen will do if it is their misfortune to be invaded and conquered by the Germans in the course of the present war.' The executions, he pointed out, were turning patriots into martyrs and handing the country over to SINN FÉIN.

Shaw then took up the defence of ROGER CASEMENT. He believed it was a lost cause (he would not allow his wife to put money into the defence fund) but suggested that the line of defence should be an admission of guilt. He wished Casement to say: 'I am an Irishman, captured in a fair attempt to achieve the independence of my country.' While this accorded with Casement's own view, the defence put forward by his counsel, A. M. Sullivan, was based on a legal technicality. Following the trial, Shaw continued to fight, presenting a petition to the Prime Minister, H. H. ASQUITH, with the message that if Britain wanted to make a martyr out of Casement, it should hang him. His letter headed 'Shall Roger Casement hang?' was rejected by the *Times* (London) but was published in the *Manchester Guardian,* 22 July 1916.

Shaw was awarded the Nobel Prize for Literature in 1925 and was joint founder (with W. B. YEATS) of the IRISH ACADEMY OF LETTERS. He declined British honours, turning down the Order of Merit and a peerage. He died following a fall received while pruning an apple tree at his home in Ayot St Lawrence, Hertfordshire (now the Shaw Museum). He bequeathed part of his estate towards the introduction of a new alphabet, based on phonetics; the winning scheme, that of Kingsley Read, was used for the publication of one edition of Shaw's play *Androcles and the Lion* but was not otherwise taken up. Under his will, royalties from *Pygmalion* (1912) accrue to the NATIONAL GALLERY OF IRELAND.

Shaw, William (1823–1895), businessman, banker, and politician (Whig); born in Cork, educated at Highbury School, Salisbury. A director of the Munster Bank, he was member of Parliament for Bandon, 1868–74, and for Co. Cork, 1874–85. He succeeded ISAAC BUTT as chairman of the IRISH PARTY, 1879. Having lost the leadership to CHARLES STEWART PARNELL, May 1990, he formally seceded from the party, followed by eleven other Whigs, January

1881, but continued to support Gladstone and the Liberals on home rule. After his bank failed in 1885 he played no further part in public affairs.

shebeen (Irish *síbín,* a vessel of 2–3 quarts' capacity used to exact grain tolls, later used to measure drink), an illicit public-house. According to MARIA EDGEWORTH in *Castle Rackrent* (1800), 'taplash' or weak beer was commonly available in shebeens, as was POITÍN. The owner also dispensed some legal whiskey, the permit for which served as a cover for his illicit trade. The legal trade raised little objection to the shebeens, which catered for a less desirable clientele. Shebeens were rarely visited by the police: a warrant was needed to enter the building (which was a private dwelling), and they were then faced with the task of proving whether the drink found was legal or illicit spirit.

Sheehy, David (1843–1932), politician (Irish Party) and land agitator; born in Broadford, Co. Limerick, brother of FATHER EUGENE SHEEHY. He established a milling business at Loughmore, near Templemore, Co. Tipperary, where he raised his family. A supporter of the IRB and of the LAND LEAGUE, he was elected to Parliament for Co. Galway, 1885–1900, and South Meath, 1903–08. He served eighteen months in prison during the PLAN OF CAMPAIGN. During the crisis over the leadership of CHARLES STEWART PARNELL, December 1890, he opposed Parnell's continuance in office, believing it would endanger the tenant-farmers' fight for fair rent. HANNA SHEEHY-SKEFFINGTON was his daughter.

Sheehy, Rev. Eugene (1841–1917), clergyman (Catholic) and land agitator; born in Broadford, Co. Limerick, educated at the Irish College, Paris, and ordained in 1868. While a curate in Kilmallock, Co. Limerick, 1868–84, he was president of the local branch of the LAND LEAGUE; his support for the land agitation earned him the popular title of 'the Land League Priest' as well as a period of imprisonment, May 1881. He ministered in Bruree, Co. Limerick, 1884–1909, where ÉAMON DE VALERA was among his altar-boys. He organised a boycott of the local landlord family of Gubbins because of its policy of eviction. Following his resignation he moved to Dublin, where his nieces—daughters of DAVID SHEEHY, including HANNA SHEEHY-SKEFFINGTON—were active in nationalist organisations and the suffrage movement. He was close to leaders of the IRB and visited the United States on behalf of the Supreme Council, 1910. A founder-member of the IRISH VOLUNTEERS, he visited the GPO garrison to give spiritual aid during the EASTER RISING (1916), though in very poor health.

Sheehy-Skeffington, Francis (1878–1916), journalist, socialist, feminist, and pacifist; born Francis Skeffington in Bailieborough, Co. Cavan, educated at UCD, where his friends included JAMES JOYCE, who portrayed him as McCann in *A Portrait of the Artist as a Young Man* (1916). He was registrar of University College, Dublin, from 1902 until 1904, when he resigned after a public dispute with the president, Father William Delany, over the rights of women to academic status. On his marriage to Hanna Sheehy (HANNA SHEEHY-SKEFFINGTON), 1903, he adopted her surname in addition to his own to show that marriage was no barrier to equality between the sexes, and they worked together in a wide number of radical causes.

He was joint founder, manager and editor of the *Irish Citizen,* 1912. He supported the SOCIALIST PARTY OF IRELAND, 1908, and Independent Labour Party of Ireland. During a lecture tour of the United States, 1915, he was entertained by CLAN NA GAEL, though as a pacifist he disapproved of republican violence. He supported the (third) HOME RULE BILL and disapproved of the EASTER RISING (1916). While attempting to prevent looting during the rising he was arrested by Captain J. C. Bowen-Colthurst, who had him summarily shot in Portobello Barracks. Bowen-Colthurst was subsequently adjudged guilty of murder but held to be insane and was detained for a period in Broadmoor Asylum for the Criminally Insane, Berkshire; he later emigrated to Canada, where he became a banker. An investigation by a royal commission into the circumstances of Sheehy-Skeffington's death led to an offer of £10,000 compensation, which his widow rejected.

Sheehy-Skeffington published 'Michael Davitt's unfinished campaign' in *Independent Review,* 1906, and a *Life of Michael Davitt* (1908). His novel *In Dark and Evil Days* was published in 1919.

Sheehy-Skeffington, Hanna (1877–1946), teacher and feminist; born Hanna Sheehy in Kanturk, Co. Cork, daughter of DAVID SHEEHY and niece of REV. EUGENE SHEEHY, educated at Dominican Convent, Eccles Street, Dublin, and St Mary's University College. A language teacher at the School of Commerce, Rathmines, she jointly founded the Women Graduates' and Candidate Graduates' Association, 1901. She married Francis Sheehy (FRANCIS SHEEHY-SKEFFINGTON), 1903, with whom she founded the IRISH WOMEN'S FRANCHISE LEAGUE, 1908. She wrote theatre reviews for the *Irish Review.* In 1912 she was imprisoned for breaking windows in protest at the exclusion of women from the franchise in the (third) HOME RULE BILL. During the EASTER RISING (1916) she carried messages to the GPO. She refused compensation of £10,000 from the British army for the killing of her husband during the rising. She undertook a lecture tour of the United States, December 1916, and during the next two years called for support for SINN FÉIN and succeeded, where other republicans failed, in meeting President Wilson, January 1918. On her return to Ireland she was arrested and imprisoned, together with KATHLEEN CLARKE, CONSTANCE MARKIEVICZ, and MAUD GONNE; they were released following a hunger strike. A member of the Executive Committee of Sinn Féin, she was a judge of the Dáil Courts in South Dublin. Rejecting the ANGLO-IRISH TREATY (1921), she supported the Republicans during the CIVIL WAR. She later visited Soviet Russia, 1929, and was a founder of the Women's Social and Progressive League.

Her sisters, Mary and Kathleen Sheehy, were married to THOMAS KETTLE and Frank Cruise O'Brien, respectively. Her son Owen Sheehy-Skeffington (1908–1970), was a prominent academic and humanist.

Sheil, Richard Lalor (1791–1851), lawyer and politician (Repeal); born in Drumdowney, Co. Kilkenny, educated at TCD. While studying law at Lincoln's Inn, London, 1811–17, he paid his way by writing plays. Having opposed DANIEL O'CONNELL over the VETO, 1813–15, after becoming a member of the CATHOLIC BOARD, 1813, he was closely associated with the struggle for CATHOLIC EMANCIPATION. He attacked O'Connell in 1821 for subordinating emancipation to the demand for parliamentary reform but two years later helped him to found the CATHOLIC ASSOCIATION and was active in the Co. Clare by-election of 1828, when O'Connell won the seat.

Among the first Catholics called to the inner bar, 1830, he won the Co. Tipperary parliamentary seat, 1833–41, and, as a member of the Repeal Party, assisted in bringing about the LICHFIELD HOUSE COMPACT. During the next few years he enjoyed some sinecures: commissioner of Greenwich Hospital, 1838, vice-president of the Board of Trade, 1839, and Judge-Advocate, 1841. Though not averse to enjoying his own positions, he made himself unpopular by bluntly refusing to seek patronage for his supporters. As Master of the Mint, 1846–50, he was the cause of a celebrated controversy when he neglected to have the florin (2 shillings) of 1849 stamped with the inscription *Fidei Defensatrix Dei gratia* ('by the grace of God, Defender of the Faith'), causing the coin to become known as the 'godless florin'. He was replaced as Master of the Mint and completed his career as ambassador to Florence.

Siamsa Tíre, a folk theatre founded in Tralee, Co. Kerry, by Father Patrick Ahern, 1968. It was reorganised as Siamsa Tíre, the National Folk Theatre of Ireland, 1974, with Father Ahern as artistic director (until 1998). Under its auspices the first Teach Siamsa was opened in 1974 in Finuge, Co. Kerry, to encourage traditional modes of entertainment; another was opened at Carraig in Corca Dhuibhne (the Dingle Peninsula).

Siege of Great Strand Street. In March 1933 some of the congregation that had heard a sermon from a Redemptorist priest at the Pro-Cathedral, Dublin, marched from the church to the offices of the REVOLUTIONARY WORKERS' GROUP at 64 Great Strand Street. On their way they smashed windows in Unity Hall (offices of the WORKERS' UNION OF IRELAND) and were joined by members of the congregation of the Store Street Mission. They surrounded 64 Great Strand Street, harangued and intimidated those inside, then burned and looted the building. The incident was symptomatic of the prevailing anti-communist hysteria, for which over-zealous members of the Catholic clergy were held responsible.

Sigerson, Dr George (1836–1925), physician and scholar; born in Holyhill, near Strabane, Co. Tyrone, studied medicine in Cork and Galway and arts and medicine in Paris. He translated and edited Charcot on diseases of the nervous system, and his work on biology attracted the attention of Charles Darwin, among others. A fellow of the Royal University of Ireland, he was professor of biology at University College, Dublin, president of the National Library Society from 1893, and one of the founders of the Feis Cheoil. He was a member of the Senate of the Irish Free State,

1922–25. His works include *The Poets and Poetry of Munster* (1860), *A History of Land Tenures and Land Classes in Ireland* (1871), *Political Prisoners* (an anthology, 1890), *Bards of the Gael and Gall* (1897), and *The Last Independent Parliament of Ireland* (1918).

His daughter, Dora Sigerson Shorter (1866–1918), was a poet who spent most of her life in England. Her publications include *Ballads and Poems* (1899) and *Sixteen Dead Men and Other Poems of Easter Week* (1919).

'silenced priest', a Catholic clergyman who had been suspended by his superiors. Such priests were often believed to possess special powers, enabling them to cure sickness or overcome the Devil and evil spirits; when all other resources failed, a silenced priest was often approached in time of trouble. GEORGE BERNARD SHAW has a portrait of one in *John Bull's Other Island* (1904). (See also SPOILED PRIEST.)

Simms, G. O. [George Otto] (1910–1991), bishop (Church of Ireland) and scholar; born in Dublin, educated at TCD. After ministering briefly in Dublin he taught at Lincoln Theological College, 1938–39. He was dean of residence in Trinity College, Dublin, 1939–52, Dean of Cork, 1952, Bishop of Cork, Cloyne and Ross, 1952–56, Archbishop of Dublin, 1956–69, and Archbishop of Armagh and Primate of All Ireland, 1969–80. An authority on Irish illuminated manuscripts, he contributed to facsimile editions of *The Book of Kells* (1950–51) and *The Book of Durrow* (1960).

Sinn Féin, a political movement that evolved under the direction of ARTHUR GRIFFITH and BULMER HOBSON, 1905–08. Griffith founded the original Sinn Féin in 1905; a merger of CUMANN NA NGAEDHEAL and the DUNGANNON CLUBS created the Sinn Féin League, 21 April 1907, which absorbed the NATIONAL COUNCIL, 5 September 1907. Mary Lambert Butler suggested the name Sinn Féin ('ourselves'). The movement's paper, *Sinn Féin,* was edited by Griffith, 1906–14. 'Our declared object,' Griffith stated, was 'to make England take one hand from Ireland's throat and the other out of Ireland's pocket.'

Sinn Féin's anti-CONSCRIPTION stand during the Great War helped to secure popular support for the movement. Though it was not involved in the EASTER RISING (1916), the executions and arrests that followed aided Sinn Féin in becoming a mass movement, as did the death of THOMAS ASHE on hunger strike. T. M. HEALY later observed, 'The Sinn Féiners won in three years what we [the Irish Party] did not win in forty.' Reorganised by CATHAL BRUGHA and MICHAEL COLLINS during 1917, when ÉAMON DE VALERA became president, Sinn Féin became a national movement on a platform of national independence and the withdrawal of Irish members from the British Parliament.

Sinn Féin adopted the following constitution on 25 October 1917:

I

1. The name of this organisation shall be Sinn Féin.
2. Sinn Féin aims at securing the international recognition of Ireland as an independent Irish Republic. Having achieved that status the Irish people may by referendum freely choose their own form of government.
3. This object shall be attained through the Sinn Féin organisation.
4. WHEREAS no law made without the authority and consent of the Irish people is, or ever can be, binding on their conscience,

   Therefore, in accordance with the Resolution of Sinn Féin adopted in convention, 1905, a Constituent Assembly shall be convoked, comprising persons chosen by the Irish Constituencies as the supreme national authority to speak and act in the name of the Irish people and to devise and formulate measures for the welfare of the whole people of Ireland,

   Such as

   (*a*) The Introduction of a Protective System for Irish industries and commerce by combined action of the Irish County Councils, Urban Councils, Rural Councils, Poor Law Boards, Harbour Boards and other bodies directly responsible to the Irish people.

   (*b*) The establishment and maintenance under the direction of a National Assembly or other authority approved by the people of Ireland of an Irish Consular Service for the advancement of Irish commerce and Irish interests generally.

   (*c*) The re-establishment of an Irish Mercantile Marine to facilitate direct trading between Ireland and the countries of continental Europe, America, Africa and the Far East.

(*d*) The industrial survey of Ireland and the development of its mineral resources under the auspices of a National Assembly or other national authority approved by the people of Ireland.
(*e*) The establishment of a national stock exchange.
(*f*) The creation of a national civil service, embracing all the employees of the County Councils, Rural Councils, Poor Law Boards, Harbour Boards and other bodies responsible to the Irish people, by the institution of a common national qualifying examination (the latter at the discretion of local bodies).
(*g*) The establishment of Sinn Féin Courts of Arbitration for the speedy and satisfactory adjustment of disputes.
(*h*) The development of transit by rail, road and water, of waste lands for the national benefit by a national authority approved by the people of Ireland.
(*i*) The development of the Irish Sea Fisheries by National Assembly or other national authority approved by the people of Ireland.
(*j*) The reform of education, to render its basis national and industrial by the compulsory teaching of the Irish language, Irish history and Irish agricultural and manufacturing potentialities in the primary system, and, in addition, to elevate to a position of dominance in the university system Irish agriculture and economics.
(*k*) The abolition of the Poor Law system and substitution in its stead of adequate outdoor relief to the aged and infirm, and the employment of the able-bodied in the reclamation of waste lands, forestation and other national and productive works.

II

A special meeting of the Executive may be summoned on three days' notice by the President on requisition presented to him, signed by six members of the Executive specifying the object for which the meeting is called.

In case of an urgent emergency, the President shall call all members of the Executive to an urgency meeting, and may take action in the name of the Executive in case he secures the approval of an absolute majority of the entire Executive. The action taken is to be reported for confirmation at the next ordinary meeting of the Executive.

III

That where Irish resources are being developed, or where industries exist, Sinn Féiners should make it their business to secure that workers are paid a living wage.

That the equality of men and women in this organisation be emphasised in all speeches and leaflets.

Sinn Féin won 73 seats in the general election of December 1918 (the Irish Party retained 6, and Unionists won 26). The elected Sinn Féin members who formed the first DÁIL ÉIREANN, 19 January 1919, issued a DECLARATION OF INDEPENDENCE and adopted a Constitution and the DEMOCRATIC PROGRAMME. While the Dáil regarded itself as the legitimate government of Ireland, the IRA waged the WAR OF INDEPENDENCE against Crown forces. Sinn Féin won control of 172 out of 206 borough and urban district councils in the local elections of 15 June 1920.

The ANGLO-IRISH TREATY (1921) split Sinn Féin. Those who accepted the establishment of the IRISH FREE STATE formed CUMANN NA NGAEDHEAL; opponents of the Treaty retained the title Sinn Féin, rejected the legitimacy of the Free State, and gave their allegiance to the second Dáil Éireann. The IRA separated from Sinn Féin in 1925. A second split in Sinn Féin came during the period 1926–27, when de Valera left Sinn Féin to establish FIANNA FÁIL, which took its seats in the Dáil, 1927.

For forty years Sinn Féin held to its irredentist platform. It had little success in general elections but made occasional gains at local government level. It won five seats in the general election of June 1927 (but lost them in another election in September). Against the background of the IRA's BORDER CAMPAIGN, the party won four seats in the 1957 general election but lost them four years later, when, putting forward twenty candidates, its vote fell from 65,000 to 35,000.

Sinn Féin changed direction during the 1960s. Under the presidency of TOMÁS MAC GIOLLA (from 1965) and influenced by the WOLFE TONE SOCIETY, the party moved leftwards. Events in Northern Ireland raised tensions within the party: in Northern Ireland the Republican Clubs carried the undiluted message of a united Ireland, but in the Republic the party now mingled socialism with traditional republican doctrine. The split in Sinn Féin, January 1970, mirroring that in the IRA, December 1969, formally occurred over whether Sinn Féin should drop its traditional policy of not recognising parliaments in Dublin or Belfast. The minority who voted to retain the traditional abstention policy, mainly from the North and supported in the Republic by traditionalists who were hostile to the socialist tendency, walked out and reorganised in what came to be called 'Provisional' Sinn Féin (by association with the 'Provisional' IRA, after those who left the IRA had set up the 'Provisional Army Council'); the majority movement came to be called 'Official' Sinn Féin. The Official movement continued to publish the monthly paper *United Irishman*; Marxist in outlook, it offered a radical programme. It changed its name to Sinn Féin the Workers' Party in January 1977. By the end of the 1990s it had been through several changes of title: Sinn Féin the Workers' Party was renamed the WORKERS' PARTY, 1982; in 1992 all its TDs except Mac Giolla left, led by PROINSIAS DE ROSSA, to form New Agenda, which in turn became DEMOCRATIC LEFT from 28 March 1992 and was later to merge with the LABOUR PARTY, 1999.

What had at first been the minority party, 'Provisional' Sinn Féin quickly became numerically superior. It published AN PHOBLACHT, and RUAIRÍ Ó BRÁDAIGH was president until 1983. While it was abstentionist in relation to the elected assemblies in Belfast, Dublin, and London, in 1982 it decided to occupy any seats won in local elections. It had contested local elections in the Republic, where it held thirty seats on twenty-six councils in fourteen counties. By 1986 it had more than fifty councillors on district councils in Northern Ireland.

The change in the direction in the 1980s should be seen against the background of the 'blanket protest' and 'dirty protest' by republican prisoners seeking SPECIAL CATEGORY status in Northern Ireland and in particular the H BLOCK hunger strikes of 1980 and 1981. During the first hunger strike, in late 1980, Sinn Féin called for immediate British withdrawal from Northern Ireland (for a time it had seemed to favour a form of phased withdrawal). The second wave of hunger strikes, led by BOBBY SANDS—whose death on 5 May 1981 was followed by nine others—gained sympathy for the movement. In the general election in the Republic on 11 June 1981 two H block prisoners were returned. The new direction was signalled at the 1981 ard-fheis when Danny Morrison asked, 'Who here really believes that we can win the war through the ballot box? But will anyone here object if, with a ballot box in this hand and an Armalite [automatic rifle] in this hand, we take power in Ireland?' The 'ÉIRE NUA' policy of 1972 was dropped in 1982, under pressure from Northerners, led by GERRY ADAMS, when the ard-fheis ruled that in future Sinn Féin candidates must give their 'unambivalent' support to the 'armed struggle'. Sinn Féin won five seats in the 1982 Assembly elections, with 10 per cent of the vote.

Adams headed the poll in West Belfast in the elections for the British House of Commons, 1983, when the Catholic hierarchy was urging nationalists not to vote for those who supported Provisional IRA violence. At the 1983 ard-fheis Adams and Martin McGuinness won the presidency and vice-presidency, respectively. When the 1986 ard-fheis voted (429 to 161) to register Sinn Féin as a political party, ending the traditional abstentionist position, dissidents led by Ó Brádaigh again left the party, to form REPUBLICAN SINN FÉIN.

From the 1980s Sinn Féin was active in urban communities in both North and South, building its profile in areas of high unemployment and drug abuse. Adams retained the West Belfast seat in 1987, defeating the SDLP candidate. From 1988 the party supported the HUME-ADAMS TALKS, the embryo of the PEACE PROCESS. In January 1989, in an attempt to win a wider degree of nationalist support, the party appealed to the Provisional IRA to avoid accidental civilian deaths. In the period before the British parliamentary elections of 1992 Adams pointed out that Sinn Féin and the IRA 'are not as one . . . I do not agree with everything they do.' Adams in fact lost his seat to Dr Joe Hendron of the SDLP (who benefited from tactical voting by unionists, who supported him to get Adams out).

Most Sinn Féin candidates lost their deposit in the 1992 general election in the Republic. In the 1993 Northern Ireland council elections Sinn Féin had the highest vote of any party in Belfast. It rejected the DOWNING STREET DECLARATION (1993). Following the Provisional IRA ceasefire of 31 August 1994 the Taoiseach, ALBERT REYNOLDS, publicly shook hands with Adams, together with JOHN HUME, in Dublin. In October the broadcasting restrictions about which the party had complained for so long were lifted. On 9 December 1994 a Sinn Féin delegation entered Stormont Castle for the first time. The ard-fheis of 1995 was held in the Mansion House, Dublin, for the first time in four years. In August, at a meeting with government representatives in Dublin, Sinn Féin called for 'an inclusive all-party talks process.' It now held the view that there was 'no other strategy' and that there was 'no military solution' to the Northern conflict. In November 1995 the party held its first rally in the Ulster Hall, Belfast, traditional bastion of unionism.

Sinn Féin leaders met the INTERNATIONAL BODY ON DECOMMISSIONING OF ARMS and described as 'realistic' the report by GEORGE MITCHELL, January 1996. The party expressed surprise at the unexpected ending of the Provisional IRA ceasefire, 9 February 1996, as a result of which Sinn Féin representatives were turned away from the 'proximity talks' at Stormont. The party won 17 of the 100 seats in the Northern Ireland Forum, but its representatives were refused admission. Adams (West Belfast) and McGuinness (Mid-Ulster) were elected to the British House of Commons in May 1997 but were not admitted when they would not take the oath of allegiance. On 2 June, Adams and Pat Doherty were barred when they attempted to take part in talks at Stormont.

In the general election in the Republic on 6 June 1997 Sinn Féin ran fifteen candidates in fourteen constituencies, winning one seat when Caoimhghin Ó Caoláin (first elected to Monaghan County Council in 1985) tripled his vote in Cavan-Monaghan to take the first seat with 19 per cent of first-preference votes (1.16 times the quota). Nationally, Sinn Féin won 2½ per cent of first-preference votes.

The restoration of the Provisional IRA ceasefire, July 1997, enabled Sinn Féin to take up office accommodation in Stormont; two months later the party accepted the Mitchell Principles. Led by McGuinness, Sinn Féin participated in the later sessions, which produced the BELFAST AGREEMENT, 10 April 1998. At a special ard-fheis in May, 96 per cent of delegates supported the agreement, permitting Sinn Féin members to take their seats in the new Assembly; some dissidents broke away to form the 32-County Sovereignty Committee. Winning 18 seats in the 108-seat Northern Ireland Assembly entitled the party to two seats on the Executive (Bairbre de Brún as Minister for Health and Martin McGuinness as Minister for Education).

In the general election of 7 June 2001 Sinn Féin won four of the eighteen Northern Ireland seats in the British House of Commons: Adams and McGuinness retained their seats and were joined by Michelle Gildernew (Fermanagh-South Tyrone, the first woman Sinn Féin MP since CONSTANCE MARKIEVICZ in 1918) and Pat Doherty (West Tyrone). The SDLP held three seats. In the local elections on the same day Sinn Féin secured 108 seats (an increase of 34) and became the largest party on Belfast City Council.

On 17 May 2001 the general election in the Republic returned five Sinn Féin members, Ó Caoláin being joined by Seán Crowe (Dublin South-West), Martin Ferris (Kerry North), Arthur Morgan (Louth), and Aengus Ó Snodaigh (Dublin South-Central). The party secured 6.5 per cent of the first-preference vote (compared with 1.9 per cent in 1987, 1.2 per cent in 1989, 1.7 per cent in 1992, and 2.5 per cent in 1997).

Sinn Féin, a paper founded and edited by ARTHUR GRIFFITH as the organ of SINN FÉIN, 1906–14. It supported HOME RULE, opposed partition, and was critical of the pro-British stance adopted by JOHN REDMOND. It had a limited circulation and was in constant financial difficulty. Following its suppression in December 1914 Griffith replaced it with SCISSORS AND PASTE; this too was banned after a brief period.

Another paper of the same name was published by Sinn Féin in collaboration with the IRA from August 1923 until 1925, being replaced by AN PHOBLACHT.

Sirius, the first steamship to cross the Atlantic solely under steam, beating Brunel's *Great Western* to the record by a few hours. Built for the St George Steam Packet Company of Cork by Robert Menzies and Son of Leith, Midlothian, the 412-ton vessel arrived in Cork on 9 August 1837 and was engaged on the Cork–London route. At 10 a.m. on 3 April 1838 the *Sirius*, now commanded by Richard Roberts, with a crew of thirty-eight, left for New York with forty passengers; it arrived in New York at 9 p.m. on 22 April, having covered 2,897 miles in eighteen days, an average of 161 miles per day or 6.7 m.p.h. On arrival it had less than 15 tons of coal in its hold. On 15 January 1847, under the command of Captain Moffett, the *Sirius* left Cork for Dublin with ninety-one passengers aboard. In dense fog it struck a reef in Ballycotton Bay, Co. Cork, with the loss of twenty lives; a ship-to-shore line rescued the remainder. The ship was salvaged and scrapped by Mason and Company of Birmingham, 1898, but many items, including the ship's bell, found their way to various places in Cork city and county.

'Skirmishing Fund', established by the Fenians in the United States, at the suggestion of JEREMIAH O'DONOVAN ROSSA, 1875, for the purpose of undermining British rule in Ireland. JOHN DEVOY and DR WILLIAM CARROLL gained control of the fund for CLAN NA GAEL and used it to finance the NEW DEPARTURE; the money was also used to support the submarine experiments of JOHN P. HOLLAND and to help finance the campaign of the DYNAMITERS in Britain.

slane, also **slean** (Irish *sleán*), a spade used in turf-cutting. Two types were in general use, the underfoot and the breast slane, the former distinguished by the upward slant of the cutting edge of the wing, whereas that of the underfoot slane sloped downwards. The underfoot slane was provided with a two-sided foot-step and was used on tough or humified turf. The handle varied with tradition, taste, and local conditions; cowhorn was widely used, whereas a black sally splice on the handle, believed to absorb perspiration, was favoured in the Glens of Antrim.

sliding coffins. During the GREAT FAMINE (1845–49) it proved impossible to meet the demand for coffins, and various methods were employed in conveying the dead to their place of burial. Coffins with a sliding base were widely used: the coffin was placed over the grave, and when the base was drawn out, the body fell into the grave, allowing the coffin to be reused. A variation on the sliding coffin was the hinged coffin.

Canon John O'Rourke, author of *The Great Irish Famine* (1874), received a cross made from the wood of a sliding coffin from a physician at the Bantry Poor Law Union. It bore the inscription:

> During the frightful famine-plague, which devastated a large proportion of Ireland in the years 1846–47, that monstrous and unchristian machine, a 'sliding coffin', was, from necessity, used in the Bantry Union for the conveyance of the victims to one common grave. The material of this cross, the symbol of our Redemption, is a portion of one of the machines, which enclosed the remains of several hundreds of our countrymen, during their passage from the wretched huts or waysides, where they died, to the pit into which their remains were thrown.

Sloan, Thomas Henry (1870–1941), trade unionist and politician (Independent); born in Belfast, educated locally. He worked in Harland and Wolff's shipyard and was a prominent member of the ORANGE ORDER. A leading member of the BELFAST PROTESTANT ASSOCIATION, he criticised E. J. SAUNDERSON, for which he was expelled from the Orange Order. Sloan founded the INDEPENDENT ORANGE ORDER, 1902, being joined by ROBERT LINDSAY CRAWFORD, and won the South Belfast parliamentary seat, 1902. He became part of the loose alliance between nationalist, labour and independent candidates in Belfast for the 1906 general election. However, his influence within Orangeism declined on the publication of his MAGHERAMORNE MANIFESTO (July 1907), and he retired from active politics following his defeat in the general election of 1910.

Smiddy, Timothy A. (1875–1962), economist and diplomat; born in Cork, educated at Queen's College, Cork, in Paris, and at the Handelshochschule in Cologne. He was professor of economics at University College, Cork, 1909–24, economic adviser to the plenipotentiaries during the Treaty negotiations, October–December 1921, envoy and fiscal agent of the Free State to the United States, 1922–24, and chairman of the Fiscal Committee of the Senate of the Irish Free State, 1923. He was later envoy extraordinary and minister plenipotentiary in Washington, 1924–29 (the first Irish diplomat to be received by an American government), high commissioner in London, 1929–30, and a delegate to the London Naval Conference, 1930. He was chairman of the Free State Tariff Commission, 1931–33, chairman of the Free State Trade Loan Commission, 1933, chairman of the Summer Time Commission, 1939–45, director of the Central Bank of Ireland, 1943–55, and chairman of the Commission of Inquiry into Post-Emergency Agricultural Policy, 1947.

Smith-Barry, A. H. [Arthur Hugh], first Baron Barrymore (1843–1925), landowner and politician (Unionist), educated at the University of Oxford. Owner of a large estate in Co. Tipperary, part of it embracing the town of Tipperary, he was a member of Parliament, 1867–74 and 1886–1900. Opposed to HOME RULE and the LAND LEAGUE, during the PLAN OF CAMPAIGN he was agent for the PROPERTY

DEFENCE ASSOCIATION. His liberal assistance to the owners of the Ponsonby estate at Youghal, Co. Cork, helped save the estate from bankruptcy. His opposition to the Plan of Campaign brought him into conflict with his Tipperary tenants, June 1889. Archbishop T. W. CROKE denounced him as 'an aggressive busybody.' His eviction of 152 tenants led to the establishment of the TENANTS' DEFENCE LEAGUE and of 'NEW TIPPERARY'. After the collapse of the New Tipperary project he came to terms with his tenants, 1895. He was chairman of the IRISH UNIONIST ALLIANCE and later a member of the ALL-FOR-IRELAND LEAGUE.

Smyllie, R. M. [Robert Maire] (1894–1954), journalist; born in Glasgow, raised in Sligo, educated at TCD. Studying in Germany on the outbreak of the Great War, he was interned until 1918, when he escaped during the revolution in Berlin. The *Irish Times* commissioned him to cover the Paris Peace Conference (1919); on his return he was appointed assistant editor and in 1934 succeeded John E. Healy as editor. During his editorship the paper was one of the country's most influential organs of public opinion; he once described its policy as 'to advocate the maintenance of a strong Commonwealth connection, while insisting, no less strongly, on Irish political independence . . .' Smyllie was alleged to have been responsible, together with Major Bryan Cooper of Sligo, for ensuring the absence of Alderman John Jinks from the crucial vote of no confidence in the CUMANN NA NGAEDHEAL government, 16 August 1927 (see JINKS AFFAIR).

Smyth, Lieutenant-Colonel Gerald (1885–1920), British soldier; born in Dalhousie, India. He joined the British army in 1905. As divisional commander of the RIC in Munster, 1920, he was responsible for the AUXILIARIES and BLACK AND TANS in his district. At Listowel RIC Barracks he addressed the police, 19 June 1920, telling them that in dealing with the IRA and Sinn Féin, 'the more you shoot the better I will like it, and I assure you no policeman will get into trouble for shooting any man.' This led to resignations from the RIC and an airing of general dissatisfaction within the police. Representations on behalf of the constabulary were made by T. J. MCELLIGOTT and JEREMIAH MEE. Shortly afterwards, Smyth was killed by the IRA in the Cork County Club.

Smyth, Patrick James (1823–1885), Young Irelander and politician (Home Rule); born in Dublin, educated at Clongowes Wood College, Co. Kildare. A member of YOUNG IRELAND and of the IRISH CONFEDERATION, he made his way to the United States following the rising of 1848. He planned the escape of the Young Ireland leaders from Tasmania, including JOHN MITCHEL, 1854.

He returned to Ireland, 1856, rejected revolution, and was called to the bar. For his services in organising an ambulance brigade during the Franco-Prussian War (1870–71) he was awarded membership of the Legion of Honour. Member of Parliament for Co. Westmeath, 1871, he was considered a possible candidate for the leadership of the IRISH PARTY. He won the Co. Tipperary seat in the general election of 1880, after which CHARLES STEWART PARNELL became leader of the party. Smyth's opposition to the LAND LEAGUE lost him popularity, and in 1882 he resigned his seat, after which be lived in poverty for some time. He died within a few weeks of accepting the secretaryship of the Irish Loan Representative Fund, for which he had been severely criticised in nationalist circles.

Social Democratic and Labour Party, founded 21 August 1970 by members of the NATIONALIST PARTY OF NORTHERN IRELAND, the NORTHERN IRELAND LABOUR PARTY, the REPUBLICAN LABOUR PARTY, the NATIONAL DEMOCRATIC PARTY, and civil rights activists (see NORTHERN IRELAND CIVIL RIGHTS ASSOCIATION). The members of the executive included GERRY FITT (chairman), JOHN HUME (vice-chairman), and PADDY DEVLIN. The party's constitution stated as its aims:

> To organise and maintain in Northern Ireland a socialist party . . .
> To co-operate with the Irish Congress of Trade Unions in joint political or other action . . .
> To promote the cause of Irish unity based on the consent of the majority of people in Northern Ireland . . .
> To contest elections in Northern Ireland with a view to forming a government which will implement the following principles: (*a*) the abolition of all forms of religious, political, class or sex discrimination; the promotion of culture and the arts with a special responsibility to cherish and develop all aspects of our native culture; (*b*) the public ownership and democratic control of such essential industries and services as the common good requires; (*c*) the utilisation of its powers by

the state, when and where necessary, to provide employment, by the establishment of publicly-owned industries.

The SDLP led the opposition in the Parliament of Northern Ireland, pressing the ULSTER UNIONIST PARTY for reform and concessions to the civil rights movement. It withdrew in protest at the failure to inquire into killings by the British army in Derry, July 1971. A month later the Prime Minister, BRIAN FAULKNER, introduced INTERNMENT in an attempt to destroy the Provisional IRA; in protest, the SDLP supported a rent and rates strike and established the 'Dungiven Parliament' as an 'alternative assembly of the Northern People'. The British government suspended the Northern parliament and introduced direct rule from London, March 1972.

The SDLP called for a policy of co-operation with the Secretary of State for Northern Ireland, WILLIAM WHITELAW, 'as a gesture of our confidence that meaningful political progress is now possible.' In *Towards a New Ireland* it advocated a system of joint sovereignty over Northern Ireland by the British and Irish governments, with an assembly and an executive elected by proportional representation. It won 83 seats in the local elections of May 1973 and 19 seats in the Northern Ireland Assembly, 28 June 1973. Following talks with the Faulknerite Unionists and the ALLIANCE PARTY, 5 October, it was allocated four posts in the power-sharing Northern Ireland Executive: Fitt (Deputy Chief Executive), Hume (Commerce), Devlin (Health and Social Security), and Austin Currie (Local Government); in addition, Edward McGrady (Economic Planning) and Ivan Cooper (Community Relations) were non-voting member of the Executive.

The SDLP was represented at the talks leading to the SUNNINGDALE AGREEMENT (December 1973). It was critical of the British government for not confronting the ULSTER WORKERS' COUNCIL, which brought down the Executive with a strike. Northern Ireland again reverted to direct rule from London, May 1974.

The SDLP's seventeen seats made it the second-largest party in the 1975 Constitutional Convention. Following the dissolution of the Convention the party, disillusioned with the British government's refusal to confront loyalists, represented moderate nationalist opinion in seeking power-sharing (multi-party government) and the rejection of the IRA armed campaign.

In August 1977 Paddy Devlin claimed that the SDLP was moving away from socialism, and he was expelled; Ivan Cooper also questioned the direction in which the party was moving. In the 1977 district council elections the party won 113 seats (compared with 83 in 1973). In 1978 the party conference called again for the British and Irish governments and both communities in Northern Ireland to come together to find a settlement, stating that eventual British withdrawal was 'desirable and inevitable.' While Fitt retained his British House of Commons seat for Belfast West in the general election of 3 May 1979, the party did not do well otherwise. A month later, however, its morale received a boost when Hume won the second Northern Ireland seat in the European Parliament. Fitt left the party over its refusal to attend a constitutional conference on Northern Ireland, being succeeded by Hume, December 1979. During the republican hunger strikes of 1980 and 1981 the party called for concessions to the hunger-strikers (but not for SPECIAL CATEGORY status).

The SDLP won 103 seats in the 1981 local elections (a drop of 3 per cent). A year later it contested the elections but would not participate in the Assembly (1982–86); instead it advocated a 'Council for a New Ireland', to enable politicians from Northern Ireland and the Republic to discuss the implications of Irish unity. The party won fourteen seats in the Assembly. It participated in the NEW IRELAND FORUM in Dublin, May 1983. In June it fared poorly in the British parliamentary elections. There were now seventeen Northern Ireland seats (an increase of five); the SDLP contested all seventeen but its only victory was John Hume's in the Foyle constituency. In 1984 Hume retained his European Parliament seat with 22 per cent of first-preference votes (Sinn Féin won 13 per cent). By the end of the year the party was dismayed at Margaret Thatcher's dismissal of the findings of the NEW IRELAND FORUM.

The SDLP won 101 seats in the 1986 local elections (in which Sinn Féin won 59 seats). In 1986 Séamus Mallon won the Armagh and Newry seat in the British House of Commons in the spate of by-elections that followed Unionist resignations in protest at the ANGLO-IRISH AGREEMENT. The party's hopes that the agreement would lead to inter-party talks were disappointed. In the general election of 1987, when the SDLP won 21 per cent of the vote (compared with Sinn Féin's 11 per cent), Mallon held his seat, as did Hume, while Eddie

McGrady won in Down South, but Dr Joe Hendron lost to GERRY ADAMS in Belfast West for the second time.

During 1988 the HUME-ADAMS TALKS, a milestone in the PEACE PROCESS, began. In May 1989 the SDLP secured an additional 20 seats (for a total of 121) in the local elections, making it the second-largest party both in votes and in council seats. It supported initiatives by PETER BROOKE and later by SIR PATRICK MAYHEW to find a road to the restoration of self-government for Northern Ireland. Unionists rejected Hume's position that neither 'majority' (i.e. single-party) nor 'power-sharing' (i.e. multi-party) government would work in Northern Ireland. The party enjoyed a notable victory in Belfast West in the 1992 British parliamentary election when Dr Joe Hendron, supported by tactical voting by unionists, recovered his seat from Gerry Adams. In the 1993 local elections the party had its highest number returned (127 seats, an increase of four, with 22 per cent of the vote). In West Belfast the party took three seats (compared with Sinn Féin's seven).

The SDLP welcomed the DOWNING STREET DECLARATION (1993). The Provisional IRA announced a ceasefire on 31 August 1994, followed by a loyalist ceasefire in October. The party welcomed the FRAMEWORK DOCUMENTS (February 1995) and over the next few months held talks with the UUP and DUP, mainly on social and economic issues. It was critical of calls by DAVID TRIMBLE for a new Northern Ireland Assembly.

Divisions within the SDLP emerged at the annual conference in November 1995 when a motion ruling out an electoral pact with Sinn Féin was referred back to the Executive. Welcoming the Mitchell Report (January 1996), the party became involved in 'twin-track' meetings with the ULSTER DEMOCRATIC PARTY and PROGRESSIVE UNIONIST PARTY. When the Provisional IRA ceasefire ended, 9 February 1996, the SDLP called for all-party talks to restore the ceasefire. It held meetings with Mayhew and DICK SPRING for 'proximity talks' at Stormont, as a preparation for multi-party talks. As the momentum towards peace talks continued, the SDLP became the second-largest party, with nineteen constituency seats and two from the regional list in the May 1996 elections to all-party talks. In October the party agreed with the UUP a joint blueprint on an agenda for the multi-party talks but stalled for months over the issue of decommissioning of arms. In the British parliamentary elections of May 1997 Hendron again lost his seat to Adams. The party also lost further ground to Sinn Féin in the local elections. In August it launched its talks agenda as 'parity of esteem, treatment and opportunity.'

The SDLP played a leading role in bringing about the BELFAST AGREEMENT (10 April 1998). During the period 2000–01 it broadly welcomed proposals of the PATTEN REPORT on policing and was critical of the British government's attempts to find a way of implementing it without alienating unionists. On 20 August, committing itself to the deadline of 21 August for a response to the implementation plan for the new POLICE SERVICE OF NORTHERN IRELAND, published a week before, the SDLP became the first Northern Ireland political party to endorse the proposals and agreed to nominate three members to the nineteen-member Police Board. This endorsement provided the degree of cross-community support that was mandatory if the new service was to work.

The SDLP again lost ground to Sinn Féin in the British parliamentary elections of 7 June 2001. It retained its three seats, while Sinn Féin gained two to make a total of four. In the local elections on the same day the party lost three seats, returning with 117 (with 19 per cent of the vote), while Sinn Féin gained 34, for a total of 108 (with 21 per cent of the vote). MARK DURKAN became the third leader of the party on 11 November 2001.

Socialist Labour Party, founded in Dublin, November 1977, by former members of the LABOUR PARTY and left-wing supporters. Its sole spokesperson in Dáil Éireann was DR NOEL BROWNE, elected as Independent Labour in June 1977. The party opposed coalition government, capitalism and imperialism and called for the withdrawal of 'the British presence in all its forms from the thirty-two counties of Ireland.'

Socialist Party, a political party founded in 1996 by Joe Higgins, formerly of the Militant Tendency within the Labour Party, who rejected the policies of the LABOUR PARTY and Democratic Left. The party advocated state-owned industry and services, a thirty-hour working week, six weeks of paid holidays per year, and guaranteed permanent employment for all. It publishes a monthly paper, *Voice*. Higgins was its sole representative in Dáil Éireann (for Dublin West) in 2003.

Socialist Party of Ireland, formed on 4 March 1904 from a merger of a remnant of the IRISH SOCIALIST REPUBLICAN PARTY, founded by JAMES CONNOLLY (then in the United States), and a dissident faction calling itself the Socialist Labour Party. It was constitutional and non-Marxist. Its small membership was taken over in 1921 by Roderic Connolly (Connolly's son) and reorganised as the first COMMUNIST PARTY OF IRELAND.

Society for the Preservation of the Irish Language, established in 1876; its early membership included David Comyn, Father John Nolan, and Thomas O'Neill Russell. It succeeded in having the Board of National Education and Board of Intermediate Education put Irish on their curriculum. The society was divided over whether Old and Middle Irish or Modern Irish should be its chief focus; many of the most prominent members, including DR DOUGLAS HYDE, left to form the GAELIC UNION to concentrate on Modern Irish. (See GAELIC LEAGUE.)

Somerville, Sir William Meredyth, first Baron Athlumney of Somerville and Dollardstown (1802–1873), politician (Liberal); born in Athlumney, Co. Meath, educated at the University of Oxford. He served in the British diplomatic corps and was elected member of Parliament for Drogheda, 1837–52. In the House of Commons he sought the repeal of the Corn Laws, 1841, and opposed COERCION, 1846. He was appointed Chief Secretary for Ireland, 1847–52, during the GREAT FAMINE (1845–49), when the Treasury was insisting that 'Irish woe should be financed by Irish wealth.' His attempt to introduce a relieving Land Bill to ease the lot of tenant-farmers was blocked by landlord interests in 1848, and he was persuaded to withdraw it in favour of the removal of legislation that precluded a Catholic from holding office as Lord Chancellor of Ireland. As Lord Athlumney (from 1863) he supported the DISESTABLISHMENT of the Church of Ireland and the Landlord and Tenant (Ireland) Act (1870) (see LAND ACTS).

'souperism', a highly pejorative term applied to the practice whereby Catholics, in exchange for food or clothing, converted to Protestantism, especially during the GREAT FAMINE (1845–49). Those who changed their religion were known as 'soupers' and also as 'JUMPERS' or 'PERVERTS'. In the west of Ireland, famine proselytisers, including REV. HYACINTH D'ARCY and REV. EDWARD NANGLE, actively engaged in a campaign to win converts by offering starving Catholics food as an inducement to change religion. The concern of the Catholic Church at the tactic was exemplified in a letter from Father William Flannelly of Ballinakill, Co. Galway, to DANIEL MURRAY, Archbishop of Dublin, 6 April 1849, in which he stated:

> It cannot be wondered if a starving people would be perverted in shoals, especially as they [proselytisers] go from cabin to cabin, and when they find the inmates naked and starved to death, they proffer food, money and raiment, on the express condition of becoming members of their conventicles.

The activities of proselytisers was generally opposed by the Church of Ireland, whose philanthropic work during the famine was sometimes misinterpreted as proselytising. The resentment of Catholic neighbours to those who changed their religion extended in many cases over several generations.

soup kitchens. The Temporary Relief of Destitute Persons Act (1847), popularly known as the Soup Kitchens or Rations Act, operated from 26 February 1847. A commission under the chairmanship of Sir John Burgoyne, Inspector of Fortifications in Ireland, oversaw the introduction of the kitchens, which were modelled on the successful operations of the Society of Friends in Cork and Dublin. However, the soup dispensed by the Friends was superior in quality to that of the government scheme. Ingredients used at the Friends' depot in Barrack Street, Cork, which produced up to 180 gallons daily, were 120 lb of 'good' beef, 27 lb of rice, 27 lb of oatmeal, 27 lb of split peas, and 14 oz of spices, to which were added various vegetables. Those who could afford to pay were charged 1 penny for a quart of soup and a portion of bread. Meat was banned under the government scheme. The 2,049 Poor Law unions involved in its operation were informed by the Commissariat: 'Of course, Meat would improve the soup, but then the price would be greatly increased; and the object is to produce a nutritious Food at the lowest price.'

Bureaucracy and mismanagement hampered the introduction of the government scheme, and when, in anticipation of the scheme being fully operational, the public works closed in May, many areas were left without any form of relief. Numbers on the scheme rose from 2.73 million on 5 June to more than 3 million in mid-August. In some areas there was physical resistance to cooked food, with demands for uncooked meal to be distributed as an alternative. There were reports of recipients collapsing within minutes of having taken soup, their debilitated systems and weakened organs unable to sustain the sudden increase in metabolism.

The quality and nutritional value of the government scheme varied widely. An outbreak of scurvy forced the intervention of Board of Health officials, who recommended that leeks, onions, scallions and shallots be added and that fresh vegetables, peas and beans be frequently included in the mixture. The scheme, having cost £1,724,631, was closed on 1 October 1847.

Alexis Benoît Soyer (1809–1858), French cook of the Reform Club, London, arrived in Ireland in 1847 at the invitation of the British government to demonstrate his 'economical soup', two gallons of which, he asserted, 'had been tried and tested by numerous noblemen, Members of Parliament and several ladies . . . who have considered it very good and nourishing.' His 'recipe no. 1' allowed for 100 gallons of soup to be produced for less than 17 shillings, including an allowance for fuel. It consisted of 4 oz of beef to every two gallons of soup, 2 oz of dripping fat, 8 oz of flour, and ½ oz of brown sugar, to which were added a few onions, turnip-tops, and celery parings. His soup kitchen was launched at the Royal Barracks (Collins Barracks), Dublin, 5 April, organised as a gala event, with an admission fee of 5 shillings, allowing observation of the destitute partaking of the soup, provoking the *Dublin Evening Packet,* 6 April 1847, to comment that 'feeding time at the zoological gardens could be observed for sixpence.' The *Lancet* declared 'without hesitation or doubt' that the concoction was 'worthless.' Offended by this evaluation, Soyer left Ireland; his 'model kitchen' was bought by the government for the Relief Committee of the South Dublin Union.

South, Seán (1928–1957), republican; born in Limerick, educated at Sexton Street Christian Brothers' School. He worked as a clerk in a local wood-importing firm. A member at times of the Gaelic League, Legion of Mary, Clann na Poblachta, FCA, and Sinn Féin, he founded the local branch of MARIA DUCE in Limerick, edited and illustrated his own magazines, *An Gath* and *An Giolla,* and designed a number of Christmas cards for the Gaelic League. A member of the IRA from 1955, he took part in the raid on Brookeborough RUC Barracks, Co. Fermanagh, on New Year's Eve, 1957, when he was killed, aged twenty-nine, together with Fergal O'Hanlon (aged eighteen). Thousands attended South's funeral in Limerick, 4 January 1957; both he and O'Hanlon were the subject of ballads, 'Seán South of Garryowen' and 'The Patriot Game'.

'Southern Ireland'. Under the GOVERNMENT OF IRELAND ACT (1920) the six north-eastern counties of Ulster were designated Northern Ireland and the twenty-six counties designated Southern Ireland. DÁIL ÉIREANN, which regarded itself as the legislative assembly for the Irish Republic, did not recognise the act. The act provided that unless at least half the members presented themselves to take an oath of allegiance, the Parliament of Southern Ireland should be dissolved and a Crown colony government established. A general election in May 1921 was treated by SINN FÉIN as an election to Dáil Éireann.

The Parliament of Southern Ireland was summoned on 28 June 1921. Fifteen out of sixty-four senators attended and four MPs (those representing the University of Dublin) out of 128; following a fifteen-minute meeting it adjourned *sine die.* In July a truce led to the suspension of the WAR OF INDEPENDENCE. There was only one other meeting of the parliament, when ARTHUR GRIFFITH, as President of Dáil Éireann, summoned the assembly to meet, 14 January 1922, for the purpose of approving the ANGLO-IRISH TREATY (1921) and transferring power to the PROVISIONAL GOVERNMENT OF SOUTHERN IRELAND. This meeting was attended by sixty pro-Treaty TDs and the four members for the University of Dublin; it was boycotted by ÉAMON DE VALERA and other opponents of the Treaty. A motion of approval of the Treaty was passed, and the assembly elected the Provisional Government. Two days later the Provisional Government met to prepare for the establishment of the IRISH FREE STATE.

Southern Unionist Committee, founded on 20 February 1918 to represent Southern Unionists, who felt they were not properly represented by the IRISH UNIONIST ALLIANCE. They believed their interests had not been upheld at the IRISH CONVENTION and that the Home Rule Act (1914) (see (third) HOME RULE BILL) could be set aside and a new settlement found. Led by William Jellett, member of Parliament for the University of Dublin, 1919–21, and HUGH DE F. MONTGOMERY, they refused to accept assurances for their future under Irish self-government and were hostile towards SINN FÉIN. The committee was dissolved after the

Anglo-Irish Treaty (1921).

Southwark Literary Club, founded in London on 4 January 1883 by Francis A. Fahy (1854–1935) for the promotion of Irish history, art, and literature. Supported by leading nationalists and politicians, it sponsored lectures, amateur dramatics, concerts and dances and also had a Junior Irish Club for young people. It became the IRISH LITERARY SOCIETY in 1891. A year later, inspired by the club's ideals, W. B. YEATS and DOUGLAS HYDE founded the IRISH NATIONAL LITERARY SOCIETY.

soviets. During the WAR OF INDEPENDENCE a number of forcible takeovers of businesses and institutions became known as 'soviets'. The first, at Monaghan Asylum in January 1919, led by PEADAR O'DONNELL, lasted two days.

The most famous was established in Limerick, 14 April 1919. A tense situation had developed earlier that month when an imprisoned union organiser and republican, Bobby Byrne, was shot dead during a rescue attempt. His funeral was attended by some 15,000 people and became the occasion of a SINN FÉIN demonstration. When martial law was invoked, protesting workers, led by the Limerick United Trades and Labour Council, established the Limerick Soviet. It received wide press coverage, as foreign journalists were in the city to cover the stopover of Major Woods on his proposed air crossing of the Atlantic. The Limerick Soviet did not have the support of the Irish labour movement, and ran into financial difficulties. It issued a newspaper, the *Daily Bulletin*. On 24 April Bishop Denis Hallinan and the mayor of Limerick, Alphonsus O'Mara, reached an agreement with the British military commander of the city, and the strike ended. The chamber of commerce estimated that employers lost £250,000 in turnover and the workers some £45,000 in wages.

There was a further development in Co. Limerick in May 1920 when the workers took over Cleeve's creamery at Knocklong after their wage demands were refused and they were subsequently locked out. Again the trade union movement, with the sole exception of the Belfast Co-Operative Society, proved apathetic, and the workers handed back control in less than a week.

Further takeovers took place in 1921. In Co. Leitrim, coal-miners established a soviet following the rejection of a wage claim; in Cork, workers took over the Harbour Board; and in Drogheda, a foundry was taken over. At Bruree, Co. Limerick, workers seized Cleeve's mill and bakery, August 1921, but they handed back control within a few hours. In Dublin, LIAM O'FLAHERTY seized the Rotunda Rooms, 18 January 1922; the small garrison was attacked by a hostile crowd and collapsed within two days. Three members of the Communist Party of Ireland, Hedley, Dowling, and McGrath, founded the Munster Council of Action, December 1921; they established two soviets, the last of which was at the Cork Flour Mills, February 1923.

spalpeen (Irish *spailpín*), a poor labourer, traditionally working for a penny a day. Carrying their scythe, spade, or loy (depending on the crop to be harvested), spalpeens presented themselves at a HIRING FAIR, where they agreed terms with an employer. A spalpeen might hold a plot of land on CONACRE, and the money received from his labours was vital to the family income. The itinerant spalpeen (*spailpín fánach*) was a regular feature of rural life until the GREAT FAMINE (1845–49); many migrant workers from the western seaboard who travelled annually for the potato-picking season in Scotland and England followed the tradition of the spalpeen. (See also ARRANMORE DISASTER, CLEW BAY DISASTER, and KIRKINTILLOCH BOTHY DISASTER.)

Spanish Civil War. Irishmen fought on opposing sides during the Spanish Civil War (1936–39). The Connolly Column, led by FRANK RYAN, consisted eventually of some two hundred volunteers who fought with the Abraham Lincoln Battalion of the International Brigade on behalf of the Spanish republican government, while EOIN O'DUFFY led some six hundred former BLUESHIRTS in support of the rebels led by General Franco. Ryan's contingent was in action at Jarama, February 1937, when nineteen Irish republicans died, including the poet Charles Donnelly (1910–1937), whose last words were said to have been 'Even the olives are bleeding.' O'Duffy's followers saw little action and were sent home in June 1937. The Irish government, having first supported a policy of neutrality and prevented Irish involvement, followed the lead of the British and French governments by announcing its recognition of Franco's government, 28 February 1939.

special category, a status granted by WILLIAM WHITELAW, 13 June 1972, after republican prisoners went on strike in Crumlin Road Prison, Belfast. It applied to those sentenced to more than nine months' imprisonment for offences relating to civil disturbances. These prisoners, who regarded themselves as prisoners of war, did not have to work or wear prison clothing and were allowed extra visits and parcels.

The number enjoying these privileges was 1,116 by the end of 1974, predominantly republicans. They ran their own affairs within the prisons. This status was condemned by the GARDINER REPORT (1975). In 1975 MERLYN REES announced that special category status no longer applied to those convicted of terrorist offences after 1 March 1976: they would be treated as common criminals. The numbers involved fell from more than 1,500 at the end of 1976 to 800 by the summer of 1978. In 1980 Humphrey Atkins blocked all new admissions to special status. Protests by some 300 republican prisoners in the Maze Prison against its removal took the form of refusing to wear prison clothes (the 'blanket protest'), refusing to wash or use toilet facilities (the 'dirty protest'), and two hunger strikes, October–December 1980 and January–October 1981, the second of which led to ten deaths. By 1983, 230 prisoners in the Maze Prison still had special category status—105 Provisional IRA and INLA, twelve Official IRA, sixty-seven UVF, and forty-six UDA. The special category was abolished in September 1991.

Special Criminal Court. The first non-jury criminal court was established in 1939 to deal with subversion. Another was set up on 23 November 1961, staffed by army officers, to deal with members of the IRA, at that time in the final stages of its BORDER CAMPAIGN. The court was reintroduced by the Minister for Justice, DESMOND O'MALLEY, in May 1972.

'special men', a designation applied to Irish political prisoners in English jails in the 1880s, most of them imprisoned under the TREASON FELONY ACT (1848). They received particularly harsh treatment: their designation as 'special' made them targets for the hostility of the prison staff, several being driven insane. Among those who suffered were THOMAS J. CLARKE, JOHN DALY, James Egan, DR THOMAS GALLAGHER, Alfred Whitehead, and JEREMIAH O'DONOVAN ROSSA. Agitation by the AMNESTY ASSOCIATION led to the release of such prisoners, the last of whom, Clarke, was freed in September 1898.

Special Powers Act, popular name for the Civil Authorities (Special Powers) Act (Northern Ireland) (1922), enacted by the Parliament of Northern Ireland and coming into force on 7 April 1922. The legislation granted the Minister of Home Affairs the power to 'take all such steps and issue all such orders as may be necessary to preserve the peace.' This included the power to arrest without warrant and intern without trial, prohibit coroners' inquests, flog, sentence to death, requisition land or property, ban any organisation, and prohibit meetings and publications. It was renewed every year until 1928, when it was renewed for five years and then became permanent. Under the act, INTERNMENT was introduced in 1922–24, 1938–45, 1956–62, and 1971–75. The Public Order Act (1951) reinforced the act. The power to flog was removed in 1968.

The Special Powers Act was examined in 1969 by a commission under the Northern Ireland Attorney-General, Basil Kelly, which recommended that the act be abrogated, January 1970, and also that internment be at the will of Parliament and not at the discretion of the Minister of Home Affairs.

From 1969 British armed forces in Northern Ireland operated under the provisions of the act. In February 1972 the Lord Chief Justice ruled that the military could not operate under the terms of the act; it was then afforded retrospective sanction through the Northern Ireland Act (1972). The act was virtually replaced by the Emergency Provisions Act (1973) and the Special Powers Act (1974).

Special Powers Act, a name sometimes given to the Constitution (Amendment No. 17) Act (1931). Under this act the Constitutional (Special Powers) Tribunal—a military tribunal—operated from 20 October 1931 to 18 March 1932. It declared AN PHOBLACHT, the *Irish World*, the *Workers' Voice*, the *Irish Worker* and *Republican File* seditious. The tribunal dealt with sixty cases, which resulted in fifty-two convictions and eight acquittals. Four charges of seditious libel against the *Irish Press* and its editor, FRANK GALLAGHER, were upheld, and a fine of £200 imposed, 25 January 1932.

'Speed the Plough', a government policy during the 'ECONOMIC WAR' (1932–38), involving import controls and a system of guaranteed prices for cereals. It succeeded in increasing the production of wheat.

Spence, Augustus (Gusty) (born 1933), loyalist; born in Belfast, educated at primary school. He served in the British army in Germany and Cyprus, 1957–61, before returning to Belfast to work in the Harland and Wolff shipyard. An associate of REV. IAN PAISLEY, with whom he was involved in ULSTER PROTESTANT ACTION, he played a role in reactivating the ULSTER VOLUNTEER FORCE, 1966. He received a twenty-year prison sentence, 14 October 1966, for the murder of a Catholic barman, Peter Ward.

While imprisoned at Long Kesh, where he commanded the UVF contingent until he resigned, 1977, Spence underwent a change of heart, rejecting violence as counter-productive. Influential within a generation of younger loyalists in prison, on whom he urged a policy of reconciliation, he influenced Billy Hutchinson, Billy Snodden and DAVID ERVINE, the nucleus of the future PROGRESSIVE UNIONIST PARTY. Released in ill-health, December 1983, he publicly opposed violence. In 1985 he criticised the ULSTER UNIONIST PARTY and the DUP for their failure to open communication with the SDLP in an effort to outflank Sinn Féin. A leading PUP strategist, he played a pivotal role in bringing about the COMBINED LOYALIST MILITARY COMMAND's ceasefire of 1994 when he stated, 'In all sincerity we offer to loved ones of all innocent victims over the past twenty-five years abject and true remorse.'

Spencer, John Poyntz Spencer, fifth Earl (1835–1910), British politician (Liberal). A member of the House of Lords from 1887, he supported W. E. GLADSTONE on the DISESTABLISHMENT of the Church of Ireland. As Lord Lieutenant of Ireland, 1869–74 and 1882–85, his plan to establish a firm but conciliatory style of government proved difficult in the prevailing political climate. An outbreak of agrarian crime by the RIBBONMEN in Co. Westmeath led to increased COERCION under the 'Westmeath Act'. Lord President of the Council, 1880–82, in Gladstone's second ministry, he supported the Land Law (Ireland) Act (1881) (see LAND ACTS) and the 'KILMAINHAM TREATY' with CHARLES STEWART PARNELL.

Following the resignation of Lord Cowper over the Kilmainham Treaty, Spencer returned as Lord Lieutenant. When the Chief Secretary for Ireland, LORD FREDERICK CAVENDISH, was assassinated, new coercion measures were introduced, May 1882, and Spencer's reputation suffered. Parnell attacked him over a miscarriage of justice in the 'MAAMTRASNA MASSACRE' trials, 1882. When he sought the renewal of sections of the Crimes Act in 1885 he was opposed by JOSEPH CHAMBERLAIN. He supported Gladstone on HOME RULE in 1886 when the Liberals returned briefly to power and assisted in drafting the first HOME RULE BILL, defeated in July.

Spender, Sir Wilfrid Bliss (1876–1960), soldier and civil servant. Sympathising with unionism, he was a signatory of the ULSTER SOLEMN LEAGUE AND COVENANT (1912) and financed a press petition against HOME RULE. After resigning from the General Staff of the British army in 1913 he served as assistant quartermaster-general in the ULSTER VOLUNTEER FORCE, 1913–14, and took part in the planning and execution of the LARNE GUN-RUNNING (1914). He rejoined the General Staff in 1914. At the invitation of SIR EDWARD CARSON he left his job at the Ministry of Pensions in London, 16 July 1920, to oversee the reorganising of the UVF. He suggested the establishment of the ULSTER SPECIAL CONSTABULARY, 1920. He described the devolved Parliament of Northern Ireland as a 'factory of grievances'. He was secretary of the Northern Ireland government, 1921–25, and was permanent secretary to the Minister of Finance and head of the Northern Ireland civil service, 1925–44, and a member of the Joint Exchequer Board, 1933–54. Opposed to sectarianism, he was appalled at the numerous instances of it he encountered in his work.

Spire of Dublin. The competition for a monument to be erected in O'Connell Street, Dublin, on the site of the former NELSON'S PILLAR was won by the British architectural firm of Ian Ritchie. Erected by GDW Engineering of Chorley, Lancashire, the structure consists of 126 tonnes of stainless steel, milled and polished in France, rolled into 'tapering half-cylinders' in Scotland, and trimmed and welded into spire sections by Radley Engineering in Dungarvan, Co. Waterford. The flanges connecting the sections are German, and the 2-tonne damper to minimise the sway (up to 1.5 m at the top) is Canadian. At a height of 120 m (394 feet), the spire is seven times the height of the nearby GPO; its widest section is 3 m across, tapering to 150 mm at the top. The shell is 35 mm thick at the base and 10 mm thick at the apex. The light from the top 12 m is diffused through 11,884 perforations, each 15 mm in diameter. The final section of the spire was installed on 21 January 2003. Its cost was estimated at €4.6 million.

'spoiled priest', one who studied for the Catholic priesthood but did not proceed to ordination. It was considered a social disgrace to have a son who studied for the priesthood but was not ordained. Sometimes disowned by family and rejected by friends, the 'spoiled priest' often became a wanderer, frequently becoming a teacher away from his native place. (See also 'SILENCED PRIEST'.)

Spring, Dick (born 1950), barrister and politician (Labour Party); born in Tralee, educated at TCD and King's Inns and called to the bar. Practising law in Dublin and on the south-western circuit, he won his late father's Kerry North seat in Dáil Éireann in the 1981 general election. On his first day in the Dáil, 30 June 1981, he was appointed Minister of State at the Department of Justice, with special responsibility for law reform. He succeeded MICHAEL O'LEARY as leader of the LABOUR PARTY and became Tánaiste when the Labour Party entered a coalition government with FINE GAEL, 1982–87. Minister for the Environment, 1982–83, and Minister for Energy, 1983–87, he was party to the NEW IRELAND FORUM and was involved with the Taoiseach, DR GARRET FITZGERALD, in negotiations leading to the ANGLO-IRISH AGREEMENT (1985).

Citing opposition to proposed spending cuts, he precipitated a general election when his party withdrew from the government, 20 January 1987. In the general election of February 1987 he retained his own seat by four votes. Within the Labour Party he outmanoeuvred the Militant Tendency (see SOCIALIST PARTY). He successfully challenged the validity of the constitutional position of the Taoiseach, CHARLES HAUGHEY, following the loss of a Dáil vote and forced Haughey to concede that he had been acting *ultra vires* (beyond his authority) and held office only in a caretaker capacity. He enjoyed a triumph when MARY ROBINSON, nominated by the Labour Party, the WORKERS' PARTY, and two independent senators, defeated Brian Lenihan (FIANNA FÁIL) in the election for the Presidency of Ireland, 7 November 1990.

In 1991 the Labour Party increased its representation in local government from 6½ per cent to 11½ per cent. The following year it returned to the Dáil with a record thirty-three seats. In January 1993 Spring entered coalition with Fianna Fáil and became Tánaiste and Minister for Foreign affairs, 1993–97. With ALBERT REYNOLDS he took part in the evolving PEACE PROCESS in Northern Ireland. He was also engaged in the negotiations that secured a reported £8.6 billion from EU structural funds. Following the DOWNING STREET DECLARATION (1993) he urged that SINN FÉIN be allowed take part in talks before the 'decommissioning' of IRA weapons.

His relationship with Reynolds, damaged as a result of the BEEF TRIBUNAL, declined sharply when Reynolds proposed the appointment of the Attorney-General, Harry Whelehan, as President of the High Court. A complicated series of events, involving accusations of undue delay in the Attorney-General's office in dealing with charges of child abuse against a number of priests, eroded political confidence, and the Labour Party withdrew from government. For the first time, the fall of a government was not followed by a general election. A 'rainbow coalition' of Fine Gael, the Labour Party and DEMOCRATIC LEFT formed a government, in which Spring retained the Department of Foreign Affairs. In October he supported the 'twin-track' approach (political talks separate from the arms issue) advocated by PATRICK MAYHEW. The Labour Party's loss of seventeen seats in the general election of June 1997 was followed by the defeat of the party's choice (Adi Roche) in the 1997 presidential election. On 5 November Spring resigned as party leader and was succeeded by RUAIRÍ QUINN.

Squad, the, an assassination unit set up by Mick McDonald in July 1919 at the direction of MICHAEL COLLINS. Five in number, the group was shortly increased to twelve (the 'Twelve Apostles'), commanded by Paddy Daly. The unit was permanently housed in Abbey Street, Dublin, under the cover of a legitimate business, 'George Moreland, cabinet-maker'; members received basic tuition in carpentry from a cabinet-maker and carpenter colleague, Vinny Byrne. Dispersed throughout the city in safe houses, they reported daily at 9 a.m., armed beneath their overalls. Selected from units of the Dublin Brigade of the IRA, members were on paid permanent duty. They also acted as Collins's unofficial bodyguard. Members of the Squad were Frank Bolster, Ben Byrne, Eddie Byrne, Vinny Byrne, Jim Conroy, Johnny Dunne, Paddy Griffin, Tom Kehoe (or Keogh), Mick Kennedy, Mick Reilly, Jim Slattery, and Bill Stapleton. Their driver was Pat McCrea.

The Squad was informed of operations through Collins's Special Intelligence Unit, which occasionally assisted the unit. IRA headquarters, through CATHAL BRUGHA, sanctioned proposed executions. The first was the killing of Detective-Sergeant 'Dog' Smyth of G Division,

DMP, 31 July 1919. Other operations included the killing of informers and the shooting of Detective Daniel Hoey, 12 September 1919, Detective John Barton, 29 November 1919, and Assistant Commissioner William Forbes-Redmond, 21 January 1920, the abduction and shooting of a resident magistrate, Alan Bell, 26 March 1920, and the killing of Sergeant Roche, 11 October 1920. The Squad took part in the virtual annihilation of the British intelligence unit known as the 'CAIRO GANG' on BLOODY SUNDAY (21 November 1920).

Stack, Austin (1880–1929), republican and politician (Sinn Féin); born in Tralee, educated locally. He was an income tax inspector for the Dingle region. A founder-member of the IRISH VOLUNTEERS, he was a commandant during the EASTER RISING (1916). Unaware that the AUD was arriving three days earlier than scheduled, he failed to make contact with it. Hearing that a stranger (ROGER CASEMENT) had been picked up on Banna Strand, he went to Tralee RIC Barracks to make inquiries and was himself arrested. During his imprisonment he was ostracised for a time by the Kerry Volunteers, who held him responsible for not attempting to rescue Casement. He was released in June 1917, having led the struggle for political prisoner status.

Elected to the first Dáil Éireann for West Kerry, December 1918, he was Substitute Minister for Home Affairs, 1920, and Minister for Home Affairs from August 1921 until January 1922. He was close to CATHAL BRUGHA. He accompanied ÉAMON DE VALERA to London for the talks with DAVID LLOYD GEORGE, July 1921, and supported de Valera's rejection of the British terms. A leading opponent of the ANGLO-IRISH TREATY (1921), he supported the anti-Treaty IRA during the CIVIL WAR. While imprisoned in Kilmainham Jail, Dublin, from April 1923 he led a hunger strike that severely weakened his health. He was again elected a Sinn Féin TD in 1923.

Staines, Michael (1885–1955), politician (Sinn Féin) and Garda Commissioner; born in Newport, Co. Mayo, educated at national school. After moving to Dublin, 1902, he joined the IRB and became a member of the Supreme Council, 1921–22. He fought in the EASTER RISING (1916) and was interned at Fron-Goch, Wales, where he was officer commanding the 1,800 Irish internees. On his release he was prominent in the reorganised IRISH VOLUNTEERS and in SINN FÉIN. He represented the St Michan's division, Dublin, for Sinn Féin and was an alderman of Dublin Corporation, 1919–25. Director of the BELFAST BOYCOTT from 4 September 1920, he was also closely associated with the ARBITRATION COURTS, for which he was arrested. Following his release he accepted the ANGLO-IRISH TREATY (1921) and was reappointed director of the Belfast Boycott, 19 January 1922. In February 1922 he became first Commissioner of the CIVIC GUARD but resigned after a mutiny. He was a member of the Senate of the Irish Free State, 1922–36, where he opposed cuts in Garda salaries.

Stalker Affair. During 1982 the RUC killed six unarmed Catholics, five of whom had alleged terrorist links. Amid accusations of what came to be known as a 'shoot to kill' (i.e. shoot on sight) policy, the Assistant Chief Constable of Manchester, John Stalker, was appointed to conduct an inquiry into such killings. After claiming that he was being hampered in his inquiries, Stalker was taken off the case and was then required to face disciplinary charges in Manchester, which were subsequently dropped. Stalker's investigation was taken over by Chief Constable Colin Sampson. The reports were not published.

In 1988 SIR PATRICK MAYHEW said that while there was evidence of attempts to pervert the course of justice, there would be no prosecution of members of the RUC, for reasons of 'national security'. The Northern Ireland Police Authority decided (by one vote) that there would be no disciplinary charges against three senior officers. Subsequently, Chief Constable Charles Kelly of Staffordshire submitted a report to the Chief Constable of the RUC, Sir John Hermon, leading to disciplinary charges against twenty members of the RUC. The coroner, John Leckey, abandoned inquests into the deaths because Chief Constable Sir Hugh Annesley refused to provide the Stalker Report, 8 September 1994. In May 1995 in the Liverpool High Court Mr Justice Owen accepted a public interest immunity certificate from Sir Patrick Mayhew preventing Stalker from giving evidence in a case involving a Manchester businessman, Kevin Taylor. (See also STEVENS INQUIRY.)

Standing Advisory Committee on Human Rights, established under the Constitution Act (1973) to monitor the effectiveness of laws against discrimination in Northern Ireland on the grounds of religion or politics. Its early recommendations included bringing the law on divorce and homosexuality into line with those in Britain (later adopted). In May 1979 it recommended ending internment without trial. It pressed for a bill of rights during the period 1980–81. It criticised the law (passed after the election of the hunger-striker BOBBY SANDS in May 1981) that prevented a convicted person from being nominated for Parliament. Following the ANGLO-IRISH AGREEMENT (1985) the committee supported the case for three-judge courts to deal with terrorist offences. It urged an end to exclusion orders under the Prevention of Terrorism Act, which banned people from Britain or Northern Ireland, and the easing of port controls. It called for a review of the law on the use of 'reasonable force' by the police and British army and proposed 'clear and comprehensive measures' on fair employment. It questioned the impartiality of the new police complaints procedure.

In January 1989 the committee accused the government of failing to consult sufficiently widely before introducing anti-terrorist measures. The government explored its recommendation for race relations laws tailored to Northern Ireland to include protection for Travellers. In the period 1990–91 the committee suggested that a bill of rights should incorporate the European Convention on Human Rights. Later that year it called for SIR PATRICK MAYHEW to institute human rights reforms in the wake of the Provisional IRA ceasefire, 31 August 1994. Two years later it asked him to launch a full inquiry into the violence in Portadown that accompanied the ORANGE ORDER march from Drumcree. It called for the establishment of an independent body to deal with contentious parades, December 1996, and criticised the government over its response to the UN report on the alleged harassment of lawyers in Northern Ireland, April 1998.

On 1 March 1999 the Standing Advisory Committee on Human Rights was replaced by the Northern Ireland Human Rights Commission, established under the terms of the BELFAST AGREEMENT (1998), with Bruce Dickson its first full-time chief commissioner, aided by nine part-time members.

Stardust Fire. The Stardust Ballroom in Artane, Dublin, was the scene of a disaster when fire broke out at a St Valentine's Day dance on 14 February 1981. Eighteen people died and 128 were injured, some horrifically. An inquiry later found that the premises had been in serious breach of fire and safety regulations, as a result of which new legislation was introduced to prevent future disasters of this nature. A memorial park was opened in Coolock, Dublin, 19 September 1993.

Staten Island, a part of the city of New York developed as a quarantine station in the early 1840s. All vessels bound for New York were obliged to put in for inspection, and the quarantine period was thirty days. From May 1847, emigrants arriving at the station paid $1.50 'hospital money' to indemnify themselves against hospital charges for a period of twelve months. The hospital complex, spread over 30 acres, included two hospitals, each with two hundred beds, an isolation hospital with accommodation for fifty patients, a workhouse for the destitute (nearly all of whom were Irish), and some ancillary buildings. To accommodate orphans and convalescents and to cater for emigrants suffering from non-infectious illness, the authorities opened another hospital at WARD'S ISLAND.

The Staten Island establishment was soon overtaxed, and temporary wooden sheds were erected to care for the infected. In 1847 there were more than 3,000 cases of typhus, 600 cases of smallpox, and more than 60 cases of cholera. The wooden shacks were by now holding more than a thousand patients. The death rate was exceedingly high. As at GROSSE ÎLE, accurate records were not maintained, but mortality was estimated at 16–20 per cent. From 1891 to 1954 Ellis Island received the great majority of immigrants wishing to enter the United States. (See also POINTE SAINT-CHARLES.)

'State of the Country' (1790–1831), a series of reports from magistrates, army commanders and private individuals (often clergymen) dealing with the situation in various parts of the country in relation to law and order. They are now in the NATIONAL ARCHIVES.

'station', the holding of religious services in selected houses, a custom peculiar to Ireland, probably dating from the eighteenth century, when it was not always possible for Catholics to have ready access to the sacraments. Stations were held twice yearly, usually during Lent and in autumn. The site of the station, which was rotated, was announced in the church, and all the people of the townland were expected to attend. The clergy heard Confession, offered Mass, and distributed the Eucharist. The parish dues were then collected, and the officiating priest or priests, altar-boys and neighbours were entertained to breakfast.

Statute of Westminster (1931), legislation enacted on 11 December 1931 to implement a resolution of the Imperial Conference of 1930, at which the IRISH FREE STATE was represented by P. J. MCGILLIGAN. It provided that no law made by the parliament of a dominion should be void and inoperative on the grounds that it was repugnant to the law of England, and that the parliament of a dominion should have the power to repeal or amend any existing or future act of the British Parliament in so far as the same was part of the law of a dominion. The parliament of a dominion was granted full power to make laws having extraterritorial operation. It was also provided that no future act of the British Parliament should extend to a dominion, unless it was expressly declared in that act that the dominion had requested and consented to its enactment. This provision was opposed by WINSTON CHURCHILL, who pointed out that this would enable Dáil Éireann to repudiate the ANGLO-IRISH TREATY (1921), and by the Secretary of State for Dominion Affairs, L. S. Amery, who said that the Irish Free State must be treated in the same way as other dominions.

Staunton, Michael (1788–1870), journalist; born in Co. Clare. Editor of the *Freeman's Journal,* he founded the short-lived *Dublin Evening Herald,* 1823–23, and, with the encouragement of DANIEL O'CONNELL, the *Dublin Morning Register,* 1824–43. Staunton, whose staff included CHARLES GAVAN DUFFY, THOMAS DAVIS, and JOHN BLAKE DILLON, did much to transform Irish newspapers from servile instruments of the government into independent organs of public opinion; he was known contemporaneously as the 'creator of the Irish press.' Eventually he fell into dispute with O'Connell, who wanted the press to be an uncritical instrument in the struggle for Repeal. Staunton denounced YOUNG IRELAND and the IRISH CONFEDERATION. He was lord mayor of Dublin in 1845.

Steele, Thomas (1788–1848), associate of DANIEL O'CONNELL; born in Derrymore, Co. Clare, educated at TCD and the University of Cambridge. A prominent landlord in Co. Clare, he bankrupted his estates providing aid for the patriot army in the Spanish War (1823). Devoted to O'Connell, Steele (a Protestant) worked in both the CATHOLIC ASSOCIATION and the REPEAL ASSOCIATION. His elaborate, grandiloquent mode of speech was incomprehensible to all but those closest to him. O'Connell, who dubbed him his 'head pacificator', encouraged him to adjudicate disputes among the association's supporters. Steele was so overcome by O'Connell's death in 1847 that he attempted suicide by jumping off Waterloo Bridge in London; though rescued, he died shortly afterwards. He is buried close to O'Connell in Glasnevin Cemetery, Dublin.

Stephens, James (1824–1901), republican; born in Kilkenny, educated at St Kieran's College. A railway engineer, he was a member of YOUNG IRELAND and the IRISH CONFEDERATION and *aide de camp* to WILLIAM SMITH O'BRIEN at BALLINGARRY, Co. Tipperary, 1848, where he was wounded and reported killed. Escaping to Paris, where he met JOHN O'MAHONY and MICHAEL DOHENY, he was influenced by French revolutionary figures. He remained there after O'Mahony went to the United States, 1853, and taught English before returning to Ireland, 1856. Over the next two years he travelled some three thousand miles around the country examining the feasibility of establishing a secret movement more durable than Young Ireland; this period earned him the title 'An Seabhac Siúlach' ('the roaming hawk'), sometimes Anglicised to 'Shooks' or 'Mr Shooks'. He earned a living teaching French to the children of JOHN BLAKE DILLON. Contacted in 1857 by Owen Considine, an emissary of the EMMET MONUMENT ASSOCIATION, he despatched JOSEPH DENIEFFE to New York to seek funds for a new movement. Instead of the several thousand dollars he expected he received $400, and with this he established the IRISH REPUBLICAN BROTHERHOOD, 17 March 1858. At the same time O'Mahony founded the FENIANS, the name by which the whole organisation was popularly known.

Appointed head centre of the IRB, Stephens spent much of the period 1859–60 in the United States or France. He established the IRISH PEOPLE, 1863, and brought together recruiting agents, including JOHN DEVOY. After the paper was suppressed and the IRB leaders imprisoned, 1865, he evaded capture until November. Devoy engineered his escape from Richmond Jail, Dublin, with the help of two sympathetic warders, Byrne and Breslin.

His relations with O'Mahony and the American wing worsened during 1864. The Americans and many Irish members disliked his dictatorial attitude. Constantly complaining that the Americans were not supplying him with promised arms and money, Stephens made no secret of his poor opinion of the American Fenians. Finally, in 1865, when the Americans expected an Irish rising, THOMAS J. KELLY arrived to examine the organisation but found no evidence of the 85,000 members of which Stephens boasted. Stephens persuaded Kelly to abandon plans for a rising for the moment. Early in 1866 they travelled to New York, where Stephens unsuccessfully attempted to reunite the fractured American movement. When he again attempted to persuade the Americans to postpone an Irish rising, they replaced him as head centre with Kelly, who returned to Ireland, January 1867, with a group of Irish-Americans to plan the ill-fated rising.

Stephens again lived in Paris until 1885, when the French authorities, concerned over his possible involvement with DYNAMITERS, expelled him. He was in Switzerland until he was permitted to return to Ireland through the intervention of CHARLES STEWART PARNELL. He spent the remainder of his life in seclusion in Dublin, with the exception of a brief appearance during the CENTENARY CELEBRATIONS, 1898.

Stevens Inquiry. John Stevens, Deputy Chief Constable of Cambridgeshire (later Commissioner of the London Metropolitan Police), was appointed on 17 May 1990 to head an inquiry into the circumstances in which security files, including photographs of republican paramilitary suspects, came into the possession of loyalist paramilitary groups. While the RUC was cleared of involvement, ten members of the ULSTER DEFENCE REGIMENT were charged; Tommy Lyttle, a member of the UDA, was sentenced to seven years' imprisonment in 1991 for the possession of documents likely to be of benefit to terrorists. The UDA was banned on 11 August 1992. The inquiry also led to the arrest of Brian Nelson, a British army spy within the UDA, for conspiracy to murder five Catholics (for which he received ten years' imprisonment).

At the request of the RUC Chief Constable, Sir Hugh Annesley, August 1993, Stevens reopened his inquiry on foot of new information. Following the murder by the UDA of Rosemary Nelson, a prominent solicitor, 15 March 1999, the Chief Constable, Sir Ronnie Flanagan, asked Stevens to reopen the case of the murdered solicitor Pat Finucane, killed on 12 February 1989 by the UDA amid allegations of collusion by the RUC and British army. While the British government deflected calls for an inquiry into the Finucane killing by claiming that Stevens had already investigated it, Stevens stated that he had never investigated it.

The Stevens Report was presented to the Chief Constable of the PSNI, Sir Hugh Orde (who had worked at one time as an investigator during the inquiry), 17 April 2003. Stevens found that his three investigations had been obstructed and misled: 'From day 1, this obstruction was cultural . . . and widespread within parts of the army and RUC, the Force Research Unit, and RUC Special Branch in particular.' This included 'wilful failure to keep records, the absence of accountability, the withholding of intelligence and evidence, [and] the extreme of agents being involved in murder.' A fire at the Stevens Inquiry incident room had been a 'deliberate act of arson.' Stevens found that the British army and RUC had colluded with loyalist paramilitary groups in the murder of innocent civilians. Nationalists known to be targets of such groups were not properly warned or protected. The murder of Pat Finucane and of Adam Lambert—a nineteen-year-old student killed on 9 November 1987 by the UDA, who had mistaken him for a Catholic—were preventable. The RUC and British army had covered up the collusion. The RUC had not dealt adequately with both sides of the community in 'threat intelligence'.

Among twenty-one recommendations, Stevens stated that an assistant chief constable answerable to the chief constable should have responsibility for the Anti-Terrorist Branch; that the senior investigating officer of murder and other serious crimes should receive full co-operation and relevant intelligence from the Special Branch, particularly where intelligence agents were suspects for murder or other serious crime; and that an internal investigation department should be established by the PSNI so that any allegations or suspicions of collusion and corruption could be actively tackled.

In March 2003 Steevens was preparing prosecution papers on approximately twenty former and serving members of the police and British army for presentation to the Director of Public Prosecutions.

stipendiary magistrates. The Lord Lieutenant of Ireland was given legislative power in 1814 and 1822 to appoint 'magistrates of police' in areas proclaimed as being in a state of disturbance. The magistrates, who had to be landowners, held office at the pleasure of the Lord Lieutenant. The imbalance between Catholic and Protestant appointees incurred the hostility of the Catholic population. DUBLIN CASTLE generally held county office-holders in low esteem, suspecting self-interest as the primary motivation for office.

Stokes, Whitley (1763–1845), physician; born in Dublin, educated at TCD, of which he became a fellow, 1788. A supporter of the UNITED IRISHMEN, he was suspended from his fellowship in 1798. Regius professor of medicine, 1830–43, he was highly praised for his exhaustive efforts during typhus epidemics in Dublin.

Stokes, Whitley (1830–1909), lawyer and scholar; born in Dublin, son of DR WILLIAM STOKES, educated at TCD and called to the bar. While working as a lawyer in India, 1862–82, where he became president of the Law Commission, he continued studies in Irish, after which he moved to England. Said later to have been the first modern Celtic scholar born in Ireland, he was a student of Old Irish and comparative languages (Breton and Cornish) and edited several translations from Irish. His extensive library was presented to University College, London.

His works include *A Mediaeval Tract on Latin Declension* (1860), for which he received a medal from the ROYAL IRISH ACADEMY, *Goidelica* (1866), *Saltar na Rann* (1883), *The Tripartite Life of Patrick* (1887), *Lives of the Saints from the Book of Lismore* (1889), *The Annals of Tigernach* (1897), *The Eulogy of Columba* (1899), and *The Martyrology of Oengus* (1905). He was associated with John Strachan (1862–1907) in publishing *Thesaurus Palaeohibernicus* (a two-volume collection of Old Irish glosses, 1901–03). He also worked with Kuno Meyer.

Stokes, William (1804–1878), physician; born in Dublin, son of WHITLEY STOKES (1763–1845). Physician at the Meath Hospital, Dublin, he was founder of the Pathological Society, 1838, Physician to the Queen in Ireland, 1851, and president of the Royal Irish Academy and of the Royal College of Physicians, 1849–50. He succeeded his father as professor of medicine at Trinity College, Dublin, 1843; he influenced the decision by Trinity College to initiate a diploma in state medicine, 1870, the first such award in the world. His name is perpetuated in the Stokes-Adams syndrome (a pulse abnormality) and in Cheyne-Stokes respiration (an irregular breathing signalling the onset of death). In addition to papers on a wide variety of medical topics, he published a life of GEORGE PETRIE (1878).

Stoney, George Johnstone (1826–1911), scientist; born at Oakleypark, Birr, Co. Offaly, educated at TCD. LORD ROSSE appointed him the first astronomical assistant at the Parsonstown [Birr] Observatory. He completed his fellowship at Trinity College while working for Lord Rosse, through whose influence he was appointed professor of natural philosophy at Queen's College, Galway. After five years' work in Galway he returned to Dublin as secretary of the Queen's University (until its dissolution in 1882). He was a fellow of the Royal Society from 1861. He gave the name 'electron' to the elementary charge of electricity, discovered by J. J. Thomson in the 1890s. He was a Visitor of the Royal Observatory at Greenwich and the Royal Institution in London and honorary secretary of the ROYAL DUBLIN SOCIETY for more than twenty years. A foreign member of the Academy of Science, Washington, and of the Philosophical Society of America, he was a member of the Joint Committee on Solar Research of the Royal Society and Royal Astronomical Society and of several international scientific committees.

Stormont, popular name for the Parliament Building, in the grounds of Stormont Castle, outside Belfast, and for the Parliament of Northern Ireland. The building was designed by Sir Arthur Thornley and opened by the Prince of Wales, later King Edward VIII, 17 November 1932. The Parliament had previously met in the Council Chamber of Belfast City Hall and in the Assembly College, Belfast. The last sitting of the Parliament of Northern Ireland was on 28 March 1972, when it adjourned until 18 April; however, before that date the Parliament was prorogued by the British government and direct rule from London was introduced, in an attempt to find a solution to the Northern conflict. The Secretary of State for Northern Ireland (with offices in Stormont Castle) became responsible for the affairs of the province.

stradogue, sleeping in (Irish *sráideog*), the custom among the rural poor of sleeping communally in a makeshift bed. In *Sketches in Erris and Tyrawley* (1851), CAESAR OTWAY described a cottage and its sleeping arrangements:

> Stripping themselves entirely the whole family lie down at once and together, covering themselves with blankets if they have them, if not, with their day clothing, but they lie down decently and in order, the eldest daughter next the wall farthest from the door, then all the sisters according to their ages, next the mother, father and sons in succession, and then the strangers, whether the travelling pedlar; or tailor or beggar. Thus the strangers are kept aloof from the female part of the family and if there be an apparent community, there is great propriety of conduct.

Strzelecki, Sir Paul Edmund (1797–1873), explorer and humanitarian; born Pawel Edmund Strzelecki in Gluszyna, Poland. After leaving his native country in 1830 he travelled widely. During the GREAT FAMINE (1845–49) he agreed to distribute relief in Connacht, on condition that part of the fund be used for the feeding and clothing of schoolchildren. Later he told the English politician John Bright, 'If the Devil were to invent a scheme to destroy Ireland he could not have thought up anything more effectual than the principle and practice upon which landed property has been held and managed in Ireland.'

Stuart de Decies, Henry Villiers-Stuart, first Baron (1803–1874), landowner and politician; educated at Eton College, Windsor. He had an estate at Dromana, near Dungarvan, Co. Waterford, and was persuaded by SIR THOMAS WYSE to stand as CATHOLIC EMANCIPATION candidate in the by-election of 1826. With the support of DANIEL O'CONNELL and the CATHOLIC ASSOCIATION he defeated the powerful Beresford family and won the seat. Lord Lieutenant of Co. Waterford, 1831–74, he was created Baron Stuart de Decies in 1839. His eldest son, Henry Windsor Villiers-Stuart, failed to succeed to the title when a parliamentary committee ruled that there were doubts about the validity of Villiers-Stuart's marriage to Therese Pauline Ott of Vienna, alleged to have taken place in a Catholic church.

Studies, a scholarly journal that succeeded NEW IRELAND REVIEW in 1912, sponsored by the Society of Jesus. Edited from 1914 to 1950 by Father Patrick J. Connolly (1875–1951), it has attracted contributions on every aspect of cultural, academic, economic and literary life.

Sub-Letting Act (1826), legislation prohibiting the sub-letting of property by a tenant except with the consent of the proprietor. Sub-letting, with the consequent division of the land, was generally held to be responsible for the poor condition of small tenant-farmers. The act also assisted landlords in their policy of consolidating landholdings at the expense of tenants, who were in many cases evicted when their lease expired. Sub-division continued until it was brought to an end by the GREAT FAMINE (1845–49).

Sullivan, Alexander (1847–1913), lawyer and Fenian; raised at Amherstburg, Ontario, where his father served with the British army. He settled in Chicago, 1872, and was active in republican politics. As a member of the 'TRIANGLE' during the 1880s he encouraged the DYNAMITERS. He was national chairman of CLAN NA GAEL, 1881–85, and president of the IRISH NATIONAL LEAGUE in America, 1883–84. His alleged responsibility for the murder of Dr P. H. Cronin, 1889, discredited his leadership of the American Fenians, but he remained an influential force in Irish-American politics.

Sullivan, A. M. [Alexander Martin] (1830–1884), journalist and politician (Nationalist); born in Bantry, Co. Cork, brother of T. D. SULLIVAN and an uncle of T. M. HEALY. He worked as a journalist in Dublin and Liverpool, 1853–55, and was proprietor and editor of the NATION, 1855. A member of YOUNG IRELAND, he opposed the IRB, which passed a death sentence on him, 1865. A founder-member of the HOME RULE LEAGUE, he entered politics as member of Parliament for Co. Louth, 1874–80. After being called to the bar he passed the *Nation* to his brother, T. D. Sullivan, 1876. Elected to Parliament for Co. Meath, 1880, he resigned following a heart attack in 1881. Using £400 collected for him during his imprisonment in 1868, he erected a statue to HENRY GRATTAN in College Green, Dublin. His most popular works were *The Story of Ireland* (1867) and *New Ireland* (2 vols., 1878). His son, A. M. Sullivan (1871–1959), was defence counsel for ROGER CASEMENT.

Sullivan, T. D. [Timothy Daniel] (1827–1914), journalist and politician (Nationalist); born in Bantry, Co. Cork, educated locally. A supporter of YOUNG IRELAND, he contributed to the *Nation,* which his brother, A. M. SULLIVAN, bought in 1855. He supported the HOME GOVERNMENT ASSOCIATION and the HOME RULE LEAGUE. After taking over editorship of the *Nation,* 1876, he employed his nephew, T. M. HEALY, as parliamentary correspondent. A supporter of the LAND LEAGUE and of CHARLES STEWART PARNELL, he entered politics as member of Parliament for Co. Westmeath, which he represented until 1885. He was lord mayor of Dublin, 1886–87, and member of Parliament for Dublin, 1885–92, and for West Donegal, 1892–1900. He was recognised as the leader of the 'Bantry Band', a group of Cork nationalists. Through his control of the *Nation* he was extremely influential, both in Ireland and in the IRISH PARTY, and was a leader of the PLAN OF CAMPAIGN. He wrote *Lays of Tullamore* while imprisoned under COERCION, 1888. He was a member of a fund-raising delegation in the United States when the crisis arose over Parnell's involvement in the O'Shea divorce case and was the only delegate to repudiate Parnell's leadership at that time. On his return he was forced to sell the *Nation*, which had lost circulation to the *Freeman's Journal*.

Sullivan was the author of a number of popular ballads, including 'God Save Ireland' (a song about the MANCHESTER MARTYRS, which became a *de facto* national anthem until 1916) and 'Song of the Canadian Woods' ('Ireland, Boys, Hurray'). His works include *Speeches from the Dock* (jointly edited with his brother, 1867), *Green Leaves* (1885), and *Recollections of Troubled Times in Irish Politics* (1905).

His son Timothy Sullivan (1874–1949), called to the bar in 1895 and a King's counsel from 1918, was the first president of the Supreme Court and Chief Justice of Ireland, 1936–46.

Sunningdale Agreement (1973), an agreement between the British and Irish governments and the incoming Executive of Northern Ireland, following tripartite talks at the Sunningdale Park Civil Service College, Ascot, Berkshire, 6–9 December 1973. Leaders in the talks were EDWARD HEATH, British Prime Minister (who presided), LIAM COSGRAVE, Taoiseach, and BRIAN FAULKNER, leader of the ULSTER UNIONIST PARTY and Chief of the Executive to be installed on 1 January 1974. GERRY FITT represented the SDLP and OLIVER NAPIER the ALLIANCE PARTY.

The talks, initiated by Heath, reached a wide measure of agreement. The British and Irish governments agreed that there should be no change in the status of Northern Ireland until a majority of the population there had expressed support for such a change; the Irish government and the SDLP upheld the aspiration to a united Ireland, but only by consent. The British government declared its support for a united Ireland in the event of a majority decision by the people of Northern Ireland; the Unionist and Alliance Parties voiced the unionist desire to remain within the United Kingdom. It was also agreed to revive the idea of a COUNCIL OF IRELAND and that there should be co-operation between Northern Ireland and the Republic on matters of law and order (the 'Irish dimension').

The Sunningdale Agreement was attacked by the Provisional IRA, loyalist paramilitary groups, and FIANNA FÁIL. When KEVIN BOLAND challenged the agreement, Mr Justice George Murnaghan in the High Court found that the Sunningdale references to Northern Ireland as a state were not in conflict with the Constitution of Ireland, 16 January 1974. The ULSTER UNIONIST COUNCIL rejected the Council of Ireland. In May, following a loyalist strike, the power-sharing Executive, over which Faulkner presided, was brought down after five months (January–May 1974).

sweat-house, a common feature of rural life up to the end of the nineteenth century. In *A Frenchman's Walk through Ireland* (1796–97), Jacques-Louis de La Tocnaye observed that 'wherever there are four or five cabins near each other there is sure to be a sweating house.' The building, usually a drystone corbelled structure some 4 to 7 feet in diameter and up to 6 feet in height, was sited, where possible, close to a source of water. After a fire had burned for at least two days, the ground was swept and strewn with rushes. Five or six people were admitted at a time. The door was then sealed with sods, and smoke was allowed to escape through a hole in the roof. The occupants sat naked, sweating profusely, and were later cooled in a stream or with buckets of water. In some houses the floor was cobbled and a huge fire allowed to burn for some days; buckets of water were then thrown upon the stones, producing an effect not unlike that of a Turkish bath. Sweat-houses were frequented by kelp-gatherers, fishermen, and those afflicted with rheumatism or similar ailments. Young women visited them either to improve their complexion or before their attendance at a HIRING FAIR.

Sweetman, John (1844–1936), philanthropist, politician, and language activist; born in Rathfarnham, Co. Dublin. The founder of the Sweetman Colony in Currie, Minnesota, he claimed that in America he had spent some forty years indulging his 'hobby' of 'abolishing ranches,' to which end he had bought 20,000 acres of grassland and divided it into small farms. Member of Parliament for Wicklow East, 1892–95, he was a joint founder of the

GAELIC LEAGUE, to which he was a generous benefactor. He provided his relative REV. JOHN SWEETMAN with £5,000 towards the Benedictine foundation of Mount St Benedict at Gorey, Co. Wexford. A benefactor also of SINN FÉIN, he was president from 1908, in succession to EDWARD MARTYN. Imprisoned after the EASTER RISING (1916), he supported the ANGLO-IRISH TREATY (1921) but also supported ÉAMON DE VALERA in 1932. His writings include *Nationality* (1907), *Liberty* (1909), and *Protection: Some Letters to the Press with Regard to the Protection of Irish Industries* (1926).

Sweetman, John Francis (1872–1953), Benedictine priest and educationalist; born in Clohamon, Enniscorthy, Co. Wexford, educated at Downside Abbey, Bath, and in Rome. During the Anglo-Boer War as a British army chaplain he studied tobacco-growing. In 1909 he established Mount St Benedict at Gorey, Co. Wexford, where students—including JAMES DILLON, SEÁN MACBRIDE, and MICHAEL O'RAHILLY—lived under austere and eccentric rule. The school encouraged self-esteem, logic, and respect for the environment; cricket and walking were the favoured pastimes. Senior boys were given a tree with which to heat their rooms if they provided ten trees for planting in return. Many of the pupils spent much of their leisure time in the manufacture of cigarettes at the Ballyowen tobacco factory run by Father Sweetman. Following the execution of the leaders of the EASTER RISING (1916), Father Sweetman's support for SINN FÉIN brought him into conflict with Bishop Codd of Ferns, who appealed to Rome for the closure of Mount St Benedict; Rome refused the request but had a new head appointed, and Father Sweetman was transferred to Liverpool, 1925.

Synge, John Millington (1871–1909), dramatist; born in Rathfarnham, Co. Dublin, educated privately and at TCD. He studied music at the Royal Irish Academy of Music, where he became a member of the orchestra in 1891. He followed the advice of W. B. YEATS to seek his subject matter in the Aran Islands. Now suffering from Hodgkin's disease, he spent his summers from 1899 to 1902 living with the islanders. Observation and the stories he heard there provided him with the material for *Riders to the Sea* and *The Playboy of the Western World*; it also provided him with the material for his book *The Aran Islands* (1907, with illustrations by JACK B. YEATS). Synge's other travels in the west of Ireland led to the creation of a new idiom, based entirely, he claimed, on the speech of the people among whom he had travelled.

He was closely associated with the founding of the ABBEY THEATRE, of which he was appointed a director. *The Shadow of the Glen* (1904), with its adulterous heroine, was denounced by nationalists as a slur on Irish womanhood; ARTHUR GRIFFITH in the *United Irishman* played a leading role in the attack on the play and its author. It was followed by *Riders to the Sea,* which PATRICK PEARSE accused of containing 'a sinister and unholy gospel'; he was later to reverse this opinion and to describe Synge in 1913 as 'one of the two or three men who have in our time made Ireland considerable in the eyes of the world.' Following *The Well of the Saints* (1905), which was again offensive to nationalists, Synge's most controversial work, *The Playboy of the Western World*—in which he created the role of Pegeen Mike for his fiancée, Molly Allgood ('Máire O'Neill')—was produced at the Abbey, 26 January 1907. The accompanying riots led to a bitter dispute between Yeats and nationalists, who claimed that the play showed the Irish people in a vicious and ridiculous light at a time when the nationalist aim was to project the image of a civilised people worthy of self-government.

The Playboy of the Western World is widely regarded as the most important play of the Irish literary revival. In recognition of Synge's contribution to Irish drama Yeats put on *The Tinker's Wedding* at the Abbey in 1908. By then the dying Synge was unable to complete *Deirdre of the Sorrows,* also written for his fiancée. His other works include *Poems and Translations* (1910) and *In Kerry, West Kerry, and Connemara* (1911).

Synod of Thurles (1850). Thurles, Co. Tipperary, was the venue for the first national synod of the Catholic hierarchy to be held in Ireland since the Middle Ages. Meeting from 22 August to 9 September 1850, it was called by the Archbishop of Armagh, PAUL CULLEN, acting under instructions from Rome, which had expressed concerns regarding the administration of the church in Ireland. The synod condemned the QUEEN'S COLLEGES and agreed to establish a Catholic university. It called on pastors to increase the number of schools and to direct 'those pious associations for the diffusing of catechetical knowledge and the caring of the poor.' It accepted that each bishop would have discretion in relation to NATIONAL EDUCATION in his diocese. SECRET SOCIETIES were condemned, and the callous treatment of the rural poor during the GREAT FAMINE (1845–49) was denounced.

Questions on which the bishops could not agree were to be referred to Rome. Priests were forbidden to issue denunciations of people or movements from the altar, or to say Mass after noon. It was decreed that the sacraments of baptism and marriage could be administered only in churches. Marriages between Catholics and non-Catholics were to be discouraged; the church's disapproval of such unions was to be expressed in withholding much of the normal marriage ritual. A register of marriages and baptisms was to he kept in each church. Catholic clergy were not to engage in public disputation with members of other religions, and the laity were forbidden to engage in discussions with non-Catholics. Priests were alerted to the dangers of proselytising (see SECOND REFORMATION); to combat this, specially commissioned preachers were to be invited to give retreats. Sodalities were to be established for the laity, and Catholic books were to be published to help strengthen the faith.

Decreta Synodi Nationalis Totius Hiberniae ('decrees of the national synod of all Ireland') was published in Dublin in 1851, but it took some time for them to win acceptance. They were not popular with the clergy, and three years after the Synod, Cullen, by then Archbishop of Dublin, complained that the decrees were not even observed in Thurles.

T

Taibhdhearc na Gaillimhe, an Irish-language theatre in Galway founded in 1927 by Máire Ní Thuathail, Dr Séamus Ó Beirn, Prof. Liam Ó Briain, and Tomás Ó Máille (who proposed the name 'Taibhdhearc', from *taibhreamh,* 'dream', and *dearc,* 'eye'). They secured a £600 subsidy from the government and a lease on the Augustinian Hall in Middle Street, and the theatre opened in the summer of 1928 with a production of *Diarmaid agus Gráinne* by Mícheál Mac Liammóir (who directed, played Diarmaid, and designed the set). The original premises were bought, with government aid, and on 17 March 1978 the renovated Taibhdhearc celebrated its golden jubilee with a production of *An Spailpín Fánach* by Críostóir Ó Floinn.

An Taisce, a voluntary body established on 15 July 1948 to 'advance the conservation and management of Ireland's natural and constructed endowments in manners which are sustainable.' It is a prescribed body under the Planning Acts.

take, as described by Edward Wakefield in *An Account of Ireland, Statistical and Political* (1812), a portion of a farm given over to tillage under the early nineteenth-century Irish land system. Divided into twenty to thirty lots, subdivided into fields and partitioned into smaller lots, each portion had one or two ridges, which were held by their owners as long as the take was given over to tillage. The take system, common in Cos. Kildare, Kilkenny, and Tyrone, was in decline before the GREAT FAMINE (1845–49).

Talbot, Matt (1856–1925), labourer and religious zealot; born in Dublin, educated at Christian Brothers' school. A heavy drinker, he took the pledge in 1884 and turned to a life of piety, modelling his penitential exercises on those of St Catherine of Siena and St Teresa of Avila. He slept on a plank bed with a wooden block as pillow and held vigils over a period of forty years. He made few friends. During the DUBLIN LOCK-OUT (1913) he gave financial assistance to the families of married colleagues. His life of self-mortification impinged on his health, leading to kidney and heart ailments, and he collapsed and died in Granby Lane on his way to Mass in Dominick Street, 7 June 1925. At Jervis Street Hospital it was discovered that chains worn about his body had channelled deep grooves on his abdomen and back, and there were additional chains on an arm and a leg. He was declared 'venerable' by the Catholic Church in 1976, a first step in the process of canonisation. A *Life of Matt Talbot* (1951) by John Aloysius Glyon was translated into thirteen languages.

tally-man, a travelling salesman who supplied goods, usually clothing or footwear, on credit and recouped the cost through regular door-to-door collections. Tally-men formed a vital element of the Irish social fabric up to the mid-1960s.

Tally-man is also the name given to a person who supplies an estimated election result, based on calculations as the votes are being counted.

tally-woman, a young woman serving as mistress to a member of the Anglo-Irish aristocracy or gentry. It was customary in the eighteenth century for landlords to select mistresses from among their tenants; they lived in the 'big house' and enjoyed the life-style of their lovers.

Those who became pregnant were compensated with money or land, and a marriage would be arranged with one of the landlord's tenants. The custom largely died out during the GREAT FAMINE (1845–49) but survived in some areas into the early twentieth century.

Tánaiste (Irish, 'heir presumptive'), deputy head of the Government, a term introduced in the CONSTITUTION OF IRELAND (1937). (See GOVERNMENTS OF IRELAND.)

Taoiseach (Irish, 'chief'), head of the Government, a term introduced in the CONSTITUTION OF IRELAND (1937). The head of the government of the Irish Free State, December 1922 to December 1937, was known as President of the Executive Council. (See GOVERNMENTS OF IRELAND.)

Tara, a secret loyalist, anti-Catholic and anti-communist organisation in the 1960s; by the end of the decade it was describing itself as 'the hard core of Protestant resistance' in Northern Ireland. Composed principally of members of the ORANGE ORDER, it sought the closure of Catholic schools and the criminalisation of the Catholic religion.

Tariff Commission, established as an independent body in 1926 to receive applications from groups desiring tariffs and to adjudicate on them. The three-member commission was headed by J. J. MCELLIGOTT, then under-secretary of the Department of Finance. Though in effective existence for only six years, it was not formally abolished until 1939.

Tartan Gangs, groups of loyalist youths who wore tartan scarves in memory of three members of the Royal Highland Fusiliers regiment of the British army killed in Belfast on 10 March 1971. The Tartan Gangs were believed to be involved in the intimidation of people who wished to work during the 1974 loyalist strike (see ULSTER WORKERS' COUNCIL).

technical education. Under the Technical Instruction Act (1889) local authorities were empowered to raise a rate of up to 1 penny in the pound (0.4 per cent) for the provision of technical or manual instruction; manual instruction was defined as instruction in the use of the tools and processes of agriculture and modelling in clay, wood, and other materials. Under the Local Government (Ireland) Act (1898) (see LOCAL GOVERNMENT) technical education was placed under the county councils. The Department of Agriculture and Technical Instruction, established 1899, assumed responsibility for technical instruction, which was also available in reformatory and industrial schools.

In 1924 technical and all other education was placed under the Department of Education. The Vocational Education Act (1930) established thirty-eight vocational education committees (VECs), with responsibility for the provision of technical schools. (See VOCATIONAL EDUCATION.)

Telesis Report (1982), a report commissioned from the Telesis consultancy firm by the NATIONAL ECONOMIC AND SOCIAL COUNCIL, July 1980, to inquire into industrial policy. The report, February 1982, found that despite improved living standards, the income gap between Ireland and other industrialised countries had widened. It queried government policy on foreign investment, criticised excessive financial inducements, and urged a greater commitment to the development of indigenous industry. Emphasising the absence of international competition necessary to foster a native entrepreneurial class, it advocated that state support be confined to firms in the 'exposed' sector. Fearing that Ireland would be perceived as a mere assembly-line for foreign firms, the consultants recommended that foreign companies establish research-and-development units in Ireland.

Temporalities Commission, established after the DISESTABLISHMENT of the Church of Ireland in 1869 to administer the revenues accruing from the property of the church. It became a voluntary body from 1 January 1871.

Tenant League, founded by CHARLES GAVAN DUFFY and FREDERICK LUCAS in Dublin at a meeting attended by representatives of the TENANTS' PROTECTION SOCIETIES, 9 August 1850. Its initial support came from the ULSTER TENANT RIGHT ASSOCIATION, led by WILLIAM SHARMAN CRAWFORD; this support, however, was soon lost, principally because of the involvement of Catholic clergymen in the south. Gavan Duffy called his movement the 'League of North and South'.

The aim of the league was to secure the 'THREE FS' (fair rent, fixity of tenure, and free sale). To the larger tenant-farmer, fixity of tenure was the priority; the league never had the support of smaller tenants, for whom fair rents were the principal concern. The founders wished to establish a parliamentary party of Irish members who would oppose any government not prepared to grant TENANT RIGHT. This brought the league into alliance with the 'IRISH BRIGADE'.

Following the general election of July 1852, when fifty Irish members, including Gavan Duffy and Lucas, had been elected, the INDEPENDENT IRISH PARTY was founded at a meeting in Dublin; but the cause of tenant right was seriously weakened when JOHN SADLEIR and WILLIAM KEOGH defected from the party in December. Supporters of the league were also intimidated by hostile landlords. The most serious blow to its success, however, was Lucas's decision to take his complaints about the Archbishop of Dublin, PAUL CULLEN, to Rome, which alienated clerical support. Lucas died in October 1855, shortly after the failure of his mission to Rome, and a month later Gavan Duffy emigrated to Australia. The Tenant League collapsed, and the Independent Irish Party had disappeared by 1860. The demand for tenant right persisted and was taken up as a popular cause by the LAND LEAGUE, which secured it in the Land Law (Ireland) Act (1881) (see LAND ACTS).

tenant right. Free sale, also known as the Ulster custom, was the right of a tenant-farmer to sell occupancy of his holding to the highest bidder, subject to the landlord's approval of the purchaser. This would allow the tenant to secure compensation for any improvements for which he was responsible. Under tenant right the tenant would be entitled to compensation for 'disturbance' (i.e. eviction), as a landlord who wished to evict would either have to allow the sale of tenant right or pay the outgoing tenant the market price. It was of importance to the larger tenant-farmers, who organised the TENANT LEAGUE. Under the Landlord and Tenant (Ireland) Act (1870) tenant right was conceded wherever the custom could be shown to prevail, but this was a failure. It received legal recognition as one of the 'THREE FS' under the Land Law (Ireland) Act (1881) (see LAND ACTS).

Tenants' Defence Association, founded 15 October 1889 in Tipperary, an inspiration of WILLIAM O'BRIEN, an organiser of the PLAN OF CAMPAIGN. The scheme had the support of CHARLES STEWART PARNELL, who was represented at the inaugural meeting by THOMAS SEXTON; the association was led by O'Brien and JOHN DILLON. While Parnell disapproved of the Plan of Campaign, he supported the Tenants' Defence Association under pressure from O'Brien, who felt it was necessary to retaliate against landlords uniting to resist the plan. Some £61,000 was raised nationally for the relief of evicted tenants, but most of the association's finances were spent on NEW TIPPERARY. It collapsed as a result of the split in the IRISH PARTY, December 1890, following Parnell's involvement in the O'Shea divorce action.

Tenants' Protection Societies. Based on a suggestion by JAMES FINTAN LALOR, the first Tenants' Protection Society was founded in Callan, Co. Kilkenny, in 1849 by two Catholic priests, Father O'Shea and Father Keeffe. Their aim was to protect tenant-farmers from the excessive demands of landlords, to secure a fair rent, and to prevent tenants from buying or renting land from which another tenant had been evicted. During 1850 the Callan example was followed in other areas as tenants, suffering from the effects of the GREAT FAMINE (1845–49), sought to secure improvements. The landlords retaliated: on Lord Derwent's estate in Callan, 442 tenants were evicted; over the country as a whole the figure was 100,000. In August 1850 CHARLES GAVAN DUFFY invited the societies to send representatives to a meeting in Dublin, where the TENANT LEAGUE was established to co-ordinate the struggle.

thatch. The use of thatch for roofing was once common throughout Ireland. Isaac Weld, while engaged on the Royal Dublin Society's Statistical Survey in 1832, noted in Co. Roscommon that 'out of 517 houses, no less than 462 are thatched.' The materials used for roofing varied from area to area—dictated by financial considerations, availability, and weather conditions.

Barley. Used in the most humble of dwellings only, and then on a limited scale.

Flax. Occasionally used in Cos. Derry, Donegal, and Fermanagh.

Heather. Used in Co. Donegal and other mountain districts; though of rough appearance it presented a sturdy and durable roofing material.

Oat-straw. Favoured in Cos. Kildare, Laois, Louth, Meath, and Westmeath; this particular straw had an attractive golden sheen when new.

Reed. Munster thatchers favoured the wild reed.

Rye. This thatch was considered extremely

durable if cut just before ripening; it was specially grown for thatching purposes in Co. Donegal.

In recent years some thatchers have used imported thatch; Tomás Collins, responsible for the upkeep of the famous Adare houses, used Turkish thatch. Climatic conditions allow the imported thatch to be cut to a greater length, which increases its durability from fifteen to thirty years.

Thatcher, Margaret (born 1925), British politician (Conservative). Prime Minister from 1979 to 1990, she was regarded as a committed unionist before becoming a member of Parliament. She suffered a serious personal blow in the year she became Prime Minister when her confidant and shadow Secretary of State for Northern Ireland, Airey Neave, was murdered by a car bomb planted by the INLA in the car park of the House of Commons, 30 March 1979. Promising tough security measures, Thatcher announced that there would be no amnesty for convicted terrorists. She was the first British Prime Minister to visit south Armagh; on meeting the Taoiseach, JACK LYNCH, she sought closer cross-border co-operation.

She led a British delegation to Dublin for talks with CHARLES HAUGHEY, December 1980, when their agreement to review 'the totality of relations' between the two countries upset Unionists, though she assured them there was no constitutional threat to Northern Ireland. Rejecting Unionist accusations that the Anglo-Irish Intergovernmental Council was a 'sell-out', she stressed the importance of close relations with the Republic on security and economic issues. Her relations with Haughey deteriorated quickly when he criticised the British war with Argentina over the Falkland Islands. In July 1982 she stated that 'no commitment exists for Her Majesty's Government to consult the Irish Government on matters affecting Northern Ireland.' Her refusal to consider any concessions during the HUNGER STRIKES of 1981 angered Sinn Féin and the SDLP.

Thatcher had a poor relationship with the Secretary of State for Northern Ireland, JIM PRIOR (it was believed she appointed him in the expectation that he would resign from the government rather than accept the post). She did not appear to support his 'rolling devolution' proposal. She survived the Provisional IRA bomb explosions at her hotel in Brighton during the Conservative Party conference, 12 October 1984. Her rejection of the three NEW IRELAND FORUM options ('that is out . . . that is out . . . that is out') embarrassed GARRET FITZGERALD and delighted Unionists, though a communiqué committed London and Dublin to reflect the identities of both communities 'in the structures and processes of Northern Ireland.' She offered no alternative to the ANGLO-IRISH AGREEMENT (November 1985), which Unionists rejected as conceding a consultative role to the Republic on Northern Ireland. She was annoyed at the Haughey government's decision that the Attorney-General must preview evidence supporting each application by the British authorities for extradition from the Republic of persons suspected of political crimes. Before resigning, November 1990, Thatcher lost another friend to republican terrorism when Ian Gow was killed by the Provisional IRA, 30 July 1990.

Third Force, a loyalist paramilitary organisation sponsored by the DEMOCRATIC UNIONIST PARTY at the end of 1981, first appearing at rallies organised by REV. IAN PAISLEY, who claimed it reduced the number of murders of Protestants in border areas. Claims of a membership of fifteen to twenty thousand were considered exaggerated, and it faded away within a year.

36th (Ulster) Division, a British army division raised and trained in Ulster, consisting principally of members of the ULSTER VOLUNTEER FORCE (though about a quarter of its Belfast recruits were Catholics). On the opening days of the Battle of the Somme the division lost more than five thousand men; only 70 out of 700 men from the West Belfast Battalion of the UVF survived the first day without injury.

Thompson, William (c. 1785–1833), political economist, social reformer, socialist, and supporter of women's emancipation; born in Ross Carbery, Co. Cork, heir to a large estate. During his travels in England and on the Continent he came into contact with leading philosophers and economists. He established a co-operative farm on his estate at Ross Carbery, where he granted long leases and taught tenants modern methods of cultivation and scientific farming. He anticipated Karl Marx in the theory of surplus value and received an acknowledgement in volume 1 of Marx's *Capital.* He bequeathed his estate to the co-operative, but his relatives challenged the will in an action that continued for twenty-five years, to the benefit neither of themselves nor of the co-operative.

He published *An Inquiry into the Principles of Distribution of Wealth Most Conducive to Human Happiness* (1824), which, while supporting the idea of a co-operative, rejected most of Robert Owen's theories, *Practical Considerations for the Speedy and Economic Establishment of Communities on the Principle of Co-operation* (1825), and *An Appeal of One Half of the Human Race, Women, Against the Pretensions of the Other Half, Men, to Retain Them in Political and Thence in Civil and Domestic Slavery* (1825).

Thompson, William (1805–1852), naturalist; born in Belfast, educated locally. Having left the family linen business, he devoted himself to nature studies and in 1832 began the systematic collection and arrangement of specimens of Irish fauna. President of the Natural History Society of Belfast from 1843, he published *Report on the Fauna of Ireland—Division Vertebrata* (1840) and his major work, *The Natural History of Ireland* (4 vols., 1849–56).

Thom's Directory, first compiled by Peter Wilson as the *Dublin Directory* (1752) and sold for 3 pence. It became the property of Alexander Thom and Company in 1844 and henceforth bore his name. Irish Press PLC bought it in October 1999.

Three Fs. Fixity of tenure, fair rent and free sale were the demands of Irish tenant-farmers since the eighteenth century. Free sale, also known as TENANT RIGHT, generally obtained in Ulster, where it was known as the ULSTER CUSTOM. The Three Fs were conceded in the Land Law (Ireland) Act (1881) (see LAND ACTS), under which Land Courts were empowered to arbitrate in disputes between landlords and tenants. While fixity of tenure and free sale were of value to the larger tenant-farmers, fair rent was of vital concern to the poorer tenants.

tithes, 'the tenth part of the increase, yearly arising and renewing from the profits of lands, the stock upon lands, and the personal industry of the inhabitants,' paid for the upkeep of the Church of Ireland. First introduced during the reign of King Henry II, tithes were not paid outside the area around Dublin until the reign of Queen Elizabeth I, when they were used for the upkeep of the established church. As they were then to be paid by the Catholic population for the upkeep of a church to whose doctrines they did not subscribe, tithes were a chronic source of complaint and unrest into the nineteenth century.

There were three sources of tithes: *praedial* (corn), *mixed* (lambs), and *personal* (money). They were divided into two major types: *great or rectoral* (corn, hay, and wood) and *small or vicarial* (flax, garden produce, and potatoes). The 'great' class made up two-thirds of the Church of Ireland's income from tithes. By an Irish act of 1735 that forbade the payment of tithes on pasturage and its produce, the main burden of paying tithes fell on those who could least afford it. This act was confirmed at the time of the ACT OF UNION (1800). Resistance by the Catholic and Presbyterian churches led to support for agrarian SECRET SOCIETIES. Assessment for tithes was carried out by tithe-proctors, who were often Catholics and held in contempt by their co-religionists. There were three methods of payment: payment in kind (tithe-proctors were notorious for taking the best-quality share of the produce), payment by fixed annual payment based on acreage, and payment by a variable tithe, depending on the output of the farm. In 1835 Church of Ireland revenues were calculated at £815,331, of which £531,782 came from tithes.

The 'Tithe War' was fought between 1830 and 1838. According to Lord Gort, speaking in the House of Lords in 1832, 242 homicides, 1,179 robberies, 401 burglaries, 568 burnings, 280 cases of cattle-maiming, 161 assaults, 203 riots and 723 attacks on houses were directly attributed to the enforcement of tithes. The Chief Secretary for Ireland, Lord Edward Stanley (see EARL OF DERBY), fought against the evasion of tithe payments. The war began in Graiguenamanagh, Co. Kilkenny, when the tithe-proctor distrained the cattle of a Catholic priest, Father Martin Doyle, who, with the approval of his bishop, JAMES WARREN DOYLE, organised a resistance that spread to the midlands. In January 1831, when a magistrate in Newtownbarry (Bunclody), Co. Wexford, ordered out the Yeomanry at a sale of cattle that had been seized for non-payment of tithes, twelve people were killed. This was followed by incidents at Castlepollard, Co. Westmeath, Knocktopher, Co. Kilkenny, and Wallstown, Co. Cork. The government issued 43,000 decrees against tithe evaders and spent £26,000 in collecting £12,316. Lord Edward Stanley secured a Tithe Composition Act, 16 August 1832, that made the leaseholder above the tenant-at-will liable for payment, but it failed to resolve the crisis. By 1833 arrears were estimated at more than £1 million, and in June that year the government advanced this sum (most of which was written off) to tithe-owners, subject to a 21 per cent reduction in the arrears for 1831/32.

Another attempt to solve the problem was made in 1834 by EDWARD JOHN LITTLETON, but the bill was defeated in the House of Lords after amendments had been secured by DANIEL O'CONNELL. In the same year there were two notorious incidents in the Tithe War, at Doon, Co. Limerick, and Rathcormack, Co. Cork. There was a riot in Doon when the Church of Ireland rector, Rev. J. Coote, seized the cow of a Catholic priest in lieu of a tithe payment and then offered the animal for sale at auction. Four thousand people attended the auction and were confronted by six companies of British soldiers and two artillery pieces. Doon became a rallying-cry in the Tithe War, which intensified when the Archdeacon of Cloyne, Rev. William Ryder, who was also a justice of the peace, attempted to collect a £2 tithe from a widow in Rathcormack. Accompanied by police and soldiers, he entered the woman's cottage by a back window, and there was a confrontation between the soldiers and local people; nineteen people were killed and thirty-five were wounded. Ryder, who had been popular in the neighbourhood before the incident, became a symbol of tithe oppression.

Another attempt to deal with the problem was made in 1837 when a bill was introduced by Lord Morpeth (later EARL CARLISLE). It was unsuccessful, but during the following year the Tithe Rentcharge (Ireland) Act (1838) removed a major grievance when the tithe became a rent charge at three-quarters of the old composition, to be paid twice yearly by the head landlord; he was allowed to add the charge to the rent of the immediate sub-tenants. By converting the tithe into a rent charge the act removed the tithe-proctor and tithe-farmer and so removed the immediate source of discontent and in effect ended the Tithe War.

tithe applotments. The Tithe Applotment Books, dating from 1823 to 1837, contain a record of the valuations assessed for each parish by the Parochial Commissioners, one of whom was appointed by the Church of Ireland bishop and the other elected by the rate-payers.

Todd, Rev. James Henthorn (1805–1869), clergyman (Church of Ireland) and scholar; born in Dublin, educated at TCD. He became a member of the Council of the ROYAL IRISH ACADEMY, 1837, secretary, 1847–55, and president, 1856–61. Founder of the IRISH ECCLESIASTICAL RECORD, 1840, and of the Irish Archaeological Society, 1841, he worked with JOHN O'DONOVAN and EUGENE O'CURRY in cataloguing Irish manuscripts while librarian at Trinity College, Dublin, from 1852. He quadrupled the library's stock and procured transcripts of several Irish manuscripts in Continental libraries. He assisted O'Donovan in the preparation of EDWARD O'REILLY's *Irish–English Dictionary* (1864). His works include *Life of St Patrick* (1864) and *The Book of the Vaudois* (1865).

Top-Level Appointments Committee, created in January 1984 by the Minister for the Public Service, John Boland, to implement the recommendations of the Devlin Report, fifteen years after it was first proposed. The report had recommended promotion on merit in the civil service and that secretaries of departments should serve a maximum of seven years and not serve beyond the age of sixty.

An Tóstal ('muster, assembly'), sub-titled 'Ireland at Home', a national festival organised in 1953, during a severe economic depression. The stimulus had come from the desire of Pan-American Airways to encourage off-season tourist traffic between the United States and Ireland; it was possibly influenced also by the Festival of Britain (1951). Running from 5 to 26 April 1953, it was not a financial success. Having been held annually until 1958, the event disappeared except in Drumshanbo, Co. Leitrim. The Dublin Theatre Festival was a successful offshoot of the festival.

Trade Union Act (1941), legislation restricting the rights of trade unions, introduced by the FIANNA FÁIL government; supported by the IRISH TRANSPORT AND GENERAL WORKERS' UNION, the biggest union in the country, it met with strong resistance from the rest of the trade union movement and especially from JAMES LARKIN. Under the act a union has to lodge a sum of money with the High Court in order to obtain a licence to participate in collective bargaining. It also specified that a tribunal would be established to determine that one union should be entitled to organise a particular category of workers if it could be demonstrated that this union had the support of the majority of workers in that category; it stipulated also that only an Irish union should receive sole negotiating rights from the tribunal (this was later held by the Supreme Court to be unconstitutional).

Travellers, an indigenous nomadic section of the Irish population, at one time generally called 'tinkers' and later officially known as 'itinerants', now designated by the name they use for themselves. They are generally believed to be descended from the dispossessed of the seventeenth and early eighteenth centuries, but this is now disputed. Many were tinsmiths (tinkers) by trade. Prominent surnames among Travellers are Cash, Coffey, Doherty, Maughan, McCarthy, MacDonagh, Reilly, and Ward. They formerly spoke their own dialect of English, sometimes called Shelta or Sheldry. As tinsmithing became an obsolete occupation, Travellers attempted to find alternative work as traders. Their attempts to integrate in the settled community and to obtain recognised halting-sites have been seriously hampered by prejudice.

Traynor, Des (1931–1994), banker; born in Dublin, educated at Westland Row Christian Brothers' School. An articled clerk at the accountancy firm of Haughey Boland and Company, 1951, he played a prominent role in the firm until 1969. He was later a member of the board of Cement-Roadstone Holdings, Guinness and Mahon (a private bank), and New Ireland Assurance Company. From 1960, when CHARLES HAUGHEY entered the government and retired from Haughey Boland, Traynor was responsible for raising the funds necessary to maintain Haughey's lavish lifestyle. Later, when Haughey became leader of FIANNA FÁIL and Taoiseach, Traynor organised a settlement through which Allied Irish Banks wrote off a considerable amount of Haughey's €1.45 million overdraft. Joint managing director of Guinness and Mahon from 1969, Traynor placed customers' funds outside the jurisdiction, including the Cayman Islands. As chairman of Cement-Roadstone from 1986, he used his offices there for his banking activities; approximately half the Cement-Roadstone board availed of the scheme. Details of Traynor's activities became public as a result of the MCCRACKEN TRIBUNAL and MORIARTY TRIBUNAL and led to the ANSBACHER INQUIRY (1999–2002).

Traynor, Oscar (1886–1963), politician (Fianna Fáil); born in Dublin, educated at Christian Brothers' school. A member of the Irish Volunteers, he was interned for his role in the EASTER RISING (1916). Following his release he became active in the reorganised SINN FÉIN and was officer commanding the Dublin Brigade of the IRA during the WAR OF INDEPENDENCE. His brigade attacked the CUSTOM HOUSE, Dublin, 25 May 1921, resulting in the destruction of important administrative and historical documents. Rejecting the ANGLO-IRISH TREATY (1921), he was active in the CIVIL WAR, when, as senior officer, he ordered the Four Courts garrison to surrender in order to let him 'carry on the fight outside.' A founder-member of Fianna Fáil, he was Minister for Posts and Telegraphs, 1936–39, Minister for Defence, 1939–48 and 1951–54, and Minister for Justice, 1957–61.

Treacy, Seán (1895–1920), Republican soldier; born in Soloheadbeg, Co. Tipperary, and raised in Lackenacreena, Hollyford, educated at Tipperary Christian Brothers' School. A member of the Gaelic League and the IRB from 1911, as head of the Tipperary Circle of the IRB he had his farmhouse adapted to conceal arms and equipment. He was a friend of DAN BREEN, with whom be joined the Irish Volunteers in 1913. After the EASTER RISING (1916) he played a central role in the reorganising of the Volunteers and Sinn Féin and was twice imprisoned. Vice-commandant of the 3rd Tipperary Brigade, he took part in the ambush at Soloheadbeg, 21 January 1919, that marked the beginning of the WAR OF INDEPENDENCE. Wounded during the rescue of Seán Hogan at Knocklong, 13 May 1919, he was subsequently on the run and worked for a time in Dublin with MICHAEL COLLINS and the SQUAD. He took part in the attempt to assassinate EARL FRENCH at Ashtown, 19 December 1919, and during 1920 took part in the raids on Hollyford Barracks, 10–11 May, Drangan Barracks, 3 June, and Rear Cross Barracks, 11 July. Having moved to Dublin in September, he was killed in a gun battle in Talbot Street on 14 October 1920 in which two of his assailants (Lieutenant Price and Sergeant Christian) were also killed.

Treason Act (1939), introduced on 30 May 1939 in response to the campaign conducted by the IRA against Northern Ireland and England; it made treason punishable by death. Shortly afterwards the government introduced the OFFENCES AGAINST THE STATE ACT (1939).

Treason Felony Act (1848), an act rushed through the British Parliament to give the Irish executive power to apprehend prominent members of YOUNG IRELAND. It permitted the prosecution of 'any person who, by open and advised speaking, compassed [brought about] the intimidation of the Crown or Parliament.' The penalty for those found guilty under the act was transportation for terms ranging from fourteen years to life. JOHN MITCHEL became the first Young Irelander to be found guilty under the at, May 1848. Those imprisoned under the act, sometimes known as 'SPECIAL MEN', were treated with great harshness in British prisons.

Treasury of Irish Poetry (1901), a collection edited by T. W. Rolleston and Stopford Brooke, published at the height of the Irish literary revival and becoming the accepted anthology of Anglo-Irish poetry.

Treaty ports. Under an annex to the ANGLO-IRISH TREATY (1921), Britain retained certain 'specific facilities' in 'Southern Ireland', including three ports: the dockyard at Bearhaven, Co. Cork, Queenstown (Cóbh), Co. Cork, and Lough Swilly, Co. Donegal. The Admiralty retained its properties and rights at those sites and undertook responsibility for harbour defences and maintenance parties. Under the agreement that ended the 'ECONOMIC WAR', and against the opposition of WINSTON CHURCHILL, Britain vacated the ports in 1938. To mark the occasion, parades were held throughout the country; at Cóbh, as British naval personnel withdrew, 11 July 1938, the Taoiseach, ÉAMON DE VALERA, arrived to reclaim the port and hoist the Tricolour over the harbour.

Trench, W. Steuart (1808–1872), land agent and author; born in Portarlington, Co. Laois, educated at TCD. Winner of the Gold Medal of the Royal Agricultural Society for an essay on land reclamation, 1841, he served as land agent for the Shirley estate, Co. Monaghan, 1843–45, the Lansdowne estate at Kenmare, Co. Kerry, from 1849, the estate of Lord Bath in Co. Monaghan from 1851, and Lord Digby's estate in the midlands from 1856, all of which he cleared of 'paupers', including, notoriously, 4,500 tenants off the Lansdowne estate at Kenmare. His implacable opposition to Ribbonism led to the suspicion that he was in the pay of Dublin Castle. Described by JOSEPH DENIEFFE as 'one of the meanest and most contemptible petty tyrants that ever held authority over poor mortals,' Trench recorded his experiences in *Realities of Irish Life* (1868), which went through five editions in its first year.

Trevelyan, Sir Charles Edward (1807–1886), British civil servant. As assistant secretary to the Treasury, 1840–59, he virtually dictated relief measures during the GREAT FAMINE (1845–49). Together with the Prime Minister, LORD JOHN RUSSELL, and Chancellor of the Exchequer, SIR CHARLES WOOD, he was totally committed to free trade; in addition he held the belief that the famine resulted both from a benign Providence seeking to reduce an expanding population and from 'the moral evil of the selfish, perverse and turbulent character of the people.' From March 1846 he controlled public works through the disbursement of public funds. He defended the export of grain from Ireland on grounds of free trade; when rioting broke out in protest at the exporting of corn he deployed mobile columns of two thousand soldiers (who were provisioned with beef, pork, and biscuits) 'to be directed on particular ports at short notice.' He was opposed to railway construction as a form of relief and successfully opposed Russell's scheme for the distribution of some £50,000 worth of seedlings to tenant-farmers. Informed by an official, 4 September 1847, that 'the face of the country is covered with ripe corn while the people dread starvation' and that 'the grain will go out of the country, sold to pay the rent,' Trevelyan (who had never visited Ireland) replied, 'It is my opinion that too much has been done for the people. Under such treatment the people have grown worse instead of better, and we must now try what independent exertion can do . . .' In 1848 he ceased Treasury grants to distressed POOR LAW unions, though by now there was an outbreak of cholera. Later in the year he was knighted for his services to Ireland.

His son George Otto Trevelyan (1838–1928) was Chief Secretary for Ireland, 1882–84, succeeding the assassinated LORD FREDERICK CAVENDISH. Having resigned over the (first) HOME RULE BILL, April 1886, he was later reconciled to home rule and rejoined W. E. GLADSTONE, 1892–94.

Triangle, the, code name for a triumvirate that dominated CLAN NA GAEL during the 1880s, consisting of ALEXANDER SULLIVAN, Michael Boland, and Denis Feeley, who affixed a triangular mark instead of signatures to notices issued on their behalf. The Triangle encouraged terrorist activities in England and provided finance for the DYNAMITERS. The principal opposition to their policy came from JOHN DEVOY. Following the murder of Dr P. H. Cronin, of which Sullivan was accused, the Triangle was discredited in 1889.

Tricolour, popular name for the national flag of

the Republic. Tricolour flags of various patterns appeared from about 1830 in imitation of that of France, with green and orange substituted for blue and red. At a meeting of the IRISH CONFEDERATION in Dublin in April 1848 at which THOMAS FRANCIS MEAGHER, recently returned from France, presented a tricolour as a gift 'from the citizens of France,' JOHN MITCHEL commented, 'I hope to see that flag one day waving as our national banner.' As the flag promoted by the IRB it was displayed during the EASTER RISING (1916), in conjunction with the traditional national flag of green with a yellow harp, and thus came to be associated with the new revolutionary Ireland. It was the *de facto* flag of the IRISH FREE STATE from 1922. Article 7 of the CONSTITUTION OF IRELAND (1937) declares: 'The national flag is the tricolour of green, white and orange.'

Trimble, David (born 1944), politician (Ulster Unionist Party); born in Belfast, educated at QUB, where he became assistant dean, 1968–90. A member of ULSTER VANGUARD, he was active in the 1974 loyalist strike. As a member of the Ulster Unionist Party from 1977 and of the ULSTER CLUBS, he opposed the ANGLO-IRISH AGREEMENT (1985). Member of Parliament for Upper Bann from 1990, he became UUP spokesperson on legal affairs. Opposed to the SDLP talks with SINN FÉIN, he insisted, following the Provisional IRA ceasefire of August 1994, that the Irish government should not have an executive role in cross-border bodies arising from the PEACE PROCESS. In July 1995 he succeeded JAMES MOLYNEAUX as leader of the UUP. Following a meeting with the DEMOCRATIC UNIONIST PARTY and the UK UNIONIST PARTY to discuss unity among the unionist parties, he called for immediate elections to a new Northern Ireland Assembly. In October he became the first UUP leader to visit Government Buildings in Dublin, where he had talks with JOHN BRUTON and BERTIE AHERN.

After the Provisional IRA ended its ceasefire, 9 February 1996, Trimble invited DICK SPRING to 'limited talks' but refused to attend 'proximity talks' in March because of Spring's presence. Following the Provisional IRA bomb explosion in Manchester, 15 June, he sought Sinn Féin's 'permanent exclusion' from multi-party talks. Though he had met BILLY WRIGHT during the Drumcree crisis, July 1996, in September he condemned the continuing loyalist pickets on the Catholic church at Harryville, Co. Antrim. In October he became the first UUP leader to address a fringe meeting of the British Labour Party. In June 1997 he had a cordial meeting with the new Prime Minister, TONY BLAIR, but had a cold relationship with the Secretary of State for Northern Ireland, MARJORIE (MO) MOWLAM.

Following the new Provisional IRA ceasefire, July 1997, Trimble accused the British government of 'duplicity' and giving 'secret promises' to Sinn Féin. In August he criticised the decision to set up an international body on decommissioning. When the talks resumed, 15 September 1997, he took part in meetings attended by GERRY ADAMS and Martin McGuinness (though he would not address them directly).

The BELFAST AGREEMENT (1998) fulfilled one of Trimble's principal ambitions: it ended the Anglo-Irish Agreement (1985). He met Gerry Adams for talks at Stormont (the first meeting between a Unionist Party leader and Sinn Féin leader for seventy-five years). While insisting that Sinn Féin could not sit in the Executive without decommissioning of arms by the IRA, he nevertheless presided over an Executive that contained two Sinn Féin members. For his contribution to the peace process Trimble shared the Nobel Prize for Peace with JOHN HUME, December 1998.

Over the next two years he was forced to seek the support of the ULSTER UNIONIST COUNCIL to keep his critics at bay. Under attack from the DUP and from within his own party, in the period before the British parliamentary elections of 7 June 2001 he stated that he would resign his post of First Minister if the Provisional IRA had not decommissioned by 1 July. In the election the party lost three of its parliamentary seats; in the local elections it lost 31 seats to secure 154. Trimble resigned his Executive position as promised, precipitating a crisis, with a risk that the institutions created under the Belfast Agreement could fall.

On 8 October 2001 Trimble lost the vote in the Assembly (54 to 45) on his motion seeking to exclude Sinn Féin from the Executive. He led the five Unionist ministers out of the Executive, 19 October, threatening the collapse of the institutions within a week, in his final protest at the failure of the Provisional IRA to decommission. On 23 October the INDEPENDENT INTERNATIONAL COMMISSION ON DECOMMISSIONING announced that it had witnessed the IRA putting some of its weapons beyond use. On 6 November Trimble and MARK DURKAN

(SDLP) were elected First Minister and Deputy First Minister, respectively, of the Executive; their election was made possible only when three members of the Alliance Party and one member of the Women's Coalition redesignated themselves 'unionists' for the purpose of the election. Shortly afterwards Trimble's position was endorsed by a majority of the Ulster Unionist Council, but he remained under constant attack from dissidents led by Jeffrey Donaldson and David Burnside.

Trinity College, Dublin, sole college of the University of Dublin, founded in 1592 and modelled on the residential colleges of Oxford and Cambridge. No part of the original college remains; much of the splendid architecture dates from the eighteenth century. As graduates were required to subscribe to the Oath of Supremacy, the college became the centre of education for the Anglo-Irish Ascendancy. Catholics were able to take degrees after 1793, but fellowships and scholarships were open only to members of the Church of Ireland.

Trinity College Library houses more than three thousand ancient manuscripts, including Egyptian papyri, the Palimpsest Codex Z of St Matthew's Gospel uncovered by Professor John 'Jacky' Barrett (1753–1821), and also Greek, Latin and ancient Irish manuscripts. Other literary treasures include the Book of Kells, Book of Durrow, Book of Armagh, Book of Leinster, and Yellow Book of Lecan. An act of Parliament of 1801 extended to Trinity the right to receive a copy of every book published in Ireland and Britain, provided the library authorities claimed it within a year of publication. The Trinity College harp, the oldest surviving Irish harp and the model for the state emblem, is also on display in the library.

Troy, John Thomas (1739–1823), bishop (Catholic); born in Porterstown, Co. Dublin, educated at Rome. As Archbishop of Dublin, 1784–1823, he was an outspoken opponent of SECRET SOCIETIES and was regarded as being close to DUBLIN CASTLE. His concern that clerical students should not go to France, where they might be influenced by republican or democratic ideas, led to the founding of St Patrick's College, MAYNOOTH, 1795. Archbishop Troy presided over a meeting held in the college, January 1799, when the hierarchy considered guarantees for the church under the proposed ACT OF UNION; the four archbishops and six bishops signed a resolution accepting CATHOLIC EMANCIPATION together with the VETO. However, the Union was not followed by Emancipation (see KING GEORGE III and WILLIAM PITT), but the issue of the veto continued through his term as Archbishop of Dublin, until it was defeated by DANIEL O'CONNELL and the populists in 1815. One of his last public appearances was to lay the foundation-stone of the Pro-Cathedral in Marlborough Street, Dublin, 1815.

Truce (1921). King George V appealed for peace between Britain and Ireland while opening the parliament of NORTHERN IRELAND, 22 June 1921. Two days later the President of Dáil Éireann, ÉAMON DE VALERA, received an invitation from the Prime Minister, DAVID LLOYD GEORGE, to attend talks. As a preliminary to the talks a truce was agreed between de Valera and GENERAL SIR NEVIL MACREADY, 9 July, to come into force on 11 July. Though discussions between Lloyd George and de Valera broke down, the uneasy truce continued throughout August and September. The deadlock was broken on 30 September when Lloyd George's 'GAIRLOCH FORMULA' was accepted as the basis for new discussions, which began on 11 October and concluded on 6 December, when the ANGLO-IRISH TREATY (1921) was signed.

truck, the payment of wages in kind rather than in money. It was outlawed by acts of 1715, 1729, 1745 and 1841 but persisted until the GREAT FAMINE (1845–49). It was replaced in some areas by payment in both kind and money.

TUAS, an acronym associated with the policy of the Provisional IRA during the 1970s, generally believed to mean 'tactical use of armed struggle'. Its strategic objectives were to alter the national and international perception of the IRA's position to one in which it appeared reasonable; to develop a Northern nationalist consensus in particular and an Irish consensus in general on constitutional change; to secure Irish-American support; to develop and mobilise an anti-imperialist peace movement; to expose the British and Unionists as the intransigent parties; to heighten the contradiction between British unionism and Ulster loyalism; to assist in the development of whatever potential existed in Britain for a movement towards peace; and to maintain the political cohesion and organisational integrity of SINN FÉIN so as to make it an effective political force. These objectives helped Sinn Féin emerge as a major political force in the 1990s under the leadership of GERRY ADAMS and Martin McGuinness.

tuberculosis, a major cause of death throughout the nineteenth and into the twentieth century, sometimes known as the 'Irish disease'. In 1906 the disease was responsible for more than 15 per cent of recorded deaths in Ireland; the largest number was in the age group 20–34. An early attempt to deal with the problem was made by Lady Aberdeen in 1907 through the establishment of the Women's National Health Association. The Tuberculosis Prevention (Ireland) Act (1908) established hospitals to treat those suffering from the disease. County councils and borough corporations were authorised to provide clinics and sanatoriums, but little impact was made, as these were inadequately staffed and financed, and the death rate from the disease continued to increase.

Infantile tuberculosis was tackled at St Ultan's Hospital for Children, Dublin, in a unit that included Dr Dorothy Price (1890–1954). On 26 January 1937 St Ultan's became the first hospital in Ireland to use the BCG (bacillus Calmette-Guérin) vaccine in the fight against the disease (later to be complemented by streptomycin). Another pioneer in the field, DR JAMES DEENY, joined the Department of Local Government and Health as chief medical adviser and was there when DR NOEL BROWNE, as Minister for Health in the first inter-party government (1948–51), inaugurated a concerted attack on the disease. Dr Browne, whose family had suffered from the disease, provided resources to establish emergency sanatoriums throughout the country. The death rate fell below 100 per 100,000 of population, until by 1952 it had been reduced to 40 per 100,000 (1,187 cases) and by 1957 to 24 per 100,000 (694 cases). The death rate in Northern Ireland fell within the same period from 30 per 100,000 (410 cases) to 13 per 100,000 (175 cases).

Concern has been expressed in recent years at an increasing incidence of the disease, especially among teenagers.

Tudor, Major-General Sir H. Hugh (1871–1965), British soldier; born in Exeter. As police adviser to the Irish executive, 1920–22, he was in effect head of police forces in Ireland, 1920–22, responsible for the co-ordination of the DUBLIN METROPOLITAN POLICE and the ROYAL IRISH CONSTABULARY during the WAR OF INDEPENDENCE. He had to replace the secret service, which had been rendered ineffective by MICHAEL COLLINS and the IRA. Tudor was criticised over the behaviour of the AUXILIARIES and the BLACK AND TANS and acknowledged that there was much drunkenness among those under his command. He was an air vice-marshal and commander in chief of British forces in Palestine in 1922.

Tuke, James Hack (1819–1896), English philanthropist; born in York, educated at the Friends' School. He accompanied his fellow-Quaker W. E. FORSTER to Ireland to distribute relief in the west of Ireland during the GREAT FAMINE (1845–49). His experiences were recorded in *A Visit to Connaught in 1847* (1847), in which he commented: 'The culminating point of man's physical degradation seems to have been reached in Erris . . .' He returned to Ireland during the famine in Connacht in 1880 at the request of Forster, now Chief Secretary for Ireland. He urged the introduction of the 'THREE FS' and family emigration to end agrarian unrest. He returned again in 1881 and 1882 to administer a fund established with government support to assist emigrants, 1,200 of whom were helped to emigrate to the United States. A year later 5,380 were assisted and 2,800 in 1884, many of them personally selected by Tuke. He distributed seed potatoes during the period 1885–86.

Tuke's comments on the west of Ireland were answered in some measure by the creation of the CONGESTED DISTRICTS BOARD in 1889–90. He was an adviser to the board that oversaw another of his suggestions, the creation of a light railway system in Connacht.

He published 'Peasant proprietors at home' in *Nineteenth Century* (1880), *Achill and the West of Ireland: Report of the Distribution of the Seed Potato Fund* (1886), and *The Condition of Donegal* (1889).

turbary right, the ancient right to cut turf in a bog. The right was dependent on landholding, but the land to which the turbary right was attached did not necessarily adjoin the bog. Turf-cutting in such bogs was a communal affair, with families pooling their resources and each in turn acting as hosts while the turf was being saved.

An Túr Gloine ('the glass tower'), the centre of the Irish stained-glass revival, established in 1903 by Sarah Purser (1849–1943) and EDWARD MARTYN at 24 Upper Pembroke Street, Dublin. It operated on co-operative lines, and its artists produced works for a variety of buildings in Ireland and abroad. The first commission was for the windows of Loughrea Cathedral, Co. Galway (1903). Artists employed by the studio included Michael Healy (1873–1941), Evie Hone (1894–1955), Wilhelmina Geddes (1887–1955), Mainie Jellett (1896–1943), and Hubert McGoldrick (1897–1967). Following the death of Sarah Purser (whose role had been largely administrative and advisory) the company was dissolved and the premises retained as a studio by one of the artists, Catherine O'Brien, until her death in 1963.

turnover tax, introduced in the 1963 budget at a rate of 2½ per cent, later replaced by value-added tax.

Tuskar Rock Air Crash (1968). An Aer Lingus Viscount aircraft, *St Phelim,* en route to Heathrow Airport, London, on 24 March 1968, piloted by Captain Barnie O'Beirne, crashed into the Irish Sea off Tuskar Rock, Co. Wexford, with the loss of all fifty-seven passengers and four crew members. No difficulty had been reported until 11:58 a.m., when a voice thought to be that of the co-pilot, Paul Heffernan, reported: '12,000 feet, descending, spinning rapidly.' No mechanical or structural faults were discovered from an examination of the wreckage. The tailplane, elevators and fuselage structure in the tail cone area were never recovered, leading to widespread speculation that the aircraft was struck by a missile or target drone.

Twomey, Maurice 'Moss' (1896–1978), republican; born in Clondulane, Fermoy, Co. Cork, educated at Christian Brothers' school. A member of the Irish Volunteers from 1914, he was intelligence officer of Cork No. 2 Brigade and later commandant of the 1st Southern Division of the IRA during the WAR OF INDEPENDENCE. A close associate of LIAM LYNCH, he rejected the ANGLO-IRISH TREATY (1921) and supported the anti-Treaty IRA during the CIVIL WAR. Following his capture in Dublin he was imprisoned on 6 April 1923 until 1924. Chief of staff of the IRA from 1927, Twomey and the IRA leadership supported FIANNA FÁIL during the period 1932–33 and helped to combat the BLUESHIRTS. He opposed the REPUBLICAN CONGRESS (1934). When the Fianna Fáil government outlawed the IRA in 1936 he went on the run but was captured and imprisoned until 1938, when he was succeeded as chief of staff by SEÁN MACBRIDE. He opposed SEÁN RUSSELL and the extremists in their 'declaration of war' on Britain in 1939. He established a grocery and newsagent's business in Dublin, where he lived for the rest of his life.

Tyrie, Andy (born 1940), loyalist paramilitary; born in Belfast. A member of the UVF before joining the UDA, he was prominent in the loyalist strikes of 1974 and 1977 and was credited with restricting violent fringe elements in the UDA. Commander of the UDA, 1973–88, in July 1974 he led the UDA delegation in talks with the SDLP, but they agreed only on opposition to internment. In 1976 he led the UDA out of the Ulster Loyalist Central Co-ordinating Committee, because some of the latter had been talking to republicans about independence. In 1979 the UDA sponsored the New Ulster Political Research Group, which, under his leadership, produced a plan for negotiated independence for Northern Ireland, a scheme they promoted in the United States. Tyrie was joint author (with John McMichael) of *Beyond the Religious Divide* (1979) and *Common Sense* (1986), which envisaged power-sharing (multi-party government). He opposed the ANGLO-IRISH AGREEMENT (1985). Tyrie rejected suggestions that the killing of his deputy, John McMichael, by the Provisional IRA, 22 December 1987, was connected with investigations into racketeering. He withdrew from the leadership in 1988 following the discovery of a booby-trap bomb attached to his car. His play *This Is It!* deals with Ulster identity.

U

Ua Buachalla, Domhnall (1866–1963), politician (Sinn Féin and Fianna Fáil); born in Maynooth, Co. Kildare, where he later owned a shop, educated at Belvedere College and Marist College, Dublin. He was active in the Gaelic League in Maynooth. A member of the Irish Volunteers, he led a detachment from his home to Dublin to fight in the GPO after the start of the EASTER RISING (1916). Following a period of internment he was active in the anti-conscription campaign and was elected for Co. Kildare in the general election of December 1918. Rejecting the ANGLO-IRISH TREATY (1921), he was in the FOUR COURTS at the outbreak of the CIVIL WAR, when he was for a time imprisoned. A founder-member of Fianna Fáil, he was a member of Dáil Éireann, 1927–32.

Appointed GOVERNOR-GENERAL OF THE IRISH FREE STATE by the de Valera government, de Valera and Ua Buachalla used an Irish title, 'Seanascal', instead of 'Governor-General'. As it was de Valera's intention to phase out the office, Ua Buachalla did not live in the Viceregal Lodge but in a suburban house in Monkstown, Co. Dublin, commuting by bicycle instead of official car; nor did he appear at official functions. He retired following de Valera's termination of the office, 11 December 1936.

Ulster Army Council, formed on 10 December 1973 from the membership of loyalist paramilitary organisations in the wake of the SUNNINGDALE AGREEMENT; it supported the UNITED ULSTER UNIONIST COALITION in calling for an end to the power-sharing Executive and a return to direct rule from London, new elections by proportional representation, and the blocking of attempts to form a Council of Ireland. It threatened a *coup d'état* in 1974 'if Westminster is not prepared to restore democracy.' Following the strike organised by the LOYALIST ASSOCIATION OF WORKERS, which brought down the power-sharing Executive in 1974, the Ulster Army Council was replaced by the ULSTER LOYALIST CENTRAL CO-ORDINATING COMMITTEE.

Ulster Citizen Army, a loyalist splinter group formed by dissidents within the UDA and UVF, February 1974. It threatened to assassinate businessmen and British army officers if the government succeeded in bringing Northern Ireland into 'vicious sectarian warfare.' In October it issued leaflets alleging that 'power-crazed animals have taken over control of the loyalist paramilitary organisations and have embarked on a programme of wanton slaughter, intimidation, robbery and extortion.' It claimed that psychopaths, acting on the orders of loyalist leaders, had butchered twelve people, and promised to supply the addresses of those involved to the police. The group was thought to have acted also under the name of the Covenanters.

Ulster Clubs, founded in 1985 following a confrontation in Portadown, Co. Armagh, where the authorities attempted to prevent the local branch of the ORANGE ORDER from marching through a Catholic area known as the Tunnel; the name commemorated clubs formed by EDWARD CARSON during the 'HOME RULE crisis' of 1912–14. The clubs organised protests against the ANGLO-IRISH AGREEMENT (1985) and asserted the right to maintain the Union as long as it was in Northern Ireland's interest and to combat the encroachment of Irish nationalism. The committee included the paramilitary leaders John McMichael (UDA) and BILLY WRIGHT (LOYALIST VOLUNTEER FORCE) as well as Orange leaders and local politicians, including DAVID TRIMBLE.

Following the anti-agreement by-elections, January 1986, the clubs organised a rally in the Ulster Hall, Belfast, 10 November 1986, when the DUP announced the formation of ULSTER RESISTANCE. This meeting in effect brought together the 'THIRD FORCE' proposed by REV. IAN PAISLEY and the Ulster Clubs. Wright told those present: 'Faced with treachery, as we are today, I cannot see anything other than the Ulster people on the streets prepared to use legitimate force—only this will bring down the agreement.' The group was said to have a membership of 12,000 by 1988. Following his imprisonment in October 1988 for non-payment of fines for car tax offences as a protest against the ANGLO-IRISH AGREEMENT and for non-payment of fines for taking part in illegal parades, Wright stood down as leader, February 1989.

The clubs' association with the UDA led to a decline in its middle-class support. During the 1990s they sought the integration of Northern Ireland with the United Kingdom.

Ulster College, Jordanstown, Co. Antrim, established in 1968. Comprising several colleges, including Belfast College of Art and Design, it offered a variety of non-degree courses. Under the direction of Derek Birley (1926–2002), rector from 1970, it was renamed the Northern Ireland Polytechnic, 1978, and subsequently incorporated in the UNIVERSITY OF ULSTER, 1984.

Ulster Constitution Defence Committee, founded by Noel Doherty and REV. IAN PAISLEY, 1966, to protest against any commemorations of the EASTER RISING (1916). Open only to 'those who have been born Protestant,' it led the opposition to any form of rapprochement between Northern Ireland and the Republic. The committee, in effect a cover for Doherty's ULSTER PROTESTANT VOLUNTEERS, stated that it was 'one united society of Protestant patriots pledged by all lawful methods to uphold and maintain the Constitution of Northern Ireland as an integral part of the United Kingdom as long as the United Kingdom maintains a Protestant Monarchy and the terms of the Revolutionary Settlement [of 1688].' In June 1966 Paisley denied that the committee had any connection with the UVF. On 12 October 1966 Doherty was sentenced to two years' imprisonment for explosives offences and expelled from the organisation. Reacting to the growth of the NORTHERN IRELAND CIVIL RIGHTS ASSOCIATION, the committee and Paisley were associated with the short-lived PROTESTANT UNIONIST PARTY and later with the DEMOCRATIC UNIONIST PARTY.

Ulster custom, also known as 'TENANT RIGHT' (one of the 'THREE FS'), the customary right of a tenant-farmer to sell his tenancy, a tacit recognition of the tenant's saleable interest in his holdings. The landlord rarely exercised his power of veto over a new tenant, as he would then have to forfeit the agreed price to the tenant, thus fixing the value of tenant right. Eviction could still take place, but before any eviction the tenant had to be compensated, either by the incoming tenant or by the landlord, for any improvements carried out during his tenancy. The custom was found principally in Ulster, as a result of which there was less land agitation there than in the rest of the country. The demand for the custom, which was of importance to the bigger tenant-farmers, grew during the 1850s (see TENANT LEAGUE), but it was not granted legal recognition until 1881 (see LAND ACTS).

Ulster Defence Association, a loyalist paramilitary organisation founded in Belfast by Charles Harding Smith of the Woodvale Defence Association, September 1971, as an umbrella group for local loyalist defence associations and Protestant vigilante groups in combating the Provisional IRA. The organisation was widely viewed as a substitute for the disbanded ULSTER SPECIAL CONSTABULARY. At first it lacked central control and was torn by leadership struggles. Smith's successor in 1972, James Anderson, reorganised the UDA on military lines, with a thirteen-member Inner Council. At its peak, membership was estimated at between forty and fifty thousand; by the end of the decade it had fallen to approximately ten thousand, and it again declined in the next decade. Its deputy leader, Tommy Herron, was killed on 16 September 1973. On marches and demonstrations members wore combat jackets, bush hats, masks, and dark glasses. It enforced its rules through kangaroo courts and beatings (in notorious 'romper rooms') and was also closely associated with racketeering: by 1988 the police believed it might be raising as much as £3 million a year from rackets.

From 1973 the UDA was involved in sporadic outbursts of violence, sometimes under the cover-name 'ULSTER FREEDOM FIGHTERS'. During the ULSTER WORKERS' COUNCIL strike, 1974, the UDA commander, ANDIE TYRIE, was on the co-ordinating committee, while UDA personnel provided manpower for roadblocks and were accused of intimidating those who desired to work. In June of that year the UDA ruled out talks with the Provisional IRA, though it was prepared to meet elected representatives of SINN FÉIN. In November, Tyrie, Tommy Lyttle and others met representatives of the SDLP, led by GERRY FITT, but apart from opposition to internment they failed to find common ground. That month also a UDA delegation led by Glenn Barr visited Libya to seek economic aid for Northern Ireland; by coincidence, a Sinn Féin delegation was also in Libya at the time. The UDA was influenced by Barr's support for WILLIAM CRAIG (who sought a voluntary coalition between loyalist organisations). The UDA supported the loyalist work stoppage in 1977 but, believing that he had used the organisation for his own purposes, rejected support for REV. IAN PAISLEY's 'day of action' and his so-called 'THIRD FORCE'.

The UDA established the NEW ULSTER POLITICAL RESEARCH GROUP, January 1978, which published *Beyond the Religious Divide,* a discussion paper by Tyrie and John McMichael, March 1978. It sought an independent Northern Ireland, claiming that only a negotiated independence was acceptable to both communities. After the killing of Lord Louis Mountbatten, 27 August 1979, the UDA claimed it had drawn up a 'death list' of known republicans in Northern Ireland, the Republic, and Britain; two years later it claimed to have another 'death list' of alleged Provisional IRA members. Tyrie threatened that UDA members might enter the Republic to 'terrorise the terrorists.' During the 1980s there was tension within the organisation between those who sought a more political role and those who saw themselves as primarily involved in the original loyalist counter-terrorist organisation. The Ulster Loyalist Democratic Party sought independence within the British Commonwealth and the EEC, believing that this would be acceptable to the Catholic community. However, the group failed to win any seats in the district council elections between 1981 and 1985 and did not contest the 1986 January by-elections in the wake of the ANGLO-IRISH AGREEMENT (1985), to which the UDA was opposed.

Tyrie set up a new organisation within the

UDA, the Ulster Defence Force, to respond to any 'doomsday' event, such as the implementing of the Anglo-Irish Agreement. In February 1986 the deputy leader, John McMichael, leaving his chequered past apparently behind him, was involved with Tyrie in attempting to move the organisation down a political path, urging that Sinn Féin be included in any constitutional conference. He was killed by a Provisional IRA car bomb on 22 December 1987. On 15 October 1988 two UDA gunmen killed Jim Craig for alleged involvement in the killing; ironically, his death coincided with the publication of *Common Sense: An Agreed Process*, of which he was a joint author (with Tyrie). This called for an assembly and an executive, to be elected by proportional representation, to produce an all-party coalition, with provision for a bill of rights and a written constitution. This was welcomed by JOHN HUME and the Northern Ireland Office; however, nothing came of it, and the UDA reverted to violence.

Three months after McMichael's murder Tyrie retired and was replaced by a collective leadership, consisting of six members of the inner council. They stated that the UDA would direct a military campaign against the Provisional IRA and build a political front on the head of their devolution proposal.

In December 1988 Mr Justice Nicholson, sentencing members on blackmail charges, urged the Protestant community to stop the UDA from 'living off them.' By the end of the year the Ulster Loyalist Democratic Party had declared itself a political party completely separate from the UDA, changing its name to the ULSTER DEMOCRATIC PARTY in 1989. One of its spokespersons was Gary McMichael, John McMichael's son.

In 1991 the trial of Tommy Lyttle led to the uncovering of information leaked from RUC and British army intelligence files to the UDA and to the establishment of the STEVENS INQUIRY. The information led also to the arrest of the double agent Brian Nelson, who received ten years' imprisonment for conspiracy to kill five Catholics. The resulting shake-up within the UDA led to more militant leaders taking control.

Most of those killed by loyalist gunmen during the period 1991–92 were victims of the 'Ulster Freedom Fighters'. On 5 February 1992 five Catholics were shot dead in a bookmaker's shop on Lower Ormeau Road, Belfast (a response to the Provisional IRA killing of eight Protestants in Co. Tyrone three weeks earlier). The Secretary of State for Northern Ireland, SIR PATRICK MAYHEW, proscribed the UDA on 10 August 1992 (the UFF was already banned). In that year the UDA carried out more punishment shootings than the Provisional IRA and, according to police sources, was operating very profitable rackets. Under the cover-name Ulster Freedom Fighters it killed three Catholics in a bookmaker's shop in the Oldpark Road, Belfast (a retaliation for the Provisional IRA bomb explosion at Coleraine town centre). During the period January–March 1993 it was responsible for nearly fourteen murders and in March killed six Catholics within two days, including four building workers at Castlerock, Co. Derry, 25 March. By the end of the year the organisation was claiming thirty-one killings. Its favoured weapon was the 'pipe bomb'. Members were also responsible for a campaign against prison officers, often attacked in their homes. The UDA was mobilised after the Provisional IRA's bomb explosion in the Shankill Road area, Belfast, 23 October 1993; the bomber killed himself and nine customers in Frizzell's fish shop. The UDA retaliated at the Rising Sun bar and restaurant in Gresteel, Co. Derry, shooting dead seven people and wounding thirteen (one of whom died later).

The UDA continued its campaign against the background of the PEACE PROCESS. Following the DOWNING STREET DECLARATION (1993), in January 1994 a Queen's University academic, Liam Kennedy, revealed that he had seen a UDA 'doomsday plan' proposing repartition and 'ethnic cleansing' in the event of a civil war in Northern Ireland.

More UDA killings followed during February. In late May, rioting erupted in loyalist areas of Belfast when Johnny 'Mad Dog' Adair was charged with 'directing the activities' of the UFF. Following the Provisional IRA ceasefire, July 1994, the COMBINED LOYALIST MILITARY COMMAND declared a ceasefire in October. Loyalists had killed 38 of the 69 people who died that year (republicans killed 27). The conflict was responsible for nine deaths in 1995. The UDA went on 'full alert' after the Provisional IRA ceasefire ended with the bomb explosion at Canary Wharf, London, 9 February. While the amount of violence increased (with a total of 22 deaths), against the increasing momentum of the peace process the year remained comparatively quiet. In January 1998 UDA prisoners in the Maze Prison withdrew support for the political process, blaming the government's 'constant pandering' to Sinn

Féin and the IRA. However, the UDA renewed its ceasefire. It supported the BELFAST AGREEMENT (10 April 1998). The next month UDA leaders in the Maze Prison announced that 'the war is over' and apologised to all victims of UDA violence.

In July the UDA and UFF were declared officially inactive, to enable imprisoned members to avail of early release under the Belfast Agreement. During 1999, observers believed that some dissidents were joining anti-agreement organisations. During 2000 there were several clashes between the UDA and the UVF. Members of both organisations used the title RED HAND DEFENDERS.

Ulster Defence Regiment, a British army regiment established on 1 January 1970, following the recommendations of the HUNT COMMISSION and the disbanding of the B Specials (see ULSTER SPECIAL CONSTABULARY). The UDR, which was divided into full-time and part-time sections, assisted the RUC and British army in the fight against the IRA.

Catholics made up 18 per cent of the force. Contrary to the intentions of the Hunt Commission, some former B Specials were recruited, earning the suspicion of many Catholics. The UDR was frequently accused of colluding with paramilitary groups in attacking republican activists, for which some members were successfully prosecuted. In October 1976 two members of the UDR were convicted together with the UVF gang responsible for the murder of three members of the Miami Showband near Newry, Co. Down, 31 July 1975.

The UDR was merged with the ROYAL IRISH RANGERS to form the ROYAL IRISH REGIMENT, July 1992. By that time 197 members and 47 former members of the UDR had been killed by republican activists.

Ulster Defence Union, founded in 1894 by E. J. SAUNDERSON for the purpose of collecting funds and organising resistance to HOME RULE. In the event the (second) HOME RULE BILL was defeated in the House of Lords. (See also UNION DEFENCE LEAGUE, ULSTER UNIONIST COUNCIL, and ULSTER UNIONIST PARTY.)

Ulster Democratic Party, formed in December 1989 out of the Ulster Loyalist Democratic Party (established by the ULSTER DEFENCE ASSOCIATION in June 1981). Though its predecessor claimed to have no paramilitary links, the UDP was the political wing of the UDA. GARY MCMICHAEL won a council seat for the UDP in Lisburn in 1993. The party chairman, Raymond Smallwood, was killed by the Provisional IRA outside his home in Lisburn, Co. Antrim, 11 July 1994. The party played a central role in promoting the loyalist ceasefire of October 1994 to loyalist prisoners in the Maze Prison. A spokesman also attended meetings in Washington and met PRESIDENT MARY ROBINSON in Dublin. In November the party advised people to take policing problems to the RUC and not to paramilitary groups. In December party leaders held their first formal meeting with government representatives, after which they declared that the Union was safe. They also met SDLP leaders but rejected any Council of Ireland. They called for dialogue after the publication of the FRAMEWORK DOCUMENTS (February 1995). The party rejected a suggestion by DAVID TRIMBLE that loyalists should hand in some weapons to put pressure on the Provisional IRA to decommission its arms. It welcomed the report on decommissioning by GEORGE MITCHELL, January 1996, and in the same month held its first 'twin-track' meeting with the SDLP.

After the Provisional IRA broke its ceasefire, February 1996, the UDP appealed for calm among loyalists. A month later it was the only unionist party to attend 'proximity talks' at Stormont. Members met the Prime Minister, JOHN MAJOR, in July; in November the party warned Major that the loyalist ceasefire was 'in jeopardy' if the talks were further delayed by the impasse over decommissioning. In January 1998 the party withdrew from the Lancaster House talks before it could be expelled because of recent killings by the 'ULSTER FREEDOM FIGHTERS' (i.e. the UDA) but rejoined the talks in late February. Gary McMichael attacked the DUP and the UK UNIONIST PARTY over their approach to the talks. The UDP supported the BELFAST AGREEMENT (1998); however, its links with paramilitary groups became clear at a party rally in Belfast, May 1998, from the warmth of the reception for Michael Stone (who had murdered three mourners and injured sixty others in a one-man attack on a funeral in Milltown Cemetery, Belfast, but was released under the Belfast Agreement). A UDP spokesperson, John White, said that he would now recommend the decommissioning of arms to the UDA, to put pressure on the Provisional IRA.

None of the party's candidates was elected to the new Assembly (Gary McMichael lost to the SDLP in Lagan Valley), whereas the

Progressive Unionist Party, political wing of the UVF, won two seats. The UDA rejected the Belfast Agreement in July 2001, and on 28 November the UDP announced that it was dissolved.

Ulster Independence Association, established in the 1970s to campaign for a sovereign assembly as a solution to the Northern conflict, with 100 members elected by proportional representation. It sought consensus government, with a negotiated transfer of power from London to Belfast, and was active in seeking American support. Claiming Catholic support also, it looked for a declaration from the republican movement that it would respect a sovereign independent Northern Ireland.

Ulster Independence Committee, founded in 1988 by Rev. Hugh Ross, a Presbyterian minister and member of the ORANGE ORDER, to seek an end to sectarian politics by agreement on a common Ulster identity. The committee sought a written constitution and a bill of rights in a sovereign independent Northern Ireland as an alternative to what it called the 'tyrannical and arbitrary rule of the London-Dublin coalition,' leading to a united Ireland. The Queen would remain head of state. In 1990 Ross accused the unionist political leaders of betraying Northern Ireland through concessions to Dublin. On 12 July 1993 the committee claimed that the Queen now shared the post of head of state with President Robinson, while the Irish government had a share in running Northern Ireland. Opposed to the BELFAST AGREEMENT (1998), party candidates stood in all eighteen constituencies on a united unionist 'no' platform in the post-agreement referendum in May 1998 but failed to secure any seats.

Ulster Independence Party, launched in October 1977 to secure 'by democratic means, a sovereign, free and independent Ulster.' It sought a government based on proportional power-sharing at all levels and called on Protestants and Catholics to join hands in a spirit of friendship.

Ulster Liberal Unionist Committee, established on 4 June 1886 following a meeting between Ulster Liberals and Conservatives, April 1886, a month before the vote on the (first) HOME RULE BILL. The committee organised opposition to home rule by providing speakers for meetings in Britain. The bill was defeated in the House of Commons a month later. The Liberal Unionists remained a strong force in Ulster politics and helped to organise the Unionist Convention of 1892. The Ulster Liberal Unionist Committee had twelve delegates to the ULSTER UNIONIST COUNCIL, 1905–29.

Ulster Literary Theatre, founded in Belfast by BULMER HOBSON and David Parkhill ('Lewis Purcell') as the Ulster branch of the IRISH LITERARY THEATRE; following a challenge from the ABBEY THEATRE at the use of the title 'Irish Literary Theatre' it was renamed Ulster Literary Theatre. It opened in November 1902 with productions of *Cathleen ni Houlihan* by W. B. YEATS and *The Racing Log* by James Cousins. From its first full season, starting on 7 December 1904 with Hobson's *Brian of Banba* and Purcell's *The Reformers,* it emulated the Abbey Theatre policy of 'peasant drama'. Other writers associated with the theatre were Joseph Campbell, Rutherford Mayne, and Gerald MacNamara. Its journal *Uladh* appeared from November 1904 to September 1905; the theatre survived until 1934.

Ulster Loyalist Anti-Repeal Union, founded in Belfast on 8 January 1886 as the Ulster Loyalist Anti-Repeal Committee, a rival to the IRISH LOYAL AND PATRIOTIC UNION. Supported by landowners, businessmen, and Protestant clergymen, it opposed self-government for Ireland and was dedicated to fighting the (first) HOME RULE BILL, to be introduced by W. E. GLADSTONE in April. The committee was supported by the *News Letter* (Belfast), the editor of which was its treasurer. By March there were twenty local associations, and a series of meetings was organised throughout Ireland and Britain. The union helped to organise the visit to Belfast of LORD RANDOLPH CHURCHILL, who declared, 'Ulster will fight; Ulster will be right,' 23 February 1886. It was involved in sectarian rioting in Belfast during the summer of 1886. Following the defeat of the Home Rule Bill, July 1886, leaders of the union remained active in the unionist interest and were prominent in the ULSTER UNIONIST PARTY. The union was dissolved in 1911.

Ulster Loyalist Association, a group prominent during the period 1969–72 in opposing any interference with the constitutional status of Northern Ireland, led by WILLIAM CRAIG, Rev. Martin Smyth of the Orange Order, and Austin Ardill. With a membership mainly drawn from the ORANGE ORDER, the association called for stronger security policies, in particular against the Provisional IRA. It held a series of rallies calling for the sealing of the border and an end to diplomatic relations with the Republic.

Ulster Loyalist Central Co-ordinating Committee, established after the 1974 loyalist strike to act as a forum for loyalist paramilitary organisations, replacing the ULSTER ARMY COUNCIL; it included the ULSTER DEFENCE ASSOCIATION, ULSTER VOLUNTEER FORCE, RED HAND COMMANDO, LOYALIST ASSOCIATION OF WORKERS, Orange Volunteers, and Down Orange Welfare. In 1976 the UDA and Down Orange Welfare withdrew after suggestions that some of the constituent organisations were talking to the Provisional IRA about the possibility of an independent Northern Ireland. The joint chairman of the committee, John McKeague, was killed by the INLA, 29 January 1982.

A reformed ULCCC was active in 1991 in the period before the inter-party talks. In April that year it stated that there could be no role for the Republic in the affairs of Northern Ireland. A spokesperson, Raymond Smallwood (killed by the Provisional IRA, 11 July 1994), urged the establishment of a pan-unionist convention to lead 'the fight for democracy in Northern Ireland.'

Ulster Popular Unionist Party, founded as the Ulster Progressive Unionist Party, 17 January 1980, by Sir James Kilfedder MP, formerly of the Ulster Unionist Party; the name was changed in March to Popular Unionist Party to avoid confusion with the Progressive Unionist Party. It won five seats in the 1981 district council elections. Kilfedder won Down North in the 1983 British House of Commons election. Three Popular Unionist councillors were elected in the 1985 district elections. The group opposed the ANGLO-IRISH AGREEMENT (1985). Kilfedder retained his seat in 1987 but with a much reduced majority (eroded by ROBERT MCCARTNEY, who ran as a 'Real Unionist'). The party's representation in the 1989 district elections fell to two seats, but it gained one more in 1993. Despite formidable opposition, Kilfedder again held the seat in 1992, but his sudden death in March 1995 was a prelude to the demise of the party. McCartney took the Down North seat for the UK UNIONIST PARTY.

Ulster Protestant Action, a loyalist movement active in the 1950s, based on the ULSTER PROTESTANT LEAGUE of the 1930s. During a period of economic depression it encouraged the employment of Protestants only and discrimination against the Catholic population. In the late 1950s REV. IAN PAISLEY dominated the organisation. Members who continued careers as militant unionists were Noel Doherty, later active in the ULSTER PROTESTANT VOLUNTEERS, and GUSTY SPENCE, founder of the revived ULSTER VOLUNTEER FORCE in 1966.

Ulster Protestant Action Committee, a nebulous paramilitary group at first believed to contain dissident members of the ULSTER DEFENCE ASSOCIATION in 1974. It was responsible for the murder of Catholics, claiming in October that such killings would continue until the Provisional IRA was eliminated.

The name Protestant Action reappeared in 1981 when a group using this name threatened to kill 'active republicans'. In the following year it claimed the murders of several people, at which time it was thought to have connections with the RED HAND COMMANDO.

Ulster Protestant League, founded in 1931, in the midst of economic depression, to foster discrimination against the Catholic population of Northern Ireland. It called on Protestant employers not to employ Catholic workers and asked Protestants not to work with or do business with Catholics. Leading apologists for the movement included the Belfast Unionist MP Major Henry McCormack. In three weeks of sectarian violence, July–August 1935, thirteen people died, hundreds were injured, and several hundred Catholic families were driven from their homes. Responding to these events, Cahir Healy, a leading Nationalist politician, claimed in a letter to the British Solicitor-General, Sir Thomas Inskip, 16 August 1935, that 'the identification of certain Northern Ministers with the Ulster Protestant League, whose watch word is "Protestants employ Protestants," indicates that they have been . . . the moving spirits in a most intolerant and reactionary effort to stir up old animosities amongst the most ignorant and excitable classes in the community.' He complained that a government minister, Sir Basil Brooke (later VISCOUNT BROOKEBOROUGH), was a principal speaker at a UPL meeting in the Ulster Hall, Belfast. Improving economic conditions led to a decline in support. ULSTER PROTESTANT ACTION was revived for similar purposes in the 1950s.

Ulster Protestant Volunteers, founded in 1966 by Noel Doherty and REV. IAN PAISLEY as a subsidiary of the ULSTER CONSTITUTION DEFENCE COMMITTEE. It organised counter-demonstrations to civil rights meetings.

Described by Paisley as 'constitutional, democratic, open and legal,' it barred members of the RUC from membership but was open to members of the B Specials (see ULSTER SPECIAL CONSTABULARY). A prominent figure in the organisation was Major Ronald Bunting, who also claimed leadership of a number of one-man and sometimes fictitious organisations. The group was briefly connected, through Doherty, to the ULSTER VOLUNTEER FORCE. Members saw themselves as guardians of the Union, which they claimed was under attack from republicans and 'Lundyite' (renegade) Unionist politicians, led by the Prime Minister, TERENCE O'NEILL. Bunting led the attack on the PEOPLE'S DEMOCRACY at Burntollet Bridge, Co. Derry, 4 January 1969, under the eyes of the international press. The organisation collapsed during the early 1970s.

Ulster Reform Club, founded in 1880 by Ulster Liberals as the centre of the Ulster Liberal organisation and to mark the return of W. E. GLADSTONE as Prime Minister. Following the defeat of the (first) HOME RULE BILL, July 1886, the club came under the control of the Liberal Unionists, led by FREDERICK CRAWFORD. Members, dedicated to the preservation of the Union, included many industrial and commercial leaders, who identified the prosperity of Ulster with the Union. After 1905 the club was affiliated to the ULSTER UNIONIST COUNCIL, on which it had a strong influence.

Ulster Resistance, an organisation founded by Noel Little, REV. IAN PAISLEY and Peter Robinson of the DEMOCRATIC UNIONIST PARTY and Rev. Ivan Foster to oppose the ANGLO-IRISH AGREEMENT (1985), launched on 10 November 1986 at an invitation-only rally in the Ulster Hall, Belfast. Relations with the DUP cooled when its politicians opted for talks rather than a more direct campaign against the agreement. Weapons similar to those used by the UDA and UVF, uncovered in Armagh in November 1988, were linked to the group through the discovery of its uniform red berets at the site and the arrest of a former DUP district council candidate. In April 1989 Noel Little, James King and Sammy Quinn were arrested in Paris in the company of a South African diplomat, Daniel Storm, with pieces of a demonstration missile from Short Brothers of Belfast; they were believed to be seeking weapons from South Africa in return for Shorts' military technology. Loyalists mounted a campaign for the release of the three, who denied paramilitary involvement; following fines and suspended sentences they were released in October 1991. Ulster Resistance was listed as a member of the COMBINED LOYALIST MILITARY COMMAND in 1991.

Ulster Service Corps, a loyalist vigilante group formed in 1977 with the support of the UNITED UNIONIST ACTION COUNCIL. Members established roadblocks in parts of Cos. Derry, Armagh, and Tyrone. Its claimed a membership of five hundred, believed to contain many former members of the B Specials (see ULSTER SPECIAL CONSTABULARY). The authorities denied its claim to have liaison with the RUC and the ULSTER DEFENCE REGIMENT; however, the SDLP claimed that members of the group engaged in joint patrols with the UDR in some parts of mid-Ulster.

Ulster Special Constabulary, established on 2 September 1920 to assist the RUC, then under increasing attack from the IRA during the WAR OF INDEPENDENCE. Sir James Craig (see VISCOUNT CRAIGAVON) proposed that a part-time force of special constables should be raised 'from the loyal population.' In October 1920 DUBLIN CASTLE announced the formation of a Special Constabulary under the Constabulary and Police (Ireland) Acts (1832 and 1914). All law-abiding citizens between the ages of twenty-one and forty-five were invited to apply; no indication was given that the new force would operate exclusively in the new state of Northern Ireland. Recruitment was mainly from among the ULSTER VOLUNTEER FORCE and former members of the British army. Nationalist politicians and the ANCIENT ORDER OF HIBERNIANS actively discouraged Catholics from joining the new force, of which there were three categories, A, B, and C.

The Constabulary was required to swear an oath before a justice of the peace. The text of the oath was:

> I do swear that I will well and truly serve our Sovereign Lord the King in the Office of Special Constable without favour or affection, malice or ill-will, and that I will to the best of my power cause the Peace to be kept and preserved, and prevent all offences against the persons and properties of his Majesty's subjects; and that while I continue to hold the said office I will to the best of my skill and knowledge discharge all the duties thereof faithfully according to law. So help me God.

The A Constables, uniformed and armed, operated under six-month contracts with the

RUC. The more numerous B Specials did not face a compulsory medical inspection (nor did class C); they selected their own officers and while on duty were uniformed and armed. The requirement that they surrender their arms at the end of a tour of duty was rarely enforced, and they routinely retained arms in their homes. The B Specials performed a half-night's duty per week, or one full night per fortnight. They were not paid, except for an allowance of 4 shillings per half-night or 8 shillings per full night, to cover dress, meals, and travelling expenses. They served in their home districts, operating in patrols of three to four with an RUC constable. C constables were considered a general reserve, to be called on only in an emergency.

The new force was commanded by Lieutenant-Colonel C. G. Wickham, divisional commissioner for Ulster of the RIC. He was responsible to both MAJOR-GENERAL SIR H. HUGH TUDOR in Dublin and to the Under-Secretary for Ireland, Sir Ernest Clark, in Belfast. Six county commandants were appointed to complement the county inspectors of the RIC, with whom they were expected to co-operate. The force was further divided into districts and sub-districts.

The Special Constabulary remained almost exclusively Protestant, and many members were also active in the ORANGE ORDER. The B Specials attracted the particular ire of the Catholic population, who saw them as protectors of the loyalist interest. They were particularly active in attempts to contain the NORTHERN IRELAND CIVIL RIGHTS ASSOCIATION and PEOPLE'S DEMOCRACY in the 1960s. Violent clashes involving the RUC, B Specials, loyalists and civil rights marchers during the period 1968–69 were captured by the international press; as a result of the ensuing controversy the HUNT COMMISSION recommended the disbanding of the force, which was stood down on 30 April 1970, though many former members were absorbed into the new ULSTER DEFENCE REGIMENT. The Ulster Special Constabulary Association, consisting of former members of the force, was subsequently formed; with an estimated ten thousand members it became a significant pressure group within loyalism and was active in support of the ULSTER WORKERS' COUNCIL strike of 1974.

Ulster Solemn League and Covenant, signed on 28 September 1912 as loyalists pledged themselves to resist HOME RULE. The leader in the signing ceremony was SIR EDWARD CARSON. Within a few days 218,206 men had signed the Covenant (women were not invited to sign it, but 228,991 women signed a declaration pledging support to the men in opposition to home rule). The text of the covenant was:

> Ulster's Solemn League and Covenant
>
> Being convinced in our consciences that Home Rule would be disastrous to the material well-being of Ulster as well as of the whole of Ireland, subversive of our civil and religious freedom, destructive of our citizenship and perilous to the unity of the Empire, we, whose names are underwritten, men of Ulster, loyal subjects of His Gracious Majesty King George V, humbly relying on the God whom our fathers in days of stress and trial confidently trusted, do hereby pledge ourselves in solemn Covenant throughout this our time of threatened calamity to stand by one another in defending for ourselves and our children our cherished position of equal citizenship in the United Kingdom and in using all means which may be found necessary to defeat the present conspiracy to set up a Home Rule Parliament in Ireland. And in the event of such a Parliament being forced upon us we further solemnly and mutually pledge ourselves to refuse to recognise its authority. In sure confidence that God will defend the right we hereto subscribe our names. And further, we individually declare that we have not already signed this Covenant.
>
> The above was signed by me at ....
>
> "Ulster Day," Saturday, 28th September 1912
>
> God Save the King.

Ulster Tenant Right Association, founded in 1847 by WILLIAM SHARMAN CRAWFORD, Edward Maginn (Catholic Bishop of Derry) and James McKnight following the defeat of Crawford's Tenant Right Bill, which had sought to legalise the ULSTER CUSTOM. Representatives of the Ulster movement attended a conference called by CHARLES GAVAN DUFFY in Dublin, August 1850, at which the TENANT LEAGUE was established. Though the new movement was sometimes called the 'League of North and South', the Northern tenants took little part.

Ulster Unionist Council. Following the devolution proposal of August 1904, a Unionist Council was proposed on 2 December. The governing body of the ULSTER UNIONIST PARTY, it was formally constituted at a meeting in the Ulster Hall, Belfast, 3 March 1905, with the aim of acting 'as a further connecting link between Ulster Unionists and their parliamentary representatives; to settle in consultation with them the parliamentary policy,' and 'generally to advance and defend the interests of Ulster Unionists.' Its first president was the Duke of Abercorn and the first chairman E. J. SAUNDERSON, leader of the UUP. The original two hundred members were drawn from local Unionist associations, the ORANGE ORDER, members of Parliament, and peers. Saunderson was succeeded by WALTER LONG in 1906, and a year later the Council organised the Joint Committee of Unionist Associations of Ireland. SIR EDWARD CARSON became leader in 1910. It was the first such organisation to have full-time staff; the secretary from 1906 to 1921 was RICHARD DAWSON BATES.

Membership of the UUC expanded to meet changing circumstances. As it prepared to fight the (third) HOME RULE BILL, 1912–14, it was increased to 370 members in 1911. As part of the campaign to resist home rule, the council organised the ULSTER SOLEMN LEAGUE AND COVENANT, September 1912, and the ULSTER VOLUNTEER FORCE, January 1913. It appointed a 'Provisional Government' for Ulster, September 1913, and organised the LARNE GUN-RUNNING, April 1914. The council was represented at the IRISH CONVENTION (1917–18), after which its membership was expanded to 432.

Having reluctantly accepted the GOVERNMENT OF IRELAND ACT (1920), the council played a leading role in the creation of the state of Northern Ireland, all governments of which were subsequently formed by the UUP; all Unionist members of Parliament for northern constituencies were members of the council's Standing Committee. In 1946 the council adopted a new constitution 'to maintain Northern Ireland as an integral part of the United Kingdom and to uphold and defend the Constitution and Parliament of Northern Ireland.'

Organisations affiliated to the Ulster Unionist Council, which by 2003 had 860 members, include the ULSTER UNIONIST LABOUR ASSOCIATION, ULSTER WOMEN'S UNIONIST COUNCIL, and ULSTER YOUNG UNIONIST COUNCIL.

Ulster Unionist Labour Association, founded in June 1918 to increase the involvement by trade unionists in the Ulster Unionist Party. SIR EDWARD CARSON (president) and JOHN MILLER ANDREWS (chairman), the only two members of its committee who were not trade unionists, were anxious to have trade union support within the unionist movement to counter criticism that it was a movement dominated by Conservative landlords.

In the general election of December 1918 three Labour Unionists were elected for the Shankill division (north Belfast), St Andrew's (south Belfast), and Victoria (east Belfast). They sat on the Conservative benches in the British House of Commons but in 1925 lost their seats to candidates of the NORTHERN IRELAND LABOUR PARTY. The association, which opened two working men's clubs (east Belfast, 1921, and north Belfast, 1924), lost members during the economic depression of the 1920s and 30s. There was a small revival during the 1950s, but the association did not lead to a noticeable increase in working-class influence within the Unionist Party.

Ulster Unionist Party. The Ulster Unionists were the strongest element of the Unionist Party from 1886. Led by E. J. SAUNDERSON, they formed the ULSTER UNIONIST COUNCIL, 1905, as a central body through which to fight HOME RULE. Following Saunderson's death, 1906, the Ulster Unionists were led by WALTER LONG until 1910 and from then until 1921 by SIR EDWARD CARSON. Carson was succeeded by Sir James Craig (see VISCOUNT CRAIGAVON), who became the first Prime Minister of the state of Northern Ireland, 1921. The UUP provided all governments of Northern Ireland until the introduction of direct rule from London, March 1972, and had a strong association with the ORANGE ORDER, of which all Unionist leaders were members. Between 1921 and 1972 the UUP held up to 40 of the 52 seats in the Parliament of Northern Ireland. It dominated Northern Ireland representation in the British House of Commons until the 1970s, holding eleven out of thirteen seats (1922 and 1923), all thirteen (1924), eleven again (1929, 1931 and 1935), nine (1945), ten out of twelve (1950), nine (1951), ten (1955), all twelve (1959 and 1964), and eleven again (1966); the fragmentation in unionism showed in 1966 when its representation fell to eight seats. It never recovered its former predominance: by 1983, when there were seventeen Northern Ireland seats, the Official Unionist Party (as it was known for a while) held eleven and in the 1987 general election took ten.

Closely associated with the British

Conservative Party since 1886, the UUP was a branch of the British party, with full voting entitlements at the annual conference. EDWARD HEATH's introduction of direct rule from London in 1972 strained the relationship.

The Unionist Party remained united until the late 1960s, when, under the premiership of TERENCE O'NEILL, the rise of the NORTHERN IRELAND CIVIL RIGHTS ASSOCIATION and the demand by the Catholic population for full civil rights placed the party under considerable strain. The split came when BRIAN FAULKNER accepted the SUNNINGDALE AGREEMENT (1973) and led the party into the Northern Ireland Assembly's power-sharing Executive with the ALLIANCE PARTY and SDLP, 1974. The UNITED ULSTER UNIONIST COUNCIL, a coalition of traditionalists opposed to Sunningdale, was then set up. When the Executive fell, May 1974, Faulkner resigned the leadership of the party to form the UNIONIST PARTY OF NORTHERN IRELAND. HARRY WEST became new leader of the Unionist Party. Many anti-reformist unionists moved to the DEMOCRATIC UNIONIST PARTY and ULSTER VANGUARD.

Further fragmentation occurred over the next two decades, the more prominent entities including the PROGRESSIVE UNIONIST PARTY and ULSTER DEMOCRATIC PARTY. The former Conservative MP Enoch Powell represented Down South in the British House of Commons, 1974–87. In the election to the Constitutional Convention, 1975, the party won nineteen seats with 26 per cent of the vote. Opposed to power-sharing (multi-party government), the UUP joined the DUP and Vanguard to support a majority Convention report seeking 'majority' (all-unionist) government; this was rejected by London, as it did not meet the criterion of devolved government. The UUP then opposed a proposal by WILLIAM CRAIG to secure a voluntary coalition that would include the SDLP.

The UUP's relationship with its erstwhile partners deteriorated further in 1977 when the party did not participate in the loyalist strike in a demand for tougher security policies and in protest at the continuation of direct rule. In the district elections in May the UUP secured 30 per cent of first-preference votes, to win 178 seats. In the British House of Commons the six UUP members, led by JAMES MOLYNEAUX, were no longer in the Unionist Coalition; WILLIAM CRAIG joined them in 1978. In the 1979 elections to the European Parliament, John Taylor of the UUP won a seat with 22 per cent of first-preference votes (by contrast, REV. IAN PAISLEY of the DUP won 30 per cent and JOHN HUME of the SDLP 25 per cent.)

Molyneaux succeeded HARRY WEST, who had been eliminated in the election for the European Parliament. The UUP boycotted the Constitutional Conference at Stormont, November 1979. It also rejected the proposal for a fifty-member Advisory Council. The party was hostile to a review by the Prime Minister, MARGARET THATCHER, with the Taoiseach, CHARLES HAUGHEY, of the 'totality of relations' between the two countries at a meeting in DUBLIN CASTLE, December 1980. Unionists rejected a role for the Republic in a Northern Ireland settlement (the 'Irish dimension').

Following the killing by republicans of a UUP member of Parliament, Rev. Robert Bradford, 14 November 1981, the party joined the DUP in sponsoring the 'day of action', 23 November 1981, to demand a tougher security policy; however, it was soon distancing itself from its arch-rival. It rejected a DUP proposal that an agreed Unionist candidate should run in the South Belfast by-election, 4 March 1982, which was won by Rev. Martin Smyth of the UUP. The party was divided over the 'rolling devolution' proposal and regarded an Assembly as a revival of power-sharing and Sunningdale; it feared the British government was attempting to co-operate with proposals to allow the Republic a say in the government of Northern Ireland. Jim Prior secured an Assembly, despite UUP opposition. The UUP won twenty-six seats in the Assembly with 30 per cent of the vote (the DUP secured 21). It conceded a deal on three seats with Paisley (who had wanted a deal on six) in the 1983 British parliamentary elections; the UUP won 34 per cent of the vote to take eleven out of seventeen seats (its best result since 1972); the DUP won three seats. However, in the 1984 European Parliament elections John Taylor secured only 20 per cent, compared with Paisley's 34 per cent. The party maintained its lead in the district council elections in 1985, winning 180 seats with 30 per cent of the vote (compared with the DUP's 142 seats with 24 per cent).

The parties co-operated in opposition to the ANGLO-IRISH AGREEMENT (1985). Fifteen Unionists resigned their seats to force a series of by-elections as a test of support for the agreement. The UUP won ten seats (compared with three for the DUP). Following the March 1986 'day of action' in protest at the agreement, the gap between the UUP and DUP widened. In the 1987 general election the UUP secured 38 per cent of the vote, compared with the DUP's 12 per cent. However, the Conservative majority of 101 forced the two main unionist parties into a degree of co-operation, starting with 'talks about talks' on whether the Major government was prepared to consider an alternative to the Anglo-Irish Agreement. The earlier policy of boycotting district council business gradually petered out. In the 1989 council elections the UUP won three extra seats (bringing it to 193), took control of three councils, and was the largest party in three others.

Molyneaux attended the resumed BROOKE-MAYHEW TALKS in Dublin, 1992. At the end of the talks the party suggested a settlement including a bill of rights, a 'meaningful role' for the SDLP in a new Assembly, and an inter-Irish relations committee. When Paisley condemned this as a breach of the 'agreed joint unionist position', Molyneaux accused the DUP of 'gross hypocrisy in unilaterally leaving the talks.' Though Sinn Féin was the biggest vote-winner in Belfast, the UUP also recorded an increase in the general election. It entered into an understanding with the Conservatives in 1993, allowing the Treaty of Maastricht to pass. Party delegates met the American Morrison delegation in September.

The UUP was suspicious of the Hume-Adams agreement the same month, viewing it as the possible basis for change in government policy. It did not oppose the DOWNING STREET DECLARATION (1993), and the membership was mollified by the announcement of a House of Commons Select Committee on Northern Ireland Affairs. Republican opposition to the declaration led the UUP to press for new security measures. Amid widespread speculation about a Provisional IRA ceasefire, the UUP declined an opportunity to meet another Morrison delegation from the United States. The ceasefire came in August 1994. The UUP saved the Major government in the House of Commons (on Spanish fishing rights). In February 1995 it rejected the FRAMEWORKS DOCUMENTS as 'nationalist'. Dissatisfaction with Molyneaux became public when Lee Reynolds stood as a 'stalking horse' and received eighty-eight votes in a leadership challenge. Molyneaux led the party into talks with the SDLP on social and economic issues in May.

DAVID TRIMBLE became party leader in August 1995, defeating John Taylor (466 to 333) and then appointing him deputy leader. In October there was a proposal for 'a sensitive and radical review of party structure,' which would involve loosening the traditionally tight ties with the Orange Order. The party then issued the document *Unionism Restated,* in which it called for Northern Ireland to be treated as a region of the United Kingdom and also rejected cross-border executive bodies.

The UUP helped defeat the British government in the House of Commons on EU fishing policy. It rejected an invitation to meet the Irish government as part of the 'twin-track' negotiations. Following the collapse of the Provisional IRA ceasefire with the bomb explosion at Canary Wharf, London, 9 February 1996, the UUP stated that it had been right on decommissioning all along. It then published proposals for a ninety-member body, to be elected by proportional representation in the eighteen parliamentary constituencies. In March, Trimble led a delegation to meet the Irish government, to which it emphasised the importance of Irish legislation to deal with decommissioning. As talks began on 10 June, the party expressed reservations on the role of the proposed chairman, the former US senator GEORGE MITCHELL, viewing him as too close to the Irish-American lobby in Washington. However, it agreed a compromise to reduce his 'supreme role' and 'discretionary powers', though this led to disputes with the other unionists parties. The UUP withdrew from the talks after the confrontation over the Orange Order march in Portadown (in the heart of Trimble's constituency). It issued the document *Addressing Decommissioning,* in which it argued that Sinn Féin should be admitted to the talks but only in the event of a 'genuine IRA ceasefire' and 'instalments' in the handing over of arms. It opposed the proposal for a special commission to deal with decommissioning separately from the talks. In October the party agreed a joint blueprint with the SDLP on an agenda for talks but stalled over decommissioning.

In the general election of May 1997 the UUP gained one extra seat. Jeffrey Donaldson, soon a prominent opponent of Trimble's leadership, replaced Molyneaux as member of Parliament for the Lagan Valley constituency. The party had a poor relationship with the new Secretary of State for Northern Ireland, MARJORIE (MO) MOWLAM. It complained about 'concessions' to Sinn Féin in December. In February 1998 party leaders met the main parties in the Republic during a visit to Dublin. They pressed for an extension of Sinn Féin's temporary exclusion from the talks in March, but stayed in the talks.

In April the party executive voted (55 to 23) in favour of the BELFAST AGREEMENT, which Trimble stated was 'as good and as far as it gets.' He became First Minister of the Executive of the new Northern Ireland Assembly in July. Within a month the party was telling the Blair government that it would not participate in an Executive containing Sinn Féin without the actual handing over of Provisional IRA weapons. Members launched a campaign to press for a ballot of the Ulster Unionist Council on involvement by the UUP with Sinn Féin in the Executive. The executive voted (70 to 30) in favour of the proposal for ten ministerial departments and six North-South bodies. Decommissioning continued to be an issue, but Trimble won enough support within the UUC to survive. But the issue of decommissioning remained, and Trimble lost patience with what he considered prevarication by the Provisional IRA. He stated on 7 May 2001 that he would resign the office of First Minister on 1 July if the Provisional IRA had not decommissioned weapons. This coincided with Blair's announcement of a general election on 7 June. The UUP lost three seats. Lady Sylvia Hermon became the party's first woman member in the House of Commons and the first woman since 1969 to represent a Northern Ireland constituency. In the local elections on the same day the UUP lost 31 seats, dropping to 154 (the DUP gained 40, for a total of 131). On 8 October 2001 David Trimble lost the vote (54 to 45) in the Assembly on his motion seeking to exclude Sinn Féin from the Executive. Following a number of crises, the Northern Assembly and Executive were suspended.

The party's share of seats in Northern Ireland general elections since 1921 was:

1921	40
1925	37
1933	36
1938	39
1945	33
1949	37
1953	38
1958	37
1962	34
1965	36
1969	36

In the 1969 election, in addition to the thirty-six officially sponsored Unionists elected, a further three Unofficial Unionists were returned. These were candidates who ran against official party nominees who had declared their opposition to the O'Neill reform programme. Out of a total of thirty-nine Unionist MPs, official and unofficial, returned in this election, twenty-seven were pro-O'Neill, ten anti-O'Neill, and two unclear in their attitude to the Prime Minister.

The leaders of the Ulster Unionist Party since 1921 have been:

Lord Craigavon (1921–40)
John Miller Andrews (1940–43)
Sir Basil Brooke, Lord Brookeborough (1953–63)
Terence O'Neill (1963–69)
James Chichester-Clark (1969–71)
Brian Faulkner (1971–74)
Harry West (1974–79)
James Molyneaux (1979–95)
David Trimble (1995–)

(For a list of the governments of Northern Ireland formed by the Ulster Unionist Party see NORTHERN IRELAND.)

Ulster Vanguard, a movement launched by WILLIAM CRAIG, 9 February 1972, as a pressure group within the ULSTER UNIONIST PARTY to oppose British government proposals for reforms in Northern Ireland. At first supported by the Prime Minister, BRIAN FAULKNER, Vanguard demanded the maintenance of Northern Ireland, under its own government, within the United Kingdom, sought the restoration of internal security, and expressed total opposition to a united Ireland. Moderates were alarmed when Craig attended demonstrations accompanied by motorcycle escorts, making speeches that appeared to call for a pogrom of those suspected of disloyalty to Northern Ireland ('If the politicians fail, it will be our duty to liquidate the enemy'). Vanguard was supported for a time by loyalist paramilitary groups, including the Vanguard Service Corps and the ULSTER DEFENCE ASSOCIATION.

On the introduction of direct rule from London, March 1972, Craig broke with Faulkner. He established the anti-reformist Vanguard Unionist Progressive Party early in 1973, with the support of the UDA and LOYALIST ASSOCIATION OF WORKERS, to fight forthcoming elections in alliance with the DEMOCRATIC UNIONIST PARTY. Vanguard candidates won seven seats in the Assembly of Northern Ireland, June 1973, and, as part of the UNITED ULSTER UNIONIST COUNCIL, destroyed the power-sharing Executive, 1974. At one point the party advocated an independent

Ulster rather than direct rule from London; but when Craig expressed support for an emergency coalition between the SDLP and loyalists he was expelled from the council and lost the leadership of Vanguard.

Vanguard secured fourteen seats in the Constitutional Convention (1975) but, like other small political parties, became for the moment largely irrelevant. DAVID TRIMBLE was for a time deputy leader. Ernest Baird broke with Craig to establish the UNITED ULSTER UNIONIST MOVEMENT. Vanguard members were subsequently absorbed back into the Official Unionist Party. Craig, standing for the Vanguard Unionist Party in Belfast East in the election to the Northern Ireland Assembly, 20 October 1982, won only 2,274 votes.

Ulster Volunteer Force (UVF), founded on 31 January 1913 by the ULSTER UNIONIST COUNCIL from among local corps in Ulster for the purpose of resisting the implementation of HOME RULE (due to become law in September 1914). Businessmen and the landed gentry provided finance; aid also came from England, with Rudyard Kipling contributing £50,000 (and a poem, 'Ulster, 1913') and contributions also made by the Duke of Bedford, Lord Iveagh (Edward Cecil Guinness), and Lord Rothschild. Leaders of the movement were James Craig (see VISCOUNT CRAIGAVON), SIR EDWARD CARSON, and FREDERICK CRAWFORD. Sir George Richardson was appointed commander (July 1913) after he was nominated for the post by Field-Marshal Lord Roberts, while Lord Milner selected British army officers to train the force. GENERAL SIR HENRY WILSON, attached to British army headquarters in London, showed his support, as did army officers stationed at the Curragh, Co. Kildare (see CURRAGH INCIDENT). Numbers were limited to 100,000 men between the ages of seventeen and sixty-five who had been signatories of the ULSTER SOLEMN LEAGUE AND COVENANT (September 1912). In September 1913 the Volunteers became the 'Army of Ulster' when the ULSTER UNIONIST COUNCIL appointed a 'Provisional Government'.

The UVF was able to operate in the open because drilling was legal when authorised by two magistrates, and most magistrates were either members of the UVF or sympathetic to its aims. However, Carson (a lawyer) admitted that 'drilling is illegal, the Volunteers are illegal, and the government knows they are illegal, and the government does not interfere with them,' and he told his followers, 'Don't be afraid of illegalities.' Their example was followed in Dublin, where nationalists established the IRISH VOLUNTEERS.

The UVF was armed after the LARNE GUN-RUNNING (April 1914), which secured it 25,000 guns and 3 million rounds of ammunition. By that time the CURRAGH INCIDENT had demonstrated to the Prime Minister, H. H. ASQUITH, and the Liberal government that the British army in Ireland could not be relied upon to act against Ulster.

On the outbreak of the Great War, August 1914, the UVF responded to Carson's call to join in the defence of the British Empire, and the UVF was incorporated in the British army as the 36TH (ULSTER) DIVISION. A month later HOME RULE became law, allowing for temporary partition, but with the act suspended for the duration of the war. In July 1916 the Ulster Division was virtually wiped out at the Battle of the Somme. By the end of the war the Irish situation had changed as a result of the EASTER RISING (1916) and the rise of SINN FÉIN. DAVID LLOYD GEORGE sought to solve the 'Irish question' by means of the GOVERNMENT OF IRELAND ACT (1920), dividing the country into Northern Ireland and Southern Ireland. At Carson's request, SIR WILLIAM SPENDER arranged that UVF members should have preference in recruitment for the new ULSTER SPECIAL CONSTABULARY. The UVF was then disbanded.

The name Ulster Volunteer Force was revived in 1966 by GUSTY SPENCE as a loyalist paramilitary force to oppose republican attempts to commemorate the fiftieth anniversary of the Easter Rising. On 21 May a statement was published in Belfast newspapers:

> From this day we declare war against the IRA and its splinter group . . . Known IRA men will be executed mercilessly and without hesitation . . . We will not tolerate any interference from any source and we solemnly warn the authorities to make no more speeches of appeasement. We are heavily armed Protestants dedicated to this cause.

The Northern Ireland government proscribed the UVF, described by the Prime Minister, TERENCE O'NEILL, 28 June 1966, as 'this evil thing in our midst . . . a dangerous conspiracy . . .' On the same day Spence and two others were found guilty of the murder of an eighteen-year-old Catholic, Peter Ward, for which they were subsequently sentenced to life imprisonment.

The rise of the NORTHERN IRELAND CIVIL RIGHTS ASSOCIATION revitalised the UVF, which was believed responsible for some of the bombings during 1969. O'Neill, unable to satisfy the civil rights movement and to contain the loyalist reaction, fell from power, 28 April. His successor, JAMES CHICHESTER-CLARK, failed to suppress the violence as the Catholic and Protestant populations moved towards civil war. Additional British soldiers arrived in August. The UVF was disorganised during 1971, though violent acts were carried out in its name. A new paramilitary force, the ULSTER DEFENCE ASSOCIATION, was founded in August 1971; fearing a loss of support, the UVF reorganised. The tone was set by a warning published in the *News Letter* (Belfast), 8 March 1972: for every member of the armed forces who was killed, the UVF would kill ten republicans. By this time it was believed that the UVF numbered 1,500, many of them former soldiers. As political initiatives failed and unionism fragmented, 1972–74, paramilitary groups on both sides filled the vacuum, setting a pattern of violence—bombings, murder, reprisal, and counter-reprisal—that lasted until the end of the century.

Following the fall of the power-sharing Executive, 1974, there were attempts to establish a Constitutional Convention, and the ban on the UVF was lifted in an effort to induce members to join the political process. The Volunteer Political Party was founded in October, and members held meetings with government ministers. There were also secret meetings between the UVF and both wings of the IRA amid calls for peace and reconciliation.

The UVF leadership changed during 1975, a move believed to herald an undeviating military policy, which took its biggest toll on 2 October when the organisation was responsible for a wave of violence, including thirteen bomb explosions in many parts of Northern Ireland, killing twelve people and wounding forty. The UVF was again banned. On 5 October, aided by inside information, the RUC and British army raided the homes of UVF members in east Belfast and east Antrim, wrecking the organisation in those areas. In March 1977 twenty-six UVF members received a total of seven hundred years' imprisonment (including eight life sentences) on fifty-five charges, including five murders. The movement's Scottish section took a severe blow in June 1979 when nine members were imprisoned for plotting to buy arms for the UVF. Four of them were convicted of bomb explosions in two Glasgow public houses; as a result the Glasgow UVF (believed to have sixty members) was broken up.

Eighteen members of the UVF arrested in Co. Armagh in 1982, on information supplied by Clifford McKeown, pleaded guilty to a variety of terrorist offences. The following year the UVF commander Joseph Bennett became an informer and provided evidence leading to the conviction of fourteen leading members, including John Graham; they were freed on appeal. More arrests followed during the summer on foot of evidence provided by other informers. In June 1985 six members were sentenced for eighty crimes, including a number of murders.

During the 1990s the UVF was mainly active in Belfast and Cos. Armagh and Tyrone, with lesser activity in east Antrim and north Down. The most active units were believed to be in Portadown, Co. Armagh (where they were led by BILLY WRIGHT), and north Belfast.

The UVF was a party to the COMBINED LOYALIST MILITARY COMMAND, 1991. This coalition called a ceasefire for nine weeks during the BROOKE-MAYHEW TALKS, though the following year the UVF was believed to be responsible for eleven murders and during 1993 for twelve. The killing continued until the CLMC ceasefire of 13 October 1993 (announced by the founder of the UVF, Gusty Spence).

In April 1996 a bitter feud broke out between the UVF and its Mid-Ulster unit, commanded by Billy Wright. Wright and Alex Kerr rejected an order that the unit disband and an order to leave Northern Ireland. Wright then set up the LOYALIST VOLUNTEER FORCE. Following the BELFAST AGREEMENT (1998), in May the UVF named Billy Hutchinson of the PROGRESSIVE UNIONIST PARTY as its link with the arms decommissioning body. The Secretary of State for Northern Ireland, MO MOWLAM, declared officially that the UVF was inactive, thus enabling UVF prisoners to benefit from early release under the Belfast Agreement. However, during July 1999 there was speculation that the UVF had reorganised in Portadown, a loyalist flashpoint each summer when the Orange Order attempted to hold a march from Drumcree Church down the (Catholic) Garvaghy Road. During 2000 there were a number of deaths when the UVF engaged in a bloody feud with the UDA.

Ulster Women's Unionist Council, founded on 23 January 1911 for 'the maintenance of the legislative Union between Great Britain and Ireland on the unimpaired integrity of which we believe our civil and religious liberties depend.' Mainly upper and middle-class in membership, its first president was the Duchess of Abercorn; another leader was the

Marchioness of Londonderry. The council, which had a membership of forty to fifty thousand during its early years, declared it support for the ULSTER UNIONIST PARTY, 18 January 1912: 'We will stand by our husbands, our brothers, and our sons, in whatever steps they may be forced to take in defending our liberties against the tyranny of Home Rule.' The council organised signatures for the ULSTER SOLEMN LEAGUE AND COVENANT (1912), supported the ULSTER VOLUNTEER FORCE, January 1913, and addressed meetings in Britain during the passing of the (third) HOME RULE BILL, 1913–14. By 1913 it claimed a membership of 200,000.

The council had twelve representatives on the ULSTER UNIONIST COUNCIL from 1918 to 1929. From 1944 it had six representatives and was active in organising weekend seminars for the study of unionism. It was also active in fund-raising and maintaining an up-to-date electoral register.

Ulster Workers' Council, a loyalist group formed in 1974 to oppose direct rule from London, the power-sharing Executive of the Assembly of Northern Ireland, and the SUNNINGDALE AGREEMENT. It called a general strike, which began with power cuts on 15 May. The co-ordinating committee was led by Glenn Barr, an ULSTER VANGUARD member of the Assembly, and included HARRY WEST (Ulster Unionist Party), REV. IAN PAISLEY (Democratic Unionist Party), WILIAM CRAIG (Vanguard), Andy Tyrie (UDA), and Ken Gibson (UVF). Supported by paramilitary groups, the strike paralysed Northern Ireland and two weeks later brought down the Executive and the Assembly. On 22 March 1987 a former agent of the Security Service (commonly called MI5), James Miller, alleged that British intelligence, in an effort to destabilise the government of HAROLD WILSON, had helped to promote the strike. Paisley's followers were influential within the council, but attempts in 1977 to elicit support for another strike failed, as the UWC failed to involve the power workers. In February 1981 the former chairman of the council, Harry Murray, announced that the UWC was being reformed to campaign for jobs and to promote the unity of workers, with no paramilitary links.

Ulster Young Unionist Council, the youth branch of the ULSTER UNIONIST PARTY, established in Belfast in 1946. It organised weekend seminars for the study of economic, social and political questions. In May 1964 it was reorganised to play a more positive role within the Unionist party. By 1970 it had sixty-eight branches. Among those who emerged from the youth movement to political careers were WILLIAM CRAIG, John Taylor, and ANNE DICKSON.

Ultimate Financial Agreement (1926), an agreement between the government of the IRISH FREE STATE and the British Government whereby the Free State ratified its undertaking to pay LAND ANNUITIES to the British exchequer and also took responsibility for pensions payable to former members of the RIC. The agreement was signed on the Free State's behalf by W. T. COSGRAVE and the Minister for Finance, ERNEST BLYTHE. The financial commitments, to the total of £5 million, were never presented to Dáil Éireann for ratification and became a matter of extreme political importance when the agreement was attacked by FIANNA FÁIL, 1929–32.

ultramontanism (meaning 'beyond the mountains,' i.e. the Alps), the doctrine that recognises the absolute authority of the Pope on matters of faith and morals. It was introduced into the Irish Catholic Church by PAUL CULLEN, who was appointed Archbishop of Armagh in 1849 and became Archbishop of Dublin three years later, with a brief from the Vatican to bring the Irish church into line with Roman practice. It was opposed by GALLICANISM.

unbaptised children. Catholic children who died without being baptised were not permitted burial in consecrated ground. Most parishes had a special place, known as a 'killeen' or 'little graveyard', for their interment. The unbaptised were also sometimes buried on the north side of a graveyard or on boundary lines. The practice ceased in the late 1940s.

Under-Secretary for Ireland, a post created in 1767 in a reorganisation of responsibilities at DUBLIN CASTLE. Two such posts were created, one for civil and the other for military affairs. Both were answerable to the CHIEF SECRETARY FOR IRELAND and replaced archaic structures over which the Chief Secretary previously had little control. In the nineteenth century the Under-Secretary was the head of the civil service in Ireland.

Union Defence League, founded in London in 1907 by WALTER LONG to combat HOME RULE; its first secretary was Ian Malcolm. Anticipating the (third) HOME RULE BILL (1912), the league entered into the LONDONDERRY HOUSE AGREEMENT with the Joint Committee of Unionist

Associations of Ireland, 6 April 1911. It placed staff and a special committee at the disposal of Lord Milner (1854–1925) in a crusade that involved financing the purchase of arms (see LARNE GUN-RUNNING) and supporting the officers involved in the CURRAGH INCIDENT. Home rule became law in September 1914 but was suspended for the duration of the First World War.

Unionist Anti-Partition League, formed in 1919 by an influential group of southern Unionists, following secession from the IRISH UNIONIST ALLIANCE, to seek a solution to the Irish demand for HOME RULE that would leave Unionists with a role in an independent Ireland. Meetings with ÉAMON DE VALERA and ARTHUR GRIFFITH confirmed the group's hopes. Opposed to the ANGLO-IRISH TREATY (1921), members were granted generous representation in the first Senate of the Free State, established in December 1922.

Unionist Clubs, founded by Lord Templetown to oppose the second HOME RULE BILL (1893). A central body, the Association of Unionist Clubs of Ireland, was later established in Belfast. Members formed a large proportion of the twelve thousand who attended a convention in Belfast, June 1893. Though the Home Rule Bill was defeated in the House of Lords, the Unionist Clubs remained vigilant on behalf of Ulster unionists. Represented on the ULSTER UNIONIST COUNCIL from 1905, their influence extended, in the words of the *News Letter* (Belfast), 3 March 1914, 'to the extreme of His Majesty's domain,' when it reported that a Vancouver affiliate of the clubs had declared: 'We will to the utmost limit support our brother loyalists in their resistance.'

Unionist Party. Organised unionism began in the south of Ireland with the founding of the IRISH LOYAL AND PATRIOTIC UNION, May 1885, known as the IRISH UNIONIST ALLIANCE from 1891. Eighteen Irish Unionists were returned in the general election of November 1885, sixteen of them representing Ulster constituencies. The Liberal Party returned to power in January 1886, aided by the IRISH PARTY, led by CHARLES STEWART PARNELL, the price for his support being the commitment of W. E. GLADSTONE to HOME RULE. This led to the formation of the ULSTER LOYALIST ANTI-REPEAL UNION, 8 January, and later that month of the Irish Unionist Party, pledged to support the Conservatives in opposition to the (first) HOME RULE BILL. The bill was defeated in June, and the Liberals lost the ensuing election in July, which returned nineteen Unionists, seventeen in Ulster constituencies.

The twenty-three Unionists (including four southern Unionists) successful in the 1892 general election organised resistance to Gladstone's (second) Home Rule Bill through the formation of UNIONIST CLUBS, January 1893. The bill passed the House of Commons but was defeated in the House of Lords. The Liberals lost the 1895 general election, in which twenty-one Unionists were returned, eighteen for Ulster constituencies. Unionist figures remained the same following the 1900 general election, in which the party was led by E. J. SAUNDERSON.

The ULSTER UNIONIST COUNCIL was formed in 1905 as a centre for northern opposition to home rule. The success of the Liberals in the 1906 general election led to the establishment of the Joint Committee of Unionist Associations, 1907. Saunderson was replaced as leader by WALTER LONG in 1906. Twenty-one Unionists were returned in the general election of January 1910, eighteen for Ulster constituencies. In February SIR EDWARD CARSON became leader. In the general election of December 1910 the Unionists lost two seats, one of them in Ulster. The PARLIAMENT ACT (1911) removed the House of Lords veto and substituted the power to delay legislation for a maximum of two years; this ensured the success of the (third) Home Rule Bill, introduced by Asquith in 1912.

Southern Unionists were now concerned to seek protection within a home rule framework, while the Ulster Unionists were determined to prevent home rule. At a demonstration at the home of James Craig in Co. Armagh, Unionists threatened open defiance of Asquith's policy and were publicly supported by the Conservative leader, ANDREW BONAR LAW, 23 September 1911. Two days later the Ulster Unionist Council prepared the establishment of an Ulster provisional government in the event of home rule.

The Ulster Unionists formed the ULSTER VOLUNTEER FORCE, January 1913. The CURRAGH INCIDENT, March 1914, alerted Asquith to the possibility that the British army in Ireland could not be relied on to act against Ulster if required to do so. Unionists were represented at the unsuccessful BUCKINGHAM PALACE CONFERENCE in July, when European considerations were occupying the government's attention. By agreement with Carson and Redmond, the Home Rule Act became law on 18 September 1914, accompanied by a suspensory act and a proviso that presented Parliament with a further opportunity to make separate provision for Ulster. Northern Unionists were determined to exclude the six north-eastern counties of Ulster from home rule.

The executions and mass arrests following the EASTER RISING (1916) hardened nationalist opinion, and full independence rather than home rule became the majority aspiration. SINN FÉIN, under the leadership of ÉAMON DE VALERA, became a mass movement. The IRISH CONVENTION (1917–18) was attended by the Unionists but was boycotted by Sinn Féin. The general election of December 1918 resulted in a sweeping victory for Sinn Féin (with seventy-three seats) and a crushing defeat for the Irish Party (six seats). Twenty-six Unionists were elected, twenty-three of them in Ulster. The SINN FÉIN representatives formed the first Dáil Éireann, 21 January 1919, and proclaimed an all-Ireland republic; the WAR OF INDEPENDENCE, waged by the IRA against Crown forces, started on the same day. The IRISH UNIONIST ALLIANCE split, allowing Lord Midleton and his supporters, mainly southern Unionists, to form the UNIONIST ANTI-PARTITION LEAGUE, representative in the main of southern Unionists. DAVID LLOYD GEORGE attempted to solve the 'Irish question' with the GOVERNMENT OF IRELAND ACT (1920) by creating two Irish states, Northern Ireland and Southern Ireland. Sinn Féin recognised only the all-Ireland assembly in Dublin, which claimed to legislate for the Irish Republic.

Through the Unionist Anti-Partition League the southern Unionists held discussions with de Valera in Dublin, 2–8 July 1921. A TRUCE in the War of Independence was reached, 11 July, and in October negotiations opened between the representatives of Dáil Éireann and the British government. During these negotiations, which resulted in the ANGLO-IRISH TREATY (6 December), the leader of the Irish delegation, ARTHUR GRIFFITH, met representatives of the southern Unionists, including Lord Midleton and Archbishop Bernard of Dublin, and discussed safeguards for the unionist population under home rule. Their requirements, which included a senate to protect their interests, were reported to de Valera. Lloyd George assured the southern Unionists that they would be protected in their property and religion and that they would have a voice in the IRISH FREE STATE. The ANTI-PARTITION LEAGUE was dissolved in early 1922, and the Irish Unionist Alliance wound up its affairs.

Southern Unionists were given generous representation in the Senate of the Free State, appointed in December 1922. The CIVIL WAR, however, revived Unionist fears, and they were the object of attacks on their persons and property by the anti-Treaty IRA. Many of them left the country; those who remained were allowed to pursue their interests unhindered. (See also ULSTER UNIONIST PARTY.)

Unionist Party of Northern Ireland, founded by BRIAN FAULKNER and former members of the ULSTER UNIONIST PARTY, 24 June 1974, following the collapse of the Assembly of Northern Ireland. It was formally launched in September, a further step in the fragmentation of the unionist movement. It held five of the seventy-eight seats in the Constitutional Convention (1975), where it pressed for a power-sharing (multi-party) administration with strong links to Britain. ANNE DICKSON succeeded Faulkner as leader in 1976. In the 1977 district council elections the party stood twenty-four candidates and won six seats. In the 1979 British parliamentary elections its three candidates lost their deposits. It made a negligible impact in the European Parliament election the same year. The UPNI was wound up following its abject showing in the 1981 district council elections.

United Ireland, a paper established by CHARLES STEWART PARNELL from the *Flag of Ireland* (bought from RICHARD PIGOTT), the first number appearing on 13 August 1881. Edited by WILLIAM O'BRIEN until 1890, it was the official organ of the LAND LEAGUE and of the IRISH PARTY. During O'Brien's imprisonment, October 1881, the paper was published by the LADIES' LAND LEAGUE. An article by Timothy Harrington headed 'A plan of campaign', 23 October 1886, heralded a new land agitation, the PLAN OF CAMPAIGN (1886–91).

United Ireland provoked a bitter dispute with the Catholic hierarchy for defending JOHN DILLON from an attack by EDWARD O'DWYER, Bishop of Limerick, who condemned the boycotting tactics of the plan, August 1890. Parnell seized control of the paper when O'Brien's deputy, Matthew Bodkin, criticised his continuing leadership of the party, 6 December 1890. Bodkin edited a substitute, *'Suppressed' United Ireland*, later *Insuppressible*, which ceased publication on 24 January 1891. *United Ireland* ceased publication in 1898.

CUMANN NA NGAEDHEAL published a paper called *United Ireland* in the early 1930s.

United Ireland Party, the original name of the party generally known as FINE GAEL, founded 8 September 1933 from an amalgamation of CUMANN NA NGAEDHEAL, the CENTRE PARTY, and the National Guard (BLUESHIRTS).

United Irish League, founded by WILLIAM O'BRIEN at Westport, Co. Mayo, 23 January 1898, as a response to the depressed condition of agriculture in the west. Its name commemorated the UNITED IRISHMEN, whose centenary was celebrated during the year. With MICHAEL DAVITT as president and under the slogan 'The land for the people,' it called for the redistribution of large estates among small farmers and attacked land-grabbers. It quickly gained support and by October had fifty-three branches, mainly in Co. Mayo. The league spread beyond Connacht and by April 1900 was claiming 462 branches, with more than sixty thousand members in twenty-five counties. Its paper, the IRISH PEOPLE, was edited by O'Brien, 1899–1908.

The rapid growth of the UIL alarmed the various factions of the IRISH PARTY, fragmented since the crisis over the leadership of CHARLES STEWART PARNELL, December 1890. Fearing a loss of the political initiative to O'Brien, JOHN DILLON and JOHN REDMOND reunited the party in 1900 and invited O'Brien to join them. Redmond then assumed the presidency of the UIL, which became the new constituency organisation of the Irish Party. By 1901 there were 100,000 members, and Redmond carried the League to the United States (despite opposition from JOHN DEVOY and CLAN NA GAEL).

The league lost much of its influence and support in 1914 when Redmond called on the IRISH VOLUNTEERS to aid Britain's war effort. Four years later it was destroyed outside Ulster when SINN FÉIN annihilated the Irish Party at the polls. It closed its Dublin office in 1920 but continued to operate until 1928 in Ulster, where it was the organisation of JOSEPH DEVLIN.

United Irishman, a paper founded on 12 February 1848 by JOHN MITCHEL following his break with the *Nation* and the principal organ for advanced republican views. Despite its price of 2 shillings, it sold 5,000 copies on its first day of issue. Mitchel, influenced by JAMES FINTAN LALOR on the land issue, sought an armed insurrection and called on tenant-farmers, suffering from the GREAT FAMINE (1845–49), to withhold the payment of rent and Poor Law rate, to boycott those who did pay, and to withhold the harvest. He published instructions on street warfare. The paper was suppressed in May 1848, and Mitchel was tried and transported for fourteen years.

ARTHUR GRIFFITH, who had been deeply influenced by Mitchel, revived the title *United Irishman* for his own weekly paper, 1899–1906. First issued on 4 March 1899, it became the organ of CUMANN NA NGAEDHEAL, advocating self-government; contributors included W. B. YEATS and GEORGE RUSSELL. Griffith's series of articles 'The resurrection of Hungary' was published in the *United Irishman* during 1904. Two years later he replaced the paper with *Sinn Féin.*

The *United Irishman* was also the title of the monthly paper of the IRA and Sinn Féin from 1948; by 1957 its circulation was believed to be 120,000. Following the split in the republican movement, January 1970, it became the organ of the 'Official' IRA and Sinn Féin but ceased publication during the 1970s.

United Irishmen. The Society of United Irishmen was founded in Belfast on 18 October 1791 by a group of young radicals, including Hamilton Rowan, Thomas Russell, Samuel Neilson, and Theobald Wolfe Tone, and in Dublin on 9 November, when James Napper Tandy was among the founder-members. Smaller clubs were founded in other centres. The movement attracted support at first from Ulster Presbyterians and from Protestants and liberals seeking parliamentary reform. Others, including Tone, inspired by the French Revolution, sought to establish a republic. When the government moved to suppress it, May 1794, the movement went underground; reconstituted in 1795 as a secret, oath-bound society dedicated to the establishment of a republic, it took root among rural Catholics. The repressive measures undertaken by Lieutenant-General Gerard Lake drove the society into revolt in 1798. The rising was suppressed with great savagery and the movement destroyed. The government, alarmed by the rising, set about implementing the legislative union of the Irish and English parliaments (see ACT OF UNION). The unsuccessful attempt by ROBERT EMMET to organise a rising in 1803 spelt the death of the movement.

The ideals of Wolfe Tone and the United Irishmen continued to be a potent force. They influenced THOMAS DAVIS, JOHN MITCHEL, the IRB, and JAMES CONNOLLY. The CENTENARY CELEBRATIONS in 1898, organised by the IRB, became a rallying-point for all shades of nationalist opinion.

United Irishwomen, the women's branch of the co-operative movement, founded in 1910 by SIR HORACE PLUNKETT and Ellice Pilkington. It became the IRISH COUNTRYWOMEN'S ASSOCIATION (ICA) in 1934.

United Kingdom Unionist Party, founded in 1996 by ROBERT MCCARTNEY, a former member of the ULSTER UNIONIST PARTY. It won three seats in the elections to the Northern Ireland Forum in 1996 (McCartney, Cedric Walker, and DR CONOR CRUISE O'BRIEN). It accused the UUP leader DAVID TRIMBLE of 'selling out the Union' for accepting GEORGE MITCHELL as chairman of the multi-party talks that led to the BELFAST AGREEMENT (1998). It withdrew from the talks in July and then returned in September, when it tried to have the ULSTER DEMOCRATIC PARTY and PROGRESSIVE UNIONIST PARTY ejected over threats by the UVF to the dissident BILLY WRIGHT. In January 1997 SIR PATRICK MAYHEW rejected demands by the UKUP for the expulsion of other loyalist parties. In June the party again withdrew while the government held talks with SINN FÉIN. Opposed to the Belfast Agreement, the UKUP won five seats in the post-agreement Assembly. During December there was a rift within the party over an exit strategy from the talks if Sinn Féin took seats in the Executive. McCartney was opposed by his four colleagues; in their absence he called a meeting at which their 'position and privileges' were removed. The expelled members then formed the Northern Ireland Unionist Party, leaving the founder of the UKUP as the sole representative in the Assembly.

United Labour Party, launched in 1978 with the aim of establishing a government in Northern Ireland based on democratic socialism; founder-members included the veteran republican socialist PADDY DEVLIN. The party advocated co-operation between labour movements throughout Ireland and Britain. Devlin was unsuccessful in the 1979 European Parliament election, with 6,000 first-preference votes. The party's candidate in the South Belfast by-election for the British House of Commons, 4 March 1982, Brian Patrick Caul, came sixth, with 303 votes. The ULP was later absorbed into LABOUR '87.

United Nations and Ireland. Under its Charter (26 June 1945) the United Nations is determined 'to save succeeding generations from the scourge of war . . . and to reaffirm faith in fundamental human rights . . . and to promote social progress and better standards of life in larger freedom.' Ireland's application for membership was consistently opposed by the Soviet Union, on the grounds that it had contributed no assistance to the Allies in the Second World War. ÉAMON DE VALERA retorted that the Soviet Union had supported Germany in the early years of the war and that its attacks on the Baltic states and Poland were not compatible with membership of a peace-loving organisation; he also cited Sweden's neutrality during the war.

Ireland became a member, with fourteen other countries, on 14 December 1955. Irish policy in relation to the United Nations, as laid down by the Minister for External Affairs, LIAM COSGRAVE, was an independent stance, so as not to be 'associated with particular blocs or groups so far as possible,' while at the same time pledging support for 'those powers which were dedicated to preserving freedom from communism.'

The first Irish delegation, led by F. H. BOLAND, later president of the General Assembly, took its place in 1956. FRANK AIKEN, Minister for External Affairs, 1957–69, was unsuccessful in efforts to secure agreement on the non-proliferation of nuclear arms. He repeatedly argued for the admission of the People's Republic of China, though when it was finally admitted, in 1961, Ireland opposed it. In 1961 DR CONOR CRUISE O'BRIEN, a member of the Irish delegation, was chosen to represent the secretary-general, Dag Hammarskjöld, in the breakaway Congolese province of Katanga.

Irish soldiers have served in UN peacekeeping missions throughout the world. Nine Irish soldiers were killed in an ambush at Niemba in the Congo, 8 November 1960. SEÁN MACBRIDE was UN Commissioner in Namibia until 1977. MARY ROBINSON resigned as President of Ireland in 1997 to become UN Commissioner for Human Rights. Following an intensive lobbying campaign, Ireland became a member of the Security Council in January 2001.

United Trades Association, formed in 1863 from the amalgamation of thirty Dublin trade unions. Seeking to protect labour and to encourage native manufactures, it did not propose 'to interfere with the legitimate progress of trade' but rather 'to push trade in every manner possible.' Unsuccessful in its attempt to form a federated Irish trade union alliance, 1864, it joined the (British) Trades Union Congress soon after that body was established in 1868. The IRISH TRADE UNION CONGRESS was founded in 1894.

United Ulster Unionist Council, also known as the Loyalist Coalition, founded in January 1974 to oppose the SUNNINGDALE AGREEMENT and to bring down the power-sharing Executive and Assembly of Northern Ireland. Parties represented on the council were the Official Unionist Party, led by HARRY WEST, the Democratic Unionist Party, led by REV. IAN PAISLEY, and the Vanguard Unionist Party, led by WILIAM CRAIG. Supported by loyalist paramilitary groups, the UUUC co-operated with the ULSTER WORKERS' COUNCIL in organising a strike that brought down the Assembly. The coalition won 47 out of 78 seats in the election to the Convention to draft a constitution for Northern Ireland, 1 May 1975. Craig, hitherto one of the most hard-line loyalists, suggested that loyalists might form an emergency coalition with the SDLP if devolved government returned to Northern Ireland. The rejection of this proposal (37 to 1) led to Craig's expulsion from the coalition, 23 October.

The coalition's report for the consideration of the Convention condemned the SDLP and demanded 'majority rule' (i.e. no power-sharing) through a Westminster-style parliament in Northern Ireland. Though this stand was rejected by other parties, the UUUC report was accepted in the Convention (42 to 31). The British government then rejected it but extended the life of the Convention to 7 May 1976. The coalition disintegrated following the unsuccessful attempt to organise another loyalist strike in 1977.

United Ulster Unionist Movement, formed in 1975 by members of the Vanguard Unionist Progressive Party (see ULSTER VANGUARD) following the expulsion of WILLIAM CRAIG from the UNITED ULSTER UNIONIST COUNCIL. Led by Ernest Baird, it campaigned for a united Unionist Party; when this proved unattainable, Baird announced that the UUUM would become the United Ulster Unionist Party. The party secured twelve seats in the district council elections of May 1977. John Dunlop, who had been Vanguard member of Parliament for mid-Ulster, held the seat for the UUUP in the British parliamentary elections, 3 May 1979, when he was not opposed by the Official Unionist Party. Baird came fourth in Fermanagh-South Tyrone. The party won five of the seven seats it contested in the 1981 district council elections. A year later all twelve candidates failed in the Assembly elections. Some of the more prominent members, including Reg Empey, were later active in the ULSTER UNIONIST PARTY.

United Unionist Action Council, a coalition that promoted the unsuccessful loyalist strike of 1977. Leading figures included REV. IAN PAISLEY and Ernest Baird. It organised vigilante patrols under the name of the Ulster Service Corps. It was in effect a sub-committee of the Steering Committee of the UNITED ULSTER UNIONIST COUNCIL.

United Unionists, a coalition formed to oppose the BELFAST AGREEMENT (1998), supported by the DEMOCRATIC UNIONIST PARTY, UNITED KINGDOM UNIONIST PARTY, and dissident elements within the ULSTER UNIONIST PARTY. It campaigned unsuccessfully for a 'no' vote in the referendum on the agreement in May and won three seats in the June elections (East Londonderry, North Belfast, and Upper Bann). In September it launched the United Unionists Assembly Party, led by Denis Watson.

Unity Movement, an anti-Unionist group formed in April 1973 by Frank McManus MP (Fermanagh-South Tyrone). In May it issued a manifesto calling for an amnesty for all political prisoners, the disbanding of the RUC and its replacement with a new force acceptable to the nationalist community, and the repeal of 'offensive and repressive' legislation. McManus lost his seat in the general election of February 1974, and the second Unity candidate came last, with 1,364 votes, in Co. Armagh. Frank Maguire took a seat for Unity in Fermanagh-South Tyrone in November 1974. In 1977 McManus was a joint founder of the IRISH INDEPENDENCE PARTY.

Unity Proposals (May 1922), an attempt by officers of the IRA to bridge the gap between the pro-Treaty and anti-Treaty factions. (See ANGLO-IRISH TREATY.) The proposals read:

> We, the undersigned officers of the IRA, realising the gravity of the present situation in Ireland, and appreciating the fact that if the present drift is maintained a conflict of comrades is inevitable, declare that this would be the greatest calamity in Irish history, and would leave Ireland broken for generations.
>
> To avert this catastrophe we believe that a closing of the ranks all round is necessary.
>
> We suggest to all leaders, army and polit-

ical, and all citizens and soldiers of Ireland the advisability of a unification of forces on the basis of acceptance and utilisation of our present national position in the best interests of Ireland; and we require that nothing shall be done which would prejudice our position or dissipate our strength. We feel that on this basis alone can the situation best be faced, viz:

(1) The acceptance of that fact—admitted by all sides—that the majority of the people of Ireland are willing to accept the Treaty.

(2) An agreed election with a view to

(3) Forming a government which will have the confidence of the whole country.

(4) Army unification on above basis.

Signed

Tom Hales, S. O'Hegarty, Seán Moylan, Eoin O'Duffy, Micheál Ó Coileáin [Michael Collins], Dan Breen, H. Murphy, F. O'Donoghue, R. J. Mulcahy, Gearóid O'Sullivan.

University of Ulster, formed in 1984 from a merger of the Northern Ireland Polytechnic (formerly the ULSTER COLLEGE) and the new UNIVERSITY OF ULSTER, the largest university in Northern Ireland, with colleges at Belfast, Coleraine, Derry (MAGEE COLLEGE), and Jordanstown. The merger was overseen by Derek Birley (1926–2002), who became the first vice-chancellor of the university.

V

vaccination, introduced to Ireland in 1800, when JOHN MILNER BARRY used it in his native Cork. In the same year the Dispensary for Infant Poor, Exchequer Street, Dublin, vaccinated more than nine thousand children against smallpox.

Vesey-Fitzgerald, William (1783–1843), landowner and politician (Conservative); born in Ennis, Co. Clare; educated at the University of Oxford. Member of Parliament for Ennis, 1808–12, 1813–18, and 1831–32, and for Co. Clare, 1818–28; after serving as Lord of the Irish Treasury and Privy Councillor, 1810, and English Privy Councillor, 1812, he was envoy extraordinary to Sweden, 1820–23, and Paymaster-General of the Forces, 1826. On appointment as President of the Board of Trade, 1828, he had to seek re-election to his Co. Clare seat. Though his sympathies were with CATHOLIC EMANCIPATION and he was a popular landlord, the CATHOLIC ASSOCIATION put DANIEL O'CONNELL forward to contest Co. Clare. O'Connell's victory (2,057 to 982), 5 July 1828, marked the closing stage of the struggle for emancipation, which was granted a year later. The government found Vesey-Fitzgerald another seat (Newport, Cornwall); he was re-elected for Ennis, 11 May 1831. Sir Robert Peel made him Baron Fitzgerald of Desmond and Clan Gibbon, 1835.

veto. As an accompaniment to CATHOLIC EMANCIPATION, a veto by the Crown on the appointment of Catholic bishops and archbishops was mooted. In return, the state would provide for the payment of Catholic clergymen. At a meeting in Maynooth, January 1799, acceptance of the veto was favoured by the four archbishops, including JOHN THOMAS TROY, Archbishop of Dublin, and six bishops, who hoped that Catholic Emancipation would accompany the Union. After the Union, however, KING GEORGE III extracted from WILLIAM PITT a promise that Emancipation would not be raised. The controversy over the veto continued for more than two decades.

Sir John Cox Hippisley raised the issue of the veto in 1805, and three years later it had the support of the Whigs when HENRY GRATTAN introduced a Catholic Relief Bill that included it. It had clerical support in the early stages, but later in the year the bishops rejected it. While Emancipation accompanied by the veto had support from the aristocratic and propertied elements on the CATHOLIC COMMITTEE, a strong opposition was led by DANIEL O'CONNELL. He had clerical and episcopal support in rejecting the veto when it was again raised in 1810. Grattan introduced another bill in 1813, this time without the veto. When VISCOUNT CASTLEREAGH attempted to amend it to include securities, Grattan rejected it. The bill, in any event, was lost.

The battle between the aristocratic leadership of the movement for Emancipation and the populists led by O'Connell reached a crisis in 1814 when the vice-prefect of the Congregation for the Propagation of the Faith, Monsignor Quarantotti, supported by Pope Pius VII, issued a rescript (decree) favouring the veto. The rescript was denounced by the bishops and O'Connell and led to the rout of the aristocratic leadership of the emancipationists. The Pope announced his acceptance of the veto, 1815; in February 1816 he pointed out to the Irish bishops that he was acting in accordance with established custom in not appointing bishops who were 'displeasing to the powers under whom the dioceses to be administered were situated.' A Relief Bill introduced by Sir Francis Burdett, supported by O'Connell, 1825, included two 'wings' instead of the old veto: state payment of the clergy, and the disfranchisement of the FORTY-SHILLING FREEHOLDERS. The bill was lost in the House of Lords. Catholic Emancipation was granted, without the veto, in 1829.

Victoria, Queen (1819–1901), Queen of the United Kingdom of Great Britain and Ireland, 1837–1901. Distressed by the agitation of DANIEL O'CONNELL and the REPEAL ASSOCIATION, she encouraged SIR ROBERT PEEL on the Maynooth Grant, 1845 (see MAYNOOTH), and also supported him on the repeal of the Corn Laws. Though she contributed £2,000 to the BRITISH ASSOCIATION FOR THE RELIEF OF EXTREME DISTRESS during the GREAT FAMINE (1845–49), she became known to generations of nationalists as the 'Famine Queen'. Shortly after William Hamilton of Adare, Co. Limerick, fired a blank charge at her carriage in London, 19 May 1849, she paid her first visit to Ireland. Her party arrived at Cóbh, Co. Cork (renamed Queenstown in August). After travelling by yacht to Kingstown (Dún Laoghaire) she spent four days at the Viceregal Lodge in the Phoenix Park. She was enthusiastically received during her visit; before moving to Belfast she created her eldest son Earl of Dublin, 10 September, and gave the name Patrick to her third son, Prince Arthur, 22 June 1850. Returning to Ireland in August, she opened the DUBLIN EXHIBITION (1853); the organiser of the exhibition, WILLIAM DARGAN, declined her offer of a knighthood. She made a third visit to Ireland in August 1858.

She considered W. E. GLADSTONE a dangerous radical (she said of him that he addressed her as though she were a public meeting) and opposed his DISESTABLISHMENT of the Church of Ireland. She rejected his suggestion that the office of Lord Lieutenant of Ireland should he abolished and replaced by the Prince of Wales (the monarch's eldest son) in permanent residence in Dublin. She was profoundly affected by the death of her husband, Prince Albert of Saxe-Coburg-Gotha, 1861, after which she became a virtual recluse, to the point where her absence from the public eye led to temporary unpopularity.

She urged strong government for Ireland during the LAND WAR, encouraging W. E. FORSTER to break the LAND LEAGUE. Forster and the Queen both disapproved of the 'KILMAINHAM TREATY' (1882). She held a poor opinion of CHARLES STEWART PARNELL and the IRISH PARTY, calling its members 'low, disreputable men, who were elected by order of Parnell.' She opposed HOME RULE for Ireland, on the grounds that to break the Union would be repugnant to her Coronation Oath. Having celebrated her diamond jubilee, 1897, she again visited Ireland, 4–25 April 1900, when, despite protests organised by MAUD GONNE and JAMES CONNOLLY, she was well received.

vigilance committees, established in Limerick and then in other towns as a result of a lecture to the Catholic Truth Society by the English Catholic writer Canon William Barry as part of a Crusade Against Evil Literature, 1911. The committees gradually faded away until by 1918 only two survived (Dublin and Limerick). They were revived after the War of Independence and played a leading role in the agitation for the CENSORSHIP OF PUBLICATIONS ACT (1929).

vocational education. The Vocational Education Act (1930) reorganised technical education, providing instruction at a low cost for pupils whose needs were not catered for in the existing secondary education system. This form of education had been the responsibility of the Technical Instruction Section of the Department of Agriculture and Technical Instruction since 1899. Vocational education was designed for 'trades, manufactures, commerce and other industrial pursuits.' Apprenticeship courses were offered, some leading to professional qualifications, and much of the teaching was through night classes. The system was largely geared to the needs of a rural community. The vocational schools were financed from central funds and local rates. Co-educational and non-denominational, they were administered by thirty-eight vocational education committees, whose purpose was to oversee the provision of continuing education, to 'supplement education provided in elementary schools,' and to include general and practical training in preparation for employment. Membership of the VECs was selected by local authorities to be representative of commercial, industrial, educational and cultural interests; eight of the fourteen seats on each committee were to be filled by the local authority.

The distinction that obtained between secondary and vocational schools was broken to a large extent when the latter offered Intermediate and Leaving Certificate courses from 1967.

Voice of Labour, an organ of the LABOUR PARTY and trade union movement, published from October 1922 until 1927 and edited by CATHAL O'SHANNON. It was succeeded by the *Irishman*, 1927–30, and the *Watchword of Labour*, 1930–32.

Voluntary Health Insurance (VHI) Board, established under the Voluntary Health Insurance Act (1957) as a statutory corporation to operate various voluntary health insurance schemes.

Volunteer Political Party, founded in April 1974 by Kenneth Gibson as the political wing of the ULSTER VOLUNTEER FORCE. It sought to continue links with Britain, claiming that any weakening of the Union would be reflected in higher taxes and lower social welfare benefits. Gibson secured 2,690 votes (6 per cent of the vote) when he contested West Belfast in the British parliamentary election of October 1974. In the same month the UVF was again proscribed, and the VPP disappeared.

W

Wages Standstill Order (1941), a government order introduced in May 1941 in an effort to protect the economy. The order, steered through Dáil Éireann by SEÁN LEMASS, prevented trade unions from striking for higher wages by removing legal protection for strike action. Strongly resisted by JAMES LARKIN, the order was repealed in 1946.

wake, the custom of keeping a body in the family home until its removal to the church. Female neighbours usually laid out the body, clothing it in a habit, placing a crucifix on the breast, and entwining rosary beads in the fingers; in some areas it was customary to place a prayer book or Bible under the chin. Candles were lit near the body, and the relatives were led formally into the presence. A KEEN or lament was then performed. The chief mourners provided food, drink, snuff and pipes. Visitors prayed silently by the body before sympathising with the relatives. Drink was freely available and sometimes (particularly if the deceased was aged) dancing and merrymaking, including the playing of special 'wake games'. Some of these were of pre-Christian origin and had sexual undertones; it was said that in rural Ireland 'many a wedding was made at a wake.'

The Catholic Church on numerous occasions condemned the custom of drinking at wakes. By decree of the Synod of Dublin (July 1831) priests were ordered to forbid their congregations to provide tobacco at wakes or to spend money on anything that would lead people to commit sin. The Synod of Ardagh (1835) condemned the custom of making alcoholic drinks available at wakes and funerals, as did the Synod of Maynooth (1875), which described it as a 'disgrace to Christian communities.' Bishops were exhorted to penalise those found guilty of such misbehaviour. It was not unknown for a family to become impoverished as a result of expenses incurred in a wake. Wakes in the west of Ireland were known to last for a week, provoking Mary Little to comment that 'the sleep which knows no waking is always followed by a wake which knows no sleeping.'

Walker, William (1870–1918), trade unionist; born in Belfast, educated at St George's National School. A union organiser at the Harland and Wolff shipyard, he was a delegate to the first IRISH TRADE UNION CONGRESS, 1894, of which he was appointed secretary. As a full-time official of the Textile Operatives' Society of Ireland he was recognised as the most important labour leader in Ireland, but his support for unionism kindled a bitter feud with JAMES CONNOLLY. A prominent member of the British Labour Party, he failed in three attempts to gain a Belfast parliamentary seat, 1905–07. He lost much support and influence following his appointment as a national insurance inspector, 1911. His pamphlet *The Irish Question* (1908) stated his belief that HOME RULE would hamper economic progress.

Walkerites, followers of the Church of God, a fundamentalist sect founded by Rev. John Walker (1768–1833), who broke from the Church of Ireland in 1804.

Walsh, Edward (1805–1850), folklorist and language activist; born in Derry, educated chiefly at a hedge school in Millstreet, Co. Cork. He worked as a tutor, a hedge schoolmaster and national school teacher and was briefly imprisoned for participating in the TITHES agitation. He lost his teaching post at Glounthane, Co. Cork, for publishing 'What is Repeal, Papa?' in the *Nation*; through his friend CHARLES GAVAN DUFFY he found a post as subeditor on the *Dublin Monitor*. In Dublin he met the poet, bookseller and publisher John O'Daly (1800–1878), who arranged the publication of Walsh's *Reliques of Irish Jacobite Poetry* (1844) in weekly parts. Returning to Cork, he worked as a schoolmaster at the convict settlement on Spike Island, where, in November 1848, he met JOHN MITCHEL and lost his job for associating with him. He spent his last days as a schoolteacher in the Cork workhouse. As a folklorist Walsh is considered second only to T. CROFTON CROKER, while his lyrical gift earned him the admiration of W. B. YEATS. His *Irish Popular Songs, Translated with Notes* was published in 1847.

Walsh, William Joseph (1841–1921), bishop (Catholic); born in Dublin, educated at the Catholic University and St Patrick's College, Maynooth. He was professor of dogmatic and moral theology at Maynooth, 1867–78, vice-president, 1878–80, and president from 1880 until his appointment as Archbishop of Dublin, 1885, an appointment opposed by the British government. A member of the Senate of the ROYAL UNIVERSITY OF IRELAND, 1883–84, he pressed for a Catholic system of national, intermediate and university education.

Walsh supported the PLAN OF CAMPAIGN. When the crisis arose over Parnell's involvement in the O'Shea divorce case, November–December 1890, he played a leading role in restraining his fellow-bishops from becoming immediately embroiled in the leadership crisis within the IRISH PARTY. He remained publicly aloof from the leadership struggle until 3 December, when he sent a telegram to the party calling on it to 'act manfully.' Later that day the Standing Committee of the Catholic bishops recommended that the Irish people reject Parnell's continuing leadership; three days later the party split on the issue.

During the 1890s Walsh was closely connected with the controversy over 'bimetallism' (the policy that silver should be used as well as gold as a monetary standard), on which he was an authority; he published *Bimetallism and Monometallism* (1893), which was translated into German and French. He supported SINN FÉIN and opposed the GOVERNMENT OF IRELAND ACT (1920), which partitioned the country. A member of several charitable and educational bodies, he was a member of the Senate of the National University of Ireland, of which he became the first chancellor, 1908.

He was a prolific writer; his works include *A Plain Exposition of the Land Act of 1881* (1881), *The Queen's Colleges and the Royal University* (1883 and 1884), *Addresses on Irish Education* (1890), *Statement of the Chief Grievances of Irish Catholics in the Matter of Education* (1890), *The Irish University Question* (1897), *Trinity College and the University of Dublin* (1902), and *The Irish University Question: Trinity College and its Medical School* (1906)

Walton, Ernest (1903–1995), scientist; born in Dungarvan, Co. Waterford, educated at Methodist College, Belfast, and TCD. He worked for his doctorate, 1931, under Ernest Rutherford at Cambridge and stayed on in the Cavendish Laboratory as Clerk Maxwell scholar. With John Cockcroft he performed a crucial experiment on 14 April 1932, the transmutation of an element by artificial means, the first experimental splitting of the atomic nucleus, for which they were awarded the Nobel Prize for Physics, 1951. He returned to Trinity College, Dublin, shortly after the epoch-making experiment, working there until his retirement, as a fellow from 1934 and as Erasmus Smith professor of natural and experimental philosophy, 1946–74. He was chairman of the School of Cosmic Physics at the DUBLIN INSTITUTE OF ADVANCED STUDIES from 1952 and a supporter of the Pugwash movement (international scientists' group for peace).

Ward's Island, a part of the city of New York developed as a quarantine station in the early 1840s. Covering 225 acres on the East River, it became an ancillary centre to STATEN ISLAND in the period 1846–47, intended to cater for convalescents, the old, orphans, and those suffering from non-infectious complaints. Six unpaid interns worked at the hospital complex, supervised by six visiting New York physicians and surgeons. Like GROSSE ÎLE, Ward's Island was wholly unprepared for the influx of thousands of Irish emigrants brought by the GREAT FAMINE (1845–49). Testifying before a committee of the New York Assembly of Doctors in 1852, Dr John Grissom, who had worked at the island's hospitals, described the complex as a 'dreadful place' and said that the shanties on the island were filthy. A colleague, Dr Emmet, stated that he had on occasion put as many as five patients into three beds, and fever patients had sometimes to sleep on the floor. Dr Alexander Hosack submitted that many patients were in a worse condition on discharge than on arrival. After a snowstorm he had observed beds—in which people were dying of typhus—covered with snow because of badly fitting windows. He noted that 'the meat, when landed, was frequently thrown into dirt carts, and when delivered to the cook was found covered with dirt and horse manure.' (See also POINTE SAINT-CHARLES.)

War of Independence (1919–21). The ambush of an RIC party at Soloheadbeg, Co. Tipperary, 21 January 1919, is often taken to be the first important co-ordinated action of the War of Independence. As the ambush was taking place, 21 January 1919, SINN FÉIN members returned in the general election of December 1918 constituted themselves the first DÁIL ÉIREANN, through which they proclaimed the Irish Republic and issued the DECLARATION OF INDEPENDENCE. Before this there had been isolated attacks on the ROYAL IRISH CONSTABULARY, notably the abortive attempt on the RIC barracks at Gortatlea, Co. Kerry, when two members of the IRISH VOLUNTEERS (John Browne and Richard Laide) were killed; but following Soloheadbeg, the attacks against Crown forces intensified.

As the year progressed, small bands of Volunteers made lightning raids against the RIC and against banks, post offices, and tax offices. Squads of soldiers and police were ambushed, and the attackers then faded into the rural background, where they were protected in 'safe houses'. Volunteer leaders, including FRANK AIKEN, TOM BARRY, LIAM LYNCH, SEÁN MAC EOIN, and ERNIE O'MALLEY, became folk heroes as an estimated two thousand Volunteers took part in the struggle against fifty thousand soldiers and policemen by 1921. The Volunteers came to be called the IRISH REPUBLICAN ARMY after taking an oath of allegiance to Dáil Éireann, August 1919. Their actions were condemned by the British Prime Minister, DAVID LLOYD GEORGE. While the Dáil's Minister for Defence was CATHAL BRUGHA, it was his colleague MICHAEL COLLINS who, as director of intelligence, enjoyed the confidence of the IRA.

The British government's attempt to solve the 'Irish problem' through the GOVERNMENT OF IRELAND ACT (1920) was ignored in the south during the war but led to the establishment of the six-county state of NORTHERN IRELAND, 1921. Lloyd George refused to recognise the existence of a war between Ireland and Britain, though he was increasingly embarrassed by the financial and military demands made by the struggle. The policy of reprisals adopted by the RIC and its reinforcements, the AUXILIARIES and BLACK AND TANS, after the summer of 1920 led to questions in the House of Commons and to calls on the government by the British press for a solution to the 'Irish question'.

DÁIL COURTS and ARBITRATION COURTS took over from Crown courts. As these courts spread, the IRA acted as a police force, and British law ceased to operate in parts of the country. The IRA inflicted a further blow to the British administration in Ireland when it raided and destroyed tax offices around the country, 3–4 April 1920; no further taxes were collected until 1923, after the establishment of the IRISH FREE STATE. Sir Henry Grattan Bellew, a magistrate and Deputy Lord Lieutenant of Co. Galway, together with 148 other magistrates, resigned in August 1920 when civil law was subordinated to military law. The IRA strengthened its hold over the population as police and military counter-measures alienated the civilian population. ARTHUR GRIFFITH estimated that between 1 January 1919 and 31 July 1920 there had been 38,720 armed raids on private houses, 1,604 armed assaults, 102 sackings and shootings in towns, and 77 murders, including those of children, by Crown forces.

The IRA used hunger strikes as a weapon to focus attention on Ireland when prisoners in Mountjoy Jail, Dublin, refused food, 5 April 1920; they were released within ten days following calls for a general strike by the IRISH TRADE UNION CONGRESS. Later in the year the hunger strike became a deadly weapon and emphasised the Irish demand for independence when TERENCE MACSWINEY died in Brixton Prison, London, 25 October 1920, having survived for seventy-four days without food.

Crown forces rampaged through the countryside; the IRA burned loyalist houses. The Catholic hierarchy condemned the violence. While individual bishops such as MICHAEL FOGARTY of Killaloe (himself the victim of an attempt on his life by the police) showed sympathy for Dáil Éireann and the republican cause, the hierarchy as a body never granted formal recognition to the struggle for independence. A plot to murder Arthur Griffith, uncovered by an agent of Collins in early October, set in train the events that resulted in BLOODY SUNDAY (21 November 1920). The RIC suffered heavy losses: 165 killed and some 251 wounded during 1920. There were mass resignations, resulting in an increased role for the Black and Tans and Auxiliaries.

As atrocities on both sides mounted there were attempts to secure a peace in the second half of 1920, in which the Assistant Under-Secretary for Ireland, SIR ALFRED COPE, played a leading role. Other attempts were made by the Archbishop of Perth, Patrick Clune, who came to Ireland to attend the funeral of his nephew, CONOR CLUNE, murdered in prison on Bloody Sunday. Testing the Irish attitude towards peace negotiations, Clune failed to make any progress, as the IRA refused to lay down arms as a preliminary to talks. ÉAMON DE VALERA, President of Dáil Éireann, having returned from the United States, December 1920, secured permission from the Dáil to announce a formal 'state of war with England', 11 March 1921. This announcement demonstrated that the Dáil was now assuming responsibility for the actions of the IRA, while also showing a determination to press ahead with the struggle. Meanwhile the British press intensified its attacks on the government's failure to find a solution.

A new initiative presented itself when KING GEORGE V, opening the PARLIAMENT OF NORTHERN IRELAND, 22 June 1921, pleaded for an end to the war. The diplomatic manoeuvring that followed was conducted by de Valera, Lloyd George, Sir James Craig (see VISCOUNT CRAIGAVON), Lord Midleton, General Jan Smuts, and Cope. Following de Valera's response to Lloyd George's invitation to London, details of a TRUCE were worked out between GENERAL SIR NEVIL MACREADY and the IRA, 8 July 1921; it came into force on 11 July 1921 and, though an uneasy peace, held until Dáil Éireann sent a team of plenipotentiaries, headed by Griffith and Collins, to London in October. The ANGLO-IRISH TREATY, under which the 26-county state became the IRISH FREE STATE, with 'dominion status' within the British Commonwealth, was signed on 6 December 1921.

The following incidents illustrate the nature of the struggle.

Soloheadbeg, Co. Tipperary, 21 January 1919. Members of the South Tipperary Brigade of the IRA, commanded by Séamus Robinson and including DAN BREEN and SEÁN TREACY, ambushed an RIC gelignite patrol near Soloheadbeg Quarry. Following a brief encounter, during which Constables MacDonnell and O'Connell were killed, the attackers made off with three boxes of gelignite, some rifles, a carbine, and a small quantity of ammunition.

Knocklong, Co. Limerick, 13 May 1919. Sections of the 3rd Tipperary Brigade, led by Dan Breen and Seán Treacy, rescued Volunteer Seán Hogan, a prisoner under escort, from the Cork–Dublin train. During the rescue attempt two RIC men (Sergeant Peter Wallace and Constable Enright) were killed and another (Constable Reilly) wounded. Both Breen and Treacy were seriously wounded. On 7 June 1921 Edward Foley and Patrick Maher were hanged on charges arising from the rescue, though Maher had not been present and Foley, though present, was said to be unarmed.

Fermoy, Co. Cork, 7 September 1919. Under the command of Liam Lynch, a party of twenty-five Volunteers surrounded soldiers of the King's Shropshire Light Infantry on parade at the Wesleyan Church and fired on them when they refused to surrender their arms. One soldier was killed and two others wounded. The IRA unit seized all the weapons and escaped unharmed. This first killing of a British soldier in Ireland provoked the first reprisal when the town was subjected to looting and burnings and the indiscriminate discharge of weapons.

Bantry Bay, Co. Cork, 17 November 1919. A party of the 5th (Bantry) Battalion of Cork No. 3 (West) Brigade, commanded by Maurice Donegan, raided a British motor torpedo boat and made away with six rifles, ten pistols, and a quantity of ammunition.

Carrigtwohill, Co. Cork, 2 January 1920. Under the general command of Michael Leahy, vice-commandant of Cork No. 1 Brigade, members of the Cóbh Company under Dáithí O'Brien and the Midleton Company commanded by Diarmuid Hurley attacked Carrigtwohill RIC Barracks. The RIC surrendered when the gable end of the building was breached; no casualties were recorded. The attacking party took possession of all station records, carbines, shotguns, grenades, and a large quantity of ammunition. Carrigtwohill was the first RIC barracks to be captured during the War of Independence, resulting in the closure of a large number of smaller posts and the concentration of garrisons in towns and larger villages.

Drumbane, Co. Tipperary, 18 January 1920. Using gelignite captured at Soloheadbeg, members of the 2nd Tipperary Brigade attacked a local hall that was in use as an RIC barracks. The attack was repulsed, but the building was extensively damaged and ceased to function as a barracks.

Shantonagh, Co. Monaghan, 15 February 1920. Members of the Monaghan Brigade under EOIN O'DUFFY and Ernie O'Malley destroyed the RIC barracks. Several arrests were made, but following a hunger strike organised by O'Duffy all prisoners were released and taken to hospital.

Mile Bush, Midleton, Co. Cork, 5 June 1920. Eight members of the Midleton Company, Cork No. 1 Brigade, under Diarmuid Hurley disarmed a cycle patrol of twelve Cameron Highlanders and an RIC constable. The IRA unit had set up a bowls game and disarmed the patrol, without casualty, as they cycled through the players. Midleton was the scene of a reprisal by British soldiers later that day.

Rear Cross, Co. Tipperary, 11 July 1920. The last RIC outpost of consequence in the area was attacked by units of three Tipperary brigades, assisted by a unit of the East Limerick Brigade. In the fighting, described by Dan Breen as 'a desperate battle,' Sergeant O'Sullivan was killed and several constables wounded. Breen, Seán Treacy and Jim Gorman of the attacking party were also wounded. RIC casualties were not disclosed, but it was believed that several others died when the building was burned.

Tuam, Co. Galway, 19–20 July 1920. Following the killing of two RIC men in an ambush at nearby Newtown Darcy, Black and Tans rampaged through the town all night, looting, burning, and discharging weapons. Head Constable Bowles and Constable Colleran prevented several murders by placing themselves in front of intended victims. Sir Nevil Macready, commander in chief of British forces in Ireland, failed to respond to demands for a public inquiry into the destruction of the town.

Oola, Co. Limerick, 30 July 1920. An armed party of the Oxfordshire Regiment en route by lorry to Limerick Junction was ambushed at Oola. Two soldiers (Lance-Corporal Parker and Private Bayliss) were killed and three wounded. The town of Tipperary was sacked in reprisal.

Dungarvan, Co. Waterford, 8 August 1920. While awaiting the arrival of the mail train, five members of the RIC were disarmed (and released unharmed) by Volunteers of the West Waterford flying column under Pat Keating. The mail was sent on to its destination bearing the legend 'Censored by the IRA'. As a consequence, light aeroplanes replaced the normal mail service.

Rineen, near Milltown Malbay, Co. Clare, 22 September 1920. Ignatius O'Neill commanded the 4th Battalion, Mid-Clare Brigade, when it ambushed a tender travelling to Milltown Malbay, killing its occupants. While retiring from the scene of the ambush they were confronted by 150 soldiers from a passing convoy. Several members of the Crown forces were killed during the fighting; the IRA had two members wounded. Six rifles, a revolver and several thousand rounds of ammunition were captured. Later that evening the towns of Ennistimon, Lehinch and Milltown Malbay were attacked in reprisal, and six local people were killed.

Mallow, Co. Cork, 28 September 1920. Units of Cork No. 2 (North) Brigade led by Liam Lynch and Ernie O'Malley occupied the barracks of the 17th Lancers. Informed by Dick Willis, a civilian painter, and Jack Bolster, a carpenter on the maintenance staff, that two-thirds of the garrison, including the officer in charge, exercised their horses daily outside the town, the attacking party took possession of the barracks without difficulty. The only casualty was Sergeant Gibbs, shot as he ran towards the guardroom. During the twenty-minute operation twenty-seven rifles, two machine-guns, a revolver, bayonets and a large quantity of ammunition were taken. There were severe reprisals as a result of the raid. Mallow was sacked, and Cleeve's factory, a hotel and several shops were gutted. There was widespread looting by British military, who raked the streets with rifle fire. The *Times* (London) commented:

> The accounts of arson and destruction by the military at Mallow, as revenge for the Sinn Féin raid which caught the 17th Lancers napping, must fill English readers with a sense of shame. The authorities would have been fully entitled, after the raid, to arrest on suspicion of complicity any townsfolk against whom a case could be established . . . They were not entitled to reduce the chief buildings of the township and to destroy the property of the inhabitants merely as an act of terrorism.

Mallow barracks was the only military barracks to be taken by the IRA during the War of Independence.

Trim, Co. Meath, 30 September 1920. Acting on intelligence provided by T. J. MCELLIGOTT, forty-four members of the Trim Battalion, Meath Brigade, under Michael Hynes and Séamus Finn, attacked the RIC barracks. Head Constable White was shot dead during the operation. The IRA took all available arms and destroyed the barracks. The town was later sacked by Auxiliaries and Black and Tans.

Thomastown, Co. Tipperary, 28 October 1920. The flying column of the 3rd Tipperary Brigade, led by DINNY LACEY, ambushed a party of Royal Engineers and Northamptonshire Regiment. Three soldiers were killed and five wounded, as was one of the attackers. Following a forty-minute exchange the IRA withdrew on the approach of reinforcements from Cashel and Tipperary. There were police reprisals in the area later that day.

Chaffpool, Co. Sligo, 30 September 1920. District Inspector Brady was killed and several constables wounded when some fifty IRA members ambushed an RIC party. The nature of the wounds suggested that the attackers were using dumdum bullets. That evening Black and Tans and soldiers, together with an officer sent to investigate the incident, set fire to three creameries and several houses in the vicinity.

Ballinalee, Co. Longford, 2–9 November 1920. Aided by a unit from Roscommon, the 1st Battalion, Longford Brigade, under SEÁN MAC EOIN attacked an RIC party engaged in burning the paternal home of the parish priest of Granard. After a sharp engagement the RIC withdrew with their wounded. Anticipating reprisal, Mac Eoin organised the defence of Ballinalee, which was largely vacated, 3 November, and prevented its sacking over the ensuing days. Following one engagement the military withdrew, abandoning thousands of rounds of ammunition. After a pitched battle with military forces on the night of 8/9 November, Mac Eoin withdrew his units from the town, which was later looted and burned.

Lisnagall, Glen of Aherlow, Co. Tipperary, 13 November 1920. The flying column of Tipperary No. 1 (South) Brigade under Dinny Lacey ambushed a lorryload of Black and Tans travelling from Galbally to Bansha. Five soldiers were killed. The attackers suffered no casualties and made off with all available arms and ammunition. Over the following days Tipperary and surrounding towns were subjected to destruction and violence.

Kilmichael, Co. Cork, 28 November 1920. In the first engagement between Auxiliaries and the IRA, Cork No. 3 (West) Brigade, led by TOM BARRY, ambushed two tenders of Auxiliaries, killing all eighteen, including their leader, Lieutenant-Colonel Crake. The IRA lost three, including Pat Deasy (aged sixteen), who had followed the column in defiance of instructions. Eighteen rifles, thirty revolvers, grenades and 1,800 rounds of ammunition were taken.

Cork, 11 December 1920. Following an IRA ambush at Dillon's Cross, Auxiliaries and Black and Tans rampaged through the city, looting and burning, principally in the main thoroughfare, Patrick Street. As a consequence, several thousand workers were unemployed. The efforts of the fire brigade, assisted by units from Dublin, were hampered by the cutting of their hoses by members of the British military. The City Hall, a mile distant across the River Lee, was also burned. The Chief Secretary for Ireland, SIR HAMAR GREENWOOD, replying to a question in the House of Commons about how the City Hall came to be burned, stated that the blaze had 'spread across the city and set the City Hall on fire.' A military inquiry under Major-General Peter Strickland produced a report, but it was suppressed by the Cabinet.

Glenwood, Co. Clare, 20 January 1921. A detachment of the East Clare Brigade under Commandant Michael Brennan ambushed a party of police at Glenwood House, killing District Inspector Clarke, a sergeant and four constables and wounding two others. Over the next forty-eight hours Crown forces fired Broadford, Kilkishen, Lissane, O'Brien's Bridge, and Sixmilebridge.

Tureengarriffe, near Ballydesmond, Co. Kerry, 28 January 1921. The Newmarket Battalion, Cork No. 2 Brigade, and East Kerry Volunteers under SEÁN MOYLAN ambushed Major-General Philip Armstrong-Holmes (Munster divisional commander of the RIC) and his escort. One policeman was killed and the remainder wounded. The attackers transferred the police casualties to the County Infirmary, where Holmes died from his wounds. The ambush sparked police reprisals at Ballydesmond and Knocknagree.

Dromkeen, Co. Limerick, 3 February 1921. Units of the East Limerick Brigade flying column and the Mid-Limerick Brigade, led by Commandant Denis Hannigan, ambushed a thirteen-strong detachment of RIC and Black and Tans, killing eleven.

Clonbanin, Co. Cork, 5 March 1921. Liam Lynch led the Cork No. 2 (North) Brigade and Seán Moylan the Kerry No. 2 Brigade in an ambush on a convoy of the East Lancashire Regiment, during which General H. R Cumming was killed and thirteen of the escort wounded. The IRA escaped without casualty. Cumming had originated the practice of conveying civilian hostages in military vehicles.

Selton Hill, Co. Leitrim, 11 March 1921. Crown forces ambushed a party of the South Leitrim Brigade flying column, killing six, including their commander and GHQ Staff Officer, Seán Connolly.

Cross Barry, Co. Cork, 19 March 1921. In one of the biggest engagements in the War of Independence, General Tom Barry led 104 members of the flying column of the Cork No. 3 (West) Brigade in a battle with more than a thousand soldiers of the Essex and Hampshire

Regiments, killing thirty-nine and wounding forty-seven. IRA losses were three dead and four wounded. The IRA captured a light machine-gun, rifles, and a large quantity of ammunition.

Headford, Co. Kerry, 21 March 1921. A column of the Kerry No. 2 Brigade led by Commandant Dan Allman, Tom McEllistrim and Johnny O'Connor attacked soldiers of the 1st Battalion, Royal Fusiliers, aboard the Kenmare train at Headford Junction. The hand-to-hand fighting that ensued resulted in the deaths of Allman and Volunteer James Bailey. Twenty-four British casualties were reported. The IRA failed in its objective of disarming the soldiers.

Scramoge, Co. Roscommon, 23 March 1921. Members of the 3rd North and 3rd South Roscommon Brigades under Martin Fallon, Seán Leavy and Pat Madden ambushed a company of the 9th Lancers under Captain Sir Alfred Peek, escorting two members of the Black and Tans who had been charged with misbehaviour. Captain Peek was killed and Lieutenant Tennant mortally wounded. There were no casualties on the attacking side, whose captured weapons included a machine-gun.

Tourmakeady, Co. Mayo, 3 May 1921. Thirty members of the flying column of the South Mayo Brigade under Commandant Tom Maguire (who was wounded during the action) ambushed a party of RIC and then retreated to the Partry Mountains, where they were attacked by British reinforcements. The flying column of the 1st (Castlebar) Battalion, West Mayo Brigade, under Commandant Michael Kilroy came to the assistance. Following a day of intense fighting the British forces withdrew. The IRA suffered one casualty (Volunteer M. J. O'Brien), while British casualties were not disclosed. Following the encounter the RIC barracks at Cuilmore, Derrypark and Kinnury were vacated.

Ballyturin, near Gort, Co. Galway, 15 May 1921. Following the murder of Father Michael Griffin of Gorteen, the IRA attacked a party leaving Ballyturin House, home of J. G. Baggott. Captain B. A. Cornwallis, 17th Lancers, was shot dead as he alighted to open the gates. When the attackers called on the two women in the party, Mrs Gregory and Mrs Blake, to return to the house, Mrs Gregory complied, but Mrs Blake refused. Captain Blake (district inspector of Gort) and Lieutenant McCreery (17th Lancers) were killed. Using her husband's revolver, Mrs Blake, who was several months pregnant, pinned down the attackers until she was also shot dead. Reinforcements arrived, and Constable John Kearney was mortally wounded. The attackers suffered no losses. There were reprisals in Gort, where shops were looted and some fourteen houses and inhabitants assaulted.

Castlemaine, Co. Kerry, 1 June 1921. The 6th Battalion, Kerry No. 1 Brigade, under Tom O'Connor, assisted by Tadhg Brosnan, Kerry No. 1 Brigade flying column, ambushed a detachment of Black and Tans and RIC, three of whom, including District Inspector McAughey, were killed. The IRA lost Jerry Myles, Kerry No. 1 Brigade.

Modreeney, Cloughjordan, Co. Tipperary, 2 June 1921. A 43-strong joint military and RIC detachment en route to a court hearing at Cloughjordan was ambushed by units of the Tipperary No. 1 Brigade under Commandant Seán Gaynor and Jack Collison. Constables Briggs, Cantlon, Feeney and Walsh were killed and fourteen wounded. The attacking party escaped unscathed, largely as a result of a chance shot that put the gun on the military lorry out of action. Some half-dozen houses of republican sympathisers were later burned in reprisal.

Bandon, Co. Cork, 21 June 1921. Castle Bernard, home of Lord Bandon, Lord Lieutenant of Co. Cork, was raided by a detachment of the 1st Bandon Battalion, Cork No. 3 (West) Brigade, under Commandant Seán Hales. As a surety against the execution of IRA prisoners, Lord Bandon and three local magistrates were taken hostage. The kidnapping of Lord Bandon posed a serious threat to proposed truce negotiations. Leslie Price, head of Cumann na mBan and de Valera's personal emissary, was despatched to west Cork to ensure the well-being of the prisoners, who were released unharmed following assurances on the treatment of imprisoned IRA members.

When a truce was agreed, the following general order to all IRA units was issued, signed by General Richard Mulcahy:

> In view of the conversations now being entered into by our Government with the Government of Great Britain, and in pursuance of mutual understandings to suspend hostilities during these conversations, active operations by our troops will be suspended as from noon Monday, July 11th.

Webb, Alfred John (1834–1908), writer and politician; born in Dublin. He inherited the family printing business. Close to MICHAEL DAVITT, he supported the DISESTABLISHMENT of the Church of Ireland and was an early member of the HOME RULE LEAGUE. He presided over the Tenth Indian Congress in Madras (1867), campaigned on behalf of women's' suffrage, opposed anti-Jewish prejudice, and supported the Boers. A member of Dublin Corporation and the Dublin Port and Docks Board, he sought an improved domestic water supply for the city. While in Australia for reasons of health, 1853–55, he tried his hand at prospecting but earned more from his writings. He was member of Parliament for West Waterford, 1890–95. *A Compendium of Irish Biography* (1878) remained a standard reference until superseded by *Compendium of Irish Biography* (1928) by JOHN SMYTH CRONE.

Wellesley, Richard Colley Wellesley, second Earl of Mornington and Marquess (1760–1842), landowner and politician; born in Dangan, Co. Meath, educated at the University of Oxford. As Lord Lieutenant of Ireland, 1821–28, his attempts to steer a neutral course between nationalists and the ORANGE ORDER earned him the suspicion of the Anglo-Irish ASCENDANCY. After he ordered the lord mayor of Dublin to ban an Orange demonstration to King William's statue in College Green, 4 December 1822, a bottle was thrown at him in the Theatre Royal, 14 December. He suspended *habeas corpus* during WHITEBOY agitation over TITHES and CONACRE. He reorganised the police and reformed the magistracy. During the famine of the 1820s he organised famine relief in Ireland and England. His brother, the DUKE OF WELLINGTON, Prime Minister from January 1828, did not intend to concede CATHOLIC EMANCIPATION and recalled Wellesley from office, replacing him with the MARQUESS OF ANGLESEY (who also had to be recalled because he favoured it). Wellesley returned as Lord Lieutenant in 1833 but was recalled when Lord Grey's ministry fell, 1834. After failing to secure the post from VISCOUNT MELBOURNE, he retired from public life.

Wellesley-Pole, William, third Earl of Mornington (1763–1845), politician (Conservative); born William Wellesley in Dangan, Co. Meath, a brother of RICHARD COLLEY WELLESLEY; educated at Eton College, Windsor. He assumed the additional surname Pole on inheriting the estate of his uncle, William Pole, in Co. Laois. He chose the title for his brother Arthur when he was created DUKE OF WELLINGTON, 1814. Clerk of the Ordnance, 1802, and secretary of the Admiralty, 1807, he succeeded his brother Arthur as Chief Secretary for Ireland, 1809–12. At first opposed to CATHOLIC EMANCIPATION, he made himself unpopular in Ireland for his use of the Convention Act. Under the influence of his brother Richard he turned to support Emancipation. His suggestions for quelling the unrest over Repeal were incorporated in the legislation introduced by HENRY GOULBURN, 1823.

Wellington, Arthur Wellesley, Duke of (1769–1852), soldier and politician; born in Dublin, a brother of RICHARD COLLEY WELLESLEY and William Wellesley; educated at Eton College, Windsor. Member of Parliament for Rye, Sussex, 1806, as Chief Secretary for Ireland, 1807–09, he criticised absentee landlords and forbade triumphalist processions on the anniversary of the defeat of the UNITED IRISHMEN. Alarmed by the Treaty of Tilsit between Napoléon Bonaparte and the Tsar of Russia and fearful of a French invasion, he devoted his attention to Irish defences. During the summer of 1807, when he heard rumours of a British expedition to the Continent, he demanded to be relieved of the Irish Office, which he officially vacated in April 1809 (being succeeded by his brother WILLIAM WELLESLEY-POLE). For his services as commander in the Iberian Peninsula during the Napoleonic Wars he was created Duke of Wellington, 3 May 1814. He was appointed ambassador to the French court in August and attended the Congress of Vienna (1814–15). Known as the 'Iron Duke', he was appointed commander in chief of the allied force that defeated Bonaparte at the Battle of Waterloo (18 June 1815).

He became Prime Minister in January 1828, at the height of the agitation for CATHOLIC EMANCIPATION led by DANIEL O'CONNELL. Supported by the Secretary of State for Home Affairs, SIR ROBERT PEEL, he agreed to the condition laid down by KING GEORGE IV that emancipation should not become a Cabinet issue; however, the appointment of WILLIAM VESEY-FITZGERALD to the Board of Trade led to the Co. Clare by-election and a victory for O'Connell. Wellington believed that the right of Catholic members of Parliament to take their seats without subscribing to the Oath of Supremacy could no longer he denied without the risk of civil war in Ireland. Emancipation became law in April 1829. Following defeat in 1830, Wellington became the elder statesman of the Tory party. With reference to his being Irish by birth he was reputed to have remarked that being born in a stable did not make one a horse.

West, Henry (Harry) (born 1917), politician (Ulster Unionist Party); born in Enniskillen, Co. Fermanagh. President of the Ulster Farmers' Union, 1955–56, he was first elected to the Parliament of Northern Ireland, 1958, when he became Parliamentary Secretary to the Minister of Agriculture; he was Minister of Agriculture, 1960–67 and 1971–72. Critical of the reformist tendency in the Unionist Party, 1968–71, he resigned from the West Ulster Unionist Council but returned to the post of Minister of Agriculture, June 1971. He opposed both power-sharing (multi-party government) and the SUNNINGDALE AGREEMENT.

Succeeding BRIAN FAULKNER as leader of the UUP, January 1974, he joined the UNITED ULSTER UNIONIST COUNCIL to oppose the three-party Executive led by Faulkner in the Northern Ireland Assembly. He supported the ULSTER WORKERS' COUNCIL strike, which brought down the Executive and Assembly, May 1974. He lost his seat in the second election of 1974 in October but regained it in the election to the Constitutional Convention, 1975–76, in which he was leader of the Official Unionist Party. Differences within the UUUC centred in the main on the Unionist Action Council, which mounted an unsuccessful strike in May 1977 against direct rule from London and for a tougher security policy. West refused to support the strike. Unsuccessful in the 1979 European Parliament elections, he resigned the leadership, 2 July, and was succeeded by JAMES MOLYNEAUX. He was defeated by the IRA hunger-striker BOBBY SANDS in Fermanagh-South Tyrone, April 1981.

Wexford Opera Festival, opened on 21 October 1951 as Wexford Festival of Music and the Arts with a performance in the Theatre Royal, Wexford, of Balfe's *Rose of Castile.* The English writer Sir Compton Mackenzie, founder of the magazine *Gramophone,* inspired the idea, which went on to establish an international reputation for its sponsorship of more obscure operas. The founding director of the festival was Dr Tom Walsh, 1951–66.

Whately, Richard (1787–1863), theologian and bishop (Church of Ireland); born in London, educated at Oriel College, Oxford, where he was Drummond professor of political economy, 1829–31. Appointed Archbishop of Dublin, 1831, he quickly involved himself in its social, cultural and political life. He supported CATHOLIC EMANCIPATION and sought reforms in the POOR LAW and NATIONAL EDUCATION. He supported the Maynooth Grant and the state endowment of Catholic clergy. An outspoken critic of evangelicalism, he was critical of the method by which TITHES were collected, though he disapproved of the widespread agitation they aroused.

He was connected with most of the leading scientific associations of the period, including the Royal Irish Academy, of which he was vice-president, 1848. He was a prolific writer; his works include *Introductory Lectures in Political Economics* (1831), *Easy Lessons on Money Matters* (1837), and *Introductory Lessons on the British Constitution* (1854).

Whiddy Island Disaster (8 January 1979). Following a fire on board, the 150,000-ton *Betelgeuse* exploded at the Gulf Oil terminal on Whiddy Island, Bantry Bay, Co. Cork, causing fifty deaths (forty-three crew members and seven local workers). 80,000 tons of oil, two-thirds of the cargo, had been unloaded into the terminal when the accident occurred. The inquiry, under Mr Justice Declan Costello, heard from more than a hundred witnesses over some seventy days; in its report (July 1980) it laid the blame on the two oil companies involved, Total, owners of the *Betelgeuse,* and Gulf.

Whitaker, T. K. [Kenneth] (born 1916), civil servant and economist; born in Rostrevor, Co. Down, educated at the University of London. Taking first place in the clerical officer examination, he joined the civil service in 1934. An assistant inspector of taxes, 1937, and administrative officer, 1938, his subsequent career was meteoric for the time: the Minister for Finance, Gerry Sweetman, broke with the precedent of promotion by seniority to make him secretary of the Department of Finance (and *de facto* head of the civil service), 30 May 1956. Five days before his appointment he delivered a paper, 'Capital Formation, Savings and Economic Progress', to the Statistical and Social Inquiry Society of Ireland. His economic analysis 'Has Ireland a Future?' was presented to the Government, 9 December 1957. Developed into a memorandum (the 'Whitaker Memorandum'), it was the basis of 'Economic Development', which he delivered to the Government, 29 May 1958. The basis of the white paper *Programme for Economic Expansion* (11 November 1958), his paper was published under his own name eleven days later.

Whitaker's rapport with his Northern Ireland counterpart, James Malley, was a significant factor in the organising of the two meetings between SEÁN LEMASS and TERENCE O'NEILL in 1965. A director of the CENTRAL BANK OF IRELAND, 1958–69, and governor, 1969–76, he played a crucial role as an adviser to the Taoiseach, JACK LYNCH, when the Northern conflict erupted, 1968–69. In 1977 he was nominated by Lynch as a member of Seanad Éireann, where he became increasingly critical of FIANNA FÁIL economic policy. A senator until 1982, he was president of the Economic and Social Research Institute, a member of the governing body of the School of Celtic Studies, and a member of the Council of the Statistical and Social Inquiry Society of Ireland. He was chancellor of the National University of Ireland, chairman of Bord na Gaeilge, 1975–78, and president of the Royal Irish Academy. In 2002 he was presented with the award of Man of the Century by RTE television.

White, Captain James ('Jack') (1879–1946), soldier; born in Broughshane, Co. Antrim, educated at Winchester College, Hampshire. A veteran of the Anglo-Boer War, in which he was decorated for bravery, he returned to Ireland, where he supported HOME RULE. On 24 October 1913 he spoke alongside ROGER CASEMENT at Ballymoney, Co. Antrim. Horrified by conditions in the Dublin slums, he supported JAMES LARKIN during the DUBLIN LOCK-OUT (1913) and organised the IRISH CITIZEN ARMY to boost the workers' morale and protect them from employer and police intimidation. In May 1914 he left the Citizen Army and became an organiser in Cos. Derry and Tyrone for the IRISH VOLUNTEERS but was dismissed when he called on Britain to recognise the Volunteers as an Irish defence force. He served in France with an ambulance unit, 1914–16. Following the EASTER RISING (1916) he organised a Welsh miners' strike in an attempt to save JAMES CONNOLLY from execution and was imprisoned at Pentonville Prison, London (where he arrived the day before Casement was hanged). He later settled in Belfast, where he was once more arrested following involvement in the protests concerning outdoor relief, October 1932. He published his autobiography, *Misfit,* in 1930.

Whiteboys, an oath-bound agrarian secret society originating in Co. Tipperary, 1761, where members wore white smocks to identify each other at night. Their principal grievances were landlord exactions, TITHES, the price of CONACRE, insecurity of tenure, wages, hearth money, tolls, and unemployment. Leaders used names such as Captain Lightfoot, Slasher, Cropper, Echo, Fear-Not, and Burnstack, names that in many instances were quite apposite: driving off or maiming cattle, levelling fences and burning property were common methods employed to intimidate landlords and their agents.

The Whiteboy movement was strongest in Cos. Cork, Kilkenny, Limerick, and Waterford. Its association with atrocities earned the condemnation of the Catholic Church and the secular authorities during the 1770s. A series of repressive 'Whiteboy Acts' were passed, under which participation in Whiteboy activity was a capital offence. Later the Whiteboys and other organisations, such as the RIBBONMEN, which modelled themselves on the Whiteboys in their oaths of allegiance and methods, were condemned by DANIEL O'CONNELL. In *Principles of Political Economy* (1848) John Stuart Mill wrote: 'Rockism and Whiteboyism are the determination of a people who have nothing that can be called theirs, but a daily meal of the lowest description of food, not to submit to being deprived of that for other people's convenience.' (See also SECRET SOCIETIES and DONERAILE CONSPIRACY.)

White Cross, a Sinn Féin organisation founded in Dublin, 1 February 1921, to distribute the (American) White Cross Fund. It assisted republicans and their families suffering hardship through involvement in the WAR OF INDEPENDENCE; funds were also applied to aid Catholic workers expelled from Northern Ireland and others not otherwise entitled to compensation. Accounts published on 31 August 1921 revealed that it had collected £1,374,795. The principal contributions came from private American sources (£1,250,000), John McCormack (£35,000), American Red Cross Fund (£12,500), private English sources (£9,517), Canadian sources (£8,659), Pope Benedict XV (£5,000), and Scottish sources (£3,814). White Cross activists included ARTHUR GRIFFITH and MAUD GONNE; its patrons included CARDINAL LOGUE.

Whitelaw, William (1918–1999), British politician (Conservative). As the first Secretary of State for Northern Ireland, March 1972 to November 1973, from the introduction of direct rule from London in March 1972 he faced two serious problems: the deep-seated resentment of Unionists at the loss of power, and the rise of the Provisional IRA. He met the

Provisional IRA leadership, including SEÁN MAC STIOFÁIN, Martin McGuinness, and GERRY ADAMS, in London, July 1972, but was unable to accommodate their demands—a public declaration that the Irish people as a whole should decide the future of Ireland, the withdrawal of British soldiers from Irish soil within three years, and pending the withdrawal that all British soldiers be withdrawn from 'sensitive areas', and a general amnesty for all political prisoners, internees, and persons on the wanted list. Whitelaw later admitted that he erred by agreeing to SPECIAL CATEGORY status for convicted terrorists, a concession he had granted in response to a hunger-striker in Belfast Prison (the Provisional IRA leader Billy McKee, who was close to death).

Responding to Belfast's 'Bloody Friday' (21 July 1972), when ten civilians and three soldiers died during a series of attacks, he ordered OPERATION MOTORMAN—the takeover by the military of the 'no-go areas', mainly in Belfast and Derry. He failed to bring the Northern Ireland constitutional parties together in conference at Darlington, September 1972. His discussion paper in November 1972 pointed towards the need to recognise both the British and Irish dimensions in Northern Ireland if a solution was to be found. This was followed in March 1973 by a white paper proposing the establishment of a 78-member Assembly with a power-sharing (multi-party) Executive, to be elected by proportional representation. The movement away from 'majority' (all-unionist) rule was anathema to the anti-reformist tendency within unionism but was welcomed by the SDLP and Alliance Party.

Whitelaw sponsored an agreement between the ULSTER UNIONIST PARTY, SDLP and ALLIANCE PARTY, leading on 21 November 1973 to a formula for a three-party Executive, the first coalition administration in the history of Northern Ireland. The details were worked out in the SUNNINGDALE AGREEMENT, in effect a recognition of what became known as the 'Irish dimension' (conceding a role to the government of the Republic), to the fury of many traditional unionists.

One of Whitelaw's last acts as Home Secretary in 1983 was to remove the ban on Gerry Adams, who had been elected to the British House of Commons for West Belfast.

Widgery Tribunal (the 'tribunal appointed to inquire into the events on Sunday, 30 January 1972 which led to loss of life in connection with the procession in Londonderry on that day'), appointed by the British government on 2 February 1972. Lord Widgery's interpretation of his terms of reference was that 'the Inquiry was essentially a fact-finding exercise . . . to reconstruct, with as much detail as was necessary, the events which led up to the shooting,' in which thirteen people were shot by the British army on 'BLOODY SUNDAY'. The first substantive hearing was on 21 February, after which Widgery continued to sit in Coleraine until 14 March; during seventeen sessions, 114 witnesses, including priests, people from Derry, press and television reporters, photographers, cameramen and sound recordists, British soldiers, policemen, doctors, forensic scientists, and pathologists, gave evidence and were cross-examined. Three further sessions were held in the Royal Courts of Justice, London, 16, 17 and 20 March, when Widgery heard the closing speeches of counsel for the relatives of the deceased, for the British army, and for the tribunal.

In his report (19 April 1972) Widgery found that though soldiers recalled seeing weapons or bombs in the hands of civilians at the march, none was recovered by the army, nor was there any supporting photographic evidence; nor had any soldiers suffered injuries from firearms or bombs. Eyewitnesses did not see any such evidence, and the clothing of eleven of the deceased showed no traces of gelignite. Widgery concluded that there would have been no deaths in Derry on 30 January if those who organised the illegal march had not created a highly dangerous situation in which a clash between demonstrators and the RUC and British army was almost inevitable. He concluded that there was no reason to suppose that the soldiers would have opened fire if they had not been fired upon first, and that soldiers who identified armed gunmen fired on them in accordance with standing orders on the 'yellow card'.

> None of the deceased or wounded is proved to have been shot whilst handling a firearm or bomb. Some are wholly acquitted of complicity in such action; but there is a strong suspicion that some others had been firing weapons or handling bombs in the course of the afternoon and that yet others had been closely supporting them.

The latter findings outraged Northern nationalists and public opinion in the Republic. The British government rejected demands over the next two decades for a new inquiry into 'Bloody Sunday', until 30 January 1998, when the Prime Minister, TONY BLAIR, moved a motion in the House of Commons for a new inquiry on the grounds of 'compelling new evidence'.

The SAVILLE INQUIRY opened in the Guildhall, Derry, on 27 March 2000. On 3 September 2002 Dr John Martin, retired principal scientific officer with the Department of Industrial and Forensic Science, stated that he now disputed his original finding that most of the thirteen victims had been linked to the use of weapons on Bloody Sunday. He had concluded in 1972 that seven of the victims fired a gun, had handled a gun, or had been beside a gunman when they were killed. He stated that 'it would be unwise to interpret my findings as anything other than contamination.' He agreed that it was 'probably fair enough' to say that at the time he did the original scientific tests he was 'invited' to produce evidence that the victims had been associated with firearms, but he denied that this amounted to 'a corruption of the process.' 'They were extraordinary times, and we were making extraordinary decisions.' He denied he was 'under pressure from anybody to produce a report that favoured the conclusion that some of the victims had been associated with firearms use.' He had never been involved before in a case in which thirteen people were shot dead on the same day, when 108 bullets (not the twenty to thirty he had originally thought) had been fired and when some of the victims had been exposed to substantial fire. 'I think that it is very likely that all the findings that I got on hands and clothing were due to contamination.'

Wilde, Sir William Robert Wills (1815–1876), surgeon, antiquarian, and writer; born in Castlerea, Co. Roscommon, educated at London, Berlin and Vienna and apprenticed to Dr Abraham Colles at Dr Steevens' Hospital, Dublin, before being awarded his licence by the Royal College of Surgeons, 1837. Wilde, who tabulated fifty-seven diseases from Irish manuscripts, identified the crannóg at a former lake at Lagore, Co. Meath, which he excavated with DR GEORGE PETRIE; his findings appeared in the *Proceedings of the Royal Irish Academy*, 1840.

After travelling to the Mediterranean as private doctor to a millionaire, Robert Meiklam, on the *Crusader*, he published *Narrative of a Voyage to Madeira, Tenerife and Along the Shores of the Mediterranean* (2 vols., 1840) and used the proceeds to further his medical studies in London, Vienna, Prague, and Berlin. He then published *Austria: Its Literary, Scientific and Medical Institutions* (1843). Wilde financed St Mark's Hospital, Dublin, for eye and ear diseases, giving his services free to the poor; it later became St Mark's Hospital and in 1898 the Royal Victoria Eye and Ear Hospital. Under Wilde it was the only hospital in Ireland to teach aural surgery, and its reputation was such that it became compulsory for medical students at Trinity College, Dublin, to attend there from 1870.

In his capacity as medical commissioner to the census of 1841 and 1851 Wilde produced a ground-breaking report on the 1841 census, in which he introduced tables of causes of death that included a 94-item classification of disease, equating standard English medical terms with their Irish equivalents and with explanations of many Irish derivations. The inventor of an ophthalmoscope, Wilde's forceps, and Wilde's angled snare, he introduced a new form of treatment for mastoiditis ('Wilde's incision'); 'Wilde's cord', an area of the brain, is also named after him. Appointed Surgeon Oculist to the Queen in Ireland (at the age of thirty-eight), he was knighted in 1864. In the same year he was the centre of a famous libel action when a patient, Mary Travers, alleged that he had behaved improperly towards her. The jury found for the plaintiff but awarded the minimum possible damages of one farthing. The bill for costs nearly ruined him, and his practice fell into decline; when he died his widow was financially insecure.

His works include *Beauties of the Boyne and Blackwater* (1849), *The Epidemics of Ireland* (1851), *The Nature and Treatment of Diseases of the Eye* (1853), *Catalogue of the Contents of the Museum of the Royal Irish Academy* (3 vols., 1858–62), for which he was awarded the RIA's Cunningham Gold Medal in 1873, and *Lough Corrib and Lough Mask* (1867).

Wilde's wife, Jane Francesca Wilde, née Elgee (1826–1896), poet and folklorist, was born in Wexford. Influenced by THOMAS DAVIS and RICHARD D'ALTON WILLIAMS, she was a national figure for her contributions to the NATION under the pen-name 'Speranza'. Her best-known poem was 'The Famine Year'. Following her husband's death, 1876, she moved to London, where she maintained a renowned and unconventional salon; but despite the international success of her son Oscar Wilde (1854–1900) her later years were spent in poor circumstances. Awarded a civil list pension of £300 a year, she died during Oscar's imprisonment and was buried in an unmarked grave in Kensal Green Cemetery, London. Her works include *Ancient Legends of Ireland* (1887), *Ancient Cures* (1891), and *Men, Women, and Books* (1891). She completed her husband's biography of the eighteenth-century illustrator Gabriel Beranger.

Williams, Richard D'Alton (1822–1862), Young Irelander and poet; born in Dublin, spending his childhood at Grenanstown, Co. Tipperary, educated at St Patrick's College, Carlow. He studied medicine in Dublin from 1843 and in that year also published the first of his many contributions to the *Nation,* 'The Munster War Song' (under the pen-name 'Shamrock'). As a student attached to St Vincent's Hospital, Dublin, he wrote some of his most popular poetry: 'The Dying Girl', 'The Sister of Charity', and the humorous series 'Misadventures of a Medical Student'. A founder-member of the Dublin Society of St Vincent de Paul, he was active in the treatment of cholera victims in the city during the GREAT FAMINE (1845–49). A member of YOUNG IRELAND and of the Council of the IRISH CONFEDERATION, he assisted his friend KEVIN IZOD O'DOHERTY in founding the IRISH TRIBUNE, to which he also contributed. He was acquitted of treason in the wake of the 1848 rising following an eloquent defence by SIR SAMUEL FERGUSON. Graduating from the University of Edinburgh, 1850, he worked briefly at Dr Steevens' Hospital, Dublin, before emigrating to the United States, 1851. He was professor of *belles-lettres* at the Jesuit University in Mobile, Alabama, before establishing a medical practice in New Orleans, where he died of tuberculosis after writing his last work, 'Song of the Irish-American Regiments'.

Wills, Rev. James (1790–1868), clergyman (Church of Ireland), poet, and biographer; born in Castlerea, Co. Roscommon, educated at TCD. On taking holy orders, 1822, he was not offered a parish and began writing. Living for some time in Dublin, he contributed to various magazines, including DUBLIN UNIVERSITY MAGAZINE, of which he was editor, 1822–38. After a spendthrift brother squandered their inheritance, Wills, for a payment of £500, enabled Rev. Charles Robert Maturin to publish 'The Universe' as his own poem. With REV. CAESAR OTWAY he founded the *Irish Quarterly Review.* He was appointed Donnellan lecturer in Trinity College, Dublin, 1855. His chief work, *Lives of Illustrious Irish Men* (6 vols., 1839–45), earned him £1,000 in royalties. An enlarged work, *The Irish Nation, Its History and Biography,* was posthumously reissued (8 vols., 1875), completed by F. Willis.

Wilson, Gordon (1927–1995), peace campaigner; born in Manorhamilton, Co. Leitrim. Moving to Enniskillen, Co. Fermanagh, he worked in the drapery trade. His account of holding the hand of his dying daughter Marie Wilson, aged twenty, in Enniskillen after the Provisional IRA set off an explosion at the Remembrance Day ceremony, 8 November 1987, made him an international figure. The Taoiseach, ALBERT REYNOLDS, appointed him to Seanad Éireann to 'help to build bridges.' In April 1993 he met Provisional IRA representatives at a secret venue to dissuade them from the 'armed struggle' but later admitted that it was a 'pointless meeting'. A tireless campaigner for peace, he eventually came to believe that INTERNMENT should be considered for both parts of Ireland. In February 1994 he attended a SINN FÉIN Peace Commission meeting in Dublin, where he made a plea for an end to violence. In the same year the Taoiseach appointed him a delegate to the FORUM FOR PEACE AND RECONCILIATION.

Wilson, Harold (1916–1995), British politician (Labour Party). As Prime Minister, 1964–70, he was in office when the civil rights campaign began and had decided to send soldiers to Northern Ireland before the request from the Northern Ireland Prime Minister, JAMES CHICHESTER-CLARK, August 1969. He handled the critical talks with Northern Ireland ministers, setting the agenda for reforms. A supporter of a united Ireland with the consent of the majority in Northern Ireland, he stated: 'If men of moderation have nothing to hope for, men of violence will have something to shoot for.' He suggested talks between the London, Dublin and Belfast parliaments to lead to a constitutional commission to work out arrangements for a united Ireland, to come into effect fifteen years after agreement had been reached, provided that violence had ceased. His proposal for the participation of Catholics at all levels of government and the transfer of all security powers to London, rejected by Unionists and the NILP, was welcomed by Catholic politicians.

He returned to power, 1974–76, and was faced by a loyalist strike; he was criticised by both reformist unionists and the SDLP for his failure to prevent the fall of the power-sharing Executive led by BRIAN FAULKNER. On 25 May 1974 he was vilified by loyalists for a speech in which he condemned the strike organisers as people 'purporting to act as though they were an elected government, spending their lives sponging on Westminster.' His next initiative, the Constitutional Convention (1975), had failed before he unexpectedly resigned in 1976.

Wilson, General Sir Henry (1864–1922), soldier and politician (Conservative); born in Currygrane, Granard, Co. Longford, educated at Marlborough College, Wiltshire. He was assistant chief of staff of the British Expeditionary Force in France, 1914. A supporter of the ORANGE ORDER, opposed to HOME RULE, and described by H. H. ASQUITH as 'voluble, impetuous and an indefatigable intriguer,' he supported officers in the CURRAGH INCIDENT. Highly regarded by DAVID LLOYD GEORGE, he became Chief of the Imperial General Staff, 1918–22, and pressed for CONSCRIPTION for Ireland in 1918. He was promoted to field-marshal and knighted in July 1919.

Proposing the use of COERCION during the WAR OF INDEPENDENCE, he suggested that one solution to the conflict would be to shoot five SINN FÉIN leaders every time a policeman was murdered. He established the British intelligence 'CAIRO GANG' in 1920. He opposed the TRUCE (11 July 1921), stating that 'we are having more success than usual killing rebels, and now is the time to reinforce and not to parley.' He was security adviser to the new government of Northern Ireland, 1921, and Unionist member of Parliament for Down North, February–June 1922. He was killed on the steps of his home in London, 22 June 1922, by two republicans, Reginald Dunne and Joseph O'Sullivan (the latter had lost a leg at Ypres), for which they were hanged at Wandsworth Prison, London, 10 August 1922.

Wimborne, Ivor Churchill Guest, first Viscount (1873–1939), British politician (Conservative). As Lord Lieutenant of Ireland, 1915–18, he was lulled into complacency by the spilt in the IRISH VOLUNTEERS, when thousands of members responded to an appeal by JOHN REDMOND to enlist in the British army. The EASTER RISING (1916) took the Irish administration by surprise. Harsh measures, including the execution of the leaders, were taken to suppress it. Wimborne commented: 'Sternest measures are being taken and will be taken for the prompt suppression of the existing disturbances and the restoration of order.' Public reaction to the methods used by GENERAL MAXWELL to restore order caused widespread support for the reconstituted Sinn Féin movement. The Hardinge Commission (to investigate the rising) exonerated Wimborne, declaring that he was not answerable for government policy.

During 1917 the British government was under strong pressure to extend CONSCRIPTION to Ireland. It was felt that such a measure would require a stronger personality than Wimborne, and he was replaced by EARL FRENCH OF YPRES.

'wise person', usually an old person, of either sex, held to have special powers and knowledge, including the gift of prophecy, and held in great awe by the community. Consulted in times of sickness, trouble or doubt, wise persons were often posthumous children or the seventh son of a seventh son, believed to have the gift of healing. Hereditary cures and knowledge of the curative powers of plants and flowers made them efficacious where medicine had failed. Their methods were closely guarded, leading to a belief in supernatural intervention—a belief not discouraged by the practitioners. Many were denounced by the clergy, who were apprehensive of the wise person's influence and standing in the community. The most famous 'wise person' was BIDDY EARLY.

Wolfe Tone Society, founded in 1963 by Dr Roy Johnston 'to work out a synthesis between traditional republican populism and socialism.' The society played a leading role in moving the IRA and Sinn Féin to the left during the 1960s. The civil rights campaign in Northern Ireland had its genesis in a Dublin conference of Wolfe Tone Societies, when Johnston and Anthony Coughlan led a discussion on discrimination and the artificial divisions between Protestant and Catholic workers. They argued that when Protestant and Catholic workers no longer opposed each other, bigotry, discrimination and the lack of civil rights for the Catholic-nationalist community would cease. Civil rights demands should be brought to the attention of 'as wide a section of the community as possible.' On 29 January 1967 the Belfast Wolfe Tone Society was represented on the thirteen-member committee responsible for the formation of the NORTHERN IRELAND CIVIL RIGHTS ASSOCIATION.

Women's International League for Peace and Freedom, founded following the Hague Congress of Women (1915) as the Committee of Women for Permanent Peace, adopting its new title in 1919. A branch established in Dublin lasted until 1932. The fifth annual congress was held in Dublin, July 1926, when there were twenty-two delegates, including HANNA SHEEHY-SKEFFINGTON.

Women's Prisoners' Defence League, established in 1922, with CHARLOTTE DESPARD as president and MAUD GONNE as secretary, to give financial aid to families of republican prisoners. They ignored a government ban that declared the organisation illegal, January 1923; their Sunday meetings and marches in O'Connell Street, Dublin, were constantly harassed by the authorities.

women's rights. The first Irish suffrage society was founded in Belfast in 1872 by Isabella M. S. Tod; two years later Anna and Thomas Haslam founded a society in Dublin. A year later the Royal College of Physicians in Ireland admitted women. Women students were admitted to Queen's College, Belfast, in 1882. In October 1884 nine women received degrees from the Royal University of Ireland. The Royal College of Surgeons in Ireland—an examining body only—admitted women as graduates in 1885. Women were admitted to Queen's College, Cork, in 1886.

The municipal franchise was extended to women ratepayers in Belfast in 1887. SHAN VAN VOCHT, a feminist republican journal, was published in Belfast by Alice Milligan and Anna Johnston (Ethna Carbery) until 1899. In March 1898 the Registration (Ireland) Act conferred the municipal franchise on Irish women. The Local Government (Ireland) Act (1898) permitted women to become members of rural district councils and urban district councils, but they could not become county councillors until 1911. The Women Graduates' and Candidate Graduates' Association (later the Women Graduates' Association) was founded in 1902. In 1904 women students were admitted to Trinity College, Dublin.

The IRISH WOMEN'S FRANCHISE LEAGUE was formed in 1908; a year later the Irish Branch of the Conservative and Unionist Women's Suffrage Association was established in Dublin. United Irishwomen, later the IRISH COUNTRYWOMEN'S ASSOCIATION, was established in 1910. The Irish Women's Suffrage Society was founded in Belfast, and in 1911 the ULSTER WOMEN'S UNIONIST COUNCIL was established. Other organisations pursuing women's franchise included the Munster Women's Franchise League, the Irish Women's Suffrage Federation (an umbrella organisation), the Irish Women Workers' Union, and the Irish Women's Reform League.

A Women Suffrage Bill was defeated in the British House of Commons, 1912. The Women's Social and Political Union formed branches in Belfast and Dublin. An Irish branch of the Church League for Women's Suffrage for Anglican Women was established in Dublin in 1913. On 2 April 1914 CUMANN NA MBAN was founded as a women's auxiliary to the IRISH VOLUNTEERS. The Irish Catholic Women's Suffrage Association was established in Dublin in 1915. The LEAGUE OF WOMEN DELEGATES was founded to safeguard the political rights of Irish women in 1917, later adopting the name Cumann na dTeachtaí.

The Representation of the People Act (1918) granted votes to women over the age of thirty. CONSTANCE MARKIEVICZ (Dublin) and WINIFRID CARNEY (Belfast), both representing SINN FÉIN, were the only women candidates in the general election, in which Markievicz became the first woman elected to Parliament, though as an abstentionist she did not take her seat, sitting instead in the first DÁIL ÉIREANN, 21 January 1919. St Ultan's Hospital for Children, Dublin, founded by DR KATHLEEN LYNN, administered and staffed by women, opened in 1919. The WOMEN'S PRISONERS' DEFENCE LEAGUE was set up in 1922.

The CONSTITUTION OF THE IRISH FREE STATE (1922) enfranchised all citizens over the age of twenty-one. The National Council of Women of Ireland was established in 1924; a year later the Irish Federation of University Women was formed from branches of the Women Graduates' Association. The Civil Service Regulation Act empowered the government to bar women from certain civil service examinations. The Matrimonial Act outlawed divorce. The Juries Act (1927) in effect barred most women from jury service. In 1932 a ban on hiring married women teachers, which was eventually extended to all the civil service, was introduced. The Criminal Law Amendment Act (1934) imposed a complete ban on the importing of contraceptives. The Women's Social and Progressive League was established in 1937. The IRISH HOUSEWIVES' ASSOCIATION was founded in 1942.

The Irish Women's Liberation Movement demonstrated on 22 May 1971 against the law banning the importing of contraceptives. Members travelled from Dublin to Belfast by train to buy contraceptives and, on their return, openly paraded their purchases at Connolly Station, Dublin. The law was changed following the Supreme Court decision in the MCGEE CASE.

On 31 July 1973 the Government conceded to trade union demands to ratify

Convention 100 of the International Labour Organisation, which provided for equal pay for men and women.

Máire Geoghegan-Quinn and Eileen Desmond were the first women to hold ministerial office. Máire Geoghegan-Quinn was appointed Minister for the Gaeltacht in 1979, and Eileen Desmond became Minister for Health and Social Welfare in 1981. MARY HARNEY became the first woman to lead a political party in the Republic when elected leader of the Progressive Democrats, 12 October 1993; she became Tánaiste on 26 June 1997.

Women's Social and Progressive League, a non-party organisation founded in November 1937 by Mary Kettle, MARY HAYDEN, Mary Macken and DOROTHY MACARDLE to promote the political, economic and social status of women. It sought to organise women voters to secure equal opportunities and equal pay for equal work (not conceded until 1973) and opposed discrimination against women in the work-place. It also promoted the candidature of women as independent members of Dáil Éireann, Seanad Éireann, and public boards and commissions. It acted as a watchdog on legislation affecting the interests of women. The league published an 'Open Letter to Women Voters', 1938. In the 1943 general election it endorsed HANNA SHEEHY-SKEFFINGTON, who stood as an independent in Dublin South but secured only 917 first-preference votes.

Wood, Sir Charles, first Viscount Halifax (1800–1885), British politician (Liberal). Chancellor of the Exchequer in the government formed by LORD JOHN RUSSELL, 1846–51, as a supporter of *laissez-faire* he resolutely opposed new expenditure and the raising of additional taxes during the GREAT FAMINE (1845–49). As a Malthusian he held that the famine would be beneficial, in reducing the population of Ireland to manageable proportions. He was influenced by SIR CHARLES EDWARD TREVELYAN, assistant secretary of the Treasury, with whom he agreed that should the potato crop again fail in 1846, market forces must be allowed to operate without interference.

As famine conditions worsened, Wood announced, 8 July, that £4½ million (half the money advanced to Ireland from the Treasury) would be forgiven but that there would be no further aid. In September he insisted that the Poor Law rate should be collected, regardless of hardship; it was reduced from 5 shillings to 3 shillings in the pound (i.e. from 25 to 15 per cent of rateable valuation). He also supported forced emigration.

Early in 1848 the *Times* (London) published a series of articles critical of the Irish Poor Law unions, drawing attention to their lack of independent financing, which led to a constant drain on the Treasury. This argument was reinforced by the humorous magazine *Punch,* which lampooned the rural Irish as lazy buffoons. Designed to foster a hostile public reaction to the Irish situation, the articles were based on selective statistics leaked by Wood and Trevelyan. Wood welcomed the ENCUMBERED ESTATES ACTS, describing them to Russell, 20 May 1848, as a means by which 'substantial proprietors possessed of capital and the will to improve their estates are introduced into the country.'

A despised figure in Ireland (where it was not generally known that he had subscribed £200 from his own pocket for famine relief), Wood held various offices under Lord Aberdeen and Lord Palmerston, 1853–59, and was created Lord Halifax in 1866, having retired from politics following a serious accident.

Workers' Defence Corps, founded in June 1929, drawing its principal support from among Dublin trade unionists and left-wing elements of the IRA. Following its first convention, 7 July, attended by prominent left-wing members of the IRA, including FRANK RYAN, Michael Price, and Geoffrey Coulter, it was renamed the IRISH LABOUR DEFENCE LEAGUE. On 17 October 1931 it was outlawed, together with SAOR ÉIRE, the WORKERS' REVOLUTIONARY PARTY, the IRISH WORKING FARMERS' COMMITTEE, and several other radical and communist organisations.

Workers' Party. The party known as 'Official' Sinn Féin from January 1970 was reconstituted as Sinn Féin the Workers' Party in 1977. A left-wing party with branches in both Northern Ireland and the Republic, it won three of the fourteen seats it contested in the general election in the Republic, 18 February 1982; its three TDs then supported CHARLES HAUGHEY as head of a FIANNA FÁIL minority government. To remove its association with the Official IRA in Northern Ireland, where Official Sinn Féin and the Republican Clubs were regarded as its counterparts, the party dropped 'Sinn Féin' to become the Workers' Party the following April. It supported the ANGLO-IRISH AGREEMENT in Dáil Éireann, November 1985. It was adamant that devolution for Northern Ireland should be in the hands of local parties. It dismissed claims that it had any links with the Official IRA and crime in 1987, but this contention resurfaced periodically and was a factor in the split in February 1992, when PROINSIAS DE ROSSA and a majority of party activists left to form New Agenda, renamed DEMOCRATIC LEFT, 28 March, leaving TOMÁS MAC GIOLLA as the sole Workers' Party member of the Dáil. He lost his seat in November 1992. The party supported the BELFAST AGREEMENT (1998) but failed to secure a seat in the Northern Ireland Assembly.

Workers' Party of Ireland, founded in May 1926 by RODERIC CONNOLLY, JACK WHITE and members of the defunct Communist Party of Ireland with the aim of establishing a workers' state. Failing to secure affiliation to the Comintern, they were advised by Moscow to join James Larkin's IRISH WORKER LEAGUE. The party published a weekly paper, *Irish Hammer and Plough,* 22 May to 16 October 1926. Former members founded the James Connolly Workers' Education Club in 1928; the club founded the Irish National Unemployed Movement, which lasted into the 1930s. They were later active in the REVOLUTIONARY WORKERS' GROUP and the revived COMMUNIST PARTY OF IRELAND.

Workers' Republic, a weekly socialist paper founded by JAMES CONNOLLY as the organ of the IRISH SOCIALIST REPUBLICAN PARTY, August 1898. It made an uncompromising stand for the rights of labour, failed after eleven issues, and ceased publication temporarily in October. It appeared irregularly, depending on Connolly's financial circumstances; a second series ran from May 1899 until the presses were smashed by the DUBLIN METROPOLITAN POLICE in December after Connolly had organised a pro-Boer rally. He again revived it, May 1900, but it collapsed shortly afterwards. Another series ran from October 1900 until January 1902, and yet another from March to June 1903. Following the collapse of the *Irish Worker,* Connolly revived the *Workers' Republic* again, May 1915–16. His son, RODERIC CONNOLLY, published a paper of the same name during the period 1921–22.

Workers' Revolutionary Party, a socialist organisation founded by PEADAR O'DONNELL, 13 March 1930, who edited its paper, the WORKERS' VOICE. Many prominent members were also members of the IRA. The party was part of an upsurge of radical activity, which alarmed the government during the economic depression of the late 1920s; it was among a number of organisations banned, 17 October 1931.

Workers' Union of Ireland, a syndicalist trade union founded by Peter Larkin, 15 June 1924, while his brother, JAMES LARKIN (who objected to the idea while he was still trying to regain control of the IRISH TRANSPORT AND GENERAL WORKERS' UNION) was in the Soviet Union. Following his return, faced with a *fait accompli* and unsuccessful in his attempt to regain control of the ITGWU, he made the WUI his new vehicle. It succeeded in attracting thousands of Dublin members from the ITGWU but made little impact outside the city. Through the influence of WILLIAM O'BRIEN the WUI was excluded from the IRISH TRADE UNION CONGRESS until 1945, when it became affiliated; the ITGWU disaffiliated in protest. In 1947 the WUI expanded and accepted members from the ESB, Aer Lingus, Guinness, and other large companies. It was affiliated to the new IRISH CONGRESS OF TRADE UNIONS, 1959, when the breach in the labour movement was healed. By 1977 the WUI had some 35,000 members. The first general secretaries were James Larkin, 1924–47, James Larkin junior, 1947–69, and Denis Larkin, 1969–77. Renamed the Federated Workers' Union of Ireland after its merger with the Federation of Rural Workers, it amalgamated with the ITGWU in January 1990 to form the SERVICES, INDUSTRIAL, PROFESSIONAL AND TECHNICAL UNION (SIPTU).

Workers' Voice, a communist paper published from April 1932; it changed to the *Irish Workers' Voice* in 1933 and became the organ of the COMMUNIST PARTY OF IRELAND when it was relaunched in June 1933.

workhouse. While the workhouse system had its genesis in an act of 1772, it was not until 1834 that 'an act for the amendment and better administration of the laws relating to the poor in England and Wales' was passed. Following a report by the English Poor Law commissioner Sir George Nicholls (1781–1865), certain provisions of the act were extended to Ireland (see POOR LAW). Nicholls engaged George Wilkinson, who had designed English workhouses. He completed 163 buildings, 1840–53 (28 of which were in Connacht, 49 in Munster, 40 in Leinster, and 46 in Ulster). The first workhouse opened in Cork, 1 March 1840. The workhouse at Youghal, Co. Cork, was the largest of the seven institutions opened in the final phase, 1853. The buildings were intended to accommodate a total of 80,000 inmates, with provision for emergency extension to 100,000. The following table shows the occupancy from the GREAT FAMINE (1845–49) to 1855:

1845	38,497
1846	42,089
1847	83,283
1848	128,020
1849	193,650
1850	211,040
1851	217,388
1852	166,855
1853	129,390
1854	95,197
1855	75,599

Mortality in the workhouse was particularly high, because of the impoverished circumstances of those admitted and the generally appalling conditions of the institutions. In Cork alone, 3,329 inmates died in 1847 (757 of them in a single week in March). In the allocation of food, which was barely at subsistence level, a distinction was drawn between the able-bodied, infirm, children under twelve, infants under two, and the sick. Those considered able-bodied were expected to work, on the grounds that 'no pauper shall work on his own account; and no pauper shall receive any compensation for his labour.' Poor Law guardians were empowered to ease pressure on the system by arranging the emigration of 'deadweight paupers'—single mothers, deserted wives, and orphan children. Some 4,100 such emigrants were landed in Australia, May 1848 to April 1870, while sixty-one orphans from the Wexford Poor Law Union were sent to the Cape of Good Hope during the same period. With the appointment of the Sisters of Mercy as nurses, 1861, conditions in the workhouses improved and their role began to change as they began to cater for the aged, infirm, and mendicant. The spectre of the workhouse, however, continued to loom large in the conscience of post-famine Ireland, and few would admit to the stigma of having had relatives in such institutions.

Wright, Billy (1960–1997), loyalist paramilitary (Ulster Volunteer Force and Loyalist Volunteer Force); born in Wolverhampton. Following his parents' separation he was brought to Co. Armagh and raised in fosterage in Mountnorris, a strongly republican area, where he was brought up as a Presbyterian while learning about Irish culture and playing Gaelic football with Catholic children. He joined the UVF in Portadown, 31 July 1975. Following interrogation at Castlereagh RIC Barracks he was sentenced to six years' imprisonment for possession of arms and hijacking. He served part of his sentence in the UVF wing of the Maze Prison, Lisburn, where he took part in the 'blanket protest' until it was called off by the UVF leadership. Deported from Scotland, he returned to Portadown, where he resumed his activities with the UVF. He was acquitted of a murder charge at the age of twenty-one. For a time he was a Christian preacher, at one time preaching in Cork, but allegedly broke with the Christian faith over the ANGLO-IRISH AGREEMENT (1985). An uncle, his father-in-law and a brother-in-law were killed by the IRA. Espousing armed resistance, he reorganised the Portadown UVF and became leader of the Mid-Ulster UVF, the most notorious part of the organisation, believed responsible for some of the worst sectarian killings during the Northern conflict.

In October 1994 Wright opposed the ceasefire called by the COMBINED LOYALIST MILITARY COMMAND. He also opposed the FRAMEWORK DOCUMENTS. During July 1996 he led loyalist resistance at Drumcree, Co. Armagh, in defence of the Orange march; the RUC capitulated and forced the march through the (Catholic) Garvaghy Road. In August, Wright and six others were dismissed from the UVF over allegations of drug-dealing and involvement in the murder of a taxi-driver during the Drumcree confrontation. Wright was believed to have financed activities by dealing in the drug 'ecstasy'. He broke with the UVF (which issued a death threat) and set up the LOYALIST VOLUNTEER FORCE. There was a public rally on his behalf in Portadown to protest at the UVF death threat, at least one of them organised by leaders of the ORANGE ORDER, Harold Gracey and Rev. William McCrea.

Under Wright's leadership the LVF was believed responsible for attacks on Catholic churches and other buildings as well as the murder of two GAA officials, 1997. In March 1997 he was jailed for threatening to kill Gwen Reed during a punishment attack on her daughter's boy-friend in a field in Portadown, August 1995; he was also found guilty of perverting the course of justice by threatening Reed's son. It was widely believed that Wright had been involved in the murder of some two dozen people. On 27 December 1997 he was killed by the INLA in the Maze Prison; his killing set off a series of sectarian murders.

Writ of Prohibition, a writ applied for in 1920 by Michael Comyn, senior counsel for the IRA, to test the legality of the British military courts, which had rejected all applications for *habeas corpus,* on the grounds that a state of war existed, though the British government denied this. Comyn applied for the writ on behalf of two republican prisoners, Clifford and O'Sullivan, to prevent the further functioning of the military courts, which, he submitted, were illegal. Judgment by the House of Lords, 28 July 1920, was in favour of the appellant, and the military courts and executions ordered by them were declared illegal. Forty-two republican prisoners under sentence of death by military courts were subsequently released.

Wyndham, George (1863–1913), British politician (Conservative). His mother was a granddaughter of Edward Fitzgerald, and he was also related to the EARL OF DUNRAVEN. As Chief Secretary for Ireland, 1900–05, he supported the policy of constructive legislation—'killing home rule with kindness'—inaugurated by ARTHUR J. BALFOUR. Wyndham's approach, however, incurred the hostility of Ulster Unionists, particularly when he encouraged Lord Dunraven and the LAND CONFERENCE (1902). In discussions leading to the Irish Land Act (1903) (see LAND ACTS) his cousin, WILFRID SCAWEN BLUNT, acted as intermediary between the Chief Secretary and JOHN REDMOND. Wyndham failed in his effort to solve the university question (see NATIONAL UNIVERSITY OF IRELAND). Unionist pressure forced his resignation, 6 March 1905, and he left the Irish Office with his health impaired.

Wyse, Thomas (1791–1862), politician (Liberal) and reformer; born in Waterford, educated at TCD and Lincoln's Inn, London. An early supporter of the CATHOLIC ASSOCIATION, in 1825 he played a leading role in the campaign for CATHOLIC EMANCIPATION. A talented organiser, he led the campaign against the powerful Beresford faction in the Waterford by-election of 1826, securing the return of the emancipationist HENRY VILLIERS-STUART by marshalling the FORTY-SHILLING FREEHOLDERS (a tactic that proved successful when adopted by DANIEL O'CONNELL in Co. Clare two years later). On the eve of Emancipation in 1829 he published *A Letter to My Fellow Countrymen,* calling for the dissolution of the Catholic Association. In the same year he published *Historical Sketch of the Late Catholic Association* (2 vols.). After his election to Parliament for Co. Tipperary, 1830, he supported the Reform Bill (1832).

Passionately interested in education, Wyse proposed a progressive plan for NATIONAL EDUCATION to Lord Edward Stanley (see EARL OF DERBY), some of which was incorporated in the scheme introduced in 1831 (though without acknowledgment). Retiring from his Tipperary seat in 1832, he unsuccessfully contested Waterford but was returned for the constituency in 1835, though in dispute with Daniel O'Connell, for whom he had a personal dislike. He was chairman of the Commission of Inquiry into National Education; his report anticipated intermediate education (see SECONDARY EDUCATION), provincial colleges (see QUEEN'S COLLEGES), and a second university (see UNIVERSITY EDUCATION). He published *Educational Reform* (1837) and was joint founder of the Central Society for Education. He sought the release of O'Connell from prison in 1844.

X

X Case. On 24 February 1992 the Attorney-General, Harry Whelehan, sought an interim High Court injunction to prevent a fourteen-year old girl (identified only as X) travelling to England for an abortion following rape by a family friend. Mr Justice Declan Costello in the High Court supported the Attorney-General. The girl's family appealed to the Supreme Court, which ruled (4 to 1) that article 40.3.3 of the Constitution of Ireland allowed for abortion when there was a substantial risk to the life of the mother (X was reported to have threatened suicide). The Supreme Court lifted the High Court injunction, though ruling that there was no absolute right to travel or to abortion information. A referendum on 25 November 1992 removed the ambiguity concerning the right to provide information and the right to travel; but the electorate, for diverse reasons, rejected the wording of the final part of the amendment:

> It shall be unlawful to terminate the life of an unborn unless such termination is necessary to save the life, as distinct from the health, of the mother where there is an illness or disorder of the mother giving risk to her life, not being a risk of self-destruction.

This was defeated by 65 to 35 per cent, leaving the legislature with a dilemma.

Y

Yeats, Jack Butler (1871–1957), artist and writer; born in London, son of the portrait-painter John Butler Years (1839–1922) and younger brother of W. B. YEATS; educated privately and with his maternal grandparents in Co. Sligo. He trained at art school in London from 1888. His first commercial work was published in the *Vegetarian,* 1888, and he subsequently worked for the *Daily Graphic* and *Manchester Guardian.* Returning to Ireland, 1900, he began a career as a watercolourist and also worked as an illustrator for the family business, Cuala Press. He exhibited throughout America and Europe and at the Armory Exhibition of Modern Art in New York, 1913, where his fellow-exhibitors included Duchamp, Matisse, and Picasso. Elected to the ROYAL HIBERNIAN ACADEMY, 1915, he took up oil painting and became celebrated for his romantic landscapes and in particular his depiction of life in the west of Ireland. The EASTER RISING (1916), the WAR OF INDEPENDENCE and the CIVIL WAR inspired some of his finest work. His best-known paintings include *The Tinker, The Country Jockey, Bachelor's Walk, The Circus Clown, The Rake, Man from Aranmore, Empty Creels, Face in the Shadow,* and *The Funeral of Harry Boland.* He published a monthly *Broadsheet,* 1902–03 and 1908–15. During his career he had sixty-two individual exhibitions, including frequent showings at the Victor Waddington galleries, Dublin; he also exhibited at the National Gallery (London), 1942, and the Tate Gallery (London), 1948. A retrospective exhibition toured the United States and Canada, 1951–52. Honours included membership of the Legion of Honour, 1950.

He published *Life in the West of Ireland* (1912), *Sailing and Sailing Swiftly* (1933), *Ah Well!* (1942), and *And to You Also* (1944). His plays included *Apparitions* (1933), *Harlequin's Positions* (1939), *La La Noo* (1943), and *In Sand* (1949).

Yeats, W. B. [William Butler] (1865–1939), poet and dramatist; born in Dublin, eldest son of the portrait-painter John Butler Yeats (1839–1922) and brother of JACK BUTLER YEATS; educated by his father, at the Godolphin School, London, and Erasmus Smith High School, Dublin. While studying at the Metropolitan School of Art, Dublin, 1884, he befriended GEORGE W. RUSSELL. He was studying at the ROYAL HIBERNIAN ACADEMY when his first published work, 'Song of the Faeries', appeared in *Dublin University Review,* March 1885. He was joint founder (with Russell) of the Dublin Hermetic Society, 16 June 1885. Following the publication of *Mosada: A Dramatic Poem* (1886) he turned to full-time writing. Returning to London, he joined the Blavatsky Lodge of the Theosophical Society. He worked for some time as literary correspondent for American newspapers. His interest in Irish myth was stimulated by living in the west of Ireland and through contact with JOHN O'LEARY, to whom he dedicated *Poems and Ballads of Young Ireland* (jointly edited with DOUGLAS HYDE, 1888), the first major work of the literary revival. *Fairy and Folk Tales of the Irish Peasantry* was also published in 1888, the year in which he published his most popular lyric, 'The Lake Isle of Inishfree'. His first volume of poetry, *The Wanderings of Oisin,* was published together with *Crossways* in 1889.

Yeats first met MAUD GONNE at his father's home in London, 30 January 1889; she declined his proposal of marriage, 1891. His only novel, *John Sherman,* and *Dhoya,* a prose tale influenced by research for his fairy and folk tale collection, appeared pseudonymously in 1891. He was a founder-member of the IRISH LITERARY SOCIETY and the IRISH NATIONAL LITERARY SOCIETY, 1892. He completed his first poetic play, *The Countess Kathleen,* in 1892. His first collection of folk tales, *The Celtic Twilight,* was published in 1893, as was his three-volume edition of *The Works of William Blake,* in collaboration with Edwin J. Ellis. His interest in spiritualism led to membership of the Order of the Golden Dawn, 1894. *The Land of Heart's Desire* (1894) was one of his first plays to be staged.

His friendship with LADY AUGUSTA GREGORY began in 1896. He encouraged JOHN MILLINGTON SYNGE to look for inspiration in the west of Ireland. Under Maud Gonne's influence he became involved in republicanism to the extent of playing a prominent part in organising the CENTENARY CELEBRATIONS for the UNITED IRISHMEN. His *Cathleen ni Houlihan* (staged on 2 April 1902, with Maud Gonne in the title role) was written expressly for the IRISH LITERARY THEATRE, of which he was a founder-member. He was later to ask, 'Did that play of mine send out | Certain men the English shot?' He had a very successful forty-lecture tour of the United States, November 1903 to March 1904, but was shocked on his return to learn of MAUD GONNE

MACBRIDE's marriage to JOHN MACBRIDE.

He was a founder-director of the ABBEY THEATRE; the opening double bill included his play *On Baile's Strand,* 27 December 1904. He confronted a rioting audience during Synge's *Playboy of the Western World* with the words 'The author of *Cathleen ni Houlihan* addresses you,' January 1907. Ezra Pound, whom he met in 1908, became his part-time secretary, 1913–16, and introduced Yeats to the Japanese *noh* theatre.

The pre-1916 period found Yeats disillusioned by the mercenary concerns of the Irish bourgeoisie and a spirit of narrow-minded nationalism, which he viewed with distaste. He refused the offer of a knighthood, 1915, and a year later proposed again to Maud Gonne (whose husband had been executed for his part in the Easter Rising). When his offer was again declined he married Georgie Hyde-Lees, 1917. They lived in Thoor Ballylee, near Lady Gregory's estate of Coole Park, Gort, Co. Galway, from 1922.

The CIVIL WAR (1922–23) horrified Yeats. He became a member of the Senate of the Free State, where, until 1928, he proved a constant source of irritation to the highly conservative political and church establishment, proposing a number of liberal measures, including divorce legislation. In 1923 he became the first Irish person to be awarded the Nobel Prize for Literature. From 1924 he spent a considerable time abroad, particularly in France. His health suffered in his last years, and he underwent a Steinach 'rejuvenation' operation in 1933. One of his last major literary undertakings was his editorship of the controversial *Oxford Book of Poetry* (1936). He moved to France in 1938 and died at Cap Martin. The Second World War delayed the return of his body to Ireland; he was returned aboard the corvette *Macha*, which left Nice on 6 September 1948, and re-interred in Drumcliff Churchyard, Co. Sligo, 17 September 1948, under a self-composed epitaph:

Cast a cold Eye
On Life, on Death.
Horseman pass by!

A crater on Mercury was named in his honour, 21 February 1977.

Young, Rev. Henry (1786–1869), clergyman (Catholic); born in Dublin; educated at Rome, ordained in 1810. Returning to Ireland, he became curate at St Michan's and Harold's Cross, Dublin, 1819–27. Noted for his charity and piety, he travelled throughout Leinster preaching at fairs, missions, and retreats. He was an outspoken opponent of intemperance and of FACTION-FIGHTING. A friend and supporter of DANIEL O'CONNELL, he spoke and celebrated Mass at many of his meetings. Despite a self-imposed life of austerity, during which he frequently partook of only one meal a day and slept in barns and outhouses, he lived to be the oldest priest in Ireland. He made several translations of religious works and was joint author of a Breviary, 1822.

Young Ireland, a nationalist movement led by THOMAS DAVIS, JOHN BLAKE DILLON, and CHARLES GAVAN DUFFY. Through the *Nation,* from October 1842 the movement attracted a middle-class following, many of whom supported DANIEL O'CONNELL and the REPEAL ASSOCIATION but whose aspirations went further than simple Repeal. Davis sought a nationalism that would 'establish internal union and external independence.' Relations between O'Connell's 'Old Ireland' and the younger movement were uneasy. Young Ireland disapproved of his alliance with the Whigs, 1835–40. In 1844, when O'Connell gave his acceptance to a proposal for a federal solution to the demand for Repeal, Young Ireland attacked him and continued to remain suspicious of him after he had long abandoned the idea. O'Connell also had a poor relationship with WILLIAM SMITH O'BRIEN, the parliamentary spokesman for Young Ireland, while the Liberator's son, John O'Connell, displayed an open contempt for the movement. Young Ireland's support for the QUEEN'S COLLEGES, 1845, further widened the breach, and relations between O'Connell and Young Ireland quickly deteriorated.

The onset of the GREAT FAMINE (1845–49) attracted more radical people to the movement, including JOHN MITCHEL (who replaced Davis on the *Nation*), MICHAEL DOHENY, THOMAS D'ARCY MCGEE, THOMAS FRANCIS MEAGHER, and JOHN MARTIN. Mitchel's strident militancy alarmed O'Connell, who demanded that members of the Repeal Association pledge that under no circumstances could physical force be justified. O'Brien and Mitchel led Young Ireland out of the Repeal Association, 28 July 1846.

As famine conditions continued through 1846, the tenant-farmers became desperate. The government was perceived to be insensitive to the Irish crisis. Young Ireland split in 1847, and Gavan Duffy and O'Brien organised the

IRISH CONFEDERATION. Mitchel openly preached sedition in his new paper, the UNITED IRISHMAN, which was suppressed, and he was transported for fourteen years to Van Diemen's Land (Tasmania), May 1848. The confederation, impressed by the revolution in France, February 1848, now sought an armed uprising in Ireland. Smith O'Brien led a badly armed and disorganised insurrection at BALLINGARRY, Co. Tipperary, July 1848; its collapse was followed by the arrest or flight of the Young Ireland leaders, and the movement quickly disintegrated.

Young Ireland Association, a new title assumed by the National Guard (BLUESHIRTS) after it was banned by the FIANNA FÁIL government, 8 December 1933. A youth organisation on the lines of contemporary right-wing movements on the Continent, it was closely associated with FINE GAEL. When the association was declared illegal, Fine Gael replaced it with a new organisation, the LEAGUE OF YOUTH.

Young Ulster, a secret movement dedicated to the maintenance of the union and opposition to HOME RULE, founded in 1892 by FREDERICK CRAWFORD. Members had to possess either a revolver, a Martini-Henry rifle or a Winchester cavalry carbine in addition to a hundred rounds of ammunition. The group was absorbed by larger Unionist organisations when the (second) HOME RULE BILL was defeated in the House of Lords, 1893. (See UNIONIST PARTY and ULSTER UNIONIST PARTY.)

Z

Zozimus, nickname of Michael Moran (1794–1846), balladeer and song-writer; born in Faddle Alley, off Lower Clanbrassil Street, Dublin. Blinded by illness in infancy, he turned to street singing and recitations for a livelihood. The last of the Dublin 'gleemen', possessed of an extraordinary memory and a powerful voice, he performed at Essex Bridge, Wood Quay, Church Street, Dame Street, Capel Street, Sackville Street (O'Connell Street), Grafton Street, Henry Street, and Conciliation Hall (Burgh Quay). His most popular ballads were 'St Patrick was a Gintleman', 'The Life of St Mary of Egypt', 'Maguire's Triumph', and 'The Finding of Moses'. When arriving at his chosen pitch he began each performance with

> Ye sons and daughters of Erin, attend,
> Gather round poor Zozimus, yer friend;
> Listen boys, until yez hear,
> My charming song so dear.

He was not above plagiarism. In 1822 a fellow-balladeer had written a tract against the Protestant Archbishop of Dublin, which went through three printings. Within a few days Zozimus was reciting the work from memory and peddling it for a quarter of the price. For many years after his death an enterprising contemporary, McGee, made 'a pretty penny' by having himself led through the streets of Dublin labelled as 'the Real, Identical, Irish Zozimus'.